TeamSAP. Success assured, rest assured. Unknown cost, time, and support are major concerns for any company when implementing a total enterprise software solution. That's why SAP has launched a new initiative called TeamSAP,™ the driving force behind the successful implementation of R/3™ software. It's a coordinated network of people, processes, and products that defines the responsibility and commitment needed to achieve faster results for businesses worldwide. And, to assure *A Better Return On Information,*℠ TeamSAP puts SAP in the role of coach throughout the life cycle of your R/3 investment. Which puts all of your concerns completely to rest. For more information about how you can benefit from TeamSAP, visit us at http://www.sap.com or call 1-888-Team-SAP.

A Better Return On Information.℠

 TeamSAP is a new initiative of people, processes and products representing SAP's total commitment to customer success.

How to smile when stiff competition, constant pressure and changing conditions are par for the course. In golf and in business, the challenges never let up. PGA Tour golfer Jesper Parnevik succeeds on the course with practice, planning and skill. SAP R/3™ software takes the same approach in helping over 8,000 companies worldwide succeed. By working with industry leaders, focusing on business issues, and anticipating what's ahead, SAP gives customers a competitive advantage, today and in the future. Jesper Parnevik works hard to ensure he can win against anyone, in any conditions. We work hard so our customers can do the same. For more information, please visit us at www.sap.com or call 1-800-283-1SAP.

A Better Return On Information.℠

Proud Sponsor of Jesper Parnevik.

A Better Return On Information℠

PRESENTS

The World of Professional Golf
Mark H. McCormack
1998

An IMG PUBLISHING Book

An IMG PUBLISHING Book

All rights reserved
First published 1998
© IMG Operations, Inc. 1998

Designed and produced by Davis Design

ISBN 1-878843-20-6

Printed and bound in the United States of America.

Contents

1	The World Ranking	1
2	The Year In Retrospect	12

MAJOR CHAMPIONSHIPS

3	Masters Tournament	28
4	U.S. Open Championship	42
5	British Open Championship	55
6	PGA Championship	67

OTHER SIGNIFICANT EVENTS

7	The Players Championship	80
8	Ryder Cup	87
9	Toyota World Match Play	93
10	Alfred Dunhill Cup	98

WORLDWIDE TOURS

11	American Tours	103
12	European Tours	144
13	Asia/Japan Tours	167
14	Australasian Tour	205
15	African Tours	212
16	Senior Tours	221
17	Women's Tours	262

APPENDIXES

The World Ranking	306
World's Winners of 1997	310
Multiple Winners of 1997	318
World Money List	319
World Money List Leaders	325
Career World Money List	326
Senior World Money List	327
Women's World Money List	329
U.S. PGA Tour	332

Special Events	395
Nike Tour	409
Canadian Tour	429
South American Tour	437
PGA European Tour	443
Challenge Tour	492
Asia Tour	522
China Tour	533
Japan Tour	536
Omega Tour	562
Australasian Tour	577
African Tours	585
U.S. Senior Tour	603
European Seniors Tour	638
Japan Senior Tour	650
South Africa Senior Tour	656
U.S. LPGA Tour	658
Women's European Tour	684
Women's Australasian Tours	695
Japan LPGA Tour	701

1. The World Ranking

An unprecedented meeting occurred on July 15, 1997, at the Turnberry Hotel in Scotland. Never before had representatives of all the world's major golf organizations gathered together as they did to endorse the World Ranking. As founder of the system, formerly the Sony Ranking, I was the chairman of this group which also consisted of Tim Finchem (Commissioner, United States PGA Tour), Ken Schofield (Executive Director, PGA European Tour), Brian Allen (Chief Executive, PGA Tour of Australasia), Kosaku Shimada (Executive Director, PGA Tour of Japan), Arnold Mentz (Commissioner, Southern African PGA Tour), Will Nicholson (Chairman, Competition Committees, Augusta National Golf Club), Colin Maclaine (Past Captain and Chairman of the Championship Committee of the Royal and Ancient Golf Club of St. Andrews), Pat Rielly (Past President, PGA of America), Jim Awtrey (Chief Executive Officer, PGA of America) and Frank Tatum (Past President, United States Golf Association).

The concept of a world ranking for men's professional golf was first expressed in this annual for the year 1968, and that was the exclusive source until 1986 when the Sony Ranking, based upon my original guidelines, was launched during the week of the Masters Tournament with the sanction of the R and A's Championship Committee. Over the next decade, the Sony Ranking came to be endorsed (or informally utilized in making player invitations) by the professional tours and major championships.

The World Ranking was finally and formally approved by all that day at Turnberry.

Briefly, the World Ranking, which is issued every Monday, consists of events of the five professional tours which make up the PGA Tours International Federation (United States, Europe, Japan, Australasia and Southern Africa). Points are generally awarded according to the players' finishing positions, and the points are related to the number and ranking of the players in the respective tournament fields. The four major championships — Masters, United States Open, British Open and PGA Championship — are rated separately to reflect the higher quality of the events. The Players Championship in the United States, Volvo PGA Championship in Europe, Australian Open and Japan Open are allocated higher minimum points levels to reflect their status.

The World Ranking points for each player are accumulated over a two-year "rolling" period, and the points awarded in the most recent 52-week period are doubled. Each player is then ranked according to his average points per tournament, which is determined by dividing his total number of points by the number of tournaments he has played over that two-year period. There is a minimum requirement of 20 tournaments for each 52-week period.

The winners of the four major championships are awarded 50 points, and there are 30 points for second place, 20 points for third place, 15 points for fourth place, and down to one point for a player completing the final round. The winner of The Players Championship is awarded 40 points, and points are awarded down to 50th place. The Volvo PGA Championship has a minimum of 32 points for the winner, and points are awarded down to 40th place.

Minimum points levels for official tour events have been set at six points for winners in Southern Africa (other points are awarded down to ninth place), eight points for winners in Australasia and Japan (other points down to 12th place), and 10 points for Europe and the United States (other points down to 14th place). The Australian Open and Japan Open have minimums of 16 points for winners (other points down to 21st place).

Points are reduced proportionately for tournaments curtailed from 72 holes to 36 or 54 holes because of inclement weather or other reasons.

The Turnberry meeting aside, the year 1997 was eventful for the World Ranking. Greg Norman began and ended the year as No. 1 in the world, but yielded the ranking for a total of 12 weeks to three players: Tom Lehman, Ernie Els and Tiger Woods. Lehman and Els were ranked No. 1 for one week each, and Woods held the top position for one week, then nine weeks, before Norman regained it for the last 17 weeks of the year.

Before 1986 the ranking was only published annually, and Jack Nicklaus was ranked No. 1 for the first 10 years. Then Tom Watson led for five years and Seve Ballesteros, for three years. Norman has been dominant since then, in the era of weekly updates, holding No. 1 for 330 weeks out of the total of 611 weeks. He is the only player never to have been out of the top 10 since 1986. Watson and Bernhard Langer are the only players also to never have been out of the top 50 in that time.

Special note should also be made of Masashi (Jumbo) Ozaki, who made the top 10 in 1974 with the No. 6 ranking and 23 years later, at age 50, was ranked No. 8 in the world.

When the Sony Ranking was introduced, Langer was No. 1 for the first three weeks. These were other top-ranked players and their time spans from then through 1997: Ballesteros (60 weeks), Nick Faldo (97 weeks), Ian Woosnam (50 weeks), Fred Couples (16 weeks), Nick Price (43 weeks), Lehman (one week), Els (one week) and Woods (10 weeks).

Norman had a record of 96 consecutive weeks as No. 1 before he was replaced by Lehman on April 20, then Norman went back to the top for seven weeks, until June 15, when Woods became the youngest-ever No. 1 player at the age of 21 years, 24 weeks. Just one week later, Els took over for a week, then Norman was back for a week before Woods returned for nine more weeks at the top.

Woods, who became a professional at the end of August, 1996, broke all records in his rise from amateur status. He took just six weeks to reach the top 100 and eight weeks to reach the top 50, whereas the previous best was 31 weeks for both by Robert Gamez. Woods ended 1996 with the No. 33 ranking. He reached the top 10 in his 33rd week and the previous best was 177 weeks by Jose Maria Olazabal.

The emergence of Woods, along with the the fall of Couples from No. 5 to No. 20, meant there were still five Americans among the world's top 10. Others were No. 5 Davis Love III, No. 6 Phil Mickelson, No. 9 Lehman and No. 10 Mark O'Meara. In addition to Norman (Australia) and Ozaki (Japan), others in the top 10 were No. 3 Price (Zimbabwe), No. 4 Els (South Africa) and No. 7 Colin Montgomerie (Scotland). Americans also held the next four positions: No. 11 Justin Leonard, No. 12 David Duval, No. 13 Scott Hoch and No. 14 Brad Faxon.

Els earned the most points in 1997, a total of 394 points in 28 events (14.07 average), and Woods had the best average, 17.09, with 376 points in 22 events. A total of seven players earned more than 300 points for the year, and 21 players earned more than 200 points.

As a by-product, the World Ranking system is able to identify the strongest tournaments in the world. Following were the highest-rated tournaments in the world for 1997:

	Event	\multicolumn{5}{c}{No. of World Ranked Players Participating}	World Rating Points
		Top 5	Top 15	Top 30	Top 50	Top 100	
1	PGA Championship	5	14	28	47	83	755
2	The Players Championship	5	15	30	50	73	740
3	British Open Championship	5	13	28	45	75	711
4	U.S. Open Championship	5	15	30	45	65	687
5	Masters Tournament	5	15	30	46	58	674
6	Bay Hill Invitational	4	12	21	34	55	523
7	Doral-Ryder Open	4	10	19	32	51	511
8	Memorial Tournament	3	8	18	33	55	495
9	NEC World Series of Golf	4	11	18	27	37	453
10	Kemper Open	3	9	18	27	47	445
11	Tour Championship	4	11	22	28	30	440
12	MCI Classic	2	9	19	29	44	433
13	AT&T Pebble Beach Pro-Am	2	6	18	27	46	403
14	Sprint International	3	8	15	26	45	400
15	MasterCard Colonial	3	6	14	25	45	394
16	Motorola Western Open	1	5	16	26	46	366
17	Nissan Open	2	8	15	24	40	364
18	GTE Byron Nelson Classic	2	6	13	25	42	360
19	Phoenix Open	1	5	14	23	42	342
20	Buick Open	2	7	15	21	35	326
21	Mercedes Championships	3	10	15	19	27	321
22	Bell Canadian Open	2	5	9	17	32	296
22	Gulfstream Loch Lomond	3	6	10	15	35	296
24	Greensboro Chrysler Classic	1	6	10	19	37	286
25	Honda Classic	4	4	8	18	36	275
25	Buick Invitational	1	6	10	20	37	275
27	Las Vegas Invitational	1	4	8	18	36	271
28	Bob Hope Chrysler Classic	1	4	9	20	36	265
29	Freeport McDermott Classic	2	4	9	15	27	256
30	Buick Classic	2	4	8	17	25	254

Age Groups of Top 100 World Ranked Players

Under 25	25-27	28-30	31-33	34-36	37-39	40-42	43-45	Over 45
					Lehman			
					Couples			
			Love		S.Jones			
			Parnevik		Woosnam			
			Maggert		Nobilo			
			Tolles		Calcavecchia	Norman		
			Janzen		Glasson	Price		
			Watts	Montgomerie	Tway	O'Meara		
	Mickelson		Olazabal	Faxon	Frost	Hoch		
	Leonard		McCarron	Singh	K.Perry	Faldo		
	Duval		Parry	Elkington	Minoza	Langer		
	Furyk	Els	Johansson	Waldorf	Pavin	Roberts		
	Appleby	Stankowski	Bradley	Brooks	Forsman	Cook		
	Allenby	Maruyama	Franco	Triplett	T.Byrum	N.Ozaki		
	Herron	Clarke	Andrade	Magee	Lowery	Stewart	McNulty	
	Bjorn	Stricker	Jobe	Turner	Senior	Rocca	Stadler	
	Harrington	Goosen	Goydos	M.Martin	Sutton	Sluman	Romero	M.Ozaki
Woods	Garrido	Lonard	Ames	Fehr	Blake	Ogrin	Haas	Watson
Westwood	Coltart	D.Hart	O'Malley	Mediate	Mize	Funk	T.Ozaki	Kite
Cink	R.Russell	R.Karlsson	Herrera	Kaneko	Cochran	Blackmar	James	Nelson

Although players in their 20s attracted most of the attention in 1997, professional golf was still very much a game for 30-somethings, as the graph above illustrates. Of the top 100 players in the world, 51 were ages 31 through 39, with the largest group being the 20 players at ages 37-39. Add the 15 players at ages 40-42, and two-thirds of the top 100 were from ages 31 to 42. There also were more players over age 45 (four) than under age 25 (three).

The top 200 players on the World Ranking as of December 31, 1997 are to be found on pages 6 and 7, and in greater detail in the Appendixes. The opposite page makes note of the trends which occurred during the year.

Woods was foremost among the 10 Americans (out of 14 players) who made the largest gains within the top 50, followed by Price, who climbed 10 positions to No. 3. Americans were also prominent among those falling in the top 50, with Steve Stricker dropping from No. 12 to No. 43 and Couples from No. 5 to No. 20. Faldo (England) also dropped in the ranking, from No. 6 to No. 17.

Lee Westwood (England), Stuart Appleby (Australia) and Olazabal (Spain) made the greatest gains into the top 50. Westwood went from No. 64 to No. 23; Appleby, from No. 282 to No. 44, and Olazabal, from No. 220 to No. 42. Americans Corey Pavin and Mark Brooks experienced the greatest falls out of the top 50, Pavin from No. 11 to No. 76, and Brooks from No. 18 to No. 62.

American rookies Stewart Cink and Robert Damron, along with Tateo Ozaki (Japan), were leaders outside the top 50. Cink climbed from No. 220 to No. 55, Ozaki from No. 268 to No. 71, and Damron from unranked to No. 124. On the other side, American Woody Austin dropped from No. 63 to No. 206 and Michael Campbell (New Zealand) from No. 78 to No. 418.

1997 World Ranking Review

Major Movements Within Top 50

Upward

Name	Net Points Gained	Position 1996	Position 1997
Tiger Woods	297	33	2
Nick Price	174	13	3
Justin Leonard	160	29	11
Jim Furyk	120	49	22
Jesper Parnevik	107	39	18
Davis Love III	98	9	5
David Duval	96	19	12
Ernie Els	64	4	4
Brad Faxon	63	23	14
Steve Jones	63	28	24
Tommy Tolles	51	48	32

Downward

Name	Net Points Lost	Position 1996	Position 1997
Steve Stricker	152	12	43
Fred Couples	116	5	20
Nick Faldo	82	6	17
Tom Lehman	62	2	9
Robert Allenby	44	37	50
Payne Stewart	43	34	47
Bob Tway	43	35	49

Major Movements Into Top 50

Name	Net Points Gained	Position 1996	Position 1997
Lee Westwood	183	64	23
Stuart Appleby	174	282	44
Jose Maria Olazabal	113	220	42
Scott McCarron	94	103	44
Shigeki Maruyama	78	56	33
Bill Glasson	78	122	41
Paul Stankowski	73	59	31
Tom Kite	70	84	38
Darren Clarke	69	62	36
John Cook	66	60	35
Naomiki (Joe) Ozaki	55	66	46
Per-Ulrik Johansson	32	69	48
Craig Parry	15	52	40

Major Movements Out of Top 50

Name	Net Points Lost	Position 1996	Position 1997
Corey Pavin	247	11	76
Mark Brooks	167	18	62
Sam Torrance	120	40	118
Kenny Perry	114	25	64
Jim Gallagher, Jr.	112	45	201
Billy Mayfair	103	43	120
Mark McCumber	103	30	104
Peter Senior	95	47	95
Costantino Rocca	95	24	53
Peter Jacobsen	77	46	128
Jay Haas	53	36	57
Duffy Waldorf	34	41	58
Michael Bradley	12	44	51

Other Major Movements

Upward

Name	Net Points Gained	Position 1996	Position 1997
Stewart Cink	112	220	55
Tateo (Jet) Ozaki	83	268	71
Robert Damron	78	–	124
Phil Blackmar	75	212	74
Retief Goosen	71	110	60
Peter Lonard	68	161	65
Kevin Sutherland	68	405	114
Tom Byrum	67	277	89
Brent Geiberger	64	–	136
David Toms	62	303	101
Tim Herron	57	99	70
Chris Perry	56	332	103
Robert Karlsson	51	245	80

Downward

Name	Net Points Lost	Position 1996	Position 1997
Woody Austin	114	63	206
Michael Campbell	106	78	418
Ben Crenshaw	102	58	262
Scott Simpson	88	54	177
John Daly	73	91	227
D.A. Weibring	72	55	143
Barry Lane	71	100	318
Wayne Riley	70	75	174
Masahiro Kuramoto	69	118	349
John Huston	54	68	140
John Morse	52	79	187
Alexander Cejka	51	93	202
Miguel Angel Jimenez	50	75	126

The World Ranking
(As of December 31, 1997)

POS.	NAME, COUNTRY	POINTS AVERAGE	POS.	NAME, COUNTRY	POINTS AVERAGE
1	Greg Norman, Australia	11.49	51	Michael Bradley, USA	2.96
2	Tiger Woods, USA	10.76	52	David Frost, South Africa	2.93
3	Nick Price, Zimbabwe	9.93	53	Costantino Rocca, Italy	2.92
4	Ernie Els, South Africa	9.89	54	Eduardo Romero, Argentina	2.84
5	Davis Love III, USA	9.09	55	Stewart Cink, USA	2.79
6	Phil Mickelson, USA	8.73	56	Jeff Sluman, USA	2.78
7	Colin Montgomerie, Scotland	8.58	57	Jay Haas, USA	2.72
8	Masashi Ozaki, Japan	8.05	58	Duffy Waldorf, USA	2.65
9	Tom Lehman, USA	8.02	59	Carlos Franco, Paraguay	2.58
10	Mark O'Meara, USA	7.98	60	Retief Goosen, South Africa	2.56
11	Justin Leonard, USA	7.00	61	David Ogrin, USA	2.56
12	David Duval, USA	6.87	62	Mark Brooks, USA	2.54
13	Scott Hoch, USA	6.85	63	Billy Andrade, USA	2.48
14	Brad Faxon, USA	6.66	64	Kenny Perry, USA	2.41
15	Vijay Singh, Fiji	6.54	65	Peter Lonard, Australia	2.38
16	Steve Elkington, Australia	6.49	66	Brandt Jobe, USA	2.36
17	Nick Faldo, England	6.44	67	Kirk Triplett, USA	2.36
18	Jesper Parnevik, Sweden	5.70	68	Fred Funk, USA	2.30
19	Tom Watson, USA	5.47	69	Frankie Minoza, Philippines	2.23
20	Fred Couples, USA	5.47	70	Tim Herron, USA	2.23
21	Bernhard Langer, Germany	5.39	71	Tateo Ozaki, Japan	2.22
22	Jim Furyk, USA	5.34	72	Andrew Magee, USA	2.22
23	Lee Westwood, England	5.26	73	Thomas Bjorn, Denmark	2.18
24	Steve Jones, USA	5.21	74	Phil Blackmar, USA	2.15
25	Ian Woosnam, Wales	5.06	75	Paul Goydos, USA	2.15
26	Frank Nobilo, New Zealand	4.92	76	Corey Pavin, USA	2.13
27	Loren Roberts, USA	4.88	77	Greg Turner, New Zealand	2.04
28	Mark Calcavecchia, USA	4.42	78	Padraig Harrington, Ireland	2.03
29	Jeff Maggert, USA	4.38	79	Dudley Hart, USA	2.02
30	Mark McNulty, Zimbabwe	4.22	80	Robert Karlsson, Sweden	2.00
31	Paul Stankowski, USA	4.09	81	Ignacio Garrido, Spain	1.94
32	Tommy Tolles, USA	3.96	82	Stephen Ames, Trinidad &Tobago	1.94
33	Shigeki Maruyama, Japan	3.89	83	Miguel Angel Martin, Spain	1.87
34	Lee Janzen, USA	3.79	84	Peter O'Malley, Australia	1.87
35	John Cook, USA	3.70	85	Andrew Coltart, Scotland	1.84
36	Darren Clarke, N. Ireland	3.65	86	Rick Fehr, USA	1.84
37	Brian Watts, USA	3.64	87	Dan Forsman, USA	1.82
38	Tom Kite, USA	3.59	88	Rocco Mediate, USA	1.80
39	Craig Stadler, USA	3.51	89	Tom Byrum, USA	1.78
40	Craig Parry, Australia	3.49	90	Mark James, England	1.77
41	Bill Glasson, USA	3.47	91	Eduardo Herrera, Colombia	1.72
42	Jose Maria Olazabal, Spain	3.40	92	Yoshinori Kaneko, Japan	1.70
43	Steve Stricker, USA	3.30	93	Larry Nelson, USA	1.70
44T	Scott McCarron, USA	3.29	94	Steve Lowery, USA	1.67
44T	Stuart Appleby, Australia	3.29	95	Peter Senior, Australia	1.66
46	Naomichi Ozaki, Japan	3.22	96	Hal Sutton, USA	1.64
47	Payne Stewart, USA	3.15	97	Jay Don Blake, USA	1.64
48	Per-Ulrik Johansson, Sweden	3.13	98	Larry Mize, USA	1.63
49	Bob Tway, USA	2.98	99	Raymond Russell, Scotland	1.62
50	Robert Allenby, Australia	2.96	100	Russ Cochran, USA	1.61

THE WORLD RANKING / 7

POS.	NAME, COUNTRY	POINTS AVERAGE
101	David Toms, USA	1.58
102	Paul McGinley, Ireland	1.57
103	Chris Perry, USA	1.55
104	Mark McCumber, USA	1.52
105	Paul Broadhurst, England	1.52
106	Jose Coceres, Argentina	1.52
107	Paul Azinger, USA	1.51
108	Wayne Westner, South Africa	1.51
109	Fulton Allem, South Africa	1.48
110	Michael Long, New Zealand	1.48
111	Tom Purtzer, USA	1.47
112	Joakim Haeggman, Sweden	1.47
113	Mark Wiebe, USA	1.46
114	Kevin Sutherland, USA	1.45
115	Hajime Meshiai, Japan	1.45
116	Brad Bryant, USA	1.44
117	Don Pooley, USA	1.44
118	Sam Torrance, Scotland	1.43
119	Doug Martin, USA	1.42
120	Billy Mayfair, USA	1.41
121	Hisayuki Sasaki, Japan	1.40
122T	Shoichi Kuwabara, Japan	1.40
122T	Clarence Rose, USA	1.40
124	Robert Damron, USA	1.39
125	Richard Green, Australia	1.39
126	Miguel Angel Jimenez, Spain	1.39
127	Brandel Chamblee, USA	1.38
128	Peter Jacobsen, USA	1.38
129	Hiroyuki Fujita, Japan	1.38
130	Bob Estes, USA	1.36
131	Mike Brisky, USA	1.35
132	Todd Hamilton, USA	1.32
133	Patrik Sjoland, Sweden	1.31
134	Brad Fabel, USA	1.29
135	Jamie Spence, England	1.29
136	Brent Geiberger, USA	1.28
137	Stephen Leaney, Australia	1.27
138	Jarmo Sandelin, Sweden	1.27
139	Peter Mitchell, England	1.26
140	John Huston, USA	1.25
141	Edward Fryatt, England	1.25
142	David Ishii, USA	1.25
143	D.A. Weibring, USA	1.23
144	Mike Reid, USA	1.21
145	Mike Hulbert, USA	1.21
146	David Gilford, England	1.20
147	Keiichiro Fukabori, Japan	1.20
148	Glen Day, USA	1.19
149	Steve Alker, New Zealand	1.17
150	Hirofumi Miyase, Japan	1.17
151	Nolan Henke, USA	1.16
152	Toshiaki Odate, Japan	1.16
153	Fuzzy Zoeller, USA	1.15
154	Grant Waite, New Zealand	1.14
155T	Paul Lawrie, Scotland	1.14
155T	Lennie Clements, USA	1.14
157	Roger Chapman, England	1.13
158	Olin Browne, USA	1.13
159	Kazuhiko Hosokawa, Japan	1.13
160	David Edwards, USA	1.13
161	Angel Cabrera, Argentina	1.12
162	Brian Henninger, USA	1.11
163	Jean Van de Velde, France	1.09
164	Tsukasa Watanabe, Japan	1.08
165	Lee Rinker, USA	1.08
166	Toru Suzuki, Japan	1.08
167T	Eiji Mizoguchi, Japan	1.07
167T	Sven Struver, Germany	1.07
169	Peter Teravainen, USA	1.07
170	Mitsutaka Kusakabe, Japan	1.07
171T	Greg Chalmers, Australia	1.06
171T	Phil Tataurangi, New Zealand	1.06
173	Jerry Kelly, USA	1.06
174	Wayne Riley, Australia	1.05
175	Wayne Levi, USA	1.05
176	Len Mattiace, USA	1.05
177	Scott Simpson, USA	1.02
178	Russell Claydon, England	1.02
179	David Carter, England	1.02
180T	Robert Gamez, USA	1.00
180T	Donnie Hammond, USA	1.00
182	Jean Louis Guepy, France	0.98
183	Toshimitsu Izawa, Japan	0.96
184	Curtis Strange, USA	0.95
185	Kenichi Kuboya, Japan	0.95
186	Peter Baker, England	0.95
187	John Morse, USA	0.95
188	Shinichi Yokota, Japan	0.95
189	Ronnie Black, USA	0.94
190	Hidemichi Tanaka, Japan	0.94
191T	Pete Jordan, USA	0.93
191T	Joey Sindelar, USA	0.93
193	Clinton Whitelaw, South Africa	0.93
194	Katsunori Kuwabara, Japan	0.92
195	Jim Carter, USA	0.92
196	Ross McFarlane, England	0.92
197	Yoshinori Mizumaki, Japan	0.91
198T	Kevin Wentworth, USA	0.90
198T	Anthony Painter, Australia	0.90
200	Bradley Hughes, Australia	0.89

Detailed Structure For Allocation of World Ranking Points

Pos.	0-3 (not currently used)	4-5 S.Africa Minimum	6-15	16-25 Austr/NZ & Japan Minimum	26-35	36-45 Eur & USA Minimum	46-55	56-65	66-75	76-85	86-95	96-105 Austr & Japan Opens Minimum	106-115	116-125	126-150	151-175	176-200	201-225	226-250	251-275	276-300	301-325	326-350	351-375	376-400	401-425	426-450	451-475 Volvo PGA Champ. Minimum	476-500	501-525	526-575	576-625	626-675	676-725	726-775	776-825	776-825 Players Champ.	MAJOR CHAMPIONSHIPS
1st	5	6	7	8	9	10	11	12	13	14	15	16	17	18	19	20	21	22	23	24	25	26	27	28	29	30	31	32	33	34	35	36	37	38	39	40	40	50
2nd	3	4	4	5	5	6	7	7	13	14	15	16	17	18	19	20	21	22	23	24	25	26	27	28	29	30	31	32	33	34	35	36	37	38	39	40	40	30
3rd	2	2	3	3	4	4	4	5	5	6	6	6	7	7	8	8	8	9	9	9	10	10	10	11	11	12	12	13	13	14	14	14	15	15	16	16	24	20
4th	1	2	2	2	3	3	3	3	4	4	5	5	5	5	6	6	8	8	9	9	10	10	10	11	11	12	12	13	13	14	14	14	15	15	16	16	16	15
5th	1	2	2	2	2	2	2	3	3	3	4	4	4	5	5	5	6	6	7	7	7	8	8	8	9	9	10	10	10	11	11	11	11	11	12	12	12	12
6th	1		2	2	2	2	2	2	3	3	3	3	4	4	4	5	5	5	6	6	6	6	7	7	7	7	8	8	8	8	9	9	9	9	9	10	10	10
7th	1		1	1	2	2	2	2	2	2	3	3	3	3	3	4	4	4	5	5	5	5	5	6	6	6	6	6	7	7	7	7	7	8	8	8	8	9
8th			1	1	1	1	2	2	2	2	2	2	2	3	3	3	3	4	4	4	4	4	4	4	4	5	5	5	5	5	5	5	5	6	6	6	6	8
9th			1	1	1	1	1	1	2	2	2	2	2	2	3	3	3	3	3	3	4	4	4	4	4	4	4	4	4	4	5	5	5	5	5	5	6	8
10th			1	1	1	1	1	1	1	1	2	2	2	2	2	3	3	3	3	3	3	3	3	3	4	4	4	4	4	4	4	4	4	4	5	5	5	7
11th						1	1	1	1	1	1	2	2	2	2	2	2	2	3	3	3	3	3	3	3	3	3	3	3	3	3	4	4	4	4	4	5	6
12th							1	1	1	1	1	2	2	2	2	2	2	2	2	3	3	3	3	3	3	3	3	3	3	3	3	3	3	3	3	4	5	6
13th										1	1	2	2	2	2	2	2	2	2	2	2	2	2	2	3	3	3	3	3	3	3	3	3	3	3	4	4	5
14th												2	2	2	2	2	2	2	2	2	2	2	2	2	2	3	3	3	3	3	3	3	3	3	3	3	4	5
15th													1	1	2	2	2	2	2	2	2	2	2	2	2	2	2	2	3	3	3	3	3	3	3	3	3	5
16th				1	1	1	1	1	1	1	1	1	1	1	1	2	2	2	2	2	2	2	2	2	2	2	2	2	2	2	3	3	3	3	3	3	3	4
17th														1	1	1	2	2	2	2	2	2	2	2	2	2	2	2	2	2	2	3	3	3	3	3	3	4
18th														1	1	1	1	1	2	2	2	2	2	2	2	2	2	2	2	2	2	2	3	3	3	3	3	4
19th															1	1	1	1	1	1	2	2	2	2	2	2	2	2	2	2	2	2	2	3	3	3	3	4

TOTAL RATING POINTS

RATING POINTS

Current Rank of Players	Rating Points
1st	50
2nd	34
3rd	30
4th	27
5th	24
6th	21
7th	20
8th	19
9th	18
10th	17
11th	16
12th	15
13th	14
14th	13
15th	12
16th to 30th	11
31st to 34th	10
35th to 38th	9
39th to 43rd	8
44th to 50th	7
51st to 55th	6
56th to 60th	5
61st to 70th	4
71st to 80th	3
81st to 100th	2
Total Available	825

51st plus all completing final round in major championships

World Golf Rankings 1968-1997

Year	No. 1	No. 2	No. 3	No. 4	No. 5	No. 6	No. 7	No. 8	No. 9	No. 10
1968	Nicklaus	Palmer	Casper	Player	Charles	Boros	Coles	Thomson	Beard	Nagle
1969	Nicklaus	Player	Casper	Palmer	Charles	Beard	Archer	Trevino	Barber	Sikes
1970	Nicklaus	Player	Casper	Trevino	Charles	Devlin	Coles	Jacklin	Beard	Huggett
1971	Nicklaus	Trevino	Player	Palmer	Casper	Barber	Crampton	Charles	Devlin	Weiskopf
1972	Nicklaus	Player	Trevino	Crampton	Palmer	Jacklin	Weiskopf	Oosterhuis	Heard	Devlin
1973	Nicklaus	Weiskopf	Trevino	Player	Crampton	Miller	Oosterhuis	Wadkins	Heard	Brewer
1974	Nicklaus	Miller	Player	Weiskopf	Trevino	M. Ozaki	Crampton	Irwin	Green	Heard
1975	Nicklaus	Miller	Weiskopf	Irwin	Player	Green	Trevino	Casper	Crampton	Watson
1976	Nicklaus	Irwin	Miller	Player	Green	Watson	Weiskopf	Marsh	Crenshaw	Geiberger
1977	Nicklaus	Watson	Green	Irwin	Crenshaw	Marsh	Player	Weiskopf	Floyd	Ballesteros
1978	Watson	Nicklaus	Irwin	Green	Player	Crenshaw	Marsh	Ballesteros	Trevino	Aoki
1979	Watson	Nicklaus	Irwin	Trevino	Player	Aoki	Green	Crenshaw	Ballesteros	Wadkins
1980	Watson	Trevino	Aoki	Crenshaw	Nicklaus	Pate	Ballesteros	Bean	Irwin	Player
1981	Watson	Rogers	Aoki	Pate	Trevino	Ballesteros	Graham	Crenshaw	Floyd	Lietzke
1982	Watson	Floyd	Ballesteros	Kite	Stadler	Pate	Nicklaus	Rogers	Aoki	Strange
1983	Ballesteros	Watson	Floyd	Norman	Kite	Nicklaus	Nakajima	Stadler	Aoki	Wadkins
1984	Ballesteros	Watson	Norman	Wadkins	Langer	Faldo	Nakajima	Stadler	Kite	Peete
1985	Ballesteros	Langer	Norman	Watson	Nakajima	Wadkins	O'Meara	Strange	Pavin	Sutton
1986	Norman	Langer	Ballesteros	Nakajima	Bean	Tway	Sutton	Strange	Stewart	O'Meara
1987	Ballesteros	Langer	Langer	Lyle	Strange	Woosnam	Stewart	Wadkins	McNulty	Crenshaw
1988	Ballesteros	Norman	Lyle	Faldo	Strange	Crenshaw	Olazabal	Frost	Azinger	Calcavecchia
1989	Norman	Faldo	Ballesteros	Strange	Stewart	Kite	Woosnam	Calcavecchia	Woosnam	Azinger
1990	Norman	Faldo	Olazabal	Woosnam	Stewart	Azinger	Olazabal	Kite	McNulty	Calcavecchia
1991	Woosnam	Faldo	Olazabal	Ballesteros	Norman	Couples	Ballesteros	Stewart	Azinger	Davis
1992	Faldo	Couples	Woosnam	Olazabal	Norman	Langer	Langer	Price	Azinger	Love
1993	Faldo	Norman	Langer	Price	Couples	Azinger	Cook	Kite	Love	Pavin
1994	Price	Norman	Faldo	Langer	Olazabal	Els	Woosnam	Montgomerie	Love	Pavin
1995	Norman	Price	Langer	Els	Montgomerie	Pavin	Couples	Couples	M. Ozaki	Elkington
1996	Norman	Lehman	Montgomerie	Els	Couples	Faldo	Faldo	M. Ozaki	M. Ozaki	O'Meara
1997	Norman	Woods	Price	Els	Love	Mickelson	Montgomerie	M. Ozaki	Lehman	O'Meara

THE WORLD RANKING / 11

World Ranking of Leading Players 1986-1997

Player	1st Ranking	1986 Aug 31	1986 Dec 28	1987 Aug 30	1987 Dec 27	1988 Aug 28	1988 Dec 25	1989 Aug 27	1989 Dec 31	1990 Aug 26	1990 Dec 30	1991 Aug 25	1991 Dec 29	1992 Aug 30	1992 Dec 27	1993 Aug 29	1993 Dec 26	1994 Aug 28	1994 Dec 25	1995 Aug 27	1995 1st 2-Year Ranking	1996 Sep 1	1996 Dec 31	1997 Aug 31	1997 Dec 31
Norman	6	2	1	1	1	1	2	1	1	1	1	4	5	7	5	2	2	2	2	1	1	1	1	2	1
Woods	52																						33	1	2
Price		40	54	46	47	33	41	43	38	47	38	17	24	10	8	4	4	1	1	2	2	11	13	4	3
Els			147	60	60	82	91	62	65	59	44	25	23	80	40	27	20	7	6	5	3	2	4	3	4
Love	96	35	23	19	18	18	11	13	12	107	81	36	36	163	145	11	9	18	25	17	20	14	9	10	5
Mickelson												22	30	24	20	68	47	22	22	25	24	9	7	7	6
Montgomerie						30	29	27	27	30	22	15	14	20	15	16	14	9	8	6	6	6	3	5	7
M. Ozaki	5	36	33	24	27	26	41	24	24	39	39	42	41	101	116	87	88	36	30	10	10	5	8	8	8
Lehman																50	36	34	26	12	11	3	2	6	9
O'Meara	37	28	48	22	183	116	132	137	106	114	120	38	91	35	33	20	16	19	15	61	41	10	10	9	10
Leonard																				91	54	28	29	11	11
Duval																				40	33	20	19	28	12
Hoch	24	9	10	25	16	19	17	18	20	64	62	56	77	37	38	18	19	40	43	26	19	18	15	12	13
Faxon										80		46	44	27	18	88	36	3	3	27	31	25	23	16	14
Singh				169		175	163	143	142					1	1	50	16	33	39	13	16	17	20	18	15
Elkington					14	5	4	3	2	2	2	3	2	175	196	20	19	26	23	11	9	13	14	14	16
Faldo	4		18	16	17	19		18	20	33	43	29	33	32	30	18	1	5	7	3	8	4	6	15	17
Parnevik					46	27	19	16	15	11	11	9	6	2	2	6	5	5	7	43	37	59	39	17	18
Watson	42		73	53		27										28	26	26	23	35	34	22	17	23	19
Couples		62														6	5	5	7	8	7	7	5	13	20

2. The Year in Retrospect

That grammatically incorrect phrase "You ain't seen nothing yet" was a perfect description of professional golf in 1997 as Tiger Woods continued to exceed expectations until after a while, it was better to exaggerate predictions rather than to be so terribly wrong again. So Tiger didn't win $4 million in prize money on the United States PGA Tour or become the first to complete the Grand Slam of professional major championships in one year. He's human, after all.

After simply taking over the game in the autumn of 1996, Tiger — who became known by one name faster than Arnold Palmer became Arnie, yet another record — was expected to dominate this year, but who could have forecast this: a stunning 12-stroke victory with 24 records broken or tied in the Masters Tournament, three other PGA Tour victories plus another in Thailand, and record PGA Tour earnings of $2,066,833. Most of that was done in merely six months, his last victory coming in the first week of July.

Those accomplishments are not insignificant, but they are merely figures and statistics which do not reveal his impact on the sport and society at age 21 as golf's first major champion of African or Asian heritage. It was written that golf had been "hot" before but never had it been "cool." He continued to bring in new audiences, young and old, people of various ethnic and economic backgrounds. Television ratings and attendances soared whenever he played, or remained unchanged when he did not. He was a prime topic in media of every sort. The Associated Press figured his economic boost for golf in 1997 was $653.5 million.

He also was scrutinized like no golfer before, and like few people outside the highest public offices. The observations and criticisms were of little or no consequence, some were intrusions into his privacy, some were opinions of reporters who did not understand Tiger's perspective, and none bear repeating here.

In the autumn of 1996, Woods earned $932,244 worldwide in 11 tournaments, including $790,594 on the PGA Tour, finishing 25th on the money list, while winning two tournaments. He was the first PGA Tour player since 1990 to win twice in his first year and the first player, rookie or otherwise, since 1982 to have five consecutive top-five finishes. He was the *Sports Illustrated* Sportsman of the Year.

In 1997, Woods became just the fifth golfer to be selected by America's sports editors as the Associated Press Male Athlete of the Year since the award was started in 1931, following Gene Sarazen (1935), Byron Nelson (1944-45), Ben Hogan (1953) and Lee Trevino (1971). He was everyone's Player of the Year including honors from the PGA Tour, PGA of America and Golf Writers Association of America, and was the youngest-ever winner in each case.

He achieved No. 1 on the World Ranking on June 15, in his 42nd week as a professional, and became the youngest-ever No. 1 player (21 years, 24 weeks), ahead of Bernhard Langer (29 years, 31 weeks) in 1986. He spent a total of 10 weeks as No. 1, finishing the year ranked No. 2.

In his first year as a professional, ending with the NEC World Series of

Golf, Woods won $2,740,514 on the PGA Tour ($2,946,163 worldwide) with six victories and 14 top-10 finishes in 25 events (seven victories and 19 top-10 finishes in 30 events worldwide). "It seems like it's been about five," Woods said in Akron, Ohio, of his first year. "My life has changed dramatically. I honestly never thought I would receive this much attention this early."

What Woods had possibly done was to launch a new era in golf, arguably the seventh since Harry Vardon, in the words of Bernard Darwin, "blazed out in full glory" by winning the first of his six British Open titles in 1896. The mantle passed from the British to the Americans in 1913 with Francis Ouimet's U.S. Open victory over Vardon and Ted Ray. Then came Bobby Jones, winning his first U.S. Open in 1923 and retiring in 1930. Ben Hogan ruled from 1946 through 1955, Palmer commanded from 1958 until 1965, then Jack Nicklaus took over until the 1980s.

As Nicklaus observed at the end of 1996, "I don't think we've had a whole lot happen in what, 10 years? I mean, some guys have come on and won a few tournaments, but no one has sustained and dominated. I think we might have somebody now."

Woods' emergence provided a springboard for Tim Finchem, commissioner of the U.S. PGA Tour, to conclude new television contracts in May which will take effect in 1999, increase annual coverage from 350 hours to 400-plus hours and provide gross revenues of close to $400 million through 2002, more than double the previous package. Finchem projected that official prize money would grow from $78 million in 1997 to over $93 million in 1998 and escalate to over $150 million by 2002. The average prize money per event was projected to increase from $1.7 million in 1997 to over $3 million in 2000 and $3.5 million in 2002.

The increases could result in events being moved from smaller markets into larger ones such as Seattle, Philadelphia, Minneapolis and St. Louis. Some organizers were restive, and words such as "carnage" and "not going down without a fight" were being heard. Asked by *Golfweek* if he had made enemies, Finchem said, "I may have, but I suspect it's not making enemies so much as it is making tough choices that disappointed people. This was a time in which we had to make some hard changes. It just was time."

In March 1996, in an American-led initiative, five of the world's leading golf tours — U.S. PGA Tour, PGA European Tour, Southern Africa PGA Tour, PGA Tour of Australasia and PGA Tour of Japan — announced the formation of the PGA Tours International Federation. In late October, details were announced for a three-event World Golf Championships (WGC) series to begin in 1999, with a fourth event, a World Cup-style team competition, to be added in 2000. The tournaments are projected to each have $4 million purses.

The WGC events will start with the 64-player Andersen Consulting Match Play at LaCosta in February, replacing the Mercedes Championship, which will move to Hawaii to replace the unofficial Lincoln-Mercury Kapalua Invitational. The unofficial Andersen Consulting World Championship will be discontinued. There will be an Invitational in August with 36 to 48 players, members of the Ryder Cup and Presidents Cup teams, to replace the NEC World Series of Golf, and will be held in Akron for three of the four years, and there will be a Stroke Play event with 60 to 65 players in November, the first to be held in Spain.

The announcement was considered by some as a redemption for Greg Norman, whose world tour proposal was repelled by Finchem late in 1994. "Let them have it," Norman said of the announcement. "Let them go with it. Let them see what they can do with it." Nick Price said, "It's good that Greg's getting some of the credit. The tour needed a wake-up call. They had always been very territorial in their thinking. You've got some people who are thinking locally and others thinking globally. I can remember fighting with (former commissioner Deane) Beman over this stuff all the time."

Despite being hailed as innovative, the WGC announcement offered nothing that was new and only one additional tournament, not three. The U.S. PGA Tour has failed previously in attempts to stage a match-play event — and apparently never understood why — and the Invitational will be little more than a reformatted World Series.

The Stroke Play event will be an addition to the schedule, but all the WGC dates are based upon the presumption that the star players will be willing to crisscross six or more time zones for those events, which by no means will be assured. Also left unanswered was how the WGC series will affect season-ending events such as the Tour Championship and Volvo Masters and other highly regarded tournaments around the world.

The announcements of the U.S. television contracts and the WGC events came at a critical time for the other golf tours, in particular the PGA European Tour. Colin Montgomerie, Europe's leading player, said, "My first reaction when I saw the television money being agreed to in America was one of complete shock, then to wonder how on earth Europe could compete. It is going to be very, very difficult."

There was speculation that Montgomerie would take up residence in America for 1998 but at the conclusion of the European season, Montgomerie announced that he was staying there. "We have undeniable talent in Europe," Montgomerie said in his prepared statement. "It is inconceivable that I should choose to leave at this crucial stage ...

"There is a big challenge to win here. We have some very, very good young players. Three years ago when Nick Faldo left, we were looking for good young players and there weren't any. Now there are Westwood, Clarke, Bjorn, Garrido and Harrington. I'm sure the European Tour will go from strength to strength."

In a *Golf Magazine* article, Montgomerie made this comparison: "We have to make sure that, while we're not the NBA, we can offer a level of basketball that appeals to everybody; we may not be the NFL, but we can still offer a standard of football where players can take pride in their achievements. If we do that we'll be all right."

A worrisome trend in the late 1990s has been an effort by the U.S. PGA Tour to in effect "take over" professional golf and some of its initiatives. Actually, the U.S. PGA Tour appears to be trying to take over the entire sport whether professional or not. This, I think, is a dangerous trend. The guardians of the game are the Royal and Ancient Golf Club of St. Andrews, which controls golf in most parts of the world, and the United States Golf Association, in North America, and the various national golf unions and federations who have created the very foundation of the sport. Their authority and their power should not be challenged either overtly or covertly.

I also think that from the standpoint of the professional game, the non-U.S. tours led by the PGA European Tour should unite to develop a global alternate tour to the U.S. PGA Tour. If they do not do this, they will find themselves all in a secondary position, if not a tertiary position, and they will be totally submerged by the U.S. PGA Tour and its ever increasingly restrictive rules and regulations.

Youth was a primary theme of 1997, highlighted in the major championships by the 21-year-old Woods, then 27-year-old Ernie Els in the U.S. Open and 25-year-old Justin Leonard in the British Open. Only the victory by 33-year-old Davis Love III in the PGA Championship, with Leonard placing second, prevented a sweep of the major titles by the 20-something generation. Those three — Woods, Els and Leonard — got most of the attention, but equally impressive was the depth of talent under the age of 30.

They included five of the top 10 on the U.S. PGA Tour money list (Woods, Els, Leonard, David Duval and Jim Furyk) and six of the top 10 on the PGA European Tour money list (Lee Westwood, Darren Clarke, Ignacio Garrido, Retief Goosen, Padraig Harrington and Robert Karlsson). Beneath them were such notables as, in America, Phil Mickelson, Stuart Appleby, Paul Stankowski, Stewart Cink and Robert Damron. In Europe, there were Raymond Russell, Thomas Bjorn, Patrick Sjoland, Joakim Haeggman and Robert Allenby.

To this list, Japan added Shigeki Maruyama for an extensive roll of nations that featured the United States, Australia, England, Spain, South Africa, Ireland, Sweden, Denmark and Scotland.

"There's a changing of the guard right now," Tom Watson told *Sports Illustrated.* Part was talent and part was attitude. "It's gravy if you win a major in your 20s," said Appleby, 26 years old, "so maybe we don't get so frightened, so caught up with all that. We can just play the game. We can be in the attack mode." Frank Nobilo, age 37, agreed, saying "With older players, there is so much more pressure because you know you're running out of opportunities. If you let one slip away, there's no telling when you'll have another." And part was equipment, as Nobilo noted. "There have been two major developments, the metal driver with the more advanced shafts and the lob wedge," Nobilo said. "Older players didn't grow up with either, while these kids did. Their games are built around the advantages that come with them."

Nevertheless, the players who had ruled professional golf did not slip away. Norman remained No. 1 on the World Ranking despite several challenges and Montgomerie won his record fifth consecutive PGA European Tour money title and repeated as the leader of the World Money List. Masashi (Jumbo) Ozaki, at age 50, was again Japan's leading player and outstanding years were turned in by many others including Price, Nobilo, Elkington, Mark O'Meara, Vijay Singh, Brad Faxon, Tom Lehman, Jesper Parnevik, Mark Calcavecchia, Bernhard Langer, Ian Woosnam and Jose Maria Olazabal.

Seve Ballesteros made his mark not as a player but as captain of the victorious European team over the United States in the Ryder Cup matches, which was the most enthralling tournament of the year, and a setback for America's three major champions of 1997, who had a combined 1-9-3 record.

Following were my top five players of 1997:

TIGER WOODS

Event	Position
Mercedes Championship	1
Phoenix Open	T-18
AT&T Pebble Beach National Pro-Am	T-2
Asian Honda Classic	1
Australian Masters	T-8
Nissan Open	T-20
Bay Hill Invitational	T-9
The Players Championship	T-31
Masters Tournament	1
GTE Byron Nelson Classic	1
MasterCard Colonial	T-4
Memorial Tournament	T-67
U.S. Open Championship	T-19
Buick Classic	T-43
Motorola Western Open	1
British Open Championship	T-24
Buick Open	T-8
PGA Championship	T-29
NEC World Series of Golf	T-3
Bell Canadian Open	MC
Disney World/Oldsmobile Classic	T-26
Las Vegas Invitational	T-36
Tour Championship	T-12
MasterCard PGA Grand Slam	2

The tone was set for Tiger Woods' first full year as a professional in the Mercedes Championship, the tournament for the previous year's U.S. PGA Tour winners, when Woods and Tom Lehman, tied for first place after 54 holes, were sent to a playoff as the event was shortened by rain to three rounds. Woods was in the playoff only because he had birdied the last four holes in the third round.

Lehman, who that week had received 1996 Player of the Year honors, was up first in the playoff during a steady rain and hooked a six-iron shot into a pond bordering the 188-yard, par-three seventh hole, which was the only hole officials deemed playable. Woods then launched a six-iron shot that drew perfectly to the flag, landing two feet to the right of the hole and spinning back to within about 10 inches.

The crowd erupted as the 1997 Year of the Tiger, extended from the previous August, was underway. The volume was turned up again at Phoenix two weeks later when, before a boisterous crowd estimated to be 20,000 people on the 16th hole, Woods cut a nine-iron shot that took two small hops then settled into the hole for an ace, setting off a celebration worthy of a touchdown in the Super Bowl. He tied for 18th place there, but won again before the Masters in the Asian Honda Classic in Thailand, his mother's home country, where he was greeted like royalty.

His performance in the Masters Tournament will go down as one of the most significant in golf history, made even more amazing by the fact he took

40 strokes on the first nine holes. He blazed back in 30, having a first-round 70 to hold fourth place, three strokes off the lead. Then came rounds of 66, 65 and 69 for a record total of 270, 18 under par, and a 12-stroke victory, the largest margin in a major championship in this century.

He won the next time out in the GTE Byron Nelson Classic and in early July in the Motorola Western Open, but came away short in the other major championships, placing tied for 19th in the U.S. Open, tied for 24th in the British Open and tied for 29th in the PGA Championship. His mistakes and some bad luck cost him more shots than he should have taken. He made three double bogeys in the U.S. Open, a quadruple bogey and two triple bogeys in the British Open and four double bogeys in the PGA Championship.

Later in the year, he was worn down. His totals were five victories, four on the U.S. PGA Tour with record earnings of $2,066,833, and fifth place on the World Money List with $2,380,831.

"I learned lessons at every tournament," Woods said. "I hit some real loose shots at the majors, and you just can't do that at the majors and win. But if you don't learn from every experience, you are a fool." In the process, he was learning to handle the grind of a year-long professional schedule, far more demanding than his previous three-month amateur circuits. "Overall, it's been a great year," he said. "For my first full year out, not bad."

ERNIE ELS

Event	Position
Mercedes Championship	T-14
Johnnie Walker Classic	1
Heineken Classic	T-8
South African Open	T-3
Nissan Open	MC
Doral-Ryder Open	MC
Honda Classic	T-23
Bay Hill Invitational	MC
The Players Championship	T-10
Masters Tournament	T-17
MCI Classic	T-68
Greater Greensboro Chrysler Classic	T-9
Volvo PGA Championship	T-2
Memorial Tournament	T-38
Kemper Open	MC
U.S. Open Championship	1
Buick Classic	1
Family House Invitational	T-5
Gulfstream Loch Lomond World Invitational	2
British Open Championship	T-10
Sprint International	T-7
Buick Open	T-2
PGA Championship	T-53
NEC World Series of Golf	T-16
BMW International	T-26

Toyota World Match Play	2
Tour Championship	T-26
MasterCard PGA Grand Slam	1
Nedbank Million Dollar Challenge	T-2
Andersen Consulting World Championship	3

Lest we forget, five years ago there was another player barely in his 20s who had a sensational start, winning six times in 1992. That was Ernie Els, from South Africa, and he completed the first hat-trick of winning the South African Open, PGA and Masters titles since Gary Player did it back in 1979. He won the Dunlop Phoenix in Japan in 1993, then took on the PGA European Tour in 1994, the year he was discovered by most of the world. He came over and won the U.S. Open Championship at age 24.

Els won his second U.S. Open title in 1997 and was the first man to have won two Opens in his 20s since Jack Nicklaus won his second in 1967. Between those two victories, Els had maintained a top-10 position in the World Ranking, including a record three consecutive victories in the Toyota World Match Play, and he finished the year just as he started, holding the No. 4 ranking.

He won the Buick Classic for the second consecutive year the week after the U.S. Open, and also had an early-year win in the Johnnie Walker Classic in Australia and a late-season triumph in the MasterCard PGA Grand Slam, raising his career total to 24 victories. He was second or tied for second five times, one of those when Vijay Singh ended his run at the Toyota World Match Play 1-up in the final. He also led South Africa to its first victory in the Alfred Dunhill Cup.

On the World Money List, Els placed second with $3,188,962, the second-highest total ever achieved.

The U.S. Open victory required 22 holes on the last day, including four holes to complete the storm-delayed third round. Els put himself in position to win that morning, making birdies on three of the four holes to enter the final round tied for second place with Jeff Maggert, two strokes behind Tom Lehman. He closed with 69 to outlast both, as well as Colin Montgomerie, who took second.

DAVIS LOVE III

Event	Position
Mercedes Championship	T-6
AT&T Pebble Beach National Pro-Am	T-58
Buick Invitational	T-59
Nissan Open	WD
Bay Hill Invitational	T-9
The Players Championship	DQ
Freeport-McDermott Classic	T-11
Masters Tournament	T-7
MCI Classic	T-9
Greater Greensboro Chrysler Classic	6
GTE Byron Nelson Classic	T-64
MasterCard Colonial	T-70

Memorial Tournament	T-10
Kemper Open	T-19
U.S. Open Championship	T-16
Motorola Western Open	T-7
British Open Championship	T-10
Fred Couples Invitational	T-7
Sprint International	12
Buick Open	MC
PGA Championship	1
NEC World Series of Golf	T-9
Bell Canadian Open	T-6
Buick Challenge	1
Las Vegas Invitational	T-30
Tour Championship	3
Lincoln-Mercury Kapalua International	1
MasterCard PGA Grand Slam	3
Nedbank Million Dollar Challenge	T-2
Andersen Consulting World Championship	2

There probably was not a more popular victory among the U.S. PGA Tour professionals than that of Davis Love III in the PGA Championship, his first major title after 12 years of trying. Much had been expected of the long-hitting Love when he started in 1986. He had won 10 tournaments but the most important came in 1992 when he won The Players Championship, which lacks the essential prestige of the four traditional events.

Before Love finally won he had to shed the reputation of a chronic underachiever. Through 1994 Love had played in 27 major championships, had missed the 36-hole cut in 10, had never been among the top-10 finishers, and had been among the top-20 finishers only twice. The breakthrough came when he placed second in the 1995 Masters, then tied for fourth and tied for second in the 1995 and 1996 U.S. Opens.

Any question of whether Love had the will to win on the big occasions was answered on the 13th hole of the final round at Winged Foot during the PGA Championship. After starting the round tied with Justin Leonard, Love moved five strokes ahead then had the margin cut to three. He was in danger of losing another stroke at the 13th, with his ball in tangled rough alongside a bunker. The hole was set close to the edge, and Love had only a tiny target, but he almost holed the shot. Leonard two-putted there from 15 feet, and Love cruised to a five-stroke victory.

Later in the year, Love also won the Buick Challenge and Lincoln-Mercury Kapalua International. He placed second in two big-money events, the Nedbank Million Dollar Challenge and Andersen Consulting World Championship, and was third on the World Money List with $2,861,953. He improved four positions to No. 5 on the World Ranking.

COLIN MONTGOMERIE

Event	Position
Johnnie Walker Classic	T-15
Heineken Classic	T-22
Dubai Desert Classic	T-6
Doral-Ryder Open	T-20
Honda Classic	4
Bay Hill Invitational	T-19
The Players Championship	T-7
Masters Tournament	T-30
MCI Classic	T-20
Benson and Hedges International Open	T-59
Alamo English Open	T-12
Volvo PGA Championship	5
Compaq European Grand Prix	1
U.S. Open Championship	2
Peugeot Open de France	T-11
Murphy's Irish Open	1
Gulfstream Loch Lomond World Invitational	T-10
British Open Championship	T-24
Volvo Scandinavian Masters	T-8
PGA Championship	T-13
Smurfit European Open	T-22
BMW International Open	3
Canon European Masters	T-10
Trophee Lancome	T-22
One 2 One British Masters	2
Linde German Masters	2
Toyota World Match Play	T-5
Volvo Masters	8
Hassan II Trophy	1
World Cup of Golf (Individual)	1
Nedbank Million Dollar Challenge	T-7
Andersen Consulting World Championship	1

Reaching two goals and falling short of another, Colin Montgomerie had a year much like his most recent ones. He led the PGA European Tour money list for the fifth successive year, won more money than any other player in the world for the second time in a row, and came agonizingly close to winning his first major championship for the fourth time.

Victories in the Compaq European Grand Prix and Murphy's Irish Open enabled Montgomerie to win the European money title with £798,947, more than £100,000 ahead of second-place Bernhard Langer. Additional wins in the World Cup of Golf, Hassan II Trophy in Morocco and, more importantly, Andersen Consulting World Championship enabled Montgomerie to repeat at the top of the World Money List with $3,366,900, nearly $200,000 more than Ernie Els, the runner-up. Montgomerie had been the first to reach $3 million in 1996, when he earned $3,071,442.

Ranked No. 7 in the world, with 17 career victories at age 34, Montgomerie needs only to win a major title to stand alongside the best golfers of his generation. A bogey on the next-to-last hole, when he missed a five-foot par putt, cost him in the U.S. Open, where he finished one stroke behind Els.

Earlier, Montgomerie narrowly lost in the 1992 U.S. Open and fell in a playoff, along with Loren Roberts, to Els in the 1994 U.S. Open, then lost in a playoff to Steve Elkington in the 1995 PGA Championship.

JUSTIN LEONARD

Event	Position
Mercedes Championship	T-22
Phoenix Open	MC
AT&T Pebble Beach National Pro-Am	MC
Buick Invitational	MC
Tucson Chrysler Classic	T-27
Nissan Open	T-51
Doral-Ryder Open	MC
Bay Hill Invitational	T-38
The Players Championship	T-37
Freeport-McDermott Classic	T-43
Masters Tournament	T-7
MCI Classic	T-30
Shell Houston Open	T-15
GTE Byron Nelson Classic	T-27
MasterCard Colonial	T-13
Memorial Tournament	T-46
Kemper Open	1
U.S. Open Championship	T-36
FedEx St. Jude Classic	T-5
Family House Invitational	T-14
Motorola Western Open	T-3
British Open Championship	1
Sprint International	T-39
Buick Open	T-49
PGA Championship	2
NEC World Series of Golf	T-19
Bell Canadian Open	T-6
CVS Charity Classic	T-23
Michelob Championship	MC
Tour Championship	T-8
MasterCard PGA Grand Slam	4
Nedbank Million Dollar Challenge	6

Justin Leonard came to the U.S. PGA Tour after Phil Mickelson and before Tiger Woods, and received far less publicity than either of them. That probably was to Leonard's benefit. He had an outstanding amateur record, won the U.S. Amateur and NCAA titles, but was under less pressure to have immediate success as a professional. While Leonard did not match Woods' start, he went one better than Mickelson by winning his first major championship.

The British Open title came on a final-round 65 that enabled Leonard to overtake Jesper Parnevik from five strokes behind and to win by three strokes. The five-stroke comeback equalled the championship record set by Jim Barnes in 1925 and tied by Tommy Armour in 1931.

Leonard won his first professional event in the 1996 Buick Open, then took the Kemper Open title six weeks before his triumph at Royal Troon. He also was runner-up in the PGA Championship, after a slow start to the year in which he had only one top-10 finish in 16 events before the Kemper Open.

He finished seventh on the World Money List with $2,022,963, and advanced from No. 29 to No. 11 on the World Ranking.

Ask the casual observer about Greg Norman or Nick Price in 1997, and the response might be that they didn't have very good years. That probably was the impression, and how wrong it was. It was an indication of how well they have played in the past, that anything less was regarded as poor performance.

Norman raised some eyebrows when he missed 36-hole cuts in the year's first two major championships, the Masters and U.S. Open, following his six-stroke collapse in the final round of the 1996 Masters. He remained the No. 1 player on the World Ranking, however, because of the consistency which has been a hallmark of his career. Rare were the weeks when the 42-year-old Australian was not in contention, and those two major events were the only cuts he missed.

There were two victories in the FedEx St. Jude Classic and NEC World Series of Golf, plus an unofficial team triumph with Brad Faxon in the Fred Meyer Challenge, for the third consecutive year, raising Norman's career total to 77 wins, 82 including team events.

Equally impressive was that Norman finished second or third in eight events around the world, including three tournaments that he lost in playoffs. Early in the year, Norman lost the Peugeot Open de Espana to Mark James and the Dubai Desert Classic to young countryman Richard Green. Later in the Holden Australian Open, he went four playoff holes before losing to Lee Westwood.

He was seventh on the U.S. PGA Tour money list with $1,345,856 and eighth on the World Money List with $1,949,508 while pushing his record total on the Career World Money List past $20 million to $20,621,287.

Price's decline was real, not imagined, then the 40-year-old Zimbabwean got his life and game in better order. Ranked No. 1 in the world from August 1994 through June 1995, Price had stumbled to No. 13 by the end of 1996 through a combination of illness, business problems and troubles on the golf course. He had not won in America since 1994, although he won twice in Africa late in 1995.

Nine top-10 finishes worldwide in 1996 were indicative that not all was wrong with Price, and he proved it this year by surging back to No. 3 in the world. He won in the United States at the MCI Classic, which he dedicated to his former caddie, Jeff (Squeeky) Medlen, who would later die of leukemia.

Although that was his only victory in America, Price felt he was playing as well from tee to green as he had three to five years ago, when he won the British Open and the PGA Championship twice, but not putting as well. This was borne out by his 68.98 scoring average, which earned him the Vardon Trophy.

In his home region of Southern Africa, Price won four times, twice in events co-sanctioned by the PGA European Tour — Dimension Data Pro-Am and Alfred Dunhill South African PGA — plus the Zimbabwe Open and Nedbank Million Dollar Challenge, with a $1 million first prize, which pushed him to fourth place on the World Money List with $2,517,716. He also was runner-up in the South African Open.

David Duval did something that Norman and Price could not — take the headlines from Tiger Woods. In the closing tournaments of the U.S. PGA Tour season, Duval won three tournaments in succession to climb all the way to second place on the final money list with $1,885,308.

At age 25, Duval was also in the company of his contemporaries — Woods, Ernie Els and Justin Leonard — as the four under-30 players to earn more than $2 million on the World Money List. Duval was sixth among the seven $2 million winners with $2,044,808. His growing international stature was also evident by his No. 12 position on the World Ranking, up seven places from 1996.

Despite his youth, Duval would have been justified to think his success was overdue. After an outstanding amateur career which ended in 1993, Duval played the rest of that year and the next on the developmental Nike Tour. He qualified for the main circuit in 1995 and had seven second-place finishes, including two this year, before breaking through in his 93rd professional start.

He won twice in playoffs, at the Michelob Championship and Walt Disney World/Oldsmobile Classic, took the next week off, then won again in the season-ending Tour Championship. He was the first player in four years to win three consecutive tournaments. "Three victories in a year, no matter how they are spaced out, is a great year," Duval said. He had a one-word explanation for the difference between not winning and winning: "Breaks."

Duval's success left Phil Mickelson, age 27, less prominent among the young stars, even though Mickelson finished the year ranked No. 6 in the world. After having four victories in 1996, Mickelson won two in 1997, the Bay Hill Invitational and Sprint International, and did not crack the top 20 of the major championships. He was 12th on the World Money List with $1,707,335.

Jim Furyk and Stuart Appleby, other players in their 20s on the American circuit, also won more than $1 million worldwide and Paul Stankowski just missed that mark. Furyk, who had three second-place finishes and was fourth on the U.S. PGA Tour money list, won $1,942,574 for ninth place worldwide. He had victories in the Argentina Open and Family House Invitational. Appleby, an Australian, won the Honda Classic and $1,072,083 worldwide. Stankowski, winner of the United Airlines Hawaiian Open, had a $998,446 worldwide total.

Stewart Cink, with a victory in the Canon Greater Hartford Open, was the Rookie of the Year over Robert Damron, who also had a solid first year. Cink's worldwide earnings were $967,157 while Damron won $483,336.

There were 11 players in America who won two or more tournaments. Four of those have not been identified so far: Steve Elkington, Mark O'Meara,

Vijay Singh and Steve Jones. Elkington, age 34, and O'Meara, 40, started as if they might have really sensational years.

O'Meara won the AT&T Pebble Beach National Pro-Am for the fifth time among his 13 U.S. victories, beating Woods and Duval, then won the Buick Invitational the next week. He had one more victory in Europe in the autumn, winning the Trophee Lancome for the 20th triumph of his career. His worldwide earnings were $1,531,412 and he held No. 10 on the World Ranking.

Elkington won twice in the Florida swing, at the Doral-Ryder Open and by seven strokes in The Players Championship, his second title in that event. He also won the unofficial Diners Club Matches with Jeff Maggert, held the No. 16 World Ranking and won a worldwide total of $1,732,111 for 10th place.

While Vijay Singh won twice in America, he will remember as well or better his two victories elsewhere, in the South African Open and the Toyota World Match Play, where he ended Els' three-year reign. The U.S. triumphs were at the Memorial Tournament and Buick Open, as Singh, a 34-year-old Fijian and the world's No. 15 ranked player, won a total of $1,674,188.

Jones, the 1996 U.S. Open champion, won the Phoenix Open and Bell Canadian Open, providing further evidence of his recovery from the dirtbike accident in 1991 which kept him off the circuit for nearly three years. The 40-year-old Jones, ranked No. 24, had earnings of $1,090,743.

Other especially notable performers in America included Scott Hoch and Brad Faxon, who were among the top 10 on the money list and had victories, tournament winners Mark Calcavecchia and Frank Nobilo, who also won elsewhere, and Jesper Parnevik, who earned a captain's choice for the European Ryder Cup team and tied for second place in the British Open.

Aside from Jones, the 1996 major championship winners had a mixed bag of results. Tom Lehman came the closest to winning another and suffered the greatest heartache. For the third consecutive year, Lehman did not win the U.S. Open after holding or sharing the lead through 54 holes. This year, he had a two-stroke lead but finished third, two strokes behind, doomed by an approach shot into the water on the 17th hole.

Lehman, who lost a playoff to Woods in the season-opening Mercedes Championship, had one victory outside America in the Gulfstream Loch Lomond World Invitational. He won $1,574,319 around the world but dropped seven positions on the World Ranking to No. 9.

Both Nick Faldo and Mark Brooks performed miserably, although Faldo did win the Nissan Open. A man whose career is based upon winning major titles, having secured six, Faldo missed cuts in the Masters and PGA Championship, tied for 48th in the U.S. Open and tied for 51st in the British Open. Brooks became the first to miss the cuts in all four major events after winning one the previous year.

Faldo dropped from No. 6 to No. 17 on the World Ranking, and Brooks, from No. 18 to No. 62. They were joined in decline by two other recent major champions, Fred Couples (No. 5 to No. 20) and Corey Pavin (No. 11 to No. 76).

John Daly, the 1995 British Open champion, was at year's end determined to overcome his problems with alcohol, which had led to a binge in March during The Players Championship that resulted in Daly entering the Betty Ford Clinic and his wife seeking a divorce. By all reports, Daly was doing well, receiving therapy and involved in a fitness program.

There was a balance of old and new faces on the PGA European Tour, as well. In addition to Montgomerie, Europe's established stars included Bernhard Langer, Ian Woosnam, Costantino Rocca and, in a welcomed return, Jose Maria Olazabal.

Langer was in the running to overtake Montgomerie for the money title until the final event. The 40-year-old German won four times in Europe, plus the Argentina Masters, and secured the point that retained the Ryder Cup for Europe. Ranked No. 21 in the world, Langer earned $1,501,988.

Woosnam's one victory in Europe was an important title, the Volvo PGA Championship, and he also triumphed in the Hyundai Motors Open on the Omega Tour in Asia. He went over $1 million with $1,207,365 and was ranked No. 25. Rocca, 39, the same age as Woosnam, was the Canon European Masters winner and held the No. 53 ranking.

Olazabal rejoined the PGA European Tour in late February for the first time since September 1995. The 31-year-old Spaniard, who won the 1994 Masters, had been out because of a foot ailment, originally diagnosed as rheumatoid arthritis, which threatened even his ability to walk. Finally, a German doctor decided the cause was a hernia, and prescribed a exercise regimen which enabled Olazabal to return. In just his third tournament, Olazabal won the Turespana Masters-Open de Canarias, and went on to earn a place on the Ryder Cup team.

The best of the young Europeans were good friends Lee Westwood, 24 years of age and from England, and Darren Clarke, 28, from Northern Ireland.

Westwood won the season-ending Volvo Masters along with three overseas events, the Benson and Hedges Malaysian Open, Sumitomo Visa Taiheiyo Masters in Japan and Holden Australian Open. Rising from No. 64 to No. 23 on the World Ranking, Westwood earned $1,723,603 worldwide.

Clarke, with two victories in his career, did not add to that total but had 12 top-10 finishes around the world and came close to two big prizes with his runner-up finishes in the British Open and Volvo PGA Championship. He won over $1 million and gained the world's top 50 with his No. 36 ranking.

Joining Westwood and Clarke among the top 10 of the European money leaders were Ignacio Garrido (age 25), Retief Goosen (28), Padraig Harrington (26) and Robert Karlsson (28). Garrido, Goosen and Karlsson won tournaments.

Japan, as usual, was the domain of Masashi (Jumbo) Ozaki, the world's No. 8 ranked player, who had five victories while earning $1,420,207 for 21st place on the World Money List. Next behind Ozaki was Shigeki Maruyama, age 28, with $1,380,821 and the No. 33 ranking. Maruyama had four Japanese victories and was an early-round contender for a major title in the PGA Championship. Naomichi (Joe) Ozaki, Kenichi Kuboya, and two Americans, Brandt Jobe and Brian Watts, each won twice.

In Southern Africa and Australasia, other winners of particular note included three-time champion Craig Parry, whose most important prize was the Japan Open, between victories in the Satelindo Indonesia Open and, in the season finale at home in Australia, the Schweppes Coolum Classic. Des Terblanche won three times in Asia and South Africa, including the Volvo Asian Match Play; Mark McNulty and Desvonde Botes each won twice in

South Africa; Greg Chalmers, in the European Challenge Tour and Australasia; and Greg Turner, in Europe and Japan.

Turning now to senior golf, after winning twice and having seven runner-up finishes in 1996, Hale Irwin hit his stride this year with a record-equalling nine victories on the U.S. Senior PGA Tour. According to Irwin, the difference was patience. "I'm hitting the same shots this year as I did last year," Irwin, age 51, said in September. "It's just that last year I tried to hit them too early in the round."

Irwin's nine titles included his second consecutive PGA Seniors' Championship, which he won by 12 strokes, as he tied the Senior Tour record set by Peter Thomson in 1985.

Such were the purses in those early years that Thomson won only $386,724 for his nine titles, while Irwin became the first senior to exceed the $2 million mark. His official earnings were $2,343,364 and his worldwide total was $2,736,628, including a 10th victory in the Senior Slam. That worldwide total meant he earned more money playing golf than anyone in 1997 except for Montgomerie, Els and Love.

Senior golf has always been ruled by the younger players, and second place to Irwin went to Gil Morgan, who became eligible to play at age 50 the previous September. Morgan won six times plus the unofficial Diners Club Matches, earning $2,160,562 officially and $2,441,016 overall. He won one of the major titles, The Tradition, and beat Irwin in the season-ending Energizer Senior Tour Championship.

Five other seniors won more than $1 million officially — Isao Aoki, Jay Sigel, David Graham, John Bland and Graham Marsh — and Dave Stockton reached that mark when other earnings were add to compile our Senior World Money List.

There was a significant list of prominent players who did not win in 1997, including Jim Colbert, the leading money winner in 1995 and 1996, Jack Nicklaus, Gary Player, Lee Trevino, Raymond Floyd, Chi Chi Rodriguez, Bob Charles and Tom Weiskopf. Six seniors won for the first time: Graham, Bud Allin, Bruce Summerhays, Dana Quigley, Hugh Baiocchi and Bob Eastwood. Graham had three victories, and the two-time winners were Eastwood, Sigel and Marsh, who had an unofficial third in the Liberty Mutual Legends of Golf.

Marsh, one of the best players of his generation not to win a major championship, got a major senior title in the U.S. Senior Open. The other senior title, the Ford Senior Players Championship, was won by Larry Gilbert, who was later diagnosed with inoperable lung cancer.

It was a shocking year for medical news, from the early days of January, when Arnold Palmer had to undergo surgery for prostate cancer. He was able to return to golf in March for his Bay Hill Invitational. In the middle of the year, Colbert also underwent prostate surgery, Player had double-hernia surgery and Bruce Devlin had to have a kidney removed.

On the European Seniors Tour, Tommy Horton continued to be the star, following a four-victory season in 1996 with six more titles plus one in South Africa. Player won the Senior British Open and one other European event, as well as one in Japan. Aoki won the Japan PGA Senior Open along with one event in America.

In women's golf, it appeared that Karrie Webb, a 22-year-old Australian, and Annika Sorenstam, a 26-year-old Swede, were destined to be rivals for a long, long time. Webb won the Vare Trophy for the lowest scoring average on the U.S. LPGA Tour from Sorenstam. But Sorenstam snared two of Webb's 1996 awards, becoming Player of the Year and the leading money winner.

It was the second Player of the Year award in three years for Sorenstam, who won six tournaments but failed in her quest for a third consecutive U.S. Women's Open victory. She won $1,236,789 on the LPGA Tour and $1,460,252 worldwide, breaking the Women's World Money List record of $1,383,003 set by Laura Davies in 1996. Sorenstam also had victories in Europe and Japan for a total eight.

Webb was second in LPGA earnings with $987,606 and her worldwide total was over $1 million for the second time with $1,048,687, some $82,284 short of her 1996 figure. She won the Weetabix Women's British Open title in addition to two tournaments in America. Kelly Robbins, who had two LPGA victories, was third on both money lists, having $910,907 for her LPGA play and $964,907 worldwide.

The LPGA's major championships were won by older players. Betsy King, age 42, won the Nabisco Dinah Shore; then Chris Johnson, 39, took the McDonald's LPGA Championship; followed by Alison Nicholas, 35, in the U.S. Women's Open, and Colleen Walker, 41, in the du Maurier Classic. Nancy Lopez, 40, almost was in that group, falling short in the U.S. Women's Open while setting a tournament record with four rounds in the 60s.

Seven players won two LPGA events: Walker, Robbins, Terry-Jo Myers, Tammie Green, Chris Johnson, Michelle McGann and Liselotte Neumann. Davies had only one victory in America but won twice in Europe. Her worldwide earnings were $694,531, roughly half her 1996 total. Karen Lunn also won twice in Europe and Pernilla Sterner had two victories in Australasia.

Once again, Akiko Fukushima was the leader in Japan, and she was fourth on the Women's World Money List with $841,326. Fukushima had six victories, including the Japan LPGA Championship, and there were six two-time winners.

Before turning in detail to the year in professional golf, we recall these who passed away during 1997: Skip Alexander, 79, two-time former Ryder Cup player; Ed Furgol, 79, winner of the 1954 U.S. Open; Jay Hebert, 74, winner of the 1960 PGA Championship; Ben Hogan, 84, one of only four players to win all four major professional titles; Dave Marr, 63, international broadcaster and winner of the 1965 PGA Championship; Henry Picard, 90, winner of the 1938 Masters Tournament and 1939 PGA Championship, and one of the best players of all, the former Joyce Wethered, Lady Heathcoat-Amory, 96, winner of four British Women's Amateur titles.

3. Masters Tournament

The 1997 Masters Tournament opened with a scene unheard of in the world of golf for these past nine months — galleries swarming not to follow Tiger Woods, but to leave him.

This was more than just another glorious Masters. This was Tiger Woods' first Masters as a professional. It was a pivotal moment in golf history. Jack Nicklaus had already predicted that Woods would win more Masters than he and Arnold Palmer put together, and that figure was an intimidating 10. This was a kind of coronation by Nicklaus, and so for that, and because Woods was already a phenomenon, the galleries had been gathering by the thousands at every tournament he played since turning professional in August, 1996.

The Masters magnified the attraction. They swarmed him again by the thousands, six deep and maybe more, through every practice day, and again when the first round started. Then an amazing thing happened. They were soon turning away by the thousands. For the first time in his young career, his gallery was leaving. Woods had opened the Masters with a thud. He was playing like anything but a winner, much less someone who could win the Masters. Nicklaus might be right with his prediction. Woods indeed might win more than 10 Masters. But this certainly wasn't looking like the first one.

History, with its appetite for minutiae, may want to note that Woods began this historic Masters with a bogey. You could say he was in good company. The first hole, a par-four of 405 yards, with a big bunker on the right crest of the hill and bunkers at the green, took 29 bogeys out of the 86 starters in the first round. There were also three double bogeys, and even a triple bogey. For Woods or for anyone else, there was nothing comforting about this kind of company. He had bogeyed the hole only once before in his six previous rounds. Woods, in fact, was on his way to shooting 40 on the first nine. He was playing with Nick Faldo, who had three Masters titles to his credit, and who was the defending champion. Faldo himself was on his way to 41. The crowd was thinning fast. Before long, they would come racing back.

Woods had embarked on a course that would change golf history, and that would expand the universality of the game. From the start of this grand invitation tournament in 1934, it had always been won by whites. It had been won by a South African (Gary Player), an Englishman (Faldo), a Scot (Sandy Lyle), a German (Bernhard Langer) and two Spaniards (Seve Ballesteros and Jose Maria Olazabal). They were all white. In fact, until Lee Elder played in 1975, no black had ever even been invited.

Now came Woods, a young American of African and Asian heritage. He would be the first person of color and of other than a Caucasian background to win the Masters, and he would become the youngest ever to win, at age 21 years, three months and 14 days, succeeding Ballesteros (23 years, four days with his first victory in 1980). He was not the youngest to win a major championship. Three others were younger. John McDermott won the 1911 U.S. Open at 19 years, 10 months, 14 days; Gene Sarazen won the 1922

PGA Championship at 20 years, 22 days, and Young Tom Morris won the 1868 British Open at 17 years, five months, eight days.

Woods would shoot rounds of 70, 66, 65 and 69 for a 270 total, 18 under par, and win by 12 strokes and set or tie practically every champion's record in the books. The record total had been 271 by Nicklaus in 1965 and by Raymond Floyd in 1976. The record margins of victory had been nine strokes by Nicklaus in 1965 and eight strokes by Floyd in 1976. Twelve strokes was the largest margin in a major championship in this century and the largest ever for a major championship played over 72 holes.

In the early British Opens, played over 36 holes, Old Tom Morris won by 13 strokes in 1862 and his son, Young Tom, won by 12 strokes in 1870. The record for the U.S. Open is 11 strokes by Willie Smith in 1899, and the record for the PGA Championship is seven strokes by Nicklaus in 1980.

These were the 18 Masters records that Woods would set, as compiled by tournament historian Bill Inglish:

- Low 72-hole score: 270 (70-66-65-69), 18 under par
- Youngest champion: Age 21
- Widest margin of victory: 12 strokes
- Low score for last 54 holes: 200 (66-65-69), 16 under par
- Largest lead, first 54 holes: nine strokes
- Youngest leader, first 54 holes: Age 21
- Low score, middle 36 holes: 131 (66-65)
- Youngest leader, first 36 holes: Age 21
- Most strokes under par, second nine holes: 16 (30-32-33-33)
- Second nine in pars or better: two eagles, 12 birdies, 22 pars
- Most strokes under par, final 63 holes: 22
- Worst start by champion, first nine holes: 40, four over par
- Champion in first professional start as participant
- Most threes by champion: 26 (14 birdies, two eagles, 10 pars)
- Youngest participant to score 65: Age 21
- Youngest participant to score 66: Age 21
- Youngest participant to score 30 on second nine: Age 21
- 19 under par in 45-hole span beginning with 10th hole: (30-66-65)

These were the six Masters records that Woods would tie:

- Low score, first 54 holes: 201 (70-66-65), 15 under par
- Three rounds in the 60s: (66-65-69)
- Most threes: 26
- Most holes under par, four-round totals: 11 (eight on second nine)
- Most rounds better than field: Two (66-65)
- Best performance by champion at hole No. 11: Two under par (four-round total)

Augusta, Georgia, in April is noted for its balmy, gentle weather, but the 61st Masters Tournament opened that Thursday, April 11, on a chill, windy day that found honorary starters Sarazen, Byron Nelson and Sam Snead bundled in sweaters. The wind also created something of a controversy. Some players complained that the course had been set up in anticipation of benign weather. The greens were already hard from lack of rain, and some pins were in positions veterans said they had never seen before. The wind made the greens even harder and faster.

U.S. Amateur runner-up Steve Scott, after posting 79, said, "If it weren't for the greens out there, this course would be nothing." How tough were the greens? "Like putting down the hood of your car," he said. Said veteran John Cook, after shooting 75, "They must be planning on some weather coming in here soon. If we don't get any weather tomorrow in this place, you guys are going to be laughing at us. I'm already laughing."

Before long, the atmosphere warmed to Masters temperatures on a miracle eagle by John Huston, a breathtaking turnaround by Woods and a surge by the unlikely Paul Stankowski, one of the most light-hearted golfers to come along for years.

Huston had the last laugh on Augusta National Golf Club that first day, thanks to a stunning eagle at the 18th hole that gave him the first-round lead on a five-under-par 67. He had jumped by one stroke over Stankowski, who had an eagle of his own, but a routine one. Stankowski got his at the par-five No. 8, on in two, one putt. Huston got his the hard and accidental way. The 18th, an uphill par-four hole of 405 yards, is a dogleg to the right. Golfers try to thread their tee shots through the slot. Too far to the left, and you may end up in one of the fairway bunkers at the elbow, as Sandy Lyle did, setting up his winning birdie in 1988. Too far to the right and you catch the trees, which many have done.

But who can remember the last one to put his ball where Huston did? He "overcut" his tee shot, and it got away from him to the right. It knocked around in the trees, and glanced farther to the right, and out almost into the 10th fairway behind. He had just turned the dogleg right into a dogleg left. His lie, of course, was good, there being no rough at Augusta National. Huston had 190 yards to a flag he couldn't see from behind a tree up ahead. But he did have a clear shot. He hit his five iron. The ball homed right in on the hole. He couldn't see it, but he could hear it from the thunderous gallery.

The shot came too early in the round, and too early in the tournament, to rank with other dramatic Masters shots, such as Sarazen's double eagle at the 15th in the final round in 1935, or Larry Mize's chip-in at the 11th to beat Greg Norman in a playoff in 1987. But it sure looked good on Huston's card. His best finish in the Masters was a tie for third place in his first, in 1990, and he had at least had one round in the books toward another good finish.

The fairway eagle wasn't his only break in the round. He got a big one at the par-five 15th, with its close-cropped banks around the pond in front of the green. His approach shot cleared the pond, but was starting to trickle back down the bank, heading for doom. Then it stopped about three feet above the water, much like Olazabal's approach shot when he went on to beat Tom Lehman in 1994. Huston birdied from there, and then the eagle at the 18th gave him a back-nine 31. No question, he said. It was one of his luckiest rounds ever.

"But I feel I had it coming," he said, thinking back on missing the cut five times in nine starts so far this season. "This year hasn't been too kind to me."

A lot of players did not feel the warm smile of Lady Luck, which helps explain why the 86-man field averaged a stunning 76.09 against a par of 72. But it didn't threaten the record 77.32 set in 1982. There was a landslide of 13 scores in the 80s, and only six of those were by former champions not in their prime. Seven were by players who might be challenging.

There was Loren Roberts, for one. He's nicknamed the "Boss of the Moss" for his proficiency with the putter, but he gave almost all of it back on Augusta National's greens. He had a staggering 40 putts for the day. He had a four-putt green and four three-putts. His woes began at No. 1, where his second shot rolled over the green and down a slope. Putting from the slope, he rolled the ball 30 feet past the hole. On the green, his first putt went two feet past, and his comeback lipped out and ended up four feet away on the other side. When he finished, he had used his putter four times and suffered a triple-bogey seven.

"I was kind of shellshocked," Roberts said.

Slippery greens? At the par-three 16th, Roberts' tee shot hit the green, but trickled 45 feet from the pin. His first putt got within five feet of the hole, then turned and slowly rolled away, stopping 25 feet from the hole. It took him two more to get down. Another bogey. "I just had one of those bad days," Roberts said, "and this is not the place to have a bad day."

Roberts certainly wasn't alone. Ken Green, playing in his first Masters in six years, got blistered on the greens with six three-putts, one four-putt and even one five-putt. He shot 87, second-worst only to the 89 posted by Arnold Palmer, who still hadn't fully recovered from prostate cancer surgery earlier in the year. "It was one of the most embarrassing days in my life," Green said. "From the sense that I wasn't scared or nervous, I was trying. But it was so unbelievable."

David Duval, playing in his second Masters, found his trouble packed into two holes. After a birdie at the 10th, he was one under par coming to the celebrated par-three 12th, and there he got stung for a double-bogey five. Then he got crushed by the par-five 15th. He was playing it in the classical way, with a drive and a prudent lay-up. All was calm. He was comfortably short of the pond, 64 yards from the green. Then he was just a tad short with his wedge, and hit the bank. He didn't have Huston's luck. The ball didn't stick on the bank. It trickled back down into the water.

He walked back 16 yards for his drop — to get to 80 yards, his favorite sand wedge distance — but then duplicated the error. The shot was short, and the ball hit the bank and rolled back into the water. He dropped again, and this time got to the green. He two-putted for a nine. He was baffled. "Eighty yards is a good distance for my sand wedge, but I caught that one fat, too," Duval said. "It's one thing to do it once, but it's inexcusable to do it again." He paid with 78, his worst Masters score.

Duval was just one of many victims of Augusta's par-fives. Ed Fiori, playing in his fifth Masters and on his way to his fourth straight missed cut, was even-par coming to No. 8, and made a triple-bogey eight. Then he double-bogeyed the 15th and shot 78. Norman, the marked man who blew the six-stroke lead the year before, made a double bogey at the 15th in his 77. Ballesteros, a two-time Masters champion, made eight there in shooting 81.

"That's by far the toughest I've ever seen the course play without strong wind or unusual conditions," said former U.S. Open champion Lee Janzen, after a three-birdie, three-bogey, par 72.

The statistics sheet was gloomy. Only three players broke 70, only four others broke the par of 72. Ten matched par, and 69 were over par, including the 13 at 80 and more.

At about noon, Paul Azinger, who has never won the Masters, took the lead with 69. It was his best start in 10 visits. The pivotal point of his round, he said, was a par at the par-three No. 6, which went on to play the fourth hardest hole of the day.

"They should put that pin a little farther back," Azinger said, meaning that there was little room for the ball. His playing partner, Tom Kite, had an uphill putt, and the ball came back down to him. He bogeyed. Azinger was worse off. His tee shot ended 25 feet from the hole, and his first putt went 25 feet past. Now he was looking at a dangerous return putt that could go back down the hill, but he dropped it for a saving par. "That," Azinger said, "was the key."

Then came Stankowski, who missed the cut in his only other Masters, the year before. He bogeyed No. 4, then got the eagle at No. 8 on a drive, a three-wood shot to 12 feet, the putt. The fireworks came on the second nine. He made birdies at the 11th and 13th holes, a bogey at the 14th, then a birdie-birdie finish that only one other player, Sweden's Jesper Parnevik, could boast. Stankowski put a pitching wedge to 10 feet at the 17th, and an eight-iron shot to four feet at the 18th for his 68.

No one could question his ability, but his desire was suspect, as his preparation showed. "I went fishing last week," Stankowski said. "Kind of a bonehead plan, because I came out here stale." Even so, he had the lead with 68, and was grateful. "I've been blessed," he said. "A year ago I'm playing the Nike Tour in New Orleans, and then I win in Atlanta. If you guys," he said to the media, "can remind me this is just a game, that will help me for the rest of the week."

Before long, the attention would shift back to Woods, but only after he came through that first nine. At the first hole, he had the crowd ooohing when he out-drove Faldo by some 70 yards. Unfortunately, Woods ended up in a bunker and behind a tree on the left. He punched the ball out, and caught a greenside bunker, and bogeyed from there. He was on his way to a four-over-par 40. Faldo was in the same boat. A repeat championship started to drift away early. He was out in 41 and couldn't make up the ground. He shot 75.

"I couldn't keep the ball in the fairway," Woods said. "I knew what I was doing wrong, but I couldn't stop it. I was pretty hot at the way I was playing." He would compound the bogey at No. 1 with bogeys at Nos. 4, 8 and 9 for the no-birdie 40.

Woods was coming back too far on his backswing. "It's long for me," he said. "If I get to parallel, then I'm way too long. I need to stay a lot shorter, a lot wider. From there, I can just zip the club through and take advantage of the speed of my golf swing. I can't do that when I'm long."

He solved the problem, and then some, and the gallery came rushing back. He exploded coming home for 30, just one stroke short of the second-nine record 29 set by Mark Calcavecchia in 1992.

What a dramatic turnaround. Remember, Woods had just bogeyed the eighth and ninth holes, and now he faced the tough, downhill 10th, a brute of a par-four at 485 yards. Woods hit it with a two iron and an eight iron, and sank a 15-foot putt for a birdie. At the 12th, both he and Faldo missed the green, and both chipped in for birdies. Woods bumped a nine-iron shot some 40 feet, and Faldo putted in from 30 feet.

Then at the 13th, Woods hit a driver, six iron, and had two putts for a birdie. He saved par at the 14th with a chip to 10 feet, then eagled the 15th with a stupendous driver and a wedge shot 151 yards to four feet from the hole. He closed the streak with a birdie at the 17th, hitting a wedge shot to 12 feet. A par at the 18th made it a 40-30–70 day and put him in fourth place, just three shots out of the lead. It was the first time in six Masters rounds that he had broken par.

Looking back, it might have been a bogey that set up Woods' round. It came at No. 8. He drove into the trees on the left. His ball rested on pine straw. "I didn't really have a whole lot of options," he said. "When I looked at it initially, I thought I could go through the trees on the lefthand side. Then I saw a little gap when I looked a little more right. I took the chance and tried to go through this gap, and it went right through."

He punched out, then hit a four iron over the green, and finally got down for his six. It could have been a lot worse. He bogeyed the ninth, and then fixed what he was doing wrong. "I was just playing real defensive golf," he said, "and that's not exactly what you want to do when you're struggling. It was a tough day initially, but I got through it."

The first-round leaderboard:

John Huston	67
Paul Stankowski	68
Paul Azinger	69
Tiger Woods	70
Jose Maria Olazabal	71
Costantino Rocca	71
Nick Price	71

The Masters had opened with two major questions. Could Faldo repeat and chalk up his fourth Masters? Could Norman rebound from the devastation of blowing a six-stroke lead in the final round the year before? Both answers were no. In an astonishing development, neither even made the 36-hole cut. When the cut came in at 150, both the 1996 champion and runner-up were gone.

Norman shot 77-74–151. Three straight bogeys from the 15th hole in the second round did him in. Faldo wasn't even close. He shot 75-81–156. This was his 14th Masters, his first missed cut. Faldo, playing the PGA Tour full time, won the Nissan Open four starts earlier, and was tied for 40th, 59th and 24th in his three outings since. He may not have been playing like Nick Faldo, but an 81?

Faldo started the second round with a double bogey, then two bogeys, and then suffered a nine at the 15th. He had practically nothing to say. "I'm shellshocked," he said. "No, I'm sorry. I'm flabbergasted." What had happened to his game? Here's one possibility. In winning the 1996 Masters, he averaged 29 putts per round. Here, he averaged 34.5 for his two rounds.

Then there was the shock of Norman. He was lackluster in his three U.S.

tournaments so far in 1997, finishing tied for ninth, 53rd and 22nd. Maybe the collapse in the 1996 Masters was still preying on his mind. He said no. "I wasn't nervous," Norman said. "I tried to play my game. I didn't change anything."

They were merely the most prominent players to miss the cut. The casualty list contained some other names generally found among the contenders: Duval, Phil Mickelson, Brad Faxon, Jeff Maggert and 1996 U.S. Open champion Steve Jones. Said Jones, winner of the Phoenix Open in January and Tucson Chrysler Classic runner-up in February, "I was aggressive, I was defensive, and then I was gone. This is the most disappointed I've been in my career. Nothing is going right."

Things went wrong in a big way for Huston, the first-round leader. He made 77 the hard way. He was out in 37, which didn't really hurt him, but then he crashed to an awful 10 at the par-five 13th hole. It was the fifth-highest score there in Masters history. Huston was four under par for the tournament coming to the 13th. He laid up with his second shot, then plunked his third into the creek in front of the green.

In almost a repeat of Duval's stumble at the 15th the day before, Huston opted to move from his original spot for his drop, and he chose the adjacent 14th tee. Then he pitched two more shots into the creek. He eventually got on the green, and two-putted for his 10. Rattled, he bogeyed the 14th, then pulled himself together and birdied the 16th and 18th (the hole he had eagled the day before). As for the 10, he took it philosophically, saying, "All I can say is, it's pretty embarrassing. I mean, if you're afraid to embarrass yourself, then I guess you're at the wrong tournament."

Augusta National's par-fives had reverted to their soft-touch status, particularly the 13th and the 15th holes. They took an awful beating from the 46 players who made the cut. It was easier to count the pars on those two holes, seven at the 13th, 15 at the 15th. It took disasters to remind everyone how dangerous they could be. Huston's 10, for example. And Vijay Singh made eight at the 13th, and it nearly cost him the cut. He just made it at 74–149. Then there was Faldo with his nine at the 13th.

The 13th hole was where this Masters turned around. Woods was four under par and tied for the lead with Colin Montgomerie when he reached the 13th tee. He hit a three wood off the tee and an eight iron from 170 yards to 20 feet past the hole. He made the putt for an eagle.

Woods started his move in the second round with an odd birdie at No. 2. "Missed the green and flubbed my chip shot," he said. Then he chipped in from 12 feet It was the start of a brilliant day on the par-fives. He would play those holes in five under par. At No. 8, he two-putted from 30 feet for a birdie, and after the eagle at the 13th, he birdied the 15th on two putts from eight feet. He bogeyed the tough par-four No. 3 when he missed the green, then two-putted from six feet. At No. 5, also a tough par-four, he lofted a sand wedge to two feet and made that for a birdie. The birdie at No. 8 had him out in 34. He parred his way to the mid-stretch burst on the back — the eagle at the 13th, followed by two birdies, a tap-in at the 14th and the two-putt at the 15th. He came home in 32 for 66.

Woods was at 136, eight under par for the tournament and leading Montgomerie by three strokes. Italy's Costantino Rocca was third at 67–140, and three were tied at 141 — Jeff Sluman, whose 67 included an eagle at No.

2; 1992 champion Fred Couples, with a three-bogey 69, and 1994 champion Olazabal (70), who had missed 18 months, including the 1996 Masters, because of severe foot problems.

If Woods' head was spinning at the thought of leading the Masters after 36 holes, it didn't show. "I'm in the lead, which is nice," he said. "But it's only the halfway point. I've got to shoot a good number tomorrow and put myself in position where I'm in good shape for Sunday. There are so many guys to beat. It's supposed to rain, and the course will play easier, and they'll attack the pins. The greens won't be so scary."

While Woods was grabbing the spotlight, there was a lot of golf going on in the second round. Take Nicklaus, for example. The owner of a record six Masters titles, he set another record. When he made the cut, that meant the fourth round Sunday would be his 147th round in the Masters, breaking Sam Snead's record of 146. Nicklaus was in danger after shooting 77 in the first round, but he made the cut with room to spare with 70 in the second round for a 147 total. He did it in heroic fashion. His status was still in doubt coming down the stretch. He needed to make some birdies.

He started at the par-four 14th. He holed a six-foot putt for the birdie. Hard to believe, but this was his first one-putt green of the tournament. Then he came to the 15th, and there he faced a 25-footer. Son Jackie, his caddie, picked this moment to remind him that he had promised son Steve a 70 for a 34th birthday present. The 70 was very much in doubt, but Nicklaus holed the 25-footer for an eagle. After two par-saving putts at the 16th and 17th, he faced another 25-footer at the 18th. Jackie reminded him that he needed this one for Steve's 70. Nicklaus got it.

Nicklaus played alongside Norman and was unhappy for him. By his observation, Norman was doing what he said he did, trying his best. Then he hit his approach shot to the green at the 15th hole — a good shot, Nicklaus said — and the wind shifted at that instant and the ball rolled back into the water, costing him a bogey. "He didn't want to play after that, it appeared," Nicklaus said. Norman bogeyed the next two holes as well.

But the principal subject was Woods, his game, and his lead. Everyone agreed he was excellent, but no one was conceding anything.

"This tournament is far from over," said Stankowski, after 74 left him at 142, tied for seventh place and six shots behind Woods. "Tiger's got a three-shot lead over Colin Montgomerie, but it doesn't matter. It's Augusta, and anything can happen on the PGA Tour. I don't know if he's comfortable with his lead, but we saw what happened last year. There is no lead too big here."

"Nobody runs away here," said Paul Azinger, who played with Woods and fell six strokes behind with his 73–142 total. "But I wouldn't put it past him. You don't know what the pressure will do, and this course has a history of doing some funny things. But I think he'll be hard to beat. He's really good."

The final word came down to Montgomerie, No. 1 in Europe, for whom a victory in America — and a victory in any of the four majors — has become something like the quest for the Holy Grail. Here he was, right up there again. He shot 67, his best score in six Masters, and was in second place at 139, three behind Woods. He had played some dazzling iron shots. He birdied No. 2 from six feet, chipped in at No. 6, and birdied No. 7 from eight feet. He birdied the 10th from 20 feet, and the 11th from 18 inches. The par-three holes on the second nine hurt him, however. He three-putted both for his only bogeys. Then came the big question.

"Can I win?" Montgomerie said. "It depends on how Mr. Woods fares. The way he plays this course tends to suit him more than anyone else playing right now. If he decides to do what he's doing, well, more credit to him. We'll all shake his hand and say well done. But at the same time, there's more to it than hitting the ball a long way. The pressure's mounting, more and more."

The second-round leaderboard:

Tiger Woods	66 - 136	
Colin Montgomerie	67 - 139	
Costantino Rocca	69 - 140	
Jeff Sluman	67 - 141	
Fred Couples	69 - 141	
Jose Maria Olazabal	70 - 141	

If there was one way to sum up this Masters, it was Montgomerie's unabashed statement after the third round. Keeping in mind, of course, that some in the media thought after the second round that Montgomerie was itching to get a crack at Woods. Montgomerie came into Augusta National's interview room, and took his seat at the table beside Dan Yates, the interview moderator. The episode said more than all the analysis in the world.

"Just a few brief questions, because Tiger's waiting in the wings," Yates said. "Who wants to know what?"

Before anyone could offer a question, Montgomerie leaned into the microphone.

"All I have to say is one brief comment today," Montgomerie said. "There is no chance. We're all human beings here. There's no way does Tiger Woods not win tomorrow."

"What makes you say that," came a voice from the media.

Montgomerie stared at the man. "Did you just arrive?" he asked, with an inflection of disbelief. "Have you been on holiday?"

The man reminded Montgomerie that a year ago, Greg Norman blew a six-shot lead in the final round and that Nick Faldo picked up that surrendered green jacket.

"This is different — very different," Montgomerie said. "Costantino Rocca is not Nick Faldo and Tiger Woods is not Greg Norman."

Woods heard of this a little later, this combination of praise for him and a harpoon for the Shark, and just shrugged. "Just kind words," Woods said. "Obviously bold statements. But the tournament's not over yet."

There were those who would disagree.

"Everybody might as well go home," Nicklaus said.

What brought about all this was Woods' performance in the third round. He polished off a no-bogey 65, for a 15-under-par total of 201. That was nine strokes better than the man in second place, Rocca, the good-natured Italian. Rocca shot 70 and was at six-under 210. Stankowski was third at 69–211, and Tom Watson, a two-time winner, calmed his putting problems for 69 to tie with Kite (66) at 212. Montgomerie, who was paired with Woods, strained to keep up but could only manage 74 and slip 12 strokes behind at 213.

Woods, in his third Masters, his first as a professional, was — as they say — blowing away the field. He started the day with a three-stroke lead over Montgomerie and ended with a nine-stroke lead over Rocca, and in between, wrote one reporter, "he was so casual you expected him to stop for a burger and fries at the turn."

The question was on the point. Tiger, the reporter said, are you as comfortable out there as you've ever been in any competition?

"I'll have to say yes," Woods said, "because when you're thinking well and playing well at the same time, you're going to feel a little comfortable. And that's exactly what's happening right now. I feel comfortable off the tee. When that's the case out here, I'm going to have wedges into some of these holes. "I came in here playing really well, and it didn't show for the first nine holes on Thursday. But it finally clicked in, and I've been playing basically the way I've been playing all last week at home."

A performance like this, at Augusta, does it amaze you?

"Not really," Woods said. "To be honest with you, if I drive the ball like I'm doing now — I mean, look at the irons I'm using. With that in mind, I can be aggressive. I can spin the ball, hold my distances a lot — I'll say a little easier than the guys who hit seven irons in at some of these par-fours. That's a great advantage. And right now I'm capitalizing on my advantage."

It spelled a direct threat to Nicklaus' and Floyd's record of 17-under-par 271. All Woods needed in the final round was a two-under-par 70 to tie, 69 to break the record. The way he was playing, the record was within reach.

"My record's held up for 32 years," Nicklaus said. "Raymond's held up for 21 years. Tiger has a good shot at it now, and the golf course is a lot tougher than it was then." How would a 21-year-old react in the final round, faced not only with the chance to win the Masters but also break the record? "He could play terribly tomorrow," Nicklaus said, "and still not shoot a bad score." Nicklaus noted that Woods' ability to overpower Augusta was the key factor.

Woods' advantage was immense At the par-five second, for an excellent example — and it's a 555-yard downhill hole — he hit driver and a nine iron over the green. He chipped back to one foot and tapped in for his first birdie. At the par-four fifth, one of the course's toughest holes, a 435-yarder, he hit driver off the tee, then a pitching wedge to 15 feet and made that putt.

He didn't need his driver at the 360-yard No. 7. He hit his two iron off the tee, then a sand wedge to 12 feet for his third birdie. The fourth came at the par-five eighth, the 535-yard uphill hole. A driver and a two iron put him on the front third of the green, just 18 feet from the hole. He two-putted for the birdie, his fourth on the first nine, and he made the turn in 32.

It took accuracy as much as length, and Augusta National's wide-open fairways, free of rough, were the perfect targets. At the dangerous, downhill 11th hole, 455 yards, he positioned his drive perfectly, then hit a nine iron to eight feet and dropped the putt for another birdie. The par-five 13th escaped him for the first and last time. He made only a par there. He got the 15th again, and again impressively.

Long ago, in 1935, Sarazen hit a driver and a four wood on this hole. That was his famous double eagle. The average-length professional of today hits driver and then a lay-up shot. A big hitter will go with a driver and a long iron, some with a medium iron. Woods was hitting a driver and wedge shot.

Not this time, though. He had hit his driver down the left side. "I was a little blocked out by the tree," he said, "so I had to start the ball at the bunker, then turn it back." Meaning he had to hit a hook, and he used a six iron. He put it on the green, 35 feet from the hole, and two-putted for the birdie.

At the 18th, a 405-yard uphill hole, he hit a driver, and came into the hole with a breathtaking shot — a sand wedge from 109 yards that stopped a foot from the hole.

But power and accuracy were only part of his game.

"I appreciate that he hit long and straight, and I appreciate that his iron shots were very accurate," Montgomerie said, marvelling. "I did not appreciate how he putted." As for his own game, Montgomerie said, "It doesn't really take much talking about today, really. It was quite poor. I played the par-fives badly." Badly was right. Montgomerie bogeyed both on the first nine, and only parred the two on the second nine. Woods played those holes in three birdies and a par. That's a net gain of five shots on the par-fives.

Rocca, on the other hand, had what had to be one of the wildest 70s ever in the Masters. He had a par-birdie start, then blew sky-high. He double-bogeyed No. 3 and bogeyed the fourth and fifth, birdied the seventh, bogeyed the eighth, and bogeyed the 10th. He was four over par through the 10th. Then he blazed home in six under par. He birdied the 11th and 12th, eagled the 13th with a 20-foot putt, and birdied the 14th for a five-under-par run through four holes. He put a seven-iron shot to 15 feet at the 18th, and birdied for the 70 and second place. This was a 19th hole story if there ever was one.

"What do you want, birdies and bogeys, eagles?" Dan Yates asked the media.

"Pars will go quicker," Rocca said.

The question for Woods was academic at this point — would he have a number in mind, a goal, for Sunday's final round? "Whether I shoot 69, 62 or 72, it really doesn't matter," Woods said. "The only thing I want is a green jacket in my closet. Winning the Masters would mean a lot to me, for a number of reasons. I would be the youngest, and that means no one else has ever accomplished that. More importantly, in my estimation, it would open up a lot of doors and opportunities for others who never thought of playing the game. It's going to do a lot for the game as far as minority golf is concerned."

Did the challengers really stand a chance, with Woods leading by nine?

Kite, ever the gutsy competitor, was conceding nothing, "Last year, we gave this tournament away Saturday night," he said. "I promise you that Nick Faldo is not going to award that green jacket tonight."

Rocca knew Woods' figures as well as anyone. Woods had started with 40 on the first nine on Thursday. Here he was, Saturday evening, 19 under par over the last 45 holes. Rocca figured he had a chance. "I can win maybe if I play nine holes, and under par, too," he said.

Stankowski also wasn't conceding. He said he might be able to catch Woods if he could just get off to a quick start in the final round. "If I can made five, six, seven birdies early," he said, with a grin. "Like in the first three holes ..."

The third-round leaderboard:

Tiger Woods	65 - 201	Tom Kite	66 - 212
Costantino Rocca	70 - 210	Jeff Sluman	72 - 213
Paul Stankowski	69 - 211	Colin Montgomerie	74 - 213
Tom Watson	69 - 212		

Nicklaus was trying to find a way to describe Woods and borrowed from what an earlier champion once said about him. "It's a shame Bob Jones isn't here," Nicklaus said. "He could have saved the words he used for me in 1963 for this young man, because he's certainly playing a game with which we're not familiar."

What was left to this Masters? Kite, who has done everything but win in his 24 Masters, made his mark again. Now age 47, he closed with 70 and finished second for the third time, and registered his ninth top-five finish, his 12th top-10 finish, and this after missing the cut in three of his last four Masters. Even in second place, he was 12 shots behind Woods.

Tommy Tolles, the Floridian who had fled to the quaintness of a small mountain town in North Carolina, tied the day's best, 67, and rose to third place, a memorable achievement for a man in his first Masters. He had this assessment of Woods, "He's in a different league than I am. This is a tournament he can probably win for the next 20 years if he is on his game."

Rocca shot his worst round, 75, and slipped to a tie for fifth place with Stankowski (74), who said he had figured out what to do in the Tiger Woods era. Said Stankowski, who is age 27, "When I get on the Senior Tour, I'm going to have six years out there before Tiger Woods is there."

Then there was the crash of Ben Crenshaw. He suffered an 11 at the 15th hole and shot 80. Interestingly enough, it wasn't the all-time Masters worst for the often mercurial Crenshaw. He merely tied his all-time worst. He had shot 80 in 1979 and another in 1982. This 80 dropped him to 45th place, one position over Frank Nobilo, who closed with 81 and finished 46th and last.

Kite came out a winner in a way. He was captain of the U.S. Ryder Cup team, and he badly wanted this prodigy on his team. He finished his round 10 minutes before Woods, and waited at the 18th. "I obviously wanted to see him finish," Kite said, "and also to congratulate him on making the Ryder Cup team. Certainly, I'm pleased to have him on the team."

That pretty much was Sunday at the Masters, a tidbit here, a tidbit there as Woods turned the fourth round into a mere formality. This one was over. It would have taken a catastrophe to get this one out of Woods' hands. Still, it could happen. See John Huston, taking 10 in the second round. Take Crenshaw, taking 11 in this round. See Nick Faldo shooting 81. It needn't take bad golf, necessarily. A couple of bad breaks would do the trick. Or even letting one's mind wander to the scoring record just within reach. Was he ever so comfortable with his huge lead that that's what he was thinking about?

"No," Woods said. "I knew I had to get through the Amen Corner with par at the worst. I couldn't afford to let up on my concentration or anything. All you have to do is put your ball in the water at 11 or 12, and there it goes. "After I got by what I would say are the water holes on the last nine, after I hit the tee shot at 16 — even though I screwed up and hit it to the right — I knew it was pretty much over. Because I knew I could bogey in. Those water holes, you know, can creep up and hurt you in a heartbeat."

Masters historian Bill Inglish provided a numerical portrait of the new champion. First, what little trouble Woods had came on Augusta's first nine. He made only seven bogeys in the entire tournament, and all of them were on the first nine. He did not bogey any hole more than once. Four of the bogeys came in that first-round 40. Overall, he made nine birdies on the first nine, playing it at an average of 35.5 — a half-stroke under par. He played the second nine in an average of four-under-par 32, logging two eagles and 12 birdies. He breezed through the dreaded Amen Corner — the 11th, 12th and 13th holes — in an eagle and five birdies, seven under par. He played Augusta National's par-five holes in 13 under par. He bogeyed only once at No. 8 in the first round, and he had 10 birdies and two eagles (13th and 15th). Some final tidbits for the statistical buffs: He hit 55 of 72 greens (76.39 percent), 47 of 56 fairways (83.93 percent), was 0-for-3 in sand saves, used 117 putts (1.63 per hole), and drove the ball an average of 323.13 yards.

Woods painted the rest of the picture on the course.

Woods began the final round, his triumphal march, with a birdie at No. 2, his third in the four rounds. It was with a driver and eight iron this time, and a chip to eight feet to go to 16 under par. Coming to No. 5, he hadn't bogeyed since No. 3 in the second round, 37 holes without a bogey. Now he got two quick bogeys. At No. 5, he hit a wedge over the green to the back bunker. He came out to 12 feet and two-putted. And at the 360-yard No. 7, he hit a three iron into the left trees. He punched out with an eight iron, but into a bunker, and came out to eight feet and two-putted. So much for the damage.

Woods went back to 15 under par with a sparkling birdie out of bogey territory at the par-five No. 8. Off a perfect drive, he pulled a four-iron shot into the trees on the left. He was still 35 yards from the pin, with a big mound in the way. He bumped his way over it with a brilliant eight iron to within two feet of the hole. He was back to 15 under.

He got to 16 under par with his second straight birdie at the 11th, this one off a drive and a wedge to 20 feet. At the par-five 13th, he put a six-iron shot to 15 feet and two-putted for the birdie that got him to 17 under, tying the Nicklaus-Floyd record. He needed one more birdie to break the record, and he got it on the next hole, the 14th, hitting a three wood, then a sand wedge to eight feet. He was 18 under par, and he parred home with the record. The record — that was the only question. The victory was a foregone conclusion, especially after he cleared the dangerous Amen Corner in two under.

At the 18th, Woods sank a four-footer for par, his 69, the 270 total, and the record. Then he made straight for the man who began teaching him this game when he was just a tyke, his father, Earl. He wrapped him up in a big, quiet hug. And he remembered his dad's words Saturday night, as they contemplated the historic finale.

"Son," Earl Woods said, "this will probably be one of the toughest rounds of golf you've ever had to play in your life. Just go out there and be yourself, and it will be one of the most rewarding rounds you've ever played in your life."

"He was right," the son said, "because I had to deal with a lot of different thoughts and emotions that were going through my head."

Others were going through it with him. There was Lee Elder, for one, the first black ever invited to play in the Masters. His invitation, in 1975, ended a long and acrimonious episode in which the late Clifford Roberts, co-founder and chairman of the tournament, contended that it wasn't race, but a lack of qualifications that kept Elder away from Magnolia Lane.

Elder had not planned on attending this Masters, but changed his mind when Woods took that nine-stroke lead in the third round. He and his wife, Rose, drove from their home in Pompano Beach, Florida. Elder followed Woods much of the way, then went to the clubhouse to watch him on television, then returned and was in the gallery as the young champion made his way up the 18th fairway. Elder was crying.

"He's been making me cry more and more," Elder said. "I made history here, and I came back to see more history made today. To have a black champion of a major is something that makes my heart feel very, very good. Tiger winning here, it could have more potential than Jackie Robinson breaking baseball's color barrier. No one will turn their head when a black man walks to the first tee."

Elder was the first black to play at Augusta, and was followed by Jim Thorpe, Calvin Peete and now Woods. Charlie Sifford, prominent black golfer of a generation ago, had accused Roberts of twisting the invitation rules to keep him out.

"I'm glad it's over with," said Sifford, who was reached by the media at his home at Kingwood, Texas. "I took a lot of knocks when I started talking about the Masters. It's all over with now. Lee Elder played, and now Tiger has won it. I'm proud of them both."

Woods was proud of them, and all the black golfers who had gone before him. "I wasn't the pioneer," Woods said. "Charlie Sifford, Lee Elder, Ted Rhodes — those are the guys who paved the way. All night I was thinking about them, what they've done for me and the game of golf. Coming up 18, I said a little prayer of thanks to those guys. Those guys are the ones who did it."

4. U.S. Open Championship

Partway through the Masters Tournament's third round, when Tiger Woods was making a shambles of the opposition, the thought occurred to me, as I'm sure it did to many others, that if anyone were ever to win the Masters, the U.S. and British Opens and the PGA Championship in the same season, it could be this man this year. His next step towards the Grand Slam would be the U.S. Open, at Congressional Country Club in Bethesda, Maryland, a suburb of Washington, D.C.

Of course he didn't win. His mistakes and some bad luck cost him more strokes than he should have taken, and Ernie Els, not Tiger Woods, became the champion. Woods shot 286 and tied for 19th place. Over a difficult course with vicious rough compounding its excessive length, Els shot rounds of 71, 67, 69 and 69 for a 276 total to beat Colin Montgomerie by one stroke and Tom Lehman by two. Jeff Maggert held on until a mis-hit drive led to a bogey on the 16th.

Finishing 10 strokes behind the winner of the U.S. Open is no disgrace. At least Woods played all four rounds. Nick Faldo and Greg Norman didn't. After playing-off for the 1996 Masters, they missed the cut in the 1997 Open. Norman had missed in the Masters as well.

No matter that Woods had fallen too far behind to have any reasonable hope of catching the leaders Sunday afternoon, he drew his usual large and enthusiastic gallery. As his fans followed after him, racing to find good views, he shot 72, completing what would have been a first-class performance for any other first-year professional but disappointing to him.

So much has been expected of him — indeed he had accomplished so much — that anything less than winning, or at least challenging until the very end, seemed a letdown.

There can be no dispute that he had been the biggest attraction in golf in a generation. He had drawn a following of new fans, a great many young and a great many unschooled in the decorum of watching golf. They yelled and raced after him, occasionally upsetting other players. Davis Love III compared them to football and baseball fans, and he didn't like it. Nevertheless, he would have to deal with it because the fans weren't going away unless Woods faded into the U.S. Open rough.

In the era of Tigermania, inquiring minds wanted to know, so the U.S. Golf Association staged a press conference for Woods on Tuesday, two days before the Open was to begin. It was a scene that had been repeated at every tournament Woods had played since becoming a professional. Staged in the mammoth interview segment of the press facility — actually the club's indoor tennis courts — it drew amazing coverage, which was no surprise. Woods had come to the interview straight from a practice round. As he stepped onto the first tee, his fans encircled the hole and stood seven- and eight-deep along the gallery ropes. Then he went directly to the press interview. It was standing room only, a condition once reserved for champions — and now for Tiger every Tuesday afternoon.

To begin with, the USGA had approved 1,100 applications for press credentials, about 300 more than usual. When Woods showed up, all the 280 seats in the interview room were filled, and an overflow stood behind the chairs and along the walls. Those who were there estimated 350 reporters, columnists and radio and television commentators were in the room. On a raised platform at the back of the room, 33 television cameras beamed the event to local stations and the networks.

The mass interview began at 1 o'clock and lasted until 1:45. CNN interrupted its normal programming, and along with the Golf Channel showed the whole 45 minutes. ESPN had planned to show the complete spectacle but somehow couldn't arrange connections in time.

Throughout his interview, Woods answered questions ranging from what was the longest iron he had hit into any of Congressional's greens to how can he agree to play at a club (Lochinvar, in Houston) that has no women members. He fielded the first question precisely and the second deftly. He had hit nothing longer than a three iron into any green, including the 15th, a par-five of 583 yards (no one thought to ask if he meant the 607-yard ninth as well). As for Lochinvar, where he went to work on his swing with Butch Harmon, the club's professional, he answered quite rightly that he can't champion every cause.

When the interview ended, Woods walked out through a gauntlet of security guards. Because the tennis courts were so far from the clubhouse, cars brought the players to the building and back to the clubhouse. As Woods left, seven other television cameras and a number of still photographers shot him climbing into the car.

Earlier in the day only 40 reporters had sat for an interview with Steve Jones, the defending champion. Then Justin Leonard appeared an hour or so after Woods had left. Even though Leonard had won the Kemper Open the previous week, only seven reporters waited for him, a turnout so low that USGA people approached other writers and asked them to sit in to avoid embarrassing Leonard.

Woods had played in two previous Opens as an amateur without distinguishing himself. He had withdrawn because of an injured wrist partway through the second round at Shinnecock Hills in 1995, and he had played poorly in the first round at Oakland Hills in 1996 after reaching the 14th tee three under par. He tied for 82nd place. Corey Pavin had won at Shinnecock with 280 and Jones had shot 278 at Oakland Hills.

Oakland Hills had held six Opens by then, and 1995's had been the second at Shinnecock within nine years. The players were fairly familiar with those two. Congressional was another matter. The Open hadn't come back since 1964, and even though the Kemper Open had been played at Congressional from 1980 through 1986, no one knew quite what to expect. Between the last Kemper Open and the 1995 U.S. Senior Open, the golf course had been rebuilt.

Responding to the tremendous distance the modern golfer of championship quality hits the ball, Rees Jones added new tees that lengthened Congressional to 7,213 yards, the longest Open course ever and probably the longest of any of the four major championships. Nothing unusual in that, though; when Trent stretched Congressional to 7,053 yards in 1964 he created the longest Open course ever, and a year later he lengthened Bellerive in St. Louis to 7,191 yards.

As Jones rebuilt it, he made Congressional into a first-class test of golf for players of Open caliber. With five of its 12 par-four holes measuring 450 yards or more, its two par-fives stretching 607 and 583 yards, and the second, a par-three, reaching 235 yards, Congressional demanded the best of everyone. The sixth and the 10th, two of its lengthiest par-fours were actually three-shot holes for members, but the tees were moved up to bring the greens within reach of iron-shot approaches. Even so, the sixth measured 475 yards to a green set behind a pond bordered by a rocky bulwark, and the 10th measured 466 yards and ran beside a narrow creek that blossomed into another pond alongside the green. They were formidable holes, indeed, and they played critical roles in the championship.

Add narrow fairways, punishing rough and slick greens and Jones had turned Congressional into an extreme examination of golf skill. Mitigating the demands, though, every problem had been laid open to the players; it was up to them to play it as best they could.

From my point of view there was one hitch. Until Congressional, no Open course had ended with a par-three hole since the Englewood (New Jersey) Golf Club, back in 1910. Important championships like the 1964 U.S. Open and the 1976 PGA Championship had avoided the 18th by adding two holes from a third nine and finishing on the normal 17th, a wonderful par-four that measured 480 downhill yards to a cape green reaching into a broad pond.

The club balked at using the 17th as the finishing hole again and insisted that since it had cost it so much to bring Congressional up to Open standards, the course should be played as it was designed. The USGA accepted the club's position. Now the Open would end with a ball played with a medium iron from a peg.

As it played out, though, except for Woods' missing the green and making five in the first round, the 18th played a minor part in the outcome. Everything that mattered the last day happened on the 17th. This was the hole where Els played a marvelous iron into a dangerous position and saved the Open, and where both Montgomerie and Lehman ended their pursuit of Els. Lehman needed a birdie three to catch him but bogeyed instead, and Montgomerie needed a par four to carry the issue to the final hole, but he bogeyed as well.

Els opened the championship with 71, a sound score but one that left him six strokes behind Montgomerie, who shot a blistering 65. When the day ended, Monty led by one stroke over Hal Sutton, who hadn't been heard of in years, and Steve Stricker, who hadn't yet reached his potential. Both shot 66s. Lehman and Mark McNulty stood another stroke back at 67, and Hideki Kase, a 38-year-old Japanese who had qualified by shooting 138 at Woodmont, another Washington club, shot 68, along with Dave Schreyer. Another stroke back at 69 stood Jeff Sluman and Leonard.

Meantime, Maggert shot 73 and Woods a maddening 74 that upset him terribly.

While higher scores might have been expected because of the severity of the course, one circumstance suggested Congressional might be ripe for a battering. A rainy spring that had helped the rough grow straight and tall had softened the greens as well and made them easier to hold than the USGA had hoped. As a countermeasure the club had installed powerful fans that shot streams of drying wind across every green for two solid weeks.

As the championship developed, Congressional held up extremely well. It gave up strokes to superior ball-striking and it claimed an expensive price for loose and indifferent golf and for flawed thinking. Early scores the first day showed Congressional was playing tough. With only a few exceptions, birdies won on the early holes were being taken back later in the round.

Chris Perry stood two under par after 13 holes, but played the last five in two over for his 70. Loren Roberts birdied the first two holes, then played the fourth, fifth and sixth in bogey-birdie-bogey, double-bogeyed the dangerous 10th, and shot 72. Nick Price shot 34 on the first nine but came back in 37. Jack Nicklaus went out in 34 as well, but double-bogeyed the innocent 11th, bogeyed the 13th, and shot 73.

Others were having bad days as well. Both Greg Norman and Phil Mickelson went out in 39, lost another stroke coming in and shot 75. After opening with a birdie, Vijay Singh bogeyed the next three and shot 71, Nick Faldo shot an erratic 72 with two double bogeys, and Curtis Strange went out in 38, double-bogeyed the 10th, and shot 79.

At the end of the day only nine men had finished in the 60s and eight more had come in with even-par 70. In a field of 156 of the game's best players, only 17 had managed par or better. Two years earlier, at Shinnecock Hills, 10 men had shot in the 60s and 15 others matched par.

The sixth, the 10th and the 16th, a regulation 441-yard par-four, had been especially troubling. During the first round, the sixth claimed 15 double bogeys, the 16th 12, and the 10th had 11. Over the course of the four days the sixth counted 49 double bogeys or higher, the 10th had 44, and the 17th had 37.

Under conditions like these, Montgomerie's 65 stood out like a beacon. While it had been matched by T.C. Chen in 1985, only Nicklaus and Tom Weiskopf, with 63s at Baltusrol in 1980, and Lee Mackey, with 64 at Merion in 1950, had opened with lower scores.

Like most low rounds, Colin's could have been better. He had legitimate birdie openings on nearly every hole. One of the early starters, beginning at 8 o'clock, he shaved two strokes from par with 33 on the first nine, then raced back in 32.

The formula for playing any U.S. Open course is simple: hit the fairways and hit the greens. Montgomerie followed the formula almost perfectly. Even though he is probably the straightest driver of all the leading players, Monty left his driver in his bag and drove with his three wood. He was deadly. He hit 13 of the 14 fairways on driving holes and 16 of the 18 greens.

His virtuoso performance left his playing partners breathless. Mickelson, a witness to every shot, said it was the finest example of ball-striking he had ever seen. Ben Crenshaw exclaimed, "My God. He's so straight!" Montgomerie himself said, "This is possibly the best round I've ever put together in major championship golf."

Only one missed green cost him a stroke. He bunkered his approach to the 17th and bogeyed. Ironically, the other missed green might have saved his round.

He had begun with an annoying string of botched birdie openings, missing from eight, six and four feet on the first three holes after sparkling approaches. Then he pulled his drive into the left rough on the intimidating sixth. An experienced player, Montgomerie recognized futility when he saw it. Standing ankle-deep in the wiry, unyielding grass, he knew he had no chance of reaching the green and instead tried nothing more dangerous than chopping his ball back into play. From a decent lie in the fairway now, Monty played a stunning eight iron that nearly knocked the flagstick from the hole. His ball braked little more than a foot from the hole and he saved his par four.

That was all he needed. His confidence buoyed, he ran off five birdies over the next 12 holes and lost only the stroke on the 17th. His distance control was impeccable. He said that, "If I had 158 yards to the pin, I'd hit it 158 yards. If I had 178, I'd hit it 178."

Montgomerie finished a few minutes after 1 o'clock. By then Woods had been out for an hour and getting nowhere. By tradition, as the current U.S. Amateur champion, he played along with Jones, the U.S. Open champion, and Lehman, the British Open champion. Their huge gallery made Montgomerie's seem like little more than friends and acquaintances. All three walked onto the first tee close behind one another, with Woods last. After the crowd's cheers died down, Jones, pretending the crowd was cheering him as the defending champion, called, "Now let's hear it for Tiger Woods." The gallery obliged.

Woods began as if he might play as well at Congressional as he had at Augusta. Hitting superb irons, he might have birdied the first two holes, but his putt on the first lipped out and he birdied only the second after a marvelous two iron inside two feet.

Out in 34 with a couple of bogeys from three-putting the third and fifth, Woods birdied the difficult 10th and stood two under par. Now, though, his game unraveled. While it isn't easy, the 11th measures just 411 yards, and the hole was cut toward the back left of the green perhaps 25 feet from the edge, not a difficult position. Woods misjudged the distance and flew his approach over the green and into the trees, pitched over the green again, and made six. He had lost both strokes he had taken.

Now his inexperience cost him more strokes. After a routine par three on the 12th, he jerked his drive into the left rough of the 13th and tried to play an iron to the green. It couldn't be done. His shot ran no more than halfway and he bogeyed again.

This was the first of a series of mis-played shots. He drove into the right rough on the 14th and back to the left rough on the 15th. He escaped with his par only on the 14th. As he had on the 13th, Woods had thrown away another stroke by playing an almost impossible shot on the 15th. As Tiger strained for distance from that deep and treacherous rough, the grass tore the club from his hands and the ball flew across the fairway into the right rough.

His frustration broke through again on the 16th. When he overshot still another green he cried, "You're kidding me." Nevertheless he saved his par there and again on the 17th, but his tee shot to the 18th started left of the flagstick, curled farther left, caught the steep bank, and tumbled into the water. It was his second double bogey in eight holes. Out in 34, he came back in 40.

Lehman, a man with not a hint of Woods' flair, very quietly birdied four holes on the home nine, shot 67, picked up nearly a stroke a hole on Tiger with his closing 32, and placed himself in position to challenge for the lead.

The first-round leaderboard:

Colin Montgomerie	65	Hideki Kase	68
Hal Sutton	66	Dave Schreyer	68
Steve Stricker	66	Jeff Sluman	69
Mark McNulty	67	Justin Leonard	69
Tom Lehman	67		

Golf is a strange game. What works one day doesn't necessarily work the next. Conversely, what didn't work one day might work another. Montgomerie and Woods proved it in the second round. Montgomerie had been a model of sound, Open-style golf the first day, hitting fairways and hitting greens, while Woods had stumbled through the second nine, hitting only four fairways and four greens.

Something happened overnight. Playing loose shots, missing more fairways and greens than he hit, and complaining of a headache, Monty slipped to 76. Woods, meantime, regained his poise, played as he had at Augusta, shot 67, and climbed from a tie for 80th place into a tie for ninth.

While those two exchanged roles, Lehman, an unexciting golfer, shot an unexciting 70 and slipped into first place with 137, three strokes under par. Both Stewart Cink, a tall, 24-year-old former Nike Tour player, and Els, the 1994 champion, thrust themselves into the chase by shooting 67s and climbing into second place, at 138. They stood one stroke ahead of Scott Hoch, with 68; David Ogrin, with 69; Sutton, who went from 66 to 73, and Maggert, who played the day's low round of 66. McNulty went from 67 to 73, and Stricker slipped from 66 to 76.

This was an eventful day. Not only did the lead change hands, but lightning caused a two-hour interruption, wrecking the tournament schedule. This was the day when the 156-man field would be trimmed to the low 60 and anyone within 10 strokes of the leader. When play resumed after 2 o'clock, it was obvious the entire field couldn't finish. Then, when daylight ran out and play called off at 8:30 p.m., 45 men were still on the course. They would complete their rounds the following morning.

Then there was John Daly's episode. Playing in his third tournament since an eight-week stay for alcohol rehabilitation at the Betty Ford Clinic, Daly shot 77 in the first round. After playing the first nine of the second round in 38, he walked off the course and drove away, leaving Els and Payne Stewart, whom he was with, waiting on the 10th tee. Els and Stewart finished without him.

The lightning interruption came at a time when the players were taking the measure of Congressional, as trying an Open course as anyone could remember. Where only eight men had matched or bettered par in the opening round, 20 men shot in the 60s in the second, and five others shot 70.

Rain had fallen briefly in early morning, stopped for a few hours, and began again just before lunchtime. Sirens screamed when weathermen detected lightning, leading the USGA to suspend play a few minutes before noon.

Even Lehman, Woods and Jones were caught, and they had begun at 7 o'clock in the morning. The siren blew just as Lehman teed his ball on the 17th. By then he stood one under par for the round and had played extraordinarily sound golf. After a rocky start — he three-putted the second and missed both the fairway and green of the third, costing him two strokes — Lehman settled down, played a series of first-class irons, birdied three of the next seven holes, and went out in 34. Starting back he three-putted the 10th, then nearly holed his pitch to the 14th, setting up his last birdie of the day.

Something seemed to be missing after the rainstorm passed; none of the three looked as sharp as they had been. After missing just two fairways and two greens over the first 16 holes, Lehman missed both the fairway and green of the 17th but still scraped out his par, missed the 18th green as well and bogeyed, and ended with an even-par round of 70 and the Open lead. Woods three-putted the 17th from 35 feet for a bogey five, and Jones made seven.

Once again the gallery had flocked to Woods, and this time he rewarded the fans with exceptional golf. Sticking to his plan to use his driver only occasionally and rely instead on his two iron and three wood, he missed only the 13th and 17th fairways. While he bogeyed them both, he had the round under control by then.

He began by birdieing four of the first seven holes, mainly through deadly irons that left him little to do on the greens. For example, he hit an eight iron to six feet on the first, a six iron to eight feet on the third, another eight iron to three feet at the fifth, and a seven iron to four feet at the seventh. Four under par, he made the turn in 31.

The 13th cost him one stroke when he pushed his two-iron tee shot into the rough and couldn't recover, but he followed up with another precisely played seven iron to 12 feet on the 14th. Better was coming. Facing the 583-yard 15th, Woods inspired clamorous cheers with two Brobdingnagian shots — a driver and a six iron to the back of the green. He birdied, of course, his seventh of the day, dropping him to five under par. Three more pars and he would shoot 65.

He didn't make them. He lost one stroke at the 16th, another at the 17th, and nearly at least one more on the 18th. When the wind caught his eight iron, the ball fell short of the green. Had the grass not been wet, it might have tumbled down the bank and into the water. It hung up, though, and Woods saved his par three, came back in 36, and shot 67.

Not the glorious player he had been in the first round, Montgomerie, meantime, was having all sorts of problems. Colin had never stood up well to the heat and humidity of an American summer. His caddie said that Monty felt faint every time he leaned over to putt, and on the eighth hole he walked to the gallery ropes and asked his wife, Eimear, to find him an aspirin.

He drove into the rough on the 16th and made his fifth bogey of the day, followed with still another on the 17th, and struggled to save his par three from off the 18th green. He finished with 76. Later, he admitted, "I didn't play well. I've got to regroup and try to find what I was doing Thursday. If I do, I can still win."

When the round finally ended the following morning, 84 players had shot 147 or better and got to play the last two rounds.

Nicklaus was among them. After his opening 73, he came back with 71 and 144, tying for 36th place, along with Tom Kite, the 1992 champion; Stewart, who had won in 1991; Paul Azinger, the 1993 PGA champion, and Larry Mize, the 1987 Masters winner.

Norman played two poor rounds and left. His mind evidently not so concentrated on his golf as on his father, who had heart surgery in Australia, Greg went from 75 to 79, and for the first time missed the cut in both the Masters and the Open. After winning the Volvo PGA Championship in Europe a month or so earlier, Ian Woosnam missed as well, along with Corey Pavin, the 1995 champion; Bernhard Langer, usually a reliable player who had won the Masters twice; Mark Brooks, the current PGA champion; Curtis Strange, the last to win successive Opens, and Steve Hart, who had been called early Thursday morning to replace Costantino Rocca, who withdrew.

The second-round leaderboard:

Tom Lehman	70 - 137	David Ogrin	69 - 139
Ernie Els	67 - 138	Hal Sutton	73 - 139
Stewart Cink	67 - 138	Scott Hoch	68 - 139
Jeff Maggert	66 - 139	Mark McNulty	73 - 140

By Saturday, the day of the third round, the weather had become critical. After another thunderstorm set back the schedule more than two hours once again, skeptics predicted that with luck the Open might end by the following Wednesday. The storm dumped more than half an inch of rain on already wet grounds and forced 21 players, the tournament leaders, to come back Sunday morning to finish. This was to have a profound effect on the outcome. The day had begun with overcast skies. When menacing black clouds threatened lightning, officials posted danger warnings on scoreboards scattered around the course and sirens wailed a little after 5 o'clock. Rain gushed down a few minutes later, turning a few holes into bogs, the club's paved roads and parking lots into rivers, and soaking the 30,000 spectators, many of whom squeezed into food and merchandise tents for shelter.

The storm passed and the round resumed a little after 7 o'clock, but with so little daylight left, even the small field couldn't complete the round. When the light grew dim, the USGA suspended play at 8:20 p.m. Those with holes to play would complete their rounds Sunday morning, then wait for their afternoon starting times.

This was another bewildering day when no one could be certain who held command. Maggert held first place at the rain delay, Lehman led overnight, and Els moved into a tie with Maggert following a string of three birdies Sunday morning.

When the round eventually ended the next day, Lehman had shot 68 and led with 205, five under par, two strokes ahead of Maggert and Els at 207. Montgomerie had recovered from his loose second round and shot 67, the best round of the day, jumping him to fourth place at 208, only three strokes behind now. No one else had broken par for the 54 holes.

Woods could do nothing. Beginning the round at one over par, he shot 73 and lost three more strokes. With 214, he would play no further part in deciding the championship.

Meantime, scoring improved. At the end of the round, 21 men had broken par 70 and five others had matched it. Nine of the 11 men at 211 or better had shot in the 60s. Maggert might have done better, but after shooting his second 31 on the first nine, he came back in 37 and shot 68.

Els, though, made the biggest statement. When the USGA suspended the round Saturday evening, he had played 14 holes in two over par, putting him at risk of dropping far down in the standings. He evidently found his game overnight, because when he returned Sunday morning, he birdied the 15th, birdied the 16th, and birdied the demanding 17th, a truly difficult hole. With a par three on the 18th, he had played four tough holes in 4-3-3-3, just 13 strokes. These would become critical.

With the second round's overnight delay and the need to regroup the players, the third didn't begin until 10:10 Saturday morning, much later than the usual time. Because of the late start, the field had to be grouped in threes rather than the customary pairs. As the 36-hole leader, Lehman went off last, along with Els and Stewart Cink, just behind Maggert, Sutton and Ogrin.

Playing exceptional irons that left him only short putts for birdies on the fourth and fifth, Lehman moved quickly to five under par and opened a five-stroke gap over Els, who had double-bogeyed the second, a par-three, and remained two ahead of Maggert, even though Jeff birdied two of the first three holes.

Now Lehman made a mistake. He pulled his drive into the deep rough lining the sixth fairway, played a safe shot back to the fairway, and nearly saved his par with a lovely pitch to five feet. The putt missed. He went back to four under par for 42 holes, one under for the round. He recovered by birdieing the seventh with another blistering iron to six feet, eased past the eighth, the easiest par-four at Congressional, then pushed his drive into the right rough on the ninth.

Taking the prudent approach once again, Lehman pitched back to the fairway, but now he stood miles from the green with a one iron in his hand. Just then the sirens sounded and Lehman ducked into the clubhouse to think it over.

The grounds crew, meanwhile, went to work at warp speed to make Congressional playable. Men with squeegees swooshed water off greens and fairways, others carrying portable blowers whooshed away debris, while bucket-wielding crews bailed out bunkers and rebuilt their washed-out faces.

When play began again after 7 p.m., Congressional was certainly playable but terribly difficult. Balls plugged in bunkers, and the rough had become savage. One good result of the rain: It had softened the greens.

Congressional lay under a wispy fog when the players returned to the course. It was eerie. Unconnected voices carried through the mist, but the haze blocked everyone's vision. Players could see a shot start off, but they couldn't follow its flight. Lehman said later, "I didn't see a single shot I hit." Perhaps not, but he saw the ninth green well enough to drill his one iron into the rough just short, chop it out, and save his par five.

Maggert, meantime, birdied both the eighth and ninth and caught Lehman. Jeff seemed to have the combination to Congressional's first nine. Playing just ahead of Lehman, he had shot his second consecutive 31 and just before the suspension had driven 25 yards past Sutton and Ogrin, his playing partners.

While Maggert was playing his best golf, Montgomerie had found his game as well and had started even better than in his first round. He had gone out in 33 then, and now he shot 31. Where he had birdied only two holes on the first nine on Thursday, he birdied four on Saturday, one that will be remembered by everyone who saw it.

After a nice tee shot into the seventh, the 174-yard par-three, Monty faced a perplexing 20-foot downhill putt with a huge break. He lined himself up to start his ball perhaps 20 feet left of the hole, then, grinning at the absurdity of it, he backed off. Shaking his head, he re-set himself and holed the putt. When the ball fell, he dropped his putter, turned to the gallery, and held out his hands, obviously surprised.

The birdie gave him life. He made another at the eighth and still another on the ninth. Three under for 45 holes, he began the long slog home by bogeying the 10th. Back to two under par.

The rain interrupted his round on the 13th, which frustrated him enough, but then he was further irritated when, soaked with perspiration, he tried to buy a shirt in the golf shop but couldn't find his size.

In the failing light, Lehman and Maggert continued their battle for first place. Tied at five under par after the storm, Lehman botched the 10th and 11th while Maggert ran off three pars and moved two strokes ahead. Maggert gave one stroke away at the 13th, and when play ended for the day, Jeff held first place at four under after 14 holes. Lehman stood three under after 13, Montgomerie two under, Sutton one under, and Els even par, tied with Ogrin and Jay Haas in seventh place.

The fog had flown by the next morning, along with Maggert's lead. Beginning with pars on the 15th and 16th, he pushed his approach to the 17th into the rough and bogeyed, but he nearly won back the stroke with a fine putt on the 18th that hit the hole and spun out.

Montgomerie, on the other hand, did indeed hole from 25 feet or so for a birdie on the 18th, and Sutton doomed himself with a pulled tee shot that skidded off the left side of the green and into the water. Once within three strokes of the lead after holing his pitch for an eagle two on the eighth, Sutton played the last six holes in 5-5-5-5-5-4, five over par.

Lehman, meantime, birdied the 14th with a marvelous pitch less than a yard from the hole and finished with a nice draw to about seven feet on the 18th. When the putt fell he had picked up three strokes on Maggert over those last five holes and reclaimed first place.

The third-round leaderboard:

Tom Lehman	68 - 205	Jay Haas	68 - 210
Jeff Maggert	68 - 207	Tommy Tolles	69 - 210
Ernie Els	69 - 207	David Ogrin	71 - 210
Colin Montgomerie	67 - 208		

The sun had burned away the morning overcast by the time the early starters teed off for the final round, and for once Congressional held no threat of rain. Off early, Nicklaus drew a good crowd as he completed his 41st Open with a round of 74 and tied for 52nd place at 293. At 57 he might have been the oldest man ever to play 72 holes in the Open. Statisticians tell us as well that on Saturday he played his 10,000th hole in the four major championships.

Woods drew his usual following, but most spectators either hung around to follow the last two groups or found space near strategic points, many of them lining the hillsides overlooking the final two greens.

President Clinton and his daughter Chelsea arrived late in the day, watched for a while from a tower behind the 16th green, then moved to the television facility by the 17th and 18th. As far as anyone knows, Mr. Clinton was the first sitting president to have seen a U.S. Open since 1921, when Warren Harding, a dedicated golfer himself, presented the trophy to Jim Barnes at the Columbia Country Club, a few miles from Congressional in Chevy Chase, Maryland, another Washington suburb.

Those who chose to walk with the leaders had let themselves in for a session of day-long tension watching Els, Montgomerie, Lehman and Maggert play their hearts out over an unforgiving course that tolerated no loose shots.

Those four made up an interesting combination. Els had won the Open, Lehman had placed second a year earlier, and Montgomerie had lost a play-off to Els in 1994. Maggert, though, had never placed higher than fourth.

Montgomerie and Lehman had suffered most. This was the third straight year Lehman had either held or shared the 54-hole lead, and yet he hadn't won. He had slipped to 74 in the closing round at Shinnecock Hills in 1995 and dropped to third place, and he had driven into a fairway bunker on the 18th at Oakland Hills in 1996 and lost by one stroke to Steve Jones. Montgomerie looked for a time as if he might have won in 1992 when he shot 288 at Pebble Beach, but Tom Kite beat him with 285. Two years later he tied Els and Loren Roberts at Oakmont but played miserably on the first nine of the playoff, shot 78, and didn't figure. Els had won that playoff, but he had missed the cut the following year and tied for fifth in 1996.

Still, after he had played such indifferent golf through much of the season and had missed the cut in the Buick Open the previous week, it seemed surprising to find him in position to win at Congressional. He was paired with Montgomerie and played just ahead of Lehman and Maggert. The four of them created tension all afternoon with stirring shots, wonderful recoveries and laser-guided putting.

The standing changed throughout the day. Els played steady golf through the early holes, but Montgomerie caught him with a nice nine iron to four feet on the first hole. When Lehman bungled both the third and fourth, driving into the rough on the third for the fourth consecutive day, and then missed the fourth green with a seven-iron approach, he slipped to three under par, tied with Els and Montgomerie. At four under now, Maggert led once again.

Lehman birdied the fifth and caught Maggert at four under, and now all four men bogeyed the difficult sixth. At that stage Lehman and Maggert led at three under and Els and Montgomerie stood at two under. Three holes later, after Lehman birdied the eighth, Montgomerie birdied the seventh and ninth, and Els bogeyed the ninth, Montgomerie had tied Lehman and Maggert at four under, one stroke ahead of Els. One hole later Els played one of the shots that won the Open.

The 10th is a very hard hole. It measures 466 yards, its green sits alongside a pond, and the fairway tilts toward a stream that feeds the pond. With 180 yards to go after a quite useful drive, Els played a six iron that didn't have enough steam and pulled up perhaps five yards short. In trouble now, Ernie took a lofted club and pitched to the front of the green. The ball ran directly toward the hole, hit the flagstick, and dropped into the cup. A birdie; now all four men were tied at four under par.

They were playing one great shot after another. Montgomerie had pitched within six feet to set up his birdie on the ninth. Lehman followed with a 180-

yard six iron into the 10th and then an even better pitch on the 11th, within four feet of a hole tucked behind a bunker on the front right. Maggert covered the flag with a five iron to the 12th, the par-three, after Els had played his five iron to 10 feet. Then Lehman nearly holed a sand-wedge third shot into the 15th, the last of the par-fives. Aside from Montgomerie's on the ninth, only two of those shots won birdies: Els made his two on the 12th and Lehman his four on the 15th.

At that point, with everyone through the 15th, Els, Montgomerie and Lehman were still tied at four under, with Maggert lagging one stroke behind. Now both Maggert and Lehman stumbled. Maggert missed the 16th fairway and green and Lehman missed the green as well. Their bogeys left Montgomerie and Els battling for the lead.

Now they came to the 17th, the defining hole of the championship, 480 yards downhill to a treacherous green jutting into the pond with the hole cut in the left rear, its most dangerous position. It was the key. It ruined both Lehman and Montgomerie, and it showed that even when his heart must have been racing, Els could still play the shot he had to play.

Montgomerie and Els first. Both men drove well, but Monty, perhaps wary of the pond, pushed his approach onto the bank of a greenside bunker, off to the right, safely away from the water. Els, though, after smashing a three wood far down the fairway, gambled and played a stunning 212-yard five iron that started off right of the flagstick, took a gentle turn to the left, cleared the trouble, and nestled on the back of the green within 15 feet of the hole. It was as fine a shot as anyone within memory had played into a vital hole of the Open.

Now Montgomerie grew agitated because of the noise coming from the big gallery watching Haas and Tolles hole out on the 18th, just across the lake from the 17th. Monty eventually played a nice pitch to about five feet, and Els rolled his putt just past the cup. Then Montgomerie waited until Haas and Tolles had begun their climb to the clubhouse. Asked later why he waited so long, he said, "I didn't want to rush the most important putt of my life."

With the gallery quiet once again, Montgomerie stepped up to his ball and tapped it just right. It ran toward the cup, broke left, and looked as if it would hit dead center. Suddenly it straightened out and ran past. A bogey five. Monty stared at his ball with despair, but it was all over. Monty made a gallant attempt to force a playoff, but his 25-footer on the 18th slipped past the cup.

Because of the delay, Lehman had seen everything from the 17th fairway. He knew he needed a birdie, but he also knew he might never have a better chance. He had ripped a driver into just the right position, less than 190 yards to the hole, and he had just the shot in mind — a slight right-to-left draw with a seven iron, the perfect shot for him, he said.

As soon as he made contact he knew he had lost the Open. Caught a little heavy, the ball curled too far left, hit the bank beside the green, and dived into the water.

As he saw the ball swerve off line, Lehman moaned, "Oh, no," then covered his head with his hand and stood still as a statue. When, after an endless pause, Lehman took off his cap, his face wore a doleful expression, as if that one mis-played shot had torn the heart from him. He had been so close those last three years, he wondered if something might be missing inside him.

The Open belonged to Els, his second in four years. He had won first as a 24-year-old at Oakmont in 1994 and now again at 27. By winning he became the first man to have won two Opens in his twenties since Nicklaus had won in 1962 and 1967.

A week after winning the Open, Els shot 64-68-67-69–268 at Westchester Country Club in New York, led every round for the second consecutive year, and beat Maggert by two strokes in the Buick Classic. With those two victories, Els bolted to first place in the World Ranking.

His sudden rise revived the question of whether he had reached his best level of golf or if he could become better. Fascinating speculation. Since he first made himself known as a young golfer of immeasurable potential, he had been an enigma. Take 1997, for example. He played especially well in Europe early in the year, winning the Johnnie Walker Classic and placing second to Ian Woosnam in the Volvo PGA, and he won the Open Championship of South Africa, his native land. But when he came to the United States he didn't play nearly as well. In his best finish, he placed ninth at Greensboro. Of the 11 tournaments he entered, he missed the cut in four. Then he won the national championship for the second time.

At the same time, he bothers those who follow the game closely because he had openings to win other important competitions and tossed them away. He had the 1995 PGA Championship within reach, three strokes in front with 18 holes to play, but after rounds of 66, 65 and 66, he appeared to lose his poise after a couple of mistakes, closed with a weak 72, and fell into a tie for third behind Steve Elkington, who won, and Montgomerie, who lost the playoff.

Again, at Royal Lytham and St. Annes, he chased Lehman through the final 18 holes of the British Open, and even though Lehman didn't play at his best, closing with 73, Ernie made his move too late. Even with 67 he finished two strokes behind.

There is no question he has formidable talent. Thirty years had passed since Nicklaus had won his second Open. He eventually won four. Els might win four as well. He seems to have everything he needs — power, finesse, a sound putting touch and stainless steel nerves. Only a player with supreme confidence in his swing could have taken the dare and gone for the pin on the 17th in those last tense moments on Sunday. Outwardly he seemed relaxed and loose, perhaps even lethargic. It's an illusion. Inwardly, he said, he was boiling under the pressure.

"I think any player will tell you they're pretty intense," he said. "I was quite intense today, but I had confidence in my game. I think that just comes with experience."

5. British Open Championship

If, after playing the sixth hole at Royal Troon Golf Club on Scotland's west coast, you walk to the top of the hill behind the green and look southward toward the old town of Prestwick, you can see the holes of the Prestwick Golf Club winding through the rough dunesland. It was over this quirky 12-hole course that championship golf was born. In October of 1860, six months before the opening shots of the American Civil War, Prestwick invited other clubs to send their two best professionals to play for a championship belt of red Morocco leather trimmed in silver.

Only eight men showed up on a chilly autumn morning and plodded three times around Prestwick's 12 holes. In a classic struggle between two giants of the game, Willie Park of Musselburgh beat Old Tom Morris, based in Prestwick at the time, 174-176. No one else was close.

The tournament arranged by Prestwick and played over its grounds the first 12 years eventually became known as the British Open Championship. It continued to be played periodically at Prestwick after other clubs joined not only in the rota but in the tournament's administration as well. The championship developed into the highlight of the year in most of the golfing world.

By the beginning of the century, Prestwick had been turned into a conventional 18-hole course and the Open into a 72-hole test, but even with its new design, the club had been cramped into too little acreage to handle galleries safely. It held its last British Open in 1925, when Jim Barnes made up five strokes in the last round. Over the next 71 years only Tommy Armour in 1931 made up so much ground after 54 holes.

Then, on a warm summer afternoon at Royal Troon in July of 1997, within sight of Barnes' great moment, Justin Leonard began the final 18 holes of the 1997 championship five strokes behind the Swede Jesper Parnevik. With precise shotmaking and deadly putting he caught and passed Parnevik with a round of 65 and claimed the 126th British Open. He shot 272 for the 72 holes, an exceptional score over so difficult a course.

Parnevik, meantime, shot 73 and dropped from first place into a tie for second with the Northern Irishman Darren Clarke, three strokes behind Leonard, at 275. Jim Furyk took fourth place, but with 279 he lagged four strokes behind Parnevik and Clarke and seven behind Leonard. Tom Lehman, the defending champion, played indifferent golf until his closing 66 and tied for 24th place. Ruined by an opening 75, Ernie Els, the U.S. Open champion, tied for 10th with 282, and Tiger Woods, winner of the Masters Tournament, tied for 24th, along with Colin Montgomerie, who played exceptionally well over the last three rounds but not well enough to wipe out his opening 76.

Leonard's 65 matched the second lowest finishing round in all the British Opens. Greg Norman had closed with 64 in winning the 1993 championship, at Royal St. George's, the best ever, but Leonard's had matched the 65s shot by Tom Watson in his unparalleled duel with Jack Nicklaus at Turnberry in 1977 and Seve Ballesteros in his tight battle with Nick Price in 1988.

Neither Turnberry nor Royal Lytham and St. Anne's ranked as so difficult a course as Troon in 1997. Not only did it measure 7,079 yards, easily within reach of the modern championship golfer, but the design of the holes added a further note of terror.

Separated from the Firth of Clyde by only a few yards of sandy beach and exposed to high winds that often sweep in from the Irish Sea, Troon begins gently enough with three short par-four holes of less than 400 yards, two par-fives reachable in two on the hard British turf, and a 210-yard par-three. Then it toughens up.

Colin Montgomerie, a native of Troon whose father had been club secretary, summed it up by saying, "From the seventh tee onward you're really just hanging on."

Nevertheless, whether even a course so strong as Troon could take the measure of the British Open field seemed questionable, because so many of the game's leading players had been playing so well. Nick Faldo, who had won this championship three times, looked over the field and said, "I can't remember a major championship with so many of the leading players in top form."

They were indeed. Lehman, for example, had come to Troon at the peak of his game, along with Els, who had won the U.S. Open just three weeks earlier, Montgomerie, Norman and, of course, Woods.

Lehman seemed the most impressive of them all. He had hung on until the 71st hole of the U.S. Open, and the week before the British Open he had shot 65-66-67-67–265 and won the Gulfstream Loch Lomond World Invitational, beating Els by five strokes. For his part, Els had won at Westchester the week after the U.S. Open and, of course, placed second to Lehman at Loch Lomond.

Montgomerie, meanwhile, had not only finished second to Els at the U.S. Open, but he had won the Compaq European Grand Prix in early June and the Murphy's Irish Open two weeks before Troon.

As everyone knows, Woods had won the Masters with a record score and had followed what for him had been a disappointing tie for 19th place in the U.S. Open by winning the Motorola Western Open two weeks later, his fifth victory of the season.

Norman had sprung to life as well by winning the FedEx St. Jude Classic in Memphis, Tennessee, with 268, rather sensational scoring.

Indicators like this, though, can't be taken too seriously because golf is the least formful of games; the best players don't necessarily win or even come close. Consider that three of the game's leading figures practically played themselves out of contention in Troon's opening round. Having a bad ball-striking day, Lehman shot 74, Els shot 75, and Montgomerie was worst of all. Usually the straightest of drivers, he rarely hit a fairway and shot 76, matching the highest score he had ever shot in six previous British Opens. Woods, meantime, shot a ragged 72 that could have been much better or much worse.

The high scoring was certainly understandable because of the weather. It was foul. Any score under par represented superb golf on a chilly, dreary day like this. Thick gray clouds blocked out the sun through most of the day, and the wind blew in from the sea at strengths from 20 to 30 miles an hour, turning Royal Troon into as difficult an examination of shotmaking as anyone could remember. From a field of 156 of the world's best golfers, only five men shot in the 60s, five others shot 70, and six more matched the course par of 71.

Difficult under benign conditions, the homeward nine played directly into the wind, turning this normally hard course into a brutal test of the game. Only the best ball-striking could wring results from Troon. Norman, who shot 69, said Troon was like two courses — one going out, the other coming in. Nicklaus said, "Par on the second nine today is 39 or 40. There were about six par-fives on that nine, par-four holes I could not reach in two shots." Nicklaus had played nine irons for his third shots to the 13th and 15th, both par-fours. Hardly short hitters, Strange couldn't reach the 15th with a three wood nor could Lehman reach the 13th with a wooden-club second.

At the same time, as Faldo pointed out, playing downwind wasn't a picnic, either, "You have to judge your shots really well. It's a weird feeling trying to land a wedge shot short of the green. I bogeyed the second hole because I hit the drive too far. I had a shot from about 80 yards and I didn't have a club for it."

The 18th caused real problems for those who hit the ball only moderate distances. A band of rough extended so far out from the tee that many of them couldn't reach the fairway. Leonard was among them. He estimated the deep rough swallowed his ball 10 or 15 yards short of the fairway. He made his par-four nevertheless.

When the round ended, Leonard said, "I used my one iron from most of the tees on the first nine and for most of my second shots on the second."

Of course, the wind led to some sensational drives on the outward nine, not all of them good. The first hole measured 369 yards. Woods hit a very hot tee shot that caught a greenside bunker. Had it been straight, it would have gone yards over the green. Three holes later, playing the fourth, a par-five of 557 yards, he was left with a second shot of about 120 to 125 yards. His drive had covered approximately 435 yards.

Nevertheless, the home nine caused most of the agony by consistently taking away strokes won on the first nine. Fred Couples went out in 31 with the wind at his back, but struggled home in 38. Both Clarke and Furyk went out in 32 and came back in 35. Norman came back in 37 after an outward 32.

Those were the good scores. Lehman went out in 34, two strokes under par, but after turning into the wind he missed nearly every green and came back in 40. Even so, he did better than lots of others. Els, Jose Maria Olazabal and Costantino Rocca all went out in 35, one under par, and came back in 40, five over. Peter Lonard, a husky Australian who had lost four years of competitive golf because of a malaria-like disease, went out in 32 and back in 40; Peter Hedblom, the Swede who had played so well at Lytham the previous year, shot 33-43; Phil Mickelson shot 35-41; Mike Bradley went out in 34 and back in 43, and Klas Erickson played the first nine in even-par 36 and mangled the home nine with 49.

Ninety-three players, 60 percent of the field, shot 40 or higher on the second nine and only seven men shot 35 or better. It had been a hard day.

Through all the chaos, some golfers managed to cope. Furyk, of the bizarre swing, and Clarke, a big, chunky, round-faced Irishman, shot extraordinary 67s, beat par by four strokes and led the field by two. In spite of his problems with length, and even though he did not hit a green in regulation through those last difficult nine holes, Leonard shot 69 and tied for third place with Couples and Norman, who alone among those who came into the championship in top form showed any spark at all.

With his closing 34, Parnevik shot 70, along with Love, Andrew Magee, Angel Cabrera and the 43-year-old amateur Barclay Howard. Of those, only Parnevik would stay in the hunt until the end, although Howard finished as low amateur.

Incredibly, both Furyk and Clarke birdied the 11th hole. With their birdies, Furyk jumped to five under par and Clarke to four under, after losing a stroke on the 10th.

They played in successive groups, Furyk at 12:15 p.m. and Clarke 10 minutes later. Furyk began with a bold drive that pulled up 20 yards short of the green, pitched to four feet and birdied, and three holes later had a chance to eagle the fourth, the first of the par-fives. A drive and a stunning six iron pulled up just eight feet from the cup, but he missed the putt. It was a birdie four though, and he was two under par.

Quickly, Furyk birdied two more. He drove with a four iron on the seventh and pitched to four feet and followed with an eight iron that rolled just off the eighth green. No problem. He holed from 35 feet. Out in 32, he began the torturous home nine by drilling a two iron to five feet on the 11th. If he parred in he would shoot 66.

He couldn't hold on. Poor driving cost him bogeys on the 13th and 18th, but he had one further birdie. Into the full force of the wind, he ripped a three iron to 20 feet on the 14th, the 179-yard par-three, and holed the putt.

When it was over, Furyk claimed he liked this kind of golf because, "You need a lot of imagination, especially downwind. We're not used to landing the ball maybe 30 yards short of the green and letting it run to the hole."

Clarke, on the other hand, had played under these conditions often. He played the first nine in 32 as well, with birdies on the two par-five holes, where he hit ridiculous clubs for his second shots — a nine iron to the fourth and a five iron to the sixth. Both shots fell into bunkers, though, and he saved his birdies by holing from five feet on each.

He had begun his run of birdies by holing from 20 feet on the second and from 25 feet on the seventh. After losing a stroke at the 10th, like Furyk he rifled a two iron onto the 11th green and holed an outrageous putt from perhaps 70 feet. He birdied the 16th as well, taking three strokes to reach the green and running in his putt from 12 feet. Again like Furyk, he bogeyed the 18th after driving into the rough.

As solidly as both Clarke and Furyk played the homeward nine, no one's finish compared to Parnevik's. Jesper had gone out in 36, even par, and started back with a double-bogey six at the 11th. Still two over after the 13th, he suddenly began playing superb golf. He birdied the 14th, lost another stroke at the 15th, then birdied the last three holes — four birdies in five holes. He came back in 34, and with 70 saved himself for the greater challenges ahead.

As everyone expected, Woods carried the largest gallery, and for a time he rewarded the fans with solid golf. It didn't last. The 11th destroyed his round. He drove into gorse along the right, hacked his ball out, tried a risky shot with a two iron that didn't work, pitched on with his fifth shot, and made seven. Only a strong finish — two birdies on the last three holes — saved him for another day.

The first-round leaderboard:

Jim Furyk	67	Angel Cabrera	70
Darren Clarke	67	Davis Love III	70
Greg Norman	69	Andrew Magee	70
Fred Couples	69	Jesper Parnevik	70
Justin Leonard	69	*Barclay Howard	70

The weather had eased somewhat late Thursday. The sun had broken through, the wind slackened, and the temperature climbed. Conditions had improved even more by the next morning. Where dark clouds had hung overhead through most of the opening round, a bright sun warmed Troon the following day. With only a moderate breeze, the course had lost most of its sting. It was still tough, although less impossible. No one claimed he couldn't reach the fairways with well-struck shots, and the scoring reflected the more forgiving conditions. Just 10 men had broken par in the first round, but 45 shot under 71 in the second. Where 140 had shot 72 or higher in the first, only 92 had failed to match or better par in the second.

Five men shot 66, five others shot 67, seven shot 68, and 13 more shot 69. It was quite a change and it helped a number of players. Clarke, for example, was among those at 66, along with Leonard, Parnevik and David Tapping. With 133 for 36 holes, Clarke took over the lead by two strokes over Leonard, at 135, and by three over Parnevik, at 136.

Furyk fell six strokes behind with 72. Couples improved by one stroke with 68 and shared fourth place, at 137, with Tapping, a 22-year-old Englishman playing in his first British Open. Lehman, meanwhile, shot 72 and fell 13 strokes behind, and Norman shot 73 and dropped from two strokes behind to nine back.

Never comfortable in the wind, Montgomerie rebounded from his grim opening 76 with 69; Tom Kite moved among the leaders with 67; Mark James shot 67 as well, and so did Brad Faxon, Mark McNulty and Mark Calcavecchia, who won the 1989 Open at Troon. Els made a slight upward move with 69, but it wasn't enough; Faldo couldn't hole a putt and shot a dull 73, and Price, who had been playing well lately, shot 78 and missed the cut.

Among the early starters, going off a few minutes after 8 o'clock, Clarke raced through the first nine in 32, four under par, running off six birdies but losing strokes on each of the two par-three holes, where he missed the greens. He played every bit as well coming back, but the demands of Troon's closing holes asked for much more than the outward nine. Even so, Clarke played first-class golf, and except for a bogey on the 10th, he hit the middle of nearly every green.

He had played intelligent, mature golf, eliminating risk where he could. For example, had he used his driver he might have driven the greens of the first two holes, but he might also have driven into bunkers. "As soon as you go into bunkers here it's a penalty stroke," he explained. "There's no going forward. Just get it out." Instead he drove with a four iron on the first and a three iron on the second, stayed short of the bunkers and birdied both holes.

He putted immaculately as well. He had come to Troon unsure of his stroke, but he solved his inconsistency by switching putters and shortening his stroke to avoid hitting up on the ball. The changes paid dividends. Five times he holed from 20 feet, made another from 10 feet, and still another from eight feet. All of them were birdies. He made his other birdie on the fourth, where he reached the green with a three-wood second and two-putted from 40 feet.

He might have made another, but after a stunning iron to the 18th, perhaps his best iron shot of the day, he missed a putt from little more than four feet.

Clarke had hardly been in for half an hour when Parnevik came home with a 66 of his own and climbed within three strokes with half the championship still to be played.

Jesper had putted sublimely in birdieing three of the last four holes of the opening round, but he wasn't satisfied. Claiming his putting felt terrible, Parnevik switched to a new putter with a rubber insert on its face. Then he knocked a putt 12 feet past the hole and bogeyed the first. Except for a wild drive on the 18th, that was his last mistake. He hit every green but the last, and he eagled the fourth after a three iron to six feet. He followed with birdies on both the seventh and eighth with fine pitches to eight feet and six feet and went out in 33.

After holing from 25 feet for another birdie on the difficult 11th, Parnevik played routine pars to the 16th, a birdie hole, where he hooked his second shot badly. From the rough he lofted a nice pitch to less than three feet and birdied once more. He looked as if he would bogey the 18th after driving behind a grandstand about 200 yards short of the green, but he lofted an eight iron over the stands and into a pot bunker. From about 30 yards, he hit his third as hard as he could and felt lucky to reach the front edge of the green 50 feet from the hole. He rolled his putt dead into the cup for the par four.

Clarke and Parnevik had finished long before Leonard teed off, just after 2 o'clock, knowing what he had to do to stay afloat. Not much had been expected of Leonard when the championship began. Some felt he didn't have the game for this level of competition, even though he had won twice since joining the PGA Tour in 1994. Obviously they were wrong.

In punishing conditions the previous day, Leonard had played the first nine in 34. Now, with the wind eased, he went out in 31 with one bogey, two birdies and, for the first time since his amateur days, two eagles. Even without the full force of the previous day's blow, he reached both the fourth and sixth greens with five-iron seconds and holed both putts. He nearly holed his eight-iron pitch to the seventh and birdied from only a foot or so and fell to five under par.

Turning homeward, Leonard bogeyed the 11th, one of 70 scores over par that day, but he had some luck on the formidable 13th. From a good lie on the high ground on the left side of the fairway, Justin played a three iron that started left but deflected off a little mound and rolled within 20 feet of the hole. He holed it, birdied the 16th with a 20-yard pitch to four feet, and after a steady par three on the 17th, he three-putted the 18th from about 40 feet.

As Leonard made his move, Mickelson and Woods were going nowhere. Mickelson has never been at his best in the British Open. Now, in danger of missing the cut after his opening 76, he saved himself with 68, only his third round in the 60s in the five British Opens he had played.

Woods, meantime, played another erratic round. Out in 36, once again he let a single hole wreck his round. He overshot the 10th green with his approach, and with his ball lying almost against a gorse bush, he tried to hack it out. That was a mistake. His club hit a branch on the downswing and slipped under the ball. It barely moved. He dug at it again and once more left it short, and before calming down, took another swipe and knocked it over the green. He made eight, four over par, shot 74, and fell into a tie for 49th place, along with Lehman.

At least they qualified for the last two rounds. The 36-hole cut fell at 147 and eliminated two of the British Open's finest champions of the past — Gary Player and Seve Ballesteros.

Never approaching his best golf, Elkington missed by one stroke. Price and Rocca went out as well, along with Lee Janzen, Craig Stadler, John Cook, who came so close at Muirfield in 1992, Sam Torrance, Sandy Lyle, the 1935 champion, Paul Azinger and Mark Brooks. Brooks was struggling through a bleak year. After winning the PGA Championship the previous August, he had now missed the cut in the Masters, U.S. Open and the British Open.

The second-round leaderboard:

Darren Clarke	66 - 133	David Tapping	66 - 137
Justin Leonard	66 - 135	Jim Furyk	72 - 139
Jesper Parnevik	66 - 136	Tom Kite	67 - 139
Fred Couples	68 - 137		

Some big occasions stimulate memories of particular shots, like Bobby Jones' two iron into the 18th at Inwood in 1923 or Gene Sarazen's four wood for a double-eagle two in the 1935 Masters, Palmer's slashing six iron from the rough at Royal Birkdale in 1961 or perhaps Nicklaus's one iron that hit the flagstick at Pebble Beach in 1972. Those are all positive memories. The 1982 British Open, though, is remembered best for Bobby Clampett.

Once a budding star, Clampett had played the first 36 holes in 133 and led the field by seven strokes going into the sixth hole of the third round. Within the next 20 minutes or so his game, and indeed his career, collapsed utterly and completely. Going from bunker to bunker he made eight and began a slide that didn't end. Eventually he dropped out of championship golf.

Thoughts of Clampett surfaced as Clarke headed into the third round of the 1997 championship. He had shot 66-67–133, the same scores Clampett had shot 15 years earlier, leading to speculation he might be headed for disappointment as well.

In his last full year as an amateur, Clarke played with great confidence, consistency and elan and won every tournament he entered. He brought so much talent onto the PGA European Tour he nearly guaranteed immediate success. Assumptions of this sort don't always work out. Faced with stiffer competition, he lost his consistency and along with it his confidence. Rudderless, he lost faith in himself as the shots that once flew to their target veered off line, and instead of putting for birdies he putted for survival.

It took Clarke three years to win his first tournament and three more to win his second. Now he stood at the brink of winning one of the game's greatest prizes. Still, thoughts of Clampett surfaced persistently. While everyone held his breath, Clarke eased past the sixth at two under par and made the turn for home in 32, but he lost the magic on the home nine, stumbled back in 39 when he needed something better, shot 71, and dropped from two strokes ahead to two strokes behind.

Parnevik shot another 66 and jumped into the lead at 202, Clarke followed with 204, and Leonard and Couples came next at 207. Couples shot 70 and Leonard a shaky 72. Furyk hung around the edges with 70 and 209, the same as Stephen Ames and Eduardo Romero. Tapping fell behind with 78 and 215, and Woods finally played as everyone knew he could. Tiger shot 64, equaling the course record, one stroke over the championship record of 63, shared by seven men. His 64 was the best round of the week.

On another balmy day, Troon basked under a bright, blue sky broken only by a milky white cloud bank in the distance. The sun sparkled on the Clyde, and off shore a lone sailboat sought the wind that would carry her to harbor. Barely a puff of breeze rippled the calm sea, not nearly strong enough to influence the flight of the ball. Hardly ever had Troon lain so open to low scoring.

The players took advantage of its lowered defenses. Of the 70 men who had survived the cut, 29 shot under-par golf and five played the course in even-par 71, one less than half the field. Besides Woods with his 64, Parnevik, Ames and Robert Allenby shot 66s, Romero and Lee Westwood shot 67s, and Stuart Appleby, Frank Nobilo, Steve Jones and David Russell shot 68s. Eight men shot 69s, among them a second straight by Montgomerie, which boosted him to 214, one over par and 12 strokes behind Parnevik, far too many to make up in the one round he had left.

A number of old as well as new heroes had the same problem. Watson, still a wonderful tee-to-green player, shot 70 and with 211 had nine strokes to make up. Both Norman and Curtis Strange shot 70s for 212, and Mickelson, Els and Ian Woosnam each shot 69 and stood at 213, level par.

Lehman lost whatever slim hopes he had to repeat with another 72, but he remained a favorite of the galleries. Even though he played loose and indifferent golf, the fans willed him on, applauding and cheering him on every green.

The cheers for Lehman, though, didn't approach the frenzy around Woods. He arrived for his 11 o'clock starting time intending to attack the course, and attack it he did, birdieing three of the first four holes. When he made the turn in 32, he had fought back to even par for the championship.

This was not the time to relax, though. He still had lots of ground to make up, and he had come to the heart of the golf course, the uncompromising 3,650 yards of the second nine. He may have saved his round on the 11th, where he had taken seven strokes on Thursday. He drove into the gorse as he had then, found his ball playable, and hit a wedge into even more gorse. At that point Woods looked as if he might make anything. Luckily, his ball sat in grass clear of the bushes. He made it to the green in four and holed a four-foot putt for a bogey five, the kind of bogey that can save a round.

Quickly Woods regained the lost stroke with a birdie at the 12th, made pars on the next three holes, then played two remarkable holes. Left with a second shot of 280 yards to the front of the 16th green, the last of the par-five holes, Tiger took his driver and from bare ground played a marvelous shot within 15 feet of the cup and eagled. Then, after missing the green of the 17th, a par-three of 223 yards, he holed a treacherous chip from a downhill lie to a hole cut no more than 18 feet from the green's edge for a birdie two. He had played a par-five and a par-three in a total of five strokes.

Even though he had been guilty of some erratic golf, missing fairways and missing greens, he had played the second nine in 32 and finished seven under par and climbed back into the race.

Woods had almost finished when Couples, Parnevik and Leonard began. Couples didn't birdie once in his round of 70, but he holed a full-blooded 168-yard six iron for an eagle two on the pitiless 11th and hung within five strokes of Parnevik.

Nor could Leonard make headway. He parred the first 10 holes but lost strokes on both the 11th and the easier 12th, where he drove into the rough. Strangely enough, his putting, usually the strength of his game, let him down. Leonard had putted nicely throughout the first two rounds, but he holed only one putt of any length in the third, a 25-footer for a birdie on the 17th. It looked irrelevant at the time because by then Leonard had been left far behind the leaders, for both Clarke and Parnevik were playing at the top of their games through the first nine.

At first Clarke looked unbeatable. When Parnevik birdied the first two holes, Clarke answered by laying a sand wedge to two feet and birdieing the third and recovering from a bunker to five feet on the fourth. At 11 under par, Clarke had moved five strokes ahead of Parnevik, who had bogeyed the fifth.

Still, Clarke wasn't through. Short of the sixth green with his second shot, he putted along the close-cropped fairway dead to the hole for another birdie, and added still another with a nine-iron pitch to 10 feet on the eighth. Now Clarke stood 13 under par.

Parnevik, meantime, had recovered from his bogey on the fifth with birdies on the sixth and seventh. When his drive on the seventh ran within 50 yards of the green, like Clarke on the sixth, Jesper rapped the ball with his putter. It scooted along the ground, climbed the upslope, and pulled up within 15 feet of the cup. He holed it and finished the first nine in 33.

A terrific score, but he had lost a stroke to Clarke, who looked not at all like quitting. Now they were coming to Parnevik's part of the course. He owned the second nine. While it had been a mystery to everyone else, Parnevik had shot 34 and 33 in the first two rounds, and now he began eating away at Clarke's lead.

Jesper picked up one stroke with a birdie on the 10th and another when Clarke hooked his drive into the gorse on the 11th. Parnevik gave one back with a loose bogey on the 12th, missing both the green and a four-foot putt, but bounced back with birdies on the 16th, with a pitch to six feet, and the 17th, after one of the finest iron shots of the week, a three iron drilled three feet from the cup.

With a routine par four on the 18th, Parnevik had come back in 33 once again and shot 66 for the round. Amazingly, with his second straight 33 he had played the second nine five under par in the first three rounds. Nor had he done badly on the first nine, shooting one 36 and two 33s, six under an easier par.

While Parnevik had held onto his game, Clarke lost control of his shots, hitting nearly everything to the right, and lost five strokes to Jesper. At the same time, he stood only two strokes behind him with 18 holes to play.

Looking ahead to the last round, Clarke said, "If I can get off to a good start tomorrow, maybe I'll play the back nine better than I did today."

The third-round leaderboard:

Jesper Parnevik	66 - 202	Stephen Ames	66 - 209
Darren Clarke	71 - 204	Eduardo Romero	67 - 209
Fred Couples	70 - 207	Jim Furyk	70 - 209
Justin Leonard	72 - 207		

After arriving at Troon for the last round, Parnevik reflected on the 1994 championship, when he led playing the last hole at Turnberry, tried a risky pitch that failed, and lost to Nick Price. "I have already finished second," he said, "so it's not like I don't know what to expect. I've done that. I've finished second, so it doesn't matter to me to finish second again. I'm going out to win." For most of the day it looked as if his determination might carry the day.

After birdieing the 11th and climbing two strokes ahead of Justin Leonard, Parnevik seemed to have won, but his game unraveled under Leonard's constant pressure.

Leonard was relentless, never wavering and playing one glorious shot after another. Of the last 18 golfers to tee off, only he shot in the 60s. Those who saw his round will never forget the series of putts he holed at the end. Nor will they forget his precise approaches that consistently put him in position to birdie. Over the first nine holes he laid seven pitches within 15 feet of the hole. From the sixth through the ninth he was awesome. He pitched to four feet on the sixth, to two-and-a-half feet on the seventh and to six feet on the ninth. He holed every putt.

Leonard played nearly flawless and nerveless golf, especially on the greens. A sensational putter as an amateur — he had won the 1992 U.S. Amateur — Justin holed everything he looked at, most tellingly at the end, when he played the last three holes in two under par.

His resolute, attacking golf drove Parnevik to commit errors he had avoided through the first three rounds. Where he had played the second nine in 33 in the first three rounds, Parnevik played it in 38 in the last.

Only one player scored within a stroke of Leonard. Lehman closed the disappointing defense of his championship with 66 and 284, which, aside from soothing his spirits, lifted him into a tie for 24th place with Montgomerie, Mickelson, Woosnam and Woods, who slipped backward with 74.

Troon was much the same as it had been the previous two days, although clouds blocked out the sun through much of the day and the wind picked up just a little. It was warm and pleasant, the sun broke through in the afternoon, and it was a delightful day for golf.

Playing under such mild conditions, 26 men broke par 71 and 11 others matched it. Some scores are worth mentioning. Els shot his third consecutive 69, but he had been ruined by his opening 75; Nobilo shot a second consecutive 68; Love, Olazabal and Faxon shot 67s, and Watson closed with 71 and tied for 10th place with nine others, among them Els, Love, Kite and Calcavecchia.

Once again Woods hurt himself with a bad hole, needing two shots to recover from a bunker on the little eighth and then three-putting for six. He played listless golf the rest of the way. It really didn't matter, because with Leonard playing as he was, Woods had no chance at all.

While Woods struggled and Clarke fumbled, Parnevik and Leonard moved steadily ahead. With only the homeward nine to play, they had pulled so far ahead they had the championship to themselves.

Beginning at 11 under par, Parnevik started slowly by parring the first two holes, went 12 under with a birdie on the third, and then committed the sin of bogeying a par-five hole. After a nice drive on the sixth, he hit his well-struck second shot into a fairway bunker that left him no opening to the green. He pitched out to perhaps 25 yards short of the green, and once again putted along the hard ground. The shot didn't turn out nearly as well as it had from the seventh fairway the previous day and ran more than 20 feet past the hole. He two-putted and walked off with a six.

He made up that stroke on the seventh, where his approach tangled itself in the flag and dropped beside the cup. He was back to 12 under par. Two more pars and he made the turn in 35.

Playing along with Parnevik, Clarke had about given up hope. He had birdied the first and then hit what he called the worst shank of his career. The ball squirted off toward the beach and out of bounds. He made six with a nice recovery from a bunker and never again threatened to win.

Leonard, meanwhile, had been playing up ahead and making one birdie after another. Six under par at the start, he birdied the second, third and fourth holes, lost a stroke at the par-three fifth, where he three-putted, then played the first in his series of telling pitches.

From bare ground short of the sixth green he played a sand wedge to four feet. His wedge to the seventh looked as if it might jump into the hole but stopped about two feet away. His 25-foot putt on the eighth hung over the lip of the cup but wouldn't fall, and his eight iron to the ninth came down just off the green, took the roll of the ground and curled perhaps six feet away.

He birdied all but the eighth. In an instruction-book first nine, he had hit every green, birdied six holes, and with his lone bogey had shot 31. From six under par at the start, he had gone to 11 under and climbed within a stroke of Parnevik.

Leonard's threat appeared even more serious because Parnevik had been playing loose golf, pulling his shots throughout the day and saving himself with deft work around the greens. Even though he had hit only four greens going out, he had shaved par by one stroke mainly because he had had only 11 putts. His short game had been deadly.

After both Parnevik and Leonard bogeyed the 10th, Jesper looked as if he had saved himself on the 11th, Troon's most difficult hole. The 11th had given up only two birdies all day, but from light rough on the left, Parnevik played a terrific shot that pulled up hole high about 18 or 20 feet from the cup and holed the putt. Twelve under par again, he led Leonard by two strokes with the hardest part of the course coming up.

Leonard's putting had been hard to believe through the early holes, and now he seemed to hole everything. He took three shots to reach the 11th green but holed from 10 feet, missed the 12th green from the rough but chipped to a foot and saved another par, and made routine pars on the 13th and 14th.

Parnevik then lost a stroke when his approach to the 13th hit a mound and rolled down a hill, away from the green, and he missed from 10 feet. Back to 11 under par, still one stroke in hand.

The 15th probably turned the championship around. Leonard pushed his drive into the wispy rough, couldn't reach the green with his second, and played an indifferent pitch to 15 feet. Trailing Parnevik by one stroke and with the holes running out, he simply had to hole the putt. Taking his time finding the line, he rolled the ball into the center of the hole. He was still 10 under par.

Now he began the string of holes that won the championship for him. Short of the 16th green with his second, Leonard played another indifferent pitch 15 feet short of the hole again, and again he rolled it home. With the birdie he had caught Parnevik, who saw it all standing back in the 16th fairway. A few minutes later, Parnevik heard another roar from the 17th and knew Leonard had birdied again and gone to 12 under par.

Parnevik wasn't worried yet. He had played a lovely pitch to three feet on the 16th and seemed assured of a birdie of his own, which would drop him to 12 under as well. He set himself carefully and struck the putt gently. Just as it reached the hole it moved slightly right, grazed the edge of the cup and eased past. For the first time, Leonard had climbed into first place.

Up ahead on the 18th tee, knowing he had to avoid the fairway bunkers, Leonard drove with his three wood. Championships are often decided by narrow margins. Parnevik's putt might have fallen but didn't and Leonard's drive could have run into a bunker but didn't. It missed the first fairway bunker on the left by less than a foot. From there he played a safe shot to the green and got down in two putts for a par four.

By the time Leonard struck his first putt it was all over. Parnevik had pulled another shot left and bogeyed the 17th. When he bogeyed the 18th as well, he finished three strokes out of first place, tied with Clarke, who had picked up four strokes on him over the last three holes.

Leonard had played his best golf when he needed it most, and he gave the rest of the field a post-graduate course in pressure putting.

At 25 years of age, he was the third successive American to win the British Open, the fifth successive American to have won at Troon, and the third man in his 20s to have won the major championships of 1997.

6. PGA Championship

While the little pitch Davis Love III played into Winged Foot's 13th hole during the last round of the PGA Championship doesn't qualify as the Shot of the Year, it boosted his confidence nevertheless at a time when it might have been sagging and spurred him on to a five-stroke victory over Justin Leonard, the British Open champion.

In the context of the 1997 season, Love's delicate lob stood as one of three shots played at critical moments of the last rounds by the winners of the U.S. Open, the British Open and the PGA Championship. Ernie Els played the first of those three when he holed a pitch-and-run from off the 10th green at Congressional in the last round of the U.S. Open. Justin Leonard played the other, holing a 15-foot putt on Royal Troon's 15th green that saved a vital par. Each of those shots followed mistakes that might have cost both Leonard and Els their championships.

While Love's margin over Leonard seemed substantial at the end, it was certainly in danger at the 13th. With the two men tied after 54 holes, Davis had moved four strokes ahead after five holes and five ahead after eight. Then Love bogeyed the 12th, one of two par-five holes at Winged Foot. When Leonard birdied, he picked up two strokes. Only three behind now, he looked as if he might easily win back one more and possibly two when his three iron into the 13th, a 212-yard par-three, settled within holing distance and Love's four iron curled left into tangled rough alongside a bunker.

Now Love played a decisive shot. There was no question he would hit the green, but to save a stroke he would have to leave himself a makeable putt. It wouldn't be easy. He had a chancy lie, and the hole was set just four paces from the green's near edge.

As he set himself for what might be the most important shot of his career, I couldn't help remembering Love at Oakland Hills the previous year when, with a golden chance to win the U.S. Open, he let a five iron get away from him and bogeyed the 17th and followed by missing a short, downhill putt on Oakland Hills' home green. He tied for second place behind Steve Jones. Memories like this and of previous drab showings in important tournaments led some of us to wonder if Love had the will to win on the big occasions.

With the hole set so close to the edge, Davis had only a tiny target. His shot would have to carry to the green, land short of the hole, then run a few feet. Taking his stance, Love drew back his sand wedge slowly and with what seemed to be a lento motion, popped the ball from the grass. It cleared the bunker, hit the green, caught a piece of the cup, and stopped so close he couldn't possibly miss. Perhaps unsettled by Love's fine shot, Leonard missed his birdie.

It was over. After another mistake, Leonard had dropped four strokes behind through the 17th, and Love birdied the 18th. He shot 66, his third 66 of the championship, and finished with 269. Justin shot 71 and 274.

Speaking later, Love said he made his worst swing of the day on the 13th tee. But he insisted his 10-yard pitch, "Saved the tournament for me.

"It gave me confidence that I could get up and down from anywhere and handle anything."

From midway through the third round, Love and Leonard had had the championship to themselves. Jeff Maggert closed with 65 and still fell two strokes short of Leonard, with 276, and Lee Janzen, with 279, became the only other player to score under 280.

Scoring in general had been unexpectedly low. Among the nation's best and more demanding courses, Winged Foot, outside New York City in Mamaroneck, New York, had never yielded so many exceptional rounds. In the club's last major championship, the 1984 U.S. Open, Fuzzy Zoeller, the eventual winner, and Greg Norman tied at 276, four under par. Ten years earlier, Hale Irwin had won the first of his three Opens by shooting 287, seven over par. Now Love had played such forceful, attacking golf he had finished 11 under par.

When Love joined the PGA Tour in 1986 at the age of 21, he seemed certain to play a major role in tournament golf for years. It hadn't worked out that way. In his 12-year career he had come close to winning one of the four major championships only twice — in 1995, when he finished one stroke behind Ben Crenshaw in the Masters, and in 1996, when he finished one stroke behind Jones in the U.S. Open. Until that 1995 Masters, he had never placed among the top 10 in any of the four big events, and most often played such mediocre golf he created the impression he lacked the fire, the overwhelming determination to win, that drives the game's great players. His stoic, expressionless reaction left the impression he felt contented to spend his career as a runner-up.

He won tournaments, to be sure — 10 victories in 12 years, which isn't bad — but he won nothing that had raised players of lesser ability to a higher level.

No one could understand not only why Love hadn't won one of the major championships but seldom finished within reach of first place. Taught the game by his father, Davis came onto the PGA Tour endowed with a glorious swing. Tall and lean at 6-foot-3 and 175 pounds, he draws the club back in a wide arc and then moves into the ball with effortless ease. Like the hub of a wheel, his head never moves until the ball is on its way.

His legato tempo masks a swing of abnormal power; he is among the game's longest drivers. Those impressed with the rhythm of his swing might miss the hand action at impact, where he generates exceptional clubhead speed. During 1996 he averaged slightly over 285 yards with his drives, about three yards less than John Daly, the leader, with 288. Love ranked fourth, behind Daly, John Adams and Fred Couples. Since Daly's arrival, only Love had broken his monopoly on the long-driving records. Love averaged a fraction under 284 yards in 1994, when Daly played very little.

A month before the PGA, Love closed the British Open with 67. That may have lighted a spark, because in his next round in an important event, Love blistered Winged Foot by shooting 66 in the PGA's opening round, matching the lowest score he had ever shot in a major championship. He had closed the 1995 Masters with 66. It also matched the lowest score ever shot under tournament conditions over Winged Foot's West Course. Zoeller shot 66 in the second round of the 1984 U.S. Open and then 67 in his playoff with Norman.

Had Davis teed off early, instead of at 1:25 in the afternoon, he'd have been the first to tie the Winged Foot record; in one of his periodic flashes of superb golf, Daly finished with 66 an hour or more before Love started.

By the time Love finished, it was evident this was not the Winged Foot of 1974, where par golf would have won the U.S. Open by seven strokes. Winged Foot had never been so badly mauled. Where only seven men had shot in the 60s throughout the 1974 Open, none of them in the first round, 22 had broken par 70 in 1997 and 10 others had matched it.

Robert Allenby, a tall and wiry 26-year-old Australian, bogeyed the 18th late in the day and shot 67; Norman, Leonard and Tom Kite were among eight players at 68, and Maggert, Tom Lehman, Phil Mickelson and Jim Furyk were among 11 men at 69. Tiger Woods followed with 70, along with Els and eight others, including Mark Brooks, the defending champion.

Among the disappointed, Colin Montgomerie shot 74, the same as Jack Nicklaus; Nick Faldo shot 75, and Jesper Parnevik shot 76. Both Irwin, the 1974 Open champion, and Zoeller shot 73s.

A wet spring had softened the greens, and wider fairways offered more generous targets. Nevertheless, this was outstanding scoring. It was an especially encouraging performance for Daly, who had walked off halfway through the second round of the U.S. Open, complaining he had the shakes. He hadn't survived the 36-hole cut in the last three PGA Championships, and he didn't even play in the British Open, the championship he had won in 1995.

His troubles with alcohol may have ruined his impressive golf game, although he has made periodic attempts to fight it. He entered the Betty Ford Clinic in March, lost 40 pounds, went on a fitness kick with help from a personal trainer, and had seen a psychologist regularly after leaving his partners stranded on the 10th tee at Congressional.

Talking about his condition, Daly said, "I feel more focused, and physically I feel great. Before, when I would play 18 holes, I would go into the clubhouse, eat four cheeseburgers, and go to bed. Now the guys are telling me they've never seen me hit it farther."

He had seldom hit it better, either, running off seven birdies after a slow start. One over after two holes, he traded birdies and bogeys through the first nine and turned for home in 35, even par.

Suddenly seeing the line on nearly ever putt, he holed for birdies from 20 feet on the 10th and from six feet on the 11th. Two under par then, he eased past the 12th and 13th in routine pars, and then played one of the finest recovery shots he could remember. After pushing his drive into the right rough of the 14th, he hit a faded seven iron to the green. When the ball pulled up about 15 feet from the hole, the gallery cheered.

Still two under, he bogeyed the 15th and dropped to one under par with that brutal finish coming up. Over the years it had defeated nearly everyone. Bobby Jones had stumbled over them in 1929 and only saved a place in a playoff by holing a breaking 12-foot par putt on the 18th. Irwin had played them in four over par in 1974, and 10 years later Zoeller played them in two over.

Daly birdied all three by playing some terrific approaches — nine iron to five feet on the 16th, wedge to four feet on the 17th, and a nine iron to about a foot on the 18th. Even driving with his three wood, he had very little yardage left — he estimated 156 yards to the flag on both the 16th and 18th and 137 yards on the 17th.

How the times had changed. When Irwin won at Winged Foot he drilled a two iron into the 18th green, and Greg Norman needed a six iron in the last round in 1984.

Out in 35, Daly had played the home nine in 31.

When it was over, he said he was shocked.

"Every time I got on the green I just saw the line and the putts started going in. It gave me confidence. When you make putts you tend to play aggressive shots off the tee. I started hitting a lot of fairways, and that made it fun."

While Daly made his move late in the round, Love's game meshed on the early holes. With three birdies and an eagle, he played the first six in five under par, shot his 31 on the first nine, and after some loose holes starting back, birdied the 17th and 18th for his closing 35.

After routine pars on the first two holes, Love went on his spree. He drew a very good three iron into the third, a par-three of 216 yards, and holed from 20 feet for his first birdie, ripped a six iron to six feet on the fourth, a really long par-four of 460 yards, and birdied again. Reaching the fifth, a 515-yard par-five, he hit a driver and another three iron to the back fringe of the green and holed from 25 feet for an eagle three. Love finished his run with another birdie on the sixth, at 324 yards among the shortest par-four holes in championship golf. Playing safely, he drove with a three iron, lofted a sand wedge to 15 feet and made the putt.

One stroke slipped away on the eighth, where his drive plowed into such deep rough he had to lay up, but he thought he could make up ground coming back, figuring the 11th and 12th as birdie holes. Instead, he parred them and bogeyed both of the second nine's par-threes, hitting his tee shot to the right on the 10th, and to the left on the 13th. Now he stood at two under par with Winged Foot's hardest holes coming up.

It was there he made his birdies — a driver and eight iron to 10 feet on the 17th and a three wood and a 170-yard six iron to 12 feet on the 18th.

By the time Love was teeing off, the day's glamour group was finishing. Els, Leonard and Woods had been sent off together a little before 9 o'clock that morning, drawing the day's biggest gallery, and at first looking as if both Woods and Els might set course records themselves. Feeding off one another, Woods birdied the fourth, fifth and sixth and Els birdied the fourth, fifth and seventh. They drew cheers on the fourth where Els rolled in a putt from 30 feet, and then Woods rolled in on top of him from 25 feet.

Suddenly they cooled off. Els made six on the eighth. His drive sank into deep rough on the right, and he nearly whiffed his second, moving a seven iron barely five yards. He wasted another stroke chopping the ball back into play and double-bogeyed.

Woods hurt himself as well on the 12th, the 540-yard par-five. Straining to reach the green after another Promethean 300-yard drive, he pushed his three-wood shot behind a tree alongside the green. Thinking he might have the room to run his third shot on if he could hit it hard enough, he squeezed into a cramped position and took a vicious swipe. The ball climbed more quickly than he expected, rattled around in the branches, and dropped into the rough again. He made seven on a hole he should figure to birdie, and came back in 38 after going out in 32.

Els, too, played through a very rough series of holes. After his double bogey on the eighth, he bogeyed the 10th, 11th and 14th, losing five strokes in seven holes, but he picked up strokes with birdies on the 16th and 18th and, like Woods, finished at even par.

Leonard, meantime, played erratic golf, but he continually saved himself with a succession of astonishing recoveries. At a dinner the previous evening, Byron Nelson told him, "You know I've played that course before. You have to realize you're going to make bogeys, and so is everybody else. When you hit it in the rough, just get it to where you've got an eight or nine iron or a wedge in your hands and you'll get a few up and down. Just avoid making big mistakes."

After he finished, Leonard said, "I had hoped I wouldn't have to remember his words as often as I did today — like every hole."

Leonard did indeed play some loose stuff. He hit only half the fairways and just seven greens, but he saved pars on five holes where he missed the green. Some of those recoveries are worth mentioning — a chip to 10 feet on the third, a 60-yard sand wedge to three feet on the fourth, a 103-yard sand wedge to three feet on the 11th, a chip to about a foot on the 14th, a 50-yard sand wedge to four feet on the 16th, and an 80-yard sand wedge to five feet on the 18th.

Overall he birdied four holes, bogeyed just two in spite of his wild driving, and shot 34-34–68.

"It wasn't a pretty 68," Leonard said, "but it looked good on the scoreboard."

The first-round leaderboard:

Davis Love III	66	Justin Leonard	68
John Daly	66	Tom Kite	68
Robert Allenby	67	Paul Stankowski	68
Bob Tway	68	Greg Norman	68
Paul Azinger	68	Shigeki Maruyama	68

Had Love followed Nelson's advice the following day he might have held the lead instead of falling behind Janzen, who shot 67 and moved to the top at 136, four under par. Love dropped to second at 137 after a double bogey on the 16th, where he tried to save one stroke but lost two instead.

Playing under more testing conditions than opening day, the field became bunched. When it ended, 20 men stood at even par or better, all within four strokes of first place. Among them were eight who accounted for 11 major championships. Janzen, Kite and Payne Stewart had won the U.S. Open, Couples and Woods the Masters, Leonard, Daly and Norman the British Open, and Daly and Stewart the PGA Championship.

Leonard held steady, two strokes out of first with a second-round 70, and with 138 tied Couples, Maggert, Phil Mickelson, Shigeki Maruyama, Costantino Rocca and Phil Blackmar. Six others tied at 139, including Vijay Singh, who shot another 66, the lowest score of the day; Daly, who slipped behind with 73, and Kite. With another 70, Woods shot 140, along with Stewart.

Els played himself out of the championship with 76, and after losing three strokes over the first three holes, Allenby shot 77.

A breeze had helped dry the ground and turn Winged Foot into a more demanding test than it had been on opening day. The greens had firmed up and become more difficult to hold, and the rough had grown higher, in some spots up to six inches. The wind had its effect as well. Daly noticed a difference in club selection.

"Yesterday," he said, "I hit a lot of approach shots with nine irons and wedges. Today I was hitting five and six and seven irons. With the wind, the last three holes were playing tough."

As a consequence, only 17 men broke par, five fewer than on opening day. Beside Singh's 66 and Janzen's 67, Couples eagled the 11th by holing a 140-yard nine iron and shot 67, six others shot 68, and eight more shot 69. At the end, none of them mattered.

On a confusing day when the progress of the championship was hard to follow, four men held first place at different stages. At one time or another, Janzen, Love, Daly and Kite stood alone at the top; Maruyama and Maggert shared first place at four under par, and then Leonard joined Kite after Maruyama and Maggert dropped back when Maggert bogeyed two of the last four holes and Maruyama two of the last six.

Love threw away his opportunity to hold first place by playing an impulsive shot on the 16th. Teeing off at 9:13, he had bogeyed two of the first three holes, but fought back to four under for the tournament after birdieing the 12th. When he birdied the 15th as well, he stood at five under, alone in first place.

His lead lasted only one hole. The 16th swings gently from right to left, and its fairway, like most of those at Winged Foot, is narrowed by stands of trees bordering both sides. At 457 yards, it is the third longest of the par-fours. Feeling confident after birdieing three holes since the third, Love reached for a little more distance. His timing off, he pushed his drive into the trees beyond the rough.

Had he followed not only Nelson's strategy but advice from Jack Lumpkin, his coach, he would have pitched back into play and tried to save his par from there. He had already done it on the 14th, where he hacked an eight iron to the front of the green from deep rough, but now Davis felt he could save himself by threading a one iron through a narrow gap in the trees. Of course it didn't work. The ball fell short, leaving him still in the rough, only now with a bunker between his ball and the green. With no shot, he tried to scoot the ball on with a 30-yard five iron, but it caught the bunker's lip and dropped into the sand. Love made six; back to three under par for 34 holes. With pars on 17 and 18, he shot 71 and held first place alone for the moment.

Still, he couldn't forgive himself for gambling on the 16th, admitting, "It just wasn't very smart."

Daly seemed to have everything under control through the first nine, hitting fairways and greens and dipping to five under with a birdie two on the seventh. Out in 34, he held first place through the 10th, but then he went into a tailspin. He began missing those five- and six-footers you simply must hole at this level of competition, bogeyed five of the next eight, birdied one, came back in 39, and shot his 73. It was nearly 74. Facing a three-foot putt for a par four on the 18th, Daly knocked it five feet past and barely snaked it in coming back.

It spite of his ragged homeward nine, Daly said he felt encouraged, adding, "If you'd told me I would be one under after two days, I would have taken it."

With Daly at 139, Love was safe from him, and with Winged Foot playing so hard, for most of the day Davis looked as if he might carry his lead into the third round. Then Janzen teed off at 2 o'clock, in the sixth group from the end, along with Singh and Ian Woosnam.

Janzen and Singh played the course differently. While Janzen ripped through the first nine in 31, Singh shot 34, and where Singh sped back in 32, Janzen stumbled over the closing holes and shot 36.

Playing aggressively since beginning the second nine the previous day, Janzen played the first two holes in routine pars, and then, firing at the pins, he birdied four of the next five. He rifled a three iron to 15 feet on the third, reached the fifth with a three wood for a two-putt birdie, nearly drove the sixth green and chipped within a foot, and with that birdie moved ahead of Love into first place. Next he floated a six iron to five feet on the seventh and opened his lead to two strokes.

Four under for the day through the first nine, and five under for the tournament, he had played his last 18 holes — the second nine in the first round and the first in the second — in 62. Now Janzen opened his lead to three strokes by holing from 15 feet on the 10th, an over-rated par-three of 190 yards with a house behind it, a hole Ben Hogan described as "a three iron into some guy's bedroom." Janzen, though, hit a six iron.

Sailing along with everything going his way, Janzen suddenly fell on hard times. He missed the 13th green and bogeyed, played a lovely pitch to two feet on the 15th and birdied, and after making a routine par on the 16th, drove into the rough on the last two holes and bogeyed both. His 25-foot par putt on the 17th sat on the lip of the cup but wouldn't fall, and his 20-footer on the last stopped inches short.

Even with his weak finish, Janzen said he wasn't all that disappointed. "I'm still leading and they've still got to shoot a better score than me."

Several old favorites wouldn't get that chance. Nicklaus had made the cut in the Masters, U.S. Open and British Open earlier in the year and needed at worst 72 to survive in the PGA. Having a dismal day, climaxed by losing a ball on the 14th where his drive hit a tree and disappeared, he struggled to 76 and 150. He hadn't made all four cuts since 1991.

Faldo disappointed himself as well, shooting 78 to go with his opening 75. Three years after moving from England to Florida for the practice facilities and tournament conditioning he felt he needed to prepare himself for the four major events, he hadn't threatened in 1997 to win one of them. In fact, in the 12 rounds Nick played at Augusta, Congressional, Troon and Winged Foot, he missed two cuts and shot an abysmal 43 over par.

Zoeller went out as well, with 148, along with Tom Watson, Ian Woosnam and Jose Maria Olazabal. Ben Crenshaw shot 77-80 and missed, along with Curtis Strange, who shot 76-77.

And then there was Mark Brooks, who had played so well on the big occasions for two years and finally broke through at Valhalla in the 1996 PGA Championship. Something happened after 1996, and Brooks laid claim to a dubious record. He became the first man to miss the cut in all four major championships after winning one of them the previous year. After a scrambling 70 in the first round, he shot 79 and missed by three strokes.

The second-round leaderboard:

Lee Janzen	67 - 136	Justin Leonard	70 - 138
Davis Love III	71 - 137	Jeff Maggert	69 - 138
Phil Mickelson	69 - 138	Shigeki Maruyama	68 - 138
Fred Couples	67 - 138	Phil Blackmar	68 - 138

The sun blazed down on Winged Foot the morning of the third round, the temperature climbed into the middle 90s, and the heat index reached 105. Some of the players were just as hot. Leonard shot 65 and set the course record, Love shot his second 66, and three others shot 67. Leonard's great day reshuffled the standings, leaving him and Love tied for first place and the rest of the field so far behind they wondered where they had gone.

It was a perplexing day, a day when Janzen couldn't hole a putt and fell out of the race, when Woods would climb within two strokes of first but play a few holes like a handicapper and drop back, and when Mickelson would play 14 holes in three under par but the other four in seven over and ruin his hopes.

It was also a day when Daly would erupt over a bad drive and set an Olympic-style record for the driver-throw, shoot 77, and drop from sight.

It was another day of interrupted play, like the two at the U.S. Open, when a thunderstorm passed through, causing a delay of about two hours. Fortunately, only 16 men were left on the course, but they had enough time to finish when play resumed after 7 o'clock.

Once again Winged Foot played a little harder than it had the previous day. Only eight men finished under 70, and the number of players under par for the holes played had dwindled from 22 after the first round to 15 after the second, to just two after the third.

Twenty men had been bunched within four strokes of the leaders after the first round, no one was that close after the third. Behind Love and Leonard, who shared first place at 203, Kite and Janzen trailed at 210, Mickelson, Couples, Maggert, Woods, Scott Hoch and David Duval had 211.

Of those who were in position to challenge when the day began, Woods went off first, at 12:50, paired with Stewart. Both men had shot two rounds of 70, but Stewart lost two strokes on the first nine and steadily fell back. After struggling through the first nine, too, Woods fought back, birdied the 11th, eagled the 12th, and at two under par might have climbed even higher. He had already double-bogeyed the fourth, and now he bungled the 17th badly, driving into the deep rough and leaving his approach short and deep in the rough. His recovery ran across the green, he chunked his next shot no more than a foot, chipped, and holed from about a foot. Another double-bogey six. A bogey on the 18th and he finished with 71 and 211.

Eight strokes behind now, Woods had played himself out of the championship with an erratic round made up of two double bogeys, three bogeys, four birdies and one eagle. He parred eight holes. So far he had made three double bogeys in three days. He had not found the key to consistency.

Nor had Daly. He didn't last as long as Woods, but he gave spectators at the 12th a little entertainment.

Things hadn't been going well for John that day. He had started at one under par, just five strokes behind Janzen, and dropped further back from the start. With 39, he had lost four strokes going out, another at the 10th, and reached the 12th tee expecting salvation. He knew he could reach the green with two good shots and perhaps recover some of those lost strokes with an eagle three. A good enough drive might even bring the green within nine-iron range. But he blocked it out. His ball soared over the trees and into the 17th fairway.

Then Daly exploded. With his face a glowing crimson, he gripped his driver and flung it over a fence. Some say it was the longest club throw since the 1960 U.S. Open, when Tommy Bolt hurled his driver into a lake in front of the 17th tee at Cherry Hills.

As Daly fumed toward his ball, two marshals of doubtful sanity scaled the fence, picked up the club from a patch of undergrowth that looked suspiciously like poison ivy, and raced ahead to give it back. As angry as he felt, Daly was luckier than Bolt. A young boy had dived into the water at Cherry Hills, found Tommy's driver gathering barnacles on the bottom, and brought it back to dry dock. When Tommy grinned and reached for it, the boy ran, climbed a fence, and disappeared, still clutching his prize.

Daly at least had his club returned, even though it didn't help. With a bogey on 12 and another on 16, he disappeared into a tie for 38th place, and the galleries were safely out of harm's way.

Mickelson had his troubles as well. Three under par after the fourth, he survived a double bogey on the fifth, struggled back to three under through the 15th, and then triple-bogeyed the 16th, a hole that claimed heavy penalties for mis-played shots. His drive drifted into the rough and he couldn't get out. Four more shots and he had reached the green, and two putts later he had his seven. At 211 for 54 holes he lagged eight strokes out of first place.

Janzen not only couldn't make a move, he couldn't hold on to what he had. He birdied just one hole and steadily slipped backwards, finishing at even par, seven strokes back.

Nor could Couples. Beginning the day at two under par, three strokes behind Janzen and two behind Love, Couples bogeyed the first two holes and had to struggle to salvage 71 and save sinking lower than a tie for fifth.

While everyone else was losing the battle with Winged Foot, Leonard and Love perked along without a care. Playing last, with Janzen, Love played the first four holes comfortably before ripping a four-iron second shot onto the fifth green for one birdie and adding another at the sixth by playing conservatively. Davis was strong enough to drive the green, but with the hole set behind a bunker in the right rear corner of the green, he played a safe three iron and followed with a sand wedge that cleared the bunker, braked about 10 feet past the hole, then trickled back to about four feet. When he holed the putt, Love stood at five under par and had drawn two strokes ahead of both Janzen and Leonard.

Two holes later Love found trouble. On the eighth his drive hit a tall birch tree about 120 yards out and dropped into the deep rough. Remembering Lumpkin's advice, Love lofted a 100-yard pitch to the fairway and then a seven iron to 10 feet. It was the shot of the day. It saved his par, and he made the turn in 33.

Leonard, meanwhile, was doing nothing but hitting fairways and greens and getting very little from it. Usually a sensational putter, Justin missed four putts from 15 feet, another from 20, and one from six feet. He birdied only the eighth on the first nine, rifling a four iron to the heart of the green and holing from eight feet. He turned in 34, one under for the day and two strokes behind Love.

Starting back, Davis improved to six under with a mammoth drive on the 12th that left him within six-iron range of the green and two-putting from 50 feet. He was three under for the day and three ahead of Leonard, by now his only rival. Everyone else had fallen back, except for Mickelson, who was about to wreck himself on the 16th.

Now Leonard began his stretch run. He began with a pitch to two feet on the 14th and a seven iron to 12 feet on the 15th. Five under now, he had climbed within one stroke of Love, just as they had started the day.

Love gave away a stroke by bogeying the 13th, but he won it back by birdieing the 14th with a glorious nine iron to less than a foot. He was six under and ahead once more. Leonard caught him with a stunning seven iron into the 17th that ran within two feet of the hole. Just then the sirens wailed signaling suspension of play, and players and spectators alike headed for shelter.

Winged Foot had mobilized for the possibility of dangerous storms. Warnings were posted on scoreboards, and evacuation procedures began.

Ever since two men had been killed by lightning strikes in 1991, organizations that conduct tournaments have had meteorologists on the site to monitor the weather. The PGA's man had been watching this storm since 8 o'clock in the morning. By 5:22 it had reached within 20 miles of Winged Foot, close enough to suspend play.

A fleet of 106 busses staged at Westchester County Community College and Yonkers Raceway rushed to Winged Foot and ferried spectators to temporary parking lots several miles away. Officials estimated their busses moved nearly 17,000 spectators in the first 35 minutes.

Before everyone could be evacuated, the skies turned black, the wind rose, gusting occasionally to 50 or 60 miles an hour, and the rain pelted down. Torn loose and broken by the vicious winds, branches and leaves littered the ground, but workmen were already clearing away the debris before the storm ended.

Play resumed at 7:17 with Leonard on the 18th tee and Love on the 15th green. Four under for the day, Justin could tie the course record with a par four or break it with a birdie three. He had been playing with great confidence in his swing, and now he drew his driver, ripped it down the middle of the fairway, flew a five iron to the green, and coaxed in a 10-foot downhill putt. When the putt fell he had birdied four of the last five holes, come back in 31, and shot 65, not only setting the course record but taking over first place as well, for now he stood at seven under par against Love's six under.

His lead didn't last very long. A few minutes after saving one par by holing from four feet on the 15th, another from 10 feet on the 16th, and still another after bunkering his approach to the 17th, but still one stroke behind, Love ripped a six iron to 10 feet and birdied the 18th — three successive 10-footers when he needed them all.

Love had come back in 33 and shot his second 66 of the week, and once again had tied for first place. Leonard had played the better golf, though.

From tee to green he had been superb. He had hit every fairway and missed just three greens, only one of them badly. Fooled by the wind, he pulled a seven iron that rattled in the trees bordering the 16th before dropping to the fairway about 40 yards short. After a pitch to 10 feet, he holed a dangerous downhill putt.

This had been his best day of golf, of course. In his first two rounds he had hit only 19 of 36 greens and 19 of 28 fairways.

His 65 reminded everyone of his 65 finish in the the British Open only a few weeks earlier. Asked to compare the two, Leonard said he considered the round at Troon the better, "but this is right up there."

"You know," he went on, "my goal at the beginning of the week was to be in good position to win going into the last round. Now I can look ahead to a few more things tomorrow."

The third-round leaderboard:

David Love III	66 - 203	Jeff Maggert	73 - 211
Justin Leonard	65 - 203	Fred Couples	73 - 211
Tom Kite	71 - 210	Scott Hoch	68 - 211
Lee Janzen	74 - 210	David Duval	71 - 211
Phil Mickelson	73 - 211	Tiger Woods	71 - 211

As the last round began on another hot and humid morning, only Love and Leonard mattered. With such a big lead, both men would have to break down to give someone else an opening. But even if Love and Leonard blundered, someone close enough would have to shoot an exceptional score.

It had been done, of course. Jack Burke had picked up nine strokes on Ken Venturi in the 1956 Masters, and Arnold Palmer had stormed back from seven strokes behind in the 1960 U.S. Open by closing with 65. Both Burke and Palmer had help, though. On a blustery Sunday, while Burke was shooting 71, Venturi shot 80, and those ahead of Palmer played such loose golf, Arnold passed 14 men at Cherry Hills. There was no Arnold Palmer at Winged Foot nor was there a Billy Casper, who made up seven strokes in nine holes on Palmer in the 1966 Open, and neither were the leaders nervous amateurs like the Venturi of 1956.

To thwart Love and Leonard, someone had to lower the course record by a stroke or more while Love and Leonard stumbled. As it played out, no one had a chance, with Love shooting 66. Either Kite or Janzen would have had to shoot 59, and either Maggert, Mickelson, Couples, Hoch, Duval or Woods would have needed 58. Maggert did his best by shooting 65, and Janzen shot 69, but they weren't nearly good enough, only a stroke better than the 70s by Kite, Daly and Hoch. Couples, Mickelson and Woods fell apart with 75s. Of the 15 men who shot in the 60s, only Janzen, Maggert and Hoch had begun the round within eight strokes of the leaders.

Leonard, who was had just turned 25 in June, had played in only two previous PGA Championships. In his 11 rounds he had never scored above par. Counting his three rounds at Winged Foot, he had five scores in the 60s, including 66s at Riviera in 1995 and Valhalla in 1996 to go with his 65 at Winged Foot.

Love, on the other hand, hadn't made the cut since Paul Azinger won at Toledo in 1993. If a choice had to be made, it would have been Leonard.

It would have been wrong. By the end of five holes, Love had pulled four strokes ahead and was never caught.

Justin wasn't playing the kind of golf we had seen through the first three rounds. Missing fairways and missing greens, he had bogeyed the second and fourth and slipped back to five under par while Love played precision golf. His birdie on the third was particularly telling.

A long hole at 216 yards, it has tree branches overhanging the green, two long and deep bunkers bunched against its sides, and out of bounds behind it. When he won the 1959 U.S. Open at Winged Foot, Casper never once went for the flag; he laid up short of the bunkers and made his par every day.

Love's three iron barely trickled to the front left edge, at least 35 feet from the cup. He holed it. Then Leonard, facing the kind of putt he had gobbled up both at Troon and at Winged Foot earlier in the week, missed from 15 feet. Two strokes behind after three holes, Leonard lost another when he drove into the rough on the fourth and bogeyed, and still another when Love rifled a 215-yard four iron to the heart of the fifth green and birdied.

Four behind, Leonard wasted one chance to cut into Love's lead by missing from four feet on the sixth, but he holed from 40 feet on the seventh. Love struck back by picking up two strokes on the eighth. When Leonard pushed his six-iron approach into deep rough right of the green, Love played a better six iron just above the hole. From a heavy lie, Leonard chipped across the green to the collar on the opposite side, took two putts and bogeyed. Love holed his putt. Five ahead now, Love made a cast-iron four on the ninth and turned for home in 32 against Leonard's 37.

With the holes running out, Leonard picked up one stroke by birdieing the 10th, and another when Love bungled the 12th, a par-five he had birdied his previous two rounds. Once again the rough cost a stroke. Love's drive settled so deep in the rough he could do no more than hack it out. A seven iron fell short, and he chipped on and missed from seven feet. At the same time Leonard played the hole perfectly — a driver into the fairway, a seven iron 120 yards short, a nine iron to 12 feet, and a bold putt.

Love admitted that at that point he was feeling emotional strain.

"Literally I was choking up a lot. Every time I thought about winning, every time I thought about what it would mean, every time I was three or four strokes ahead, I had to remind myself to keep playing the game. I think that bogey on 12 got me a little more focused and back into the tournament."

Now Leonard had closed within three strokes, and Love looked shaky. He looked shakier still when his four iron veered left and missed the green badly.

Then Davis played the shot he had to play — the lob that saved his par.

Still, he wasn't safe, because if Leonard birdied he would have climbed within two strokes with five holes to play. But he missed.

Now it really was all over. Although he fought off a minor crisis facing a 195-yard shot into the 18th green, Love made no more mistakes. His nerve ends a trifle frayed, Davis told his caddie — his younger brother Mark — "Help me stay in there another 10 minutes."

He did indeed hold together. From the center of the fairway he flew a five iron onto the green and holed from 12 feet for the birdie. He had come back in 33, shot 66 for the day, and with 269 posted the lowest 72-hole score ever shot at Winged Foot, beating the 1984 U.S. Open score by seven strokes. At the same time, Leonard shot 71, his first round over par in his PGA Championship career. He finished with 274, two strokes under the old record and safely in second place, two strokes ahead of Maggert.

Love had played first-class golf through that nerve-wrenching last round, when he had to prove to himself that he could play his best when it mattered most. He drove well, hitting 10 of the 14 fairways on driving holes, and missed just three greens; one of those was no farther off than the collar. Only one missed green cost him a bogey.

Over the four days, Davis had hit 42 of 56 fairways and 53 of 72 greens. He also averaged a fraction over 307 yards on the two holes measured each day, the best in the field.

Love had owned three of Winged Foot's holes. In four rounds he had played the fifth, sixth and the demanding 18th in 11 under par. While he had birdied each of them three times, he had eagled the fifth as well, giving him a combined score of five under par in the four times he had played it.

No one had played more consistently. He had shot three 66s and one 71.

Slightly off his game, Leonard couldn't respond. Had he put pressure on Davis, he might have made a difference, but he lost too many strokes too early, and when Love nearly holed his pitch on the 13th and Justin missed his birdie, Leonard had run out of holes.

It was a blessed relief for Love, who had finally won something of lasting significance. When the final putt fell, he flung his arms around his brother and with tears overflowing, embraced his wife, Robin, and his mother, Penta.

There was a sense of mysticism about the finish as well. Heavy rain had begun falling at the 15th, but it had stopped by the time they reached the 18th, and as Love stepped onto the final green, a vivid rainbow arched across the pale blue sky. Love had seen the same kind of rainbow the day he won The Players Championship.

There was also a sense of something missing. Love's father had died in a private plane that crashed near Jacksonville, Florida, in February of 1988. He was only 53 years old.

Davis Love III was born April 13, 1964, the day after his father tied for 34th place in the Masters. He had opened with 69 and shared first place with Palmer, who eventually won, Gary Player, Kel Nagle and Bob Goalby. He had also played in the 1974 U.S. Open at Winged Foot and missed the cut. An unsteady putter, he eventually drifted away from tournament golf and became a respected teacher.

His son still missed him. He thought about him throughout the championship and after he had won, he thought back to the 1987 Heritage Classic at Hilton Head Island, South Carolina, the first tournament he won as a professional. His father was with him for the first three days, but he had to miss the last round because of his teaching responsibilities.

"It's hard to believe that's the only tournament he saw me win or saw me have a chance to win. He was proud of me no matter what I did, but I sure would have liked to share one with him."

7. The Players Championship

As golf tournaments go, there are victories and then there are victories. And then there was Steve Elkington's frolic in the The Players Championship. If it was hard to find the words to describe it, you could always ask Elkington. He put it straight in 10 words: "I basically blew away the best field we've ever had."

That was pretty much it — he just blew them away. He could hardly have asked for a better stage for such a performance. Just consider the field. For the first time ever, all 50 of the top-ranked players in the world were in the same tournament. And on an outstanding golf course, the Tournament Players Club at Sawgrass in Ponte Vedra Beach, Florida. It figured to be a wild free-for-all. But Elkington — who had won the Doral-Ryder Open just three weeks earlier — ruined the show. He just kept getting tougher. He led by one stroke in the first round, one in the second round, two in the third round, and then he ran away and won by seven strokes. The runner-up, in case you were wondering, was Scott Hoch.

So, high drama The Players wasn't, but high theater it was, and high comedy it could have been if it hadn't been so painful for some. You had John Daly falling again to his alcoholism; Fred Couples, the defending champion, in another affair of the heart gone south, and Davis Love III committing a silly and fatally expensive rules violation. Whether any of them could have put enough pressure on Elkington to change the outcome is strictly material for the 19th hole. But they never had the chance to find out.

Couples, who won with such flair in 1996, simply wasn't on his game. For one thing, there was his chronic back problem. It would reoccur from time to time, and you didn't always know when unless you asked him. And then, on the heels of a messy and very public divorce, came the failed romance. Who can measure what effect this might have had on him? True, such personal things are generally left unsaid, but it was Couples who brought it up, explaining why he wasn't in the best of spirits for playing golf.

Daly, wrestling with alcoholism, had resumed "social" drinking in the autumn of 1996. But he slipped badly at The Players. He shot a four-over-par 76 in the first round — who can say whether this precipitated things? — and then spent that night drinking and singing at a Jacksonville nightspot. When he got back to his hotel later, he flew into a rage in an argument with his wife and damaged the room. Police were summoned. So was Fuzzy Zoeller, his best friend on the PGA Tour, and they took him to a hospital. The next day he was on his way to a rehabilitation center in California. "I apologize to others who struggle with me in fighting this disease," Daly said. The story began to leak out during the second round, but didn't emerge fully until the final day.

Then there was the presence of the prodigious Tiger Woods. He had turned professional only some eight months earlier, and he was automatically the favorite to win every time. The golf world was especially watching The Players. This was his first time out against the full force of professional golf. Woods, as usual, drew most of the attention, but the first day belonged to

Elkington — barely. He found 18 players within three strokes of him.
The TPC at Sawgrass, that Pete Dye-designed dragon, took an awful beating in the first round. The course was soft and the breezes manageable. So manageable, in fact, that it was no fun for the crowds who perched on the bank along the notorious 17th hole just to watch the disasters. This time, only two players hit shots into the water, Sam Torrance and John Morse, and the hole played as the third-easiest on the course. The players jumped on the course. Elkington was at 66, five were tied at 67, 10 were at 68. All told, 19 players were in the 60s, and 57 broke the par of 72.

Elkington has either a very wry sense of humor or a great gift for understatement, or perhaps a combination of the two. Note how he described the start of his 66. "That's usually the makings of a decent round," Elkington began. He was talking about starting off with four straight birdies. He had a point. Four consecutive birdies do not a round make, but they're sure like money in the bank. Anyway, the 66 was a good sign. When Elkington won The Players in 1991, guess what his opening score was?

This was a rejuvenated Elkington, or at least a re-armed one. His favorite clubs had been stolen back home in Houston, and then his replacement set was stolen in the San Francisco airport. He finally got another set that suited him, and he won the Doral-Ryder Open with them. That was just four weeks before The Players. So there was good reason to believe that this was the real Steve Elkington, the one who won the Mercedes Championship and PGA Championship in 1995. But Elkington also had another problem, a very human one.

He missed his family. Annie Elizabeth, two years old, and Samuel, barely two months old, were back home with his wife in Houston, and the thought tugged at him. "Half of me feels like I should be home at the moment," he said, "and the other half knows I should be out here playing." The realities of the breadwinner had to be faced. Golf was his life and his livelihood, and so here he was.

He started on the second nine, and it was immediately clear that everything was in very good order. The driving was accurate, the irons precise, the putting sharp. Those four quick birdies were on the 10th (his first) from 20 feet, the 11th from a mere foot and the 12th and 13th from eight feet each. That's what you call the makings of a decent round. But just the makings. He had been around too long to be deceived by such a start. He was also prepared for the other, and it came at his ninth hole (No. 18), where he skied his three-wood tee shot, then pulled a 220-yard two wood into the water on the left and suffered a double-bogey six. This must have hurt. Right. He promptly birdied the next two holes, his 10th and 11th, and then his 15th to take the lead by a stroke.

Zoeller was already in with his 67, off seven birdies and two bogeys. And he wasn't deceived, either. Who could forget him in The Players in 1994? "I broke the course record by four shots — and got beat by four shots," he said. "Something wasn't right with that picture, folks." That, of course, was Greg Norman's 24-under-par year. What about his 67? "The scores might even go lower this afternoon," he said.

He wasn't thinking of just 66, but if there was a 65 or less out there, no one could produce it. That's because The Players course was not a total pussycat. There was the rough.

"I've never seen it this thick or this high," said Mark Calcavecchia, also at 67. "They're trying to do a U.S. Open thing. A one-shot penalty. I wouldn't be surprised if someone blows out his back or shoulder trying to lash it out of there."

There were no reports of injuries, except to the course, and Calcavecchia was a chief villain. For a half-round, anyway. This was the Calcavecchia of old, with no adventure left untouched.

"Long time since I made a par," Calcavecchia said, meaning none over his last eight holes, actually. This was Calc's wild back nine: He parred the 10th, birdied the next three, bogeyed the 14th out of the rough, went birdie, eagle, birdie, then bogeyed the 18th. The eagle came at the par-five 16th. He faded a three-wood approach to 12 feet.

David Edwards ran off four birdies in his first five holes for 67. Russ Cochran, also at 67, had an interesting perspective about the soft course. Yes, you didn't get as much roll on the soft fairways. But then, that made them more "gracious." When was anything in golf called gracious? "Hit it in the edge of the fairway," he explained, "and it's going to stay there." So the ball doesn't roll much, but it doesn't roll into the rough, either.

Tom Lehman, the 1996 Player of the Year, also was at 67, but not with his normally solid game. "Usually, my bad shots aren't all that bad," Lehman said. "But today I hit some really lousy ones. That's the way I've been playing for the last few weeks, so I need to iron that out." Case in point: He shot 32 on his second nine (the real first nine), but with a double bogey at his 12th hole. "The strongest part of my game is generally my iron play," he said, "and today it was the worst."

The Tiger Woods report: He shot a one-under 71 and found himself in good company, tied with Couples, Nick Faldo and Greg Norman, among others. And also in lots of company. A total of 26 players shot 71 in the first round.

The surprise of the day was Taylor Smith, famed for tying Woods in the 1996 Walt Disney World/Oldsmobile Classic, then being disqualified for having a non-conforming grip on his long putter. This was Smith's first Players, and — now with a legal putter grip — he leaped at the chance with an opening 68. It included birdies at the 11th and 16th, both par-fives, the easiest holes in the first round, and thereby hung the tale of the pencils. Smith gets extra yardage off the tee at par-fives by teeing his ball on a tall tee. Except that this time, his kid brother, in the gallery, had the only one and was saving it for his own match. "So I use the scoring pencils," he said. And how do you get the ball to stay on a pencil? You take the eraser off.

So Smith left the TPC vowing to get more long tees, and Elkington left a contented man, no longer worried about someone stealing his clubs. "I've got plenty of sets now, so if you feel like stealing them, be my guest," he said. "My caddie may chop your head off, though."

Maybe the golfers were taken by surprise, but beachcombers and the hotel people could have told them that The Players course was in for a beating. They could tell by the sandflies — the beachcombers for obvious reasons, and the hotel folks because they had to guard against an infestation. The tipoff was the message left on the beds. Said one: "Due to the abundance of rain that we have experienced, the sandfly population is high. Please do not leave towels on your balcony." So there were sandflies on the beaches, and birdies at Sawgrass. But help was on the way for the course in the second round — wind.

"The rough was tough, but the wind was tougher," Lehman said, after a 71 that tied him for fifth place at 138. It had looked pretty tame on television in the morning, he said, but tame is a relative term. This was hardly the kind of killer wind that can come ripping in off the Atlantic, but at 15 miles an hour, it was enough to keep the guys guessing. The morning players had the better of it.

Elkington shot an easy 69 and held on to his one-stroke lead at nine-under 135. "Once you get playing well," he said, "it gets to be less of a race." He made two bogeys, but they didn't indicate that any cracks were showing in his game. His five birdies were holidays — all on one-putts, including two in the five-foot range at the two second-nine par-fives, the 11th and 16th. He seemed to be at ease with himself, and being the halfway leader posed no problems for him. "I've won from behind and I've won from in front," he said. "I'm just happy to be playing well."

Larry Mize moved up to second place at 136, and attributed his improved play to a new frame of mind. He said a friend told him he played better when he was relaxed and smiling. "So I've been working on trying to be more relaxed, and smile," he said. He has not done well in The Players. He missed the cut six times in 14 visits, and he would rather forget his best finish. That was a second in 1986 — after blowing a four-shot lead in the final round. "That did gnaw at me a little bit," he admitted.

Tommy Tolles also had a finish to forget, and that was just a year ago. He first came to prominence with some strong play in The Players. His first PGA Tour victory was almost in his bag, but he let it get away. He led David Duval by two shots, and Fred Couples (the eventual winner) by four. But he closed with 72, including two bogeys over the final four holes, and tied for second. "There was a lot of self-doubt creeping in," Tolles said. "I had one hand on the ball, a 10-year exemption, $630,000, and I just let it go by the wayside." No doubts this time. He eagled the par-five 16th from 20 feet, and birdied the 17th and 18th, each from 12 feet. "I would probably give a little over $300,000 to have had that finish last year," Tolles said, grinning. This time it was worth 67 and a tie for third place with David Edwards (70) at 137. Love had the day's low, 66, with a wild stretch on the back nine. Starting at the 14th, he went birdie, double bogey, birdie, birdie, and tied for fifth.

Mark Brooks, the 1996 PGA champion, outwitted the wind at the eighth, the longest par-three hole on the course at 215 yards. "I thought we were going to have some help from the wind, and maybe it was a three iron," Brooks said. But the wind switched, and so did he, to a one iron, and got only the second ace ever at the hole. It helped him to 68 and a tie for 15th place at 140.

Never mind who was shooting what. The attraction here and everywhere on the Tour remained Tiger Woods. The unrelenting attention paid to him was never better illustrated than at The Players. Take the *Florida Times-Union* of Jacksonville. The newspaper carried a daily feature, "Tiger Time Line," chronicling him from opening tee shot to final putt. The entry for 4:47 p.m. tells of how Tim Herron outdrove him, and a young girl in the gallery said, "Oh, my gosh, Tiger's behind somebody. That's a first." He was also behind someone on the scoreboard, shooting one-over 73 for an even-par 144 total and a tie for 50th place.

The second round ended with some smiles, a lot more wounds. The troubled Daly had already withdrawn, and was joined by four others. Guy Boros and Ian Woosnam withdrew with aches and pains after starting, and Patrick Burke and David Frost left without starting.

Ben Crenshaw had pain of a different kind. He missed the 36-hole cut for the sixth time in six starts. He shot 81-79 and tied for dead last with Robert Allenby (83-77) at 160, the worst totals at the course in the 1990s. This wasn't like Crenshaw. His longest drive was 232 yards, he hit only seven out of 18 greens, and just 13 out of 36 greens for the two rounds. "I have no confidence at all," Crenshaw said. Fred Couples made the cut (74–145), but he wouldn't be repeating, not from 10 strokes off the lead. Nick Faldo shot 72, and at 143 he was also too far back. No matter. "I made the cut," he announced, with relief, "and that's something."

The story of the third round was the story of two men talking. There was Elkington. He calmly sat back and munched on an orange while he spoke of how he staggered in and lost two strokes of a four-stroke lead. If it was a surprise that Elkington could be so casual, it was as much a surprise that Hoch was speaking at all. Hoch was upset at something someone had written earlier in the year, and vowed he would no longer speak to the press. But how can you stay silent after a superb seven-under 65 — seven birdies and no bogeys on a tough course that got a even tougher with the gusting winds. "Did you think a 65 was likely under those conditions?" someone asked.

Hoch, not known for overpowering length, answered simply, "Not by me." Someone offered that he was known as a good ball-striker. "That's the funny thing about being known for something," Hoch said, playing off the media theme and his image. "I'm known for a lot of things that aren't necessarily true."

Things didn't look promising when Hoch stepped to the first tee. Hoch, a seven-time winner in his 17 years on the Tour, looked at the dark sky and swaying trees, and decided to make the best of it, and the best it was. His birdies came on two 15-foot putts, one 12-footer and the rest in the three-foot range.

It had become a two-man race, but there were some stubborn souls out there.

"Any time you get a great player who's on a roll the way Steve is," said Billy Andrade, "those guys are unbeatable sometimes. But it takes 72 holes, and on this course, anything can happen, especially on those last few holes." Andrade would know. He left a 25-foot birdie putt fully 15 feet short. Maybe it's because he was playing under a different kind of pressure. His wife, Jody, was expecting their second child any day. "I talked to her before I teed off and everything was OK," Andrade said. "So I told her just hang in there, just one more day." Andrade dropped that clutch 15-footer for his par and a 68 that put him in a tie for third place with Tom Purtzer (69) at 208. Purtzer had a spotless round going, including an eagle at No. 5, until he bogeyed the 18th. That ended a run of 27 holes without a bogey.

Back to Elkington and his orange — he came walking into the press room and took the interview seat, and he proceeded to chomp on that orange while he told about how, when he just about had the championship by the throat, he dropped two shots of his lead.

"My bogey-bogey finish didn't spoil my day," Elkington said. "But it almost did." This happened after a six-birdie surge had put him at 15 under par and five shots to the good through the 11th. So what would have been a near-lock ended up as 68 for a 13-under total of 203 and a two-stroke lead on Hoch.

Elkington opened the day with three straight birdies. He was this much on his game — his putts were from two, six and 10 feet. Then, after two pars, he got three more birdies over six holes, from two, four and 10 feet. The wind had calmed, then kicked up as he headed home. At the par-four 12th, he put his approach over the green and bogeyed. Then he parred through the 16th. Then came the 17th, Fantasy Island, the little par-three hole.

"The 17th is real tricky," Elkington said. "You never know what to do there." Actually, conditions were fairly benign. It gave up 16 birdies in the third round, and only seven bogeys. One of the bogeys was Elkington's. He left a nine-iron shot 50 feet from the hole and three-putted. Worse, he had left himself a three-footer for par and missed it. Then came the 18th, which gave up only two birdies in the entire third round. It was an act of sheer craftsmanship that Elkington escaped a mean situation with just a bogey. He put his approach shot up on a bank next to a cart path. He got a free drop, but his shot was of the utmost delicacy — a downhill pitch. He got it to 10 feet and two-putted.

Actually, Elkington said, what looked like a predicament on that bank was really nothing more than an inconvenience. "I figure the worst I can make is five, so I'm still in good shape," he said. "I mean, at this point, I'm not really protecting my lead, I'm just trying to finish my round. I'm not going to ruin my round with a double, or whatever."

If this wasn't confidence talking, nothing was. So his lead had been chopped in half, and he hadn't even flinched. He just munched away on that orange. The bogey-bogey finish left Elkington with 68 and at 13-under 203 for the three rounds. The shaky finish failed to shake him.

"I'm playing well," said Elkington, looking ahead to the final round. "And there's no reason I won't play well. You know I'll let it rip. Don't worry about that."

Someone had asked Scott Hoch what it would take in the final round for him to win this thing. "Probably one of my best rounds," he said. Unfortunately, he played one of the other kind. It was 74, his worst score of the tournament. But it might not have mattered. Elkington was not about to be turned back. In fact, he even finished with a flourish, chipping in at the 18th for an embarrassment of riches. It gave him a closing 69 and a 272 total, 16 under par, and a seven-stroke victory over Hoch. Elkington spent an untroubled Sunday. It was a day at the beach. In fact, the only thing to put a ripple on the calm of the day was a huge and expensive gaffe committed by Love.

Love had a six-foot birdie putt at the island 17th. He accidentally brushed his ball on a practice swing, knocking it a short distance away. He assessed himself a one-stroke penalty and continued to play, two-putting for what he thought was a bogey four. But under the rules, he should have replaced the ball. He didn't, meaning he had played from an incorrect place — another violation of the rule. Then he signed for 73, which turned out to be an incorrect scorecard, and so was disqualified. Then things really got painful. If Love had replaced the ball and then two-putted for his bogey four, he would have tied for seventh, and that would have been worth $105,437.

That was the only thing that interrupted Elkington's day. "You know, it was an unbelievable day," he said. "I must say that leading this tournament from wire to wire is the most difficult thing that I've had to do in golf."

Well, he made it look easy. And he thanked his putter. Coming into the tournament, he ranked a distant 127th in PGA Tour putting statistics, with an average of 1.83 per hole. He averaged only 1.45 in The Players.

"The putting was super all week," Elkington said. "I think it was probably the best putting performance I've had since I've played the Tour."

We have Hoch's word for that, too.

"Maybe if he would've missed all the putts I did, and I would've made all the putts he did, then we might have had a good horse race going," Hoch said. "I felt like it would almost take an act of God for me to catch him after the 14th hole."

As a final round, it was just an exercise in bookkeeping. Elkington had one bogey, that at No. 11, and four birdies. Yes, Elkington really did just blow away the toughest field in golf.

"And I don't know if I was capable," he said.

Well, how about this for proof: Figures don't lie.

8. Ryder Cup

Late in the afternoon of a spectacular Sunday on Spain's Andalucian coast, a sudden rainstorm swept in off the Mediterranean Sea. It couldn't dampen the spirits of the Europeans. The Ryder Cup was still theirs. Seve Ballesteros, the European captain, was congratulating his team, and being congratulated, on the steps of the clubhouse at the Valderrama Golf Club in Sotogrande. Then came a special telephone call. King Juan Carlos wanted to salute this native son for steering the Europeans to victory over the favored Americans in the first playing of the Ryder Cup matches on the Continent. There was another part to the king's message. "I got very nervous," he said, "when things looked complicated."

He wasn't alone. All of Europe drew a deep breath of relief. Thus ended one of the wildest of all Ryder Cup matches. Things had looked so simple. It was a European runaway — until the Americans staged one of the best rallies in Ryder Cup history the last day.

Colin Montgomeri clinched the European victory with a sporting concession to halve with Scott Hoch on the 18th hole of the final singles match. "At the 10th, I was happy because it looked like we might get a walk in the park," he said. "But it didn't turn out that way. It was a nerve-wracking experience."

Said Ballesteros, "They nearly took the cup away from us."

The Americans trailed by a prohibitive five points, 10½-5½, going into the 12 singles matches, worth one point each, on the third day. Their position was hopeless. Then they fought their way back, but Europe hung on for a thrilling 14½-13½ victory and stretched their dominance. That may sound strange. The United States, after all, leads with 23 victories, six losses and two ties, going back to 1927. In the modern matches — with the expansion of the Great Britain-Ireland team to include all of Europe in 1979 — the United States has only a 5-4-1 edge. Europe now is 4-2-1 in the last seven meetings.

The Americans were generally the favorites this time. Tom Kite, the American captain, who had a 15-9-4 record in seven Ryder Cup competitions knew better. Kite said the Europeans ought to be favored, for their course knowledge at the least. After all, he said, they played at Valderrama every year in the PGA European Tour's Volvo Masters. Ballesteros also thought his men were the favorites, but he wasn't thinking about local knowledge.

At any rate, on paper, the Americans were clearly stronger. To begin with, they had three of the four reigning major champions — Justin Leonard (British Open), Davis Love III (PGA Championship) and the phenomenal Tiger Woods, age 21, who had won the Masters and three other U.S. PGA Tour events.

Not that this Ryder Cup needed any more hype, but it got some anyway from Ian Woosnam, the feisty little Welshman. "Because I've never won a singles, I've never experienced the honor of sinking the putt which wins the Ryder Cup," Woosie said. "So give me Tiger Woods in the last match on the last day and I'll whip his butt, as the Americans say."

Said Ballesteros, "I think any of my 12 men can compete against Tiger Woods, and beat Tiger Woods."

"Valderrama," Montgomerie said, "isn't Augusta."

It was a prophetic attitude. Tiger was doomed not to live up to his billing. He would finish with a 1-3-1 record. "It's called golf," he would say.

The Ryder Cup opened dramatically that Friday morning to a ferocious storm, said to be the worst in September in eight years. It delayed play for about 90 minutes, and forced the last two afternoon matches over into Saturday morning. The matches also opened deceptively, with a 2-2 tie in the Friday morning better-ball, itself a big switch. Ballesteros insisted on starting with fourballs (better-ball) instead of the usual foursomes (alternate shot).

"Why?" he said, laughing. "That's a good question. But not a good answer. Just to make sure I do something different."

"It doesn't make much difference to me," Kite said.

Perhaps the painstaking Ballesteros had noted that in the seven Ryder Cup matches since 1983, the Europeans outscored the United States 32½-24½ in better-ball. Maybe there was an edge here. At any rate, the move was completely in character for the dashing young man whose sheer brilliance saved the Ryder Cup from extinction when the Great Britain-Ireland team was expanded, primarily in order to bring him in. In eight Ryder Cups, he amassed a 20-12-5 record and 22½ points, just a half-point behind Nick Faldo's European then-record 23 points.

In the opening better-ball matches Friday morning, Jose Maria Olazabal and Costantino Rocca shook off a two-hole deficit through the 12th and beat Love and Phil Mickelson 1 up. A fatal flaw had been exposed. The Americans would show a maddening inability to hold the lead on the second nine. Rocca birdied the 13th, and Olazabal backed him up by holing a 131-yard wedge shot for an eagle at the par-four 14th. Rocca then birdied the 16th from about four feet for a 1-up lead, and Love and Mickelson missed chances to tie at the 18th. Said Kite, "They played very, very well but didn't make any putts." The words would become familiar.

The Americans squared the better-ball in the next pairing, with Fred Couples and Brad Faxon beating Faldo and Lee Westwood 1 up. Ironically, the match came down to Faxon holing a six-footer for a par at the 17th for a halve and the win. It was almost identical to the clutch putt Faxon had missed on the final hole against David Gilford in the 1995 Ryder Cup matches at Oak Hill. "That was with the Ryder Cup on the line," Faxon said. "This time we were just trying to grab a point."

The Swedish twosome of Per-Ulrik Johansson and Jesper Parnevik brushed off an early 2-down deficit to beat Tom Lehman and Jim Furyk 1 up. The key moment was Johansson's birdie at No. 8, where he hit a 122-yard wedge shot through a small opening in the gnarled cork oaks to within about one foot of the hole. Then Parnevik birdied the par-five 17th, flipping his third shot across the pond to 15 feet, and then the 18th, from nine feet.

The long-awaited debut of Woods had arrived and proved profitable. Woods teamed with his Orlando, Florida, neighbor Mark O'Meara to beat Montgomerie and Bernhard Langer, 3 and 2, and square the better-ball at 2-2. Montgomerie and Langer had not made a birdie. "It was embarrassing," Montgomerie said.

Woods, with former U.S. President George Bush and wife Barbara in his gallery, made two birdies. Adjusting to a course that took the driver out of his hands much of the time, he used a two iron off the tee at the 535-yard No. 4, then hit a nine-iron layup shot, then a sand wedge to 20 feet. He holed the birdie putt for a 1-up lead. After Langer bogeyed No. 6, Woods put the Americans 3 up at the par-four 10th on a 10-foot putt. O'Meara birdied the 14th, then closed out the match with a 36-footer at the 16th.

The question came: It had been said that Woods couldn't handle Valderrama. Were he and O'Meara trying to prove something? "Not really," Woods said. "Mark and I just want to go out there and play. If we both played our good games, we both figured we would be on top." That was a big "if." It would come back to taunt him.

And so the opening better-ball on Friday ended in a 2-2 tie. Who could have dreamed that this was the closest the Americans would come to winning. The Europeans took command in the alternate-shot matches that began Friday afternoon and ran over to Saturday morning, thanks to the rain delay.

Woods had been informed that he and O'Meara would be playing Montgomerie and Langer again. "Perfect," he said, with a confident smile. Not so perfect. Montgomerie and Langer, restoring Ballesteros' faith in his pairings, went ahead on the American team's bogey at No. 2 and stayed there, winning 5 and 3. Montgomerie ended it by holing the 15-foot putt Langer left him at No. 15. "I had to hole that putt for him," Monty said. "I loved it."

Hoch and Lee Janzen were 2 up on three occasions but had to scramble for a 1-up win over Rocca and Olazabal. The Europeans tied it with a birdie at the 17th. At the 18th, Rocca hit a dazzling approach from the left rough to about 10 feet. Janzen responded with a 165-yard six iron to six feet. Hoch dropped that putt for the winning birdie, and for the first Ryder Cup point for both.

A minor flap occurred later in the afternoon. Faldo and Westwood were 2 up on Leonard and Jeff Maggert at the 16th hole, with darkness falling. Faldo argued that both teams had agreed to finish the hole. Maggert stopped play at the green, saying it had become too dark. "We wanted to be fresh, and let them think about it overnight," Maggert said, with Faldo crying foul. Then on Saturday morning, Leonard's 20-foot birdie try hung near the edge, but Westwood rolled his 11-footer right in for the 3-and-2 win.

"My partner just put me in the record book," said Faldo, now with his record 24th Ryder Cup point. "Yes, it means a lot to me. That's what it's all about." He would get his 25th point before this week was over.

Then it was Mickelson and Lehman against Parnevik and Ignacio Garrido, the young Spaniard, and once again the Americans were found wanting on the second nine. At the 14th, Parnevik put an eight-iron shot to about one foot, and Garrido dropped the birdie putt to square the match. They halved out from there for a halved match and 4½-3½ European lead.

Then came contrasting strategies. For the Friday afternoon alternate shot, Kite sent out his four remaining players, pairing Hoch with Janzen, and Leonard with Maggert. "I felt it was important to get all 12 of my guys out," he said. "Now they all have Ryder Cup experience."

Ballesteros stuck with his strengths. Garrido was his only change for Friday afternoon. It wasn't until the Saturday better-ball that he used the rest of his men — Denmark's Thomas Bjorn and Northern Ireland's Darren Clarke, both rookies, and Woosnam, who hadn't been playing well.

This would turn into Black Saturday for the Americans — an entire day without a win, and this included two carried-over Friday matches. It was only the third time in history a team did not win, but the first for the United States. Woosnam stoked the fire some more. "It's nerve and bottle and whether you've got it or not," he said. "The U.S. has a very good team, a very good lineup, but that doesn't come down to anything in match play."

The Europeans took a strangle hold on the Ryder Cup by taking 3½ of a possible four points in the Saturday morning better-ball. The answer was on the greens. The Europeans could putt, the Americans could not.

Olazabal and Garrido scratched out a halve against Mickelson and Lehman in a match that showcased two remarkable shots at the par-five 17th — Mickelson's two iron out of the right rough, across the waiting pond to six feet, and Garrido's exquisite floater from the back bunker that trickled lazily to a stop 10 feet from the hole, cheating the water just beyond. Garrido made his birdie, and Mickelson missed his winning eagle. They halved the match.

Chalk up another U.S. defeat. Couples and Love, who practically owned the World Cup of Golf as a team, couldn't hold a lead on the second nine and lost to Montgomerie and Clarke. The U.S. went 2 up on Couples' eagle at the par-four eighth, a 76-yard wedge shot, and his birdie at the 10th. Ultimately, the match came down to the 17th. Clarke gambled for the green and lost his second shot in the water, but Montgomerie laid up, hit a wedge to eight feet, and made the birdie. A halve at the 18th gave the Europeans a 1-up win.

Woods and O'Meara were partners for the third time, against Faldo and Westwood this time, and they seemed to have something going. O'Meara birdied the fourth hole and Woods, the seventh, and they were 2 up. But Westwood birdied the 10th, 11th and 15th holes from eight, 10 and five feet, and the Europeans were 1 up. Faldo's birdie from 18 feet at the 16th set up their 2-and-1 win.

Sometimes, when things go bad, they just seem to get worse. Leonard, playing with Faxon, set a blistering pace. He holed an 86-yard pitch for an eagle at the par-five No. 4, then birdied Nos. 5 and 6, then Nos. 9 and 10. He had gone six under par over a six-hole stretch. And they lost to Woosnam and Bjorn, 2 and 1. Leonard was asked if he had ever played so well and lost. "Well, not too many times," he said. "In fact, never." Bjorn and Woosnam had shot an approximate eight-under-par 63. Faxon still had not made a birdie. "Justin Leonard," Bjorn said, "did everything but win."

In the Saturday afternoon foursomes (alternate shot), Ballesteros sent Montgomerie and Langer out again, against Janzen and Furyk. The Europeans trailed just once, to Janzen's birdie at No. 1. Montgomerie left Langer a 10-foot putt at No. 9, which he downed for a 2-up lead. The Americans missed a birdie try that would have squared the match at the 14th. "And then we hung on," Monty said. "That's all we did." Darkness forced a halt. They returned early Sunday, halved the 18th in bogeys, and Montgomerie and Langer had a 1-up win. Europe was now leading 9-4.

This time it was the Europeans who couldn't hold a lead. Ballesteros sent Faldo and Westwood out again, for the fourth time, and they rushed to a 3-up lead through No. 5. Then Hoch drew the Americans even with a par putt at the ninth from 24 feet and a birdie putt at the 10th from 21 feet. At the

12th, Maggert's bunker shot to three feet set up the winning par for a 1-up lead.

Darkness soon fell, and they had to come back Sunday morning. They were at the 15th, an imposing par-three hole of 200 yards. "I had all night to think about it," Maggert said. "I just wanted to hit a good shot …" It was a four-iron shot to two feet. The birdie was conceded, and the Americans had a 2-and-1 victory, the only American come-from-behind-win from more than 1 down.

Couples and Love still were cold. They led briefly, then Olazabal and Rocca took over for an easy 5-and 4-win. "They have helped us," Olazabal said. "They have not played very well." Olazabal could have said that about a lot of Americans as the Europeans went into the singles with a five-point lead, 10½-5½.

Some felt the Europeans actually won this Ryder Cup some weeks earlier when Ballesteros and other officials dismissed Miguel Angel Martin from the team. Martin had won a berth on points early in the season, but he had injured a wrist and couldn't play. He still wouldn't withdraw.

Martin was dropped in an acrimonious episode, and Ballesteros got the three men he wanted — Olazabal, recovered from his foot problem, who moved up on the points list on Martin's departure, and his two captain's picks, Faldo and Parnevik, who were playing the U.S. PGA Tour and so couldn't earn European points. Olazabal went 2-2-1, Faldo 2-3, and Parnevik 1-1-2. All together, they accounted for 6½ of Europe's 14½ points. In an awkward move, Martin was allowed to retain his status as a team member, which entitled him to certain benefits from his endorsement contracts.

The Americans' last chance was more like a task out of Greek mythology No team had ever come back from more than two points down. They were trailing by five. They would have to win nine of the 12 singles matches on Sunday. Kite, facing early defeat, loaded the top of his lineup with experience, going with Couples, Love, O'Meara, Woods and Mickelson, in that order. Ballesteros saved his strength for later. He needed it. The American charge (in order of finish) was ferocious:

Couples triggered the explosion by blowing away Woosnam, 8 and 7. Couples went eagle-birdie-birdie from No. 5 and was seven under par when he closed out Woosnam at the 11th. This was Woosnam's eighth Ryder Cup and he had yet to win in the singles. Johansson got the point back, and kept Love pointless, with a 3-and-2 victory.

O'Meara birdied five of the first eight holes and whipped Parnevik, 5 and 4. The American gloom deepened when Woods, the super match-player, fell easily, 4 and 2, to Rocca, who birdied three of the first five holes. Woods' debut ended with a disappointing 1-2-1 record. Europe was still ahead by five, 12½-7½.

Mickelson eagled the first two par-fives and turned back Clarke, 2 and 1, but then Leonard went through a weird experience. He exploded to a 4-up lead with birdies on the first four holes, then got only a tie when Bjorn bogeyed the 18th. The scheduled 12th singles match ended early when Lehman walloped Garrido, 7 and 6, cutting Europe's lead to 13-10.

Now King Juan Carlos began to get edgy. Maggert sidetracked Westwood, 3 and 2. The U.S. was within two points, at 13-11. And then the king could relax. In the eighth match (the ninth to finish), Langer assured Europe of a tie, and of keeping the Ryder Cup, getting the 14th point (14-11) with a 2-and-1 win over Faxon. After 45 holes on his own ball, 36 in better-ball and nine in singles, Faxon finally made a birdie, but it was far too little and too late.

A tie was still possible, and Janzen did his part with a clutch rally against Olazabal. Janzen, 2 down at the 15th, swept the last three holes — the 16th with a par, the 17th with a birdie from 14 feet and the 18th with a birdie from three feet for a 1-up win.

Furyk finally broke through, and he did it in high spirits. Faldo, 2 down, fired a seven-iron shot to within three inches at the 14th. "Pick it up," Furyk said. And he proceeded to match him by chipping in from 12 feet for a halve. At the 15th, Faldo put a brilliant four-iron shot to three feet. "Pick it up," said Furyk. And, incredibly, he holed a bunker shot, matching Faldo again. At the 16th, an official was trying to determine who was away in the fairway. "It doesn't matter," Faldo said. "He'll probably hole it anyway." Furyk won 3 and 2, and Europe led 14-13.

That set the stage for the Montgomerie-Hoch finish, the 10th match on the schedule but the last of the day as Sunday was fading in the rainy twilight. Hoch's chance to beat Montgomerie ended when he drove into the rough. He got to the green in three, 15 feet from the hole. Montgomerie was on in two shots, 20 feet away from a certain par.

The Ryder Cup was already in hand, the victory all but assured. There was no need to put Hoch through the pressure of a meaningless putt. Monty conceded for the halve. The only person he hurt was himself. He might have had a full point. After losing his opener, he finished with a 3-1-1 record and 3½ points, one point more than anyone else.

That still left the question. It used to be, why can't the Europeans win the Ryder Cup? Now it is why can't the Americans? "The American guys may have a fantastic team," Woosnam offered, "but maybe they aren't in contention enough at times to be able to control their emotions under the pressure of it."

"I'm still totally convinced we have the 12 best players, today proved that," Lehman insisted. "But put their guys together, and they have magic at their fingertips."

Maybe it's that simple. Maybe there's nothing like playing the Americans to bring the fire out in them.

Kite blamed himself for not having urged the Americans before the British Open to go play at Valderrama, for local knowledge. How important was it? The Americans knew Muirfield Village from the Memorial Tournament, yet the Europeans won there in 1987. The three Americans who did play Valderrama in advance — Love, Woods and O'Meara — had a combined 1-9-3 record.

"Maybe if we had got blown out," Kite said, "it would have been easier to take."

Said Ballesteros, "I have won the Masters and I have won the British Open, and I have won all over the world, and this was the greatest."

9. Toyota World Match Play

"Any game is going to be tough," said Ernie Els, prophetically, as it turned out. "It is a quality field," the South African added. "You have to take it as it comes, hole by hole. I don't think I want to start thinking about the final or Sunday afternoon or speeches or anything."

Els had won the Toyota World Match Play Championship three times in a row, but he knew there were no guarantees about making it four. Els slipped past Ian Woosnam in his first match, and then survived his longest ever match at the 37th hole against Nick Price, but his 12th contest on Wentworth's West Course proved beyond him.

It took until the 36th hole before Els gave up his crown, but Vijay Singh eventually wrestled it away. Singh had been the third of Els' final victims the year before. "This is sweet," said the Fijian. "Having lost to him last year. To beat Ernie is a big achievement, especially as he hasn't lost to anyone before. I've had a few good wins in the States, but this is one of the bigger ones today."

This was Singh's fourth victory of the year — his first had involved defeating Els in his home country at the South African Open — and the 21st of his career. He is truly a world-class player and has won in every corner of the globe, in Africa, Asia, Europe and America. Now he could call himself the World Match Play champion. As this was the 34th playing of the tournament, at the Wentworth Club near London, he could also claim to be a part of the history that had initially inspired him in the game.

"I have read about this tournament and I remember the Players and Irwins winning it," Singh said. "That was when it was the Piccadilly World Match Play. I dreamed of playing in it one day and here I am. Not only playing in it, but winning it, too. It is an achievement I have always looked forward to personally. It is a big event, one of the biggest in the world. It is the World Match Play."

If Singh was clearly enjoying getting used to the idea, then why not? His had not been the traditional route to golf stardom. He was born of Indian descent in Fiji. His name, Vijay, means "victory" in Hindi. He learned the game from his father, an airplane technician who also taught the game. One of his heroes was Tom Weiskopf and he possesses one of the most graceful swings to prove it. At one time he was a club pro in Borneo, but wherever the game has taken him, one thing has been constant. His work ethic is simply stated: practice, practice, practice.

Singh spent a lot of time on the West Course in all kinds of weather during the World Match Play. He played 134 holes over four days. Not only was his the first name other than Els' to go on the trophy since 1993, but also he was the first player since Corey Pavin that year to win from the opening round. In each of his four appearances in the event, Els has been seeded into the second round. "It is a lot of golf when it is cold and raining and the course is playing long," Singh said.

"It was disappointing last year because I played very well all week, but not as good on the final day," Singh said. "I think fatigue has something to do with it. I was in much better condition this year." Singh has a personal trainer to work with him whenever he is at home. "When you are still in your 20s you are still quite fit, but most players, when they reach the 30 mark, have to do some sort of exercise. I have a trainer and it is working."

The 34-year-old Fijian began his fifth campaign in the event with a first-round match against Tsukasa Watanabe of Japan and cruised to a 4-and-3 victory. "I did what I needed to do," Singh said. "I didn't need to play too smart."

The best match of the first day featured Frank Nobilo and Phil Mickelson. After 12 holes, Mickelson found himself 4 down, but he fought back magnificently to be 2 down at lunch and to square the match at the 21st hole. "Phil's short game can demoralize people in match play," Nobilo said.

Nobilo did not think his opponent could keep his run going, but Mickelson went 1 up with one to play when Nobilo drove out of bounds for the second time of the day at the 17th hole. "In the morning I hit my worst shot all day and I joked with myself that I couldn't do it again," Nobilo admitted. "I hit it as hard as I could, and it was worse."

But Mickelson found sand off the tee at the last hole, and while Nobilo two-putted for his birdie, the American faced a 12-footer for his four. It looked in all the way, but then lipped out. "I thought I had made the putt at 18," he said, "but as I look back on it, it was the drive and not the putt that hurt me."

It was not to be Mickelson's day and for the second year running he lost in the first round. The year before, his bunker shot at the 18th had flown into the hole and then bounced out again as he lost by one hole to Singh. This time, he got as far as the 38th, when Nobilo hit his seven iron at the short second to one foot.

"It was a classic match play game," Nobilo said. "In stroke play, we would not have got away with what we were doing. Each player forced the other to play shots they probably didn't want to play. I am very proud to have Phil's scalp, but at the 18th I thought his ball had to go in the hole. Phil is tremendous with the blade and you just have to stand and watch."

Mickelson's American Ryder Cup teammate Brad Faxon did make it through to the second round, and at the expense of a member of the winning European team at Valderrama, Darren Clarke. The Northern Irishman won the first hole and maintained the advantage until the American levelled the match at the 10th. From there, Faxon took command and won 2 and 1.

Neither man was happy with his putting, but Faxon is a bad man to have an off-putting day against, even if he is not at his usual high standard. "It is nice to win any match," said Faxon, who denied he was on a mission of vengeance. "There wasn't quite the tension there was at Valderrama. It is not going to get the Ryder Cup back to the States."

As far as the home crowd was concerned, the match of most interest centered on the battle between two European team members, Woosnam and Jesper Parnevik. Woosnam, after an indifferent Ryder Cup, was back to the look of a man who had won two World Match Play titles. In the early windy conditions, the Welshman played the best golf of the morning with an approximate 68, although that was only good enough to put him 1 up against the Swede. But when Woosnam won three holes in a row from the sixth, he was set fair for what was eventually a 4-and-3 win.

Parnevik was playing his first golf since the final day at Valderrama. That night, with the European celebration in full swing, he had gone down with food poisoning. The stomach virus turned out to be so serious that he needed to spend 24 hours in a Stockholm hospital. The doctor wanted to keep Parnevik in for further observation, but the Swede had other ideas, such as not wanting to miss his regular Friday bridge session with some friends, so he checked himself out.

Woosnam's victory was also helped by a new driver, the club that had let him down in the second half of the season. The new club, designed by a former NASA scientist, had a more centrally located shaft. "It is meant to help amateurs stop slicing the ball," Woosnam explained, "and it is just what I need."

The inconsistency that had plagued Woosnam's game all year returned the following day in his match against Els. The South African was 4 up after only six holes, held the same advantage at lunch and by the turn in the afternoon was seven in front. From there it did not take long to confirm the 7-and-6 result. "It is not the driver, is it," Woosnam said. "It is obviously me."

Els had arrived at Wentworth after a five-week break at home in South Africa. "It was beautiful," he said. "I didn't do much." He played a little social golf, and watched the Ryder Cup for three straight days. He would not say who he was supporting but did reveal he had won some money in bets from his friends. Els had two weeks off in May and then also returned to action on the West Course, finishing second in the Volvo PGA Championship.

"This is probably the best course I could come back on," Els said. "It is probably the second course where I play most golf. And Wentworth has been good to me in the past." At a dinner before the tournament, he was presented with honorary membership in the club.

Els was at a loss to explain his success in winning the championship for an unprecedented three successive years. "I have no idea," he said. "I can only say that I enjoy the course. I get a good feeling when I go out there. I know the greens well, I know what irons to play. I just go out there and try and beat the other guy, try to make more birdies. My strategy is to try to go out from the first hole and play as well as I can, and if I make a mistake at least it is just one hole. Sure, I have a lot of good memories here, but you almost have to forget about the good times and try and get your mind ready on the present."

That meant some work on the practice range if Els, just short of his 28th birthday, was to win his 11th consecutive match, against Price, the following day. "Maybe I will have to play better to beat Nick Price," he said, "but in match play you play as good as you have to play."

As defending champion, as well as the U.S. Open champion, Els was naturally seeded first. In the absence of any of the other 1997 major winners, Steve Elkington was seeded second, Colin Montgomerie, third, and Price, fourth. Like Els, they all joined the action on the second day with Price taking on Nobilo. The Kiwi could not live up to his dramatics of the previous round and was 4 down as Price shot an approximate 68 in the morning. The Zimbabwean won 6 and 5. "It was the sort of day where I was just happy to get ahead early on and stay there," Price said.

For Elkington and Montgomerie, the extra rest proved to no avail. In fact, the Scot awoke with the flu, the result of his exertions in the previous few weeks when he had twice finished second on the PGA European Tour and, in between, played in the Ryder Cup, including gaining the vital extra half point which gave Europe an outright victory.

This was Montgomerie's ninth week in a row, and having not missed a cut all year, he probably needed a week off. "But I'm not saying this is a blessing in disguise," he said of his defeat to Faxon by 2 and 1. "My mind was always keen to play, but unfortunately my body was saying 'no' today."

The match was always close and the first time anyone went 2 up was when Montgomerie won the fourth, fifth and sixth holes after lunch. At the next, Montgomerie's putt from the fringe stopped on the edge of the hole, while Faxon chipped 25 feet past but holed that for a half. Faxon then holed from 30 feet for another half at the ninth before winning the next four holes. Montgomerie had no answer.

"The seventh hole was pivotal because I didn't want to lose four holes in a row," Faxon said. "I was just trying to hang on. He didn't play as well on the back nine as I have seen him and I knew he was sick so I wanted to make sure I kept the match going."

Elkington and Singh provided a contest between the immediate past losing finalists, but Singh was 4 up at lunch and was never worse than 3 in front afterwards. "I didn't play well in the morning, but I thought I had a chance after lunch. I was 3 under and Vijay matched me," Elkington said after losing 5 and 4.

Although this was one day the rains stayed away and the sun came out, a strong breeze presented its own problems. "It's probably the trickiest I have ever seen Wentworth," Singh said. "Club selection was critical. You had to hit a lot of half-shots and a lot of knockdown shots."

With the two British players out, the nearest "home" connections rested with Singh, who, in addition to his house in Florida, has a residence in London, where he takes his son Qass to the local driving range, and Price, whose mother lives in Norwich.

Singh was 8 up on Faxon after 16 holes and, although the American fought back tenaciously in the afternoon, Singh always had a bit too much in hand and won 4 and 3. "It took a bit longer than I thought," Singh said. "I played really well in the morning before the rains came." His morning round was estimated at 65, although that would have included a couple of large concessions.

When the rain came, it never let up and by mid-afternoon, a team of 20 grounds-staff were squeegeeing the greens on most putts and did a remarkable job to allow the two semi-finals to finish. Els and Price both shot 67s to be tied at lunch, but the South African went 2 up on the first nine in the afternoon, before a three-stroke swing went against him between the 12th and 15th holes. Els had two opportunities to even the match, missing from six feet at the 16th and then at No. 17, exactly the same putt he had had in the morning to even the match then. He thought his number was up then, but a birdie at the last hole, where he holed from five feet, meant he survived.

Price missed the fairway at the 37th hole but hit a brilliant three wood inside Els, but the South African holed his putt from 40 feet, while Price missed from half the distance.

"Walking down the 18th, I thought I had lost," Els said. "I thought I would be playing off for third and fourth. These great players are hard to shake off. But Nick left the door open for me when he missed the green with his third shot and I holed the putt. At the first, it was straight up the hill. That's the longest putt I've holed all week."

Price, before going on to lose 5 and 4 to Faxon in the third-place playoff, said, "I don't mind losing when it has been a great match with good scoring. It was superb match play — nip and tuck, going one way and then the other."

Els hoped he had got his toughest match out of the way, but it was not to be. At lunch, Singh was 3 up. Els got exactly the start he wanted in the afternoon, hitting an eight iron to eight feet for a birdie at the second, sinking a 40-footer for eagle at the fourth and another monster, from 35 feet, at the 10th. The match was not even for long, since Singh hit his eight-iron approach at the 11th to 18 inches, which was conceded before Els missed from four feet.

Els birdied the par-five 12th to square the match again, but finding a greenside bunker at the 15th, he went 1 down with three to play. The South African then drove into the trees on the 16th but made a par, but when Singh pitched from rough to 20 feet at the 17th, Els, sensing a chance, let it slip by leaving his chip even shorter.

The putt, from 25 feet, looked to be in all the way, but did not catch enough of the right lip to fall. Singh could not hole his putt for the match, however, so they went to the last. Their drives finished virtually side by side, but Els was just in the long rough and found a greenside bunker. Singh then hit his five iron onto the green. "I knew it was pretty much done then," he said.

Needing to hole his bunker shot, Els came out 10 feet short, but would not concede Singh's two-footer for a four until he had missed his putt. "It would have been interesting if I had holed it," Els said. "I wanted to make him work for the win." Singh all but won the hole, but the referee gave the official result as a one-hole margin of victory.

"I never felt comfortable with my swing all day," Els said. "It is a pity it should have ended this way. It would have been different if I had played well and he had beaten me playing great. But congratulations to Vijay. Maybe he'll win it a couple of times now."

"The course was playing longer than I have ever known," said Singh. "We didn't play as well as we can, but it was match play and you only need to play better than your opponent. I was two under in the morning and one under in the afternoon and that is what I needed to do to win the tournament."

10. Alfred Dunhill Cup

For a nation with such talented golfers, South Africa's record in the Alfred Dunhill Cup was good, but not as good as one might have thought it could have been. The Rainbow Nation only joined the competition in 1991, and got to the final then, but since had managed two appearances in the semi-finals. Sometime, surely, they would improve on that record.

And so they did in 1997, when the team of David Frost, Ernie Els and Retief Goosen won the 13th staging of the Alfred Dunhill Cup over the Old Course in St. Andrews, Scotland. A dramatic final day started with the trio avenging their defeat to New Zealand in the semi-finals in 1996, and then reversing the result of the 1991 final, when South Africa's debut had ended in defeat at the last stage to Sweden.

On that occasion, Sweden was represented by Anders Forsbrand, Mats Lanner and Per-Ulrik Johansson, and South Africa by Frost, John Bland and Gary Player. Frost, in fact, had played on all seven South African teams. "He was telling me," Els said, "that in 1991, he was the youngest in the team, and now he's the oldest guy." That 1991 final was a close affair, hinging on the last match which went to the 19th hole before Lanner's birdie putt shook off the ever-tenacious Player.

As well as South Africa's return to team competition, that tournament marked the emergence of Sweden as a genuine power in European golf. Six years later, they were back in the final for the first time since, but with a team of high pedigree. Joakim Haeggman had become the first Swede to play in the Ryder Cup in 1993, while Johansson and Jesper Parnevik had recently played a substantial part in Europe's victory at Valderrama.

They swept through the qualifying stage by topping a group that also included twice-former winners Australia and then defeated the defending champions America in the semi-finals. This was helped in no little part by Haeggman's 27 for the first nine, a record for the Old Course.

As the weather turned from a balmy autumn morning to a viciously cold afternoon as the wind started howling, it was the southern hemisphere team, rather than that from the northern reaches of Europe, which claimed the victory.

Johansson and Frost were matched, as they were six years earlier, but the Swede was the winner this time to complete a record of five wins in five matches. South Africa then won the other two. Goosen beat Parnevik and with Els taking care of the record-breaking Haeggman, South Africa won 2-1.

"We have been coming here for seven years and it is wonderful finally to win this trophy," said Frost, the South African captain. "It is always a pleasure to come back to St. Andrews, and it will be even more so to defend next year."

This was the a "new" Old Course that the 48 players from the 16 countries found when they assembled this year. At the instigation for the Royal & Ancient Golf Club, whose magnificent clubhouse is the backdrop for the most famous first tee in the world, six holes had new tees, extending the course by 161 yards. Its total length was now 7,094, with the significant changes being to the 15th, where the tee was moved back 46 yards, and to the 16th, which was extended by 44 yards.

The idea was to bring back into play some of the great features of the Old Course, such as the Coffin bunker on the sixth hole, and the Principal's Nose bunker at the 16th, as the feeling was that the big hitters of the modern game were bypassing all the trouble and finding wide-open landing areas well past all the perilous bunkers.

The reaction of the players was mixed. Many applauded the changes, principally Els and Colin Montgomerie, the Scot commending the R&A on their foresight in testing the revisions prior to the 2000 British Open at St. Andrews.

Others, including the American Mark O'Meara, took the view that the Old Course had stood the test of time. The previous year, O'Meara, the only member of the winning United States team to return, had scored 63 on a calm day in which he went to the turn in 28, birdieing the first eight holes. He had Curtis Strange's course record of 62 in his sights before he took a double-bogey six at the 17th, the Road Hole.

O'Meara's teammate Justin Leonard similarly showed what can be achieved on the Old Course in tranquil conditions when he went eight under par after 12 holes on the opening day. Back-to-back bogeys at the 14th and 15th holes followed, however, before the British Open champion birdied the last hole for 65. Leonard hurried to a telephone to tell his parents. "I never thought I would be eight under on this golf course," said Leonard, who first played the Old Course as a 14-year-old with his father, breaking 80 in the process.

An eagle at the 14th hole took Scotland's Raymond Russell to eight under par, but he then double-bogeyed the 15th, triple-bogeyed the 17th and finished with 68. Parnevik matched Leonard with 65 later in the day. Any feeling that the Old Course was still a pushover evaporated the following day when the wind got up and only two players broke 70, as opposed to 14 in the first round.

Despite Leonard's performance on the first day, when he beat Jose Coceres by seven strokes, America almost lost to Argentina. Angel Cabrera defeated Brad Faxon 68-72, leaving the top match to decide the outcome. It was a good one, too, with Eduardo Romero birdieing the 17th, hitting a six iron to 12 feet, to square a match with O'Meara he had earlier led. A pair of 67s meant they had to return to the first hole, where Romero hit into the Swilcan Burn with his approach shot.

After that, the Americans were rarely in trouble and defeated both Japan and then England, which had lost to Argentina on the second day, 2-1. As the No. 1 seeds, the Americans thus secured their expected place in the semi-finals. There they might have expected to face the No. 4 seeds, Australia, but instead Sweden, the No. 5 seeds, topped their group after winning all their matches and dropping only one game.

The Swedes swept away Chinese Taipei and France, both 3-0, to almost guarantee them a semi-final place but not quite. Australia still had a chance, despite their indifferent progress. On the opening day, they lost to France when Jean Van de Velde holed from 25 feet at the first extra hole of his match against Steve Elkington. This was especially galling for Elkington since he had led until he bogeyed the 17th, while Van de Velde birdied it. He had also missed a six-footer for the match at the 18th. Elkington redeemed himself with a playoff win against Chen Liang-hsi the following day to give Australia a narrow 2-1 win over Chinese Taipei.

That left Sweden needing just one win in their match against the Australians to go through. The Aussies, however, could proceed by winning 3-0. Australia had been in the same situation as the Swedes in each of the previous two years, and managed to lose 3-0 on each occasion. Haeggman's 66 against Stuart Appleby made sure the same fate did not lie in store for the Swedes, and just to complete Elkington's unfortunate week, Johansson beat him at the second extra hole.

The strongest group seemed to be the one containing South Africa, the No. 3 seeds; Scotland, winners two years before; Ireland and Germany. The Germans were without Bernhard Langer, but in Sven Struver, Thomas Gogele and Alexander Cejka, featured the new breed of golfers whom Langer helped to inspire.

Ireland, too, had a strong young trio of Darren Clarke, a Ryder Cup player, Padraig Harrington, who narrowed missed out on a place at Valderrama, and Paul McGinley. Scotland could call upon Montgomerie, a talented youngster in Raymond Russell and an old hand in Gordon Brand, Jr. In beating Clarke on the second day, Brand took his number of wins in the competition to 20, two behind the record-holder, Greg Norman.

As it turned out, all the matches went according to their seeding, and they all finished in 2-1 results, except the third-day decider between South Africa and Scotland, which was left with a 2-0 win for the South Africans with one game undecided. That was the encounter between Els and Montgomerie, eagerly anticipated given their past tussles in two U.S. Opens and a World Match Play final. Montgomerie was in front until he found the Road Hole bunker and bogeyed the 17th.

The status of their match depended on what was happening ahead. In the top match, Frost had the measure of Russell, winning 68-71, and Goosen was in front of Brand until the last hole, where the South African three-putted for a bogey and Brand birdied. As they went back up the first hole, the Els-Montgomerie affair was very much alive and both birdied the 18th, Els from 18 feet and then the Scot following him from 12 feet, to tie with a pair of 68s.

As they waited on the first tee, watching the action on a giant video screen, the other tie was decided. Brand had found a tight lie for his approach to the first green and came up 30 feet short of the pin. His first putt was still eight feet short and when he missed that, Goosen and South Africa kept up their winning records.

"To be 13 under par is a fine team performance," said a generous Montgomerie of the South Africans. "I'm glad Ernie and I finished all square, but at the end of the day, it did not matter."

In the final group Zimbabwe was competing with one hand tied behind the back, as it were, since an injury to Nick Price required him to withdraw. This occurrence was the first time it had happened in the event's history and left Tony Johnstone and Mark McNulty to fight alone.

Price had pulled a muscle during his World Match Play semi-final against Els the previous week and aggravated the injury while losing the third-place playoff at Wentworth to Faxon. Had it been an individual event, Price would not even have travelled to St. Andrews. However, he played on the opening day and, with Tony Johnstone losing to Kang Wook-soon at the 19th, his win over Kim Jong-duk ensured that Zimbabwe beat Korea 2-1.

The following day, Price could not play more than 12 holes against Miguel Angel Jimenez and had to withdraw. With Johnstone and McNulty winning their matches, Zimbabwe beat Spain 2-1 and Price gained the support and sympathy from his teammates for his decision. "Nick is not one to complain about pain, so his must be severe," Johnstone said. "He has carried us for so long, but it is our turn."

But Zimbabwe had no margin for error in their group-decider against New Zealand, who had also won their first two matches. Under the rules of the competition, the higher-placed seed got to select one match first, and Zimbabwe used this to pair Price with the Kiwi captain Frank Nobilo, while hoping Johnstone could beat Steve Alker and McNulty could beat Michael Long. In the event, neither could, Alker winning by five and Long edging his opponent 67-68.

"It was almost harder on our two guys having one point on the board already and I was pleased for them that both won," Nobilo said.

Having had to sit out on Saturday, Nobilo made up for it by scoring 66 on Sunday morning to beat Els by four strokes. While the Kiwis had beaten their great rugby-playing rivals in the previous year's semi-final, the South Africans were too strong this time as Goosen's 67 bettered Long by five and Frost beat Alker 72-76. "We did all we could," said Nobilo. "South Africa are a tough team and to lose 2-1 to the team that could win the Cup, you can't hope for much better than that."

The dramatics, however, were all occurring in the other semi-final, also a repeat of 1996, but with the result reversed, the Swedes beating the Americans for the first time in four meetings. Quickly, it became clear that Haeggman was up to something special in his match against Leonard.

At the first hole, Haeggman holed from 15 feet for a birdie. At the next, he missed from 18 feet, but that was the last time that was to happen. He made up for only having a par at the second hole by holing his wedge shot from 133 yards for an eagle two at the third. He birdied the rest of the first nine by hitting a six iron to four feet at the fourth, taking two putts from off the green at the fifth and holing from 10 feet, sinking a 24-footer at the sixth, holing from 16 feet at the seventh, hitting an eight iron to four feet at the eighth, and holing from 23 feet at the ninth.

Leonard could only stand and watch Haeggman's 27. "I saw a lot of putts made," Leonard said, "but I wasn't standing over the ball at the time. All I said was, 'good putt,' 'good shot,' 'nice drive,' 'that's perfect,' 'no, you are still on the tee.' I made sure I kept the card real neat because I knew it was going on a wall somewhere."

Understandably, Haeggman could not keep it up. Pars at the 10th and 11th holes were followed by a triple-bogey seven at the 12th, where he lost his ball in a gorse bush and took three putts on the green. He finished with 68 and, having been 10 ahead after 11 holes, won by four. "It is hard to find a better place to do this than here," Haeggman said. "I suppose the message is that it is possible to shoot 54, but I lost focus on the back nine."

O'Meara beat Parnevik by one stroke, 68-69. Johansson was always in command against Faxon and his 71 gave him a three-stroke win. "We knew the Swedes were playing well, and they started hot and we got too far behind," O'Meara said.

The South Africans had the first choice of pairings in the final and picked Els to play Haeggman in the bottom match. "Our trump card all week was to have Ernie at the back of the field," Frost said. "If there was going to be pressure, he was the guy I wanted to be there. We put our strongest guy against their strongest guy."

Els admitted he thought he ought to play Parnevik. "The whole of the Swedish team was quality as they showed by beating America," Els said. "When a guy makes 27 on the first nine, I guess he is either in very good form or has used up all his putts." The former was the case.

Haeggman was not playing badly by any means. He went to the turn in 36, nine worse than the morning, and shot an even-par 72, but Els was always ahead of him and eventually won by three strokes to clinch the winning point. Goosen's 70 was four better than Parnevik, and Johansson beat Frost 71-74.

"My win was good, but it's a team thing and it didn't matter in the end," Johansson said. "We had high hopes and are disappointed that we could not pull it off, but that's the way it goes. It was like summer one minute, and when we turned it was very tough."

The warm sunshine gave way to an ever-strengthening and freezing gale on the second nine, making it difficult for the player down in a match to mount a charge. "We do not have weather like this in South Africa, and when we do, you don't play golf in it," Els said.

Frost added, "When the weather turned, we could not have had two stronger guys in Ernie and Retief to hold the reins. The odds were with us to do well with the strength of our team."

The win meant, at least for a month, that South Africa held both the Alfred Dunhill Cup and the World Cup. "That's nice for South Africa," Els said. "It is a good feeling."

11. American Tours

Experts have been trying to assess the impact of Tiger Woods since he entered the scene. While they go through their piles of facts and figures, here's the best way of all to measure him: By the second half of the 1997 season, folks were wondering what was wrong with him. He wasn't winning any more. After all, he had only won four times on the United States PGA Tour by July.

Well, that still made it the Year of the Tiger, or maybe the Year and a Half of the Tiger. Woods didn't miss a beat with the change of the seasons. He turned professional in late August 1996, won twice, then launched 1997 by winning the season-opening Mercedes Championships. He won a non-PGA Tour event, the Asian Honda Classic in Thailand in February. He won his first major championship as a professional at the Masters in April, winning by a record 12 shots and breaking a number of other records as well, then won the GTE Byron Nelson Classic in May and the Motorola Western Open in July. He didn't threaten after that, and showed he had trouble on tight courses, was a bust in the Ryder Cup, but totalled $2,066,833 in winnings and took PGA Tour Player of the Year honors.

There's a signature everything else these days, so if there's such a thing as a signature moment, then there were two for the 1997 PGA Tour, both authored by Woods. The first came late in January at the Phoenix Open, when he aced the 16th hole. It set off a frenzied celebration in the huge gallery behind the green. It was more like something at a football or basketball game. Steve Jones would go on to win the tournament, the first of his two, but Woods had left his mark on it The next one was all Woods. When he won the Masters, the hug he gave his father, Earl, said it all.

Of his "failures," Woods merely said, "It's called golf."

Davis Love III pointed out what should be obvious to anyone, that Woods couldn't win every major, as so many expected, but he would be a factor in almost every tournament he enters. "That's where we're going to be from now on," Love said.

There was more to the PGA Tour in 1997 than Tiger Woods, of course. There was his good buddy, for example, leading the parade of double-winners.

The Prince of the Monterrey Peninsula struck again. Mark O'Meara, holding off Woods, won the AT&T Pebble Beach National Pro-Am for the fifth time. "You might hit it 50 yards by me," O'Meara chided Woods, "but I might find a way to clip you." The following week, with Woods in Thailand, O'Meara won the Buick Invitational, becoming the first of 11 multiple winners of the season. Woods had four and the other 10 had two each.

The 1997 season wasn't all glory. There were two unfortunate incidents. John Daly slipped back into his alcohol problems during The Players Championship in March and returned to rehabilitation. He returned at the Memorial Tournament. And Fuzzy Zoeller, trying to make a wisecrack, uttered what some believed was a racist comment after Woods' win in the Masters. Both episodes made headlines for days. There were two big breakthroughs in 1997, both by men who carried the heavy label "... the best never to have won (fill in the blank)." Love, a 12-year veteran, was "the best never to have won a major." He scraped that off when he took the PGA Championship at Winged Foot in a dramatic finish, with a rainbow arching across the sky as he finished the last hole.

He added the Buick Challenge about two months later. The other was David Duval, a 25-year-old of such promise that be had become suspect. He was "the best never to have won a tournament." He collected that and then some with three victories late in the season. First, he took the Michelob Championship on the first extra hole of a three-way playoff with Duffy Waldorf and Grant Waite. "I felt my time would come," Duval said. "Other people made a bigger deal out of it than I would let it be." In case the message was lost, he won the Walt Disney World/Oldsmobile Classic the next week, then his third consecutive at the Tour Championship to place second behind Woods on the money list with $1,885,308.

Greg Norman rebounded from his crash in the 1996 Masters with two victories — the FedEx St. Jude Classic in June "... elation more than relief ..." he said — and the NEC World Series of Golf in August. Justin Leonard, another young player of great promise, benefited from Mark Weibe's crash down the stretch to score his first win in the Kemper Open in June, then a month later took the British Open at Royal Troon. Ernie Els won the U.S. Open at Congressional dramatically over the last few holes, then took the Buick Classic the following week.

History of a kind was made when the first Swedish victory was scored, but it wasn't one of the familiar names. It was little-known Gabriel Hjertstedt, who came to America in the best of traditions — no money and no certain future, and he wasn't even sure he could play the next week. "That's all changed now," he said, after winning the B.C. Open in September. And New Zealand's Frank Nobilo, long expected to crack the winner's circle, finally did so in the Greater Greensboro Chrysler Classic.

The year had its oddities and its benchmarks. The oddest oddity: Nick Faldo won the Nissan Open in March, then made barely a ripple the rest of the year. Was he running dry? And benchmarks: Love was 33 when he won the PGA, but the other three majors went to players in their 20s — Woods, 21; Leonard, 25, and Els, 28. Rookie Stewart Cink, 24, scored his first win in the Canon Greater Hartford Open, and Tim Herron, 27, a second-year player, notched his second victory, this in the LaCantera Texas Open. Had the youth movement arrived? The 1998 season might tell us.

U.S. PGA Tour

Mercedes Championships—$1,200,000
Winner: Tiger Woods

The PGA Tour started the 1997 season with the Mercedes Championships the second week of January at the La Costa Resort in Carlsbad, California. Tiger Woods merely picked up where he left off. When heavy rains cut the tournament to three rounds, Woods and Tom Lehman, the 1996 Player of the Year, had to play off. Officials found a playable hole, the 186-yard, par-three No. 7. Lehman, hitting first, knocked his shot into the pond in front of the green. Woods, with a six iron, coolly hit a gentle draw that nearly holed out. The ball stopped about 10 inches away. The playoff had ended not only on the first extra hole, but almost on his first extra shot.

Woods was now age 21 years and 14 days. He had turned professional and joined the Tour only some five months earlier, late in August. He won twice in what little was left of 1996, and here he was, winning his first time out in 1997. That's three wins in nine starts. Was he surprised?

"No," Woods said. "This is what I set out to do — win every tournament. If my mindset was to make the cut, then it would be different. I would be ecstatic. But I try to go out and win."

He didn't look like a winner for the first 50 holes. That's two rounds and 14 holes of the third round. Lehman opened with 66 for a one-stroke lead over Paul Goydos and Jim Furyk. Woods was four strokes behind. Lehman upped his lead with 67 in the second round, and was 11 under par and two ahead of Furyk (68). Woods was still four behind, but in the third round (which would prove to be the last), he picked up the pace and had taken the lead, and was heading for home when he stumbled to bogeys at the 12th and 13th holes.

"They got me more focused," Woods said. "I felt I lost three shots there, and I wanted to get them back." He did, with a vengeance. He birdied the last four holes — the 15th from 18 feet, the 16th from 12, the 17th on two putts (he was the first in tournament history to reach the 569-yarder in two), and the 18th from 12. The burst gave him a seven-under-par 65 and the lead.

Now it was Lehman, playing behind Woods, who had to produce the heroics. And he did, dropping a 35-foot putt at the 18th for a birdie and a tie at 14-under-par 202. Woods shot 70-67-65, Lehman 66-67-69. Then it was on to the playoff, and Woods' near-ace for the win and a high tribute.

Said Lehman: "Tom Lehman was the Player of the Year, but Tiger Woods is probably the player of the next two decades."

Bob Hope Chrysler Classic—$1,500,000
Winner: John Cook

Tiger Woods' fans had to be content that he did not play in the Bob Hope Chrysler Classic in Indian Wells, California, but he probably wouldn't have won anyway. How do you counter a 62-63 finish? Which is how John Cook played to overrun Mark Calcavecchia and score not only his second Hope victory in five years, but his third PGA Tour win in six months. Cook's rampage makes most sense when seen through Calcavecchia's eyes. After all, he saw it best.

"If you can't win shooting 32 under, what can you say?" Calcavecchia said. "He can really play, and he did. He hit every wedge straight at the hole, and every putt straight in."

The answer, Cook said, lay in his regeneration of 1995. First, he had to hit bottom. He had gone four years without a victory, and in 1995 he missed the cut in six of his first eight starts. "I got tired of looking at the board on Friday, trying to figure out whether I made the cut," Cook said. "I was just physically and mentally beat up." He was thinking of giving up the game, but first he decided to check with Ken Venturi, the television commentator and an old friend. Before long, John Cook was back. And never more so than in this 1997 event. A lot happened in those five rounds.

Larry Rinker, 39, who had to go back to the Tour qualifying tournament, shot 63 to take the first-round lead by one stroke over Calcavecchia and Steve Jones. Rinker hung on to a share of the lead with 68 in the second round, and was caught by Calcavecchia (67) at 131. Cook was four shots off. Calcavecchia took over the lead in the third round with 66, for a one-stroke edge over Jay Don Blake, but not without a touch of magic. He turned a potential double bogey into a breathtaking birdie at the 13th, hooking a 161-yard eight iron from nearly out of bounds, around some trees and onto the green. He made the putt. Cook was five behind. Calcavecchia, with a 64 in the fourth round, tied the Tour's record for 72 holes, 27 under par, and he led Cook and Pooley by three. But it wasn't enough. Cook wrapped it up with 63, for a five-round total of 66-69-67-62-63–327 for the ninth win of his career.

His reaction: "Twenty birdies in two days," Cook said. "I hope I didn't blow my quota for the rest of the year."

Phoenix Open—$1,500,000
Winner: Steve Jones

How can you lead a man by 10 strokes and still get upstaged by him? When the man is Tiger Woods and he's just scored a hole-in-one. It was the third round of the Phoenix Open, and Woods holed a nine-iron shot at the 155-yard 16th hole at the TPC of Scottsdale, Arizona. It set off a frenzied celebration around the hole. For all of the fireworks it generated, the ace merely got Woods within 10 strokes of the leader, Steve Jones. When Jones came to the interview area, he found a thin media corps waiting. "Where did everybody go?" Jones cracked. "To the Super Bowl?"

Jones had his consolation, a wire-to-wire runaway victory. He shot 62, 64,

65 and 67 for a 258 total, 26 under par, and just one stroke off the PGA Tour's 72-hole record, which has stood for 42 years. This from someone who almost missed his first tee time. Jones, forgetting how long the walk was from the practice range, arrived at the first tee with only seconds to spare. It almost cost him a two-stroke penalty. Jones rushed his tee shot and skied it almost out of bounds to the right. "I almost whiffed," he said. Then he sliced a two iron around a tree and scrambled to a par from out of the rough. He went on to make nine birdies and shoot 62. The rout was on. It was all over but the tributes.

"It was definitely a second-place tournament," said Jesper Parnevik. "I won that one." Said 1996 Phoenix winner Phil Mickelson, "Take Steve out and it would've been an excellent tournament."

Jones knew the reason. It wasn't his driving. He hit only 29 of the 56 fairways for the week, and in fact only six in his first-round 62. It was his putting that did it. He needed only 99 putts all week, an average of only 24.7 per round. "That putter bailed me out every time," he said. "I ought to bronze that thing when I'm done with my career."

AT&T Pebble Beach National Pro-Am—$1,900,000
Winner: Mark O'Meara

He didn't exactly win one for the Gipper, but he figures he scored one for the 40-year-olds. This was Mark O'Meara, 40, holding off his friend, Tiger Woods, to win the AT&T Pebble Beach National Pro-Am by one stroke in Pebble Beach, California. He did this with a set of four 67s for a 20-under-par 268 total, breaking the tournament record by three strokes, although with the benefit of a lift-clean-and-place rule because of rainy weather. Even so, it was a splendid example of performance under pressure. O'Meara told of how Woods would needle him about going head-to-head. O'Meara had his answer. "You might hit it 50 yards by me," he said, "but I might find a way to clip you."

In a tournament brightened by show biz and shenanigans, O'Meara and Woods put on the best show of all in the final round. O'Meara started three strokes off the lead. Woods, after 63 in the third round, was five strokes off the lead and two behind O'Meara, and looking for his fourth victory in 11 PGA Tour starts as a pro. But O'Meara was the king of Pebble Beach. He had won there four times.

The decks had been cleared. Jesper Parnevik and David Duval shared the first-round lead, Jim Furyk took over in the second, and Duval grabbed the lead in the third, tying the Pebble Beach course record with 62. In the fourth round, Duval missed nine greens and slipped to a one-under 71. It opened the door. He would be a runner-up for the sixth time. Furyk birdied the 11th and 12th holes and got to 17 under par, but bogeyed the 13th and 18th. It was O'Meara and Woods, center stage.

O'Meara birdied four of the first seven holes, then cooled off and was one over par for the next eight. Woods jumped at the chance. He birdied the 16th and 17th, firing deadly shots to within four feet at each. O'Meara, who could tell what Woods was doing from the gallery roars, missed the green at the 16th, but chipped in from 15 feet for his birdie. "That was a huge shot," he said. At the par-three 17th, he put a six iron to 12 feet. Woods played the par-five 18th dramatically, booming a three-wood second shot 265 yards to 25 feet and two-putting for the birdie. It gave him 64 but only a share of second place, because O'Meara, as he said he would, found a way to clip him. At the 18th, he coolly got up and down for the par he needed.

He also got in the final needle. "Maybe I didn't knock the flags down like my little Tiger Woods did," he said, "but I stayed focused and held my composure."

Buick Invitational—$1,500,000
Winner: Mark O'Meara

To borrow an expression, Mark O'Meara didn't have his friend Tiger Woods to kick around any more. Woods went off to Thailand to win the Asian Honda Classic, so O'Meara had to win the Buick Invitational in La Jolla, California, all by himself. Not that it came easily. He won by two strokes, but had to outrun a crowd of seven players to do it. In fact, all seven tied for second place. It was outstanding work. O'Meara shot 67, 66, 71 and 71 for a 275 total, 13 under par, and that first 71 (one under par) was his highest score in 13 rounds.

"I was mentally tough today," O'Meara said after the final round. "I think I'm a wiser player, you might say. I don't consider myself a dominant player. And I've always thrived on the fact that when I've had a chance to win, I get the job done."

He showed what he meant coming down the stretch. First, he needed an opening, and he got it when Jay Don Blake, the third-round leader, bogeyed five of the first six holes. O'Meara himself seemed headed in the same direction, but he stopped the damage at two bogeys over the first four. Then what looked like a shootout between the ubiquitous Swede, Jesper Parnevik, and Craig Stadler down the stretch, evaporated in errors. Stadler bogeyed the 16th and 18th, and Parnevik bogeyed the 17th. "I felt like I lost this one," said Parnevik, who hadn't finished out of the top five yet this season. Said Stadler of his play: "It was a pretty pitiful effort."

O'Meara, on the other hand, took the lead at the par-five 13th hole with a brilliant eagle, off a four-wood shot to 22 feet. He three-putted the 16th for a bogey, but bounced back for a birdie at the 17th on a 16-footer. That put him back at 13 under par. He locked up the victory with an inspired finish. At the 18th, he pulled his tee shot far to the left. How to get out of this fix? Simple — hook an iron back into the fairway, and from there, clear a pond in front of the green.

United Airlines Hawaiian Open—$1,200,000
Winner: Paul Stankowski

Paul Stankowski was so far out of this United Airlines Hawaiian Open in Honolulu, he was in another area code. First, he had the memory of missing the cut in the past three tournaments. This time he started with a one-under-par 71. Not only was he in 70th place, he was also nine shots behind leaders

Mike Reid and Brian Claar, who shot 10-under 62s. ("I've never had a locker number this low," Reid said.) Stankowski was also 21 places behind defending champion Jim Furyk, who was 48th at 70. There were such perfect conditions at Waialae Country Club that 90 of the 143 starters broke par. Given all of this, what chance did Stankowski have? Excellent, as things turned out.

He rocketed through the ranks with some spectacular play, ran off rounds of 66, 64 and 70, tied Reid and Furyk at 17-under-par 271, then won on the fourth extra hole. For all of his heroics, his key shot, he said, was the eight-foot birdie putt at the 18th in the final round. "That was the big one," he said, "because it got me in the playoff."

Yet, until that last hole, the tournament was a duel between Reid and Furyk. Reid led by two strokes going into the final round, faltered, then birdied the 18th for 71. Furyk, trailing by three to start the day, dropped a shot, then made four straight birdies and had a two-stroke lead coming down the stretch. He four-putted the 15th from 50 feet for a double-bogey six and closed with a bogey and two birdies for 68.

Reid, who last won on the PGA Tour in 1986, was ousted on the first extra hole but was not crushed. His game had turned sour, he almost didn't start. At the third extra hole, Stankowski needed a 30-foot putt for birdie to stay alive. He got it. At the fourth, the par-five 18th, Stankowski's eagle putt from the edge left him a tap-in. Furyk had a 10-footer for birdie. He missed, and Stankowski had his second PGA Tour victory.

Tucson Chrysler Classic—$1,300,000
Winner: Jeff Sluman

If patience is the name of the game in golf, Jeff Sluman is an expert. It was nine years and 241 tournaments between victories for Sluman. He scored his first in the 1988 PGA Championship. He got his second in the Tucson Chrysler Classic late in February, 1997. His reaction? "It's just been a long time coming," Sluman said. "Maybe the monkey's off my back now."

Golf is rarely ever that simple, though. Sluman's next wait was even longer. He had finished, and was leading the tournament. Now he had to watch for Steve Jones, in the final group, and playing the 18th hole. He needed a birdie to beat Sluman or a par to tie him. The answer finally came. Jones pulled his six-iron second shot to the left. "I should've hit the seven iron again," Jones was to say. "I wasn't thinking, I guess." He bunkered the shot and bogeyed. Sluman, who also had bogeyed the hole, had his victory.

He looked like anything but a winner at first. He opened with a three-over-par 75, tying for the worst first round of the 75 players who went on to make the cut. And at that moment, he was in 107th place. He rolled from there, shooting 68, 65 and 67 for a 275 total, 13 under par, to edge Jones by a stroke.

Sluman took the lead with a birdie at the 14th hole on the final day, and there he stayed. Jones was tough all the way, shooting 66-68-72-70–276. He and Jeff Maggert tied for a one-stroke lead in the first round, and by three strokes through the second round on another bogey-free round. Brad Bryant took the lead with 67 in the third round, and Sluman made his move. He zoomed from 36th place to fifth with the low round of the day, a 65 that included two chip-ins.

The fates cleared the way for Sluman in the final round. The leaders dropped like flies, Bryant double-bogeying the 10th, then Mike Reid the 13th. Jones wouldn't let up, though. He birdied three straight from the 13th. Sluman inched ahead with a tap-in birdie at the par-three 17th, nearly holing a four-iron tee shot. Then he bogeyed the 18th out of a bunker, and sat back to sweat and wait.

Nissan Open—$1,400,000
Winner: Nick Faldo

A number of remarkable events occurred at the Nissan Open at Riviera Country Club in Pacific Palisades, California. For example, Hal Sutton, who won the 1983 PGA Championship at Riviera, shot 80 in the first round. He would miss the cut. Also in the first round, Jerry Kelly two-putted from one inch at the 18th and triple-bogeyed. He missed the cut by three shots. Don Pooley, at age 45, led through the second round. Scott McCarron made back-to-back eagles at the 10th and 11th holes in the third round, and shot the tournament-low 64. It was all overshadowed by one event that was completely unremarkable: Nick Faldo won.

"This week I played as solidly as I've ever played," Faldo said, after taking his first victory since the 1996 Masters, some 11 months earlier. It was Faldo at his precise, relentless, methodical best. In a total of 66-70-68-68—272, 12 under par, he made just four bogeys and one double bogey. He won by three strokes over Craig Stadler, the defending champion. The double bogey came in the second round, when he hit just eight greens but needed only 23 putts. And he hit just two bunkers all week.

Faldo was only one stroke off the lead in the first two rounds, behind Scott Hoch and Payne Stewart (65s) in the first round, then behind Pooley (68–135). He seemed about to break free of the pack when he made his only double bogey, that at No. 12. Then he took the lead in the third round by one stroke. It was in the final round, more than any other time, that Faldo showed how strong and steady his game was. Stadler started the round only a stroke behind, but then could get no closer than three, and that was at the 15th, where Faldo took a three-putt bogey. The decisiveness of his win and his play, of course, raised questions about the Masters, just some six weeks away. Was his game ready?

"I feel very close," Faldo said. "Let's see if this is going to be the start of a good run."

Doral-Ryder Open—$1,800,000
Winner: Steve Elkington

Maybe the real story of the 1997 Doral-Ryder Open in Miami, Florida, lay in two areas — Raymond Floyd's re-design that put fangs back into the famed Blue Monster course, and the crash on the second nine that helped pave the way for Steve Elkington. Crash is the word.

David Duval led through the second round, and then the third despite a pyrotechnic display. He shot an amazing two-under-par 70 in the third round. He made three pars, nine birdies, five bogeys and a double bogey. On the second nine, he bogeyed four of the last six holes. Nick Price bogeyed three of the last six, and Greg Norman bogeyed the 13th and 16th and double-bogeyed the 18th. And while the three of them were a combined nine over on the last six holes, Elkington was two under.

Elkington trailed by two strokes going into the final round, and he made up the ground in a hurry. The key was No. 3, a 430-yard par-four. He had 150 yards to the hole, into a brisk wind. He hit a six iron, and he thought it was short. Then he discovered it went into the hole on the fly for an eagle two. "As I walked up there," he said, "I thought this was going to be my day. I said, 'I'm going to make it my day.'" Then he birdied the ninth and 10th holes to go three up on Duval and four up on Price.

Winning for the first time since he took the 1995 PGA Championship, Elkington played the par-72 course in 70, 66, 70 and 69 for a 275 total, 13 under par. He won by two over Nick Price and Senior Tour-bound Larry Nelson, 49, who enjoyed his best finish in 128 starts in the 1990s. Duval's wildness continued. He made five bogeys in a closing 74 and finished alone in fourth place. He had led after 54 holes for the fourth time, and had not won. He finished second six times, third twice, and fourth twice. Price encouraged him. "Just keep doing what you've been doing," he said, "and someday it's going to turn out right."

Honda Classic—$1,500,000
Winner: Stuart Appleby

The PGA Tour got its first first-time winner of the season in the person of Stuart Appleby, 25, a slender Australian who had the stamina for a 36-hole wrap-up and who also figured an easy and profitable way out of the deep rough in the Honda Classic in Coral Springs, Florida. The stage for this drama was set on Friday, when rains washed out the second round. Officials decided that rather than cut the tournament to 54 holes, they would play 36 holes on Sunday.

"It was one day to go, but a long way to go," Appleby said. "I knew it was Sunday, but I knew it was really Saturday." At one point during the 36 holes, eight players were tied for the lead. Appleby finally resolved things. After playing tag with Payne Stewart, among others, much of the long day, Appleby found himself in ankle-deep rough 65 yards from the hole at the par-five 14th. He was trying to get his ball within 20 feet, but the ball hit the fringe and rolled in for an eagle. He had tied Stewart. "That's golf," Stewart said. "You've got to take the good with the bad."

Then it got worse. Appleby holed a six-footer for a birdie at the par-five 16th. That got him the lead, and two pars got him a two-stroke victory. He shot 68, 68, 67 and 71 for a 274 total, 14 under par. Stewart closed with 71, Michael Bradley shot 68, and they tied for second at 275.

"I had some opportunities to win," Stewart said, but he wouldn't dwell on them. In the final stretch, he missed a 30-inch par putt at the 12th, chunked a chip from the collar at the 16th and cost himself a birdie, and at the 17th he three-putted from the fringe, from 40 feet.

When it came to nerves, Appleby may have had a bad case of them, watching to see whether Bradley would catch him. Bradley had birdied the 16th, saved par from 20 feet at the 17th, and had a 22-footer for a tying birdie at the 18th. When Bradley missed that putt, Appleby finally could relax. "It's never easy," Appleby said. "It's never going to be easy."

Bay Hill Invitational—$1,500,000
Winner: Phil Mickelson

It only made sense: This was Arnold Palmer's golf course and his tournament, and the game was vintage Palmer. But it wasn't Palmer playing it. It was that easy-smiling left-hander Phil Mickelson. He had been fairly quiet in the Bay Hill Invitational in Orlando, Florida, but suddenly, on the final nine ... "With this being Arnold's tournament, and having seen a couple of pictures in the locker room with Arnold holding that putter up and giving it the 'Arnie charge,'" Mickelson said, "I thought it would be kind of cool if I was able to do that."

He was spectacularly able. He electrified everyone, going five under par on a four-hole stretch, and six under on six holes for the 10th victory of his career but his first in Florida and only his second east of the Mississippi River.

"I didn't really notice he was making a big move until I stepped on the 16th tee," said Stewart Appleby, co-leader through the turn, playing behind Mickelson, and now suddenly trailing him. "It was sort of stimulating," he said. It came without warning.

Mickelson was one under par for the day through the turn and was three behind Appleby and Omar Uresti. It started routinely, with a birdie at the par-four 11th. The big boom came at the 570-yard 12th. Using his driver off the fairway, he hit a 283-yard second shot to the fringe, 50 feet from the cup. He holed the eagle putt and was tied for the lead. He took the lead at the par-four 13th with a birdie from 10 feet, then went ahead by two with a 10-footer at the par-three 14th. He completed the charge at the par-five 16th with another birdie, and parred in for a seven-under-par 65 and a total of 72, 65, 70 and 65 for 272, 16 under, for a three-stroke victory.

Palmer was wearing a huge grin. "Not bad," he said. This was, by the way, Palmer's first tournament since having surgery for prostate cancer on January 15. He shot 81 in the first round, and was five over par through the 15th hole when darkness halted the second round. He withdrew. "I didn't figure there was anything I could accomplish," Palmer said.

The Players Championship—$3,500,000
Winner: Steve Elkington

See Chapter 7.

Freeport-McDermott Classic—$1,500,000
Winner: Brad Faxon

"You drive for show, but you putt for dough." Brad Faxon didn't compose that little ditty, but he lives by it. Faxon set a PGA Tour record in 1996 for the most money won without a victory —$1,055,050. This time his touch paid off in a win, too, his first since 1992. He needed just 105 putts, an average of 25.75 per round, in winning the Freeport-McDermott Classic by three strokes. It put an end to a perplexing streak. Faxon, who didn't miss a cut in 22 starts in 1996, had missed three in his first seven tournaments this year.

"I would love to hit precision shots every time," said Faxon, who admits he's sometimes irritated by the attention paid to big hitters. "No matter how good you hit the ball, you always have to use your short game." He certainly used his in ringing up a total of 68, 69, 66 and 69 for a 272 total, 16 under par on the tough English Turn course near New Orleans. Defending champion Scott McCarron and Larry Rinker matched each other with 65-69s and shared the lead through the first two rounds. Faxon trailed them by three strokes through each round, then shot 66 to move into a one-stroke lead through the third round. Faxon said he didn't feel he had control until he made a sensational putt at the 11th.

"I sank a 30-foot putt with a double break there," Faxon said, "and thought that was the swing hole." He maintained his steady pace, and eventually the pursuit became futile.

There was Jesper Parnevik, for one. "I thought I had a chance until I three-putted the 14th," Parnevik said. "After that, Faxon was too far ahead." Parnevik finished with 66 and tied for second with Bill Glasson, who closed with a pair of 66s, the lowest back-to-back rounds of the tournament.

The tournament was also noteworthy for the presence of Jose Maria Olazabal, making his first American appearance since the 1995 NEC World Series of Golf. Olazabal, coming back from foot problems, had won a PGA European Tour event two weeks earlier and tied for seventh place here at 10-under 278.

Masters Tournament—$2,500,000
Winner: Tiger Woods

See Chapter 3.

MCI Classic—$1,500,000
Winner: Nick Price

Nick Price played like a man on a mission. And he was. He wanted to win the MCI Classic in Hilton Head Island, South Carolina, for his longtime caddie and friend, Jeff "Squeeky" Medlen, who was back in Columbus, Ohio, preparing to undergo a second bone marrow transplant in his desperate battle against leukemia. "It is important for me to win, but it is more important for me to know, for Squeeky to know how many people are pulling for him," Price said. "I think he knows that now." Price did win, and the way his challengers came to grief, it wouldn't be hard to believe he got help from somewhere else.

Surely word got back to Medlen that pleasant April weekend that his old friend raced wire-to-wire to score his first victory since their good old days together when they won 12 times from 1992 through 1994. And this was Price's first PGA Tour win since then, the last being the 1994 Canadian Open. And what style. Price played the classic par-71 Harbour Town course in rounds of 65, 69, 69, 66 for a 269 total, 15 under par. He led the first and second rounds by one stroke, the third by two, and then won by five over Brad Faxon and Jesper Parnevik. The wreckage in Price's wake was stunning.

In the first round, Price made five straight birdies from the 10th hole en route to 65. Faxon shot a six-under-par 29 on his first nine holes, but finished with 66. Rick Fehr had a chance for 64 and a two-stroke lead, but he hit the cart path at the 18th and double-bogeyed. Phil Mickelson tied for the lead, then doubled the 17th.

It was more of the same in the second round. Price was vulnerable. He got to 10 under par through the 16th hole, then bogeyed the 17th and 18th. Faxon caught him with a birdie at the 16th, then missed a short par putt at the 17th. Lennie Clements birdied three of the first four holes on the second nine and tied Price, then bogeyed the 17th. Fehr also caught Price, then bogeyed the last hole off a short approach. The real disaster was saved for Mickelson. He made an eagle and three birdies to catch Price, then went six over par on his last six holes with five bogeys, a double bogey and a par for 72. It knocked him back to 10th place.

In the third round, Tom Lehman birdied six holes on the first nine but cooled off and moved up to third place with 67. In the final round, Faxon started with three straight birdies, but Price wouldn't budge. Faxon holed a 50-footer at No. 1. Price followed him in with a 15-footer. Faxon wedged to tap-in range at No. 3 and got to 11 under par. Price rolled in a downhill 30-footer. And finally at No. 7, Faxon bogeyed from a bunker and Price birdied from four feet. Now he was four ahead. A bright moment was on its way to a hospital room in Columbus, Ohio. "It's been pretty tough," Price said. "I just hope this gives him a boost."

Greater Greensboro Chrysler Classic—$1,900,000
Winner: Frank Nobilo

Frank Nobilo, an amiable New Zealander, a veteran with 10 wins around the world but a rookie on the American circuit, had missed three cuts in his last five starts. Discouraged, he was going to skip the Greater Greensboro Chrysler Classic to recharge his batteries until his friend, Ernie Els, said, "You're playing." That was an idea whose time had come. Nobilo never led, and had to birdie six of his last 11 holes to tie Brad Faxon. Then he beat him in a playoff for his first American victory.

"If you want to improve your game, you have to play against the best," Nobilo said. "I stuck with it, so it makes me the happiest guy in the world."
Nobilo played the Forest Oaks Country Club course in Greensboro, North

Carolina, in 69, 69, 69 and 67 for a 14-under-par 274 total to catch Faxon (67-70-65-72). Faxon made a spectacular finish of his own. After going 45 holes without a bogey, he bogeyed two of the last five holes and needed a brilliant par at the 18th. Coming out of the rough, he was approximately 100 feet short of the green, but wide open. He gambled, using his putter, and got within two feet of the hole, and tapped in for his par and a tie.

At the first playoff hole, No. 18, Nobilo drove into the left rough, and could get his second shot only within 75 yards of the green. Then he lobbed his third shot to eight feet from the hole. Faxon, meanwhile, had driven well but put his second shot on the green in a place where he would have to putt through the fringe. He chose to drop in the light rough so that he could chip. (They were playing lift-clean-and-place on the rain-soaked course.) He chipped 12 feet past, then missed his par. Nobilo then sank his eight-footer for his par and the victory.

It was a week of surprises. The first round, for example, went to Sandy Lyle, who revived his once-formidable game and shot 66 to tie for the lead. He shot 77 the next day. Tom Kite, who was also struggling, shot middle rounds of 68 and 67 to share the lead, first with Mike Hulbert, next with Faxon. But 76 in the final round took Kite out of contention.

Shell Houston Open—$1,600,000
Winner: Phil Blackmar

If this a rut, Phil Blackmar will take more of the same every week. The Shell Houston Open was his third victory, and all three were by playoffs — the 1985 Greater Hartford Open, the 1988 Provident Classic and now this. "All the wins have meaning," he said, "but this one is extremely special. It's been a long time, and it's the first time my dad has seen me win." It had to be tough on both.

Blackmar and Kevin Sutherland were tied for the lead at 10 under par going into the final round, and Blackmar nearly won in regulation. He made four birdies coming home and was leading by two strokes going to the par-four 17th hole at the TPC at The Woodlands. His approach went just over the back of the green. His delicate chip shot hit three feet in front of the flagstick, but the ball rolled off into the water. He double-bogeyed.

"I was more in shock than anything else," Blackmar said. "I went to No. 18 thinking this is not a time to go berserk." He held himself together for a par at the 18th, dropping a five-footer to match Sutherland's eight-footer. They returned to the 18th for the playoff. Sutherland, seeking his first PGA Tour win, put his approach shot 15 feet from the hole. His birdie try just missed. Blackmar hit his approach to five feet, about the same putt he had for the tie minutes earlier. He made this one, too, and had his third victory. Blackmar played the par-72 course in 68-71-67-70, and Sutherland in 68-72-66-70 to tie at 12-under-par 276.

Both stepped past the frustrated David Duval. Victory continued to elude him. He led through the first two rounds with 65 and 71, then shot 75 in the third round, clearing the way for Blackmar, who birdied three of the first four holes on his way to 67. Sutherland birdied two of the last three holes for 66 to tie Blackmar at 10 under par.

BellSouth Classic—$1,500,000
Winner: Scott McCarron

When you can drive the green on a 310-yard hole under pressure for one birdie and hole a 75-foot putt for another, you know it's your week. So it was for Scott McCarron, breaking from a tie down the stretch to make the BellSouth Classic in Duluth, Georgia, the second victory in two years in his young career. It came a tad easier.

"The first time, you don't know what to expect," McCarron said. "It's a lot calmer the second time, no question." McCarron, who gave up golf after college because he thought he wasn't good enough, proved himself all over again when he stood up under the intense pressure of the stretch drive.

McCarron was tied with Nick Price and David Duval through No. 12 in the final round when the break came. He drove the green at the 310-yard 13th hole, and tapped in for a birdie. He was in front to stay. Then he drained a 75-footer for a birdie at the 15th to go two ahead. He parred the last three holes for a three-under-par 69 and a three-stroke victory over David Duval, Brian Henninger and Lee Janzen. McCarron opened with 70 that left him in 20th place, then shot 69 and tied Duval for the lead with 66 in the third round. He finished with a 14-under-par 274 total.

The tournament started on a refreshing and unexpected note with the veteran Don Pooley running off eight birdies and 10 pars for the first-round lead with 64. Duval took the second-round lead when he launched a 66 with a hole-out eagle and five birdies. In the third round, when 77 knocked Pooley out of the picture, Duval's one-shot lead disappeared in a watery bogey at the 18th, and McCarron caught him. Greg Norman, who designed the course, made a move in the final round and was just one stroke out of the lead until he found the woods and water at the 17th, and ended up with a double-bogey six and a tie for fifth place.

GTE Byron Nelson Classic—$1,800,000
Winner: Tiger Woods

Tiger Woods took off after winning the Masters and reappeared in mid-May at the GTE Byron Nelson Classic in Irving, Texas, well-rested but with his golf game slightly rusted. He wasn't pleased by his club position or his posture. He said did not have his "A" game. If he were grading himself, he would have given a C-plus or B-minus. Then, all Woods did was tie for the lead in the second round, lead outright for the last two rounds, shake off a challenge, and win by two strokes at 17-under-par 263. It was his third victory in eight starts on the PGA Tour this year and his fifth victory in his 16 starts since joining the Tour in August, 1996. He became the second-youngest player to win five times on the Tour, at age 21 years, five months and 20 days. Horton Smith, in 1929, was the youngest at 20 years, 10 months and one day.

"My swing is kind of on the 'iffy' side," said Woods, after he tied Lee Rinker for the second-round lead with 64. After his 67 in the third round tied the tournament record of 15-under-par 195 and gave him a two-stroke lead, Woods said, "I need work on the range. My swing is getting stuck. My game is not great right now."

Woods lost the lead briefly on the first nine in the final round. He hit his drive into the water at No. 3 and bogeyed, and fell two behind when Rinker got to 16 under par on birdies at the first, fifth and seventh holes. Woods righted things in short order. He birdied the par-five No. 7, saved par at the par-four 10th, and reclaimed the lead on a two-stroke swing when he dropped a 10-foot birdie putt at the 12th and Rinker two-putted from eight feet for a bogey ahead at the 15th. Woods finished with rounds of 64, 64, 67 and 68 for a 263 total.

For all of their flamboyance, Woods' accomplishments had to be kept in perspective. The tournament was played over two courses in the first two rounds. In the second round, the average score at Cottonwood Valley was 68.079, and at the TPC at Las Colinas, 69.526.

Still, Woods, as he said, did not have his "A" game, which raised an interesting question. Said Rinker, "What is his 'A' game — 40 under par?"

MasterCard Colonial—$1,600,000
Winner: David Frost

Free-spirited David Ogrin decided he could use little extra help against Tiger Woods. As they came down the fifth fairway as the final pairing in the final round of the MasterCard Colonial in Ft. Worth, Texas, battling for the lead, Ogrin — mugging for the camera — raised both arms and fired a two-handed "whammy" at Woods just ahead. The "whammy" was so strong it hit him, too. While they struggled the rest of the way, David Frost coolly slipped up from behind and made off with the red plaid winner's jacket, his first victory since 1984 and the 10th PGA Tour win of his career.

"It always seems to happen at the least-expected time," Frost said. "So many times I've expected to do well and then shot 75. Now I win and all of a sudden I'm a party-crasher." He was referring to Woods. The young phenomenon again drew huge crowds, sellouts for the final three days. They went home disappointed as Woods' imposing game misfired and he fell back to a tie for fourth place with a final-round 72. Ogrin also shot 72 and tied for second with Brad Faxon. Frost, meantime, on rounds of 66, 63, 69 and 67, won by two strokes with a 15-under par 265 total.

The tournament opened on an oddity. Faxon, who was penalized two strokes for missing his tee time in the Wednesday pro-am, almost missed his tee time again. But he birdied five of his last eight holes for 63 and the first-round lead. Frost tied him in the second round with another 63, and Ogrin shot 62 in the third round to lead Woods by one and Frost by three going into the fourth round.

Ogrin and Woods were tied for the lead at 16 under par through No. 8 and were two strokes ahead of Frost. Then a crack appeared in Woods' game. For the day, he was long on 10 approach shots, but at No. 9 he was short and in the pond with an eight iron and double-bogeyed. He was 30 yards long at the 17th and double-bogeyed again. With a bogey thrown in, he played his last 10 holes in four over par. Ogrin's putter went sour, and he played the second nine in 38. Although hardly anyone was there to see it, Frost played the last eight holes in one under par, got up-and-down for par three times over the last seven holes, and holed a 25-footer for birdie at the 17th to lock up the victory.

Memorial Tournament—$1,900,000
Winner: Vijay Singh

There's nothing new about rain-shortened, three-round tournaments, but this may have been one for the books: One round took three days to play. When this Memorial Tournament in Dublin, Ohio, finally was over, the golf writers were typing, "Singhing in the Rain." Chalk up PGA Tour win No. 4 for Vijay Singh.

Which shot would you rather have after a rain delay? A delicate chip? A drive? For Singh, it was a 236-yard three-wood shot. That's what he faced when he came back Monday at Muirfield Village's daunting par-five 11th hole, and Singh bombed the shot to within 18 inches of the hole. The eagle carried Singh two strokes clear of Scott Hoch and on his way to his first victory since the 1995 Buick Classic.

"I didn't have that much expectation of doing well, so what can I say? I can't be any more pleased," said Singh after posting rounds of 70, 65 and 67 for a 202 total, 14 under par, for a two-stroke victory over Jim Furyk and Greg Norman. And Hoch couldn't have been more displeased. He was tied with Singh when play resumed Monday, and hurt his back with his first swing. He shot 73 and tied for fourth place. Tim Herron, Billy Andrade, Glen Day and Jesper Parnevik shared the first-round lead with 66s, and Hoch broke through for the second-round lead with 65.

The third round was spread over three days. Singh played three holes on Saturday, seven on Sunday and eight on Monday. The tournament was noteworthy for other reasons. Jack Nicklaus, tournament founder and two-time winner, made the 36-hole cut for the first time in four years. He tied for eighth place. Tiger Woods had his worst moments so far this year: a second-nine 42 for 75 in the second round, nine at the par-four No. 9, and he tied for 67th place, his worst finish as a professional. John Daly, making his first start after undergoing alcohol rehabilitation, made the cut but shot 80 in the final round and finished last.

Kemper Open—$1,500,000
Winner: Justin Leonard

It's said that no one remembers who finished second, but Mark Wiebe was wishing he could forget the Kemper Open in Potomac, Maryland. "It was my tournament to win or lose, and I lost," he said. "When you hit putts like that, it's probably not to be." It was a stunning collapse. Wiebe, winless for 11 years, led by three strokes going into the final round, and by four coming to the eighth hole. He missed three-foot putts at No. 8 and No. 9, then an agonizing pair of two-footers at the 17th and 18th.

A victory had fallen into Justin Leonard's lap, but he was not about to apologize. "You've got to take every victory you can get," Leonard said. "I'm not going to put an asterisk on the tournament because of what happened on the last hole." He did do his part, shooting 69, 69, 69 and 67 for a 10-under-par 274 total at the TPC at Avenel, winning by one over Wiebe, who shot 69, 67 and 66 then closed with 73.

The tournament, the week before the U.S. Open, looked like a dogfight at first. Greg Norman eagled the par-five No. 2, then got five birdies on the back for 66. That tied him for the first-round lead with Nick Price, who had five birdies coming in. Wiebe, three strokes behind after the first round, led through the middle rounds with a pair of 69s without a bogey. In the third round, he holed three birdie putts from 25 feet and two others from 15 feet. It was the short ones that bothered him, he said, because of a nervous "buzz" brought on by allergy shots.

The victory, Leonard's second on the PGA Tour, did not come easily. He birdied the 15th hole after a brilliant eight iron to two feet, but he bogeyed the 16th after driving near a cart path. There went his chances, it seemed. Then came Wiebe's closing collapse. Leonard was happy to win, but he preferred a different ending. "I really would have rather seen him make that putt (on the 18th) and us go into a playoff," he said.

U.S. Open Championship—$2,600,000
Winner: Ernie Els

See Chapter 4.

Buick Classic—$1,500,000
Winner: Ernie Els

What's the South African phrase for "courses for horses"? Whatever it is, Ernie Els can give it new meaning. He owns Westchester Country Club in Rye, New York. When he ran off with the Buick Classic title in mid-June, that gave him a record of second, fourth, first and first in four consecutive appearances. This was just one week after he won the U.S. Open. How did he do it? Simple.

"For two weeks, I've kept the ball in play," Els said.

It couldn't have been that simple, considering the way Els handled the 6,722-yard, par-71 course — a wire-to-wire victory on rounds of 64, 68, 67 and 69, tying the tournament record with a 16-under-par 268 total. He won by two strokes over Jeff Maggert, but it really wasn't that close. Els led by two in the first round, three through the second and third rounds, and he was up by eight strokes at one point in the third round. He was threatened only briefly, early in the final round, when Maggert came within one stroke.

Els wondered whether he would have a post-Open letdown. His first-round 64 was the answer. In the second round, he birdied three of the first five holes, and shot 68 which he called "mediocre." And in the third round, he opened that eight-stroke lead. He cooled off, bogeyed twice on the second nine and still shot 67 for a tournament-record 199 total. Maggert birdied three of his last five holes for 66 to climb into second place, three strokes behind.

In the fourth round, it was catch me if you can. Els turned conservative.

"That was my strategy," he said. "To play sensibly and make the other guys come after me." Maggert tried. He got within one stroke on the first nine, but just couldn't close the gap, and settled for 68 and a runner-up position by four strokes over Jim Furyk and Robert Damron. "It's no fun to play well and finish second," Maggert said. "Well, I guess it's fun to play well, but it's tiring to keep coming up short."

FedEx St. Jude Classic—$1,500,000
Winner: Greg Norman

Fate couldn't have been meaner to rookie Robert Damron than to let him dangle in the lead for three rounds, and then snatch victory from his fingertips in the FedEx St. Jude Classic in Memphis, Tennessee, when a veteran charged in.

Greg Norman had not gone away, although he had his troubles on the PGA Tour after his crash in the 1996 Masters. He missed six cuts early in 1997, including the Masters and the U.S. Open. Anyone who thought that was the end of him had only to watch his dynamite finish at the TPC at Southwind. He emerged from the pack and birdied the last three holes for a thrilling one-stroke victory over Dudley Hart. Norman, who was in 23rd place after the first round, shot 68, 65, 69 and 66 for a 268 total, 16 under par.

Damron, who looked like a breakthrough winner for three rounds, leading on scores of 65, 66 and 69, shot 70 in the fourth round, tied for third place, and won $87,000.

Rain fragmented the tournament. Like the rest of the field, Norman had to complete the third round Sunday morning. He played 15 holes Sunday and shot a 69 that dropped him one notch to fourth place. He had an hour's rest, then went back out. A balky putter cost him some birdie chances early in the round, and after nine straight pars, his game sprang to life down the closing stretch. At the 16th, he came out of a bunker to a tap-in birdie. At the par-four 17th, he put a four iron to four feet and birdied again. And at the 18th, he fired a six iron to 30 feet right of the pin, and rolled it in. The big scramble was over and so were rumors of his demise.

"I don't know whether it's relief," Norman said. "I think it's elation more than relief, because I knew I was playing well."

Motorola Western Open—$2,000,000
Winner: Tiger Woods

The scene was reminiscent of the British Open. The crowd was swarming up the 18th fairway, almost engulfing the conquering hero. That said it all about Tiger Woods. Unable to contain themselves, the spectators at the Motorola Western Open in Lemont, Illinois, broke through gallery ropes to escort Woods to his fourth PGA Tour victory of the year (and sixth of his career). The $360,000 first prize lifted him to $1.7 million for the year.

"I don't think about the money," Woods said. "The money takes care of itself. I just want to win tournaments." This he did with authority, playing the Cog Hill course near Chicago in rounds of 67, 72, 68 and 68 for a 275 total, 13 under par, for a three-stoke victory over Frank Nobilo. What little Woods couldn't do for himself was done for him. "The golfing gods were looking down on me," he said, with a grin, meaning the shot he got away with at No. 14 on the final day. The outcome of the tournament was in doubt for only a few minutes. Nobilo had birdied the 14th and 15th holes to tie Woods at 11 under par. Moments later, Woods came to the 14th. His approach shot, a nine iron from 167 yards, got away from him and hit in tangled grass near the slope of a bunker. Did it stop and leave him a tough shot? No, it caromed to the left and rolled to within a foot of the hole.

"That," said Nobilo, "was like a knife in the heart. That seems to be happening the last 12 months. The holes Woods needs to birdie, he birdies. When he's in a position to win, he very rarely goes backward."

Quad City Classic—$1,350,000
Winner: David Toms

The Quad City Classic would be a birthday present — almost literally — for young Mr. Toms, after his father, David Toms, ended about 150 tournaments of frustration at Oakwood Country Club in Coal Valley, Illinois. "He gave me incentive to play well," said Toms, his mind on the son who was due to arrive any day now.

Toms, the third first-time winner of the year, was a PGA Tour player for three years, lost his card in 1994, and regained it by finishing third on the Nike Tour in 1995. He led the 1996 Nortel Open after three rounds, and closed with 74. In the 1996 Kemper Open, he pulled within one stroke after three rounds, then shot 72.

This time, Toms wouldn't be denied. He was high on the leaderboard with a 67-66 start, tied for the lead with Brad Fabel in the third round with 67, then closed with a five-under-par 65 for a 15-under 265 total and a three-stroke victory over Brandel Chamblee (67), Robert Gamez (67) and Jimmy Johnston (62). Toms had an uncertain moment, missing a four-footer for a bogey at the 13th, but he rebounded with two strong birdies, a 12-foot putt at the 14th and a 30-footer at the 15th, and he cruised in from there.

"I've had people tell me — 'It's your time, it's your time, it's your time,'" Toms said. "It finally was." There was one sour note, however. As usual, it was noted that many of the PGA Tour's big names weren't playing. No matter, Toms said, "I could finish second 20 times and make Ryder Cup teams, but to win a PGA Tour event, that's something they can never take away from you."

Deposit Guaranty Golf Classic—$1,000,000
Winner: Billy Ray Brown

The rest of the golf world might have been thinking about the British Open, but Billy Ray Brown, trying to come back from wrist surgery for five years, was thinking of only one thing, the 18th hole. The Deposit Guaranty Golf Classic at Annandale Golf Club in Madison, Mississippi, the PGA Tour stop opposite the British Open, was hanging by a thread.

Brown had just lost a two-stroke lead with a double bogey at the par-four 17th hole. His first victory since 1992 was about to slip away. He needed a birdie at the 532-yard 18th hole, where he'd already found the front water twice. But his mind was made up. "When I hit the fairway on 18, I knew I had to go for it," Brown said. "I could go to sleep at night if I hit it in the water trying to win, but I can't sleep if I lay up and lose in a playoff."

Brown had worked his way up. Mike Brisky led the first round with 64, and Don Pooley (68) and Steve Jurgensen (67) shared the second-round lead. Jurgensen (69) was the solo leader after three rounds. Brown, shooting 69, 66 and 69, moved from 40th place to second, two strokes off the pace, going into the final round.

Jurgensen double-bogeyed the first hole, and Brown broke from the pack with five birdies over the first seven holes. After a rain delay, he birdied the 16th to get to 18 under par, then crashed at the 17th, where his double bogey began with a drive into the rough behind a tree. That dropped him into a tie with Mike Standly, who had already finished at 16 under par.

This time, at the stubborn 18th, he slugged his four wood to about 70 feet right of the flag. His first putt left him five feet from home. He dropped that one for the birdie, 67, a 17-under-par 271 total and a one-stroke victory. "I'll cherish this victory," Brown said. "This one means more than any other."

Canon Greater Hartford Open—$1,500,000
Winner: Stewart Cink

The PGA Tour got its fourth first-time winner of the year and Jeff Maggert got his 10th second place in five years when he unraveled down the stretch at the Canon Greater Hartford Open.

"I feel sorry for him," said Stewart Cink, the 6-foot-4 rookie from Atlanta. "You hate to see it end like that. But it's over." And so it was. Cink got his victory when Maggert went four over par on the last three holes.

Maggert started the final round leading by two strokes, and coming to the par-four 18th hole he was tied with Cink, who had already finished. Maggert needed a birdie to win, a par to tie. He drove into the left rough, bounced his second shot through a greenside bunker and into the rough, and couldn't get up and down. "Angry? Yes," Maggert said. "Angry at myself." He closed with a one-over-par 71 and dropped into a tie for second place with Tom Byrum (69) and Brandel Chamblee (66) at 268.

Cink had put himself in position to win. The key was his daring execution at the par-four 17th hole. His tee shot left him facing a shot over water from a downhill lie in the rough. Smart money said lay up, but Cink went for it. "It was a tough shot, a tough lie," he said. "But you never know if you're going to be in that situation again. You've got to go for it." The ball just cleared the water and ended up on the green, leaving him two putts for par. He shot 69, 67, 65 and 66 for a 13-under-par 267 total, tying the tournament record since it moved to the TPC at River Highlands in 1984.

The door was opened when Wayne Levi, after setting the 36-hole record of 129 (64 and 65), shot 70 in the third round while 53 players were scoring in the 60s. Said Levi, who last won in 1990, "I played like a wimp."

Sprint International—$1,700,000
Winner: Phil Mickelson

One way to understand the Sprint International in Castle Rock, Colorado, is to see what happened to Nick Faldo in the first round. He ran off 18 straight pars — for nothing. "The last time I did that, they gave me the (British) Open jug," Faldo said. That was in 1987. But pars count for nothing in the International, and so all he got was the weekend off. He went on to miss the halfway cut.

The International is scored on a point system — five for an eagle, two for a birdie, minus one for a bogey and minus three for a double bogey or worse. Phil Mickelson, scoring his second victory of the season, rang up several tournament records — 27 points for 36 holes, 39 points for 54 holes, and finally 48 points for 72 holes. With his second International title, he became the first multiple winner of the event in its 12 years.

"Colorado has been good to me," Mickelson said. He dominated this International. The first round was the only one he didn't lead. He was third with 14 points behind co-leaders Jay Haas and Larry Mize, who had 15 points each. Tom Purtzer made the biggest move in the second round. After going minus four in the first round, Purtzer scored 21 points over 12 holes on Friday and tied the single-day record of 20 points. But Mickelson added 13 points for a total of 27 and a three-point lead after 36 holes.

In a bogey-free third round, Mickelson carded six birdies for a 54-hole total of 39 points. In the final round, the only pressure came from Skip Kendall. Mickelson led him by five points to start, and got to 11 by the turn. Then Kendall went on a spree, with birdies at the 10th, 11th and 13th, getting within five. But Kendall never went lower, and after Mickelson birdied the 14th on a downhill 18-foot putt, Kendall crashed. He bogeyed the 15th with three putts and double-bogeyed the par-three 16th.

Buick Open—$1,500,000
Winner: Vijay Singh

The Buick Open started with one of the cruelest stories of the year. Never mind that Sonny Skinner, a Nike Tour player, tied for 59th place. The thing is, he shot 10-under-par 62 for the first-round lead — and then 76 in the second round. Then the tournament belonged to U.S. Open champion Ernie Els, until he bogged down in the final round. And then it was Vijay Singh's, for his second victory of the season. It was a four-stroke win on scores of 67, 73, 67 and 66 for a 273 total, 15 under par at Warwick Hills.

"I thought Ernie would win this today," Singh said, "but after the front nine, we were all bunched up. So on the back, I just got my tail up."

Singh started the final round five strokes behind Els. Singh birdied the fifth and seventh and made the turn in 34, and then got off to a blistering start on the second nine, with birdies on three of the first five holes. He parred the 17th, then holed a 25-foot putt for a birdie at the 18th to wrap up a six-under-par 66. Els, playing two groups behind Singh, bogeyed No. 8 and No. 11. He birdied the 13th, but bogeyed the par-three 17th, shot a two-over-par 74, and slipped into a six-way tie for second place.

Els exploded for 63 in the second round and a four-stroke lead at the halfway point at 13-under-par 131. He carded 72 in the third round and was still up by three strokes. Then came the struggle in the fourth. "This golf course," he said, "just wouldn't give me anything."

Singh attributed his win at least partly to a new putter he got from a person near the putting green Wednesday, then recalled he picked up a new putter before the Memorial, and won that, too. "Maybe I should get more new putters," Singh said.

PGA Championship—$2,400,000
Winner: Davis Love III

See Chapter 6.

NEC World Series of Golf—$2,200,000
Winner: Greg Norman

It was, to coin an expression, a piece of pavlova, that being an Australian cake. Greg Norman said he had been having a poor year, despite winning the FedEx St. Jude Classic. Winning the NEC World Series of Golf in Akron, Ohio, would make it, well, poor-plus, at best. He started the final round trailing two men — leader John Cook by two strokes and Phil Mickelson by one. Then with Cook faltering and Mickelson frustrated, Norman went zipping by with a thrilling if ragged three-under-par 67 for a four-stroke win. Never mind that it was worth $396,000 and a 10-year exemption. "Like I said yesterday, if I win, it will be a poor-plus year," Norman said. "So it's a poor-plus."

Norman played the long and soggy Firestone South course in rounds of 68, 68, 70 and 67 for a 273 total, seven under par, finally taking the lead on the last day. He was even par on the first nine with two birdies and two bogeys, and was blistering with his irons with four birdies on the second nine on an 18-foot putt and three seven-footers. It would have been a five-shot margin except for a spectacular bogey at the 18th. A poor drive forced him to lay up in the adjoining 10th fairway, and from there he hit a brilliant seven iron over trees and skyboxes at the green, and two-putted, he said, "from downtown."

Defending champion Phil Mickelson and Tiger Woods led the first round with 67s. Dudley Hart took over in the second round with a no-bogey 65 that required only 24 putts, and then John Cook led the third round with a 67. The fourth round was his undoing. "When I needed something to go right, it went wrong," Cook said. A four-over 74 dropped him to a tie for third place. Mickelson finished second with a no-birdie 72.

Greater Vancouver Open—$1,500,000
Winner: Mark Calcavecchia

"I was very successful in the late '80s. I putted better than anyone in the world for about four years," Mark Calcavecchia was saying. "That is not the case anymore." Perhaps. But it was for a while at the Greater Vancouver Open, soon after Calcavecchia commandeered a putter from Jeff Maggert before the third round. He really needed a new putter. He had twisted the head off his own putter in disgust when he missed a short putt in the second round. He couldn't find one he liked in the pro shop, and couldn't borrow one he liked. Then he spotted Maggert's.

"I lifted it right out of his locker and away I went," Calcavecchia said. He holed a 25-footer for a birdie at No. 1 and a 15-footer on the second. After a 68-66 start that had him back in the pack, he took the lead with a six-under-par 65 in the third round and added 66 in the fourth round for his first victory in almost 16 months. His 19-under-par total of 265 at Northview gave him a one-stroke win over Andrew Magee, who finished with two 65s. "It felt nice to be out there in the heat of the battle," Magee said. He turned up the heat at the final hole when he hit a driver and a seven iron to 12 feet and narrowly missed the putt that would have tied them.

Tom Byrum took the first-round lead when he lowered his own course record to 63, and the trio of Richard Zokol (64), Steve Pate (who birdied eight of the last 12 holes for 64) and Len Mattiace (67) shared the second-round lead. Then Calcavecchia spotted that putter. In the final round, he picked up where he left off. He birdied No. 6 from 30 feet, tapped in after a 66-yard wedge shot at No. 7, holed a 12-footer at the 10th, a 20-footer at the 11th, and eagled the 12th from 16 feet.

Will Maggert get that putter back? "It depends," Calcavecchia said, "on how bad he wants it."

Greater Milwaukee Open—$1,300,000
Winner: Scott Hoch

Does a golfer really know when a ball's going in the hole? Check Scott Hoch in the Greater Milwaukee Open. He had a 70-foot chip shot on the final hole, the par-five 18th. The ball was still rolling when he lifted his arms in triumph. "It got about 10 feet away, and I was licking my chops," Hoch said. Ten feet later, he had an eagle, his second Milwaukee title in three years, and his eighth PGA Tour victory, winning by one stroke on rounds of 70, 66, 66 and 66 for a 16-under-par 268 total.

Hoch broke two hearts with that shot. First was Loren Roberts. He was the leader in the clubhouse by one stroke. "I wasn't stunned," Roberts said, "because I knew I needed to make birdie on the 18th." He had made a par. The other was David Sutherland, who was seeking his first career win. He was in the final group, and he had wasted a healthy lead, and now needed a 60-foot putt at the 18th for an eagle to tie Hoch. It lipped out. He sagged to his knees and held his head in his hand.

The tournament opened like a stampede, with seven players tied for the first-round lead at five-under-par 66 at Brown Deer Park. Clarence Rose took over in the second round with 66-133, one shot ahead of Nike Tour veteran Spike McRoy, who eagled No. 4 en route to 63. Neither would last. In the third round, Sutherland shot his second consecutive 65, and Fulton Allem, recovering from a wrist injury, shot 64 to share a one-stroke lead. Through this all, Hoch was practically out of sight. He was in 53rd place after his opening 70, then climbed to ninth and fourth on consecutive 66s. When he birdied the 16th on Sunday, he was just one behind Roberts, who had taken the lead from the sinking Sutherland.

"I was slowly losing my confidence," Sutherland said. He had led by three through the turn, bogeyed the 10th and 13th, and came to the 18th needing an eagle that eluded him. He fell to second place with Roberts, one stroke behind Hoch.

Bell Canadian Open—$1,500,000
Winner: Steve Jones

This one needed an asterisk. To begin with, the Bell Canadian Open in Ils Bizard, Quebec, was a tournament of extremes. Rookie Robert Damron shot a bogey-free 65 for the first-round lead, then shot 75 in the second round. Rocco Mediate, still struggling to return from back surgery, took the halfway lead with 68 in the second round, then shot 78 in the third round. Then Steve Jones, after taking the lead in the third round, came to the 72nd hole leading by one stroke over Greg Norman. Jones bogeyed that last hole — and still won by a stroke. Norman, of course, also bogeyed.

Jones credited his win to a looser attitude. He had been grinding so hard to try to make the U.S. Ryder Cup team, and when he didn't, he decided it was time to smile. Said Jones, "I told myself, 'I'm 38. I don't care if I shoot 80, I'm just going to have fun.'" Jones' fun took the form of numbers: 71-68-67-69–275, five under par at the par-70 Royal Montreal course.

Jones started the final round one stroke up on Norman, and immediately got to two with a three-foot birdie putt at No. 1. Norman, who had won two weeks earlier, was thwarted by lip-outs on the first nine, then double-bogeyed the 11th from the trees and fell four behind. He battled back and got the deficit down to one with a curling 45-foot birdie putt at the 16th. Both parred the 17th. Then came the final test.

At the uphill, 444-yard 18th, both drove into the right rough. Jones, 203 yards from home, couldn't get his club fully on his ball down in the rough. He topped it about 30 yards. Then he lofted an eight iron to the green, 35 feet from the hole. The door was open to Norman. But his four-iron approach shot nicked a tree and came down short, and he pitched on and ran the putt 20 feet past. Then both two-putted for bogeys, and Jones had his second win of the year.

One final asterisk: Tiger Woods shot 70-76–146 and missed the cut for the first time as a professional.

CVS Charity Classic—$1,200,000
Winner: Loren Roberts

"When you've got a great putter like Loren and someone who's not so great, like me," Bill Glasson was saying, "you'll always bet on the great putter." This was Glasson, explaining why, after leading through the middle two rounds, he finished second in the CVS Charity Classic in Sutton, Massachusetts. Loren Roberts, known as the "Boss of the Moss," simply out-putted him at the par-71 Pleasant Valley Country Club. Roberts, moving steadily up from his eighth-place start, shot 67, 67, 68 and 64 for a 266 total, 18 under par. Glasson finished one stroke back. Peter Jacobsen, who had tied for the second-round lead, charged with six birdies through the 16th hole and got to 16 under par, but a bogey at the par-four 17th ruined his chances. He finished third.

"I'm not going to beat anybody off the tee," Roberts said. "I'm going to have to beat them off the green. That's the best part of my game. That's what I'm going to play to." That's what won for him in a real scramble. Dave Rummells and Charlie Rymer tied for the first-round lead with 64s. Jacobsen shot 65 to tie Glasson for the 36-hole lead at nine-under-par 133. Then it was Glasson in the lead alone in the third round.

Roberts came down the final stretch with a fresh memory he could do without, of how he didn't birdie the 18th hole at the Greater Milwaukee Open and Scott Hoch chipped in for an eagle there and beat him. "What happened two weeks ago was going through my mind," said Roberts, envisioning a similar duel with Glasson, who lost the lead on a three-putt at the 14th hole. Roberts thought he had to birdie the 18th to beat Glasson, but it didn't work out that way. Roberts parred the 18th, but Glasson couldn't cash in this opportunity. He birdied the 18th, but he had only parred the par-three 17th, and one stroke wasn't enough.

"The difference was, I had a two-shot lead this time," Roberts said. "So I figured the worst thing that's going to happen is a playoff."

LaCantera Texas Open—$1,400,000
Winner: Tim Herron

It was a tough week for American Ryder Cup players in the LaCantera Texas Open in San Antonio, their last competition before heading for Spain. Lee Janzen tied for 31st, Jeff Maggert for 49th, and Tom Lehman missed the 36-hole cut. It was a great time for Tim Herron, who wasn't going to the Ryder Cup. He was busy notching his second victory in two years on the PGA Tour.

Herron, after a 71-67 start, took command in the third round. On the second nine, he made four birdies and an eagle for 30 and an eight-under-par 64 that carried him to a one-stroke lead. He kept up the pace in the fourth round. He eagled No. 5 and counted his blessings. "You need some breaks to win out here," he said, "and when that eagle putt went in from 15 feet, I told my caddie it would have gone at least 10 feet past if it didn't find the hole." He birdied No. 8 and led by three strokes through the turn, and wasn't challenged after that. His closing 69 gave him a 17-under-par

271 and a two-shot victory over Rick Fehr and Brent Geiberger.

Herron, who broke through to win the 1996 Honda Classic as a rookie, put his second win in perspective. "When you've won before," he said, "you get used to the big checks, so I was happy to win again."

B.C. Open—$1,300,000
Winner: Gabriel Hjertstedt

Everyone knew it was a matter of time before a Swede won on the PGA Tour, but it was supposed to be Jesper Parnevik, or before him, Anders Forsbrand. Not many Americans had even heard of Gabriel Hjertstedt, but it was a case of Swedes beating Americans on both sides of the Atlantic that September weekend.

While Parnevik and Per-Ulrik Johansson were helping the Europeans beat the Americans in the Ryder Cup, Hjertstedt, a most uncertain rookie on the PGA Tour, was busy winning the B.C. Open at Endicott, New York. In fact, Hjertstedt got up early that Sunday and watched the Europeans win.

"My emotions were running high," he said. "That was an inspiration for me." First the stage had to be set. Greg Kraft, the first-round leader with 66, was out of contention. Second-round co-leaders Bruce Fleisher, Grant Waite and Jim McGovern had slipped. Stewart Cink led going into the final round but crashed to four bogeys in the first six holes. Hjertstedt, trailing Cink by one stroke, bogeyed the first hole and double-bogeyed the second. He re-grouped and birdied three of his next four holes. A nine iron to three feet at the 10th set him up for another birdie, and victory became a possibility.

Andrew Magee, leading by one stroke with four holes to play, bounced his sand wedge approach shot off the back of the 16th green and bogeyed. "I went for it on No. 16 because of that," Hjertstedt said. He hit driver at the nasty 312-yard hole whose green sits amid nine bunkers. Off his bold tee shot, he chipped to six feet and got the birdie for the lead. He held on for the win, shooting 275 on rounds of 70, 69, 66 and 70.

"Last year, I had no money, and coming into this week I wasn't sure I was going to be able to play next week because my ranking wasn't good enough," he said. "That's all changed now."

Buick Challenge—$1,200,000
Winner: Davis Love III

From disaster one week to smashing triumph the next, that was Davis Love III, following his 0-4 shutout in Ryder Cup play with a victory in the Buick Challenge in Pine Mountain, Georgia. Not that it eased the hurt that much. "I could win the next 10 tournaments, but we still lost the Ryder Cup," Love said. "I'm going to be hard on myself, no matter what, for the way I played last week." Not so hard that he couldn't dominate the Buick Challenge, shooting rounds of 67, 65, 67 and 68 for a tournament-record and 21-under-par 267 total and a four-stroke win over Stewart Cink.

In the final round, Cink, playing with Love, got to within one stroke with a birdie at No. 5. Love went back in front by two with a birdie at No. 7, and then came the decisive moment at the par-five 11th. Cink bogeyed, Love birdied, and it was all but over. Cink got one more glimmer of hope when Love suffered his only bogey, that at the 14th hole, but he bounced back with a birdie at the 15th. Then it was time for two assessments. Said Cink: "I'm not embarrassed by the way I played. I played solid all week." Said Love, with his 12th career victory tucked away: "Playing that well after not playing so well last week means a lot for my confidence."

Love set the course and 54-hole tournament record of 199 with a six-birdie 67. Among other noteworthy accomplishments, Love had six birdies and an eagle in his second-round 65. Hal Sutton, co-leader with 65, birdied seven of his first 11 holes. In the final round, Steve Lowery rocketed from 47th to a third-place finish with a stunning course-record 60, the lowest score of the year.

Michelob Championship at Kingsmill—$1,550,000
Winner: David Duval

It was beginning to look as if David Duval would go through another year without a victory, then he beat Duffy Waldorf, who led through the first three rounds, and Grant Waite on the first hole of a playoff in the Michelob Championship at Kingsmill in Williamsburg, Virginia. Duval was a heralded player when he came out of Georgia Tech and joined the Tour in 1993. Victory kept eluding him — until now. "I don't know what to say," Duval said. "I guess the anticipation was great, obviously. At the same time, I felt my time would come. Other people made a bigger deal out of it than I would let it be."

The three tied with 271 totals, 13 under par at Kingsmill's River Course. Duval had moved from eighth place in the first round to second place in the middle two rounds and finally into the tie on scores of 67, 66, 71 and 67 on the par-71 course.

For a while in the third round, it seemed another of Duval's crippling rounds was going to sink him again. He started to slip with bogeys at the fourth and fifth holes, but righted himself quickly. He dropped a 15-footer for a birdie at No. 7, then birdied the 15th from four feet and the 16th from 18 inches for 71 and a tie with Waite, three strokes behind Waldorf. In the final round, Duval edged into the lead with an 18-foot birdie at the 12th, and he charged to three strokes ahead with an eagle at the 15th, holing a 24-footer. But it wasn't over yet. Duval dropped a stroke when he missed the green at the 16th. Then Waldorf birdied three straight holes, the last a 30-foot curler at the 14th, and tied Duval. Waite charged back with five birdies in six holes, the last a 12-foot putt at the 16th that got him into the tie at 13 under par.

The playoff started and ended at the 18th. Waldorf drove into the rough and bogeyed. Waite left his long birdie try 18 inches short. Duval, who had gone 92 starts without winning and who had finished second seven times, ended his long, frustrating journey with a 10-foot birdie.

Walt Disney World/Oldsmobile Classic—$1,500,000
Winner: David Duval

After three years of explaining why he wasn't winning, now David Duval was having to explain why he was. The answer, as he had said earlier, was simple: "Breaks," he said. "Basically, that's what it boils down to."

If so, then the fates owed him a few more, and they paid him handsomely in the Walt Disney World/Oldsmobile Classic in Lake Buena Vista, Florida. He won for the second straight week, and again in a playoff. He did it by holing a 15-foot par putt on the first extra hole against Dan Forsman, who bogeyed out of a scruffy lie.

"I came down here after my first victory and didn't know what to expect," Duval said. "It seemed to carry over a bit." Talk about breaks. In the final round at the Magnolia Course, Duval came to the par-four 17th hole tied with Forsman at 18 under par. He promptly pulled his drive, and his ball was heading for the lake on the left. It hit a tree and caromed safely back into the fairway. "Those," Duval was to say, "are the breaks you get when you're winning." He converted, with a wedge and a six-foot birdie putt. Earlier, at the 11th hole, he was trying to get down in two from 60 feet across a green grown fast and crusty by whipping winds. Instead, the ball dropped for a birdie.

Duval could have won in regulation play. At the 18th he drove into the right rough, put his second shot into a bunker, came out poorly to 15 feet, and then just grazed the hole with his par putt. The bogey gave him 70 and dropped him into a tie with with Forsman at 18-under-par 270. Duval did it on rounds of 65, 70, 65 and 70.

The fates were not as kind to some other challengers. Len Mattiace shot 65 in the third round and was in the final pairing for the first time in his two years on the PGA Tour. He was leading by two strokes, but bogeyed three of the first five holes, shot 74, and tied for third place. Payne Stewart, who led through the first two rounds, posted 70 in the third round. He was putting for birdie 16 times, but made only two. Then he hurt his back on the practice tee and shot 75 in the final round.

Las Vegas Invitational—$1,800,000
Winner: Bill Glasson

All eyes were on Tiger Woods. He scored his first win as a professional in October, 1996, proceeded to set the PGA Tour on fire, and was the favorite at the Las Vegas Invitational, the last official full-field event. No, he did not repeat. He did not even threaten. That, as Woods has said, is golf.

So Bill Glasson, who admitted he was looking over his shoulder, was left to his own devices, which were plenty good. He shared the lead through the first two rounds of this five-round tournament, trailed in the next two rounds, and regained the lead late in the final round and held on to score his seventh victory in his injury-plagued 14 years on the PGA Tour.

Despite a bone spur in his left elbow (he would have surgery in a few weeks), Glasson shot rounds of 63, 65, 75, 71 and 66 for a 340 total, 20 under par on three courses — TPC at Summerlin, Desert Inn and Las Vegas

Country Club. He shared the first-round lead on an amazing 63, in which he hit 18 greens in regulation, but only eight of the 14 driving fairways. Phil Mickelson got hot in the second round. "I was thinking 59," he admitted. Little wonder. He started on the 10th hole at Summerlin and birdied eight of the first nine holes. He cooled to 63, then shot 79 the next day. Billy Mayfair and Duffy Waldorf also shot 63s and tied Glasson for the 36-hole lead.

In the third round, with winds gusting to 45 miles an hour, Waldorf was one of only eight players to break 70, taking a four-stroke lead with his 69. With more wind in the fourth round, no one broke 70, and Waldorf held on to a two-shot lead with 75.

Glasson started the final round two strokes behind Waldorf. He birdied three holes in a row from No. 7, the jewel a chip-in at the 247-yard eighth that he said "turned a four into a two." Glasson then got to 20 under par at the par-five 16th, where he ran his 60-foot eagle try six feet past, then made the putt coming back for a birdie. Mayfair reached the 16th in two but three-putted. Waldorf also failed to birdie it, then bogeyed the last two holes. Glasson parred in for his first win since the 1994 Phoenix Open.

Noticeable by his absence was David Duval, the hottest man on the PGA Tour, winner of the previous two tournaments. He withdrew before the start, saying he was exhausted.

Tour Championship—$4,000,000
Winner: David Duval

The rest did David Duval a world of good. He was worn out after winning two tournaments in a row, both in playoffs. He had entered the Las Vegas Invitational but withdrew, citing exhaustion. So he came out refreshed the following week for the season-ending Tour Championship — and he won again. Suddenly Duval, who had gone 92 tournaments before he could win, who was a runner-up seven times, had won three times in four weeks, but in three straight starts, the first to do that since Nick Price in 1993. He was the first ever to make his first three victories consecutive.

"Three victories in a year, no matter how they are spaced out, is a great year," Duval said. This also made it a great year: His $720,000 first prize lifted him to second place on the final PGA Tour money list with $1,885,308. Tiger Woods, who finished 12th in the tournament, topped the list with a record $2,066,833.

Duval played the par-71 Champions course in Houston, Texas, in rounds of 66, 69, 70 and 68 for a 273 total, 11 under par, for a one-stroke win. It was a scramble all the way. Duval, Jim Furyk and Jesper Parnevik shared the first-round lead with 66s. Scott Hoch, making only one bogey, shot a tournament-low 65 for a nine-under-par total of 133 and a one-stroke lead over Furyk after 36 holes. Then, in a wind-blown third round, Duval (70), Bill Glasson (68), Davis Love III (69) and Brad Faxon (69) tied for a two-stroke lead going into the fourth round.

Love took the early lead, but faded on the second nine when his iron play faltered. Duval, on the other hand, put on a show. He struck at the par-five 13th hole, firing a three iron 257 yards to 40 feet from the pin. He got the eagle. At the 17th, he saved himself twice, first getting out of deep rough off his drive, then holing a 12-foot putt for his par. He also recovered from the rough at the 18th, and saved par again. Love, playing behind him, needed a birdie to tie. He bogeyed, leaving Furyk in second place.

Special Events

Family House Invitational—$850,000
Winner: Jim Furyk

Jim Furyk, who traces his roots to western Pennsylvania, overtook faltering Rocco Mediate, a native son out of Greensburg, to win the Family House Invitational at Oakmont Country Club. Mediate took the lead with a six-under-par 65 in the pro-am first round. "But when you start missing fairways, it's all over," he said. He shot 75 in the second round of the charity event.

Furyk solved the storied course for another 69 and a four-under-par 138 total to win the $170,000 first prize. The only other round under par came from Frank Nobilo, in a remarkable 77-69 turnaround. It went the other way, too. Mark Brooks, the defending PGA champion, shot 69-80. This turned out to be the last tournament for Family House, a low-cost medical housing facility in Pittsburgh. Officials of the facility cancelled it some weeks later.

Fred Couples Invitational—$565,000
Winner: Scott Simpson

It was Scott Simpson's victory in the Fred Couples Invitational, a charity event, but the big galleries belonged to Arnold Palmer, and they didn't get any smaller when he was paired for the first time ever with Laura Davies in the second round. Those who followed Simpson saw him beat out Tom Lehman with a disciplined 67-67–134 total at Inglewood Golf Club in Kenmore, Washington.

Simpson took the lead at No. 9 in the second round when Tom Lehman bogeyed. Simpson birdied the final two holes, the last a clutch 12-footer at the 18th hole. Lehman had one last chance. He had to eagle the par-five 18th to force a playoff. He reached the green in two, but faced a 40-footer. "I was nervous watching him putt," Simpson said. "I would rather not go into a playoff with Tom Lehman, that's for sure. I was happy when it went by the hole." Lehman's eagle try just missed.

Fred Meyer Challenge—$700,000
Winners: Greg Norman and Brad Faxon

"I walked up to him on the first tee, and I said, 'Are you ready to win three in a row?'" Greg Norman was saying. Said his partner, Brad Faxon, "Yes, I am. Let's go." And so the Fred Meyer Challenge, with its field of 12 two-man teams, has become the Norman-Faxon early-August private party at the Oregon Golf Club in Linn, Oregon. They opened with five straight birdies, and were 10 under par through the 12th hole before they slowed down. They shot an 11-under-par 60 in the first round for a two-stroke lead over Fred Couples and John Cook, then added 63 for a 123 total and a three-stroke win over Jay Haas and Phil Mickelson, who closed with a tournament-best 61.

Lincoln-Mercury Kapalua International—$1,200,000
Winner: Davis Love III

Forgive the pun, but the Lincoln-Mercury Kapalua International had truly been a love affair — as in Davis Love III. He won again, and now consider this record: In 10 appearances, he won twice, was second three times and third twice. He won this time going away, and it would be his last. After 16 playings, the tournament came to an end. It will be replaced by the Mercedes Championships at Kapalua, the Hawaiian resort, in 1999. Love had a rousing introduction to the tournament in 1986, when he finished as runner-up to Andy Bean. And now he gave it a rousing sendoff. On rounds of 67-66-67-68, Love trailed David Toms by four strokes in the first round, was tied with Toms in the second and third rounds, then won by three with a 22-under-par 268 total.

Love, who had quite a year with victories in the PGA Championship and the Buick Challenge, then reflected on his career since his first Kapalua International. "I was a young guy trying to beat the veterans," he said. "To see how far I've come and all the great things that have happened to me, it's been amazing. It's hard to believe this is the last time around."

Subaru Sarazen World Open—$2,000,000
Winner: Mark Calcavecchia

The classy field in the Subaru Sarazen World Open wasn't what scared Mark Calcavecchia. It was his back, and things looked "iffy" by the sixth hole of the final round. "I was having some light spasms, and immediately started praying that I could finish," he said. He had been crushing the field at the par-72 Chateau Elan course at Braselton, Georgia.

It would be a shame to waste a performance that began with a 10-under-par 62. And Calcavecchia didn't. His scores were 62, 67, 71 and 71 for a 271 total, 17 under par. He led, successively, by six strokes, seven, six and finally three.

Calcavecchia was ahead by a forbidding 10 strokes through No. 6 when the back problems started. He had to put on a back brace at No. 9. His lead shrank dangerously as he was hobbling to a clutch of bogeys while England's

Lee Westwood was getting birdies at the 14th and 16th holes. He still felt "a couple of big jolts" at the 13th and 17th.

Calcavecchia stopped the drain at two with a clutch 10-foot bogey putt at the 17th. "The big putt of the day," he said. He went to the 18th up by two, and dropped a 40-foot putt for a birdie for the three-stroke win.

Franklin Templeton Shark Shootout—$1,100,000
Winners: Scott McCarron and Bruce Lietzke

In the question of dream pairings for the Franklin Templeton Shark Shootout, host Greg Norman and fellow Aussie Steve Elkington come to mind. Brad Faxon and Lee Janzen are an impressive pair. How about Bruce Lietzke, a veteran, and Scott McCarron, a newcomer? This falls under the label of "unlikely." Lietzke rarely plays anywhere and McCarron had the thinnest credentials in the field.

At the end of the frolic, however, it was Lietzke saying, "This was a dream pairing for both of us. Scott can really launch the ball and I can keep it in play." This led to a decisive outing. The two were fifth in the 10-team field after the alternate-shot first round with 68, six strokes behind Peter Jacobsen and John Cook who shot 62. Lietzke and McCarron vaulted into a two-stroke lead in the second round with a better-ball 13-under-par 59 and a 127 total. In the final round, played as a scramble, they ripped off another 59 for a 186 total, 30 under par at Sherwood Country Club in Thousand Oaks, California.

"Our strategy from the very beginning was for me to hit first on every shot," Lietzke said. "I played here in the previous eight tournaments and I have a pretty good feel for the course, especially the greens. It worked perfectly." And the dreamiest dream pairing? Norman and Elkington finished next-to-last.

MasterCard PGA Grand Slam—$1,000,000
Winner: Ernie Els

That was a pretty good three-headed problem facing U.S. Open champion Ernie Els in the MasterCard PGA Grand Slam, an event for winners of the major championships at Poipu Bay, Hawaii. There was formidable Masters champion Tiger Woods, the first-round leader; PGA champion Davis Love, mounting a charge, and to complicate things, a soggy course.

Woods led Els by two strokes in the first round, and Love by five. Woods couldn't hold off Els in the second round. Els caught him by No. 6 and went ahead at No. 7. Els led by three through No. 10, three-putted the 16th for a bogey, then settled for a birdie at the 18th after his eagle try just missed. With a 68-65–133 total, 11 under par, he won by three over Woods (66-70–136). Love (71-67–138) birdied four of the first five holes, then ran out of steam. British Open champion Justin Leonard (77-72–149) was not a factor.

World Cup of Golf—$1,500,000
Winners: Ireland/Colin Montgomerie

You say Ireland won the World Cup of Golf, and people may say, sure, Christy O'Connor and Harry Bradshaw. But that was in 1958. Now there's a new breed of Irishmen, this pair named Padraig Harrington, age 25, and Paul McGinley, 30, and they came from out of the crowd of the 32-team field to run away with the World Cup by five strokes.

Scotland's Colin Montgomerie, who played the Ocean Course at Kiawah Island, South Carolina, in the 1991 Ryder Cup, won the individual championship with a splendid card of 68, 66, 66 and 66, for a 22-under-par 266 total. (The last time Monty played the par-three 17th hole was in singles in the Ryder Cup, and he won the hole over Mark Calcavecchia with a double bogey. In his next visit, the first round of the World Cup, he hit a five iron to eight feet and holed the birdie.)

Harrington and McGinley started with 66-71–137, seven shots off the lead of 130 by Sweden's Per-Ulrik Johansson and Joakim Haeggman. The Scots were up next. Montgomerie and Raymond Russell shot 66-72 in the second round and stood at 272, two ahead of the second-place Irishmen (66-71–274). In the third round, the Germans moved up, with Alexander Cejka shooting his second bogey-free round in three days, 63, and Sven Struver, 70, for 408 total. The Irish were still two strokes behind, with 410, on McGinley's 66 and Harrington's 71.

Then came the runaway. McGinley closed with 68, Harrington 67 for a 545 total, while the Germans sank to a tie for fourth place, and the Scots, spurred by Montgomerie's 66, took second, five strokes behind at 550. Reminded of O'Connor and Bradshaw of 39 years earlier, "There were a lot of Irish golfers between us and them," McGinley said, "and that makes us proud."

General Motors Mexican Open—$300,000
Winner: Frank Nobilo

Frank Nobilo, the amiable New Zealander who broke through on the American PGA Tour in the Greater Greensboro Chrysler Classic in April, expanded his conquests in the General Motors Mexican Open in Mexico City in November. Nobilo rallied in the final round to outrun a faltering Jeff Maggert for a two-stroke victory. Stewart Cink, the bright young American, and Argentine veteran Eduardo Romero shared the first-round lead at 69 over the par-72, 7,333-yard Golf Club of Mexico course. Nobilo, Maggert and Kawika Cotner were one stroke behind at 69.

Maggert vaulted into the lead with 68 in the second round, and was looking good after the third round, when 66 carried him two strokes clear of Nobilo. The other challengers faded fast, Cotner worst of all. One stroke back after two rounds, he eliminated himself with 79 in the third. Nobilo wrapped up his Mexican holiday with a closing 68 and a 15-under-par 273 total. Maggert slid to 73 and dropped to a tie for third with Cink, behind Tommy Armour III, who rose to second on a closing 68.

Callaway Golf Pebble Beach Invitational—$300,000
Winner: Loren Roberts

Loren Roberts opened with a two-stroke lead and stayed in front — if barely at one point — to take the Callaway Golf Pebble Beach Invitational by three strokes. Roberts shot rounds of 64, 68, 74 and 70 for a 276 total, 12 under par, to win by three strokes over a field of 51 that included men and women professionals playing for the same purse.

Roberts was hardly coasting. He expanded his lead to five with the 68 in the second round, but 74 in the third round dropped him into a tie with Johnny Miller (69-68-69). Miller's chase ended with 73 and a tie for second place with defending champion Kirk Triplett (70). John Daly was closing in hard. He trailed by four strokes in the first round, then three, then two in the third round with his 67-68-73 scores. He was still in contention until he hit his second shot out of bounds at the 14th hole. He shot 73 and tied for fifth place.

JCPenney Classic—$1,500,000
Winners: Clarence Rose and Amy Fruhwirth

The key to the championship in the JCPenney Classic was Bob Low, a caddie. He had worked for both Clarence Rose and Amy Fruhwirth. When he heard Rose was looking for a partner in this 52-team event, he recommended Fruhwirth. Said Rose, "I didn't know what she looked like and she didn't know what I looked like." They were soon good friends and happy winners.

Mike Brisky and Barb Mucha were the first to turn compatibility into a golf asset. They shot a better-ball, nine-under-par 62 and led the first round by one stroke over Jeff Sluman and Dottie Pepper, who had 29 on their first nine. Dan Forsman and Catriona Matthew took over in the second round with 64 in modified alternate-shot play. Then they were caught in the third round by Steve Pate and Meg Mallon with 64.

Rose and Fruhwirth finished with a five-under-par 66 for a 20-under 264 total, then had to wait and fret. Forsman and Matthew gave them cause. Forsman fired a three iron to within four feet of the cup at the par-three 17th, but Matthew missed the putt. At the 18th, Forsman had one last shot at them. His chip from off the green just missed. "That watching," Rose said, "is tough."

Office Depot Father-Son Challenge—$860,000
Winners: Raymond Floyd and Raymond Floyd, Jr.

If ever a name ought to be changed, this is it — from the Office Depot Father-Son Challenge to the Raymond Floyds' Invitational. Raymond Floyd and son Raymond, Jr., are three-for-three in the early December event. Dave and Ron Stockton shot 60 for the first-round lead, then the Floyds took over in the second round, making birdies on 14 holes for a 14-under-par 58 and a 120 total at Windsor in Vero Beach, Florida. The first two events were played at better-ball the first day, a scramble format the second day, but this tournament was a scramble both days.

"The scramble format is so aggressive," the elder Floyd said. "If your partner has hit first and is in good shape, you may even try shots you would never consider in a tournament." The field was gaining on the Floyds, though. They won by six strokes in 1995, by two in 1996, and they beat the Stocktons by only one this time.

Diners Club Matches—$2,100,000
Winners: Steve Elkington and Jeff Maggert
Gil Morgan and Jay Sigel
Juli Inkster and Dottie Pepper

In a classic nip-and-tuck duel, the last nip went to Steve Elkington and Jeff Maggert, ending the two-year reign of Duffy Waldorf and Tom Lehman in the PGA Tour segment of the Diners Club Matches on the Jack Nicklaus Course at PGA West in La Quinta, California. Neither team was more than 1 up until late in the second nine. The key moment? Maybe Elkington's eagle at the par-five 13th, off a two-iron shot to six feet. "When he birdied the 14th, I knew it was our match to win or lose," Maggert said. Elkington rolled in a 20-footer for a halve, preserving their 1-up lead. Then Maggert hit the winning shot at the par-three 17th, a five iron to four feet, and the clinching birdie putt for the 2-and-1 victory.

In the taxing round-robin format, Jay Sigel and Gil Morgan had gone 24 holes to win one match and five extra holes in a playoff to reach the final of the Senior PGA Tour segment, then they beat Bob Eastwood and Walter Morgan 1 up. "Those 11 playoff holes had tired us out," Sigel said. "It seemed like we were trying to salvage pars much of the day," Morgan said. They took the lead on Sigel's eagle three at No. 8.

Juli Inkster and Dottie Pepper repeated as LPGA champions, beating the formidable combination of Laura Davies and Nancy Lopez, 3 and 2. Pepper's birdie from 25 feet at No. 5 gave them the lead. "The key," Pepper said, "was that we didn't let them get any momentum. We were able to make birdies when they made birdies."

Lexus Challenge—$1,000,000
Winners: Raymond Floyd and William Devane

Raymond Floyd had built up a good reputation as a closer in his years on the pro tours, but it was his partner, actor William Devane, who did the trick in the $1 million Lexus Challenge, the pro-celebrity event at La Quinta, California. Devane sank a four-foot putt at the par-five 17th hole for a net eagle (the celebrities played at full handicap), then sank a three-footer for a net birdie at the 18th for a team total of 12-under-par 60 and a two-round total of 20-under 124. "That was an incredible finish," Floyd said. "He was just incredible when it meant a lot."

What it meant was a one-stroke victory over two other teams — Jim Colbert and actor Kevin Costner, and Gil Morgan and baseball pitcher Roger

Clemens. Morgan and Clemens, playing behind Floyd and Devane, led them by three going to No. 16. But that lead quickly shrank to one when Morgan bogeyed and Floyd birdied. Morgan needed a birdie at the 18th to force a playoff, but missed his 15-footer.

Oddly enough, in the first round, Costner made a real eagle at the 17th — for a net double-eagle two — to spark him and Colbert to the opening lead on 60. Floyd and Devane were four strokes back. "We were totally out of it," Floyd said. "But then we caught fire. I probably played the best stretch of holes I've played in 10 or 15 years."

Andersen Consulting World Championship—$3,650,000
Winner: Colin Montgomerie

Colin Montgomerie won his second successive World Money List title by claiming $1 million for his 2-up victory over Davis Love III in the 36-hole final of the Andersen Consulting World Championship at the Grayhawk Golf Club's Raptor course in Scottsdale, Arizona, four days into 1998.

Montgomerie's fifth victory of the year gave him a total of $3,366,900. Ernie Els was second with $3,188,962 and Love, with $500,000 for second place, took third with $2,861,953. In 1996, Montgomerie became the first to earn more than $3 million in a year with $3,071,442, then in 1997 he won his record fifth consecutive PGA European Tour money title.

There were 32 players in the tournament which began with four regional events from March through May. Montgomerie came out of the European section; Love, from the United States; Els, from the International, and Hajime Meshiai, from the Japan qualifier.

In the semi-finals at Grayhawk, Montgomerie defeated Els 3 and 2, and Love won 1 up over Meshiai. Montgomerie led 4 up with four holes to play in the final. Love birdied the next two holes and then Montgomerie bogeyed, sending their match to the 36th hole. Montgomerie put his second shot 10 feet from the hole and Love finished 60 feet away. After missing the putt, Love conceded the match. In the third-place match, Els beat Meshiai 4 and 3.

Nike Tour

The Nike Tour for 1997 added up to 30 tournaments and $6.6 million in purses, but on closer examination, it was a lot of other things. Among them: the first "battlefield promotion," five straight first-time winners, 16 first-timers overall, a proliferation of Bates and Batemans, a 52-hole tournament, and achieving a dream at age 45.

"Battlefield promotion" — the very expression evokes images of John Wayne swaggering through a hail of bullets, helmet at a rakish angle, being promoted for working yet another miracle. Fortunately, Chris Smith was in no such peril. He won a different kind of battlefield promotion. Under a new policy that went into effect in 1997, a player who wins three Nike events in one year automatically wins his PGA Tour playing card. Smith, 28, an Ohio State graduate out of Peru, Indiana, became the first to do it.

It may not have been John Wayne-ish, but it was something of a miracle in its own right. Winning three is tough enough, but Smith won his three with authority — the Upstate Classic early in June by three strokes, at 21 under par, then seven weeks later, back-to-back tournaments, the Dakota Dunes Open by two strokes, at 20 under par, and then his masterpiece, the Omaha Classic by 11 strokes, with a record 26-under-par 258 total.

"I wasn't trying to shoot a certain score," Smith said. "When I finished and totaled up my score, I was 26 under par." And he didn't want to dwell on his success. "I'm not going to think about the battlefield promotion right now," Smith said. "But whether it's this fall or next year, I'm excited about getting back to the PGA Tour. I just hope I have more success than last year." Smith was on the "big tour" in 1996, and finished 206th on the money list.

Two men fell a victory short of a battlefield promotion. Mike Small, 27, of Danville, Illinois, won the Monterrey Open in March (his career first) and took the Cleveland Open in June with an inspired rally. Small began the final round five strokes off the lead, and was six behind leader Pat Bates through the final turn, and took the lead when Bates double-bogeyed the 17th. Small credited going back to his old driver. "I don't hit it as far," he said, "but I can hit it straight." Todd Gleaton, a Nike Tour rookie, also won two.

The Nike Tour had a confusion of names, and Tour resources didn't say whether anybody was related to anybody here. There was Pat Bates, who won the Colorado Classic, and Ben Bates, the Wichita Open. And Dan Bateman, who won the Carolina Classic, and Brian Bateman, who won nothing.

R.W. Eaks, a member of the Nike Tour since it started in 1990, and making a record 191st start, won the San Jose Open, his first victory since 1993. But why was he still plugging away at 45, twice the age of some of his fellow golfers? "It's the only way I know how to make a living," Eaks said. "The only other thing I ever wanted to be was a basketball coach." But he didn't have to try the courts this time. Eaks finished ninth on the money list and won his PGA Tour card.

Elsewhere on the Nike Tour:

Mark Carnevale, who had suffered through several difficult years on the PGA Tour, won the Inland Empire Open. He assessed the sensation, "I've won on the PGA Tour, but this may feel even better because of the way I've played the past couple of years."

Not all of golf's good breaks come on the golf course. Some come from the sky. John Elliott was trying to sleep on the third-round lead of the Alabama Classic. Sleep was hard to come by, and would become even more difficult. "I woke at 3 this morning, looked at the Weather Channel, and saw this big blob coming at us," Elliott said. That meant a storm cell headed their way. "And after that I couldn't go back to sleep thinking about winning," he said. Would the storm get there in time? Yes — and it washed out the final round and left Elliott the winner.

Speaking of weather, the Puget Sound Open, won by Kevin Johnson, was a 52-hole tournament. The first round was shortened to 17 holes when No. 1 became unplayable because of rain. And then one round was cancelled when the first two took three days to complete. At that, Johnson tied with Steve Jurgensen and defending champion Michael Clark, and went two extra holes to win. "I wanted to make it an official 54-hole event," Johnson cracked.

Gleaton, 28, won both the St. Louis Classic and the Tri-Cities Open, but he won his first with a flourish. He shot a final-round 64 for a 261 total at St. Louis, tying the Nike Tour record of 23 under par, and won by three. Even so, he was upstaged. Everyone was watching Clark Dennis, 31, a veteran out of Houston, who was busy trying to shoot 59 in the final round. "I started thinking 59 when I hit it two feet at the 17th," Dennis said. Finally, he needed a 20-footer at the 18th for the 59. "There wasn't any way you can be more nervous than I was standing over that putt," Dennis said. He missed. But he two-putted for a 60, tied the Nike 18-hole record, and finished third.

Steve Flesch, 30, who took six fruitless cracks at the qualifying tournament, this time needed only a top-15 finish in the season-ending Nike Tour Championship in October to get his 1998 PGA Tour card. He did better than that. He became the first player in Nike history to get to 10 under, at 278, and won by three. "I've never even seen a Tour card," Flesch said. Now he could look at one any time he wanted to, and so could the entire Nike graduating class (top 15, up from top 10), in order of finish: Smith, Carnevale, Chris DiMarco, Flesch, Barry Cheesman, J.L. Lewis, Brian Kamm, Eaks, Glen Hnatiuk, Joe Daley, Ben Bates, Harrison Frazar, Mike Small and Bobby Wadkins.

Canadian Tour

When it comes to dramatic flourishes, Mike Weir was his own cavalry, riding to his own rescue. The Canadian Tour thus gained a star and lost one at the same time, with the rise of Weir in 1997, to be followed by his departure for the U.S. PGA Tour in 1998. Weir, 27, of Bright's Grove, Ontario, ruled the 10-event Canadian Tour in 1997. He won twice — once by one stroke, once in a runaway — finished second in a playoff, became the first Canadian to lead the money list since 1989, with $80,696 in winnings, and with a scoring average of 69.29 also became the first Canadian since 1989 to win that award. "I have to admit that it was a goal of mine from the start of the year to win the Order of Merit," Weir said. He proceeded into the American tour qualifying tournament in December, and there won a berth the same way he had ruled the Canadian Tour — with a heroic finish.

First, Weir prevailed in the BC Tel Pacific Open at Mayfair Lakes in Richmond, British Columbia, early in June, the second event of the year. Weir, who trailed by three strokes through the final turn, was tied with American Ken Duke and Australian Ken Druce coming to the last hole, a par-five. He hit a 322-yard drive, then put a seven iron to 25 feet, and two-putted for a birdie and 69. When Duke missed a 15-footer for his birdie and parred for 71, and Druce fell short with 68, Weir had his first win of the year, and his first since his rookie year of 1993.

In the Canadian Masters late in July, Weir began enjoying himself with five holes to play. Talk about cautious optimism. He checked the leaderboard after making a birdie on the 13th, and saw that he had an eight-shot lead. "It was a lot of fun from then on," he said. It was a notable card: 64-67-66-69–266, a tournament-record 18 under par at Heron Point.

It was American Guy Hill to the rescue this time — his own rescue, denying Weir a third win, this at the Canadian PGA Championship in August. They were coming down the stretch, Hill playing two groups ahead of Weir. "I knew Mike was going to get to eight under," Hill said, and so he knew he needed an eagle three at the 18th. He got it, holing a 10-foot putt. When Weir then missed his eagle putt from 20 feet, they were tied. Hill won on the first playoff hole, tapping in for a par after Weir put his second into a hazard, next to a drainage pipe.

That was the third and final playoff of the season, and by far not the most complicated. That distinction had been left to the Telus Edmonton Open at Windermere. It ended in a four-way tie, with Manny Zerman, a Tucson-based South African, Canadian Todd Fanning and Americans Chris Tidland and Mike Grob all at 10-under-par 274. Zerman untied it by holing a 30-foot bunker shot on the second extra hole. "That's not the way I wanted to play that hole," Zerman said, "but you take what you can get." In the other playoff, American Ray Freeman dropped a 25-foot birdie putt on the fourth extra hole at Wolf Creek to beat Canadian Stuart Hendley in the Henry Singer Alberta Open, shortened to three rounds because of heavy rains.

The season opened with the Payless Open at Gorge Vale, Victoria, in June, and with Canadian Philip Jonas losing as much as fellow Canadian Rick Todd winning it. Jonas birdied five of his first seven holes to barge into the lead in the final round, but he called a penalty on himself at the 13th when his ball moved as he was addressing it. When he missed the green at the 18th and bogeyed for 67, he lost by one shot to Todd, who also finished with 67. "That last hole was the killer, not the penalty," Jonas said. Said Todd, "If Phil didn't get penalized, we would be in a playoff, and who knows what would have happened." In the Telus Calgary Open, South Africa's Ian Hutchings started getting comfortable with a four-shot lead through the 11th in the final round. "I backed off a bit," he admitted, "and you can't do that." He closed with 67 and a two-stroke victory over Americans Scott Petersen (63) and Jean-Paul Hebert (66).

Things were considerably less complicated for American Mark Wurtz in the Xerox Manitoba Open at Elmhurst, Winnipeg. He led wire-to-wire, and it took a pair of bogeys on the final nine to cut his margin to two. The following week, Petersen, who fell short despite a closing 63 at Calgary, this time saw a brilliant rally rewarded in the Infiniti Championship at Diamondback, at Richmond Hill, Ontario. He started the last round four shots off the lead, was tied with South Africa's Marco Gortana through the 17th, and wrapped up a two-stroke victory with a 12-foot birdie putt at the 18th. American Mike Grob moved up to second and Gortana faded to fifth place.

Finally, it was Grob's turn. Grob, 33, from Billings, Montana, had yet to win since joining the tour in 1988. He had gotten close this season — co-playoff runner-up in the Edmonton, runner-up at the Infiniti, fourth at Calgary and Manitoba. And now the winner in the season finale, the Montclair PEI Classic at Mill River, Woodstock. Grob took the lead in the second round and stayed there to win by two strokes over American Perry Parker. "You just never know when it's finally going to happen," Grob said.

The same could be said, finally, for Weir. After performing heroics for his two victories and a playoff runner-up, he headed for the American qualifying event. In the sixth and final round, he was all but out of the running. Then he holed a 40-foot birdie putt at the 14th, nearly holed out at the 16th, and closed with two pars for a seven-under-par 422 total to win his player's card with a tie for 26th place. He ended the season the way he started it — with a rescue.

South American Tour

The eight-event, $1.24 million South American Tour came to a bizarre conclusion in the circuit's biggest event, the Argentina Open, when American Jim Furyk was handed the title after two Argentine challengers were disqualified. Furyk had birdied the last hole for 70 and a 275 total and, he thought, a playoff with Eduardo Romero, who had just finished with 69. Unknown to Furyk, Romero and Vicente Fernandez, who shot 276, had just been disqualified because they had forgotten to swap scorecards at the beginning of the round, and had incorrectly scored both.

"These things happen," said Furyk, whose victory in the 92nd Argentine championship was worth $70,000 and also was his second title of the year, the other being the unofficial Family House Invitational. "I was prepared for the playoff and who knows how it would have come out. I have every sympathy for these two truly great players. Beyond that, it's a tremendous honor to win an Open with such history."

Second place, three strokes behind Furyk, was shared by Mathias Gronberg of Sweden and two Americans, Chris DiMarco and Tim Hegna.

The October-to-December tour through Brazil, Ecuador, Peru, Chile and Argentina also featured the victory by Germany's Bernhard Langer, his fifth of the year after four on the PGA European Tour, in the Argentina Masters over Romero and American Payne Stewart. In the other tournaments, Argentines Ricardo Gonzalez and Gustavo Rojas won twice each and Armando Saavedra, once, along with Canadian Philip Jonas, once.

12. European Tours

It would be almost impossible to sum up the European season in 1997 in just a few words. It defies one description, but instead encapsulated all possible emotions.

Joyfully, there was the return to the game of Jose Maria Olazabal. The Spaniard's foot injuries had kept him sidelined at his home in Fuenterrabia in the Basque country since September, 1995. The first steps back came in the Dubai Desert Classic and they were hardly faltering ones: He finished 12th. Two tournaments later, at the Turespana Masters in the Canaries, Olazabal did something he wondered whether he would ever do again. He won.

There were tears in Olazabal's eyes on the 18th green and later in the aftermath of Europe's Ryder Cup victory at Valderrama. "I didn't think I would walk again," he said before breaking down when trying to explain the moment.

The win at Valderrama gave the PGA European Tour's administrators renewed heart. The events of the week were a triumph for the man for whom the Ryder Cup was taken to Spain in the first place. Much of the year had been a trial for Seve Ballesteros as he struggled with his own game, to the extent that he admitted losing desire. But his passion brought a "hands on" approach to his captaincy that had so much to do with Europe winning the Ryder Cup again. He was even feeling better about his own game by the end of the year.

For perseverance, Bernhard Langer deserved all the accolades he received. After conquering the yips for the fourth time in his career by turning to the long putter, the German was wielding his broomhandle to such good effect that he won four times.

At the other end of the career-scale, new talent continued to emerge and impress. Darren Clarke was a runner-up in the British Open and the Volvo PGA Championship and made his Ryder Cup debut alongside Thomas Bjorn, Denmark's first representative, Ignacio Garrido and Lee Westwood. At only 24, Westwood won the Volvo Masters and was one of only 16 players — and three Europeans, the others being Colin Montgomerie and Jesper Parnevik — to make the cut in all four major championships.

Not everything went according to plan. Some courses fell below an acceptable standard either in terms of condition or in the way they were set up for tournament play. Off the course, there were arguments about the number of wild cards that should awarded for the Ryder Cup team, and then the manner of the exclusion of the injured Miguel Angel Martin after the Spaniard had qualified on merit.

But in terms of news-making, one man stood head and shoulders above everyone and everything else. Montgomerie played some exquisite golf during the year. His record makes for impressive reading. He led the European money list for the fifth consecutive time, surpassing Peter Oosterhuis' feat of winning the money title four times in a row in the early 1970s.

Montgomerie, who ensured that Europe came away with a win rather than a tie at Valderrama, won twice, at the Compaq European Grand Prix with a closing round of 65, and at the Murphy's Irish Open, where he shot a course-record 62 on the final day to come from three behind Westwood to win by seven. He earned £798,947 on the money list, clinching his position ahead of Langer in the final event, and was 177 under par with a stroke average of 69.37, both personal bests.

"To stay No. 1 in any business, whether it is golf or anything else, is difficult because the competition is increasing all the time," Montgomerie said. "I feel I have improved every year in all aspects of my game, and knowing I've achieved that is very satisfying. If I had stood still, I would have been overtaken."

Having narrowly missed out on another major championship when he lost by one stroke to Ernie Els in the U.S. Open, Montgomerie was expected to take his U.S. PGA Tour card. Instead, he decided to continue playing a worldwide schedule from his base on the PGA European Tour.

"We have undeniable talent in Europe," he said. "It is inconceivable that I should choose to leave at this crucial stage. I only won twice in Europe this year and there is a big challenge to win here. We have some very, very good young players. Three years ago when Nick Faldo left, we were looking for good young players and there weren't any. Now there are Westwood, Clarke, Bjorn, Garrido and Harrington. I'm sure the European Tour will go from strength to strength."

PGA European Tour

Dubai Desert Classic—£700,000
Winner: Richard Green

Take two superstars and an underdog, remember this is golf, and bet on the unknown. Richard Green of Australia proved himself no respecter of reputations when he defeated Greg Norman and Ian Woosnam, on his 39th birthday, in a playoff at the Dubai Desert Classic.

Woosnam, the third-round leader, should have clinched a regulation victory when he led by two strokes playing the par-five 18th hole. Having laid up in front of the water, Woosnam dunked his sand wedge from 73 yards into the drink. He then got down in two for a bogey six which, after a 69, dropped him back into a tie at 16 under par with Green and Norman.

Norman, playing his first tournament of the year, had improved every round to close with 66, including a birdie at the 18th. Green, playing with Woosnam, also birdied the last in his 68 by holing from 20 feet. In the playoff at the 17th, both Norman and Woosnam, who had holed out for an eagle two in the third round, found the back fringe.

Only Green was able to get enough spin on his approach to stop his ball within 12 feet, a birdie putt he promptly rolled in to become the first left-hander to win on the PGA European Tour since Bob Charles in the 1974 Swiss Open. Age 26, he only had previous wins at home twice at the New Caledonian Open.

"Greg has been a huge idol of mine since I was young," Green said. "I admire him so much for what he has done and I had not met him properly until we met in the scorer's hut. I was nervous then and my heart was pumping against my chest in the playoff. To win against guys like Greg and Ian is an unbelievable feeling."

The tournament saw the return to the Tour of Jose Maria Olazabal, who had not played since the Lancome Trophy in September, 1995, due to foot injuries that were originally diagnosed as rheumatoid arthritis. A doctor in German refuted that and, with exercise and physiotherapy, Olazabal was able to return to playing golf after times in which he had only been able to crawl in the mornings. Although not quite in contention, it was a remarkable comeback for the Spaniard as he finished tied for 12th place following a third-round 65.

Moroccan Open—£350,000
Winner: Clinton Whitelaw

For a man who has not enjoyed playing golf, Clinton Whitelaw made a fair impression of someone who cannot get enough of the game. While three players had got stuck on nine under par, Whitelaw, a 26-year-old South African, swept to his first PGA European Tour victory with a birdie-eagle-par finish in the Moroccan Open. He became the sixth non-European winner in seven tournaments, including the co-sponsored events in South Africa and Australasia.

That title earlier appeared to be going to Australian Darren Cole, who caught everyone by surprise by posting 64, the best score of the week, when the leaders were barely underway.

Roger Chapman, who was destined to chalk up his sixth runner-up finish on the PGA European Tour without a win, bogeyed the 18th for 67 to join Cole at 279, and another Australian, Wayne Riley, matched the mark after his 68.

Whitelaw sped to the victory by holing from 25 feet at the 16th, and then, after a huge drive at the next, his five-iron shot finished 10 feet away, which he holed for the eagle. His 69 took him to 277, 11 under par.

Whitelaw had won the 1993 South African Open before becoming disillusioned with the game. "I hated going to the practice range to hit shots," he said, "so my dad advised me to try a change of scene. I took myself off to the Canadian Tour for three months. The experience gave me a new enthusiasm and I went home and won my first two tournaments."

David A. Russell, an Englishman who is based in Los Angeles, showed he has recovered from two years of treatment for lymphatic cancer despite a 51-hour journey after he got a last-minute call-up for the tournament. He led after the second and third rounds, and despite going to the turn in 40 on Sunday, he responded with an eagle and four birdies coming home, and only two more dropped shots dropped him to fifth place.

Portuguese Open—£350,000
Winner: Michael Jonzon

Informed that a British bookmaker had made him the 14-1 favorite to win the Portuguese Open, Jose Maria Olazabal described the odds as "a little bit insane." It was, after all, only the second tournament of his comeback after 18 months out, but the faith placed in him looked justified when the Spaniard shot a third-round 65. Following previous rounds of 70 and 67, that put Olazabal only two strokes behind the 54-hole leader, Sweden's Michael Jonzon. Olazabal even birdied two of the first four holes in his final round, but thereafter Jonzon took control. The 24-year-old, who rated himself a two-handicap downhill and cross-country skier, went to the turn at Aroeira in 32.

His five-shot advantage over Olazabal could have been severely cut when he lost a ball in the trees off the 10th tee, but the Swede holed a 20-foot putt to limit the damage to a bogey six. Jonzon, with rounds of 67, 65, 68 and 69 for a 19-under-par total of 269, went on to win by three shots over another Spaniard, Ignacio Garrido, who closed with a charging 65.

England's Paul Broadhurst was third, and Olazabal, who came home in 39 for 74, tied for fourth, seven strokes back, with Darren Clarke, Wayne Riley and Stephen Allan. "I never felt comfortable over the ball all week, but my short game saved me the first three days," Olazabal said. This was being a bit hard on himself, but then he always was, but it was true that he took 18 putts over the back nine on Sunday. "I can feel my feet, of course, but I am making no excuses."

"I knew most people wanted him to win," Jonzon admitted. "Jose Maria is a hero of mine. I love his attitude and the way he goes right for the flag. But I was focused on my own game. I felt surprisingly calm and relaxed and got off to a great start."

Turespana Masters - Open de Canarias—£350,000
Winner: Jose Maria Olazabal

The moment was only delayed by seven days, but when it came, it was accompanied by tears of joy. Jose Maria Olazabal had not won a tournament since the 1994 World Series of Golf. Amazingly, the Turespana Masters - Open de Canarias was only his third tournament after being forced out of the game for a year and a half. At times, he thought he might not be able to play again. At times, he could hardly walk. What was originally diagnosed as rheumatoid arthritis by three specialists in Spain and America, was later treated as a hernia by a Munich doctor, Hans-Wilhelm Muller-Wohlfahrt, whose clients include Boris Becker and Steffi Graf. A course of exercise and physiotherapy, including many a paddle in the sea on the Basque coastline, enabled Olazabal to regain his life as well as his golf.

But not even the 31-year-old Spaniard could believe the quality of golf, after only four weeks of serious practice, he produced in his comeback. At Maspalomas, Olazabal shot rounds of 70, 67, 68 and 67 for a 20-under score of 272 and a two-shot victory over England's Lee Westwood.

"It was a very special moment for me on the 18th green," said an emotional Olazabal. "The memories came flooding back of all the hard times I have been through. There were times in the darkest days between April and September last year when I feared I might never play again. I even thought that I would end my days in a wheelchair.

"Nothing was going right for me. The treatment was not working and there seemed no light at the end of the tunnel. But as soon as I went to see the doctor in Munich things started to improve. I didn't know how it would be when I came back in Dubai after 18 months away from the game. But now I've finished 12th there and fourth in Portugal and my physical condition has gotten no worse."

His driving was not quite as he would want it, but the old genius was there as he went to the turn in 32 on the final day to move into a comfortable lead. Westwood, who had led by five strokes with four holes to play in the third round, rallied with three birdies in the last eight holes to beat Paul Broadhurst and Argentina's Eduardo Romero for second place. "I can't be disgruntled with second place to Ollie," Westwood said. "It's wonderful to have him back."

Madeira Island Open—£300,000
Winner: Peter Mitchell

Peter Mitchell is accustomed to shooting low scores. The problem has been developing that happy knack into a winning habit. In 1992, Mitchell won the Austrian Open with two rounds of 62. Five years later, the 38-year-old Londoner added his second Tour win with a one-shot victory in the Madeira Island Open.

Mitchell raced to a four-stroke lead with a second-round 63, and a final-round 71 meant he held off the stunning charge of young Swede Fredrik Jacobsen, whose 64 almost caught Mitchell's 12-under-par 204 total.

Low clouds and then high winds had meant less than two hours' play on the opening day and the tournament had to be cut to 54 holes. "It was difficult defending a four-stroke lead. I got a bit protective," admitted Mitchell, who enjoyed his best year in 1996, his 12th season as a card holder, as he finished 12th on the money list.

Mitchell completed the victory with a birdie at the 18th achieved by hitting his wedge approach shot to within tap-in range. "The last few holes were terrifying," he said. "I thought I was leading outright coming to the 18th. If I had known that Jacobsen was at 11-under with me, I would probably have duffed my second completely. Hopefully, it will be a little easier next time."

Jacobsen, a former ice hockey ace in his country, climbed the leaderboard to overtake Andrew Coltart, who missed birdie chances on the last two holes, by one and Andrew Sherborne by two.

Europe 1 Cannes Open—£300,000
Winner: Stuart Cage

David Carter did not win the Europe 1 Cannes Open, but the fact that he was merely teeing up at Royal Mougins was remarkable in itself. Carter had collapsed before the Dubai Desert Classic at the end of February and, after being found unconscious in his hotel room, underwent emergency surgery to remove fluid from his brain.

Carter, 24, who was born in South Africa of British parents, spent three weeks in a Dubai hospital, but soon after returning home was again playing golf with his father Bryan, a club pro and player on the European Seniors Tour. Seven weeks after the operation, Carter played on the Tour again, the only after-effects being short-term memory loss which made practicing or taking a golf lesson pointless.

For the opening rounds, Carter played with Raymond Russell, who had beaten him the year before, and he was immediately on the leaderboard with 68 on the first day. By the final round, Carter matched his course-record 62 of 1996, although preferred lies were in effect, and Carter finished tied for second with Paul Broadhurst, five shots behind Stuart Cage.

Jamie Spence fired a last-round 61 to tie for fourth, with Paul Eales, Cage's last round playing companion and nearest challenger until he fell away at the end. Cage, a 23-year-old from Yorkshire and a member of the 1993 Great Britain and Ireland Walker Cup team, never gave a hint of losing his lead and came home in 32 for a closing 66. His first Tour title, in his third year on the circuit, arrived with a 14-under score of 270. The run started with a nine iron to two feet at the 10th and then a sand iron to 18 inches at the 12th.

"After what I've been through this year, it's a dream come true," said Cage, who had suffered for weeks with a vicious stomach bug he picked up in South Africa. "When you come out, you think the top guys are unbeatable. Now I know they are not."

Peugeot Open de Espana—£550,000
Winner: Mark James

It took until the third extra hole of the playoff in the Peugeot Open de Espana for a couple of forty-somethings to settle their argument. Mark James had not won for two years. Greg Norman had just missed the cut in the Masters and had lost his place at the top of the World Ranking.

For one week, at least, golf was not about the youngsters. James, 43, and Norman, 42, tied at 277, 11 under par, to prolong their battle. In regulation play, Norman had bogeyed the 17th, then seen the Englishman three-putt the final green before the Great White Shark holed his 24-foot birdie putt to force the playoff.

Twice the 18th hole was halved, which meant returning to the par-three 17th. Neither man threatened the flag, but while Norman missed the green, found a horrible lie and left his chip 10 feet short, James was on the putting surface and two-putted from 40 feet for his 18th win in a PGA European Tour career that dates back to 1976.

James coped with the grainy La Moraleja greens, having reverted to a conventional putter from a long putter a couple of months previously. "I have never putted better for four rounds," James said. "The greens got fast, like Augusta, and for me to putt well on them was miraculous. This win means a tremendous amount because it gives me more confidence in my ability to carry on playing, which I was beginning to doubt last year."

In 1996, James slumped to 116th on the European money list, where his previous worst had been 32nd. "I keep myself pretty fit and I don't feel my nerve has gone, but you can get lost mentally and technically," he said. "The older you get, the less inclination there is to get it back. Last year I thought poorly, swung poorly, had bad luck, and didn't chip and putt well." As for Norman, his second playoff defeat in Europe this season nevertheless sent him back to the top of the World Ranking.

Conte of Florence Italian Open—£500,000
Winner: Bernhard Langer

With Jose Maria Olazabal leading by one stroke with a round to go, the Conte of Florence Italian Open looked to be a continuation of the Spaniard's brilliant return to form after his season away. The events of the final day at Gardagolf, in the foothills of the Alps and above the glories of Lake Garda, did just that, because Olazabal did not do anything wrong, but he did not earn his second win of the year.

Instead, Bernhard Langer shot a final-round 64, a course record, to post another brilliant victory in his 48-win career. In 1996, Langer failed to win on the PGA European Tour for the first time in 17 years. Having turned to the long putter to cure a fourth plague of the yips, the German did win in Asia in November, but his win in Italy came 17 months after his last in Europe.

The resilience of the man who would turn 40 later in the year was confirmed as he showed there was not too much wrong with his putting. The last five greens saw just one swish of his putter each, four of those putts producing birdies and the other making a vital par-saver at the short 17th.

When Langer holed from 15 feet at the 18th for a 15-under-par total of 273, he went into the lead for the very first time. His battle with Olazabal had been a classic, and made all the more special by the fact that it would have been inconceivable a year before.

Before his flying finish, Langer had caught the Spaniard three times, but each time Olazabal had responded with a birdie to restore his advantage. Still, his closing 68 left him one shot behind. "I did not lose the tournament," Olazabal said. "I made four birdies and was never over par. Bernhard's 64 was an unbelievable score and all credit to him. I'm not disappointed."

Langer, who switched from a metal driver back to his usual persimmon driver for the last two rounds, said, "The way Jose Maria was playing, I knew he was the man to beat and I was really aggressive. I felt I needed 66 or 65 to win, but I underestimated."

Darren Clarke finished three shots behind Olazabal, with Philip Walton and Steve Webster one further back, and local hero Costantino Rocca, after a last-round 66, among those tied in sixth place.

Benson and Hedges International Open—£700,000
Winner: Bernhard Langer

Before he left Florida to return to Europe for the first time in seven months, Bernhard Langer had turned to his wife, Vikki, and offered the thought that he was playing well enough to win one of his first three tournaments. Langer was doubly right, as he followed his victory in Italy by also claiming the Benson and Hedges International Open.

While he had played in the Florida-like sunshine the week before, at The Oxfordshire conditions were very different. The wind howled, the rain bucketed down, it was freezing cold — Tuesday's practice round had been interrupted by snow — and, on Sunday, the threat of thunder and lightning delayed the finish until darkness was falling, but none of this worried the tenacious German.

While some had suggested that golf in Britain should be confined to July and August, Langer, who confirmed a ninth Ryder Cup appearance with his back-to-back wins, got on with business. "If you think positively and keep your mind on what's right, it gives you a better attitude," he said. "If you moan and groan and are disgusted, you play miserably, too."

No one is better prepared to play in these types of conditions than Langer, who also won this tournament in waterproofs and a wool hat at St. Mellion in 1991. "My course strategy comes out better in bad conditions, and also how I manage myself. I don't go out there screaming at the weather. What's that good for anyway? I accept what happens if it blows or not."

Apart from a dropped shot at the second, Langer was almost perfect through a final round of 69, the only score under 70 that day. His 12-under-par total of 276 gave him a two-shot win over Ian Woosnam, with Lee Westwood four behind. Woosnam finished with five birdies in the last eight holes, including the last two, but had resumed after one of the two stoppages on the final day by dumping his nine-iron approach to the 10th into the water for a double-bogey six.

Westwood, 24, was paired with Langer in the final group and had not dropped a shot — a feat no one else had achieved — until he came to the 17th. Going for the green in two with his driver from 224 yards, Westwood, two behind Langer, found the water. "I had a great drive and that gave me a chance to go for it, but I caught it a bit thick," he said. "That was my chance gone."

Langer, though, was impressed. "He was thinking of winning and he probably would not have done that by laying up. He needed an eagle or a birdie. I would probably have done the same if I was in that position."

Alamo English Open—£650,000
Winner: Per-Ulrik Johansson

Per-Ulrik Johansson was on a run with destiny in the Alamo English Open. His previous finishes in the event had been sixth, fourth, second — and now first. It was Johansson's experience which counted when most on the leaderboard were seeking a way to claim their first-ever victory. This was his fourth win since he came onto the Tour in 1991, and his second in the current Ryder

Cup qualifying period after his European Open win in September 1996.

Johansson, a 30-year-old Swede, lives for most of the year in Marbella and was planning to be at Valderrama anyway, but his victory in the Alamo English Open suggested it would be as a player and not a spectator.

Johansson did not putt as he would have liked for the first two rounds at Hanbury Manor, the Jack Nicklaus II-designed layout, but he got full reward over the weekend. He shot 64 on Saturday and closed with 67 which gave him a 19-under-par 269 total and a two-shot win over his countryman Dennis Edlund.

Edlund became the surprise leader when he birdied the second, third and fourth, the last with a four iron to four feet. But Johansson took over when he first chipped in at the 10th from an awkward lie just above a bunker, and then eagled the 12th from 12 feet. "I hit a perfect five iron and it was nice to hole the putt," he said. "That was the big turnaround. I was very pleased for Dennis. He's a good player and he belongs out here. He was disappointed but he did give me a little smile."

Edlund almost gave up the game after he failed at the qualifying tournament for the seventh time in eight attempts at the end of the 1995 season. "My sponsors persuaded me to continue for another year and I'm glad I went to the Challenge Tour and got my card that way," said the 31-year-old.

He was not the only one after a first title. Steve Webster, winner of the qualifying tournament in 1995, capitalized on his fine form with a closing 68 to tie for third with American Jay Townsend, who set the course record of 63 in the second round. David Howell set his best-ever score for 72 holes of 15 under to finish fifth alongside Roger Chapman. The 38-year-old Kenyan-born Chapman had become a tour millionaire without winning in 16 years, but led at the halfway mark after two rounds of 66.

Volvo PGA Championship—£1,100,000
Winner: Ian Woosnam

The setting was perfect, Wentworth's West Course playing longer, narrower and greener than Nick Faldo could remember. The weather was fair, too, with the glorious sunshine drying out the greens and making them even trickier. And a record crowd of over 20,000 was in place on the Bank Holiday Monday.

What was that about not playing golf in England in May? The leaderboard carried some of the biggest names in European golf. What more fitting way for the richest ever event on the PGA European Tour to climax than in a victory for Ian Woosnam. It was one of the best wins of the Welshman's career and not for his usual aggressive style, but for being patient while all around were unable to mount a sustained challenge.

Woosnam won the PGA title for the second time with a last-round 70 for 275 total, 13 under par. Darren Clarke, his nearest challenger overnight, shot a 71. Neither Nick Faldo nor Ernie Els could break 70. The trio shared second place, two behind Woosnam, and only Colin Montgomerie got a score going. His last-round 64 was one off Wayne Riley's course record and 12 strokes better than his third round and it brought him up to fifth place.

"I wouldn't say it was one of my spectacular rounds, but I hung on," said

Woosnam, who had twice been second this year. "It gives your confidence a boost to win against one of our stronger fields and it is nice to still be winning tournaments coming up to 40."

The victory, the 32nd of his career, took Woosnam to the top of the European money list and the Ryder Cup qualifying points list, confirming his place in the European team with Colin Montgomerie, Bernhard Langer and Clarke.

"The Ryder Cup is taken care of now. I'd love to win the order of merit now," said the Welshman. "It was difficult today with the wind into you one moment and against you the next, and the greens were getting bouncy. Wentworth does fetch the best out of the best players. You need experience here."

Woosnam was caught by Clarke when the 28-year-old birdied the par-five fourth and the Irishman went into the lead when he added another at the eighth. Woosnam's patience must have been wearing thin until he finally picked up his first birdie of the day by holing from 12 feet at the 12th. A bogey from Clarke at the next followed by a five iron to 20 feet at the 14th for a birdie by Woosnam took him into the lead by two.

Faldo, thwarted again in his attempt to win a fifth PGA title, was playing with Els on the final day, but neither could quite spark each other off. The South African almost chipped in at the last, but that would not quite have been enough.

Deutsche Bank Open–TPC of Europe—£750,000
Winner: Ross McFarlane

Ross McFarlane winced at being called a "journeyman." He winced again on being described as a "veteran." Finally he had to admit that "veteran journeyman" just about summed him up. Finally, after 14 years on the Tour, McFarlane found it was a journey well travelled as he collected his first win in the Deutsche Bank Open–TPC of Europe. As the title doubles as the European Tournament Players' Championship, McFarlane earned a five-year exemption, as well as the first prize of £125,000, a sum bigger than any of his yearly earnings before 1996.

The son of a former Manchester United soccer player, age 36, McFarlane had to go back to the qualifying tournament in 1993, before rising to 43rd on the money list in 1996, his best-ever finish. The season included his best previous finish, tied for second at the English Open. "It's unbelievable," McFarlane said. "I'm just glad I stuck with the game."

He had been thinking about a job in television when severe tendinitis in his left arm and shoulder almost forced him to quit in the early 1990s. "The pain was right up from my wrist to my neck. I could see my career coming to a swift end. I had talks with a television company about doing a bit of commentary work, which is something I have always fancied doing."

Switching to graphite shafts reduced the shock effects on his arm and allowed McFarlane to start practicing again. Of more immediate benefit, McFarlane had spent the previous week working with Bill Ferguson, the man initially behind Colin Montgomerie and later Ian Woosnam. "I had been trying to book lessons with Bill for about a year," McFarlane said. "It's paid handsome dividends."

McFarlane shot rounds of 70, 73, 68 and 71 for a six-under-par total of 282 to beat former Ryder Cup player Gordon Brand, Jr. and Swede Anders Forsbrand by one stroke. Darren Clarke was two back.

McFarlane looked to be out of the tournament when he dropped three strokes behind after driving into a ditch at the 10th. He had to take a penalty and the hole cost him a double bogey. At the next, he drew a four iron into 10 feet for the first of three birdies in a row. "Dropping those two strokes at the 10th gave me a kick up the backside," he said. "I told myself that I was a good enough golfer to win and just to concentrate extra hard. In the high wind, I knew it would be very difficult for anybody to catch me. The conditions were difficult, but that seems to bring out the best in me."

Compaq European Grand Prix—£650,000
Winner: Colin Montgomerie

If it is June, Colin Montgomerie is probably playing good golf. It is the month that for him contains the most important date of the year, the U.S. Open, and Monty made sure he left for America in the best form possible by winning the Compaq European Grand Prix at Slaley Hall.

After rounds of 69, 68, 68, Montgomerie closed with a 65 for an 18-under-par 270 score and to win by five strokes over defending champion Retief Goosen, with Lee Westwood one stroke further back. Goosen shot 69 and Westwood 70, but both were eclipsed by the form of Montgomerie as the four-time European No. 1 money winner claimed his first European win of the year.

Montgomerie played the last nine in 30 on the final day, birdieing four of the last five holes from 25, 35, 20 and 12 feet. Westwood had briefly caught Montgomerie with a birdie at the fourth, but he hooked his shot into the woods at the seventh and the Scot was in front to stay.

"I filed a late entry because I thought I could win," said Montgomerie, who had withdrawn from the previous week's tournament. "I desperately wanted the competition and the feeling of being in contention before going to the States. No one will be going to the U.S. Open with more confidence than me. I cannot wait for Thursday."

Montgomerie dropped only two strokes to par during the week. One was due to a misclubbing and the other came in near darkness after a two-hour storm delay on Saturday evening. "Slaley Hall was ideal preparation for Congressional with narrow fairways and pretty penal rough," he said. "I gave myself a talking to on Saturday night about the need to get the putts up to the hole. But putting and golf are about confidence and I feel very confident about the way I'm doing my job right now."

Volvo German Open—£700,000
Winner: Ignacio Garrido

At the Ryder Collingtree Seniors Classic, Antonio Garrido shot a final-round 68 to finish tied for second behind Neil Coles and then rushed to a television. There he saw his son, Ignacio, go one better by winning the Volvo

German Open, his first PGA European Tour success. "This is wonderful," said the elder Garrido, who won five times in Europe, including the 1972 Spanish Open, after turning professional in 1961. "I am so proud. Ignacio hung on very well and he will be an even better player now."

The young Garrido's victory put him in contention for a place in the European Ryder Cup team for the match at Valderrama. Antonio Garrido, with Seve Ballesteros, became the first continentals to compete for Europe in the match in 1979. The family would have a further place in history should Ignacio, whose aim had been to contend for a Ryder Cup place in 1999, make the team. Percy and Peter Alliss were the only previous father and son to feature in the matches.

The 25-year-old Garrido played brilliantly over the Schloss Nippenburg course near Stuttgart for the first three rounds with scores of 65, 67, 67. The Spaniard led by five and could afford a one over 72 on the final day to still record a four-stroke win with a 13-under-par total of 271. Russell Claydon added to his lengthy list of second places by closing with a 66 to push Mark James into third, while Bernhard Langer was among those tied for fourth.

"I am pleased with the way I handled the pressure to increase my lead to five on Saturday and then stay in front on the final day," said Garrido, a fluent English speaker after his father sent him to stay with an English family for a month each summer for seven years. "It was all new to me and I didn't know how I would react. When you haven't been there before, you don't know what to expect."

Peugeot Open de France—£600,000
Winner: Retief Goosen

With four holes to play, Retief Goosen led the Peugeot Open de France by one stroke. Yet, at the 18th, the 28-year-old South African was able to afford a double-bogey seven and still win by three.

His fortune was the result of misfortune for Martin Gates, an Englishman who started the tournament in 177th place on the money list. Gates had produced a superb run of birdies with five in seven holes from the fifth and another at the 14th. But then he bogeyed the 15th, found water at the par-three 16th for a double bogey, and in all lost five shots in the last four holes.

"It was a pity Martin let it slip so badly because he played great all day," said Goosen. "He had put in a fantastic challenge and I thought it was going to go to the wire. But suddenly, after the 16th, the pressure was off and I was coasting after that."

Goosen's seven at the 18th came when he decided to lay up at the par-five and then put his pitch from 66 yards into the water. If that was his most inaccurate shot of the week, his most accurate came at his very first hole, the 10th in the first round, when he holed out from 126 yards with a wedge. "It's the first time I've won a tournament starting with an eagle two and finishing with a double bogey," Goosen added after his second European win.

Gates said, "I feel gutted. I hit only one bad shot, at the 15th, and it knocked me for six. I was challenging so strongly, but I never recovered my momentum." Gates shot a final-round 71 to tie with Raymond Russell, Darren

Clarke and Van Phillips for third place, one behind Jamie Spence who slipped into second with 68. Goosen's scores were 64, 67, 70 and 70 for a 17-under-par total of 271.

Murphy's Irish Open—£681,818
Winner: Colin Montgomerie

So good was Colin Montgomerie's performance in the final round of the Murphy's Irish Open, Lee Westwood would have to have shot 65, the mark he set as the course record in the first round and two shots better than all but one competitor scored on the last day, just to get into a playoff.

Given that Westwood started the day with a three-stroke advantage, it is still hard to believe Montgomerie won by seven strokes as he retained his title. Michael Jonzon had lowered the course record to 64 on Friday, but on Sunday Montgomerie sliced two further shots off that to impose a 10-stroke reversal on the young Englishman who Montgomerie called the "best player under 30 in Europe" and who learned again, as at the European Grand Prix, that it was no disgrace to finish second to the Scot.

Montgomerie's nine-under-par effort gave him a 15-under score of 269. Westwood shot a 72, and was left holding off Nick Faldo for second place. Faldo, with 68, finished two shots further back, with Ian Woosnam and Jonzon two more, and Jose Maria Olazabal another stroke behind.

Montgomerie capped his stunning show by rolling in a 40-footer at the 17th for his eighth birdie of the day. "I didn't even look at the line, just stood up and hit it," Monty said. "That sort of thing happens when you are leading by six shots."

"I found out the tournament is returning here next year and that put me in a good mood before I went out," he said. "It is a nice feeling to defend a title. From the Portuguese Open (when he won by 11 shots) this is my best performance over four rounds in Europe. I have shot lower, but today's round has to be up there with the best I've ever played."

Montgomerie had banned talk of a five letter word beginning with "T" — Troon, his home club where the British Open would take place in two weeks' time. "Forget what is coming up," Monty said, "I want to savour this. To be three behind and to win by seven is good effort, especially with some good names on the leaderboard.

"I am very confident and everything is going well at an important time of the year. I've been playing very well since the Andersen Consulting in May. The ball is going the right distance and I'm putting well. I holed out very well in the last round of the U.S. Open, and that is the secret. You can't shoot in the low and mid 60s if you are not putting well and I hope it holds up. If I can be as relaxed as I was today, it is amazing how low you can score."

Gulfstream Loch Lomond World Invitational—£800,000
Winner: Tom Lehman

Even Tom Lehman, winning the week before he set out to defend his British Open title at Royal Troon, was impressed with his victory in the Gulfstream Loch Lomond World Invitational by five strokes over Ernie Els.

Lehman completed a final round of 67 (after scores of 65, 66 and 67) for a 19-under-par total of 265, while Els, the man who was runner-up to the American at Lytham a year ago but who reversed roles to win the U.S. Open the previous month, shot 66 to be 14 under par. Retief Goosen, after a course-record 62, was third, with Greg Norman and Pierre Fulke tying for fourth.

"Any time you win is special," Lehman said. "To win in Scotland is special and to win against this quality of field is special too. And to be 19 under on this golf course is very satisfying. To play this well for four straight days is not something you do very often. I only had two bogeys in 72 holes and I have not done that before."

He was briefly tied by Fulke, the Swede who was lying three shots behind overnight, but a run of three birdies in a row from the seventh put the American back in control. "When you are being chased by Ernie Els, Greg Norman, Steve Jones, the list goes on, there is always a little bit of anxiety," said Lehman. "The birdie at the 16th was the clincher. I knew Ernie was on a run and you never know what can happen over the last four holes. If you look at my victories, they have all been when I have been putting well and they have all been decisive.

"I'm not sure I can do any better, but going into a big tournament like the Open requires you to be going in with belief in your game. You need to approach it in a positive frame of mind and I know I am at the top of my game. It feels very similar to last year. A few people said to me after the U.S. Open that I was in a bit of a slump, but I said that but for a couple of putts at tournaments like the Mercedes Championship and the U.S. Open, then I would be having a great year."

Goosen, the recent Peugeot Open de France winner, looked like breaking the magical 60 barrier. He bogeyed the first hole, but from there collected seven birdies and an eagle in the next 11 holes. One more birdie at the 17th, from 20 feet his longest of the day, edged him a stroke inside of the mark set by Joakim Haeggman and equalled by Paul Curry on the first day.

British Open Championship—£1,600,000
Winner: Justin Leonard

See Chapter 5.

Sun Microsystems Dutch Open—£700,000
Winner: Sven Struver

Sven Struver won his first tournament on the PGA European Tour in 1996. At the end of the season he changed his clubs for a new set, but after missing

10 cuts in 13 events, the old faithfuls went back in the bag. Only a matter of weeks later and Struver won his second title, the Sun Microsystems Dutch Open at Hilversum.

This was the first time Struver had scored all four rounds in the 60s — 67, 64, 69 and 66 for a 266 total, 18 under par, which equalled the course record. "Golf is an amazing game," said the 29-year-old from Hamburg. "You go through a rough time like I've had and then suddenly you are on top of everything and walking off with the trophy.

"This win means so much to me after the way I have been playing in the last few months. But I played four excellent rounds of golf and I can't remember when I was so solid every day."

Struver's father is a professional, as is his uncle. But for an idol to follow, Struver had Bernhard Langer, who also won the Dutch title, which dates back to 1919, in 1984 and 1992. "I am very proud to follow Bernhard in winning this title," he said. "He helped me a lot when I first started out and he has stayed a good friend."

Struver went into the final round tied with Russell Claydon, but was helped to a three-stroke victory by two eagles on the last day. The first came with a three wood to eight feet at the fourth hole, the second from a 25-foot putt at the 12th. Claydon had briefly led early in the round but, in closing with 69, finished two strokes ahead of Roger Chapman and Angel Cabrera.

Chapman had six runner-up finishes and Claydon had now made it four, plus two as an amateur in professional events. "I can't complain," Claydon said. "Sven played much better than I did."

Volvo Scandinavian Masters—£750,000
Winner: Joakim Haeggman

It took 22 years for a Swede to win a PGA European Tour event in Sweden, but with the great success their players have had on the Tour, it was inevitable they would not wait as long for a second home winner. Jesper Parnevik won at Barseback in 1995, and when the Scandinavian Masters returned in 1997 the course did the trick again.

Joakim Haeggman beat Parnevik to another distinction, being the first Swedish Ryder Cup player in 1993. That was also the year he won his only title, the Spanish Open. But a dislocated shoulder and broken ribs from an ice hockey accident in 1994 interrupted his success. Since then he has turned to fishing as a pastime.

After Parnevik ended his run of bogey-free holes on the Barseback course at 114 when he bogeyed the sixth hole of the third round, Haeggman took control. At the halfway point, Haeggman was in a tie with seven others for the lead. A third-round 65, which included a chip-in birdie at the last, put Haeggman well clear, and the 27-year-old from Kalmar was never threatened on the final day. He shot a closing 69, in which he hit a superb recovery from the trees at the 18th to set up a birdie that was greeted with rapturous applause. That gave him a four-shot victory at 270, 18 under par, over Ignacio Garrido and by five strokes over Mats Hallberg and Peter Baker.

Part of Haeggman's success was being confident putting on the greens.

"The people turned out to watch Jesper repeat his 1995 victory but he's used to putting on great surfaces on the U.S. Tour," Haeggman said. "These greens are more like the ones I grew up on. It wasn't a week for great putters to shine. They were my kind of surfaces."

Chemapol Trophy Czech Open—£800,000
Winner: Bernhard Langer

Just to prove that his back-to-back wins earlier in the season were no flukes, Bernhard Langer won the Chemapol Trophy Czech Open by four strokes with a superb display over the weekend. In his final two rounds, Langer claimed 15 birdies and did not drop a shot to par.

His first two rounds had been 70 and 67, but he swept into the lead with closing efforts of 64 and 63 for a 20-under-par score of 264 on the new Karlstein course near Prague. The hilltop setting was overlooked by a 14th century fortress which added a backdrop as beautiful as the way the German played to claim his 50th worldwide victory.

"I can't remember the last time I shot 127 for two rounds," said Langer. With his 40th birthday only a few weeks away, Langer closed with five birdies in seven holes on the back nine. "My short game is as sharp as ever. I'm stuck with a few bad habits. Sometimes I can do it on the range and not on the course and sometimes I can't even do it on the range, but the results seem to be okay."

Langer and Jose Maria Olazabal were heroes to Ignacio Garrido, and ones that the young Spaniard now thought he could beat. Garrido finished second for the second week running to virtually assure himself of a place on the European Ryder Cup team, following his father Antonio.

But he was not going to beat Langer in Prague. "When I asked my caddie on the 16th what I needed to do, he said I shouldn't worry because Langer was 20 under," Garrido said. Rounds of 65, 67 and 66 on the last three days brought Garrido his second place alongside Niclas Fasth. Miguel Jimenez was fourth, five strokes back, and Czech-born Alexander Cejka shared fifth place.

Smurfit European Open—£850,000
Winner: Per-Ulrik Johansson

Per-Ulrik Johansson played some impressive golf to retain his Smurfit European Open title in Ireland at the K Club near Dublin. A second-round 64, which equalled the course record set by Colin Montgomerie the day before, even impressed the Swede. "Today was almost better than sex," he said. When questioned about this statement later by his girlfriend, he added, "I did say 'almost.'"

What so excited Johansson about his eight-birdie round was this. "I cannot remember hitting so many good shots," he said. "Usually in a good round you only have about three shots which you hit perfect. But today there must have been around 10 shots that came off exactly how I visualized them."

Having opened with 68, the 30-year-old did not go over par in the last three days, which were rounded out with efforts of 66 and 69. Johansson's second victory of the season was achieved by six strokes over Peter Baker. His 267 total, 21 under par, was 10 better than he managed on the same course the previous year.

"It was difficult playing with such a big lead. I started putting a bit defensively, but it is nice to know you can hole those six and seven footers when you do make a mistake," Johansson said after securing his Ryder Cup place. "It is the first time I can remember not dropping a shot for three rounds. You are only happy with your game for two percent of the time so I am going to enjoy that two percent."

Merely setting foot on the Emerald Isle seems to lift Johansson's spirits. "I love playing in Ireland. Everything went right this week — from the bread to the fresh orange juice. I am still trying to find a bakery that will deliver me a loaf every week wherever I am in the world."

Despite the Swede's runaway success, there was what appeared to be a crucial putt holed at the 18th. Jose Maria Olazabal sank his effort from 10 feet and punched the air, the first time he could remember doing such a thing since the 1994 NEC World Series of Golf. It meant the Spaniard finished third, in a tie with Raymond Russell, and overtook Padraig Harrington to go to 11th place on the Ryder Cup standings with a week left in the qualifying.

BMW International Open—£750,000
Winner: Robert Karlsson

Many were the implications of performances in the BMW International Open. Robert Karlsson needed to prove that exhaustive sessions of "body psychotherapy" could help him regain his winning form. Carl Watts, starting the week in 149th place on the European money list, needed to secure his tour card, while Colin Montgomerie continued his search for a fifth money title.

Overshadowing everything was the race for Ryder Cup points. The last qualifying event, however, produced little change. Thomas Bjorn, who finished fifth in Munich, Costantino Rocca and Ignacio Garrido were confirmed on the team, while Jose Maria Olazabal finished 11th on the list, ahead of Padraig Harrington. With Olazabal 31st and the Irishman ninth in the tournament, neither could dislodge the injured Miguel Angel Martin from the 10th and last automatic qualifying place, although a few days later Olazabal was dramatically handed Martin's place when the latter refused a fitness test on his wrist.

At the top of the leaderboard, Montgomerie appeared to be on course for another victory when he was second after three rounds and closed with 66 to finish at 23 under par. That was only good enough for third place as Karlsson and Watts tied at 264 after final rounds of 66 and 65 respectively.

Karlsson lost confidence after winning for the first time in 1995, and had undergone sessions of "body psychotherapy" — counselling which takes place with the patient's body in unnatural, "stressed" configurations — to regain his belief. Watts, an Englishman in his first year on the tour, holed from six feet at the last to force the playoff and lipped out from 30 feet at the second extra hole. Back at the 18th for the third playoff hole, he hooked his drive into a pond and this time missed his par putt.

"It was one of my most enjoyable rounds of golf," said the Swede. "I had gone out with a one-shot lead and won before and I just tried to concentrate on my own game."

Canon European Masters—£800,000
Winner: Costantino Rocca

Breathtaking as the views are from the Crans-sur-Sierre course, high in the Swiss Alps, taking deep breaths was very much the order of the week at the Canon European Masters. In a nightmare sequel for the PGA European Tour after what happened at the One 2 One British Masters in 1996, the greens at Crans were in such poor condition that the tournament was in danger of being cancelled.

Waterlogged by torrential summer rains, a greenskeeping mistake led to the greens being treated with the wrong fertilizer. The result was surfaces which were bare and cracked, with two temporary greens having to be employed. Yet someone had to win, and Costantino Rocca did so in spectacular style.

Rocca shot a closing round of 62 which included an eagle and seven birdies. His 266 total, 18 under par, gave the Italian his fourth win of his career, by one stroke over the hot Robert Karlsson, who closed with 64, and the Scottish rookie Scott Henderson. "I have never shot a 62 in my life before," Rocca said, "not even playing with friends."

Clear of the shoulder injury that had plagued him during the summer — "the pain has gone like magic," he said — Rocca thought he was on course for the PGA European Tour's first 59. He missed from 12 feet at the eighth, from three feet at the 11th, four feet at the 12th and 12 feet at the 16th. "But I'm happy," he added. "This is the best I've played since my first victory in Lyon four years ago, and just what I wanted two weeks before the Ryder Cup."

Nick Faldo was the 54-hole leader, but slipped to 70 in the final round, which left him tied for sixth. Playing with the Englishman, plus coping with the air at the 5,000-foot altitude, left Henderson, a few days short of his 28th birthday, with some bad headaches. After his opening 62, Henderson's third-round 73 was cancelled out with a closing 66.

Another Italian, Aldo Casera, winner of the title in 1950 and playing for the 49th consecutive time, equalled his age with 78 in the first round, and then beat it by five strokes on day two. Also missing the cut was 17-year-old Justin Rose, just returned from playing for Great Britain and Ireland in the Walker Cup, who shot rounds of 71 and 73 to outscore Seve Ballesteros by a stroke.

Trophee Lancome—£700,000
Winner: Mark O'Meara

As a smash-and-grab raid it was startlingly effective. Mark O'Meara came across to Europe early for a week's reconnaissance prior to the Ryder Cup and walked off with the bronzed torso which is the Trophee Lancome.

This was O'Meara's second win in Europe — 10 years after his Lawrence

Batley International victory at Royal Birkdale — his third of the season, his sixth outside America and the 20th of his career. It added, despite an otherwise sunny weekend in Paris, to the depressing nature of the PGA European Tour of late. "I don't know about captain Tom Kite," O'Meara said, "but it certainly brings a big smile to my face."

O'Meara, extending his career earnings to over $10 million with the first prize of £116,660, compiled a final-round 69. It was good enough to hold off the two 54-hole leaders from Australia, Greg Norman and Peter O'Malley, and a late charge from Swede Jarmo Sandelin, who finished one behind after 67 that included three bogeys in his first four holes. Sandelin finished second at 272, with the Aussies one stroke further back.

"Obviously, I'm proud and pleased to win the Trophee Lancome," said O'Meara, the former U.S. Amateur champion. "I was not playing absolutely sterling and I wanted to be ready for Valderrama, so this will help."

O'Meara suffered two sixes in his first nine, in between a run of five birdies in seven holes. But he pulled his tee shots at all of the last three holes. He was to chip and single putt on each occasion. At both the 16th and 17th, he had to recover from the trees, but claimed a birdie at the 16th from 12 feet and a par at the 17th from 18 feet.

"My tee shot at the 17th was really ugly," O'Meara admitted. "I've played enough golf to know that. Usually, it is in the pressure situations when your technique can come up short. My game was not 100 percent, but my putting saved me. The putt at the 17th was the big one because I still had a one-stroke lead going to the last."

The leading European Ryder Cup player was Lee Westwood in eighth place, but captain Seve Ballesteros reproduced his brilliance of past summer in an opening 65 during which he hit a wonderful four wood from behind a tree and off his knees. "It was like old times," he admitted.

One 2 One British Masters—£750,000
Winner: Greg Turner

Greg Turner, a New Zealander with a partial interest in the Ryder Cup, having spent 12 years in Europe, was the victor in the One 2 One British Masters at the Forest of Arden. But only just. A par from a bunker at the 18th gave him a one-stroke win over Colin Montgomerie. That was the same Montgomerie who only just made the cut on the mark, then went on to post rounds of 67 and 63 over the weekend to jump from 57th to second place. His final round equalled his own course record, on a course where he had previously finished first once and second twice.

Turner, whose wife Jane was expecting their first child the following week, scored a closing 70 to finish at 13 under par. For much of the day his closest challenger had been Thomas Bjorn, who finished tied for fourth with Raymond Russell, behind Mark Roe.

At the 15th green, the 34-year-old New Zealander knew that Montgomerie was the man to beat. "It was a two-horse race, but then the horse changed. Monty suddenly came through and it is different over the last few holes when you know there is a target to beat," he said.

Turner went over the back of the 17th green and could not save par, leaving him with a one-stroke advantage going to the 18th, a par-three. His four-iron tee shot came up short in a bunker, but he came out to six feet and holed the putt.

Montgomerie had earlier holed 15-footers at each of the last two holes for an eagle-three, birdie-two finish, but he was most pleased with having saved par from under a tree, holing from six feet, at his last hole on make the cut. "I might not have been here but for that, so all this is a bonus," he said. "I'm very proud of the way I played over the weekend. To be 14 under on a tough course which is playing long is a good effort.

"I started to relax and I play my best golf when I am relaxed. I am not frightened to go low and I have had a lot of low scores this year, especially on Sundays. Sunday is payday and you don't want to go backwards."

Ryder Cup
Winner: Europe

See Chapter 8.

Linde German Masters—£750,000
Winner: Bernhard Langer

Not for the first time, the Linde German Masters took place the week after a dramatic Ryder Cup. In 1991, after missing a putt to retain the Ryder Cup for Europe at Kiawah Island, Bernhard Langer showed his resolve and strength of character by returning home to win the following week.

In happier circumstances, Langer won the European Open the week after the 1995 Ryder Cup. Then, having been the man who made sure Europe kept the Ryder Cup this year at Valderrama, Langer did his trick again.

This was Langer's third win in the event he helps to promote, his fourth of the year, and his 10th in Germany in front of an adoring gallery. Exhausted, but inspired as always to be playing at home, Langer won by six strokes with a 267 total, 21 under par. For three of the four rounds he was his usual efficient self. But in the third round, he was brilliant, scoring the eighth 60 ever seen on the PGA European Tour.

The 60 came on the back of his last hole in the second round, actually the ninth, where his perfect drive finished in a divot and he pitched into a pond. The next day he made up for it by chipping in at the fifth for an eagle and then going on to record 11 birdies. His only bogey was at the sixth, where he three-putted, and he also had a three-footer at the 14th spin out, otherwise Europe could have seen its first 59.

"This is the lowest round of my career, but my best round was the 62 to win the Spanish Open at El Saler in 1984, and then there was my 62 at Valderrama in 1994," said Langer. "It was a great thrill to do it in front of a German gallery."

With his lead at the top of the money list threatened, Colin Montgomerie hauled himself into second place with three birdies in the last six holes. That kept him in front of Langer by £45,000 with only the Volvo Masters to go for the two of them. Other Ryder Cup players were high on the leaderboard with Thomas Bjorn third, Jose Maria Olazabal and Costantino Rocca tied for fourth, Darren Clarke tied for seventh and Per-Ulrik Johansson tied for 11th. Phil Mickelson and Tom Lehman tied for 30th.

Toyota World Match Play—£650,000
Winner: Vijay Singh

See Chapter 9.

Open Novotel Perrier—£350,000
Winners: Anders Forsbrand and Michael Jonzon

Anders Forsbrand had been due to play with Per-Ulrik Johansson in the Open Novotel Perrier, the PGA European Tour's unofficial two-man team tournament. But when Johansson declined the invitation, pleading too many commitments, Forsbrand was happy to hook up with another countryman, Michael Jonzon.

He was even happier after Jonzon had holed two crucial putts to give the Swedes a victory after a playoff against Spaniards Santiago Luna and Jose Rivero. With both players playing their own ball on the final day — after three days of fourballs, foursomes and greensomes — Forsbrand gave his team a chance of winning by holing a 35-footer at the 17th hole at Golf du Medoc.

Then at the 18th, Jonzon holed from 15 feet to clinch a place in the playoff. Jonzon had scored 71 and Forsbrand 69 to tie Luna and Rivero's 12-under total of 343. At the first extra hole, Jonzon rolled in a 30-footer for the win. "Michael's two birdie putts were fantastic," Forsbrand said. "We combined great together."

Ryder Cup captain Seve Ballesteros and Jose Maria Olazabal, former winners of the event, tied for third place, five strokes back, along with Mark Roe and Marc Farry and Peter Hedblom and Patrik Sjoland.

Alfred Dunhill Cup—£1,000,000
Winner: South Africa

See Chapter 10.

Oki Pro-Am—£450,000
Winner: Paul McGinley

Paul McGinley's second PGA European Tour win came in contrasting fashion to his first. At the Hohe Brucke Open in Austria in 1996, the Irishman scored a final-round 62 to take the title from seven strokes back. At La Moraleja for this year's Oki Pro-Am, the 30-year-old McGinley did all the hard work over the first three rounds.

His 54-hole score of 197, in which he did not make a bogey, equalled the year's best in Europe and gave him a six-shot lead going into the final round. An outward 32 extended his lead even further before he settled for 69 and a four-stroke win over Iain Pyman with a 22-under-par 266 total.

"That's the best I've played for 54 holes," McGinley said of his 66-67-64 opening scores. "But I was determined neither to protect my lead nor to be complacent. I knew a lot of guys behind me were capable of shooting scores between 61 and 64, so to go out on the front nine the way I did was important."

McGinley had borrowed a putter from his Alfred Dunhill Cup teammate Darren Clarke at St. Andrews the previous week. "My father advised me to switch to a long putter from the 31-inch club that I was using, so I borrowed a 34-inch putter from Darren, which is much heavier, and it transformed my touch. It was a marvellous feeling to putt so well."

Pyman, a former British Amateur champion, went into the last full-field event of the year ranked 116th on the money list, with only the top 117 retaining their cards. A closing 64 gave him the biggest check of his career, £50,000, and clinched his card. Greg Turner was third, three strokes further behind.

Volvo Masters—£1,000,000
Winner: Lee Westwood

In a dismal end to the year, a storm across Andalucia reduced the Volvo Masters to 54 holes with only a couple of hours' play possible on the final day. Lee Westwood never got the chance to tee it up, but gained his first PGA European Tour victory of the year, while Colin Montgomerie was confirmed as the leading European money winner for the fifth consecutive time, a unique feat.

Westwood's three-round total of 200, 16 under par, gave him a three-stroke win over Padraig Harrington, and Jose Maria Olazabal was third, a further shot behind. It was the 24-year-old from Worksop, England's second European win, and his fourth worldwide.

"I was confident of holding onto a three-stroke lead," Westwood said. "This was the first time this year I have hit the ball well and putted well in the same week. I have achieved a lot this year, in the majors and the Ryder Cup was the highlight, but I felt a bit empty without having won."

Westwood's 67 came on the second day when the wind was starting to blow, and his 68 on the final afternoon came in the height of a gale, an impressive display. He enjoyed a four-stroke lead at one point, only for Harrington to finish eagle, birdie, birdie to move within one before Westwood played the last three holes in two under par to re-establish his lead.

Montgomerie could have been overhauled by two players going into the last event. Bernhard Langer needed to finish first or second to take the No. 1 spot, while anything worse than fourth meant he was out of the running. Darren Clarke needed to win to have any hope.

There was a nervous moment for Montgomerie when he went out of bounds at the 16th hole, finishing in a plowed field. The error led to a triple-bogey eight and allowed Clarke to slip past him. On the third day, Clarke's 77 and Langer's 74 left them tied for 15th place, while Montgomerie was ninth. The champagne was on ice, but was watered down slightly by the cancellation of the last day. Montgomerie said, "It's a season-long schedule and winning for the fifth successive time is not an anti-climax."

Challenge Tour

Michele Reale needed no further motivation for playing on the European Challenge Tour in 1997. For one thing, his countryman Costantino Rocca, who qualified from what was then the satellite tour in 1989, was again one of the main stars on the PGA European Tour and in the Ryder Cup at Valderrama. Secondly, Reale had finished 16th on the 1996 Challenge Tour, missing out on his card by just £690.

The 26-year-old Italian made sure of gaining a promotion as one of the top 15 on the Challenge Tour's money list by winning two tournaments. He was the leading money winner with £51,679, a record. Reale admitted to being "devastated" at missing out the year before, but added, "It was difficult to come back this year, but perhaps I wasn't ready for the main tour, but I hope to have proved I am now by winning twice."

Reale has much in common with Rocca, not least his northern Italian upbringing in Biella, near Turin. He has a similar solid build, and his game is also solid in all departments, rather than spectacular in any one area. Prior to this year, Reale had been second five times on the Challenge Tour. But in 1997, his 26 tournaments included eight top 10s and only five missed cuts, his two wins both coming in playoffs at the Canarias Challenge in Las Palmas and the Sovereign Russian Open in Moscow.

By the time the tour reached the Grand Final at Estoril in Portugal, Reale had sewn up the No. 1 spot. "That was important because it shows the other players that you are a good golfer," Reale said. "I enjoyed the Challenge Tour because the competition is so good and the standard is so high. You have to play under pressure and I am sure that will help me next year."

Just like the Volvo Masters on the main tour, the final round of the Grand Final was washed out, leaving Nicolas Joakimides, who scored 62 in the third round, as the winner. That lifted the Frenchman into the top 15 on the money list, while the eighth place by Bradley Dredge of Wales was good enough for him to jump into 15th place and claim the last card.

Denmark, for whom Thomas Bjorn became their first Ryder Cup player in 1997, confirmed its position as the emerging Scandinavian country in golf with three players in the top 15, Steen Tinning, Knud Storegaard and Soren Hjeldsen. The other qualifiers were Kalle Brink (Sweden), Greg Chalmers (Australia), Raphael Jacquelin (France), Anssi Kankkonen (Finland), David Lynn (England), Craig Hainline (U.S.), Stephen Leaney (Australia), Heinz P. Thul (Germany) and Nicolas Vanhootegem (Belgium).

13. Asia/Japan Tours

It has gotten so that, as each new year unfolds on the Japan PGA Tour, the question no longer is: Who will be No. 1? Now it is: Who will be finishing second to the remarkable Masashi (Jumbo) Ozaki? Nothing seems to slow down Ozaki, not the opposition and certainly not age. Ozaki turned 50 during 1997, played a few less tournaments, but did nothing to suggest that he is or should be considering a switch to senior golf.

Why should he when, in just 19 starts in Japan, he won five times and finished second in four others? Why should he when, in the last 11 starts, he placed 10th or better? Why should he when he led the money list for the fourth straight year and eighth time in the last 10 years, taking ¥170,847,633 to the bank?

Shigeki Maruyama took his turn in the No. 2 slot on the money list. In fact, the 28-year-old Maruyama took a serious run at Ozaki's hold on the top position and had a shot at it in the final tournament of the season. He won four times, including the Japan PGA Championship and Japan Match Play, one more than he had won in his previous five years, and collected ¥152,774,420.

It seems probable that Maruyama faces a better future than the previous two runners-up, Yoshinori Kaneko and Satoshi Higashi, who did little in 1997. American Brian Watts, the 1994 runner-up, had another strong season, though, winning twice, losing a playoff and being the only other player to top ¥100 million with his ¥111,153,198

Three other players landed two 1997 titles — fellow American Brandt Jobe, Kenichi Kuboya and Naomichi (Joe) Ozaki, who scored back-to-back victories in mid-summer after announcing that he would be a full-time player in Japan in 1998 after playing the U.S. PGA Tour regularly since 1993. With the two wins, Naomichi became just the sixth man in Japanese history with at least 25 victories, the watermark for lifetime exemption.

Tateo (Jet) Ozaki, the third member of golf's most famous brother act, didn't win, but was a strong contender time and again, finishing fifth on the money list behind Naomichi with ¥77,555,311. Naomichi collected ¥96,994,361 in Japan and, with his U.S. winnings, placed 30th on the World Money List with $1,006,936. Masashi was 21st with $1,420,207 and Maruyama 22nd with $1,380,821. On the other side of the coin, one of those six lifetime exemptees, Tsuneyuki (Tommy) Nakajima, went winless for a second year in a row and never seriously threatened in the late stages of any tournament.

Foreign players took 11 of the 36 titles, including the two each by Watts and Jobe. The most attention-getting of those was the victory of 48-year-old Hall-of-Famer Tom Watson in the rich Dunlop Masters. Singapore-based Peter Teravainen was a fourth American winner. England's Lee Westwood repeated in the Taiheiyo Masters and Craig Parry of Australia captured the Japan Open.

Asia Tour

Mitsubishi Motors - Southwoods Open—US$250,000
Winner: Takao Nogami

With his challengers already in the clubhouse, Japan's Takao Nogami, 25, was a safe par from his first victory on the Asian Tour in the Mitsubishi Motors - Southwoods Open in Manila. Nogami hadn't got this far playing conservatively, so after finding the fairway with his drive at the final hole, he declined to lay up and instead ripped a three wood to the green. Then he two-putted for a birdie and a two-stroke victory over Canada's Jim Rutledge and American Kevin Wentworth. It was more than just Nogami's own first win. With an eight-under-par total of 281, Nogami became the first Japanese to win on the Asian Tour outside of Japan since 1986.

It was a battle with England's Peter Alabaster for the first three rounds. Alabaster led the first round with 65, one shot ahead of Nogami. Nogami leapfrogged him by two in the second round with 72, and was tied with him after shooting 73 in the third round. Both were one ahead of India's Arjun Atwal. The path cleared quickly. Alabaster self-destructed with a closing 78, and Atwal sank with 74, leaving Rutledge and Wentworth to get to the clubhouse and await their chances with Nogami at the 18th. It was a short wait, as Nogami shot 70 to win.

Konica U-Bix Manila Open—US$200,000
Winner: Yasuharu Imano

Japan's Yasuharu Imano, who emerged from the Asian Tour qualifying early in February, gave himself a terrific boost two weeks later, winning the Konica U-Bix Manila Open at Wack Wack Golf and Country Club. He won with the flourish of a veteran, coming from three strokes off the lead to wrap up a 286 total on rounds of 70, 74, 71 and 71. He had the only under-par score in the field for a two-stroke victory over Paraguay's Pedro Martinez, the Philippines' Danny Zarate and American Kevin Wentworth.

Imano, tied for fourth place coming into the final round, took the lead with 34 on the first nine, and stayed there when his challengers fell short. Canadian Ian Leggatt, the third-round leader, soared to 77. American Don Walsworth, one stroke off the lead, blew to 78. And Argentina's Gustavo Rojas, who was third, slipped with 75. Zarate made a move, but missed the green at the par-five 13th and made seven. Imano doubled-bogeyed the par-four 11th, but at the par-three 16th, he hit a five iron to three feet and birdied for a two-shot lead, then parred in. Imano speaks little English, but said it all with his acceptance speech. "Play good," he said. "Very happy."

Benson and Hedges Malaysian Open—US$300,000
Winner: Lee Westwood

Britain's rising Lee Westwood didn't know when he was beaten in the Benson and Hedges Malaysian Open. "When I was five behind, I just told myself to keep plugging away," he said. This was in the final round, about the time leader Harumitsu Hamano had reached the fifth tee. "I knew Hamano wasn't going to pull clear," Westwood added. Westwood was right, but Hamano was only the first obstacle. Next came American Larry Barber. Barber rose from third place at the start of the day and took the lead with four holes to play. Westwood caught him with a birdie at No. 15, and went ahead when Barber three-putted the 16th for a bogey that dropped him to second place.

Westwood birdied the par-four 18th to win by two strokes. He played the Saujana course in Kuala Lumpur in rounds of 64, 72, 69 and 69 for a 274 total. Hamano fell to fifth place on a closing 75. Westwood, who opened with a course-record 64, was one stroke behind Hamano starting the final round. That deficit increased to five strokes when Hamano birdied three of the first four holes and Westwood bogeyed. "Patience was the key to this win," said Westwood, making it his second victory in Asia in four months. The previous November, he won the Sumitomo Taiheiyo Masters in Japan.

Thai Airways International Thailand Open—US$300,000
Winner: Christian Chernock

With the Thai Airways International Thailand Open being snatched away from him at the last instant, American Don Walsworth must have been feeling more like Captain Ahab than a golfer trying for his first victory. A closing 65 ought to be good enough. Not so. This time it was fellow-American Christian Chernock getting that one last birdie for 64 to beat him by one stroke. Chernock, who won only $11,280 on the Asian Tour the year before, played the Sriracha International course in rounds of 70, 66, 68 and 64 for a 268 total, 20 under par.

The tournament was a horse race at the halfway point. Japan's Tsuneyuki Nakajima led at 10-under-par 134. Walsworth and Argentina's Gustavo Rojas were one stroke behind, and Chernock and seven others were two behind at 136. American Brian Wilson took the third-round lead with 65–202, but faded to a tie for sixth place. Walsworth shot 65 and took the lead, but along came Chernock. So the Walsworth watch continued.

Rolex Masters—US$289,000
Winner: Kyi Hla Han

Birth and victory seem to mean the same thing to Myanmar's Kyi Hla Han. He won three straight tournaments in the autumn of 1994, when his wife Marlene was about to give birth to their first child. Now, with his wife eight months pregnant in late March, he took the Rolex Masters at Singapore Island Country Club. "Well, it does seem that the pregnancies have been lucky for me," Han said. It took more than just luck, of course, for rounds of 67, 68, 65 and 68 for a tournament-record 16-under-par 268 total.

American Dean Wilson, who tied for fourth place, shot a course-record nine-under-par 62 in the second round. It included a gambling birdie at the par-five 18th to break the previous record of 64. More than a record was at stake, he said, "so I decided not to be conservative." He got his ninth birdie of the day, the 62, and the halfway lead. In the third round, the Philippines' Danny Zarate, fighting a painful stomach ailment, shot 68 to tie Han for the lead. In the final round, Zarate birdied two of the first three holes for a two-stroke lead, but the edge was wiped out when Han birdied No. 5 and Zarate bogeyed No. 7. Zarate went on to bogey four of the next six holes, leaving second place to Taiwan's Yeh Chang-ting and England's Edward Fryatt, both two strokes back.

Classic India Open—US$300,000
Winner: Edward Fryatt

England's Edward Fryatt broke away from the start, was tied for the lead after the second round, then shook off all challengers for a runaway six-stroke victory in the Classic India Open. Fryatt opened with a nine-under-par 63 at the par-72 Royal Calcutta Golf Club, playing at 7,195 yards, which was shortened by the warm, dry weather of late March. Fryatt toured it in 63-69-67-73—272, 16 under par.

American Gary Rusnak closed with a rush and took second place with the best round in the finale, 67 for a 278 total. Although 20 finishers broke the par of 288, only Paraguay's Pedro Martinez was a threat to Fryatt, and then only briefly. Martinez trailed Fryatt by two strokes after the first round, 63-65, then tied him after the second round with 67–132. A 74 in the third round ended Martinez's hopes of catching him. At that, he was still second, but a closing 75 dropped him to fifth place at seven-under 281.

Mobiline Philippine Open—US$300,000
Winner: Kevin Wentworth

At first glance, the scoring summary looked scary. There were four 62s. Of the 11 finishers through the top eight places, there were 42 rounds in the 60s and only two 70s. It seemed Camp John Hay at Baguio City, Philippines, had been trampled in the Mobiline Philippine Open. Not quite. This was a 5,252-yard course, par 68, so the scoring wasn't what it seemed.

Six players tied for the first-round lead at 65 — American Tim Straub, Australian Stephen Leaney, Japan's Hideto Shigenobu, Germany's Uli Zilg and the Philippines' Richard Sinfuego and Roger Cabajar. Then American Kevin Wentworth turned the traffic jam into a sprint with a pair of 62s in the middle rounds. He shot 67-62-62-68—259, 13 under par, to win by three strokes over Straub, who started the final round eight behind, and slashed the deficit with 63.

Maekyung LG Fashion Open—US$400,000
Winner: Shin Yong-jin

Korea's Shin Yong-jin looked like anything but a winner when the Maekyung LG Fashion Open started. Not that a first-round 69 was out of the picture, but it looked like a two-man race between India's Jeev Milkha Singh and Canada's Danny Mijovic. Both shot seven-under-par 65s in clear, calm weather at the Nam Seoul Golf Club in Seoul. Korea's Cho Chul-sang was one stroke behind at 66, but would soon drift out of contention. Singh would have to rebound to get back into the race after the second round. A 71 dropped him to 136, three strokes behind Korea's Choi Kyung-ju, whose 66 set the pace at 11-under 133.

The third round was harsh. Choi slipped with 73, and Mijovic, two strokes off the lead after the second round, was knocked out by 75. And rebound Singh did, with 67 that carried him back to the top at 13-under 203. It was here that Shin emerged, climbing out of the pack to second place. Then in the final round, Singh stumbled to 73, his only round over par, and Shin had the victory. He shot 69-67-68-68–272, 16 under par, to win by one stroke over American Tim Balmer. Singh tied for fifth at 276.

Volvo China Open—US$400,000
Winner: Cheng Jun

Cheng Jun, of whom much was expected after he won two China Amateur Opens, ended three years of frustration as a professional with his breakout victory in the Volvo China Open at Beijing International Golf Club. "It feels like nothing I have ever felt before," Cheng said. "It's a surprise and a shock to have won. I don't know what to say." He shot 72, 70, 68 and 70 for a 280 total, eight under par, for a breezy five-stroke victory. But it didn't come without stress.

Cheng started the final round six strokes ahead of Korea's Mo Joong-kyung and American Mike Cunning. Mo climbed to within two of Cheng with four straight birdies from No. 2. "I really felt the pressure for the first five holes," Cheng said, "but I always felt that there was no way Mo could continue his form. After the seventh, I began to feel much more confident."

Cheng all but won when he holed a 20-footer for a birdie at No. 10, and he got to six strokes ahead with seven holes to play. Only a second-nine 33 by Australian Adrian Percey, the runner-up, cut his margin to five.

Hyundai Motors Open—US$500,000
Winner: Ian Woosnam

Victory was sweet for Ian Woosnam, but not as sweet as it might have been. The man he defeated in the Hyundai Motors Open on the second playoff hole was old friend and former Ryder Cup teammate Sandy Lyle, who has been in a prolonged slump. "I feel very sorry for Sandy," Woosnam said, "and I would have liked to see him win today. On the evidence of his performance this week, I'm sure that he will win again very soon."

The tournament at Lakeside Country Club in Seoul, South Korea, became a battle of the two old friends soon after third-round leader Choi Kyung-ju bogeyed the first hole and double-bogeyed the second. Lyle had finished the sixth hole and was six under par and in the lead when lightning delayed play. When they came back out, Woosnam finished a bogey-free 68 to tie Lyle. Woosnam shot 71, 74, 67 and 68 for a 280 total, eight under par, and Lyle tied him with rounds of 74, 70, 67 and 69. Both parred the first playoff hole. Woosnam won with a 15-foot birdie on the second.

Lyle, who hadn't won since the 1992 Volvo Masters, was encouraged rather than crushed. "Overall, I'm very pleased with my performance this week," he said. "To shoot 69 on this golf course in conditions like we had today is as good a score as I could have hoped for. I'm very happy indeed."

Chinese Taipei Open—US$275,000
Winner: Tsai Chi-huang

Important numbers come in pairs for Tsai Chi-huang. That was bad news in the 1996 Chinese Taipei Open. He started with 76 and closed with 76 and finished out of sight. It was a different story in 1997 at the Sunrise Golf and Country Club in July. Tsai left the field breathless, opening with a set of 66s, and he cruised in from there with a pair of 71s for a 274 total and a seven-stroke victory over South Africa's Andre Cruse.

Taiwan PGA Golf Championship—US$436,000
Winner: Gerry Norquist

The Taiwan PGA Golf Championship was an odd one. What was more interesting, American Gerry Norquist's playoff victory or the collapse of the challengers? The failures were unusually pronounced this time. Take the first round, for example. India's Vivek Bhandari, America's Ted Purdy and Taiwan's Yu Chin-han tied for the lead at Pearl Heights Golf Club in Taipei. Bhandari shot 72 in the second round — not a high score, but he couldn't get below it the rest of the way. Yu shot 75 in the second round, and as if that hadn't hurt enough, he finished with 86. Purdy didn't wait that long. He came back from his 68 with 79, then 77.

It came down to the final chase. American Christian Chernock, leading through the third round by two strokes, closed with nothing worse than 72. It was enough to keep him from an outright win. Taiwan's Chou Hung-nan shot 67 and tied him at 280. And Norquist, second after the third round, joined the tie with 70. Norquist, who won the DFS Galleria Guam Open by three strokes in April, won on the first extra hole this time.

Shinhan Donghae Open—US$400,000
Winner: Edward Fryatt

Edward Fryatt, known as an Englishman who speaks like an American — this from growing up in the United States — took a big step towards establishing his identity with a playoff victory over Kevin Wentworth in the Shinhan Donghae Open at Seoul, Korea. But Fryatt squandered a comfortable cushion on the way. Fryatt, who won the Classic India Open in March, bolted into the lead with an opening six-under-par 66, one stroke ahead of Wentworth. He shot 68 in the second round and was tied at 135 by Japan's Takao Nogami (66), both one stroke ahead of Wentworth. Then came what looked like the decisive third round. Fryatt bolted five strokes ahead with 68, while Wentworth, the Mobiline Philippine Open champion, shot 72 and Nogami 73. Fryatt's cushion was wiped out when he closed with 72 and Wentworth rallied for 67. Nogami, the Mitsubishi-Southwoods Open winner in February, fell short of the playoff with 70.

Korea Open—US$400,000
Winner: Kim Jong-duk

The Korea Open started off with Australia's John Senden leading at 70, four players at 71, and 10 at 72 at the par-72 Han Yang Country Club at Goyang City. Then it turned into a real tussle that ended in a four-way playoff that did not include Senden. He was part of a five-way tie going into the final round, but a closing 74 knocked him back to seventh place. Korea's Kim Jong-duk picked off the title in the playoff, beating countrymen Choi Kwang-soo, Shin Yong-jin and American Andrew Pitts. All shot 71 in the final round and tied at three-under-par 285.

Mercuries Cup Masters—US$350,000
Winner: Gerry Norquist

American Gerry Norquist seemed to be making a name for himself as a come-from-behind player. Norquist, who came from four strokes behind to win the DFS Galleria Guam Open in April, was only one stroke behind this time in the Mercuries Cup Masters at Tamsui Golf and Country Club in Taiwan. He rallied for a final-round 68, the best score of the day, for a five-stroke victory that wasn't as easy as it looked. In fact, he had trailed all the way.

Taiwan's Lee Wen-sheng led the first round with a five-under-par 67, and Norquist was one shot behind, tied with Taiwan's Ho Ming-chung. A 70 in the second round left him one stroke off again, this time behind Taiwan's Lu Wen-ter and Thailand's Thammanoon Sriroj, the Pakistan Open champion, both with 66–138 totals. Lu kept the edge with a third-round 71, and Norquist stayed a shot behind with his own 71, while Thammanoon was knocked out by 76. The final round was almost gift-wrapped. The challengers self-destructed. While Norquist was shooting that 68, Lu blew to a 76, and Kuo Chie-hsiung, who had been two off the lead, shot 78. Norquist had his 10-under-par victory.

Johnnie Walker Super Tour—US$350,000
Winner: Jesper Parnevik

Playing in four Asian countries in six days took its toll on Jesper Parnevik, but the talented Swede won the Johnnie Walker Super Tour and its US$100,000 first prize by four strokes over Nick Faldo. The tournament, featuring four international players and four players from the region, was played in Indonesia, Thailand, the Philippines and Taiwan.

Parnevik and Faldo were tied at 138, six under par, through two rounds, then Parnevik shot 68 in the third round to go ahead by four strokes. Both shot 70s in the last round. "I did not know what to expect," Parnevik said of the final round at Taipei's Ta Shee course. "I had a cough and fever when I arrived last night, but I managed to get off to a good start with birdies at the first and third holes."

China Tour

The Volvo China Tour enjoyed its third year in 1997 and had another good international mix as golf continued to expand in China. This time, the four winners were an Argentine, an Australian born in Wales, an American, and all led by the local favorite, Zhang Lian-wei. The year before the winners were a Chinese (Zhang, of course), a Scot, an Australian and a Malaysian.

The tour is a series of four 36-hole events, played at three different courses (Shenzhen Golf Club hosted two). Zhang played in all four, and had one victory, a second, a tie for third and a tie for ninth.

It began in 1997 with the Volvo Open at Shenzhen, and the victory went to Adrian Percey, a Welsh-born Aussie, on a 15-foot birdie putt on the second playoff hole against American Robin Byrd. Percey shot 68-69 and Byrd 69-68 to tie at 137. Byrd had the win in his sights until he bogeyed the last two holes. "I lost my concentration a little," he said. Percey, on the other hand, finishing a half-hour later, birdied the last two holes to tie him.

Zhang, who tied for third in the Volvo Open, thrilled the gallery the following week at Shenzhen in the Hugo Boss Open with a bogey-free 65 the second day for a one-stroke win over American Jerry Smith (66) and Taipei's Wang Ter-chang (67). "At the start of the day I thought a 68 would be good enough," said Zhang, who started one shot out of the lead, tied with Smith at 67. They duelled through to the end, and were tied at 11 under par coming to the par-five 18th. Smith hit the green in two, but Zhang chipped to 10 feet and dropped the putt for a birdie and 65. Smith three-putted for a par and 66, and Wang, the first-round leader, missed an eagle putt to tie and had to settle for a birdie for 67 to join Smith in second place.

It was a first for both Argentina's Gustavo Rojas and the Volvo China Tour in the Coca-Cola Open at Guangzhou. It was Rojas' first victory on the circuit. "I'm delighted I've been playing well this year," said Rojas, 29, who turned professional in 1983. He was in a five-way tie for the lead in the first round at 69, then shot another for a two-stroke victory over Korea's Charlie Wi, despite bogeys at the 16th and 18th holes. Rojas credited a birdie at the 10th — "That got me going" — then pulled ahead with birdies at the 13th and 14th while others were having their problems on the second nine.

Smith, co-runner-up at the Hugo Boss Open, put together two 66s for a two-stroke victory over Zhang in the Founder Open at Chengdu. Smith was tied with Byrd after the first round, then pulled ahead with 32 on the first nine. Australian Justin Cooper eagled the par-five 10th to get within two strokes of him, but couldn't close the gap. It was more than just a victory for Smith. It was a kind of liberation. "I've been in the lead going into the back nine on the last day of several tournaments, but I haven't managed to get the job done," Smith said. "I hope this might be the breakthrough I've been looking for."

Japan Tour

Token Corporation Cup—¥100,000,000
Winner: Masashi Ozaki

Masashi (Jumbo) Ozaki picked up where he left off when the new year began with the Token Corporation Cup. He won again. The remarkable Ozaki, who had scored his eighth and final win of 1996 in his season-ending appearance in the Japan Series of Golf, rolled to his 83rd official victory, although not without a serious challenge from Paraguay's Carlos Franco.

Ozaki fired a course-record 61 in the third round at Kedoin Golf Club, Kagoshima, to take a five-stroke lead, then barely held off Franco the last day to win by one shot with his 19-under-par 269 total.

Franco, a three-time winner in Japan, led by three strokes after a first-round 65 and shared the top spot after 36 holes at 133 with Tsukasa Watanabe (69-64). Then, after Ozaki's brilliant 61, the product of nine birdies and an eagle that equalled the all-time tour mark for 18 holes in a 72-hole event, Franco fought back with a closing 68. He missed an eight-foot birdie putt for a tie at the 72nd hole when Ozaki came back to the field with a par round for what Japanese records-keepers say was the 102nd overall victory of his career.

Daido Drinko Shizuoka Open—¥100,000,000
Winner: Hisayuki Sasaki

Hisayuki Sasaki, who spent most of 1996 chasing success elsewhere in the world, found it back home early in 1997. The 32-year-old Sasaki scored his first victory in three years when he broke open a tight battle in the final round of the 26th Daido Drinko Shizuoka Open and rolled to a three-stroke win. He closed with 68 for a 274 total, 14 under par on the Hamaoka course of Shizuoka Country Club.

Sasaki had only moderate success on the U.S. PGA Tour in 1996, but carried American star Davis Love III five extra holes before losing in a playoff for the individual title in the 1995 World Cup. He placed third in the Andersen Consulting World Championship the first week of January.

He overcame a slow start to take his third title. He opened with 71, five shots off the pace of Keiji Teshima, age 39, winless in 15 seasons. Winless Teshima was to remain as Frankie Minoza took a two-stroke lead with 65 for a 134 total. Sasaki was still four back despite 67, but overtook the Philippine veteran on the third day when he shot 68 and Minoza managed just a par round. Carlos Franco of Paraguay and Shigemasa Higaki were just a stroke behind the leaders at 207.

Sasaki rang up four birdies in the middle of the final round to establish the three-shot final margin that he never relinquished the rest of the way. Franco had 71 and finished as the runner-up for the second week in a row as Minoza took 73 and dropped into a five-way tie for third.

Just System KSB Open—¥70,000,000
Winner: Keiichiro Fukabori

Keiichiro Fukabori, an exempt player for the first time in his five years, emerged from a strange final round in the Just System KSB Open with his first victory. On a day when no one could take advantage, a grateful Fukabori had a two-over-par 74 hold up for a two-stroke victory at the Kinojo Golf Club at Okayama.

While the 28-year-old Fukabori was struggling himself, several others in the thick of the fight ran into disasters. Yutaka Hagawa, the veteran lefthander, who twice was tied for the lead, took a nine at the short 14th hole. Mitsuo Harada, who had middle rounds of 63-66 to climb into second place, collapsed to 81. And Katsunori Kuwabara, who moved into a one-stroke lead over Fukabori at the 14th hole, then went bogey, double bogey. He shot 73 and tied for second with Toshiaki Odate.

Fukabori and Kuwabara, one or the other or both, were on top all of the way. Kuwabara, who won the 1995 Acom International and represented Japan in the 1996 World Cup, led the first day with 66. Fukabori caught Katsunori in the second round with 64 that included an eagle, eight birdies and pars on the last five holes. They were at 133. Fukabori edged two strokes in front of Harada and Hagawa, who had an eagle-birdie-eagle spurt, with 69 for 202. The 74 finish for 276 gave him his first official victory, although he won the non-tour Kanto Open in 1996.

Descente Classic—¥100,000,000
Winner: Peter Teravainen

The Americans made their presence felt for the first time in 1997 at the Descente Classic. After Japanese pros captured the first three titles of the season, Peter Teravainen and Todd Hamilton finished one-two at Edosaki Country Club.

The victory tended to validate the credentials of the globe-trotting Teravainen, who scored the biggest victory of his career when he won the 1996 Japan Open. Later in the year he added the Merlion Masters on the Omega Tour, which was staged in Singapore, his home base.

The 40-year-old Yale graduate, who has played virtually all of his professional golf in Asia and Europe, led the pack in the Descente Classic from the second round on, finishing with a 14-under-par 270 total and a two-stroke victory over Hamilton, the younger American, the 1992 Asia champion who has won six times in Japan during the ensuing six years.

Teravainen seized the lead in the second round with his second of three consecutive 67s as Kenichi Kuboya, 25, opened with 66 and followed with 70 on his way out of contention. Shingo Katayama, Samson Gimson of Singapore and Brandt Jobe of the U.S. trailed by one, Hamilton, Kuboya and three others by two.

The third 67 for 201 maintained Teravainen's one-stroke margin, then over Hamilton, whose 66 for 202 matched the day's best round. Teravainen shot 69 and Hamilton 70, settling it between themselves in the final grouping on a rainy Sunday.

Tsuruya Open—¥100,000,000
Winner: Mitsuo Harada

Mitsuo Harada wiped out nine years of frustration and bitter memories of a final-round collapse three weeks earlier with a strong finish and an impressive victory in the Tsuruya Open at Sports Shinko Country Club's Yamanohara course at Hyogo.

Harada, who had never done well enough to earn a full-time playing card during those nine years, outshot the highly regarded Shigeki Maruyama as they went head-to-head, winning by four strokes with his 68 for a 279 total, nine under par. Maruyama, four over par after eight holes, wound up with 74.

Harada, who had plunged from 54-hole runner-up to remote also-ran with a closing 81 in the Just System KSB Open in March, lingered not far off the lead through the first three rounds at Sports Shinko.

Peter Teravainen got two more good rounds from his game following his Descente win. He claimed first place in the opening round with 67, then shared the top spot with Maruyama at 138. Harada, who had begun with 72, followed with 67 and was just a shot off the lead. The American finally ran out of gas, shooting 78 in the third round, and Maruyama had first place to himself when he produced 71 for a 209 total and the two-stroke lead over Harada, setting up the final-round duel.

Kirin Open—¥100,000,000
Winner: Kim Jong-duk

It would be hard to match the drama and impact of the finish of the Kirin Open, what it meant to the golfing life of South Korea's Kim Jong-duk. Besides being the sixth event on the Japan PGA Tour schedule, the tournament on the West course of Ibaraki Golf Club was the final Asian event to decide the 1997 winner of the money list and its lucrative rewards.

The title seemed to be destined for either American Kevin Wentworth or Britain's Edward Fryatt, the point leaders, certainly not for Kim Jong-duk, 45th in the standings at the start of the Kirin Open. However, when the Korean ran in a 30-foot chip shot at the 18th hole for 68 and a 278 total, he not only won the Kirin Open by one stroke over four other players but also jumped into first place on the money list.

It meant that, in addition to the ¥18 million first prize, nearly six times his total winnings in 1996, Kim received a two-year exemption to play on the Japan PGA Tour and an invitation to the British Open.

For the second week in a row, Shigeki Maruyama appeared headed for his first win of the year. Hot on the heels of leader Zaw Moe of Myanmar (67-69) through the first two rounds, Maruyama edged a stroke in front of him with his rounds of 69-68-67 for his 12-under-par 204. Moe holed a wedge shot from 133 yards at the 18th to stay close. But Kim's hole-out there the next day meant so much more. With rounds of 69-73-68, he trailed Maruyama by six.

Maruyama and Moe both struggled on the final day en route to 75s and, when Kim bounced back from bogeys at 15 and 16 with the birdie chip-in at 18, he was tied for the lead with those two, who were playing 16. Moe bogeyed from the sand at 17 and Maruyama drove into the trees at 18, was over the green in three and missed the tying chip. He tied for second at 279 with Hirofumi Miyase, Brian Watts and Tateo (Jet) Ozaki, who fell just short with a closing 65.

Chunichi Crowns—¥120,000,000
Winner: Masashi Ozaki

It takes more than a touch of controversy to interfere with Masashi (Jumbo) Ozaki's comfort zone when he plays in the Chunichi Crowns, the oldest non-major on the Japan PGA Tour. Brushing off criticism from playing companion Greg Norman about his club placement behind the ball early in the final round of the 38th Chunichi Crowns, Ozaki went on to post a three-under-par 67 and win the rich tournament for the third year in a row and fifth time overall.

It was Ozaki's second win in just three starts in Japan in 1997, the 84th official title and 103rd victory of his brilliant career.

Ozaki bided his time at Nagoya as lightly regarded Taichi Teshima, winless in five seasons, stole the show with his record-tying 62 on opening day, taking a four-stroke lead over Norman, David Smail of New Zealand, Masayuki Kawamura and Ikuo Shirahama. Ozaki shot 67.

American Brian Watts, an eight-time winner in Japan since 1992, overtook

Teshima with 65–132 as Teshima settled for par after matching the record 62s of Haruo Yasuda in 1970 and Anthony Gilligan of Australia in 1995. Ozaki, Norman and two others were at 134. Ozaki then forged a stroke in front with 66, leading Norman (67) and Watts (69) by one, Teshima (70) by two.

Ozaki and Norman were tied for the lead Sunday until the eighth hole after Norman took his complaint to a tour official at the second, suggesting that Ozaki improved his lie behind the ball by pressing down with his club. Ozaki then birdied the eighth and went on to 67 while Norman was shooting 70. Watts got within a stroke on the second nine, but eventually shot 68 and took the runner-up slot two behind Ozaki at 269.

Fuji Sankei Classic—¥120,000,000
Winner: Kenichi Kuboya

Kenichi Kuboya signaled future stardom with the way he won his first title on the Japan PGA Tour. A professional for less than two years, the 25-year-old Kuboya led the strong Fuji Sankei field from start to finish and did it with Masashi Ozaki, a six-time winner of the event, and several other experienced pros on his heels. He had never played with Ozaki before.

Indicative of how much Kuboya had progressed in reaching the victory: He had never placed higher than 13th, even earlier in the year when he led the Descente Classic the first day but finished tied for 33rd. He was 113th on the 1996 money list with ¥6 million in earnings, less than a third of the winner's check of ¥21.6 million he received at the Fuji Sankei.

Kuboya was one of just five players in the 120-man field who broke par on a windy opening day on the Fuji course at Ito's Kawana Hotel in Shizuoka. He shot a three-under-par 68 to lead Nobuo Serizawa and Nobuhito Sato by one, Ozaki and Hisashi Nakase by two. Kuboya followed with 69 and opened a two-stroke edge over Ozaki on another breezy day. The cut came at eight over par, the highest of the season.

Kuboya slipped to 73 for 210 but remained a shot ahead of Ozaki (72) and Carlos Franco, who shot a day's-best 68 as he sought to better two second-place finishes earlier in the season.

Kuboya survived pressure right to the final putt, first from Yoshinori Kaneko, the No. 2 money winner in 1996, and at the end from Ozaki, who birdied the last three holes. Eventually, Kuboya sank a five-foot putt on the 18th green for 69 and a 279 total and a one-stroke win over Ozaki and Kaneko.

Japan PGA Championship—¥100,000,000
Winner: Shigeki Maruyama

It was just a matter of time. After twice failing to capitalize on third-round leads earlier in the season, Shigeki Maruyama went a different route and nailed down his first win of the year in the prestigious Japan PGA Championship. The 28-year-old Maruyama bolted from two strokes off the pace with a blistering back nine on the West course of the Central Golf Club, Ibaraki, his 67 for a 272 total giving him a two-stroke victory. It was Maruyama's fourth win in his sixth professional season.

Until the end, the leaderboard carried mostly lesser-known names. At the opposite extreme, Masashi Ozaki missed the 36-hole cut shockingly with a pair of 74s. The first day belonged to Masayuki Kawamura and Toshiaki Odate. They shot 66s to lead Taisei Inagaki by one shot, Maruyama, Australia's Peter Senior and six others by two. Odate fell back in the second round, but Kawamura, with 68 for 134, remained on top, tied for first with Shusaku Sugimoto (68-66), two ahead of Maruyama and Masanobu Kimura.

Kawamura and Sugimoto held onto their leading position with 69s for 203 totals, but were joined by Shinichi Yokota, who fired 66. Maruyama remained two back with his 69, then came alive in the last round after a par first nine, ringing up five birdies on the first six holes of the incoming side to go ahead to stay. Sugimoto shot 71 for 274 and second place, the highest finish of his career.

Ube Kosan Open—¥100,000,000
Winner: Shigenori Mori

Shigenori Mori, who has a good idea what it takes to win tournaments after 13 seasons, made a prediction as he headed into the final round of the Ube Kosan Open with a two-stroke lead and a 14-under-par score of 199. "If I can improve my score to 17-under tomorrow," he remarked, "I think that will be good enough to win."

That's exactly what he did — shot 68 — and actually it was more than enough to carry him to victory, just the second of his long career. None of the closest contenders could mount a threat and the 39-year-old Mori rolled to a four-stroke victory. He had scored his only other win in the 1995 Daiwa International.

Eagles abounded in the opening round at Ube Country Club. Kaname Yokoo, 24, had two of them plus five birdies in compiling a 63 for a one-stroke lead over Kiyoshi Murota, who had one eagle in his 64 round. Taisei Inagaki, tied for third at 65 with Toru Taniguchi and Shigemasa Higaki, matched a tour record with three eagles.

Mori blew into the picture with 64 for 131 in the second round, staking himself to a two-stroke lead over Singapore's Samson Gimson (66-67) as Yokoo and Murota faded. Mori then shot a pair of 68s to secure the victory. Higaki bounced back into second place with 64–201. Gimson was at 202 and Tsuneyuki Nakajima, a two-time winner at Ube, made his first contending appearance of the season with 64 for 203. Mori bogeyed the first hole on the last day, but had no further problems. Out in one-under 34, Mori birdied 11 and 12, then parred in with the second 68 and his 267 total. Higaki finished second with 70–271. Nakajima shot 69 and finished fourth.

Mitsubishi Galant—¥120,000,000
Winner: Masashi Ozaki

Masashi (Jumbo) Ozaki was "on the defensive" as he got off to another outstanding start in 1997. He won three times in his first six starts, piling up ¥71 million in the process, and the latter two victories were successful title defenses — the Chunichi Crowns for the third year in a row and the Mitsubishi Galant for a second straight time.

The Mitsubishi Galant lead bounced around for three days before Ozaki took charge with a closing 68 for 278, 10 under par on the Rokko course of the Taiheiyo Club at Hyogo.

First up was Keiichiro Fukabori, the Just System KSB Open winner in March. He shot a six-under 66 to lead Mitsutaka Kusakabe by a stroke. The course record fell in the second round when New Zealand rookie David Smail shot the best score of his life — 62 — to leap-frog 73 players and take the lead at 136 by one over Kaname Yokoo.

The shakeup continued in the third round, which ended with the veteran Toru Nakamura (winless since 1992), Koki Idoki and Taiwan's Lin Keng-chi tied for the lead at 208 with four players at 209 and four others, including Ozaki, at 210. Ozaki, who had shot three consecutive 70s, rumbled into the lead and to his 85th official victory with the 68 and unwilling assists from the third-round leaders, none of whom broke par. Satoshi Higashi joined Nakamura and Idoki in the runner-up spot at 280.

JCB Classic Sendai—¥100,000,000
Winner: Nobuhito Sato

Nobuhito Sato capped an eventful year with a four-stroke victory in the JCB Classic Sendai. The win, the first for the 27-year old professional, came in his first full season on the Japan PGA Tour. He had gained that opportunity by leading the money list on the secondary Growing Tour in 1996.

Sato poor-mouthed his game after the triumph at the Omotezao Kokusai Golf Club at Miyagi in Northern Japan, claiming "it was mostly putting and luck that brought me where I am." The middle rounds really insured the win. After Tsukasa Watanabe opened the tournament with a six-under-par 65, three better than Sato's start, Sato moved within a stroke of the lead in the second round.

He posted 65 for a 133 total, along with Taichi Teshima and Eduardo Herrera trailing Yoshinori Kaneko by the shot, then took charge in the third round with an eight-birdie 64 for his 197 total, racing four strokes in front of Kaneko (69) and Toshiaki Odate (65). A one-under-par 70 carried Sato to a 267 total, 17 under par, and his four-stroke victory. He was never threatened, at one point leading by six strokes, as Odate shot 71, Kaneko 74.

Naomichi Ozaki, making his first Japanese start of the year, tied for second at 201 with Toshimitsu Izawa, who closed with 67. Brother Masashi, nursing a sore left hand, tied for seventh at eight-under 276 and headed for America and the U.S. Open with a secure hold on the top spot on the money list.

Sapporo Tokyu Open—¥100,000,000
Winner: Hirofumi Miyase

The Japan PGA Tour had a first-time winner for the second week in a row when Hirofumi Miyase ended nine frustrating years of trying with a wire-to-wire victory in the Sapporo Tokyu Open in Hokkaido in mid-June. Following on the heels of Nobuhito Sato's breakthrough win in the JCB Classic Sendai, the 28-year-old Miyase overwhelmed the opposition through the first 54 holes of the Sapporo Tokyu and eased home with a par 72 and a five-stroke victory on Sapporo Kokusai Country Club's Shimamatsu course. A professional since 1989, Miyase lost full playing privileges only in 1992 in his futile quest for victory.

Miyase set up the week with his opening, five-under 67 that put him in front to stay. He led Yoshinori Kaneko, Katsunori Kuwabara and Hisao Inoue by one stroke. A 70 in the second round widened the margin to two, then over Katsumasa Miyamoto, Takeshi Oyama and Kuwabara, and Miyase moved virtually out of reach with 66 in the third round.

Frankie Minoza of the Philippines, his nearest pursuer, was four behind at 207, but fell back with 76. Hajime Meshiai, the defending champion, finished with 70 that gave him second place at 280.

Yomiuri Open—¥100,000,000
Winner: Shigeki Maruyama

Shigeki Maruyama made a victorious return after a four-week absence, picking up his second title of the season at the Yomiuri Open in his first appearance in his homeland since winning the Japan PGA Championship in mid-May.

In between, he aborted a playing visit to the United States when he came up with a shoulder injury and spent two weeks at home treating and resting it. Either leading or sitting close throughout the week at Yomiuri Country Club, Maruyama prevailed by two strokes at the end, carding a 17-under-par 267 total for his fifth career victory.

Maruyama showed no effects of the injury when he opened the tournament with a four-under 67 for a one-stroke edge over 10 players at 68. Brian Watts, the American who has established a fine career in Japan, was one of those 68 shooters and he seized first place with 66–134 in the second round. Maruyama, with 68 just one shot back, regained the lead in the third round, using five back-nine birdies to shoot a five-under 66 for 201 that created a three-stroke margin over Watts (70), Brandt Jobe (65), Frankie Minoza and Naomichi (Joe) Ozaki.

Maruyama virtually duplicated the effort in putting away the two-stroke victory. Tightening up his pursuit of Masashi Ozaki on the money list, Maruyama shot another 66 and again had five birdies on the incoming stretch, making the final one at the 18th after Naomichi Ozaki had closed to within a stroke. Admirably, he shook off a double bogey at No. 6. Ozaki, playing in just his third Japanese event of the year, shot 65 and took second place two strokes ahead of Minoza and Jobe.

Mizuno Open—¥100,000,000
Winner: Brian Watts

The "horses for courses" axiom applies nicely to Brian Watts and the Mizuno Open. The American, who found a "home" on the Japan PGA Tour, has won nine times in his five years and three of the victories have been scored on the Bijodai course of Tokinodai Country Club, site of the Mizuno Open in Ishikawa.

To no one's surprise, the 31-year-old Oklahoma State University graduate remarked after registering the third one there at the end of June, "I think Tokinodai Country Club is the best course in Japan."

Watts, a native Canadian from Montreal who won the U.S. collegiate championship in 1987, did not have an easy time of it in 1997 at Tokinodai, squeezing out a two-stroke win over Toshimitsu Izawa that came down to the final hole. His total was 10-under-par 278.

Watts stayed close with a pair of 69s in the first two rounds as Hirofumi Miyase, the Sapporo Tokyu winner two weeks earlier, and Myanmar's Zaw Moe opened on top with 65s and shared the second-round lead at 137 with Izawa, the 1995 Japan Open champion.

The cut survivors had to battle the fringe winds and rain from a typhoon. The best score was 69 and Watts' 71 propped him into first place by one stroke over Izawa, who shot 73. Watts carded his third 69 on a still-blustery final day. He led by three with three holes to play, but Izawa benefited from a two-shot swing there. Watts established the final margin when he rolled in his third birdie putt of the day from 12 feet on the 18th green.

PGA Philanthropy—¥70,000,000
Winner: Naomichi Ozaki

Naomichi (Joe) Ozaki made a major career decision in the spring of 1997, announcing that he would forsake the U.S. PGA Tour next season and play full time on the home circuit on which he had achieved most of his fame and fortune. He had returned to Japan after playing in the early months of a fourth winless season in the U.S. and validated his decision by capturing the PGA Philanthropy title in just his fourth start back in Japan.

Ozaki, at 41 the youngest of the three golfer brothers, monopolized the competition in the PGA Philanthropy tournament at the Maple Point Golf Club in Yamanashi, sharing the lead with Eiji Mizoguchi at 66 in the first round before keeping it to himself and expanding the margin the rest of the way.

Ozaki scorched Maple Point with 64 in the second round to go three in front of Yoshinori Mizumaki, increased the advantage to six over Mizoguchi in the third with 68, his third straight round without a bogey, and finished with 69 for a 17-under-par 267 total and a nine-stroke victory over Mizoguchi and Tsuyoshi Yoneyama. The bogeyless string ended as he took four, three in the last six holes when it didn't matter.

The win was the 24th of Ozaki's career, moving him just one victory away from a lifetime exemption on the Japan PGA Tour, certainly one factor that had influenced his decision to concentrate on Japan.

Yonex Open Hiroshima—¥80,000,000
Winner: Naomichi Ozaki

Naomichi (Joe) Ozaki wasted little time in achieving one of the goals he designated when he announced his intentions to direct his attention to the Japan rather than the U.S. PGA Tour from now on. In short order, Ozaki scored the 24th and 25th victories of his career on successive Sundays in July and thereby became just the sixth player in Japan PGA Tour history to earn a lifetime exemption on the circuit.

With the latter victory, a come-from-behind triumph in the Yonex Open Hiroshima, Ozaki joined brother Masashi, Tsuneyuki Nakajima, Isao Aoki, Masahiro Kuramoto and Teruo Sugihara in that exclusive group, a figurative Japanese Golf Hall of Fame. Interestingly, Masashi Ozaki has won the Yonex seven times since its inception in 1971.

Shigemasa Higaki carried a five-stroke lead into the final round at Niigata Yonex Country Club, but succumbed to the pressure of trying to gain his first victory and of going head to head with Ozaki. Naomichi chipped away at Higaki and took the lead for the first time when he birdied the par-three 16th. Higaki drove out of bounds and took a triple bogey at the 17th.

That made the wrap-up easy for Ozaki, who finished with 68 to Higaki's 76 and won with his 12-under-par 276 total. Hiroyuki Fujita slipped into second place with 68-278, a shot ahead of Higaki, who missed his best chance for that first win since his runner-up finish in the Ube Kosan in May.

For the record, Koichi Nogami and Harumitsu Hamano, neither of whom survived the second round, led the first day with 68s before Higaki fired a brilliant 64 to assume a three-stroke lead over Shoichi Kuwabara and Yeh Chang-ting of Taiwan, from whom much more would come the following week.

Nikkei Cup—¥100,000,000
Winner: Yeh Chang-ting

Another country was heard from at the Nikkei Cup. Taiwan got its first representative win of the season in Japan and its Yeh Chang-ting his first-ever victory in Japan at the Fuji Country Dejima Club in Ibaraki. The achievement took two extra holes in the first playoff of the year as Yeh defeated Tsukasa Watanabe for the title. He was the fourth foreign winner of the year.

A star of the recent past — Satoshi Higashi — emerged as the first-round leader. Higashi, winless since 1995 when he took four titles and finished second to Masashi Ozaki on the money list, put up an eight-under-par 64 that included a run of six straight birdies and took a two-stroke lead. However, with 72 in the second round, he relinquished first place to Watanabe and his 10-under-par 68-66—134. Akio Nishizawa had 10 birdies in shooting 64 for 135 and the runner-up slot.

Masashi Ozaki joined the fray in the third round, shooting 67 for 203 to tie for the lead with Watanabe (69), seeking his first win in three years, and Kiyoshi Maita (67). Only Watanabe stayed alive on the last day as Ozaki, seeking his fourth win of the year, shot 72 and Maita 71.

Watanabe's 69 for 272 was matched by Yeh's 68—272, bringing about the playoff. The Taiwanese had a two-stroke lead after he birdied the 17th, but he bogeyed the 18th as Watanabe was birdieing the 17th behind him. Watanabe drove wildly at the second playoff hole and Yeh grabbed his first title with a two-putt par.

NST Niigata Open—¥60,000,000
Winner: Kazuhiko Hosokawa

Some like it hot, and one golfer who does is Kazuhiko Hosokawa. The 26-year-old Hosokawa has won four times and every one of the first three victories — the Sanko Grand Summer and Acom International in 1996 and the KBC Augusta in 1995 — was achieved in the summer heat of August. The latest triumph was on the third of August in the NST Niigata Open, in which he jumped into the lead in the third round and fended off the charge of Hisayuki Sasaki to score a one-stroke victory with his 11-under-par 277 total.

Until Hosokawa entered the picture in the third round, the headlines went to Naoya Sugiyama, Toru Suzuki, Noboru Sugai and Hisashi Sawada, who was playing in just his fourth tournament. Sugiyama, who had never before led a tournament, did so on the first day, starting a stroke in front of Suzuki with his opening 67. He was replaced at the top by Sugai and Sawada, who shot 65 and 66, respectively, for 135s and a four-stroke advantage on Sugiyama, Suzuki and Hosokawa, who had rounds of 71-68.

Hosokawa, who finished third the previous week in the Nikkei Cup, then produced a sharp 67 in the third round and zipped past Sawada (74) and Sugai (80) into a two-stroke lead over Naoki Hattori, a fruitless campaigner since 1989. Sasaki, who has designs on trying to qualify for the U.S. PGA Tour, was five shots off the pace, but made a strong bid. In fact, Hosokawa needed his two-putt birdie on the par-five 18th to secure the one-stroke victory.

Sanko Grand Summer—¥100,000,000
Winner: Shoichi Kuwabara

Shoichi Kuwabara joined the ranks of 1997's first-time winners in Japan when he put two hot rounds together at the end of the week and won the Sanko Grand Summer crown. Kuwabara, the eighth newcomer of the year to enter the winner's circle, was floundering in 28th place after 36 holes, then shot 64 and 66, each day's lowest scores, back to back, to gain a one-stroke victory over Taichi Teshima and Masashi Shimada, the overnight leader, with his 17-under-par 271 total.

Low scoring was the norm all week. Sixty-one players were under par at Sanko 72 Country Club, Gunma Prefecture, the first day with two 1997 winners — Nobuhito Sato (JCB Classic Sendai) and Yeh Chang-ting (Nikkei Cup) — in front at six-under 66 with Tsukasa Watanabe and Satoshi Higashi. A new cast took over in the third round. Kiyoshi Maita went two strokes in front when he shot 66 for 133. Shimada seized the runner-up spot with an erratic 67 — seven birdies, three bogeys. Kuwabara, then eight back at

70-71–141, made his big charge as the 64 jumped him into fourth place, four behind Shimada's 201.

Kuwabara caught up quickly on the last day as he birdied four of the first five holes. He ran off three more birdies and had a two-stroke lead until he bogeyed the 18th. Both Shimada and Teshima then could tie with birdies there, but Shimada overshot the green and Teshima missed his vital putt from 20 feet.

Acom International—¥100,000,000
Winner: Kazuo Kanayama

The parade of new champions in Japan continued at the Acom International, the distinctive tournament that is scored with a modified version of the Stableford system, and for the newest member of the club, it was a very long time in coming.

When Kazuo Kanayama defeated Colombia's Eduardo Herrera on the second hole of a playoff, he ended a victory drought of 22 years. He was the ninth first-time winner of the season.

Considerable jockeying transpired in the early rounds. Shingo Katayama, also a non-winner, piled up 17 points with an eagle and six birdies at the Seve Ballesteros Golf Club in Fukushima to lead by three after the first round, then fell three points behind Hiroyuki Fujita and his 25 points after the second round. Kanayama then had 23 points and Herrera, thanks to making two eagle deuces, a rare feat, had 20.

Though adding only nine points the next day, Kanayama moved into the lead at 32 as Fujita drew a blank and remained at 25. Herrera picked up 11 and climbed into second place with Tateo (Jet) Ozaki.

The outcome narrowed to a duel between Kanayama and Herrera on the final holes. Kanayama cut the South American's four-point lead in half with a two-putt birdie at the par-five 16th. Both then bogeyed the 17th and, at the par-three 18th, Kanayama holed from 15 feet, the two points for the birdie forging the tie at 41. They both parred the first extra hole, then Kanayama birdied the second — the 18th again — to win the tournament.

KBC Augusta—¥100,000,000
Winner: Masashi Ozaki

Masashi (Jumbo) Ozaki, a professional baseball player as a young man, raised his "batting average" on the Japan PGA Tour to .400, an impressive figure in either sport, with his fourth victory in just 10 starts in 1997.

Returning after a month away from competition, Ozaki ran roughshod over the field in the KBC Augusta tournament and steamrollered to a 12 stroke victory, the biggest margin of the season. His score was 266, 22 under par on the Keya Golf Club at Shima in Fukuoka. It was Ozaki's third successful title defense of the year and third KBC Augusta victory.

The 50-year-old Ozaki was on medication for an attack of the gout, but one would never know it the way he played from the word go. Ozaki launched his run to his 86th official victory with a seven-under-par 65 and never looked back. American Brandt Jobe and Kunihiko Masuda were second at 67, not realizing that even that good a score was hopeless. Ozaki then followed with three consecutive 67s. The first extended his lead to six strokes over Hiroyuki Fujita, Katsunari Kuwabara and Masuda. Takaaki Fukuzawa shot 65 in the third round to reduce Ozaki's margin to five. No one else was even near Fukuzawa and, when he dropped to 74 on the last day, Ozaki's last 67 created the final margin and the 105th victory of his career. Taichi Teshima also shot 67 and tied Fukuzawa for second place. Ozaki had six birdies and a bogey at the par-three 12th that ended a 24-hole stretch in which he did not give up a stroke.

Japan Match Play—¥80,000,000
Winner: Shigeki Maruyama

Shigeki Maruyama enhanced his hold on second place in the money standings and his fast-rising prestige when he won the Japan Match Play. In landing his third victory of the year, the reigning Japan PGA champion moved within ¥11 million of top-running Masashi Ozaki, who elected to skip the Match Play event, one of three recognized major tournaments on the circuit.

Maruyama's victim in the final match at the rain-swept Nidom Classic course in Hokkaido was American expatriate Peter Teravainen, the 1996 Japan Open champion, whose Descente Classic victory in April helped him qualify for the Match Play as one of the current leading 31 money winners.

Maruyama took Teravainen's measure, 3 and 2, in a back-and-forth match. Maruyama built a 4-up lead over the first 18 holes, only to have Teravainen catch him in the afternoon with four front-nine birdies and take the lead for the only time with an eagle at the 12th hole. The 41-year-old American then put his tee shot in the water at the par-three 13th. Maruyama birdied the 14th and the match ended two holes later after Teravainen drove out of bounds at the 15th and three-putted the 16th.

Maruyama's march to the finals included victories over Eiji Mizoguchi, 21 holes; Hirofumi Miyase, 3 and 2; Keiichiro Fukabori, 2 up, and Tateo (Jet) Ozaki, 4 and 3. Teravainen's victims were Shigenori Mori, 3 and 2; Masanobu Kimura, 1 up, 19 holes; Satoshi Higashi, 6 and 5, and Shoichi Kuwabara, 5 and 4.

Suntory Open—¥100,000,000
Winner: Hiroyuki Fujita

Hiroyuki Fujita, a career non-winner, stood tall against the hands-on challenge of Masashi Ozaki, who was playing on his home course, and walked off with a convincing, three-stroke victory in the venerable Suntory Open. The 28-year-old from Fukuoka had built a four-stroke lead over the first three days and finished with a par 72 at the Narashino Country Club course for his 14-under-par 274 total. Ozaki, seeking his fifth win of the season, had to settle for second place at 277.

Masashi's brother, Tateo (Jet), who won at Narashino twice in the 1980s, started with an eight-birdie 65 and a one-stroke lead over Hawaiian David Ishii, Tatsuo Takasaki and defending champion Hajime Meshiai. Tateo's afterburners failed the rest of the way and Fujita went in front with his second 68. At 136, Fujita led Masashi Ozaki, Takasaki, Kiyoshi Murota and Teruo Sugihara, the age-defying 59-year-old.

Fujita extended a bogey-less streak through 54 holes as he established the four-stroke margin over Mitsutaka Kusakabe with 66 for 202. Masashi lurked at 207 and made enough birdies Sunday, five in a row beginning at the 12th, but three bogeys and a double bogey cancelled them out and he shot 70 for the 277 and second place. With the comfortable par, Fujita became the 10th first-time winner of the season, his sixth on the tour.

ANA Open—¥100,000,000
Winner: Shinichi Yokota

New names kept popping up at the top on the 1997 Japan PGA Tour. The extraordinary number of first-time winners reached 11 in just 25 tournaments as Shinichi Yokota, a five-year man on the tour, came up with an impressive, three-stroke victory in the ANA Open in Hokkaido in late September.

A more likely victor would have been Masashi Ozaki, who has won the ANA seven times since 1972, but he had to settle for a sixth-place finish with Hajime Meshiai, who had led after the first round, scoring two eagles en route to a 66 as he sought his first victory of the year.

Meshiai, 43, whose biggest achievement in 1997 was to win the Japanese berth in the rich, four-player Andersen Consulting World Championship, led Yokota, Shinichi Akiba and Satoshi Higashi by two strokes.

Yokota was strongly in the picture the rest of the way. He fired 65 in the second round on Sapporo Golf Club's Wattsu course and went two strokes in front of Akiba, three ahead of Myanmar's Zaw Moe, as Meshiai took 73 and dropped into a tie for fourth with defending champion Carlos Franco and four others.

Akiba, also winless on the circuit, overtook Yokota in the third round with 70 to Yokota's 72 and the two carried 11-under-par 205s into the final round. The 25-year-old Yokota responded to the challenge with 68 for his winning 273 total, while Akiba went the other way with 76. Tateo (Jet) Ozaki (68), a frequent contender but non-winner in 1997, vaulted into a second-place tie with Moe (70).

Jun Classic—¥110,000,000
Winner: Eduardo Herrera

It wasn't that Eduardo Herrera hadn't won before in Japan, but the odds were clearly against him as he tried to capture his first victory of the year. The Colombian regular on the Japan PGA Tour since 1993 went into the final round of the Jun Classic at the Rope Club in Tochigi one stroke behind and playing with leader Masashi (Jumbo) Ozaki, the defending champion and five-time winner of the tournament.

Aided and abetted by an unnatural collapse by Ozaki, Herrera beat those odds and landed that title with a final-round 70 and a 12-under-par 276 total for his third win in Japan.

Herrera, who won the season-ending Daikyo Open in 1996 but lost in a playoff in August in the Acom International, made his presence known but not particularly felt in the Jun Classic the second day when he shot 66 and moved into a first-place tie at 137 with Shigeki Maruyama, second on the money list with three victories, and one stroke ahead of Ozaki, the money leader with four wins, and Carlos Franco, his fellow South American, who had led the first day with 66.

Ozaki shot a mixed-bag 67 in the third round to take a one-stroke lead at 205 over Herrera (69) as Maruyama slumped to 74. Ozaki's card showed an eagle, six birdies, a bogey, a double bogey and just nine pars. He four-putted a green. Perhaps the inconsistency was an indication of what was to come at the end. While the 32-year-old Herrera was accumulating his 70, Ozaki bungled the last two holes, took 75 and dropped into a four-way tie for fourth. Toshiaki Odate took the runner-up slot with 69–277.

Japan Open—¥120,000,000
Winner: Craig Parry

Craig Parry drops into Japan occasionally, especially for the big-money events in the autumn, as he globe-trots through his effective international career. He visited in 1989 and won the Bridgestone Open. This year Parry came for the Japan Open, the only foreigner in the field other than the group of regulars from all parts of the world. It was a most-worthwhile trip as Parry made off with the championship.

Coming from four strokes off the lead in the final round, the stocky little Australian registered a one-shot victory with his two-over-par 286 total at Koga Golf Club in Fukuoka Prefecture. Now, the 31-year-old Parry can play in Japan almost any time he wants thanks to the 10-year exemption that accompanied the ¥24 million first prize.

For much of the time that week, it had looked as though Masashi (Jumbo) Ozaki was on the verge of snagging his sixth Japan Open title. Shaking off a disastrous finish in the previous week's Jun Classic, Masashi shot 67 in the opening round at Koga and shared the lead with Frankie Minoza of the Philippines, a four-time winner in Japan.

Sitting at 69 were Tateo (Jet) Ozaki, Australia's Peter Senior, Yoshinori Mizumaki and Eduardo Herrera, the Jun winner. Masashi shot a one-over 72 in strong winds on the second day and led by one over brother Tateo with his 139. Minoza had a 74 and slipped to third at 141.

Enter a new leader, Seiki Okuda, who said "(it) is such a scary tournament that I myself wonder how I was able to win (in 1993)." The 37-year-old veteran was the only player under par after rounds of 70-72-70–212 as Masashi Ozaki stumbled to 77–216, tied for fifth with Parry, who shot 70 after two earlier 73s. In between were Minoza at 73–214, Eiji Mizoguchi (68) and Tateo Ozaki (75) at 215.

Parry took an early bogey in the final round, then ran off nothing but pars until he birdied the 16th and 18th to nail the victory. Masashi had a playoff chance in hand until he bogeyed the 18th for 71–287 and dropped into a second-place tie with Okuda (75) and Minoza (73).

Tokai Classic—¥110,000,000
Winner: Brandt Jobe

Two of the most successful players in America in 1996 — Player-of-the-Year Tom Lehman and U.S. Open Champion Steve Jones — arrived from the U.S. for the Tokai Classic, but wound up playing second fiddle to another American, lesser-known Brandt Jobe, at week's end.

Jobe, who has played almost all of his tournament golf in Japan since getting an exemption as the Asia Tour champion in 1995, picked up his second title on the Japan PGA Tour when he defeated fellow American Brian Watts in the season's second playoff. Jobe won the 1995 Mitsubishi Galant with a tour-record 262.

Foreign professionals dominated the Tokai in 1997. The 31-year-old Jobe, an Oklahoma-born collegiate All-American at UCLA, shared the first-round lead at Miyoshi Country Club with Naoya Sugiyama. They shot four-under-par 68s on Miyoshi's West course and led Tsuneyuki Nakajima, suffering through a meager season, by one stroke.

Canadian Rick Todd then had a day in the sun, taking a one-shot lead with 67–139 as Jobe had 72–140 and Sugiyama 74–142. Watts, the Mizuno Open winner in June, joined Jobe in the runner-up slot with 68, and the two Americans moved into the lead together in the third round with 69s for 209 totals as Todd crashed with 83.

Jobe and Watts both had 69s again on the last day for 278 totals, distancing themselves from the rest of the field — Eiji Mizoguchi and Toru Taniguchi tied for third at 283 — and bringing about the playoff. It ended quickly at the 18th green on the first extra hole. Jobe holed a 10-foot putt for birdie and the win after Watts missed his birdie try from 33 feet. Lehman and Jones finished eight shots off the pace.

Golf Digest Tournament—¥100,000,000
Winner: Brandt Jobe

From Sunday to Sunday, it was another playoff and another victory for American Brandt Jobe as titles fell into foreign hands for the fourth week in a row. Jobe, who defeated Brian Watts in overtime in the Tokai Classic, picked off veteran Toru Suzuki when the Golf Digest Tournament went extra holes for the first time since 1981.

The leaderboards were all red from the start as the field blitzed the Tome Country Club course with birdies and eagles. It started with Tsuyoshi Yoneyama in the first round. Yoneyama, although nursing a flu-like illness, tied the course record with a nine-under-par 62 and took a two-stroke lead over Hajime Meshiai and Kiyoshi Maita with three others at 65.

Yoneyama, a non-winner over his 10 years on the tour, followed in the second round with 66 for 128, widening his margin to four over Hiroyuki Fujita, the Suntory champion, five over Meshiai and three others. The to ranks shuffled drastically on the third day as Suzuki shot 64 to take the lead and Jobe, nine off the pace after 36 holes, got back in it with a 63 that put him just two behind. Yoneyama (71) was one back with Shusaku Sugimoto.

Jobe, a Colorado resident when he is in America, fashioned 67 in the final round, polishing it off with a two-foot birdie putt on the 18th green. Suzuki followed him in with 69 for his 267 to go into a playoff. As he did the previous week, Jobe finished the job quickly with a 10-foot birdie putt at 18, the first extra hole. The ¥18 million check lifted Jobe to third place on the money list behind Masashi Ozaki and Shigeki Maruyama, who did not play.

Bridgestone Open—¥120,000,000
Winner: Masashi Ozaki

Masashi (Jumbo) Ozaki had done everything but win his fifth tournament of the Japan PGA Tour season in his four starts since putting No. 4 on his record — two seconds, a fourth and a sixth — but one poor round had kept him out of the winner's circle.

When Ozaki returned to action in the Bridgestone Open after a two-week hiatus, he avoided any high scores, but still needed to make up five strokes in the final round. Which he did as he annexed the fifth victory and ran his official total to 87 and his overall number to 106. He mustered a closing six-under par 66 for 273 and a one-stroke victory. Interestingly, he had taken time off just before his fourth win, too.

Brother Tateo (Jet), who had been frustrated time and again as he sought his first victory in four years, was the major victim of Masashi's charge. Tateo had led the tournament after the second and third rounds as he shot 68-66-68 for a 202 total at Sodegaura Country Club, Chiba, after Masashi had started the tournament on top with Masatoshi Horikawa at 66. After 54 holes, though, rounds of 70-71 had brought him to 207. Shigeki Maruyama, the Bridgestone champion in 1995 and 1996, had a shot at a three-peat after shooting 64–205.

Spurred by an eagle at the second hole, Masashi birdied the 18th for the closing 66. When Tateo and Maruyama reached there shortly thereafter, both men needed eagles to catch Masashi but had to settle for birdies. Maruyama hit the pin with a bunker shot and Tateo missed a chip from the back of the green.

Philip Morris Championship—¥200,000,000
Winner: Brian Watts

It seemed to take the likes of Masashi (Jumbo) Ozaki to keep the titles out of the hands of the foreign professionals in the autumn segment of the season. Ozaki had broken a four-tournament streak of non-Japanese winners the week before at the Bridgestone, but American Brian Watts restored the foreign domination at the Philip Morris Championship with his second victory of the year.

Watts, a playoff loser to Brandt Jobe three weeks earlier, commanded the

Philip Morris the final two rounds and closed out his 10th victory in Japan with 70 for a 280 total, eight under par, and a two-stroke final edge.

Veteran Seiki Okuda, 37, who had made a strong run at his second Japan Open championship a month earlier, tried again in the Philip Morris, one of the two richest tournaments in Japan with ¥200 million purses. He, Eiji Mizoguchi and Taichi Teshima shot opening 69s at the ABC Golf Club, Hyogo, with the field bunched closely behind.

Roger Mackay, the 41-year-old Australian regular in Japan, seized first place in the second round with 67–140, four under par, with Americans in hot pursuit. Pete Jordan was at 141, Watts and Todd Hamilton at 143, with Mizoguchi and Russ Cochran at 144 with, among six others, Masashi Ozaki.

Watts took over in the third round. His bogey-free 67 put him in first place with a three-stroke lead over Maruyama (69), Mackay (73) and Jordan (72), and his subsequent 70–280 total gave him the final two-stroke margin over Kaname Yokoo, 25, the best finish of his young career for the former collegiate champion. Jordan and Mackay had 70s for 283 while Maruyama took a 71 for 284.

Sumitomo Visa Taiheiyo Masters—¥150,000,000
Winner: Lee Westwood

Lee Westwood, clearly a bright new star on the European PGA Tour horizon, reinforced his credentials in the eyes of Japanese observers when he successfully defended his championship in the Sumitomo Visa Taiheiyo Masters, the grandfather of the big-money late-autumn events on the Japan PGA Tour which draw strong international fields.

Westwood protected a three-stroke 54-hole lead with a one-under-par 71 that held off late charges by Ozaki brothers Naomichi and Masashi, the latter a two-time winner of the 25-year-old event. Westwood's final score was 272, 16 under par, one better than the Ozakis'.

A sparkling performer for the Europeans in their Ryder Cup victory in September, Westwood had won the Benson and Hedges Malaysian Open on the Asian Tour and the Volvo Masters, the season-ending tournament in Europe earlier in the season.

The field took advantage of rain-softened greens on the Taiheiyo Club's Gotemba course with 45 of the 87 starters breaking par in the first round. Australian Peter McWhinney, Yoshinori Mizumaki and Yoshitaka Yamamoto led the way with 66s. Westwood avoided a bad start when he birdied his last five holes for 68 and joined an elite pack at the top of the standings when he shot another 68.

Naomichi Ozaki led with 67-68–135, but with Westwood at 136 were brother Masashi, American star Mark O'Meara, Irish Ryder Cupper Darren Clarke, former winner Roger Mackay and Mizumaki. Naomichi shot a bogey free 65.

Westwood greased the way for his victory when he pieced together a sterling, seven-birdie 65 and charged to a three-stroke lead over Naomich Ozaki with his 15-under-par 201. Masashi Ozaki, O'Meara, Clarke and Taiwan's Chen Tze-chung finished at 205, still hopeful.

In fact, O'Meara overtook the British standout at one point, but two late bogeys consigned him to a tie for fourth with Toru Suzuki. A bogey at 17 spoiled Naomichi Ozaki's chances and his brother forced Westwood to shape out a careful par at 18 for the win when Masashi eagled the home hole.

Dunlop Phoenix Tournament—¥200,000,000
Winner: Tom Watson

Tom Watson was so elated with his second victory in the Dunlop Phoenix Tournament in mid-November that he drew upon an apt figure of speech to describe the accomplishment. "It just shows this old bottle of wine hasn't turned to vinegar yet," said the 48-year-old American great after easing home with a two-stroke victory in the Japan PGA Tour's second of two ¥200,000,000 tournaments, the richest of the season.

Watson's win, 17 years after his first in the Dunlop Phoenix and five years after his last victory in Asia in the Hong Kong Open, ended Masashi (Jumbo) Ozaki's mastery at Phoenix Country Club after three straight triumphs, although the Japanese star took a good run at the title.

Watson made his key move in the second round, coming up with eight birdies that translated into 65 and the lead at 135 as first-day leader Retief Goosen of South Africa (66) slipped to 72–138, tying for third with Frankie Minoza of the Philippines and Keiichiro Fukabori behind Australia's Craig Parry (70-66), who hadn't played in more than a month since winning the Japan Open.

At the end of 54 holes, Watson (70) and Parry (69) were tied for the lead eight-under-par at 205 with Masashi Ozaki threatening in third place at 208.

Shaky putting led to another 70 and 275 total for Watson, but it was good enough to hold off Naomichi (Joe) Ozaki's blazing finish with 65–277 as both Parry and Masashi Ozaki came a cropper late in the final round. Parry (73–278) double-bogeyed the par-three 17th and Masashi Ozaki took three consecutive bogeys on the second nine that led to 71 and a fourth-place tie with Spaniard Jose Maria Olazabal. The win was the 42nd of Watson's career.

Casio World Open—¥150,000,000
Winner: Mitsutaka Kusakabe

Just when it was looking like Mitsutaka Kusakabe was headed for the qualifying tournament for the 1998 Japan PGA Tour, he earned his way instead into the exclusive Japan Series of Golf field by winning the Casio World Open. Just when it was looking like Masashi (Jumbo) Ozaki would finally win that tournament and add a sixth 1997 title to his record, he blew the lead with bogeys on the last three holes and finished fifth.

Kusakabe, who had won just ¥13 million through a disappointing season after winning the Pepsi Ube in 1996, birdied the final hole for 70, a 10-under-par 278 total and a one-stroke victory over Naomichi (Joe) Ozaki, Hirofumi Miyase and Keiichiro Fukabori.

The Ozaki brothers, Hitoshi Kato and American Chris Smith, a three-time winner on the Nike Tour, started the Casio event in front of the pack with

67s as most of the top foreign players who competed in the Dunlop Phoenix the week before had gone. Naomichi Ozaki birdied four of the first five holes and took a two-stroke lead in the second round with 68–135 in his bid for his third win of the year.

Kusakabe entered the picture there, also shooting 68 for 137 and second place. He remained in that position with 71–208 on a blustery third day, but then trailed Miyase (68–207), who replaced Naomichi Ozaki on top. Naomichi and Masashi were well-positioned for the final round, though, with 209 totals.

Kusakabe rang up four birdies and two bogeys, the decisive birdie coming when he two-putted the 18th green to clinch the victory. Masashi Ozaki made four birdies on the first 13 holes to take the lead and was ahead by two before the concluding three bogeys. Miyase shot 72, Naomichi Ozaki 70 and Fukabori 69 in tying for second.

Japan Series of Golf—¥100,000,000
Winner: Shigeki Maruyama

It had been a long season. Masashi (Jumbo) Ozaki's 50-year-old back was aching badly, so the Japan PGA Tour's leading money winner, a five-time victor during the season, withdrew before his final scheduled 1997 start in the Japan Series of Golf, which he had won the last two years and seven times since 1971. Obviously, he thought his ¥50 million lead was safe.

Not quite so, as it turned out, when No. 2 Shigeki Maruyama, feeling so badly with a cold and a stomach ailment that he thought he might have to drop out himself, soldiered through it with a strong 67 and won the tournament by two strokes. Interestingly, the ¥30 million check for his fourth win of the season and seventh of his short career moved Maruyama close enough to Ozaki that a win in the Daikyo Open finale the next week would give him the coveted money title.

Keiichiro Fukabori, winner of the Just System KSB Open in March, paced the elite field of 30 top winners and money leaders with his opening-round, six-under-par 65, one in front of Hirofumi Miyase and two ahead of Tateo (Jet) Ozaki and Mitsuo Harada.

Craig Parry, the Japan Open champion who made a strong bid in the Dunlop Phoenix two weeks earlier, then roared three strokes in front with a dazzling, nine-under-par 62 for a 130 total. Maruyama did almost as well, climbing into second place with Eduardo Herrera with 63–133. Herrera had 65.

A battle royal in the final round was in prospect after Parry (71), Maruyama (68), Herrera (68) and Fukabori (66) wound up in a four-way tie for the lead at 201 after the third round at the Tokyo Yomiuri Country Club. The ailing Maruyama emerged the victor with a stout 67 — five birdies and a bogey — for 268, finishing two shots ahead of Tateo Ozaki, who raced home with 65.

Daikyo Open—¥120,000,000
Winner: Kenichi Kuboya

Most eyes were on Shigeki Maruyama at the start of the Daikyo Open, the 1997 finale, as he launched his last-ditch effort to snatch the money title from Masashi Ozaki. By the last day, with Maruyama's victory hopes gone, attention had shifted to a crowded leaderboard. Young Kenichi Kuboya broke away from the pack that day to make it two wins in his second tour year.

The 25-year-old birdied two of his last three holes and needed them to edge Katsunori Kuwabara and Brian Watts by a stroke with his 65 and 21-under-par 263 total, the lowest score of the year. Kuwabara shot the week's second 61, while the American, Watts, shot 65 as he solidified his third-place finish on the money list with ¥111,153,198. Maruyama, who ran out of gas after an opening 66, tied for 20th place.

David Ishii, the Hawaiian-born American who was the tour's No. 1 performer in 1987, made an early run at Okinawa's Daikyo Country Club. Ishii, a 14-time winner in Japan who hasn't won since the 1994 Suntory Open, shared the first-round lead with once-promising Ryoken (Ricky) Kawagishi, a non-winner since 1995. They had 63s, Kuwabara 65.

The Hawaiian standout added a 66 for 129, on top alone and a stroke ahead of Kuboya (64), but fell back into a four-way tie at 198 with Watts (66), Kuboya (68) and Toru Suzuki, who had the initial, course/tour-record 61 that day. Ishii shot 69. By then, Maruyama was five back and finished with 72 for 275.

Omega Tour

Asian Honda Classic—US$300,000
Winner: Tiger Woods

Tiger Woods had been invited to come help open the 1997 season of the Omega Tour in Thailand, the homeland of his mother. He arrived to a welcome that some said outdid those that greeted Queen Elizabeth II and President Bill Clinton, and he was honored by the Thai government. Then he proceeded to turn the Asian Honda Classic into a one-man show.

A problem with the heat did set Woods back briefly. He had to withdraw from the pro-am after 13 holes, and he trailed by four strokes in the first round. Then he was on his way. He played the par-72 Thai Country Club in rounds of 70, 64, 66 and 68 for a 20-under 268 total and a 10-stroke win. He led by six strokes going into the final round, and he was five under par for the day until the 17th when he took his only bogey of the day. Second place went to Korea's Mo Joong-kyung (68–278).

"I've not won in this fashion for a long time, not since my junior or amateur days," Woods said. "My swing was actually not quite there today. It was a little loose. But I made some key putts, which is what wins tournaments."

Vietnam Open—US$200,000
Winner: Andrew Bonhomme

With the gift of Chang Tse-peng's big error, Australia's Andrew Bonhomme scored his first Omega Tour win in the Vietnam Open at the Vietnam Golf and Country Club in Ho Chi Minh City.

Chang, from Taiwan, who led the tournament through the second and third rounds, came to the par-four 14th hole in the final round leading by one stroke. He drove into a fairway bunker, then tried to hit a four iron out to the green. His ball hit a tree and came down well short. He tried for the green again and the ball hit another tree and bounced out of bounds. "That was a stupid shot," Chang said. "I wanted to play safe, but then I changed my mind and decided to attack the green." He took a quadruple-bogey eight.

Chang stormed back and played the last four holes in four under par, including an eagle at the par-five 17th, where he hit a four-iron second shot to three feet. Bonhomme chipped to two feet and birdied. Then, at the 18th, after watching Chang hole a 15-footer for birdie, Bonhomme faced a 12-footer for a par and the win. "I didn't feel comfortable over that last putt," Bonhomme said. "Luckily, a leaf blew in my way and I stepped away. I felt more confident when I addressed the ball again." He sank the putt, wrapping up rounds of 68, 70, 66 and 69 for a 273 total, 15 under par, for a one-stroke victory.

London Myanmar Open—US$200,000
Winner: Boonchu Ruangkit

Big John Senden, 6-foot-3 Australian, streaked to four birdies over the last four holes for 66 to catch Thailand's Boonchu Ruangkit at 15-under-par 273 in the London Myanmar Open at City Golf Resort in Yangon. Boonchu, who closed with four straight pars for 68, then needed some brilliance of his own.

On the first playoff hole, Boonchu lay two in a shallow fairway bunker at the 527-yard 18th hole, just 50 yards from the green. He came out with a low running nine iron that stopped just two feet from the cup. "I think people thought it was a lucky shot, but it was intentional," he said. Senden was in the same bunker, and came out to 12 feet. He just missed his birdie attempt, and Boonchu tapped in to become the first to do two things on the Omega Tour: successfully defend a title and win four events.

Boonchu, who started the final day one stroke behind leader Jamnian Chitprasong of Thailand, bogeyed No. 1, then birdied the next three and Nos. 8 and 9 as well. He held a three-shot lead through the turn over Jamnian, Senden and Australian Scott Laycock. Jamnian dropped to fourth place and Laycock to 13th, both with closing 72s.

DFS Galleria Guam Open—US$250,000
Winner: Gerry Norquist

American Gerry Norquist chalked up his third Omega Tour victory in the DFS Galleria Guam Open, but that might have been the least of his worries those mid-April days. First, there was Typhoon Isa, which reduced the tournament to three rounds, and then there were several minor early morning earthquakes on the third day. "I am very surprised to win," Norquist said. "I wasn't feeling particularly good at the start of the round. But I managed to be patient and stay focused."

Norquist, who gave away a victory to Craig Parry with a shaky finish in the Satelindo Indonesian Open in April, this time got a similar gift in return. Norquist started the final round four strokes behind Taiwan's Tsai Chi-huang, who was leading at five under par. Then Tsai shot 76. Norquist, meanwhile, closed in on him with 33 on the first nine, getting to within one stroke.

"I was not feeling so confident about my game," Norquist confessed. "I was almost laughing at the turn when I was three under for my round." The big turnaround came at the 11th hole. Tsai hit his drive out of bounds and suffered a double-bogey seven, and Norquist was ahead by two. He shot 74, 69 and 67 for a 210 total, six under par for the abbreviated tournament, winning by three over American Mike Cunning, who closed with 69.

Satelindo Indonesia Open—US$250,000
Winner: Craig Parry

When a man loses six balls in the pro-am, this is not considered a good sign. "It didn't do much for my confidence," Australia's Craig Parry said, "but it was the first time I ever played the course, and I wasn't too concerned." It seemed he might have been along the way. In his 67-70-74-69–280 total, eight under par at Jagorawi Golf and Country Club, he didn't lead until he birdied No. 13 in the final round while American Gerry Norquist was unraveling and slipping out of the lead.

Norquist birdied the first two holes of the final round and got to 10 under par for the tournament by No. 8. He led Parry by three strokes and South Africa's Des Terblanche by five. Then it was all over. Norquist caught a fairway bunker and double-bogeyed No. 9, then double-bogeyed the 11th and fell into a tie with Parry and Terblanche at six under.

Parry took the lead for the first time in the last round with a birdie at the 13th, and with five holes to play he led Norquist and Terblanche by two. He won by two over Terblanche, who closed with 70, and by three over Norquist (74). "I just feel frustrated," Norquist said. "I handed someone a present today."

Sabah Masters—US$200,000
Winner: Des Terblanche

Any man who birdies the same hole four times in the same day deserves to win, and that was South Africa's Des Terblanche in the Sabah Masters. The hole was the 513-yard 18th at the Sabah Golf and Country Club in Malaysia. His first birdie came at the end of regulation, completing a six-under-par 66 that gave him the lead with a seven-under-par 281 total. Then came the chase to catch him.

Singapore's Mardan Mamat got to eight under par, but then took seven on the par-four 16th hole. He shot 74 and dropped to a tie for fourth place. Thailand's Thammanoon Sriroj caught Terblanche with a 50-yard chip shot to a foot for 73. They played the 18th three more times in the playoff, and Terblanche finally broke the stalemate by dropping a 20-foot putt for another birdie and Thammanoon missed his putt from 10 feet. "I never thought about winning the whole way around," Terblanche said.

SingTel Ericsson Singapore Open—US$500,000
Winner: Zaw Moe

The excitement finally got to Myanmar's Zaw Moe at the 18th hole, where a 10-foot birdie putt stood between him and a victory on the Omega Tour. He charged the putt three feet past the hole, then missed coming back. "I got a little excited," Moe said. "I should have lagged it." He bogeyed, but it was a luxury he could afford. The closing par-72 at Jurong Country Club left him at 11-under-par 277 for a three-stroke victory over American Fran Quinn in the SingTel Ericsson Singapore Open.

Moe was nervous early, too. He started the last round with a four-shot lead over a number of challengers, but the lead shrunk to two coming down the second nine. Then he righted himself, birdied the 15th and 16th holes, and had a four-stroke cushion for the close. "I really struggled for much of the day," he said, "and only got my swing going on the 15th." This was Moe's first win since 1993.

Philip Morris Asia Cup—US$500,000
Winner: Park No-seok

Korea's Park No-seok admitted he was just trying to lag that putt at the final hole. "I just wanted to two-putt," he said. "I was really gearing myself for a playoff." The 25-footer found the cup for a birdie, and he had a one-stroke victory over countryman Park Nam-sin in the Philip Morris Asia Cup.

Their duel made it a two-man race at Woo Jung Hills Country Club at A-San City, Korea. Park No-seok had rounds of 71, 71, 66 and 71 for a 279 total. He edged into a one-stroke lead at the turn, and before he could really pull away, Park Nam-sin caught him with an eagle at the 11th. They matched each other the rest of the way, with Park No-seok getting a big lift with nothing more dramatic than a par at the par-three 16th.

"That hole had been my worst hole all week," he said, "so to make three there at such an important moment felt so good. I was really nervous all day."

Asia Pacific Ericsson Masters—US$500,000
Winner: Darren Cole

The Asia Pacific Ericsson Masters essentially was the story of two missed putts. Australia's Darren Cole missed a three-footer on the final hole that would have won for him in regulation, and then he won in a playoff minutes later when India's Jeev Milkha Singh missed a four-footer for par on the second extra hole.

"I was handed a second chance," said Cole. "I felt the pressure when I missed that putt on the last for the win." It was a question of nerves for Singh, too, when he missed the four-footer. "I made a big mistake," he said. "I rushed the putt. I felt very uncomfortable over the putt."

Singh seemed on the way to his fourth Omega Tour win, leading Cole by three strokes at the turn. Then he went three over par on the second nine. India's Arjun Atwal looked like the winner before that. He led by one stroke through the third round, then closed with 76. Cole, who played the Bintan Lagoon course in rounds of 72, 64, 68 and 71 for a 275 total, 13 under par, had entered the tournament on a hunch — his wife's. "I wasn't sure I was going to play," he said. "And my wife said that if I played, I would probably win."

Mild Seven Kuala Lumpur Open—US$300,000
Winner: Charlie Wi

"I could feel Zhang breathing down my neck," Charlie Wi was saying. "I know what he is capable of and just how well he can putt." Actually, not to worry. China's Zhang Lian-wei never got closer than two strokes down the home stretch, and when he bogeyed the 14th and 16th holes, Wi coasted in for a four-stroke victory in the Mild Seven Kuala Lumpur Open in Malaysia. Wi, scoring his first victory on the Omega Tour, played the Saujana Golf and Country Club course in rounds of 67, 73, 69 and 68 for a 277 total, 11 under par. Zhang (67) and Taiwan's Lu Wen-teh (69) tied for second place at 281.

Wi had to wait for the victory, sitting out a storm for over an hour and stewing over the thought of success being at hand. "I was thinking about all the things that could go wrong," he said. "I would then start thinking something like, if I win, how it would change my life." The daydreaming proved expensive. When play resumed, he immediately bogeyed the eighth hole. He bounced back and birdied the ninth, and he was relieved. Wi said he had been off his game. "The thing that saved me this week was my putter," he said.

Yokohama Singapore PGA—US$200,000
Winner: Prayad Marksaeng

The Yokohama Singapore PGA was pretty much up for grabs all the way. First, Thailand's Thammanoon Sriroj led through the first and second rounds by four strokes at the halfway point. He was tied by countryman Prayad Marksaeng in the third round, and down the stretch Indonesia's Kasiadi barged into the race. It came down to the final hole, and Prayad made the par he needed to for a one-stroke win over Kasiadi on rounds of 71, 71, 65 and 70 for a 277 total, 11 under par at Raffles Country Club.

Prayad hit a two iron off the tee on the 18th hole for safety but caught the left rough, and then hit an eight iron to within 15 feet of the pin. This was the crucial moment. Kasiadi had already parred the 18th and Thammanoon had bogeyed. Prayad needed two putts to win. The shaky putter that had troubled him all week left him a four-footer for the par and the victory. He got it and won by one stroke over Kasiadi and by two over Thammanoon and American Eric Meeks. Kasiadi started his move at the par-five No. 8, where he holed out a 40-yard wedge shot for an eagle. He then birdied the 10th, 11th and 16th holes for 69 and second place.

ABN-AMRO Pakistan Masters—US$200,000
Winner: Thammanoon Sriroj

You could say the ABN-AMRO Pakistan Masters ended in a prickly situation. Thailand's Thammanoon Sriroj won on the second playoff hole after Australia's Scott Laycock hit his drive into a cactus bush and had to take a drop under penalty. Thammanoon had thought his chances were gone when he missed a six-footer for an eagle at the 14th in the final round. "Even coming down the 18th fairway, I thought I was going to have to hole out with my second shot to force a playoff," he said.

His deliverance was more involved than that. It came at the 18th, where he birdied from eight feet for 69, and where Laycock dropped only his third shot of the week, two-putting from six feet for 71. Thammanoon shot rounds of 67, 70, 68 and 69 at the Karachi Golf Club to tie Laycock with 14-under-par 274 totals.

This was his third Omega Tour victory, and the most satisfying, he said. "Not only because I thought I was out of it with a few holes left to play," he said, "but also because I played some very good golf throughout the week."

Dubai Creek Open—US$250,000
Winner: Adrian Percey

The Dubai Creek Open came down to a match-play situation between Australia's Adrian Percey, who led going into the fourth round, and South Africa's Des Terblanche, who caught him. They came to the 18th hole tied. Both hit their second shots to the fringe of the green. Percey chipped weakly and came up 12 feet short of the hole. Terblanche was a little more successful, leaving his chip within four feet. Then Percey ran his 12-footer in for his par, and Terblanche missed. Percey had his first victory on the Omega Tour.

Percey, who shot 69-68-66-69—272, 16 under par, led by two strokes going into the final round, and was on his way to victory until Terblanche (68) caught him with three birdies on the first nine, caught him again with birdies at the 12th and 13th holes, then went ahead with another at the 15th. Now it was Percey's turn to catch up, and he did, with an eight iron to six feet for a birdie at the 17th, setting up the finish.

Hero Honda Masters—US$200,000
Winner: Ted Purdy

American Ted Purdy, age 24, figured he aged fast when he bogeyed the 14th and 15th holes in the final round of the Hero Honda Masters. "I think I lost a couple of years of my life then and there," Purdy said. He pulled himself together and parred in for the first win of his career by one stroke over India's Gaurav Ghei at the Delhi Golf Club in Delhi, India. He did it with an 11-under-par 277 total, shooting rounds of 72, 68, 66 and 71. "If there's such a thing as a good bogey, then it's the one I had at the 15th," Purdy said. "It was a great motivator not to have made a much bigger number."

Purdy, who trailed by five strokes after the first round, made up ground fast in the next two rounds, and was leading by three strokes going into the final round. He was out in 34 on three birdies and a bogey, and led by four shots through the 13th hole. His lead was abruptly cut to one when he missed the fairway at the 14th and 15th for bogeys and Ghei birdied the 16th. Fate denied Ghei, however. "When I sank that 25-foot putt on the 16th," he said, "I knew I could make another birdie on 18. But unfortunately, I blocked my drive and had to take a drop from an unplayable lie." At that, he got his third shot to the green, 20 feet from the hole, but left the birdie putt short.

Ta Shee Open—US$250,000
Winner: Wang Ter-chang

The par-four 18th hole at Ta Shee Golf and Country Club in Taiwan had vexed Wang Ter-chang all week, and then it almost destroyed him in the final round. He came to the 18th leading by two strokes, flirted with disaster, but hung on to make a clutch bogey and win the Ta Shee Open by one stroke over Australian Leith Wastle and American Eric Meeks. "I played it terribly all week," Wang said. "My tee shot was bad and my approach was even worse ... my worst shot all week."

He hit his three-wood tee shot into the lake on the right, took a penalty drop, and hit a seven-iron second short of the green. He chipped poorly, to seven feet, but holed the putt for a bogey five, wrapping up a six-under-par 282 total on rounds of 71, 70, 70 and 71. Wang's chief threat going into the final round was countryman Tseng Wen-chi. They were tied at 211. Tseng was soon on his way to 79, and Wang was well in command, leading by three strokes with four holes to play. He bogeyed the 15th and 16th, recovered for a birdie at the 17th to get his lead back to two strokes, then escaped the 18th with nothing worse than a bogey.

Volvo Masters of Malaysia—US$200,000
Winner: Christian Pena

The Volvo Masters at Kuala Lumpur, Malaysia, was largely the story of two poor putts. The first was by American Christian Pena. He missed a two-footer for par on the final hole in the third round. It seemed it would be a costly miss.

It was still on his mind the next day when the second occurred, also at the final hole. This time, it was Taiwan's Hsieh Yu-shu who made the poor putt, leaving a 15-footer four feet short. That set up Pena, a 24-year-old from Tucson, Arizona, whose best previous finish was a tie for seventh place. He was short of the green, and chipped up to five feet. He made it for 69, a 12-under-par total of 276, and a one-stroke victory over Hsieh.

The 201-yard, par-three 17th proved to be the pivotal hole. Pena hit a six iron to 10 feet, then holed the putt for a one-stroke lead going to the 18th after Hsieh's tee shot went long. Pena thanked his good fortune. He had hit the green, but off target. "But the steep slope on the green brought the ball down to the hole," he said. "It wasn't a deliberate shot."

Lexus International—US$200,000
Winner: Prayad Marksaeng

The Lexus International at Bangpoo Country Club in Bangkok, Thailand, opened as a full-fledged tournament but ended in one of the hottest match-play events. Thailand's Prayad Marksaeng had shot 70, 69 and 65 through the first three rounds, and India's Arjun Atwal matched him with 67, 69 and 68. They were tied at 204 going into the final round. Then the fun began. Both birdied No. 1, pulling away from the field. Prayad went two ahead through No. 6. "I was very confident of winning," Prayad said. "But then Arjun made a terrific eagle at No. 7, and I thought, 'Here we go again. It's going to be another long day.'"

Atwal took the lead with a birdie on No. 9, and Prayad tied him with a six-foot birdie at the 10th. At the 13th, it was Prayad's turn. He took the lead on a three-foot birdie. He didn't stay long. Atwal went one ahead on a two-shot swing at the 15th, his birdie to Prayad's bogey. And at the 16th, Prayad caught him with a six-foot birdie putt. Finally, it came down to the 18th. And Prayad, who had made one bogey, made his seventh and final birdie with a two-foot putt for a six-under-par 66 and an 18-under total of 270. He won by one shot over Atwal (67–271), who wasn't too disappointed. "I played the best golf of my life this week," he said, "and there wasn't really much more I could do — on the day the best player won."

Tugu Pratama PGA—US$300,000
Winner: Clay Devers

American Clay Devers had the distinction of winning the Tugu Pratama PGA with a broken foot. The pain-killers didn't affect his thinking, however. With 11 under par already in as a target not to be missed, Devers chose not to challenge the dangerous par-five 18th hole at Damai Indah Golf and Country Club. He opted to play away from the water down the left side. "I stayed right all the way on 18," Devers said, "and chose not to go for the green in two." He laid up 60 yards short, and put his third shot 30 feet right of the flag. A two-putt par would send him into a four-man playoff.

Swaziland's Paul Friedlander, who took the third-round lead with an Omega Tour-record 62, was paired with Devers and finished with 73. Two others had finished earlier, both with 68s after getting birdies at the 18th — Korea's Kwon Young-suk and American Mike Cunning, who gambled for an eagle. He reached the 18th in two shots, but missed his 15-foot eagle putt and settled for the birdie.

Devers, who got to 11 under par at the 15th, put his third shot 30 feet from the cup at the 18th. "I was just thinking about getting a par and not doing anything stupid," he said. The putt was uphill, and he gave it a rap, to be sure not to leave it short. It dropped for a two-under-par 70, a 12-under 276 total, and a one-shot win.

Andersen Consulting Hong Kong Open—US$350,000
Winner: Frank Nobilo

Mexico one week, Hong Kong the next — that was the itinerary for Frank Nobilo as the 1997 year in golf neared its end. Not long after he took the Mexican Open, he added the Andersen Consulting Hong Kong Open, breezing to a five-stroke victory. Nobilo came out of the pack in the second round to take control. American Dean Wilson had the first-round lead with a five-under-par 66. Nobilo and Costantino Rocca were locked in a six-man tie for second place at 67.

American Tim Straub became the curiosity piece in the second round. Here was a man who, at age 30, had abandoned a favorite old pet, his putter. "I'd had that old putter since I was 13," Straub said. "And this is the first tournament I've played since I stopped using it. I putted real well today." It helped him to 64 for a 10-under-par 132 total and a one-stroke lead over Nobilo.

It was all Nobilo from there. A 66 in the third round carried him to a 14-under-par 214 total and a three-stroke lead on Straub (70). South Korea's Kang Wook-soon closed with 69 to finish in second place by five strokes, and Straub slipped to third with 72.

Omega PGA Championship—US$500,000
Winner: Rodrigo Cuello

A funny thing happened to Filipino Rodrigo Cuello when he completed the final hole. Someone had to tell him he had taken the lead. "I didn't think about what any of the other players were doing," Cuello said. "I never looked at the leaderboards." A few minutes later, he got the rest of the message — he had won the the Omega PGA Championship again, the Omega Tour's final stroke-play event of the season.

Cuello closed with a four-under-par 66 for a 10-under-par 270 total at Clearwater Bay in Hong Kong for a one-stroke victory over Taiwan's Lu Wen-teh. Cuello made what proved to be the decisive move when he birdied the 15th hole. That put him 10 under par and three strokes ahead of Lu and Korea's Park No-seok. Lu, playing ahead of him, charged to two birdies over the last three holes. But Cuello, playing in his own world, calmly parred in.

He also overran Scotland's Kenny Walker, who climbed into a one-stroke lead with 66 in the third round. "I am not really used to such pressure," Walker said, after fading to 73. Neither was Korea's Choi Kyung-ju, who was within one stroke but blew to 79. It all took Cuello by surprise. "I don't know why Hong Kong has been so good to me," he said. "I like it here, but I think I am just lucky."

Volvo Asian Match Play—US$250,000
Winner: Des Terblanche

"Obviously it's not the best way to win a tournament," South Africa's Des Terblanche conceded. But then, it wasn't as though he had backed into the title at the Volvo Asian Match Play, the last event on the 1997 Omega Tour schedule. In the 36-hole finale, Terblanche was 2 up when Australia's Brett Partridge withdrew with a hurt forearm at the 27th hole. "Although the match was by no means over," Terblanche said, "I felt in control and thought I had an excellent chance of winning."

Terblanche played solidly the entire week at the Mimosa Golf and Country Club in the Philippines. In the first round, he came from behind to catch Thailand's Boonchu Ruangkit at the 10th hole, then breezed to a 4-and-3 win. The second day, he beat England's Peter Mitchell, 4 and 3, then American Jerry Smith, 3 and 2.

Against Partridge, Terblanche was 3 up with pars at Nos. 7 and 8, and was well on his way. If Partridge's injury denied Terblanche the satisfaction of winning on the course, it spared him the possibility of losing, and winning is always better. "It's a great way to round off what has been my best year as a professional," Terblanche said. "It's a great Christmas present."

14. Australasian Tour

Greg Norman started the year in the No. 1 place on the World Ranking, and ended the year in his familiar position. Three players — Tom Lehman, Tiger Woods and Ernie Els — each took over for brief spells as the game's leading player, but Norman's victories in the FedEx St. Jude Classic and the NEC World Series of Golf meant he retained the top position.

Norman's consistency around the world was the key to his continued presence at the top of the game. In 22 events, he finished in the top three in 10. Three times he lost in playoffs, to young Australian Richard Green in the Dubai Desert Classic, to Mark James in the Peugeot Open de Espana and to Lee Westwood in the Holden Australian Open.

Green, a young left-hander, proved no respecter of reputations as he won at the first extra hole. A photo of Norman adorned Green's wall as a child and meeting Norman for the first time before the playoff was almost as thrilling for Green as his victory.

That was the only Australian win in Europe, although New Zealander Greg Turner won the One 2 One British Masters and finished 18th on the money list. In America, Norman apart, March was the time for the Aussies as Steve Elkington won the Doral-Ryder Classic and The Players Championship — his seven-stroke victory being one of the best performances of the year — and Stuart Appleby claimed the Honda Classic.

Frank Nobilo of New Zealand, having moved to the U.S. PGA Tour from Europe, won the Greater Greensboro Chrysler Classic in April, and won late in the year in Mexico and Hong Kong.

The emergence of younger players like Appleby and Green was matched at home by victories for Stephen Leaney, Darren Cole, Greg Chalmers and New Zealander Steve Alker. Peter Lonard, with a string of consistent finishes, topped by a victory in the Ericsson Australian Masters, took the money list title.

Lonard has fully recovered from Ross River Fever, an energy-sapping condition he had caught from a mosquito bite, and which threatened to end his career.

In the major championships, the Australasian interest does not seem to have been as great recently as in previous years, although when Craig Parry ended the year with a win in the Schweppes Coolum Classic he thought he was getting back to the level he was when he was a contender at the Masters. "Back then we did not know how good we were," Parry said, also alluding to Ian Baker-Finch's heart-breaking loss of form. "Finchy and I were winning tournaments and were in the top 20 in the world and Greg (Norman) was No. 1. We kept trying to improve and we all seem to have gone backwards. I can feel myself coming back to the way we were."

Victorian Open—A$200,000
Winner: Stephen Leaney

With a course-record 64 in the first round at the Victoria Golf Club in Melbourne, Stephen Leaney simply picked up where he left off the year before. Leaney's only previous professional victory had been the same title 12 months earlier, and improving the course record by three strokes set him up to become the first to win successive Victorian Open titles for 34 years.

Three even-par rounds of 72 was good enough to give the 27-year-old from West Australia the victory, and he only lost the lead briefly on the final day when he dropped three shots in four holes early in the round. "I was in front for about 60 holes but it didn't worry me when I lost the lead," Leaney said. "Actually, to have someone go in front helped settled me down. The difference in the two wins was that this year I was mentally tougher."

Darren Cole and Euan Walters both had the chance to tie Leaney but missed 10-foot birdie chances at the last hole. They tied for second, with amateur Geoff Ogilvy and Peter Lonard one shot further back.

Johnnie Walker Classic—A$1,400,000
Winner: Ernie Els

The PGA European Tour opened on Australia's Gold Coast with a South African and a New Zealander making the headlines. And it rained. It was a fairly typical European event, then. Ernie Els gained the victory, but honor in defeat went to Michael Long. The 28-year-old New Zealander was tied for the lead going into the final round with Australians Peter Lonard and Anthony Painter, but Els, with four birdies in six holes from the fifth, burst out for the victory.

Long came to the 15th green at Hope Island with a 30-foot birdie putt to share the lead. Having marked and replaced his ball, which was touching the fringe, Long then called a one-shot penalty on himself after seeing his ball move.

"It was resting on a piece of kikuyu and after addressing the ball I looked up one last time, only to look down again and see the ball was against the putter blade," Long explained. "It had only moved half a roll, but I had placed it with the writing up and it was blank on top. No one could have seen that it had moved, but if I had gone on to win, I would have known it was a hollow victory."

Els, who saved Long from another penalty shot when he told his playing companion to replace his ball to where it was originally, said, "In golf, the players have to call penalties on themselves and that is why it is a great game played by gentlemen. That incident was the turning point. I didn't play well down the stretch and it is not often that you bogey the last to win, but I am thrilled to start the year with a victory."

Els, who had only just switched to Taylor Made clubs, closed with 69 for a 10-under total of 278. Long shot 72, as did Lonard, who holed a huge putt on the last green. The pair tied for second place, with Painter, Nick Faldo and Fred Couples three strokes further behind.

Heineken Classic—A$1,200,000
Winner: Miguel Angel Martin

Miguel Angel Martin is far from being one of the biggest men in golf, but that does not mean a good small one cannot have his day. That's something the Spaniard took awhile to realize, but having done so, he took full advantage in the Heineken Classic at The Vines course in Perth.

"I always thought golf was a game for the big boys, but the small ones can win sometimes," Martin said after saving par from a bunker at the last hole for a birdie. His 71 gave him a total of 273, 15 under par, and a one-stroke win over Fred Couples, who himself is not quite a giant.

The American had taken advantage of a Sunday afternoon on which most people seemed to forget there was a golf tournament to win. He shot 67 and raced out of the pack. Yet he was left kicking himself for finishing five, five (bogey, par).

Martin, following 65 in a third round which was played in sweltering heat, led by three going into the final round. He left his second shot in a bunker on the 12th fairway and took a bogey, and Couples was in front by two strokes with two to play. By holing a 20-footer on the 16th, the American had claimed his fifth birdie in seven holes.

From the middle of the 17th fairway, Couples pushed his nine-iron shot into a bunker on the right and that cost him a bogey. "I've hit some bad shots, but not one that easy," Couples said. Driving into a bunker at the 18th put an end to his chances of a closing birdie. "I knew that's what I needed," he added. "When you get a lead, you should bury it. But Miguel hung in there all day and birdied the last hole where I didn't."

Martin still needed to get in front of Couples and did so by holing from 20 feet at the 14th for a birdie. He made par-saving putts at the 16th and 17th, then grabbed a four at the 18th. "I am very confident with the putter," Martin said of his hot play on the greens.

Ford Open—A$300,000
Winner: Steve Alker

With two major champions still out on the course when Steve Alker reached the safety of the Kooyonga clubhouse, the New Zealander may not have thought that his 15-under-par 273 total was going to be enough to win the Ford Open. Alker won after posting a course-record 65 in the final round, but it was only after a little help from Wayne Grady and Tom Lehman.

Lehman, the reigning British Open champion, had to find a local caddie on arriving in Adelaide, after his wife, Melissa, who was to have been his bag carrier, learned she was pregnant with their fourth child. Lehman followed his local advice to good effect until he three-putted the eighth in the final round for a bogey and then double-bogeyed the ninth.

That put Grady, the 1990 U.S. PGA champion, into the lead until disaster struck at the 17th. Grady, who had not won since the 1991 Australian PGA Championship, took a triple bogey, and his closing 70 and 274 total was one more than Alker. The 25-year-old Alker gained his second win of the season, having earlier won the Queensland Open the previous October.

Lehman, who closed with a 72, tied for third place with Brett Ogle, Craig Parry and Alker's fellow New Zealander Michael Long.

Ericsson Australian Masters—A$750,000
Winner: Peter Lonard

Peter Lonard had to be patient before recording his first Australasian Tour win, but when it came it was a good one. No one could deny Lonard's consistency as he had finished runner-up no less than four times during the season, including at the Johnnie Walker Classic. But at Huntingdale in the Ericsson Australian Masters, his seventh top-10 finish in 11 starts finally provided the win he was looking for.

Lonard had had to quit the Tour almost five years before after contracting Ross River fever, a form of malaria, from a mosquito bite during a tournament in Queensland. He had thought he would not play competitively again and tried everything from visiting leading specialists to Chinese herbal medicine before the energy-sapping disease was properly diagnosed.

Consistent to a tee, Lonard posted four successive rounds of four under par to catch Peter O'Malley, who had opened in sparkling fashion with rounds of 65 and 66. O'Malley, who missed from two and three feet to save par at the ninth and 10th, then had no answer to Lonard's birdie at the second extra hole. With his putter sweeping him to victory, Lonard secured the top spot on the 1996-97 Australasian money list.

Tiger Woods, a week after winning by 10 shots in Thailand, finished tied for eighth place in his second appearance as a professional in Australia.

Canon Challenge—A$450,000
Winner: Peter Senior

Seldom does a paying spectator know better than the sports person they are watching, yet it never stops them from offering an opinion. Thus was Peter Senior accosted as he walked from the ninth green to the 10th tee during the final round of the Canon Challenge: "You're finished now," he was told in a voice that wanted everyone to hear. The voice was wrong.

Senior, who had started the day with a two-shot advantage, had indeed just double-bogeyed the ninth to fall three behind the leaders, but he responded by grasping five birdies on the back nine to tie Steve Alker. The New Zealander had closed with another 65, holing from 40 feet at the last, and was looking to win his third event of the season.

Senior, who went around in 68, 70, 66 and 70 for a 274 total, instead ended up by winning the tournament for the third time in four years. Their playoff went to the fourth extra hole, where Senior used his long putter to hole from six feet for a birdie. "I don't know whether the remark spurred me on or not, but I got on the 10th and hit two of the best shots there that I had hit all round," Senior said.

His victory boosted Senior (A$359,051) into second place on the Australasian money list behind winner Peter Lonard (A$484,534), who continued his consistent play by sharing third place with Robert Allenby at 276.

MasterCard PGA Championship—A$500,000
Winner: Andrew Coltart

It is not often a winner has the luxury of scoring a final-round 76 and winning by four shots, but that was the case with Andrew Coltart's victory in the MasterCard PGA Championship at the New South Wales course in Sydney.

Coltart was the only player to finish under par for the tournament, his 285 total being three under par. Stuart Appleby and Stephen Allan tied for second place at 289, and Rodger Davis and Paul Devenport were one stroke further back.

It was the second time Coltart, the 27-year-old Scot who had yet to win in Europe, had won the tournament. He also claimed the title in 1994. The blustery conditions over the weekend made life difficult, but Coltart was able to maintain the cushion he had established on the third day with a brilliant 66.

Coltart, however, denied his birthplace gave him an advantage in the wind. "I have no advantage in these conditions," he said. "We have links golf in Scotland and here in Australia. The reason that I came out on top today was that I was more patient. I did not try to push things. When it was windy back home in Scotland, I wouldn't go out and play. You'd have to be off your head to do that."

Holden Australian Open—A$1,000,000
Winner: Lee Westwood

Even for a man on a roll like Lee Westwood, taking on Greg Norman on his home turf and going for a third consecutive Holden Australian Open title and sixth in all, would seem a tall order. Not so. The 24-year-old Westwood had just won the Volvo Masters, finished second in the Sarazen World Open, retained his title at the Visa Taiheiyo tournament in Japan, and finished 20th in the Dunlop Phoenix. He completed a five-week run which earned him over £500,000 by beating Norman in a four-hole playoff at the Metropolitan club in Melbourne.

After rounds of 68, 67 and 66, Norman led Westwood (68, 66, 68) by one stroke with one round to go. Although Craig Parry eventually finished one stroke outside the playoff with a late charge, the event was essentially a match-play situation between Norman and Westwood.

Westwood, disturbed by a mobile phone, three-putted the first hole to give Norman a two-stroke cushion and it was not until the 18th that Westwood drew even. Two behind with two to play, the young Englishman parred the remaining two holes, while Norman bogeyed both, being blocked out by trees at the 17th and three-putting the last. Norman closed with a one-over-par 73 and they tied at 274, 14 under par.

At the first playoff hole, the 17th, Norman had to get up and down from a bunker to make his par, while at the next, the 18th, Westwood's long putt from the front of the green crashed into the flagstick and stopped on the edge of the hole. Back at the 17th again, Norman almost holed out from the sand, and Westwood two-putted from long range.

The 18th hole was finally decisive. Both players left their approaches 30 feet right of the hole, almost in the same place Norman had been in regulation. He did exactly the same, running his birdie attempt five feet past and missing the one back, while Westwood two-putted.

In contrast to Norman's playoff record, Westwood had now won three out of three. "I had nothing to lose," he said, "but Greg had everything to lose as he was the defending champion in front of his home crowd. To say I am pleased with the finish of the year is an understatement. This is such a prestigious title. You look at the great names on the trophy and now mine will be added to it."

ANZ Players Championship—A$1,012,500
Winner: Greg Chalmers

Greg Chalmers was 11 months old when John Davis won the 1974 Victorian Open. That was the last time a left-hander had won in Australia until Chalmers came from four strokes behind with a final-round 68 to win the ANZ Players Championship at Royal Queensland.

It was Chalmers' first victory since the 24-year-old former Australian Amateur champion turned professional in 1995. His 276 total was 12 under par and gave him a one-stroke win over Peter Lonard. Robert Allenby was third, a further stroke behind. Allenby and Stuart Appleby had shared the third-round lead, but closed with rounds of 74 and 75, respectively.

Chalmers drew even with Appleby by birdieing the 10th hole and then eagling the 11th and he withstood the late challenge of Lonard, who birdied five of the last 10 holes, by birdieing the 15th and 17th, where his drive rebounded off a television tower back onto the fairway.

"You need a bit of luck," Chalmers said. "It is great to win. I think at the back of most players' minds is the question: 'Am I good enough?' I don't feel as if I have done anything differently this week. I worked very hard at staying calm. That is difficult because it is very exciting. Your natural reaction after each shot is to run down the fairway and hit it again."

AMP - Air New Zealand Open—NZ$500,000
Winner: Greg Turner

Greg Turner comes from an impressive sports family, and his victory for the second time in his national Open brought him alongside Bob Charles as the only home players to achieve that feat. Turner's brother Glenn was a New Zealand Test cricket captain and coach, while his other brother Bryan was an international soccer player who caddied for Greg at Auckland Golf Club.

Three rounds of 69, plus a third-round 71, saw Turner at his front-running best as he converted a one-stroke third-round lead into a seven-shot winning margin. It was his second win of the year, following his victory in the One 2 One British Masters. "Any time you win more than once in a season, it's a successful season," Turner said.

Andrew Coltart, the Australian PGA champion, shared second place with

Jean-Louis Guepy and Lucas Parsons, while Frank Nobilo was tied for fifth with Brett Partridge.

Schweppes Coolum Classic—A$275,000
Winner: Craig Parry

Craig Parry saved his best round for last. His 67 gave him a 12-under-par 276 total and three-stroke victory over Robert Allenby, who closed with 66.

It was an early Christmas present for Parry, who decided to return to Australia after giving up his base in America to allow his eldest daughter April to attend school in her native country. It also completed an eight-event run in which he also won in Japan and never finished lower than seventh despite also playing in America and New Zealand.

"I've played pretty darn good for the past two months," Parry said. "I could have won every tournament. I have eliminated a couple of little errors from my game, and it is exciting to go out and play again. I guess I am playing a lot safer and hitting irons off the tee more often. I am taking the bogeys out of it.

"The game is so much easier when you play safe and you know what you are going to do. If you don't know, you end up with all the trouble in the world. When I need to play aggressively, and I have the right shot, I will go for it."

Ian Baker-Finch played for the first time since shooting 92 in the British Open, but he withdrew after being six over par for eight holes of the first round and then finding the water with two tee shots at the ninth.

15. African Tours

For Nick Price, anything that happened after his glory years of the early 1990s, when he won three majors championships between 1992 and 1994 and became the No. 1 golfer on the World Ranking, was going to be a letdown. But by anyone's standards, things have not been easy for the amiable Zimbabwean.

His 1996 season was affected by a sinus problem he spent most of the year trying to shrug off. Then came the news that his caddie, Squeeky Medlen, was diagnosed with chronic myelogenous leukaemia. No one could have been more supportive while losing a friend than Price. After ending the year by winning the Nedbank Million Dollar Challenge at Sun City, Price dedicated the victory to the memory of his companion. "We shared some very special moments which can never be forgotten," Price said.

In 1997, Price rediscovered his very best form to dominate the short season in South Africa. In the most important three-week segment — the events co-sanctioned with the PGA European Tour — Price finished second to Vijay Singh in the South African Open, beat David Frost in a playoff at the Alfred Dunhill South African PGA, then won the Dimension Data Pro-Am by eight strokes.

These were Price's first wins since the 1995 Zimbabwe Open. In America, where he had not added to his victory list since five triumphs in 1994, he won the MCI Classic. Although he was not to win again in the United States, his consistency enabled him to place 17th on the money list and win the Vardon Trophy for having the lowest stroke average.

Despite a side injury suffered at the Toyota World Match Play, Price later returned home to win the Zimbabwe Open and the Million Dollar event in successive weeks. "I feel that my long tee-to-green game is probably more consistent than it was in 1993 and 1994," Price said. "I'm just not putting as well as I did then. I putted so well those two years and I think that's why I won so many tournaments."

While Price did not add to his major achievements, Ernie Els certainly did. Els had won the U.S. Open at the age of 24 in 1994, and the theory was that other youngsters, such as Tiger Woods, had overtaken the young South African. But three years later, Els once more became the U.S. Open champion in a thrilling four-way battle with Tom Lehman, Jeff Maggert and Colin Montgomerie.

"Ernie is so laid-back it is frightening," said Montgomerie. "I have only admiration for him." In his next appearance Els retained his Buick Classic title, winning from wire-to-wire for the second year running. Els also won in Australia. A fourth successive World Match Play title was denied by Singh, but Els led South Africa to its first victory in the Alfred Dunhill Cup.

San Lameer South African Masters—R750,000
Winner: Mark McNulty

Having won his last event of 1996, the Zimbabwe Open, by four shots, Mark McNulty started 1997 by winning his first tournament, the San Lameer South African Masters, also by four shots. The only difference between the two victories for the 43-year-old Zimbabwean was that while he was experimenting with his new Callaway clubs in Harare. He had signed up with the company over the Christmas break before arriving at the San Lameer Country Club.

McNulty, who won four times in 1996 including the Volvo Masters on the PGA European Tour, shot a closing round of 67 after earlier efforts of 71, 68 and 70. Birdies at the 12th and 13th finally distanced him from the field in general, and Adilson da Silva in particular. The Brazilian, who had led at the halfway stage, went to the turn in 32 on the final day but dropped two shots in his last four holes. His 70 left him four behind McNulty's 12-under 276, while South African Deane Pappas and American Bruce Vaughan shared third place six shots further back.

Nashua Wild Coast Sun Challenge—R750,000
Winner: Mark McNulty

If his victory had been sun-kissed the week before, Mark McNulty had to contend with strong southwesterly winds to win the Nashua Wild Coast Sun Challenge. Safe to say, the Zimbabwean did so better than anyone else as he cruised home by nine shots with a 10-under-par 270 total. Justin Hobday was the only other man to break par for the week at 279.

It was McNulty's third win on the Southern African Tour in three starts, his fourth in five outings anywhere and the fourth time he had won the title. "I reckon I'm now playing the best golf of my career," McNulty, 43, said. "I am really enjoying my new Callaway clubs. They have added a bit of distance and trajectory to my game. I had a very productive run in the mid-1980s, but now I'm a more experienced player and that makes a difference."

McNulty, who led by four strokes going to his final round of 66, has also relied more on strategy than strength but has never stopped trying to elevate his game to a higher level. "I've been in consistent form for the last four years and I just wish I could take this sort of form onto a U.S. Open course and into the other majors."

FNB Players Championship—R750,000
Winner: Warren Schutte

Clearly, the man to beat at the Durban Country Club was Mark McNulty, but it was his playing companion for three rounds, Warren Schutte, who became the FNB Players Championship winner. Schutte went to college in America and beat Phil Mickelson to be the 1991 NCAA champion.

But the 25-year-old South African, who is still based in the U.S. despite not having any playing privileges there now that he is a professional, reckoned his golfing education was not complete until he had observed McNulty at close quarters. The Zimbabwean had undergone minor surgery on the day before the tournament and eventually finished tied for 10th place.

Schutte said of McNulty, "He wasn't on top of his game this week, otherwise he would have probably won at a canter. He just didn't look at ease with himself. But just watching how he conducts himself on the golf course is an education. He hits every shot the same and I tried to emulate him on the final day."

He did so to the tune of a closing 65 for a total of 274 and a two-shot victory over Nico van Rensburg, who stayed with his burly rival until Schutte produced four birdies in five holes from the 10th. Andre Cruse, the third-round leader, was third at 279 and Richard Kaplan was a further shot back.

South African Open—R3,375,000
Winner: Vijay Singh

Vijay Singh had two "thank yous" to make after his first victory for 14 months in the South African Open at Glendower in Johannesburg. First, it was his wife, Ardena, who persuaded Singh to discard his long putter the previous autumn. "I don't regret switching (to the long putter)," Singh said. "I had slipped to 165th in the putting statistics on the U.S. Tour and I needed a chance. It helped me with my long putting, but I stopped holing the 10-footers. I never won a thing with it."

Then, it was Bruce Vaughan, the veteran African campaigner from America, who stepped in and handed Singh a driver when the eventual winner's exploded on the practice range five minutes before he was to tee off in the first round. "Bruce offered me his spare and I kept it for four days," Singh said.

Singh won with rounds of 69, 66, 66, 69 for an 18-under-par total of 270, which was only one shot better than Nick Price's 72-66-65-68. It was not until the 17th that Singh knew he was going to win. Having earlier been in trouble on the hole, Singh holed from 15 feet for a par, and Price missed from eight feet for his birdie.

That kept the margin at two strokes, but Price did hole from 35 feet at the 18th. Ernie Els, Mark McNulty and Fulton Allem all shared third place, five strokes behind Singh.

Dimension Data Pro-Am—£400,000
Winner Nick Price

Nick Price had not won for 15 months, but he only had to wait a week longer to end his winless drought at the Dimension Data Pro-Am at Sun City. He did it in style by a matter of eight strokes.

It was probably good that Price had such an advantage, since an 80-minute lightning delay on the final afternoon meant that the final groups had to run over the last couple of holes to beat the fall of darkness.

Price, who shot rounds of 67, 66, 66, 69 for a 20-under-par 268 total, could not have cared less. He had not won since the Zimbabwe Open in 1995 and had spent most of 1996 fighting a sinus problem. "It is great to get this monkey off my back," said Price, a month past his 40th birthday. "It's been a long time, but all my illness worries are behind me and I've felt this win coming for a while. I've stayed patient and it's paid off. I didn't have any three-putts all week and that has given me my confidence back. This was a very good field and a very trying week."

Apart from the weather, Price was one of the players who was first penalized two shots, then had the penalty nullified, when, under a local rule, they were given rides from the 14th tee on the Lost City course.

David Frost, along with Thomas Bjorn, was only one shot behind Price after two rounds, but a pair of 71s meant he was second with 276, and Bjorn finished at 277.

Alfred Dunhill South African PGA—£300,000
Winner: Nick Price

For the third and final PGA European Tour co-sanctioned event in South Africa, it looked like there would be an overdue win for a third successive player. David Frost had not won since the 1994 Hong Kong Open, and with a second-round 63, he led by three strokes going into the final round of the Alfred Dunhill South African PGA.

But Frost dropped four shots over the first five holes of the final round, and it took five birdies on the back nine, including a 15-footer at the 18th, for Frost to tie Nick Price. Frost's closing 71 was for a 269 score, which Price reached with 66 that contained five birdies and an eagle.

With the first extra hole being a rerun of the 18th hole, Frost could not match his earlier effort and a bogey handed Price his second consecutive win. "I feel as if I've gone 15 rounds with Mike Tyson," Price said.

"I was operating on my last sinews. I never expected to win from five behind, but I just somehow made it. I thought I was fully over my sinus problems, but I may have overdone it this week. It's wonderful to be playing well again and to have found my old putting touch."

In fact, it was a three-putt at the third hole in the final round that got him going. He birdied the next two holes and holed from 20 feet for the eagle at the seventh. "It was like a wake-up call," Price said. "I was so angry and upset."

Nico van Rensburg, with a closing 68, was third, one shot out of the playoff, with Retief Goosen two strokes further back. His second-first-first run meant Price secured first place on the Southern African money list with R1,223,026, almost double the earnings of the next man.

Hollard Insurance Royal Swazi Sun Open—R500,000
Winner: Warrick Druian

With the Southern African money list title tied up by Nick Price with his victories in the previous two weeks, the Hollard Insurance Royal Swazi Sun Open provided a chance for someone to make themselves a star. That is just what Warrick Druian did in claiming his first professional title.

The 27-year-old South African was two strokes ahead going into the final day after rounds of 70, 64 and 65, and despite slipping to 70 hung on for victory by one shot over Chris Davison and Nic Henning. Davison closed with 67, while Henning, son of Graham, fired 69 but could not quite catch Druian.

Playing the par-three last hole one stroke ahead, Druian found heavy rough with his tee shot, but chipped and one-putted for total of 269 which was 10 shots less than his previous best. "I had to contend with a stiff challenge from Nic and Chris over the back and it was a good lesson for me," Druian said. "They both stayed cooler than I was under pressure, but I just sneaked through in the end."

Kalahari Classic—R75,000
Winner: Sean Pappas

Sean Pappas won the Kalahari Classic at the Sishen Club in Kathu. Pappas, one of four golfing brothers, scored a final-round 69 for a seven-under-par total of 209 to win by one stroke over Justin Hobday, Andrew McLardy and Tjaart van der Walt.

Vodacom Series: Eastern Cape—R150,000
Winner: Des Terblanche

Played on the Humewood course in Port Elizabeth, the nearest approximation to a links layout in South Africa, Des Terblanche beat Andre Cruse by two strokes in the Vodacom Series: Eastern Cape tournament. Terblanche recovered from opening with a 75 to record two 68s for a five-under total of 211. Cruse closed with an even-par 72.

Bosveld Classic—R80,000
Winner: Desvonde Botes

Having opened with 66, Desvonde Botes added 72 in the second round to fall one stroke behind James Kingston before closing with 67 for a total of 205, 11 under par, and a three-stroke victory over Darren Fichardt in the Bosveld Classic. Kingston, who scored 72 in the final round, shared third place with Sean Pappas and Steve van Vuuren at seven under par.

Vodacom Series: Mpumalanga—R150,000
Winner: Robbie Stewart

If there was only one way Robbie Stewart's scores were going to go after a six-under-par 65 in the first round at White River, Nelspruit, then rounds of 68 and 69 were good enough for a one-stroke win over Steve van Vuuren in the Vodacom Series: Mpumalanga event. The runner-up only differed in his scoring from the winner by taking a 69 in the second round.

Trustbank Gauteng Classic—R120,000
Winner: Bradford Vaughan

Des Terblanche just failed to claim his second win of the season in the Trustbank Gauteng Classic when he lost by a stroke to Bradford Vaughan. Both players shot final rounds of 70, but Vaughan's 66 on the second day proved decisive as he finished at 209, seven under par. Brett Liddle and Ashley Roestoff shared third place two strokes behind Terblanche.

Vodacom Series: Gauteng—R150,000
Winner: John Nelson

Bradford Vaughan was denied back-to-back victories as John Nelson triumphed at Royal Johannesburg with rounds of 71, 68 and 72 for a five-under-par total of 211 in the Vodacom Series: Gauteng tournament. Vaughan finished one stroke back, sharing second place with John Mashego.

FNB Botswana Open—R150,000
Winner: Nasho Kamungeremu

In a battle of two players attached to the Chapman Club in Harare, Zimbabwe, Nasho Kamungeremu beat Marc Cayeux at Gaborone by a stroke in the Botswana Open with rounds of 72, 65 and 68 for a total of eight-under-par 205. Third place was shared by Justin Hobday, James Kingston and Hennie Otto.

FNB Namibia Open—R150,000
Winner: Wallie Coetsee

A final round of 65, six under par, brought victory in the Namibia Open for Wallie Coetsee at Windhoek, but only by one shot over Brett Liddle, who, like the winner, completed three rounds in the 60s. Coetsee's total was 203, 10 under par, while James Kingston and Bradford Vaughan tied for third place at eight under par.

Bearing Man Highveld Classic—R75,000
Winner: Darren Fichardt

Wallie Coetsee went one better in the Bearing Man Highveld Classic at Witbank, completing a three-round total of 202, 14 under par, but could only share third place with Ashley Roestoff as Darren Fichardt beat Sean Pappas by one stroke. Fichardt scored rounds of 65, 66 and 69 to Pappas' 65, 67, 69 to win with a 16-under-par total of 200.

Vodacom Series: Free State—R150,000
Winner: Dean van Staden

Roger Wessels got off to a flying start in the Vodacom Series: Free State event with an opening 64, but could not break 70 again, something Dean van Staden had no trouble with. Rounds of 67, 69 and 69 at the Bloemfontein Club gave the winner an 11-under-par total of 205 and a two-stroke victory over Wessels. Nico van Rensburg took third place at 208.

Vodacom Series: Western Cape—R150,000
Winner: Desvonde Botes

For the fourth event running, the Vodacom Series: Western Cape, the winner had three rounds in the 60s, but Desvonde Botes had to go into extra holes before securing his second win of the season. Botes compiled rounds of 69, 66 and 68, but was tied at 203, 13 under par, by the previous week's winner Dean van Staden. Brenden Pappas, brother of Sean, finished two strokes outside the playoff after a closing 65.

Vodacom Series: Kwazulu-Natal—R150,000
Winner: Grant Muller

Consistent scoring of 71, 70, 70 left Grant Muller as the only player who was able to break par in the Vodacom Series: Kwazulu-Natal event at the Selborne Club. Muller won by five strokes over Hennie Otto, who matched par 216 for three rounds. Brett Liddle, Bobby Lincoln, Brenden Pappas and Darran Warner shared third place at one over par.

Lombard Tyres Classic—R120,000
Winner: Andrew McLardy

Matching middle rounds of 66 brought Andrew McLardy into contention for the Lombard Tyres Classic title at the Krugersdorp Club, but it was a closing 70 which secured a one-stroke win over Justin Hobday at 273, 15 under par. Hobday was highly consistent with rounds of 69, 68, 68 and 69, while eight players shared third place.

Hassan II Trophy—US$415,000
Winner: Colin Montgomerie

Having secured a fifth consecutive money title in Europe, Colin Montgomerie was in relaxed mood when he teed up in the Hassan II Trophy at the Dar-es-Salam course in Rabat, Morocco. Montgomerie can play some pretty good golf under pressure, but admits to playing his best when he is relaxed.

With new irons in his bag, Montgomerie added to his two official 1997 wins in Europe with a three-stroke victory over England's David Howell and Henrik Nystrom of Sweden. Montgomerie moved up a gear on the second nine on the last day to claim five birdies starting with two back-to-back at the 10th and 11th holes. Two more followed at the 14th and 15th and the last at the 17th. He had rounds of 73, 68, 67 and 69 for a 15-under-par total of 277.

Donnie Hammond was fourth, along with Tom Lehman, and defending champion Ignacio Garrido tied for fifth, five strokes back.

Leopard Rock Classic—R100,000
Winner: Adilson da Silva

High in the mountains overlooking the Zimbabwe-Mozambique border, Adilson da Silva claimed a four-stroke victory in the Leopard Rock Classic with rounds of 64, 69 and 66. His 199 total was 14 under par, while at 10 under, Mark Murless and Sean Pappas shared second place.

Zambia Open—R250,000
Winner: James Loughnane

At a Lusaka course with a par of 73 for the Zambia Open, James Loughnane's 273 total was 19 under par and his 65 and 66 on the second and third days represented 15 under par for two rounds. But on the final day when he scored 71, Loughnane came under attack from Colin Sorour, whose 66 allowed him to finish one behind, and from Hennie Otto, whose 63 took him up to third place, three behind.

Zimbabwe Open—R400,000
Winner: Nick Price

Convinced he was playing close to his best again, Nick Price suffered a rib injury at the Toyota World Match Play in October that made the end of the year highly frustrating. But returning home seemed to do the trick and, for the second time in three years, Price won his national title, the Zimbabwe Open, at the Chapman Club in Harare.

Price shot rounds of 68, 67, 66 and 68 that gave him a 19-under-par total of 269 and a two-stroke win over Brenden Pappas and Mark McNulty, who came home in 32.

"As always with me, it is the putting which is the critical factor, but I felt confident on the bent-grass greens here all week," said Price, who was an irresistible force in the game in 1993 and 1994. He added, "If anything, I reckon my game from tee to green is even better than it was then."

Nedbank Million Dollar Challenge—US$2,510,000
Winner: Nick Price

Ending the year with back-to-back wins, Nick Price claimed his second victory at the Nedbank Million Dollar Challenge. A final-round 68 gave Price a 13-under-par total of 275, 11 strokes higher than his record score for Sun City of 24 under par posted during his first win in 1993.

This proved a tighter affair, with the Zimbabwean having to hole a 12-foot par putt on the final green to win. In a thrilling climax at the par-four finishing hole, Davis Love III hit his approach shot to within tap-in birdie range for 67 that took the U.S. PGA champion into the clubhouse at 12 under par.

Then, playing with Price, local favorite Ernie Els, who has yet to win this event and lost in a playoff to Colin Montgomerie in 1996, holed a monster putt across the final green for another 67 to tie Love. Price's second shot had trickled through behind the green and, after playing a tricky chip as well as he could have hoped, he had to wait for the roars of the gallery to subside after Els' putt before he holed his right-to-left putt.

Phil Mickelson started the final round with a three-stroke lead and eagled the second hole before he gave it back with a double bogey on the eighth. A bogey at the 16th dropped him into a share of the lead with Price. Needing to hole a long birdie chance to tie at the last, Mickelson three-putted to drop to fourth place.

"There were no real holes in my game," said Price. "The pins were in very tough positions, but this is the type of course one has to play with what I call cautious aggression. I only went one under on the back nine and that is indicative of how tough the course is and the pressure that builds." Turning his thoughts to his 1994 British Open victory, he added, "Holing that putt on the 18th, though, was like the one I sank at the 17th at Turnberry."

Mycom Mafunyane Trophy—R200,000
Winner: Kevin Stone

Kevin Stone ended the year victorious in the Mycom Mafunyane Trophy after a closing 64, eight under par, brought him a two-stroke victory over Gavin Levenson and Brenden Pappas, the local hero who is attached to the Hans Merensky Country Club and was born in Phalaborwa. After rounds of 68 and 66, Pappas' last-day 71 left him two strokes behind Stone's 13-under-par 203 total.

16. Senior Tours

The wonders of senior professional golf haven't ceased. Not by a long shot, even though there is some validity to the observations of some magazine and newspaper pundits that fading star power is starting to affect the gates and the television appeal.

By and large, followers of the game are reluctant to invest Hale Irwin with the mantle of stardom worn by such of his dominating predecessors on the Senior PGA Tour as Arnold Palmer, Gary Player, Lee Trevino, Raymond Floyd, Chi Chi Rodriguez and, in his infrequent appearances, Jack Nicklaus.

Irwin may not have the flair that contributed to their popularity with the galleries and television viewers, but his accomplishments in 1997 surpassed anything any of them achieved in their best years on the circuit.

With a record-tying nine victories around an assortment of nine other top-10 finishes in his 23 official starts on the Senior PGA Tour, Irwin accumulated $2,343,364 in prize money, not only a record amount for the seniors, but more than anyone ever won on any single tour.

Not even Tiger Woods, playing on the PGA Tour with its bigger purses, could match Irwin's tournament income, although Woods and senior Gil Morgan also topped the heretofore-unscathed $2 million mark in 1997. Irwin's nine triumphs, including the PGA Seniors' Championship, spanned the schedule of 37 tournaments as he equalled Peter Thomson's nine-win season of 1985. In a way, Irwin went Thomson one better since he also had a 10th victory in 1997. He won the unofficial Senior Slam, the 36-hole event for the winners of the Senior PGA Tour's four major championships.

Morgan was the other attention-getter on the U.S. circuit during the season. Morgan, who won the 1996 Ralphs Senior Classic 11 days after his 50th birthday, gave Irwin his stiffest competition and finished the season on a high note by repeating in the Ralphs event and outshooting Irwin in the year-ending Energizer Senior Tour Championship, winning his fifth and sixth titles of 1997 and climbing over the $2 million mark. He also had a seventh, unofficial victory in the Diners Club Matches. His big victory came in The Tradition, which he won by six strokes.

The "changing of the guard" was quite evident in 1997. None of the aforementioned leading lights — Nicklaus, Player, Trevino, Floyd, Rodriguez — won a tournament, Trevino for the first time as a senior, nor did such other 1996 victors and standouts as Jim Colbert, the leading money winner the previous two years; Bob Charles, the No. 2 money winner in senior golf, and Tom Weiskopf, who played in just five tournaments.

Six seniors won for the first time, including, as expected, David Graham, shedding the controversy surrounding his 1996 ouster as captain of the Internationals in the Presidents Cup. The others were Bud Allin, Bruce Summerhays, Dana Quigley, Hugh Baiocchi and Bob Eastwood. Eastwood (two) joined Irwin (nine), Gil Morgan (six), Graham (three), Graham Marsh (two) and Jay Sigel (two) as multiple winners.

The most shocking developments of the season, though, were medical. Even before the first tournament, the golf world was stunned by the news that Palmer had undergone prostate cancer surgery. Five months later, Colbert had the same ailment and operation. Bruce Devlin had a kidney removed and Player was on the shelf for six weeks after double-hernia surgery. The most disturbing report came in September when Larry Gilbert, who emerged from the club pro ranks to become a standout on the Senior PGA Tour, was diagnosed with inoperable lung cancer.

As impressive in its own scale was Tommy Horton's domination of the European Seniors Tour again in 1997. The Englishman, who was the No. 1 performer on the circuit the previous season with four victories, manhandled the 1997 fields, taking six of the 17 titles.

Horton added a seventh title in November in South Africa in the ICI John Bland Invitational, the concluding event of that country's brief senior tour in Johannesburg. Bland, winless in America after an outstanding four-victory season in 1996, and Simon Hobday, also without a 1997 title on the U.S. circuit, took the other two late-year victories.

Elsewhere in the final months, an unmatched senior streak was extended as the ever-challenging Isao Aoki won the last tournament of the eight-event Japan Senior Tour — the Senior Open — for the fourth year in a row. It capped another excellent year for Aoki in America, where he won his seventh title on the Senior PGA Tour.

Although shut out in America, Player picked off a victory in Japan, then landed his third Senior British Open and the Shell Wentworth Masters on the European Seniors Tour, running his list of career victories to 162.

U.S. Senior PGA Tour

MasterCard Championship—$1,000,000
Winner: Hale Irwin

A recurring theme was established for the Senior PGA Tour when Hale Irwin and Gil Morgan battled down the stretch in the MasterCard Championship. The two sparred on even terms through most of the final round at the Hualalai Golf Resort at Kailua-Kona until Irwin, starting his second full season on the senior circuit, ran in a 28-foot birdie putt at the 17th and tour rookie Morgan three-putted there from 50 feet. That two-shot swing gave Irwin a two-stroke victory with a seven-under-par 209. Bob Charles birdied the last two holes to finish third at 212.

The tournament began in a gale. With winds gusting up to 40 miles an hour, par was unsullied. Morgan, who gained his spot in the exclusive field of 24 tournament winners of 1996 with a victory in the Ralphs Classic 11 days after turning 50, matched par to lead Irwin, Dave Eichelberger and Dave Stockton by one shot. Morgan followed with 69 and Irwin, 68, to share the second-round lead at 139, two in front of Eichelberger (70) and Charles (69), as the weather calmed.

With birdies on three of the par-fives in the last round, Irwin and Morgan shed the other challengers, including Jay Sigel, who had bounced back from an opening 80 with 67 and a first-nine 31 before running out of birdies. Morgan lost his last opportunity to move ahead of Irwin when he missed a six-foot birdie putt at the 16th just before the decisive 17th.

Royal Caribbean Classic—$850,000
Winner: Gibby Gilbert

Gibby Gilbert righted a faltering game when the Senior PGA Tour staged the Royal Caribbean Classic, its first full-field tournament of 1997, at Key Biscayne, Florida. Even though he had won the previous September, the 56-year-old native Tennesseean felt that his game had not been up to snuff since his prime senior period of 1992-93, when he won four times. Whatever the reason, his game — and his putting — were solid at Crandon Park, and he marched to a four-stroke victory. He posted an 11-under-par 202 total.

Gilbert and the field deferred to Chi Chi Rodriguez the first day. Rodriguez, who admitted that he had lost his enthusiasm after three mediocre seasons, mustered a recharged 67 and took a one-stroke lead over Jack Kiefer, J.C. Snead and Bruce Summerhays. Gilbert, who opened with 70, came back with 66 for a 136 total and a one-stroke lead over Dave Eichelberger.

Gilbert began his move at the ninth hole in the last round with his first of six birdies on the final 10 holes. He scored another 66 for a four-stroke triumph over David Graham, who closed with 68 for 206, one shot ahead Isao Aoki and John Schroeder.

LG Championship—$1,000,000
Winner: Hale Irwin

Hale Irwin made it two for two in Naples, Florida. Irwin, who won the season-opening MasterCard Championship and skipped the Royal Caribbean Classic, captured another stretch duel in the LG Championship, this time against a surprised Bob Murphy, who had started the day just two strokes off the pace and was in the process of shooting 65, a combination that usually wins tournaments. Hearing little noise behind him, Murphy had no idea until he finished that Irwin had taken the lead at the 15th hole and would finish with 65, too, and win by one shot.

Neither man got in front in the earlier rounds. Al Geiberger was the first-round leader at 66, trailed by one stroke by Chi Chi Rodriguez, Rocky Thompson, Isao Aoki, Vicente Fernandez and David Graham as Murphy opened with 68 and Irwin had 70. Dave Stockton, with 67 for 135, went in front in the second round as Irwin, with a seven-birdie 66, moved into the runner-up slot with Jack Kiefer and Fernandez. Murphy was at 137 with Jerry McGee and Bruce Summerhays.

Fernandez and Murphy had the hot hands early in the final round, making the turn at 13 under par. Fernandez led momentarily when he eagled the par-five 10th to Murphy's birdie, but Murphy went ahead when he birdied the 13th. Meanwhile, Irwin was coming on strong. He birdied the 10th, 12th and

14th, then took the lead when he holed a 40-foot bunker shot at the 15th. He created a cushion when he birdied the 17th. That covered a bogey at the last hole that made it 65 and the winning 201 total, 15 under par.

GTE Classic—$900,000
Winner: David Graham

David Graham finally found a way to effect a change of public subject from the painful one he had been stuck with for the better part of a year, that of the man who had been forced out of his Presidents Cup captaincy. He became a winner again, landing his first victory on the Senior PGA Tour in the GTE Classic at the TPC of Tampa Bay.

It had been a long time between wins, too, for the Australian who has U.S. Open (1981) and PGA Championship (1979) titles on his impressive career record. Graham hadn't won a 72-hole tournament since the 1985 Queensland Open in his homeland, two years after his last PGA Tour victory in the Houston Open.

Unlike most name players coming onto the Senior PGA Tour, Graham had dropped out of competitive golf in the 1990s while concentrating on course design projects. It took awhile for him to regain his competitive touch after turning 50 in May of 1996. In 13 starts the remainder of the year, he lost in a five-way playoff at Pensacola, but had only two other top-10 finishes.

Graham indicated the win was coming with a runner-up finish at Key Biscayne and a fourth-place showing at Naples. He put himself in good position just off the pace of John Schroeder, the first-round leader at 67, and Bob Eastwood, the second-day front-runner with 136 after a sparkling 65. Graham was at 139 at that point after rounds of 71-68.

He was smoking Sunday, running off seven birdies on the first 14 holes to take a firm grasp on the lead. A par save from a horrid bunker lie was critical during that spell. His only bogey at the 15th merely reduced his final-round score to 65, his winning total to 204, 12 under par, and his margin to three over Bob Dickson, who closed with 67.

American Express Invitational—$1,200,000
Winner: Bud Allin

The Senior PGA Tour had its second consecutive first-time winner in Sarasota, Florida, at the TPC at Prestancia in the rich American Express Invitational. Bud Allin, starting his third full season, followed the footsteps of David Graham into the winner's circle on the course where the Senior PGA Tour staged the now-defunct Chrysler Cup from 1987 to 1994.

Allin experienced a much longer and more severe victory drought than Graham did. He scored his last of five PGA Tour victories in the 1976 Pleasant Valley Classic. He was out of competitive golf and struggling to make ends meet during much of the intervening time. Nor had things gone that well for him on the Senior PGA Tour. Until the victory, he was a non-exempt player and he got into the $1.2 million American Express event as a last-minute replacement.

The white-haired 52-year-old took immediate advantage of the opportunity, shooting an opening-round 68 that tied him for the lead with Jim Colbert, Butch Baird and Simon Hobday. Despite strong winds, 26 players broke Prestancia's par 72. Thirty-three did it in the second round, but Allin was still able to open a three-stroke lead with another 68. Trailing him then were Colbert, Jim Albus, Mike Hill, Isao Aoki, Graham Marsh and Bob Eastwood.

"My nerves stayed in pretty good check, except for the putter," said Allin of the final round. He maintained his lead with four birdies on the first 10 holes, but had to work hard at the finish. He led Colbert and Hill by two strokes through 16, but hooked his tee shot into the trees and bogeyed the 17th. Then, at the 18th, he left himself a 60-footer to two-putt for the win. He rolled the first one just two feet from the cup. The par gave him 69 for a 205 total, one better than Colbert.

Senior Slam—$500,000
Winner: Hale Irwin

Appropriately, Hale Irwin prevailed when the winners of 1996's four designated PGA Senior Tour major championships convened in Mexico for the two-day Senior Slam in late February. Playing without benefit of a practice round, Irwin made a shambles of the competition against his three colleagues at Palmilla Golf Club at Los Cabos, breezing to a nine-stroke victory with a smashing, 13-under-par, 65-66–131 total.

Irwin, the 1996 PGA Seniors' champion who already had won twice in 1997 and was far in front on the Senior PGA Tour money list, made only one bogey over the 36 holes and quickly had the others thinking about runner-up money. With the 65 Monday, Irwin staked out a five-stroke lead over Raymond Floyd, seven on Dave Stockton and eight on Jack Nicklaus. He was just as sharp in the second round. He missed only one fairway and two greens en route to the 66 and the $250,000 winner's check. Stockton shot 68 for 140, edging Floyd for second place and its $125,000 payoff. Floyd, with 70-71–141, collected $75,000 and Nicklaus (73-70) received $50,000 for his last-place finish.

Toshiba Senior Classic—$1,000,000
Winner: Bob Murphy

You could call it not-so-sudden death, or perhaps prolonged agony. When Bob Murphy missed a seven-foot birdie putt on the 54th hole of the Toshiba Senior Classic, he and Jay Sigel headed back to the 18th tee for some overtime work. Little did they think that they would still be playing two hours later, prompting Murphy to crack afterward that "we were out there so long I thought they moved the clubhouse." It finally ended in a stunning way as Murphy, in imminent danger of three-putting, instead watched his putt from 80 feet dive into the cup at the ninth extra hole. It was the longest playoff in Senior PGA Tour history, going one more hole than Orville Moody went before beating Bob Betley in Salt Lake City in 1992.

Murphy, a 10-time winner on the Senior PGA Tour, never expected to be in a position to add the 11th when he arrived at Newport Beach Country Club in California, having no confidence in his swing. His first surprise of the week was his opening 65 that put him in a tie for the lead with David Graham and J.C. Snead. He was just one stroke off the pace of Graham when he followed with 70 to David's 69 Saturday.

The Aussie faded early in Sunday's final round and Murphy was in the driver's seat coming down the stretch. Sigel, playing ahead of him after rounds of 69 and 68 but seemingly out of the picture after a three-over first nine of 38, birdied four of the last six holes for a one-under 70 and 207. That was enough for the tie when Murphy bogeyed the 17th and missed the seven-footer for the win at the 18th. The two men went in circles — 18-16-17-18-16-17-18-16-17 — matching birdies twice at 18 and parring everything else until Murphy made the monster putt.

Liberty Mutual Legends of Golf—$1,100,000
Winners: John Bland and Graham Marsh

Prompted by criticism about the credentials of several players in the 1996 tournament, the organizers of the Liberty Mutual Legends of Golf established some specific guidelines for the invitations to the 1997 event. Graham Marsh and John Bland, the winners, clearly belonged in the tournament despite Marsh's self-deprecating remarks about their stature compared to "the true legends of the game ... John and I are competent players, but we don't have the great records of those guys." Over the last decade, Lee Trevino is really the only player among all the winners with a record clearly superior to those of either of the 1997 champions.

Bland, the South African who won five times in his first year in America, and Marsh, the Australian with a huge collection of victories around the world, broke away from the other contenders to score a three-stroke triumph on the Palmer course of PGA West. They never trailed as they posted scores of 63, 64 and 65 for a 192 total, 24 under par and three better than runners-up Gil Morgan and Hubert Green.

An opening 63 put them in a first-place tie with old hands Don January and Gene Littler, who won twice as a team and two other times with different partners in the 1980s. The Bland/Marsh twosome's 127 Saturday edged them a stroke in front of Littler/January, Green/Morgan, Dave Stockton/Al Geiberger and Gibby Gilbert/J.C. Snead. The winners started well in the last round with birdies on two of the first four holes, then almost self-destructed at the par-three fifth when they both put tee shots in the water and took a double bogey, dropping out of the lead. By the 11th hole, though, they were among five teams tied for the lead at 19 under. Bland's 10-foot par putt at 13 kept them there, then Marsh went on a rampage — eagle, birdie, birdie — to wrap up the victory.

Southwestern Bell Dominion—$800,000
Winner: David Graham

"Finally," John Jacobs must have been thinking, "a win in America." The 52-year-old Californian, whose four victories during his younger globe-trotting days all came in the Far East, had just finished his final round in the Southwestern Bell Dominion one stroke ahead of the field with a three-under-par 69 and 207 total.

Unfortunately for Jacobs, the player one stroke behind was David Graham, who promptly snatched the victory away from him with a 365-yard tee shot on the par-five finishing hole — "I don't drive that far on vacation," quipped Chi Chi Rodriguez — an eight iron to 10 feet and a solid putt for the week's only eagle there, a 69 and a one-stroke victory. Expecting no worse than a playoff chance, Jacobs, a big hitter, rued his failure to at least birdie the hole himself.

Graham joined the absent Hale Irwin as the only players with two 1997 victories, and the check carried Graham to the top of the Senior PGA Tour's money list with well over $400,000, all of which provided solid evidence that the Australian had overcome a rusty game and the Presidents Cup fall-out that led to a mediocre first season in 1996.

Both Graham and Jacobs were contenders from the start at The Dominion Country Club in San Antonio, Texas, the long-time site of one of the circuit's oldest events. Jacobs shared the first-day lead at 67 with Graham Marsh, who aced the 17th in his first round since winning the Legends of Golf with John Bland. Graham was at 68. Dave Stockton shot 66 in the second round and surged into a one-stroke lead over Rodriguez, the 1987 winner, at 135, nine under. Graham had 69 for 137 and Jacobs 71 for 138. Both Stockton (74) and Rodriguez (73) faded on the last day, setting up the dazzling finish at the home hole, where Jacobs' put his second shot in a greenside bunker, blasted to 10 feet and didn't come close with the putt.

The Tradition—$1,200,000
Winner: Gil Morgan

With his late-season victory in the 1996 Ralphs Classic in the second start of his Senior PGA Tour career, Gil Morgan showed that he could win. In the prestigious Tradition tournament six months later, the 50-year-old Oklahoman showed that he could win the big ones, too. He devastated the classy Tradition field with a tournament-record 266 total and won his second senior title by six strokes on the very reputable Cochise course at the Desert Mountain Country Club.

What made it particularly impressive was that Morgan did it in much-less-than-ideal conditions — cold, damp weather, abnormal for Scottsdale, Arizona, in early April, that plagued the tournament through the first three rounds. Typical of the impression he made on his fellow competitors was the observation of Gary Player: "I'd like to see anybody in the world beat that under those conditions."

Looking like a beardless Santa Claus with his red sweater and red-and-white stocking cap in the 40-degree weather, Morgan opened the tournament with a six-under 66, matched by J.C. Snead, Simon Hobday, Isao Aoki and John Jacobs, shaking off his disappointing second-place finish the previous week in San Antonio. It was pretty much all Morgan the rest of the way. He repeated the 66 in similar weather, moving two strokes ahead of Aoki, Jacobs and Terry Dill. A 67 came next, putting him 17 under par for the 54 holes and five strokes up on Aoki and Jacobs and more on the rest of the field.

No one could get closer than four as he concluded the rout with a second 67. The key to Morgan's victory was his mastery of the five par-five holes. One of the game's big hitters, Morgan was 15 under on the par-fives, climaxing it all with an eagle on the final hole.

PGA Seniors' Championship—$1,200,000
Winner: Hale Irwin

Put an important tournament at a demanding course in front of Hale Irwin and he figuratively salivates. He's made an outstanding career out of dealing with such situations ... U.S. Opens at Winged Foot, Inverness and Medinah, three times the Heritage at Harbour Town and twice in the Memorial at Muirfield Village. Then, of course, there was the Champion course at PGA National in 1996 and here he was back as defending champion. A month earlier, he had won the 36-hole Senior Slam by nine. At Palm Beach Gardens, Florida, in the season's second major, his pinpoint game and course management intense and razor-sharp, Irwin rolled to a 12-shot victory, 14 under par at 274, the margin breaking the Senior PGA Tour by one stroke. Arnold Palmer won the 1985 Senior TPC and Orville Moody the 1988 Vantage by 11 strokes.

Irwin, who in his first eight events of 1997 matched his first four senior victories in 1995 and 1996, if you count the Senior Slam, took charge of the tournament in the second round. He followed his opening 69 — three off the pace of leader John Bland — with a sizzling 65 that included an eagle two at the 13th, where he holed a 115-yard pitching wedge shot. The 134 shot him seven strokes in front of runner-up Bob Charles, leading him to remark, "I had a remarkable day and the rest of the field didn't."

Irwin struggled to a par-72 in the second round, three-putting twice for two of his three bogeys, but maintained the seven-stroke lead at 10 under as again no one else could do much with the Champion course. Jack Nicklaus, who was to finish in a second-place tie with Dale Douglass at 286, made a bit of a move on the first nine, but eventually shot 73. Larry Gilbert moved into second place at 213, and Bland and John Morgan were the only others under par at 215. Irwin summed up his finishing 68 succinctly, "I would have hated to have been chasing me today."

Las Vegas Senior Classic—$1,000,000
Winner: Hale Irwin

When Hale Irwin put the Las Vegas Senior Classic title back to back with his PGA Seniors' Championship to make it four official victories in his first eight starts of the 1997 season, he set himself squarely on the pace of Peter

Thomson, who established the Senior PGA Tour record with nine victories in 1985. The win at the new TPC at The Canyons course was certainly the most arduous and tightest of the four. Irwin battled Isao Aoki and 40 mile-an-hour winds to the final putt before claiming his eighth senior title.

The weather played a major role all week, as only 23 rounds in the 60s were posted. The winds blew so hard that the pro-am was cancelled and it didn't really calm down until midway through the opening round. That was a help to late-starting Isao Aoki, who matched Gil Morgan's earlier 66 to share a big lead. No one else was better than the 70s of Irwin, Raymond Floyd, John Bland, Orville Moody and John Jacobs. Benign weather greeted the field in the second round and a batch of low scores tightened things up. Irwin led the 14 players shooting in the 60s with 65 and took a two-stroke lead over Jacobs and Aoki with his 135 total.

The gales returned on the final day and Irwin had his hands full securing the victory, primarily because his putting was faulty. Even though he three-putted for the third time in the round at the 14th hole to go one over for the day, Irwin still led Aoki by two strokes. When Aoki birdied the 15th and he missed a seven-foot par putt at the 17th, Irwin dropped back into a deadlock with the Japanese star. Both drove into the rough at the home hole, but reached the green with their approaches. Aoki missed from 20 feet, then Irwin, getting a read from Isao's putt, rolled his in for 72–207 and the victory. "I saved the best putt for last," he remarked. "I'm glad it's over. I sure didn't want to get in a playoff. I was leaking oil."

Bruno's Memorial Classic—$1,150,000
Winner: Jay Sigel

The way he had lost the Toshiba Classic in March to an 80-foot putt, Jay Sigel could easily have lost heart as well. Instead, he was philosophic. "When it happened, I thought, hopefully, my day will come again," said Sigel, "and it has." The salvation came in the Bruno's Memorial Classic in Birmingham, Alabama, where he outplayed Hale Irwin, the Senior PGA Tour's dominating player, and others in the final round and registered a three-stroke victory with his 11-under-par 205 total. The win, the third for the long-time amateur standout, was his first since he captured the Senior Tour Championship the previous November.

Aided by an eagle two, Gil Morgan took the first-round lead at Greystone Golf Club with 67, one shot ahead of Sigel, Tom Shaw and Bob Charles, then yielded front-and-center to Sigel, who raced to nine under par with 67 for a 135 total, three shots ahead of Bob Eastwood. Irwin and Morgan lurked in third place at 139.

For the second Sunday in a row, the seniors had to battle strong winds, but Sigel's big game was equal to the task. He reached the green at the par-five second in two with a six iron and dropped the four-foot eagle putt. When he followed with a birdie at the fifth, Sigel had the tournament well in hand. Morgan got within three strokes at the 15th hole, but Sigel fired back with a birdie at 16 and led by four until he made just his third bogey of the tournament at the final hole. That gave him a 70 for the 205 total. His putting, in particular, was solid. He didn't three-putt in the tournament.

Irwin, on the other hand, again experienced trouble on the greens. Seeking his third straight victory and fifth of the season, Irwin slipped to 75 and finished nine shots off the pace in a tie for seventh. Morgan shot 69 to claim second place, two ahead of Isao Aoki.

Home Depot Invitational—$900,000
Winner: Jim Dent

Lee Trevino has never been one to keep his thoughts to himself nor has Jim Dent had a reputation for not paying attention. That combination was played out at the Home Depot Invitational, the new name for the long-time Senior PGA Tour tournament in Charlotte, North Carolina, as Dent won the season's second playoff, beating Trevino and Larry Gilbert for the 11th title of his senior career.

"I should have kept my mouth shut," quipped Trevino after Dent carefully surveyed, then holed the winning putt on the green of the par-three 17th at the TPC at Piper Glen, the second extra hole. Trevino was referring to his remark to Dent after Jim had typically taken little time and missed a three-foot birdie putt at the 18th hole earlier that would have given him the victory without the overtime exercise. "When you've got a putt to win a tournament, you'd better take your time with it," Trevino had said to him.

DeWitt Weaver, seeking his first victory in six years, carried a three-stroke lead into the final round with a 68-66–134 total, and remained in the lead until he drove out of bounds and put another ball in the water en route to an eight at No. 10. John Morgan, the first-round leader (66), and Walter Morgan, the joint runners-up entering the round, also came a cropper on the second nine.

Abruptly, Dent, who had started the day four back with 68-70 and trailed by six strokes at one point, had the lead. Trevino, who was to finish the season winless, posted 67 and a 208 total early. Gilbert matched that total with a 70 just before Dent's surprising miss that gave him a 70 and set up the playoff. Gilbert went out when Dent and Trevino birdied the par-five 16th. Trevino missed the green on the short 17th before Dent put his nine-iron tee shot three feet from the cup. Then, with the second chance, he carefully holed the putt.

Cadillac NFL Classic—$950,000
Winner: Bruce Crampton

It's a compelling statistic: More than 75 percent of the winners on the Senior PGA Tour have been under 55 years of age. With that in mind, what were the odds that Bruce Crampton, 61 and five years beyond his last victory, would win the Cadillac NFL Classic? Whatever they were, Crampton defied them with an overtime victory over South African newcomer Hugh Baiocchi at New Jersey's Upper Montclair Country Club in mid May. He was the oldest winner of the season to date and one of only three 1997 winners past that figurative 55 dividing line. Jim Dent, 58 (Home Depot), and Gibby Gilbert, 56 (Royal Caribbean), were the others.

George Archer, who has played through a variety of serious physical ailments for years and had a hip replacement in 1996, led the tournament the first two days. Archer, 57, calling it "probably the finest wind round in my entire life," opened with 67 amid 30 mile-per-hour gusts. Baiocchi and Mike McCullough, with 71s, were the only other sub-par shooters. In more benevolent conditions in the second round, Archer shot 72 but held onto a one-stroke lead over Rik Massengale, who shot 72-68—140. Meanwhile, Crampton had recovered from an opening 76 with his first of two 67s to get within four shots of the lead.

Dave Stockton took over first place on the last day when Archer faltered to an outgoing 38. However, after a bogey at the 12th, he yielded to Crampton's eagle deuce at the 14th, where Bruce holed a 110-yard pitching wedge shot. Crampton parred in for the 67 and 210, joined moments later by Baiocchi when he holed a 25-foot birdie putt at 18. Stockton, needing a birdie at the 18th to get into the playoff, went for the green in two with a driver and faded the ball into the water. Baiocchi missed birdie chances on the first two playoff holes, then Crampton snagged his 20th senior title with an eight-foot birdie putt.

Bell Atlantic Classic—$1,000,000
Winner: Bob Eastwood

Little did Bob Eastwood realize at the time just how big were two long putts he made at the conclusion of his second round in the Bell Atlantic Classic in suburban Philadelphia. Eastwood, winless since his three victories in the mid-1980s on the regular tour, ran in a 25-foot birdie putt at the 17th hole and a 27-footer for another at the 18th. That gave him 69 and a 135 total and a one-stroke lead over John Bland and Bob E. Smith with one round to go. Which never went. A heavy rain first delayed, then wiped out the final round at Chester Valley Golf Club and Eastwood had his first Senior PGA Tour victory in his second season.

Eastwood, 51, played with thoughts of his seriously ill father on his mind. When he learned in the Chester Valley locker room that he was the winner, he dedicated the victory to the man who had opened a driving range and got him started in golf. Fred Eastwood had had a stroke the previous week.

Bob Eastwood bogeyed his first hole of the tournament, but mustered five birdies afterward to score a four-under-par 66 and take a one-shot lead over Bland and Bob Dickson. Eastwood took two bogeys on the front nine in the second round, then got one back at the 11th before his birdies on the last two holes restored the lead and gave him the victory. He had expected to win on the senior tour. "I was a good enough player on the PGA Tour that I felt I would eventually win out here," he said. Smith, whose only win in his long career was in Japan in 1993, was happy with his $80,000 runner-up check but disappointed with the rainout. "I'm not in this position very often, so I would have liked to have gone out there and given it a shot."

Ameritech Senior Open—$1,200,000
Winner: Gil Morgan

Gil Morgan had a brief description of his second victory on the season on the Senior PGA Tour: "Pretty brutal." Although he led from start to finish in the Ameritech Senior Open, the first winner to do that in 1997, Morgan staggered home with a one-stroke victory over Hale Irwin, almost giving it away on the tough finishing stretch at Kemper Lakes Golf Course. "I'm a little disappointed with the close," said Morgan after finishing with 74 and six-under-par 210 total, "but it's always good to win."

Fortunately for Morgan, who succeeded another Morgan — Walter — as the Ameritech winner, he had a big cushion going into the final three holes and rival Irwin, in another head-to-head battle, was also in the process of shooting 74. Morgan, who opened the tournament with 67 and a one-stroke lead over Hugh Baiocchi, had Irwin right on his heels going into the final round. Irwin shot 66–137, Morgan 69–136 to set up the shootout. While Irwin was struggling without birdies, long-hitting Morgan was picking up three on par-fives. When he went to the 16th tee, Morgan had a five-stroke lead.

Morgan anticipated trouble on the final holes and it came. A poor drive cost him a bogey at 16, where another challenger, Bob Eastwood, headed back toward third place with a double bogey. Another bogey came when he missed the 17th green and he put his second shot from the rough into the water at the 18th. By then, Irwin had his ball just into the heavy fringe at the green. Had he holed from there, Morgan would have needed his eight-footer to tie. Irwin missed and Morgan solidified his runner-up position on the season's money list with the $180,000 check. It pushed his winnings to $754,342, some $50,000 more than he won in 1990, his best year on the PGA Tour.

BellSouth Senior Classic—$1,300,000
Winner: Gil Morgan

One would not have thought that Gil Morgan had required an "adjustment period" of nine months before he reached a confidence level that, at the BellSouth Senior Classic, carried him to his second win in two weeks on the Senior PGA Tour, two tournaments in which he was out of the lead only once. That's what he said about his early months on the senior circuit, even though he won twice and was a high finisher almost every start. In fact, he had done so well along with the three 1997 wins that he pulled within $12,000 of leader Hale Irwin on the money list with his two-stroke victory at Springhouse Golf Club.

Walter Morgan stole his thunder for a day in Nashville, Tennessee. Morgan, who had placed 16th or better in his last nine starts, opened with an eight-under-par 64 and jumped off to a three-stroke lead over David Graham and J.C. Snead. Gil Morgan then tacked 66 onto his first-round 69 and took a one-shot lead on John Bland, two on Brian Barnes and Dave Stockton.

Several players, including Irwin, made challenging motions Sunday, but only Bland had a chance at the end. Morgan birdied two of the first three

Masters Tournament

The new Master, Tiger Woods, won by 12 strokes, the largest margin in a major championship in this century, and he set or tied 24 tournament records.

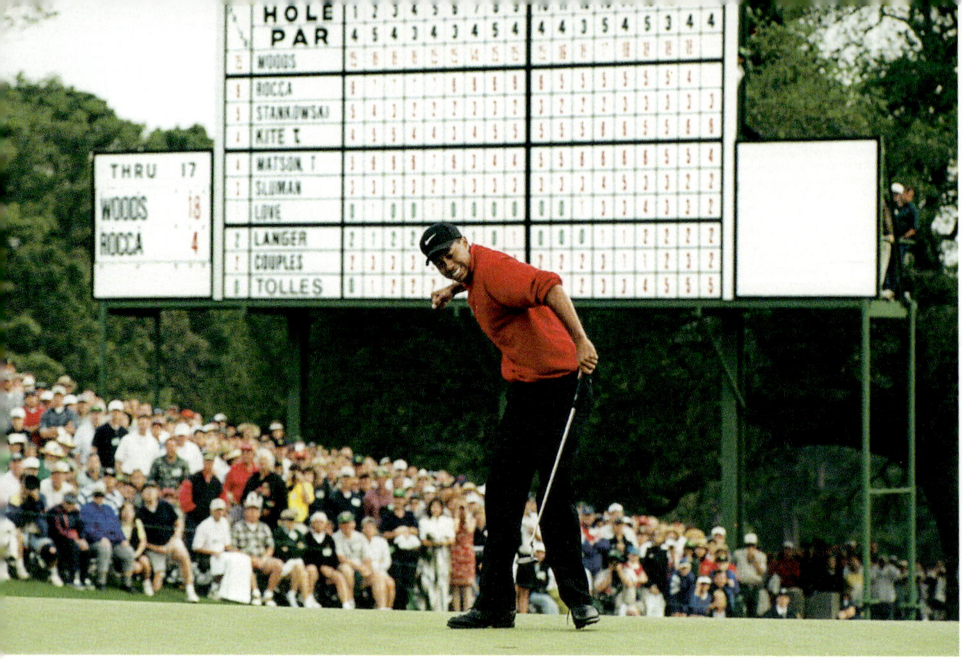

Among his records, Woods' 270 score was the Masters' lowest total ever.

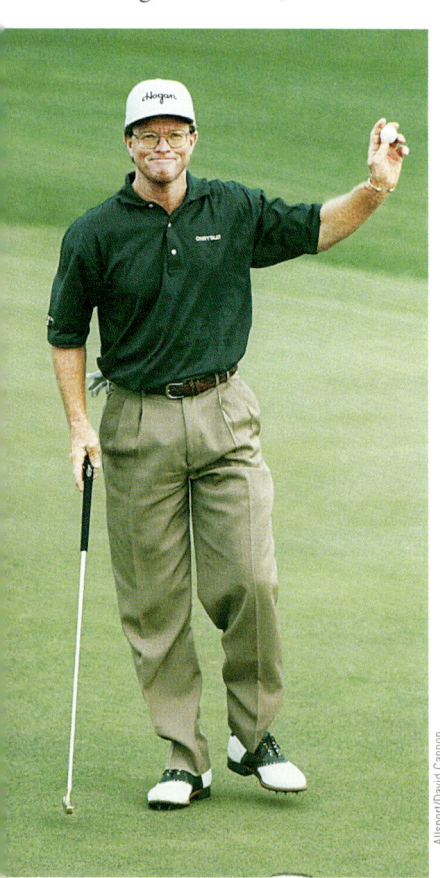

Tom Kite took second place.

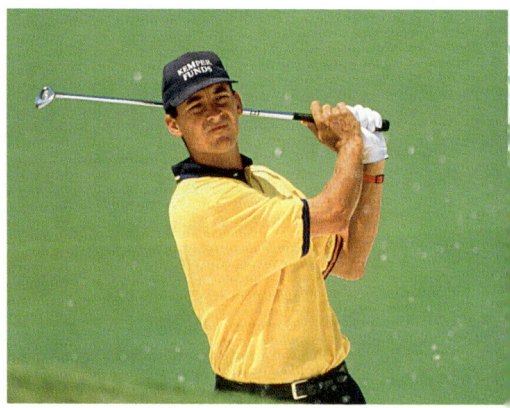

Tommy Tolles closed with 67 for third.

Allsport/David Cannon

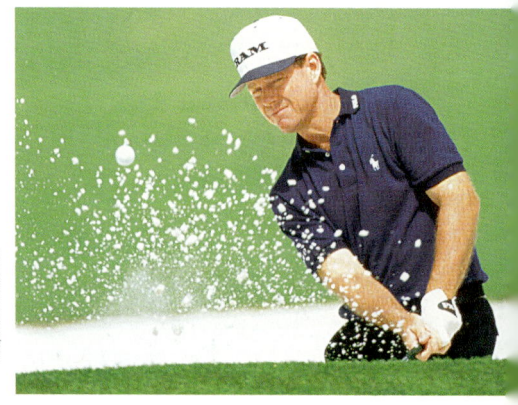

Tom Watson was fourth, 14 strokes back.

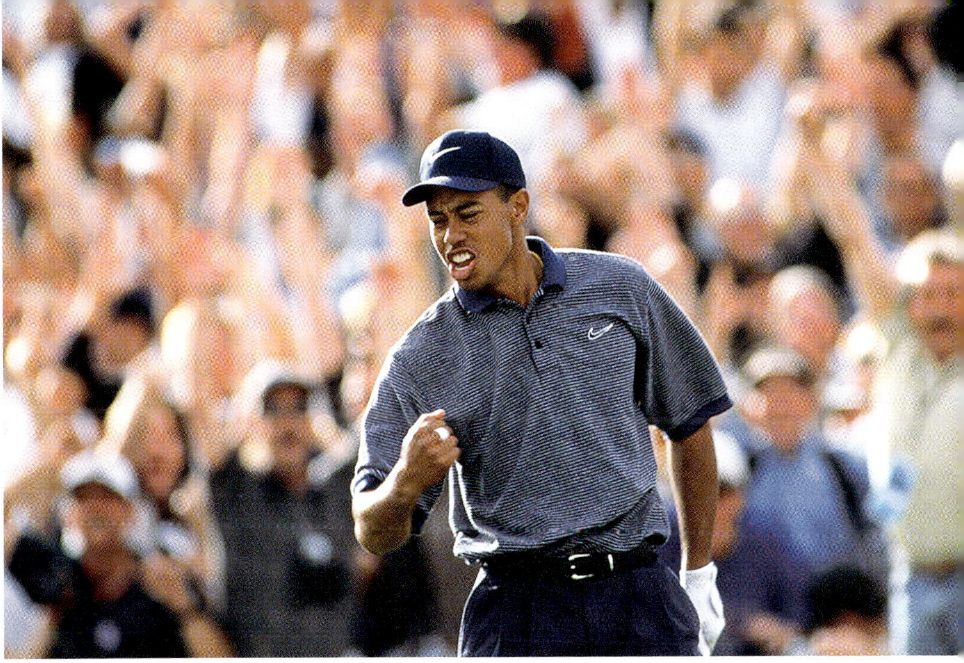

Even in defeat Woods generated excitement, such as with his hole-in-one at Phoenix.

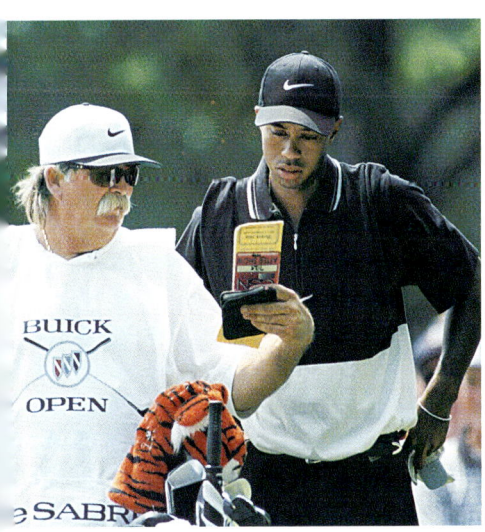

Mike (Fluff) Cowan became golf's most celebrated caddie.

Allsport/Craig Jones

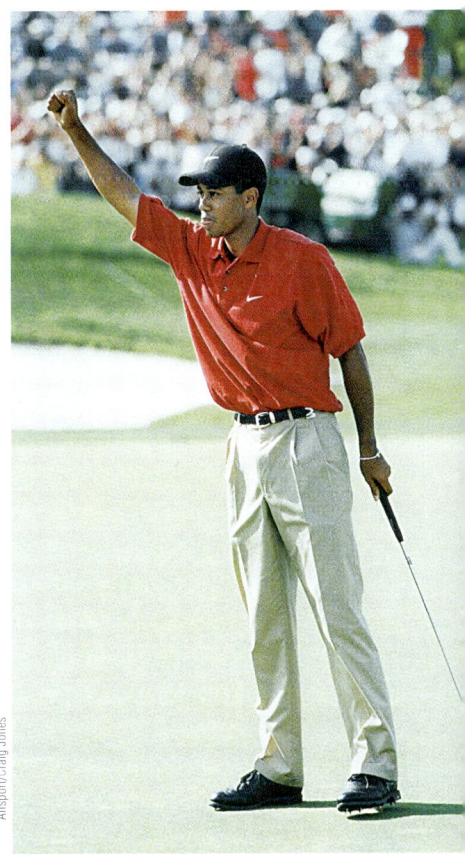

The GTE Byron Nelson Classic was one of four PGA Tour wins.

U.S. Open

Only 27 years of age, Ernie Els won his second U.S. Open Championship.

Colin Montgomerie came one stroke short.

Jeff Maggert settled for fourth place.

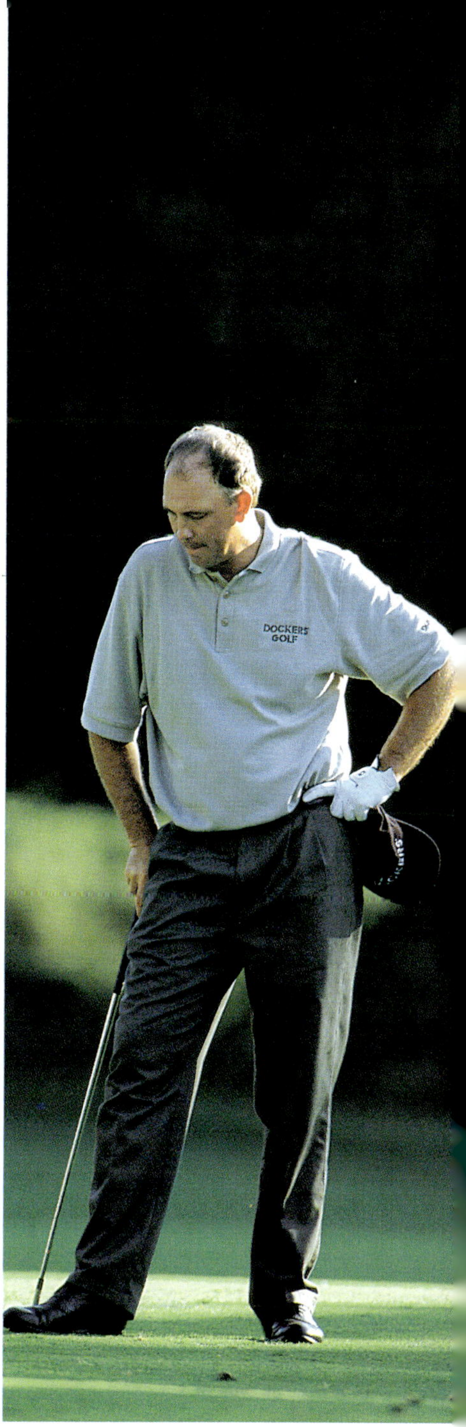

Tom Lehman was disappointed again.

British Open

Justin Leonard, age 25, became the British Open's third consecutive American winner.

Tiger Woods, who tied for 24th place, tied the course record with 64 in the third round.

Ahead after 54 holes, Jesper Parnevik tied for second place, three strokes behind.

Ireland's Darren Clarke led after 36 holes.

im Furyk's 70-70 finish took fourth place.

Colin Montgomerie tied for 24th on his home course.

PGA Championship

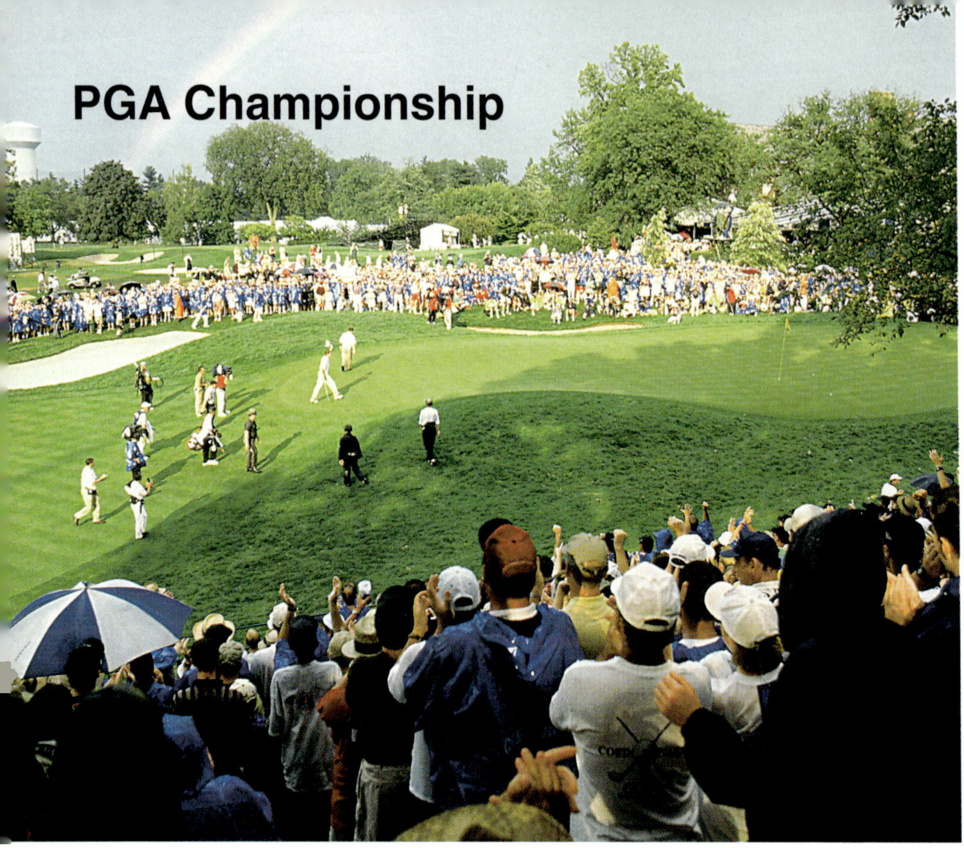

A rainbow framed the 18th hole as Davis Love III won his first major title.

Allsport/David Cannon

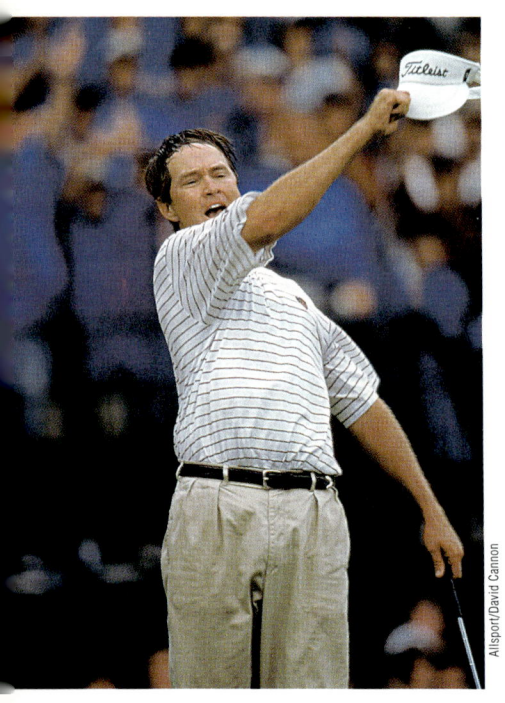

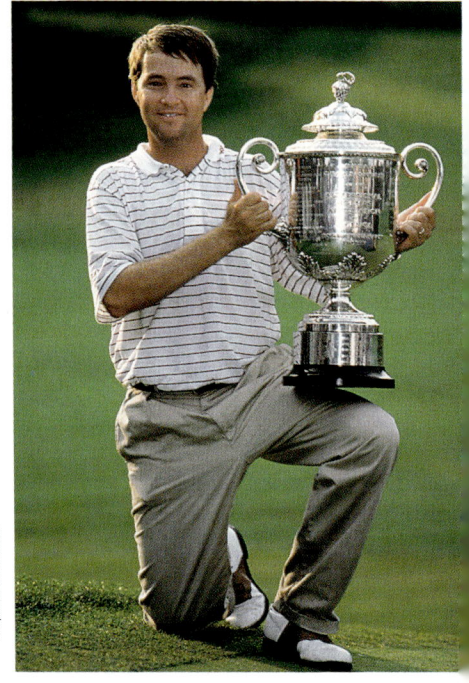

Love's rousing finish for 66 and a 269 total secured the PGA trophy.

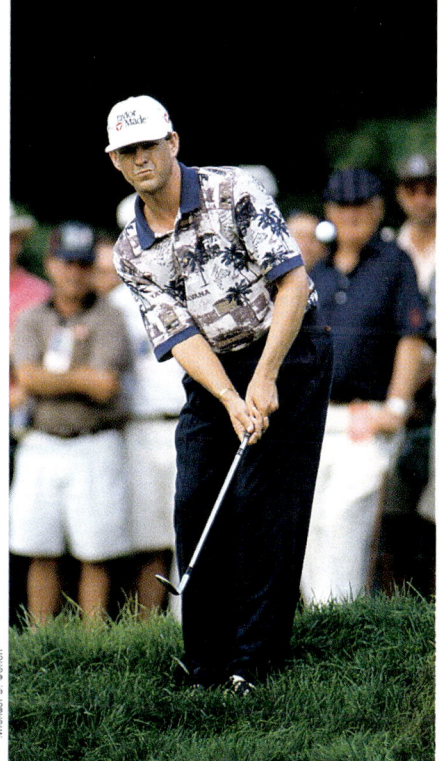

Lee Janzen had the 36-hole lead.

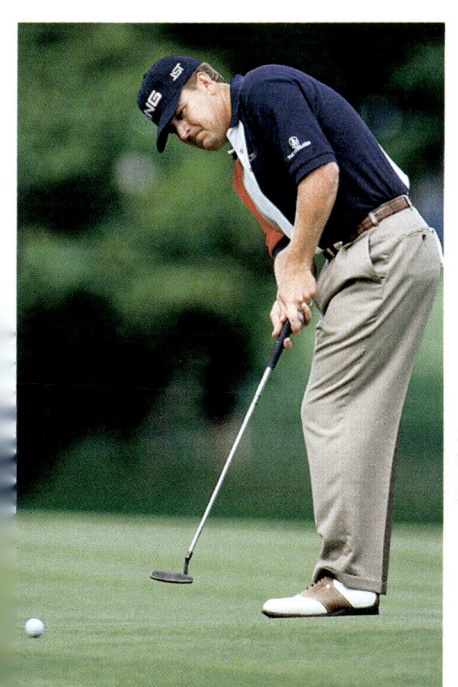

Jeff Maggert finished with 65 for third.

Michael C. Cohen

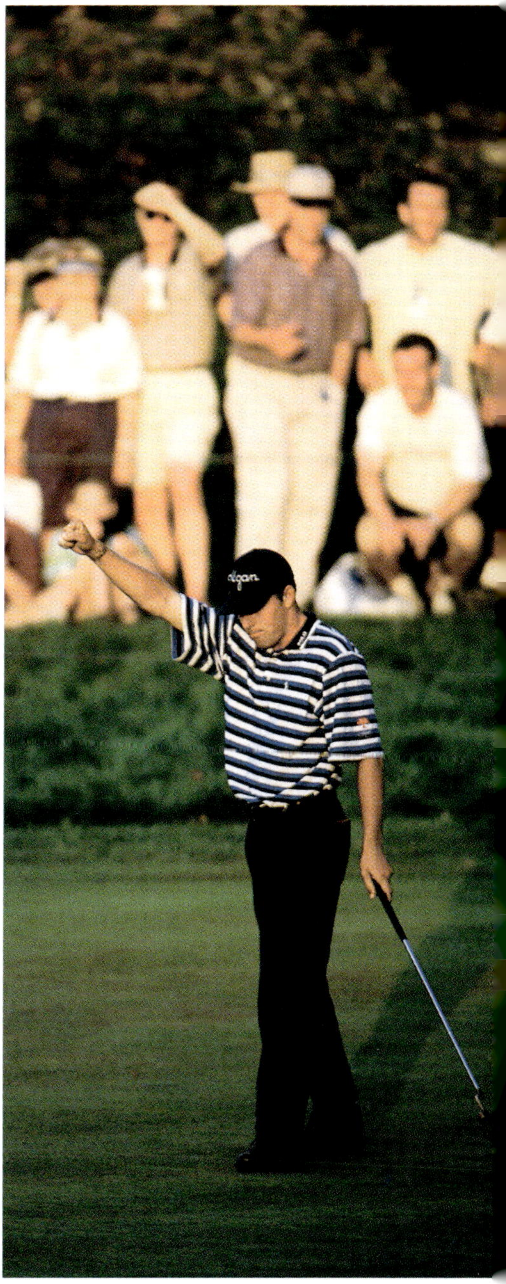

Justin Leonard tied for the lead with his course-record 64 in the third round.

Ryder Cup

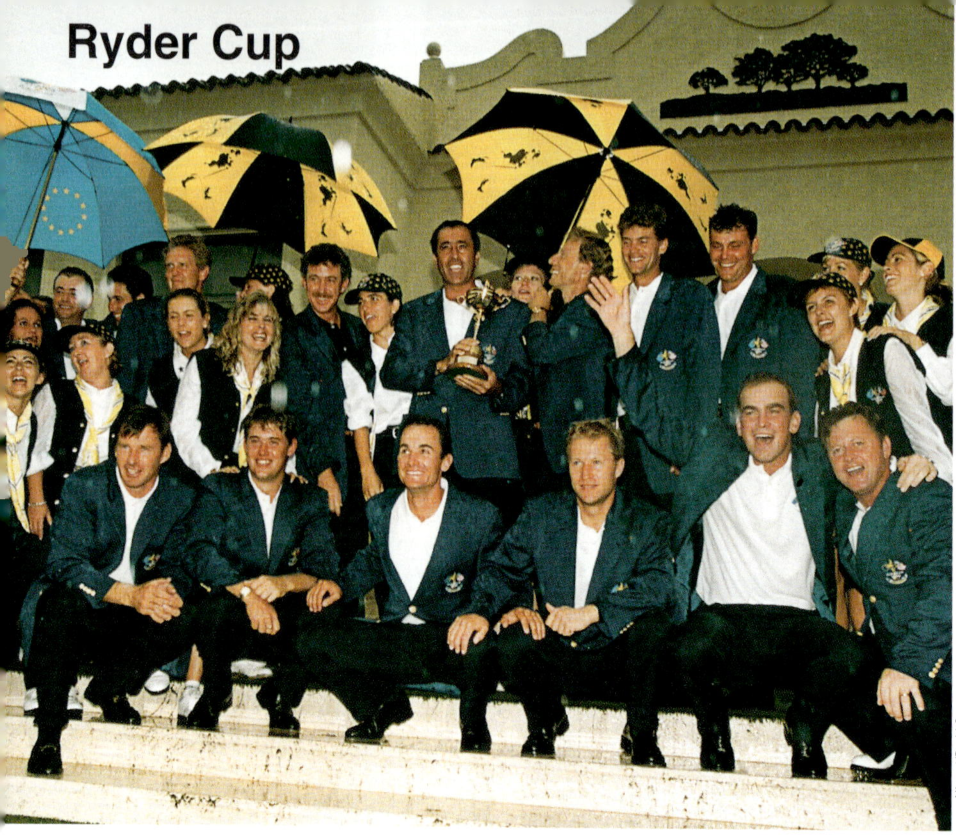

Allsport/David Cannon

The European team celebrated a 14½-13½ victory in the rain at Valderrama.

Allsport/Craig Jones

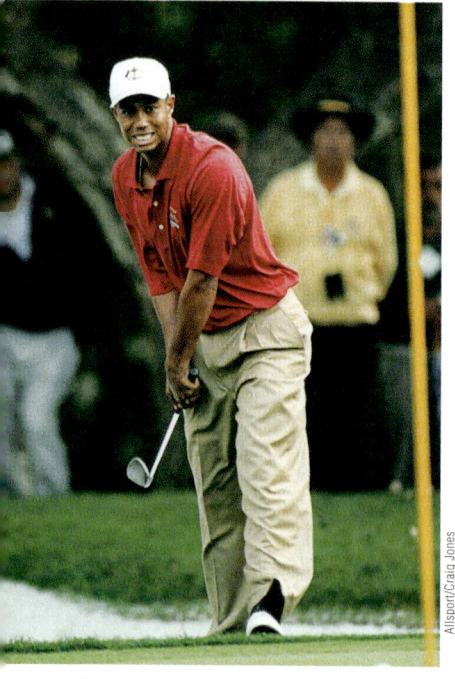

Tiger Woods had a disappointing 1-3-1 record.

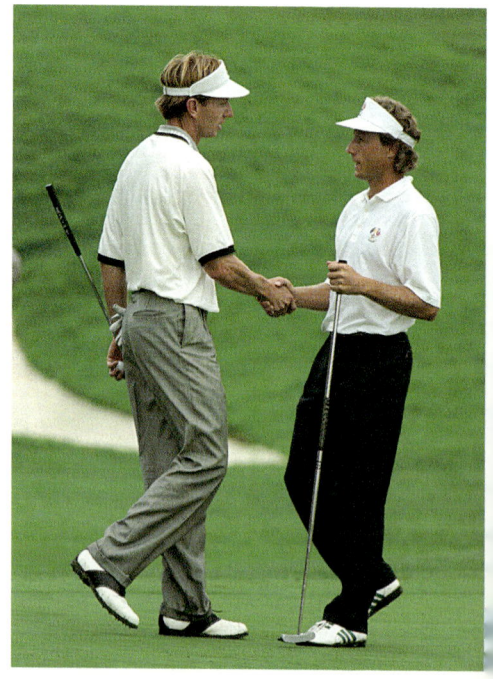

Brad Faxon (left) surrendered the Ryder Cup after losing to Bernhard Langer.

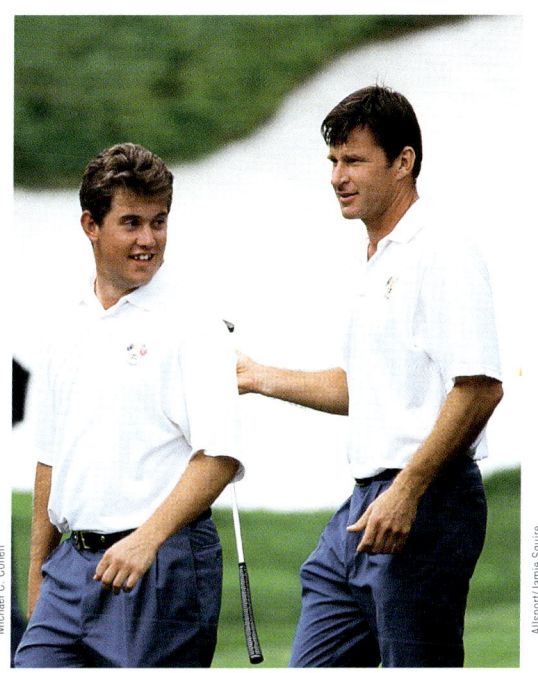

Lee Westwood (left) was guided by Nick Faldo, Europe's most experienced player.

Allsport/Jamie Squire

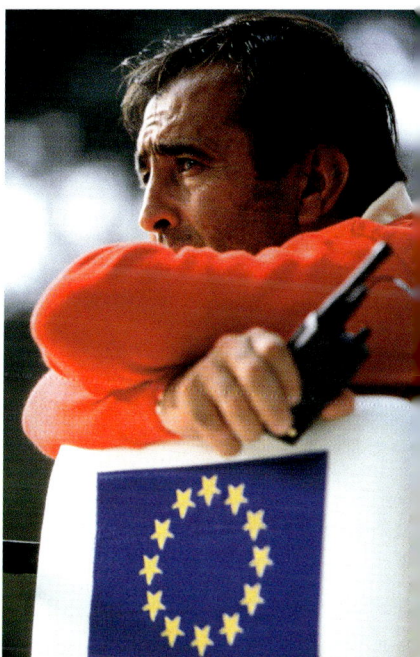

Seve Ballesteros was a hands-on captain for the Europeans.

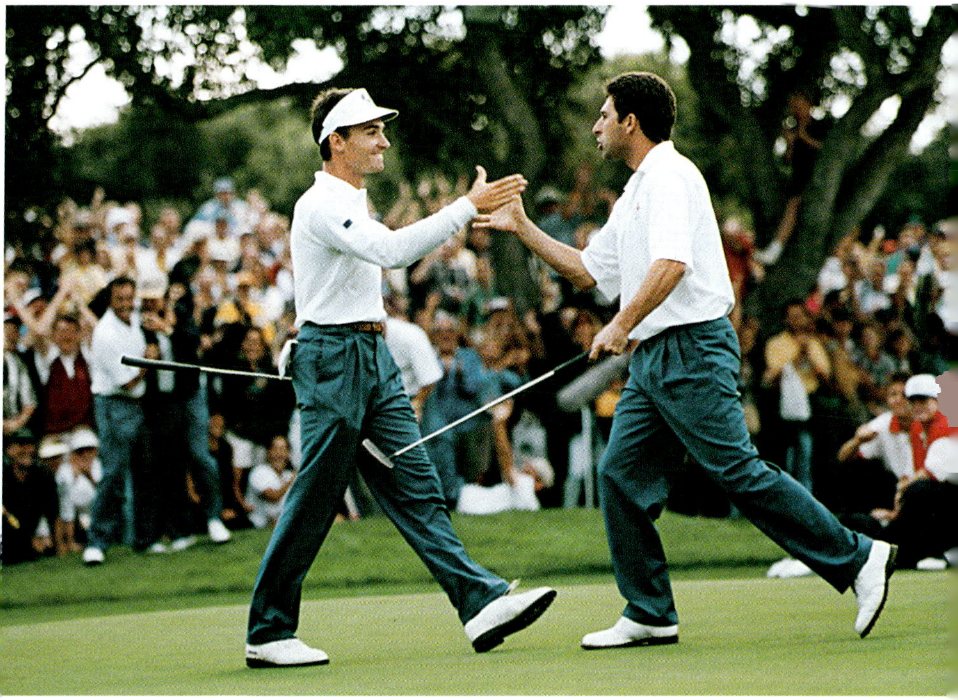

Ignacio Garrido (left) and Jose Maria Olazabal were heroes in Spain.

Toyota World Match Play

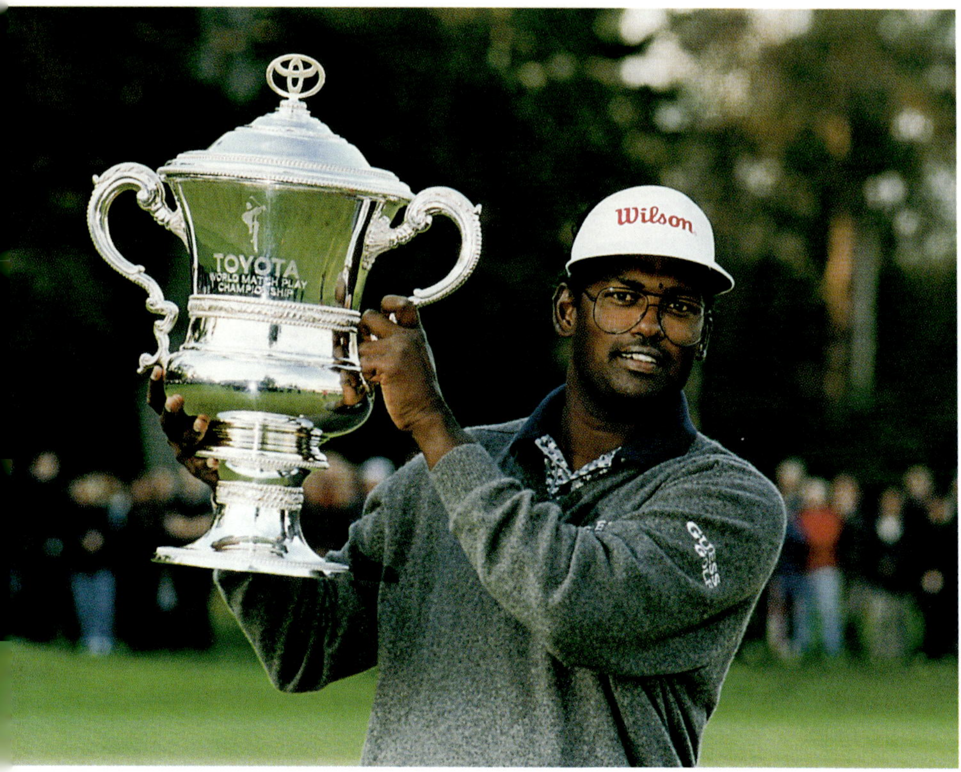

Allsport/David Cannon

Vijay Singh became the first to stop Ernie Els in the World Match Play.

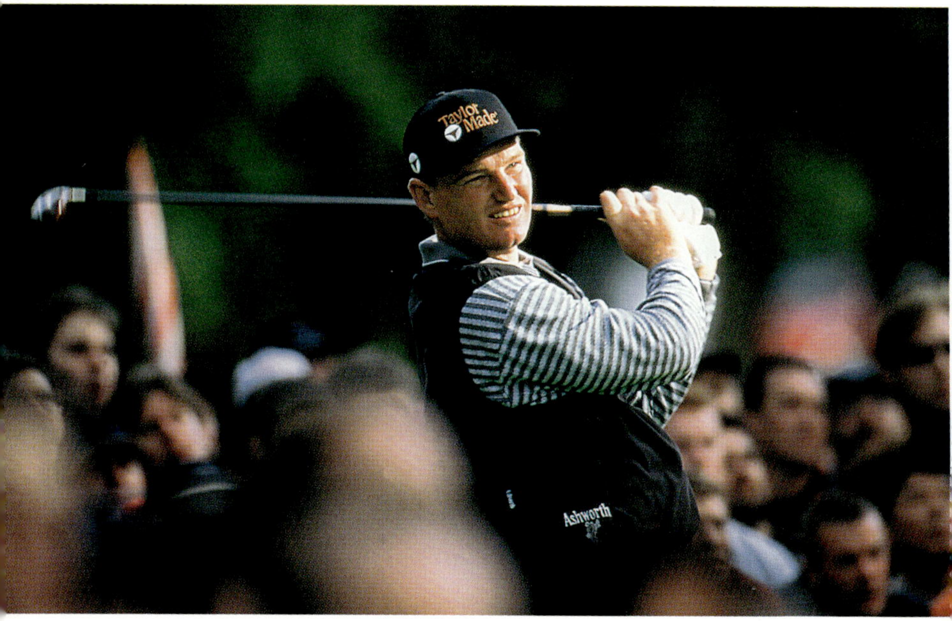

Els had won a record three consecutive titles before losing in the final.

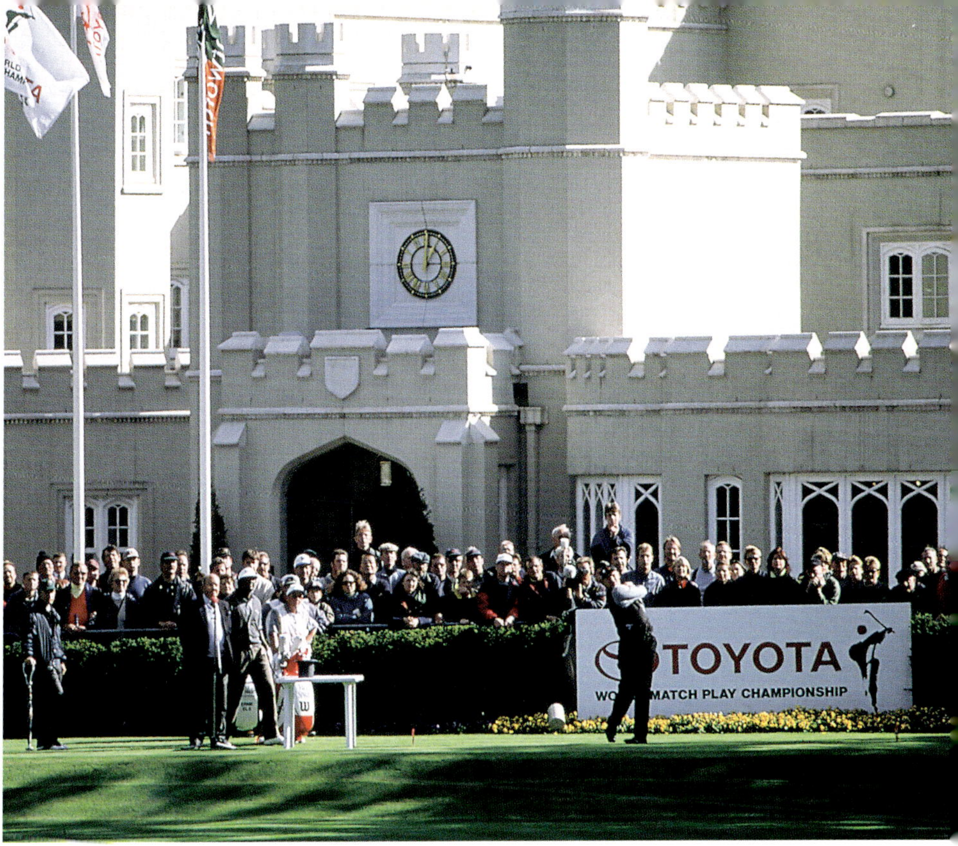

Allsport/Stephen Munday

Els teed off at the Wentworth Club, host to 34 World Match Play events.

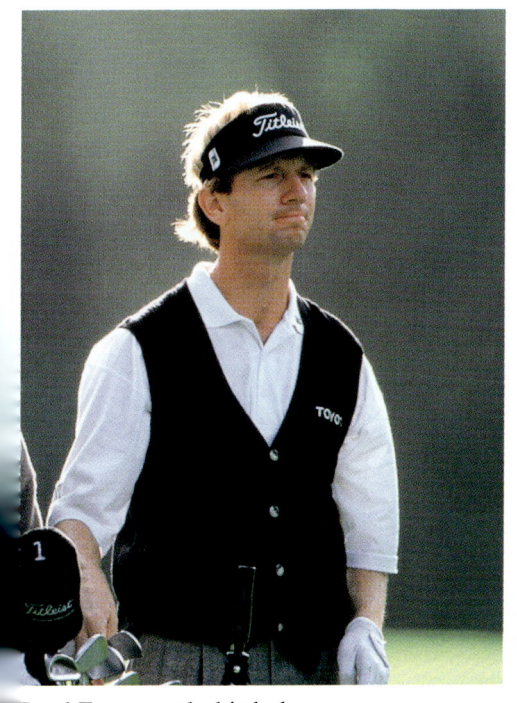

Brad Faxon took third place.

Allsport/Andrew Redington

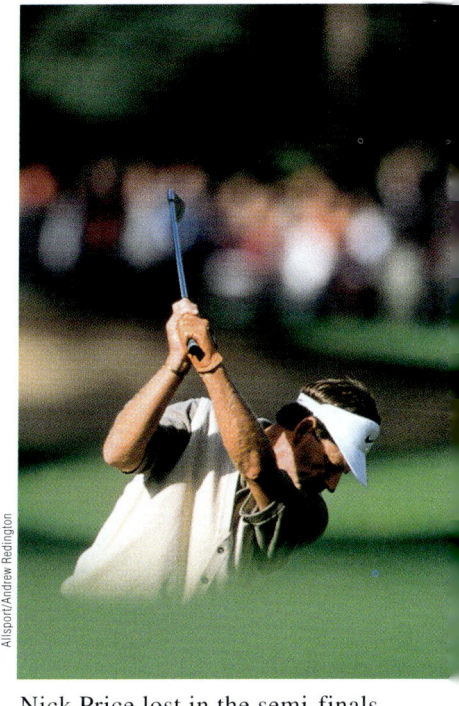

Nick Price lost in the semi-finals.

Alfred Dunhill Cup

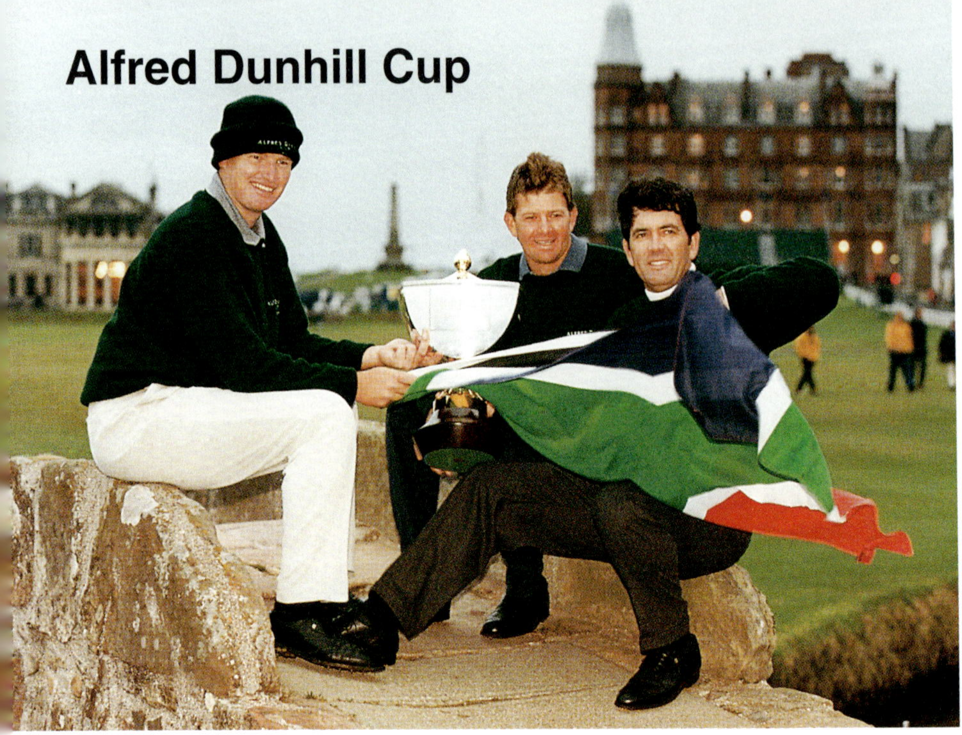

Allsport/Andrew Redington

Draped in the South African flag, the Alfred Dunhill Cup winners were (from left) Ernie Els, Retief Goosen and David Frost.

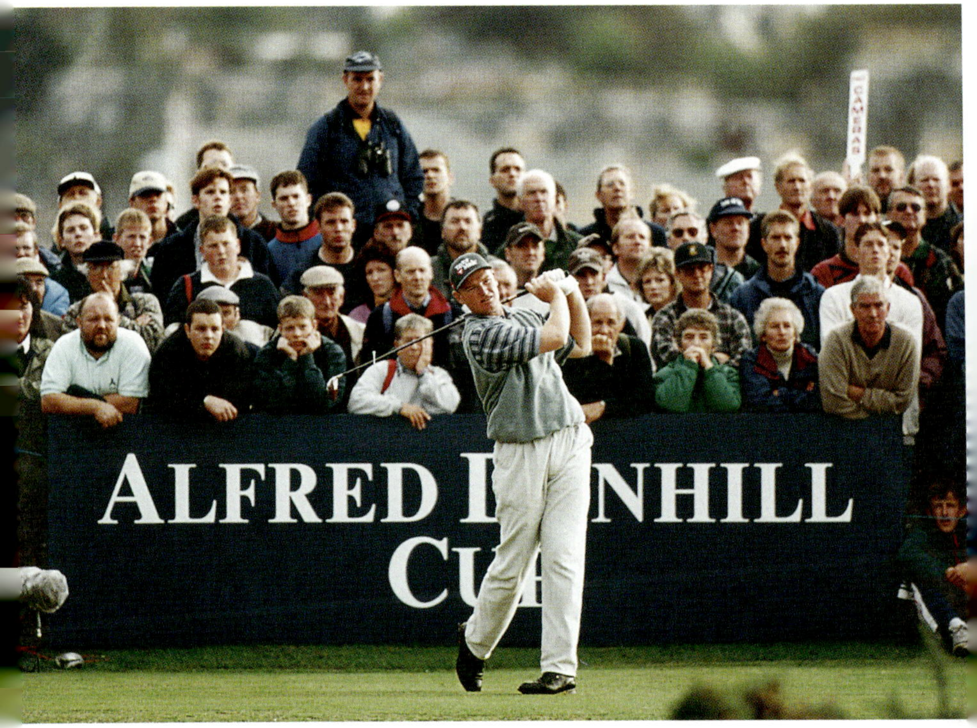

Els helped steer South Africa past Ireland, Germany, Scotland, New Zealand and Sweden for their first victory in the Alfred Dunhill Cup.

Goosen won in the semi-finals and final.

Joakim Haeggman fell to Els.

Per-Ulrik Johansson scored Sweden's only point in the final.

Jesper Parnevik played backwards from the notorious Road Bunker.

The Players Championship

Steve Elkington won his second title in The Players Championship.

Scott Hoch stumbled but took second place.

Holding a seven-stroke lead, Elkington could celebrate along the 18th hole.

holes and established a two-stroke lead that he never relinquished the rest of the way. Irwin, who had started the day four back, pulled within two when he birdied the 13th. But a bogey on the next hole crimped his bid. Larry Gilbert was five under par for the round and within two strokes before bogeying the 18th. Bland birdied the 16th and 17th to get within two. He saw a chance for a two-shot swing at the 18th when Morgan's approach came up short of the green, but the South African bunkered his approach and Morgan wrapped up the win when he saved par with a pitch to two feet, posting 67 and a 14-under-par 202 total. Bland parred, too, for 68–204 and the runner-up spot.

du Maurier Champions—$1,100,000
Winner: Jack Kiefer

Jack Kiefer, Jim Colbert and Graham Marsh shared the first-round lead in the du Maurier Champions with 65s and that set the tone for the rest of the week at St. George's Golf and Country Club in Etobicoke, Canada. The three men occupied the top three positions in the standings each day with Kiefer, the unlikeliest of the three, winding up with the victory. The long-time club pro shot a final-round 68 and won by two strokes with his 15-under-par 269 total in the only Canadian event on the Senior PGA Tour and one of only five contested over 72 holes on the schedule.

It looked like Colbert's tournament for two days. The tour's No. 1 player in 1995 and 1996, Colbert went to St. George's winless in 1997. He shot a second 65 in the second round, yet at 130 he only led Marsh (65-66) by a stroke and Kiefer (65-67) by two. Vicente Fernandez was fourth but four strokes behind Kiefer. Things didn't change much in the third round. Colbert had 70 for 200 and led Marsh (70) and Kiefer (69) by one shot, everybody else by five or more going into the final round, with a little help from Kiefer. Jack, who led by two with three holes left, bogeyed all three.

Not a good thing for the least experienced of the three players, who qualified for the tour in 1991 and scored his only victory in the Ralphs Senior Classic in 1994. He handled it well, remarking afterward, "I'll forget about it and get on with it tomorrow. It would have bothered me in years past but not now. At least now I have a shot at it."

The 57-year-old Florida resident took the lead from Colbert Sunday when he birdied the 11th and rode it to the finish. He got a cushion when Colbert bogeyed the next two holes. Colbert got one back with a birdie at the 15th and just missed another from 15 feet on the final green before Kiefer dropped a par putt to secure the victory.

Nationwide Championship—$1,300,000
Winner: Graham Marsh

Graham Marsh had good feelings about his game when he arrived in Georgia for the Nationwide Championship, even though he had come out third best to Jack Kiefer and Jim Colbert a few days earlier in the du Maurier Champions in Canada. The vibes were right, as the Australian carved out a one-stroke victory over Hale Irwin at the Golf Club of Georgia in suburban Atlanta with a 205 total, 11 under par. It was his fourth individual win in his three years on the Senior PGA Tour — he won the Legends earlier in the year with John Bland — and sent him, full of confidence, to Chicago for the U.S. Senior Open.

Marsh took the lead in the second round of the Nationwide event when he, Bob Murphy and Bob Charles, the final group, finished a few minutes after 9 o'clock after spending a long time on the course on the year's longest day — June 21 — thanks to weather delays of more than two hours. Marsh shot 68 for a 135 total to go two strokes ahead of Irwin and Murphy, who had returned to action after a two-week rest and opened the tournament with 64, one shot off the course record. Murphy had a card full of birdies and bogeys in shooting 73. Irwin, gunning for his fifth victory of the season, had 68-69 the first two days.

Shooting a steady 70 in the final round, Marsh remained in front all day. Murphy shot himself out of it with a seven at the par-three 13th and Irwin trailed by three going to the 17th hole. However, Irwin, tabbed the man to beat by the winner before the round began, almost forced a tie with some help from Marsh. Graham bogeyed the 17th and left himself more than 35 feet from the cup facing a difficult two-putt over a hump for par at the long 18th, knowing that Irwin had a sure birdie after a wedge third to two feet on the hole. With a playoff looming against the man he called "the best senior player in the world," Marsh rolled the tester two feet from the hole to clinch the victory.

U.S. Senior Open—$1,300,000
Winner: Graham Marsh

Graham Marsh had memories and momentum going for him when he teed it up in the U.S. Senior Open and he fed on that to fulfill a goal he had when he came to America on a full-time basis for the first time three years earlier "I had a very express purpose in coming to the U.S. and the Senior Tour I came to win a major," said the Australian whose 60 earlier victories worldwide never included one.

Marsh shot an even-par 280 total on the testing Olympia Fields course for a one-stroke triumph over John Bland, his partner in a Legends of Golf victory earlier in the season. Marsh had come into the Senior Open off his Nationwide win the previous Sunday and finishes of sixth and third the two weeks before that. That was the momentum. The memories were of consecutive high finishes in his three earlier appearances in the Senior Opens at Canterbury, Congressional and Pinehurst.

Olympia Fields, in suburban Chicago, proved to be as tough as advertised the first day as just five players broke par, all with 69s — Gil Morgan, Tom Wargo, Steve Veriato, Kermit Zarley and Bland. Zarley shot 69 again Friday making five birdies on the incoming nine, and took a one-shot lead over Wargo, Marsh (72-67), Bland and Dave Eichelberger (70-69). Marsh fired another 67 Saturday and moved two strokes in front of Bland as Zarley soared to 80.

The final round became essentially a head-to-head duel between Marsh and Bland, who got the upper hand early when Marsh began with three bogeys in a row. Marsh fought back and the lead see-sawed until Marsh bogeyed the 16th and dropped into a tie with the South African. They both parred the 17th. Bland bunkered his approach at 18, while Marsh drove perfectly, put an eight iron 18 feet from the cup, and two-putted for the victory as Bland missed the tying putt.

Kroger Senior Classic—$1,000,000
Winner: Jay Sigel

Bracketed by the final two senior majors of the season, the Kroger Senior Classic had problems as most of the top players got some rest between the two 72-hole tournaments and their demanding playing conditions. Those who did show up at the 6,673-yard course at the Golf Center at Kings Island had a picnic themselves, especially Jay Sigel, the winner. His victory was a superlative performance — lowest round of the season, lowest 54-hole score of the year, fewest putts ever at Kings Island and lowest 36- and 54-hole scores in the history of the eight-year-old event on the outskirts of Cincinnati, Ohio. Forty-eight of the 74 players finished at par or better with 108 sub-par rounds posted.

Sigel cashed in an 18-under-par 195 total — the fifth time in six years that the winning score was under 200 — for his second win of the year. Bob Eastwood, the Bell Atlantic winner, and David Ojala, in the field as the sixth alternate, broke out of the box with 65s, one stroke in front of Sigel and Jimmy Powell, but it was Sigel's show after that. His 63 in the second round jumped him into a four-stroke lead over Ojala. He achieved the eight-under score without benefit of a birdie on any of the three par-fives. As he said afterward, "I was very efficient around the greens." He took only 74 putts.

Sigel discouraged the challengers on the last day with a four-under-par first nine that he capped with an eagle at the par-five ninth. That moved him six strokes ahead of Ojala, who faded to 71 on the second nine and tied for third with Larry Gilbert and John Jacobs. Sigel, playing conservatively coming in, was one under to finish with another 66 for the 195 that bested the tournament record set by Mike Hill in 1995 by one stroke. Isao Aoki, the defending champion, shot a final-round 67 to finish second. Graham Marsh, seeking a third straight win, tied for 21st.

Ford Senior Players Championship—$1,800,000
Winner: Larry Gilbert

In retrospect, could any one begrudge Larry Gilbert his emotional victory in the Ford Senior Players Championship, the year's richest tournament? Surely not for a man who was to learn just two months later that he had inoperable lung cancer. Gilbert, the fifth former club pro to win one of the Senior PGA Tour's major titles, emerged from a pack of contenders with a strong 67 on the demanding TPC of Michigan course at Dearborn, Michigan, that gave him a three-stroke victory.

"This is incredible," said a teary-eyed Gilbert, who passed up a playing career on the PGA Tour in the early 1970s in favor of a club job in his native Kentucky but has become a $3 million winner since joining the Senior PGA Tour in 1993.

Gilbert had solid rounds the first two days. He opened the tournament with his first of two 67s, sharing first place with Dana Quigley, one shot ahead of former winner Dave Stockton and John Bland. Jack Nicklaus, the 1990 champion who designed and toughened the TPC of Michigan course, shot 67 in the second round and climbed into second place, one stroke behind Gilbert, who had 68 for a 135 total. There were then 16 players within four strokes of the lead.

Things got even tighter in the third round. When both Gilbert and Nicklaus shot 72s, the 16 players at four back became 22. Gilbert shared the top spot — 207 — with Stockton, Bland and Bob Dickson, but "wouldn't give a plugged nickel for my chances" off his play. However, he started with a birdie at No. 1 when he hit the flagstick with his approach and never trailed. He made three more birdies on the first nine to go 13 under. Stockton caught him with birdies at 10 and 13, but bogeyed the next two holes. When Gilbert rolled in a long birdie putt at 16, he was back in front by three and that's how he finished with his 14-under 274. Stockton and Dickson shared second place with Isao Aoki and Jack Kiefer.

Burnet Senior Classic—$1,350,000
Winner: Hale Irwin

For most players, it takes a long run of poor performances or even a winless season before they consider themselves to be in a slump. For a player of the calibre of Hale Irwin, it takes only a couple of months without a victory to plant that thought in his mind.

Irwin had had a couple of second-place finishes since he scored his fourth victory of 1997 at Las Vegas in April and still led the money list when he arrived in Minneapolis, Minnesota, for the Burnet Senior Classic, but was particularly dissatisfied with his play in the two recent majors — fifth in the Senior Open, 19th in the Senior Players. He had the answer, though. He had determined how to turn his putting around and it paid off with his fifth triumph of the season, a two-stroke victory in a stretch duel with Lee Trevino at Bunker Hills Golf Club. Irwin shot 66–199, and Trevino, 67–201.

Reverting to the putting grip that had brought him such success early in the year, Irwin opened the Burnet Classic with seven birdies and an eagle for 65, trailing leader Jimmy Powell by one stroke. Indicative of the improved putting, all of the birdie putts were 10 feet or longer and he eagled the par-five 18th from 15 feet. Irwin moved into the lead on the rain-delayed second day with 68–133, one ahead of Trevino, who also shot 68.

The two left the rest of the field behind in the last round. They were tied seven times during the confrontation, the last going to the 17th tee. "It became a matter of who would make the mistake first," noted Irwin. It happened there when Trevino, battling for his first win of the season, three putted from the back fringe. Irwin birdied from from 20 feet and led by two. Trevino made a game try to catch him, hitting his three-wood second sho

10 feet from the cup at 18. Irwin, putting from the fringe, left it six feet short before Trevino's eagle putt died on line but just short, too. Both birdied.

Franklin Quest Championship—$1,000,000
Winner: Dave Stockton

For the second week in a row, one of the Senior PGA Tour's leading players emerged from a self-described slump when Dave Stockton scored his first victory of the season in the Franklin Quest Championship at Park Meadows Golf Club outside of Salt Lake City, Utah. Stockton, the leading money winner in 1993 and 1994 with 13 senior victories in his first five full seasons, had gone much longer without a win — since the autumn of 1996 — than had Hale Irwin before his victory in the Burnet Classic.

His two tour-playing sons pushed Stockton to the triumph at Park Meadows, Ron with some technique observations three weeks earlier and Dave Jr. with a telephone challenge during a weather break in the action on the last day. Stockton also had past performances going for him. He owned the tournament (197) and 18-hole (63) course records from his previous Franklin Quest win in 1993 as well as the low tournament scoring average.

A record seven players — Bruce Devlin, Mike McCullough, Kermit Zarley, Hugh Baiocchi, Tom Shaw, Frank Conner and Bobby Stroble — shared the first-round lead at 67 as Stockton opened with 69. Stockton then surged three strokes ahead in the second round with an eight-under-par 64 and 133 total, the product of nine birdies and a bogey. He had his hands full in the final round.

Zarley, Baiocchi and Larry Ziegler, who was en route to a 64 himself, caught him at 12-under-par before a second lightning storm brought a two-hour suspension of play. That's when Dave Jr., on the road between stops on the regular tour, caught him on the telephone in the locker room and challenged him to beat his 68 earlier that day in Hartford. After play resumed, Stockton ran off three consecutive birdies to match his son's 68, shoot 201 and win by two strokes over Zarley and three over Baiocchi and Ziegler.

Johnny Miller made his first start on the Senior Tour there, debuting inauspiciously with a 215 total, tying for 44th place.

BankBoston Classic—$1,000,000
Winner: Hale Irwin

Put Hale Irwin in or tied for the lead going into the final round of a Senior PGA Tour tournament nowadays and you can mark up another victory on his record. Irwin displayed his successful finishing talents for the fifth straight time in the BankBoston Classic when he recorded his sixth victory of 1997. He broke from a 36-hole-leading deadlock with Bob Betley to gain a two-stroke win at Nashawtuc Country Club in Concord, Massachusetts, with a 13-under-par 203 total. Irwin was the first to score six victories on the Senior PGA Tour since Lee Trevino in 1994.

The sixth did not come easily, though. He started the tournament three strokes off the pace of Kermit Zarley, who limped to 66 after aggravating an old knee injury on the eve of the event. Irwin then forged the second-round tie with a 67–136 total to Betley's 70-66 as Zarley faded with a 75. Betley, the 1993 winner, was in the tournament on a sponsor's exemption.

So was Bob Wynn, who, along with Jerry McGee, gave the winner a run for his money. The two, playing together just ahead of Irwin, found themselves in a deadlock with Irwin after he bogeyed the 16th to drop to 11 under par. Wynn and McGee parred the short 17th and the tie seemed likely to remain when Irwin pulled his tee shot, leaving himself with a difficult 50-foot putt. "I had the same putt last year and I made it back then," Irwin recalled after he repeated the feat to take a one-stroke lead.

Irwin drove into a fairway bunker on the 18th, but played out safely after learning that neither Wynn nor McGee birdied that final hole. He did after a wedge to nine feet for 67 and the 203 total. Wynn and McGee tied for second at 205, Wynn closing with 66 and McGee with 67.

Northville Long Island Classic—$1,000,000
Winner: Dana Quigley

Never has the final day of a tournament ended on a more somber note than the 1997 Northville Long Island Classic. Within an hour after Dana Quigley won his first tournament ever at the Meadow Brook Club, he learned that his father had died while he was fighting for the Northville title that Sunday afternoon. It was a crushing blow to Quigley, who had just won a three-hole playoff duel against the formidable Jay Sigel.

Quigley could easily not have been on Long Island that weekend at all. He got into the Northville tournament through the Monday qualifier, then drove home to Providence to see his ailing 82-year-old father. He returned to play only at the insistence of his father and other family members. They must have known something.

Quigley, who played the regular tour from 1978 through 1982, began the tournament with 67, three shots off the pace of leader Jose Maria Canizares one of Spain's leading players on the PGA European Tour for years. Quigley shot another 67 in the second round and moved into a three-way tie for first place with Canizares and Walter Hall, also a Monday qualifier who was to win two weeks later on the European Seniors Tour. On the last day, Quigley struggled to a 70–204 total, and Sigel caught him with 66 despite bogeys on two of the last four holes. Canizares missed a four-foot par putt on the last green to miss the playoff and join Raymond Floyd and Hubert Green at 205.

The decision came after Quigley and Sigel matched bogeys and pars on the first two extra holes. Both had long birdie putts at the par-five third and Quigley got down in two from 75 feet while Sigel, losing his second playoff of the year, three-putted from 35 feet. Quigley became the fourth first-time Senior PGA Tour winner of the season, following David Graham, Bud Allin and Bob Eastwood, and the first Monday qualifier victor.

First of America Classic—$1,000,000
Winner: Gil Morgan

If history held sway, it was easy to predict who wouldn't win the First of America Classic: None of the 11 players who had been victorious in the 11 previous Grand Rapids tournaments. Gil Morgan would have been a good choice, though. With Hale Irwin playing that week in the PGA Championship, Morgan, second on the money list, was the only man besides Irwin with more than two 1997 wins on the books. Morgan lived up to the billing, squeezing out a one-stroke victory over Bob Duval at Egypt Valley Country Club, his fourth of the season. His nine-under-par 207 total was the highest winning score in tournament history.

Rainy weather through much of the tournament contributed to the high scores. Play started more than two hours late in the first round because of a heavy downpour and, when the long day ended, first-year players Duval and Englishman John Morgan led with 68s, one stroke ahead of Gil Morgan and three others. Morgan leaped into the lead on a calmer second day with 67–136, two in front of Duval (70) and four or more ahead of the rest of the field.

Birdies were scarce as rain returned in the final round. Gil Morgan, playing "somewhat conservative," ran off 11 pars to start the final round and stay ahead of Duval, trying to beat his more-famous son to a tour winner's circle. Duval had a three-birdie string on the first nine and was even with Gil until Morgan birdied and he bogeyed at the 12th. A two-shot swing went the other way at 15, then Morgan went ahead again with a birdie at 17. He got a break at 18 when his errant tee shot hit a tree and stayed out of the woods. Both he and Duval missed the green and got up and down for pars, the winner from 50 feet for 71. Duval had 70–208, two in front of John Morgan.

Saint Luke's Classic—$1,000,000
Winner: Bruce Summerhays

The frustration of Bruce Summerhays was approaching the 100 mark when lightning struck. Although a solid performer, Summerhays, who had played in every event for which he was eligible since joining the Senior PGA Tour full time at the start of the 1995 season, had gone through 96 tournaments without a victory until fortune smiled on him in the Saint Luke's Classic at Kansas City, Missouri, in late August. Summerhays capitalized on a good bounce on a bad tee shot at the 54th hole to get into a playoff and claimed his first victory on the second extra hole, the fifth first-time senior tour winner of the season.

The players who battled it out at the end in overtime — Summerhays and Hugh Baiocchi — began the tournament excitingly with seven-under-par 63s over the 6,539 yards of Loch Lloyd Country Club. South African Baiocchi followed with a 65 in the second round for 128, the lowest 36-hole score of the season, but Jay Sigel, a two-time winner in 1997, pulled within one stroke with 65-64, as Summerhays gave up a lot of ground with 71.

Summerhays, a club pro who never qualified for the regular PGA Tour, had four birdies on the first nine, but made up just one stroke as Baiocchi shot 32. Baiocchi's game came untracked on the second nine. He bogeyed 10 and double-bogeyed 12, opening the door to 53-year-old Summerhays and fast-finishing Dave Stockton, who shot 64 for 200 and just missed the playoff. Summerhays birdied the 16th and the 18th, the latter with a 24-foot putt after his wild tee shot ricocheted off a spectator. He shot 65 for 199. Baiocchi struggled to 38 on the second nine and had to make a six-footer at 18 for 71 and the deadlock.

Both parred the first extra hole and missed the green on the second, Baiocchi after driving into the trees. Summerhays pitched to two feet and holed for the victory after Baiocchi missed his par putt from 20 feet.

Pittsburgh Senior Classic—$1,100,000
Winner: Hugh Baiocchi

Hugh Baiocchi, who followed fellow South African John Bland to America and the Senior PGA Tour, followed him into the winner's circle at the Pittsburgh Senior Classic after eight frustrating months in the non-exempt maelstrom and two Sundays on the short end of title playoffs.

Baiocchi, a long-time standout on the European and South African Tours, didn't even qualify for a tournament until the PGA Seniors' in late April, but once he got into the fields he showed his talent with frequent top-10 finishes, including two playoff losses.

He finally broke through at Quicksilver, where he overtook a fading Bob Duval in the final round, but it took six extra holes to land the all-important initial U.S. victory. He joined Summerhays and four others before him as a first-time winner of the 1997 season.

Baiocchi wasn't really noticed the first two days as he shot a pair of 70s and stood four strokes off the lead of Duval, who posted two 68s to lead the field into a final round for the first time. Duval was in a five-way tie for the lead the first day with John Jacobs, Dan Wood, Kermit Zarley and John Rech. At 136, Duval had two shots on Jacobs, Tom Wargo and David Graham.

He seemed to have the situation well in hand Sunday when he birdied the 12th hole to go 12 under, but "I was leaking oil out there after that." He bogeyed 13 and 15, opening the door for Baiocchi, who birded the 18th for 66 and the tie with Duval at 206. After the two men matched pars through five playoff holes, Duval bogeyed from a fairway bunker on Quicksilver's 10th hole and lost to Baiocchi's two-putt par.

Bank One Classic—$800,000
Winner: Vicente Fernandez

There was something appropriate about the victory of Vicente Fernandez in the farewell staging of the Bank One Classic in Lexington, Kentucky. One of the Senior PGA Tour's oldest existing tournaments, the Bank One even produced an inordinate number of overseas winners over its 15-year existence. Gary Player (two), Isao Aoki, Bruce Crampton and Bob Charles pre

ceded Fernandez as winners in the PGA's only regular stop in the Bluegrass State.
  In fact, if anyone hated to see the tournament go by the boards, it was Aoki, who battled Fernandez to the wire, losing by one stroke to Fernandez's 203 total. In his four previous appearances in Lexington, Aoki finished first, second, third and fourth and, with 1997's runner-up money of $70,400, he won more than $260,000 in his five visits to Kentucky.
  Fernandez, Argentina's most successful golfer since the great Roberto de Vicenzo, scored his second victory in America. He was in a more comfortable position for this one as an exempt regular. He won his first in his rookie 1996 season at Minneapolis as a Monday qualifier.
  Vicente ran a par-or-better scoring streak to 19 rounds at Kearney Hills — 67-69-67 — as he contended from the start. Walter Hall, himself a Monday qualifier who had won the Beltry PGA Seniors in England on the European Seniors Tour two weeks earlier, was the leader with an opening 66. Al Geiberger, just a few days beyond his 60th birthday, went in front in the second round with 67–135, one shot better than Fernandez and Jay Sigel (68-68) and two in front of Aoki, who shot 65, and Hall (71).
  The drama came at the end. Fernandez went two strokes in front with sizeable birdie putts at 16 and 17 after leader Aoki drove into the water and bogeyed 16, then missed a three-foot tiddler at 17. Aoki birdied 18 to cut the final margin to one as Fernandez parred for his 69 and the victory.

Boone Valley Classic—$1,300,000
Winner: Hale Irwin

Hale Irwin, who had played only once in the previous five weeks, made amends to his hometown fans by winning the second Boone Valley Classic, scoring his seventh victory of a remarkable season and setting a new single-season money-winning record in the process. Irwin, who lives in the St. Louis suburbs, had lost ingloriously to Gibby Gilbert in a playoff in the inaugural in 1996 and confirmed that he "had an extra surge of desire to do well" in the second edition.
  Irwin couldn't have done much better, shooting a pair of seven-under-par 65s after an opening 70 for a 200 total and a two-stroke victory, his third in his last four starts. The $195,000 first prize jumped Irwin's earnings to $1,706,989, exceeding the record $1,627,890 collected by Jim Colbert in 1996.
  Rocky Thompson, who hadn't won in more than three years, had his moment with a first-round 66 that staked him to a one-stroke lead over David Graham and Mike McCullough. Then Irwin and money runner-up Gil Morgan entered the picture. Irwin's first 65, in which he birdied five of the last six holes, projected him into a first-place tie after the second round with Graham, who shot 68, while Morgan, with 70-67, joined John Bland and Dale Douglass two off the lead.
  Graham, a two-time winner in his first full season, held Irwin at bay until Irwin birdied the par-three 12th. He followed with "my shot of the week" at the 13th, an eight-iron shot out of a divot to nine feet that set up another birdie and established his winning two-stroke margin, as he birdied four of

the last six holes. Morgan also shot 65 Sunday to nail second place, three strokes ahead of Bland and four in front of Graham, who faded to a 71 on the back nine. Irwin never made a bogey during the tournament.

Comfort Classic—$1,050,000
Winner: David Graham

David Graham bounced back from a disappointing finish in St. Louis one Sunday to victory in Indianapolis seven days later. Graham picked off his third victory of the Senior PGA Tour season in the Comfort Classic, the renamed tournament at the Brickyard Crossing course that winds in and out of the famous racetrack, joining Hale Irwin and Gil Morgan as the only players with more than two victories on the 1997 tour.

The Aussie's finish at Brickyard was in striking contrast to his final nine at Boone Valley, a stretch during which he went from leader to fourth place at the end. This time, he came from behind on the incoming nine and won with a birdie on the 18th green. He had a 31 coming in for 65 and the winning 16-under-par 200 total.

David positioned himself one stroke off the pace Saturday night with rounds of 67-68–135, tied for second place with Raymond Floyd and Bud Allin, the first-time winner at Sarasota in the spring. The leader was Larry Nelson, the latest star to come off the PGA Tour and enter the senior ranks. Playing in just his second event on the Senior PGA Tour, Nelson began 69-65 for the 134 total. Simon Hobday, the 1995 winner and 1996 first-round leader at Indianapolis, led again on opening day, but faded after that.

Allin wrested the lead from Nelson at the sixth hole and never trailed until the 18th. Graham shot into contention when he eagled the 15th hole with a huge drive, a six-iron second and a four-foot putt. That put him at 15 under par, one shot behind Allin. He parred the next two holes, hit another big drive at the 18th, wedged to six feet and sank the birdie putt, the winner as it turned out when Allin was in the rough with his first two shots, pitched over the green and missed the tying chip. That dropped him into a second-place tie at 201 with Nelson. Irwin, seeking his eighth win, "hit the proverbial wall" and tied for 21st.

Emerald Coast Classic—$1,100,000
Winner: Isao Aoki

Isao Aoki finally figured how to escape those second-place finishes and get a 1997 victory onto the record: resurrect a faithful old putter and shoot the lowest round in the 18-year history of the Senior PGA Tour. Those were two of the major ingredients that spurred the great Japanese golfer to his playoff triumph in the Emerald Coast Classic at Pensacola, Florida, after winding up the runner-up in five events earlier in the year. With the old putter, the 55-year-old Aoki sank a short birdie putt to force the playoff and a much longer one to secure his seventh Senior Tour victory. The record 60 in the second round put him back in the game and made the Sunday deadlock possible.

Aoki had taken a two-week break prior to the Emerald Coast Classic and decided to reactivate a putter he had stopped using even though it had helped him produce some 60 wins in his earlier career. It didn't help much in the first round at Pensacola's The Moors Golf Club in Milton, as he shot 71 and trailed leader Vicente Fernandez by eight strokes.

Then came the 10-under-par 60 with 10 birdies on the first 16 holes and a try for 59 at No. 18 coming up one foot short. Five players — Lee Elder, Rocky Thompson, Jim Colbert, Dale Douglass and Bud Allin — had shared the record with 61s. The 60 lifted Aoki into a tie for third place with Hale Irwin and Douglass, one shot behind leaders Fernandez and Simon Hobday at 130.

Aoki made six more birdies in the last round, the last two earning the tie and winning the tournament, his first U.S. victory in a playoff in three tries. Gil Morgan, who had started the day two strokes off the lead, birdied the 18th from 15 feet for 64—196 before Aoki made his four-footer for 65 to force the playoff, the third in the three-year history of the tournament. Morgan, seeking his fifth 1997 victory, missed the green on the first extra hole and Aoki holed an 18-footer for the win.

Vantage Championship—$1,500,000
Winner: Hale Irwin

Another hallmark of the astonishing success of the PGA Senior Tour was etched into the record book when Hale Irwin registered his eighth victory of the season in the Vantage Championship at Winston-Salem, North Carolina, the first week of October. Who would have thought that, 17 years after the four-tournament inaugural season, a senior player would pile up winnings of more than $2 million and be the first on any tour in the world to do it. That's what the talented Irwin accomplished with his one-stroke victory at Tanglewood Park Golf Course, the winner's check of $225,000 running his earnings in 20 Senior Tour events to $2,003,864.

Irwin had to shed the conservative mantle he wore through most of the final round to beat the unpredictable Dave Eichelberger, who birdied the 18th hole for a nine-under-par 62 with Irwin watching from the fairway. Irwin then drilled his three-wood second shot 245 yards onto the green at the par-five hole and two-putted for the win, his second in three years in the Vantage. "It was maybe my best shot of the year," he concluded.

He "didn't anticipate playing this conservatively" when he ran off 15 consecutive pars after taking a five-stroke lead with a dazzling 62 himself in Saturday's second round on top of an opening 64. The 126 tied the tour's 36-hole record set by Jim Colbert in the 1994 GTE West Classic.

Any challenge in the last round it appeared, would come from runner-up Larry Nelson, whose 66-65 start would have led most tournaments. Instead, Eichelberger made up nine strokes as Irwin spun his wheels with the pars. Starting the final day eight back at 66-68—134, Eichelberger bogeyed the first hole, then birdied 10 of the remaining 17 holes, including the last four, to force Irwin's hand. Irwin birdied 16 and 18 for 69 and 195 total. As with his last previous win at St. Louis, he went the distance without a bogey.

The Transamerica—$800,000
Winner: Dave Eichelberger

How often a near-miss one week turns into a victory the next week in tournament golf, particularly when it wasn't one a player gave away. Carry-over momentum, you could call it. Whatever, that's how it went at The Transamerica for Dave Eichelberger, who had closed with 62 but lost to Hale Irwin by a stroke the previous Sunday. He kept it going when the Senior PGA Tour moved cross-country to Napa, California, and became the 20th different winner of 1997, scoring a four-stroke victory at Silverado Country Club that was tighter than the final margin would indicate.

"The Senior Tour saved me from I'm not sure what, pumping gas or something," said Eichelberger, whose game deserted him in the late 1980s and early 1990s on the PGA Tour but whose senior earnings have topped $3.4 million. A hot-and-cold player, Eichelberger felt his game getting away from him early in the final round at Silverado. He had taken a one-stroke lead after a 67-68 start, as new senior Larry Nelson fell back after a leading 64 in the first round, a tournament record for an opening day.

Eichelberger bogeyed three of the first four holes and dropped three strokes off the pace of DeWitt Weaver. A birdie at the par-five fifth settled him down and he eventually regained the lead at the 15th, where Weaver missed a short putt for a bogey. Eichelberger birdied the 17th to insure the victory after watching from the tee at the par-three hole as Weaver and Jimmy Powell, both just one back, self-destructed.

Weaver three-putted and Powell triple-bogeyed as he thoughtlessly slammed a club to the ground inside a hazard where his ball wound up unplayable against a tree. Eichelberger added a final birdie at 18 for 70 and a 205 total, 11 under par for the distance. Weaver finished in the four-man runner-up deadlock at 209 with Frank Conner, Terry Dill and John Jacobs.

Hyatt Regency Maui Kaanapali Classic—$850,000
Winner: Hale Irwin

In September, Hale Irwin won the Boone Valley Classic in his St. Louis hometown. A month later, Irwin won the Hyatt Regency Maui Kaanapali Classic in his Hawaiian home-away-from-home, down the road from the Kapalua Resort he has represented for two decades. The one in the Islands had special significance. It was the ninth win of his sensational season and tied the record for wins in a single season set by Peter Thomson in 1985, immediately inviting comparisons. Irwin declined to do so, observing, "We played at different times under different circumstances. If it was as difficult for him as it was for me, then I know how difficult it was."

A middle round of 63, eight under, keyed Irwin's victory on Kaanapali Golf Club's North Course, where Irwin may have lost the 1996 money title and end-of-season honors to Jim Colbert when he finished second to Bob Charles by a stroke. He had opened with 67, three strokes off the pace of Bruce Summerhays and J.C. Snead. Although the 63 didn't project him into the lead, it put him in excellent position one shot behind Summerhays (64-65—129).

Playing in strong, gusty winds on the last day, neither player was doing much until the sixth hole, where Summerhays hooked his tee shot out of bounds, took a triple bogey and lost four strokes to Irwin when Hale birdied from seven feet. Irwin lost two shots before the turn, but Summerhays couldn't capitalize in the tough conditions. Irwin then wrapped up the victory with birdies at 13 and 15, finishing with a 70 for a 200 total. Summerhays shot 74 and dropped into a second-place tie at 203 with Mike Hill, nearing the end of his first winless season since 1989.

Raley's Gold Rush Classic—$900,000
Winner: Bob Eastwood

Bob Eastwood completed a coast-to-coast double when he won the Raley's Gold Rush Classic in his old stomping grounds in Northern California with a host of family and old friends in the gallery. Eastwood, who grew up in the Stockton area and while a teenager helped his father build a golf course there, picked up his earlier victory in the Bell Atlantic Classic at Philadelphia in May.

Both were wire-to-wire wins, but the East Coast triumph was in the year's only rain-shortened, 36-hole event. Eastwood, 51, who won three times in the 1980s on the PGA Tour, prevailed by two strokes over Rick Acton, also a second-year player on the Senior PGA Tour, at Serrano Country Club in El Dorado Hills. He shot a 12-under-par 204 total as he became just the sixth multiple winner of the season.

Eastwood began his run with 67 in strong winds that gave him a two-stroke lead on Gary Player, John Morgan, Jim Dent, Bruce Summerhays and Tom Wargo. When he followed with 69 for 136, he retained the two-stroke margin, then over Player, Dent, Summerhays and Acton, who joined the contenders with 65 and was to be Eastwood's strongest challenger in the last round. Eastwood birdied the third and fourth holes to get to 10 under, then ran off 11 straight pars. Acton took advantage and moved a stroke ahead before falling victim to a strong finish by Eastwood.

"To be in the lead with four holes to play and not win is disappointing," he said afterward. "But Bob didn't flinch." Eastwood had birdied the 15th, went ahead when Acton missed a short par putt at the 16th and opened the final two-stroke margin with a 20-footer at the 17th. He shot a 68 for the 204 total and admitted to "getting choked up out there on the last few holes."

Ralphs Senior Classic—$1,000,000
Winner: Gil Morgan

When Gil Morgan won the Ralphs Senior Classic 11 days after his 50th birthday in 1996, the quickest any newcomer ever won on the Senior PGA Tour, he hinted to his fellow competitors that he would be a major player in the years to come. When Morgan won the Los Angeles tournament again a year later, he had proved the point. The victory, by one stroke over George Archer, was his fifth of a fine season.

The spotlight was on others, though, until the final round. Hale Irwin, gunning for a record 10th victory of the year, put his foot in the doorway with a course-record, eight-under-par 63 at Wilshire Country Club, but perhaps talked himself out of the win with his complaints about fatigue at the end of a long season. He shot 72 and 73 the next two days to fall back to a tie-for-ninth finish.

The second round belonged to Jim Colbert, making just his third start since his prostate cancer surgery in June. Colbert, who trailed Irwin and Dave Stockton (64) after Thursday's round, fired his second straight 65 to move into a three-stroke lead over Morgan (67-66).

Colbert, understandably wilting in the 90-degree weather, drifted back into a tie with Morgan through the first nine on the last day, and fell from contention with double bogeys at the 13th and 16th holes, finishing fifth. Archer, another player coming back from surgery — a hip replacement in 1996 — remained in the hunt, though.

The 58-year-old Californian, who had 17 victories on the Senior Tour but none since the operation, had started the round two strokes back of Morgan with 67-68–135. He shot 64 and had a glimmer of hope for a playoff when Morgan bogeyed the 17th and led by just one. But he parred the 18th for 65–198 and the one-stroke victory. Archer was nearly as pleased with his performance as Morgan was with the triumph. "I'm really happy that I can still play this well," he said.

Energizer Senior Tour Championship—$1,850,000
Winner: Gil Morgan

Even though he couldn't steal Hale Irwin's 1997 thunder with his rich and prestigious victory in the Energizer Senior Tour Championship, Gil Morgan made a lot of noise with his tournament-record performance in the concluding event of the Senior PGA Tour's season at the Dunes Golf and Beach Club in chilly early November weather in Myrtle Beach, South Carolina. His 16-under-par 272 total and the $328,000 first-place check left him nearly $200,000 short of Irwin's all-time-record $2,343,364.

The finish of the tournament that was contested by the season's 31 top money winners was certainly appropriate — Morgan vs. Irwin the last two days with no one else in serious contention. Bob Murphy, who won in March in the Toshiba, had another moment in the first round, shooting 65, but followed with three rounds in the 70s. The Morgan-Irwin confrontation was set up Friday when they both recorded 135s and, along with promising newcomer Bob Duval, led the field.

Morgan shot his second consecutive 66 to edge two strokes ahead of Irwin with 201 as Duval fell back with 74. Morgan, playing bogey-less golf, had a four-stroke lead on Irwin before Irwin birdied three of the last four holes to keep it tight going into the final round. The two-man shootout was virtually insured as runner-up Irwin was five strokes ahead of Mike Hill, Hubert Green and Dave Eichelberger after the 54 holes.

As it turned out, it really was no contest. Morgan made three first-nine birdies and by the 14th hole had opened a five-stroke lead. Bogeys at 15 and 18 narrowed the final margin back to the two shots that separated them at the start of the day, both men finishing with 71s. The ever-present Isao Aoki shot 67 and finished third — in the tournament and on the final money list

European Seniors Tour

Beko Turkish Seniors Open—£150,000
Winner: Tommy Horton

Tommy Horton picked up where he left off in 1996 when he captured the Beko Turkish Open, the opening event of the 1997 European Seniors Tour in early May. Horton, who had four victories in 1996, held off a pack of challengers with a three-under-par 69 in the final round at the National Golf Club at Antalya, Turkey, to post a two-stroke victory. Maurice Bembridge also closed with 69 to snare runner-up honors at 210, one shot ahead of American Joe Carr, who also finished with 69.

Carr, who tied for 12th in the qualifying tournament for 1997, opened play with a five-birdie 68, taking a one-stroke lead over Horton, Bembridge and fellow American Chick Evans. Horton's 70 in the second round moved him into first place as Carr slipped to 74. Holland's Jan Dorrestein drew much of the attention that day. The Dutchman, who quit the regular tour in 1975 because of putting yips, set a course record on the resort course designed by David Feherty and David Jones when he took just 25 strokes on the greens en route to his 66 for a 140 total, one back of Horton.

Bembridge gave Horton a run for his money. "Maurice played the better golf tee to green," Horton remarked after his scrambling final round. "I really felt nervous out there." Shaky or not, the Royal Jersey star, runner-up to Bobby Verwey in Turkey in 1996, put a 12th victory on his Seniors Tour record. That equalled his total in all of his pre-seniors years.

AIB Irish Seniors Open—£75,000
Winner: Tommy Horton

Tommy Horton will play in Ireland any time. When he won the AIB Irish Seniors Open in mid-May, it was his fifth professional victory on the Emerald Isle among the 24 on his overall career record and his third as a senior. The triumph extended his winning streak on the circuit to three straight, starting with the Players Championship, the concluding tournament on the 1996 tour, and added a 13th title to his Seniors Tour chart.

Horton wound up with the same score — 208 — as he registered the previous week in Turkey, but the task was a bit more formidable. He entered the final round at the four-year-old St. Margarets Golf Club course trailing Australian Noel Ratcliffe by two strokes. Ratcliffe had raced to a four-shot lead in the first round with a splendid 66 as nippy winds whipped off Dublin Bay, then added a par 72 in the second round for a 138 total. Horton moved into second place at 71-69–140.

Horton and Ratcliffe waged a stirring battle on the second nine in the last round. Horton took his only bogey of the week at the 14th hole to fall one stroke behind, then birdied the next three holes to set up a victorious 68. He dropped a 14-footer for two at the par-three 15th, then birdied the back-to-back par-fives, a 240-yard, three-wood carry at the 16th "my shot of the week." The 52-year-old Ratcliffe managed only one birdie all day and had to settle for 72 and second place. Malcolm Gregson birdied the 16th and 17th holes for 69–212 and third place.

Philips PFA Golf Classic—£80,000
Winner: DeRay Simon

DeRay Simon, the beneficiary of a rare gaffe by streaking Tommy Horton, landed his first professional title of any description — the Philips PFA Golf Classic at the Marriott St. Pierre Hotel and Country Club in Wales. The 58-year-old American, who has played spottily on the European Seniors Tour since 1991, won going away, winning by six strokes with his one-under-par 212 total.

Simon, 59, who plays out of Las Vegas, had put together a pair of 69s the first two days, sharing the first-round lead with Horton and Jim Rhodes, then moving three strokes in front. He had particular cause for concern when he teed off for the last round, since Horton was the runner-up and had added an off-tour victory during the preceding open week on the schedule to remain unbeaten in three 1997 starts. (He won the Scottish Life/Ben Sayers Club Professional Championship at Coventry by nine strokes, his third successive win in that event.)

Any pressure Simon felt surely lessened greatly when Horton mis-hit a six-iron tee shot at the par-three sixth, found heavy rough and took a quadruple bogey on the hole. Simon went on to a 74 in blustery conditions for the 212 total. With that, the American, whose biggest victories until then had been state open titles in California and Nevada and two wins in Canada, exulted, "It's been a long time coming but, boy, it was worth it." Horton retained his composure after the disaster at the sixth, finished with 77 amid a bevy of over-par scores to take second place at 218, one shot ahead of Rhodes, Malcolm Gregson, Antonio Garrido, Tienie Britz and Brian Huggett.

Jersey Seniors Open—£100,000
Winner: Tommy Horton

"I don't know when this wonderful dream is going to end," enthused a delighted Tommy Horton after he won the Jersey Seniors Open, his third victory in four starts, and fulfilled a life-long ambition in the process. Until this early June week at La Moye Golf Club, Horton had never won a tournament on his home island, a feat that had been "one of my two remaining ambitions." (The other is to win the Senior British Open.)

Horton capped his decisive victory deliciously when he swept in a 25-foot birdie with his broom-handle putter on the final green for 68 and a six-stroke victory. He was 12-under-par at 204 with earlier rounds of 69 and 67, the latter score giving him a three-stroke lead after he had shared first place Friday with Northern Ireland's Paul Leonard and Australia's Randall Vines.

Only Leonard was within five strokes entering the final round and any hopes he had of his first Seniors Tour victory died when he went double bogey, bogey at the end of the first nine. Horton followed with birdies at the 11th and 12th that opened his ultimate six-shot margin. He had 15 birdies the last two rounds. The runner-up was Welshman Craig Defoy, a newcomer on the circuit who also finished second to Horton two weeks earlier in the Senior Club Professional Championship. Defoy, a former World Cup player for Wales, made five birdies and closed with 69 for 210, two shots ahead of Leonard and Jose Maria Canizares, the Spanish Ryder Cupper and PGA European Tour veteran who turned 50 in February and was making his first Seniors Tour start where he won the regular tour Jersey Open in 1980.

De Vere Hotels Seniors Classic—£80,000
Winner: T.R. Jones

An appropriate catch-all caption for the first five weeks would have been — Tommy Horton and the Americans. Horton won three of the tournaments during that period and, when he slipped all the way to second place the other two weeks, the titles were claimed by players from the United States.

The victory of journeyman pro DeRay Simon in the Philips PFA Classic was not particularly surprising, but the other American winner certainly came out of the blue, both literally and figuratively. T.R. Jones, who nipped Horton by a stroke to win the De Vere Hotels Seniors Classic at Grantham's Belton Woods Golf Club, flies into the wild blue yonder for Continental Airlines for a living and just turned professional in 1995 at age 51 to take a crack at senior golf in his spare time. He missed qualifying for the U.S. Senior Tour, but made it in Europe. The De Vere event was just his second start.

Thomas Richard Jones shared the first-round lead with Peter Townsend at 68, then slipped one stroke behind Noel Ratcliffe of Australia (69-71) with 73 on the second day. Horton and David Creamer joined Jones at 141 with 71-70 scores. Three early bogeys blunted Horton's chances, but all three of the other Saturday contenders had opportunities to catch Jones at the par-five finishing hole. Horton reached the green in two but missed the 15-foot eagle putt that would have tied him with Jones. Creamer, tied with the pilot, put his second shot in the water in front of the 18th green, as did Ratcliffe when he came to the final hole needing a birdie to tie. They finished third with Arnold O'Connor at 214. Jones shot 71 for 212, four under par.

Ryder Collingtree Seniors Classic—£90,000
Winner: Neil Coles

Neil Coles became the oldest winner ever on the PGA European Tour when he won the 1982 Sanyo Open at age 48. Fifteen years later, he achieved the same distinction on the European Seniors Tour when, at age 62, he captured the Ryder Collingtree Classic at Collingtree in Northampton, the 41st victory of his illustrious 47-year professional career.

"I'm delighted to score one again for the old boys," Coles said after posting his eight-under-par 208 total, his third victory at Collingtree and

10th as a senior. It was a record score for the event and his seven-stroke winning margin equalled the tour record, which had been shared by Bob Charles (Senior British Open) and Maurice Bembridge (Jersey Open). Coles ranks behind only Tommy Horton in career wins and money on the Seniors Tour.

Coles led from start to finish at Collingtree. He opened with 68, one shot better than Brian Waites and Matt McCrorie, and widened his margin to two in the second round with 71–139. Waites and Agim Bardha, the Albania-born pro who migrated to America years ago and has played on the U.S. Senior PGA Tour, were at 141. The battle was over almost before it started Sunday. Coles birdied the first hole off a crisp eight iron to six feet while Waites was making a bogey after missing the green at No. 1 and Bardha a six after leaving a bunker shot in the sand there. Coles was then four ahead, increased it to seven by the turn and had it to eight after 11 holes before finishing with 69. Waites recovered with 34 on the second nine for 74 and a share of second place at 215 with Antonio Garrido, who closed with 68. Horton tied for sixth, shooting a final-round 73 for a 218 total.

Manadans Affarer Seniors—£75,000
Winner: Noel Ratcliffe

Noel Ratcliffe, who had been knocking at the door on frequent occasions over two seasons plus, finally gained admission to the winner's circle when the circuit made its only stop of the year in Sweden for the Manadans Affarer Seniors at Stockholm. Ratcliffe, who had finished second in four events since joining the Seniors Tour, duplicated Neil Coles' record-tying feat of the previous week with a seven-stroke victory. He shot a nine-under 204 total on the par-71 Fagelbro Golf Club course.

The Sydney pro, who enjoyed moderate international success in his younger days, was not about to let opportunity escape him this time. For two days, he dogged the heels of Steve Wild, a leading British amateur who had just turned pro and gained Seniors Tour privileges at the 1996 fall qualifier. Wild, a Midlander, had opened the tournament with a 67 to lead Ratcliffe and Scot Norman Wood by a stroke. He followed Saturday with 68, Ratcliffe shot 67 for 136 and Wood slipped to 74–140, leaving the title race to Wild and Ratcliffe.

Ratcliffe's experience paid off after he fell two behind when he three-putted the first green. He followed quickly with a birdie and went in front to stay when Wild dropped three strokes at the third and fourth holes. Wild made one last bid with three birdies in a row, starting at the sixth, but Ratcliffe matched two of them and took full charge on the second nine on his way to 68 and the 204 total. Wild shot 76 for 211, but he held onto second place, one stroke in front of Wood. Ratcliffe and the rest of the field didn't have to contend with Tommy Horton, who played instead in the U.S. Senior Open.

Lawrence Batley Seniors—£80,000
Winner: Antonio Garrido

Antonio Garrido completed a "family double" when he squeezed out a one-stroke victory in the Lawrence Batley Seniors at Huddersfield Golf Club. The victory, his second on the European Seniors Tour, came just two weeks after his son Ignacio won the Volvo German Open on the PGA European Tour, following in the footsteps of his father. Antonio's other son, Daniel, caddied for him at Huddersfield. Garrido closed with two birdies to nip Italy's Renato Campagnoli for the Batley title with his seven-under-par 206 total as 12 players finished within four shots of the winning score.

Neil Coles, Brian Huggett and Malcolm Gregson took the first-round lead with three-under 68s as Garrido opened with 70. Then the second day, Brian Waites shot a course-record 65 and joined Huggett in the lead at 136. Canada's Bill Hardwick, who started the day three off the pace, had two birdies and an eagle in an outgoing 32 in the final round. Another birdie at the par-five 14th put Hardwick into the lead, but he bogeyed the last hole for 67, which ultimately left him in a three-way tie for third at 208 with Gregson and Waites.

Meanwhile, Garrido and Campagnoli, playing together, were locked in an exciting battle. Campagnoli birdied the 15th to go a stroke ahead of the Spaniard, but gave it back when he bogeyed the 16th. Garrido then birdied the 17th to take the lead and matched birdies with Campagnoli at the 18th to score his one-stroke victory. Garrido won five times on the regular tour in earlier years, once on the Challenge Tour in 1990 and took his first Seniors Tour victory in the 1994 Shell Scottish Seniors Open.

Senior German Open—£100,000
Winner: Noel Ratcliffe

Noel Ratcliffe became the second multiple winner of 1997 when he won the Senior German Open two weeks after scoring his initial victory in Sweden. While he led from start to finish at the Owingen-Uberlingen Golf Club just as he did in the Manadans Affarer Seniors at Stockholm, Ratcliffe had more of a fight on his hands to collect the second triumph. He didn't shake off his final pursuer until he birdied the 16th hole to establish a three-under-par 69, a 204 total and a two-stroke victory over David Creamer.

Ratcliffe opened the tournament with a stout 66, good for a one-stroke lead over Northern Ireland's David Jones, playing in just his second tournament after turning 50 in late June. Both Ratcliffe and Jones shot 69s in the second round to remain one-two in the standings, while the venerable Neil Coles, a winner a month earlier, threatened three back at 137.

Coles made his run early. Two birdies on the first five holes jumped him a stroke ahead of the Australian, but his chances ended when he found bushes twice on the par-four 12th hole and the necessary penalty strokes led him to a nine. Creamer, who had started the day six strokes off the pace, produced a splendid 65 off an outgoing 32 and posted a 206 total. Ratcliffe dropped a 15-foot putt for the birdie at No. 16, Jones missed his from four feet, and the issue was settled. Jones weighing his future between concentrating on a playing role and continuing his work as a commentator and course designer, finished with 71 and took third place at 207, three shots in front of Maurice Bembridge and Renato Campagnoli. Coles wound up with 77 and tied for 12th.

Senior British Open—£350,000
Winner: Gary Player

Gary Player added another prestigious title to his remarkable collection of victories when he bested fellow South African John Bland in a playoff for the Senior British Open Championship in late July at Royal Portrush Golf Club in Northern Ireland. Player achieved his 161st professional victory and third Senior British Open win as his ninth senior major title, matching the nine major championships he won in his prime years.

Player, never shy with the superlatives, considered the closing 68 that raised him into a tie with Bland "one of the best two rounds I have played as a senior." The 62-year-old Hall-of-Famer missed only one green all day and made his first putt longer than three feet on the second playoff hole — a 15-footer for the deciding birdie.

Bland traded the lead back and forth with Australian Noel Ratcliffe, who continued his hot pace at Portrush. Bland opened with a six-under-par 66 to lead Player and Dave Eichelberger by two shots, then Ratcliffe jumped three strokes in front with a course-record-tying 65 for 135. Ratcliffe faltered with 75 in the third round as Player caught him with 72 and Bland regained the lead by two with 70 for a 208 total.

The final round produced a wonderful finish as all three birdied the par-five 17th and went to the 18th in a three-way deadlock with British club pro Jim Rhodes just one shot off the pace. Ratcliffe nearly drove out of bounds there and bogeyed as the other three parred the hole. Tommy Horton, the season's leading player, finished a respectable 10th, seven shots behind the winners, but never got into serious contention.

Player won his earlier Senior British Opens in 1988 and 1990 at Turnberry.

Shell Wentworth Senior Masters—£125,000
Winner: Gary Player

It doesn't always help, but Gary Player had a bit of an edge on the field as he posted his second victory in eight days at the inaugural Shell Wentworth Senior Masters, at which galleries walked the fairways as in the old days. In concert with John Jacobs and Bernard Gallacher, Player designed the new Edinburgh course at the famed Wentworth Club in England where he won the World Match Play Championship five times in his younger years on its West course, so it was fair to expect him to have some extra course knowledge going for him.

Player needed that advantage, since he had to hold off several challenges in registering his 162nd career triumph by a single stroke a week after winning the Senior British Open for a third time. Player closed with 70 for a 207 total, nine under par, bogeying the last hole to nip David Creamer and

Jose Maria Canizares. He had shared the lead with Creamer at 137 going into the final round, one stroke in front of Guy Hunt, the former Ryder Cupper taking time off from his duties as a referee on the PGA European Tour.

Neither of those two mounted as serious a threat in the last round as those of Australian Terry Gale, who shot 65, the week's best score, to put a seven-under-par 209 on the scoreboard, and Canizares, who finished eight under at 208 with 68. Those became challenging scores only because Player backed up on the incoming nine after establishing a four-stroke lead with five birdies and a 31 on the first nine. His lead was down to two before he failed to save par from in front of the 18th green. Creamer grabbed a share of the runner-up slot with Canizares by holing a 12-footer there. Hunt shot 72 to join tour leader Tommy Horton, Jose Maria Roca and David Jones in fifth place. Northern Ireland's Hugh Jackson, the first-round leader with 67, tied for 10th place.

Credit Suisse Private Banking Seniors Open—£100,000
Winner: Brian Waites

Brian Waites changed putters for the Credit Suisse Private Banking Seniors Open in Switzerland and it spurred him to his first victory in two years. Waites dropped a six-footer for a birdie with a new putter on the second hole of a playoff against Malcolm Gregson to land his fifth Seniors Tour title and first since the 1995 Northern Electric Seniors. The two had tied for first place that final afternoon with seven-under-par 203 totals to bring on the overtime work.

That the short — 5,740 yards — Bad Ragaz Golf Club layout near Zurich would yield generally low scores was indicated the first day when Waites charged to a course-record 63, matching the circuit's all-time low 18-hole mark. (Antonio Garrido shot 63 in the 1995 Shell Scottish Senior Open.) Even at 63 Waites led the consistently challenging Noel Ratcliffe and South African Hugh Inggs by only one shot.

Waites followed with 69 for a 132 total and still led by one stroke as Inggs matched the 69 and Ratcliffe shot 70 for 134. However, Gregson emerged from five strokes behind with 66 in the last round to overtake Waites, who shot 71. Ratcliffe, a two-time winner earlier in the season, missed the playoff by a stroke when, as he did two weeks earlier in the Senior British Open, he bogeyed the final hole. Inggs also finished at 204 despite birdies on two of the last three holes. A costly oversight cost Inggs a two-stroke penalty and the title. He had moved his marker to clear Waites' putting line on the eighth green and failed to return it to the right spot before putting. Tommy Horton missed a shot at his fourth 1997 title when he double-bogeyed the last hole and joined Neil Coles, Jim Rhodes and Paul Leonard in fifth place at 205 as 22 players put up sub-par final scores.

The Belfry PGA Seniors Championship—£150,000
Winner: Walter Hall

An unheralded American again stole the thunder of much better known professionals in the PGA Seniors Championship at The Belfry, site of three Ryder Cups. With a golf background similar to that of T.R. Jones, one of two American winners earlier in the season, long-time amateur Hall emerged from relative obscurity for an impressive three-stroke victory in the important event.

Only close observers had noted that Hall, a tall North Carolinian who spent most of his adult life as an engineering salesman after abandoning a pro career in the early 1970s for family reasons, had tied for eighth at Royal Portrush in the Senior British Open. Those few weren't overly surprised when Hall, just three months past his 50th birthday, launched his victory run at The Belfry with the first of three consecutive 69s, one shot off the lead shared by Tommy Horton, Jose Maria Canizares, Antonio Garrido and Noel Ratcliffe. The second one put him into a first-place tie with Garrido and both stayed on top the third day with their 69s that took them nine under par and five strokes ahead of nearest pursuers Horton and David Huish.

Undaunted by this position that was a new experience for him, Hall continued his solid play in the last round and, when Garrido faltered a bit on the first nine, opened a six-stroke lead with his outgoing 33. Horton, gunning for his fourth win of the season, shot 34 to overtake Garrido and moved ahead of him with birdies at the 10th and 11th. Horton's chances of catching Hall dissolved, though, when he bogeyed the par-threes while Hall was methodically posting pars. Horton got the two strokes back on the par-fives and shot 68 as Hall finished with a three-putt bogey at the 18th for a 277 total and the three-stroke victory. Garrido and Canizares tied for third at 282.

Motor Senior Classic—£75,000
Winner: Ian Richardson

The European Seniors Tour had rookie winners back to back when Englishman Ian Richardson nipped Eddie Polland and DeRay Simon by one stroke in an exciting climax of the Motor Senior Classic at the Marriott Goodwood Park Hotel and Golf Club.

Like American Walter Hall, the previous week's winner, Richardson, 51, just returned to the professional ranks to play senior tournament golf and qualified for the 1997 European season. He had done well earlier in the year, tying for fourth at Dublin in his best showing, but was never in serious contention until his first two rounds — 70-67 — in the Motor Senior Classic lodged him just one shot behind leader Eddie Polland. The former Ryder Cup player had opened with a six-under-par 66, one of only three players in the 60s that day.

Six players mounted challenges in the last round, but it came down to Richardson and Polland at the end. Polland kept his hopes alive when he holed a 24-foot par putt at the 17th after having to drop out of a ditch and Ian missed his par putt from a mere three feet. They were then tied at seven under and both reached a bunker near the green in two at the par-five 18th.

Richardson put his 30-yard sand shot two feet from the cup and birdied for his 71–208 total before Polland came out short and missed from 35 feet for his 73–209. Simon birdied the last hole to tie Polland for second place. Tommy Horton had his worst tournament of the season, tying for 31st place.

Scottish Seniors Open—£100,000
Winner: Tommy Horton

Tommy Horton returned to the winner's circle with a vengeance at the Scottish Seniors Open. Even though the tournament was shortened to 36 holes to avoid playing on the day of Princess Diana's funeral, Horton rolled to a nine-stroke victory with a 12-under-par 132 total the next day and set a few records in the process.

Horton opened the tournament at the Newmachar Golf Club in Aberdeen comfortably with 70, one shot off the pace of Michael Murphy of Dublin and in a second-place tie with Brian Waites. The cancellation — "my first day off from golf since April" — seemed to charge Horton's batteries.

He turned the competition into a shambles with 62 on the last day. The 132 total was the best 36-hole score against par ever recorded on the circuit and just one stroke short of the record 131 shot by Gary Player at Turnberry in the first two rounds of the 1988 Senior British Open. The nine-stroke victory margin also was a record — by two — and those were achieved over 54 holes.

Murphy scored two early birdies and led by two after four holes, but Horton whipped past him with five first-nine birdies for 31 as Murphy, with straying tee shots, lost five strokes by the turn. Horton wrapped up his fourth 1997 victory with another 31 on the second nine, finishing the brilliant round eagle-birdie-birdie. J.R. Delich, an American pro attached to the Tryall Club in Jamaica, was the only other player under 70. A qualifying school graduate, Delich achieved his best finish of the season as his 69–141 total carried him into second place. Murphy managed a 74 despite his first-nine woes and tied for third with Jim Rhodes and Jose Maria Roca of Spain.

Clubhaus Seniors Classic—£75,000
Winner: Tommy Horton

Tommy Horton ended the regular season as he had started it — with back-to-back victories. Horton polished off that remarkable achievement with a victory in the Clubhaus Seniors Classic at Benton Hall in Essex. He staged a brilliant rally to overtake David Jones and record his fifth win of the season. He smashed another record of his own as well. The first-place check of £12,450 increased his 1997 earnings to £138,427, more than £5,000 better than his winnings of 1996.

The win at Benton Hall had similarities to his performance the previous week at Aberdeen, especially the final round. Horton hovered just off the pace the first two days. Norman Wood, the former Ryder Cupper who just joined the European Seniors Tour for the 1997 season, shot 66 Friday, one of eight players in the 60s, among them Horton at 68. David Jones moved ahead in the second round with 69-68—137, while Horton added 71 for 139.

Horton didn't quite equal the tour-record 62 he shot at Aberdeen in the final round at Benton Hall, but he didn't miss by much. He shot 64 for a 203 total, 13 under par, and won by two. Jones built a four-stroke lead through 12 holes, but a Horton birdie to Jones' three-putt at the 13th turned the momentum. Horton's 40-foot eagle putt from just off the green at the 15th squared things and he established the winning margin with a birdie-bogey swing at the 17th. He was five under par on the final six holes. Malcolm Gregson birdied three of the last four holes for 68 and finished third at 207.

Senior Tournament of Champions—£120,000
Winner: Tommy Horton

Five weeks after the weekly run of the European Seniors Tour had ended, the leading 36 available money winners of the season reassembled at Buckinghamshire Golf Club in Denham for the Senior Tournament of Champions. The other 35 might as well have stayed at home, because Tommy Horton came. Displaying no loss of sharpness from the layoff, Horton marched to a solid three-stroke victory, the sixth of his splendid season and 17th of his senior career.

Horton came from two strokes behind leader Jose Maria Canizares, fresh from a good stretch of play in America and seeking his first European victory in senior golf, to win the title. The Spaniard shared the first-round lead with Steve Wild at 68, one stroke in front of Horton and J.R. Delich. Wild and Delich faded in the second round, setting up a duel between Canizares at 134 and Horton at 136.

A two-stroke swing at the sixth hole on the last day got Horton going and his birdie at the ninth gave him the lead for the first time. Canizares regained first place one final time at the 10th with a birdie-bogey swing, then fell hopelessly behind as he took a double bogey while watching Horton run off three consecutive birdies and build a four-stroke lead at 12 under par. Horton eventually shot 68 to 73 by the Spaniard for the three-stroke victory at 204. Alberto Croce of Italy and David Huish of Scotland tied for third but were five behind Canizares at 212. Neil Coles, Noel Ratcliffe and Eddie Polland were at 213.

Japan Senior Tour

Daiichi Seimei Cup—¥50,000,000
Winner: Gary Player

Age has not slowed Gary Player's international globe-trotting. The 62-year-old Hall-of-Famer, just getting over a double-hernia operation, took a quick trip to Japan at the end of May and left the country as the winner of the Daiichi Seimei Cup tournament, the opening event on the Japan Senior Tour's short 1997 schedule. The victory at Tomisato Golf Club, Sammu, came in a three-man playoff after he, Teruo Sugihara and Terry Gale of Australia finished the 54-hole event with matching eight-under-par 208 totals.

Tadao Nakamura launched the tournament with 65 and a two-stroke lead over Taiwan's Kuo Chie-hsiung. Then Player took over on the way to his 160th career title, shooting 68 for 137. He led Lee Trevino (68-71), another well-traveled star, by two and Gale (69-71) by three going into the final round. When Player managed only 71 Sunday, Gale, with 68, and Sugihara, one of Japan's all-time greats, with 66, caught him and forced the playoff.

TPC Starts Senior Golf—¥50,000,000
Winner: Seiji Ogawa

Seiji Ogawa scored his first win on the Japan Senior Tour in early June, coming from one stroke off the pace in the final round of the 72-hole tournament to register a one-shot win. Ogawa had made steady progress up the leaderboard and finally overtook Toru Nakayama with his closing 71 for a 280 total, eight under par.

Nakayama led for two days after Tadao Furuichi opened the event with 67, then plunged from contention with following rounds of 78-76-77. Nakayama went in front with 70-68–138, one shot ahead of Akira Kawamata and Toshiharu Horimoto. He followed with 70 and Ogawa moved within a stroke with his 69-71-69–209. The 71 brought the victory when Nakayama could muster only 74. Nakayama finished third behind Seiichi Kanai, a nine-time winner on the Japan Senior Tour, who grabbed the runner-up slot with a final-round 68.

Castlehill Senior Open—¥30,000,000
Winner: Toru Nakayama

Toru Nakayama didn't let victory slip away again when it beckoned for the second week in a row in the Castlehill Senior Open at Castlehill Country Club. A poor final round had cost him the TPC Starts title the previous Sunday. At Castlehill, he won a final-round duel with Ichiro Teramoto and recorded a one-stroke victory.

Nakayama and Teramoto were co-leaders after 36 holes with 139s, but reached that score in much different ways. Nakayama, who trailed first-round leader Yutaka Suzuki by one shot with 69, added 70, while Teramoto, seemingly out of the picture for the week after his starting 76, rebounded with a dazzling 63. Nakayama's 69 for a 208 total, eight under par, edged Teramoto, who had 70. Hiroshi Kazami finished third at 210, one shot in front of Akira Yabe.

Japan Media System Cup—¥30,000,000
Winner: Katsuji Hasegawa

Katsuji Hasegawa captured his first senior title, the Japan Media System Cup, although in a tournament of only 18 holes. Hasegawa and Koji Nakajima, a two-time winner, tied for first place at Tsu Country Club with one-under-par 71s and Katsuji won the subsequent playoff. Akira Yabe had another high finish, shooting 72 and tying for third with Fumio Tanaka.

HTB Senior Classic—¥15,000,000
Winner: Kesahiko Uchida

The HTB Senior Classic went 36 holes rather than the 18 of the previous Japan Media System Cup and produced another first-time winner for the over-50 ranks from among former titleholders on the regular Japan PGA Tour. Kesahiko Uchida fired a pair of 69s at Mitsui Kanko Iris Golf Club and his 138 gave him a two-stroke victory over the omnipresent Toru Nakayama and Hiroshi Ishii.

Komatsu Nagoya TV Open—¥40,000,000
Winner: Seiji Ogawa

Seiji Ogawa became the season's only double winner when he won the Komatsu Nagoya TV Open at Hananoki Golf Club. Ogawa, the TPC Starts victor in June, led from start to finish, but had to contend with Toru Nakayama once again.

Those two players had the only sub-70 rounds on the first day, Ogawa shooting 68 and Nakayama 69. Ogawa widened his lead to three strokes with 69 as Nakayama shot 71 and was tied at 140 by Yamotsu Ito, who posted a six-under 66. Ogawa shot a par 72 Sunday for 209, barely enough to edge Nakayama, who came within one shot with 70–210. Seiichi Kanai, Katsuji Hasegawa and amateur Yukio Imada tied for third at 211.

Japan PGA Senior Championship—¥50,000,000
Winner: Ichiro Teramoto

Ichiro Teramoto, a frequent contender in earlier tournaments on the Japan Senior Tour, cashed in with a victory in the Japan PGA Senior Championship at Shimoakima Country Club at the expense of Toru Nakayama. Teramoto won by four strokes, though trailing Nakayama by three going into the final round.

Teramoto benefitted from Nakayama's worst round of the year, 79, scoring the easy victory with a par-72 for a 286 total, the only sub-par score for the distance. In fact, the scores were so high that Nakayama still placed second by three strokes despite the feeble finish. It was his third runner-up showing to go with his victory in the Castlehill tournament and third in the TPC Starts.

Japan PGA Senior Open—¥50,000,000
Winner: Isao Aoki

Isao Aoki wouldn't miss the Japan PGA Senior Open. Aoki, who had another splendid season on the Senior PGA Tour in America, returned home in time to win his fourth Senior Open title in a row. This time, he won by five strokes at Morihaga Takataki Country Club at Ichihara, where they lost a round to rainy weather. He shot a 54-hole 210 total, five better than Yuji Ishii, first-round leader Teruo Sugihara (68) and Australian Graham Marsh, who played regularly and successfully in Japan in his younger days and, like Aoki, had a good year in the United States.

Aoki, long recognized as Japan's most successful international player ever, trailed Sugihara by two strokes after the first round, but his second-round 69 established a two-stroke lead over Sugihara (73) and Hiroshi Ishii. That proved more than enough of a cushion Sunday as he closed with 71 for the 210. Marsh gained his runner-up position with a 68, Sunday's low round. The win was Aoki's second of 1997, going with the Emerald Coast Classic title in America and a host of high finishes that put him third on the Senior PGA Tour money list with $1,410,499.

South Africa Senior Tour

Vodacom Senior Classic—R400,000
Winner: Simon Hobday

The South African contingent that had just wound up the Senior PGA Tour campaign in America returned home for the country's brief senior circuit in and around Johannesburg and, led by Simon Hobday, they dominated the Vodacom Senior Classic, the first of three events on the schedule.

Hobday, whose game tailed off on the U.S. circuit in 1997 as he dropped to 47th on the money list, sank a dramatic, 20-foot birdie on the final hole to nip Hugh Baiocchi by one stroke in the Vodacom event at Dainfern Country Club. He shot 69 for a 205 total, 11 under par, in scoring his first victory since the 1995 Brickyard Crossing Seniors at Indianapolis, Indiana.

Gary Player, also winless in America in 1997, shared the first-round lead at 68 with Allan Henning, the stay-at-home brother of player Harold and tournament director Brian, who live in America. Baiocchi and little-known Gabriel Putsoe were at 69. The colorful Hobday injected himself into the picture with a sparkling 65 for a 136 total, tying him for the lead with Baiocchi, who shot 67. They had three strokes on Henning, their nearest pursuer.

The two men sparred all afternoon in the rain on the last day, with Baiocchi holding the upper hand most of the day. Birdies at the second and fourth holes gave Baiocchi a two-stroke lead and he remained in front until birdies by Hobday the 11th and 13th tied it up again. Baiocchi, who had an excellent first year in America with a victory in Pittsburgh, edged one stroke in front when he birdied the 14th, but Hobday squared it again with a birdie at the par-five 17th. Baiocchi bunkered his tee shot at the 18th and missed the green, as Hobday put his approach 20 feet from the cup and, without hesitation, holed the putt.

Templeton South African Senior Open—R125,000
Winner: John Bland

John Bland, who never won the South African Open during his 30-year career in his native land, did "the next best thing" at Houghton Golf Club when he won the Templeton South African Senior Open. Bland, who had displayed his talent convincingly in America with five victories over the previous two years, scored a crushing six-stroke victory at Houghton. He closed with 69, the low round of the day, for his four-under-par 212 total and the six-shot margin over Allen Henning, a third-place finisher a week earlier at Dainfern.

Bland was coming off a hot finish himself the previous week — a closing 66. He opened with 71, the only sub-par round of the day, on his way to the wire-to-wire victory at Houghton. A second-round 72 staked Bland to a three-stroke lead over Hugh Baiocchi and he took it from there after a start Sunday that he, in his own words, "played disgracefully." Although still even par for the round after four holes, Bland had bogeyed the second and cancelled it out only by holing from the sand at the short third. He pulled away from pursuers Baiocchi and Henning when he scrambled for a birdie to match theirs at the par-five ninth and added two more at the 10th and 14th en route to his 69. Henning closed with 71 for his 218, one stroke better than Bobby Verwey, who also shot 71. Baiocchi slipped to 74-220 and tied Tommy Horton, who had dominated the European Seniors Tour and just arrived in South Africa. No one else was within six strokes of them.

ICI John Bland Invitational—R100,000
Winner: Tommy Horton

Tommy Horton quickly rekindled the form that carried him through a wonderful season on the European Seniors Tour when he traveled to South Africa in mid-November. The Englishman, who has the 1970 South African Open on his impressive record, added the ICI John Bland Invitational to cap the best season by a senior outside of the United States. That victory in the concluding event in Johannesburg was Horton's seventh of 1997, following six wins in Europe earlier in the year.

Horton edged the tournament's namesake by one stroke at Royal Johannesburg Golf Club with his 10-under-par 206 total, but Bland, by virtue of his victory in the Senior Open and fifth-place finish in the Vodacom Classic, collected an extra R31,000 as the leader of the rankings for the three tournament swing. Horton was still playing in Europe the week of the Vodacom event.

Horton led from start to finish at Royal Johannesburg, posting 69, the only sub-70 score of the opening round. He repeated that score for a 138 total, and was joined by Bland (71-67) and Allan Henning (70-68). Horton fell a stroke behind the other two on the first nine in the final round as he ran off seven pars before snagging a birdie at the par-five eighth. He drew even with a birdie at the 10th and forged a two-stroke lead over Bland with two more at the 13th and 14th.

Henning put a ball in the water and fell out of contention at the 11th. When Horton bogeyed the 17th, Bland had a shot at a tie at the par-five 18th. But he didn't get the requisite eagle there and Horton birdied to insure the one-stroke victory. He shot 68 to Bland's 69. Henning slipped to a par round and tied for third with Hugh Baiocchi, three strokes behind Bland.

17. Women's Tours

Karrie Webb's breakthrough rookie year in 1996 — when she won four tournaments and became the first player to earn $1 million in a single LPGA season in the United States — might have done even more for Annika Sorenstam than it did for Webb. Sorenstam, who did not particularly embrace the spotlight when it first found her in 1995 when she won her first U.S. Women's Open and was named LPGA's Rolex Player of the Year, made the discovery that she missed what she once had after a relatively quiet 1996 season while still winning four times including a second U.S. Women's Open. She yearned to return to the top. The arrival of Webb on the scene proved to be the perfect motivator.

In 1997, Sorenstam recaptured the limelight, not to mention a lot more hardware, dominating women's golf by winning six events in 22 starts and setting an LPGA earnings record with $1,236,789. "I knew if I worked really hard, I could do it," said Sorenstam of her monster year, which began with victory at the Chrysler-Plymouth Tournament of Champions in January, finished in victory at the ITT LPGA Tour Championship in November, and included four triumphs in between, plus victories in Europe and Japan for a total of eight and $1,460,252 in worldwide earnings.

"I have a lot of respect for Karrie," Sorenstam said. "She's really young, but she has a lot of experience. She's someone that I want to beat. When I watch good players, I ask myself, 'Why are they good?' and 'What can I do to get better?' To be the best, I've got to beat the best. I'm always looking for challenges like that."

Webb, who at age 22 is four years younger than Sorenstam, was the player providing Sorenstam's toughest competition in 1997. Webb followed up a sensational rookie year by winning three times, including the Weetabix Women's British Open, falling less than $13,000 shy of back-to-back $1 million LPGA seasons, and earning $1,048,687 worldwide. Webb captured the Vare Trophy for low scoring average, edging Sorenstam, 70.00 to 70.04. But it was Sorenstam who collected Player of the Year honors for the second time in three seasons.

"She won't make mistakes," Webb said of Sorenstam. "You know that you have to play your best to beat her."

There were many bright moments on the LPGA Tour in 1997. Terry-Jo Myers overcame a longtime battle with interstitial cystitis, a bladder disease which frustrated her to the point she nearly took her own life, to win not once, but twice, prevailing at the Los Angeles Women's Championship and Sara Lee Classic. She was presented with the LPGA's Heather Farr Award in recognition of her "perseverance and spirit."

While many young stars continued to blossom in 1997, the LPGA's major championships were captured by players who had considerable experience to lean upon. Betsy King, age 42, won the Nabisco Dinah Shore; Chris Johnson, 39, won the McDonald's LPGA Championship; and Colleen Walker, 41, who one year earlier gave birth to her first son, captured the du Maurier Classic.

In July, Nancy Lopez came painstakingly close to winning the one championship that has somehow eluded her through the years, finishing second to Alison Nicholas at the U.S. Women's Open. Lopez was left in tears at the 18th green when her potential tying birdie putt slipped past the hole. In defeat, Lopez, who celebrated her 40th birthday in January, became the first woman to shoot four consecutive rounds in the 60s (69-68-69-69) at the Open.

Kelly Robbins, who hit nearly 79 percent of her greens in regulation — a new standard on any tour — finished third on the LPGA money list, eclipsing $900,000. She also led in eagles (17) and birdies (383).

Five of the top 10 players on the LPGA money list were 35 or older — Johnson (fourth), Tammie Green (fifth), Juli Inkster (sixth), Lopez (ninth) and King (10th). In addition to Sorenstam and Webb, who won six and three tournaments respectively, there were seven others who won more than once in 1997: Myers, Green, Johnson, Walker, Robbins, Michelle McGann and Liselotte Neumann.

Laura Davies, the LPGA's Player of the Year in 1996, struggled with her putting throughout most of the year, and finished eighth on the money list. She did manage to capture the Standard Register Ping in March, winning that tournament for a fourth consecutive year. Davies also won twice on the WPG European Tour. Karen Lunn also won twice in Europe, while Pernilla Sterner had two victories in Australasia.

The Japan LPGA Tour was dominated by Akiko Fukushima with six victories, including the Japan LPGA Championship, and earnings of ¥99,594,094 ($841,326 worldwide). There were seven two-time winners in Japan: Woo-Soon Ko, Suzuko Maeda, Aki Takamura, Michiko Hattori, Aiko Takasu, Liselotte Neumann and Ok-Hee Ku. At age 46, Japan's greatest-ever female golfer, Ayako Okamoto, won the Japan Women's Open for the second time.

U.S. LPGA Tour

Chrysler-Plymouth Tournament of Champions—$700,000
Winner: Annika Sorenstam

Playing alongside Karrie Webb in what would prove to be a sign of things to come on the LPGA Tour in 1997, Annika Sorenstam — whose putter arrived at the LPGA's Chrysler-Plymouth Tournament of Champions a day late and mangled by airport handlers — literally rolled her way to a season-opening victory. Sorenstam shot six-under-par 66 to break away from Webb and win by four shots in the fourth round at Weston Hills Country Club in Ft. Lauderdale, Florida. Sorenstam finished at 16-under-par 272 and won $115,000, which came in handy for her honeymoon, which began the day after the tournament.

Webb, the LPGA's leading money winner in 1996, shot four sub-par rounds, but it wasn't enough to stay up with Sorenstam. Webb was left to play for what she termed a "mini-victory" at the par-five 18th, where a 15-footer for birdie allowed her to claim second place by herself. Barb Mucha (70–277) finished third, one shot behind Webb at 11 under par.

Early in the week, Sorenstam, who was both LPGA Player of the Year and leading money winner in 1995, thanked Webb for Webb's tremendous season of 1996. Sorenstam said Webb's performance helped remove her from the intense media spotlight, giving her some needed peace of mind after a hectic 1995 season. At Weston Hills, Sorenstam had a funny way of showing her appreciation. Both players left knowing they would meet again.

HealthSouth Inaugural—$600,000
Winner: Michelle McGann

Karrie Webb's aggressive style first put her in position to win, and then cost her victory at the HealthSouth Inaugural, where a three-putt bogey in a playoff left Michelle McGann hoisting the championship trophy at Walt Disney World's Lake Buena Vista course in Orlando, Florida. The victory, McGann's sixth as a professional, was worth $90,000, and she improved her record in playoffs to 4-0.

Webb made some big shots down the stretch to force the playoff, ramming in a fist-pumping 18-footer for birdie at the last regulation hole to tie McGann at nine-under-par 207. She then knocked her approach inside McGann's on the playoff hole at No. 18. But Webb's aggressive run at a downhill 20-footer to win caught the right edge of the cup and didn't stop until it slid six feet past. She pulled her comeback attempt for par, giving the advantage to McGann, who then stepped up and made a three-foot par putt for the victory.

McGann, who also fired 69, and Webb began the day tied for the lead at six under par. By the time they made the turn — at seven and six under, respectively — it was clear nobody from the pack was going to catch them.

"I have a lot more confidence in my game," McGann said. "I have a chance to win every week. My game is good enough and consistent enough. I've matured out here. My first seven years on tour were a learning experience. I came out at 19, and you can't expect to have instant success. At least I didn't."

Diet Dr. Pepper National Pro-Am—$500,000
Winner: Kelly Robbins

Kelly Robins broke into the 1997 winner's circle when she parred the second hole of a playoff to defeat Emilee Klein and capture the inaugural Diet Dr. Pepper National Pro-Am in West Palm Beach, Florida. Klein missed the green at the second extra hole, chipped long and missed her par putt, setting up Robbins for the victory when the latter two-putted from 10 feet. Robbins shot rounds of 66, 69, 69 and 67 for a 271 total to finish 17 under par.

It was Klein who came up with the round of the tournament, however, making nine birdies en route to shooting 63 to catch Robbins, who was the third-round leader.

Chris Johnson finished third, four shots off the pace, and Kate Golden finished fourth, her best finish in more than three seasons on the LPGA Tour. Golden was an unlikely contender. She got into the field as an alternate when Kim Williams, who was first off the tee, withdrew. And Golden competed with a new set of clubs she had never used in tournament play.

The Diet Dr. Pepper National Pro-Am was designed after the PGA Tour's Pebble Beach stop, bringing together the LPGA's top players with celebrities from other fields. Among the stars who turned out to play: actress Cheryl Ladd, baseball Hall of Famer Ernie Banks and former hockey player Cam Neely.

Los Angeles Women's Championship—$650,000
Winner: Terry-Jo Myers

Terry-Jo Myers stood by the 18th green at Oakmont Country Club in Glendale, California, not really worried about finishing first or second. The bigger picture was her persevering battle over a bladder disease that had driven her to such frustration she nearly took her own life. Myers captured the Los Angeles Women's Championship by two strokes over Annika Sorenstam, shooting rounds of 74, 66 and 66 for a 206 total. When she stood over her final birdie putt on the 18th green, her vision was blurred by tears. To reach that point, she had traveled an incredible, arduous journey.

Myers was diagnosed in 1984 with interstitial cystitis, an incurable bladder disease that caused her to urinate as often as 60 times a day, and kept her awake at night. The pain was described as having the equivalent of paper cuts on the lining of her bladder. Playing a round of golf became a difficult challenge in itself, and in 1992, after she earned only $13,587, she was ready to surrender.

Four years earlier, Myers had taken a knife out in her kitchen and planned to take her own life. Only an 11th-hour visit to her daughter's room to say goodbye kept her from performing the act. She know she could not leave her daughter alone.

In February, her troubles seemed a lifetime ago. Myers, who has been helped by the experimental drug Elmiron, shot back-to-back 66s, equaling the course record. She started five shots behind Sorenstam in the final round, then caught up when Sorenstam struggled uncharacteristically by shooting 73. The tears Myers shed were caused by deeper sentiments than anything caused by victory. "I'm very proud of myself for being able to concentrate again," she said. "I overcame a lot of obstacles."

Cup Noodles Hawaiian Ladies Open—$650,000
Winner: Annika Sorenstam

When she reached the second tee in the final round of the Cup Noodles Hawaiian Open at Kapolei Golf Course in Oahu, Annika Sorenstam already was ready for a self-prescribed pep talk.

One week after losing a final-round lead at the Los Angeles Women's Championship, Sorenstam had just four-putted the first hole for a double-bogey seven that gave back two shots of the four-shot lead she had worked so hard to build in firing 67 and 66 out of the gates. "I couldn't believe it," she said. "I though about last week and I said, 'Oh, no.'"

Usually, that's what Sorenstam's opponents are left to mutter when she seizes a lead in the final round of the tournament. This time was no different. Sorenstam regained her composure and her putting stroke in time to rebound for a one-shot victory over Meg Mallon. Sorenstam shot 73 in the final round, but conditions weren't exactly ideal for scoring. Only five players in the field shot in the 60s, so Sorenstam was in no danger of anybody making a great move.

Mallon, who was defending champion, had a chance, getting to the 17th tee at four under par for the day and 11 under for the tournament, but a bogey-bogey finish left her wondering what might have been. Betsy King finished third, followed by Gail Graham.

Welch's/Circle K Championship—$500,000
Winner: Donna Andrews

Nothing is guaranteed in professional golf, greatness included. Just ask Donna Andrews. Her career was rolling along quite impressively as the 1990s were picking up steam. She won three times in 1994, winning her first major (Nabisco Dinah Shore), had 12 top-10 finishes, and played on the victorious U.S. Solheim Cup team. But in 1995, her golf game left her. Back problems began to bother her, and she won $25,346 in 24 starts. In 1996, thing began to improve, but not to the level she once achieved. In 26 starts, her best finish was fifth place.

Andrews' victory at the Welch's/Circle K Championship in Tucson, Arizona, was the starting point to getting everything turned around. It was nice to have her old confidence back. Andrews' final-round 68 was enough to catch final-round leader Annika Sorenstam, who squandered most of a four-stroke lead when she knocked an approach shot into water fronting the ninth green, then three-putted to add further insult.

Sorenstam, in fact, fell from first to third, passed not only by Andrews, but by Tina Barrett as well. Andrews won $75,000 for her 15-under-par 273 effort, but the victory meant far more than any financial windfall.

Andrews finished strongly, making birdies at the 14th and 15th holes to build a little cushion at Randolph North Golf Course. "I was just trying not to do anything stupid at that point and let the excitement get to me," Andrews said.

Sorenstam was disappointed in her finish. It was the second time in three tournaments she surrendered a lead on the final day, and this time, she chalked the error up to strategy. Instead of hitting a five wood to lay up at the par-five ninth hole, she instead hit seven wood, leaving a longer and more difficult approach.

Standard Register PING—$850,000
Winner: Laura Davies

If Laura Davies was going to do something abut her dismal record in American playoffs, there was no better place to address the issue than Moon Valley Country Club in Phoenix, Arizona, which by now might as well be renamed Laura's Place.

Davies rolled in a four-foot par putt on the first playoff hole to defeat Kelly Robbins and capture her fourth consecutive Standard Register PING title, shooting 70, 69, 70 and 68 for a 277 total. It was Davies' first playoff triumph after losing her first six. Robbins had been 4-0 in playoffs, having already won earlier in the season at the Diet Dr. Pepper National Pro-Am.

The victory was Davies' 50th triumph around the world, and paid her $127,500. Since 1994, Davies had played 16 rounds at Moon Valley in a combined 50 under par.

In the playoff, Robbins boomed a drive down the fairway, while Davies hooked a two iron off the tee and was fortunate to find an opening through a patch of trees that allowed her an approach to the green. Robbins hit a wedge shot into a back bunker and made bogey, and Davies lagged a first putt to four feet, then sank the winning par putt. In winning, Davies became the first LPGA player to win the same golf tournament four times consecutively.

Nabisco Dinah Shore—$900,000
Winner: Betsy King

Golf became a difficult game for Betsy King once she collected her 30th victory to gain entry into the LPGA's venerable Hall of Fame. But King emerged from the valley with a magnificent victory at the Nabisco Dinah Shore at Mission Hills Country Club in Rancho Mirage, California, on a picturesque Easter Sunday. King shot rounds of 71, 67, 67 and 71 for a 276 total to finish 12 under par and edge Kris Tschetter by two strokes. It was King's third victory at the Dinah Shore, and her sixth major title overall.

"Last year I struggled all year, and now I feel much better," said King, whose best finish in 1996 was fifth place. "This is the best I've played for a year and a half. I struggled with my swing and didn't hit the ball well during that time. Golf became a hard game."

Kelly Robbins, who tied for third place, held a three-shot lead with eight holes to go, but struggled down the homestretch, shooting 40 on Mission Hills' second nine. Robbins finished with a round of 74. "I thought Kelly was going to win," said King. "I was down three at the 10th hole and thought I would not win the tournament."

King broke a winless drought that had stretched 46 events covering 21 months. During that time, she finished in the top three four times. At Mission Hills, she turned her fortunes around as if she had found some old magic in a lantern.

Said King, "Once in a while, the old guard can still do it."

Longs Drugs Challenge—$500,000
Winner: Annika Sorenstam

The finish in the Longs Drugs Challenge in Lincoln, California, had one player that people were surprised to see near the top and another who was no surprise at all. At Twelve Bridges Golf Club, Annika Sorenstam held off Pam Kometani by making a par at the second playoff hole, the 74th hole of the tournament.

Kometani, age 32, never had higher than 27th place in an LPGA event, and despite her position and a chance to enter the winner's circle, stayed surprisingly calm throughout the final day. On a narrow golf course that featured speedy greens, Kometani closed by shooting two-under-par 70, catching up to Sorenstam, who finished with 73.

Of the players at or near the lead beginning the final round, Kometani was the only one who managed to break par. In one of the highest scoring events of the year, she and Sorenstam tied through 72 holes at three-under-par 285.

Sorenstam, who had to make a four-footer on the first playoff hole to force one more hole, lagged a 25-foot birdie putt to within inches of the hole at the par-three 13th, which she reached with a seven iron. Kometani knocked a five iron over the green, ran a chip past the hole, and missed the par putt coming back. "It's really just a matter of survival," said Sorenstam, who had done just that in shooting 73, 68, 71 and 73 for a 285 total. "It's not a course where you shoot really low."

Jan Stephenson and Juli Inkster tied for third at 286.

Susan G. Komen International—$500,000
Winner: Karrie Webb

Following a series of close calls that began her second year on the LPGA Tour, Karrie Webb broke away to victory at the Susan G. Komen International in Myrtle Beach, South Carolina, firing back-to-back rounds of six-under-par 66 on the weekend.

Webb displayed the ability that elevates her game among the best in the world when she ran off six consecutive birdies in the final round in a stretch that began at the 11th hole of Wachesaw Plantation East Golf Club. "Through the first 10 holes, I was down on myself," she said. "I took a look at the leaderboard and I was surprised that nine under was leading the tournament. I figured if I could make some putts, I still had a good chance to win." So she began to make a putt or two. Then another, and another, and another, and one more for good measure at 16.

"I like to come from behind because I can play aggressively and go for broke," she said. "I have nothing to lose."

And everything to gain, of course. Webb won $75,000 for the victory. Second place was shared by Cathy Johnston-Forbes, whose brother, Clyde, actually designed the course, and Nanci Bowen. Both players shot 70 to finish at 278, two shots behind Webb, who opened rather unimpressively with consecutive 72s. This time, Webb saved her best for last.

Chick-fil-A Charity Championship—$550,000
Winner: Nancy Lopez

The fact the Chick-fil-A Charity Championship was shortened to 36 holes because of thunderstorms in Stockbridge, Georgia, may have left the winner feeling a little awkward, but before long, all the emotions of victory began to return to Nancy Lopez. A strict regimen of conditioning and diet not only helped Lopez lose 40 pounds, but it helped to add yet another piece of hardware to a mantel that must be about to give way by now. The triumph was Lopez's 48th as a member of the LPGA Tour.

"A year and a half ago, when I really didn't feel I could win again, I wondered whether I really needed to stay out here anymore," said Lopez, who lost in her battle to fight back tears in the press room following the tournament. "I resigned myself to either get more prepared and get in shape or quit playing golf."

Lopez wasn't alone in being thankful she chose the former, not the latter. Her victory was a popular one among her peers, who realize all that Lopez, age 40, has done for the game in her storied career.

When rains washed out play on Sunday, Lopez's hot 66 a day earlier proved enough to taste victory once again. For 36 holes, Lopez was seven under par, two shots better than Tina Barrett, Deb Richard and Karrie Webb. Lopez's 66 included an 83-yard sand wedge shot she holed for eagle from the 13th fairway on Saturday. The field tried to get in Sunday's round, to no avail. Laura Davies was on the golf course ahead of Lopez, and an eagle-birdie spurt on the third and fourth holes let her climb to four under par. Lopez was six under at the time, and on the green at the par-five third hole in two shots.

"If I were in the shoes of some of the other players, being a shot back, I'm sure I'd wish that we could go out and play again," said Lopez. "But I really played yesterday (Saturday) with the thought that we might not be able to play again."

Sprint Titleholders Championship—$1,200,000
Winner: Tammie Green

Tammie Green, age 37, ended a winless string of almost three years by holding off some of the game's elite names to win the Sprint Titleholders Championship by two shots over two-time defending U.S. Open champion Annika Sorenstam, who closed by shooting six-under-par 66.

Among the others giving chase in the last round were Kelly Robbins and Karrie Webb, two of the LPGA's brightest young stars, as well as Nancy Lopez, winner of 48 LPGA events. Increasing Green's challenge were demanding first-round conditions. Winds gusting as high as 20 miles an hour made club selection difficult and made the course play tougher than it had all week. In the end, Green simply proved tougher.

A two-foot birdie putt set up by a brilliant wedge shot from 89 yards at the 452-yard, par-five 18th hole produced a round of even-par 72 and a four-round score of 14-under-par 274, a personal best.

"Well, it has been a long time since I won, and to win a championship such as this one — you know, I feel like it is a major championship — that makes it even more special," said Green. "It's really hard to describe. You get a little nervous. But this is one thing about winning; you've got to get through all that. You try to get the negatives away from you and try to think positively. You believe in yourself and have the confidence that you can win and are good enough to play against these players."

Green underwent emergency surgery for a ruptured ovarian cyst early in 1996, and struggled to regain the consistency with which she played from 1993-95, when she finished no lower than 13th on the LPGA's money list and played in the Solheim Cup. At the Sprint Titleholders, she showed she was back in top form.

Sara Lee Classic—$675,000
Winner: Terry-Jo Myers

Terry-Jo Myers had waited nine years between winning the 1988 Mayflower Classic and the 1997 Los Angeles Women's Championship. She did not wait quite so long to win again. Myers, one of golf's top comeback stories of 1997, tapped in for par from one foot on the fifth hole of a playoff to defeat Laurel Kean and Nancy Harvey and win the Sara Lee Classic in Nashville, Tennessee.

All three players had shots to win. Myers had an 18-foot birdie putt to try to win in regulation, but slid the putt past the left edge of the cup. Kean shot 66 on the last day but missed a three-footer for par on the final playoff hole. Harvey had a one-shot lead heading down the final hole of regulation but missed a four-footer for par, bogeyed, and slipped back to nine-under 207.

Myers sandwiched a second-round 67 between a pair of 70s. Kelly Robbins, who held the lead after two rounds, three-putted the par-four 15th hole for double bogey and eventually missed the playoff by one shot after a round of 72. In the press room after her victory, Myers admitted she did not expect to be back in the winner's circle so soon. "It's kind of a neat habit, if it becomes a habit," she said.

McDonald's LPGA Championship—$1,200,000
Winner: Chris Johnson

In her 18th season on the LPGA Tour, Chris Johnson captured her first major title, outduelling Leta Lindley to capture the McDonald's LPGA Championship at DuPont Country Club in Wilmington, Delaware. Johnson prevailed on the second hole of a playoff when she was able to get up and down from behind the green at the 10th hole, making a putt of six feet. Lindley made bogey after pushing her drive under a tree.

Johnson had won six times in her career, but seldom had played with a great deal of consistency. She knew if she kept plugging along, however, her moment would arrive. It arrived in Wilmington in late May. "There was a time when I realized I could wait for my week to come along, and when everything goes your way, God comes down and says it's your week," Johnson said.

For a time, it appeared to be Lindley's week. She had an opportunity to seize the limelight on the first playoff hole, as Johnson had pried open the door by making her second consecutive bogey at the 18th hole. However, Lindley's putt for victory from just outside three feet failed to drop. Lindley, whose best finish of the season had been a tie for 28th place in Los Angeles, got into the hunt by shooting 69 in the second round in arduous conditions that featured winds gusting to 30 miles an hour. Lindley was the only player in the field to break par, and 26 players shot in the 80s.

Annika Sorenstam played her way into contention in the final round with a brilliant closing score of 67, but missed a chance to join the playoff when she pushed a 30-inch putt for par at the last hole.

Johnson, who was on the leaderboard from the start, shot rounds of 68, 73, 69 and 71 for a 281 total to finish three under par, earning $180,000. Sorenstam finished third. Laura Davies, who four-putted the first hole of her second round en route to 75, battled back to finish tied for fourth with Sherri Steinhauer.

Corning Classic—$650,000
Winner: Rosie Jones

For some players, 10 birdies would constitute a pretty fair week of tournament golf. Rosie Jones made 10 birdies in a day in Corning, New York, nine in regulation and one more in a playoff against Tammie Green on the final day to win the Corning Classic for the second consecutive year. Jones earlier shot rounds of 72, 69 and 71, and closed with 65 to clinch her victory, the eighth of her career. Green, who started the final round with a two-shot lead, played well, shooting 69 on a wet, drizzly day, but it wasn't enough to match Jones' 11th-hour heroics.

In the playoff, Jones hit a three wood off the tee at the par-four 18th hole, her ball finishing 30 yards behind Green, who hit a driver. Jones barely hit her second shot on the green, and then, facing a 50-foot putt with a double break, rolled her ball right into the cup. Green, shocked, missed her birdie attempt from 10 feet.

The playoff was strange from the start. Jones actually won the coin toss, but instead of electing to hit first, deferred to Green, who had been struggling with her driver. Green then stepped up to the tee and smashed a drive right down the middle of the fairway. "So much for my great plans," said Jones. In the end, however, she had no complaints about the way things sorted out.

Michelob Light Classic—$600,000
Winner: Annika Sorenstam

Annika Sorenstam continued her domination of women's golf in 1997, collecting her fourth victory of the year with a steady performance at the Michelob Light Classic in St. Louis, Missouri. A final round of 72 on a damp, drizzly day when only one player (Rachel Hetherington) was able to dip into the 60s carried Sorenstam to a three-shot lead over Hiromi Kobayashi.

Instead of hitting a wall in the middle of the schedule, as she had after winning her second U.S. Open in 1996, Sorenstam was still hitting her peak. Sorenstam shot 11-under-par 277, one stroke off the tournament record.

Sorenstam and Kobayashi broke from the pack in the last round, with Kobayashi, who was seeking her first victory since 1993, doing a decent job of keeping pace on a difficult day to play. In the end, Sorenstam would prove too steady, and Kobayashi fell back to the pack by shooting two-over 74. "Annika is such a good player," she said. "I knew I couldn't make any mistakes."

Sorenstam led the tournament in greens in regulation (56 of 72) and was second in putting (115 putts), which is a lethal combination. She shot rounds of 70, 69, 66 and 72 for a 277 total, and the victory was her 10th on the LPGA Tour.

Oldsmobile Classic—$600,000
Winner: Pat Hurst

The Oldsmobile Classic in East Lansing, Michigan, turned into a battle between San Jose State graduates Pat Hurst and Juli Inkster, with Hurst registering her first LPGA victory when she sank a 20-foot birdie putt at the final hole. Hurst, age 28, who had an impressive amateur record, once put her golf clubs away for a year, citing burnout, but gradually worked herself back into the game. At Walnut Hills Country Club, she was glad she had.

The final round proved to be quite a shootout. Five players were tied atop the leaderboard at one point on the second nine — Hurst, Kim Saiki, Susie Redman, Elaine Crosby and Lisa Hackney. In the end, it was Hurst and Inkster, and Inkster dropped back with a bogey at the short, 286-yard, par-four 17th hole, where she hit her second shot over the green and did not recover. Both players finished by shooting 70 on a day when the lowest score was 68.

Hurst became the fourth former NCAA champion since 1996 to win on the LPGA Tour, joining Melissa McNamara, Annika Sorenstam and Emilee Klein. Hurst was the NCAA champion in 1989, and the LPGA Rookie of the Year in 1995. After rounds of 68, 70, 71 and 70 for a 279 total, she was able to add LPGA tournament champion to the resume.

Edina Realty Classic—$600,000
Winner: Danielle Ammaccapane

Danielle Ammaccapane, who had not won on the LPGA Tour in five years, battled back from a final-round deficit of five shots to capture the Edina Realty Classic in Maple Grove, Minnesota. In one of the more closely contested events of the year, Ammaccapane posted a bogey-free final round of four-under-par 68 at Rush Creek Golf Club to edge Hiromi Kobayashi, Catriona Matthew, Mayumi Hirase and Jane Geddes by one shot. Ammaccapane shot rounds of 70, 70 and 68 to finish 54 holes at eight-under-par 208.

Kobayashi had a chance to force a playoff but made a bogey at the 18th hole, and Geddes narrowly missed a chip for birdie at the final green in her attempt to tie for the lead. Ammaccapane won three times in 1992, but struggled after that. She earned $65,578 in 1996 — finishing 84th on the money list — then opened 1997 by missing the cut in her first sixth events. "It crossed my mind to quit," she said. "I wasn't having any fun out here, and I said if that ever happened, I would quit. I came as close to quitting as you can."

Making her LPGA debut was Kelly Kuehne, the two-time U.S. Women's Amateur champion from McKinney, Texas. She shot 73 and 75 and missed the cut by one shot. Afterward, she downplayed a comparison to Tiger Woods. "The comparisons don't bother me at all," she said, "but they are a little far-fetched."

Rochester International—$600,000
Winner: Penny Hammel

Penny Hammel had to wait for a few groups to finish before she could collect the winner's check at the Rochester International. After waiting six years between victories, what was another 30 minutes? Hammel was ready for a playoff after watching Dottie Pepper's chip shot come to rest two feet from the flagstick at the 18th hole. But Pepper, who had a spike mark between her ball and the hole, missed the putt, and Hammel didn't even have to put in overtime for the victory.

Pepper's reaction? "I'm shocked," she said.

Hammel was more than a little surprised herself at the way everything sorted itself out at Locust Hill Country Club in Pittsford, New York. She began the final day three shots out of the lead on a crowded leaderboard, but began to pass others with a solid closing round of 68. Her winning score was nine-under-par 279.

The LPGA's Rookie of the Year in 1985, Hammel struggled from 1992 to 1995, finishing no higher than 16th. She lost a brother to AIDS, and golf became less important to her. In 1996, she decided to rededicate herself to the game, and won $260,000. At Rochester, given Pepper's final-putt misfortune, Hammel wondered if she had earned the victory. She had.

ShopRite Classic—$900,000
Winner: Michelle McGann

It took Michelle McGann seven years to put all the pieces together and become a champion on the LPGA Tour, accomplishing that feat with a victory at the 1995 Sara Lee Classic. Now that she has found the winning mix and broken through, she is finding that winning is a hard habit to break.

A week that started rather unspectacularly with a round of 72 turned into something special on the weekend at Greate Bay Resort and Country Club in Somers Point, New Jersey. A second-round 65 and a tournament-record-tying 64 a day later produced McGann's seventh LPGA victory. She finished at 12-under-par 201 — a tournament record — to catch second-round leader Annika Sorenstam and win by three strokes.

"You shoot 72 in the first round of the tournament and it tells you something," McGann said. "It tells you to never give up. Golf is a game of patience, bounces and some luck. You've just got to keep hanging in."

Sorenstam, who would finish second for the third time in the 1997 season, had little luck getting her round energized on the last day, when she shot 71. Sorenstam watched her lead slip away, then climbed back into a tie for the lead with a birdie on the 16th hole. The outcome was decided at No. 17, where McGann punched a seven iron from beneath a tree to seven feet, and Sorenstam made bogey after dumping a nine iron into a bunker.

The victory was McGann's second of 1997.

Jamie Farr Kroger Classic—$700,000
Winner: Kelly Robbins

Kelly Robbins set a four-round LPGA scoring record at Highland Meadows Golf Club, blistering the course in 19-under-par 265 to capture the Jamie Farr Kroger Classic in Sylvania, Ohio, in the final tune-up before the U.S. Women's Open.

The previous LPGA low had been Betsy King's 267 total, which was shot at the Mazda LPGA Championship in 1992, also on a par-71 layout. The record score for 72 holes on a par-72 course was 266, shared by Nancy Lopez and Beth Daniel. "To be recognized as someone that can shoot numbers like that, that's great," said Robbins. "I put together four really good days of golf. It was a very rewarding week."

Robbins shot rounds of 67, 64, 67 and 67 to win by eight strokes over Tammie Green. Lopez finished third at 274, nine shots back.

Robbins birdied three of her final five holes in the third round to shoot 67 and build her lead to six shots over Karrie Webb and seven shots over Lopez and Vickie Odegard. One day earlier, Robbins had birdied three of the last four holes in shooting seven-under 64.

After getting her name in the record books, Robbins confessed she does not get too caught up in such achievements. "But for those who do," she said, "they'll see my name."

U.S. Women's Open—$1,300,000
Winner: Alison Nicholas

The chance of a lifetime had just eluded Nancy Lopez, and standing on the 18th green at Pumpkin Ridge Golf Club in Cornelius, Oregon, she didn't quite know what to do. A putt remained, but she could not see the golf ball near her feet. The tears forming a reservoir in her eyes didn't allow it.

Talk about bad timing. Just when Nancy Lopez figured out how to play the U.S. Women's Open — she's been trying since 1977 — along came a player who did it just a little better. Alison Nicholas, a pint-sized but powerful British player whom friends in England call "the pocket battleship," sank Lopez's longtime quest to capture the U.S. Women's Open, surviving a pressure-filled showdown with one of the game's greats to shoot 71 and hang on for a one-stroke triumph.

The two players broke from the field early — combined, they played thei first four holes in six under par — and staged an entertaining duel that did not end until Lopez slid a downhill 15-footer for birdie past the right side of the cup at the 494-yard closing hole on Pumpkin Ridge's Witch Hollow course.

Lopez, age 40, who shot nine-under-par 275 for the tournament, established a U.S. Women's Open record by shooting four rounds in the 60s (69-68-69-69), making a final five-footer made cloudy by tears. But Lopez did not travel home to Georgia with the trophy she covets like no other in her Hall of Fame career. "It's a tough thing, because I've always wanted to win the U.S. Open, and this was, really, my time to do it," said Lopez, who has been runner-up four times. "I probably won't sleep tonight because I'll be thinking about every shot and what went on and what we did and what I could have done.

"I played well. I can't take anything away from me, because I think Alison won it. She went out there and played her best. She won the U.S. Open today."

For Nicholas, age 35, the mere idea of being U.S. Women's Open champion did not sink in right away. Although her aggregate total of 274 was not an Open record, Nicholas, who has won 17 times around the world, became the first player in a U.S. Women's Open to finish 10 under par. Kelly Robbins (66–277) was third, followed by Karrie Webb, who shot 65-68 on the weekend to finish fourth at 278.

When Lopez tried to put heat on Nicholas early in the round, Nicholas responded beautifully, matching her shot-for-shot. In fact, she even upstaged Lopez. Lopez birdied the first hole and added an eight-footer for birdie at No. 3, but Nicholas matched the second birdie, canning a putt of six feet to keep a two-shot edge. At the 501-yard fourth hole, Nicholas then produced the shot of the tournament. Both players had less than 60 yards to the par-five green on their third shots, and Lopez hit first, knocking her ball to 18 inches. Nicholas followed with a low, hard-spinning wedge that hit once, twice, thrice, and short-hopped into the cup for eagle. The lead was back to three.

"My shot looked terrible after that," Lopez said.

Nicholas built the cushion to four shots on the second nine, but it slipped to three after Lopez birdied the 13th and shrunk to one shot when Nicholas, pumped up by adrenalin, powered a wedge over the 14th green and made double bogey. Lopez gave one back when she went for the pin at the par-three 15th, slid a five iron right of the green, and made bogey — her lone regret of the round. But she rallied once more with a five-foot birdie at the difficult, 405-yard 16th hole.

The championship came down to the 18th, where Nicholas' ball was one foot away for par and Lopez, trailing by one shot, faced 15 feet to force a playoff. But her putt died off right, to the low side of the cup, and with it died Lopez's chances of filling out an LPGA resume that already boasts 48 victories. "It was just a wonderful day," Nicholas said. "Playing with Nancy was a privilege. She's a great champion. I shall just remember this forever, really."

JAL Big Apple Classic—$750,000
Winner: Michele Redman

There is some sort of correlation between Wykagyl Country Club in New Rochelle, New York, home of the JAL Big Apple Classic, and first-time winners on the LPGA Tour. For the third consecutive year, the player left to formulate a victory speech on the 18th green was doing something she had never done before. In 1997, that champion was Michele Redman, who won in style, leading from wire to wire and outdistancing runner-up Annika Sorenstam by three strokes. Meg Mallon finished third, and Karrie Webb and Chris Johnson tied for fourth.

Sorenstam knows a little something about winning golf tournaments, and she walked away impressed with what she saw of Redman, who briefly let Sorenstam back into the hunt in the final round, then slammed the door closed when Sorenstam could not make a birdie in her final seven holes. Redman protected her slim lead with a nice save at the 16th hole, made par at the 17th, and clinched victory with one last birdie at the final hole.

"I'm so relieved right now," said Redman, who has been to the LPGA's qualifying tournament four times. "Annika was right behind me, and she has been there before."

Giant Eagle Classic—$600,000
Winner: Tammie Green

Tammie Green took home a nice trophy for winning the Giant Eagle Classic in Warren, Ohio. It would have been more fitting if tournament organizers tied a big red bow around the 471-yard, par-five 18th hole and found a way to stuff it into her car.

Green saw plenty of the 18th hole, playing it three times in regulation and three more times in a playoff against long-hitting Laura Davies. Green played the hole in eight under par, making a pair of eagles in a five-hole playoff, the last one finally landing the victory.

Through 54 holes, Green and Davies were deadlocked at 13-under-par 203. Davies had a shot to win in regulation, reaching the 18th hole with a driver and nine iron, but she three-putted from 40 feet, missing a five-footer for the victory. Back to the 18th they went.

Both players birdied the 18th to start the playoff, halved the par-four 10th with pars, then headed back to 18 again, where both made eagles — Green from 10 feet, Davies from four. They each parred No. 10 once more, and returned to 18 once last time. This time, only one of the players would manage to make an eagle, and it was Green. As Davies flailed away on the hole, Green hit a six-iron approach to three feet and sank the putt for her second victory of the season.

du Maurier Classic—$1,200,000
Winner: Colleen Walker

The LPGA's major championships of 1997 were not made for the young and the restless. Instead, experience paid dividends. Colleen Walker captured the first major title of her 16-year LPGA career, firing a course-record-tying 65, eight under par at Glen Abbey Golf Club in Oakville, Ontario, to edge Liselotte Neumann by two shots.

Walker, age 40, who 10 months earlier had given birth to a son, zoomed past eight players who began the final round ahead of her on the leaderboard. When others began to encounter difficulty in Glen Abbey's 11th through 15th holes, dubbed the Valley holes, Walker made her move. Walker birdied the par-three 12th hole and the par-five 13th to get to 13 under par. The clincher came at 18, where she curled in a 20-foot birdie putt, walked off the green, then realized just what she had done. "Every player's dream out here is to win a major," said Walker.

Neumann played well from tee to green, but had a difficult time getting key putts to fall in the final round, when she shot 69. Betsy King, trying to become only the second player to capture all four LPGA majors, also shot 69, and finished tied for third with Kelly Robbins at 281, three shots back.

Because of her pregnancy, Walker played in only seven events in 1996, and the time away from the game answered a few doubts she harbored regarding whether she still had the fire to compete. She hadn't won since 1992, and had only two top-20 finishes in the last 17 events she had played before the break.

In her final 18 holes at Glen Abbey, Walker learned she still had plenty of fire. Her closing eight-under-par 65 was one stroke short of the best round ever recorded in the final round of a women's major championship. JoAnne Carner holds that distinction with a last-round, nine-under-par 64 at the du Maurier Classic in Toronto in 1978.

Friendly's Classic—$550,000
Winner: Deb Richard

For Deb Richard, the physical barriers of enduring once-excruciating spasms between her shoulder blades had been knocked down and conquered. What was left was the matter of turning away the mental ghosts that had stayed with her, the doubts that kept creeping in that made her wonder if she ever would be the player she once was.

By winning the Friendly's Classic in Agawam, Massachusetts, Richard hoped she had received a significant sign of better times to come. There had been a couple of close calls earlier in the year, some top-10 finishes. But in winning, Richard proved to herself she had come all the way back from a career-threatening injury.

A final round of five-under-par 67 was good enough to hold off hard-charging Chris Johnson, whose eagle three at the 17th hole pulled her to within one shot of the lead at 10 under par. Johnson's late charge would not be enough to thwart Richard's triumphant moment at Crestview Country Club.

Three years earlier, Richard had to withdraw from the Safeco Classic — where she was defending champion — because spasms between her shoulder blades became so painful that they actually took her breath away. There was bone-on-bone grinding between her rib cage and shoulder blade, and surgery was unavoidable if she was going to save her career.

The victory at Friendly's Classic was the fifth of her career for Richard, a former University of Florida standout. She shot rounds of 72, 70, 68 and 67 for a 277 total. Johnson finished alone in second. Brandie Burton, who closed with 68, was third at 280. "I guess this means I'm really back," Richard said.

Star Bank Classic—$550,000
Winner: Colleen Walker

Colleen Walker, who had not won an event on the LPGA Tour in five years before capturing the du Maurier Classic in August, captured her second title in as many starts at the waterlogged Star Bank Classic in Beavercreek, Ohio.

By shooting 13-under-par 203, Walker not only walked away with first-place money of $82,500, but also collected a bonus of $100,000 offered to any winner who already had won in 1997. Walker turned in rounds of 67, 69 and 67, pulling away from a packed leaderboard when she made birdies at the 15th (sand wedge, eight feet), 16th (six iron, three feet) and 17th holes (five iron, five feet).

Terry-Jo Myers was tied for the lead at one point at 11 under par, but finished in second, two shots behind Walker. A group at eight under par included Laura Davies, Tammie Green, Kim Williams and Dottie Pepper.

Walker won for the ninth time as a member of the LPGA Tour. "I did miss playing when I was sitting at home last summer," she said. "I don't know if there is anything in the world I'd rather do than play golf.

"They say life begins at 40," she added. "I guess it's true. It's happening."

State Farm Rail Classic—$600,000
Winner: Cindy Figg-Currier

As the axiom goes, good things come to those who wait. Well, Cindy Figg Currier waited and waited and waited, and then waited some more. Fourteen years and 314 LPGA tournaments to be exact. Finally at the State Farm Rail Classic in Springfield, Illinois, Figg-Currier enjoyed her brilliant day in the sun.

By sinking a three-footer for birdie on the first playoff hole, Figg-Currie not only edged Kris Tschetter and Lorie Kane, but ended one of the longest winless droughts on the LPGA Tour. "It's a feeling of relief because it's been so long," she said. "I think it's a matter of having perseverance and believing in yourself."

Figg-Currier entered the final round with a one-shot lead, but it was all she could do to hold on with several players making strong moves up the leaderboard. Tschetter, seeking her first LPGA victory, fired 64, and Kane a rookie, shot 65. All three players birdied the 18th hole in regulation to ge to 16 under par. In the playoff, also staged at the 376-yard finishing hole, Tschetter lipped out a long birdie putt, Kane left a birdie putt short, and Figg-Currier then stepped up and rolled in her short birdie effort for the victory.

Scotland's Kathryn Marshall equaled an LPGA scoring record by shooting 10-under-par 62 in the second round at the Rail Golf Course. She was the fifth player on the LPGA Tour to shoot 62, and the second to do so at the Rail Classic, joining Laura Davies, who did so in 1991.

Safeway Golf Championship—$550,000
Winner: Chris Johnson

Chris Johnson had a chance to win the 1996 Safeway Golf Championship but stumbled down the stretch, making bogeys at the last two holes as Dottie Pepper walked off with the victory. A year later, Johnson would put herself in a similar position. This time, the results were far different.

This time, Johnson birdied the final two holes to pull out a one-shot triumph over Kim Saiki and Lisa Hackney. Johnson hit approaches to five and eight feet, respectively, at the final two holes, and cashed in with the putter to shoot 66 and finish at 10-under-par 206.

Saiki did all she could to keep it close, making birdies at her final three holes to shoot 66, the best score of her career. Hackney didn't finish as strongly. At the 17th hole, she hit a four wood that caught a cedar tree and led to a bogey that dropped her from 10 to nine under par and surrendered any momentum gained from a 15-foot birdie putt at the 16th.

For Johnson, who earlier in the season had captured the McDonald's LPGA Championship, the victory was more icing on what already had been a career season. The winner's check for $82,500 pushed Johnson's 1997 earnings past $612,000, nearly triple her previous best season. "At the beginning of the year, I knew I was capable of doing something like this," said Johnson. "But I'm exceeding everything I thought."

Safeco Classic—$550,000
Winner: Karrie Webb

Karrie Webb came from three strokes behind at Meridian Valley Country Club in Kent, Washington, to win her second consecutive Safeco Classic, edging Annika Sorenstam by one shot. Webb shot rounds of 67, 67, 71 and 67 to finish at 16-under-par 272 on the 6,241-yard Meridian Valley layout. Webb clinched the victory when she reached the 470-yard, par-five 18th hole with a drive and a five wood, then two-putted for birdie from 20 feet.

Webb said the turning point in her final round arrived at the 363-yard 14th hole, where she missed the green with her second shot and the ball plugged in a bunker. She managed to blast the shot to four feet, then made the putt for par. She also chipped in at the par-five ninth hole for birdie. The victory was Webb's fourth of the year, and her 18th top-10 finish in 21 starts.

Patty Sheehan entered the final round with the lead, but got off to a cold start and shot 75. Because it was Sheehan's final event of 1997, it brought to an end her streak of eight years with at least one victory. Still, her third-place finish was her best effort of the season.

Welch's Championship—$550,000
Winner: Liselotte Neumann

Liselotte Neumann, who began her 1996 season with a victory at the Chrysler-Plymouth Tournament of Champions, had to be a little more patient in 1997. In late September at the Welch's Championship in Canton, Massachusetts, Neumann prevailed for her first victory of the season, breaking out of a final-round tie with Nancy Harvey to win her ninth LPGA title.

Neumann, who shot rounds of 67, 70, 69 and 70 for a 12-under-par 276 total at Blue Hill Country Club, birdied two of her first three holes on the last day and never released the lead. Harvey, who was seeking her first LPGA victory, shot 73 and finished second, three shots ahead of Karrie Webb. After Neumann birdied the 12th hole and Harvey bogeyed the 13th, Neumann's lead swelled to five shots. She coasted home from there.

"My goal starting the round was to make sure I didn't get caught up in a match-play situation with Nancy," said Neumann. "There's a tendency to do that when you're playing with the person you are tied with, and then someone from the field catches you."

Neumann pocketed $82,500 for her victory. Harvey earned $51,201, which was more money than she had won in any of her previous eight seasons on the LPGA Tour. Before 1997, her top finish was a tie for sixth at the 1990 Stratton Mountain LPGA Classic.

Fieldcrest Cannon Classic—$550,000
Winner: Wendy Ward

Former Arizona State star Wendy Ward was expected to be an instant success when she earned her LPGA Tour card in 1995, graduating alongside Karrie Webb. People expected quite a rookie race. Instead, Webb took the LPGA by storm, winning four times, and Ward struggled to keep her playing card.

At the Fieldcrest Cannon Classic in Charlotte, North Carolina, in September, the golf world got a glimpse of Ward's potential. Not only did she break through to capture her first LPGA event, she did so in record-breaking style, setting the LPGA's all-time-to-par scoring record by blistering the Peninsula Club in 23-under-par 265.

Ward, who had broken 70 only five times in 74 previous rounds in 1997, shot rounds of 66, 65, 64 and 70 to defeat Jane Geddes and Rosie Jones by two shots. Ward made 24 birdies and only one bogey, that arriving on the fifth hole of her opening round. Ward's effort matched the LPGA's all-time scoring mark (265) established earlier in the season by Kelly Robbins on par-71 course at the Jamie Farr Kroger Classic.

"I'm 21 under par and two shots back," Geddes said afterward, somewhat stunned by Ward's performance. "That's a pretty good indication of what this tour is all about today. That's good news and bad news. It's bad news for us older players."

CoreStates Betsy King Classic—$600,000
Winner: Annika Sorenstam

Annika Sorenstam continued her torrid 1997 year by collecting her fifth victory, successfully defending her championship at the CoreStates Betsy King Classic in Kutztown, Pennsylvania. The winner's check for $90,000 pushed Sorenstam past the $1 million mark in season earnings, becoming the second LPGA player (Karrie Webb was the first in 1996) to reach the plateau.

"I personally feel inside I can improve even more," said Sorenstam, who shot rounds of 70, 67, 68 and 69 to finish at 14-under-par 274 for 72 holes. "I really look forward to climbing the ladder even higher."

Kelly Robbins finished second, two shots behind Sorenstam. Betsy King, the tournament host and a local favorite, began the final round tied for the lead and eventually finished in a four-way tie for third.

Sorenstam was in a three-way tie for the lead on the final nine holes, but continued to make pars and was handed the lead for good when King bogeyed the 14th hole and Catriona Matthew bogeyed No. 15.

Samsung World Championship of Women's Golf—$525,000
Winner: Juli Inkster

Feeling fortunate just to make it to a playoff with Helen Alfredsson at the Samsung World Championship of Women's Golf, Juli Inkster made the most of her opportunity, rolling in a 12-foot birdie putt to win the limited field event in Seoul, South Korea.

Alfredsson had a chance to win in regulation, but slid a three-foot putt for birdie past the cup. Alfredsson, Inkster and Kelly Robbins — all of whom finished 72 holes in eight-under-par 280 — then proceeded to a playoff, where Inkster prevailed for the 16th LPGA victory of her career. It marked Inkster's first victory since 1992. "To win against those two players is a great feeling for me," she said. "It's been awhile since I won."

Inkster moved into contention with an eagle at the par-five 11th hole, but still needed a little help down the stretch from Alfredsson to gain a shot at victory. Inkster shot 67 at Lakeside Country Club's West Course in the final round, compared to 69 for Robbins and 73 for Alfredsson.

ITT LPGA Tour Championship—$750,000
Winner: Annika Sorenstam

The 1997 LPGA Tour season faded to black just the way it opened in January, with Annika Sorenstam standing on the 18th green at a tournament, hoisting another winner's trophy. Sorenstam proved to be the class of the field amid one of the best fields of the year in the ITT LPGA Tour Championship, shooting rounds of 72, 68, 67 and 70 for a 277 total and then edging Lorie Kane and Pat Hurst in a playoff for her sixth win of the season. The victory also catapulted Sorenstam to $1,236,789 in season earnings, an LPGA record.

Sorenstam, whose trademark is her consistency, made pars at each of the three playoff holes to outlast Hurst, who made a bogey on the first playoff hole, and Kane, who missed a five-foot chance to force a fourth extra hole. "She's the best we have," said Kane, "and she's the best in the world."

The victory capped a remarkable season for Sorenstam, 27, who was the LPGA's Player of the Year for the second time in three seasons. In 22 starts, she won six times, finished runner-up five times, had 14 finishes in the top three and 16 top-10 efforts. Her scoring average of 70.04 was second only to Karrie Webb's 70.00. In the end, Sorenstam didn't want to see the season end. Nobody could blame her.

"Too bad it's the last tournament of the season," Sorenstam said. "I'd like to play some more."

Women's European Tour

Estoril Ladies' Open—£90,000
Winner: Mandy Sutton

Mandy Sutton could not have opened her third Women's Professional Golf European Tour season in more impressive fashion than in the Estoril Ladies' Open in Estoril, Portugal. Sutton, who is attached to the Sherwood Forest Club in the heart of Nottinghamshire's Robin Hood country, set a course record of 63 in the first round.

The 33-year-old led by three strokes and though Karina Orum cut her advantage to one after the second round, Sutton maintained the margin over the Dane with a final-round 71. Her first professional victory came with a five-under-par 202 total, while Shani Waugh finished third at even par.

American Express Tour Players' Classic—£100,000
Winner: Karen Lunn

The biggest of Karen Lunn's five previous victories had been the Weetabix British Open in 1993. Since then, however, the 31-year-old Australian has struggled with a herniated disc in her back and lost confidence trying to play on both the European and the LPGA Tours. Her 1996 season was also marred by the death of her father. "I lost interest in playing," Lunn said. "It is great to be back in Europe. It is beyond my wildest expectations to win my second tournament back."

Lunn did so by overtaking her final-round playing companions, Patricia Meunier Lebouc and Tina Fischer, in the American Express Tour Players' Classic at the Tytherington Club in Cheshire, England. Lunn shot 71 for five-under-par 283 total to win by one stroke, with Wales' Helen Wadsworth fourth at even par.

Ford-Stimorol Danish Open—£90,000
Winner: Laura Davies

In leading the 1996 European money list, Laura Davies won her last two events of the season. She played in Denmark in her first appearance on the tour in 1997 and immediately completed a three-stroke victory over Sweden's Maria Hjorth in the Ford-Stimorol Danish Open in Vejle.

Davies shared the lead with an opening 68, but a second-round 70 put her three ahead of the field and her closing 69 could have been better but for a double-bogey seven at the 18th. Hjorth, who made an impressive charge with a final-round 64, equalling the course record, cut the deficit to two strokes before Davies claimed three consecutive birdies starting from the 12th.

It was the remarkable Englishwoman's second win of the year, having already won the Standard Register Ping, her 26th in Europe and the 51st of her career. She has also won every year in Europe since she joined the tour in 1985. "It's great that the streak continues," she said.

Deesse Ladies' Swiss Open—£90,000
Winner: Marie-Laure de Lorenzi

With a six-stroke lead over Trish Johnson with five holes to play, Marie-Laure de Lorenzi must have been fairly confident of victory in the Deesse Ladies' Swiss Open in Lausanne. But her 19th tour success, and her first for two years, was not a runaway affair.

The 36-year-old Frenchwoman was one ahead of Johnson going into the final round, but swept to the turn in 32. Her lead started to unravel at the 14th, where there was a two-stroke swing. De Lorenzi then bogeyed the 16th after hitting into a bunker, while Johnson birdied the 17th and holed from 20 feet for a birdie four at the 18th. De Lorenzi pulled her drive into trees and found a awkward spot in a bunker with a third.

Another bogey left her at eight-under-par 280 after a closing 70, while the Englishwoman had tied her with 69. The first playoff hole was back at the 18th and Johnson parred the hole, while de Lorenzi holed from 20 feet for the birdie for the hard-earned victory. Karen Lunn continued her good play to finish third, two strokes behind.

Evian Masters—£425,000
Winner: Hiromi Kobayashi

Another playoff scenario a week later in the Evian Masters in Evians-les-Bains, France, saw the chaser catch the hunted and then take the glory in the playoff. Hiromi Kobayashi certainly enjoyed it, she never stopped smiling or laughing all evening, after winning over Alison Nicholas.

Nicholas had led by one stroke going into the final round and was in command for virtually all of the final round. But the 465-yard, par-five 18th hole belonged to Kobayashi.

On the final hole of regulation play, Kobayashi hit a three wood from 223 yards onto the green and two-putted for a birdie. Nicholas saw her birdie attempt shave the hole but not fall. Kobayashi had scored a closing 69 and they were tied at 274, 14 under par. They had separated themselves from the rest of the field, the best of whom was Marie-Laure de Lorenzi who finished six shots back.

Nicholas blocked out her second shot and put her third into a greenside bunker. Kobayashi hit a perfect drive and then again played her trusty three wood, ending up on the front fringe, 30 feet from the hole. Holing the putt for an eagle was her crowning moment.

"I was just trying to get it close and I was so happy when it went in," Kobayashi said. She was playing with an invitation from the sponsors and had not won for two years. Having won nine times in Japan and twice on the LPGA Tour, she became the first Japanese player to win in Europe in seven years.

Guardian Irish Open—£110,000
Winner: Patricia Meunier Lebouc

Having narrowly missed out the previous week, Alison Nicholas was also close to retaining her Guardian Irish Open title in Dublin. Nicholas was tied with Laura Navarro and 54-hole leader Patricia Meunier Lebouc playing the 17th hole at Luttrellstown Castle. Meunier Lebouc had already had to recover from a double bogey at the 10th and a shank two holes later which dropped her two strokes behind Navarro.

Now the Frenchwoman, who is married to Challenge Tour player Antoine Lebouc, holed from 25 feet for an eagle at the 17th to claim her second career victory. Her final-round 71, two worse than her two rivals, gave her a four-under-par 284 total, with Navarro finishing one stroke back and Nicholas two behind.

"I told myself that I mustn't lose my mind," Meunier Lebouc said. "This is a better win than my first one. Then it was a big shock. This time, I knew I could win."

Ladies' German Open—£100,000
Winner: Joanne Mills

The Ladies' German Open in Hamburg turned into an exclusively Australasian occasion when Australia's Joanne Mills tied with Lynnette Brooky of New Zealand. The water that fronts the 18th green at Treudelberg Golf Club may not be as big as the Tasman Sea which separates their countries, but it might well have been when Brooky reached the green at the par-five hole in two shots in the playoff at the first extra hole.

Then Mills, like her opponent seeking her first professional title, holed her wedge shot from 70 yards for an eagle. Stunned, Brooky could not make her 30-footer to continue the playoff. "I can't believe it went in," Mills said. "I've always dreamed of winning, but to do it this way is unbelievable."

Earlier, Mills had found the pond at the 18th with her second shot at the hole in regulation, but pitched and one-putted for a par. Brooky came to the hole needing a birdie to win, but three-putted from 10 feet. Both scored final-round 71s to tie at 283, nine under par. Joanne Morley, the defending champion, was the third-round leader but fell to third place, one behind the playoff with a closing 74.

McDonald's WPGA Championship of Europe—£300,000
Winner: Helen Alfredsson

Helen Alfredsson had been playing in pain for years, the result of a childhood bicycle accident, before she underwent a back and pelvic operation in 1996. Her doctor suggested she take a whole year away from golf, but the bubbly Swede could not be kept down for long.

Although Alfredsson admitted a return to the LPGA Tour in November had probably been too early, gradually her play improved until at the beginning of August, in the glorious setting of the Kings Course at Gleneagles, Alfredsson returned to winning form in the McDonald's WPGA Championship of Europe.

Her play was not exactly consistent, with a second-round 65 following an opening 74, then with 67 and 70 to close, but it did not need to be. With a 276 total, 12 under par, the 32-year-old Alfredsson won by four strokes over Kathryn Marshall and Charlotta Sorenstam, Annika's sister. Her closest challenger was Lora Fairclough, who got within one stroke with nine holes to play, but faded to share fourth place with Marie-Laure de Lorenzi and Trish Johnson six shots back.

"It's the first time in ages I have played so well," Alfredsson said. "My swing has had to be re-modelled and it has been a very tough mental battle. A year ago I was as down as I have ever been. It was very difficult to picture good shots again, so to win is really a bonus."

Weetabix Women's British Open—£525,000
Winner: Karrie Webb

When she won the Weetabix Women's British Open at Woburn two years before, Karrie Webb had been an unheralded rookie. That success, achieved by six strokes, was a big warning for what was to follow as the Australian took the LPGA Tour by storm in 1996. After many years at Woburn, the tournament was switched to a rota of venues, the first of which was the historic Sunningdale Golf Club, near London. Webb returned to the event only 22 years old but now a major star and she lived up to her billing.

Webb opened with 65 to lead by three stokes over Trish Johnson and Liselotte Neumann. A second-round 70 kept her advantage, this time over Johnson and Kathryn Marshall, but then she really set to work.

Her 63 in the third round was a women's record for Sunningdale and left Webb eight shots ahead of American Rosie Jones. A bad start to her final round and a heavy downpour could not unsettle the Australian and 71 gave her a record total for the event of 269, 19 under par. Jones birdied the last hole to claim second place, eight stroke behind, by one from Annika Sorenstam.

"I was wondering when everything was going to come together," Webb said. "And it was this week. I played brilliantly. I am over the moon to win the British Open again. It is such a special tournament for me because it was the first one I ever won."

Compaq Open—£300,000
Winner: Annika Sorenstam

Just in case there was any doubt who the star of women's golf in Sweden is, Annika Sorenstam won for the second successive time on home soil. A year after claiming the Trygg Hansa title, Sorenstam was cheered to a four-stroke victory in the Compaq Open.

All week, the current queen of women's golf battled a former holder of the title. Nancy Lopez took the first-round lead with 66, one better than Sorenstam. While the Swede added an identical score on day two, Lopez slipped three behind with 71. The margin widened a stroke after the third round, but the American eagled the opening hole on the final day.

It could not last, however. Lopez stumbled to 74, and with 70, Sorenstam claimed a winning total of 277, 11 under par. Catrin Nilsmark, two months before she was due to give birth, closed with 71 to take second place six strokes behind her countrywoman. Helen Alfredsson finished fourth, one behind Lopez.

"This victory means a lot to me," Sorenstam said. "To win in front of the Swedish fans and in a duel with Nancy Lopez has been great. Now I feel I am back to my best form."

Although Sorenstam had won four times on the LPGA Tour up to this point, this was her first win since missing the cut at the U.S. Women's Open, where she had been the two-time defending champion.

Ladies' French Open—£100,000
Winner: Karen Lunn

A second victory of the season, becoming the first double winner of the year proved Karen Lunn right in her assertion that she prefers playing in Europe. Nevertheless, a day after claiming the Ladies' French Open title by four strokes over Laurette Maritz, Lunn travelled to America to take part in the pre-qualifying for the LPGA Tour tournament.

"I don't really enjoy playing in America and if we had more tournament in Europe I wouldn't go. But I just want the chance to play more golf," Lunn said.

Rounds of 72, 70, 69 and 70 showed she can do that very nicely at the Jack Nicklaus-designed Paris International course and her 281 total was seven under par. Maritz closed with 73, while defending champion Trish Johnson continued her consistent season in third place, one stroke further back.

Hennessy Cup—£300,000
Winner: Laura Davies

By her own high standards, the year had not been a raging success for Laura Davies, with only two victories. Putting problems had plagued her all year, and three-putting the first green in her final round was not the start Davies wanted in trying to claim the Hennessy Cup, a title that had always eluded her.

But Davies needed no better than a last-round 74 in claiming a one-stroke victory over Australian Anne-Marie Knight, while U.S. Open champion Alison Nicholas, Lisa Hackney and Helen Alfredsson were one stroke further back.

Alfredsson (three times), Liselotte Neumann (twice) and Annika Sorenstam had made the event the private property of the Swedes for the previous six years. "It's great to have broken the jinx," Davies said. "I've been waiting 13 years for this moment."

Sicilian/Italian Open—£100,000
Winner: Valerie Van Ryckeghem

This event was both the 11th Italian Open and the first Sicilian Open, played at the Il Picciolo course in the foothills of Mount Etna. While there was no eruption from the "smoking mountain," there certainly was from Belgium's Valerie Van Ryckeghem. She became the fourth first-time winner of the season by holing a five-foot putt at the first extra hole of a playoff with Patricia Gonzalez. The veteran Colombian, looking for her first win after 12 years on the WPG European Tour, had led by four strokes with six holes to play.

Gonzalez was still two in front playing the 17th, but had a lost ball when she hooked her drive into trees. The triple bogey put her one stroke behind Van Ryckeghem, who had completed a last-round 76 to set the target with a total of 288, four under par. Gonzalez birdied the last hole from 18 feet to force the playoff, but Van Ryckeghem, in her second year on tour, claimed the win that saved her from a trip back to the qualifying tournament. Marie-Laure de Lorenzi and Karina Orum shared third place, one back.

Air France Madame Open—£60,000
Winner: Loraine Lambert

Winning the Air France Madame Open became less important than finishing second. While Loraine Lambert posted her first victory in Europe, Alison Nicholas took second place to win the money list title for the first time.

Nicholas, the U.S. Women's Open champion, returned to compete in the last event of the season to try to pass Helen Alfredsson at the top of the money list. To do so, the Englishwoman needed to finish in the top two in Deauville. With three holes to play, this was not about to happen. But Nicholas, for whom the putts had refused to drop, then birdied the 16th, where she chipped to one foot, then the 17th, holing from 12 feet, and completed the hat-trick at the last hole, where she hit a drive and a seven iron to 10 feet and holed the putt.

With a closing 73, Nicholas, having a 215 total, went ahead of Shani Waugh by one stroke but only claimed outright second place when local player Valerie Michaud dropped four shots in the last three holes to tie Waugh. Unconcerned with such matters, Lambert, who carried her own clubs for all three rounds, finished with 69 to win by two strokes.

With a prize of £6,090, Nicholas finished a European season in which she did not win, but had seven top 10s in her nine events, with £94,589 to finish £1,662 ahead of Alfredsson. Marie-Laure de Lorenzi was third and Laura Davies, fourth.

Princess Lalla Meriem Cup—US$70,000
Winner: Diane Barnard

The Princess Lalla Meriem Cup, a concurrent event with the Hassan II Trophy in Rabat, Morocco, featured 17 women professionals and saw England's Diane Barnard win by four strokes over Spain's Amaia Arruti. Barnard, whose one victory on the WPG European Tour came in 1990, led from start to finish with rounds of 71, 75 and 71 for a 217 total. Arruti, who caught the winner on the 12th hole of the final round before slipping back, squeezed home one ahead of Gillian Stewart and Lora Fairclough.

Praia D'El Rey European Cup—£150,000
Winners: European Seniors Tour

The last organized event on the European professional golf scene in 1997 brought most of the leading ladies and senior men to Portugal for the Praia D'El Rey European Cup, a new competition, at the Praia D'El Rey links, a new course on the Atlantic north of Lisbon. Not surprisingly, the cream of the European Seniors Tour, led by seven-time winner Tommy Horton, scored a 13-7 victory over the prime players of the WPG European Tour in the Ryder Cup-style competition.

Although the seniors needed only three victories from the 10 singles matches on the final day, the women stayed alive until late in the day. The WPGET players matched the men in the opening foursomes for a 2½-2½ start, but the European Seniors shut out the ladies in the fourballs to take a 7½-2½ lead into the final day.

Noel Ratcliffe scored the only victory for the men in the early going on the last day and at one point the women led in eight of the 10 singles matches. However, Jose Maria Canizares, Malcolm Gregson, John Morgan and Horton swept the final four matches to establish the final margin.

Women's Australasian Tours

Republic of China Open—US$120,000
Winner: Ai-Yu Tu

A last-round 69, nine strokes better than her score the previous day, gave Taiwan's Ai-Yu Tu a win in the Republic of China Open for the Cosmos Bank Cup. Her 218 total, two over par, was shared by amateur Hung Chin Hei, who was ineligible for prize money and not included in the official results. American Jean Bartholomew was listed as second, two strokes behind.

Toyota Philippine Open—US$110,000
Winner: Pernilla Sterner

The second event of the Women's Asian Tour, the Toyota Philippine Open, pointed the way for the rest of the short series of events as Swedish golfers filled the first three places at Sta. Elena. Just days after celebrating her 29th birthday, Pernilla Sterner scored a final-round 73 for an even-par total of 216 to beat Asa Gottmo by one stroke and Anna Carin Jonasson by two.

Thailand Open—US$120,000
Winner: Sophie Gustafson

Having collected her first victory in Europe at the Swiss Open in 1996, Sweden's Sophie Gustafson started her season in the best possible way by winning the Thailand Open. Gustafson closed with a two-under-par 70 for a 214 total which left her one stroke in front of China's Tseng Hsiu-Feng and American Jean Bartholomew.

JAL Malaysian Open—US$90,000
Winner: Petra Rigby-Jinglov

An opening-round 66 by Sweden's Petra Rigby-Jinglov a day after her 28th birthday set her up for victory in the JAL Malaysian Open. After a second-round 74, the Malmo golfer had to battle Japan's Masako Ishihara for the title, a tussle she won, 71 to 72. Tina Fischer of Germany was third, four shots behind.

Indonesian Open—US$110,000
Winner: Pernilla Sterner

Pernilla Sterner gained her second and Sweden's fourth win in four weeks on the Asian Ladies Tour by beating Wendy Dicks of England in a playoff at the Indonesian Open. Dicks came back from seven shots down on the last day with a 69 to Sterner's 76 to tie at 215, but the Swede recovered her composure to sneak the victory in extra time and topped the Asian money list.

Alpine Australian Ladies Masters—A$650,000
Winner: Gail Graham

No Australian had won the Alpine Australian Ladies Masters in its eight-year history. Karrie Webb looked set to change that as the new star of the LPGA Tour, but instead Canadian Gail Graham claimed her second career title.

Webb, the local hero at the Royal Pines course on Queensland's Gold Coast, had only one bogey in her first 54 holes and led Graham by six strokes with 12 holes to play on the final day. But by the 17th tee her advantage was down to a single shot, which disappeared when she three-putted. Watched by some 40 family members, Webb then left her first putt from the back fringe 15 feet short at the 18th and when she missed the next one, Graham two-putted from 20 feet for the win. Her last-round 68 gave her a 273 total, 15 under par, one ahead of Webb, who closed with 73 after earlier rounds of 69, 66 and 66, and two ahead of Laura Davies.

"The pressure was on Karrie today as the hometown hero," Graham said. "And I tried to put more pressure on her by shooting for the flag on a few occasions when I wouldn't normally. I feel I beat one of the best players in the game."

Toyota Australian Women's Open—A$350,000
Winner: Jane Crafter

Not since Jan Stephenson in 1977 had an Australian won her country's national women's Open. Karrie Webb was expected to break the trend, but the home favorite did not feature in the local one-two at the top of the leaderboards in the Toyota Australian Women's Open, as Jane Crafter beat Joanne Mills by three strokes. Webb finished fifth.

The veteran Crafter has been based on the U.S. LPGA Tour since 1981 and needed all her experience in compiling rounds of 65, 72, 72 and a closing 70 for a 13-under-par total of 279. Mills, who gained her first victory in Europe earlier in the year at the German Open, scored a final-round 68 to take second place by a stroke from Korea's Kang Soo-Yun.

It was Kang and not Mills who gave Crafter the most trouble on the last day. As her playing companion, Crafter had to watch as Kang birdied five holes in a row from the sixth and briefly took the lead. Then at the 11th a par-three, Crafter holed a birdie putt from 25 feet for a two-shot swing and was never caught again. "I told my caddie that she could not keep going like that," Crafter said. "I was in shock witnessing all those birdies. Her relentlessness pulled me back to reality and I decided that to win, I had to play the golf course. No one was going to give me the title."

Japan LPGA Tour

Daikin Orchid Ladies—¥60,000,000
Winner: Woo-Soon Ko

The Japan LPGA Tour season got off to an unusual start in the Daikin Orchid Ladies tournament when two experienced members of the relatively small Korean contingent wound up in a first-place tie at the end of regulation play. Woo-Soon Ko, who holds 16 domestic titles in Korea, captured her fourth in Japan when she defeated Ok-Hee Ku in the subsequent playoff.

Two of Japan's strongest players — Kaori Harada and Ikuyo Shiotani — had the upper hand the first two days. Harada opened with 66, then Shiotani blazed in front with 64 Saturday for a 134 total and a three-stroke lead over Ko (69-68) and Natsuko Noro (70-67). Ku was another shot back and overtook Ko in the last round with 68 and her compatriot shot 69 for her 206. Shiotani skidded to 74, missing the playoff by two strokes.

Saishunkan Ladies—¥60,000,000
Winner: Chikayo Yamazaki

Chikayo Yamazaki, who scored her first victory in 1996, picked up her second by one stroke in the Saishunkan Ladies at Kumamoto Kukoh Country Club at Kikuchi, winning in much the same fashion as she did the year before in the Goyo Kensetsu, where she shot just a par final round. At Kumamoto, Yamazaki managed only a one-over 73 in the last round, but it was enough to hold off Huang Yu-Chen, Yuko Moriguchi and Ikuyo Shiotani, near-missing for the second week in a row.

Yamazaki took a two-stroke lead into the final round with her 73-69–142 total after Fuki Kido had self-destructed with 78, yielding a four-stroke lead she had over eight players with her opening 68. Shiotani, Moriguchi and Aki Takamura were two behind Yamazaki going into the final round.

Yellow Hat Tokyo Ladies Open—¥50,000,000
Winner: Suzuko Maeda

Suzuko Maeda posted her third victory in the last five years in the Yellow Hat Tokyo Ladies Open and did it the hard way. Maeda, whose last win was in the 1996 Katokichi Queen's Cup, came from five strokes off the pace with 68 to pick up the win with her two-under-par 214 total.

The victory came with unusual circumstances aiding her. Yuko Saitoh, Kyoko Ono and Akane Ohshiro shared the 36-hole lead at 141, then all three shot 74s to wind up in a five-way tie for second place at 215. Maeda birdied her first two holes in the final round, added two more on the second nine and avoided bogeys on Tokyo's Wakasu Golf Links as she passed 19 players on her way to the victory.

Kenshoen Ladies—¥50,000,000
Winner: Kaori Harada

Kaori Harada put a lot of overtime on the clock before securing her fifth career victory. It took five extra holes and a birdie on the sixth for her to defeat Mitsuyo Hirata in the Kenshoen Ladies tournament at Dohgo Golf Club. The two had tied after 54 holes with even-par 216 totals.

Yuko Saitoh, who had blown a victory chance the previous week in Tokyo, tried to make amends at Dohgo, when she started with 68 and a one-stroke lead. But she followed with 74-77 and yielded first place to Hirata (70-71) Saturday. Harada was at 71-72–143. She shot 73 and Hirata 75 Sunday to force the playoff.

Mitsukoshi Cup Ladies Open—¥60,000,000
Winner: Akemi Yamaoka

Akemi Yamaoka, who claimed her first two victories in 1994 at age 43, returned to the winner's circle in the Mitsukoshi Cup Ladies Open as the playoff trend continued. Yamaoka defeated Akiko Fukushima in the overtime battle, the second extra-hole decision in a row and third among the first five tournaments of the season.

Yamaoka began the year's first 72-hole event with 71, three strokes off the lead of Akane Ohshiro. She moved within one shot of the top with 71-70–141 as New Zealand's Marnie McGuire took the lead, then tied for first with Keiko Arai at 213, shooting 72. Her final-round 71 forged the tie with Fukushima at 284, Fukushima catching her with a closing 69.

Nasu Ogawa Ladies—¥50,000,000
Winner: Woo-Soon Ko

Korea's Woo-Soon Ko picked up her second victory in seven weeks with a strong come-from-behind effort in the final round of the Nasu Ogawa Ladies tournament. Ko, who won the season-opening Daikin Orchid, came from four strokes off the lead to register her fifth career win, shooting a final-round 69 for a 213 total.

Ko's victory came at the particular expense of Mikino Kubo, who led Marnie McGuire by two after 36 holes with her 72-68–140 total. Kubo, who scored her first victory in 1996, plunged to 80 and a 12th-place finish. Ko birdied the last two holes for her 69 to nip McGuire by one stroke. McGuire's three-putt at the 17th cost her a playoff opportunity. Ikuyo Shiotani had the best final round, 67, to tie for third with Kumiko Hiyoshi.

Katokichi Queen's Cup—¥50,000,000
Winner: Jae-Sook Won

Korean golfers claimed back-to-back victories in early May when Jae-Sook Won captured the Katokichi Queen's Cup on the heels of Woo-Soon Ko's win at Nasu Ogawa. Won, landing her fifth career victory, came from three strokes off the lead and won by two at Sakaide Country Club in Kagawa. Shaking off an in-and-out start, the 27-year-old Korean shot 69, one of just four sub-par rounds on the windy day, for a six-under-par 210 total.

Chieko Nishida, seeking her first victory in three years, shared the first-round lead with Won at 66, then moved two strokes in front despite 72 on a day of high scoring. Won, for instance, took 75 before her closing rush in the final round. Nishida had her hopes dashed when she bogeyed three of the first six holes en route to an outgoing 40. She rallied with 34 on the second nine to take second place at 212, one stroke better than three others.

Gunze Cup World Ladies—¥60,000,000
Winner: Tseng Hsiu-Feng

Pros from abroad continued to hold sway on the Japan LPGA Tour when the circuit returned to Tokyo for the Gunze Cup World Ladies. Despite the presence of more likely winners — international stars Laura Davies and Liselotte Neumann — in the field, Tseng Hsiu-Feng of Taiwan became the third straight foreign victor in the year's fourth playoff. It was her third win in Japan. The defeat, on the first extra hole, was especially frustrating for Michiko Okada, a 30-year veteran who is not likely to get many more chances.

Another Taiwanese pro, Mei-Chi Cheng, led the Gunze Cup for two rounds before yielding first place to Tseng. Cheng's 72 gave her a one-stroke lead over Tseng, Okada and Kasumi Adachi and she hung on by that margin with a 74–146 total. Okada and Yuko Motoyama were at 147 and Tseng was another shot back. She shot 69 to lead Okada by two after the third round, but fell into the playoff deadlock with 74 to Okada's 72 Sunday. Neumann never was a contender, tying for 10th place, and Davies, a five-time winner in Japan, missed the cut.

Yakult Ladies—¥60,000,000
Winner: Tomiko Ikebuchi

Tomiko Ikebuchi walked off with her first victory in the Yakult Ladies at Fukuoka Kokusai Country Club. She outplayed the experienced, young Aki Takamura in the final round to score a one-stroke victory with her nine-under-par 207 total.

Actually, the two players dueled for the title from the start. The 24-year-old Takamura began the week with a seven-under-par 65 to lead Ikebuchi by two strokes and the margin remained the same between the two as they both shot 70s in the second round. Tomiko gained the victory with another 70 as Takamura slipped to 73 and a 208 total. The ever-present Akiko Fukushima and Toshimi Kimura shot 68s to tie for third at 209.

Chukyo TV Bridgestone Ladies—¥50,000,000
Winner: Aki Takamura

Aki Takamura could not have had a better follow-up procedure. Determined to do something to rectify her final-round loss to Tomiko Ikebuchi the previous week, Takamura nailed a one-stroke victory in the Chukyo TV Bridgestone Ladies at Kasugai Country Club.

This time, Takamura was the one to stage a winning rally. The young standout, who has Japan Open and Japan PGA Championships on her five-victory record, trailed Bie-Shyun Huang of Taiwan for two days. The Taiwanese pro, a three-time winner in Japan, started with 66 to lead Mitsuko Hamada by one shot and Takamura by six. Takamura moved into a second-place tie at 141 with dual 1997 winner Woo-Soon Ko, cutting her deficit in half as Huang had a 72 for 138. A one-under 71 got the job done in the final round for Takamura as Huang shot 75 to lose by one stroke.

Toto Motors Ladies—¥50,000,000
Winner: Yoko Inoue

Yoko Inoue, who broke the victory ice big-time at the end of the 1996 Japan LPGA season, acquired her second title with a one-stroke triumph in the Toto Motors Ladies at Saitama's Toto Hannoh Country Club. Inoue, winner of the Meiji Nyugyo Cup last year, nipped Kaori Higo by one stroke in the Toto Motors, posting an eight-under-par 208 total.

The 25-year-old Inoue trailed leading money winner Woo-Soon Ko by one with her first-round 66 and Higo by one with her 36-hole score of 70–136. Higo shot 66 for her 135 total. Yoko grabbed the victory with a two-birdie two-bogey 72 as Higo shot 74 in the last round.

Mitsubishi Denki Ladies—¥50,000,000
Winner: Akiko Fukushima

Akiko Fukushima was not where she expected to be at this point, one-third of the way through the 1997 Japan LPGA season. The leading money winner and dominant player of 1996, Fukushima had not won in 1997 and was fifth on the money list. Her move back to the top began with her two-stroke victory in the Mitsubishi Denki Ladies at Kitarokkoh Country Club, where she fashioned a consistent seven-under-par 209 total.

The 24-year-old daughter of a pro baseball player, who won her first tour title when she was just 20, hovered just off the lead the first two days. She opened with 70 and was among seven players in second place two strokes behind Junko Yasui. Another 70 left her alone in the runner-up slot, one shot behind Young-Mc Lee of Korea as Yasui took a 73. Finally, 69 gave the long-hitting Fukushima her sixth tour win when Lee shot 72 and dropped into a second-place tie with Yasui (70).

We Love Kobe Suntory Ladies Open—¥50,000,000
Winner: Ikuyo Shiotani

Like Akiko Fukushima before the preceding tournament, the veteran star Ikuyo Shiotani had gone surprisingly long without a victory on the Japan LPGA Tour. Like Fukushima, she took care of that omission. With one difference. Shiotani made a shambles of the competition with a seven-stroke victory, the biggest margin of the 1997 season to that point. The 34-year-old Shiotani built a 16-under-par 272 total over the 72-hole distance of the Suntory Ladies Open at Arima Royal Country Club in Kobe.

Shiotani's middle rounds of 64 and 66 broke the backs of the opposition. The 64 brought her from four strokes off the first-round pace of Yuki Yamana into a five-stroke lead over Yamana (73), Toshimi Kimura (72) and Woo-Soon Ko (68). The 66 widened the gap to a yawning 10 strokes over Fuki Kido and she coasted to a seven-stroke final margin over Chikayo Yamazaki and Miyuki Shimabukuro. It was her 17th career victory.

Dunlop Twin Lakes Ladies Open—¥50,000,000
Winner: Ok-Hee Ku

Ok-Hee Ku, South Korea's leading woman pro since the early 1980s, joined compatriots Woo-Soon Ko and Jae-Sook Won as 1997 winners in Japan with a two-stroke victory in the Dunlop Twin Lakes Ladies Open at Twin Lakes Country Club in Gunma Prefecture. Ku staged a rousing rally in the final round, coming from four strokes off the pace to record the win, her 12th in Japan. The closing, five-under-par 67 established the winning 211 total in the weather-shortened tournament.

The 40-year-old Ku put up her first of two par rounds to start, falling three strokes behind leader Keiko Motoyama. Typhoon-spawned wind and rain forced cancellation of the second round. With 72-68–140, Toshiko Fujisaki edged a stroke in front of Motoyama when action resumed. Ku won in spectacular fashion on the last day. She made up three strokes with six birdies and three bogeys before she ran in a 50-foot eagle putt on the final green to create the final margin with the course-record-tying 67. Fujisaki and Young-Me Lee finished second at 213.

Japan Women's Open—¥70,000,000
Winner: Ayako Okamoto

Ayako Okamoto, perhaps Japan's greatest female golfer ever, keeps rolling along. At age 46, she plays sparingly but still so well that, at the end of June, she won the Japan Women's Open for the second time, surviving a postponement that ran the tournament over to Monday for the first time ever. A final-round 73 carried her easily to a three-stroke victory over Akiko Fukushima, perhaps her heir-apparent, who jumped into second place with a final-round 71. The victory was Okamoto's 43rd in Japan and 61st of her career, 19 of those on the U.S. LPGA Tour.

Okamoto didn't have the look of a winner when she started with 78, six behind leader Tomoko Ueda. However, she handled the weather better than everybody else in the second round when her 71 vaulted her all the way into a one-stroke lead over 19-year-old amateur Hee-Won Han. The typhoon effects worsened Saturday and forced the postponement. Okamoto remained a stroke in front, then of Ok-Hee Ku, with a 73–222 Sunday, then coasted home with the final 73 Monday.

Tohato Ladies—¥50,000,000
Winner: Suzuko Maeda

Suzuko Maeda became just the second multiple winner of the season in Japan and she did it with an exclamation point. The weather improved somewhat for the Tohato Ladies tournament after blistering the Dunlop and Women's Open the two preceding weeks, but affected everyone else much more than it did Maeda. The result was that she won her second of the year and sixth of her career by nine strokes, the biggest margin of the year.

Suzuko never trailed at the Oak Village Golf Club. She shared the first-round lead at 67 with Miki Furuya in relatively calm weather. Then, when the weather started to get nasty, her par 72 was good enough to open a six-stroke lead on Ok-Hee Ku and Kumiko Hiyoshi at 145. Maeda was so much in command in the strong winds of the last day that a double bogey at the 16th hole merely narrowed the final margin to nine. She had three birdies and three bogeys otherwise for 74 and her three-under-par 213 total. The day's lowest score was 72 and Kozue Azuma, winless in four seasons, used it to finish second by three strokes at 222.

Toyo Suisan Ladies Hokkaido—¥50,000,000
Winner: Kaori Higo

Six weeks earlier, Kaori Higo couldn't muster the finishing touches and lost the Toto Motors tournament with a poor final round. The reverse was true at the Toyo Suisan Ladies Hokkaido event at Kosaido Sapporo Country Club in mid-July. Higo overpowered the field with a closing 67 that gave her a six-stroke victory, the fifth of her career and first since 1995.

The 28-year-old Higo was a leader all the way. She shared the first-round lead with Kayo Yamada at 69. Yamada fell back with 77 and Kaori set up a three-stroke lead over Ikuyo Shiotani with a 68–137 total. The dangerous Shiotani (71-69) was the one to falter in the final round, taking 74 to drop into a tie for sixth. Higo's 67 gave her a 12-under-par 204 total over Marnie McGuire. The New Zealander's 69–210 gained second place by three strokes over three other players.

Resort Trust Ladies—¥50,000,000
Winner: Fumiko Muraguchi

Fumiko Muraguchi picked up her first victory in nearly two years when she led from wire to wire in the Resort Trust Ladies tournament at St. Creek Golf Club, Aichi. In fact, it was just her second win since she arrived on the Japan LPGA Tour with a bang — two wins in her rookie 1991 season. Her winning total at St. Creek was 204, 12 under par, and she won by three, the third week in a row of decisive victories.

Muraguchi opened with 66, one of just four rounds in the 60s that first day. Jae-Sook Won shot 67, Aki Takamura 68 and Yuri Kawanami 69. Muraguchi followed with 69 for 135, creating a four-stroke lead over Kawanami (70), with two-time winner Woo-Soon Ko next at 140. Another 69 did the trick for Muraguchi, creating the three-shot margin over Kawanami, five over Mayumi Murai and at least eight over the rest of the field.

Golf 5 Ladies—¥50,000,000
Winner: Akiko Fukushima

Akiko Fukushima returned to the Japan LPGA Tour refreshed after a month's respite and promptly won the first time out in the Golf 5 Ladies tournament at Mizunami Country Club at Gifu. Snatching her second victory of 1997 — the third multiple winner — Fukushima hung on to beat Chieko Nishida by a shot with her 11-under-par 205.

Nishida led Fukushima and Ikuyo Shiotani by one stroke with her first-round 66, a course record. Then Fukushima traded places with her, shooting another 67 while Nishida was carding 69 for 135. Shiotani slipped back with 71–138. Fukushima's second 67 was a hot one in more ways than one. She didn't make a bogey in the torrid weather and remarked, "It was so hot out there that I had difficulty concentrating. My head hurt and I was only about half-conscious from about No. 12." Both Fukushima and Nishida shot 71s in the last round to finish one-two.

Mizuno Ladies—¥60,000,000
Winner: Akio Takasu

Akio Takasu, a frequent winner in her earlier seasons, had gone four years without a victory until she captured the Mizuno Ladies tournament in mid-August. Takasu, age 44, in her 24th season of professional golf, had not won since landing her 13th and 14th titles early in 1993.

Takasu led all the way at the Hamamura Onsen Golf Club in scoring a one-stroke victory with her five-under-par 211 total. She shot 69 the first day and led seven players — Chieko Nishida, Junko Yasui, Yueh-Chyn Huang, Misayo Fujisawa, Yuri Fudoh, Jean Bartholomew and Kumiko Fuchi — by two strokes. The margin narrowed to one shot as Takasu had 72-141 and Yasui, Kaori Higo (73-69) and Yoko Inoue (72-70) were at 142. A 70 gave Takasu the one-shot triumph over Inoue.

NEC Karuizawa 72—¥60,000,000
Winner: Yuka Irie

Yuka Irie has three wins on the Japan LPGA Tour, one in each of the last three seasons, and none has been conventional or easy. In the Chiyoda Ladies in 1995, she won with a final-round 78 and a four-over-par 220 total. In the Golf 5 in 1996, she finished bogey, double bogey and was forced into a playoff. In the NEC Karuizawa 72 in 1997, heavy fog bedeviled play and forced a 45-hole final result. Irie's winning total was 181, one over par at Karuizawa 72 Golf Club in Nagano Prefecture.

The tournament didn't have a first-round leader — Marnie McGuire at 70 — until mid-day Saturday because of two fog delays Friday. The domino effect brought about a Sunday finish of the second round, McGuire shooting 73 for 143 and a two-stroke lead over Irie and Kyoko Isoda. With insufficient time for a full third round, tournament officials decided to go with nine holes. When McGuire took 39 strokes to conclude her play, she slipped into a five-way tie for second behind Irie, who shot 36. Tied with McGuire at 182 were Akiko Fukushima, Kasumi Fujii, Nobuko Kizawa and Sachiko Ohshima.

Shin Caterpillar Mitsubishi Ladies—¥60,000,000
Winner: Takayo Bandoh

Mishima's Grand Fields Country Club, venue of the Shin Caterpillar Mitsubishi Ladies tournament, turned into a playground for two of the youngest players, especially for Takayo Bandoh, a four-season veteran although just 22 years old. Bandoh came from two strokes off the lead with a final-round 69 that rewarded her with her first victory. Three strokes back in second place was Yuri Fudoh, at 20 the youngest player on the circuit.

Taiwan's Huang Yu-Chen led for two days. She shot 69 to take a one-stroke lead on Bandoh and Toshiko Fujisaki, then moved two in front of Bandoh (70-72) and Fudoh (72-70) when she had 71 for a 140 total. Her game fizzled to 75 in the last round, opening the door to Bandoh. Bandoh had six birdies, including a five-in-a-row run on the second nine, to go with a bogey and double bogey on the way to the 69 and five-under-par 211 total. Fudoh shot 72 for 214 and her highest professional finish. Huang was third at 215. Bandoh was just the second first-time winner of the JLPGA season.

Goyo Kensetsu Ladies—¥60,000,000
Winner: Michiko Hattori

Michiko Hattori had drawn a victory blank for nearly three years after two splendid seasons with five wins in 1993 and 1994 before landing the sixth title of her career in the Goyo Kensetsu Ladies at the end of August. Hattori, holder of both the Japan Women's Amateur (1985) and Open (1994), struggled in the last round at the Privilege Golf Club at Narita, but her 71 was just enough to hold off the charge of Yuri Kawanami.

Michiko deferred to Akiko Fukushima by one stroke in the first round, shooting 67 to tie for second with Natsuko Noro and Nobuko Kizawa, then rode a fine 66 to a one-shot lead over Fukushima. Kawanami was virtually out of sight, seven strokes off the lead at 140. She caught fire on the final day, though, and posted a 65–205 total early. Hattori bogeyed the last hole for the 71 and 12-under-par 204 total.

Fuji Sankei Ladies Classic—¥60,000,000
Winner Aki Takamura

Aki Takamura's victories did not come easily in 1997. A one-stroke winner in the Chukyo TV Bridgestone earlier in the season, the 24-year-old Takamura went four extra holes in the Fuji Sankei Ladies Classic before besting Yu-Chuan Tai of Taiwan to take her sixth title.

Takamura shared first place for two days at Yamanashi's Fujizakura Country Club, on Friday with Wen-Lin Li at 69 and on Saturday with Ikuyo Shiotani at 140. She shot another 71 in the last round and Tai caught her with a 68 for her two-under-par 211. Mitsuyo Hirata, Mayumi Murai and Fumiko Muraguchi tied for third with 214s.

Japan LPGA Championship—¥70,000,000
Winner: Akiko Fukushima

The victories and the money had been coming Akiko Fukushima's way in impressive numbers over the past four years. Fukushima began the infusion of the additional ingredient that sets the great players apart from the rest — major titles — when she rambled to a decisive victory in the Japan LPGA Championship and acquired the emblematic Konika Cup at Gifu's Fuji Country Syuga Club in mid-September. It was the 24-year-old's first major among her eight victories since the start of the 1994 season and solidified her bid for the money-winning title of the Japan LPGA Tour for a second year in a row.

The powerful young star went in front to stay on the second day after beginning the championship on the par-73 course with 72, two back of Yuko Moriguchi, Yukiko Ishiguro and Yukiko Koyama. Her 69 in the second round placed her one stroke in front of Ishiguro and her 70 in the third round extended her lead to four strokes over Huang Yu-Chen. Ae-Sook Kim, in third place, was six off the pace. Feeling little pressure under the circumstances, Fukushima coasted to a five-stroke victory with a four-birdie, three-bogey 72 for a 283 total, nine under par. Veteran Miyuki Shimabukuro jumped into second place with 69–288.

Yukijirushi Ladies Tokai Classic—¥60,000,000
Winner: Akiko Fukushima

Not even a weak start slowed down Akiko Fukushima. Coming off her high-profile win of the Japan PGA Championship, the tour's hottest player began the Yukijirushi Ladies Tokai Classic with 75, well off the starting pace of Ikuyo Shiotani and her 70. But Fukushima bounced back resiliently the next two days and made it two victories in a row with a three-stroke win, her fourth of the season.

The second round was key to the triumph. Fukushima roared back into contention with a six-under-par 66 that vaulted her into a first-place tie with Shiotani at 141. Then, in the final round, she carded 70 and won by three with her 211 total when the veteran Shiotani slipped to 73, just edging Yoko Inoue for second place by one stroke.

Miyagi TV Cup Ladies Open—¥50,000,000
Winner: Michiko Hattori

Bad weather enabled Michiko Hattori to make short work of the field in the Miyagi TV Cup Ladies Open at Hananomori Golf Club at Ohira at the end of September. She only had 36 holes to negotiate on her way to her second win of the season when heavy rains washed out the scheduled first round Friday. She covered that ground in 142 strokes and scored a two-shot victory.

Hattori, winner of six previous titles, established the two-stroke margin when play got underway Saturday. She shot 67 and Kaori Higo and Chieko Nishida were next at 69. Even though she mustered only 75 Sunday, the 142 total was the winner. On a day of high scores, Aki Takamura, Yumi Kokubo and Nishida tied for second place at even-par 144.

Kosaido Ladies Golf Cup—¥60,000,000
Winner: Akiko Fukushima

There was no stopping Akiko Fukushima during the early-autumn segment of the Japan LPGA Tour. The current top player on the circuit rolled to her third victory in a row in the Kosaido Ladies Golf Cup tournament at Ichihara. She skipped the Miyagi TV Cup event the preceding week after posting back-to-back victories in the Japan LPGA Championship and the Tokai Classic

The Kosaido Cup triumph, her fifth of the season and 10th of her relatively short career, came fairly easily. Fukushima never trailed on the Chiba Kosaido Country Club course en route to her two-stroke victory. She shared first place the first day with little-known Man-Soo Kim and Ayako Shibata at 69, then took sole possession of the lead Saturday. Her 72–141 total led Nayoko Yoshikawa (74-68), Kyoko Ono (70-72) and Mikino Kubo (70-72) by a stroke. Yoshikawa's 68 was the day's low round. Fukushima polished things off with 70, her five-under-par 211 total giving her a two-stroke victory margin over Ono, who finished with a 71. Fukushima's soaring earnings reached ¥83.8 million.

TaKaRa World Invitational—¥80,000,000
Winner: Liselotte Neumann

The TaKaRa World Invitational must rank as Liselotte Neumann's favorite tournament in the world, even though it takes a lot of traveling to get there from one of the other women's tours. She has won the richest tournament on the Japan LPGA Tour twice — in 1993 and 1997 — collecting more than ¥25 million in the process. The more recent victory came by a slightly shaky two strokes at Caledonian Golf Club at Yokoshiba as the Swedish internationalist, who first gained prominence when she won the 1988 U.S. Women's Open, finished with a six-under-par 282 total for her third win in Japan.

Neumann and Yuko Motoyama, winless in six years on the Japan circuit, dominated the TaKaRa throughout. Motoyama opened with 67 to lead Neumann and Akane Ohshiro by two. Neumann led the rest of the way, but Motoyama stayed close to the end and finished second, eight strokes clear of the next players. Neumann shot 68 in the second round for 137, Motoyama 73 for 140. Neumann shot 73 the next day for 210, Motoyama 75 for 215. Two early bogeys cost Neumann the lead in the final round as Motoyama rang up three birdies on the first nine, but birdies at 15 and 16 got Neumann back in front and to par for the round and the 282 finish. Motoyama had 69 for 284.

Fujitsu Ladies—¥60,000,000
Winner: Aiko Takasu

Akio Takasu, who broke a four-year dry spell earlier in the year, registered her 15th career victory in the Fujitsu Ladies in mid-October at Hamano Golf Club in the second 1997 visit to the Ichihara region. The 44-year-old Takasu, who has played professional golf nearly half her life, moved from three strokes off the pace in the last round to score a two-stroke victory. She shot 68 for a 210 total, six under par.

Tomiko Ikebuchi, who had done little since scoring her first victory in the Yakult Ladies in May, made a good run at her second win of the year. She shot 68 in the first round and led Mikino Kubo and Jae-Sook Won by one stroke and retained first place with a 71 for 139, then trailed by Kubo and Ann Wilson at 140. Takasu was at 142. Ikebuchi's game came apart in the last round and she plummeted to a tie for 21st when she fumbled to 81. In contrast, Takasu shot 68 for 210, finishing two strokes ahead of Hiromi Kobayashi, back in Japan after campaigning on the LPGA Tour in the United States.

Higuchi Hisako Kibun Classic—¥70,000,000
Winner: Annika Sorenstam

Attendees at the Higuchi Hisako Kibun Classic saw firsthand what made Annika Sorenstam the best woman player in the world in 1997. The soft-spoken Swedish star traveled to Japan for the tournament and added it to her list of 1997 spoils as she won more than $1 million and six tournaments on the U.S. LPGA Tour. But the win at Manju Golf Club at Yamazoe required a strong rally in the final round before she could claim a one-stroke victory with her one-under-par 287 total.

The Kibun Classic was a tight battle full of contenders from the start, when five players — Natsuko Noro, Chikayo Yamazaki, Yuri Fudoh, Kozue Azuma and Yuka Shiroto — shared the first-round lead with 69s. Fudoh nosed in front of five other players by one stroke with a 70–139. Ok-Hee Ku, Young-Me Lee, Suzuko Maeda, Fuki Kido and Noro were at 140. Ku took over the lead with 71–211, two ahead of Lee and Fudoh. Sorenstam and Akiko Fukushima, Japan's No. 1 player of 1997, settled at 215, Sorenstam with rounds of 72, 70 and 73. Par was all the 27-year-old Stockholm native needed in a cold, windy final round to annex the victory as Ku took 77 and wound up tied with Noro at 288.

Nichirei International—US$675,000
Winners: United States

It was a long time coming, but Cindy Figg-Currier finally experienced the kind of season she had been seeking for 14 years on the LPGA Tour. Figg-Currier, who won her first tournament in the State Farm Rail Classic in September, capped that by leading the United States team to victory in the annual Nichirei International competition in Japan against the best of the women pros of that country.

Figg-Currier won all three of her matches in the Ryder Cup-style event at Tsukuba Country Club north of Tokyo as the American LPGA team defeated its counterparts from the Japan LPGA Tour for the 13th year in a row and improved the overall record to 17-2. The score was a decisive 23-13 as the Americans built a sizeable lead in the first two days of better-ball stroke play and enhanced the margin in the concluding singles matches.

The first day was a sign of things to come. The American team jumped off to a 7½-1½ lead as the efforts of Japan's two leading players helped avert a shutout. Akiko Fukushima teamed with Kaori Harada and the two scored the only win that day — they won again the second day — and Ikuyo Shiotani, who went undefeated, and her partner, Fumiko Muraguchi, tied with Liselotte Neumann and Kelly Robbins. Figg-Currier and Jane Geddes won their second match as the U.S. built its margin to 12½-5½ with three victories and four ties in the nine matches.

The U.S. took 10 of the 18 singles matches and tied another Sunday, Figg-Currier completing her sweep with a 70-75 victory over Harada. Japan won three of the last four matches, but Fukushima lost to Chris Johnson, 68-70. Interestingly, the U.S. LPGA team included players from Sweden (Neumann), Canada (Gail Graham and Lorie Kane), Great Britain (Alison Nicholas and Lisa Hackney) and even Japan (U.S. tour regular Hiromi Kobayashi).

Toray Japan Queen's Cup—US$750,000
Winner: Liselotte Neumann

Liselotte Neumann made yet another lucrative visit to Japan when the U.S. LPGA Tour joined forces with the Japan LPGA Tour in the annual late-season stop at Otsu's Seta Golf Course for the Toray Japan Queen's Cup. Neumann, finishing the season with a flurry of success, added the Toray Queen's to earlier 1997 victories in the Welch's Championship in September and the TaKaRa Invitational, also in Japan in October.

Neumann had won both of these Japanese events earlier, the Toray Queen's in 1991 and the TaKaRa in 1993. This time at Seta, she came from two strokes off the pace with a final-round 67 to win by one over Canadian Lorie Kane as foreign players from the American circuit monopolized the top spots.

Neumann hovered just off the lead for two days before making her final-round move. She trailed by a stroke after the first round as Sherri Steinhauer, Helen Dobson, Yuko Moriguchi and Chris Johnson opened with 67s. Leta Lindley shot 65 and stormed to a one-stroke lead with her eight-under-par 136. Neumann had a 70 for 138, tied with Steinhauer, Michele Redman and Akiko Fukushima, Japan's leading money winner, a shot behind Jane Crafter and Yoko Inoue.

Only Neumann emerged from that pack on the last day. She had four consecutive birdies early, but came to the par-five 18th knowing she needed a birdie to avoid a playoff with Kane, who also shot 67. Neumann responded with 60-yard sand wedge shot to three feet and knocked in the winning putt.

Although she shot an unlikely 75 and plunged to 29th place, Fukushima clinched the Japan LPGA money title. The check boosted her earnings over ¥88 million.

Itoen Ladies—¥80,000,000
Winner: Helen Alfredsson

Helen Alfredsson extended her stay in Japan after the Toray Japan Queen's Cup and extended the Swedish presence in the winner's circle as well. Following in the victorious footsteps of compatriots Liselotte Neumann and Annika Sorenstam, Alfredsson put a Japan LPGA Tour tournament win on her record — the Itoen Ladies at the Great Island Club at Chosei. It went to a playoff and Alfredsson bested Akemi Yamaoka on the first extra hole.

Kaori Higo had the upper hand going into the final round. She and Alfredsson had jointly held the opening-day lead with 68s before Higo moved three strokes in front of Alfredsson and Yamaoka, winner of the Mitsukoshi Cup

Ladies in April, with 67 for 135 Saturday. However, Higo took a 75 Sunday while Alfredsson and Yamaoka were shooting 69s to forge the 54-hole deadlock at 208, Alfredsson getting hers with a birdie at the last hole.

Daio Seishi Elleair Ladies Open—¥65,000,000
Winner: Ok-Hee Ku

Ok-Hee Ku became the season's only successful title defender when she repeated as the winner of the Daio Seishi Elleair Ladies Open and claimed her 13th victory in Japan. The 12th came earlier in the season in the Dunlop Twin Lakes Open, in which she came from four strokes off the lead to win.

The Elleair triumph also was a comebacker. Ku (69-69), Tseng Hsiu-Feng (68-70) and Yukiyo Haga, the first-round leader (65-73), trailed young Takayo Bandoh by a stroke going into the final round. Bandoh, who won her first tournament in August, shot 69-68 for her 137, but could do no better than par in the last round. Ku, on the other hand, put together a solid, five-birdie 67 to finish with an 11-under-par 205 and a four-stroke victory over Bandoh.

JLPGA Meiji Nyugyo Cup—¥60,000,000
Winner: Akiko Fukushima

It seemed perfectly appropriate when Akiko Fukushima capped her outstanding season with her victory in the limited-field JLPGA Meiji Nyugyo Cup tournament, the third major on the JLPGA schedule. Fukushima clearly was the best performer in Japan in 1997 by all standards but particularly with money (¥99,594,094) and tournaments won (six). She was the best by two strokes in the Meiji Nyugyo Cup at Aoshima Golf Club in Miyazaki.

Mikino Kubo, the first-round leader (69) by one over Fukushima and Ikuyo Shiotani, finished dead last at week's end. Shiotani, the Suntory winner, shot 68 in the second round and led Fukushima by two, Yuko Motoyama by three. Fukushima went in front to stay with her third straight 70 the next day as Shiotani suffered 75 for 213. Motoyama, promising but winless as a professional, was at 214. She had her second runner-up finish when she closed with 71 to Fukushima's 73. Fukushima's total was 283, five under par; Motoyama's 285.

APPENDIXES

The World Ranking
(As of December 31, 1997)

Pos.		Player	Country	Points Average	Total Points	No. of Events	95/96 Total	95/96 Minus	1997 Plus
1	(1)	Greg Norman	Aus	11.49	517	45	485	-350	382
2	(33)	Tiger Woods	USA	10.76	452	42	155	-79	376
3	(13)	Nick Price	Zim	9.93	437	44	263	-186	360
4	(4)	Ernie Els	SAf	9.89	554	56	490	-330	394
5	(9)	Davis Love III	USA	9.09	482	53	384	-248	346
6	(7)	Phil Mickelson	USA	8.73	419	48	404	-237	252
7	(3)	Colin Montgomerie	Sco	8.58	489	57	528	-359	320
8	(8)	Masashi Ozaki	Jpn	8.05	346	43	341	-227	232
9	(2)	Tom Lehman	USA	8.02	425	53	487	-302	240
10	(10)	Mark O'Meara	USA	7.98	383	48	363	-228	248
11	(29)	Justin Leonard	USA	7.00	413	59	253	-162	322
12	(19)	David Duval	USA	6.87	364	53	268	-180	276
13	(15)	Scott Hoch	USA	6.85	377	55	332	-217	262
14	(23)	Brad Faxon	USA	6.66	313	47	250	-161	224
15	(20)	Vijay Singh	Fij	6.54	366	56	317	-223	272
16	(14)	Steve Elkington	Aus	6.49	266	41	263	-211	214
17	(6)	Nick Faldo	Eng	6.44	277	43	359	-236	154
18	(39)	Jesper Parnevik	Swe	5.70	285	50	178	-121	228
19	(17)	Tom Watson	USA	5.47	219	40	211	-128	136
20	(5)	Fred Couples	USA	5.47	235	43	351	-228	112
21	(16)	Bernhard Langer	Ger	5.39	264	49	260	-214	218
22	(49)	Jim Furyk	USA	5.34	326	61	206	-136	256
23	(64)	Lee Westwood	Eng	5.26	342	65	159	-85	268
24	(28)	Steve Jones	USA	5.21	297	57	234	-129	192
25	(26)	Ian Woosnam	Wal	5.06	268	53	238	-134	164
26	(31)	Frank Nobilo	NZl	4.92	256	52	229	-147	174
27	(22)	Loren Roberts	USA	4.88	244	50	241	-169	172
28	(38)	Mark Calcavecchia	USA	4.42	265	60	221	-158	202
29	(27)	Jeff Maggert	USA	4.38	232	53	224	-142	150
30	(21)	Mark McNulty	Zim	4.22	169	40	204	-121	86
31	(59)	Paul Stankowski	USA	4.09	229	56	156	-83	156
32	(48)	Tommy Tolles	USA	3.96	214	54	163	-87	138
33	(56)	Shigeki Maruyama	Jpn	3.89	237	61	159	-106	184
34	(32)	Lee Janzen	USA	3.79	212	56	236	-184	160
35	(60)	John Cook	USA	3.70	207	56	141	-78	144
36	(62)	Darren Clarke	NIr	3.65	219	60	150	-95	164
37	(50)	Brian Watts	USA	3.64	182	50	156	-100	126
38	(84T)	Tom Kite	USA	3.59	158	44	88	-52	122
39	(42)	Craig Stadler	USA	3.51	151	43	143	-98	106
40	(52)	Craig Parry	Aus	3.49	227	65	212	-147	162
41	(122)	Bill Glasson	USA	3.47	139	40	61	-54	132
42	(220T)	Jose Maria Olazabal	Spn	3.40	146	43	33	-33	146
43	(12)	Steve Stricker	USA	3.30	145	44	297	-172	20
44T	(103T)	Scott McCarron	USA	3.29	184	56	90	-50	144
44T	(282)	Stuart Appleby	Aus	3.29	207	63	33	-24	198
46	(66)	Naomichi Ozaki	Jpn	3.22	206	64	151	-97	152
47	(34)	Payne Stewart	USA	3.15	167	53	210	-147	104
48	(69)	Per-Ulrik Johansson	Swe	3.13	141	45	109	-74	106
49	(35)	Bob Tway	USA	2.98	152	51	195	-137	94
50	(37)	Robert Allenby	Aus	2.96	166	56	210	-130	86

( ) : Figures in brackets indicate 95/96 positions

Pos.		Player	Country	Points Average	Total Points	No. of Events	95/96 Total	95/96 Minus	1997 Plus
51	(44)	Michael Bradley	USA	2.96	151	51	163	-90	78
52	(57)	David Frost	SAf	2.93	170	58	156	-112	126
53	(24)	Costantino Rocca	Ity	2.92	190	65	285	-201	106
54	(107)	Eduardo Romero	Arg	2.84	122	43	77	-49	94
55	(220T)	Stewart Cink	USA	2.79	145	52	33	-20	132
56	(53)	Jeff Sluman	USA	2.78	178	64	193	-129	114
57	(36)	Jay Haas	USA	2.72	136	50	189	-141	88
58	(41)	Duffy Waldorf	USA	2.65	130	49	164	-110	76
59	(86)	Carlos Franco	Par	2.58	111	43	75	-48	84
60	(110)	Retief Goosen	SAf	2.56	174	68	103	-65	136
61	(98)	David Ogrin	USA	2.56	156	61	107	-59	108
62	(18)	Mark Brooks	USA	2.54	170	67	337	-191	24
63	(103T)	Billy Andrade	USA	2.48	144	58	100	-62	106
64	(25)	Kenny Perry	USA	2.41	123	51	237	-156	42
65	(161)	Peter Lonard	Aus	2.38	114	48	46	-26	94
66	(73)	Brandt Jobe	USA	2.36	104	44	100	-76	80
67	(70)	Kirk Triplett	USA	2.36	118	50	113	-87	92
68	(51)	Fred Funk	USA	2.30	159	69	200	-133	92
69	(74)	Frankie Minoza	Phi	2.23	107	48	104	-67	70
70	(99)	Tim Herron	USA	2.23	147	66	90	-45	102
71	(268)	Tateo Ozaki	Jpn	2.22	109	49	26	-15	98
72	(124)	Andrew Magee	USA	2.22	129	58	81	-52	100
73	(112)	Thomas Bjorn	Den	2.18	120	55	76	-38	82
74	(218T)	Phil Blackmar	USA	2.15	118	55	43	-27	102
75	(87)	Paul Goydos	USA	2.15	133	62	118	-65	80
76	(11)	Corey Pavin	USA	2.13	100	47	347	-261	14
77	(94)	Greg Turner	NZl	2.04	100	49	86	-58	72
78	(95T)	Padraig Harrington	Ire	2.03	122	60	84	-42	80
79	(133T)	Dudley Hart	USA	2.02	99	49	68	-37	68
80	(245)	Robert Karlsson	Swe	2.00	86	43	35	-29	80
81	(155)	Ignacio Garrido	Spn	1.94	99	51	61	-42	80
82	(80)	Stephen Ames	T&T	1.94	97	50	97	-54	54
83	(131)	Miguel Angel Martin	Spn	1.87	86	46	71	-37	52
84	(92)	Peter O'Malley	Aus	1.87	112	60	106	-82	88
85	(71)	Andrew Coltart	Sco	1.84	118	64	130	-78	66
86	(150)	Rick Fehr	USA	1.84	81	44	58	-35	58
87	(178)	Dan Forsman	USA	1.82	89	49	46	-31	74
88	(61)	Rocco Mediate	USA	1.80	81	45	103	-56	34
89	(277T)	Tom Byrum	USA	1.78	96	54	29	-21	88
90	(138)	Mark James	Eng	1.77	85	48	64	-57	78
91	(146T)	Eduardo Herrera	Col	1.72	79	46	60	-39	58
92	(67)	Yoshinori Kaneko	Jpn	1.70	104	61	136	-74	42
93	(116)	Larry Nelson	USA	1.70	73	43	68	-37	42
94	(118T)	Steve Lowery	USA	1.67	105	63	92	-69	82
95	(47)	Peter Senior	Aus	1.66	93	56	188	-131	36
96	(128)	Hal Sutton	USA	1.64	95	58	83	-68	80
97	(111)	Jay Don Blake	USA	1.64	90	55	84	-58	64
98	(88)	Larry Mize	USA	1.63	78	48	90	-60	48
99	(146T)	Raymond Russell	Sco	1.62	94	58	60	-30	64
100	(139)	Russ Cochran	USA	1.61	100	62	75	-45	70

( ) : Figures in brackets indicate 95/96 positions

Pos.		Player	Country	Points Average	Total Points	No. of Events	95/96 Total	95/96 Minus	1997 Plus
101	(303)	David Toms	USA	1.58	90	57	28	-14	76
102	(81)	Paul McGinley	Ire	1.57	96	61	112	-66	50
103	(332T)	Chris Perry	USA	1.55	82	53	26	-16	72
104	(30)	Mark McCumber	USA	1.52	61	40	164	-109	6
105	(103T)	Paul Broadhurst	Eng	1.52	96	63	105	-67	58
106	(106)	Jose Coceres	Arg	1.52	76	50	82	-52	46
107	(125)	Paul Azinger	USA	1.51	65	43	67	-46	44
108	(65)	Wayne Westner	SAf	1.51	83	55	121	-70	32
109	(229)	Fulton Allem	SAf	1.48	65	44	34	-19	50
110	(179)	Michael Long	NZl	1.48	62	42	41	-21	42
111	(83)	Tom Purtzer	USA	1.47	72	49	82	-46	36
112	(188)	Joakim Haeggman	Swe	1.47	69	47	49	-34	54
113	(167)	Mark Wiebe	USA	1.46	73	50	53	-34	54
114	(405T)	Kevin Sutherland	USA	1.45	84	58	16	-8	76
115	(117)	Hajime Meshiai	Jpn	1.45	81	56	78	-47	50
116	(90)	Brad Bryant	USA	1.44	75	52	102	-79	52
117	(261)	Don Pooley	USA	1.44	59	41	29	-24	54
118	(40)	Sam Torrance	Sco	1.43	80	56	200	-168	48
119	(206)	Doug Martin	USA	1.42	85	60	52	-35	68
120	(43)	Billy Mayfair	USA	1.41	83	59	186	-151	48
121	(130)	Hisayuki Sasaki	Jpn	1.40	87	62	89	-60	58
122T	(181)	Shoichi Kuwabara	Jpn	1.40	77	55	44	-23	56
122T	(84T)	Clarence Rose	USA	1.40	84	60	88	-44	40
124	(738T)	Robert Damron	USA	1.39	78	56	0	0	78
125	(162)	Richard Green	Aus	1.39	71	51	47	-26	50
126	(72)	Miguel Angel Jimenez	Spn	1.39	75	54	125	-88	38
127	(149)	Brandel Chamblee	USA	1.38	72	52	66	-42	48
128	(46)	Peter Jacobsen	USA	1.38	65	47	142	-129	52
129	(428T)	Hiroyuki Fujita	Jpn	1.38	55	40	11	-8	52
130	(127)	Bob Estes	USA	1.36	64	47	71	-57	50
131	(156)	Mike Brisky	USA	1.35	77	57	68	-43	52
132	(77)	Todd Hamilton	USA	1.32	70	53	112	-74	32
133	(296T)	Patrik Sjoland	Swe	1.31	67	51	26	-13	54
134	(273T)	Brad Fabel	USA	1.29	75	58	30	-15	60
135	(187)	Jamie Spence	Eng	1.29	62	48	51	-35	46
136	(738T)	Brent Geiberger	USA	1.28	64	50	0	0	64
137	(246)	Stephen Leaney	Aus	1.27	51	40	29	-20	42
138	(159)	Jarmo Sandelin	Swe	1.27	71	56	70	-51	52
139	(97)	Peter Mitchell	Eng	1.26	73	58	102	-61	32
140	(68)	John Huston	USA	1.25	69	55	123	-76	22
141	(332T)	Edward Fryatt	Eng	1.25	50	40	20	-10	40
142	(121)	David Ishii	USA	1.25	71	57	77	-44	38
143	(55)	D.A. Weibring	USA	1.23	49	40	121	-84	12
144	(302)	Mike Reid	USA	1.21	58	48	27	-17	48
145	(175)	Mike Hulbert	USA	1.21	76	63	68	-48	56
146	(144)	David Gilford	Eng	1.20	59	49	67	-54	46
147	(354T)	Keiichiro Fukabori	Jpn	1.20	66	55	20	-10	56
148	(148)	Glen Day	USA	1.19	70	59	80	-48	38
149	(351T)	Steve Alker	NZl	1.17	47	40	18	-9	38
150	(203)	Hirofumi Miyase	Jpn	1.17	69	59	41	-26	54

( ) : Figures in brackets indicate 95/96 positions

THE WORLD RANKING / 309

Pos.		Player	Country	Points Average	Total Points	No. of Events	95/96 Total	95/96 Minus	1997 Plus
151	(108)	Nolan Henke	USA	1.16	58	50	82	-54	30
152	(499T)	Toshiaki Odate	Jpn	1.16	51	44	7	-4	48
153	(89)	Fuzzy Zoeller	USA	1.15	46	40	71	-45	20
154	(145)	Grant Waite	NZl	1.14	72	63	78	-54	48
155T	(102)	Paul Lawrie	Sco	1.14	58	51	79	-43	22
155T	(82)	Lennie Clements	USA	1.14	58	51	92	-62	28
157	(210)	Roger Chapman	Eng	1.13	61	54	47	-30	44
158	(264T)	Olin Browne	USA	1.13	70	62	32	-16	54
159	(95T)	Kazuhiko Hosokawa	Jpn	1.13	79	70	96	-61	44
160	(172)	David Edwards	USA	1.13	54	48	51	-37	40
161	(309T)	Angel Cabrera	Arg	1.12	47	42	22	-11	36
162	(341T)	Brian Henninger	USA	1.11	60	54	27	-21	54
163	(113)	Jean Van de Velde	Frn	1.09	59	54	85	-48	22
164	(201)	Tsukasa Watanabe	Jpn	1.08	68	63	59	-39	48
165	(272)	Lee Rinker	USA	1.08	69	64	39	-26	56
166	(177)	Toru Suzuki	Jpn	1.08	70	65	64	-46	52
167T	(403)	Eiji Mizoguchi	Jpn	1.07	60	56	20	-14	54
167T	(170)	Sven Struver	Ger	1.07	60	56	58	-40	42
169	(153)	Peter Teravainen	USA	1.07	61	57	67	-42	36
170	(332T)	Mitsutaka Kusakabe	Jpn	1.07	46	43	20	-16	42
171T	(241)	Greg Chalmers	Aus	1.06	54	51	38	-22	38
171T	(238T)	Phil Tataurangi	NZl	1.06	54	51	30	-16	40
173	(143)	Jerry Kelly	USA	1.06	73	69	71	-36	38
174	(75)	Wayne Riley	Aus	1.05	62	59	132	-94	24
175	(224)	Wayne Levi	USA	1.05	43	41	34	-19	28
176	(256)	Len Mattiace	USA	1.05	67	64	34	-17	50
177	(54)	Scott Simpson	USA	1.02	50	49	138	-104	16
178	(185)	Russell Claydon	Eng	1.02	52	51	54	-36	34
179	(264T)	David Carter	Eng	1.02	58	57	40	-22	40
180T	(123)	Robert Gamez	USA	1.00	57	57	85	-58	30
180T	(364)	Donnie Hammond	USA	1.00	42	42	19	-15	38
182	(189T)	Jean Louis Guepy	Frn	0.98	42	43	44	-34	32
183	(166)	Toshimitsu Izawa	Jpn	0.96	44	46	52	-40	32
184	(141)	Curtis Strange	USA	0.95	42	44	64	-50	28
185	(738T)	Kenichi Kuboya	Jpn	0.95	38	40	0	0	38
186	(171)	Peter Baker	Eng	0.95	56	59	63	-45	38
187	(79)	John Morse	USA	0.95	55	58	107	-74	22
188	(238T)	Shinichi Yokota	Jpn	0.95	53	56	36	-25	42
189	(263)	Ronnie Black	USA	0.94	51	54	37	-22	36
190	(76)	Hidemichi Tanaka	Jpn	0.94	61	65	104	-71	28
191T	(232)	Pete Jordan	USA	0.93	55	59	36	-23	42
191T	(137)	Joey Sindelar	USA	0.93	55	59	70	-45	30
193	(516T)	Clinton Whitelaw	SAf	0.93	39	42	6	-3	36
194	(183)	Katsunori Kuwabara	Jpn	0.92	59	64	59	-40	40
195	(257)	Jim Carter	USA	0.92	55	60	42	-27	40
196	(194)	Ross McFarlane	Eng	0.92	54	59	53	-33	34
197	(259)	Yoshinori Mizumaki	Jpn	0.91	50	55	44	-30	36
198T	(289T)	Kevin Wentworth	USA	0.90	36	40	24	-16	28
198T	(151)	Anthony Painter	Aus	0.90	36	40	50	-28	14
200	(114)	Bradley Hughes	Aus	0.89	47	53	65	-34	16

( ) : Figures in brackets indicate 95/96 positions

World's Winners of 1997

U.S. PGA TOUR

Mercedes Championships	Tiger Woods
Bob Hope Chrysler Classic	John Cook
Phoenix Open	Steve Jones
AT&T Pebble Beach National Pro-Am	Mark O'Meara
Buick Invitational	Mark O'Meara (2)
United Airlines Hawaiian Open	Paul Stankowski
Tucson Chrysler Classic	Jeff Sluman
Nissan Open	Nick Faldo
Doral-Ryder Open	Steve Elkington
Honda Classic	Stuart Appleby
Bay Hill Invitational	Phil Mickelson
The Players Championship	Steve Elkington (2)
Freeport-McDermott Classic	Brad Faxon
Masters Tournament	Tiger Woods (3)
MCI Classic	Nick Price (3)
Greater Greensboro Chrysler Classic	Frank Nobilo
Shell Houston Open	Phil Blackmar
BellSouth Classic	Scott McCarron
GTE Byron Nelson Classic	Tiger Woods (4)
MasterCard Colonial	David Frost
Memorial Tournament	Vijay Singh (2)
Kemper Open	Justin Leonard
U.S. Open Championship	Ernie Els (2)
Buick Classic	Ernie Els (3)
FedEx St. Jude Classic	Greg Norman
Motorola Western Open	Tiger Woods (5)
Quad City Classic	David Toms
Deposit Guaranty Golf Classic	Billy Ray Brown
Canon Greater Hartford Open	Stewart Cink
Sprint International	Phil Mickelson (2)
Buick Open	Vijay Singh (3)
PGA Championship	Davis Love III
NEC World Series of Golf	Greg Norman (3)
Greater Vancouver Open	Mark Calcavecchia
Greater Milwaukee Open	Scott Hoch
Bell Canadian Open	Steve Jones (2)
CVS Charity Classic	Loren Roberts
LaCantera Texas Open	Tim Herron
B.C. Open	Gabriel Hjertstedt
Buick Challenge	Davis Love III (2)
Michelob Championship at Kingsmill	David Duval
Walt Disney World/Oldsmobile Classic	David Duval (2)
Las Vegas Invitational	Bill Glasson
Tour Championship	David Duval (3)

SPECIAL EVENTS

Family House Invitational	Jim Furyk
Fred Couples Invitational	Scott Simpson
Fred Meyer Challenge	Greg Norman (2)/Brad Faxon (2)
Lincoln-Mercury Kapalua International	Davis Love III (3)
Subaru Sarazen World Open	Mark Calcavecchia (2)
Franklin Templeton Shark Shootout	Scott McCarron (2)/Bruce Lietzke
MasterCard PGA Grand Slam	Ernie Els (4)
World Cup of Golf	Ireland/Colin Montgomerie (4)
General Motors Mexican Open	Frank Nobilo (2)

WORLD'S WINNERS OF 1997 / 311

Callaway Golf Pebble Beach Invitational — Loren Roberts (2)
JCPenney Classic — Clarence Rose/Amy Fruhwirth
Office Depot Father-Son Challenge — Raymond Floyd/Raymond Floyd, Jr.
Diners Club Matches — Steve Elkington (3)/Jeff Maggert
Lexus Challenge — Raymond Floyd (2)/William Devane
Andersen Consulting World Championship — Colin Montgomerie (5)

NIKE TOUR

Lakeland Classic — Ryan Howison
Inland Empire Open — Mark Carnevale
Monterrey Open — Mike Small
Louisiana Open — Joe Daley
Greater Austin Open — Eric Booker
Mississippi Gulf Coast Classic — Jeff Brehaut
Alabama Classic — John Elliott
South Carolina Classic — Harrison Frazar
Carolina Classic — Dan Bateman
Dominion Open — Jeff Julian
Upstate Classic — Chris Smith
Knoxville Open — Dave Rummells
Miami Valley Open — Trevor Dodds
Cleveland Open — Mike Small (2)
Hershey Open — Barry Cheesman
Laurel Creek Classic — Matt Gogel
St. Louis Golf Classic — Todd Gleaton
Wichita Open — Ben Bates
Dakota Dunes Open — Chris Smith (2)
Omaha Classic — Chris Smith (3)
Ozarks Open — Chris DiMarco
Permian Basin Open — Paul Gow
Colorado Classic — Pat Bates
San Jose Open — R.W. Eaks
Boise Open — Iain Steel
Tri-Cities Open — Todd Gleaton (2)
Puget Sound Open — Kevin Johnson
Shreveport Open — Mark Wurtz (2)
Nike Tour Championship — Steve Flesch

CANADIAN TOUR

Payless Open — Rick Todd
BC Tel Pacific Open — Mike Weir
Henry Singer Alberta Open — Ray Freeman
Telus Calgary Open — Ian Hutchings
Telus Edmonton Open — Manny Zerman
Xerox Manitoba Open — Mark Wurtz
Infiniti Championship — Scott Petersen
Canadian Masters — Mike Weir (2)
CPGA Championship — Guy Hill
Montclair PEI Classic — Mike Grob

SOUTH AMERICAN TOUR

World Nature Games — Ricardo Gonzalez
TC Ecuador Open — Gustavo Rojas (2)
Peru Open — Philip Jonas
Litoral Open — Armando Saavedra
Argentina Masters — Bernhard Langer (5)
Los Leones - Chile Open — Gustavo Rojas (3)
Prince of Wales Open — Ricardo Gonzalez (2)
Argentina Open — Jim Furyk (2)

PGA EUROPEAN TOUR

Dubai Desert Classic	Richard Green
Moroccan Open	Clinton Whitelaw
Portuguese Open	Michael Jonzon
Turespana Masters - Open de Canarias	Jose Maria Olazabal
Madeira Island Open	Peter Mitchell
Europe 1 Cannes Open	Stuart Cage
Peugeot Open de Espana	Mark James
Conte of Florence Italian Open	Bernhard Langer
Benson and Hedges International Open	Bernhard Langer (2)
Alamo English Open	Per-Ulrik Johansson
Volvo PGA Championship	Ian Woosnam
Deutsche Bank Open–TPC of Europe	Ross McFarlane
Compaq European Grand Prix	Colin Montgomerie
Volvo German Open	Ignacio Garrido (2)
Peugeot Open de France	Retief Goosen
Murphy's Irish Open	Colin Montgomerie (2)
Gulfstream Loch Lomond World Invitational	Tom Lehman
British Open Championship	Justin Leonard (2)
Sun Microsystems Dutch Open	Sven Struver
Volvo Scandinavian Masters	Joakim Haeggman
Chemapol Trophy Czech Open	Bernhard Langer (3)
Smurfit European Open	Per-Ulrik Johansson (2)
BMW International Open	Robert Karlsson
Canon European Masters	Costantino Rocca
Trophee Lancome	Mark O'Meara (3)
One 2 One British Masters	Greg Turner
Ryder Cup	Europe
Linde German Masters	Bernhard Langer (4)
Toyota World Match Play	Vijay Singh (4)
Open Novotel Perrier	Anders Forsbrand/Michael Jonzon (2)
Alfred Dunhill Cup	South Africa
Oki Pro-Am	Paul McGinley
Volvo Masters	Lee Westwood (2)

CHALLENGE TOUR

Open de Cote D'Ivoire	Knud Storegaard
Lonrho Kenya Open	Jorge Berendt
Is Molas Challenge	Andrew Collison
Campeonato de Espana de Pro	Ignacio Garrido
Le Pavoniere Superal Challenge	Andrew Collison (2)
Alianca UAP Challenge	Anssi Kankkonen
Canarias Challenge	Michele Reale
Modena Classic Open	Jesus Maria Arruti
Matchmaker Austrian Open	Erol Simsek
Himmerland Open	Mikael Lundberg
KB Golf Challenge	Alex Cejka
Siab Open	Joakim Rask
Nedcar National Open	Brian Gee
Italian Native Open	Massimo Florioli
STG Coopers & Lybrand ASPG	Juan Ciola
Husqvarna Open	Mikael Lundberg (2)
Championnat de France Pro	Raphael Jacquelin
Lancia Golf Pokal	Erol Simsek (2)
Czech Republic	Ondrej Trupl
Team Erhverv Danish Open	David Lynn
Memorial Olivier Barras	Raphael Jacquelin (2)
Audi Quattro Trophy	David A. Russell
Open dei Tessali	Ivo Giner
Open des Volcans	Mark Litton
Neuchatel Open	Erol Simsek (3)

Volvo Finnish Open	Soren Kjeldsen
Rolex Trophy Pro-Am	Anssi Kankkonen (2)
Interlaken Open	Cancelled
BTC Slovenian Open	Kalle Brink
Klassis Turkish Open	Bradley Dredge
Challenge Tour Championship	Greg Chalmers
Norwegian PGA Championship	Morten Hagen
Terracottem Omnium of Belgium	Didier de Vooght
Esbjerg Danish Closed	Knud Storegaard (2)
Finnish PGA Championship	Mikael Piltz
Netcom Norwegian Open	Dimitri Bieri
Steelcover Dutch Challenge	Raphael Jacquelin (3)
Toyota PGA Championship	Fredrik Henge
Sovereign Russian Open	Michele Reale (2)
Ohrlings Swedish Match Play	Gregory Garbero
Perrier European Pro-Am	Craig Hainline
Eulen Open Galea	Warren Bennett
BPGT Challenge	Olivier Edmond
Polish Open	Cancelled
Telia InfoMedia Grand Prix	Fredrik Henge (2)
San Paolo Vita Open	Mathew Goggin
Estoril Challenge	Jose Carriles
Estoril Grand Final	Nicolas Joakimides

ASIA TOUR

Mitsubishi Motors - Southwoods Open	Takao Nogami
Konica U-Bix Manila Open	Yasuharu Imano
Benson and Hedges Malaysian Open	Lee Westwood
Thai Airways International Thailand Open	Christian Chernock
Rolex Masters	Kyi Hla Han
Classic India Open	Edward Fryatt
Mobiline Philippine Open	Kevin Wentworth
Maekyung LG Fashion Open	Shin Yong-jin
Volvo China Open	Cheng Jun
Hyundai Motors Open	Ian Woosnam (2)
Chinese Taipei Open	Tsai Chi-huang
Taiwan PGA Golf Championship	Gerry Norquist (2)
Shinhan Donghae Open	Edward Fryatt (2)
Korea Open	Kim Jong-duk (2)
Mercuries Cup Masters	Gerry Norquist (3)
Johnnie Walker Super Tour	Jesper Parnevik

CHINA TOUR

Volvo Open	Adrian Percey
Hugo Boss Open	Zhang Lian-wei
Coca-Cola Open	Gustavo Rojas
Founder Open	Jerry Smith

JAPAN TOUR

Token Corporation Cup	Masashi Ozaki
Daido Drinko Shizuoka Open	Hisayuki Sasaki
Just System KSB Open	Keiichiro Fukabori
Descente Classic	Peter Teravainen
Tsuruya Open	Mitsuo Harada
Kirin Open	Kim Jong-duk
Chunichi Crowns	Masashi Ozaki (2)
Fuji Sankei Classic	Kenichi Kuboya
Japan PGA Championship	Shigeki Maruyama
Ube Kosan Open	Shigenori Mori
Mitsubishi Galant	Masashi Ozaki (3)
JCB Classic Sendai	Nobuhito Sato

Sapporo Tokyu Open	Hirofumi Miyase
Yomiuri Open	Shigeki Maruyama (2)
Mizuno Open	Brian Watts
PGA Philanthropy	Naomichi Ozaki
Yonex Open Hiroshima	Naomichi Ozaki (2)
Nikkei Cup	Yeh Chang-ting
NST Niigata Open	Kazuhiko Hosokawa
Sanko Grand Summer	Shoichi Kuwabara
Acom International	Kazuo Kanayama
KBC Augusta	Masashi Ozaki (4)
Japan Match Play	Shigeki Maruyama (3)
Suntory Open	Hiroyuki Fujita
ANA Open	Shinichi Yokota
Jun Classic	Eduardo Herrera
Japan Open	Craig Parry (2)
Tokai Classic	Brandt Jobe
Golf Digest Tournament	Brandt Jobe (2)
Bridgestone Open	Masashi Ozaki (5)
Philip Morris Championship	Brian Watts (2)
Sumitomo Visa Taiheiyo Masters	Lee Westwood (3)
Dunlop Phoenix Tournament	Tom Watson
Casio World Open	Mitsutaka Kusakabe
Japan Series of Golf	Shigeki Maruyama (4)
Daikyo Open	Kenichi Kuboya (2)

OMEGA TOUR

Asian Honda Classic	Tiger Woods (2)
Vietnam Open	Andrew Bonhomme
London Myanmar Open	Boonchu Ruangkit
DFS Galleria Guam Open	Gerry Norquist
Satelindo Indonesia Open	Craig Parry
Sabah Masters	Des Terblanche
SingTel Ericsson Singapore Open	Zaw Moe
Philip Morris Asia Cup	Park No-seok
Asia Pacific Ericsson Masters	Darren Cole
Mild Seven Kuala Lumpur Open	Charlie Wi
Yokohama Singapore PGA	Prayad Marksaeng
ABN-AMRO Pakistan Masters	Thammanoon Sriroj
Dubai Creek Open	Adrian Percey (2)
Hero Honda Masters	Ted Purdy
Ta Shee Open	Wang Ter-chang
Volvo Masters of Malaysia	Christian Pena
Lexus International	Prayad Marksaeng (2)
Tugu Pratama PGA	Clay Devers
Andersen Consulting Hong Kong Open	Frank Nobilo (3)
Omega PGA Championship	Rodrigo Cuello
Volvo Asian Match Play	Des Terblanche (3)

AUSTRALASIAN TOUR

Victorian Open	Stephen Leaney
Johnnie Walker Classic	Ernie Els
Heineken Classic	Miguel Angel Martin
Ford Open	Steve Alker
Ericsson Australian Masters	Peter Lonard
Canon Challenge	Peter Senior
MasterCard PGA Championship	Andrew Coltart
Holden Australian Open	Lee Westwood (4)
ANZ Players Championship	Greg Chalmers (2)
AMP - Air New Zealand Open	Greg Turner (2)
Schweppes Coolum Classic	Craig Parry (3)

AFRICAN TOURS

San Lameer South African Masters	Mark McNulty
Nashua Wild Coast Sun Challenge	Mark McNulty (2)
FNB Players Championship	Warren Schutte
South African Open	Vijay Singh
Dimension Data Pro-Am	Nick Price
Alfred Dunhill South African PGA	Nick Price (2)
Hollard Insurance Royal Swazi Sun Open	Warrick Druian
Kalahari Classic	Sean Pappas
Vodacom Series: Eastern Cape	Des Terblanche (2)
Bosveld Classic	Desvonde Botes
Vodacom Series: Mpumalanga	Robbie Stewart
Trustbank Gauteng Classic	Bradford Vaughan
Vodacom Series: Gauteng	John Nelson
FNB Botswana Open	Nasho Kamungeremu
FNB Namibia Open	Wallie Coetsee
Bearing Man Highveld Classic	Darren Fichardt
Vodacom Series: Free State	Dean van Staden
Vodacom Series: Western Cape	Desvonde Botes (2)
Vodacom Series: Kwazulu-Natal	Grant Muller
Lombard Tyres Classic	Andrew McLardy
Hassan II Trophy	Colin Montgomerie (3)
Leopard Rock Classic	Adilson da Silva
Zambia Open	James Loughnane
Zimbabwe Open	Nick Price (4)
Nedbank Million Dollar Challenge	Nick Price (5)
Mycom Mafunyane Trophy	Kevin Stone

U.S. SENIOR PGA TOUR

MasterCard Championship	Hale Irwin
Royal Caribbean Classic	Gibby Gilbert
LG Championship	Hale Irwin (2)
GTE Classic	David Graham
American Express Invitational	Bud Allin
Senior Slam	Hale Irwin (3)
Toshiba Senior Classic	Bob Murphy
Liberty Mutual Legends of Golf	John Bland/Graham Marsh
Southwestern Bell Dominion	David Graham (2)
The Tradition	Gil Morgan
PGA Seniors' Championship	Hale Irwin (4)
Las Vegas Senior Classic	Hale Irwin (5)
Bruno's Memorial Classic	Jay Sigel
Home Depot Invitational	Jim Dent
Cadillac NFL Classic	Bruce Crampton
Bell Atlantic Classic	Bob Eastwood
Ameritech Senior Open	Gil Morgan (2)
BellSouth Senior Classic	Gil Morgan (3)
du Maurier Champions	Jack Kiefer
Nationwide Championship	Graham Marsh (2)
U.S. Senior Open	Graham Marsh (3)
Kroger Senior Classic	Jay Sigel (2)
Ford Senior Players Championship	Larry Gilbert
Burnet Senior Classic	Hale Irwin (6)
Franklin Quest Championship	Dave Stockton
BankBoston Classic	Hale Irwin (7)
Northville Long Island Classic	Dana Quigley
First of America Classic	Gil Morgan (4)
Saint Luke's Classic	Bruce Summerhays
Pittsburgh Senior Classic	Hugh Baiocchi
Bank One Classic	Vicente Fernandez
Boone Valley Classic	Hale Irwin (8)
Comfort Classic	David Graham (3)

Emerald Coast Classic — Isao Aoki
Vantage Championship — Hale Irwin (9)
The Transamerica — Dave Eichelberger
Hyatt Regency Maui Kaanapali Classic — Hale Irwin (10)
Raley's Gold Rush Classic — Bob Eastwood (2)
Ralphs Senior Classic — Gil Morgan (5)
Energizer Senior Tour Championship — Gil Morgan (6)
Diners Club Matches — Gil Morgan (7)/Jay Sigel (3)

EUROPEAN SENIORS TOUR

Beko Turkish Seniors Open — Tommy Horton
AIB Irish Seniors Open — Tommy Horton (2)
Philips PFA Golf Classic — DeRay Simon
Jersey Seniors Open — Tommy Horton (3)
De Vere Hotels Seniors Classic — T.R. Jones
Ryder Collingtree Seniors Classic — Neil Coles
Manadans Affarer Seniors — Noel Ratcliffe
Lawrence Batley Seniors — Antonio Garrido
Senior German Open — Noel Ratcliffe (2)
Senior British Open — Gary Player (2)
Shell Wentworth Senior Masters — Gary Player (3)
Credit Suisse Private Banking Seniors Open — Brian Waites
The Belfry PGA Seniors Championship — Walter Hall
Motor Senior Classic — Ian Richardson
Scottish Seniors Open — Tommy Horton (4)
Clubhaus Seniors Classic — Tommy Horton (5)
Senior Tournament of Champions — Tommy Horton (6)

JAPAN SENIOR TOUR

Daiichi Seimei Cup — Gary Player
TPC Starts Senior Golf — Seiji Ogawa
Castlehill Senior Open — Toru Nakayama
Japan Media System Cup — Katsuji Hasegawa
HTB Senior Classic — Kesahiko Uchida
Komatsu Nagoya TV Open — Seiji Ogawa (2)
Japan PGA Senior Championship — Ichiro Teramoto
Japan PGA Senior Open — Isao Aoki (2)

SOUTH AFRICA SENIOR TOUR

Vodacom Senior Classic — Simon Hobday
Templeton South African Senior Open — John Bland (2)
ICI John Bland Invitational — Tommy Horton (7)

U.S. LPGA TOUR

Chrysler-Plymouth Tournament of Champions — Annika Sorenstam
HealthSouth Inaugural — Michelle McGann
Diet Dr. Pepper National Pro-Am — Kelly Robbins
Los Angeles Women's Championship — Terry-Jo Myers
Cup Noodles Hawaiian Ladies Open — Annika Sorenstam (2)
Welch's/Circle K Championship — Donna Andrews
Standard Register PING — Laura Davies
Nabisco Dinah Shore — Betsy King
Longs Drugs Challenge — Annika Sorenstam (3)
Susan G. Komen International — Karrie Webb
Chick-fil-A Charity Championship — Nancy Lopez
Sprint Titleholders Championship — Tammie Green
Sara Lee Classic — Terry-Jo Myers (2)
McDonald's LPGA Championship — Chris Johnson
Corning Classic — Rosie Jones
Michelob Light Classic — Annika Sorenstam (4)
Oldsmobile Classic — Pat Hurst
Edina Realty Classic — Danielle Ammaccapane
Rochester International — Penny Hammel

ShopRite Classic | Michelle McGann (2)
Jamie Farr Kroger Classic | Kelly Robbins (2)
U.S. Women's Open | Alison Nicholas
JAL Big Apple Classic | Michele Redman
Giant Eagle Classic | Tammie Green (2)
du Maurier Classic | Colleen Walker
Friendly's Classic | Deb Richard
Star Bank Classic | Colleen Walker (2)
State Farm Rail Classic | Cindy Figg-Currier
Safeway Golf Championship | Chris Johnson (2)
Safeco Classic | Karrie Webb (3)
Welch's Championship | Liselotte Neumann
Fieldcrest Cannon Classic | Wendy Ward
CoreStates Betsy King Classic | Annika Sorenstam (6)
Samsung World Championship | Juli Inkster
ITT LPGA Tour Championship | Annika Sorenstam (8)
Diners Club Matches | Juli Inkster (2)/Dottie Pepper

WOMEN'S EUROPEAN TOUR

Estoril Ladies' Open | Mandy Sutton
American Express Tour Players' Classic | Karen Lunn
Ford-Stimorol Danish Open | Laura Davies (2)
Deesse Ladies' Swiss Open | Marie-Laure de Lorenzi
Evian Masters | Hiromi Kobayashi
Guardian Irish Open | Patricia Meunier Lebouc
Ladies' German Open | Joanne Mills
McDonald's WPGA Championship of Europe | Helen Alfredsson
Weetabix Women's British Open | Karrie Webb (2)
Compaq Open | Annika Sorenstam (5)
Ladies' French Open | Karen Lunn (2)
Hennessy Cup | Laura Davies (3)
Sicilian/Italian Open | Valerie Van Ryckeghem
Air France Madame Open | Loraine Lambert
Princess Lalla Meriem Cup | Diane Barnard
Praia D'El Rey European Cup | European Seniors Tour

WOMEN'S AUSTRALASIAN TOURS

Republic of China Open | Ai-Yu Tu
Toyota Philippine Open | Pernilla Sterner
Thailand Open | Sophie Gustafson
JAL Malaysian Open | Petra Rigby-Jinglov
Indonesian Open | Pernilla Sterner (2)
Alpine Australian Ladies Masters | Gail Graham
Toyota Australian Women's Open | Jane Crafter

JAPAN LPGA TOUR

Daikin Orchid Ladies | Woo-Soon Ko
Saishunkan Ladies | Chikayo Yamazaki
Yellow Hat Tokyo Ladies Open | Suzuko Maeda
Kenshoen Ladies | Kaori Harada
Mitsukoshi Cup Ladies Open | Akemi Yamaoka
Nasu Ogawa Ladies | Woo-Soon Ko (2)
Katokichi Queen's Cup | Jae-Sook Won
Gunze Cup World Ladies | Tseng Hsiu-Feng
Yakult Ladies | Tomiko Ikebuchi
Chukyo TV Bridgestone Ladies | Aki Takamura
Toto Motors Ladies | Yoko Inoue
Mitsubishi Denki Ladies | Akiko Fukushima
We Love Kobe Suntory Ladies Open | Ikuyo Shiotani
Dunlop Twin Lakes Ladies Open | Ok-Hee Ku
Japan Women's Open | Ayako Okamoto
Tohato Ladies | Suzuko Maeda (2)

Toyo Suisan Ladies Hokkaido	Kaori Higo
Resort Trust Ladies	Fumiko Muraguchi
Golf 5 Ladies	Akiko Fukushima (2)
Mizuno Ladies	Aiko Takasu
NEC Karuizawa 72	Yuka Irie
Shin Caterpillar Mitsubishi Ladies	Takayo Bandoh
Goyo Kensetsu Ladies	Michiko Hattori
Fuji Sankei Ladies Classic	Aki Takamura (2)
Japan LPGA Championship	Akiko Fukushima (3)
Yukijirushi Ladies Tokai Classic	Akiko Fukushima (4)
Miyagi TV Cup Ladies Open	Michiko Hattori (2)
Kosaido Ladies Golf Cup	Akiko Fukushima (5)
TaKaRa World Invitational	Liselotte Neumann (2)
Fujitsu Ladies	Aiko Takasu (2)
Higuchi Hisako Kibun Classic	Annika Sorenstam (7)
Nichirei International	United States
Toray Japan Queen's Cup	Liselotte Neumann (3)
Itoen Ladies	Helen Alfredsson (2)
Daio Seishi Elleair Ladies Open	Ok-Hee Ku (2)
JLPGA Meiji Nyugyo Cup	Akiko Fukushima (6)

Multiple Winners of 1997

PLAYER	WINS	PLAYER	WINS	PLAYER	WINS
Hale Irwin	10	Chris Smith	3	Kenichi Kuboya	2
Annika Sorenstam	8	Des Terblanche	3	Justin Leonard	2
Tommy Horton	7	Karrie Webb	3	Mikael Lundberg	2
Gil Morgan	7	Helen Alfredsson	2	Karen Lunn	2
Akiko Fukushima	6	Isao Aoki	2	Suzuko Maeda	2
Bernhard Langer	5	John Bland	2	Prayad Marksaeng	2
Colin Montgomerie	5	Desvonde Botes	2	Scott McCarron	2
Masashi Ozaki	5	Mark Calcavecchia	2	Michelle McGann	2
Nick Price	5	Greg Chalmers	2	Mark McNulty	2
Tiger Woods	5	Andrew Collison	2	Phil Mickelson	2
Ernie Els	4	Bob Eastwood	2	Terry-Jo Myers	2
Shigeki Maruyama	4	Brad Faxon	2	Seiji Ogawa	2
Vijay Singh	4	Raymond Floyd	2	Naomichi Ozaki	2
Lee Westwood	4	Edward Fryatt	2	Adrian Percey	2
Laura Davies	3	Jim Furyk	2	Noel Ratcliffe	2
David Duval	3	Ignacio Garrido	2	Michele Reale	2
Steve Elkington	3	Todd Gleaton	2	Kelly Robbins	2
David Graham	3	Ricardo Gonzalez	2	Loren Roberts	2
Raphael Jacquelin	3	Tammie Green	2	Mike Small	2
Davis Love III	3	Michiko Hattori	2	Pernilla Sterner	2
Graham Marsh	3	Fredrik Henge	2	Knud Storegaard	2
Liselotte Neumann	3	Juli Inkster	2	Aki Takamura	2
Frank Nobilo	3	Brandt Jobe	2	Aiko Takasu	2
Greg Norman	3	Per-Ulrik Johansson	2	Greg Turner	2
Gerry Norquist	3	Chris Johnson	2	Colleen Walker	2
Mark O'Meara	3	Steve Jones	2	Brian Watts	2
Craig Parry	3	Michael Jonzon	2	Mike Weir	2
Gary Player	3	Anssi Kankkonen	2	Ian Woosnam	2
Gustavo Rojas	3	Kim Jong-duk	2	Mark Wurtz	2
Jay Sigel	3	Woo-Soon Ko	2		
Erol Simsek	3	Ok-Hee Ku	2		

World Money List

This list of the 300 leading money winners in the world of professional golf in 1997 was compiled from the results of men's (excluding seniors) tournaments carried in the Appendixes of this edition. This list includes tournaments with a minimum of 36 holes and four contestants and does not include such competitions as skins games, pro-ams and shootouts.

In the 32 years during which World Money Lists have been compiled, the earnings of the player in the 200th position have risen from a total of $3,326 in 1966 to $248,799 in 1997. The top-200 players in 1966 earned a total of $4,680,287. In 1997, the comparable total was $128,443,429.

Because of fluctuating values of money throughout the world, it was necessary to determine an average value of non-American currency to U.S. money to prepare this listing. The conversion rates used for 1997 were: British pound = US$1.64; Japanese yen = US$0.008312; South African rand = US$0.22; Australian dollar = US$0.73; Canadian dollar = US$0.73.

POS.	PLAYER, COUNTRY	TOTAL MONEY
1	Colin Montgomerie, Scotland	$3,366,900
2	Ernie Els, South Africa	3,188,962
3	Davis Love III, USA	2,861,953
4	Nick Price, Zimbabwe	2,517,716
5	Tiger Woods, USA	2,380,831
6	David Duval, USA	2,044,808
7	Justin Leonard, USA	2,022,963
8	Greg Norman, Australia	1,949,508
9	Jim Furyk, USA	1,942,574
10	Steve Elkington, Australia	1,732,111
11	Lee Westwood, England	1,723,603
12	Phil Mickelson, USA	1,707,335
13	Vijay Singh, Fiji	1,674,188
14	Scott Hoch, USA	1,655,079
15	Jesper Parnevik, Sweden	1,612,622
16	Mark Calcavecchia, USA	1,577,695
17	Tom Lehman, USA	1,574,319
18	Brad Faxon, USA	1,536,670
19	Mark O'Meara, USA	1,531,412
20	Bernhard Langer, Germany	1,501,988
21	Masashi Ozaki, Japan	1,420,207
22	Shigeki Maruyama, Japan	1,380,821
23	Frank Nobilo, New Zealand	1,318,120
24	Ian Woosnam, Wales	1,207,365
25	Loren Roberts, USA	1,194,473
26	Darren Clarke, N. Ireland	1,115,754
27	Steve Jones, USA	1,090,743
28	Scott McCarron, USA	1,072,084
29	Stuart Appleby, Australia	1,072,083
30	Naomichi Ozaki, Japan	1,006,936
31	Paul Stankowski, USA	998,446
32	John Cook, USA	988,553

320 / WORLD MONEY LIST

POS.	PLAYER, COUNTRY	TOTAL MONEY
33	Lee Janzen, USA	981,924
34	Jeff Maggert, USA	971,384
35	Stewart Cink, USA	967,157
36	Retief Goosen, South Africa	932,822
37	Brian Watts, USA	930,347
38	Bill Glasson, USA	926,552
39	Craig Parry, Australia	908,932
40	Jose Maria Olazabal, Spain	903,760
41	Nick Faldo, England	902,533
42	Tommy Tolles, USA	899,254
43	Padraig Harrington, Ireland	869,930
44	Costantino Rocca, Italy	842,431
45	Andrew Magee, USA	807,507
46	David Frost, South Africa	793,979
47	Billy Andrade, USA	777,289
48	Tom Watson, USA	769,342
49	Ignacio Garrido, Spain	768,135
50	Per-Ulrik Johansson, Sweden	759,349
51	Jeff Sluman, USA	759,133
52	Tim Herron, USA	700,647
53	Fred Couples, USA	700,525
54	Hajime Meshiai, Japan	671,810
55	Tom Kite, USA	668,752
56	Craig Stadler, USA	655,807
57	Phil Blackmar, USA	642,400
58	Fred Funk, USA	635,141
59	Tateo Ozaki, Japan	628,725
60	Kirk Triplett, USA	611,998
61	David Ogrin, USA	611,304
62	David Toms, USA	606,659
63	Payne Stewart, USA	603,791
64	Robert Karlsson, Sweden	592,075
65	Paul McGinley, Ireland	588,576
66	Brandt Jobe, USA	575,941
67	Jay Haas, USA	570,395
68	Eduardo Romero, Argentina	542,809
69	Dan Forsman, USA	540,224
70	Tom Byrum, USA	536,174
71	Carlos Franco, Paraguay	536,034
72	Raymond Russell, Scotland	535,100
73	Duffy Waldorf, USA	529,087
74	Bob Tway, USA	523,523
75	Shoichi Kuwabara, Japan	509,728
76	Steve Lowery, USA	507,713
77	Russ Cochran, USA	504,679
78	Toru Suzuki, Japan	493,748
79	Robert Damron, USA	483,336
80	Chris Perry, USA	482,266
81	Michael Bradley, USA	482,191
82	Mark James, England	481,752
83	Kevin Sutherland, USA	479,260
84	Peter O'Malley, Australia	479,058
85	Kazuhiko Hosokawa, Japan	476,978
86	Sven Struver, Germany	473,839

POS.	PLAYER, COUNTRY	TOTAL MONEY
87	Hirofumi Miyase, Japan	460,534
88	Thomas Bjorn, Denmark	459,853
89	Clarence Rose, USA	458,981
90	Joakim Haeggman, Sweden	457,756
91	Frankie Minoza, Philippines	454,970
92	Peter Lonard, Australia	454,199
93	Hal Sutton, USA	453,928
94	Greg Turner, New Zealand	441,885
95	Doug Martin, USA	428,995
96	Lee Rinker, USA	428,451
97	Tsukasa Watanabe, Japan	428,190
98	Eduardo Herrera, Colombia	427,263
99	Peter Jacobsen, USA	426,581
100	Paul Goydos, USA	421,891
101	Mike Hulbert, USA	420,576
102	Patrik Sjoland, Sweden	419,204
103	Dudley Hart, USA	416,603
104	Keiichiro Fukabori, Japan	415,951
105	Brent Geiberger, USA	414,074
106	Kenichi Kuboya, Japan	406,711
107	Mark McNulty, Zimbabwe	405,002
108	Bob Estes, USA	390,756
109	Brad Fabel, USA	389,366
110	Robert Allenby, Australia	387,313
111	Russell Claydon, England	384,053
112	Jay Don Blake, USA	382,543
113	Billy Mayfair, USA	380,896
114	Chris Smith, USA	379,435
115	Grant Waite, New Zealand	375,961
116	Mike Brisky, USA	372,394
117	Eiji Mizoguchi, Japan	371,639
118	Hiroyuki Fujita, Japan	370,358
119	Shigemasa Higaki, Japan	369,818
120	Peter Teravainen, USA	368,646
121	Paul Broadhurst, England	366,510
122	Brian Henninger, USA	366,134
123	Brandel Chamblee, USA	353,277
124	Rick Fehr, USA	352,204
125	Miguel Angel Jimenez, Spain	350,461
126	Kim Jong-duk, Korea	347,176
127	Misutaka Kusakabe, Japan	346,005
128	Nobuhito Sato, Japan	345,348
129	Olin Browne, USA	344,653
130	Mitsuo Harada, Japan	342,556
131	Rocco Mediate, USA	341,825
132	Mike Reid, USA	341,395
133	Edward Fryatt, England	339,448
134	Miguel Angel Martin, Spain	338,156
135	Mike Standly, USA	337,122
136	Jose Coceres, Argentina	334,124
137	Skip Kendall, USA	333,605
138	Peter Baker, England	331,160
139	Richard Green, Australia	327,534
140	Don Pooley, USA	326,410

POS.	PLAYER, COUNTRY	TOTAL MONEY
141	Michael Long, New Zealand	324,261
142	Shinichi Yokota, Japan	322,324
143	Len Mattiace, USA	320,156
144	Ted Tryba, USA	319,703
145	Kaname Yokoo, Japan	317,292
146	Yeh Chang-ting, Taiwan	316,316
147	Angel Cabrera, Argentina	312,268
148	Taichi Teshima, Japan	311,578
149	Hidemichi Tanaka, Japan	311,124
150	David Ishii, USA	310,749
151	Yoshinori Kaneko, Japan	309,696
152	Ross McFarlane, England	309,139
153	Stephen Ames, Trinidad & Tobago	308,796
154	Roger Chapman, England	308,743
155	Katsunori Kuwabara, Japan	308,293
156	Brad Bryant, USA	308,227
157	Toshiaki Odate, Japan	307,857
158	David Sutherland, USA	302,663
159	Zaw Moe, Myanmar	302,564
160	Mark Wiebe, USA	301,857
161	Jarmo Sandelin, Sweden	300,351
162	Andrew Coltart, Scotland	299,177
163	Philip Price, Wales	298,358
164	David Gilford, England	295,861
165	Pete Jordan, USA	295,735
166	David Carter, England	293,747
167	David Edwards, USA	292,096
168	Michael Jonzon, Sweden	292,078
169	Toru Nakamura, Japan	292,031
170	Anders Forsbrand, Sweden	291,888
171	Jim Carter, USA	291,295
172	Steve Pate, USA	288,753
173	Robert Gamez, USA	288,716
174	Satoshi Higashi, Japan	287,617
175	Glen Day, USA	287,393
176	Scott Simpson, USA	286,661
177	Fulton Allem, South Africa	285,707
178	Gabriel Hjertstedt, Sweden	284,749
179	Sam Torrance, Scotland	283,709
180	Shigenori Mori, Japan	283,547
181	David Howell, England	283,433
182	Yoshinori Mizumaki, Japan	282,584
183	Hisayuki Sasaki, Japan	279,137
184	Larry Mize, USA	277,345
185	Kenny Perry, USA	275,920
186	Paul Azinger, USA	275,211
187	Alexander Cejka, Germany	275,208
188	Kelly Gibson, USA	272,512
189	Mark Brooks, USA	272,345
190	Todd Hamilton, USA	270,520
191	Phil Tataurangi, New Zealand	270,080
192	Jamie Spence, England	270,013
193	Gerry Norquist, USA	269,157
194	Tsuneyuki Nakajima, Japan	268,894

POS.	PLAYER, COUNTRY	TOTAL MONEY
195	Billy Ray Brown, USA	268,709
196	Peter Senior, Australia	265,067
197	Seiki Okuda, Japan	263,617
198	Niclas Fasth, Sweden	256,659
199	Kiyoshi Maita, Japan	252,638
200	Donnie Hammond, USA	248,799
201	Joe Durant, USA	246,775
202	Tsuyoshi Yoneyama, Japan	243,673
203	P.H. Horgan III, USA	243,664
204	Jerry Kelly, USA	243,257
205	Katsuyoshi Tomori, Japan	242,970
206	Peter Mitchell, England	242,182
207	Mike Cunning, USA	241,851
208	Gordon Brand, Jr., Scotland	241,458
209	Kazuo Kanayama, Japan	240,120
210	Stewart Ginn, Australia	239,994
211	Dennis Edlund, Sweden	238,993
212	Scott Henderson, Scotland	236,809
213	Wayne Westner, South Africa	236,483
214	Ronnie Black, USA	235,424
215	Tom Purtzer, USA	229,325
216	Toshimitsu Izawa, Japan	221,944
217	Frank Lickliter, USA	221,049
218	Nolan Henke, USA	220,535
219	Mark Roe, England	220,465
220	Fuzzy Zoeller, USA	210,926
221	Scott Gump, USA	209,672
222	Clinton Whitelaw, South Africa	208,998
223	Koki Idoki, Japan	208,393
224	Michael Christie, USA	207,959
225	Zhang Lian-wei, China	205,066
226	Omar Uresti, USA	203,516
227	Daniel Chopra, Sweden	202,644
228	Greg Chalmers, Australia	202,240
229	Tommy Armour III, USA	201,664
230	Brian Davis, England	201,325
231	Mike Springer, USA	200,172
232	Joey Sindelar, USA	200,069
233	Paul Lawrie, Scotland	199,258
234	Wayne Levi, USA	198,878
235	Masanobu Kimura, Japan	198,700
236	Doug Barron, USA	198,051
237	Jeev Milkha Singh, India	197,769
238	Thomas Gogele, Germany	197,087
239	Steve Alker, New Zealand	196,564
240	Kevin Wentworth, USA	196,291
241	Willie Wood, USA	195,565
242	Jim Rutledge, Canada	195,523
243	Stephen Leaney, Australia	194,816
244	Steve Stricker, USA	193,491
245	Bruce Lietzke, USA	192,880
246	Curtis Strange, USA	192,252
247	Santiago Luna, Spain	191,272
248	Guy Boros, USA	191,139

POS.	PLAYER, COUNTRY	TOTAL MONEY
249	Ronan Rafferty, N. Ireland	190,289
250	Lanny Wadkins, USA	189,962
251	Lennie Clements, USA	189,958
252	Marc Farry, France	189,647
253	John Daly, USA	189,074
254	John Adams, USA	188,986
255	Larry Rinker, USA	188,281
256	Mark Carnevale, USA	188,159
257	Katsumasa Miyamoto, Japan	186,455
258	Tom Pernice, Jr., USA	185,402
259	Wayne Riley, Australia	184,900
260	Rick Gibson, Canada	184,120
261	Shingo Katayama, Japan	182,555
262	Masayuki Kawamura, Japan	181,719
263	Ryoken Kawagishi, Japan	180,526
264	Peter Hedblom, Sweden	180,045
265	Neal Lancaster, USA	179,273
266	Carl Watts, England	178,921
267	Darren Cole, Australia	178,269
268	Mark Mouland, Wales	175,945
269	Nobumitsu Yuhara, Japan	173,975
270	Jean Van de Velde, France	172,584
271	Brett Quigley, USA	172,023
272	Toru Taniguchi, Japan	171,880
273	Robin Freeman, USA	171,547
274	Shusaku Sugimoto, Japan	171,123
275	Steve Webster, England	170,833
276	Des Terblanche, South Africa	170,134
277	Fabrice Tarnaud, France	170,019
278	Philip Walton, Ireland	168,308
279	Vanslow Phillips, England	168,020
280	Carl Suneson, England	167,567
281	Richard Boxall, England	167,266
282	Cheng Jun, China	167,194
283	Jim McGovern, USA	166,406
284	Iain Pyman, England	166,259
285	Prayad Marksaeng, Thailand	165,979
286	Chris DiMarco, USA	165,181
287	Trevor Dodds, Namibia	165,156
288	Steve Allan, Australia	164,445
289	Jimmy Johnston, USA	164,442
290	Mathias Gronberg, Sweden	164,260
291	Hideyuki Sato, Japan	163,573
292	Daisuke Serizawa, Japan	162,178
293	J.P. Hayes, USA	162,102
294	Kazuhiro Takami, Japan	161,609
295	John Morse, USA	161,363
296	Jon Robson, England	159,675
297	Blaine McCallister, USA	158,466
298	Takaaki Fukuzawa, Japan	158,223
299	Gary Orr, Scotland	157,525
300	Bruce Fleisher, USA	157,365

World Money List Leaders

YEAR	PLAYER, COUNTRY	TOTAL MONEY
1966	Jack Nicklaus, USA	$168,088
1967	Jack Nicklaus, USA	276,166
1968	Billy Casper, USA	222,436
1969	Frank Beard, USA	186,993
1970	Jack Nicklaus, USA	222,583
1971	Jack Nicklaus, USA	285,897
1972	Jack Nicklaus, USA	341,792
1973	Tom Weiskopf, USA	349,645
1974	Johnny Miller, USA	400,255
1975	Jack Nicklaus, USA	332,610
1976	Jack Nicklaus, USA	316,086
1977	Tom Watson, USA	358,034
1978	Tom Watson, USA	384,388
1979	Tom Watson, USA	506,912
1980	Tom Watson, USA	651,921
1981	Johnny Miller, USA	704,204
1982	Raymond Floyd, USA	738,699
1983	Seve Ballesteros, Spain	686,088
1984	Seve Ballesteros, Spain	688,047
1985	Bernhard Langer, Germany	860,262
1986	Greg Norman, Australia	1,146,584
1987	Ian Woosnam, Wales	1,793,268
1988	Seve Ballesteros, Spain	1,261,275
1989	David Frost, South Africa	1,650,230
1990	Jose Maria Olazabal, Spain	1,633,640
1991	Bernhard Langer, Germany	2,186,700
1992	Nick Faldo, England	2,748,248
1993	Nick Faldo, England	2,825,280
1994	Ernie Els, South Africa	2,862,854
1995	Corey Pavin, USA	2,746,340
1996	Colin Montgomerie, Scotland	3,071,442
1997	Colin Montgomerie, Scotland	3,366,900

Career World Money List

The following is a listing of the 50 leading money winners for their careers through the 1997 season. It includes players active on both the regular and senior tours of the world. The World Money List from this and the 31 previous editions of this annual and a table prepared for a companion book, *The Wonderful World of Professional Golf* (Atheneum, 1973), form the basis for this compilation. Additional figures were taken from official records of major golf associations, although the shortcomings in records-keeping in professional golf outside the United States in the 1950s and 1960s and exclusions from U.S. records in a few cases during those years prevent these figures from being completely accurate. Conversions of foreign currency figures to U.S. dollars are based on average values during the particular years involved.

POS.	PLAYER, COUNTRY	TOTAL MONEY
1	Greg Norman, Australia	$20,621,287
2	Masashi Ozaki, Japan	17,064,915
3	Bernhard Langer, Germany	16,498,735
4	Fred Couples, USA	16,186,363
5	Nick Faldo, England	15,834,208
6	Nick Price, Zimbabwe	15,459,273
7	Raymond Floyd, USA	14,489,870
8	Colin Montgomerie, Scotland	14,122,038
9	Lee Trevino, USA	13,734,812
10	Tom Kite, USA	13,144,945
11	David Frost, South Africa	12,992,600
12	Hale Irwin, USA	12,902,134
13	Isao Aoki, Japan	12,873,269
14	Ian Woosnam, Wales	12,855,431
15	Davis Love III, USA	12,633,164
16	Ernie Els, South Africa	11,547,601
17	Seve Ballesteros, Spain	11,486,633
18	Corey Pavin, USA	11,435,086
19	Payne Stewart, USA	11,325,123
20	Scott Hoch, USA	11,174,094
21	Mark O'Meara, USA	10,994,727
22	Mark Calcavecchia, USA	10,847,508
23	Tsuneyuki Nakajima, Japan	10,348,702
24	Tom Watson, USA	10,292,544
25	Bob Charles, New Zealand	10,000,647
26	Bob Murphy, USA	9,971,950
27	Jim Colbert, USA	9,930,746
28	Naomichi Ozaki, Japan	9,896,772
29	Curtis Strange, USA	9,888,453
30	Jack Nicklaus, USA	9,765,788
31	Jose Maria Olazabal, Spain	9,604,115
32	Ben Crenshaw, USA	9,275,912
33	Paul Azinger, USA	9,222,189
34	Craig Stadler, USA	9,132,243
35	Dave Stockton, USA	9,086,334
36	Gary Player, South Africa	9,078,350

POS.	PLAYER, COUNTRY	TOTAL MONEY
37	Steve Elkington, Australia	8,981,081
38	Graham Marsh, Australia	8,948,677
39	Vijay Singh, Fiji	8,669,010
40	George Archer, USA	8,632,222
41	Tom Lehman, USA	8,629,356
42	Chi Chi Rodriguez, Puerto Rico	8,425,887
43	Gil Morgan, USA	8,264,234
44	Lanny Wadkins, USA	8,148,112
45	Mike Hill, USA	7,889,700
46	John Cook, USA	7,699,577
47	Mark McNulty, Zimbabwe	7,566,165
48	Jay Haas, USA	7,503,527
49	Brad Faxon, USA	7,488,490
50	Larry Mize, USA	7,342,690

These 50 players have won $549,907,289 in their lifetimes playing professional tournament golf.

Senior World Money List

This list includes official earnings on the U.S. PGA Tour, U.S. Senior PGA Tour, European Seniors Tour and Japan Senior Tour, along with other winnings in established unofficial events when reliable figures could be obtained.

POS.	PLAYER, COUNTRY	TOTAL MONEY
1	Hale Irwin, USA	$2,736,628
2	Gil Morgan, USA	2,441,016
3	Jay Sigel, USA	1,489,838
4	Isao Aoki, Japan	1,472,839
5	John Bland, South Africa	1,345,917
6	David Graham, Australia	1,271,079
7	Graham Marsh, Australia	1,270,101
8	Dave Stockton, USA	1,186,361
9	Raymond Floyd, USA	997,566
10	Hugh Baiocchi, South Africa	942,726
11	Larry Gilbert, USA	902,816
12	Bob Eastwood, USA	893,908
13	Lee Trevino, USA	868,919
14	John Jacobs, USA	827,942
15	Bruce Summerhays, USA	812,147
16	Dave Eichelberger, USA	809,976
17	Bob Murphy, USA	782,561
18	Jack Kiefer, USA	765,235
19	Walter Morgan, USA	753,426
20	Vicente Fernandez, Argentina	723,554
21	Jim Colbert, USA	706,000

POS.	PLAYER, COUNTRY	TOTAL MONEY
22	Mike Hill, USA	695,640
23	Bob Charles, New Zealand	693,449
24	Larry Nelson, USA	631,438
25	Tom Wargo, USA	615,241
26	Jim Dent, USA	615,146
27	Hubert Green, USA	609,597
28	Bob Duval, USA	588,101
29	Jerry McGee, USA	562,794
30	Bud Allin, USA	541,294
31	Frank Conner, USA	530,396
32	Jimmy Powell, USA	524,026
33	Gary Player, South Africa	522,117
34	J.C. Snead, USA	505,316
35	Bob Dickson, USA	480,521
36	Jack Nicklaus, USA	478,315
37	Gibby Gilbert, USA	469,700
38	Chi Chi Rodriguez, Puerto Rico	465,859
39	Kermit Zarley, USA	429,442
40	Dana Quigley, USA	427,774
41	George Archer, USA	414,605
42	Bruce Crampton, Australia	404,537
43	DeWitt Weaver, USA	395,232
44	Leonard Thompson, USA	384,806
45	John Morgan, England	383,414
46	Dale Douglass, USA	376,303
47	Mike McCullough, USA	373,282
48	Brian Barnes, Scotland	354,886
49	Simon Hobday, South Africa	350,147
50	John Schroeder, USA	345,233
51	Terry Dill, USA	333,522
52	Al Geiberger, USA	317,030
53	Bobby Stroble, USA	311,970
54	Jose Maria Canizares, Spain	307,834
55	Tommy Horton, England	302,170
56	Bob E. Smith, USA	281,130
57	Charles Coody, USA	273,064
58	Rocky Thompson, USA	273,037
59	Jim Albus, USA	268,487
60	Tom Shaw, USA	263,456
61	Buddy Whitten, USA	262,133
62	Larry Laoretti, USA	244,166
63	Tony Jacklin, England	236,952
64	Rick Acton, USA	233,541
65	Dick Hendrickson, USA	220,675
66	Walter Hall, USA	216,400
67	Butch Baird, USA	196,746
68	Calvin Peete, USA	189,192
69	Bob Wynn, USA	187,374
70	Miller Barber, USA	185,113
71	Johnny Miller, USA	169,499
72	Dan Wood, USA	165,457
73	Larry Ziegler, USA	165,39
74	David Oakley, USA	164,844
75	Teruo Sugihara, Japan	161,466

WOMEN'S WORLD MONEY LIST / 329

POS.	PLAYER, COUNTRY	TOTAL MONEY
76	Noel Ratcliffe, Australia	157,538
77	Don January, USA	149,947
78	Walter Zembriski, USA	146,573
79	Harold Henning, South Africa	146,153
80	Will Sowles, USA	144,159
81	Toru Nakayama, Japan	143,089
82	David Ojala, USA	137,666
83	Ichiro Teramoto, Japan	125,220
84	Seiji Ogawa, Japan	123,839
85	Antonio Garrido, Spain	119,182
86	Brian Waites, England	118,044
87	Jim Rhodes, England	107,976
88	Bunky Henry, USA	107,178
89	Seiichi Kanai, Japan	104,321
90	Steven Veriato, USA	103,301
91	Malcolm Gregson, England	99,264
92	Dennis Coscina, USA	98,462
93	Don Bies, USA	98,426
94	Tommy Aaron, USA	97,575
95	David Creamer, England	91,235
96	Arnold Palmer, USA	90,052
97	Hsieh Min-nan, Taiwan	88,015
98	Terry Gale, Australia	86,876
99	Maurice Bembridge, England	86,661
100	Bob Betley, USA	74,597

Women's World Money List

This list includes official earnings on the U.S. LPGA Tour, Women's European Tour, Women's Australasian Tours and Japan LPGA Tour, along with other winnings in established unofficial events when reliable figures could be obtained.

POS.	PLAYER, COUNTRY	TOTAL MONEY
1	Annika Sorenstam, Sweden	$1,460,252
2	Karrie Webb, Australia	1,048,687
3	Kelly Robbins, USA	964,907
4	Akiko Fukushima, Japan	841,326
5	Chris Johnson, USA	785,076
6	Laura Davies, England	694,531
7	Juli Inkster, USA	673,270
8	Liselotte Neumann, Sweden	671,651
9	Tammie Green, USA	631,492
10	Nancy Lopez, USA	564,826
11	Alison Nicholas, England	549,694
12	Betsy King, USA	499,632
13	Ok-Hee Ku, Korea	491,588

POS.	PLAYER, COUNTRY	TOTAL MONEY
14	Michelle McGann, USA	460,633
15	Helen Alfredsson, Sweden	459,847
16	Ikuyo Shiotani, Japan	450,590
17	Colleen Walker, USA	450,186
18	Lorie Kane, Canada	449,964
19	Lisa Hackney, England	443,175
20	Donna Andrews, USA	439,871
21	Hiromi Kobayashi, Japan	437,716
22	Dottie Pepper, USA	411,398
23	Rosie Jones, USA	405,236
24	Amy Fruhwirth, USA	387,919
25	Tina Barrett, USA	375,755
26	Natsuko Noro, Japan	368,148
27	Aki Takamura, Japan	364,120
28	Woo-Soon Ko, Korea	361,868
29	Jane Geddes, USA	359,706
30	Kaori Higo, Japan	359,305
31	Pat Hurst, USA	349,299
32	Cindy Figg-Currier, USA	347,807
33	Terry-Jo Myers, USA	340,678
34	Akemi Yamaoka, Japan	339,556
35	Emilee Klein, USA	331,626
36	Brandie Burton, USA	328,974
37	Fumiko Muraguchi, Japan	325,628
38	Michele Redman, USA	321,292
39	Marnie McGuire, New Zealand	321,253
40	Barb Mucha, USA	314,966
41	Catriona Matthew, Scotland	313,531
42	Suzuko Maeda, Japan	312,272
43	Kris Tschetter, USA	311,473
44	Deb Richard, USA	296,000
45	Michiko Hattori, Japan	292,023
46	Aiko Takasu, Japan	275,811
47	Kaori Harada, Japan	275,144
48	Mayumi Murai, Japan	273,044
49	Kathryn Marshall, Scotland	267,777
50	Sherri Steinhauer, USA	267,739
51	Toshimi Kimura, Japan	260,844
52	Yuko Motoyama, Japan	258,793
53	Kumiko Hiyoshi, Japan	256,254
54	Meg Mallon, USA	255,641
55	Miyuki Shimabukuro, Japan	252,773
56	Tseng Hsiu-Feng, Taiwan	251,326
57	Gail Graham, Canada	247,046
58	Chieko Nishida, Japan	239,67
59	Ae-Sook Kim, Korea	237,69
60	Yoko Inoue, Japan	235,06
61	Young-Me Lee, Korea	233,73
62	Cindy Schreyer, USA	215,66
63	Kim Saiki, USA	210,85
64	Yuri Kawanami, Japan	208,92
65	Wendy Doolan, Australia	207,28
66	Takayo Bandoh, Japan	200,61
67	Nanci Bowen, USA	199,16

WOMEN'S WORLD MONEY LIST

POS.	PLAYER, COUNTRY	TOTAL MONEY
68	Leta Lindley, USA	198,540
69	Huang Yu-Chen, Taiwan	196,767
70	Penny Hammel, USA	195,135
71	Charlotta Sorenstam, Sweden	194,355
72	Karen Weiss, USA	193,273
73	Marie-Laure de Lorenzi, France	191,076
74	Alicia Dibos, Peru	190,991
75	Dawn Coe-Jones, Canada	190,318
76	Fuki Kido, Japan	190,299
77	Kyoko Ono, Japan	189,309
78	Ayako Okamoto, Japan	188,252
79	Nancy Harvey, Canada	187,339
80	Dana Dormann, USA	187,271
81	Nayoko Yoshikawa, Japan	186,810
82	Akane Ohshiro, Japan	186,307
83	Chikayo Yamazaki, Japan	186,303
84	Yuri Fudoh, Japan	186,190
85	Trish Johnson, England	184,659
86	Patty Sheehan, USA	184,390
87	Wendy Ward, USA	184,010
88	Junko Yasui, Japan	179,034
89	Jae-Sook Won, Korea	175,740
90	Yuko Moriguchi, Japan	173,007
91	Mikino Kubo, Japan	171,002
92	Keiko Arai, Japan	160,581
93	Rachel Hetherington, Australia	159,400
94	Susie Redman, USA	152,434
95	Danielle Ammaccapane, USA	152,411
96	Joanne Morley, England	143,447
97	Toshiko Fujisaki, Japan	143,310
98	Jane Crafter, Australia	141,049
99	Shani Waugh, Australia	136,609
100	Mayumi Hirase, Japan	136,146

American Tours

Mercedes Championships

La Costa Resort & Spa, Carlsbad, California
Par 36-36–72; 7,022 yards
(Fourth round cancelled — rain.)

January 9-12
purse, $1,200,000

	SCORES			TOTAL	MONEY
Tiger Woods	70	67	65	202	$216,000
Tom Lehman	66	67	69	202	129,600
(Woods defeated Lehman on first extra hole.)					
Guy Boros	69	68	70	207	81,600
Fred Couples	69	69	70	208	52,800
Paul Goydos	67	71	70	208	52,800
Steve Jones	70	71	68	209	41,700
Davis Love III	70	67	72	209	41,700
John Cook	70	71	69	210	35,600
Jim Furyk	67	68	75	210	35,600
Corey Pavin	70	68	72	210	35,600
Fred Funk	70	72	69	211	30,600
Scott McCarron	70	72	69	211	30,600
Phil Mickelson	71	68	72	211	30,600
Ernie Els	72	70	70	212	26,460
Mark O'Meara	71	72	69	212	26,460
Tom Watson	70	68	74	212	26,460
Michael Bradley	71	74	68	213	22,260
Mark Brooks	72	70	71	213	22,260
Tim Herron	73	72	68	213	22,260
Clarence Rose	71	71	71	213	22,260
Craig Stadler	71	70	72	213	22,260
Nick Faldo	72	71	71	214	19,560
Justin Leonard	69	71	74	214	19,560
Ed Fiori	71	71	73	215	18,160
Scott Hoch	75	69	71	215	18,160
Loren Roberts	71	73	71	215	18,160
Dudley Hart	71	73	72	216	17,316
Steve Stricker	72	73	71	216	17,316
Paul Stankowski	70	72	76	218	16,932
Willie Wood	74	71	74	219	16,692
D.A. Weibring	78	77	69	224	16,452

Bob Hope Chrysler Classic

Indian Wells, California
Indian Wells CC: Par 36-36–72; 6,478 yards
Indian Ridge CC: Par 36-36–72; 7,037 yards
Bermuda Dunes CC: Par 36-36–72; 6,927 yards
La Quinta CC: Par 36-36–72; 6,901 yards

January 15-1*
purse, $1,500,00*

	SCORES					TOTAL	MONEY
John Cook	66	69	67	62	63	327	$270,000
Mark Calcavecchia	64	67	66	64	67	328	162,000
Jesper Parnevik	66	70	68	66	62	332	102,000

AMERICAN TOURS / 333

	SCORES				TOTAL	MONEY
Mark O'Meara	68	66	68	66	65	333	72,000
Don Pooley	70	69	63	65	69	336	57,000
Tommy Tolles	65	69	73	65	64	336	57,000
John Daly	65	73	64	66	69	337	50,250
Grant Waite	68	70	64	68	68	338	46,500
Jay Don Blake	65	67	66	72	69	339	34,714.29
Stewart Cink	68	68	69	68	66	339	34,714.29
Fred Couples	71	71	64	68	65	339	34,714.29
Larry Rinker	63	68	72	70	66	339	34,714.29
Scott Hoch	71	66	67	67	68	339	34,714.28
Steve Jones	64	72	67	68	68	339	34,714.28
Craig Stadler	68	69	70	67	65	339	34,714.28
Doug Martin	70	67	69	69	65	340	25,500
Patrick Burke	69	68	70	68	66	341	22,500
Len Mattiace	66	68	69	70	68	341	22,500
Kirk Triplett	68	69	67	67	70	341	22,500
Robert Damron	67	70	68	69	68	342	16,860
Jim Furyk	68	69	70	68	67	342	16,860
Peter Jacobsen	67	72	67	67	69	342	16,860
Lee Janzen	71	70	70	66	65	342	16,860
Scott McCarron	71	71	68	69	63	342	16,860
Keith Fergus	68	68	70	72	65	343	11,700
Paul Goydos	65	68	76	69	65	343	11,700
Pete Jordan	68	70	70	68	67	343	11,700
Andrew Magee	70	66	70	71	66	343	11,700
Mark Wiebe	74	68	69	65	67	343	11,700
Doug Barron	70	66	70	68	70	344	9,525
Brad Bryant	71	66	72	70	65	344	9,525
Rick Fehr	70	71	65	68	70	344	9,525
John Huston	69	68	73	70	64	344	9,525
Mark Brooks	69	68	72	66	65	73	345	7,414.29
Michael Christie	72	69	70	66	68	345	7,414.29
Larry Mize	69	68	69	70	69	345	7,414.29
Hal Sutton	72	70	66	67	70	345	7,414.29
John Adams	68	71	68	70	68	345	7,414.28
Blaine McCallister	67	69	70	71	68	345	7,414.28
Scott Simpson	71	68	69	67	70	345	7,414.28
Russ Cochran	66	68	71	71	70	346	5,700
Jay Haas	72	64	70	73	67	346	5,700
Steve Lowery	71	67	69	70	69	346	5,700
Fuzzy Zoeller	67	70	70	68	71	346	5,700
Jimmy Green	72	67	71	66	71	347	4,204.29
Skip Kendall	68	69	69	67	74	347	4,204.29
Curtis Strange	70	72	66	71	68	347	4,204.29
David Toms	72	67	69	69	70	347	4,204.29
David Berganio, Jr.	70	71	70	70	66	347	4,204.28
Ken Green	68	68	71	73	67	347	4,204.28
Willie Wood	69	69	71	67	71	347	4,204.28
Ronnie Black	68	68	75	69	68	348	3,430
David Duval	73	70	67	69	69	348	3,430
Jim Gallagher, Jr.	67	71	71	68	71	348	3,430
Scott Gump	66	68	74	69	71	348	3,430
Jerry Kelly	69	69	71	70	69	348	3,430
Greg Kraft	72	70	70	66	70	348	3,430
Dave Rummells	74	68	67	71	68	348	3,430
Gene Sauers	68	74	68	68	70	348	3,430
Chip Sullivan	70	70	66	72	70	348	3,430
Glen Day	68	71	68	73	69	349	3,195
Hubert Green	72	71	70	68	68	349	3,195
Jeff Maggert	69	73	70	69	68	349	3,195

	SCORES	TOTAL	MONEY
Naomichi Ozaki	68 75 70 67 69	349	3,195
Steve Pate	71 70 68 71 69	349	3,195
Duffy Waldorf	69 70 66 67 77	349	3,195
Tommy Armour III	74 73 69 65 69	350	3,045
Guy Boros	67 72 72 70 69	350	3,045
Corey Pavin	69 72 70 70 69	350	3,045
Lee Rinker	66 75 67 71 71	350	3,045
Robin Freeman	72 70 66 71 72	351	2,955
Bob Tway	69 72 72 69 71	351	2,955
Bruce Lietzke	72 71 66 70 73	352	2,850
Sandy Lyle	67 74 71 69 71	352	2,850
John Mahaffey	72 72 65 72 71	352	2,850
Lee Porter	70 73 70 68 71	352	2,850
Phil Tataurangi	67 71 77 65 72	352	2,850
David Edwards	70 67 71 72 73	353	2,760
Olin Browne	68 72 72 69 73	354	2,700
Jim Carter	71 68 72 70 73	354	2,700
Larry Silveira	70 71 72 68 73	354	2,700

Phoenix Open

TPC of Scottsdale, Scottsdale, Arizona
Par 35-36–71; 6,992 yards

January 23-26
purse, $1,500,000

	SCORES	TOTAL	MONEY
Steve Jones	62 64 65 67	258	$270,000
Jesper Parnevik	66 66 70 67	269	162,000
Nick Price	64 72 65 69	270	102,000
Mark Calcavecchia	68 66 67 71	272	62,000
Rick Fehr	66 68 66 72	272	62,000
Kenny Parry	74 67 66 65	272	62,000
Scott McCarron	71 68 64 70	273	40,607.15
Phil Mickelson	70 71 66 66	273	40,607.15
Fulton Allem	67 67 66 73	273	40,607.14
Dan Forsman	69 67 65 72	273	40,607.14
Mike Hulbert	69 69 66 69	273	40,607.14
Tom Lehman	68 69 68 68	273	40,607.14
Tommy Tolles	66 65 69 73	273	40,607.14
Woody Austin	69 65 68 72	274	26,250
David Duval	66 65 65 78	274	26,250
Lee Janzen	70 67 68 69	274	26,250
Don Pooley	69 67 66 72	274	26,250
Russ Cochran	72 69 68 66	275	20,250
Andrew Magee	70 71 68 66	275	20,250
Hal Sutton	71 67 66 71	275	20,250
Tiger Woods	68 68 67 72	275	20,250
Brandel Chamblee	68 72 68 68	276	15,000
Scott Hoch	71 67 71 67	276	15,000
Len Mattiace	70 70 66 70	276	15,000
Larry Mize	68 68 68 72	276	15,000
Paul Azinger	69 63 70 75	277	11,325
Mark Brooks	69 66 72 70	277	11,325
Allen Doyle	71 65 72 69	277	11,325
Jim Furyk	71 68 66 72	277	11,325
Phil Blackmar	66 70 68 74	278	9,525
Mike Brisky	70 66 69 73	278	9,525
Jeff Maggert	68 67 70 73	278	9,525

	SCORES			TOTAL	MONEY
Ted Tryba	71	67	69	71	278	9,525
Michael Bradley	72	66	67	74	279	7,414.29
Jimmy Johnston	70	68	69	72	279	7,414.29
Steve Lowery	69	72	71	67	279	7,414.29
Lee Rinker	69	71	68	71	279	7,414.29
Ed Fiori	70	68	71	70	279	7,414.28
Tom Purtzer	69	68	72	70	279	7,414.28
Bob Tway	68	68	73	70	279	7,414.28
Jay Don Blake	69	71	69	71	280	5,550
Jim Carter	72	69	67	72	280	5,550
Scott Dunlap	67	72	70	71	280	5,550
Peter Jacobsen	72	69	68	71	280	5,550
David Ogrin	70	69	70	71	280	5,550
Guy Boros	69	69	69	74	281	4,252.50
Naomichi Ozaki	66	74	70	71	281	4,252.50
Steve Pate	71	70	69	71	281	4,252.50
Omar Uresti	68	68	68	77	281	4,252.50
Kelly Gibson	67	73	72	70	282	3,565.72
Paul Stankowski	69	70	70	73	282	3,565.72
Lanny Wadkins	71	70	69	72	282	3,565.72
Tommy Armour III	68	68	68	78	282	3,565.71
Paul Goydos	70	68	72	72	282	3,565.71
Tim Herron	69	70	70	73	282	3,565.71
David Toms	69	68	72	73	282	3,565.71
Brad Fabel	72	69	69	73	283	3,390
Doug Barron	69	72	72	71	284	3,315
Chip Beck	66	73	71	74	284	3,315
Nolan Henke	72	68	73	71	284	3,315
Scott Simpson	70	71	73	70	284	3,315
Billy Andrade	70	69	72	74	285	3,165
Patrick Burke	71	69	75	70	285	3,165
Fred Funk	71	69	71	74	285	3,165
Bob Gilder	73	65	73	74	285	3,165
Hugh Royer III	71	70	71	73	285	3,165
Steve Stricker	75	66	69	75	285	3,165
Rocco Mediate	66	72	71	77	286	3,045
Curtis Strange	73	68	72	73	286	3,045
Jim Gallagher, Jr.	67	72	73	75	287	2,985
Scott Gump	70	71	72	74	287	2,985
John Huston	68	70	73	77	288	2,940
Taylor Smith	67	73	76	76	292	2,910

AT&T Pebble Beach National Pro-Am

Pebble Beach, California
Pebble Beach GL: Par 36-36–72; 6,799 yards
Spyglass Hill GC: Par 36-36–72; 6,859 yards
Poppy Hills GC: Par 36-36–72; 6,861 yards

January 30-February 2
purse, $1,900,000

	SCORES			TOTAL	MONEY
Mark O'Meara	67	67	67	67	268	$342,000
David Duval	65	71	62	71	269	167,200
Tiger Woods	70	72	63	64	269	167,200
Jim Furyk	67	65	69	72	273	91,200
Jesper Parnevik	65	70	67	72	274	72,200
Craig Stadler	70	69	66	69	274	72,200
Billy Andrade	66	75	66	68	275	61,275

	SCORES				TOTAL	MONEY
Paul Azinger	69	70	67	69	275	61,275
Mike Brisky	69	68	68	71	276	53,200
Glen Day	70	69	67	70	276	53,200
Brian Henninger	66	69	71	71	277	41,800
Paul Stankowski	67	67	74	69	277	41,800
Ted Tryba	68	67	72	70	277	41,800
Mark Wiebe	69	68	71	69	277	41,800
Steve Elkington	70	66	69	73	278	30,400
Brad Faxon	70	69	69	70	278	30,400
Doug Martin	70	70	69	69	278	30,400
Vijay Singh	67	68	71	72	278	30,400
Tom Watson	68	71	68	71	278	30,400
Tommy Armour III	73	67	68	71	279	17,179.17
Emlyn Aubrey	68	71	71	69	279	17,179.17
Jim Carter	70	70	69	70	279	17,179.17
Jay Haas	70	69	70	70	279	17,179.17
Neal Lancaster	73	70	68	68	279	17,179.17
Tom Lehman	66	71	70	72	279	17,179.17
Jim McGovern	69	71	71	68	279	17,179.17
Rocco Mediate	71	68	71	69	279	17,179.17
Patrick Burke	71	70	70	68	279	17,179.16
Mark Calcavecchia	69	73	67	70	279	17,179.16
David Frost	70	63	74	72	279	17,179.16
Larry Silveira	68	67	75	69	279	17,179.16
Clarence Rose	70	70	69	71	280	11,780
Robert Damron	72	74	65	70	281	10,260
Fred Funk	68	74	69	70	281	10,260
Phil Mickelson	67	71	69	74	281	10,260
Naomichi Ozaki	68	72	69	72	281	10,260
Tommy Tolles	73	69	70	69	281	10,260
John Adams	70	72	70	70	282	6,862.17
Billy Ray Brown	69	68	74	71	282	6,862.17
Brad Bryant	71	74	67	70	282	6,862.17
Nick Faldo	67	70	72	73	282	6,862.17
Tim Herron	69	68	69	76	282	6,862.17
Steve Lowery	75	68	69	70	282	6,862.17
Brett Quigley	70	69	73	70	282	6,862.17
Kevin Sutherland	72	68	68	74	282	6,862.17
Joel Edwards	69	69	70	74	282	6,862.16
Mike Hulbert	68	70	74	70	282	6,862.16
Frank Lickliter	68	75	68	71	282	6,862.16
Dan Pohl	69	72	67	74	282	6,862.16
Sandy Lyle	72	67	70	74	283	4,547.34
Kenny Perry	70	74	67	72	283	4,547.34
Peter Jacobsen	70	75	67	71	283	4,547.33
Craig Kanada	68	73	69	73	283	4,547.33
Jerry Kelly	70	71	71	71	283	4,547.33
Skip Kendall	67	71	73	72	283	4,547.33
Michael Christie	69	70	71	74	284	4,313
Steve Jones	68	74	70	72	284	4,313
Joe Acosta, Jr.	70	68	70	77	285	4,218
Davis Love III	69	71	70	75	285	4,218
David Toms	73	75	64	73	285	4,218
Tom Purtzer	74	69	69	74	286	4,142
Jeff Sluman	72	69	71	76	288	4,104
Shigeki Maruyama	70	75	67	78	290	4,066
John Morse	72	68	72	79	291	4,028

Buick Invitational

Torrey Pines Golf Course, La Jolla, California
South Course: Par 36-36—72; 7,055 yards
North Course: Par 36-36—72; 6,601 yards

February 6-9
purse, $1,500,000

	SCORES				TOTAL	MONEY
Mark O'Meara	67	66	71	71	275	$270,000
Donnie Hammond	73	67	68	69	277	78,107.15
David Ogrin	67	71	70	69	277	78,107.15
Mike Hulbert	68	69	67	73	277	78,107.14
Lee Janzen	71	65	71	70	277	78,107.14
Jesper Parnevik	70	66	69	72	277	78,107.14
Craig Stadler	67	68	70	72	277	78,107.14
Duffy Waldorf	70	66	72	69	277	78,107.14
Skip Kendall	67	71	71	69	278	42,000
Steve Lowery	67	66	75	70	278	42,000
Billy Andrade	69	70	67	73	279	31,800
Jay Don Blake	65	71	66	77	279	31,800
Michael Bradley	71	63	72	73	279	31,800
Kelly Gibson	70	68	72	69	279	31,800
Bob Tway	64	72	71	72	279	31,800
Tim Herron	68	70	69	73	280	24,750
Scott Simpson	69	68	71	72	280	24,750
Tom Byrum	70	69	73	69	281	18,257.15
Sandy Lyle	71	68	72	70	281	18,257.15
David Duval	69	69	72	71	281	18,257.14
Rick Fehr	72	66	73	70	281	18,257.14
J.P. Hayes	72	70	68	71	281	18,257.14
Jimmy Johnston	73	67	72	69	281	18,257.14
Taylor Smith	65	75	69	72	281	18,257.14
Curt Byrum	68	70	71	73	282	11,962.50
Fred Funk	68	73	68	73	282	11,962.50
Brent Geiberger	71	69	71	71	282	11,962.50
Omar Uresti	68	71	72	71	282	11,962.50
Jim Carter	70	67	72	74	283	9,750
John Cook	71	67	71	74	283	9,750
Brett Quigley	70	70	74	69	283	9,750
Kevin Sutherland	71	67	70	75	283	9,750
Mark Wiebe	67	71	71	74	283	9,750
Dan Forsman	66	70	74	74	284	7,912.50
Jay Haas	71	71	71	71	284	7,912.50
Tom Pernice, Jr.	66	72	73	73	284	7,912.50
Chris Perry	72	70	72	70	284	7,912.50
Brandel Chamblee	72	67	73	73	285	6,150
Tom Kite	67	70	74	74	285	6,150
Andrew Magee	71	69	72	73	285	6,150
Jim McGovern	69	73	74	69	285	6,150
Phil Mickelson	69	67	77	72	285	6,150
Steve Pate	68	73	69	75	285	6,150
Lee Rinker	70	71	73	71	285	6,150
Howard Clark	69	72	73	72	286	4,290
Pete Jordan	68	74	72	72	286	4,290
Neal Lancaster	70	70	74	72	286	4,290
Frank Lickliter	66	68	76	76	286	4,290
Dave Stockton, Jr.	67	73	75	71	286	4,290
Kirk Triplett	71	71	71	73	286	4,290
Marco Dawson	68	71	72	76	287	3,610
Peter Jacobsen	73	68	72	74	287	3,610
Tim Simpson	69	71	73	74	287	3,610

	SCORES				TOTAL	MONEY
Todd Demsey	70	69	77	72	288	3,420
P.H. Horgan III	72	67	72	77	288	3,420
John Maginnes	71	67	74	76	288	3,420
Rocco Mediate	72	67	74	75	288	3,420
Chris Stutts	70	71	77	70	288	3,420
Scott Gump	69	69	75	76	289	3,300
Jeff Hart	72	70	70	77	289	3,300
Davis Love III	71	70	73	75	289	3,300
Ronnie Black	72	70	73	75	290	3,210
Russ Cochran	69	69	76	76	290	3,210
John Wilson	69	70	74	77	290	3,210
John Adams	72	67	75	77	291	3,090
Mike Brisky	67	75	75	74	291	3,090
Lennie Clements	69	69	76	77	291	3,090
Joel Edwards	67	75	76	73	291	3,090
Brad Faxon	70	70	77	74	291	3,090
Olin Browne	65	70	80	77	292	3,000
Brad Fabel	67	70	74	82	293	2,955
Paul Goydos	70	70	75	78	293	2,955
Chip Sullivan	69	71	77	77	294	2,910
Gary McCord	71	70	78	76	295	2,880
Doug Barron	72	69	78	77	296	2,835
Michael Fergin	70	70	75	81	296	2,835
Ed Fiori	67	75	74	81	297	2,790
Guy Boros	74	68	80	77	299	2,760

United Airlines Hawaiian Open

Waialae Country Club, Honolulu, Hawaii
Par 36-36–72; 7,012 yards

February 13-16
purse, $1,200,000

	SCORES				TOTAL	MONEY
Paul Stankowski	71	66	64	70	271	$216,000
Jim Furyk	70	67	66	68	271	105,600
Mike Reid	62	72	66	71	271	105,600
(Stankowski defeated Reid on first and Furyk on fourth extra hole.)						
Jay Don Blake	68	70	65	70	273	52,800
Donnie Hammond	70	68	66	69	273	52,800
Tom Lehman	65	69	69	71	274	43,200
Paul Goydos	70	66	71	68	275	38,700
Lee Porter	70	66	67	72	275	38,700
Stuart Appleby	67	70	69	71	277	31,200
Paul Azinger	67	70	69	71	277	31,200
Joe Durant	69	69	69	70	277	31,200
Taylor Smith	72	66	68	71	277	31,200
Brad Bryant	68	71	71	68	278	21,200
Tom Byrum	67	70	71	70	278	21,200
Brian Claar	62	75	69	72	278	21,200
Pete Jordan	63	70	73	72	278	21,200
Scott Simpson	65	66	74	73	278	21,200
Craig Stadler	71	66	72	69	278	21,200
Doug Barron	67	69	69	74	279	13,050
Shane Bertsch	68	67	72	72	279	13,050
Ed Dougherty	64	69	71	75	279	13,050
Bruce Fleisher	70	68	68	73	279	13,050
Brent Geiberger	69	69	68	73	279	13,050
Tim Herron	66	70	68	75	279	13,050

		SCORES			TOTAL	MONEY
John Maginnes	68	67	71	73	279	13,050
Len Mattiace	64	70	69	76	279	13,050
Brandel Chamblee	71	67	70	72	280	8,700
John Daly	67	69	69	75	280	8,700
David Ogrin	71	68	72	69	280	8,700
Duffy Waldorf	65	69	72	74	280	8,700
Guy Boros	69	68	72	72	281	6,805.72
John Dowdall	67	72	69	73	281	6,805.72
Billy Mayfair	70	67	71	73	281	6,805.72
Robert Gamez	70	67	73	71	281	6,805.71
Nolan Henke	69	68	68	76	281	6,805.71
Don Pooley	67	72	66	76	281	6,805.71
Anthony Rodriguez	68	69	69	75	281	6,805.71
Dave Barr	67	71	70	74	282	5,400
Kelly Gibson	65	75	70	72	282	5,400
Corey Pavin	71	68	71	72	282	5,400
Phil Blackmar	68	67	72	76	283	4,560
Keith Fergus	70	68	70	75	283	4,560
Jeff Hart	67	73	69	74	283	4,560
Frank Lickliter	68	69	71	75	283	4,560
Patrick Burke	71	68	70	75	284	3,432
Curt Byrum	69	69	71	75	284	3,432
Mark Calcavecchia	73	67	68	76	284	3,432
Paul Claxton	69	70	71	74	284	3,432
Peter Jacobsen	72	68	73	71	284	3,432
Tom Scherrer	70	68	70	76	284	3,432
Todd Demsey	72	67	73	73	285	2,841.60
Dudley Hart	70	70	71	74	285	2,841.60
Hideki Kase	71	69	70	75	285	2,841.60
Steve Stricker	69	69	74	73	285	2,841.60
Bob Wolcott	70	68	74	73	285	2,841.60
Chip Beck	70	70	71	75	286	2,688
Wayne Levi	69	69	71	77	286	2,688
Nobuo Serizawa	70	66	72	78	286	2,688
Jim Thorpe	65	70	75	76	286	2,688
Howard Twitty	71	69	75	71	286	2,688
Lennie Clements	69	69	72	77	287	2,580
Scott Dunlap	68	71	72	76	287	2,580
J.P. Hayes	67	71	74	75	287	2,580
Darrell Kestner	69	69	73	76	287	2,580
David Ishii	70	70	72	76	288	2,520
Dan Forsman	70	69	71	79	289	2,496
Joel Edwards	66	70	74	80	290	2,472
Jimmy Green	66	72	76	77	291	2,436
Mike Springer	73	67	72	79	291	2,436

Tucson Chrysler Classic

Omni Tucson National Resort, Tucson, Arizona
Par 36-36–72; 7,148 yards

February 20-23
purse, $1,300,000

	SCORES			TOTAL	MONEY
Jeff Sluman	75	68	65	67	275	$234,000
Steve Jones	66	68	72	70	276	140,400
Brad Bryant	68	69	67	73	277	75,400
Paul Stankowski	72	65	69	71	277	75,400
Lee Janzen	72	71	66	69	278	44,070

		SCORES			TOTAL	MONEY
Tom Kite	69	70	71	68	278	44,070
Jeff Maggert	66	72	70	70	278	44,070
Don Pooley	67	73	70	68	278	44,070
Clarence Rose	67	72	68	71	278	44,070
Jerry Kelly	72	68	69	70	279	32,500
Andrew Magee	70	72	67	70	279	32,500
Mike Reid	70	69	69	71	279	32,500
Scott Gump	69	74	72	65	280	24,375
Len Mattiace	71	74	71	64	280	24,375
Phil Mickelson	71	71	69	69	280	24,375
Kirk Triplett	68	69	72	71	280	24,375
Russ Cochran	69	71	70	71	281	17,011.43
Jim Gallagher, Jr.	71	70	70	70	281	17,011.43
Bob Tway	67	74	69	71	281	17,011.43
Tom Watson	73	71	67	70	281	17,011.43
Mark Wiebe	68	72	73	68	281	17,011.43
John Wilson	70	71	72	68	281	17,011.43
Michael Bradley	71	70	69	71	281	17,011.42
Joe Durant	74	68	70	70	282	11,440
David Duval	69	72	70	71	282	11,440
Chris Perry	72	70	71	69	282	11,440
Olin Browne	71	70	72	70	283	8,653.13
Stewart Cink	74	70	71	68	283	8,653.13
David Ogrin	74	70	71	68	283	8,653.13
Naomichi Ozaki	69	72	73	69	283	8,653.13
Billy Andrade	69	72	69	73	283	8,653.12
Scott Dunlap	67	73	69	74	283	8,653.12
Hideki Kase	74	69	70	70	283	8,653.12
Justin Leonard	70	69	69	75	283	8,653.12
Jim Furyk	72	72	70	70	284	6,409
Tom Purtzer	70	74	71	69	284	6,409
Payne Stewart	74	70	70	70	284	6,409
David Toms	70	72	74	68	284	6,409
Lanny Wadkins	70	74	69	71	284	6,409
Ronnie Black	73	69	73	70	285	5,330
Nolan Henke	72	73	69	71	285	5,330
Tom Kalinowski	74	71	73	67	285	5,330
Shane Bertsch	74	69	69	74	286	4,290
Jay Don Blake	68	73	74	71	286	4,290
Lennie Clements	71	73	72	70	286	4,290
Glen Day	72	73	70	71	286	4,290
Taylor Smith	74	71	69	72	286	4,290
Jim Carter	70	74	73	70	287	3,231.43
Steve Lowery	70	75	71	71	287	3,231.43
John Maginnes	74	71	71	71	287	3,231.43
Jack O'Keefe	74	69	74	70	287	3,231.43
Steve Stricker	73	71	72	71	287	3,231.43
Scott Verplank	74	70	71	72	287	3,231.43
Stuart Appleby	73	72	73	69	287	3,231.42
Tommy Armour III	74	70	72	72	288	2,925
Doug Barron	75	68	75	70	288	2,925
John Daly	71	74	73	70	288	2,925
Todd Demsey	72	72	75	69	288	2,925
Robert Gamez	70	74	74	70	288	2,925
Mike Hulbert	71	73	74	70	288	2,925
Dan Forsman	73	72	69	75	289	2,769
Jeff Hart	67	75	75	72	289	2,769
Tim Herron	70	72	73	74	289	2,769
Tim Simpson	71	72	71	75	289	2,769
Grant Waite	73	69	70	77	289	2,769

	SCORES				TOTAL	MONEY
Duffy Waldorf	73	71	74	71	289	2,769
Brandel Chamblee	73	71	73	73	290	2,652
Ken Green	71	70	75	74	290	2,652
Shaun Micheel	70	72	74	74	290	2,652
Mike Brisky	72	71	73	75	291	2,600
Allen Doyle	73	72	75	72	292	2,561
Rick Fehr	72	73	76	71	292	2,561
Gabriel Hjertstedt	70	75	75	73	293	2,522
Jim McGovern	69	71	79	75	294	2,496
Larry Nelson	73	71	76	77	297	2,470

Nissan Open

Riviera Country Club, Pacific Palisades, California
Par 35-36–71; 6,946 yards

February 27-March 2
purse, $1,400,000

	SCORES				TOTAL	MONEY
Nick Faldo	66	70	68	68	272	$252,000
Craig Stadler	71	66	68	70	275	151,200
Scott Hoch	65	71	71	69	276	95,200
Fred Funk	67	71	71	68	277	61,600
Tom Purtzer	67	71	69	70	277	61,600
Robin Freeman	69	71	68	70	278	46,900
Scott McCarron	68	73	64	73	278	46,900
Omar Uresti	70	71	69	68	278	46,900
Fred Couples	68	70	70	71	279	31,325
Paul Goydos	66	74	70	69	279	31,325
Peter Jacobsen	68	75	68	68	279	31,325
Mark O'Meara	67	69	72	71	279	31,325
David Ogrin	68	71	72	68	279	31,325
Naomichi Ozaki	73	69	68	69	279	31,325
Payne Stewart	65	72	72	70	279	31,325
Ted Tryba	70	66	74	69	279	31,325
Jeff Maggert	69	71	72	68	280	21,000
Frank Nobilo	71	70	70	69	280	21,000
Steve Pate	71	72	67	70	280	21,000
Ed Dougherty	69	75	69	68	281	14,600
Brent Geiberger	74	69	68	70	281	14,600
Larry Nelson	71	72	69	69	281	14,600
Don Pooley	67	68	75	71	281	14,600
Bob Tway	73	71	66	71	281	14,600
Willie Wood	71	68	72	70	281	14,600
Tiger Woods	70	70	72	69	281	14,600
Stewart Cink	70	74	69	69	282	9,730
Brad Faxon	73	65	73	71	282	9,730
Jay Haas	72	69	69	72	282	9,730
Jeff Hart	71	71	73	67	282	9,730
Billy Mayfair	72	70	73	67	282	9,730
Larry Rinker	71	72	72	67	282	9,730
Lennie Clements	71	68	78	66	283	6,937.78
Russ Cochran	72	70	68	73	283	6,937.78
Bob Estes	68	70	72	73	283	6,937.78
Hideki Kase	73	71	70	69	283	6,937.78
Clarence Rose	74	70	70	69	283	6,937.78
Scott Simpson	69	73	70	71	283	6,937.78
Tom Watson	67	71	76	69	283	6,937.78
David Duval	72	72	69	70	283	6,937.77

	SCORES				TOTAL	MONEY
Taylor Smith	72	72	68	71	283	6,937.77
Frank Lickliter	67	71	77	69	284	5,180
John Maginnes	72	72	69	71	284	5,180
Kenny Perry	72	67	76	69	284	5,180
Rafael Alarcon	70	69	75	71	285	4,004
Todd Demsey	71	72	74	68	285	4,004
Donnie Hammond	74	69	71	71	285	4,004
Brett Quigley	71	71	71	72	285	4,004
Mike Springer	72	72	72	69	285	4,004
Dave Stockton, Jr.	69	72	73	71	285	4,004
Justin Leonard	71	70	73	72	286	3,294.67
Corey Pavin	73	70	72	71	286	3,294.67
Tim Simpson	71	69	74	72	286	3,294.67
Duffy Waldorf	69	74	75	68	286	3,294.67
Skip Kendall	71	73	73	69	286	3,294.66
Hugh Royer III	73	71	72	70	286	3,294.66
Kevin Burton	70	73	74	70	287	3,094
Chen Tze-chung	72	71	72	72	287	3,094
Jay Delsing	69	72	74	72	287	3,094
Scott Gump	70	73	69	75	287	3,094
Yoshinori Kaneko	70	72	77	68	287	3,094
Phil Tataurangi	73	70	70	74	287	3,094
Phil Blackmar	71	69	75	73	288	2,954
Mark Brooks	71	72	73	72	288	2,954
Joe Cioe	71	72	71	74	288	2,954
Kelly Gibson	72	69	70	77	288	2,954
Patrick Boyd	72	72	73	72	289	2,842
Olin Browne	71	72	74	72	289	2,842
Jim Carter	72	68	69	80	289	2,842
J.P. Hayes	71	70	72	76	289	2,842
Michael Christie	73	71	75	71	290	2,744
Kelly Manos	73	71	73	73	290	2,744
Mike Standly	71	70	76	73	290	2,744
Jay Don Blake	74	69	74	75	292	2,674
Kirk Triplett	69	71	77	75	292	2,674
Sonny Skinner	69	73	75	77	294	2,632

Doral-Ryder Open

Doral Resort & Spa, Miami, Florida
Par 36-36–72; 6,939 yards

March 6-9
purse, $1,800,000

	SCORES				TOTAL	MONEY
Steve Elkington	70	66	70	69	275	$324,000
Nick Price	68	67	70	72	277	158,400
Larry Nelson	72	66	69	70	277	158,400
David Duval	68	66	70	74	278	86,400
Fulton Allem	70	70	70	70	280	65,700
Ronnie Black	67	71	70	72	280	65,700
Robert Damron	72	66	71	71	280	65,700
Brad Bryant	69	70	74	68	281	55,800
Wayne Levi	70	72	68	72	282	46,800
Greg Norman	66	68	74	74	282	46,800
Craig Stadler	71	72	67	72	282	46,800
Bob Tway	66	71	70	75	282	46,800
Jay Haas	67	72	74	70	283	33,750
Billy Mayfair	70	67	77	69	283	33,750

	SCORES				TOTAL	MONEY
Chris Perry	71	67	72	73	283	33,750
Vijay Singh	72	72	69	70	283	33,750
Mike Brisky	70	71	72	71	284	28,800
Michael Bradley	70	71	76	68	285	26,100
Doug Martin	67	71	74	73	285	26,100
Phil Blackmar	73	70	73	70	286	18,157.50
Stewart Cink	67	74	71	74	286	18,157.50
Scott Gump	71	68	76	71	286	18,157.50
Peter Jacobsen	70	71	68	77	286	18,157.50
Jerry Kelly	71	70	69	76	286	18,157.50
Phil Mickelson	69	68	71	78	286	18,157.50
Colin Montgomerie	69	69	73	75	286	18,157.50
Ted Tryba	70	69	72	75	286	18,157.50
Billy Andrade	68	71	74	74	287	11,712.86
Neal Lancaster	74	69	70	74	287	11,712.86
Jesper Parnevik	72	66	74	75	287	11,712.86
Kenny Perry	71	72	72	72	287	11,712.86
Larry Rinker	69	72	72	74	287	11,712.86
Steve Lowery	72	71	69	75	287	11,712.85
Lee Rinker	66	74	72	75	287	11,712.85
Scott Hoch	71	73	70	74	288	9,720
Jim Carter	72	72	73	72	289	8,662.50
John Cook	70	73	72	74	289	8,662.50
John Maginnes	71	70	74	74	289	8,662.50
Craig Parry	70	70	74	75	289	8,662.50
Keith Clearwater	71	72	71	76	290	7,200
Nick Faldo	71	68	75	76	290	7,200
Bill Glasson	71	73	71	75	290	7,200
Brett Quigley	70	72	76	72	290	7,200
*Robert Floyd	71	68	75	76	290	
Glen Day	70	73	76	72	291	5,594.40
Robin Freeman	70	74	72	75	291	5,594.40
Jim Furyk	72	71	74	74	291	5,594.40
Sandy Lyle	67	71	78	75	291	5,594.40
Clarence Rose	74	69	74	74	291	5,594.40
David Berganio, Jr.	69	75	71	77	292	4,398
Mark Brooks	72	72	74	74	292	4,398
Kelly Gibson	69	74	76	73	292	4,398
Paul Goydos	69	74	73	76	292	4,398
Joey Sindelar	72	72	75	73	292	4,398
Scott Verplank	73	71	73	75	292	4,398
Russ Cochran	71	70	77	75	293	4,068
Raymond Floyd	69	74	76	74	293	4,068
Pete Jordan	70	73	73	77	293	4,068
Skip Kendall	65	76	76	76	293	4,068
Mark O'Meara	75	69	74	75	293	4,068
Michael Christie	71	71	71	81	294	3,906
Bruce Lietzke	69	70	72	83	294	3,906
Tom Purtzer	72	71	75	76	294	3,906
Tommy Tolles	68	71	79	76	294	3,906
Grant Waite	72	68	76	79	295	3,816
Dan Forsman	74	69	72	81	296	3,762
John Morse	70	72	76	78	296	3,762
Naomichi Ozaki	70	72	76	79	297	3,690
David Toms	70	73	78	76	297	3,690
Hal Sutton	70	71	76	81	298	3,636
Pat Bates	70	72	77	80	299	3,582
Jeff Sluman	72	68	78	81	299	3,582
Andrew Magee	72	72	81	78	303	3,528

Honda Classic

TPC at Heron Bay, Coral Springs, Florida
Par 36-36–72; 7,030 yards

March 13-16
purse, $1,500,000

	SCORES				TOTAL	MONEY
Stuart Appleby	68	68	67	71	274	$270,000
Michael Bradley	69	65	73	68	275	132,000
Payne Stewart	68	68	68	71	275	132,000
Colin Montgomerie	68	68	70	71	277	72,000
Ronnie Black	69	71	68	70	278	44,250
Mike Brisky	71	66	70	71	278	44,250
Joe Durant	69	71	68	70	278	44,250
Andrew Magee	70	68	68	72	278	44,250
Doug Martin	69	66	72	71	278	44,250
Jesper Parnevik	71	69	68	70	278	44,250
Craig Parry	74	64	70	70	278	44,250
Paul Stankowski	67	66	72	73	278	44,250
Robert Gamez	70	66	70	72	278	44,250
Jim Carter	72	66	70	71	279	24,750
Marco Dawson	72	69	69	69	279	24,750
Tim Herron	73	67	67	72	279	24,750
P.H. Horgan III	69	69	68	73	279	24,750
Lee Janzen	67	68	71	73	279	24,750
Kenny Perry	71	69	71	68	279	24,750
Curt Byrum	73	66	69	72	280	18,100
Brent Geiberger	73	67	70	70	280	18,100
Hideki Kase	72	66	72	70	280	18,100
Ernie Els	72	69	71	69	281	14,400
Tim Simpson	70	70	71	70	281	14,400
Mike Standly	73	69	69	70	281	14,400
John Huston	69	65	72	76	282	11,325
Bernhard Langer	70	70	71	71	282	11,325
Bruce Lietzke	69	69	71	73	282	11,325
Dick Mast	70	71	66	75	282	11,325
Phil Blackmar	69	72	71	71	283	9,315
Greg Kraft	68	67	72	76	283	9,315
Tom Lehman	72	68	68	75	283	9,315
Len Mattiace	71	69	71	72	283	9,315
Vijay Singh	72	69	72	70	283	9,315
Guy Boros	69	69	70	76	284	7,912.50
Ian Woosnam	70	67	71	76	284	7,912.50
Mark Calcavecchia	72	67	74	72	285	6,900
Mike Hulbert	72	67	72	74	285	6,900
Brett Quigley	74	67	72	72	285	6,900
Kevin Sutherland	72	70	75	68	285	6,900
Russ Cochran	71	70	71	74	286	5,700
Robert Damron	72	68	70	76	286	5,700
Tom Kite	71	70	72	73	286	5,700
John Maginnes	71	67	74	74	286	5,700
Chip Beck	70	70	79	68	287	4,650
Billy Ray Brown	68	73	70	76	287	4,650
Olin Browne	73	67	76	71	287	4,650
Jay Delsing	72	70	72	74	288	3,870
Mark McCumber	70	70	74	74	288	3,870
Mike Springer	73	67	75	73	288	3,870
David Sutherland	72	69	71	76	288	3,870
Allen Doyle	74	67	72	76	289	3,570
Dicky Pride	75	65	78	71	289	3,570
Rafael Alarcon	69	72	71	78	290	3,480

	SCORES				TOTAL	MONEY
Tommy Armour III	73	64	77	77	291	3,390
Joel Edwards	71	70	76	74	291	3,390
Brian Henninger	72	69	74	76	291	3,390
Larry Rinker	73	69	76	73	291	3,390
Paul Trittler	73	69	74	75	291	3,390
Brandel Chamblee	72	70	75	75	292	3,270
Naomichi Ozaki	70	72	72	78	292	3,270
Tray Tyner	73	68	72	79	292	3,270
Lee Porter	72	68	77	77	294	3,210
Billy Andrade	75	67	74	80	296	3,180

Bay Hill Invitational

Bay Hill Club, Orlando, Florida
Par 36-36–72; 7,196 yards

March 20-23
purse, $1,500,000

	SCORES				TOTAL	MONEY
Phil Mickelson	72	65	70	65	272	$270,000
Stuart Appleby	73	63	70	69	275	162,000
Mark O'Meara	72	66	68	70	276	78,000
Payne Stewart	69	70	70	67	276	78,000
Omar Uresti	69	67	69	71	276	78,000
Michael Bradley	71	69	69	68	277	50,250
Tim Herron	70	70	66	71	277	50,250
Loren Roberts	70	67	70	70	277	50,250
Davis Love III	73	68	67	70	278	42,000
Tiger Woods	68	71	71	68	278	42,000
Robert Damron	70	70	69	70	279	34,500
Brian Henninger	70	68	73	68	279	34,500
Nick Price	70	68	73	68	279	34,500
Mark Calcavecchia	71	70	72	67	280	25,500
Doug Martin	71	68	71	70	280	25,500
John Morse	71	69	70	70	280	25,500
Chris Perry	69	71	68	72	280	25,500
Paul Stankowski	67	70	74	69	280	25,500
Jay Don Blake	69	70	74	68	281	19,500
Jeff Maggert	70	69	74	68	281	19,500
Colin Montgomerie	73	66	70	72	281	19,500
Rick Fehr	71	72	72	67	282	13,162.50
Paul Goydos	69	71	73	69	282	13,162.50
Peter Jacobsen	72	70	70	70	282	13,162.50
Steve Jones	68	73	72	69	282	13,162.50
Tom Kite	69	71	73	69	282	13,162.50
Bernhard Langer	69	70	72	71	282	13,162.50
Larry Mize	71	68	76	67	282	13,162.50
Don Pooley	73	65	72	72	282	13,162.50
Billy Andrade	68	73	67	75	283	9,315
Scott Gump	70	70	74	69	283	9,315
Len Mattiace	70	69	72	72	283	9,315
Scott McCarron	71	72	72	68	283	9,315
Craig Parry	72	70	69	72	283	9,315
John Daly	71	71	71	71	284	7,725
Robin Freeman	71	70	69	74	284	7,725
Vijay Singh	69	72	71	72	284	7,725
Stewart Cink	70	69	74	72	285	6,150
Kelly Gibson	71	72	71	71	285	6,150
Justin Leonard	73	70	72	70	285	6,150

	SCORES				TOTAL	MONEY
Andrew Magee	71	69	74	71	285	6,150
Mike Reid	72	70	72	71	285	6,150
Jeff Sluman	73	71	67	74	285	6,150
Ted Tryba	70	70	74	71	285	6,150
Scott Simpson	70	74	72	70	286	4,800
Kirk Triplett	72	69	73	72	286	4,800
Joe Durant	72	71	73	71	287	3,852.86
Jim Furyk	72	71	75	69	287	3,852.86
Taylor Smith	72	72	73	70	287	3,852.86
Ian Woosnam	70	73	76	68	287	3,852.86
Fuzzy Zoeller	71	70	75	71	287	3,852.86
Paul Azinger	72	69	71	75	287	3,852.85
Jay Haas	77	67	70	73	287	3,852.85
Donnie Hammond	72	71	73	72	288	3,420
Skip Kendall	70	65	79	74	288	3,420
Naomichi Ozaki	70	73	74	71	288	3,420
Steve Pate	69	70	74	75	288	3,420
Joey Sindelar	72	69	71	76	288	3,420
Nick Faldo	71	70	73	75	289	3,315
Kenny Perry	71	70	76	72	289	3,315
Mike Brisky	72	71	75	72	290	3,225
Grant Waite	71	73	74	72	290	3,225
D.A. Weibring	72	70	76	72	290	3,225
Mark Wiebe	73	70	71	76	290	3,225
Greg Kraft	70	69	78	74	291	3,150
Rocco Mediate	73	71	73	75	292	3,105
Larry Rinker	72	72	78	70	292	3,105
Scott Hoch	72	72	77	72	293	3,045
Lee Janzen	72	72	73	76	293	3,045
Fred Funk	68	74	76	76	294	3,000
Olin Browne	72	72	77	74	295	2,970
Tom Scherrer	72	70	80	76	298	2,940
Wayne Grady	72	71	76	81	300	2,910

The Players Championship

TPC at Sawgrass, Ponte Vedra Beach, Florida
Par 36-36–72; 6,896 yards

March 27-30
purse, $3,500,000

	SCORES				TOTAL	MONEY
Steve Elkington	66	69	68	69	272	$630,000
Scott Hoch	69	71	65	74	279	378,000
Loren Roberts	70	74	67	69	280	238,000
Brad Faxon	70	69	72	70	281	168,000
Billy Andrade	68	72	68	74	282	140,000
Tom Lehman	67	71	73	72	283	126,000
Mark Brooks	72	68	70	74	284	109,083.34
Colin Montgomerie	70	70	71	73	284	109,083.33
Tommy Tolles	70	67	73	74	284	109,083.33
Russ Cochran	67	74	72	72	285	84,000
Fred Couples	71	74	71	69	285	84,000
Ernie Els	68	71	72	74	285	84,000
Kirk Triplett	71	68	70	76	285	84,000
Stuart Appleby	71	71	70	74	286	54,250
Paul Azinger	72	72	71	71	286	54,250
Michael Bradley	68	74	72	72	286	54,250
David Edwards	67	70	76	73	286	54,250

	SCORES				TOTAL	MONEY
Fred Funk	71	75	68	72	286	54,250
Larry Mize	68	68	74	76	286	54,250
Paul Stankowski	73	70	71	72	286	54,250
Fuzzy Zoeller	67	72	73	74	286	54,250
John Cook	73	69	72	73	287	37,800
Craig Parry	71	67	80	69	287	37,800
Mark Calcavecchia	67	75	71	75	288	27,700
Nick Faldo	71	72	73	72	288	27,700
Robert Gamez	70	73	68	77	288	27,700
Doug Martin	72	71	75	70	288	27,700
Len Mattiace	71	72	71	74	288	27,700
Nick Price	75	68	74	71	288	27,700
Tom Purtzer	68	71	69	80	288	27,700
Rick Fehr	74	67	75	73	289	20,300
Bernhard Langer	71	73	75	70	289	20,300
Chris Perry	74	71	70	74	289	20,300
Joey Sindelar	71	73	73	72	289	20,300
Vijay Singh	71	69	74	75	289	20,300
Tiger Woods	71	73	72	73	289	20,300
Nolan Henke	72	73	73	72	290	15,400
Lee Janzen	73	73	74	70	290	15,400
Pete Jordan	72	74	73	71	290	15,400
Justin Leonard	71	71	70	78	290	15,400
Brian Watts	70	68	74	78	290	15,400
Willie Wood	74	71	70	75	290	15,400
David Duval	74	69	74	74	291	11,550
Jay Haas	68	76	74	73	291	11,550
Mark McNulty	71	73	69	78	291	11,550
Costantino Rocca	74	69	73	75	291	11,550
Duffy Waldorf	71	70	75	75	291	11,550
Peter Jacobsen	75	71	73	73	292	9,345
Omar Uresti	73	69	72	78	292	9,345
Masashi Ozaki	70	76	71	76	293	8,610
Dave Stockton, Jr.	68	71	77	77	293	8,610
Hal Sutton	70	71	74	78	293	8,610
Phil Blackmar	71	74	74	75	294	7,953.75
Robert Damron	69	72	78	75	294	7,953.75
Jim Furyk	71	74	70	79	294	7,953.75
Andrew Magee	71	71	76	76	294	7,953.75
Gil Morgan	71	72	73	78	294	7,953.75
Greg Norman	71	72	72	79	294	7,953.75
Taylor Smith	68	73	76	77	294	7,953.75
Tom Watson	70	71	79	74	294	7,953.75
Glen Day	70	72	76	77	295	7,630
Jay Don Blake	73	72	72	79	296	7,490
Mike Hulbert	70	71	77	78	296	7,490
Mike Reid	71	74	74	77	296	7,490
Scott Gump	71	75	72	79	297	7,280
Steve Lowery	73	72	74	78	297	7,280
Naomichi Ozaki	68	74	74	81	297	7,280
John Huston	72	70	77	79	298	7,105
Don Pooley	71	74	71	82	298	7,105
Jim Gallagher, Jr.	72	74	75	78	299	6,930
Sandy Lyle	68	74	77	80	299	6,930
Mark O'Meara	73	72	76	78	299	6,930
Mike Brisky	71	71	80	79	301	6,790
John Wilson	70	74	79	79	302	6,720
Lee Rinker	74	72	77	81	304	6,650

Freeport-McDermott Classic

English Turn Golf & Country Club,
New Orleans, Louisiana
Par 36-36–72; 7,116 yards

April 3-6
purse, $1,500,000

	SCORES				TOTAL	MONEY
Brad Faxon	68	69	66	69	272	$270,000
Bill Glasson	71	72	66	66	275	132,000
Jesper Parnevik	72	69	68	66	275	132,000
Scott McCarron	65	69	71	71	276	66,000
Kirk Triplett	72	68	64	72	276	66,000
Russ Cochran	70	71	67	69	277	54,000
Yoshinori Kaneko	69	74	69	66	278	45,187.50
Steve Lowery	72	71	66	69	278	45,187.50
Jose Maria Olazabal	72	67	67	72	278	45,187.50
Tommy Tolles	74	71	66	67	278	45,187.50
Marco Dawson	69	73	69	68	279	29,785.72
Joel Edwards	72	71	67	69	279	29,785.72
Steve Pate	70	73	67	69	279	29,785.72
Michael Christie	70	67	71	71	279	29,785.71
Scott Hoch	68	72	72	67	279	29,785.71
Davis Love III	69	71	70	69	279	29,785.71
Larry Rinker	65	69	72	73	279	29,785.71
Steve Elkington	71	72	69	68	280	21,750
Peter Jacobsen	70	71	70	69	280	21,750
Jerry Kelly	69	73	66	73	281	18,750
Mike Standly	70	74	68	69	281	18,750
Phil Blackmar	72	71	70	69	282	14,400
Pete Jordan	72	70	70	70	282	14,400
Billy Mayfair	68	72	67	75	282	14,400
Greg Norman	67	74	73	68	282	14,400
Bob Tway	68	72	72	70	282	14,400
Mark Brooks	70	74	69	70	283	10,875
Blaine McCallister	71	75	67	70	283	10,875
David Sutherland	72	70	73	68	283	10,875
Lanny Wadkins	69	69	72	73	283	10,875
Ronnie Black	71	71	71	71	284	8,150
Brad Bryant	71	70	68	75	284	8,150
Jay Delsing	73	73	67	71	284	8,150
Brent Geiberger	73	73	67	71	284	8,150
Brian Henninger	69	71	75	69	284	8,150
Hideki Kase	66	74	71	73	284	8,150
Chris Perry	72	72	69	71	284	8,150
Larry Silveira	67	78	69	70	284	8,150
David Toms	65	73	71	75	284	8,150
Ben Crenshaw	71	75	69	70	285	6,150
Anthony Rodriguez	72	73	69	71	285	6,150
Duffy Waldorf	70	71	72	72	285	6,150
Kevin Burton	70	73	72	71	286	4,950
Tom Byrum	76	69	73	68	286	4,950
Glen Day	72	73	70	71	286	4,950
Donnie Hammond	70	75	70	71	286	4,950
Justin Leonard	72	74	68	72	286	4,950
Robert Damron	71	74	71	71	287	3,870
Jimmy Green	72	73	67	75	287	3,870
J.P. Hayes	72	74	71	70	287	3,870
Payne Stewart	69	73	69	76	287	3,870
Eric Johnson	71	72	73	72	288	3,540
Jim McGovern	74	69	74	71	288	3,540

	SCORES				TOTAL	MONEY
Hal Sutton	72	70	75	71	288	3,540
Doug Barron	71	75	72	71	289	3,435
Ted Tryba	68	77	71	73	289	3,435
Olin Browne	73	72	72	73	290	3,390
Curt Byrum	73	72	74	72	291	3,330
Wayne Grady	73	73	73	72	291	3,330
Dave Stockton, Jr.	70	76	71	74	291	3,330
Emlyn Aubrey	74	70	72	76	292	3,255
Brian Claar	74	72	76	70	292	3,255
Craig Bowden	72	73	70	78	293	3,195
Grant Waite	73	71	74	75	293	3,195
Len Mattiace	75	70	75	74	294	3,150
Jim Gallagher, Jr.	72	74	71	78	295	3,105
Neal Lancaster	68	71	73	83	295	3,105
Lee Porter	72	74	72	78	296	3,060
Dudley Hart	72	74	79	72	297	3,000
Mike Heinen	73	73	75	76	297	3,000
Doug Tewell	70	76	74	77	297	3,000

Masters Tournament

Augusta National Golf Club, Augusta, Georgia
Par 36-36–72; 6,925 yards

April 10-13
purse, $2,500,000

	SCORES				TOTAL	MONEY
Tiger Woods	70	66	65	69	270	$486,000
Tom Kite	77	69	66	70	282	291,600
Tommy Tolles	72	72	72	67	283	183,600
Tom Watson	75	68	69	72	284	129,600
Costantino Rocca	71	69	70	75	285	102,600
Paul Stankowski	68	74	69	74	285	102,600
Fred Couples	72	69	73	72	286	78,570
Bernhard Langer	72	72	74	68	286	78,570
Justin Leonard	76	69	71	70	286	78,570
Davis Love III	72	71	72	71	286	78,570
Jeff Sluman	74	67	72	73	286	78,570
Steve Elkington	76	72	72	67	287	52,920
Per-Ulrik Johansson	72	73	73	69	287	52,920
Tom Lehman	73	76	69	69	287	52,920
Jose Maria Olazabal	71	70	74	72	287	52,920
Willie Wood	72	76	71	68	287	52,920
Mark Calcavecchia	74	73	72	69	288	39,150
Ernie Els	73	70	71	74	288	39,150
Fred Funk	73	74	69	72	288	39,150
Vijay Singh	75	74	69	70	288	39,150
Stuart Appleby	72	76	70	71	289	30,240
John Huston	67	77	75	70	289	30,240
Jesper Parnevik	73	72	71	73	289	30,240
Nick Price	71	71	75	74	291	24,840
Lee Westwood	77	71	73	70	291	24,840
Lee Janzen	72	73	74	73	292	21,195
Craig Stadler	77	72	71	72	292	21,195
Paul Azinger	69	73	77	74	293	19,575
Jim Furyk	74	75	72	72	293	19,575
Scott McCarron	77	71	72	74	294	17,145
Larry Mize	79	69	74	72	294	17,145
Colin Montgomerie	72	67	74	81	294	17,145

	SCORES	TOTAL	MONEY
Mark O'Meara	75 74 70 75	294	17,145
Sandy Lyle	73 73 74 75	295	14,918
Fuzzy Zoeller	75 73 69 78	295	14,918
Duffy Waldorf	74 75 72 75	296	13,905
David Frost	74 71 73 79	297	13,230
Scott Hoch	79 68 73 78	298	12,690
Jack Nicklaus	77 70 74 78	299	11,610
Sam Torrance	75 73 73 78	299	11,610
Ian Woosnam	77 68 75 79	299	11,610
Masashi Ozaki	74 74 74 78	300	10,530
Corey Pavin	75 74 78 74	301	9,720
Clarence Rose	73 75 79 74	301	9,720
Ben Crenshaw	75 73 74 80	302	8,910
Frank Nobilo	76 72 74 81	303	8,370

Out of Final 36 Holes

David Berganio, Jr.	72 78	150
John Cook	77 73	150
David Duval	78 72	150
Dan Forsman	74 76	150
Phil Mickelson	76 74	150
John Morse	77 73	150
*Warren Bladon	79 72	151
Brad Faxon	77 74	151
Dudley Hart	74 77	151
Greg Norman	77 74	151
David Ogrin	77 74	151
Kenny Perry	73 78	151
Gary Player	76 75	151
Bob Tway	78 73	151
D.A. Weibring	78 73	151
Stewart Cink	75 78	153
Ed Fiori	78 75	153
Jeff Maggert	77 76	153
Mark McNulty	81 72	153
Tommy Aaron	77 77	154
Raymond Floyd	79 75	154
Yoshinori Kaneko	77 77	154
Seve Ballesteros	81 74	155
Michael Bradley	79 77	156
Nick Faldo	75 81	156
Steve Stricker	77 79	156
*Steve Scott	78 79	157
Guy Boros	79 79	158
*Tim Hogarth	80 78	158
Robert Allenby	82 77	159
Mark Brooks	77 82	159
Billy Casper	83 77	160
Charles Coody	83 77	160
Steve Jones	82 78	160
Ken Green	87 74	161
Loren Roberts	85 77	162
Gay Brewer	84 79	163
*John Miller	82 81	163
Arnold Palmer	89 87	176
Doug Ford	85 94	179

(Professionals who did not complete 72 holes received $5,000.)

MCI Classic

Harbour Town Golf Links, Hilton Head Island,
South Carolina
Par 36-35–71; 6,912 yards

April 17-20
purse, $1,500,000

	SCORES				TOTAL	MONEY
Nick Price	65	69	69	66	269	$270,000
Brad Faxon	66	69	70	70	275	132,000
Jesper Parnevik	72	71	66	66	275	132,000
Lennie Clements	67	68	73	70	278	62,000
Tom Lehman	66	73	67	72	278	62,000
Hal Sutton	67	74	71	66	278	62,000
John Cook	72	74	66	67	279	48,375
Tom Watson	68	70	70	71	279	48,375
Scott Hoch	70	72	74	65	281	37,500
Davis Love III	70	73	74	64	281	37,500
Doug Martin	71	71	68	71	281	37,500
Craig Stadler	68	71	74	68	281	37,500
Willie Wood	73	69	68	71	281	37,500
David Edwards	71	73	69	69	282	25,500
Rick Fehr	66	69	77	70	282	25,500
Scott Gump	72	73	67	70	282	25,500
Joey Sindelar	70	75	70	67	282	25,500
Paul Stankowski	73	68	72	69	282	25,500
Rocco Mediate	71	73	72	67	283	21,000
Jay Haas	74	70	69	71	284	15,642.86
Donnie Hammond	71	71	70	72	284	15,642.86
Blaine McCallister	73	69	75	67	284	15,642.86
Colin Montgomerie	71	74	73	66	284	15,642.86
Bobby Wadkins	73	68	70	73	284	15,642.86
John Maginnes	68	69	77	70	284	15,642.85
Phil Mickelson	68	72	72	72	284	15,642.85
Jay Don Blake	69	71	74	71	285	11,100
Guy Boros	78	68	68	71	285	11,100
Chris Perry	72	74	69	70	285	11,100
Olin Browne	68	71	74	73	286	8,012.50
Brandel Chamblee	73	73	69	71	286	8,012.50
Brad Fabel	70	73	74	69	286	8,012.50
Lee Janzen	73	73	75	65	286	8,012.50
Justin Leonard	68	77	75	66	286	8,012.50
John Morse	75	70	69	72	286	8,012.50
Don Pooley	70	76	73	67	286	8,012.50
Loren Roberts	72	71	73	70	286	8,012.50
Jeff Sluman	71	70	73	72	286	8,012.50
Payne Stewart	71	72	72	71	286	8,012.50
Bob Tway	72	70	70	74	286	8,012.50
Scott Verplank	74	72	69	71	286	8,012.50
Michael Bradley	72	73	70	72	287	4,435
Mike Brisky	71	71	73	72	287	4,435
Brad Bryant	72	72	72	71	287	4,435
Glen Day	77	69	72	69	287	4,435
Scott Dunlap	78	67	73	69	287	4,435
Fred Funk	68	73	76	70	287	4,435
Wayne Levi	70	71	74	72	287	4,435
Steve Lowery	73	69	74	71	287	4,435
Steve Stricker	69	76	74	68	287	4,435
Omar Uresti	71	71	75	70	287	4,435
Lanny Wadkins	73	69	71	74	287	4,435
D.A. Weibring	70	75	75	67	287	4,435

	SCORES				TOTAL	MONEY
Fulton Allem	71	72	73	72	288	3,345
Stuart Appleby	70	73	72	73	288	3,345
Kelly Gibson	71	74	73	70	288	3,345
Nolan Henke	70	73	71	74	288	3,345
Tim Herron	72	74	69	73	288	3,345
Andrew Magee	72	69	74	73	288	3,345
Len Mattiace	73	73	69	73	288	3,345
Billy Mayfair	71	71	73	73	288	3,345
Gene Sauers	72	71	75	70	288	3,345
John Wilson	69	76	73	70	288	3,345
Bill Glasson	69	73	74	73	289	3,135
Peter Jacobsen	71	71	77	70	289	3,135
David Ogrin	75	71	71	72	289	3,135
Clarence Rose	73	72	70	74	289	3,135
Ernie Els	74	68	79	69	290	3,045
Vijay Singh	71	72	75	72	290	3,045
Patrick Burke	75	71	72	73	291	2,970
Robert Damron	71	74	74	72	291	2,970
Dave Stockton, Jr.	74	71	77	69	291	2,970
Emlyn Aubrey	73	71	76	73	293	2,910

Greater Greensboro Chrysler Classic

Forest Oaks Country Club, Greensboro, North Carolina
Par 36-36–72; 7,062 yards

April 24-27
purse, $1,900,000

	SCORES				TOTAL	MONEY
Frank Nobilo	69	69	69	67	274	$342,000
Brad Faxon	67	70	65	72	274	205,200
(Nobilo defeated Faxon on first extra hole.)						
Kirk Triplett	67	69	69	70	275	129,200
Billy Andrade	72	68	67	69	276	83,600
Robert Damron	66	72	67	71	276	83,600
Davis Love III	72	69	69	67	277	68,400
Tom Kite	67	68	67	76	278	61,275
Mike Standly	68	68	71	71	278	61,275
Ernie Els	69	69	67	74	279	49,400
Rocco Mediate	72	66	69	72	279	49,400
Phil Mickelson	71	68	70	70	279	49,400
Mark O'Meara	72	67	73	67	279	49,400
Lennie Clements	70	72	67	71	280	39,900
Fred Funk	69	69	72	71	281	32,300
Jim Furyk	70	72	68	71	281	32,300
Clarence Rose	70	71	68	72	281	32,300
Paul Stankowski	69	68	69	75	281	32,300
Scott Verplank	72	67	72	70	281	32,300
John Adams	71	67	70	74	282	22,230
Stuart Appleby	70	72	71	69	282	22,230
Glen Day	72	66	69	75	282	22,230
Brent Geiberger	70	70	69	73	282	22,230
Jerry Kelly	68	69	68	77	282	22,230
Doug Martin	69	72	71	70	282	22,230
Jimmy Green	71	71	69	72	283	15,152.50
Jim McGovern	70	70	71	72	283	15,152.50
David Ogrin	67	73	72	71	283	15,152.50
Naomichi Ozaki	68	71	68	76	283	15,152.50
Doug Barron	70	67	72	75	284	11,566.25

	SCORES				TOTAL	MONEY
Phil Blackmar	71	71	73	69	284	11,566.25
Russ Cochran	72	66	69	77	284	11,566.25
Dudley Hart	69	69	71	75	284	11,566.25
J.P. Hayes	71	71	68	74	284	11,566.25
Mike Hulbert	66	69	77	72	284	11,566.25
Jack O'Keefe	67	70	73	74	284	11,566.25
Hisayuki Sasaki	69	70	69	76	284	11,566.25
David Berganio	71	72	70	72	285	8,740
Guy Boros	72	66	73	74	285	8,740
Bob Estes	69	71	72	73	285	8,740
Scott Simpson	73	70	71	71	285	8,740
Eric Johnson	71	69	74	72	286	7,220
John Morse	69	71	71	75	286	7,220
Jesper Parnevik	72	70	71	73	286	7,220
Phil Tataurangi	71	69	71	75	286	7,220
Mike Brisky	69	73	74	71	287	5,719
Brad Bryant	71	66	74	76	287	5,719
Jeff Sluman	70	70	73	74	287	5,719
Dave Stockton, Jr.	70	71	70	76	287	5,719
Tom Byrum	71	71	73	73	288	4,510.60
Keith Fergus	71	72	73	72	288	4,510.60
Jeff Hart	74	69	72	73	288	4,510.60
Skip Kendall	70	67	73	78	288	4,510.60
Wayne Levi	72	71	71	74	288	4,510.60
John Maginnes	68	73	71	76	288	4,510.60
Larry Rinker	71	68	75	74	288	4,510.60
Joey Sindelar	67	72	76	73	288	4,510.60
Vijay Singh	69	69	71	79	288	4,510.60
Mike Springer	71	71	70	76	288	4,510.60
Steve Elkington	67	71	75	76	289	4,123
Brad Fabel	68	75	73	73	289	4,123
Steve Hart	71	69	72	77	289	4,123
Sandy Lyle	66	77	72	74	289	4,123
Spike McRoy	67	71	73	78	289	4,123
Omar Uresti	71	71	71	76	289	4,123
Scott Dunlap	69	72	72	77	290	3,971
P.H. Horgan III	71	72	72	75	290	3,971
Jimmy Johnston	69	73	75	74	291	3,895
Hideki Kase	73	70	71	77	291	3,895
Rafael Alarcon	73	69	73	77	292	3,838
Scott Medlin	70	73	73	77	293	3,800
Mark Wiebe	69	73	72	80	294	3,762

Shell Houston Open

TPC at The Woodlands, The Woodlands, Texas
Par 36-36–72; 7,042 yards

May 1-4
purse, $1,600,000

	SCORES				TOTAL	MONEY
Phil Blackmar	68	71	67	70	276	$288,000
Kevin Sutherland	68	72	66	70	276	172,800
(Blackmar defeated Sutherland on first extra hole.)						
Steve Elkington	69	74	70	65	278	108,800
Scott Hoch	73	68	68	70	279	70,400
Hal Sutton	68	72	71	68	279	70,400
Jerry Kelly	70	68	69	74	281	55,600
Lanny Wadkins	73	70	71	67	281	55,600

	SCORES				TOTAL	MONEY
J.P. Hayes	73	72	64	73	282	43,200
Nolan Henke	73	71	68	70	282	43,200
John Morse	68	74	69	71	282	43,200
David Ogrin	69	68	74	71	282	43,200
Larry Rinker	72	69	71	70	282	43,200
Fred Funk	69	72	70	72	283	32,000
Craig Parry	71	66	73	73	283	32,000
David Duval	65	71	75	73	284	25,600
Neal Lancaster	71	72	69	72	284	25,600
Justin Leonard	71	74	68	71	284	25,600
Scott McCarron	72	74	68	70	284	25,600
Mike Reid	73	69	70	72	284	25,600
Tom Kite	71	73	70	71	285	19,306.67
David Sutherland	69	72	73	71	285	19,306.67
Brent Geiberger	72	69	69	75	285	19,306.66
Tom Byrum	72	73	74	67	286	14,720
Jim Carter	73	68	70	75	286	14,720
Mike Hulbert	73	70	71	72	286	14,720
Grant Waite	68	72	73	73	286	14,720
Billy Andrade	74	68	72	73	287	11,360
Ronnie Black	72	70	73	72	287	11,360
John Cook	72	70	71	74	287	11,360
Wayne Levi	75	67	71	74	287	11,360
Doug Martin	76	69	72	70	287	11,360
Omar Uresti	76	70	72	70	288	8,853.34
John Wilson	73	73	72	70	288	8,853.34
Fred Couples	69	69	72	78	288	8,853.33
Brett Quigley	73	72	72	71	288	8,853.33
Mike Sullivan	76	70	71	71	288	8,853.33
Duffy Waldorf	72	74	70	72	288	8,853.33
Brad Bryant	74	72	74	69	289	6,880
Brian Henninger	71	71	78	69	289	6,880
Brad Lardon	74	72	72	71	289	6,880
Phil Tataurangi	72	72	74	71	289	6,880
Greg Twiggs	74	68	73	74	289	6,880
John Maginnes	74	71	73	72	290	5,760
Vijay Singh	71	71	71	77	290	5,760
Jeff Hart	74	72	74	71	291	4,484.58
Brad Fabel	73	68	75	75	291	4,484.57
Robin Freeman	71	71	76	73	291	4,484.57
Robert Gamez	72	70	72	77	291	4,484.57
Tom Pernice, Jr.	75	66	74	76	291	4,484.57
Lee Porter	72	73	72	74	291	4,484.57
Lee Rinker	71	72	71	77	291	4,484.57
Joel Edwards	71	72	77	72	292	3,712
Paul Goydos	72	71	71	78	292	3,712
Craig Kanada	74	71	75	72	292	3,712
Greg Kraft	76	70	71	75	292	3,712
Jeff Maggert	74	72	74	72	292	3,712
Willie Wood	70	73	75	74	292	3,712
Craig Bowden	76	70	75	72	293	3,536
Billy Ray Brown	74	72	74	73	293	3,536
Lennie Clements	71	73	72	77	293	3,536
Larry Mize	75	71	71	76	293	3,536
Payne Stewart	74	72	76	72	294	3,456
Jim Gallagher, Jr.	75	71	78	71	295	3,392
Bruce Lietzke	74	72	76	73	295	3,392
Curtis Strange	67	72	74	82	295	3,392
Patrick Burke	73	73	75	76	297	3,328
Rafael Alarcon	76	70	82	70	298	3,248

	SCORES				TOTAL	MONEY
Mark Brooks	69	75	73	81	298	3,248
Ed Dougherty	74	70	77	77	298	3,248
D.A. Weibring	72	71	79	76	298	3,248
Steve Hart	74	70	78	78	300	3,168

BellSouth Classic

TPC at Sugarloaf, Duluth, Georgia
Par 36-36–72; 7,259 yards

May 8-11
purse, $1,500,000

	SCORES				TOTAL	MONEY
Scott McCarron	70	69	66	69	274	$270,000
David Duval	66	66	73	72	277	112,000
Brian Henninger	70	71	68	68	277	112,000
Lee Janzen	69	70	70	68	277	112,000
Greg Norman	70	67	73	68	278	52,687.50
Nick Price	66	67	75	70	278	52,687.50
Hal Sutton	69	74	68	67	278	52,687.50
David Toms	69	68	70	71	278	52,687.50
Bruce Fleisher	70	72	70	68	280	37,500
Jay Haas	68	71	71	70	280	37,500
Andrew Magee	70	71	68	71	280	37,500
Don Pooley	64	70	77	69	280	37,500
Kevin Sutherland	71	71	70	68	280	37,500
Bob Estes	68	74	68	72	282	25,500
Keith Fergus	71	69	73	69	282	25,500
Robin Freeman	70	74	69	69	282	25,500
Kelly Gibson	73	69	68	72	282	25,500
Scott Gump	69	71	70	72	282	25,500
Glen Day	69	72	69	73	283	17,550
Bill Glasson	69	70	69	75	283	17,550
Larry Mize	71	70	72	71	283	17,550
Tom Pernice, Jr.	70	69	73	71	283	17,550
Kenny Perry	70	73	72	68	283	17,550
Bob Tway	72	68	74	69	283	17,550
Brandel Chamblee	75	68	69	72	284	12,250
Scott Dunlap	67	72	74	71	284	12,250
Bob Wolcott	73	68	73	70	284	12,250
Woody Austin	70	72	73	70	285	9,975
Jay Don Blake	72	71	69	73	285	9,975
Brent Geiberger	72	72	71	70	285	9,975
Craig Kanada	68	73	72	72	285	9,975
Spike McRoy	74	69	74	68	285	9,975
Steve Pate	71	69	72	73	285	9,975
John Adams	74	70	69	73	286	7,256.25
Stuart Appleby	72	71	70	73	286	7,256.25
Shane Bertsch	73	70	73	70	286	7,256.25
Craig Bowden	69	70	73	74	286	7,256.25
Dan Forsman	68	74	72	72	286	7,256.25
Donnie Hammond	66	73	75	72	286	7,256.25
Payne Stewart	75	66	72	73	286	7,256.25
Mike Sullivan	70	73	71	72	286	7,256.25
Marco Dawson	69	71	79	68	287	5,550
Nolan Henke	70	71	75	71	287	5,550
Neal Lancaster	73	68	71	75	287	5,550
Allen Doyle	72	71	76	69	288	4,290
Robert Gamez	72	68	70	78	288	4,290

	SCORES				TOTAL	MONEY
Eric Johnson	72	71	72	73	288	4,290
Jimmy Johnston	73	71	73	71	288	4,290
Scott Simpson	66	75	73	74	288	4,290
Chip Sullivan	69	72	74	73	288	4,290
Jim Gallagher, Jr.	69	75	77	68	289	3,473.34
Ted Tryba	71	72	70	76	289	3,473.34
Scott Verplank	74	70	74	71	289	3,473.34
Mark Calcavecchia	70	68	77	74	289	3,473.33
Fred Funk	71	70	76	72	289	3,473.33
Frank Nobilo	70	73	74	72	289	3,473.33
Charlie Rymer	69	67	78	75	289	3,473.33
Jeff Sluman	72	70	76	71	289	3,473.33
Bobby Wadkins	66	75	75	73	289	3,473.33
Dudley Hart	69	69	72	80	290	3,270
Jeff Hart	71	72	75	72	290	3,270
Howard Twitty	73	71	74	72	290	3,270
Brad Bryant	71	73	73	74	291	3,165
Tom Byrum	75	67	73	76	291	3,165
Jay Delsing	71	73	70	77	291	3,165
Larry Silveira	71	71	76	73	291	3,165
Billy Andrade	72	70	76	74	292	3,030
J.P. Hayes	73	70	74	75	292	3,030
Larry Nelson	70	71	76	75	292	3,030
Joey Sindelar	72	72	75	73	292	3,030
Dave Stockton, Jr.	73	70	76	73	292	3,030
Joel Edwards	71	73	76	73	293	2,925
Tommy Tolles	73	70	77	73	293	2,925
Curt Byrum	70	73	78	74	295	2,880
Naomichi Ozaki	74	68	75	79	296	2,850
Kevin Burton	73	71	78	75	297	2,805
Bradley Hughes	72	70	80	75	297	2,805
Mike Brisky	69	75	82	72	298	2,745
Hugh Royer III	71	72	77	78	298	2,745
Jim McGovern	70	74	77	78	299	2,700

GTE Byron Nelson Classic

TPC at Las Colinas: Par 35-35–70; 6,899 yards
Cottonwood Valley Golf Course: Par 34-36–70; 6,846 yards
Irving, Texas

May 15-18
purse, $1,800,000

	SCORES			TOTAL	MONEY
Tiger Woods	64	64	67	68	263	$324,000
Lee Rinker	65	63	69	68	265	194,400
Dan Forsman	67	64	66	70	267	104,400
Tom Watson	65	66	69	67	267	104,400
Andrew Magee	66	65	69	68	268	56,957.15
Bob Tway	69	65	68	66	268	56,957.15
Brad Bryant	65	67	66	70	268	56,957.14
Jim Furyk	63	67	67	71	268	56,957.14
Chris Perry	65	67	66	70	268	56,957.14
Mike Standly	66	63	68	71	268	56,957.14
Paul Stankowski	64	66	68	70	268	56,957.14
Phil Blackmar	68	63	67	71	269	33,171.43
John Cook	68	68	66	67	269	33,171.43
Eric Johnson	65	69	66	69	269	33,171.43
Neal Lancaster	70	66	64	69	269	33,171.43

	SCORES				TOTAL	MONEY
Phil Mickelson	66	67	68	68	269	33,171.43
Craig Parry	66	66	69	68	269	33,171.43
Hal Sutton	68	65	66	70	269	33,171.42
Olin Browne	74	64	63	69	270	20,314.29
Dudley Hart	64	68	69	69	270	20,314.29
Tom Kite	69	67	67	67	270	20,314.29
Loren Roberts	70	64	68	68	270	20,314.29
David Berganio	68	63	66	73	270	20,314.28
David Edwards	70	67	63	70	270	20,314.28
Nick Price	69	65	67	69	270	20,314.28
Brad Faxon	67	67	64	73	271	14,400
Brent Geiberger	69	68	67	68	272	13,320
Justin Leonard	66	69	67	70	272	13,320
Kevin Sutherland	65	69	70	68	272	13,320
Payne Stewart	69	68	65	71	273	11,700
David Sutherland	68	64	70	71	273	11,700
Kirk Triplett	67	65	66	75	273	11,700
Andy Bean	68	70	69	67	274	9,720
Tom Byrum	69	64	71	70	274	9,720
Doug Martin	66	66	70	72	274	9,720
Rocco Mediate	66	68	66	74	274	9,720
Corey Pavin	72	65	69	68	274	9,720
Shane Bertsch	70	68	67	70	275	7,740
Scott Dunlap	69	67	66	73	275	7,740
J.P. Hayes	69	66	67	73	275	7,740
John Morse	67	64	67	77	275	7,740
Mike Reid	69	66	69	71	275	7,740
Patrick Burke	69	69	71	67	276	5,940
Jim Carter	67	66	69	74	276	5,940
Brandel Chamblee	68	70	68	70	276	5,940
Nick Faldo	66	68	69	73	276	5,940
Hugh Royer III	73	65	68	70	276	5,940
Stewart Cink	68	68	74	67	277	4,524
Ben Crenshaw	66	67	72	72	277	4,524
Brad Fabel	70	68	71	68	277	4,524
Scott Gump	70	63	73	71	277	4,524
Don Pooley	68	69	71	69	277	4,524
David Toms	68	67	70	72	277	4,524
David Frost	68	68	66	76	278	4,158
Scott McCarron	68	69	72	69	278	4,158
Mike Brisky	72	65	71	71	279	4,050
Billy Ray Brown	68	69	67	75	279	4,050
Rick Fehr	68	68	70	73	279	4,050
Brett Quigley	69	66	68	76	279	4,050
Kenny Perry	68	67	71	74	280	3,906
Tommy Tolles	68	68	69	75	280	3,906
D.A. Weibring	67	71	71	71	280	3,906
Mark Wiebe	67	72	73	69	280	3,906
Mark Brooks	68	69	68	76	281	3,744
Joe Durant	71	65	74	71	281	3,744
Hideki Kase	68	70	67	76	281	3,744
Davis Love III	68	70	70	73	281	3,744
Chip Sullivan	70	68	72	71	281	3,744
Marco Dawson	67	70	68	77	282	3,636
P.H. Horgan III	66	71	73	73	283	3,600
Glen Day	67	67	71	79	284	3,546
Anthony Rodriguez	71	67	69	77	284	3,546

MasterCard Colonial

Colonial Country Club, Ft. Worth, Texas
Par 35-35—70; 7,010 yards

May 22-25
purse, $1,600,000

	SCORES				TOTAL	MONEY
David Frost	66	63	69	67	265	$288,000
Brad Faxon	63	66	70	68	267	140,800
David Ogrin	66	67	62	72	267	140,800
Paul Goydos	64	65	68	71	268	70,400
Tiger Woods	67	65	64	72	268	70,400
Dudley Hart	68	66	68	67	269	55,600
Bob Tway	65	66	69	69	269	55,600
Jim Furyk	64	67	67	72	270	49,600
John Huston	67	67	67	70	271	46,400
Glen Day	69	70	65	68	272	40,000
Steve Pate	69	66	64	73	272	40,000
Loren Roberts	67	68	66	71	272	40,000
Justin Leonard	64	67	68	74	273	32,000
Jeff Sluman	66	69	68	70	273	32,000
Stewart Cink	69	66	67	72	274	25,600
Greg Kraft	67	68	69	70	274	25,600
Jeff Maggert	71	67	68	68	274	25,600
Shigeki Maruyama	69	68	68	69	274	25,600
Kirk Triplett	69	64	67	74	274	25,600
Billy Andrade	67	70	68	70	275	20,000
Bill Glasson	67	69	70	69	275	20,000
Steve Elkington	69	71	65	71	276	13,047.28
Kazuhiko Hosokawa	71	69	66	70	276	13,047.28
Lee Janzen	71	68	67	70	276	13,047.28
Emlyn Aubrey	69	67	76	64	276	13,047.27
Mark Brooks	68	69	69	70	276	13,047.27
Billy Ray Brown	68	67	70	71	276	13,047.27
Patrick Burke	68	70	68	70	276	13,047.27
Russ Cochran	71	67	71	67	276	13,047.27
Bruce Lietzke	69	68	68	71	276	13,047.27
Phil Mickelson	70	64	70	72	276	13,047.27
Craig Stadler	73	66	67	70	276	13,047.27
Fulton Allem	67	69	67	74	277	8,100
Phil Blackmar	70	66	68	73	277	8,100
Brent Geiberger	69	65	68	75	277	8,100
Scott Hoch	70	70	69	68	277	8,100
Larry Nelson	68	69	70	70	277	8,100
Tommy Tolles	66	70	71	70	277	8,100
Lanny Wadkins	66	70	71	70	277	8,100
Fuzzy Zoeller	71	65	70	71	277	8,100
Mike Brisky	72	68	71	67	278	5,600
David Duval	65	70	66	77	278	5,600
Bob Estes	71	69	67	71	278	5,600
Mike Standly	69	67	72	70	278	5,600
Kevin Sutherland	69	69	72	68	278	5,600
Grant Waite	70	70	65	73	278	5,600
D.A. Weibring	68	66	69	75	278	5,600
Len Mattiace	73	67	67	72	279	4,021.34
Larry Rinker	66	73	65	75	279	4,021.34
Mike Hulbert	69	70	71	69	279	4,021.33
Tom Kite	70	67	69	73	279	4,021.33
John Morse	71	67	70	71	279	4,021.33
Payne Stewart	68	66	68	77	279	4,021.33
Robert Damron	71	68	67	74	280	3,584

	SCORES				TOTAL	MONEY
Brian Henninger	65	74	73	68	280	3,584
Peter Jacobsen	67	71	70	72	280	3,584
Doug Martin	72	67	70	71	280	3,584
Billy Mayfair	68	72	73	67	280	3,584
Naomichi Ozaki	72	68	69	71	280	3,584
Corey Pavin	71	68	71	70	280	3,584
Scott Simpson	68	72	71	69	280	3,584
Willie Wood	70	70	70	70	280	3,584
Marco Dawson	70	70	67	74	281	3,376
Tim Herron	67	73	71	70	281	3,376
Joey Sindelar	68	69	73	71	281	3,376
Jeff Gallagher	67	72	67	75	281	3,376
Craig Parry	70	67	64	71	282	3,296
Ed Fiori	67	71	70	76	284	3,248
Blaine McCallister	70	68	73	73	284	3,248
Kelly Gibson	70	66	72	77	285	3,184
Davis Love III	70	70	74	71	285	3,184
Mark Calcavecchia	67	70	76	74	287	3,136
Duffy Waldorf	69	71	72	76	288	3,104
Fred Funk	67	65	71		WD	

Memorial Tournament

Muirfield Village Golf Club, Dublin, Ohio
Par 36-36–72; 7,163 yards
(Fourth round cancelled — rain.)

May 29-June 1
purse, $1,900,000

	SCORES			TOTAL	MONEY
Vijay Singh	70	65	67	202	$342,000
Jim Furyk	71	66	67	204	167,200
Greg Norman	71	69	64	204	167,200
Tommy Tolles	70	64	71	205	78,533.34
Scott Hoch	67	65	73	205	78,533.33
Lee Janzen	70	67	68	205	78,533.33
Frank Nobilo	71	67	68	206	63,650
Tim Herron	66	72	70	208	57,000
Jack Nicklaus	69	70	69	208	57,000
Billy Andrade	66	72	71	209	45,600
Glen Day	66	74	69	209	45,600
Davis Love III	70	71	68	209	45,600
Bob Tway	74	66	69	209	45,600
Guy Boros	68	68	74	210	34,200
Mark Calcavecchia	73	70	67	210	34,200
Donnie Hammond	72	71	67	210	34,200
David Duval	73	69	69	211	27,550
David Frost	72	70	69	211	27,550
Peter Jacobsen	71	71	69	211	27,550
Billy Mayfair	69	74	68	211	27,550
Phil Blackmar	68	74	70	212	19,760
Robert Damron	71	70	71	212	19,760
Jay Haas	74	68	70	212	19,760
Jesper Parnevik	66	73	73	212	19,760
Don Pooley	69	71	72	212	19,760
Paul Goydos	72	69	72	213	13,775
Mike Hulbert	73	71	69	213	13,775
Greg Kraft	71	70	72	213	13,775
Tom Lehman	73	70	70	213	13,775

	SCORES	TOTAL	MONEY
Steve Lowery	74 73 66	213	13,775
Paul Stankowski	73 71 69	213	13,775
Jay Don Blake	72 71 71	214	10,513.34
Mark O'Meara	70 70 74	214	10,513.34
Mike Brisky	71 70 73	214	10,513.33
Scott Gump	71 69 74	214	10,513.33
Rocco Mediate	74 72 68	214	10,513.33
Kirk Triplett	70 72 72	214	10,513.33
Michael Bradley	72 70 73	215	7,600
Ernie Els	68 74 73	215	7,600
Dudley Hart	73 72 70	215	7,600
Andrew Magee	69 75 71	215	7,600
Lee Rinker	73 68 74	215	7,600
Curtis Strange	73 69 73	215	7,600
Steve Stricker	73 72 70	215	7,600
Hal Sutton	73 72 70	215	7,600
Paul Azinger	73 72 71	216	5,006.50
Ronnie Black	73 72 71	216	5,006.50
John Cook	75 68 73	216	5,006.50
Justin Leonard	72 71 73	216	5,006.50
Doug Martin	71 72 73	216	5,006.50
Clarence Rose	69 70 77	216	5,006.50
Mike Standly	69 74 73	216	5,006.50
Tom Watson	72 69 75	216	5,006.50
Dan Forsman	75 68 74	217	4,370
Fred Funk	70 73 74	217	4,370
Kelly Gibson	69 78 70	217	4,370
Brad Faxon	74 69 75	218	4,256
Bruce Lietzke	75 71 72	218	4,256
Chris Perry	70 73 75	218	4,256
Keith Fergus	74 71 74	219	4,104
Bill Glasson	74 71 74	219	4,104
Steve Jones	74 72 73	219	4,104
Craig Parry	73 70 76	219	4,104
Duffy Waldorf	73 71 75	219	4,104
Brian Henninger	72 71 77	220	3,971
Fuzzy Zoeller	78 69 73	220	3,971
David Edwards	73 74 74	221	3,800
Hideki Kase	72 75 74	221	3,800
Peter Lonard	73 74 74	221	3,800
Jeff Maggert	71 76 74	221	3,800
Kenny Perry	75 70 76	221	3,800
Omar Uresti	75 70 76	221	3,800
Tiger Woods	72 75 74	221	3,800
John Daly	76 71 80	227	3,648

Kemper Open

TPC at Avenel, Potomac, Maryland
Par 36-35–71; 7,005 yards

June 5-8
purse, $1,500,000

	SCORES	TOTAL	MONEY
Justin Leonard	69 69 69 67	274	$270,000
Mark Wiebe	69 67 66 73	275	162,000
Nick Faldo	73 65 68 71	277	72,000
Greg Norman	66 71 73 67	277	72,000
Nick Price	66 72 72 67	277	72,000

AMERICAN TOURS / 361

	SCORES				TOTAL	MONEY
Mike Springer	68	70	67	72	277	72,000
Tim Herron	69	70	72	67	278	45,187.50
Jim McGovern	72	69	68	69	278	45,187.50
Loren Roberts	70	69	69	70	278	45,187.50
D.A. Weibring	69	67	75	67	278	45,187.50
Dan Forsman	72	71	65	71	279	34,500
Jay Haas	69	74	69	67	279	34,500
Paul Stankowski	67	72	69	71	279	34,500
Stuart Appleby	71	69	70	70	280	25,500
Jay Don Blake	70	72	68	70	280	25,500
Lee Janzen	71	70	70	69	280	25,500
Phil Mickelson	69	73	68	70	280	25,500
Joey Sindelar	71	68	68	73	280	25,500
Pete Jordan	73	70	68	70	281	16,928.58
Rafael Alarcon	70	72	68	71	281	16,928.57
Ben Crenshaw	68	72	73	68	281	16,928.57
Jerry Kelly	69	73	69	70	281	16,928.57
Davis Love III	73	68	69	71	281	16,928.57
Jeff Maggert	72	69	68	72	281	16,928.57
Phil Tataurangi	71	71	69	70	281	16,928.57
Jim Carter	69	72	72	69	282	11,100
John Morse	69	68	71	74	282	11,100
Jose Maria Olazabal	70	69	71	72	282	11,100
Corey Pavin	71	69	73	69	282	11,100
Taylor Smith	69	71	70	72	282	11,100
Spike McRoy	69	72	71	71	283	9,525
Curtis Strange	72	67	74	70	283	9,525
Clarence Rose	72	71	71	70	284	7,757.15
Vijay Singh	73	70	71	70	284	7,757.15
Paul Azinger	69	71	70	74	284	7,757.14
Kazuhiko Hosokawa	70	70	72	72	284	7,757.14
Tom Lehman	68	69	73	74	284	7,757.14
Kenny Perry	73	67	74	70	284	7,757.14
Jeff Sluman	67	74	71	72	284	7,757.14
Russ Cochran	73	70	71	71	285	5,550
Kelly Gibson	67	74	71	73	285	5,550
Larry Rinker	72	67	74	72	285	5,550
David Sutherland	72	71	65	77	285	5,550
Kirk Triplett	71	67	79	68	285	5,550
Omar Uresti	68	69	77	71	285	5,550
Lanny Wadkins	69	73	71	72	285	5,550
Doug Barron	72	70	74	70	286	3,905
Billy Ray Brown	72	71	71	72	286	3,905
David Frost	73	68	72	73	286	3,905
Bradley Hughes	69	73	69	75	286	3,905
Steve Jones	69	70	76	71	286	3,905
Billy Mayfair	71	72	71	72	286	3,905
Mark Brooks	69	71	69	78	287	3,490
Allen Doyle	68	74	75	70	287	3,490
Lee Rinker	72	71	73	71	287	3,490
Mike Hulbert	68	74	77	69	288	3,405
Tom Pernice, Jr.	73	70	75	70	288	3,405
Olin Browne	73	70	73	73	289	3,270
Brandel Chamblee	70	68	74	77	289	3,270
John Cook	71	70	76	72	289	3,270
Nolan Henke	70	72	75	72	289	3,270
Mark O'Meara	72	69	72	76	289	3,270
Craig Parry	73	68	75	73	289	3,270
John Wilson	73	69	74	73	289	3,270
Craig Bowden	70	71	75	74	290	3,135

	SCORES	TOTAL	MONEY
Brett Quigley	72 70 76 72	290	3,135
Shane Bertsch	73 70 71 77	291	3,075
Howard Twitty	72 71 71 77	291	3,075
John Adams	72 71 74 75	292	3,030
John Daly	70 70 77 80	297	3,000

U.S. Open Championship

Congressional Country Club, Bethesda, Maryland
Par 35-35–70; 7,213 yards

June 12-15
purse, $2,600,000

	SCORES	TOTAL	MONEY
Ernie Els	71 67 69 69	276	$465,000
Colin Montgomerie	65 76 67 69	277	275,000
Tom Lehman	67 70 68 73	278	172,828
Jeff Maggert	73 66 68 74	281	120,454
Olin Browne	71 71 69 71	282	79,875.40
Jim Furyk	74 68 69 71	282	79,875.40
Jay Haas	73 69 68 72	282	79,875.40
Tommy Tolles	74 67 69 72	282	79,875.40
Bob Tway	71 71 70 70	282	79,875.40
David Ogrin	70 69 71 73	283	56,949.34
Scott Hoch	71 68 72 72	283	56,949.33
Scott McCarron	73 71 69 70	283	56,949.33
Billy Andrade	75 67 69 73	284	47,348.67
Stewart Cink	71 67 74 72	284	47,348.67
Loren Roberts	72 69 72 71	284	47,348.67
Davis Love III	75 70 69 71	285	40,086.67
Jose Maria Olazabal	71 71 72 71	285	40,086.66
Bradley Hughes	75 70 71 69	285	40,086.66
Nick Price	71 74 71 70	286	31,915.60
Paul Stankowski	75 70 68 73	286	31,915.60
Hal Sutton	66 73 73 74	286	31,915.60
Lee Westwood	71 71 73 71	286	31,915.60
Tiger Woods	74 67 73 72	286	31,915.60
Scott Dunlap	75 66 75 71	287	24,173.50
Steve Elkington	75 68 72 72	287	24,173.50
Edward Fryatt	72 73 73 69	287	24,173.50
Len Mattiace	71 75 73 68	287	24,173.50
Paul Azinger	72 72 74 70	288	17,443.25
Kelly Gibson	72 69 72 75	288	17,443.25
Paul Goydos	73 72 74 69	288	17,443.25
Hideki Kase	68 73 73 74	288	17,443.25
Mark McNulty	67 73 75 73	288	17,443.25
Jeff Sluman	69 72 72 75	288	17,443.25
Fuzzy Zoeller	72 73 69 74	288	17,443.25
Payne Stewart	71 73 73 71	288	17,443.25
John Cook	72 71 71 75	289	13,483.15
Grant Waite	72 74 72 71	289	13,483.15
Stuart Appleby	71 75 70 73	289	13,483.14
Justin Leonard	69 72 78 70	289	13,483.14
Frank Nobilo	71 74 70 74	289	13,483.14
Mark O'Meara	73 73 71 72	289	13,483.14
Steve Stricker	66 76 75 72	289	13,483.14
Darren Clarke	73 74 73 70	290	10,491.20
Fred Funk	73 70 72 75	290	10,491.20
Phil Mickelson	75 68 73 74	290	10,491.20

	SCORES			TOTAL	MONEY
Craig Parry	70 74 69 77			290	10,491.20
Chris Perry	70 73 71 76			290	10,491.20
Nick Faldo	72 74 69 76			291	8,496.67
Jesper Parnevik	72 75 73 71			291	8,496.67
David Duval	74 73 70 74			291	8,496.66
David White	70 72 73 77			292	7,786
Hale Irwin	70 73 76 74			293	7,138.84
Jack Nicklaus	73 71 75 74			293	7,138.84
Paul Broadhurst	77 69 72 75			293	7,138.83
Fred Couples	75 72 72 74			293	7,138.83
Lee Janzen	72 73 75 73			293	7,138.83
Peter Teravainen	71 73 74 75			293	7,138.83
Larry Mize	70 74 76 74			294	6,530
Clarence Rose	72 71 73 78			294	6,530
Rodney Butcher	73 74 70 78			295	6,270.50
Steve Jones	72 75 69 79			295	6,270.50
Chris Smith	77 69 74 75			295	6,270.50
Duffy Waldorf	73 73 73 76			295	6,270.50
Tom Watson	72 74 72 78			296	6,120
Ben Crenshaw	73 74 76 74			297	6,000
Brad Faxon	72 74 76 75			297	6,000
Dave Schreyer	68 73 82 74			297	6,000
Stephen Ames	73 73 75 77			298	5,742.50
Thomas Bjorn	71 75 73 79			298	5,742.50
Mike Hulbert	73 73 77 75			298	5,742.50
Tom Kite	75 69 82 72			298	5,742.50
Greg Kraft	77 69 76 76			298	5,742.50
John Morse	71 74 76 77			298	5,742.50
Jimmy Green	75 72 79 73			299	5,550
Andrew Coltart	74 71 76 79			300	5,467.50
Randy Wylie	71 76 77 76			300	5,467.50
Donnie Hammond	75 71 76 79			301	5,275
Dick Mast	73 69 83 76			301	5,275
Perry Parker	75 71 77 78			301	5,275
Vijay Singh	71 76 77 77			301	5,275
Greg Towne	71 73 83 74			301	5,275
Jack Ferenz	72 75 80 76			303	5,110
Marco Dawson	75 71 80 78			304	5,055
Slade Adams	71 74 78 83			306	5,000

Out of Final 36 Holes

Ronnie Black	76	72	148
Michael Clark	77	71	148
*Joel Kribel	70	78	148
Bernhard Langer	73	75	148
Paul McGinley	75	73	148
Corey Pavin	74	74	148
Larry Rinker	76	72	148
Lee Rinker	73	75	148
Eric Brito	74	75	149
Mark Brooks	71	78	149
Mark Calcavecchia	73	76	149
P.J. Cowan	73	76	149
Ken Green	75	74	149
John Mazza	73	76	149
Sean Murphy	75	74	149
Larry Nelson	74	75	149
Kenny Perry	76	73	149
Mike Reid	72	77	149

	SCORES		TOTAL
Larry Silveira	77	72	149
Scott Simpson	76	73	149
Mike Swartz	77	72	149
*Chris Wollmann	75	74	149
Jim Estes	74	75	149
Robert Allenby	75	75	150
Kevin Altenhof	78	72	150
Spike McRoy	73	77	150
Gary Nicklaus	73	77	150
Bill Porter	74	76	150
Curtis Strange	79	71	150
Ian Woosnam	76	74	150
Dennis Zinkon	76	74	150
Michael Bradley	77	74	151
Russ Cochran	73	78	151
Dan Forsman	77	74	151
Matt Gogel	80	71	151
*Terry Noe	75	76	151
Ken Schall	74	77	151
Mike Sposa	77	74	151
Dennis Trixler	74	77	151
Mark Wiebe	71	80	151
Tony Aguilar	77	74	151
Jay Don Blake	79	73	152
Mike Brisky	70	82	152
Steven Hart	74	78	152
Kent Jones	78	74	152
Jim McGovern	72	80	152
Masashi Ozaki	79	73	152
John Pillar	76	76	152
Gary Robison	78	74	152
Padraig Harrington	75	77	152
Rick Cramer	72	81	153
Bob Gilder	80	73	153
Frank Lickliter	71	82	153
Peter Mitchell	75	78	153
Roy Hunter	76	78	154
*Jason Semelsberger	78	76	154
Dave Stockton	76	78	154
Greg Norman	75	79	154
Rob Bradley	77	78	155
Brett Wayment	78	77	155
Roger Gunn	80	76	156
Ed Humenik	79	78	157
*Bob Kearney	76	81	157
Marty Schiene	81	78	159
Brian Tennyson	79	80	159
Ted Tryba	80	79	159
Michael Martin	87	73	160
Raymond Russell	79	81	160
Andrew Morse	87	77	164
Gregory Sweatt	78	89	167
John Daly	77		WD
David Toms	78		WD

(Professionals who did not complete 72 holes received $1,000.)

Buick Classic

Westchester Country Club, Harrison, New York
Par 36-35–71; 6,779 yards

June 19-22
purse, $1,500,000

	SCORES				TOTAL	MONEY
Ernie Els	64	68	67	69	268	$270,000
Jeff Maggert	67	69	66	68	270	162,000
Robert Damron	71	66	68	69	274	87,000
Jim Furyk	67	68	69	70	274	87,000
Jim Carter	69	70	71	65	275	60,000
Stewart Cink	73	68	66	70	277	50,250
Bob Estes	71	67	71	68	277	50,250
Clarence Rose	69	69	70	69	277	50,250
Brad Fabel	69	67	74	68	278	42,000
Pete Jordan	69	68	69	72	278	42,000
Brad Faxon	66	74	70	69	279	37,500
Billy Andrade	73	71	64	73	281	29,400
David Frost	78	67	66	70	281	29,400
Frank Nobilo	70	69	77	65	281	29,400
Mike Reid	70	69	68	74	281	29,400
Vijay Singh	67	73	69	72	281	29,400
Stuart Appleby	70	73	69	70	282	21,750
Nolan Henke	72	68	70	72	282	21,750
Lee Janzen	70	72	71	69	282	21,750
Chris Perry	71	72	67	72	282	21,750
Rafael Alarcon	69	69	73	72	283	15,000
Tom Byrum	71	67	71	74	283	15,000
Jeff Hart	72	69	72	70	283	15,000
Peter Jacobsen	72	69	72	70	283	15,000
Jeff Sluman	70	70	71	72	283	15,000
Mike Sullivan	73	71	69	70	283	15,000
Mark Calcavecchia	71	67	75	71	284	10,425
Brandel Chamblee	73	71	69	71	284	10,425
David Duval	75	68	69	72	284	10,425
Robin Freeman	70	67	74	73	284	10,425
Bob Gilder	69	74	72	69	284	10,425
Skip Kendall	73	72	69	70	284	10,425
David Berganio, Jr.	73	69	71	72	285	8,100
Mark Brooks	75	70	70	70	285	8,100
Craig Parry	70	73	73	69	285	8,100
Lee Rinker	69	73	70	73	285	8,100
Bob Wolcott	73	72	69	71	285	8,100
Fulton Allem	72	72	71	71	286	6,450
Scott Dunlap	69	73	74	70	286	6,450
Don Pooley	75	69	71	71	286	6,450
Charlie Rymer	70	75	71	70	286	6,450
Bob Tway	70	67	74	75	286	6,450
John Dowdall	76	68	73	70	287	4,567.50
Allen Doyle	71	69	73	74	287	4,567.50
Steve Elkington	74	70	70	73	287	4,567.50
Bradley Hughes	70	72	71	74	287	4,567.50
Rocco Mediate	73	66	73	75	287	4,567.50
Jim Thorpe	71	71	72	73	287	4,567.50
Willie Wood	70	71	72	74	287	4,567.50
Tiger Woods	72	72	71	72	287	4,567.50
Bruce Fleisher	74	67	74	73	288	3,610
Neal Lancaster	71	72	72	73	288	3,610
Brett Quigley	71	70	73	74	288	3,610
Doug Barron	71	73	70	75	289	3,360

	SCORES				TOTAL	MONEY
Ronnie Black	71	72	74	72	289	3,360
Fred Funk	69	70	75	75	289	3,360
Dudley Hart	74	71	73	71	289	3,360
Tim Herron	74	71	70	74	289	3,360
Gabriel Hjertstedt	73	71	75	70	289	3,360
P.H. Horgan III	74	71	71	73	289	3,360
Jack O'Keefe	71	73	72	73	289	3,360
Hugh Royer III	73	70	73	73	289	3,360
Billy Ray Brown	72	67	71	80	290	3,165
Brent Geiberger	70	73	76	71	290	3,165
Greg Kraft	74	71	75	70	290	3,165
Joey Sindelar	73	72	71	74	290	3,165
Frank Lickliter	76	68	72	75	291	3,075
Chip Sullivan	71	74	71	75	291	3,075
Jay Delsing	71	74	74	73	292	3,000
J.P. Hayes	72	72	76	72	292	3,000
Jerry Kelly	75	70	70	77	292	3,000
Ken Green	74	71	70	78	293	2,895
Kevin Sutherland	74	70	73	76	293	2,895
Howard Twitty	70	73	73	77	293	2,895
Mark Wiebe	71	73	75	74	293	2,895
Sonny Skinner	70	75	75	74	294	2,805
Tray Tyner	71	72	74	77	294	2,805
Paul Claxton	74	69	76	77	296	2,760
Tim Simpson	71	71	77	78	297	2,730
Gene Sauers	74	69	73	82	298	2,685
Phil Tataurangi	74	71	77	76	298	2,685
Ted Tryba	69	75	73	82	299	2,640

FedEx St. Jude Classic

TPC at Southwind, Germantown, Tennessee
Par 36-35–71; 7,006 yards

June 26-29
purse, $1,500,000

	SCORES				TOTAL	MONEY
Greg Norman	68	65	69	66	268	$270,000
Dudley Hart	69	68	66	66	269	162,000
Robert Damron	65	66	69	70	270	87,000
Craig Parry	69	69	66	66	270	87,000
Jay Don Blake	70	64	68	69	271	52,687.50
Michael Bradley	68	67	66	70	271	52,687.50
Justin Leonard	66	71	65	69	271	52,687.50
Nick Price	66	68	68	69	271	52,687.50
Tom Byrum	69	69	67	67	272	40,500
Mike Hulbert	67	67	67	71	272	40,500
Gene Sauers	65	67	70	70	272	40,500
Robert Gamez	71	65	72	65	273	31,500
Steve Lowery	72	68	70	63	273	31,500
Kenny Perry	66	71	70	66	273	31,500
Phil Blackmar	69	67	73	65	274	27,000
Michael Christie	70	68	65	72	275	21,750.70
Stewart Cink	68	71	68	68	275	21,750.70
Andrew Magee	68	67	69	71	275	21,750.70
Jack O'Keefe	69	66	70	70	275	21,750.70
David Toms	69	70	71	65	275	21,750.70
Fuzzy Zoeller	69	67	70	69	275	21,750.70
John Adams	70	66	69	71	276	14,400

	SCORES				TOTAL	MONEY
Brian Claar	68	71	67	70	276	14,400
Bob Estes	68	66	72	70	276	14,400
Dan Forsman	72	68	66	70	276	14,400
Skip Kendall	68	67	74	67	276	14,400
Doug Barron	69	69	68	71	277	9,775
Jim Carter	70	70	68	69	277	9,775
Peter Jacobsen	71	68	68	70	277	9,775
Pete Jordan	69	66	70	72	277	9,775
Doug Martin	66	71	72	68	277	9,775
Charlie Rymer	71	63	72	71	277	9,775
Curtis Strange	67	69	69	72	277	9,775
Ted Tryba	68	68	70	71	277	9,775
John Wilson	67	70	70	70	277	9,775
Tommy Armour III	67	67	72	72	278	7,375
Lennie Clements	65	74	70	69	278	7,375
Payne Stewart	73	63	73	69	278	7,375
John Cook	71	68	71	69	279	5,850
Kelly Gibson	67	72	67	73	279	5,850
Tom Gillis	72	67	70	70	279	5,850
Steve Hart	70	68	71	70	279	5,850
Dave Stockton, Jr.	68	70	70	71	279	5,850
Howard Twitty	70	67	70	72	279	5,850
Willie Wood	70	70	69	70	279	5,850
David Edwards	69	70	70	71	280	4,011.43
Brad Fabel	68	70	74	68	280	4,011.43
Bruce Fleisher	69	69	72	70	280	4,011.43
Scott Verplank	68	72	71	69	280	4,011.43
D.A. Weibring	67	72	71	70	280	4,011.43
Neal Lancaster	72	68	72	68	280	4,011.43
Joe Durant	71	69	70	70	280	4,011.42
Fulton Allem	68	71	71	71	281	3,408.75
Andy Bean	69	70	71	71	281	3,408.75
David Berganio, Jr.	66	73	69	73	281	3,408.75
Joel Edwards	68	68	73	72	281	3,408.75
Jay Haas	70	66	73	72	281	3,408.75
P.H. Horgan III	70	68	70	73	281	3,408.75
John Maginnes	71	68	70	72	281	3,408.75
Scott Simpson	71	69	73	68	281	3,408.75
Rafael Alarcon	71	69	70	72	282	3,225
Guy Boros	67	69	68	78	282	3,225
Loren Roberts	69	70	75	68	282	3,225
Duffy Waldorf	72	67	69	74	282	3,225
Kevin Burton	68	69	74	72	283	3,120
Tony Mollica	68	70	73	72	283	3,120
Omar Uresti	67	71	70	75	283	3,120
Emlyn Aubrey	68	70	70	76	284	3,045
Frank Lickliter	68	68	72	76	284	3,045
Woody Austin	70	69	77	69	285	2,985
Brett Quigley	69	69	75	72	285	2,985
Robin Freeman	67	73	74	72	286	2,925
Scott Gump	69	69	72	76	286	2,925
Jay Delsing	68	72	74	73	287	2,865
Dicky Pride	69	71	73	74	287	2,865

Motorola Western Open

Cog Hill Golf & Country Club, Dubsdread Course,
Lemont, Illinois
Par 36-36–72; 7,073 yards

July 3-6
purse, $2,000,000

	SCORES				TOTAL	MONEY
Tiger Woods	67	72	68	68	275	$360,000
Frank Nobilo	71	70	67	70	278	216,000
Justin Leonard	71	64	72	72	279	104,000
Steve Lowery	70	72	66	71	279	104,000
Jeff Sluman	69	69	74	67	279	104,000
Jim Furyk	67	74	67	72	280	72,000
Jay Delsing	71	67	71	72	281	56,166.67
Davis Love III	72	68	69	72	281	56,166.67
Steve Pate	75	67	67	72	281	56,166.67
Tom Watson	72	72	68	69	281	56,166.67
Stuart Appleby	71	72	70	68	281	56,166.66
Loren Roberts	70	71	66	74	281	56,166.66
Scott Hoch	71	68	71	72	282	38,666.67
Andrew Magee	69	72	70	71	282	38,666.67
Tom Byrum	75	68	69	70	282	38,666.66
Mark O'Meara	66	73	75	69	283	34,000
Billy Andrade	70	67	74	73	284	29,000
Phil Blackmar	67	74	71	72	284	29,000
Mark Calcavecchia	70	74	68	72	284	29,000
David Toms	71	71	73	69	284	29,000
John Cook	73	67	71	74	285	19,342.86
David Duval	68	73	74	70	285	19,342.86
Brian Henninger	75	70	70	70	285	19,342.86
Peter Jacobsen	75	69	71	70	285	19,342.86
Ted Tryba	71	68	75	71	285	19,342.86
P.H. Horgan III	74	70	70	71	285	19,342.85
Larry Mize	70	70	72	73	285	19,342.85
Russ Cochran	70	71	74	71	286	13,300
Brent Geiberger	70	69	73	74	286	13,300
Tom Purtzer	69	73	71	73	286	13,300
Mike Springer	70	70	75	71	286	13,300
Steve Stricker	69	73	72	72	286	13,300
John Wilson	73	70	72	71	286	13,300
Bill Glasson	73	71	70	73	287	10,320
Mike Hulbert	69	68	75	75	287	10,320
Billy Mayfair	74	70	71	72	287	10,320
Kevin Sutherland	73	72	73	69	287	10,320
Kirk Triplett	76	70	71	70	287	10,320
Lee Janzen	73	73	71	71	288	8,600
Bob Tway	73	68	75	72	288	8,600
Scott Verplank	73	71	71	73	288	8,600
Rafael Alarcon	69	71	77	72	289	6,144
Tommy Armour III	69	70	74	76	289	6,144
Jim Carter	74	68	75	72	289	6,144
Marco Dawson	71	72	71	75	289	6,144
Joe Durant	73	69	69	78	289	6,144
Robert Gamez	72	74	72	71	289	6,144
Pete Jordan	72	73	74	70	289	6,144
Tom Pernice, Jr.	70	72	74	73	289	6,144
Brett Quigley	70	74	70	75	289	6,144
Mark Wiebe	73	73	68	75	289	6,144
Kelly Gibson	73	73	71	73	290	4,664
Tom Lehman	73	71	72	74	290	4,664

	SCORES			TOTAL	MONEY
Doug Martin	73 71 72 74			290	4,664
Rocco Mediate	75 70 76 69			290	4,664
Chris Perry	74 72 72 72			290	4,664
Patrick Burke	73 71 75 72			291	4,440
Bob Estes	71 72 76 72			291	4,440
Dan Forsman	73 71 74 73			291	4,440
Vijay Singh	72 71 73 75			291	4,440
D.A. Weibring	73 70 73 75			291	4,440
Fred Couples	76 70 70 76			292	4,220
Dudley Hart	74 72 73 73			292	4,220
Steve Hart	71 70 72 79			292	4,220
Nolan Henke	74 71 71 76			292	4,220
David Ogrin	75 68 72 77			292	4,220
Scott Simpson	74 67 75 76			292	4,220
John Maginnes	75 70 70 78			293	4,040
John Morse	73 72 73 75			293	4,040
Dave Stockton, Jr.	67 78 78 70			293	4,040
Glen Day	72 73 74 75			294	3,960
Allen Doyle	72 73 71 79			295	3,900
Paul Stankowski	76 70 72 77			295	3,900
Eric Johnson	73 71 79 73			296	3,780
Jimmy Johnston	73 68 79 76			296	3,780
Omar Uresti	73 72 73 78			296	3,780
Grant Waite	73 72 77 74			296	3,780
Joey Sindelar	73 73 74 77			297	3,680
Alan Pate	74 72 78 74			298	3,640

Quad City Classic

Oakwood Country Club, Coal Valley, Illinois
Par 35-35–70; 6,672 yards

July 10-13
purse, $1,350,000

	SCORES			TOTAL	MONEY
David Toms	67 66 67 65			265	$243,000
Brandel Chamblee	71 65 65 67			268	100,800
Robert Gamez	67 65 69 67			268	100,800
Jimmy Johnston	70 67 69 62			268	100,800
Brad Fabel	68 67 65 69			269	51,300
Frank Lickliter	71 67 63 68			269	51,300
Russ Cochran	66 67 68 69			270	42,075
Dave Rummells	68 70 65 67			270	42,075
Steve Stricker	69 68 67 66			270	42,075
John Adams	69 66 68 68			271	28,012.50
Ed Dougherty	67 65 71 68			271	28,012.50
Wayne Levi	68 67 68 68			271	28,012.50
John Maginnes	71 66 67 67			271	28,012.50
Anthony Painter	70 69 65 67			271	28,012.50
Kenny Perry	67 68 68 68			271	28,012.50
Scott Verplank	67 68 67 69			271	28,012.50
Bob Wolcott	70 66 68 67			271	28,012.50
Emlyn Aubrey	67 68 69 68			272	17,604
Olin Browne	69 69 68 66			272	17,604
Skip Kendall	69 67 71 65			272	17,604
Jeff Sluman	70 68 68 66			272	17,604
Phil Tataurangi	69 70 67 66			272	17,604
Keith Clearwater	70 68 66 69			273	9,912.16
Bruce Fleisher	67 69 69 68			273	9,912.16

					SCORES		TOTAL	MONEY
Jim Gallagher, Jr.	67	70	68	68			273	9,912.16
J.P. Hayes	67	69	68	69			273	9,912.16
Mike Sullivan	67	67	71	68			273	9,912.16
Craig Bowden	69	67	66	71			273	9,912.15
David Edwards	67	69	67	70			273	9,912.15
Bob Estes	67	69	67	70			273	9,912.15
Keith Fergus	67	64	71	71			273	9,912.15
Eric Johnson	67	69	66	71			273	9,912.15
Sean McCarty	66	67	70	70			273	9,912.15
Mark Pfeil	69	69	65	70			273	9,912.15
Brad Sutterfield	68	69	65	71			273	9,912.15
Mike Brisky	71	65	69	69			274	6,084.58
Woody Austin	71	67	67	69			274	6,084.57
Shane Bertsch	68	70	69	67			274	6,084.57
Ronnie Black	67	70	68	69			274	6,084.57
Gabriel Hjertstedt	69	70	69	66			274	6,084.57
Sonny Skinner	70	67	72	65			274	6,084.57
Dave Stockton, Jr.	66	72	66	70			274	6,084.57
Marco Dawson	71	67	68	69			275	4,023
Joel Edwards	69	71	66	69			275	4,023
Jimmy Green	70	70	67	68			275	4,023
Scott Gump	68	69	69	69			275	4,023
Gary Hallberg	65	70	69	71			275	4,023
Mike Springer	72	68	68	67			275	4,023
Omar Uresti	71	66	68	70			275	4,023
Bobby Wadkins	69	71	67	68			275	4,023
Grant Waite	69	67	70	69			275	4,023
Ken Green	69	71	66	70			276	3,132
Scott Hoch	71	69	66	70			276	3,132
Jack O'Keefe	67	70	68	71			276	3,132
David Ogrin	70	70	66	70			276	3,132
Gene Sauers	69	69	68	70			276	3,132
David Sutherland	70	70	67	69			276	3,132
Guy Boros	68	69	68	72			277	2,970
Kevin Burton	70	70	67	70			277	2,970
Kelly Gibson	68	71	67	71			277	2,970
Tim Simpson	67	73	69	68			277	2,970
Willie Wood	71	66	69	71			277	2,970
Rafael Alarcon	72	68	68	70			278	2,794.50
Kevin Denike	68	70	72	68			278	2,794.50
Mike Donald	68	72	69	69			278	2,794.50
Ed Fiori	70	69	69	70			278	2,794.50
Lon Hinkle	71	68	69	70			278	2,794.50
Lanny Wadkins	70	70	70	68			278	2,794.50
D.A. Weibring	71	69	70	68			278	2,794.50
John Wilson	69	69	68	72			278	2,794.50
George Burns	72	66	71	70			279	2,632.50
Todd Demsey	68	72	70	69			279	2,632.50
Mike Smith	72	66	73	68			279	2,632.50
Richard Zokol	70	69	70	70			279	2,632.50
Brian Claar	68	70	72	70			280	2,497.50
Bobby Clampett	70	68	69	73			280	2,497.50
Greg Kraft	69	71	70	70			280	2,497.50
Billy Mayfair	67	71	71	71			280	2,497.50
Lee Rinker	76	64	69	71			280	2,497.50
Mike Standly	71	68	70	71			280	2,497.50
P.H. Horgan III	71	69	73	68			281	2,403
Bill Hoefle	67	73	70	72			282	2,335.50
Jim McGovern	69	69	69	75			282	2,335.50
Shaun Micheel	68	69	71	74			282	2,335.50

	SCORES	TOTAL	MONEY
Tom Pernice, Jr.	67 71 72 72	282	2,335.50
Dick Mast	70 67 72 76	285	2,254.50
Ben Peters	71 68 73 73	285	2,254.50
Barry Jaeckel	68 71 70 78	287	2,214

Deposit Guaranty Golf Classic

Annandale Golf Club, Madison, Mississippi
Par 36-36–72; 7,157 yards

July 17-20
purse, $1,000,000

	SCORES	TOTAL	MONEY
Billy Ray Brown	69 66 69 67	271	$180,000
Mike Standly	69 67 70 66	272	108,000
Mike Brisky	64 74 67 68	273	68,000
Brian Claar	67 69 68 70	274	36,250
Steve Jurgensen	66 67 69 72	274	36,250
Steve Lowery	69 65 70 70	274	36,250
Blaine McCallister	70 67 70 67	274	36,250
Brian Rowell	69 68 69 68	274	36,250
Mike Springer	69 69 67 69	274	36,250
Woody Austin	66 69 71 69	275	25,000
Brian Henninger	68 68 70 69	275	25,000
Don Pooley	65 68 71 71	275	25,000
Ken Green	71 68 67 70	276	17,666.67
David Ogrin	67 67 71 71	276	17,666.67
Sonny Skinner	70 69 70 67	276	17,666.67
Kirk Triplett	70 69 71 66	276	17,666.66
Skip Kendall	66 70 69 71	276	17,666.66
Jack O'Keefe	67 69 69 71	276	17,666.66
Brad Fabel	70 71 69 67	277	10,522.23
Keith Fergus	70 69 72 66	277	10,522.23
Tommy Armour III	69 68 71 69	277	10,522.22
Robin Freeman	68 70 69 70	277	10,522.22
Jimmy Green	68 72 70 67	277	10,522.22
J.P. Hayes	65 76 68 68	277	10,522.22
Frank Lickliter	73 68 69 67	277	10,522.22
Spike McRoy	67 73 66 71	277	10,522.22
Scott Verplank	67 68 70 72	277	10,522.22
Craig Bowden	68 70 69 71	278	6,650
Tom Byrum	69 70 70 69	278	6,650
David Edwards	70 70 67 71	278	6,650
Bob Estes	71 69 68 70	278	6,650
Joey Sindelar	66 70 71 71	278	6,650
Bobby Wadkins	67 69 70 72	278	6,650
Kevin Burton	71 67 72 69	279	5,050
Bobby Clampett	68 71 69 71	279	5,050
Jeff Hart	69 68 72 70	279	5,050
Brett Quigley	68 73 71 67	279	5,050
Gene Sauers	68 73 70 68	279	5,050
Hal Sutton	67 73 67 72	279	5,050
Paul Claxton	70 67 70 73	280	3,800
Robert Gamez	70 69 73 68	280	3,800
Bradley Hughes	71 70 67 72	280	3,800
Pete Jordan	69 72 69 70	280	3,800
Dave Rummells	68 70 72 70	280	3,800
David Toms	67 74 71 68	280	3,800
John Adams	67 69 77 68	281	2,543.64
Russ Cochran	69 70 71 71	281	2,543.64

	SCORES				TOTAL	MONEY
Bruce Fleisher	68	69	73	71	281	2,543.64
John Huston	68	69	74	70	281	2,543.64
Dave Stockton, Jr.	70	71	69	71	281	2,543.64
Ted Tryba	74	66	70	71	281	2,543.64
Howard Twitty	70	71	72	68	281	2,543.64
David Berganio, Jr.	66	72	70	73	281	2,543.63
Brandel Chamblee	66	73	69	73	281	2,543.63
John Dowdall	68	72	69	72	281	2,543.63
P.H. Horgan III	67	71	70	73	281	2,543.63
Bill Glasson	71	67	70	74	282	2,230
Neal Lancaster	69	72	68	73	282	2,230
David Peoples	67	71	71	73	282	2,230
Doug Tewell	67	73	72	70	282	2,230
Michael Christie	66	72	70	75	283	2,100
Jay Delsing	69	70	74	70	283	2,100
Joel Edwards	70	71	66	76	283	2,100
Kelly Gibson	71	68	69	75	283	2,100
Gabriel Hjertstedt	68	73	70	72	283	2,100
John Inman	71	70	71	71	283	2,100
Craig Kanada	64	73	74	72	283	2,100
Mike Sullivan	69	68	77	69	283	2,100
Bob Wolcott	72	68	71	72	283	2,100
Todd Demsey	69	70	71	74	284	1,980
Allen Doyle	71	70	73	70	284	1,980
Joe Durant	72	69	70	73	284	1,980
Doug Barron	72	69	74	70	285	1,940
Chip Sullivan	71	70	77	68	286	1,920
Rex Caldwell	70	71	73	74	288	1,890
Mike Donald	71	70	72	75	288	1,890
Tray Tyner	69	71	77	72	289	1,860

Canon Greater Hartford Open

TPC at River Highlands, Cromwell, Connecticut
Par 35-35–70; 6,820 yards
July 24-27
purse, $1,500,000

	SCORES				TOTAL	MONEY
Stewart Cink	69	67	65	66	267	$270,000
Tom Byrum	66	68	65	69	268	112,000
Brandel Chamblee	68	65	69	66	268	112,000
Jeff Maggert	67	66	64	71	268	112,000
Mark Calcavecchia	69	69	67	66	271	60,000
Kelly Gibson	67	74	65	66	272	50,250
P.H. Horgan III	67	71	68	66	272	50,250
Wayne Levi	64	65	70	73	272	50,250
Doug Barron	66	68	66	73	273	39,000
Mike Brisky	69	69	65	70	273	39,000
Steve Pate	65	68	70	70	273	39,000
Phil Tataurangi	69	69	68	67	273	39,000
Billy Andrade	68	70	67	69	274	28,125
Nolan Henke	68	70	68	68	274	28,125
John Huston	70	70	66	68	274	28,125
Kevin Sutherland	67	73	68	66	274	28,125
Paul Claxton	70	67	66	72	275	21,750
Joe Durant	66	69	71	69	275	21,750
Rick Fehr	72	68	70	65	275	21,750
David Ogrin	68	69	69	69	275	21,750
Michael Christie	70	69	68	69	276	14,081.2

	SCORES			TOTAL	MONEY
John Daly	71	70	67	68	276	14,081.25
Brad Fabel	72	69	66	69	276	14,081.25
Billy Mayfair	70	69	67	70	276	14,081.25
Tom Pernice, Jr.	67	71	69	69	276	14,081.25
Kenny Perry	68	69	69	70	276	14,081.25
Jeff Sluman	69	74	70	63	276	14,081.25
D.A. Weibring	69	70	69	68	276	14,081.25
Brian Claar	68	72	69	68	277	9,537.50
Lennie Clements	67	70	67	73	277	9,537.50
Scott Dunlap	71	69	70	67	277	9,537.50
Fred Funk	69	69	68	71	277	9,537.50
Doug Martin	68	71	68	70	277	9,537.50
Larry Mize	68	69	70	70	277	9,537.50
Phil Blackmar	70	73	64	71	278	7,395
Spike McRoy	71	69	71	67	278	7,395
Don Pooley	69	70	67	72	278	7,395
Mike Reid	70	71	67	70	278	7,395
Dave Stockton, Jr.	70	70	70	68	278	7,395
Mark Brooks	72	69	71	67	279	4,790.77
Patrick Burke	69	72	69	69	279	4,790.77
Tim Herron	73	68	65	73	279	4,790.77
Craig Kanada	68	72	70	69	279	4,790.77
Frank Lickliter	69	71	70	69	279	4,790.77
Jim McGovern	70	73	63	73	279	4,790.77
Sonny Skinner	68	73	69	69	279	4,790.77
Craig Stadler	70	69	69	71	279	4,790.77
Mike Standly	71	72	67	69	279	4,790.77
Chip Sullivan	71	72	67	69	279	4,790.77
Lanny Wadkins	70	69	74	66	279	4,790.77
Fuzzy Zoeller	70	73	67	69	279	4,790.77
Eduardo Herrera	71	71	63	74	279	4,790.76
Tommy Armour III	70	68	72	70	280	3,408.75
Emlyn Aubrey	72	71	67	70	280	3,408.75
Brad Faxon	67	71	69	73	280	3,408.75
J.P. Hayes	66	73	73	68	280	3,408.75
Mike Hulbert	70	72	69	69	280	3,408.75
Eric Johnson	64	70	72	74	280	3,408.75
Joey Sindelar	70	71	69	70	280	3,408.75
Jay Williamson	72	69	68	71	280	3,408.75
Rafael Alarcon	74	68	71	68	281	3,210
Craig Bowden	71	68	72	70	281	3,210
Jim Gallagher, Jr.	69	74	68	70	281	3,210
Paul Goydos	69	69	69	74	281	3,210
Bob Wolcott	68	73	72	68	281	3,210
Keith Fergus	70	70	69	73	282	3,105
Peter Jacobsen	72	70	69	71	282	3,105
Ronnie Black	69	73	67	74	283	3,000
David Edwards	73	70	67	73	283	3,000
Bradley Hughes	69	72	72	70	283	3,000
Scott Simpson	72	69	68	74	283	3,000
Willie Wood	72	70	67	74	283	3,000
John Dowdall	69	66	70	79	284	2,865
Shaun Micheel	74	69	71	70	284	2,865
John Morse	67	71	69	77	284	2,865
Grant Waite	73	69	70	72	284	2,865
Robert Damron	72	71	71	72	286	2,760
Scott Gump	70	72	73	71	286	2,760
Paul Stankowski	67	76	70	73	286	2,760
Steve Jurgensen	73	70	73	73	289	2,700
Anthony Rodriguez	67	76	71	76	290	2,670

Sprint International

Castle Pines Golf Club, Castle Rock, Colorado
Par 36-36–72; 7,559 yards

July 31-August 3
purse, $1,700,000

FINAL ROUND

	POINTS				TOTAL	MONEY
Phil Mickelson	14	13	12	9	48	$306,000
Stuart Appleby	9	10	13	9	41	183,600
Skip Kendall	10	12	12	4	38	115,600
Dudley Hart	10	10	8	6	34	81,600
Kevin Sutherland	3	14	8	8	33	62,050
Jay Haas	15	4	10	4	33	62,050
Jim Furyk	3	8	12	9	32	52,983.34
Ernie Els	5	6	14	7	32	52,983.33
Larry Mize	15	8	3	6	32	52,983.33
Nick Price	6	14	7	4	31	45,900
Scott McCarron	11	13	2	4	30	42,500
Davis Love III	5	8	9	7	29	39,100
Neal Lancaster	8	14	5	1	28	35,700
Andrew Magee	11	5	8	3	27	32,300
Hideki Kase	10	2	12	2	26	30,600
Brad Faxon	10	8	2	4	25	28,050
Pete Jordan	6	11	6	2	25	28,050
Kenny Perry	9	6	7	1	23	23,800
Steve Stricker	7	9	7	0	23	23,800
Kirk Triplett	8	10	6	-1	23	23,800
Tom Purtzer	-4	20	7	-1	22	20,400
Brent Geiberger	8	2	13	-3	20	19,040
David Sutherland	3	9	12	-7	17	17,680
Tommy Armour III	8	8	11	-13	14	16,320

IN THE MONEY

				TOTAL	MONEY
Dave Stockton, Jr.	12	3	6	21	13,883.33
Mark Calcavecchia	4	9	8	21	13,883.33
Tom Lehman	13	5	3	21	13,883.34
Olin Browne	10	6	4	20	12,070
Michael Bradley	4	6	10	20	12,070
Jim Carter	4	5	11	20	12,070
Greg Norman	9	9	1	19	10,795
Taylor Smith	6	8	5	19	10,795
Stewart Cink	9	5	4	18	9,605
Scott Gump	0	13	5	18	9,605
Tom Pernice, Jr.	4	5	9	18	9,605
Craig Stadler	6	5	6	17	8,358.34
P.H. Horgan III	6	6	5	17	8,358.33
Grant Waite	8	4	5	17	8,358.33
Tom Kite	1	9	6	16	6,970
Gary Hallberg	8	5	3	16	6,970
John Huston	6	7	3	16	6,970
Justin Leonard	3	8	5	16	6,970
Tommy Tolles	3	6	7	16	6,970
Lee Janzen	0	8	7	15	5,440
Brian Henninger	8	1	6	15	5,440
Doug Martin	2	6	7	15	5,440
Duffy Waldorf	3	9	3	15	5,440
Emlyn Aubrey	4	10	0	14	4,539
Marco Dawson	1	8	5	14	4,539

	POINTS	TOTAL	MONEY
Steve Pate	2 9 2	13	4,100.40
Corey Pavin	-1 8 6	13	4,100.40
Doug Barron	0 10 3	13	4,100.40
Michael Christie	6 2 5	13	4,100.40
David Berganio, Jr.	4 4 5	13	4,100.40
Mark Brooks	3 7 2	12	3,842
Greg Kraft	4 3 5	12	3,842
Charlie Rymer	5 4 3	12	3,842
Jimmy Johnston	5 7 0	12	3,842
Brad Fabel	2 7 3	12	3,842
D.A. Weibring	4 6 1	11	3,723
Frank Lickliter	0 7 4	11	3,723
Rick Fehr	6 5 -1	10	3,655
Scott Simpson	9 0 1	10	3,655
Dicky Pride	3 4 2	9	3,604
Ed Dougherty	3 4 1	8	3,536
Dan Forsman	3 10 -5	8	3,536
Jimmy Green	8 0 0	8	3,536
Brandel Chamblee	3 10 -2	5	3,451
Robin Freeman	6 1 -2	5	3,451
Ted Tryba	7 0 -3	4	3,400
Joe Durant	4 3 -4	3	3,366
Rocco Mediate	4 6 -16	-6	3,332

Buick Open

Warwick Hills Country Club, Flint, Michigan
Par 36-36–72; 7,105 yards

August 7-10
purse, $1,500,000

	SCORES	TOTAL	MONEY
Vijay Singh	67 73 67 66	273	$270,000
Tom Byrum	72 68 70 67	277	83,375
Russ Cochran	68 69 73 67	277	83,375
Ernie Els	68 63 72 74	277	83,375
Brad Fabel	69 67 70 71	277	83,375
Naomichi Ozaki	67 71 70 69	277	83,375
Curtis Strange	72 66 68 71	277	83,375
Dan Forsman	68 67 73 70	278	43,500
Rocco Mediate	70 71 67 70	278	43,500
Tiger Woods	72 68 70 68	278	43,500
Bob Estes	70 70 69 70	279	33,000
Brent Geiberger	69 71 69 70	279	33,000
Payne Stewart	72 65 72 70	279	33,000
Lanny Wadkins	67 69 74 69	279	33,000
Jay Don Blake	70 73 69 68	280	24,000
Jim Furyk	67 72 75 66	280	24,000
Tom Pernice, Jr.	71 68 68 73	280	24,000
David Sutherland	71 72 67 70	280	24,000
Bray Tyner	69 74 69 68	280	24,000
Nolan Henke	66 73 70 72	281	16,250
Frank Nobilo	69 71 70 71	281	16,250
Chris Perry	67 69 74 71	281	16,250
Brett Quigley	71 71 71 68	281	16,250
Dave Rummells	69 72 72 68	281	16,250
Bob Tway	71 69 71 70	281	16,250
Paul Goydos	69 72 70 71	282	11,550
Scott Gump	71 69 69 73	282	11,550

	SCORES				TOTAL	MONEY
Larry Mize	68	69	69	76	282	11,550
John Cook	73	70	69	71	283	9,332.15
Jack O'Keefe	71	72	71	69	283	9,332.15
Rafael Alarcon	67	72	72	72	283	9,332.14
Bruce Fleisher	68	73	71	71	283	9,332.14
Wayne Levi	70	71	70	72	283	9,332.14
Doug Martin	71	71	70	71	283	9,332.14
John Morse	67	69	74	73	283	9,332.14
Tommy Armour III	70	70	72	72	284	6,912.50
Lennie Clements	72	70	73	69	284	6,912.50
Allen Doyle	69	67	73	75	284	6,912.50
Eric Johnson	71	69	72	72	284	6,912.50
Gene Sauers	72	69	74	69	284	6,912.50
Jeff Sluman	69	72	69	74	284	6,912.50
Doug Tewell	72	71	74	68	285	4,958.58
Fred Couples	69	73	69	74	285	4,958.57
Scott Hoch	72	67	71	75	285	4,958.57
Greg Kraft	71	72	70	72	285	4,958.57
Jeff Maggert	71	71	74	69	285	4,958.57
Hal Sutton	67	69	73	76	285	4,958.57
Grant Waite	74	68	68	75	285	4,958.57
Paul Claxton	69	72	75	70	286	3,561
Fred Funk	67	74	76	69	286	3,561
Bill Glasson	74	69	73	70	286	3,561
Gabriel Hjertstedt	70	73	70	73	286	3,561
John Huston	71	72	74	69	286	3,561
Jimmy Johnston	71	70	71	74	286	3,561
Skip Kendall	69	70	75	72	286	3,561
Justin Leonard	70	72	73	71	286	3,561
Shaun Micheel	71	69	74	72	286	3,561
Tom Purtzer	71	71	75	69	286	3,561
Eric Booker	71	72	70	74	287	3,255
Brian Claar	71	71	72	73	287	3,255
Joe Durant	69	72	74	72	287	3,255
Lee Porter	71	72	74	70	287	3,255
Sonny Skinner	62	76	74	75	287	3,255
Tommy Tolles	69	71	72	75	287	3,255
Shane Bertsch	74	69	72	73	288	3,105
Ed Dougherty	69	69	74	76	288	3,105
Steve Elkington	70	71	75	72	288	3,105
Tony Mollica	72	68	72	76	288	3,105
John Maginnes	71	71	74	73	289	3,030
Keith Fergus	71	71	75	74	291	2,970
Larry Nelson	71	70	73	77	291	2,970
Duffy Waldorf	71	71	76	73	291	2,970
Jim Gallagher, Jr.	71	72	72	78	293	2,895
J.P. Hayes	72	69	76	76	293	2,895

PGA Championship

Winged Foot Golf Club, West Course,
Mamaroneck, New York
Par 35-35–70; 6,987 yards

August 14-1
purse, $2,400,00

	SCORES				TOTAL	MONEY
Davis Love III	66	71	66	66	269	$470,000
Justin Leonard	68	70	65	71	274	280,000
Jeff Maggert	69	69	73	65	276	175,000

	SCORES				TOTAL	MONEY
Lee Janzen	69	67	74	69	279	125,000
Tom Kite	68	71	71	70	280	105,000
Phil Blackmar	70	68	74	69	281	85,000
Jim Furyk	69	72	72	68	281	85,000
Scott Hoch	71	72	68	70	281	85,000
Tom Byrum	69	73	70	70	282	70,000
Tom Lehman	69	72	72	70	283	60,000
Scott McCarron	74	71	67	71	283	60,000
Joey Sindelar	72	71	71	69	283	60,000
David Duval	70	70	71	73	284	35,100
Tim Herron	72	73	68	71	284	35,100
Colin Montgomerie	74	71	67	72	284	35,100
Greg Norman	68	71	74	71	284	35,100
Nick Price	72	70	72	70	284	35,100
Vijay Singh	73	66	76	69	284	35,100
Tommy Tolles	75	70	73	66	284	35,100
Kirk Triplett	73	70	71	70	284	35,100
Bob Tway	68	75	72	69	284	35,100
Mark O'Meara	69	73	75	67	284	35,100
Mark Calcavecchia	71	74	73	67	285	22,500
Bernhard Langer	73	71	72	69	285	22,500
Doug Martin	69	75	74	67	285	22,500
Shigeki Maruyama	68	70	74	73	285	22,500
Kenny Perry	73	68	73	71	285	22,500
John Cook	71	71	74	69	285	22,500
Paul Azinger	68	73	71	74	286	13,625
Ronnie Black	76	69	71	70	286	13,625
Fred Couples	71	67	73	75	286	13,625
John Daly	66	73	77	70	286	13,625
Paul Goydos	70	72	71	73	286	13,625
Hale Irwin	73	70	71	72	286	13,625
Phil Mickelson	69	69	73	75	286	13,625
Frank Nobilo	72	73	67	74	286	13,625
Don Pooley	72	74	70	70	286	13,625
Payne Stewart	70	70	72	74	286	13,625
Lee Westwood	74	68	71	73	286	13,625
Tiger Woods	70	70	71	75	286	13,625
Ignacio Garrido	70	71	75	71	287	8,375
Steve Jones	69	73	75	70	287	8,375
David Ogrin	74	72	71	70	287	8,375
Eduardo Romero	71	72	72	72	287	8,375
Thomas Bjorn	72	68	77	71	288	7,375
Steve Elkington	72	72	70	74	288	7,375
Jesper Parnevik	76	70	71	71	288	7,375
Sam Torrance	74	72	70	72	288	7,375
Robert Allenby	67	77	74	71	289	6,375
Brian Henninger	74	68	75	72	289	6,375
Chris Perry	68	71	73	77	289	6,375
Loren Roberts	76	70	74	69	289	6,375
Olin Browne	70	73	74	73	290	5,280
Ernie Els	70	76	74	70	290	5,280
Billy Mayfair	75	68	75	72	290	5,280
Taylor Smith	71	71	74	74	290	5,280
Craig Stadler	72	72	74	72	290	5,280
Steve Lowery	72	69	79	71	291	4,700
Larry Mize	71	73	73	74	291	4,700
Lanny Wadkins	72	72	77	70	291	4,700
Stuart Appleby	75	70	69	78	292	4,333.34
Jay Haas	71	69	73	79	292	4,333.34
Russ Cochran	72	73	72	75	292	4,333.33

	SCORES				TOTAL	MONEY
Fred Funk	71	74	77	70	292	4,333.33
Retief Goosen	72	70	74	76	292	4,333.33
Lee Rinker	70	71	75	76	292	4,333.33
Peter Jacobsen	74	72	75	72	293	4,100
Per-Ulrik Johansson	73	69	73	78	293	4,100
Paul Stankowski	68	71	77	77	293	4,100
Carlos Franco	69	74	76	75	294	4,000
Michael Bradley	73	69	80	73	295	3,875
Yoshinori Kaneko	72	73	76	74	295	3,875
Larry Nelson	76	70	76	73	295	3,875
Costantino Rocca	69	69	79	78	295	3,875
Andrew Magee	71	70	80	75	296	3,750
Pete Jordan	76	70	75	76	297	3,675
Kevin Sutherland	73	73	73	78	297	3,675

Out of Final 36 Holes

			TOTAL
Billy Andrade	72	75	147
Bob Boyd	71	76	147
Jim Carter	73	74	147
Rick Fehr	72	75	147
David Frost	76	71	147
Len Mattiace	72	75	147
Billy Ray Brown	76	72	148
Robert Damron	76	72	148
Glen Day	76	72	148
Padraig Harrington	77	71	148
Jeffrey Lankford	72	76	148
Craig Parry	74	74	148
Ron Philo, Jr.	72	76	148
Steve Stricker	73	75	148
David Toms	73	75	148
Fuzzy Zoeller	73	75	148
Guy Boros	81	68	149
Mike Brisky	75	74	149
Paul Broadhurst	74	75	149
Mark Brooks	70	79	149
Bob Ford	74	75	149
John Mazza	71	78	149
Jay Overton	77	72	149
Chris Toulson	75	74	149
Ian Woosnam	77	72	149
Robert Gamez	74	76	150
Kelly Gibson	76	74	150
Dudley Hart	74	76	150
Mike Hulbert	75	75	150
Jack Nicklaus	74	76	150
Naomichi Ozaki	75	75	150
John Stone	75	75	150
Tom Watson	71	79	150
Jay Don Blake	73	78	151
Brandel Chamblee	77	74	151
Stewart Cink	76	75	151
Brad Faxon	73	78	151
Clarence Rose	74	77	151
Jeff Sluman	74	77	151
Bob Sowards	74	77	151
Michael Burke, Jr.	77	75	152
Ed Fiori	76	76	152
Jose Maria Olazabal	79	73	152

	SCORES		TOTAL
Duffy Waldorf	74	78	152
Darren Clarke	74	79	153
Frank Dobbs	80	73	153
Nick Faldo	75	78	153
Steve Schneiter	75	78	153
Curtis Strange	76	77	153
Chris Tucker	78	75	153
Bruce Zabriski	76	77	153
Peter Lonard	75	79	154
Bob Makoski	79	75	154
Mike Standly	76	78	154
John Lee	74	81	155
Pete Oakley	78	77	155
Brian Watts	78	77	155
Shawn Kelly	76	80	156
Hal Sutton	78	78	156
Rob Wilkin	78	78	156
Ben Crenshaw	77	80	157
Jerry Kelly	81	76	157
Jim White	82	75	157
Wayne Grady	79	79	158
James Mason	78	80	158
John Hickson	76	84	160
Darrell Kestner	79	83	162
Mark Fuller	79	84	163
John Paesani	79	85	164
Bret Taylor	82	83	165
Mark Wiebe	77		WD
John Mahaffey	78		WD
Frankie Minoza	80		WD

(Professionals who did not complete 72 holes received $1,200.)

NEC World Series of Golf

Firestone Country Club, South Course, Akron, Ohio
Par 35-35–70; 7,149 yards

August 21-24
purse, $2,200,000

	SCORES				TOTAL	MONEY
Greg Norman	68	68	70	67	273	$396,000
Phil Mickelson	67	72	66	72	277	237,600
John Cook	68	69	67	74	278	114,400
Fred Funk	70	69	71	68	278	114,400
Tiger Woods	67	72	69	70	278	114,400
Vijay Singh	71	71	71	66	279	79,200
Carlos Franco	75	67	68	70	280	70,950
Tom Lehman	74	66	69	71	280	70,950
Davis Love III	68	71	70	72	281	59,400
David Ogrin	71	70	67	73	281	59,400
Nick Price	68	71	68	74	281	59,400
Billy Ray Brown	72	72	66	72	282	44,550
Frank Nobilo	69	71	71	71	282	44,550
Phil Tataurangi	72	72	67	71	282	44,550
Lee Westwood	69	73	66	74	282	44,550
Ernie Els	68	71	74	70	283	35,200
Mark O'Meara	68	71	71	73	283	35,200
Loren Roberts	71	67	74	71	283	35,200

	SCORES	TOTAL	MONEY
Stewart Cink	69 73 73 69	284	27,700
Dudley Hart	69 65 76 74	284	27,700
Justin Leonard	73 73 66 72	284	27,700
Jeff Sluman	69 75 67 73	284	27,700
Robert Allenby	71 71 70 74	286	22,900
Scott McCarron	69 73 68 76	286	22,900
Darren Clarke	72 76 70 70	288	21,000
Shigeki Maruyama	74 72 72 72	290	18,900
Naomichi Ozaki	71 71 75 73	290	18,900
Jesper Parnevik	74 70 72 74	290	18,900
Peter Senior	73 73 71 73	290	18,900
David Toms	73 70 73 74	290	18,900
Nick Faldo	73 70 72 76	291	17,937.50
Steve Jones	72 74 73 72	291	17,937.50
Stuart Appleby	72 73 73 74	292	17,675
Guy Boros	73 73 72 75	293	17,412.50
David Frost	74 71 71 77	293	17,412.50
Michael Bradley	70 72 75 77	294	16,887.50
Ed Fiori	73 73 74 74	294	16,887.50
Yoshinori Mizumaki	73 75 72 74	294	16,887.50
Warren Schutte	73 74 74 73	294	16,887.50
Brad Faxon	74 72 74 75	295	16,375
Peter Lonard	75 68 79 73	295	16,375
Steve Elkington	74 73 74 75	296	16,150
Darrell Kestner	70 78 74 75	297	16,000
Phil Blackmar	75 70 75 79	299	15,850
Peter Teravainen	71 76 78 76	301	15,725
Paul Stankowski	72 73 79 78	302	15,600

Greater Vancouver Open

Northview Golf & Country Club, Ridge Course,
Surrey, British Columbia, Canada
Par 35-36–71; 6,817 yards

August 21-24
purse, $1,500,000

	SCORES	TOTAL	MONEY
Mark Calcavecchia	68 66 65 66	265	$270,000
Andrew Magee	65 71 65 65	266	162,000
Bob Estes	66 67 69 65	267	102,000
Russ Cochran	69 68 66 66	269	72,000
P.H. Horgan III	71 63 72 64	270	60,000
John Adams	66 68 67 70	271	45,375
Michael Christie	71 67 68 65	271	45,375
Bill Glasson	67 68 67 69	271	45,375
Tim Herron	66 69 67 69	271	45,375
Payne Stewart	64 68 68 71	271	45,375
David Sutherland	66 68 68 69	271	45,375
Joel Edwards	67 71 72 62	272	27,642.86
Brent Geiberger	68 65 70 69	272	27,642.86
Lee Janzen	67 70 69 66	272	27,642.86
Greg Kraft	66 71 68 67	272	27,642.86
Rick Todd	67 67 72 66	272	27,642.86
Brett Quigley	70 69 66 67	272	27,642.83
Richard Zokol	67 64 70 71	272	27,642.83
Skip Kendall	65 70 69 69	273	20,250
Jim Thorpe	70 66 72 65	273	20,250
Robert Damron	67 70 71 66	274	16,800

	SCORES				TOTAL	MONEY
Rick Fehr	69	67	69	69	274	16,800
Dave Rummells	67	70	66	71	274	16,800
David Berganio, Jr.	67	70	70	68	275	11,871.43
Todd Demsey	69	66	70	70	275	11,871.43
Joe Durant	66	70	69	70	275	11,871.43
Kelly Gibson	70	69	70	66	275	11,871.43
Sandy Lyle	67	69	71	68	275	11,871.43
Dicky Pride	69	69	67	70	275	11,871.43
Len Mattiace	64	67	71	73	275	11,871.42
Shane Bertsch	67	71	69	69	276	8,325
Patrick Burke	72	66	69	69	276	8,325
Bruce Fleisher	66	69	71	70	276	8,325
Steve Pate	67	64	70	75	276	8,325
Charlie Rymer	67	71	72	66	276	8,325
Chris Smith	69	70	72	65	276	8,325
Kevin Sutherland	69	68	69	70	276	8,325
Tray Tyner	67	71	70	68	276	8,325
Rafael Alarcon	66	71	68	72	277	6,000
Tom Byrum	63	69	71	74	277	6,000
Bradley Hughes	71	66	70	70	277	6,000
Philip Jonas	68	71	70	68	277	6,000
David Peoples	69	68	70	70	277	6,000
Grant Waite	69	67	74	67	277	6,000
Paul Claxton	66	68	73	71	278	4,290
Scott Dunlap	68	68	70	72	278	4,290
Glen Hnatiuk	71	67	72	68	278	4,290
Mike Reid	68	70	66	74	278	4,290
Ray Stewart	66	69	67	76	278	4,290
Chip Sullivan	70	66	70	72	278	4,290
John Dowdall	67	66	70	76	279	3,491.25
J.P. Hayes	70	66	71	72	279	3,491.25
Brian Henninger	69	66	69	75	279	3,491.25
Neal Lancaster	73	65	72	69	279	3,491.25
Jeff Maggert	69	67	71	72	279	3,491.25
Gene Sauers	73	66	72	68	279	3,491.25
Craig Stadler	66	69	72	72	279	3,491.25
Dave Stockton, Jr.	68	71	73	67	279	3,491.25
Jay Delsing	68	68	72	72	280	3,285
Robert Gamez	67	69	71	73	280	3,285
Scott Gump	69	66	74	71	280	3,285
Hal Sutton	66	69	74	71	280	3,285
Keith Clearwater	67	71	68	75	281	3,135
Lennie Clements	69	68	77	67	281	3,135
Adam Mednick	68	67	71	75	281	3,135
Larry Rinker	68	69	68	76	281	3,135
Greg Twiggs	66	72	73	70	281	3,135
Mark Wiebe	65	68	72	76	281	3,135
Craig Parry	67	70	74	71	282	3,030
George Burns	67	72	74	70	283	2,985
Mike Standly	72	67	71	73	283	2,985
Tommy Armour III	69	67	77	71	284	2,925
John Wilson	68	68	77	71	284	2,925
Kevin Burton	70	69	75	71	285	2,835
Brian Claar	70	69	73	73	285	2,835
Hideki Kase	67	70	74	74	285	2,835
Omar Uresti	69	70	73	73	285	2,835
Lee Porter	69	70	74	76	289	2,760
Jeff Hart	65	73	79	73	290	2,730

Greater Milwaukee Open

Brown Deer Park Golf Course, Milwaukee, Wisconsin
Par 35-36–71; 6,739 yards

August 28-31
purse, $1,300,000

	SCORES				TOTAL	MONEY
Scott Hoch	70	66	66	66	268	$234,000
Loren Roberts	67	69	67	66	269	114,400
David Sutherland	70	65	65	69	269	114,400
Tom Pernice, Jr.	68	69	64	69	270	62,400
Fulton Allem	67	69	64	71	271	47,450
Lee Rinker	68	69	66	68	271	47,450
Clarence Rose	67	66	71	67	271	47,450
Ronnie Black	70	68	70	64	272	36,400
Bill Glasson	66	71	68	67	272	36,400
Jerry Kelly	71	66	66	69	272	36,400
Frank Lickliter	67	71	68	66	272	36,400
Stewart Cink	70	68	68	67	273	23,237.50
Bob Estes	68	70	69	66	273	23,237.50
Brad Fabel	70	66	71	66	273	23,237.50
Ken Green	70	68	64	71	273	23,237.50
Jay Haas	70	70	69	64	273	23,237.50
Skip Kendall	69	69	64	71	273	23,237.50
Chris Smith	68	69	69	67	273	23,237.50
Steve Stricker	70	66	71	66	273	23,237.50
Andrew Magee	66	70	70	68	274	14,083.34
Brett Quigley	71	67	71	65	274	14,083.34
Billy Andrade	68	69	67	70	274	14,083.33
Mark Calcavecchia	67	69	69	69	274	14,083.33
Spike McRoy	71	63	70	70	274	14,083.33
Adam Mednick	67	69	70	68	274	14,083.33
Doug Barron	73	67	68	67	275	9,035
Mike Brisky	66	71	70	68	275	9,035
Lennie Clements	66	71	69	69	275	9,035
Fred Funk	66	69	70	70	275	9,035
Jeff Hart	69	70	66	70	275	9,035
Jeff Sluman	71	69	71	64	275	9,035
Mike Standly	68	69	69	69	275	9,035
Kevin Sutherland	69	67	71	68	275	9,035
David Berganio, Jr.	69	71	67	69	276	6,565
Brian Claar	66	70	72	68	276	6,565
Joe Durant	70	67	70	69	276	6,565
Len Mattiace	68	69	68	71	276	6,565
Chris Perry	69	71	67	69	276	6,565
Larry Rinker	71	66	68	71	276	6,565
Jay Don Blake	66	72	72	67	277	4,940
Wayne Levi	68	69	70	70	277	4,940
Dick Mast	70	70	72	65	277	4,940
Rocco Mediate	71	66	70	70	277	4,940
Curtis Strange	67	72	68	70	277	4,940
David Toms	68	69	69	71	277	4,940
Dan Forsman	67	68	73	70	278	3,536
Kelly Gibson	70	70	72	66	278	3,536
Larry Nelson	69	69	68	72	278	3,536
Anthony Painter	70	70	69	69	278	3,536
Tom Purtzer	68	68	69	73	278	3,536
Charlie Rymer	71	69	68	70	278	3,536
Olin Browne	69	69	68	73	279	2,986.7:
Jay Delsing	72	67	70	70	279	2,986.7:
Todd Demsey	69	70	67	73	279	2,986.7:

	SCORES				TOTAL	MONEY
Brent Geiberger	71	69	67	72	279	2,986.75
Eduardo Herrera	69	66	72	72	279	2,986.75
Neal Lancaster	67	71	72	69	279	2,986.75
Joey Sindelar	67	71	70	71	279	2,986.75
Duffy Waldorf	70	70	69	70	279	2,986.75
Emlyn Aubrey	68	67	74	71	280	2,834
Keith Clearwater	68	69	73	70	280	2,834
Doug Martin	69	71	70	70	280	2,834
Gabriel Hjertstedt	72	67	70	72	281	2,769
Sandy Lyle	68	69	73	71	281	2,769
Gary Hallberg	70	69	70	73	282	2,717
Anthony Rodriguez	70	70	73	69	282	2,717
Paul Goydos	71	69	74	69	283	2,678
Jim Thorpe	68	67	75	74	284	2,652
Taylor Smith	70	70	69	76	285	2,613
Chip Sullivan	69	71	75	70	285	2,613
Gene Sauers	68	71	72	75	286	2,574

Bell Canadian Open

Royal Montreal Golf Club, Ile Bizard, Quebec, Canada
Par 35-35–70; 6,737 yards

September 4-7
purse, $1,500,000

	SCORES				TOTAL	MONEY
Steve Jones	71	68	67	69	275	$270,000
Greg Norman	66	72	69	69	276	162,000
Phil Tataurangi	69	67	72	69	277	102,000
Frank Lickliter	68	72	68	70	278	66,000
David Ogrin	69	70	72	67	278	66,000
Justin Leonard	70	70	69	70	279	52,125
Davis Love III	70	67	77	65	279	52,125
Fulton Allem	69	69	73	69	280	43,500
David Frost	71	69	71	69	280	43,500
Payne Stewart	66	72	72	70	280	43,500
Chris Perry	71	72	72	67	282	36,000
Hal Sutton	71	69	71	71	282	36,000
Jay Don Blake	68	77	69	69	283	23,430
Stewart Cink	72	66	75	70	283	23,430
Scott Dunlap	72	71	69	71	283	23,430
Brad Fabel	72	69	72	70	283	23,430
Nolan Henke	71	68	69	75	283	23,430
Bradley Hughes	72	72	71	68	283	23,430
Blaine McCallister	69	72	72	70	283	23,430
Anthony Rodriguez	73	70	71	69	283	23,430
Mike Standly	71	71	71	70	283	23,430
Richard Zokol	71	71	66	75	283	23,430
Michael Christie	71	73	71	69	284	12,642.86
Scott Gump	71	71	69	73	284	12,642.86
Andrew Magee	69	72	73	70	284	12,642.86
Len Mattiace	72	73	71	68	284	12,642.86
Kevin Sutherland	69	74	74	67	284	12,642.86
Rocco Mediate	67	68	78	71	284	12,642.85
Tommy Tolles	69	71	74	70	284	12,642.85
Todd Demsey	71	72	71	71	285	9,112.50
Jimmy Johnston	72	73	70	70	285	9,112.50
Larry Mize	73	67	77	68	285	9,112.50
John Morse	70	74	71	70	285	9,112.50

	SCORES				TOTAL	MONEY
Brett Quigley	70	71	74	70	285	9,112.50
Lanny Wadkins	71	72	71	71	285	9,112.50
Jim Carter	72	71	72	71	286	6,912.50
Rick Gibson	69	74	72	71	286	6,912.50
Steve Hart	73	69	71	73	286	6,912.50
Jim McGovern	72	72	70	72	286	6,912.50
Craig Parry	73	71	72	70	286	6,912.50
Bob Tway	71	73	73	69	286	6,912.50
Joel Edwards	72	71	74	70	287	5,700
Grant Waite	68	73	79	67	287	5,700
Paul Azinger	73	69	73	73	288	4,335
Doug Barron	72	71	71	74	288	4,335
Keith Clearwater	72	71	72	73	288	4,335
Robert Damron	65	75	75	73	288	4,335
Jim Gallagher, Jr.	71	71	74	72	288	4,335
Gabriel Hjertstedt	66	74	72	76	288	4,335
Glen Hnatiuk	71	69	72	76	288	4,335
Joey Sindelar	69	73	74	72	288	4,335
Joe Durant	75	69	72	73	289	3,498
David Edwards	74	69	76	70	289	3,498
P.H. Horgan III	72	72	74	71	289	3,498
Philip Jonas	70	72	69	78	289	3,498
Vijay Singh	72	71	74	72	289	3,498
Kelly Gibson	70	74	73	73	290	3,345
Stuart Hendley	71	74	73	72	290	3,345
Mike Reid	72	70	76	72	290	3,345
Sonny Skinner	72	73	72	73	290	3,345
Adam Mednick	70	74	74	73	291	3,255
Brad Sutterfield	74	71	74	72	291	3,255
Bruce Fleisher	72	71	74	75	292	3,195
Tom Kite	69	75	75	73	292	3,195
Allen Doyle	72	73	77	71	293	3,105
John Huston	73	71	76	73	293	3,105
Shaun Micheel	70	75	74	74	293	3,105
Stephane Talbot	67	76	77	73	293	3,105
Ronnie Black	74	70	78	72	294	2,985
Lee Rinker	69	76	74	75	294	2,985
Rick Todd	70	73	76	75	294	2,985
Ted Tryba	70	74	77	73	294	2,985
Mike Springer	72	72	76	75	295	2,895
Omar Uresti	72	72	76	75	295	2,895

CVS Charity Classic

Pleasant Valley Country Club, Sutton, Massachusetts
Par 36-35–71; 7,110 yards

September 11-14
purse, $1,200,000

	SCORES				TOTAL	MONEY
Loren Roberts	67	67	68	64	266	$216,000
Bill Glasson	66	67	67	67	267	129,600
Peter Jacobsen	68	65	70	65	268	81,600
Chris Smith	68	68	66	67	269	57,600
Brian Henninger	72	67	63	68	270	48,000
Kevin Burton	66	68	69	68	271	40,200
Bob Estes	71	69	66	65	271	40,200
Craig Parry	69	66	67	69	271	40,200
John Adams	66	68	67	71	272	32,400

	SCORES				TOTAL	MONEY
Paul Azinger	69	69	69	65	272	32,400
Tim Herron	71	68	68	65	272	32,400
Paul Claxton	68	67	69	69	273	27,600
Olin Browne	70	71	67	66	274	23,200
Jim Carter	68	70	68	68	274	23,200
Charlie Rymer	64	70	69	71	274	23,200
Steve Lowery	67	69	72	67	275	18,000
Tom Pernice, Jr.	69	69	69	68	275	18,000
Dicky Pride	73	66	68	68	275	18,000
Mike Reid	65	70	73	67	275	18,000
Dave Stockton, Jr.	68	68	71	68	275	18,000
Mark Calcavecchia	70	69	66	71	276	13,920
Don Pooley	68	68	68	72	276	13,920
Doug Barron	71	67	69	70	277	9,870
Lennie Clements	70	69	67	71	277	9,870
Keith Fergus	70	70	67	70	277	9,870
Nolan Henke	65	72	67	73	277	9,870
Greg Kraft	68	68	72	69	277	9,870
Justin Leonard	70	71	71	65	277	9,870
Curtis Strange	69	71	67	70	277	9,870
Tommy Tolles	68	72	67	70	277	9,870
Guy Boros	69	72	69	68	278	7,116
Michael Bradley	67	67	69	75	278	7,116
Tom Byrum	68	72	66	72	278	7,116
John Dowdall	67	73	69	69	278	7,116
Larry Rinker	71	70	69	68	278	7,116
Fulton Allem	70	71	67	71	279	5,530
Robin Freeman	70	70	70	69	279	5,530
Neal Lancaster	67	70	69	73	279	5,530
Dave Rummells	64	72	71	72	279	5,530
Chip Sullivan	72	69	68	70	279	5,530
Willie Wood	71	69	67	72	279	5,530
Fred Funk	68	70	69	73	280	4,320
Pete Jordan	72	69	71	68	280	4,320
Lee Rinker	73	67	69	71	280	4,320
John Wilson	69	69	71	71	280	4,320
David Berganio, Jr.	72	68	71	70	281	3,209.15
Taylor Smith	70	69	71	71	281	3,209.15
Billy Andrade	67	70	70	74	281	3,209.14
John Cook	70	69	70	72	281	3,209.14
Jim Furyk	70	66	73	72	281	3,209.14
Skip Kendall	69	68	70	74	281	3,209.14
Kenny Perry	69	70	72	70	281	3,209.14
John Daly	72	69	70	71	282	2,808
Mike Springer	72	69	67	74	282	2,808
Rafael Alarcon	70	68	73	72	283	2,724
Andy Bean	71	69	74	69	283	2,724
Allen Doyle	69	68	72	74	283	2,724
Grant Waite	71	70	71	71	283	2,724
Brian Claar	69	72	70	73	284	2,628
Bruce Fleisher	72	67	71	74	284	2,628
Dick Mast	71	69	74	70	284	2,628
Blaine McCallister	68	70	76	70	284	2,628
Jimmy Green	70	71	71	73	285	2,556
Steve Pate	71	65	78	71	285	2,556
Jimmy Johnston	70	71	70	75	286	2,484
Sam Randolph	74	67	71	74	286	2,484
Hugh Royer III	70	71	72	73	286	2,484
Larry Silveira	70	71	70	75	286	2,484
Gabriel Hjertstedt	72	68	73	75	288	2,412

		SCORES			TOTAL	MONEY
Scott Trethewey	67	73	75	73	288	2,412
Woody Austin	71	69	70	79	289	2,364
Mike Hulbert	72	69	72	76	289	2,364
Hideki Kase	71	70	72	80	293	2,328
Brad Sutterfield	72	69	74	80	295	2,304

LaCantera Texas Open

LaCantera Golf Club, San Antonio, Texas
Par 36-36–72; 7,001 yards

September 18-21
purse, $1,400,000

		SCORES			TOTAL	MONEY
Tim Herron	71	67	64	69	271	$252,000
Rick Fehr	70	67	66	70	273	123,200
Brent Geiberger	67	72	69	65	273	123,200
Duffy Waldorf	66	68	70	70	274	67,200
Craig Parry	68	68	70	69	275	56,000
Doug Barron	69	68	70	70	277	45,325
Scott McCarron	68	71	71	67	277	45,325
Gene Sauers	64	73	70	70	277	45,325
Mike Springer	69	69	67	72	277	45,325
Mike Brisky	65	71	73	70	279	33,600
P.H. Horgan III	68	70	66	75	279	33,600
Steve Jones	67	71	72	69	279	33,600
Tom Byrum	70	70	69	70	279	33,600
Brad Fabel	68	68	71	73	280	23,100
Jim Gallagher, Jr.	67	71	70	72	280	23,100
Kelly Gibson	71	69	70	70	280	23,100
Steve Lowery	68	69	70	73	280	23,100
Loren Roberts	67	72	72	69	280	23,100
Paul Stankowski	72	71	67	70	280	23,100
Shane Bertsch	74	67	72	68	281	12,981.82
Michael Christie	75	67	69	70	281	12,981.82
Paul Goydos	66	70	74	71	281	12,981.82
Gary Hallberg	71	71	70	69	281	12,981.82
Rocco Mediate	71	72	71	67	281	12,981.82
David Ogrin	70	71	70	70	281	12,981.82
David Toms	68	73	70	70	281	12,981.82
Mark Wiebe	75	68	71	67	281	12,981.82
John Adams	71	72	67	71	281	12,981.81
Len Mattiace	68	70	70	73	281	12,981.81
Tommy Armour III	71	69	70	71	281	12,981.81
Andy Bean	70	70	70	72	282	7,940
Keith Clearwater	72	71	69	70	282	7,940
Brian Henninger	72	70	72	68	282	7,940
Bradley Hughes	69	64	75	74	282	7,940
Lee Janzen	69	71	73	69	282	7,940
Hideki Kase	68	71	72	71	282	7,940
D.A. Weibring	68	67	76	71	282	7,940
Bruce Fleisher	69	72	71	71	283	5,185.10
Cameron Beckman	75	66	71	71	283	5,185.09
Brad Bryant	71	68	71	73	283	5,185.09
Russ Cochran	69	70	69	75	283	5,185.09
Steve Jurgensen	73	70	68	72	283	5,185.09
Greg Kraft	70	73	67	73	283	5,185.09
Dan Pohl	70	71	69	73	283	5,185.09
Brett Quigley	68	68	75	72	283	5,185.09

	SCORES			TOTAL	MONEY
Larry Rinker	77	66	69	71	283	5,185.09
Chris Smith	69	71	71	72	283	5,185.09
Doug Tewell	71	66	73	73	283	5,185.09
Kawika Cotner	68	71	70	75	284	3,392
Scott Dunlap	68	72	73	71	284	3,392
Robin Freeman	69	71	69	75	284	3,392
Donnie Hammond	70	73	71	70	284	3,392
Jeff Maggert	70	73	70	71	284	3,392
Tim Simpson	73	68	74	69	284	3,392
Omar Uresti	69	73	70	72	284	3,392
Keith Fergus	67	73	75	70	285	3,178
Brad Sutterfield	70	72	71	72	285	3,178
Jim McGovern	71	72	70	73	286	3,094
Jack O'Keefe	73	68	71	74	286	3,094
Tom Pernice, Jr.	71	71	70	74	286	3,094
Ted Tryba	69	70	68	79	286	3,094
Mark Calcavecchia	69	70	75	73	287	2,968
Joe Durant	72	70	74	71	287	2,968
Frank Lickliter	74	68	69	76	287	2,968
Tray Tyner	67	71	71	78	287	2,968
John Wilson	71	69	73	74	287	2,968
Steve Hart	68	73	74	73	288	2,968
David Peoples	73	70	72	73	288	2,968
Ken Green	68	75	72	74	289	2,800
Charlie Rymer	75	68	79	67	289	2,800
Scott Simpson	68	74	73	74	289	2,800
Danny Edwards	71	71	73	75	290	2,688
David Frost	70	70	73	77	290	2,688
J.P. Hayes	69	72	72	77	290	2,688
Jimmy Johnston	71	69	76	74	290	2,688
Howard Twitty	72	70	75	73	290	2,688
Lon Hinkle	73	70	74	74	291	2,604
Chris Borgen	72	71	72	78	293	2,576
Taylor Smith	70	73	70	81	294	2,548
Billy Ray Brown	71	71	77	76	295	2,520
Woody Austin	74	68	73	82	297	2,492

B.C. Open

En-Joie Golf Club, Endicott, New York
Par 37-34—71; 6,920 yards

September 25-28
purse, $1,300,000

	SCORES			TOTAL	MONEY
Gabriel Hjertstedt	70	69	66	70	275	$234,000
Chris Perry	69	69	69	69	276	97,066.67
Lee Rinker	70	68	72	66	276	97,066.67
Andrew Magee	67	70	69	70	276	97,066.66
Bruce Fleisher	70	66	71	70	277	47,450
Robert Gamez	70	67	68	72	277	47,450
Richard Green	71	68	69	69	277	47,450
Bradley Hughes	70	71	69	68	278	36,400
Dick Mast	70	71	70	67	278	36,400
Dave Stockton, Jr.	68	72	69	69	278	36,400
Grant Waite	69	67	72	70	278	36,400
Billy Andrade	70	72	67	70	279	24,700
Stewart Cink	73	64	67	75	279	24,700
Jim McGovern	68	68	72	71	279	24,700

	SCORES				TOTAL	MONEY
Sean Murphy	67	72	70	70	279	24,700
Paul Stankowski	71	68	67	73	279	24,700
John Wilson	70	69	70	70	279	24,700
Brian Claar	70	70	65	75	280	18,850
Len Mattiace	69	73	68	70	280	18,850
Keith Clearwater	72	66	72	71	281	15,686.67
John Morse	72	71	69	69	281	15,686.67
Mike Hulbert	73	69	68	71	281	15,686.66
Doug Barron	71	72	70	69	282	10,692.50
Michael Christie	71	70	71	70	282	10,692.50
Barry Jaeckel	71	72	68	71	282	10,692.50
Jonathan Kaye	70	69	73	70	282	10,692.50
Greg Kraft	66	71	71	74	282	10,692.50
David Sutherland	69	72	68	73	282	10,692.50
Phil Tataurangi	73	69	74	66	282	10,692.50
Scott Verplank	73	69	72	68	282	10,692.50
Tom Byrum	73	67	73	70	283	7,709
Charlie Rymer	72	66	70	75	283	7,709
Joey Sindelar	67	71	74	71	283	7,709
Ted Tryba	69	73	71	70	283	7,709
Mike Weir	68	73	71	71	283	7,709
Keith Fergus	71	73	71	69	284	6,123
Steve Jurgensen	70	70	76	68	284	6,123
Blaine McCallister	71	70	72	71	284	6,123
Steve Rintoul	72	69	73	70	284	6,123
Tray Tyner	72	72	71	69	284	6,123
Tommy Armour III	71	70	72	72	285	4,426.50
Andy Bean	69	70	75	71	285	4,426.50
Paul Claxton	68	71	73	73	285	4,426.50
Jay Delsing	67	73	74	71	285	4,426.50
Bill Glasson	70	70	75	70	285	4,426.50
Brett Quigley	73	71	73	68	285	4,426.50
Mike Smith	67	71	75	72	285	4,426.50
Chip Sullivan	70	70	71	74	285	4,426.50
Robin Freeman	71	68	73	74	286	3,328
Adam Mednick	75	69	73	69	286	3,328
Brad Bryant	73	71	73	70	287	3,078.40
Jimmy Green	72	72	72	71	287	3,078.40
Jimmy Johnston	75	69	70	73	287	3,078.40
Mac O'Grady	76	68	67	76	287	3,078.40
Bob Wolcott	71	71	73	72	287	3,078.40
Robert Damron	75	69	71	73	288	2,951
Sonny Skinner	71	71	73	73	288	2,951
Kevin Burton	70	73	72	74	289	2,860
Gary Hallberg	67	75	73	74	289	2,860
Skip Kendall	73	71	73	72	289	2,860
Dicky Pride	72	71	75	71	289	2,860
Omar Uresti	70	72	77	70	289	2,860
Marco Dawson	68	71	75	76	290	2,756
Pete Jordan	74	66	73	77	290	2,756
Howard Twitty	70	73	72	75	290	2,756
Nolan Henke	70	70	75	76	291	2,678
Billy Mayfair	73	71	74	73	291	2,678
Larry Silveira	69	75	76	71	291	2,678
Christian Chernock	70	73	71	79	293	2,613
Neal Lancaster	74	70	75	74	293	2,613
Emlyn Aubrey	73	71	75	75	294	2,561
Ed Fiori	73	71	75	75	294	2,561
Jim Thorpe	75	69	77	74	295	2,522

Buick Challenge

Callaway Gardens Resort, Mountain View Course,
Pine Mountain, Georgia
Par 36-36–72; 7,057 yards

October 2-5
purse, $1,200,000

	SCORES				TOTAL	MONEY
Davis Love III	67	65	67	68	267	$216,000
Stewart Cink	70	64	67	70	271	129,600
Steve Lowery	69	71	72	60	272	69,600
Hal Sutton	67	65	74	66	272	69,600
Jay Haas	70	69	68	67	274	48,000
Brandel Chamblee	67	71	71	66	275	40,200
Mike Hulbert	71	69	70	65	275	40,200
Doug Martin	71	65	70	69	275	40,200
David Berganio, Jr.	69	68	69	70	276	26,850
Mike Brisky	66	71	69	70	276	26,850
Jim Carter	71	69	68	68	276	26,850
Michael Christie	69	71	69	67	276	26,850
David Duval	72	69	69	66	276	26,850
Steve Pate	68	65	75	68	276	26,850
Tommy Tolles	70	70	70	66	276	26,850
Grant Waite	71	70	65	70	276	26,850
Tommy Armour III	72	69	70	66	277	17,400
Tom Byrum	68	67	70	72	277	17,400
Fred Funk	69	67	72	69	277	17,400
Paul Goydos	69	72	66	70	277	17,400
Fulton Allem	70	69	68	71	278	12,960
Chris Perry	73	66	69	70	278	12,960
David Toms	68	72	69	69	278	12,960
Bob Tway	72	67	69	70	278	12,960
Joel Edwards	69	69	69	72	279	9,800
Dudley Hart	71	69	71	68	279	9,800
Len Mattiace	70	69	68	72	279	9,800
Michael Bradley	72	70	71	67	280	7,480
Allen Doyle	68	73	70	69	280	7,480
Joe Durant	71	71	71	67	280	7,480
Tom Gillis	71	70	68	71	280	7,480
Gary Hallberg	67	69	75	69	280	7,480
Pete Jordan	72	70	71	67	280	7,480
Don Pooley	74	66	69	71	280	7,480
Mike Reid	73	66	72	69	280	7,480
David Sutherland	70	70	65	75	280	7,480
Bob Estes	72	69	69	71	281	5,160
Bruce Fleisher	69	71	71	70	281	5,160
Gabriel Hjertstedt	67	73	69	72	281	5,160
Skip Kendall	71	71	69	70	281	5,160
David Ogrin	67	73	74	67	281	5,160
Vijay Singh	70	71	67	73	281	5,160
Craig Stadler	69	69	70	73	281	5,160
Shane Bertsch	73	68	71	70	282	3,468
Paul Claxton	70	69	70	73	282	3,468
Tim Herron	72	68	70	72	282	3,468
Eric Johnson	70	71	67	74	282	3,468
Jerry Kelly	71	71	70	70	282	3,468
Greg Kraft	72	70	70	70	282	3,468
Wayne Levi	71	69	76	66	282	3,468
Mike Standly	72	66	74	70	282	3,468
J.P. Hayes	70	69	72	72	283	2,798.40
Billy Mayfair	69	71	72	71	283	2,798.40

	SCORES				TOTAL	MONEY
Frank Nobilo	73	68	73	69	283	2,798.40
Sonny Skinner	68	72	69	74	283	2,798.40
Mark Wiebe	71	69	70	73	283	2,798.40
Rick Fehr	70	72	71	71	284	2,700
Rocco Mediate	72	68	73	71	284	2,700
David Peoples	71	68	73	73	285	2,640
Joey Sindelar	72	70	73	70	285	2,640
Willie Wood	75	66	72	72	285	2,640
Doug Barron	70	70	72	74	286	2,544
Bobby Clampett	72	70	71	73	286	2,544
Marco Dawson	70	70	70	76	286	2,544
Jay Delsing	72	69	72	73	286	2,544
Scott Gump	69	71	72	74	286	2,544
Kenny Perry	73	69	68	77	287	2,460
Dave Rummells	71	71	72	73	287	2,460
Billy Ray Brown	73	68	74	73	288	2,424
Steve Hart	74	68	75	72	289	2,388
Hugh Royer III	72	69	74	74	289	2,388

Michelob Championship at Kingsmill

Kingsmill Golf Club, Williamsburg, Virginia
Par 35-36–71; 6,797 yards

October 9-12
purse, $1,550,000

	SCORES				TOTAL	MONEY
David Duval	67	66	71	67	271	$279,000
Grant Waite	69	67	68	67	271	136,400
Duffy Waldorf	63	69	69	70	271	136,400
(Duval defeated Waite and Waldorf on first extra hole.)						
Fred Funk	69	65	70	69	273	74,400
Scott Hoch	70	66	69	69	274	62,000
Kirk Triplett	66	68	70	71	275	55,800
John Cook	69	68	68	71	276	49,987.50
Jim Gallagher	69	68	71	68	276	49,987.50
Loren Roberts	70	67	71	69	277	43,400
Payne Stewart	68	70	70	69	277	43,400
Lee Janzen	72	65	71	70	278	34,100
Steve Lowery	68	66	74	70	278	34,100
Chris Perry	68	73	68	69	278	34,100
Jeff Sluman	68	70	68	72	278	34,100
Billy Andrade	69	72	69	69	279	25,575
Brad Bryant	64	70	76	69	279	25,575
Blaine McCallister	71	68	69	71	279	25,575
David Toms	68	72	73	66	279	25,575
Tommy Armour III	67	73	73	67	280	20,150
Joe Durant	70	70	71	69	280	20,150
Chris Smith	68	72	71	69	280	20,150
Jay Don Blake	68	71	72	70	281	16,120
Kelly Gibson	69	69	74	69	281	16,120
Curtis Strange	67	68	76	70	281	16,120
Jim Carter	71	70	68	73	282	12,361.25
Donnie Hammond	71	69	71	71	282	12,361.25
J.P. Hayes	68	73	70	71	282	12,361.25
Greg Kraft	65	71	71	75	282	12,361.25
David Berganio, Jr.	71	70	71	71	283	9,643.29
Russ Cochran	71	66	78	68	283	9,643.29
Pete Jordan	72	69	71	71	283	9,643.29

	SCORES			TOTAL	MONEY
David Sutherland	68	69 75	71	283	9,643.29
Fred Couples	67	69 73	74	283	9,643.28
Ted Tryba	71	70 69	73	283	9,643.28
John Wilson	68	71 72	72	283	9,643.28
Tom Byrum	68	73 68	75	284	6,517.70
Paul Goydos	71	67 71	75	284	6,517.70
Bradley Hughes	67	73 73	71	284	6,517.70
Skip Kendall	68	72 73	71	284	6,517.70
John Maginnes	71	70 69	74	284	6,517.70
Doug Martin	72	69 73	70	284	6,517.70
Jim McGovern	69	71 74	70	284	6,517.70
Brett Quigley	66	68 75	75	284	6,517.70
Mike Reid	69	70 70	75	284	6,517.70
Dave Stockton, Jr.	68	71 76	69	284	6,517.70
Stewart Cink	72	69 69	75	285	4,030
Paul Claxton	70	70 73	72	285	4,030
Bob Estes	73	67 74	71	285	4,030
Scott Gump	66	68 75	76	285	4,030
Tom Kite	72	68 72	73	285	4,030
Neal Lancaster	67	73 70	75	285	4,030
Joey Sindelar	68	72 70	75	285	4,030
Lanny Wadkins	70	69 71	75	285	4,030
Mark Wiebe	69	68 74	74	285	4,030
Jay Delsing	70	69 74	73	286	3,549.50
Dan Forsman	72	69 77	68	286	3,549.50
Lennie Clements	66	72 76	73	287	3,425.50
Jack O'Keefe	72	69 70	76	287	3,425.50
David Ogrin	72	68 74	73	287	3,425.50
Corey Pavin	72	69 72	74	287	3,425.50
Phil Tataurangi	69	67 70	81	287	3,425.50
Willie Wood	71	68 76	72	287	3,425.50
Olin Browne	68	73 76	71	288	3,301.50
Steve Ford	72	68 77	71	288	3,301.50
Craig Bowden	69	69 77	74	289	3,224
Steve Hart	72	69 74	74	289	3,224
Tom Sieckmann	71	70 75	73	289	3,224
Mark Carnevale	75	65 76	77	293	3,162
Michael Christie	67	74 76	77	294	3,131
Gary Hallberg	67	74 79	76	296	3,100

Walt Disney World/Oldsmobile Classic

Walt Disney World Resort, Lake Buena Vista, Florida
Magnolia Course: Par 36-36–72; 7,190 yards
Palm Course: Par 36-36–72; 6,957 yards
Lake Buena Vista Course: Par 36-36–72; 6,819 yards

October 16-19
purse, $1,500,000

	SCORES			TOTAL	MONEY
David Duval	65	70 65	70	270	$270,000
Dan Forsman	67	69 65	69	270	162,000
(Duval defeated Forsman on first extra hole.)					
Len Mattiace	67	66 65	74	272	87,000
Ted Tryba	67	68 68	69	272	87,000
Paul Goydos	69	70 68	66	273	60,000
Olin Browne	74	64 66	70	274	54,000
Phil Blackmar	68	66 68	73	275	46,750
Joe Durant	68	66 71	70	275	46,750

	SCORES				TOTAL	MONEY
Lee Janzen	70	67	66	72	275	46,750
Glen Day	69	70	69	68	276	32,142.86
Tom Lehman	73	65	67	71	276	32,142.86
Andrew Magee	66	67	72	71	276	32,142.86
Jeff Maggert	67	69	70	70	276	32,142.86
Tommy Tolles	69	67	68	72	276	32,142.86
John Cook	68	66	70	72	276	32,142.85
Payne Stewart	64	67	70	75	276	32,142.85
Lennie Clements	70	68	69	70	277	18,333.34
Kelly Gibson	71	70	67	69	277	18,333.34
Chris Perry	67	68	71	71	277	18,333.34
Tommy Armour III	70	70	69	68	277	18,333.33
Brad Fabel	70	66	68	73	277	18,333.33
Scott Gump	66	72	68	71	277	18,333.33
Frank Lickliter	65	71	66	75	277	18,333.33
Bob Tway	68	69	66	74	277	18,333.33
Ronnie Black	70	69	66	72	277	18,333.33
Kevin Burton	69	68	67	74	278	10,650
Bill Glasson	67	67	68	76	278	10,650
Spike McRoy	70	65	68	75	278	10,650
Grant Waite	69	69	67	73	278	10,650
Duffy Waldorf	68	68	72	70	278	10,650
Tiger Woods	66	71	70	71	278	10,650
Allen Doyle	67	69	66	76	278	10,650
Russ Cochran	73	69	64	73	279	7,433.34
Scott Hoch	70	69	68	72	279	7,433.34
Jerry Kelly	68	71	69	71	279	7,433.34
Brad Bryant	67	67	70	75	279	7,433.33
Jim Carter	73	69	67	70	279	7,433.33
Skip Kendall	72	70	67	70	279	7,433.33
Neal Lancaster	66	71	68	74	279	7,433.33
Wayne Levi	72	67	66	74	279	7,433.33
Curtis Strange	68	67	74	70	279	7,433.33
Billy Mayfair	69	71	68	72	280	4,958.58
Steve Hart	68	71	70	71	280	4,958.57
Eric Johnson	71	69	70	70	280	4,958.57
Steve Lowery	72	71	68	69	280	4,958.57
Larry Mize	72	69	69	70	280	4,958.57
Jeff Sluman	68	70	71	71	280	4,958.57
David Sutherland	72	71	68	69	280	4,958.57
Doug Barron	69	68	70	74	281	3,702
Tim Herron	71	67	72	71	281	3,702
Mike Hulbert	71	69	70	71	281	3,702
Greg Kraft	71	69	70	71	281	3,702
Brett Quigley	70	69	72	70	281	3,702
John Adams	71	68	71	72	282	3,390
Jay Delsing	66	74	71	71	282	3,390
Donnie Hammond	71	68	70	73	282	3,390
Jeff Hart	71	65	72	74	282	3,390
Pete Jordan	73	69	66	74	282	3,390
Kirk Triplett	70	70	67	75	282	3,390
Omar Uresti	67	68	69	78	282	3,390
Jimmy Green	70	70	70	74	284	3,210
Hideki Kase	70	70	71	73	284	3,210
Rocco Mediate	72	65	73	74	284	3,210
Kevin Sutherland	70	75	66	73	284	3,210
Hal Sutton	71	69	68	76	284	3,210
Blaine McCallister	74	67	69	75	285	3,120
Dicky Pride	70	73	68	75	286	3,060
Tray Tyner	69	71	69	77	286	3,060

	SCORES	TOTAL	MONEY
Bob Wolcott	72 72 67 75	286	3,060
Lanny Wadkins	69 72 70 80	291	3,000
Robin Freeman	70 71 70 81	292	2,970

Las Vegas Invitational

TPC at Summerlin
Par 36-36–72; 7,234 yards

October 22-26
purse, $1,800,000

Las Vegas Country Club
Par 36-36–72; 7,164 yards

Desert Inn Country Club
Par 36-36–72; 7,111 yards
Las Vegas, Nevada

	SCORES	TOTAL	MONEY
Bill Glasson	63 65 75 71 66	340	$324,000
David Edwards	68 66 69 72 66	341	158,400
Billy Mayfair	65 63 73 73 67	341	158,400
Mark Calcavecchia	66 66 72 71 68	343	79,200
Duffy Waldorf	65 63 69 75 71	343	79,200
Lee Janzen	66 72 71 70 66	345	60,300
Mike Reid	67 67 70 70 71	345	60,300
Kevin Sutherland	69 63 70 73 70	345	60,300
Fred Couples	66 67 69 77 68	347	50,400
Brad Fabel	64 66 77 71 69	347	50,400
Jay Don Blake	68 69 68 71 72	348	41,400
Edward Fryatt	69 67 71 73 68	348	41,400
Ted Tryba	66 65 73 74 70	348	41,400
Brent Geiberger	68 67 75 72 67	349	30,600
Steve Jones	66 68 72 72 71	349	30,600
Rocco Mediate	68 69 72 73 67	349	30,600
Phil Mickelson	68 63 79 70 69	349	30,600
Hal Sutton	66 71 71 75 66	349	30,600
Billy Andrade	64 70 72 75 69	350	22,590
Jim Furyk	68 65 72 75 70	350	22,590
Wayne Levi	66 65 78 74 67	350	22,590
Scott Simpson	70 71 71 72 66	350	22,590
Brett Quigley	70 68 74 70 69	351	16,560
Larry Rinker	66 69 75 70 71	351	16,560
Grant Waite	67 68 73 75 68	351	16,560
J.P. Hayes	70 67 71 74 69	351	16,560
Nolan Henke	68 69 68 76 71	352	13,320
Gabriel Hjertstedt	70 70 70 70 72	352	13,320
Chris Perry	68 70 71 73 70	352	13,320
Kelly Gibson	64 65 76 73 75	353	11,430
Eric Johnson	67 65 76 73 72	353	11,430
Davis Love III	71 67 73 77 65	353	11,430
Joey Sindelar	65 68 79 71 70	353	11,430
Joel Edwards	67 70 73 73 71	354	9,945
Willie Wood	66 68 76 72 72	354	9,945
Jim Carter	70 69 73 75 68	355	8,662.50
David Frost	70 69 71 75 70	355	8,662.50
Jack O'Keefe	66 72 74 71 72	355	8,662.50
Tiger Woods	68 64 77 71 75	355	8,662.50
Tommy Armour III	71 67 74 76 68	356	6,660

	SCORES				TOTAL	MONEY
John Cook	69	68	72	75	72	356	6,660
Joe Durant	66	67	75	78	70	356	6,660
Steve Lowery	65	64	74	81	72	356	6,660
Blaine McCallister	69	64	75	76	72	356	6,660
Steve Pate	68	70	71	76	71	356	6,660
Payne Stewart	70	66	75	74	71	356	6,660
Mark Brooks	71	71	69	73	73	357	4,944
Mike Hulbert	72	69	69	72	75	357	4,944
Tray Tyner	67	68	75	74	73	357	4,944
David Berganio	68	70	67	78	75	358	4,341.60
Marco Dawson	68	69	71	72	78	358	4,341.60
Paul Goydos	69	67	74	79	69	358	4,341.60
Bradley Hughes	67	69	75	76	71	358	4,341.60
Bob Tway	67	69	74	77	71	358	4,341.60
Shane Bertsch	71	67	74	72	75	359	4,104
Tom Byrum	66	70	74	75	74	359	4,104
Bruce Lietzke	69	68	73	76	73	359	4,104
Scott Dunlap	67	71	70	80	72	360	4,014
Neal Lancaster	69	66	77	78	70	360	4,014
Phil Blackmar	70	69	72	78	72	361	3,942
Doug Martin	69	64	78	78	72	361	3,942
Jim Gallagher	69	66	77	77	73	362	3,888
Doug Barron	68	69	74	76	76	363	3,816
Skip Kendall	66	71	75	77	74	363	3,816
Lee Porter	71	70	71	79	72	363	3,816
Kirk Triplett	65	70	76	79	74	364	3,744
Olin Browne	66	68	78	79	74	365	3,690
Clarence Rose	67	68	74	76	80	365	3,690
Tim Herron	73	67	71	79	76	366	3,636

Tour Championship

Champions Golf Club, Houston, Texas
Par 36-35–71; 7,200 yards

October 30-November 2
purse, $4,000,000

	SCORES				TOTAL	MONEY
David Duval	66	69	70	68	273	$720,000
Jim Furyk	66	68	73	67	274	432,000
Davis Love III	68	68	69	70	275	276,000
Mark Calcavecchia	69	66	72	70	277	176,000
Bill Glasson	68	69	68	72	277	176,000
Brad Faxon	67	69	69	73	278	140,000
Jesper Parnevik	66	73	69	70	278	140,000
Justin Leonard	70	69	72	68	279	124,000
Loren Roberts	72	68	69	70	279	124,000
Scott Hoch	68	65	74	73	280	110,800
Vijay Singh	70	70	70	70	280	110,800
Scott McCarron	69	70	71	71	281	97,600
Greg Norman	73	69	69	70	281	97,600
Tiger Woods	69	68	75	69	281	97,600
Tom Lehman	72	71	68	71	282	86,400
Andrew Magee	69	70	70	73	282	86,400
Steve Elkington	70	69	70	75	284	80,000
Mark O'Meara	68	74	72	70	284	80,000
Paul Stankowski	70	69	72	73	284	80,000
John Cook	73	71	70	71	285	76,000
Frank Nobilo	70	72	72	71	285	76,000

	SCORES				TOTAL	MONEY
Stuart Appleby	73	70	70	73	286	72,800
Phil Mickelson	69	72	73	72	286	72,800
Stewart Cink	73	72	71	71	287	70,400
Steve Jones	72	68	70	78	288	68,800
Ernie Els	71	71	72	75	289	66,400
Lee Janzen	71	75	70	73	289	66,400
Nick Price	70	71	73	75	289	66,400
Jeff Maggert	78	72	71	70	291	64,800
Tommy Tolles	68	71	77	76	292	64,000

Special Events

Family House Invitational

Oakmont Country Club, Oakmont, Pennsylvania
Par 36-35–71; 6,946 yards

June 23-24
purse, $850,000

	SCORES		TOTAL	MONEY
Jim Furyk	69	69	138	$170,000
Rocco Mediate	65	75	140	85,000
Jeff Sluman	69	73	142	50,000
Jay Haas	67	76	143	40,000
Ernie Els	69	75	144	30,333
Loren Roberts	71	73	144	30,333
Brad Faxon	72	72	144	30,333
Paul Stankowski	73	72	145	24,000
Tom Purtzer	74	72	146	17,200
Scott Simpson	74	72	146	17,200
Bob Ford	75	71	146	17,200
Jim Gallagher, Jr.	75	71	146	17,200
Frank Nobilo	77	69	146	17,200
Justin Leonard	70	77	147	16,000
Tommy Tolles	74	73	147	16,000
Vijay Singh	75	72	147	16,000
Curtis Strange	72	75	147	16,000
Fred Funk	73	75	148	16,000
Scott Hoch	73	75	148	16,000
Stewart Cink	72	77	149	16,000
Stewart Appleby	72	77	149	16,000
David Duval	73	76	149	16,000
Mark Brooks	69	80	149	16,000
Phil Mickelson	75	75	150	16,000
Billy Andrade	73	77	150	16,000
Steve Jones	72	79	151	16,000
Craig Stadler	74	77	151	16,000
Bob Tway	77	75	151	16,000
Craig Parry	78	73	151	16,000
Scott McCarron	77	76	153	16,000
Chris Perry	73	83	156	16,000
Arnold Palmer	77	80	157	16,000

Fred Couples Invitational

Inglewood Country Club, Kenmore, Washington
Par 36-35–71; 6,543 yards

July 28-29
purse, $565,000

	SCORES		TOTAL	MONEY
Scott Simpson	67	67	134	$130,000
Tom Lehman	66	69	135	65,000
Peter Jacobsen	71	66	137	35,000
Tim Herron	71	67	138	25,000
Billy Mayfair	71	67	138	25,000
Rick Fehr	69	69	138	25,000
John Cook	70	69	139	17,500
Billy Andrade	70	69	139	17,500
Blaine McCallister	70	69	139	17,500
Davis Love III	69	70	139	17,500
Jim Furyk	72	68	140	15,000
Phil Mickelson	71	70	141	15,000
Scott McCarron	66	75	141	15,000
Fred Couples	71	71	142	15,000
Tom Purtzer	71	71	142	15,000
Jay Haas	71	71	142	15,000
Mike Hulbert	69	76	145	15,000
Arnold Palmer	72	75	147	15,000
Tommy Tolles	71	77	148	15,000
Chris Mitchell	77	72	149	15,000
David Feherty	77	75	152	15,000
Laura Davies	73	82	155	15,000

Fred Meyer Challenge

Oregon Golf Club, West Linn, Oregon
Par 35-36–71; 6,914 yards

August 4-5
purse, $700,000

	SCORES		TOTAL	MONEY (Team)
Greg Norman/Brad Faxon	60	63	123	$100,000
Jay Haas/Phil Mickelson	65	61	126	80,000
Craig Stadler/Steve Elkington	63	64	127	70,000
Peter Jacobsen/Arnold Palmer	63	65	128	60,000
Fred Couples/John Cook	62	67	129	51,250
Paul Stankowski/Scott McCarron	65	64	129	51,250
Billy Andrade/D.A. Weibring	67	62	129	51,250
Tom Lehman/Lee Janzen	67	62	129	51,250
Scott Hoch/Jim Furyk	66	64	130	47,500
Fuzzy Zoeller/Brian Henninger	65	66	131	46,500
Jack Nicklaus/Gary Nicklaus	67	65	132	46,000
Mark Calcavecchia/Billy Mayfair	67	67	134	45,000

Lincoln-Mercury Kapalua International

Kapalua Resort, Maui, Hawaii
Plantation Course: Par 36-37–73; 7,263 yards
Bay Course: Par 35-36–71; 6,531 yards

November 6-9
purse, $1,200,000

	SCORES				TOTAL	MONEY
Davis Love III	67	66	67	68	268	$216,000
David Toms	63	70	67	71	271	130,000
Olin Browne	64	72	68	69	273	80,000
John Cook	69	70	71	64	274	42,025
Bob Estes	69	68	69	68	274	42,025
Mike Hulbert	66	71	70	67	274	42,025
Kirk Triplett	70	65	71	68	274	42,025
Paul Goydos	71	67	67	71	276	25,650
Roger Maltbie	70	68	67	71	276	25,650
Billy Mayfair	67	71	66	72	276	25,650
Jim McGovern	69	69	68	70	276	25,650
Chris Smith	71	69	66	70	276	25,650
Russ Cochran	72	68	66	71	277	18,500
Steve Lowery	67	72	69	69	277	18,500
Kevin Sutherland	68	71	68	70	277	18,500
Bob Gilder	69	71	68	70	278	16,500
Loren Roberts	66	73	71	69	279	15,000
Clarence Rose	69	67	71	72	279	15,000
Billy Andrade	68	73	69	70	280	13,750
Don Pooley	73	68	70	69	280	13,750
Scott McCarron	74	68	69	70	281	13,000
Mike Standly	68	69	72	73	282	11,012.50
Tom Byrum	71	70	71	70	282	11,012.50
Brad Fabel	71	72	68	71	282	11,012.50
Dan Forsman	65	74	74	69	282	11,012.50
Nolan Henke	71	66	70	75	282	11,012.50
Steve Pate	75	73	63	71	282	11,012.50
Scott Simpson	69	71	69	73	282	11,012.50
Duffy Waldorf	68	72	74	68	282	11,012.50
Tim Herron	71	70	71	71	283	9,650
Tom Purtzer	74	67	69	73	283	9,650
Andy Bean	67	72	69	76	284	9,343.75
Jim Furyk	69	71	73	71	284	9,343.75
Brent Geiberger	69	73	68	74	284	9,343.75
David Ishii	71	72	70	71	284	9,343.75
Skip Kendall	73	70	71	70	284	9,343.75
Doug Martin	69	73	75	67	284	9,343.75
Mike Reid	75	68	70	71	284	9,343.75
Jim Thorpe	72	72	68	72	284	9,343.75
Woody Austin	69	68	73	75	285	9,187.50
Robert Damron	70	74	69	72	285	9,187.50
Peter Jacobsen	76	72	65	73	286	9,150
Thomas Bjorn	67	77	68	75	287	9,100
Fred Funk	75	70	69	73	287	9,100
Gary McCord	72	74	68	73	287	9,100
Brad Bryant	71	74	69	74	288	9,050
Brian Henninger	74	73	70	72	289	9,000
Jerry Kelly	71	69	72	77	289	9,000
Tommy Tolles	68	73	69	79	289	9,000
Lee Rinker	70	74	72	74	290	8,950
Brandel Chamblee	77	70	72	72	291	8,912.50
Sandy Lyle	72	78	70	71	291	8,912.50
David Ogrin	73	74	70	76	293	8,875

	SCORES				TOTAL	MONEY
Barry Lane	72	78	72	76	298	8,850
David Peoples	70	82	76	79	307	8,825

Subaru Sarazen World Open

Legends at Chateau Elan, Braselton, Georgia
Par 36-36–72; 7,000 yards

November 6-9
purse, $2,000,000

	SCORES				TOTAL	MONEY
Mark Calcavecchia	62	67	71	71	271	$360,000
Lee Westwood	71	65	70	68	274	216,000
Mark McNulty	74	66	70	69	279	100,500
Vijay Singh	69	69	70	71	279	100,500
Scott Hoch	69	69	69	74	281	70,000
David Duval	71	68	70	73	282	58,500
Peter O'Malley	70	66	74	72	282	58,500
Steve Jones	69	68	74	73	284	49,500
Frank Nobilo	71	69	69	75	284	49,500
Arden Knoll	72	70	71	72	285	45,000
Stewart Cink	70	77	71	68	286	40,500
Per-Ulrik Johansson	69	70	72	75	286	40,500
Retief Goosen	74	69	73	71	287	35,000
Mathias Gronberg	70	72	75	70	287	35,000
Alex Cejka	70	71	72	75	288	27,250
Edward Fryatt	70	74	70	74	288	27,250
Miguel Angel Jimenez	72	73	71	72	288	27,250
Craig Stadler	71	75	73	69	288	27,250
Sven Struver	68	72	75	73	288	27,250
Ian Woosnam	73	72	74	69	288	27,250
Desvonde Botes	75	73	74	67	289	17,670
P.J. Cowan	74	71	77	67	289	17,670
Steve Flesch	77	68	69	75	289	17,670
Jaime Gomez	69	75	74	71	289	17,670
Wayne Riley	70	74	73	72	289	17,670
Elliot Boult	73	72	74	71	290	12,600
Paul Broadhurst	75	73	70	72	290	12,600
Padraig Harrington	69	72	73	76	290	12,600
Chris Williams	69	73	76	72	290	12,600
Paul McGinley	72	76	72	71	291	9,900
Fuzzy Zoeller	76	70	73	72	291	9,900
Tony Christie	74	73	73	72	292	7,164.29
Ignacio Feliu	71	76	72	73	292	7,164.29
Ricardo Gonzalez	71	75	76	70	292	7,164.29
John Kernohan	71	76	75	70	292	7,164.29
Jorge Berendt	74	73	74	71	292	7,164.28
Sam Torrance	68	77	74	73	292	7,164.28
Clinton Whitelaw	71	73	75	73	292	7,164.28
Mike Miller	73	73	75	72	293	6,166.67
Kevin Wentworth	73	73	73	74	293	6,166.67
Andrew Bonhomme	72	73	75	73	293	6,166.66
Choi Kyung-ju	78	70	71	75	294	6,030
Michael Jonzon	73	72	73	76	294	6,030
Soren Kjeldsen	75	73	72	74	294	6,030
Fabian Montovia	73	75	71	75	294	6,030
Peter Hedblom	74	72	75	74	295	5,980
Kalle Brink	74	74	76	72	296	5,960
Raul Fretes	72	73	78	74	297	5,920
Gustavo Rojas	74	73	75	75	297	5,920

	SCORES				TOTAL	MONEY
Marcello Santi	72	74	82	69	297	5,920
Peter Lonard	73	75	75	75	298	5,880
Philip Golding	73	71	75	80	299	5,860
Mikael Lundberg	74	73	76	77	300	5,830
Steve van Vuuren	71	75	78	76	300	5,830
Payne Stewart	74	73	76	78	301	5,800
Mark Brooks	73	73	80	76	302	5,780
James Kingston	74	71	80	78	303	5,750
Anthony Musgrave	74	74	78	77	303	5,750

Franklin Templeton Shark Shootout

Sherwood Country Club, Thousand Oaks, California
Par 35-36–71; 6,914 yards

November 14-16
purse, $1,100,000

	SCORES			TOTAL	MONEY (Team)
Scott McCarron/Bruce Lietzke	68	59	59	186	$300,000
Scott Hoch/David Duval	68	62	58	188	170,000
Peter Jacobsen/John Cook	62	67	62	191	115,000
Mark Calcavecchia/Andrew Magee	65	67	60	192	86,000
Fuzzy Zoeller/John Daly	65	65	62	192	86,000
Tom Kite/Jay Haas	70	67	56	193	75,000
Brad Faxon/Lee Janzen	65	66	62	193	75,000
Lanny Wadkins/Craig Stadler	71	64	62	197	68,000
Greg Norman/Steve Elkington	71	63	64	198	64,000
Chip Beck/David Frost	71	66	62	199	60,000

MasterCard PGA Grand Slam

Poipu Bay Resort, Kauai, Hawaii
Par 36-36–72; 6,957 yards

November 17-18
purse, $1,000,000

	SCORES		TOTAL	MONEY
Ernie Els	68	65	133	$400,000
Tiger Woods	66	70	136	250,000
Davis Love III	71	67	138	200,000
Justin Leonard	77	72	149	150,000

World Cup of Golf

Kiawah Island Resort, Ocean Course,
Kiawah Island, South Carolina
Par 36-36–72; 7,273 yards

November 20-23
purse, $1,500,000

	INDIVIDUAL SCORES				TOTAL
IRELAND (545)—$400,000					
Padraig Harrington	71	67	68	67	273
Paul McGinley	66	70	68	68	272
SCOTLAND (550)—$200,000					
Colin Montgomerie	68	66	66	66	266
Raymond Russell	66	72	74	72	284

	INDIVIDUAL SCORES	TOTAL

UNITED STATES (551)—$125,000
- Davis Love III   65 69 74 65   273
- Justin Leonard   72 69 67 70   278

WALES (554)—$90,000
- Ian Woosnam   74 72 69 64   279
- Phillip Price   72 68 69 66   275

GERMANY (554)—$90,000
- Sven Struver   70 75 67 74   286
- Alex Cejka   63 68 65 72   268

SPAIN (555)—$60,000
- Ignacio Garrido   67 67 69 67   270
- Miguel Angel Martin   68 74 71 72   285

ENGLAND (559)—$45,000
- Paul Broadhurst   68 74 68 72   282
- Mark James   68 73 70 66   277

ZIMBABWE (561)—$32,000
- Tony Johnstone   73 67 72 68   280
- Mark McNulty   68 74 71 68   281

SOUTH AFRICA (562)—$26,000
- Ernie Els   73 68 69 69   279
- Wayne Westner   68 71 72 72   283

NEW ZEALAND (562)—$26,000
- Michael Long   69 75 67 75   286
- Grant Waite   70 70 69 67   276

CANADA (563)—$20,000
- Rick Gibson   68 73 71 67   279
- Mike Weir   71 69 74 70   284

MEXICO (570)—$17,000
- Rafael Alarcon   68 73 67 73   281
- Oscar Serna   70 79 68 72   289

ARGENTINA (571)—$13,000
- Jorge Berendt   71 74 74 75   294
- Jose Coceres   72 69 69 67   277

DENMARK (571)—$13,000
- Knud Storgaard   71 80 72 73   296
- Thomas Bjorn   69 72 67 67   275

MALAYSIA (571)—$13,000
- Marimuthu Ramayah   71 70 72 75   288
- Ali Kadir   66 75 71 71   283

JAPAN (572)—$9,500
- Hiroyuki Fujita   68 74 71 71   284
- Taichi Teshima   74 74 72 68   288

PUERTO RICO (572)—$9,500
- Miguel Suarez   72 72 72 70   286
- Michael Ambriz   74 72 71 69   286

	INDIVIDUAL SCORES	TOTAL
REPUBLIC OF KOREA (573)—$8,800		
Choi Kyung-ju	69 73 69 73	284
Park No-seok	71 72 73 73	289
FRANCE (577)—$8,500		
Marc Farry	72 70 77 75	294
Jean Van de Velde	68 70 70 75	283
AUSTRALIA (577)—$8,500		
Wayne Riley	67 72 74 79	292
Bradley Hughes	72 71 70 72	285
COLOMBIA (578)—$8,200		
Gustavo Mendoza	70 69 68 76	283
Jesus Amaya	73 70 79 73	295
SWITZERLAND (579)—$8,000		
Paolo Quirici	74 72 69 69	284
Juan Ciola	74 73 68 80	295
ITALY (585)—$7,700		
Massimo Florioli	77 74 70 71	292
Silvio Grappasonni	78 75 68 72	293
INDIA (585)—$7,700		
Arjun Singh	72 74 77 72	295
Gaurav Ghei	74 76 70 70	290
NAMIBIA (587)—$7,400		
Schalk van der Merwe	73 76 80 73	302
Trevor Dodds	68 73 73 71	285
PHILIPPINES (589)—$7,200		
Danilo Cabajar	73 72 74 75	294
Felix Casas	73 76 71 75	295
PARAGUAY (592)—$7,000		
Raul Fretes	70 73 71 72	286
Felix Ramon Franco	74 82 77 73	306
NORWAY (595)—$6,800		
Morten Orveland	70 78 73 70	291
Morten Hagen	81 79 72 72	304
AUSTRIA (600)—$6,600		
Gordon Manson	73 74 74 71	292
Claude Grenier	74 81 75 78	308
CHINESE TAIPEI (607)—$6,400		
Hsu Huang-lung	77 77 76 82	312
Chou Hung-nan	75 74 71 75	295
FINLAND (616)—$6,200		
Anssi Kankkonen	71 76 76 74	297
Mika Lehtinen	76 79 85 79	319
SWEDEN (WD)—$6,000		
Per-Ulrik Johansson	64 74 71	WD
Joakim Haeggman	66 70 70 72	278

INTERNATIONAL TROPHY

WINNER: Montgomerie - 266 - $100,000. RUNNER-UP: Struver - 268 - $50,000.
ORDER OF FINISH: Garrido - 270 - $25,000; Harrington, Love - 273 - $5,000 each.

General Motors Mexican Open

Golf Club of Mexico, Mexico City, Mexico
Par 36-36–72; 7,333 yards

November 20-23
purse, $300,000

	SCORES				TOTAL	MONEY
Frank Nobilo	69	69	67	68	273	$60,000
Tommy Armour III	71	68	68	68	275	38,000
Stewart Cink	68	70	71	67	276	25,500
Jeff Maggert	69	68	66	73	276	25,500
Scott Hoch	71	69	70	68	278	18,000
Eduardo Romero	68	70	73	68	279	14,500
Andrew Magee	73	65	72	71	281	12,500
*Steven Scott	71	74	68	69	282	
Carlos Pelaez	71	73	70	69	283	11,500
Brandel Chamblee	72	69	73	70	284	9,700
Grant Masson	74	67	69	74	284	9,700
Jesper Parnevik	70	73	71	71	285	7,725
Clark Dennis	73	74	67	71	285	7,725
Kory Bowman	72	71	74	69	286	5,967
Lee Janzen	71	72	74	69	286	5,967
Juan Nutt	73	71	72	70	286	5,967
Shawn Savage	70	69	77	71	287	4,550
Angel Romero	71	70	72	74	287	4,550
Keoke Cotner	77	70	71	70	288	3,550
Cesar Perez	74	71	71	72	288	3,550
Emlyn Aubrey	77	72	72	69	290	3,025
Kawika Cotner	69	69	79	73	290	3,025
Howard Twitty	78	68	76	69	291	2,725
Tommy Lewis	73	72	68	78	291	2,725
John Lewis	74	74	73	71	292	2,500
Gilberto Morales	75	75	72	71	293	2,075
Ernesto Perez Acosta	71	74	74	74	293	2,075
Rene Rangel	73	67	76	77	293	2,075
Brian Gay	72	71	72	78	293	2,075
*Eugenio Nava	74	71	70	78	293	
Rafael Ponce	75	72	76	71	294	813
Carlos Espinosa	74	73	74	73	294	813
Anai Fuentes	70	76	74	74	294	813
Octavio Gonazales	71	70	77	76	294	813

Callaway Golf Pebble Beach Invitational

Pebble Beach Golf Links, Pebble Beach, California
Par 36-36–72; 6,799 yards

November 20-23
purse, $300,000

	SCORES				TOTAL	MONEY
Loren Roberts	64	68	74	70	276	$60,000
Johnny Miller	69	68	69	73	279	24,450
Kirk Triplett	71	66	72	70	279	24,450
Dan Forsman	71	70	70	69	280	10,600
John Daly	67	68	73	73	281	8,000

	SCORES			TOTAL	MONEY
Jim Carter	68	71	69 73	281	8,000
Terry Dill	72	65	72 72	281	8,000
Mike Reid	69	69	73 71	282	6,500
Jim Dent	69	72	72 70	283	5,750
Walter Morgan	68	71	73 71	283	5,750
Ronnie Black	69	74	67 74	284	5,200
Kevin Sutherland	77	70	69 69	285	4,900
Al Geiberger	70	68	73 75	286	4,020
Chuck Milne	66	72	76 72	286	4,020
Bob Friend	74	71	69 72	286	4,020
Bob Ford	75	72	67 72	286	4,020
Brian Henninger	71	76	66 73	286	4,020
Laird Small	69	73	69 76	287	2,843
Stephen Ames	71	79	68 69	287	2,843
Brent Geiberger	73	69	73 72	287	2,843
Brian Mogg	71	72	71 73	287	2,843
Bruce Summerhays	68	71	71 77	287	2,843
Olin Browne	66	77	70 74	287	2,843
Keith Fergus	73	68	72 74	287	2,843
Joan Pitcock	76	69	69 75	289	2,250
Roger Maltbie	67	78	76 71	292	2,150
Mark Wiebe	79	71	70 72	292	2,150
Mike Christie	79	71	70 72	292	2,150
Emilee Klein	74	69	81 69	293	2,050
Frank Conner	71	69	81 72	293	2,050
Cindy Rarick	68	73	78 74	293	2,050
Dave Eichelberger	70	72	71 80	293	2,050
Jimmy Powell	78	70	73 73	294	1,950
Ted Goin	79	68	74 73	294	1,950
Lon Hinkle	73	77	71 73	294	1,950
Tommy Masters	73	70	77 74	294	1,950
Mark Pfeil	74	70	75 75	294	1,950
Bob Murphy	74	75	70 75	294	1,950
Bob Boldt	81	73	68 73	295	1,870
Brett Upper	71	74	71 79	295	1,870
Bruce Fleisher	78	76	68 74	296	1,810
Greg Powers	70	76	78 72	296	1,810
Todd Fisher	74	73	74 75	296	1,810
Marion Dantzler	68	77	73 78	296	1,810
Peter Harrison	76	70	76 75	297	1,760
Bud Allin	70	77	74 77	298	1,730
Jeff McMillan	76	74	71 79	298	1,730
Larry Ziegler	70	74	79 76	299	1,700
Andy North	78	75	70 79	302	1,700
Todd Southard	79	76	69 78	302	1,700
Rodd Cerrudo	75	77	72 79	303	1,700

JCPenney Classic

Innisbrook Resort, Copperhead Course, Palm Harbor, Florida
Par 36-35–71; 7,054 yards (men), 6,330 yards (women)

December 4-7
purse, $1,500,000

	SCORES			TOTAL	MONEY (Each)
Clarence Rose/Amy Fruhwirth	66	70	62 66	264	$187,500
Stewart Cink/Emilee Klein	65	67	68 65	265	75,577
Dan Forsman/Catriona Matthew	65	64	66 70	265	75,577
Fred Funk/Tina Barrett	68	65	64 69	266	36,058

	SCORES				TOTAL	MONEY (Each)
Vijay Singh/Marie-Laure de Lorenzi	66	67	66	67	266	36,058
Doug Martin/Carin Hj Koch	67	67	65	67	266	36,058
Michael Bradley/Colleen Walker	65	67	66	69	267	16,304
Ted Tryba/Cindy Rarick	65	69	67	66	267	16,304
David Toms/Jackie Gallagher-Smith	69	69	62	67	267	16,304
Rocco Mediate/Missie Berteotti	67	67	65	68	267	16,304
Mike Hulbert/Donna Andrews	65	65	68	69	267	16,304
Steve Pate/Meg Mallon	65	66	64	72	267	16,304
Paul Stankowski/Dana Dormann	68	68	64	68	268	10,616
Glen Day/Melissa McNamara	67	68	68	66	269	8,746
David Ogrin/Wendy Ward	64	69	68	68	269	8,746
Steve Lowery/Chris Johnson	68	66	67	68	269	8,746
Jeff Sluman/Dottie Pepper	63	68	67	71	269	8,746
Paul Azinger/Susie Redman	67	63	67	72	269	8,746
P.H. Horgan III/Cindy Figg-Currier	67	70	66	67	270	6,415
Brent Geiberger/Tammie Green	64	72	66	68	270	6,415
Dudley Hart/Dawn Coe-Jones	65	68	70	69	270	6,415
Steve Stricker/Vicki Goetze-Ackerman	67	65	69	68	271	5,839
Joe Durant/Erika Wicoff	69	69	64	69	271	5,839
Kenny Perry/Jane Crafter	69	68	67	67	271	5,839
Robert Gamez/Helen Alfredsson	66	70	69	67	272	5,282
Tom Purtzer/Juli Inkster	70	66	69	67	272	5,282
Chris Perry/Cathy Gerring	65	68	67	72	272	5,282
Kelly Gibson/Jane Geddes	68	69	68	67	272	5,282
Willie Wood/Cathy Johnston-Forbes	64	70	72	66	272	5,282
Mike Brisky/Barb Mucha	62	68	71	71	272	5,282
John Daly/Laura Davies	64	69	70	70	273	4,500
Kirk Triplett/Julie Piers	64	69	68	72	273	4,500
Jim Dent/Kim Williams	65	69	67	72	273	4,500
Chip Beck/Charlotta Sorenstam	71	70	65	67	273	4,500
Len Mattiace/Michelle McGann	66	72	70	65	273	4,500
Lee Rinker/Marianne Morris	70	67	66	71	274	4,059
Jay Don Blake/Danielle Ammaccapane	65	69	69	71	274	4,059
Brad Bryant/Marta Figueras-Dotti	69	72	62	72	275	3,812
Billy Andrade/Kris Tschetter	72	66	71	66	275	3,812
Peter Baker/Alison Nicholas	65	72	67	71	275	3,812
Nolan Henke/Terry-Jo Myers	69	71	70	66	276	3,663
Billy Mayfair/Brandie Burton	66	71	68	71	276	3,663
Mike Standly/Karen Weiss	65	70	70	72	277	3,461
Peter Kostis/Deb Richard	70	70	69	68	277	3,461
Jim Carter/Maggie Will-Halpin	67	70	68	72	277	3,461
Skip Kendall/Michele Redman	66	71	70	70	277	3,461
Tommy Tolles/Leta Lindley	68	71	73	65	277	3,461
Russ Cochran/Cindy Schreyer	69	67	67	75	278	3,289
Brad Fabel/Lisa Hackney	69	72	68	70	279	3,231
Fulton Allem/Sally Little	65	74	67	74	280	3,144
Jay Overton/Dale Eggeling	66	71	70	73	280	3,144
Wayne Levi/Amy Alcott	68				WD	3,058

Office Depot Father-Son Challenge

Windsor Club, Vero Beach, Florida
Par 36-36–72; 6,709 yards

December 6-7
purse, $860,000

	SCORES		TOTAL	MONEY (Won by professional)
Raymond and Raymond Floyd, Jr.	62	58	120	$150,000
Dave and Ron Stockton	60	61	121	100,000
Jack and Gary Nicklaus	64	59	123	80,000
Bob and David Charles	62	63	125	80,000
Jerry and Wesley Pate	64	63	127	52,500
Hale and Steve Irwin	63	64	127	52,500
Charles and Kyle Coody	65	63	128	45,000
David and Andrew Graham	66	63	129	38,333
Al and John Geiberger	64	65	129	38,333
Johnny and Andy Miller	65	64	129	38,333
Larry and Drew Nelson	65	65	130	34,500
Tom and Eric Weiskopf	64	66	130	34,500
Lee and Tony Lee Trevino	65	65	130	34,500
Gary and Wayne Player	65	65	130	34,500
Billy and Bobby Casper	68	63	131	32,000
Tony and Warren Jacklin	65	67	132	30,000

Diners Club Matches

PGA West, Nicklaus Course, La Quinta, California
Par 36-36–72; 6,900 yards

December 11-14
purse, $700,000

FIRST ROUND

Steve Elkington and Jeff Maggert defeated John Daly and Tim Herron, 1 up
Brad Faxon and Billy Andrade defeated Justin Leonard and Mike Hulbert, 1 up
Tom Lehman and Duffy Waldorf defeated Tommy Tolles and John Cook, 1 up
Jim Furyk and Lee Janzen defeated Mark Calcavecchia and Jeff Sluman, 3 and 2

SECOND ROUND

Faxon and Andrade defeated Elkington and Maggert, 1 up
Leonard and Hulbert defeated Daly and Herron, 1 up
Tolles and Cook defeated Calcavecchia and Sluman, 2 and 1
Lehman and Waldorf defeated Furyk and Janzen, 3 and 1

THIRD ROUND

Elkington and Maggert defeated Leonard and Hulbert, 1 up
Daly and Herron defeated Faxon and Andrade, 2 and 1
Furyk and Janzen defeated Tolles and Cook, 2 and 1
Lehman and Waldorf defeated Calcavecchia and Sluman, 4 and 3

(Andrade, Faxon, Furyk, Janzen, received $35,000 each; Cook, Hulbert, Leonard, Tolles, $30,000 each; Calcavecchia, Daly, Herron, Sluman, $25,000 each.)

FINAL ROUND

Elkington and Maggert defeated Lehman and Waldorf, 2 and 1

(Elkington and Maggert received $110,000 each; Lehman and Waldorf received $60,000 each.)

Lexus Challenge

La Quinta Resort & Club, Citrus Course,
La Quinta, California
Par 36-36—72; 6,825 yards

December 19-20
purse, $1,000,000

	SCORES		TOTAL	MONEY (Won by professional)
Raymond Floyd/William Devane	64	60	124	$180,000
Gil Morgan/Roger Clemens	62	63	125	112,500
Jim Colbert/Kevin Costner	60	65	125	112,500
Johnny Miller/Joe Pesci	65	62	127	95,000
Jay Sigel/Michael Chiklis	65	65	130	85,000
Lee Trevino/Glenn Frey	63	69	132	70,000
Hale Irwin/Chris O'Donnell	68	64	132	70,000
Chi Chi Rodriguez/Matthew McConaughey	65	68	133	57,500
Dave Stockton/Don Shula	66	67	133	57,500
Bob Murphy/Matt Lauer	66	67	133	57,500
Larry Nelson/Rod Laver	67	68	135	52,500
Gary Player/Clint Eastwood	68	68	136	50,000

Andersen Consulting World Championship

Grayhawk Golf Club, Raptor Course, Scottsdale, Arizona
Par 36-36—72; 7,135 yards

January 3-4, 1998
purse, $3,650,000

SEMI-FINALS

Colin Montgomerie defeated Ernie Els, 3 and 2
Davis Love III defeated Hajime Meshiai, 1 up

THIRD-PLACE PLAYOFF

Els defeated Meshiai, 4 and 3

(Els received $350,000; Meshiai received $300,000.)

FINAL

Montgomerie defeated Love, 2 up

(Montgomerie received $1,000,000; Love received $500,000.)

Japan Qualifying

Golden Palm Country Club, Kagoshima, Japan
Par 36-36—72; 6,970 yards

March 1-2

QUARTER-FINALS

Toru Suzuki defeated Shigeki Maruyama, 2 up
Hajime Meshiai defeated Hisayuki Sasaki, 1 up
Hidemichi Tanaka defeated Masanobu Kimura, 3 and 2
Kazuhiko Hosokawa defeated Masahiro Kuramoto, 2 and 1

(Each losing quarter-finalist received $20,000.)

SEMI-FINALS

Meshiai defeated Suzuki, 3 and 1
Hosokawa defeated Tanaka, 2 and 1

(Each losing semi-finalist received $70,000.)

FINAL

Meshiai defeated Hosokawa, 1 up

(Hosokawa received $150,000.)

United States Qualifying

Reynolds Plantation, Great Waters Course, April 21-22
Lake Oconee, Georgia
Par 36-36–72; 7,048 yards

QUARTER-FINALS

Tom Lehman defeated Scott Hoch, 2 and 1
Davis Love III defeated Corey Pavin, 5 and 3
Fred Couples defeated Steve Stricker, 2 and 1
Phil Mickelson defeated Mark O'Meara, 3 and 2

(Each losing quarter-finalist received $20,000.)

SEMI-FINALS

Love defeated Lehman, 3 and 2
Mickelson defeated Couples, 1 up

(Each losing semi-finalist received $70,000.)

FINAL

Love defeated Mickelson, 20 holes

(Mickelson received $150,000.)

European Qualifying

Buckinghamshire Golf Club, Denham, England May 19-20
Par 36-36–72; 6,880 yards

QUARTER-FINALS

Colin Montgomerie defeated Jose Maria Olazabal, 2 and 1
Sam Torrance defeated Ian Woosnam, 4 and 3
Darren Clarke defeated Bernhard Langer, 2 and 1
Costantino Rocca defeated Jesper Parnevik, 20 holes

(Each losing quarter-finalist received $20,000.)

SEMI-FINALS

Montgomerie defeated Torrance, 6 and 4
Rocca defeated Clarke, 19 holes

(Each losing semi-finalist received $70,000.)

FINAL

Montgomerie defeated Rocca, 5 and 4

(Rocca received $150,000.)

International Qualifying

Blackwolf Run, River Course, Kohler, Wisconsin   July 28-29
Par 37-35–72; 6,991 yards

QUARTER-FINALS

Greg Norman defeated Robert Allenby, 2 up
Steve Elkington defeated Mark McNulty, 1 up
Ernie Els defeated Frank Nobilo, 1 up
Nick Price defeated Vijay Singh, 1 up

(Each losing quarter-finalist received $20,000.)

SEMI-FINALS

Elkington defeated Norman, 2 and 1
Els defeated Price, 3 and 2

(Each losing semi-finalist received $70,000.)

FINAL

Els defeated Elkington, 2 up

(Elkington received $150,000.)

Nike Tour

Lakeland Classic

Grasslands Golf and Country Club, Lakeland, Florida
Par 36-36–72; 7,040 yards

January 30-February 2
purse, $200,000

	SCORES				TOTAL	MONEY
Ryan Howison	66	65	69	69	269	$36,000
Mark Carnevale	68	66	69	69	272	22,700
Cliff Kresge	70	69	68	66	273	13,166.67
Ray Stewart	67	68	69	69	273	13,166.67
Rob McKelvey	68	70	65	70	273	13,166.66
Brian Claar	66	69	70	69	274	7,500
Jim Estes	69	70	68	67	274	7,500
Arden Knoll	69	70	69	66	274	7,500
Gary Koch	67	66	71	70	274	7,500
Bobby Doolittle	69	68	69	69	275	4,166.67
Tom Scherrer	71	69	68	67	275	4,166.67
R.W. Eaks	68	67	69	71	275	4,166.66
Tim Conley	65	75	66	70	276	3,015
Matt Gogel	68	72	67	69	276	3,015
Carl Paulson	65	72	68	71	276	3,015
Dan Pelczarski	70	70	64	72	276	3,015
Brian Kamm	67	70	71	69	277	2,506.67
Jeff Thorsen	73	66	69	69	277	2,506.67
Bryan Gorman	68	72	66	71	277	2,506.66
Chris DiMarco	72	68	70	68	278	1,950
Jeff Gallagher	65	72	71	70	278	1,950
Buddy Gardner	71	66	69	72	278	1,950
Damon Green	65	75	71	67	278	1,950
Kevin Johnson	71	70	69	68	278	1,950
Don Reese	70	69	72	67	278	1,950
Chris Smith	72	69	71	66	278	1,950
Greg Twiggs	67	71	71	69	278	1,950
Steve Flesch	70	69	71	69	279	1,303.34
Dick Mast	69	69	72	69	279	1,303.34
Eric Booker	69	70	69	71	279	1,303.33
Eric Frishette	66	72	74	67	279	1,303.33
Mark Hensby	69	70	72	68	279	1,303.33
Bobby Wadkins	70	70	68	71	279	1,303.33

Inland Empire Open

Moreno Valley Ranch Golf Club, Moreno Valley, California
Par 36-36–72; 6,880 yards

February 20-23
purse, $200,000

	SCORES				TOTAL	MONEY
Mark Carnevale	67	71	70	66	274	$36,000
David Jackson	70	71	71	64	276	22,700
Lon Hinkle	68	71	70	69	278	14,500
Sam Randolph	70	67	70	71	278	14,500

		SCORES			TOTAL	MONEY
Michael Allen	69	68	69	73	279	8,625
Robin Freeman	71	70	70	68	279	8,625
Bob Gilder	68	71	70	70	279	8,625
Matthew Lane	73	67	68	71	279	8,625
Michael Muehr	69	67	73	71	280	5,500
Gary Webb	70	73	63	74	280	5,500
Jeff Gallagher	69	71	70	71	281	3,475
Matt Peterson	72	71	68	70	281	3,475
Dennis Trixler	69	71	70	71	281	3,475
Karl Zoller	68	71	72	70	281	3,475
Barry Conser	71	69	72	70	282	2,900
Rod Butcher	70	75	68	70	283	2,463.34
Ray Stewart	73	71	69	70	283	2,463.34
Greg Bruckner	69	70	69	75	283	2,463.33
Gary Cochran	74	66	67	76	283	2,463.33
J.L. Lewis	69	73	68	73	283	2,463.33
Chris Smith	70	73	69	71	283	2,463.33
Richard Gilkey	71	72	70	71	284	1,950
Todd Gleaton	68	75	68	73	284	1,950
Cliff Kresge	70	69	72	73	284	1,950
Tom Kroll	67	71	70	76	284	1,950
Dan Bateman	75	69	69	72	285	1,460
Cameron Beckman	69	74	68	74	285	1,460
Ashley Chinner	69	74	71	71	285	1,460
Jeff Cook	72	66	72	75	285	1,460
Brad Sherfy	75	70	69	71	285	1,460
Greg Whisman	72	72	67	74	285	1,460

Monterrey Open

Club Campestre, Monterrey, Mexico
Par 36-36–72; 6,964 yards

March 13-16
purse, $225,000

		SCORES			TOTAL	MONEY
Mike Small	68	67	68	67	270	$40,500
Mark Carnevale	67	68	68	68	271	19,387.50
Chris DiMarco	65	73	66	67	271	19,387.50
Brian Kamm	69	71	67	64	271	19,387.50
Barry Cheesman	69	71	63	69	272	10,312.50
Matt Gogel	69	66	66	71	272	10,312.50
Charlie Rymer	69	64	71	68	272	10,312.50
Brian Bateman	63	70	69	71	273	7,312.50
Bob Estes	69	70	69	65	273	7,312.50
Ben Bates	68	69	66	71	274	4,443.75
Pat Bates	69	69	70	66	274	4,443.75
Ashley Chinner	69	68	68	69	274	4,443.75
Cliff Kresge	69	69	69	67	274	4,443.75
P.J. Cowan	67	69	71	68	275	3,285
Clark Dennis	66	74	68	67	275	3,285
David Jackson	69	72	67	67	275	3,285
Dennis Paulson	71	68	71	66	276	2,534.07
Greg Towne	69	70	71	66	276	2,534.07
Michael Allen	70	69	69	68	276	2,534.06
Carlos Espinosa	69	66	68	73	276	2,534.06
Jeff Gallagher	74	67	69	66	276	2,534.06
Bryan Gorman	73	68	69	66	276	2,534.06
Tim Loustalot	66	70	68	72	276	2,534.06

	SCORES				TOTAL	MONEY
Tom Shaw	68	67	70	71	276	2,534.06
Jeff Brehaut	66	74	67	70	277	1,912.50
Greg Bruckner	69	70	65	73	277	1,912.50
Mark Hensby	68	70	65	74	277	1,912.50
Briny Baird	69	71	68	70	278	1,498.50
Mike Emery, Jr.	68	73	69	68	278	1,498.50
Sam Randolph	68	70	71	69	278	1,498.50
Howard Twitty	68	72	68	70	278	1,498.50
Ron Whittaker	69	72	69	68	278	1,498.50

Louisiana Open

Le Triomphe Country Club, Broussard, Louisiana
Par 36-36–72; 6,978 yards
(Fourth round cancelled — rain.)

March 27-30
purse, $300,000

	SCORES			TOTAL	MONEY
Joe Daley	62	67	69	198	$54,000
Bobby Wadkins	66	68	67	201	34,050
Mark Carnevale	66	66	71	203	24,750
Glen Hnatiuk	68	68	68	204	16,000
Rob McKelvey	65	75	64	204	16,000
Shaun Micheel	68	68	68	204	16,000
Dave Schreyer	71	68	66	205	11,250
Mario Tiziani	71	68	66	205	11,250
Brian Bateman	68	71	67	206	6,225
Clark Dennis	72	66	68	206	6,225
Eric Frishette	67	70	69	206	6,225
Jeff Gallagher	67	73	66	206	6,225
Cliff Kresge	68	71	67	206	6,225
Dennis Paulson	70	68	68	206	6,225
Briny Baird	69	72	66	207	3,708.75
Chris DiMarco	69	70	68	207	3,708.75
John Elliott	73	68	66	207	3,708.75
Steve Flesch	70	70	67	207	3,708.75
Todd Gleaton	66	73	68	207	3,708.75
Mike Heinen	72	68	67	207	3,708.75
Mike Standly	68	71	68	207	3,708.75
Chris Stutts	69	67	71	207	3,708.75
Dan Bateman	69	73	66	208	2,106
Michael Clark	66	71	71	208	2,106
Kawika Cotner	67	72	69	208	2,106
P.J. Cowan	68	71	69	208	2,106
Tim Estes	66	70	72	208	2,106
Keith Fergus	71	69	68	208	2,106
Matt Gogel	72	69	67	208	2,106
Kevin Johnson	64	72	72	208	2,106
Brian Kamm	68	72	68	208	2,106
J.L. Lewis	69	72	67	208	2,106
Craig Perks	69	73	66	208	2,106
Harry Rudolph	72	70	66	208	2,106
Esteban Toledo	71	70	67	208	2,106
Rocky Walcher	71	70	67	208	2,106
Greg Whisman	65	75	68	208	2,106

Greater Austin Open

The Hills Country Club, Austin, Texas
Par 36-36–72; 6,954 yards
(Third and fourth rounds cancelled — rain.)

April 3-6
purse, $200,000

	SCORES		TOTAL	MONEY
Eric Booker	69	71	140	$36,000
Brian Kamm	72	69	141	22,700
Joe Daley	70	72	142	12,125
Cliff Kresge	70	72	142	12,125
Bud Still	72	70	142	12,125
Greg Twiggs	71	71	142	12,125
Greg Whisman	73	70	143	8,000
Ben Bates	70	74	144	4,800
Cameron Beckman	73	71	144	4,800
Bryan Gorman	76	68	144	4,800
Charlie Rymer	75	69	144	4,800
Esteban Toledo	77	67	144	4,800
Mark Wurtz	71	73	144	4,800
Kyle Flinton	75	70	145	2,845
Jason Hill	72	73	145	2,845
Craig Perks	75	70	145	2,845
Gary Webb	72	73	145	2,845
Ren Budde	72	74	146	2,250
Keith Fergus	73	73	146	2,250
John Johnson	72	74	146	2,250
Matt Peterson	78	68	146	2,250
Tom Scherrer	71	75	146	2,250
Mike Small	72	74	146	2,250
Briny Baird	77	70	147	1,361.43
Greg Bruckner	73	74	147	1,361.43
Ashley Chinner	73	74	147	1,361.43
Tim Conley	75	72	147	1,361.43
Danny Edwards	77	70	147	1,361.43
Danny Ellis	75	72	147	1,361.43
Bob Estes	73	74	147	1,361.43
Bob Gilder	75	72	147	1,361.43
Dennis Paulson	71	76	147	1,361.43
Ted Schulz	75	72	147	1,361.43
Greg Sweatt	74	73	147	1,361.43
Harry Taylor	71	76	147	1,361.43
Trevor Dodds	78	69	147	1,361.42
Chris Stutts	76	71	147	1,361.42

Mississippi Gulf Coast Classic

Mississippi National Golf Club, Gautier, Mississippi
Par 36-36–72; 7,003 yards

April 17-20
purse, $200,000

	SCORES				TOTAL	MONEY
Jeff Brehaut	71	69	65	70	275	$36,000
Dan Bateman	66	72	71	72	281	19,600
Tom Scherrer	74	69	70	68	281	19,600
Jeff Barlow	74	70	69	69	282	10,666.67
Harry Rudolph	74	71	69	68	282	10,666.67
Keith Fergus	71	72	70	69	282	10,666.66
Chris DiMarco	74	69	71	69	283	6,000

	SCORES				TOTAL	MONEY
Harrison Frazar	70	72	72	69	283	6,000
J.L. Lewis	71	73	71	68	283	6,000
Mike Small	71	71	74	67	283	6,000
Greg Whisman	71	69	69	74	283	6,000
Clark Dennis	71	74	68	71	284	3,200
R.W. Eaks	75	67	73	69	284	3,200
Glen Hnatiuk	71	69	70	74	284	3,200
Sam Randolph	72	73	68	71	284	3,200
Ben Bates	71	73	71	70	285	2,570
Eric Johnson	69	70	72	74	285	2,570
Kent Jones	67	72	74	72	285	2,570
Brian Kamm	72	70	72	71	285	2,570
P.J. Cowan	71	72	73	70	286	2,050
Bruce Fleisher	75	69	71	71	286	2,050
Kevin Johnson	70	68	76	72	286	2,050
Rob McKelvey	69	75	71	71	286	2,050
Chris Smith	68	71	73	74	286	2,050
Greg Twiggs	71	71	76	68	286	2,050
Barry Cheesman	76	69	68	74	287	1,390
Joe Cioe	68	74	70	75	287	1,390
Jeff Cook	68	77	70	72	287	1,390
Spike McRoy	74	69	71	73	287	1,390
Jack O'Keefe	69	74	74	70	287	1,390
Tom Pernice, Jr.	75	70	73	69	287	1,390
Mike Smith	71	74	74	68	287	1,390
Shane Supple	73	70	71	73	287	1,390

Alabama Classic

Cherokee Ridge Country Club, Union Grove, Alabama
Par 36-36–72; 6,934 yards
(Fourth round cancelled — rain.)

April 24-27
purse, $200,000

	SCORES			TOTAL	MONEY
John Elliott	69	66	69	204	$36,000
Tom Shaw	68	66	72	206	22,700
Pat Bates	66	70	71	207	12,125
Rocky Walcher	67	69	71	207	12,125
Greg Whisman	69	68	70	207	12,125
Chris Winchip	68	69	70	207	12,125
Joe Daley	70	70	68	208	6,000
Billy Downes	70	70	68	208	6,000
Steve Flesch	67	68	73	208	6,000
Glen Hnatiuk	66	71	71	208	6,000
Gene Sauers	67	70	71	208	6,000
P.J. Cowan	69	71	69	209	3,112
Mark Hensby	73	67	69	209	3,112
Tim Loustalot	62	72	75	209	3,112
Ray Stewart	71	70	68	209	3,112
Esteban Toledo	69	68	72	209	3,112
Chris DiMarco	70	69	71	210	2,506.67
Geoffrey Sisk	70	67	73	210	2,506.67
Ben Bates	69	69	72	210	2,506.66
Briny Baird	67	70	74	211	1,950
Tim Conley	69	71	71	211	1,950
Tom Estes	71	68	72	211	1,950
Bob Gaus	70	70	71	211	1,950

	SCORES			TOTAL	MONEY
John Inman	70	68	73	211	1,950
Deane Pappas	71	68	72	211	1,950
Chris Smith	68	72	71	211	1,950
Chip Spratlin	70	70	71	211	1,950
JC Anderson	70	67	75	212	1,252.50
Richard Gilkey	67	70	75	212	1,252.50
Tom Hearn	68	73	71	212	1,252.50
Rob McKelvey	73	68	71	212	1,252.50
Dennis Paulson	70	71	71	212	1,252.50
Sam Randolph	70	69	73	212	1,252.50
Mike Sullivan	70	69	73	212	1,252.50
Greg Twiggs	69	70	73	212	1,252.50

South Carolina Classic

Country Club of South Carolina, Florence, South Carolina
Par 36-36–72; 7,150 yards

May 1-4
purse, $200,000

	SCORES				TOTAL	MONEY
Harrison Frazar	68	69	67	67	271	$36,000
R.W. Eaks	69	68	66	71	274	22,700
Chris Smith	71	65	70	69	275	16,500
Bruce Vaughan	67	70	68	72	277	10,666.67
Bobby Wadkins	69	69	68	71	277	10,666.67
Chris Couch	73	70	68	66	277	10,666.66
Dan Bateman	70	66	73	69	278	7,000
Bob Gilder	70	67	70	71	278	7,000
Esteban Toledo	69	71	68	70	278	7,000
Steve Flesch	72	70	68	69	279	3,950
Kevin Johnson	70	66	74	69	279	3,950
Sean Murphy	71	71	68	69	279	3,950
Harry Rudolph	71	70	69	69	279	3,950
David Jackson	70	71	70	69	280	2,713.34
Jeff Julian	72	69	68	71	280	2,713.34
Barry Cheesman	71	72	66	71	280	2,713.33
Mark Hensby	68	71	69	72	280	2,713.33
Glen Hnatiuk	70	70	69	71	280	2,713.33
Charlie Rymer	73	69	67	71	280	2,713.33
Jeff Cook	69	71	69	72	281	2,150
P.J. Cowan	70	66	75	70	281	2,150
Arden Knoll	68	75	68	70	281	2,150
Tom Scherrer	73	69	69	70	281	2,150
Ben Bates	71	71	69	71	282	1,602.86
Michael Clark	67	70	71	74	282	1,602.86
Bruce Fleisher	72	68	72	70	282	1,602.86
Bryan Gorman	73	69	71	69	282	1,602.86
Rob McKelvey	70	69	69	74	282	1,602.86
Phil Bland	72	71	70	69	282	1,602.85
Sam Randolph	70	67	71	74	282	1,602.85

Carolina Classic

Prestonwood Country Club, Cary, North Carolina
Par 36-36–72; 7,271 yards

May 8-11
purse, $200,000

	SCORES				TOTAL	MONEY
Dan Bateman	70	69	75	70	284	$36,000
Dennis Paulson	73	72	71	69	285	17,233.34
Steve Flesch	74	67	72	72	285	17,233.33
Terry Price	73	72	70	70	285	17,233.33
Ben Bates	70	72	72	73	287	9,166.67
Bob Friend	73	72	68	74	287	9,166.67
Trevor Dodds	68	72	74	73	287	9,166.66
Todd Gleaton	69	71	77	71	288	6,000
Tom Hearn	74	71	73	70	288	6,000
Tom Shaw	68	72	74	74	288	6,000
Mike Small	72	67	79	71	289	4,000
Jeff Brehaut	78	67	75	70	290	2,820
Greg Bruckner	73	72	74	71	290	2,820
Michael Clark	72	73	73	72	290	2,820
Chris Couch	71	66	78	75	290	2,820
Chris DiMarco	75	69	76	70	290	2,820
Roy Hunter	72	72	68	78	290	2,820
Cliff Kresge	76	67	74	73	290	2,820
Ray Stewart	72	70	72	76	290	2,820
Chris Stutts	75	67	74	74	290	2,820
Jeff Barlow	71	71	76	73	291	1,900
Joe Cioe	72	72	74	73	291	1,900
Rick Cramer	71	74	72	74	291	1,900
Barry Jaeckel	75	69	75	72	291	1,900
Carl Paulson	71	72	74	74	291	1,900
Matt Peterson	75	69	77	70	291	1,900
Harry Taylor	72	73	75	71	291	1,900
Eric Booker	73	71	74	74	292	1,332
P.J. Cowan	71	71	75	75	292	1,332
Jeff Gallagher	71	74	77	70	292	1,332
Dan Stone	75	70	71	76	292	1,332
Dennis Zinkon	78	68	72	74	292	1,332

Dominion Open

The Dominion Club, Glen Allen, Virginia
Par 36-36–72; 7,020 yards

May 15-18
purse, $225,000

	SCORES				TOTAL	MONEY
Jeff Julian	68	68	69	72	277	$40,500
Bobby Wadkins	69	71	70	68	278	25,537.50
John Elliott	65	75	69	70	279	16,312.50
Rocky Walcher	71	69	69	70	279	16,312.50
Briny Baird	68	73	72	67	280	10,312.50
Tom Scherrer	71	72	65	72	280	10,312.50
Chris Smith	71	68	73	68	280	10,312.50
Matt Gogel	71	69	70	71	281	6,750
Javier Sanchez	75	69	69	68	281	6,750
Mike Springer	70	71	64	76	281	6,750
Steve Lamontagne	72	67	72	71	282	3,470.63
Mike Sullivan	68	73	69	72	282	3,470.63
Mike Swartz	72	72	70	68	282	3,470.63

	SCORES				TOTAL	MONEY
Karl Zoller	67	73	71	71	282	3,470.63
Steve Flesch	73	66	73	70	282	3,470.62
Buddy Gardner	71	67	72	72	282	3,470.62
Dick Mast	68	71	71	72	282	3,470.62
Chris Winchip	71	68	72	71	282	3,470.62
Kent Jones	73	70	71	69	283	2,643.75
Cliff Kresge	70	70	73	70	283	2,643.75
Michael Clark	72	71	68	73	284	2,362.50
Tim Conley	72	70	68	74	284	2,362.50
Rob McKelvey	73	69	72	70	284	2,362.50
Jeff Brehaut	75	68	71	71	285	1,803.22
Chris DiMarco	71	74	68	72	285	1,803.22
Kevin Johnson	72	71	71	71	285	1,803.22
P.J. Cowan	69	70	73	73	285	1,803.21
Jerry Foltz	72	67	71	75	285	1,803.21
Matt Peterson	72	70	71	72	285	1,803.21
Greg Twiggs	71	69	77	68	285	1,803.21

Upstate Classic

Verdae Greens Golf Club, Greenville, South Carolina
Par 36-36–72; 6,773 yards

May 29-June 1
purse, $200,000

	SCORES				TOTAL	MONEY
Chris Smith	66	64	67	70	267	$36,000
Terry Price	67	67	69	67	270	22,700
Trevor Dodds	74	66	67	65	272	16,500
Shane Bertsch	68	69	70	66	273	8,833.34
R.W. Eaks	70	70	68	65	273	8,833.34
Craig Bowden	71	69	66	67	273	8,833.33
Clark Dennis	70	70	65	68	273	8,833.33
Glen Hnatiuk	66	71	68	68	273	8,833.33
Rocky Walcher	74	66	66	67	273	8,833.33
Barry Cheesman	70	67	69	68	274	5,000
Harrison Frazar	71	67	69	68	275	3,475
Gabriel Hjertstedt	71	65	68	71	275	3,475
Brian Kamm	70	66	69	70	275	3,475
Bobby Wadkins	67	70	71	67	275	3,475
Franklin Langham	65	68	69	74	276	2,900
Todd Gleaton	70	69	69	69	277	2,570
John Inman	66	69	70	72	277	2,570
Carl Paulson	70	70	68	69	277	2,570
Mike Smith	68	71	69	69	277	2,570
Cliff Kresge	70	70	68	70	278	2,100
Rob McKelvey	67	67	71	73	278	2,100
Ron Philo, Jr.	69	71	68	70	278	2,100
Bud Still	67	73	70	68	278	2,100
Fred Wadsworth	72	66	73	67	278	2,100
Marion Dantzler	69	70	72	68	279	1,650
Jim Estes	68	68	72	71	279	1,650
Shaun Micheel	72	68	66	73	279	1,650
Chris Winchip	69	70	71	69	279	1,650
Joe Cioe	71	68	71	70	280	1,240
Chris Couch	70	67	72	71	280	1,240
Mark Hensby	69	71	68	72	280	1,240
Jimmy Johnston	69	70	73	68	280	1,240
David Peoples	71	67	70	72	280	1,240
Taylor Smith	73	66	70	71	280	1,240

Knoxville Open

Three Ridges Golf Course, Knoxville, Tennessee
Par 36-36–72; 7,035 yards

June 5-8
purse, $200,000

	SCORES				TOTAL	MONEY
Dave Rummells	65	70	70	66	271	$36,000
Matt Gogel	71	67	69	66	273	19,600
Terry Price	69	68	66	70	273	19,600
Rocky Walcher	70	71	69	66	276	12,500
JC Anderson	72	70	66	69	277	9,166.67
Chris Smith	69	71	66	71	277	9,166.67
Joe Cioe	69	70	65	73	277	9,166.66
Bob Gilder	69	68	70	71	278	7,000
Ben Bates	70	71	68	70	279	4,150
Trevor Dodds	73	69	69	68	279	4,150
John Elliott	70	68	73	68	279	4,150
Harrison Frazar	72	70	66	71	279	4,150
David Jackson	69	69	71	70	279	4,150
Dennis Paulson	66	71	69	73	279	4,150
Todd Gleaton	72	71	67	70	280	2,830
Esteban Toledo	70	71	73	66	280	2,830
Jay Hobby	68	74	70	69	281	2,353.34
Fred Wadsworth	72	71	71	67	281	2,353.34
Greg Bruckner	71	71	70	69	281	2,353.33
Croy Cochran	68	70	70	73	281	2,353.33
Keith Fergus	67	71	71	72	281	2,353.33
Jay Synkelma	71	69	70	71	281	2,353.33
Chris Couch	69	70	71	72	282	1,950
Bruce Vaughan	73	68	73	68	282	1,950
Eric Booker	70	73	70	71	284	1,508.58
Todd Barranger	70	71	69	74	284	1,508.57
Joe Daley	71	72	70	71	284	1,508.57
Billy Downes	72	69	71	72	284	1,508.57
Steve Flesch	69	73	68	74	284	1,508.57
Glen Hnatiuk	69	74	67	74	284	1,508.57
John Johnson	73	67	70	74	284	1,508.57

Miami Valley Open

Heatherwoode Golf Club, Springboro, Ohio
Par 36-35–71; 6,730 yards

June 12-15
purse, $200,000

	SCORES			TOTAL	MONEY
Trevor Dodds	63	64	66	69	262	$36,000
Joe Daley	67	65	66	70	268	22,700
Glen Hnatiuk	66	68	66	69	269	14,500
J.L. Lewis	66	64	65	74	269	14,500
Ben Bates	68	68	67	67	270	10,500
Brian Kamm	64	68	72	67	271	8,500
Don Whittaker	67	68	66	70	271	8,500
Harrison Frazar	67	70	64	71	272	6,500
Jin Steel	68	67	66	71	272	6,500
John Inman	65	73	66	69	273	4,166.67
Stan Utley	69	68	68	68	273	4,166.67
Eric Johnson	64	70	69	70	273	4,166.66
Carl Paulson	68	71	66	69	274	3,300
Mike Small	69	66	72	68	275	2,713.34

	SCORES				TOTAL	MONEY
Ray Stewart	67	68	71	69	275	2,713.34
Buddy Gardner	73	65	67	70	275	2,713.33
Tim Loustalot	64	70	70	71	275	2,713.33
Dave Rummells	66	67	69	73	275	2,713.33
Esteban Toledo	65	69	71	70	275	2,713.33
Jeff Barlow	67	71	67	71	276	2,000
Craig Bowden	66	69	72	69	276	2,000
Chris DiMarco	70	68	68	70	276	2,000
Harry Rudolph	67	69	75	65	276	2,000
Mike Springer	69	67	72	68	276	2,000
Bruce Vaughan	65	69	71	71	276	2,000
John Wilson	68	68	67	73	276	2,000
JC Anderson	69	70	69	69	277	1,412
Curt Byrum	67	69	73	68	277	1,412
Barry Cheesman	71	68	69	69	277	1,412
Ron Philo, Jr.	69	70	65	73	277	1,412
Don Reese	65	68	73	71	277	1,412

Cleveland Open

Quail Hollow Resort, Devlin Course, Concord, Ohio
Par 36-36—72; 6,712 yards

June 19-22
purse, $200,000

	SCORES				TOTAL	MONEY
Mike Small	67	70	67	66	270	$36,000
Patrick Sheehan	69	68	69	65	271	22,700
Chris DiMarco	69	65	68	70	272	13,166.67
Trevor Dodds	69	68	69	66	272	13,166.67
Pat Bates	61	69	69	73	272	13,166.66
Barry Cheesman	66	66	70	71	273	8,000
Tim Conley	67	71	66	69	273	8,000
Jeff Gallagher	70	69	63	71	273	8,000
Rob Moss	71	69	68	66	274	6,000
Mike Emery	70	68	69	68	275	3,780
Glen Hnatiuk	70	66	70	69	275	3,780
Kent Jones	70	67	70	68	275	3,780
Harry Taylor	69	68	71	67	275	3,780
Chris Zambri	70	65	71	69	275	3,780
Ben Bates	69	68	71	68	276	2,760
Bob Friend	68	67	69	72	276	2,760
Michael Muehr	69	69	69	69	276	2,760
Jeff Brehaut	65	68	73	71	277	2,200
Greg Bruckner	71	68	70	68	277	2,200
J.L. Lewis	69	69	69	70	277	2,200
Ted Purdy	67	70	70	70	277	2,200
Tom Scherrer	71	67	69	70	277	2,200
Bruce Vaughan	72	68	69	68	277	2,200
Don Walsworth	68	70	69	70	277	2,200
David Jackson	67	67	74	70	278	1,700
Cliff Kresge	69	68	70	71	278	1,700
Sam Randolph	69	69	71	69	278	1,700
Clark Dennis	68	70	68	73	279	1,303.34
Dan Stone	70	68	71	70	279	1,303.3
JC Anderson	70	68	74	67	279	1,303.3
Billy Downes	69	71	70	69	279	1,303.3
Steve Lamontagne	67	70	70	72	279	1,303.3
Don Reese	65	70	70	74	279	1,303.3

Hershey Open

Country Club of Hershey, East Course,
Hershey, Pennsylvania
Par 36-35–71; 7,061 yards

July 3-6
purse, $200,000

	SCORES			TOTAL	MONEY
Barry Cheesman	71 71 70 66			278	$36,000
Billy Downes	71 71 68 69			279	19,600
Greg Lesher	73 70 68 68			279	19,600
R.W. Eaks	68 70 74 68			280	12,500
Kevin Altenhof	71 73 71 66			281	9,166.67
Mark Carnevale	70 72 71 68			281	9,166.67
Dennis Zinkon	73 69 70 69			281	9,166.66
Michael Allen	71 74 72 65			282	6,500
Chris DiMarco	69 74 71 68			282	6,500
Matt Gogel	69 72 74 68			283	4,500
Steve Lamontagne	67 74 68 74			283	4,500
Michael Clark	69 72 74 69			284	3,200
John Johnson	70 71 74 69			284	3,200
Greg Whisman	71 72 71 70			284	3,200
Ron Whittaker	70 75 72 67			284	3,200
Jeff Gallagher	71 70 71 73			285	2,516
Steve Jurgensen	73 69 72 71			285	2,516
Matthew Lane	70 74 72 69			285	2,516
Don Reese	68 72 72 73			285	2,516
Jay Synkelma	72 73 73 67			285	2,516
Dan Bateman	71 70 72 73			286	1,950
Steve Flesch	69 72 71 74			286	1,950
Harrison Frazar	69 70 77 70			286	1,950
Bob Friend	71 73 75 67			286	1,950
Darron Stiles	72 70 72 72			286	1,950
Karl Zoller	73 68 73 72			286	1,950
J.L. Lewis	78 66 74 69			287	1,412
Sam Randolph	71 74 72 70			287	1,412
Steve Schneiter	72 69 71 75			287	1,412
Patrick Sheehan	74 71 71 71			287	1,412
Bud Still	71 73 70 73			287	1,412

Laurel Creek Classic

Laurel Creek Country Club, Moorestown, New Jersey
Par 36-36–72; 6,917 yards

July 10-13
purse, $200,000

	SCORES			TOTAL	MONEY
Matt Gogel	66 68 68 67			269	$36,000
Dennis Paulson	67 67 69 67			270	22,700
Ron Whittaker	66 68 67 70			271	16,500
Chris DiMarco	67 65 72 69			273	12,500
Carl Paulson	70 70 66 68			274	9,750
Dennis Zinkon	68 67 69 70			274	9,750
John Johnson	70 66 67 72			275	7,500
Deane Pappas	70 68 69 68			275	7,500
Michael Allen	67 68 70 71			276	5,000
R.W. Eaks	69 66 71 70			276	5,000
Steve Flesch	64 70 71 71			276	5,000
Clark Dennis	65 69 69 74			277	3,200
Harrison Frazar	71 69 70 67			277	3,200

	SCORES				TOTAL	MONEY
Steve Lamontagne	68	69	69	71	277	3,200
Darron Stiles	67	69	71	70	277	3,200
Michael Clark	69	71	69	69	278	2,626.67
Croy Cochran	69	69	70	70	278	2,626.67
Matt Peterson	68	69	70	71	278	2,626.66
P.J. Cowan	70	68	72	69	279	2,200
Rick Cramer	68	71	68	72	279	2,200
Glen Hnatiuk	72	65	70	72	279	2,200
Dan Pelczarski	70	67	73	69	279	2,200
Greg Sweatt	69	70	68	72	279	2,200
Jeff Gove	68	71	69	72	280	1,900
Jeff Barlow	72	68	70	71	281	1,553.34
Barry Cheesman	73	68	70	70	281	1,553.34
Kent Jones	68	70	70	73	281	1,553.33
Heath Slocum	71	69	69	72	281	1,553.33
Dean Vomacka	68	72	69	72	281	1,553.33
Karl Zoller	73	68	67	73	281	1,553.33

St. Louis Golf Classic

Missouri Bluffs Golf Course, St. Charles, Missouri
Par 36-35–71; 7,047 yards

July 17-20
purse, $200,000

	SCORES				TOTAL	MONEY
Todd Gleaton	66	67	64	64	261	$36,000
Arden Knoll	66	66	67	65	264	22,700
Clark Dennis	67	70	68	60	265	16,500
Rocky Walcher	68	62	66	70	266	12,500
Jeff Barlow	65	70	66	66	267	9,750
Barry Cheesman	69	68	65	65	267	9,750
Dan Bateman	69	66	64	69	268	6,000
Ben Bates	70	65	67	66	268	6,000
Tim Conley	68	67	66	67	268	6,000
Cliff Kresge	73	63	65	67	268	6,000
Gary Webb	68	68	65	67	268	6,000
Chris Couch	67	68	65	69	269	3,200
Rick Cramer	68	66	68	67	269	3,200
Jay Davis	68	66	64	71	269	3,200
Dennis Trixler	67	66	67	69	269	3,200
John Elliott	70	67	67	66	270	2,690
Glen Hnatiuk	69	65	70	66	270	2,690
Michael Clark	68	69	68	66	271	2,250
R.W. Eaks	66	69	69	67	271	2,250
Franklin Langham	67	66	69	69	271	2,250
Greg Lesher	72	66	66	67	271	2,250
Jay Synkelma	67	68	69	67	271	2,250
Esteban Toledo	67	70	66	68	271	2,250
Richard Gilkey	69	66	66	71	272	1,800
J.L. Lewis	69	66	70	67	272	1,800
Matt Peterson	73	64	67	68	272	1,800
Paul Gow	66	71	69	67	273	1,455
John Johnson	70	67	67	69	273	1,455
Chris Smith	70	68	67	68	273	1,455
Karl Zoller	66	68	68	71	273	1,455

Wichita Open

Willowbend Golf Club, Wichita, Kansas
Par 36-36–72; 7,000 yards

July 24-27
purse, $200,000

	SCORES			TOTAL	MONEY
Ben Bates	67	72	64	66	269	$36,000
Carl Paulson	67	69	67	66	269	17,233.34
Jeff Brehaut	67	69	65	68	269	17,233.33
Chris Smith	64	70	65	70	269	17,233.33
(Bates won on first extra hole.)						
Bruce Vaughan	70	66	66	68	270	10,500
John Inman	68	69	68	66	271	9,000
Steve Flesch	68	70	67	67	272	7,500
Bob Friend	69	70	68	65	272	7,500
Glen Hnatiuk	66	69	69	69	273	5,000
Patrick Lee	70	68	67	68	273	5,000
Bud Still	68	67	69	69	273	5,000
Michael Clark	69	67	69	69	274	3,400
Mark Hensby	67	66	73	68	274	3,400
Jim Estes	66	67	73	69	275	2,920
Dan Pelczarski	69	69	67	70	275	2,920
Tom Shaw	72	65	69	69	275	2,920
Briny Baird	69	71	68	68	276	2,252.50
Mike Emery, Jr.	68	71	69	68	276	2,252.50
John Johnson	70	69	68	69	276	2,252.50
Jeff Julian	66	72	70	68	276	2,252.50
J.L. Lewis	70	69	67	70	276	2,252.50
Dennis Paulson	68	67	73	68	276	2,252.50
Gary Webb	69	70	65	72	276	2,252.50
Ron Whittaker	70	70	71	65	276	2,252.50
Tim Conley	67	74	67	69	277	1,600
Chris Couch	71	70	68	68	277	1,600
Joe Daley	73	68	68	68	277	1,600
Greg Lesher	72	66	67	72	277	1,600
Deane Pappas	70	70	72	65	277	1,600
Arden Knoll	68	70	72	68	278	1,165.72
Terry Price	70	70	70	68	278	1,165.72
Dean Vomacka	72	67	73	66	278	1,165.72
David Branshaw	71	68	69	70	278	1,165.71
Chris DiMarco	72	69	68	69	278	1,165.71
Matt Gogel	67	68	71	72	278	1,165.71
Shane Supple	67	71	70	70	278	1,165.71

Dakota Dunes Open

Dakota Dunes Country Club, Dakota Dunes, South Dakota
Par 36-36–72; 7,165 yards

July 31-August 3
purse, $300,000

	SCORES			TOTAL	MONEY
Chris Smith	66	67	68	67	268	$54,000
Glen Hnatiuk	68	68	63	71	270	34,050
Ian Bateman	68	69	69	66	272	19,750
Bob Gilder	69	68	68	67	272	19,750
Bruce Vaughan	66	70	67	69	272	19,750
Tim Conley	66	72	68	67	273	12,000
Arden Knoll	67	70	68	68	273	12,000
J.L. Lewis	72	69	66	66	273	12,000

	SCORES				TOTAL	MONEY
Sean Murphy	70	69	69	66	274	7,500
Terry Price	67	67	71	69	274	7,500
Tom Scherrer	68	68	67	71	274	7,500
Barry Cheesman	70	69	67	69	275	5,100
Patrick Lee	71	65	70	69	275	5,100
Ben Bates	67	68	70	71	276	3,896.25
Michael Clark	72	69	67	68	276	3,896.25
Richard Gilkey	72	68	69	67	276	3,896.25
Deane Pappas	70	69	69	68	276	3,896.25
Matt Peterson	69	67	69	71	276	3,896.25
Mike Smith	68	71	66	71	276	3,896.25
Esteban Toledo	67	69	70	70	276	3,896.25
Dennis Trixler	67	68	75	66	276	3,896.25
Harrison Frazar	73	66	69	69	277	3,000
Sam Randolph	70	70	65	72	277	3,000
Tom Shaw	73	69	67	68	277	3,000
Kevin Altenhof	76	66	67	69	278	2,330
Jeff Brehaut	70	66	71	71	278	2,330
R.W. Eaks	73	68	69	68	278	2,330
John Inman	71	70	69	68	278	2,330
Craig Perks	68	71	70	69	278	2,330
Bobby Wadkins	68	71	68	71	278	2,330

Omaha Classic

The Champions Club, Omaha, Nebraska
Par 36-36–72; 7,034 yards

August 7-10
purse, $200,000

	SCORES				TOTAL	MONEY
Chris Smith	63	65	64	66	258	$36,000
Barry Cheesman	68	66	66	69	269	22,700
Mark Carnevale	64	70	69	67	270	14,500
Esteban Toledo	65	68	64	73	270	14,500
Matt Peterson	67	65	70	69	271	10,500
Tim Conley	69	69	65	69	272	7,000
Clark Dennis	71	67	68	66	272	7,000
Bryan Gorman	68	68	69	67	272	7,000
Franklin Langham	66	71	66	69	272	7,000
Don Reese	65	72	67	68	272	7,000
Mike Emery, Jr.	65	69	70	69	273	4,000
Jeff Brehaut	67	65	69	73	274	3,300
R.W. Eaks	72	67	68	67	274	3,300
J.L. Lewis	69	65	70	70	274	3,300
Jeff Gallagher	69	67	72	67	275	2,636
Bob Gilder	67	72	66	70	275	2,636
Jeff Gove	68	70	69	68	275	2,636
Bruce Vaughan	66	66	75	68	275	2,636
Karl Zoller	67	71	64	73	275	2,636
John Elliott	66	73	71	66	276	2,050
Matt Gogel	71	63	70	72	276	2,050
Jaime Gomez	67	70	70	69	276	2,050
Jonathan Kaye	66	72	70	68	276	2,050
Ken Schall	70	69	68	69	276	2,050
Bud Still	68	70	69	69	276	2,050
Cliff Kresge	69	66	72	70	277	1,600
Ray Stewart	73	65	70	69	277	1,600
Jeff Thorsen	66	70	73	68	277	1,600
Jeff Barlow	69	69	70	70	278	1,195

	SCORES			TOTAL	MONEY
Chris DiMarco	67	71	71	69	278	1,195
Harrison Frazar	68	71	71	68	278	1,195
Kent Jones	68	69	70	71	278	1,195
Jay Synkelma	69	71	71	67	278	1,195
Dennis Trixler	67	68	71	72	278	1,195
Stan Utley	69	70	68	71	278	1,195
Dennis Zinkon	72	67	66	73	278	1,195

Ozarks Open

Highland Springs Country Club, Springfield, Missouri
Par 36-36–72; 7,058 yards
Fourth round cancelled — rain.)

August 14-17
purse, $200,000

	SCORES			TOTAL	MONEY
Chris DiMarco	66	70	68	204	$36,000
Robin Freeman	71	66	68	205	22,700
Mark Carnevale	70	73	63	206	14,500
Brian Kamm	64	69	73	206	14,500
Greg Bruckner	68	68	71	207	10,500
Clark Dennis	69	70	69	208	7,500
Matthew Lane	70	71	67	208	7,500
Darron Stiles	69	72	67	208	7,500
Karl Zoller	69	72	67	208	7,500
Tripp Isenhour	73	68	68	209	3,950
Carl Paulson	67	72	70	209	3,950
Dave Rummells	68	68	73	209	3,950
Esteban Toledo	72	71	66	209	3,950
Tim Estes	68	73	69	210	2,713.34
Jay Williamson	72	68	70	210	2,713.34
Jerry Foltz	70	68	72	210	2,713.33
Michael Muehr	68	69	73	210	2,713.33
Sean Murphy	71	69	70	210	2,713.33
Jerry Price	70	67	73	210	2,713.33
Ian Bateman	72	70	69	211	2,050
Ken Bates	72	69	70	211	2,050
Joe Cioe	71	72	68	211	2,050
John Dowdall	71	68	72	211	2,050
Harrison Frazar	67	75	69	211	2,050
Jaime Gomez	69	70	72	211	2,050
Jim Conley	70	69	73	212	1,504
Will Frantz	73	70	69	212	1,504
Bob Gilder	70	70	72	212	1,504
Tim Loustalot	73	70	69	212	1,504
Jay Synkelma	70	72	70	212	1,504

Permian Basin Open

The Club at Mission Dorado, Odessa, Texas
Par 36-36–72; 7,135 yards

August 21-24
purse, $200,000

	SCORES			TOTAL	MONEY
Paul Gow	68	69	65	65	267	$36,000
Steve Lamontagne	66	71	64	68	269	22,700
Harrison Frazar	64	77	64	65	270	16,500
Ian Kontak	68	70	66	68	272	12,500

	SCORES				TOTAL	MONEY
Jeff Gove	66	69	69	69	273	8,100
Greg Lesher	70	69	69	65	273	8,100
Dennis Paulson	66	71	67	69	273	8,100
Bud Still	71	70	65	67	273	8,100
Greg Towne	69	69	63	72	273	8,100
Pat Bates	67	69	67	71	274	4,500
Franklin Langham	68	67	69	70	274	4,500
R.W. Eaks	68	69	66	72	275	3,200
Patrick Lee	69	70	67	69	275	3,200
Dan Stone	70	69	68	68	275	3,200
Esteban Toledo	69	71	66	69	275	3,200
Barry Cheesman	65	72	66	73	276	2,626.67
Tripp Isenhour	68	68	70	70	276	2,626.67
Jim Estes	68	69	65	74	276	2,626.66
Jaxon Brigman	69	72	70	66	277	2,250
John Inman	69	71	68	69	277	2,250
Don Reese	65	67	70	75	277	2,250
Iain Steel	65	71	68	73	277	2,250
Joe Cioe	67	72	69	70	278	1,900
Kent Jones	67	70	67	74	278	1,900
Deane Pappas	69	70	65	74	278	1,900
Croy Cochran	68	71	67	73	279	1,650
Bruce Vaughan	67	74	69	69	279	1,650
Rick Cramer	64	72	73	71	280	1,332
Matthew Lane	67	73	69	71	280	1,332
Chad Magee	68	70	73	69	280	1,332
Sean Murphy	66	71	68	75	280	1,332
Rocky Walcher	70	69	71	70	280	1,332

Colorado Classic

Riverdale Golf Club, Dunes Course, Brighton, Colorado
Par 36-35–71; 7,063 yards

September 4-
purse, $200,000

	SCORES			TOTAL	MONEY
Pat Bates	71	66	64	66	267	$36,000
J.L. Lewis	65	68	67	68	268	22,700
Clark Dennis	69	67	67	66	269	16,500
Harrison Frazar	65	68	67	70	270	11,500
Jeff Gove	66	67	71	66	270	11,500
Don Walsworth	65	69	68	69	271	9,000
Michael Clark	66	69	67	70	272	7,500
Esteban Toledo	67	71	64	70	272	7,500
Ashley Chinner	71	67	70	65	273	6,000
Jeff Brehaut	69	68	70	67	274	3,297.7
Barry Cheesman	70	68	66	70	274	3,297.7
Chris DiMarco	70	67	71	66	274	3,297.7
Trevor Dodds	68	70	69	67	274	3,297.7
Eric Hoos	70	69	65	70	274	3,297.7
Steve Jurgensen	66	71	67	70	274	3,297.7
Rocky Walcher	69	67	69	69	274	3,297.7
Robin Freeman	69	66	70	69	274	3,297.7
Tom Scherrer	66	70	69	69	274	3,297.7
Mike Emery, Jr.	69	69	68	69	275	2,350
Mike Schuchart	70	69	70	66	275	2,350
Bob Friend	68	67	69	72	276	1,900
Jaime Gomez	72	65	66	73	276	1,900
Brian Guetz	69	68	66	73	276	1,900

		SCORES			TOTAL	MONEY
Greg Lesher	65	71	71	69	276	1,900
Matt Peterson	67	72	72	65	276	1,900
Harry Rudolph	71	68	67	70	276	1,900
Jay Synkelma	68	69	68	71	276	1,900
Tripp Isenhour	70	68	70	69	277	1,332
Jonathan Kaye	69	68	67	73	277	1,332
Matthew Lane	70	68	64	75	277	1,332
Chad Magee	68	69	70	70	277	1,332
Bobby Wadkins	67	67	73	70	277	1,332

San Jose Open

Almaden Country Club, San Jose, California
Par 37-35–72; 6,960 yards

September 11-14
purse, $200,000

		SCORES			TOTAL	MONEY
R.W. Eaks	68	66	71	67	272	$36,000
Mark Carnevale	67	68	71	68	274	14,240
Chris DiMarco	69	70	66	69	274	14,240
Steve Lamontagne	68	66	68	72	274	14,240
J.L. Lewis	67	70	67	70	274	14,240
Iain Steel	71	69	66	68	274	14,240
Trevor Dodds	66	72	66	71	275	7,500
Bobby Wadkins	69	71	64	71	275	7,500
Eric Booker	71	69	68	68	276	5,000
Franklin Langham	72	67	69	68	276	5,000
Steve Woods	68	69	72	67	276	5,000
Deane Pappas	68	68	72	69	277	3,500
Ben Bates	74	65	72	68	279	3,015
Jeff Gallagher	72	70	69	68	279	3,015
Glen Hnatiuk	66	71	69	73	279	3,015
Sean Murphy	70	71	70	68	279	3,015
Todd Barranger	73	69	71	67	280	2,404
Dan Bateman	71	70	66	73	280	2,404
Steve Jurgensen	71	69	72	68	280	2,404
Bud Still	69	67	73	71	280	2,404
Esteban Toledo	70	71	71	68	280	2,404
Kevin Altenhof	75	66	69	71	281	1,850
Joe Daley	71	69	70	71	281	1,850
Steve Flesch	66	73	75	67	281	1,850
Jeff Gove	70	70	69	72	281	1,850
Fred Wadsworth	69	69	75	68	281	1,850
Don Walsworth	73	69	70	69	281	1,850
Todd Gleaton	68	71	70	73	282	1,365
Brian Kamm	70	72	69	71	282	1,365
Brian Kontak	70	70	70	72	282	1,365
Jay Synkelma	68	73	63	78	282	1,365

Boise Open

Hillcrest Country Club, Boise, Idaho
Par 36-35–71; 6,685 yards

September 18-21
purse, $250,000

		SCORES			TOTAL	MONEY
Iain Steel	67	66	66	68	267	$49,500
Carl Paulson	69	67	66	68	270	31,212.50

	SCORES				TOTAL	MONEY
Trevor Dodds	64	68	69	71	272	19,937.50
Rocky Walcher	66	74	64	68	272	19,937.50
Jeff Gallagher	71	69	65	68	273	13,406.25
Bill Porter	66	72	66	69	273	13,406.25
Pat Bates	66	71	70	67	274	11,000
Mark Carnevale	72	67	71	65	275	7,562.50
Steve Flesch	68	71	69	67	275	7,562.50
Dan Pelczarski	71	70	62	72	275	7,562.50
Esteban Toledo	69	66	70	70	275	7,562.50
Briny Baird	67	74	67	68	276	4,166.25
Jeff Gove	67	70	69	70	276	4,166.25
Kent Jones	67	69	68	72	276	4,166.25
Greg Lesher	70	67	72	67	276	4,166.25
Rob Moss	65	71	72	68	276	4,166.25
Ron Whittaker	67	70	68	71	276	4,166.25
Harrison Frazar	66	71	72	68	277	3,300
Bobby Wadkins	65	71	70	71	277	3,300
Dennis Zinkon	69	69	67	72	277	3,300
Joe Cioe	69	70	69	70	278	2,818.75
Rick Cramer	71	66	69	72	278	2,818.75
Brian Kamm	70	71	66	71	278	2,818.75
Heath Slocum	67	72	68	71	278	2,818.75
R.W. Eaks	71	67	74	67	279	2,200
Cliff Kresge	75	66	70	68	279	2,200
Deane Pappas	68	72	67	72	279	2,200
Dennis Paulson	67	72	69	71	279	2,200
Garrett Willis	70	68	70	71	279	2,200
Jay Davis	67	72	72	69	280	1,723.34
John Elliott	70	70	67	73	280	1,723.33
Bruce Vaughan	73	67	70	70	280	1,723.33

Tri-Cities Open

Meadow Springs Country Club, Richland, Washington
Par 36-36—72; 6,926 yards

September 25-28
purse, $200,000

	SCORES				TOTAL	MONEY
Todd Gleaton	70	72	71	70	283	$36,000
Kent Jones	67	74	74	69	284	13,200
Patrick Lee	68	71	71	74	284	13,200
Tim Loustalot	68	70	75	71	284	13,200
Rob Moss	63	76	72	73	284	13,200
Terry Price	69	72	70	73	284	13,200
Ray Stewart	69	72	73	70	284	13,200
Greg Lesher	67	72	75	71	285	7,000
Jeff Brehaut	71	72	71	72	286	5,000
Arden Knoll	68	70	77	71	286	5,000
Deane Pappas	72	71	73	70	286	5,000
Jerry Foltz	70	73	74	71	288	3,400
Tom Shaw	71	74	73	70	288	3,400
Pat Bates	71	74	72	72	289	2,597.5
Clark Dennis	70	71	77	71	289	2,597.5
Brian Fogt	71	75	73	70	289	2,597.5
Bob Friend	69	75	73	72	289	2,597.5
Bob Gilder	71	73	78	67	289	2,597.5
Carl Paulson	69	73	76	71	289	2,597.5
Dennis Paulson	70	77	74	68	289	2,597.5

	SCORES				TOTAL	MONEY
Tom Scherrer	69	75	77	68	289	2,597.50
Michael Clark	66	77	75	72	290	1,950
J.L. Lewis	67	76	78	69	290	1,950
Matt Peterson	70	75	73	72	290	1,950
Don Reese	69	74	75	72	290	1,950
Greg Bruckner	69	76	77	69	291	1,422.86
Chris DiMarco	72	72	73	74	291	1,422.86
Trevor Dodds	72	73	72	74	291	1,422.86
Michael Muehr	72	70	76	73	291	1,422.86
Don Walsworth	76	69	75	71	291	1,422.86
Jeff Coston	66	75	77	73	291	1,422.85
Karl Zoller	71	71	75	74	291	1,422.85

Puget Sound Open

Indian Summer Golf & Country Club,
Olympia, Washington
Par 36-36–72; 7,196 yards
(Fourth round cancelled — rain.)

October 2-5
purse, $200,000

	SCORES			TOTAL	MONEY
Kevin Johnson	65	65	68	198	$36,000
Michael Clark	61	66	71	198	19,600
Steve Jurgensen	66	64	68	198	19,600

(Johnson defeated Clark and Jurgensen on second extra hole.)

	SCORES			TOTAL	MONEY
Bobby Gage	65	65	69	199	12,500
Sean Murphy	63	63	74	200	9,750
Bob Gilder	68	64	68	200	9,750
Briny Baird	66	66	69	201	5,583.34
Steve Flesch	63	68	70	201	5,583.34
Kent Jones	67	64	70	201	5,583.33
Jeff Julian	66	63	72	201	5,583.33
Rob Moss	66	69	66	201	5,583.33
Mike Swartz	63	67	71	201	5,583.33
Kevin Altenhof	65	64	73	202	3,015
Tim Conley	68	65	69	202	3,015
Keith Nolan	68	64	70	202	3,015
Dennis Paulson	70	63	69	202	3,015
Cameron Beckman	63	68	72	203	2,252.50
Barry Cheesman	68	67	68	203	2,252.50
Ashley Chinner	67	65	71	203	2,252.50
Steve Lamontagne	64	68	71	203	2,252.50
Carl Paulson	66	64	73	203	2,252.50
Stan Utley	63	64	76	203	2,252.50
Bobby Wadkins	66	65	72	203	2,252.50
Clark Dennis	66	66	71	203	2,252.50
Jeff Brehaut	67	66	71	204	1,508.58
Arden Knoll	67	68	69	204	1,508.57
L. Lewis	67	68	69	204	1,508.57
Tom Shaw	65	67	72	204	1,508.57
Greg Whisman	66	69	69	204	1,508.57
Mark Wurtz	67	64	73	204	1,508.57
Harrison Frazar	67	67	70	204	1,508.57

Shreveport Open

Southern Trace Country Club, Shreveport, Louisiana
Par 36-36–72; 6,916 yards

October 9-12
purse, $200,000

	SCORES				TOTAL	MONEY
Mark Wurtz	68	63	71	73	275	$36,000
Brian Kamm	70	71	69	66	276	22,700
Bob Friend	69	72	68	68	277	14,500
Arden Knoll	65	75	66	71	277	14,500
Steve Flesch	68	68	69	73	278	9,750
Tom Shaw	69	66	68	75	278	9,750
Billy Downes	70	71	68	70	279	7,000
R.W. Eaks	67	68	72	72	279	7,000
Ray Stewart	74	67	67	71	279	7,000
Clark Dennis	72	70	69	69	280	4,500
Kevin Johnson	73	70	68	69	280	4,500
Trevor Dodds	67	75	70	69	281	3,030
Kent Jones	66	72	69	74	281	3,030
Franklin Langham	69	71	70	71	281	3,030
Dick Mast	68	72	68	73	281	3,030
Carl Paulson	66	69	73	73	281	3,030
Dennis Zinkon	69	68	75	69	281	3,030
Mike Heinen	71	70	69	72	282	2,450
Steve Lamontagne	69	72	69	72	282	2,450
Bob Gilder	67	73	72	71	283	2,150
J.L. Lewis	69	73	70	71	283	2,150
Charlie Rymer	69	72	71	71	283	2,150
Mario Tiziani	72	70	73	68	283	2,150
Pat Bates	66	72	75	71	284	1,602.86
Eric Booker	68	72	73	71	284	1,602.86
Dennis Paulson	74	67	71	72	284	1,602.86
Rick Price	73	70	72	69	284	1,602.86
Mike Small	71	69	74	70	284	1,602.86
Sam Randolph	68	70	72	74	284	1,602.85
Tom Scherrer	70	71	70	73	284	1,602.85

Nike Tour Championship

Grand National Golf Club, Lake Course, Opelika, Alabama
Par 36-36–72; 7,149 yards

October 16-19
purse, $300,000

	SCORES				TOTAL	MONEY
Steve Flesch	69	68	68	73	278	$54,000
Chris Smith	73	70	71	68	282	34,050
J.L. Lewis	71	72	66	74	283	25,500
Mark Carnevale	69	71	71	75	286	19,500
Michael Clark	71	70	71	75	287	13,125
Trevor Dodds	73	70	71	73	287	13,125
Brian Kamm	72	68	72	75	287	13,125
Tom Shaw	72	72	71	72	287	13,125
Glen Hnatiuk	70	73	69	76	288	9,000
Ben Bates	70	70	74	75	289	6,350
Greg Lesher	69	76	69	75	289	6,350
Bobby Wadkins	74	70	69	76	289	6,350
Eric Booker	71	74	70	75	290	5,100
Barry Cheesman	76	73	72	70	291	4,380
Bob Friend	72	72	72	75	291	4,380

	SCORES				TOTAL	MONEY
Dennis Paulson	74	72	69	76	291	4,380
Steve Lamontagne	70	74	73	75	292	3,840
Mike Small	74	71	73	74	292	3,840
Clark Dennis	75	73	73	72	293	3,375
Todd Gleaton	74	72	73	74	293	3,375
Carl Paulson	74	77	72	70	293	3,375
Bruce Vaughan	74	72	71	76	293	3,375
Jeff Brehaut	75	72	76	71	294	2,925
Chris DiMarco	74	72	73	75	294	2,925
Paul Gow	75	73	73	74	295	2,700
Pat Bates	75	72	74	75	296	2,347.50
Bob Gilder	74	78	71	73	296	2,347.50
Ron Whittaker	77	73	72	74	296	2,347.50
Mark Wurtz	75	74	74	73	296	2,347.50
R.W. Eaks	76	76	71	74	297	1,872
Harrison Frazar	78	74	71	74	297	1,872
Kent Jones	73	75	74	75	297	1,872
Jeff Julian	76	73	71	77	297	1,872
Ray Stewart	72	76	78	71	297	1,872

Canadian Tour

Payless Open

Gorge Vale Golf Club, Victoria, British Columbia
Par 35-36—71; 6,382 yards

May 29-June 1
purse, C$125,000

	SCORES				TOTAL	MONEY
Rick Todd	69	66	71	67	273	C$22,500
Dave Pashko	69	71	67	67	274	10,000
Philip Jonas	67	66	73	68	274	10,000
Marco Gortana	67	73	65	71	276	4,968.75
Ian Leggatt	70	70	67	69	276	4,968.75
Tom Stankowski	68	71	67	70	276	4,968.75
Ashley Chinner	69	67	73	67	276	4,968.75
John Robertson	69	69	68	71	277	2,812.50
Marty Schiene	70	67	70	70	277	2,812.50
Mike Weir	67	70	67	73	277	2,812.50
Gary Murphy	66	71	69	71	277	2,812.50
Len Druce	69	74	67	67	277	2,812.50
Ian Hutchings	68	72	70	68	278	2,125
Chip Spratlin	74	68	68	68	278	2,125
Jay Freeman	67	70	69	72	278	2,125
Brian Kontak	70	71	69	69	279	1,812.50
Chris Anderson	69	73	68	69	279	1,812.50
Neale Smith	72	67	69	71	279	1,812.50
David Morland	71	69	71	69	280	1,656.25
Jason Shook	71	68	70	71	280	1,656.25
Stuart Hendley	69	72	72	68	281	1,411.46

	SCORES				TOTAL	MONEY
Steve Woods	69	71	68	73	281	1,411.46
Norm Jarvis	71	68	73	69	281	1,411.46
Mike Grant	73	69	69	70	281	1,411.46
Craig Poet	70	68	73	70	281	1,411.46
Brent Franklin	70	68	72	71	281	1,411.46
J.J. West	70	69	72	71	282	1,187.50
Darren Griff	70	72	70	70	282	1,187.50
Jeff Gilchrist	70	68	75	69	282	1,187.50
Rich Massey	65	73	68	76	282	1,187.50
Alan McLean	70	66	74	72	282	1,187.50

BC Tel Pacific Open

Mayfair Lakes Golf & Country Club,
Richmond, British Columbia
Par 36-35–71; 6,641 yards

June 5-8
purse, C$125,000

	SCORES				TOTAL	MONEY
Mike Weir	65	69	68	69	271	C$22,500
Ken Duke	71	65	65	71	272	10,000
Ken Druce	68	65	71	68	272	10,000
Jeff Coston	66	67	74	66	273	5,625
Steve Alker	67	67	71	68	273	5,625
Perry Parker	70	71	70	63	274	4,625
Derek Gilchrist	70	67	67	71	275	3,687.50
Chris Anderson	66	69	69	71	275	3,687.50
Jeff Schmid	68	72	67	69	276	2,510.42
Ben Walter	69	70	71	66	276	2,510.42
Jeff Bloom	70	69	69	68	276	2,510.42
Stuart Hendley	72	65	71	68	276	2,510.42
Paul Devenport	65	70	71	70	276	2,510.42
Ray Stewart	71	62	76	67	276	2,510.42
Dennis Harrington	70	71	66	70	277	1,825
Mike Grant	71	68	72	66	277	1,825
Stuart Wallace	72	65	66	74	277	1,825
Chris Tidland	66	71	71	69	277	1,825
Bruce Bulina	70	67	67	73	277	1,825
*Andrew Luke	73	68	69	68	278	
Alan McLean	72	68	67	71	278	1,441.96
Todd Spain	69	71	70	68	278	1,441.96
Marco Gortana	69	70	69	70	278	1,441.96
Ian Leggatt	70	69	68	71	278	1,441.96
Brian Kontak	69	69	67	73	278	1,441.96
Marty Schiene	69	68	70	71	278	1,441.96
Kevin Wentworth	71	65	71	71	278	1,441.96
Garry Winger	69	71	70	69	279	1,218.75
Notah Begay III	67	72	75	65	279	1,218.75
Tony Aguilar	71	68	69	71	279	1,218.75

Henry Singer Alberta Open

Wolf Creek Golf Resort, Ponoka, Alberta
Par 35-35–70; 6,516 yards
(Fourth round cancelled — rain.)

June 19-22
purse, C$150,000

	SCORES			TOTAL	MONEY
Ray Freeman	68	66	70	204	C$27,000
Stuart Hendley	69	70	65	204	15,000
(Freeman defeated Hendley on fourth extra hole.)					
Marco Gortana	67	71	68	206	9,000
Darren Griff	68	70	69	207	6,750
John Curley	70	69	68	207	6,750
Manny Zerman	68	69	71	208	5,175
Andrew Smeeth	68	71	69	208	5,175
Steve Alker	67	75	67	209	3,675
Jay Williamson	71	68	70	209	3,675
Brent Franklin	69	70	70	209	3,675
Jean-Paul Hebert	67	70	73	210	2,850
Mike Grant	68	75	67	210	2,850
Paul Devenport	72	68	70	210	2,850
Dan Halldorson	69	71	71	211	2,400
Mark Wurtz	70	72	69	211	2,400
David McKenzie	70	72	69	211	2,400
Chris Anderson	73	72	67	212	2,100
Bob Conrad	70	75	67	212	2,100
Philip Jonas	69	72	71	212	2,100
Warrick Druian	73	73	67	213	1,701.56
Duane Bock	75	70	68	213	1,701.56
Norm Jarvis	69	77	67	213	1,701.56
Dennis Harrington	73	72	68	213	1,701.56
Brad Wilson	72	70	71	213	1,701.56
Bruce Bulina	67	77	69	213	1,701.56
Bryan DeCorso	72	73	68	213	1,701.56
Nasho Kamungeremu	71	72	70	213	1,701.56
Tim Balmer	71	74	69	214	1,406.25
Ian Hutchings	74	72	68	214	1,406.25
Ian Leggatt	72	74	68	214	1,406.25
Jason Shook	73	70	71	214	1,406.25

Telus Calgary Open

Heritage Pointe Golf Club, Calgary, Alberta
Par 36-36–72; 7,064 yards

June 26-29
purse, C$150,000

	SCORES				TOTAL	MONEY
Ian Hutchings	71	66	67	67	271	C$27,000
Scott Petersen	71	69	70	63	273	12,000
Jean-Paul Hebert	71	66	70	66	273	12,000
Mike Grob	72	69	68	67	276	6,750
David Morland	67	69	68	72	276	6,750
Kelly Mitchum	69	66	70	72	277	5,550
Philip Jonas	71	69	70	69	279	4,800
Britt Pavelonis	73	69	70	68	280	3,506.25
Joe Lloyd	70	72	68	70	280	3,506.25
Tom Stankowski	70	70	71	69	280	3,506.25
Bruce Heuchan	72	68	69	71	280	3,506.25
Scott Ford	71	73	69	68	281	2,700

432 / AMERICAN TOURS

	SCORES				TOTAL	MONEY
Brent Franklin	70	68	73	70	281	2,700
Chris Tidland	69	67	71	74	281	2,700
Steve Woods	72	73	66	71	282	2,150
Ken Duke	76	69	66	71	282	2,150
Paul Devenport	74	70	69	69	282	2,150
Keith Whitecotton	68	73	69	72	282	2,150
Wes Martin	71	69	71	71	282	2,150
Frank Schiro	67	73	71	71	282	2,150
Ken Druce	76	69	70	68	283	1,725
Ray Freeman	75	69	66	73	283	1,725
Perry Parker	69	73	73	68	283	1,725
Arden Knoll	73	67	67	76	283	1,725
Brad Wilson	73	67	75	68	283	1,725
Steve Alker	75	69	71	69	284	1,518.75
Manny Zerman	75	69	73	67	284	1,518.75
Norm Jarvis	77	68	68	72	285	1,293.75
Darryl James	75	70	69	71	285	1,293.75
Todd Spain	72	72	73	68	285	1,293.75
Bob Conrad	73	70	71	71	285	1,293.75
Kris Cox	69	74	72	70	285	1,293.75
Neale Smith	74	69	74	68	285	1,293.75
Jason Samuelian	70	72	72	71	285	1,293.75
Jason Shook	70	72	70	73	285	1,293.75
Vic Wilk	71	69	71	74	285	1,293.75
David Bartman	73	64	74	74	285	1,293.75

Telus Edmonton Open

Windermere Golf and Country Club, Edmonton, Alberta
Par 71; 6,756 yards

July 3-6
purse, C$150,000

	SCORES				TOTAL	MONEY
Manny Zerman	67	70	68	69	274	C$27,000
Todd Fanning	70	70	66	68	274	10,400
Chris Tidland	69	69	66	70	274	10,400
Mike Grob	70	71	66	67	274	10,400
(Zerman won on second extra hole.)						
Bruce Bulina	71	68	67	69	275	5,175
Ben Walter	67	69	72	67	275	5,175
Mike Weir	70	65	72	68	275	5,175
David Bartman	70	65	68	72	275	5,175
Ray Freeman	70	72	66	68	276	3,675
Keith Whitecotton	71	72	70	65	278	3,050
Ken Druce	72	66	76	64	278	3,050
Doug Dunakey	69	68	73	68	278	3,050
Darren Griff	76	67	69	67	279	2,550
Guy Hill	68	71	69	71	279	2,550
Blair Philip	74	65	72	68	279	2,550
Kari Kekki	69	74	67	70	280	2,100
Ian Leggatt	73	69	71	67	280	2,100
David Morland	75	65	68	72	280	2,100
Perry Parker	68	71	72	69	280	2,100
Mark Wurtz	70	66	67	77	280	2,100
Alan McLean	73	70	69	69	281	1,666.0
Wes Martin	71	71	72	67	281	1,666.0
Kent Wiese	75	66	70	70	281	1,666.0
Marco Gortana	70	70	69	72	281	1,666.0

	SCORES				TOTAL	MONEY
Dennis Harrington	69	71	71	70	281	1,666.07
Notah Begay III	69	70	70	72	281	1,666.07
Chip Spratlin	65	72	71	73	281	1,666.07
Mike Fergin	72	71	70	69	282	1,350
Martin Price	72	70	68	72	282	1,350
Cam Emerson	69	72	71	70	282	1,350
Brennan Little	70	70	75	67	282	1,350
Derek Gilchrist	74	66	71	71	282	1,350
Bryan DeCorso	71	68	74	69	282	1,350
Paul Devenport	71	67	70	74	282	1,350

Xerox Manitoba Open

Elmhurst Golf and Country Club, Winnipeg, Manitoba
Par 71; 6,700 yards

July 10-13
purse, C$100,000

	SCORES				TOTAL	MONEY
Mark Wurtz	68	71	64	73	276	C$18,000
Perry Parker	69	73	67	69	278	8,000
Duane Bock	70	71	69	68	278	8,000
Mike Grob	75	68	71	65	279	3,720
David Bartman	75	68	68	68	279	3,720
Rick Todd	69	73	69	68	279	3,720
Kent Wiese	69	72	66	72	279	3,720
Craig Marseilles	72	68	72	67	279	3,720
Derek Gilchrist	70	72	69	69	280	2,325
Stephane Talbot	72	69	67	72	280	2,325
Paul Devenport	75	71	67	68	281	2,000
Todd Fanning	76	71	68	68	283	1,800
Britt Pavelonis	77	70	66	70	283	1,800
Notah Begay III	70	72	71	70	283	1,800
Marty Schiene	73	72	66	73	284	1,460
Philip Jonas	68	74	74	68	284	1,460
Jerry Wood	78	64	70	72	284	1,460
Rob McMillan	74	66	73	71	284	1,460
Steve Alker	71	69	73	71	284	1,460
Blair Piercy	75	72	69	69	285	1,200
Stuart Wallace	74	72	67	72	285	1,200
Matt Cole	72	73	74	66	285	1,200
Scott Ford	74	70	70	71	285	1,200
Scott Petersen	71	71	75	68	285	1,200
John Curley	72	74	72	68	286	1,012.50
Brian Wright	72	74	72	68	286	1,012.50
Bruce Bulina	75	70	72	69	286	1,012.50
Darryl James	70	74	70	72	286	1,012.50
Roy MacKenzie	75	73	71	68	287	925
Ian Hutchings	76	71	71	69	287	925
Mike Fergin	69	74	73	71	287	925

Infiniti Championship

Diamond Back Golf Club, Richmond Hill, Ontario
Par 36-36–72; 7,079 yards

July 17-20
purse, C$125,000

	SCORES				TOTAL	MONEY
Scott Petersen	68	70	71	66	275	C$22,500
Mike Grob	69	70	69	69	277	12,500
Scott Ford	70	69	69	70	278	6,750
Derek Gilchrist	63	73	74	68	278	6,750
Steve Alker	70	71	74	64	279	4,625
Marco Gortana	69	70	69	71	279	4,625
Ian Leggatt	64	72	73	70	279	4,625
Tim Balmer	68	69	70	73	280	3,218.75
David McKenzie	68	67	73	72	280	3,218.75
Dennis Harrington	69	72	74	66	281	2,625
Todd Spain	67	70	75	69	281	2,625
Matt Cole	69	73	76	64	282	2,375
Hennie Otto	71	71	69	72	283	1,968.75
Brennan Little	71	71	71	70	283	1,968.75
Tony Aguilar	68	73	71	71	283	1,968.75
Gary Cowan	70	70	73	70	283	1,968.75
Bryan DeCorso	67	72	70	74	283	1,968.75
Kari Kekki	66	72	75	70	283	1,968.75
Kelly Mitchum	70	72	72	70	284	1,562.50
Jean-Paul Hebert	69	73	77	65	284	1,562.50
Brian Kontak	68	73	73	70	284	1,562.50
Martin Price	70	71	74	69	284	1,562.50
Frank Edmonds	65	68	72	79	284	1,562.50
David Morland	71	71	71	72	285	1,287.50
Manny Zerman	73	68	77	67	285	1,287.50
Paul Devenport	74	67	70	74	285	1,287.50
Duane Bock	71	69	75	70	285	1,287.50
John Robertson	68	69	76	72	285	1,287.50
Brent Franklin	75	69	71	71	286	1,109.38
Roy MacKenzie	71	72	75	68	286	1,109.38
Jerry Springer	69	73	75	69	286	1,109.38
Ian Hutchings	71	70	79	66	286	1,109.38
Ben Walter	68	71	76	71	286	1,109.38
Paul Antenucci	69	68	77	72	286	1,109.38

Canadian Masters

Heron Point Golf Links, Ancaster, Ontario
Par 35-36–71; 6,841 yards

July 24-27
purse, C$200,000

	SCORES			TOTAL	MONEY
Mike Weir	64	67	66	69	266	C$36,000
Kari Kekki	70	70	67	67	274	12,500
Steve Alker	67	71	74	62	274	12,500
Ken Duke	66	70	66	72	274	12,500
Carlos Espinosa	66	68	66	74	274	12,500
Davidson Matyczuk	70	68	65	72	275	6,900
Dennis Harrington	70	65	70	70	275	6,900
Rick Todd	70	70	66	70	276	4,675
Craig Marseilles	70	68	68	70	276	4,675
Dan Dupuis	65	71	69	71	276	4,675
Brian Kontak	69	67	67	73	276	4,675

	SCORES				TOTAL	MONEY
Wes Martin	69	70	66	72	277	3,500
Todd Fanning	67	70	70	70	277	3,500
Ray Freeman	68	68	69	72	277	3,500
Steve Woods	67	67	73	70	277	3,500
Brent Franklin	71	70	69	68	278	2,700
Jim Rutledge	69	71	68	70	278	2,700
Ben Ferguson	69	70	69	70	278	2,700
Steve Haskins	69	70	71	68	278	2,700
Mike Grob	70	69	71	68	278	2,700
Alan McLean	68	68	66	76	278	2,700
Philip Jonas	65	69	70	74	278	2,700
Ashley Chinner	68	73	67	71	279	2,100
Marty Schiene	70	71	70	68	279	2,100
David Morland	72	67	70	70	279	2,100
Darren Griff	68	71	69	71	279	2,100
Paul Devenport	70	68	67	74	279	2,100
Bob Conrad	66	69	73	71	279	2,100
Roy MacKenzie	69	72	69	70	280	1,750
Stuart Wallace	68	73	67	72	280	1,750
Marty Scoles	69	70	70	71	280	1,750
David Bartman	70	68	74	68	280	1,750
Guy Hill	69	68	71	72	280	1,750
Matt Cole	70	67	70	73	280	1,750
Mark Wurtz	65	70	66	79	280	1,750

CPGA Championship

Mandarin Golf & Country Club, Markham, Ontario
Par 35-36–71; 6,728 yards

August 7-10
purse, C$125,000

	SCORES				TOTAL	MONEY
Guy Hill	70	64	73	69	276	C$22,500
Mike Weir	68	66	71	71	276	12,500
(Hill defeated Weir on first extra hole.)						
Chris Anderson	74	69	66	68	277	6,250
Steve Alker	71	71	67	68	277	6,250
Rick Todd	71	68	68	70	277	6,250
David Morland	68	68	69	73	278	4,000
Richard Zokol	70	65	71	72	278	4,000
Stuart Hendley	66	69	70	73	278	4,000
David McKenzie	69	69	70	71	279	3,062.50
Mark Wurtz	72	69	69	70	280	2,400
Ashley Chinner	71	70	69	70	280	2,400
Scott Petersen	69	71	73	67	280	2,400
Marcus Meloan	69	68	74	69	280	2,400
Jason Shook	64	69	76	71	280	2,400
Jean-Paul Hebert	73	71	67	70	281	1,859.38
Philip Jonas	72	71	70	68	281	1,859.38
Jason Samuelian	72	71	69	69	281	1,859.38
Tim Balmer	74	69	69	69	281	1,859.38
Craig Poet	68	72	73	69	282	1,593.75
Perry Parker	68	71	72	71	282	1,593.75
Ken Duke	67	71	77	67	282	1,593.75
Dennis Harrington	70	66	70	76	282	1,593.75
Brian Kontak	72	69	72	70	283	1,331.25
Kelly Mitchum	71	69	73	70	283	1,331.25
Stuart Wallace	66	73	72	72	283	1,331.25

	SCORES				TOTAL	MONEY
John Robertson	70	69	69	75	283	1,331.25
Todd Fanning	70	66	74	73	283	1,331.25
Dave Pashko	73	71	71	69	284	1,140.62
Derek Gilchrist	73	71	69	71	284	1,140.62
Todd Doohan	71	71	70	72	284	1,140.62
Ian Leggatt	70	69	76	69	284	1,140.62
Grant Masson	73	65	74	72	284	1,140.62
Duane Bock	70	67	72	75	284	1,140.62

Montclair PEI Classic

Mill River Golf Course, Woodstock, P.E.I. August 28-31
Par 36-36–72; 6,826 yards purse, C$125,000

	SCORES				TOTAL	MONEY
Mike Grob	68	69	71	70	278	C$22,500
Perry Parker	71	71	73	65	280	12,500
Guy Hill	71	70	71	69	281	6,750
J.J. West	73	67	70	71	281	6,750
Neale Smith	75	67	70	71	283	5,250
Ashley Chinner	71	70	74	70	285	4,000
David McKenzie	72	68	73	72	285	4,000
Todd Fanning	65	73	78	69	285	4,000
Dirk Ayers	75	70	70	71	286	2,906.25
Blair Piercy	73	71	75	67	286	2,906.25
Bruce Heuchan	73	74	69	71	287	2,437.50
Ben Ferguson	74	67	74	72	287	2,437.50
Scott Ford	75	73	73	68	289	2,012.50
Philip Jonas	73	74	71	71	289	2,012.50
David Morland	74	71	73	71	289	2,012.50
Paul Devenport	72	70	73	74	289	2,012.50
Paul Penny	69	72	76	72	289	2,012.50
Jason Bohn	69	75	76	70	290	1,750
Mike Fergin	72	77	72	70	291	1,656.25
Davidson Matyczuk	73	70	74	74	291	1,656.25
Marcus Meloan	75	75	70	72	292	1,531.25
Bruce Bulina	72	71	79	70	292	1,531.25
Trey Maples	74	76	73	70	293	1,351.56
Stephen Woodard	76	73	76	68	293	1,351.56
Jerry Wood	76	71	73	73	293	1,351.56
John Curley	75	69	75	74	293	1,351.56
Ken Duke	75	75	74	70	294	1,171.88
Pete McCutcheon	76	72	74	72	294	1,171.88
Steve Alker	77	71	76	70	294	1,171.88
Duane Bock	73	72	77	72	294	1,171.88
Blair Philip	72	72	78	72	294	1,171.88
Dave Pashko	75	68	77	74	294	1,171.88

South American Tour

World Nature Games

Iguassu Golf Club & Resort, Iguassu Falls, Brazil
Par 36-36–72; 6,983 yards

October 2-5
purse, US$200,000

	SCORES				TOTAL	MONEY
Ricardo Gonzalez	65	69	70	70	274	US$36,000
Angel Cabrera	68	67	74	70	279	22,800
Danny Mijovic	69	69	73	70	281	16,000
Pedro Martinez	69	67	73	73	282	12,800
Miguel Fernandez	71	71	75	67	284	10,400
Roberto Coceres	74	68	71	72	285	7,600
Daniel Vancsik	67	73	73	72	285	7,600
Kris Cox	69	69	76	72	286	5,400
Raul Fretes	68	71	74	73	286	5,400
Greg Green	71	73	74	69	287	4,250
Ramon Franco	69	72	74	72	287	4,250
Ruben Alvares	67	71	77	72	287	4,250
Gilberto Morales	71	72	71	73	287	4,250
Acacio Jorge Pedro	72	72	77	67	288	3,200
Bryan DeCorso	70	75	74	69	288	3,200
Ricardo Coceres	75	70	73	70	288	3,200
Sandy Morrison	70	68	76	74	288	3,200
Roy Mackenzie	69	68	77	74	288	3,200
Gustavo Rojas	72	72	73	72	289	2,310
Rodolfo Gonzalez	74	69	73	73	289	2,310
Fredrick Mansson	69	73	73	74	289	2,310
Ariel Canete	66	73	75	75	289	2,310
Jose Cantero	75	71	73	71	290	1,880
Rodolfo Rodriguez	74	68	76	72	290	1,880
Antonio Barcellos	71	74	75	71	291	1,640
Tim Hegna	71	71	76	73	291	1,640
Fabian Montovia	67	71	79	74	291	1,640
Horacio Carbonetti	69	66	79	77	291	1,640
Rafael Barcellos	71	75	76	70	292	1,380
Todd Mahovlich	69	75	75	73	292	1,380
Howie Johnson	69	73	77	73	292	1,380
Luiz Martins	72	72	74	74	292	1,380
Esteban Isasi	70	72	75	75	292	1,380
Joao Corteiz	72	73	71	76	292	1,380

TC Ecuador Open

Guayaquil Country Club, Guayaquil, Ecuador
Par 36-36–72; 6,477 yards

October 16-19
purse, US$100,000

	SCORES				TOTAL	MONEY
Gustavo Rojas	71	67	70	69	277	US$18,000
Mauricio Molina	71	68	70	68	277	9,700
Rafael Gomez	68	68	67	74	277	9,700

(Rojas defeated Gomez on first and Molina on fourth extra hole.)

	SCORES				TOTAL	MONEY
Danny Mijovic	69	68	66	76	279	6,400
Luis Graf	78	71	67	66	282	4,266.67
Ricardo Gonzalez	70	71	72	69	282	4,266.67
Ron Wuensche	71	69	72	70	282	4,266.67
Pedro Martinez	70	73	71	69	283	2,500
Sandy Morrison	73	69	68	73	283	2,500
Angel Romero	70	73	67	73	283	2,500
Jose Cantero	70	68	71	74	283	2,500
Raul Fretes	71	69	73	71	284	1,950
Fabian Montovia	69	71	72	72	284	1,950
Acacio Jorge Pedro	70	72	73	70	285	1,650
Cesar Monasterio	75	67	72	71	285	1,650
Miguel Suarez	72	72	69	72	285	1,650
Jorge Benedetti	72	70	70	73	285	1,650
Ruben Alvarez	70	71	73	72	286	1,350
Miguel Guzman	74	74	64	74	286	1,350
Sebastian Fernandez	71	69	76	71	287	1,150
Miguel Fernandez	71	71	71	74	287	1,150
Anai Fuentes	74	71	72	71	288	990
Guillermo Encina	74	72	70	72	288	990
Roy Mackenzie	77	70	70	72	289	860
Eduardo Pesenti	72	70	75	72	289	860
Esteban Isasi	72	73	71	73	289	860
Hunter Johnson	76	70	69	74	289	860
Miguel Martinez	71	73	73	73	290	760
Luiz Martinez	73	74	72	72	291	730
Jason Samuelian	71	74	72	74	291	730

Peru Open

Los Inkas Golf Club, Lima, Peru
Par 36-36—72; 6,949 yards

October 23-26
purse, US$120,000

	SCORES				TOTAL	MONEY
Philip Jonas	69	68	65	67	269	US$21,600
Esteban Isasi	65	71	70	69	275	13,680
Brian Wilson	72	68	70	66	276	7,840
Raul Fretes	69	72	68	67	276	7,840
Jose Cantero	69	72	68	67	276	7,840
Ruben Alvarez	71	66	68	72	277	5,040
Miguel Guzman	67	73	71	67	278	3,720
Ricardo Gonzalez	70	67	68	73	278	3,720
Tim Hegna	71	65	72	71	279	3,000
Cesar Monasterio	66	71	70	72	279	3,000
Rafael Gomez	75	67	71	67	280	2,440
Gustavo Mendoza	73	68	70	69	280	2,440
Roy Mackenzie	71	70	66	73	280	2,440
Demetrios Arvanetes	74	68	72	67	281	1,980
Dennis Tymosko	70	71	72	68	281	1,980
Angel Romero	69	69	75	68	281	1,980
Guillermo Encina	75	69	68	69	281	1,980
Bryan DeCorso	73	72	69	68	282	1,560
Ron Wuensche	70	73	71	68	282	1,560
Ken Duke	69	67	73	73	282	1,560
Sebastian Fernandez	75	70	72	67	284	1,171.20
Danny Mijovic	69	71	77	67	284	1,171.20
Jose Cardenas	71	74	70	69	284	1,171.20

	SCORES	TOTAL	MONEY
Rafael Barcellos	72 72 70 70	284	1,171.20
Carlos Dluhosch	71 70 73 70	284	1,171.20
Jorge Benedetti	68 73 76 68	285	898.29
Diego Ferrari	73 71 71 70	285	898.29
Brad Wilson	73 71 70 71	285	898.29
Fabian Montovia	71 71 71 72	285	898.29
Jeff Schmid	69 71 73 72	285	898.29
Acacio Jorge Pedro	71 70 69 75	285	898.29
Sandy Morrison	72 70 66 77	285	898.29

Litoral Open

Rosario Golf Club, Rosario, Argentina
Par 35-36–71; 6,377 yards

October 30-November 2
purse, US$120,000

	SCORES	TOTAL	MONEY
Armando Saavedra	66 69 65 66	266	US$21,600
David Morland	70 69 66 64	269	13,680
Ricardo Gonzalez	65 71 69 65	270	9,600
Brian Wilson	64 70 72 69	275	6,960
Scott Dunlap	66 67 71 71	275	6,960
Ruben Alvarez	70 72 67 67	276	5,040
Luis Carbonetti	72 68 68 70	278	4,080
Jeff Schmid	71 71 71 67	280	2,880
Hiroshi Matsuo	73 68 71 68	280	2,880
Adam Armagost	70 72 68 70	280	2,880
Adan Sowa	70 70 70 70	280	2,880
Esteban Isasi	69 71 69 71	280	2,880
Roy Mackenzie	71 71 70 69	281	2,100
Philip Jonas	70 70 70 71	281	2,100
Gustavo Mendoza	71 70 68 72	281	2,100
Diego Ferrari	69 71 69 72	281	2,100
Marcelo Soria	78 69 70 65	282	1,680
Raul Perez	70 73 67 72	282	1,680
Fredrick Mansson	66 71 71 74	282	1,680
Rafael Barcellos	73 71 72 68	284	1,248
Todd Mahovlich	71 74 71 68	284	1,248
Angel Romero	69 76 71 68	284	1,248
Greg Green	72 71 70 71	284	1,248
Gustavo Piovano	72 71 70 71	284	1,248
Marcelo Isla	73 73 71 68	285	964.80
Rodolfo Gonzalez	72 69 74 70	285	964.80
Dennis Tymosko	71 72 72 70	285	964.80
Bryan DeCorso	71 74 69 71	285	964.80
Tim Hegna	72 71 70 72	285	964.80
Cesar Monasterio	73 68 80 65	286	828
Davidson Matyczuk	68 75 74 69	286	828
Pablo Benzadon	74 72 70 70	286	828
Tony Aguilar	72 68 74 72	286	828

Argentina Masters

Olivos Golf Club, Buenos Aires, Argentina
Par 36-35–71; 6,659 yards

November 13-16
purse, US$170,000

	SCORES				TOTAL	MONEY
Bernhard Langer	73	69	68	67	277	US$30,600
Eduardo Romero	69	74	67	68	278	19,380
Payne Stewart	73	73	68	66	280	13,600
Angel Cabrera	75	70	68	68	281	8,160
Ariel Canete	70	73	69	69	281	8,160
Ruben Alvarez	69	73	68	71	281	8,160
Ricardo Gonzalez	73	67	69	72	281	8,160
Greg Green	70	71	71	71	283	4,760
Paul Azinger	69	72	73	70	284	4,420
Roy Mackenzie	77	71	66	72	286	4,080
Raul Fretes	73	71	74	69	287	3,357.50
Rafael Gomez	69	74	75	69	287	3,357.50
Santiago Luna	71	74	72	70	287	3,357.50
Miguel Fernandez	73	72	70	72	287	3,357.50
Jorge Berendt	74	75	71	68	288	2,720
Martin Lonardi	72	75	71	70	288	2,720
Daniel Lobos	74	71	73	70	288	2,720
Fernando Roca	71	72	76	70	289	2,210
Diego Ferrari	76	72	69	72	289	2,210
Hiroshi Matsuo	69	69	74	77	289	2,210
Ricardo Coceres	73	76	72	69	290	1,745.33
Gustavo Rojas	76	70	73	71	290	1,745.33
Jason Samuelian	74	72	72	72	290	1,745.33
Gustavo Mendoza	72	76	74	69	291	1,399.67
Acacio Jorge Pedro	75	72	74	70	291	1,399.67
Roberto Coceres	76	72	72	71	291	1,399.67
Kari Kekki	77	72	70	72	291	1,399.67
Rodolfo Gonzalez	74	71	74	72	291	1,399.67
Jose Coceres	73	70	68	80	291	1,399.67
Ken Duke	77	71	74	70	292	1,139
Jose Cantero	70	73	78	71	292	1,139
Omar Solis	73	72	75	72	292	1,139
Antonio Ortiz	74	73	73	72	292	1,139
Vicente Fernandez	71	75	74	72	292	1,139
Gustavo Acosta	76	70	73	73	292	1,139

Los Leones - Chile Open

Los Leones Golf Club, Santiago, Chile
Par 36-36–72; 6,653 yards

November 20-23
purse, US$90,000

	SCORES				TOTAL	MONEY
Gustavo Rojas	69	67	67	69	272	US$16,200
Angel Franco	66	69	73	69	277	10,260
Guillermo Encina	70	70	72	66	278	7,200
Ken Duke	65	73	73	68	279	5,220
Jose Cantero	70	69	70	70	279	5,220
Jeff Schmid	70	73	68	69	280	3,420
Mathias Gronberg	69	70	71	70	280	3,420
Sandy Morrison	71	69	72	69	281	2,520
Johan Axgren	74	71	65	73	283	2,340
Tim Hegna	72	74	67	71	284	1,980

	SCORES	TOTAL	MONEY
Kris Cox	71 68 71 74	284	1,980
Erik Andersson	70 69 71 74	284	1,980
Miguel Fernandez	72 72 73 68	285	1,395
Omar Solis	72 72 71 70	285	1,395
Ron Wuensche	68 76 71 70	285	1,395
Fabian Montovia	68 75 71 71	285	1,395
Hiroshi Matsuo	69 72 71 73	285	1,395
Adam Armagost	70 71 71 73	285	1,395
Rafael Gonzalez	70 72 68 75	285	1,395
Miguel Guzman	69 66 73 77	285	1,395
Eduardo Argiro	72 74 73 67	286	990
Francisco Franco	72 69 77 69	287	831.60
Brad Wilson	74 69 73 71	287	831.60
Roy Mackenzie	71 73 71 72	287	831.60
Diego Ferrari	71 72 71 73	287	831.60
Ruben Alvarez	72 69 72 74	287	831.60
David Morland	71 74 71 72	288	669.60
Rodolfo Gonzalez	70 69 76 73	288	669.60
Fredrick Mansson	75 70 68 75	288	669.60
Cesar Monasterio	69 69 74 76	288	669.60
Sebastian Fernandez	72 68 71 77	288	669.60

Prince of Wales Open

Prince of Wales Country Club, Santiago, Chile
Par 36-36–72; 6,681 yards

November 27-30
purse, US$100,000

	SCORES	TOTAL	MONEY
Ricardo Gonzalez	67 68 68 66	269	US$18,000
Jorge Berendt	69 65 70 67	271	11,400
Fabian Montovia	67 68 68 72	275	8,000
Roy Mackenzie	68 68 70 70	276	6,400
Pedro Martinez	74 67 67 70	278	4,700
Jeff Schmid	68 71 68 71	278	4,700
Jose Cantero	73 69 66 71	279	2,933.33
Johan Axgren	72 66 70 71	279	2,933.33
Gustavo Rojas	66 68 72 73	279	2,933.33
Miguel Guzman	74 69 67 70	280	2,400
Sandy Morrison	68 72 71 70	281	2,033.33
Hiroshi Matsuo	66 70 73 72	281	2,033.33
Miguel Fernandez	72 68 68 73	281	2,033.33
Ron Wuensche	70 70 71 71	282	1,700
Wade White	67 73 71 71	282	1,700
Bryan DeCorso	69 70 71 72	282	1,700
Sebastian Franco	71 73 69 70	283	1,350
Guillermo Encina	71 68 72 72	283	1,350
Scott Dunlap	69 75 66 73	283	1,350
Erik Andersson	72 67 67 77	283	1,350
Bob Lendzion	69 73 74 68	284	1,060
Mauricio Molina	69 72 71 72	284	1,060
Eduardo Pesenti	69 72 71 73	285	920
Esteban Isasi	68 69 75 73	285	920
Angel Romero	69 70 71 75	285	920
Anai Fuentes	71 71 75 69	286	785
Gustavo Acosta	75 69 70 72	286	785
Victor Bueno	71 72 70 73	286	785
Luis Berrios	73 68 72 73	286	785

	SCORES				TOTAL	MONEY
Greg Green	71	72	72	72	287	700
Fredrick Mansson	70	73	71	73	287	700
Rafael Barcellos	72	72	69	74	287	700

Argentina Open

The Jockey Club, Buenos Aires, Argentina
Par 35-35–70; 6,651 yards

December 4-7
purse, US$340,000

	SCORES				TOTAL	MONEY
Jim Furyk	67	70	68	70	275	US$70,000
Mathias Gronberg	73	68	68	69	278	29,668
Chris DiMarco	75	67	67	69	278	29,668
Tim Hegna	71	66	70	71	278	29,668
Ricardo Gonzalez	72	67	68	72	279	17,500
Angel Franco	72	74	69	65	280	11,600
Craig Stadler	70	69	72	69	280	11,600
Ramon Franco	69	72	66	73	280	11,600
Miguel Guzman	74	72	66	69	281	8,400
Jorge Berendt	74	71	66	70	281	8,400
Fredrick Mansson	69	68	69	75	281	8,400
Fabian Montovia	71	71	70	70	282	7,200
Bryan DeCorso	73	68	73	69	283	6,200
Miguel Suarez	73	72	68	70	283	6,200
Kris Cox	74	64	70	75	283	6,200
Tom Watson	75	70	73	66	284	5,400
Gilberto Morales	76	68	72	69	285	4,057
Adam Armagost	71	70	75	69	285	4,057
Raul Fretes	71	74	70	70	285	4,057
Raul Albarrasin	72	71	72	70	285	4,057
Scott Hoch	74	71	69	71	285	4,057
Rodolfo Rodriguez	75	69	69	72	285	4,057
Hiroshi Matsuo	71	70	72	72	285	4,057
Gustavo Acosta	77	67	74	68	286	2,800
Luis Carbonetti	73	73	70	70	286	2,800
Eduardo Argiro	74	69	72	71	286	2,800
Gustavo Rojas	70	70	71	75	286	2,800
Jeff Schmid	74	72	71	70	287	2,200
Antonio Ortiz	72	70	72	73	287	2,200
Danny Mijovic	75	70	72	71	288	1,655
Ricardo Marzorati	73	71	73	71	288	1,655
Roy Mackenzie	69	73	72	74	288	1,655
David Morland	69	70	73	76	288	1,655
Ron Wuensche	80	66	74	69	289	1,243
Ariel Canete	73	71	75	70	289	1,243
Tadahisa Inoue	70	74	74	71	289	1,243
Omar Solis	75	72	69	73	289	1,243

European Tours

Dubai Desert Classic

Emirates Golf Club, Dubai, United Arab Emirates
Par 35-37–72; 7,102 yards

February 27-March 2
purse, £700,000

	SCORES				TOTAL	MONEY
Richard Green	70	68	66	68	272	£116,660
Ian Woosnam	69	67	67	69	272	60,795
Greg Norman	71	68	67	66	272	60,795
(Green defeated Woosnam and Norman on first extra hole.)						
Bernhard Langer	66	70	68	69	273	35,000
Thomas Gogele	69	72	68	66	275	29,640
Raymond Burns	68	69	69	70	276	19,652.50
Malcolm Mackenzie	69	71	66	70	276	19,652.50
Paul McGinley	69	71	67	69	276	19,652.50
Colin Montgomerie	65	72	68	71	276	19,652.50
Angel Cabrera	73	72	70	63	278	13,440
Costantino Rocca	70	69	71	68	278	13,440
Klas Eriksson	68	71	67	73	279	10,605
Joakim Haeggman	72	71	65	71	279	10,605
Phillip Price	70	73	69	67	279	10,605
Roger Chapman	69	71	70	69	279	10,605
Jean Van de Velde	67	75	67	70	279	10,605
Jose Maria Olazabal	69	74	65	71	279	10,605
Robert Coles	69	70	69	72	280	8,855
Andrew Oldcorn	69	70	73	68	280	8,855
Prayad Marksaeng	68	71	68	74	281	7,980
Domingo Hospital	65	69	74	73	281	7,980
Mark James	66	75	69	71	281	7,980
Jose Coceres	70	73	69	69	281	7,980
Per-Ulrik Johansson	69	73	68	71	281	7,980
Mats Hallberg	68	73	73	68	282	7,140
Wayne Westner	72	69	69	72	282	7,140
Des Smyth	74	71	65	72	282	7,140
Jeev Milkha Singh	69	71	70	73	283	6,206.67
Carl Suneson	70	74	64	75	283	6,206.67
Darren Clarke	73	70	70	70	283	6,206.67
Padraig Harrington	66	72	71	74	283	6,206.67
Van Phillips	73	72	65	73	283	6,206.67
Robert Lee	69	74	68	72	283	6,206.67
Ross Drummond	71	71	71	71	284	5,460
Daniel Chopra	69	75	73	67	284	5,460
Ian Garbutt	71	71	73	69	284	5,460
Silvio Grappasonni	71	73	69	72	285	4,970
Gary Orr	72	73	67	73	285	4,970
Miguel Angel Jimenez	72	72	70	71	285	4,970
Massimo Florioli	71	73	72	69	285	4,970
Emanuele Canonica	73	72	71	70	286	4,340
Miguel Angel Martin	70	69	72	75	286	4,340
Marc Farry	71	74	68	73	286	4,340
Fernando Roca	73	72	70	71	286	4,340
Derrick Cooper	72	69	75	70	286	4,340
Dean Robertson	71	71	71	74	287	3,500
Christy O'Connor, Jr.	71	73	71	72	287	3,500

	SCORES				TOTAL	MONEY
Mark Mouland	70	74	68	75	287	3,500
Peter Mitchell	70	73	72	72	287	3,500
Andrew Coltart	73	72	70	72	287	3,500
Philip Walton	72	70	71	74	287	3,500
Steven Bottomley	75	70	72	70	287	3,500
Miles Tunnicliff	70	73	74	71	288	2,660
Michael Jonzon	72	73	68	75	288	2,660
David Howell	69	72	71	76	288	2,660
Peter Baker	69	74	73	72	288	2,660
Robert Willis	68	73	75	72	288	2,660
Jon Robson	70	74	73	72	289	2,205
Eamonn Darcy	66	77	74	72	289	2,205
David Higgins	73	71	75	71	290	1,960
Chang Tse-peng	70	72	75	73	290	1,960
Paolo Quirici	71	74	72	73	290	1,960
Ricky Willison	72	72	72	74	290	1,960
Richard Boxall	72	73	73	72	290	1,960
Gary Evans	71	74	73	73	291	1,223.50
Wayne Riley	74	70	76	71	291	1,223.50
David Gilford	69	73	73	76	291	1,223.50
Barry Lane	72	71	72	76	291	1,223.50
Zhang Lian-wei	71	73	72	76	292	1,044
Anders Forsbrand	71	74	72	76	293	1,042
Rolf Muntz	74	71	74	76	295	1,040

Moroccan Open

Royal Golf Links D'Agadir, Agadir, Morocco
Par 35-37–72; 6,657 yards

March 6-9
purse, £350,000

	SCORES				TOTAL	MONEY
Clinton Whitelaw	68	71	69	69	277	£58,330
Darren Cole	72	74	69	64	279	26,096.67
Wayne Riley	72	72	67	68	279	26,096.67
Roger Chapman	74	68	70	67	279	26,096.67
David A. Russell	69	68	71	72	280	14,830
Per-Ulrik Johansson	72	73	67	69	281	9,830
Brian Davis	70	68	71	72	281	9,830
Robert Karlsson	70	71	70	70	281	9,830
Jon Robson	73	65	70	73	281	9,830
Eduardo Romero	72	69	71	70	282	5,787.14
Tony Johnstone	71	72	71	68	282	5,787.14
Katsuyoshi Tomori	72	71	70	69	282	5,787.14
Andrew Coltart	68	73	68	73	282	5,787.14
Jose Coceres	71	67	72	72	282	5,787.14
Diego Borrego	73	71	66	72	282	5,787.14
Paul Broadhurst	70	71	71	70	282	5,787.14
Niclas Fasth	70	72	72	69	283	4,375
Gary Orr	71	73	70	69	283	4,375
Costantino Rocca	69	71	69	74	283	4,375
Wayne Westner	69	71	75	68	283	4,375
Russell Claydon	77	66	70	70	283	4,375
Alex Cejka	74	70	66	74	284	3,622.50
Miguel Angel Martin	73	68	68	75	284	3,622.50
Jim Payne	70	71	71	72	284	3,622.50
Joakim Haeggman	69	73	70	72	284	3,622.50
Carl Suneson	74	71	70	69	284	3,622.50
Domingo Hospital	69	71	71	73	284	3,622.50

	SCORES	TOTAL	MONEY
Phillip Price	72 66 70 76	284	3,622.50
Max Anglert	75 72 67 70	284	3,622.50
Anders Forsbrand	71 75 67 72	285	2,961
Adam Hunter	71 69 75 70	285	2,961
Mark James	71 67 73 74	285	2,961
Sam Torrance	74 71 68 72	285	2,961
Ross Drummond	73 68 72 72	285	2,961
Peter O'Malley	73 72 68 73	286	2,660
Santiago Luna	71 71 72 72	286	2,660
Raymond Burns	71 71 73 71	286	2,660
Padraig Harrington	69 75 74 69	287	2,450
Antoine Lebouc	69 70 74 74	287	2,450
Mark Roe	72 70 73 72	287	2,450
John Bickerton	73 72 74 69	288	2,310
Juan Carlos Pinero	69 78 67 75	289	2,205
Stephen Allan	67 76 73 73	289	2,205
Bob May	68 75 72 75	290	1,890
Fabrice Tarnaud	73 74 71 72	290	1,890
Silvio Grappasonni	73 70 73 74	290	1,890
Andrew Sandywell	76 68 71 75	290	1,890
Carl Watts	73 71 71 75	290	1,890
Daniel Chopra	75 71 71 73	290	1,890
Ronan Rafferty	76 70 71 73	290	1,890
Paul Eales	74 73 70 74	291	1,540
Ben Tinning	73 71 75 72	291	1,540
David Tapping	72 74 71 74	291	1,540
Van Phillips	71 75 74 72	292	1,400
Roger Wessels	73 71 70 79	293	1,330
Gordon Sherry	74 72 73 75	294	1,190
Francisco Valera	73 72 78 71	294	1,190
Dennis Edlund	75 69 73 77	294	1,190
Daniel Westermark	76 69 71 79	295	1,015
Massimo Florioli	75 72 75 73	295	1,015
Peter Hedblom	74 68 82 71	295	1,015
Jeff Hawkes	73 72 72 78	295	1,015
Craig Hainline	71 74 72 78	295	1,015
Duncan Muscroft	76 69 74 77	296	910
Manuel Pinero	75 71 74 77	297	700
Daren Lee	75 72 73 77	297	700
Joe Higgins	76 71 76 76	299	523

Portuguese Open

Aroeira, Lisbon, Portugal
Par 35-37–72; 6,685 yards

March 13-16
purse, £350,000

	SCORES	TOTAL	MONEY
Michael Jonzon	67 65 68 69	269	£58,330
Ignacio Garrido	69 71 67 65	272	38,880
Paul Broadhurst	68 67 67 73	275	21,910
Jose Maria Olazabal	70 67 65 74	276	13,770
Darren Clarke	70 71 68 67	276	13,770
Wayne Riley	68 66 71 71	276	13,770
Stephen Allan	69 73 67 67	276	13,770
Richard Boxall	70 71 67 69	277	8,750
Silvio Grappasonni	71 65 70 72	278	6,376.67
Peter O'Malley	65 69 72 72	278	6,376.67
Mark James	70 66 70 72	278	6,376.67

	SCORES				TOTAL	MONEY
Jose Coceres	71	69	69	69	278	6,376.67
Raymond Russell	69	69	68	72	278	6,376.67
Mark Mouland	72	69	69	68	278	6,376.67
John Wade	68	70	72	69	279	4,297.73
Mark Davis	69	69	67	74	279	4,297.73
Jose Rivero	71	69	69	70	279	4,297.73
Alex Cejka	69	70	69	71	279	4,297.73
Van Phillips	67	68	70	74	279	4,297.73
Robert Lee	71	68	67	73	279	4,297.73
Ronan Rafferty	73	69	70	67	279	4,297.73
Jean Van de Velde	73	69	66	71	279	4,297.73
Katsuyoshi Tomori	72	70	66	71	279	4,297.73
Adam Hunter	71	68	71	69	279	4,297.73
Paul Affleck	69	69	70	71	279	4,297.73
Pedro Linhart	68	71	72	69	280	3,255
Daniel Chopra	72	68	71	69	280	3,255
Miguel Angel Martin	70	70	68	72	280	3,255
Stephen McAllister	71	71	71	67	280	3,255
Jon Robson	72	70	68	70	280	3,255
Diego Borrego	69	70	68	73	280	3,255
Max Anglert	66	74	71	69	280	3,255
Paul Curry	70	71	70	70	281	2,765
Paolo Quirici	70	69	71	71	281	2,765
Jose Maria Canizares	69	73	69	70	281	2,765
Andre Bossert	70	73	69	69	281	2,765
Paul Lawrie	68	70	74	73	282	2,310
Gary Evans	72	69	68	73	282	2,310
Russell Claydon	71	72	70	69	282	2,310
Eduardo Romero	72	69	67	74	282	2,310
Massimo Florioli	73	70	68	71	282	2,310
Mike McLean	71	71	69	71	282	2,310
Paul McGinley	72	71	70	69	282	2,310
Ariel Canete	69	73	72	68	282	2,310
Andrew Sandywell	70	70	70	72	282	2,310
Angel Cabrera	72	71	71	69	283	1,960
Gary Orr	71	72	71	70	284	1,715
Tony Johnstone	70	72	74	68	284	1,715
Antonio Sobrinho	67	73	69	75	284	1,715
Domingo Hospital	67	71	74	72	284	1,715
Mathew Goggin	71	69	68	76	284	1,715
Alberto Binaghi	70	72	75	67	284	1,715
Santiago Luna	71	69	72	73	285	1,400
Peter Mitchell	70	70	70	75	285	1,400
Bob May	72	71	70	72	285	1,400
Andrew Beal	73	70	70	73	286	1,163.75
Gordon Brand, Jr.	75	68	71	72	286	1,163.75
Darren Cole	72	71	71	72	286	1,163.75
Gary Clark	69	71	74	72	286	1,163.75
John Bickerton	73	69	71	74	287	997.50
Scott Henderson	70	73	71	73	287	997.50
Ignacio Feliu	71	68	76	72	287	997.50
Fernando Roca	74	69	73	71	287	997.50
Stephen Gallacher	73	69	73	73	288	770
Marc Farry	70	73	73	72	288	770
Steve Webster	72	70	74	72	288	770
Mark Roe	68	71	76	75	290	522
Mats Hallberg	71	68	80	71	290	522
Miguel Angel Jimenez	69	68	79	75	291	519
Daniel Silva	70	72	77	76	295	517
Iain Pyman	70	69			WD	

Turespana Masters - Open de Canarias

Campo de Golf, Maspalomas, Gran Canaria
Par 36-37–73; 7,021 yards

March 20-23
purse, £350,000

	SCORES				TOTAL	MONEY
Jose Maria Olazabal	70	67	68	67	272	£61,964.63
Lee Westwood	72	63	68	71	274	41,302.72
Paul Broadhurst	69	72	67	68	276	20,932.83
Eduardo Romero	70	70	67	69	276	20,932.83
David Gilford	70	69	70	68	277	14,383.45
Jose Coceres	67	71	65	74	277	14,383.45
Diego Borrego	70	72	68	68	278	11,154.26
Ignacio Feliu	73	69	70	67	279	8,346.05
Ignacio Garrido	70	71	71	67	279	8,346.05
Retief Goosen	69	71	69	70	279	8,346.05
Domingo Hospital	71	71	68	70	280	6,072.22
Ian Garbutt	73	70	69	68	280	6,072.22
Massimo Florioli	72	69	68	71	280	6,072.22
Peter Mitchell	68	73	69	70	280	6,072.22
Scott Henderson	69	71	71	69	280	6,072.22
Andrew Sandywell	71	67	72	71	281	5,128.35
Paolo Quirici	74	64	70	73	281	5,128.35
Daniel Chopra	71	73	70	68	282	4,703.38
Francisco Cea	71	71	70	70	282	4,703.38
Fabrice Tarnaud	70	73	71	69	283	3,959.76
Andrew Oldcorn	72	71	71	69	283	3,959.76
Alex Cejka	70	74	70	69	283	3,959.76
Andrew Coltart	71	71	70	71	283	3,959.76
Robert Coles	73	69	71	70	283	3,959.76
Stephen Allan	70	70	70	73	283	3,959.76
Dennis Edlund	72	68	70	73	283	3,959.76
Katsuyoshi Tomori	68	72	71	72	283	3,959.76
Miguel Angel Jimenez	69	70	70	74	283	3,959.76
Neal Briggs	68	70	73	72	283	3,959.76
Miguel Angel Martin	71	72	69	72	284	3,104.60
Mark Davis	69	73	72	70	284	3,104.60
Padraig Harrington	72	69	71	72	284	3,104.60
Adam Hunter	67	73	73	71	284	3,104.60
Joakim Haeggman	70	69	72	73	284	3,104.60
Jonathan Lomas	69	69	72	74	284	3,104
Michael Jonzon	69	74	69	73	285	2,602.66
Michael Campbell	70	73	69	73	285	2,602.66
Brian Davis	66	77	71	71	285	2,602.66
Sven Struver	72	71	73	69	285	2,602.66
Roger Chapman	73	71	69	72	285	2,602.66
Jose Rivero	67	75	71	72	285	2,602.66
Des Smyth	70	70	72	73	285	2,602.66
Peter Baker	67	76	70	73	286	2,082.13
Pedro Linhart	75	70	74	69	286	2,082.13
Santiago Luna	72	71	74	69	286	2,082.13
Christian Cevaer	71	73	74	68	286	2,082.13
Jim Payne	70	72	72	72	286	2,082.13
Ross Drummond	72	70	70	74	286	2,082.13
Juan Carlos Pinero	70	69	71	76	286	2,082.13
Mathew Goggin	74	69	71	73	287	1,673.14
Jean Van de Velde	70	74	72	71	287	1,673.14
Carl Suneson	72	70	74	71	287	1,673.14
Mats Hallberg	67	71	73	76	287	1,673.14
Bob May	72	71	74	71	288	1,338.51

	SCORES			TOTAL	MONEY
Jon Robson	75 69 71 73			288	1,338.51
Andrew Beal	69 75 71 73			288	1,338.51
Max Anglert	72 72 70 74			288	1,338.51
Patrik Sjoland	70 70 71 77			288	1,338.51
Richard Boxall	71 72 74 72			289	1,152.61
David Higgins	72 71 72 75			290	1,078.25
Mark Mouland	71 72 73 74			290	1,078.25
Daren Lee	69 74 73 74			290	1,078.25
Stephen Field	71 72 77 71			291	1,003.88
Raymond Russell	71 72 79 70			292	948.11
Joakim Gronhagen	73 71 74 74			292	948.11
Warren Bennett	69 75 74 75			293	556.86
Raphael Jacquelin	71 73 77 72			293	556.86
Duncan Muscroft	74 70 75 75			294	553.86

Madeira Island Open

Santo da Serra Golf Club, Madeira, Portugal
Par 36-36—72; 6,606 yards
(Fourth round cancelled — fog and wind.)

March 27-30
purse, £300,000

	SCORES		TOTAL	MONEY
Peter Mitchell	70 63 71		204	£50,000
Fredrik Jacobson	68 73 64		205	33,330
Andrew Coltart	66 72 68		206	18,780
Andrew Sherborne	72 65 70		207	15,000
Carl Suneson	70 72 66		208	10,733.33
Jose Coceres	73 67 68		208	10,733.33
David Tapping	70 68 70		208	10,733.33
Thomas Gogele	71 67 71		209	7,500
Malcolm Mackenzie	69 73 68		210	5,842.50
Padraig Harrington	73 69 68		210	5,842.50
Paul Affleck	72 69 69		210	5,842.50
Dean Robertson	71 67 72		210	5,842.50
Jean Van de Velde	69 74 68		211	4,515
Anders Forsbrand	69 73 69		211	4,515
John Bickerton	72 70 69		211	4,515
Heinz P. Thul	70 68 73		211	4,515
Robert Coles	72 71 69		212	3,880
Gordon J. Brand	73 71 68		212	3,880
Bob May	69 73 70		212	3,880
David Howell	72 71 70		213	3,240
Philip Walton	74 70 69		213	3,240
Des Smyth	72 73 68		213	3,240
Van Phillips	73 70 70		213	3,240
Mark Mouland	71 71 71		213	3,240
Andrew Sandywell	69 73 71		213	3,240
Paul Lawrie	71 71 71		213	3,240
Ross McFarlane	68 73 72		213	3,240
Russell Claydon	69 71 73		213	3,240
Duncan Muscroft	72 71 71		214	2,512.50
Rolf Muntz	67 77 70		214	2,512.50
Scott Henderson	69 75 70		214	2,512.50
Richard Boxall	70 75 69		214	2,512.50
Michel Besanceney	72 71 71		214	2,512.50
Paul Broadhurst	70 72 72		214	2,512.50
Santiago Luna	70 71 73		214	2,512.50

	SCORES	TOTAL	MONEY
John Wade	72 69 73	214	2,512.50
Mark Roe	69 74 72	215	2,010
Ignacio Feliu	72 72 71	215	2,010
Stuart Cage	69 75 71	215	2,010
Mike Weir	73 72 70	215	2,010
Kalle Vainola	72 70 73	215	2,010
John McHenry	72 70 73	215	2,010
Peter Hedblom	71 71 73	215	2,010
Ignacio Garrido	68 73 74	215	2,010
Ariel Canete	71 72 73	216	1,650
Mathew Goggin	71 72 73	216	1,650
Andrew Oldcorn	73 71 72	216	1,650
Phillip Price	73 71 72	216	1,650
Martin Gates	70 73 74	217	1,290
Craig Hainline	71 73 73	217	1,290
Raphael Jacquelin	72 73 72	217	1,290
Joe Higgins	76 69 72	217	1,290
Michael Watson	72 71 74	217	1,290
Justin Hobday	73 69 75	217	1,290
Peter Baker	71 71 75	217	1,290
Fredrik Larsson	70 72 75	217	1,290
Juan Carlos Pinero	74 69 75	218	952.50
Stephen McAllister	70 75 73	218	952.50
Brian Davis	74 71 73	218	952.50
Fabrice Tarnaud	71 74 73	218	952.50
Andrew Bossert	75 70 74	219	855
Francisco Valera	70 72 77	219	855
Fredrik Andersson	72 72 76	220	795
Iain Pyman	71 73 76	220	795
*Alexandre Henriques	74 70 76	220	
Jim Payne	74 71 76	221	549.33
Antoine Lebouc	73 72 76	221	549.33
Carl Watts	75 70 76	221	549.33

Europe 1 Cannes Open

Royal Mougins Golf Club, Cannes, France
Par 35-36–71; 6,594 yards

April 17-20
purse, £300,000

	SCORES	TOTAL	MONEY
Stuart Cage	68 67 69 66	270	£50,000
Paul Broadhurst	68 70 69 68	275	26,055
David Carter	68 74 71 62	275	26,055
Paul Eales	72 65 70 69	276	13,850
Jamie Spence	74 72 69 61	276	13,850
Paul McGinley	72 68 70 68	278	9,750
Clinton Whitelaw	71 71 68 68	278	9,750
Neal Briggs	71 69 70 69	279	6,427.50
Carl Suneson	73 69 69 68	279	6,427.50
Andrew Sandywell	76 67 67 69	279	6,427.50
Andrew Coltart	71 70 69 69	279	6,427.50
Ben Tinning	72 68 73 67	280	4,747.50
Philip Walton	70 73 66 71	280	4,747.50
Andrew Sherborne	69 74 72 65	280	4,747.50
Santiago Luna	70 66 73 71	280	4,747.50
Ronan Rafferty	74 70 67 70	281	3,894
Francisco Valera	72 69 74 66	281	3,894

450 / EUROPEAN TOURS

	SCORES				TOTAL	MONEY
Michael Jonzon	72	71	69	69	281	3,894
Barry Lane	75	69	67	70	281	3,894
Paul Curry	72	72	68	69	281	3,894
Pierre Fulke	74	70	69	69	282	3,195
Howard Clark	70	75	69	68	282	3,195
Domingo Hospital	74	70	67	71	282	3,195
Pedro Linhart	71	73	73	65	282	3,195
Mathias Gronberg	71	71	66	74	282	3,195
Rolf Muntz	68	73	69	72	282	3,195
David Howell	72	72	71	67	282	3,195
Adam Mednick	75	70	72	65	282	3,195
Thomas Bjorn	71	68	73	71	283	2,745
Des Smyth	72	69	75	67	283	2,745
Peter Mitchell	73	70	71	70	284	2,409.29
Katsuyoshi Tomori	76	69	67	72	284	2,409.29
Fernando Roca	72	75	70	67	284	2,409.29
Daniel Westermark	71	73	68	72	284	2,409.29
David Gilford	79	67	67	71	284	2,409.29
Niclas Fasth	73	68	72	71	284	2,409.29
Ariel Canete	71	75	69	69	284	2,409.29
Mark Mouland	73	72	70	70	285	1,950
Sven Struver	74	71	69	71	285	1,950
John Mellor	72	72	73	68	285	1,950
Steven Bottomley	70	70	75	70	285	1,950
Fabrice Tarnaud	73	73	69	70	285	1,950
Joakim Haeggman	83	63	72	67	285	1,950
Ross McFarlane	70	72	74	69	285	1,950
Derrick Cooper	73	70	72	70	285	1,950
Bob May	72	73	71	70	286	1,620
Stephen Field	74	73	69	70	286	1,620
Ignacio Garrido	75	72	72	67	286	1,620
Dennis Edlund	77	70	71	69	287	1,500
Klas Eriksson	75	71	75	67	288	1,350
Jean Van de Velde	74	72	75	67	288	1,350
David Higgins	76	68	74	70	288	1,350
Stephen Allan	74	73	73	68	288	1,350
Raphael Jacquelin	69	77	73	70	289	1,170
Raymond Russell	72	72	72	73	289	1,170
Thomas Levet	74	73	71	72	290	1,050
Retief Goosen	74	73	71	72	290	1,050
Jarmo Sandelin	71	75	75	70	291	930
Marten Olander	75	72	68	76	291	930
Stephen Scahill	67	72	72	80	291	930
Patrik Sjoland	72	72	77	71	292	825
Mats Lanner	72	72	70	78	292	825
Matthias Debove	74	72	74	72	292	825
Warren Bennett	78	69	73	72	292	825
Darren Cole	75	72	73	74	294	750
Mark Davis	72	73	75	75	295	450
Jon Robson	74	73	77	74	298	448
Miguel Angel Martin	71	73	78	77	299	446

Peugeot Open de Espana

Golf La Moraleja II, Madrid, Spain
Par 36-36–72; 7,054 yards

April 24-27
purse, £550,000

		SCORES			TOTAL	MONEY
Mark James	67	68	73	69	277	£84,843.91
Greg Norman	69	70	68	70	277	56,506.04
(James defeated Norman on third extra hole.)						
Jarmo Sandelin	72	71	69	66	278	28,677.24
Eduardo Romero	68	70	71	69	278	28,677.24
David Howell	70	71	67	71	279	18,213.16
Jean Louis Guepy	71	68	70	70	279	18,213.16
Jose Coceres	72	69	70	68	279	18,213.16
Roger Chapman	70	67	74	69	280	11,425.65
Howard Clark	74	70	69	67	280	11,425.65
Fredrik Jacobson	73	71	69	67	280	11,425.65
Stephen Ames	68	75	70	68	281	8,590.45
Peter Mitchell	70	69	69	73	281	8,590.45
Jose Maria Olazabal	69	71	74	67	281	8,590.45
Thomas Bjorn	68	69	72	72	281	8,590.45
Costantino Rocca	70	70	71	71	282	7,466.26
Gary Clark	72	69	72	70	283	6,472.38
Adam Hunter	70	71	73	69	283	6,472.38
Jamie Spence	73	70	70	70	283	6,472.38
Miguel Angel Jimenez	68	74	71	70	283	6,472.38
Lee Westwood	69	68	73	73	283	6,472.38
Gary Emerson	67	72	70	74	283	6,472.38
Ian Garbutt	69	70	70	74	283	6,472.38
Clinton Whitelaw	69	70	71	74	284	5,599.70
Andrew Sherborne	72	71	71	70	284	5,599.70
David Carter	70	72	67	75	284	5,599.70
Greg Turner	72	71	71	71	285	4,496.73
Ross Drummond	73	69	70	73	285	4,496.73
Andrew Coltart	72	71	73	69	285	4,496.73
Rolf Muntz	70	68	70	77	285	4,496.73
Mark Roe	70	71	73	71	285	4,496.73
Ignacio Garrido	68	74	71	72	285	4,496.73
Stuart Cage	71	73	70	71	285	4,496.73
Seve Ballesteros	70	73	73	69	285	4,496.73
Dennis Edlund	73	68	75	69	285	4,496.73
Silvio Grappasonni	71	72	70	72	285	4,496.73
Iain Pyman	68	70	76	72	286	3,224.07
Ignacio Feliu	73	70	71	72	286	3,224.07
Niclas Fasth	69	74	72	71	286	3,224.07
Sam Torrance	70	70	74	72	286	3,224.07
Padraig Harrington	66	76	74	70	286	3,224.07
Bernhard Langer	72	72	74	68	286	3,224.07
Jay Townsend	73	68	75	70	286	3,224.07
Paul Eales	70	74	69	73	286	3,224.07
Gary Orr	72	69	72	73	286	3,224.07
Pierre Fulke	74	70	74	68	286	3,224.07
Carl Watts	71	69	74	72	286	3,224.07
Per Haugsrud	73	69	73	72	287	2,502.90
Patrik Sjoland	73	70	74	70	287	2,502.90
Barry Lane	68	75	76	68	287	2,502.90
Klas Eriksson	73	69	75	70	287	2,502.90
Francisco Cea	70	74	71	72	287	2,502.90
David Higgins	70	70	75	72	287	2,502.90
*Sergio Garcia	71	73	70	73	287	

452 / EUROPEAN TOURS

	SCORES				TOTAL	MONEY
Rodger Davis	70	71	77	70	288	2,078.68
Paul McGinley	72	72	71	73	288	2,078.68
Carl Suneson	74	69	75	70	288	2,078.68
Andrew Oldcorn	72	71	70	75	288	2,078.68
Carl Mason	73	71	72	73	289	1,654.46
Paul Lawrie	72	69	76	72	289	1,654.46
Santiago Luna	71	71	70	77	289	1,654.46
Jean Van de Velde	72	71	74	72	289	1,654.46
Peter Baker	73	68	77	71	289	1,654.46
Francisco Valera	69	72	75	73	289	1,654.46
Per-Ulrik Johansson	74	70	74	72	290	1,315.08
David Gilford	70	74	69	77	290	1,315.08
Emanuele Canonica	72	67	73	79	291	975.91
Miguel Angel Martin	72	72	72	75	291	975.91
Gordon Brand, Jr.	73	71	75	73	292	759
Ivo Giner	76	66	74	76	292	759
Mark McNulty	76	68	74	74	292	759
Ross McFarlane	73	71	75	73	292	759
Alex Cejka	66	73	75	79	293	754
Pedro Linhart	71	70	78	75	294	752
Jose Garcia	72	72	69	82	295	749
Jon Robson	73	71	71	80	295	749
Jose Rivero	73	71	78	74	296	746

Conte of Florence Italian Open

Gardagolf, Brescia, Italy
Par 36-36–72; 7,111 yards

May 1-4
purse, £500,000

	SCORES				TOTAL	MONEY
Bernhard Langer	71	69	69	64	273	£77,897.80
Jose Maria Olazabal	68	71	67	68	274	51,924.33
Darren Clarke	70	69	71	67	277	29,259.32
Philip Walton	71	70	70	67	278	21,583.19
Steve Webster	68	75	65	70	278	21,583.19
Lee Westwood	69	74	69	67	279	11,741.74
Costantino Rocca	71	73	69	66	279	11,741.74
Daren Lee	71	69	70	69	279	11,741.74
Raymond Russell	72	70	66	71	279	11,741.74
Brian Davis	68	70	75	66	279	11,741.74
Dean Robertson	71	69	68	71	279	11,741.74
Roger Wessels	74	69	66	71	280	7,231.69
Patrik Sjoland	68	70	70	72	280	7,231.69
Stephen Scahill	70	72	70	68	280	7,231.69
Eduardo Romero	68	69	71	72	280	7,231.69
Jarmo Sandelin	69	73	70	68	280	7,231.69
Jonathan Lomas	72	70	71	68	281	5,756.81
Manuel Pinero	70	73	70	68	281	5,756.81
Stephen Allan	70	74	69	68	281	5,756.81
Retief Goosen	66	75	69	71	281	5,756.81
Raymond Burns	70	71	70	70	281	5,756.81
Paolo Quirici	69	70	68	74	281	5,756.81
Jose Coceres	68	73	73	68	282	4,627.28
Massimo Florioli	75	69	68	70	282	4,627.28
Santiago Luna	72	67	73	70	282	4,627.28
Martin Gates	70	73	70	69	282	4,627.28
Thomas Gogele	70	71	73	68	282	4,627.28

	SCORES				TOTAL	MONEY
Mark James	69	73	71	69	282	4,627.28
Ian Woosnam	67	73	73	69	282	4,627.28
Michel Besanceney	69	72	69	72	282	4,627.28
Wayne Westner	69	74	68	71	282	4,627.28
Van Phillips	74	68	76	65	283	3,645.90
Ian Garbutt	73	70	71	69	283	3,645.90
Robert Karlsson	70	70	74	69	283	3,645.90
Padraig Harrington	70	70	71	72	283	3,645.90
Anders Gillner	71	71	70	71	283	3,645.90
Daniel Westermark	71	73	67	72	283	3,645.90
John Bickerton	71	70	71	71	283	3,645.90
David Howell	72	70	69	73	284	3,178.39
Aricl Canete	73	67	73	71	284	3,178.39
John Mellor	72	70	72	70	284	3,178.39
Emanuele Canonica	72	71	73	69	285	2,710.95
Silvio Grappasonni	71	71	71	72	285	2,710.95
Marco Gortana	72	70	71	72	285	2,710.95
Ricky Willison	72	72	69	72	285	2,710.95
Thomas Bjorn	69	70	73	73	285	2,710.95
Greg Turner	72	70	72	71	285	2,710.95
Mark Mouland	70	71	70	74	285	2,710.95
Robert Coles	71	72	74	69	286	2,243.53
Niclas Fasth	68	73	73	72	286	2,243.53
Wayne Riley	70	72	73	71	286	2,243.53
Steven Bottomley	71	72	73	71	287	2,056.56
Peter Baker	72	71	77	68	288	1,776.12
Ben Tinning	73	71	71	73	288	1,776.12
David Higgins	71	72	71	74	288	1,776.12
Mathias Gronberg	72	69	70	77	288	1,776.12
John Wade	72	72	75	69	288	1,776.12
Andre Bossert	73	70	72	74	289	1,448.98
Marco Durante	73	70	75	71	289	1,448.98
Robert Lee	76	65	73	75	289	1,448.98
Raphael Jacquelin	72	67	74	77	290	1,332.10
Stephen Gallacher	71	73	74	72	290	1,332.10
Christy O'Connor, Jr.	73	71	73	74	291	1,215.24
Gordon J. Brand	68	70	77	76	291	1,215.24
Carlos Duran	69	74	71	77	291	1,215.24
Richard Green	73	71	74	74	292	702
Alan Tait	73	71	73	76	293	700
Stuart Cage	72	71	74	77	294	698

Benson and Hedges International Open

The Oxfordshire Golf Club, Thame, Oxon, England
Par 36-36–72; 7,205 yards

May 8-11
purse, £700,000

	SCORES				TOTAL	MONEY
Bernhard Langer	70	66	71	69	276	£116,660
Ian Woosnam	70	68	70	70	278	77,770
Lee Westwood	69	69	70	72	280	43,820
Padraig Harrington	73	67	71	71	282	35,000
Kalle Vainola	70	69	71	73	283	27,070
Robert Karlsson	71	71	70	71	283	27,070
Fabrice Tarnaud	75	69	67	73	284	16,198
Darren Clarke	69	68	72	75	284	16,198
Eduardo Romero	73	65	71	75	284	16,198

	SCORES			TOTAL	MONEY
Patrik Sjoland	69 69 74 72			284	16,198
Bob May	69 72 71 72			284	16,198
Thomas Bjorn	71 70 70 74			285	12,040
Christy O'Connor, Jr.	68 74 70 74			286	10,535
David Gilford	71 72 70 73			286	10,535
Greg Turner	67 68 77 74			286	10,535
Jamie Spence	71 73 68 74			286	10,535
Retief Goosen	69 67 76 76			288	9,240
Niclas Fasth	70 72 72 74			288	9,240
Andrew Oldcorn	75 69 74 71			289	8,540
Mark Mouland	74 67 74 74			289	8,540
Wayne Westner	73 70 72 75			290	8,085
Mark James	73 70 71 76			290	8,085
Carl Suneson	70 71 74 76			291	7,245
Paul McGinley	72 71 72 76			291	7,245
Miguel Angel Jimenez	72 69 75 75			291	7,245
Peter Hedblom	71 73 73 74			291	7,245
Santiago Luna	70 70 75 76			291	7,245
Iain Pyman	72 69 75 75			291	7,245
Paul Lawrie	70 73 75 74			292	6,020
Ignacio Garrido	71 70 74 77			292	6,020
Sven Struver	73 70 74 75			292	6,020
Seve Ballesteros	72 69 76 75			292	6,020
Peter Mitchell	69 71 76 76			292	6,020
Ross McFarlane	70 66 78 78			292	6,020
Steve Webster	72 72 76 73			293	5,180
Stephen Ames	74 70 77 72			293	5,180
Richard Green	75 69 74 75			293	5,180
Derrick Cooper	71 73 73 76			293	5,180
Stephen Field	75 69 73 76			293	5,180
Ricky Willison	73 71 71 79			294	4,410
John Murray	73 69 72 80			294	4,410
Emanuele Canonica	73 71 79 71			294	4,410
Ignacio Feliu	72 71 72 79			294	4,410
Gordon Brand, Jr.	75 69 73 77			294	4,410
Gary Orr	70 74 73 77			294	4,410
Paolo Quirici	71 71 75 78			295	3,570
David Tapping	74 69 74 78			295	3,570
Philip Walton	73 71 72 79			295	3,570
Andrew Coltart	69 75 75 76			295	3,570
Olle Karlsson	75 67 80 73			295	3,570
Paul Eales	71 71 77 76			295	3,570
Thomas Gogele	76 67 75 78			296	2,800
Jonathan Lomas	69 72 75 80			296	2,800
Ian Garbutt	74 67 77 78			296	2,800
Sam Torrance	74 70 77 75			296	2,800
Rodger Davis	73 71 76 76			296	2,800
Paul Broadhurst	70 73 78 76			297	2,310
Stuart Cage	74 70 74 79			297	2,310
Jose Coceres	71 69 77 81			298	2,030
David Howell	70 71 77 80			298	2,030
Colin Montgomerie	70 71 76 81			298	2,030
Jim Payne	72 71 78 77			298	2,030
Joakim Haeggman	72 70 76 80			298	2,030
Michael Jonzon	74 70 76 79			299	1,785
Stephen Allan	72 72 76 79			299	1,785
Gary Emerson	71 71 79 80			301	1,050
Daren Lee	73 71 78 80			302	1,048
Ian Mosey	73 70 80 80			303	1,046

Alamo English Open

Marriott Hanbury Manor Hotel, Hertfordshire, England
Par 36-36–72; 7,016 yards

May 15-18
purse, £650,000

	SCORES				TOTAL	MONEY
Per-Ulrik Johansson	70	68	64	67	269	£108,330
Dennis Edlund	68	65	69	69	271	72,210
Jay Townsend	72	63	70	67	272	36,595
Steve Webster	68	66	70	68	272	36,595
David Howell	70	70	66	67	273	25,140
Roger Chapman	66	66	71	70	273	25,140
Sam Torrance	73	67	67	67	274	17,875
Russell Claydon	69	69	66	70	274	17,875
Mark James	72	67	69	67	275	14,510
Gary Emerson	68	68	65	75	276	12,480
Gary Orr	71	70	71	64	276	12,480
Ian Garbutt	75	66	67	69	277	9,091.50
Phillip Price	73	68	67	69	277	9,091.50
Colin Montgomerie	72	68	70	67	277	9,091.50
Darren Clarke	72	64	70	71	277	9,091.50
Miguel Angel Martin	73	68	66	70	277	9,091.50
Silvio Grappasonni	72	66	71	68	277	9,091.50
Stephen McAllister	71	69	67	70	277	9,091.50
Clinton Whitelaw	73	67	68	69	277	9,091.50
Stephen Ames	68	72	69	68	277	9,091.50
Niclas Fasth	70	70	68	69	277	9,091.50
Paul Lawrie	68	73	66	71	278	7,117.50
Jose Maria Olazabal	69	72	69	68	278	7,117.50
Lee Westwood	72	64	69	73	278	7,117.50
Robert Karlsson	71	67	73	67	278	7,117.50
Carl Suneson	68	74	69	68	279	6,045
Daniel Chopra	70	70	68	71	279	6,045
Peter Baker	71	69	67	72	279	6,045
Miguel Angel Jimenez	68	72	69	70	279	6,045
Eduardo Romero	73	68	65	73	279	6,045
Rodger Davis	72	68	70	69	279	6,045
David Carter	73	67	71	68	279	6,045
Thomas Gogele	67	70	68	75	280	4,875
Tony Johnstone	73	66	70	71	280	4,875
Andrew Coltart	73	67	70	70	280	4,875
Katsuyoshi Tomori	71	70	68	71	280	4,875
Peter Lonard	71	70	70	69	280	4,875
Wayne Riley	69	71	70	70	280	4,875
Raymond Burns	73	67	69	71	280	4,875
Jose Coceres	73	64	72	71	280	4,875
Mark McNulty	70	69	70	72	281	4,030
Paul Affleck	72	69	70	70	281	4,030
Stuart Cage	71	70	67	73	281	4,030
Per Haugsrud	70	69	73	69	281	4,030
Massimo Florioli	75	66	69	71	281	4,030
Ross Drummond	70	71	72	69	282	3,185
Fredrik Jacobson	72	70	72	68	282	3,185
Paolo Quirici	71	71	68	72	282	3,185
John Mellor	69	73	70	70	282	3,185
Brian Davis	68	73	69	72	282	3,185
Francisco Valera	72	68	71	71	282	3,185
Anders Forsbrand	70	72	69	71	282	3,185
Pedro Linhart	71	71	71	69	282	3,185
Peter Mitchell	72	70	68	73	283	2,600

	SCORES	TOTAL	MONEY
Iain Pyman	73 67 75 69	284	2,275
Carl Watts	71 69 72 72	284	2,275
Joakim Haeggman	73 69 69 73	284	2,275
Mats Hallberg	68 71 73 72	284	2,275
Jim Payne	70 72 67 76	285	1,885
Steven Bottomley	69 73 70 73	285	1,885
Robert Lee	69 72 69 75	285	1,885
Jarmo Sandelin	72 70 69 74	285	1,885
Santiago Luna	73 69 69 74	285	1,885
Jean Van de Velde	74 68 73 71	286	1,657.50
Gary Clark	71 68 75 72	286	1,657.50
Wayne Westner	71 71 73 72	287	975
Jamie Spence	70 72 70 77	289	973
David Higgins	71 70 73 76	290	971

Volvo PGA Championship

Wentworth Club, West Course, Surrey, England
Par 35-37–72; 6,957 yards

May 23-26
purse, £1,100,000

	SCORES	TOTAL	MONEY
Ian Woosnam	67 68 70 70	275	£183,330
Darren Clarke	66 74 66 71	277	82,023.33
Nick Faldo	70 67 70 70	277	82,023.33
Ernie Els	69 71 67 70	277	82,023.33
Colin Montgomerie	69 69 76 64	278	46,640
David Gilford	67 70 72 70	279	35,750
Angel Cabrera	73 67 70 69	279	35,750
Dennis Edlund	70 72 68 70	280	27,500
Lee Westwood	70 72 70 69	281	24,530
Barry Lane	69 72 69 72	282	22,000
Eamonn Darcy	66 75 76 67	284	18,930
Eduardo Romero	71 70 70 73	284	18,930
Frank Nobilo	68 71 77 68	284	18,930
Philip Walton	69 72 70 74	285	15,510
Raymond Burns	72 71 72 70	285	15,510
Carl Mason	73 71 69 72	285	15,510
David Carter	68 74 70 73	285	15,510
Stephen Ames	70 69 70 76	285	15,510
Peter Hedblom	73 71 75 67	286	12,388.75
Jose Maria Olazabal	72 71 73 70	286	12,388.75
Miguel Angel Martin	70 75 67 74	286	12,388.75
Thomas Bjorn	68 74 75 69	286	12,388.75
Iain Pyman	71 73 73 69	286	12,388.75
Ronan Rafferty	74 72 72 68	286	12,388.75
Jon Robson	71 71 71 73	286	12,388.75
Paul Curry	71 74 71 70	286	12,388.75
Mark Davis	70 73 73 71	287	10,230
Jose Coceres	74 72 72 69	287	10,230
Andre Bossert	73 70 75 69	287	10,230
Peter O'Malley	73 71 72 71	287	10,230
Carl Suneson	73 72 69 73	287	10,230
Andrew Oldcorn	72 71 74 71	288	8,800
Retief Goosen	73 74 69 72	288	8,800
Bernhard Langer	67 75 76 70	288	8,800
Vijay Singh	70 73 73 72	288	8,800
Gary Emerson	71 70 75 72	288	8,800

	SCORES			TOTAL	MONEY
Sam Torrance	71 75 71 72			289	7,370
Marc Farry	68 78 72 71			289	7,370
Paul Broadhurst	72 75 73 69			289	7,370
Mark Roe	72 73 71 73			289	7,370
Dean Robertson	72 74 73 70			289	7,370
Per-Ulrik Johansson	70 75 74 70			289	7,370
Diego Borrego	70 75 74 70			289	7,370
Roger Chapman	71 75 69 74			289	7,370
Emanuele Canonica	74 73 69 74			290	5,940
Ian Garbutt	71 73 72 74			290	5,940
Wayne Westner	74 70 71 75			290	5,940
Gary Evans	71 75 74 70			290	5,940
Joakim Haeggman	69 76 72 73			290	5,940
Clinton Whitelaw	69 78 71 73			291	4,950
Gary Orr	67 78 73 73			291	4,950
Ignacio Garrido	74 73 73 71			291	4,950
Peter Teravainen	74 73 71 73			291	4,950
Klas Eriksson	70 71 78 73			292	3,868.33
Stuart Cage	71 75 73 73			292	3,868.33
Miguel Angel Jimenez	75 71 70 76			292	3,868.33
Jarmo Sandelin	72 71 70 79			292	3,868.33
Robert Allenby	73 72 76 71			292	3,868.33
Manuel Pinero	73 74 75 70			292	3,868.33
Jay Townsend	74 71 73 75			293	3,080
Ross McFarlane	74 71 70 78			293	3,080
Padraig Harrington	74 73 73 73			293	3,080
Niclas Fasth	72 75 71 75			293	3,080
Anders Forsbrand	75 70 75 73			293	3,080
Robert Karlsson	67 76 80 71			294	1,867.60
Des Smyth	71 72 78 73			294	1,867.60
Gordon Brand, Jr.	76 71 73 74			294	1,867.60
Alex Cejka	74 72 74 74			294	1,867.60
Costantino Rocca	70 76 71 77			294	1,867.60
Mathias Gronberg	73 72 70 80			295	1,641
Fernando Roca	76 71 76 72			295	1,641
David Higgins	72 75 76 73			296	1,637
Juan Carlos Pinero	71 71 80 74			296	1,637
Greg Turner	74 73 79 71			297	1,634
Kevin Dickens	73 74 78 73			298	1,632
Bradley Hughes	72 75 77 75			299	1,630
Wayne Riley	72 74 78 77			301	1,628
Jonathan Lomas	73 74 78 80			305	1,625
Tony Charnley	76 71 82 76			305	1,625

Deutsche Bank Open–TPC of Europe

Gut Kaden, Hamburg, Germany
Par 36-36–72; 7,029 yards

May 29-June 1
purse, £750,000

	SCORES			TOTAL	MONEY
Ross McFarlane	70 73 68 71			282	£125,000
Anders Forsbrand	73 68 69 73			283	65,130
Gordon Brand, Jr.	72 72 67 72			283	65,130
Darren Clarke	74 72 68 70			284	37,500
Roger Wessels	70 75 70 70			285	24,817.50
Paul McGinley	72 73 66 74			285	24,817.50
Raymond Russell	72 72 70 71			285	24,817.50

		SCORES			TOTAL	MONEY
Miguel Angel Martin	69	71	76	69	285	24,817.50
Adam Hunter	73	72	68	73	286	12,632.78
Scott Henderson	73	70	71	72	286	12,632.78
Peter Mitchell	71	72	69	74	286	12,632.78
Thomas Bjorn	72	72	66	76	286	12,632.78
Robert Allenby	76	70	70	70	286	12,632.78
Howard Clark	73	69	68	76	286	12,632.78
David Carter	70	75	70	71	286	12,632.78
Ben Tinning	72	70	71	73	286	12,632.78
Katsuyoshi Tomori	73	70	72	71	286	12,632.78
Andrew Sandywell	76	70	69	72	287	8,937.50
Paul Broadhurst	68	76	71	72	287	8,937.50
Retief Goosen	70	71	72	74	287	8,937.50
Van Phillips	71	68	74	74	287	8,937.50
Santiago Luna	72	72	68	75	287	8,937.50
Michael Jonzon	72	73	69	73	287	8,937.50
Emanuele Canonica	70	70	74	74	288	7,200
Angel Cabrera	73	70	75	70	288	7,200
Jamie Spence	73	73	70	72	288	7,200
Tony Johnstone	70	73	73	72	288	7,200
Rodger Davis	72	72	72	72	288	7,200
Jon Robson	70	71	73	74	288	7,200
Paul Affleck	73	73	71	71	288	7,200
Mats Hallberg	71	72	75	70	288	7,200
Darren Cole	72	74	69	73	288	7,200
Mark Mouland	72	73	73	71	289	6,000
Malcolm Mackenzie	72	72	70	75	289	6,000
Alex Cejka	73	73	70	73	289	6,000
Niclas Fasth	71	75	73	71	290	4,950
Simon Hurley	70	76	69	75	290	4,950
Michel Besanceney	72	72	71	75	290	4,950
Silvio Grappasonni	72	71	74	73	290	4,950
Ross Drummond	72	73	70	75	290	4,950
Roger Chapman	70	73	71	76	290	4,950
Alberto Binaghi	69	73	70	78	290	4,950
Barry Lane	69	72	74	75	290	4,950
Ronan Rafferty	73	71	70	76	290	4,950
Pedro Linhart	73	71	71	75	290	4,950
Bob May	74	72	71	73	290	4,950
Diego Borrego	75	70	69	77	291	3,825
Phillip Price	75	70	71	75	291	3,825
Robert Lee	74	72	71	74	291	3,825
Thomas Gogele	79	67	70	75	291	3,825
John Wade	73	73	75	71	292	3,375
Dean Robertson	70	73	74	75	292	3,375
Francisco Valera	75	71	70	77	293	2,850
Carl Suneson	71	73	78	71	293	2,850
Gary Emerson	73	73	76	71	293	2,850
Paul Eales	74	72	74	73	293	2,850
Ignacio Garrido	71	73	74	75	293	2,850
Mats Lanner	74	72	71	77	294	2,250
Mike McLean	73	73	72	76	294	2,250
Michael Campbell	75	67	74	78	294	2,250
David Gilford	73	72	73	76	294	2,250
Mathias Gronberg	70	71	71	82	294	2,250
Gary Clark	72	73	75	75	295	1,743.75
Mark Davis	73	72	71	79	295	1,743.75
Jarmo Sandelin	72	74	72	77	295	1,743.75
Daren Lee	75	71	69	80	295	1,743.75
Jeff Hawkes	74	72	75	80	301	1,123

Compaq European Grand Prix

Slaley Hall, Northumberland, England
Par 36-36–72; 7,053 yards

June 5-8
purse, £650,000

		SCORES			TOTAL	MONEY
Colin Montgomerie	69	68	68	65	270	£108,330
Retief Goosen	69	69	68	69	275	72,210
Lee Westwood	70	70	66	70	276	40,690
David Gilford	71	69	69	69	278	30,015
Scott Henderson	69	71	68	70	278	30,015
Roger Wessels	71	69	73	67	280	17,202
Jon Robson	72	68	70	70	280	17,202
David Carter	69	70	70	71	280	17,202
John Mellor	71	72	67	70	280	17,202
Jamie Spence	69	72	67	72	280	17,202
Stephen Allan	72	71	69	69	281	11,200
Paul McGinley	73	71	67	70	281	11,200
Sam Torrance	72	71	67	71	281	11,200
Jean Louis Guepy	73	71	70	68	282	9,550
Ross McFarlane	72	69	68	73	282	9,550
Neal Briggs	70	70	70	72	282	9,550
Gordon Sherry	73	72	69	69	283	8,580
Paul Lawrie	70	69	72	72	283	8,580
Robert Coles	70	70	72	72	284	7,419.29
Barry Lane	70	68	76	70	284	7,419.29
Peter Hedblom	71	72	71	70	284	7,419.29
Gary Evans	72	68	71	73	284	7,419.29
Phil Golding	73	68	71	72	284	7,419.29
Jonathan Lomas	74	70	68	72	284	7,419.29
Emanuele Canonica	68	73	72	71	284	7,419.29
Ignacio Feliu	71	68	71	75	285	5,871.67
John Wade	71	72	71	71	285	5,871.67
Mathew Goggin	72	71	72	70	285	5,871.67
Padraig Harrington	67	74	72	72	285	5,871.67
Derrick Cooper	72	72	71	70	285	5,871.67
Fredrik Andersson	67	73	74	71	285	5,871.67
Michael Long	71	73	71	70	285	5,871.67
Miles Tunnicliff	73	69	69	74	285	5,871.67
Fredrik Jacobson	70	70	72	73	285	5,871.67
Steven Bottomley	68	71	74	73	286	4,810
Andrew Oldcorn	69	75	70	72	286	4,810
Andrew Coltart	72	72	70	72	286	4,810
Dean Robertson	72	71	73	70	286	4,810
Anders Hansen	71	73	71	71	286	4,810
Bob May	72	70	73	72	287	4,095
Gordon J. Brand	69	72	72	74	287	4,095
Massimo Florioli	73	72	70	72	287	4,095
Greg Turner	70	72	70	75	287	4,095
Russell Claydon	71	74	69	73	287	4,095
Paul Affleck	70	72	74	71	287	4,095
Jay Townsend	71	72	73	72	288	3,510
Wayne Westner	71	69	72	76	288	3,510
Steve Webster	66	76	72	74	288	3,510
Paolo Quirici	72	73	68	76	289	2,860
Van Phillips	74	70	71	74	289	2,860
Carl Mason	71	73	72	73	289	2,860
Patrik Sjoland	70	73	75	71	289	2,860
Paul Broadhurst	69	76	71	73	289	2,860
Gordon Brand, Jr.	74	71	72	72	289	2,860

	SCORES				TOTAL	MONEY
Mathias Gronberg	73	71	72	73	289	2,860
Per Haugsrud	69	73	74	74	290	2,119
Andrew Beal	69	73	74	74	290	2,119
Andrew Sandywell	75	69	74	72	290	2,119
Ross Drummond	71	71	75	73	290	2,119
Carl Suneson	70	73	71	76	290	2,119
Juan Carlos Pinero	68	74	76	73	291	1,787.50
Stephen Gallacher	72	72	74	73	291	1,787.50
Mats Hallberg	68	76	75	72	291	1,787.50
Wayne Riley	70	73	71	77	291	1,787.50
Peter O'Malley	71	72	73	76	292	1,300
Pedro Linhart	72	73	73	74	292	1,300
Daniel Westermark	75	70	73	75	293	970
Alan Tait	69	76	73	75	293	970
Daren Lee	75	69	72	77	293	970
Tony Johnstone	72	72	74	75	293	970
Christian Cevaer	73	72	72	77	294	965
David Higgins	73	72	75	77	297	962
Ben Tinning	73	72	72	80	297	962
Brian Davis	72	73	76	77	298	959
Mark Mouland	73	70	80	77	300	957
Raymond Burns	70	75	76	80	301	955

Volvo German Open

Schloss Nippenburg ETC, Stuttgart, Germany
Par 36-35–71; 6,850 yards

June 19-22
purse, £700,000

	SCORES				TOTAL	MONEY
Ignacio Garrido	65	67	67	72	271	£116,660
Russell Claydon	68	69	72	66	275	77,770
Mark James	68	67	69	72	276	43,820
Richard Green	71	66	71	69	277	25,528
Bernhard Langer	70	69	69	69	277	25,528
Eduardo Romero	67	67	73	70	277	25,528
Per Haugsrud	70	68	68	71	277	25,528
Brian Davis	68	70	66	73	277	25,528
Alex Cejka	66	76	69	67	278	14,163.33
Sam Torrance	70	68	70	70	278	14,163.33
Barry Lane	68	70	68	72	278	14,163.33
Max Anglert	70	70	71	68	279	12,040
Robert Karlsson	68	67	73	72	280	10,990
Ian Woosnam	71	69	68	72	280	10,990
Jim Payne	66	71	75	69	281	10,080
Domingo Hospital	70	71	69	71	281	10,080
Johan Skold	68	71	74	69	282	9,053.33
Greg Turner	70	72	70	70	282	9,053.33
Phillip Price	71	70	69	72	282	9,053.33
Mike Weir	65	75	72	71	283	7,980
Mark Mouland	72	67	72	72	283	7,980
Daniel Chopra	71	72	68	72	283	7,980
Van Phillips	65	70	74	74	283	7,980
Bob May	67	70	72	74	283	7,980
Ross McFarlane	71	71	71	71	284	7,035
Heinz P. Thul	70	70	74	70	284	7,035
Richard Boxall	71	72	72	69	284	7,035
Derrick Cooper	72	68	69	75	284	7,035

	SCORES			TOTAL	MONEY
Padraig Harrington	71 71 71 72			285	5,940
Philip Walton	72 70 72 71			285	5,940
Anders Forsbrand	68 73 73 71			285	5,940
Stephen Field	73 68 75 69			285	5,940
Per-Ulrik Johansson	72 71 69 73			285	5,940
David Howell	72 71 69 73			285	5,940
Zhang Lian-wei	72 71 67 75			285	5,940
Miguel Angel Jimenez	70 71 72 73			286	5,040
Jeff Remesy	68 73 74 71			286	5,040
Joakim Rask	73 70 70 73			286	5,040
Andrew Sherborne	69 68 75 74			286	5,040
Thomas Gogele	69 71 71 75			286	5,040
Massimo Florioli	70 72 71 74			287	4,340
Stephen Allan	68 71 74 74			287	4,340
Andrew Oldcorn	72 71 71 73			287	4,340
Carl Suneson	69 72 73 73			287	4,340
Stephen Leaney	68 71 73 75			287	4,340
Mark Roe	69 71 73 75			288	3,640
Paul Eales	68 74 74 72			288	3,640
Daren Lee	70 71 75 72			288	3,640
Stuart Cage	66 72 73 77			288	3,640
Klas Eriksson	73 70 68 77			288	3,640
Paul Affleck	67 76 73 73			289	3,010
Angel Cabrera	69 71 76 73			289	3,010
Jeff Hawkes	73 70 70 76			289	3,010
Rolf Muntz	65 74 72 78			289	3,010
Anders Hansen	70 71 72 77			290	2,520
Patrik Sjoland	73 68 74 75			290	2,520
Darren Cole	69 72 78 71			290	2,520
Katsuyoshi Tomori	71 71 73 76			291	2,170
Silvio Grappasonni	70 71 74 76			291	2,170
Santiago Luna	71 71 77 72			291	2,170
Jarmo Sandelin	74 68 72 79			293	1,925
Patrik Platz	70 73 73 77			293	1,925
Miles Tunnicliff	71 72 73 77			293	1,925
John Mellor	71 71 75 76			293	1,925
Gordon J. Brand	71 71 78 74			294	1,400
Paolo Quirici	71 71 78 74			294	1,400
Niclas Fasth	69 74 71 82			296	1,048
Marc Farry	70 73 76 78			297	1,046

Peugeot Open de France

National Golf Club, Paris, France
Par 36-36–72; 7,122 yards

June 26-29
purse, £600,000

	SCORES			TOTAL	MONEY
Retief Goosen	64 67 70 70			271	£100,000
Jamie Spence	68 71 67 68			274	66,660
Raymond Russell	75 68 66 66			275	28,490
Darren Clarke	70 69 67 69			275	28,490
Van Phillips	70 68 71 66			275	28,490
Martin Gates	68 67 69 71			275	28,490
Steve Webster	67 71 69 69			276	18,000
Ross McFarlane	70 70 69 68			277	13,480
Robert Coles	72 66 69 70			277	13,480
Eduardo Romero	68 70 71 68			277	13,480

	SCORES				TOTAL	MONEY
Robert Karlsson	72	67	67	72	278	10,320
Peter Lonard	68	71	72	67	278	10,320
Colin Montgomerie	66	70	73	69	278	10,320
Jarmo Sandelin	68	68	73	70	279	9,180
Des Smyth	73	70	69	68	280	8,460
Dean Robertson	71	68	72	69	280	8,460
Jose Coceres	68	68	70	74	280	8,460
Costantino Rocca	70	71	71	69	281	7,248
Jeff Remesy	70	72	68	71	281	7,248
Thomas Bjorn	70	69	71	71	281	7,248
Carl Suneson	70	68	72	71	281	7,248
Lee Westwood	67	70	73	71	281	7,248
Michael Jonzon	69	72	70	71	282	6,390
Peter Mitchell	73	70	69	70	282	6,390
Stephen Field	70	69	70	73	282	6,390
David Howell	70	68	71	73	282	6,390
Santiago Luna	68	73	72	70	283	5,580
Katsuyoshi Tomori	71	71	71	70	283	5,580
Raphael Jacquelin	73	67	72	71	283	5,580
Anders Forsbrand	68	71	73	71	283	5,580
Roger Chapman	69	69	72	73	283	5,580
Stuart Cage	68	73	70	73	284	4,320
Stephen Ames	71	70	71	72	284	4,320
Tony Johnstone	72	69	70	73	284	4,320
Derrick Cooper	71	71	69	73	284	4,320
Alex Cejka	73	69	70	72	284	4,320
Mark James	70	72	67	75	284	4,320
Steven Richardson	74	68	70	72	284	4,320
Daniel Chopra	73	70	69	72	284	4,320
Thomas Gogele	75	66	72	71	284	4,320
Paul Affleck	71	69	72	72	284	4,320
Bob May	70	69	75	70	284	4,320
Diego Borrego	69	69	71	75	284	4,320
John Wade	68	68	73	75	284	4,320
Raymond Burns	72	68	71	74	285	3,420
Sandy Lyle	68	71	70	76	285	3,420
Philip Walton	73	69	73	71	286	2,940
Paul Eales	73	69	70	74	286	2,940
Jean Van de Velde	70	73	72	71	286	2,940
Paolo Quirici	72	71	73	70	286	2,940
Paul Broadhurst	70	71	72	73	286	2,940
Jim Payne	69	71	74	72	286	2,940
Olivier Edmond	71	71	71	74	287	2,460
Marc Farry	67	68	75	77	287	2,460
Antoine Lebouc	68	73	76	71	288	2,160
Gordon Brand, Jr.	70	72	76	70	288	2,160
Gary Evans	72	71	74	71	288	2,160
Niclas Joakimides	69	72	79	69	289	1,860
Gary Orr	70	73	74	72	289	1,860
Robert Lee	71	72	72	74	289	1,860
Massimo Florioli	67	74	76	73	290	1,680
Silvio Grappasonni	71	71	73	75	290	1,680
Brian Davis	68	72	75	75	290	1,680
Richard Green	76	67	73	75	291	1,560
Mats Hallberg	71	71	75	75	292	1,500
Steven Bottomley	70	73	74	76	293	900
Ignacio Garrido	70	69	80	75	294	898
Adam Hunter	68	74	75	78	295	896

Murphy's Irish Open

Druids Glen Golf Club, Dublin, Ireland
Par 35-36–71; 6,982 yards

July 3-6
purse, £681,818

	SCORES				TOTAL	MONEY
Colin Montgomerie	68	70	69	62	269	£113,636.36
Lee Westwood	65	69	70	72	276	75,745.45
Nick Faldo	69	73	68	68	278	42,672.73
Ian Woosnam	71	70	70	69	280	31,486.37
Michael Jonzon	72	64	75	69	280	31,486.37
Jose Maria Olazabal	74	71	65	71	283	23,863.64
Daniel Chopra	71	69	71	72	283	14,003.41
David Tapping	72	68	69	74	283	14,003.41
Wayne Westner	70	70	70	73	283	14,003.41
Padraig Harrington	71	72	71	69	283	14,003.41
Paul Lawrie	72	72	72	67	283	14,003.41
Thomas Bjorn	66	70	74	73	283	14,003.41
Philip Walton	76	69	70	68	283	14,003.41
Peter Hedblom	72	73	68	70	283	14,003.41
David Carter	71	71	74	68	284	8,751.71
Ronan Rafferty	72	72	72	68	284	8,751.71
Van Phillips	72	73	71	68	284	8,751.71
Darren Clarke	72	73	71	68	284	8,751.71
Eduardo Romero	72	67	76	69	284	8,751.71
Katsuyoshi Tomori	72	69	73	70	284	8,751.71
Carl Watts	74	69	73	68	284	8,751.71
Klas Eriksson	71	71	72	70	284	8,751.71
Barry Lane	73	71	66	75	285	7,363.64
Eamonn Darcy	70	71	69	75	285	7,363.64
Rolf Muntz	70	73	71	71	285	7,363.64
John Wade	73	71	73	69	286	6,545.45
Roger Chapman	69	73	70	74	286	6,545.45
Joakim Rask	76	70	72	68	286	6,545.45
Miguel Angel Martin	74	71	73	68	286	6,545.45
Carl Mason	75	70	71	70	286	6,545.45
Daren Lee	71	73	69	74	287	5,534.09
Peter O'Malley	73	71	72	71	287	5,534.09
Gordon Brand, Jr.	73	70	70	74	287	5,534.09
Niclas Fasth	72	74	71	70	287	5,534.09
Diego Borrego	72	73	73	69	287	5,534.09
Michael Long	76	70	72	69	287	5,534.09
Phillip Price	70	73	69	76	288	4,909.09
Richard Green	72	70	75	71	288	4,909.09
Mathias Gronberg	71	71	75	71	288	4,909.09
Tony Johnstone	73	70	70	76	289	4,363.64
David Gilford	68	75	72	74	289	4,363.64
Paul McGinley	72	73	75	69	289	4,363.64
Anders Forsbrand	71	70	76	72	289	4,363.64
David Howell	71	73	73	72	289	4,363.64
Gary Murphy	74	72	72	72	290	3,613.64
Sam Torrance	71	73	70	76	290	3,613.64
Rodger Davis	68	75	74	73	290	3,613.64
Mark Roe	71	73	69	77	290	3,613.64
Steven Richardson	67	75	72	76	290	3,613.64
Miles Tunnicliff	73	67	75	75	290	3,613.64
Jose Coceres	72	72	75	72	291	2,931.82
Costantino Rocca	69	74	74	74	291	2,931.82
Robert Allenby	68	72	73	78	291	2,931.82
Alberto Binaghi	70	76	73	72	291	2,931.82

	SCORES				TOTAL	MONEY
Eoghan O'Connell	71	72	75	74	292	2,159.09
Neal Briggs	77	69	74	72	292	2,159.09
Darren Cole	72	74	75	71	292	2,159.09
Damian McGrane	73	72	76	72	292	2,159.09
Robert Lee	70	72	73	77	292	2,159.09
Wayne Riley	74	70	75	73	292	2,159.09
Jim Payne	72	73	72	75	292	2,159.09
Jonathan Lomas	72	70	76	74	292	2,159.09
Andrew Sherborne	71	73	75	73	292	2,159.09
Ross Drummond	73	71	76	73	293	1,772.73
Per Haugsrud	73	73	74	75	295	1,363.64
Ross McFarlane	67	76	77	75	295	1,363.64
Malcolm Mackenzie	73	72	78	76	299	1,020.91
Emanuele Canonica	75	70	75	80	300	1,019.09

Gulfstream Loch Lomond World Invitational

Loch Lomond Golf Club, Glasgow, Scotland
Par 36-35–71; 7,050 yards

July 9-12
purse, £800,000

	SCORES				TOTAL	MONEY
Tom Lehman	65	66	67	67	265	£133,330
Ernie Els	70	69	65	66	270	88,880
Retief Goosen	71	70	69	62	272	50,070
Greg Norman	68	68	69	68	273	36,940
Pierre Fulke	70	64	66	73	273	36,940
Payne Stewart	73	67	66	68	274	24,000
Mats Hallberg	67	71	71	65	274	24,000
Paul Broadhurst	68	70	68	68	274	24,000
Steve Jones	69	65	68	73	275	17,840
Colin Montgomerie	69	70	70	67	276	15,360
Peter O'Malley	71	68	68	69	276	15,360
Joakim Haeggman	63	72	71	71	277	13,760
Robert Allenby	68	72	70	68	278	12,293.33
Thomas Bjorn	72	67	70	69	278	12,293.33
Tom Purtzer	68	69	70	71	278	12,293.33
Jesper Parnevik	70	71	68	70	279	10,384
Mark James	72	71	65	71	279	10,384
Joakim Rask	70	70	68	71	279	10,384
Angel Cabrera	67	72	67	73	279	10,384
Glen Day	66	72	68	73	279	10,384
Nick Faldo	67	73	72	68	280	9,360
Lee Westwood	70	73	66	72	281	8,880
Larry Mize	70	69	70	72	281	8,880
Stephen McAllister	69	68	77	67	281	8,880
Patrik Sjoland	75	67	72	68	282	7,800
Costantino Rocca	70	71	66	75	282	7,800
Robert Lee	70	71	73	68	282	7,800
Darren Clarke	72	68	72	70	282	7,800
Mathias Gronberg	68	69	69	76	282	7,800
Paul Curry	63	72	70	77	282	7,800
Andrew Coltart	73	69	68	73	283	6,330
Paul Eales	68	74	71	70	283	6,330
Miguel Angel Jimenez	69	73	70	71	283	6,330
Per-Ulrik Johansson	72	71	68	72	283	6,330
Rolf Muntz	69	74	73	67	283	6,330
Derrick Cooper	71	70	69	73	283	6,330

	SCORES				TOTAL	MONEY
Raymond Russell	70	70	72	71	283	6,330
David Tapping	71	67	72	73	283	6,330
Peter Hedblom	73	70	66	75	284	5,360
Dean Robertson	71	72	67	74	284	5,360
Ian Woosnam	72	71	74	67	284	5,360
Ronan Rafferty	69	68	74	73	284	5,360
Paul McGinley	72	69	70	74	285	4,560
David Howell	67	75	72	71	285	4,560
Richard Boxall	71	72	70	72	285	4,560
Robert Karlsson	70	71	73	71	285	4,560
Peter Mitchell	69	72	70	74	285	4,560
Carl Suneson	70	70	72	73	285	4,560
Wayne Westner	72	70	70	74	286	3,440
Emanuele Canonica	72	70	71	73	286	3,440
Stephen Ames	70	72	71	73	286	3,440
Silvio Grappasonni	70	73	75	68	286	3,440
Klas Eriksson	68	75	71	72	286	3,440
Ian Garbutt	69	71	75	71	286	3,440
Robert Damron	70	69	75	72	286	3,440
Jarmo Sandelin	67	72	71	76	286	3,440
Jeff Hawkes	72	70	70	75	287	2,540
Peter Baker	70	72	76	69	287	2,540
Padraig Harrington	71	72	71	73	287	2,540
Stephen Field	68	68	73	78	287	2,540
David Carter	70	73	75	70	288	2,280
Russell Claydon	72	71	75	70	288	2,280
Mark Roe	73	70	73	73	289	2,120
Ricky Willison	73	70	72	74	289	2,120
Gary Nicklaus	70	73	75	72	290	1,600
Howard Twitty	72	68	75	75	290	1,600
Paolo Quirici	69	74	74	74	291	1,198
Gary Clark	68	74	77	73	292	1,196
Howard Clark	72	70	71	80	293	1,192
Martin Gates	69	73	77	74	293	1,192
David Gilford	71	72	79	71	293	1,192
Miles Tunnicliff	68	75	78	75	296	1,188
Jamie Spence	73	70	79	76	298	1,186

British Open Championship

Royal Troon Golf Club, Troon, Scotland
Par 36-35–71; 7,079 yards

July 17-20
purse, £1,600,000

	SCORES				TOTAL	MONEY
Justin Leonard	69	66	72	65	272	£250,000
Darren Clarke	67	66	71	71	275	150,000
Jesper Parnevik	70	66	66	73	275	150,000
Jim Furyk	67	72	70	70	279	90,000
Stephen Ames	74	69	66	71	280	62,500
Padraig Harrington	75	69	69	67	280	62,500
Fred Couples	69	68	70	74	281	40,666.67
Eduardo Romero	74	68	67	72	281	40,666.67
Peter O'Malley	73	70	70	68	281	40,666.67
Retief Goosen	75	69	70	68	282	24,300
Lee Westwood	73	70	67	72	282	24,300
Tom Watson	71	70	70	71	282	24,300
Mark Calcavecchia	74	67	72	69	282	24,300

	SCORES				TOTAL	MONEY
Robert Allenby	76	68	66	72	282	24,300
Shigeki Maruyama	74	69	70	69	282	24,300
Tom Kite	72	67	74	69	282	24,300
Davis Love III	70	71	74	67	282	24,300
Ernie Els	75	69	69	69	282	24,300
Frank Nobilo	74	72	68	68	282	24,300
Jose Maria Olazabal	75	68	73	67	283	14,500
Mark James	76	67	70	70	283	14,500
Brad Faxon	77	67	72	67	283	14,500
Stuart Appleby	72	72	68	71	283	14,500
Peter Lonard	72	70	69	73	284	10,362.50
Colin Montgomerie	76	69	69	70	284	10,362.50
Ian Woosnam	71	73	69	71	284	10,362.50
David A. Russell	75	72	68	69	284	10,362.50
Tiger Woods	72	74	64	74	284	10,362.50
Tom Lehman	74	72	72	66	284	10,362.50
Jay Haas	71	70	73	70	284	10,362.50
Phil Mickelson	76	68	69	71	284	10,362.50
Mark McNulty	78	67	72	68	285	8,750
Jonathan Lomas	72	71	69	74	286	8,283.33
David Duval	73	69	73	71	286	8,283.33
Rodger Davis	73	73	70	70	286	8,283.33
Andrew Magee	70	75	72	69	287	7,950
Greg Norman	69	73	70	75	287	7,950
Raymond Russell	72	72	74	70	288	7,550
Mark O'Meara	73	73	74	68	288	7,550
John Kernohan	76	70	74	68	288	7,550
Michael Bradley	72	73	73	70	288	7,550
Bernhard Langer	72	74	69	73	288	7,550
Vijay Singh	77	69	70	72	288	7,550
Jose Coceres	76	70	71	72	289	7,050
David Tapping	71	66	78	74	289	7,050
Curtis Strange	71	71	70	77	289	7,050
Jerry Kelly	76	68	72	73	289	7,050
Steve Jones	76	71	68	75	290	6,700
Jim Payne	74	71	74	71	290	6,700
Richard Boxall	75	71	72	72	290	6,700
Angel Cabrera	70	70	76	75	291	6,156.25
Jeff Maggert	76	69	71	75	291	6,156.25
Wayne Riley	74	71	75	71	291	6,156.25
Peter Senior	76	70	73	72	291	6,156.25
Corey Pavin	78	69	76	68	291	6,156.25
Peter Mitchell	75	69	76	71	291	6,156.25
Nick Faldo	71	73	75	72	291	6,156.25
Greg Turner	76	71	72	72	291	6,156.25
Payne Stewart	73	74	71	74	292	5,800
Jack Nicklaus	73	74	71	75	293	5,750
*Barclay Howard	70	74	76	73	293	
Tom Purtzer	72	71	73	78	294	5,625
Jamie Spence	78	69	72	75	294	5,625
Steve Stricker	72	73	74	75	294	5,625
Peter Teravainen	74	72	73	75	294	5,625
Paul McGinley	76	71	77	71	295	5,450
Per-Ulrik Johansson	72	75	73	75	295	5,450
Gary Clark	74	72	72	77	295	5,450
Tommy Tolles	77	68	75	76	296	5,350
Billy Andrade	72	72	78	76	298	5,300

Out of Final 36 Holes

	SCORES		TOTAL	MONEY
David Howell	75	73	148	1,000
Wayne Westner	75	73	148	1,000
Andrew Coltart	76	72	148	1,000
Dean Robertson	76	72	148	1,000
Seve Ballesteros	77	71	148	1,000
Paul Curry	79	69	148	1,000
Robert Karlsson	76	72	148	1,000
Gary Orr	76	72	148	1,000
Mark Wiebe	73	75	148	1,000
Michael Long	78	70	148	1,000
Steve Elkington	76	72	148	1,000
Peter Hedblom	76	72	148	1,000
Gordon Brand, Jr.	76	72	148	1,000
Carl Mason	78	70	148	1,000
Pierre Fulke	73	75	148	1,000
Brian Watts	75	74	149	800
Thomas Bjorn	76	73	149	800
Paul Broadhurst	75	74	149	800
Loren Roberts	76	73	149	800
Lee Janzen	78	71	149	800
Craig Parry	79	70	149	800
Craig Stadler	78	71	149	800
Gary Player	78	71	149	800
Robert Damron	76	73	149	800
Peter Baker	79	70	149	800
*Craig Watson	73	76	149	
Scott McCarron	73	77	150	800
Costantino Rocca	75	75	150	800
Mark Brooks	80	70	150	800
Nick Price	78	72	150	800
Glen Day	78	72	150	800
Scott Dunlap	77	73	150	800
Philip Blackmar	76	75	151	800
John Cook	76	75	151	800
Bob Tway	78	73	151	800
Van Phillips	80	71	151	800
Thomas Gogele	76	75	151	800
Ignacio Garrido	79	72	151	800
Miguel Angel Martin	79	72	151	800
Joost Steenkamer	78	73	151	800
Sam Torrance	78	74	152	700
Russell Claydon	79	73	152	700
Warren Bladon	78	74	152	700
Miguel Angel Jimenez	82	70	152	700
Kim Jong-duk	77	75	152	700
Larry Batchelor	77	75	152	700
Cameron Clark	79	73	152	700
Sandy Lyle	78	75	153	700
Jean Van de Velde	77	76	153	700
Andrew Crerar	76	77	153	700
Mike Bradley	77	76	153	700
Grant Dodd	78	75	153	700
Shaun Webster	75	78	153	
Daniel Olsson	80	73	153	
Hirofumi Miyase	79	75	154	700
Ross McFarlane	80	74	154	700
Jeff Remesy	79	75	154	700
Per Haugsrud	79	75	154	700

	SCORES				TOTAL	MONEY
Mike Miller	82	72			154	700
Mark Roe	79	76			155	700
Andrew Sandywell	80	75			155	700
Phil Hinton	78	77			155	700
Dudley Hart	78	77			155	700
Richard Green	80	75			155	700
Klas Eriksson	85	70			155	700
Paul Stankowski	80	76			156	650
Shigenori Mori	80	76			156	650
Ken Duke	80	76			156	650
Gary Murphy	84	72			156	650
Paul Azinger	79	78			157	650
*Yestyn Taylor	81	76			157	
Brendan McGovern	84	74			158	650
David Frost	81	77			158	650
Mardan Mamat	83	75			158	650
Raphael Jacquelin	81	78			159	650
*Steven Young	79	80			159	
Steven Bottomley	79	81			160	650
Alexander Cejka	81	80			161	650
Gaurav Ghei	81	81			162	650
Nobuhito Sato	85	78			163	650
Dennis Edlund	87	77			164	650
*James Miller	80	84			164	
Naomichi Ozaki	76				WD	650
Ian Baker-Finch	92				WD	650
Christopher Perry	80				WD	650
Yoshinori Kaneko	84				WD	650

Sun Microsystems Dutch Open

Hilversumsche Golf Club, Hilversum, Netherlands
Par 36-35–71; 6,636 yards

July 24-27
purse, £700,000

	SCORES				TOTAL	MONEY
Sven Struver	67	64	69	66	266	£116,660
Russell Claydon	67	68	65	69	269	77,770
Roger Chapman	65	71	68	67	271	39,410
Angel Cabrera	71	66	67	67	271	39,410
Richard Boxall	68	70	67	67	272	27,070
Jose Coceres	69	70	69	64	272	27,070
Raymond Russell	70	70	68	65	273	19,250
Mark James	69	69	70	65	273	19,250
Gordon Brand, Jr.	67	70	69	68	274	13,632.50
Wayne Westner	67	67	68	72	274	13,632.50
Michael Long	69	71	65	69	274	13,632.50
David Gilford	65	69	71	69	274	13,632.50
Sam Torrance	74	68	65	68	275	11,270
Daren Lee	67	69	68	72	276	10,290
Philip Walton	72	70	65	69	276	10,290
Alex Cejka	70	71	68	67	276	10,290
Mark Wiebe	69	69	69	70	277	8,750
Mark Mouland	70	72	68	67	277	8,750
Roger Wessels	67	69	67	74	277	8,750
Robert Karlsson	69	71	67	70	277	8,750
Miguel Angel Jimenez	67	68	71	71	277	8,750
Stuart Cage	70	70	68	70	278	7,245

	SCORES				TOTAL	MONEY
David Tapping	68	69	71	70	278	7,245
Pierre Fulke	71	68	71	68	278	7,245
Ian Garbutt	69	70	69	70	278	7,245
Robert Coles	64	70	73	71	278	7,245
Pedro Linhart	70	71	68	69	278	7,245
Gary Clark	72	70	66	70	278	7,245
Patrik Sjoland	69	72	72	65	278	7,245
Costantino Rocca	68	72	66	73	279	6,090
David A. Russell	76	67	69	67	279	6,090
Jarmo Sandelin	70	69	70	70	279	6,090
*Maarten Lafeber	72	69	67	71	279	
Andrew Sandywell	72	71	68	69	280	5,390
Daniel Chopra	71	67	65	77	280	5,390
Van Phillips	71	70	70	69	280	5,390
Mark Roe	70	71	66	73	280	5,390
Paul McGinley	67	69	72	72	280	5,390
David Carter	71	69	68	72	280	5,390
Brian Davis	70	66	74	71	281	4,760
Paul Way	70	72	72	67	281	4,760
Miles Tunnicliff	65	70	75	71	281	4,760
Tony Johnstone	69	72	71	70	282	4,480
Scott Henderson	69	73	70	71	283	4,060
Max Anglert	72	65	74	72	283	4,060
Joakim Haeggman	72	70	71	70	283	4,060
Ronan Rafferty	70	72	69	72	283	4,060
Paul Curry	71	71	71	70	283	4,060
*Maarten Van den Berg	69	74	70	70	283	
Jose Rivero	70	71	68	75	284	3,500
Rolf Muntz	69	71	73	71	284	3,500
Steve Webster	70	67	74	73	284	3,500
*Jack Boeckx	71	72	70	71	284	
Emanuele Canonica	73	68	71	73	285	2,940
Gordon Sherry	67	74	74	70	285	2,940
Klas Eriksson	67	70	69	79	285	2,940
Andrew Coltart	73	70	71	71	285	2,940
Ross Drummond	71	70	72	72	285	2,940
Howard Clark	70	71	73	72	286	2,380
Fernando Roca	69	72	72	73	286	2,380
Jeff Hawkes	71	70	70	75	286	2,380
Robert Lee	69	74	69	75	287	2,030
Marc Farry	71	71	71	74	287	2,030
Darren Cole	69	74	74	70	287	2,030
Chris Van der Velde	71	71	72	73	287	2,030
Raymond Burns	72	71	69	75	287	2,030
Thomas Gogele	70	70	79	69	288	1,785
Jamie Spence	69	68	73	78	288	1,785
Ignacio Feliu	69	72	73	76	290	1,050
Anders Hansen	68	74	72	77	291	1,046
Fredrik Andersson	68	75	74	74	291	1,046
Massimo Florioli	73	70	72	76	291	1,046
Alan Saddington	71	72	78	74	295	1,042
Ariel Canete	71	72	74	81	298	1,039
Malcolm Mackenzie	69	72	79	78	298	1,039

Volvo Scandinavian Masters

Barseback Golf & Country Club, Malmo, Sweden
Par 36-36–72; 7,301 yards

July 31-August 3
purse, £750,000

	SCORES				TOTAL	MONEY
Joakim Haeggman	67	69	65	69	270	£125,000
Ignacio Garrido	67	69	71	67	274	83,320
Mats Hallberg	72	68	67	68	275	42,220
Peter Baker	70	66	69	70	275	42,220
Mark Mouland	68	72	67	69	276	31,770
Padraig Harrington	66	71	72	68	277	24,375
Jose Rivero	66	70	70	71	277	24,375
Miles Tunnicliff	68	68	74	68	278	16,830
Colin Montgomerie	72	71	69	66	278	16,830
Roger Chapman	72	69	71	66	278	16,830
Miguel Angel Jimenez	71	71	69	68	279	12,923.33
David Gilford	70	73	66	70	279	12,923.33
Stephen Allan	72	67	66	74	279	12,923.33
Stephen Field	69	70	70	71	280	10,360
Steve Webster	70	71	70	69	280	10,360
Lee Westwood	72	69	71	68	280	10,360
Gordon J. Brand	70	73	70	67	280	10,360
Kalle Vainola	73	68	68	71	280	10,360
Daniel Chopra	71	71	72	66	280	10,360
Darren Clarke	69	71	69	72	281	8,100
Gary Evans	68	68	73	72	281	8,100
Dennis Edlund	70	70	70	71	281	8,100
Anders Gillner	72	68	73	68	281	8,100
Iain Pyman	70	70	68	73	281	8,100
David Carter	70	71	70	70	281	8,100
Greg Turner	71	70	70	70	281	8,100
Mark James	70	69	72	70	281	8,100
Van Phillips	70	67	71	73	281	8,100
Eamonn Darcy	71	71	71	69	282	6,540
Jeff Remesy	69	74	70	69	282	6,540
Adam Mednick	71	72	66	73	282	6,540
Jesper Parnevik	70	68	71	73	282	6,540
Adam Hunter	70	70	71	71	282	6,540
Paul McGinley	71	69	74	69	283	5,775
Carl Suneson	68	74	71	70	283	5,775
Raymond Russell	69	73	73	68	283	5,775
Derrick Cooper	75	66	72	70	283	5,775
Domingo Hospital	68	68	72	76	284	4,950
Robert Karlsson	68	71	71	74	284	4,950
Costantino Rocca	65	75	72	72	284	4,950
Silvio Grappasonni	68	71	73	72	284	4,950
Des Smyth	71	70	72	71	284	4,950
Jose Maria Olazabal	69	74	71	70	284	4,950
Phillip Price	72	70	71	71	284	4,950
*Henrik Stensson	69	72	73	70	284	
Steven Bottomley	68	74	72	71	285	3,675
Mark Roe	67	74	72	72	285	3,675
Alex Cejka	73	69	71	72	285	3,675
Michael Jonzon	69	67	74	75	285	3,675
Per Haugsrud	73	69	71	72	285	3,675
Marc Farry	72	69	72	72	285	3,675
Roger Wessels	72	71	71	71	285	3,675
Paolo Quirici	69	70	78	68	285	3,675
Dean Robertson	71	68	73	73	285	3,675

	SCORES				TOTAL	MONEY
Per-Ulrik Johansson	69	72	73	71	285	3,675
Paul Eales	71	70	74	71	286	2,464.29
Andrew Oldcorn	73	70	71	72	286	2,464.29
Peter Hedblom	70	72	74	70	286	2,464.29
Santiago Luna	71	72	73	70	286	2,464.29
Brian Davis	72	69	72	73	286	2,464.29
Jay Townsend	72	71	73	70	286	2,464.29
Ronan Rafferty	70	68	75	73	286	2,464.29
Neal Briggs	74	68	72	73	287	1,815
Marten Olander	70	69	77	71	287	1,815
Raymond Burns	72	70	76	69	287	1,815
Bob May	74	69	73	71	287	1,815
Alberto Binaghi	70	73	71	73	287	1,815
John Mellor	69	73	73	73	288	1,123
Sam Torrance	72	70	75	72	289	1,119
Fernando Roca	71	71	73	74	289	1,119
Ben Tinning	73	68	72	76	289	1,119
Joakim Rask	72	70	72	78	292	1,115
Klas Eriksson	74	67	76	76	293	1,113

Chemapol Trophy Czech Open

Prague Karlstein Golf Club, Prague, Czech Republic
Par 35-36–71; 6,803 yards
August 7-10
purse, £800,000

	SCORES				TOTAL	MONEY
Bernhard Langer	70	67	64	63	264	£133,330
Niclas Fasth	70	65	67	66	268	69,475
Ignacio Garrido	66	65	66	71	268	69,475
Miguel Angel Jimenez	67	64	67	71	269	40,000
Alex Cejka	71	67	67	65	270	30,990
Patrik Sjoland	70	61	70	69	270	30,990
Andrew Coltart	72	67	68	64	271	18,512
Peter Hedblom	67	71	66	67	271	18,512
Michael Long	66	71	67	67	271	18,512
Lee Westwood	67	68	68	68	271	18,512
Joakim Haeggman	69	66	67	69	271	18,512
Fredrik Jacobson	68	68	69	67	272	12,960
Scott Henderson	64	68	71	69	272	12,960
Stephen Allan	69	66	65	72	272	12,960
Jonathan Lomas	69	70	66	68	273	10,816
Raymond Russell	66	69	69	69	273	10,816
Jose Rivero	68	68	68	69	273	10,816
Clinton Whitelaw	68	66	67	72	273	10,816
David Howell	68	65	67	73	273	10,816
Darren Clarke	69	67	70	68	274	9,000
Paul Lawrie	70	64	71	69	274	9,000
Klas Eriksson	69	67	69	69	274	9,000
Peter O'Malley	66	72	67	69	274	9,000
Stephen Gallacher	68	66	70	70	274	9,000
Richard Boxall	67	68	69	70	274	9,000
Simon Hurley	65	72	70	68	275	7,560
Rodger Davis	69	68	70	68	275	7,560
Martin Gates	70	67	69	69	275	7,560
Anders Forsbrand	67	72	66	70	275	7,560
Daniel Chopra	70	63	70	72	275	7,560
Dennis Edlund	70	65	68	72	275	7,560

	SCORES				TOTAL	MONEY
Padraig Harrington	69	68	70	69	276	6,480
Stephen Field	68	66	70	72	276	6,480
Brian Davis	71	66	67	72	276	6,480
Santiago Luna	68	71	65	72	276	6,480
Stephen Scahill	72	67	68	70	277	5,680
Dean Robertson	67	69	71	70	277	5,680
Andrew Oldcorn	67	69	71	70	277	5,680
Jean Van de Velde	69	68	74	66	277	5,680
Juan Carlos Pinero	71	68	67	71	277	5,680
Gordon Brand, Jr.	69	69	67	72	277	5,680
Domingo Hospital	68	68	70	72	278	4,720
Phillip Price	68	67	71	72	278	4,720
Wayne Riley	67	70	71	70	278	4,720
Sam Torrance	71	68	70	69	278	4,720
Van Phillips	70	67	72	69	278	4,720
Massimo Florioli	67	68	70	73	278	4,720
Barry Lane	72	64	70	73	279	3,520
John Mellor	70	68	69	72	279	3,520
Olle Nordberg	69	69	69	72	279	3,520
Paul McGinley	72	67	69	71	279	3,520
Roger Chapman	69	68	72	70	279	3,520
Thomas Gogele	72	67	72	68	279	3,520
Gary Orr	73	66	73	67	279	3,520
Steven Richardson	71	66	69	73	279	3,520
Adam Hunter	71	66	69	73	279	3,520
Sven Struver	66	69	71	74	280	2,586.67
Robert Lee	73	66	70	71	280	2,586.67
Kalle Vainola	70	69	70	71	280	2,586.67
Andrew Sandywell	70	67	70	74	281	2,320
Raymond Burns	72	67	70	72	281	2,320
Philip Walton	69	70	70	72	281	2,320
Peter Mitchell	70	69	68	75	282	1,860
Greg Turner	68	71	70	73	282	1,860
Jamie Spence	68	71	74	69	282	1,860
Andrew Sherborne	70	69	67	76	282	1,860
Ross McFarlane	72	67	69	75	283	1,198
Paul Eales	69	67	73	77	286	1,196
Tony Johnstone	68	69	75	75	287	1,194

Smurfit European Open

The K Club, Dublin, Ireland
Par 36-36–72; 7,179 yards

August 21-2
purse, £850,00

	SCORES				TOTAL	MONEY
Per-Ulrik Johansson	68	64	66	69	267	£141,660
Peter Baker	70	67	68	68	273	94,440
Raymond Russell	72	69	67	66	274	47,855
Jose Maria Olazabal	69	73	67	65	274	47,855
Brian Davis	69	70	68	68	275	28,125
Costantino Rocca	67	68	67	73	275	28,125
David Carter	68	73	67	67	275	28,125
Marten Olander	69	68	71	67	275	28,125
Steven Richardson	65	72	73	66	276	18,970
Per Haugsrud	68	67	70	72	277	15,235
Eduardo Romero	70	66	70	71	277	15,235
Paul Broadhurst	70	71	69	67	277	15,235

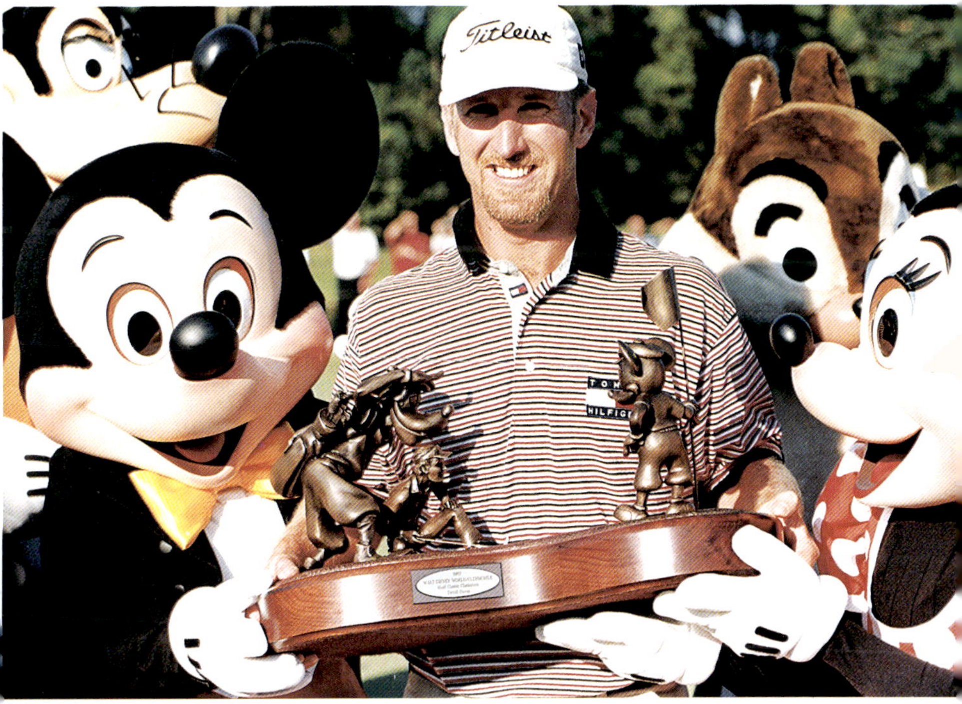

U.S. Tour

David Duval swept his last three events, including a playoff at Disney, to take second place on the PGA Tour money list.

m Furyk was fourth on the money list.

Scott Hoch won at Milwaukee.

Brad Faxon tipped his cap in winning at New Orleans.

Steve Elkington took two Florida titles.

Greg Norman posted two victories.

Phil Mickelson got Arnie's trophy.

Mark Calcavecchia won at Vancouver.

Mark O'Meara won back-to-back titles.

Jesper Parnevik earned a Ryder Cup berth for the European team.

Loren Roberts earned over $1 million.

Vijay Singh had four titles worldwide.

Steve Jones won at Phoenix, Canada.

MCI winner Nick Price had five victories.

Paul Stankowski won in Hawaii.

Stuart Appleby was Honda champion.

David Frost had a huge Colonial trophy.

Frank Nobilo won three times overall.

Bill Glasson took the Las Vegas title.

Stewart Cink was Rookie of the Year.

Robert Damron had a solid start.

European Tour

For a record fifth year, Colin Montgomerie led the PGA European Tour.

Allsport/David Cannon

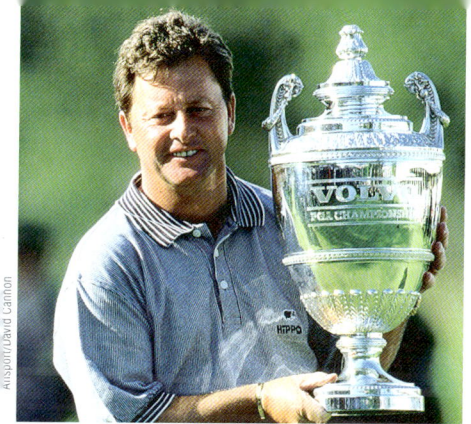

Ian Woosnam was Volvo PGA champion.

Allsport/Paul Severn

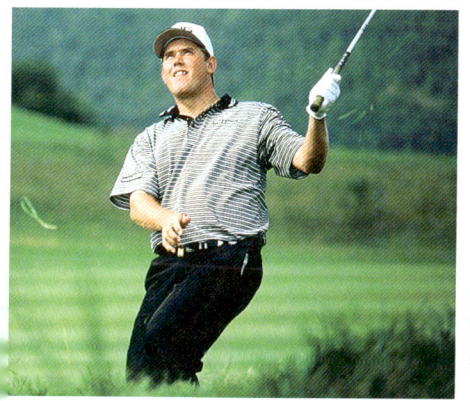

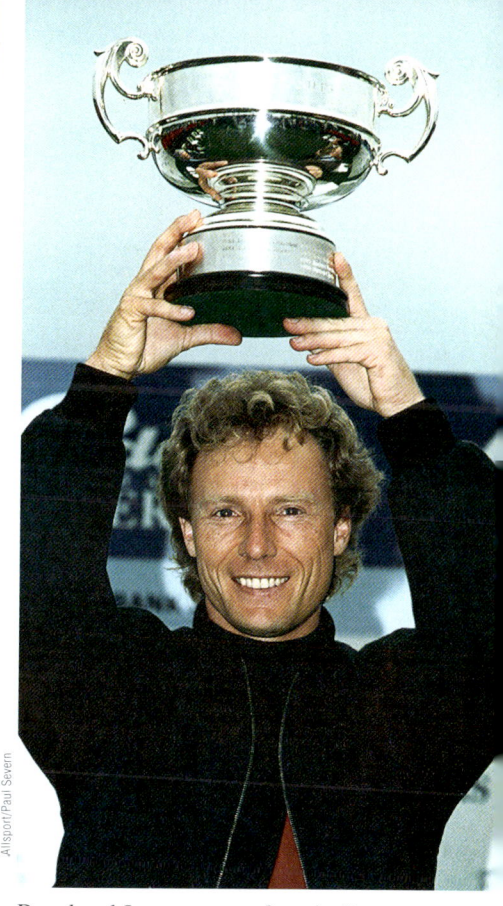

Bernhard Langer won four in Europe.

Lee Westwood took the Volvo Masters.

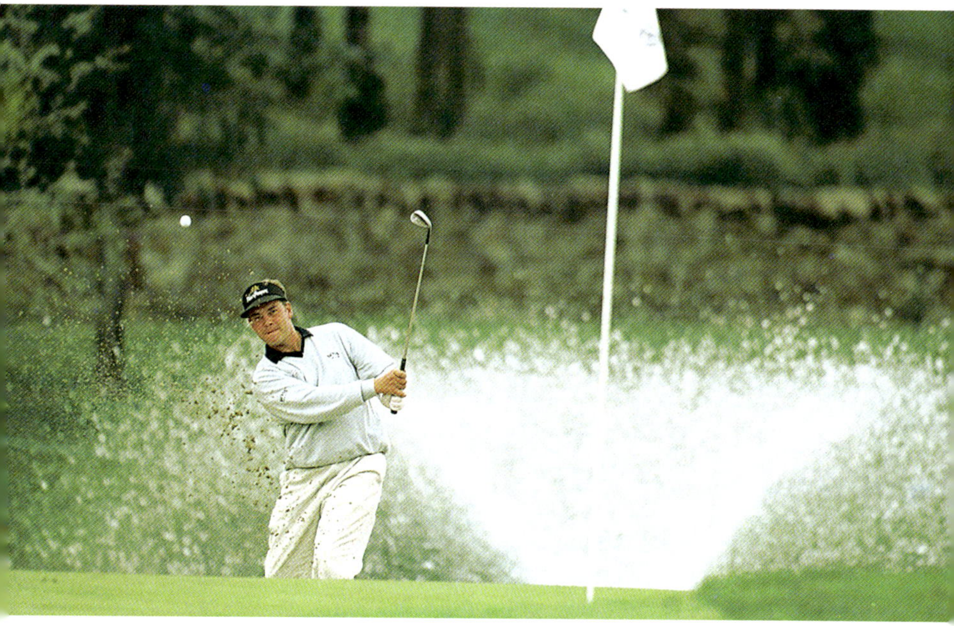

arren Clarke was among Europe's impressive young players.

Retief Goosen took seventh.

Padraig Harrington continued to impress.

Ignacio Garrido won in Germany.

Robert Karlsson took the BMW title.

Jose Maria Olazabal made a great comeback

Per-Ulrik Johansson won twice.

Costantino Rocca earned a title.

Thomas Bjorn gained the top 15.

Gabriel Hjertstedt had a U.S. win.

Mark James had a Spanish victory.

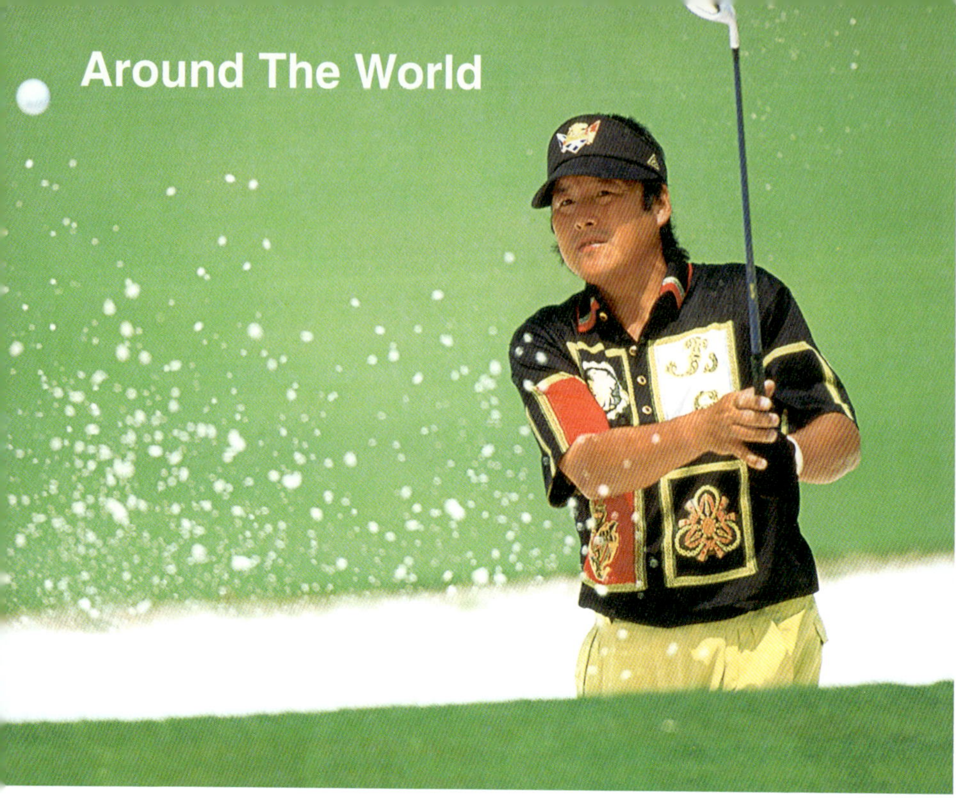

Around The World

At age 50, Masashi (Jumbo) Ozaki continued to lead in Japan with five victories.

Naomichi (Joe) Ozaki won two.

Shigeki Maruyama was a close second.

Craig Parry won in three countries.

Mark McNulty started with two wins.

Peter Lonard took the Australian Masters.

Vijay Singh won in South Africa.

Senior Tours

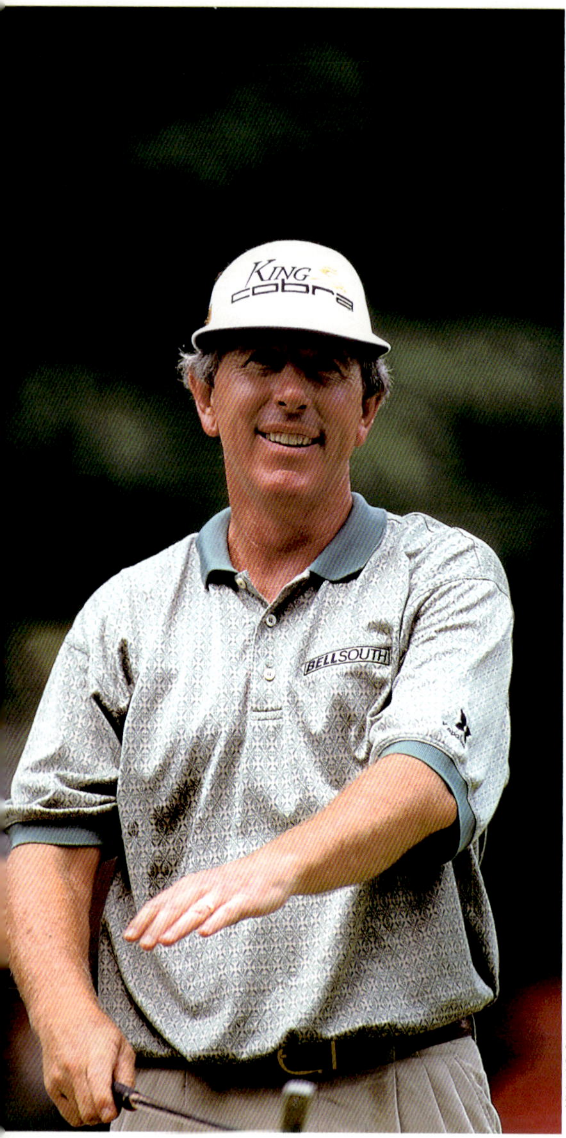

Michael C. Cohen

Hale Irwin had nine official victories.

Michael C. Cohen

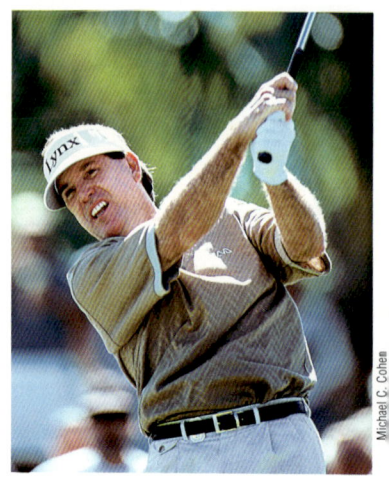

Gil Morgan won over $2 million.

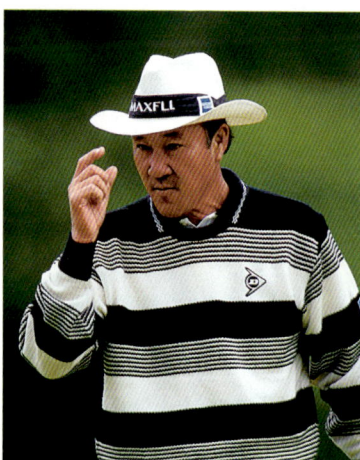

Isao Aoki took the Japan Seniors.

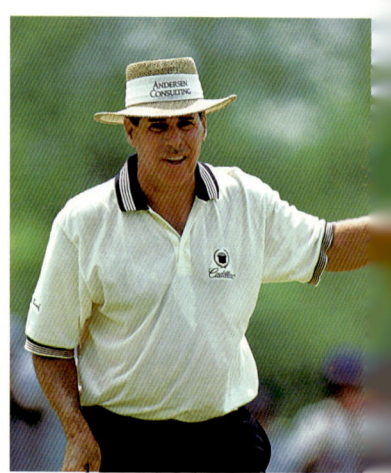

Jay Sigel had three victories.

John Bland was sixth on the money list.

Graham Marsh won the Senior Open.

Gary Player was British champion.

Tommy Horton had six European titles.

Women's Tours

Annika Sorenstam won six times and led the LPGA money list.

Karrie Webb took the British title and won twice in America.

Kelly Robbins had two victories.

Chris Johnson won the LPGA title.

Alison Nicholas claimed the U.S. Women's Open.

Betsy King celebrated her Nabisco Dinah Shore win.

Colleen Walker won the du Maurier.

Michelle McGann won twice.

Laura Davies had three victories.

Akiko Fukushima had six wins.

Gail Graham won in Australia.

	SCORES				TOTAL	MONEY
Anders Forsbrand	70	67	73	67	277	15,235
Paul Lawrie	69	71	69	69	278	11,980
Jon Robson	70	67	69	72	278	11,980
Ronan Rafferty	73	67	71	67	278	11,980
Daniel Chopra	66	69	75	68	278	11,980
Paul McGinley	69	70	68	71	278	11,980
Michael Long	71	67	74	67	279	10,228.33
Andrew Oldcorn	71	68	72	68	279	10,228.33
Santiago Luna	70	71	70	68	279	10,228.33
Niclas Fasth	65	73	69	73	280	9,180
Jonathan Lomas	67	74	66	73	280	9,180
Russell Claydon	67	70	71	72	280	9,180
Colin Montgomerie	64	69	72	75	280	9,180
Derrick Cooper	68	69	73	70	280	9,180
Patrik Sjoland	68	71	71	71	281	7,662.14
Jarmo Sandelin	70	72	70	69	281	7,662.14
Andrew Coltart	68	73	69	71	281	7,662.14
Massimo Florioli	70	68	75	68	281	7,662.14
Miguel Angel Jimenez	69	68	67	77	281	7,662.14
Ian Woosnam	71	71	70	69	281	7,662.14
Peter Mitchell	70	67	73	71	281	7,662.14
Joakim Haeggman	71	69	76	66	282	6,290
Stephen Field	69	69	74	70	282	6,290
John Mellor	70	69	71	72	282	6,290
Michael Campbell	68	72	71	71	282	6,290
Ben Tinning	70	68	72	72	282	6,290
Gary Nicklaus	72	69	71	70	282	6,290
Miles Tunnicliff	68	74	74	66	282	6,290
Klas Eriksson	70	71	72	70	283	5,185
Wayne Westner	72	70	72	69	283	5,185
Sven Struver	73	67	72	71	283	5,185
David Gilford	69	70	72	72	283	5,185
Greg Turner	69	72	71	71	283	5,185
Daren Lee	69	72	70	72	283	5,185
Peter Hedblom	70	72	69	73	284	4,420
Rodger Davis	71	71	74	68	284	4,420
Philip Walton	68	68	79	69	284	4,420
Domingo Hospital	71	70	71	73	285	3,825
Padraig Harrington	70	71	72	72	285	3,825
Paul Affleck	70	71	72	72	285	3,825
Dean Robertson	69	67	78	71	285	3,825
Jose Coceres	71	71	69	75	286	3,145
Clinton Whitelaw	69	71	76	70	286	3,145
Mark Roe	71	71	70	74	286	3,145
Ry Townsend	71	66	75	74	286	3,145
Andrew Sherborne	71	70	71	75	287	2,635
Mark James	71	70	70	76	287	2,635
Stephen Allan	70	71	72	74	287	2,635
Fredrik Jacobson	75	64	78	71	288	2,465
Paolo Quirici	75	67	75	73	290	2,337.50
Ross McFarlane	74	67	73	76	290	2,337.50
Earl Watts	70	71	73	78	292	2,167.50
Iff Hawkes	69	73	75	75	292	2,167.50
David Higgins	76	66	77	76	295	1,275

BMW International Open

Golfclub Munchen Nord-Eichenreid, Munich, Germany
Par 36-36–72; 6,923 yards

August 28-31
purse, £750,000

		SCORES			TOTAL	MONEY
Robert Karlsson	67	67	64	66	264	£125,000
Carl Watts	64	68	67	65	264	83,320
(Karlsson defeated Watts on third extra hole.)						
Colin Montgomerie	65	67	67	66	265	46,940
Fabrice Tarnaud	63	68	68	67	266	37,500
Thomas Bjorn	68	65	68	66	267	31,770
Phillip Price	65	69	68	66	268	22,500
Paul Broadhurst	68	67	67	66	268	22,500
Jose Coceres	69	66	66	67	268	22,500
Miguel Angel Jimenez	67	70	69	63	269	15,180
Padraig Harrington	66	64	71	68	269	15,180
Eduardo Romero	67	70	64	68	269	15,180
Stephen Scahill	66	71	69	64	270	10,490.50
Niclas Fasth	66	71	63	70	270	10,490.50
Mark Mouland	67	68	71	64	270	10,490.50
Bernhard Langer	68	69	68	65	270	10,490.50
Jarmo Sandelin	67	69	68	66	270	10,490.50
Marc Farry	68	69	66	67	270	10,490.50
Wayne Westner	64	70	68	68	270	10,490.50
Paul Lawrie	66	69	67	68	270	10,490.50
Ronan Rafferty	69	70	64	67	270	10,490.50
Greg Turner	68	68	72	62	270	10,490.50
Jay Townsend	66	70	66	69	271	8,212.50
Gary Orr	69	69	64	69	271	8,212.50
Domingo Hospital	71	65	64	71	271	8,212.50
Paul Curry	65	69	72	65	271	8,212.50
Mark Roe	70	68	66	68	272	7,200
Mathias Gronberg	65	69	66	72	272	7,200
Costantino Rocca	69	70	65	68	272	7,200
Stephen Ames	69	63	72	68	272	7,200
Ernie Els	67	70	70	65	272	7,200
Daniel Chopra	67	71	69	66	273	5,934.38
Patrik Sjoland	64	71	69	69	273	5,934.38
Peter Mitchell	69	68	67	69	273	5,934.38
Jose Maria Olazabal	67	72	67	67	273	5,934.38
Angel Cabrera	67	71	68	67	273	5,934.37
Per Haugsrud	68	71	66	68	273	5,934.34
Christy O'Connor, Jr.	69	69	69	66	273	5,934.37
Jon Robson	69	68	66	70	273	5,934.37
Paolo Quirici	68	66	69	71	274	4,875
Scott Henderson	69	70	69	66	274	4,875
Roger Chapman	66	70	68	70	274	4,875
Mark James	70	64	69	71	274	4,875
Ross McFarlane	71	68	65	70	274	4,875
Steve Webster	68	71	67	68	274	4,875
Iain Pyman	69	70	68	68	275	3,975
Michael Long	65	72	68	70	275	3,975
Carl Suneson	65	70	69	71	275	3,975
Peter O'Malley	69	69	70	67	275	3,975
Russell Claydon	68	69	68	70	275	3,975
Adam Hunter	70	69	69	67	275	3,975
Dennis Edlund	66	70	69	71	276	3,075
Stephen Field	68	68	70	70	276	3,075
Per-Ulrik Johansson	68	70	69	69	276	3,075

	SCORES	TOTAL	MONEY
Thomas Gogele	69 70 68 69	276	3,075
Gary Clark	68 70 65 73	276	3,075
Derrick Cooper	69 68 72 67	276	3,075
Fredrik Jacobson	66 67 73 71	277	2,300
Gordon Brand, Jr.	69 69 71 68	277	2,300
Paul McGinley	70 69 67 71	277	2,300
Raymond Russell	65 69 70 73	277	2,300
Jim Payne	72 67 67 71	277	2,300
Diego Borrego	71 67 68 71	277	2,300
Rodger Davis	70 69 70 69	278	1,743.75
Peter Baker	64 68 70 76	278	1,743.75
Andrew Coltart	67 72 72 67	278	1,743.75
Daren Lee	69 69 74 66	278	1,743.75
Peter Hedblom	64 72 74 69	279	1,121
Steven Richardson	73 66 71 69	279	1,121
Martin Gates	71 68 75 65	279	1,121
Clinton Whitelaw	70 69 71 70	280	1,115
Darren Cole	71 66 74 69	280	1,115
Katsuyoshi Tomori	68 69 69 74	280	1,115
Marten Olander	69 70 74 69	282	1,111
Jonathan Lomas	66 70 74 73	283	1,109

Canon European Masters

Crans-sur-Sierre Golf Club, Crans-sur-Sierre, Switzerland
Par 36-35–71; 6,663 yards

September 4-7
purse, £800,000

	SCORES	TOTAL	MONEY
Costantino Rocca	72 64 68 62	266	£133,330
Robert Karlsson	68 66 69 64	267	69,475
Scott Henderson	62 66 73 66	267	69,475
Patrik Sjoland	71 66 65 66	268	36,940
Peter Lonard	66 67 67 68	268	36,940
Zhang Lian-wei	67 67 67 68	269	22,460
Ronan Rafferty	65 66 69 69	269	22,460
Darren Clarke	67 66 67 69	269	22,460
Nick Faldo	66 65 68 70	269	22,460
Scott Hoch	73 66 67 65	271	15,360
Colin Montgomerie	65 72 64 70	271	15,360
Mathias Gronberg	68 71 69 64	272	11,395.56
Alex Cejka	68 70 68 66	272	11,395.56
Domingo Hospital	68 69 68 67	272	11,395.56
Ian Robson	68 69 68 67	272	11,395.56
Mathew Goggin	66 69 69 68	272	11,395.56
Stephen Scahill	71 67 66 68	272	11,395.56
Santiago Luna	69 66 68 69	272	11,395.56
Gordon Brand, Jr.	69 67 67 69	272	11,395.56
Niclas Fasth	67 67 68 70	272	11,395.56
Joakim Haeggman	66 69 70 68	273	9,000
Jeff Hawkes	69 70 65 69	273	9,000
Silvio Grappasonni	67 65 71 70	273	9,000
Phil Golding	66 68 68 71	273	9,000
Stephen Allan	71 68 70 65	274	7,680
Ignacio Garrido	71 66 72 65	274	7,680
Michael Long	66 71 68 69	274	7,680
Gordon J. Brand	71 68 66 69	274	7,680
Retief Goosen	66 68 69 71	274	7,680

	SCORES				TOTAL	MONEY
Gary Orr	61	68	72	73	274	7,680
Thomas Gogele	66	65	70	73	274	7,680
Max Anglert	67	66	73	69	275	6,160
Martin Gates	69	70	68	68	275	6,160
Steven Bottomley	71	68	68	68	275	6,160
Fredrik Jacobsen	66	69	72	68	275	6,160
Ian Garbutt	70	68	70	67	275	6,160
Richard Boxall	68	71	67	69	275	6,160
Phillip Price	67	68	70	70	275	6,160
Robert Lee	66	73	66	70	275	6,160
Jarmo Sandelin	69	68	70	69	276	5,200
Barry Lane	67	69	72	68	276	5,200
Wayne Westner	71	66	68	71	276	5,200
Jean Van de Velde	68	69	67	72	276	5,200
Michael Campbell	69	66	71	71	277	4,240
Roger Chapman	67	71	70	69	277	4,240
Daniel Chopra	72	64	72	69	277	4,240
Anders Hansen	68	71	70	68	277	4,240
Paul Affleck	70	68	72	67	277	4,240
Klas Eriksson	72	65	73	67	277	4,240
Mark Roe	68	68	69	72	277	4,240
John Bickerton	68	70	67	72	277	4,240
Alberto Binaghi	70	67	72	69	278	3,520
Eduardo Romero	70	69	68	72	279	3,280
Francisco Valera	69	67	70	73	279	3,280
Peter O'Malley	68	69	70	73	280	2,628.57
Gary Emerson	69	67	72	72	280	2,628.57
Miguel Angel Jimenez	67	72	70	71	280	2,628.57
David Higgins	70	68	71	71	280	2,628.57
Emanuele Canonica	68	69	72	71	280	2,628.57
Daren Lee	68	70	73	69	280	2,628.57
Carl Suneson	71	67	73	69	280	2,628.57
Massimo Florioli	71	68	71	71	281	2,240
Gary Evans	70	67	71	74	282	1,727.60
Ignacio Feliu	66	73	71	72	282	1,727.60
Martin Olander	69	69	74	70	282	1,727.60
Padraig Harrington	68	69	75	70	282	1,727.60
Fernando Roca	65	74	74	69	282	1,727.60
John Mellor	66	72	72	74	284	1,196
Per Haugsrud	70	69	74	72	285	1,194
Jose Maria Canizares	69	69	75	74	287	1,192
Marc Farry	69	70	75	74	288	1,190
Mark Davis	69	69	75	76	289	1,188

Trophee Lancome

Saint-Nom-La-Breteche, Paris, France
Par 36-35–71; 6,903 yards

September 11-1
purse, £700,000

	SCORES				TOTAL	MONEY
Mark O'Meara	69	67	66	69	271	£116,660
Jarmo Sandelin	70	70	65	67	272	77,770
Peter O'Malley	65	68	68	72	273	39,410
Greg Norman	67	66	68	72	273	39,410
Sven Struver	71	65	68	72	276	25,046.6
Eduardo Romero	68	68	68	72	276	25,046.6
Patrik Sjoland	75	66	69	66	276	25,046.6

	SCORES				TOTAL	MONEY
David Gilford	69	68	73	67	277	15,703.33
Paul Lawrie	68	71	70	68	277	15,703.33
Lee Westwood	68	68	74	67	277	15,703.33
Silvio Grappasonni	66	69	72	71	278	12,460
Rolf Muntz	72	70	69	67	278	12,460
Bernhard Langer	72	65	67	75	279	10,318
Retief Goosen	70	67	73	69	279	10,318
Jose Coceres	67	74	70	68	279	10,318
Paul Affleck	67	72	71	69	279	10,318
Phillip Price	69	68	71	71	279	10,318
Martin Gates	73	69	68	70	280	8,575
Per-Ulrik Johansson	71	68	69	72	280	8,575
Fabrice Tarnaud	69	70	73	68	280	8,575
Stephen Ames	69	70	71	70	280	8,575
Rodger Davis	71	71	68	71	281	7,560
Colin Montgomerie	71	72	69	69	281	7,560
Ronan Rafferty	69	73	72	67	281	7,560
Jonathan Lomas	69	70	74	68	281	7,560
Andrew Oldcorn	71	66	70	74	281	7,560
Peter Mitchell	69	69	74	70	282	6,510
Mathias Gronberg	74	67	67	74	282	6,510
Tony Johnstone	67	65	76	74	282	6,510
Miguel Angel Jimenez	70	71	70	71	282	6,510
Peter Hedblom	71	68	71	72	282	6,510
Raymond Russell	69	71	71	72	283	5,670
Iain Pyman	72	68	70	73	283	5,670
Greg Turner	69	71	72	71	283	5,670
Adam Hunter	68	69	71	75	283	5,670
Jim Payne	74	67	71	72	284	4,900
Dennis Edlund	73	70	72	69	284	4,900
Jesper Parnevik	73	69	69	73	284	4,900
Ian Woosnam	68	73	70	73	284	4,900
Joakim Haeggman	72	71	72	69	284	4,900
David Howell	66	72	72	74	284	4,900
Paolo Quirici	70	71	72	71	284	4,900
Gary Evans	69	71	74	71	285	4,130
Seve Ballesteros	65	73	74	73	285	4,130
Ian Garbutt	74	68	70	73	285	4,130
Mark Roe	71	69	73	72	285	4,130
Stephen Field	69	68	76	73	286	3,360
Diego Borrego	72	71	71	72	286	3,360
Richard Green	72	71	68	75	286	3,360
Philip Walton	70	71	75	70	286	3,360
Russell Claydon	69	70	74	73	286	3,360
Paul Broadhurst	71	71	72	72	286	3,360
Pedro Linhart	73	68	73	72	286	3,360
Eamonn Darcy	76	66	70	75	287	2,461.67
David Carter	73	70	74	70	287	2,461.67
Michael Jonzon	67	71	75	74	287	2,461.67
Sam Torrance	71	70	73	73	287	2,461.67
Robert Allenby	74	69	74	70	287	2,461.67
Mark Mouland	73	69	74	71	287	2,461.67
Barry Lane	72	69	73	74	288	2,030
Ross Drummond	73	68	73	74	288	2,030
Andrew Sherborne	71	72	78	67	288	2,030
Robert Coles	73	69	73	74	289	1,855
Daniel Chopra	68	74	73	74	289	1,855
Des Smyth	69	67	78	76	290	1,400
Peter Lonard	72	71	71	76	290	1,400

	SCORES				TOTAL	MONEY
*Sergio Garcia	71	72	73	74	290	
Jeff Remesy	73	69	79	70	291	1,045
Malcolm Mackenzie	71	71	75	74	291	1,045
Steven Bottomley	70	71	76	74	291	1,045
Wayne Riley	68	75	77	71	291	1,045
Marc Farry	76	67	73	76	292	1,038
Carl Suneson	71	66	78	77	292	1,038
Emanuele Canonica	71	70	75	76	292	1,038
Miles Tunnicliff	72	71	72	78	293	1,033
Gary Clark	71	69	77	76	293	1,033
Mark Davis	73	70	73	78	294	1,030
Paul Eales	70	69	79	77	295	1,027
Pierre Fulke	71	72	75	77	295	1,027
Gordon Brand, Jr.	72	71	80	78	301	1,024

One 2 One British Masters

Marriott Forest of Arden Hotel & Country Club, England
Par 36-36–72; 7,134 yards

September 18-21
purse, £750,000

	SCORES				TOTAL	MONEY
Greg Turner	68	71	66	70	275	£125,000
Colin Montgomerie	72	74	67	63	276	83,320
Mark Roe	65	74	70	70	279	46,940
Thomas Bjorn	69	72	66	73	280	34,635
Raymond Russell	64	75	71	70	280	34,635
Sam Torrance	69	75	66	71	281	24,375
Phillip Price	71	68	72	70	281	24,375
Robert Allenby	71	73	69	69	282	16,072.50
Angel Cabrera	71	75	67	69	282	16,072.50
Alberto Binaghi	72	74	70	66	282	16,072.50
Patrik Sjoland	68	74	71	69	282	16,072.50
Darren Clarke	71	72	70	70	283	12,146.67
Michael Jonzon	70	72	67	74	283	12,146.67
Peter O'Malley	69	69	72	73	283	12,146.67
Paolo Quirici	70	74	70	70	284	10,138
Klas Eriksson	70	73	73	68	284	10,138
Sven Struver	69	73	71	71	284	10,138
Mark James	71	71	67	75	284	10,138
Retief Goosen	72	69	73	70	284	10,138
Russell Claydon	68	76	69	72	285	8,775
Jean Louis Guepy	74	70	69	72	285	8,775
Richard Boxall	71	72	75	67	285	8,775
Dennis Edlund	69	75	70	72	286	7,650
Thomas Gogele	73	72	68	73	286	7,650
Stephen Ames	71	72	71	72	286	7,650
Peter Hedblom	67	75	75	69	286	7,650
Jay Townsend	71	71	72	72	286	7,650
Gary Orr	70	71	72	73	286	7,650
David Gilford	71	70	69	76	286	7,650
Santiago Luna	72	72	70	73	287	6,345
Jose Maria Olazabal	72	73	70	72	287	6,345
Brian Davis	69	73	72	73	287	6,345
Stephen Scahill	70	72	73	72	287	6,345
Daniel Chopra	67	75	74	71	287	6,345
Gordon Brand, Jr.	71	73	73	71	288	5,325
Gary Evans	71	73	68	76	288	5,325

	SCORES				TOTAL	MONEY
Ian Garbutt	73	72	73	70	288	5,325
Peter Baker	74	72	72	70	288	5,325
David J. Russell	72	71	70	75	288	5,325
Wayne Westner	69	74	72	73	288	5,325
Ronan Rafferty	71	71	75	71	288	5,325
Mark Davis	71	69	75	73	288	5,325
Paul Lawrie	69	76	72	72	289	4,275
Ignacio Garrido	76	70	76	67	289	4,275
Carl Mason	70	76	70	73	289	4,275
Andrew Sandywell	71	75	74	71	289	4,275
Ross Drummond	72	74	71	72	289	4,275
Emanuele Canonica	71	70	76	72	289	4,275
Jonathan Lomas	68	77	71	74	290	3,525
Peter Lonard	75	70	73	72	290	3,525
Eamonn Darcy	70	76	72	72	290	3,525
Marten Olander	68	71	78	73	290	3,525
Jean Van de Velde	73	71	72	75	291	2,775
Robert Coles	72	74	73	72	291	2,775
Costantino Rocca	75	71	73	72	291	2,775
Roger Chapman	75	68	74	74	291	2,775
Wayne Riley	70	72	78	71	291	2,775
Jarmo Sandelin	69	73	71	78	291	2,775
Diego Borrego	72	72	75	73	292	2,175
Andrew Sherborne	72	74	74	72	292	2,175
Ian Woosnam	73	73	75	71	292	2,175
Tony Johnstone	70	73	74	75	292	2,175
Richard Green	72	71	76	73	292	2,175
Andrew Coltart	71	73	75	74	293	1,518.25
Phil Golding	70	74	72	77	293	1,518.25
Jose Rivero	71	72	75	75	293	1,518.25
Darren Cole	72	70	77	74	293	1,518.25
Max Anglert	73	72	73	76	294	1,121
Peter Mitchell	75	71	74	75	295	1,119
Ben Tinning	70	75	80	73	298	1,117

Ryder Cup

Valderrama Golf Club, Sotogrande, Spain September 26-28
Par 443 543 444–35; 453 443 454–36–71; 6,734 yards

FIRST DAY
Morning Fourball

Jose Maria Olazabal and Costantino Rocca (Europe) defeated Davis Love III and Phil Mickelson (USA), 1 up

Olazabal	4		5 4 3	4		4 5 3	2		4 4
Rocca		4 2			4 4			3 3 3	
Love	3 3		5 4	4			4 C		4 4 4
Mickelson		4		3 4	4	3 4 3		3	

Fred Couples and Brad Faxon (USA) defeated Nick Faldo and Lee Westwood (Europe), 1 up

Faldo			5 4		4 4 3		4 6 3	4 4 4	4 4 4
Westwood	4 3 2		3						
Couples	4 3 3		4		4 3 4		4 5 3	3	4 4
Faxon				5 3				4 4	4

Jesper Parnevik and Per-Ulrik Johansson (Europe) defeated Tom Lehman and Jim Furyk (USA), 1 up

Parnevik	4 3		4 4 4		3 5 3			4 4 4		3								
Johansson	4			2		3 4						3 3						
Lehman	3	2	4 4			5		3 3		4 4 2			5					
Furyk	4			3	4 4			5						3 3				

Tiger Woods and Mark O'Meara (USA) defeated Colin Montgomerie and Bernhard Langer (Europe), 3 and 2

Montgomerie				5		4		5 3				
Langer	4 4 3		4 4	4 4			4		4 4 3	3		
Woods			4		4 4		3			3		
O'Meara	4 4 3		4 3		4			5 3	5 3	3		

POINTS: Europe 2, United States 2

Afternoon Foursomes

Scott Hoch and Lee Janzen (USA) defeated Costantino Rocca and Jose Maria Olazabal (Europe), 1 up

Rocca/Olazabal	4 4 3	5 5 3	3 5 5	4 6 W	5 4 3	4 4 4
Hoch/Janzen	3 3 3	6 5 4	4 4 4	4 5 C	4 4 3	5 5 3

Nick Faldo and Lee Westwood (Europe) defeated Justin Leonard and Jeff Maggert (USA), 3 and 2

Faldo/Westwood	3 5 3	4 C3	4 3 4	C4 3	4 4 3	3
Leonard/Maggert	4 4 2	5 W3	5 4 5	3 5 2	5 4 3	4

Jesper Parnevik and Ignacio Garrido (Europe) halved with Tom Lehman and Phil Mickelson (USA)

Parnevik/Garrido	4 4 4	6 4 3	5 3 4	4 5 3	4 3 3	4 5 4
Lehman/Mickelson	4 4 4	4 4 3	4 4 4	4 5 4	3 4 3	4 5 4

Bernhard Langer and Colin Montgomerie (Europe) defeated Mark O'Meara and Tiger Woods (USA), 5 and 3

Langer/Montgomerie	4 4 2	C4 3	5 3 3	4 4 3	4 4 2
O'Meara/Woods	4 5 3	4 4 3	5 4 4	4 4 3	4 5 3

POINTS: Europe 4½, United States 3½

SECOND DAY
Morning Fourball

Colin Montgomerie and Darren Clarke (Europe) defeated Fred Couples and Davis Love III (USA), 1 up

Montgomerie	4		5 3 3	4 C4	4 2		3 4 4
Clarke		4 3			4	5 3 3	
Couples	4			4 2 4	3 5 3	4	3 5
Love		4 3	4 4 3			4 3	4

Ian Woosnam and Thomas Bjorn (Europe) defeated Justin Leonard and Brad Faxon (USA), 2 and 1

Woosnam		3	3 2	4	3 4 2		
Bjorn	4 4		C	4 3	3 4	4	4 4
Leonard			3 3 2	4 3	3 3	5 4 3	4 4
Faxon	4 4 3			4	5		

Nick Faldo and Lee Westwood (Europe) defeated Tiger Woods and Mark O'Meara (USA), 2 and 1

```
Faldo          4 3     3   4 3             4 4   3 4
Westwood       4     5 3     3     3 4 3     2
Woods          4 3   3     3   4   4 4     4 4 3   4
O'Meara        4     4 3   3         3           4
```

Jose Maria Olazabal and Ignacio Garrido (Europe) halved with Phil Mickelson and Tom Lehman (USA)

```
Olazabal           3   5 3   3       4 5 3         3   4
Garrido        4   2   4     4 4             4 4 3   4
Mickelson            4 4     4       3         3   4 4
Lehman         4 3 3     3   4   4       4 3 4 4       4
```

POINTS: Europe 8, United States 4

Afternoon Foursomes

Colin Montgomerie and Bernhard Langer (Europe) defeated Lee Janzen and Jim Furyk (USA), 1 up

```
Montgomerie/Langer    4 3 3   5 4 3   5 4 3   3 4 3   5 4 3   4 5 5
Janzen/Furyk          3 4 3   6 4 3   5 4 4   3 4 3   4 4 3   5 4 5
```

Scott Hoch and Jeff Maggert (USA) defeated Nick Faldo and Lee Westwood (Europe), 2 and 1

```
Faldo/Westwood        4 3 3   5 3 3   5 4 5   4 5 4   4 4 C   4 5
Hoch/Maggert          4 4 3   6 4 2   5 4 4   3 5 3   4 4 2   4 5
```

Jesper Parnevik and Ignacio Garrido (Europe) halved with Justin Leonard and Tiger Woods (USA)

```
Parnevik/Garrido      5 4 3   5 4 3   3 4 3   C 5 3   4 4 2   5 5 4
Leonard/Woods         3 4 3   5 4 3   4 4 4   3 5 3   4 4 3   4 5 4
```

Jose Maria Olazabal and Costantino Rocca (Europe) defeated Davis Love III and Fred Couples (USA), 5 and 4

```
Olazabal/Rocca        4 4 3   4 3 3   3 4 3   4 5 3   3 3
Love/Couples          4 3 3   4 4 3   4 5 5   5 5 3   4 3
```

POINTS: Europe 10½, United States 5½

THIRD DAY
Singles

Fred Couples (USA) defeated Ian Woosnam (Europe), 8 and 7

```
Woosnam        5 4 3   4 4 3   4 5 4   4 5
Couples        4 4 3   3 3 2   4 4 3   3 4
```

Per-Ulrik Johansson (Europe) defeated Davis Love III (USA), 3 and 2

```
Johansson      4 3 3   5 3 3   6 3 5   4 4 3   4 3 3   4
Love           3 4 3   5 4 3   3 4 5   3 4 3   6 4 4   4
```

Costantino Rocca (Europe) defeated Tiger Woods (USA), 4 and 2

```
Rocca          3 4 3   5 3 3   4 4 4   4 5 3   4 4 3   4
Woods          4 4 4   5 4 3   4 4 5   4 4 3   4 4 3   5
```

Thomas Bjorn (Europe) halved with Justin Leonard (USA)

```
Bjorn          4 5 3   5 3 3   4 4 3   4 5 3   4 3 4   4 4 5
Leonard        3 4 2   4 4 3   4 5 4   5 4 4   3 5 3   5 5 4
```

Phil Mickelson (USA) defeated Darren Clarke (Europe), 2 and 1
Clarke   4 4 4   4 4 3   5 4 3   4 C 3   4 4 3   4 4
Mickelson 4 3 3   3 4 3   5 5 5   4 3 3   4 5 3   3 4

Mark O'Meara (USA) defeated Jesper Parnevik (Europe), 5 and 4
Parnevik   4 4 2   5 5 3   4 4 4   4 4 3   5 3
O'Meara   4 3 3   4 3 3   3 3 4   4 4 3   4 3

Lee Janzen (USA) defeated Jose Maria Olazabal (Europe), 1 up
Olazabal   4 4 2   5 4 3   5 4 4   3 5 3   3 4 3   5 5 4
Janzen   4 4 3   5 3 4   4 3 5   4 5 2   4 4 4   4 4 3

Bernhard Langer (Europe) defeated Brad Faxon (USA), 2 and 1
Langer   4 4 2   5 4 3   4 4 5   4 5 5   4 4 3   4 5
Faxon   4 4 3   5 4 3   5 5 4   3 5 2   5 5 3   4 5

Jeff Maggert (USA) defeated Lee Westwood (Europe), 3 and 2
Westwood   4 3 3   4 5 3   4 4 4   3 5 3   3 4 3   3
Maggert   3 3 3   4 5 2   4 4 3   4 4 3   3 4 3   3

Colin Montgomerie (Europe) halved with Scott Hoch (USA)
Montgomerie 4 4 3   5 5 4   3 4 5   4 5 3   4 4 3   4 5 4
Hoch   4 4 3   5 3 3   4 4 5   4 5 3   4 5 3   5 4 4

Jim Furyk (USA) defeated Nick Faldo (Europe), 3 and 2
Faldo   3 C 2   5 4 4   4 4 5   3 5 3   4 3 2   5
Furyk   4 4 3   5 4 3   4 3 5   3 4 3   4 3 2   4

Tom Lehman (USA) defeated Ignacio Garrido (Europe), 7 and 6
Garrido   4 4 4   5 4 3   5 3 4   4 5 4
Lehman   4 3 3   5 3 2   5 3 3   4 4 3

TOTAL POINTS: Europe 14½, United States 13½

LEGEND: C—conceded hole to opponent; W—won hole by concession without holing out; X—no total score.

Linde German Masters

Berliner Golf and Country Club, Motzener See, Berlin, Germany
Par 37-35—72; 6,848 yards

October 2-5
purse, £750,000

	SCORES				TOTAL	MONEY
Bernhard Langer	68	69	60	70	267	£125,000
Colin Montgomerie	71	68	66	68	273	83,320
Thomas Bjorn	71	68	66	69	274	46,940
Patrik Sjoland	71	68	67	70	276	31,840
Jose Maria Olazabal	69	69	66	72	276	31,840
Costantino Rocca	75	71	66	64	276	31,840
Jamie Spence	71	68	67	71	277	18,247.50
Gary Orr	69	71	69	68	277	18,247.50
Darren Clarke	73	69	65	70	277	18,247.50
Andrew Coltart	71	68	70	68	277	18,247.50
Per-Ulrik Johansson	72	67	71	68	278	13,350
Peter Baker	74	67	68	69	278	13,350
David Howell	68	72	66	73	279	11,520
Martin Gates	68	75	67	69	279	11,520
Phillip Price	75	68	68	68	279	11,520

		SCORES			TOTAL	MONEY
Max Anglert	72	69	69	71	281	9,734
Eamonn Darcy	72	68	71	70	281	9,734
Thomas Gogele	73	65	72	71	281	9,734
Phil Mickelson	73	71	69	68	281	9,734
Alberto Binaghi	70	71	71	69	281	9,734
Richard Boxall	75	70	68	69	282	8,212.50
Retief Goosen	74	72	68	68	282	8,212.50
Des Smyth	77	67	69	69	282	8,212.50
Sven Struver	74	71	67	70	282	8,212.50
Seve Ballesteros	74	70	70	68	282	8,212.50
Steve Jones	74	67	70	71	282	8,212.50
Padraig Harrington	72	70	70	71	283	7,200
Philip Walton	72	68	73	70	283	7,200
Paul McGinley	71	71	73	68	283	7,200
Paul Lawrie	76	71	66	71	284	6,431.25
Robert Karlsson	77	69	69	69	284	6,431.25
Tom Lehman	73	70	69	72	284	6,431.25
Fabrice Tarnaud	72	72	70	70	284	6,431.25
Rolf Muntz	72	69	75	69	285	5,550
Gordon Brand, Jr.	75	73	68	69	285	5,550
Andrew Sherborne	75	70	70	70	285	5,550
David Carter	73	69	70	73	285	5,550
Mark Roe	78	66	70	71	285	5,550
Paul Curry	74	73	69	69	285	5,550
Russell Claydon	74	74	66	71	285	5,550
Henrik Bjornstadt	77	71	69	69	286	4,575
Gary Evans	77	68	69	72	286	4,575
Mark Mouland	75	71	69	71	286	4,575
Adam Hunter	75	72	69	70	286	4,575
Steven Richardson	72	73	70	71	286	4,575
Mathias Gronberg	75	73	67	71	286	4,575
Derrick Cooper	74	67	72	74	287	3,900
Santiago Luna	74	72	72	69	287	3,900
Wayne Riley	75	68	69	75	287	3,900
Peter Hedblom	78	69	69	72	288	3,600
Jim Payne	76	71	73	69	289	3,075
Andrew Oldcorn	76	72	69	72	289	3,075
Peter Mitchell	77	70	68	74	289	3,075
Alex Cejka	75	72	73	69	289	3,075
Mark Davis	76	69	72	72	289	3,075
Howard Clark	77	71	73	68	289	3,075
Jeff Hawkes	78	70	73	69	290	2,381.25
Sam Torrance	71	69	73	77	290	2,381.25
Ricky Willison	76	72	72	70	290	2,381.25
Raymond Russell	74	73	72	71	290	2,381.25
Stuart Cage	73	75	72	72	292	2,025
Jose Rivero	77	71	69	75	292	2,025
Malcolm Mackenzie	73	72	76	71	292	2,025
Tony Johnstone	75	69	73	75	292	2,025
Michael Jonzon	76	71	70	75	292	2,025
Per Haugsrud	70	75	72	76	293	1,124
Paul Broadhurst	75	71	75	72	293	1,124
Paul Eales	78	70	74	73	295	1,120
Pedro Linhart	75	71	74	75	295	1,120
Wayne Westner	76	72	76	80	304	1,117

Toyota World Match Play

Wentworth Club, West Course, Surrey, England
Par 434 534 444–35; 345 434 455–37–72; 7,006 yards

October 9-12
purse, £650,000

FIRST ROUND

Ian Woosnam defeated Jesper Parvenik, 4 and 3
Parvenik	4 2 4	4 3 4	4 5 3	33	3 4 5	4 3 4	5 5 4	37	70
Woosnam	4 3 4	4 3 4	4 4 4	34	4 3 5	3 3 4	3 5 4	34	68

Woosnam leads, 1 up
Parvenik	5 3 3	3 4 5	5 4 4	36	3 4 5	4 3 4
Woosnam	4 3 5	4 4 3	4 3 4	34	3 4 4	4 3 4

Frank Nobilo defeated Phil Mickelson, 38 holes
Mickelson	4 4 4	4 3 4	4 4 5	36	3 4 5	C3 4	4 4 4	X	X
Nobilo	4 3 4	4 4 3	3 4 4	33	3 4 5	3 3 5	4 7 4	38	71

Nobilo leads, 2 up
Mickelson	4 2 3	4 3 4	5 4 6	35	3 4 4	4 3 4	4 4 5	35	70
Nobilo	4 3 4	5 3 4	4 5 4	36	3 4 C	4 3 3	4 6 4	X	X

Match all-square
Mickelson	4 3
Nobilo	4 2

Brad Faxon defeated Darren Clarke, 2 and 1
Faxon	4 3 5	4 3 4	4 4 4	35	3 4 5	4 3 3	3 5 5	35	70
Clarke	3 3 5	4 3 4	4 4 4	34	4 4 5	4 3 4	4 4 5	37	71

Faxon leads, 1 up
Faxon	4 2 4	5 3 4	4 4 5	35	3 4 5	3 3 4	4 4
Clarke	5 3 4	5 3 4	4 4 5	37	3 4 4	4 3 3	4 4

Vijay Singh defeated Tsukasa Watanabe, 4 and 3
Singh	4 4 5	4 3 4	3 4 4	35	3 4 4	4 3 4	4 4 4	34	69
Watanabe	5 3 4	4 3 5	4 5 4	37	4 4 4	4 3 4	3 5 4	35	72

Singh leads, 3 up
Singh	5 3 4	3 3 4	4 5 4	35	3 4 6	4 3 4
Watanabe	5 3 5	4 3 4	4 4 4	36	3 4 5	4 4 4

SECOND ROUND

Ernie Els defeated Ian Woosnam, 7 and 6
Els	4 2 4	3 3 4	4 4 4	32	3 4 5	5 3 4	3 4 4	35	67
Woosnam	5 2 5	5 3 5	4 3 5	37	3 4 5	4 3 4	5 4 4	36	72

Els leads, 4 up
Els	5 4 4	4 3 4	4 3 4	35	3 4 4
Woosnam	5 4 4	4 4 4	4 4 5	38	3 4 4

Nick Price defeated Frank Nobilo, 6 and 5
Price	4 4 5	3 2 4	4 3 4	33	3 4 4	5 2 4	3 6 4	35	68
Nobilo	4 3 5	4 3 4	4 4 4	35	3 3 5	4 3 5	4 5 5	37	75

Price leads, 4 up
Price	4 4 5	4 3 4	5 4 5	38	2 3 4	4
Nobilo	5 4 5	4 4 3	4 4 5	38	3 4 4	4

Brad Faxon defeated Colin Montgomerie, 2 and 1
Montgomerie	4 3 4	5 3 3	4 5 4	35	3 4 5	4 3 4	4 4 4	35	7
Faxon	4 3 4	5 3 4	4 4 5	36	3 4 5	4 2 4	4 4 4	34	7

Match all-square
Montgomerie	5 3 4	4 2 4	4 4 4	34	4 4 5	5 3 4	4 5
Faxon	4 3 4	5 3 5	4 4 4	36	3 3 4	3 3 4	4 5

Vijay Singh defeated Steve Elkington, 5 and 4
```
Elkington         4 3 5   5 3 5   5 4 5   39   3 4 5   4 3 4   4 4 5   36   75
Singh             5 3 5   3 3 4   5 4 4   36   3 4 5   4 3 3   3 5 4   34   70
Singh leads, 4 up
Elkington         4 2 4   4 3 4   4 4 4   33   2 4 5   4 3
Singh             4 3 4   3 4 3   4 4 4   33   3 3 4   4 3
```

SEMI-FINALS

Ernie Els defeated Nick Price, 37 holes
```
Els               4 4 4   4 3 3   3 3 4   32   3 4 4   5 3 4   4 4 4   35   67
Price             4 3 4   3 3 4   4 4 3   32   3 3 5   5 2 4   4 5 4   35   67
Match all-square
Els               4 3 4   5 3 4   3 3 4   33   3 4 5   4 3 5   4 5 4   37   70
Price             4 3 4   5 3 4   4 4 4   35   3 4 4   3 3 4   4 5 5   35   70
Match all-square
Els               3
Price             4
```

Vijay Singh defeated Brad Faxon, 4 and 3
```
Faxon             5 3 5   5 3 3   4 4 5   37   3 4 5   4 3 4   4 4 4   35   72
Singh             4 3 3   4 2 4   3 4 4   31   3 4 4   4 2 4   3 5 5   34   65
Singh leads, 6 up
Faxon             4 2 4   4 2 4   4 4 5   33   3 3 4   4 3 5
Singh             4 2 4   4 3 3   4 4 4   32   4 4 5   4 4 4
```

FINAL

Vijay Singh defeated Ernie Els, 1 up
```
Els               4 4 4   4 3 5   3 3 5   35   4 4 5   4 4 4   4 4 5   38   73
Singh             5 3 5   4 2 4   3 4 4   34   3 4 4   4 3 4   5 4 5   36   70
Singh leads, 3 up
Els               4 2 4   3 3 4   4 4 5   33   2 4 4   4 3 5   4 5 5   36   69
Singh             4 3 3   4 3 5   4 4 5   35   3 3 5   4 3 4   4 5 5   36   71
```

THIRD-PLACE PLAYOFF

Brad Faxon defeated Nick Price, 5 and 4
```
Price             5 3 5   5 3 3   4 4 4   36   4 4 5   4 4
Faxon             4 3 4   4 3 4   3 3 4   32   3 5 5   4 3
```

PRIZE MONEY: Singh £170,000; Els £90,000; Faxon £60,000; Price £50,000; Woosnam, Nobilo, Montgomerie, Elkington £40,000 each; Parnevik, Mickelson, Clarke, Watanabe £30,000 each.

LEGEND: C—conceded hole to opponent; W—won hole by concession without holing out; X—no total score.

Open Novotel Perrier

Golf du Medoc, Bordeaux, France
Par 35-36–71; 6,909 yards

October 9-12
purse, £350,000

	SCORES				TOTAL	MONEY (Each)
Anders Forsbrand/Michael Jonzon	65	74	64	140	343	£35,000
Santiago Luna/Jose Rivero	64	71	69	139	343	25,000
(Forsbrand/Jonzon defeated Luna/Rivero at first extra hole.)						
Mark Roe/Marc Farry	66	73	68	141	348	13,000
Seve Ballesteros/Jose Maria Olazabal	67	73	67	141	348	13,000
Peter Hedblom/Patrik Sjoland	66	70	68	144	348	13,000
Jeff Remesy/Raphael Jacquelin	64	69	66	150	349	6,500
Jim Payne/Phillip Price	68	74	70	139	351	4,916.66
Alex Cejka/Fabrice Tarnaud	69	73	69	140	351	4,916.66
Domingo Hospital/Fernando Roca	68	73	66	144	351	4,916.66
Paul Lawrie/Ross Drummond	66	74	68	144	352	4,250
Wayne Riley/Carl Mason	69	71	67	146	353	3,875
Barry Lane/Jean Van de Velde	65	74	66	148	353	3,875
Thomas Gogele/Mathias Gronberg	68	75	68	143	354	3,090
Iain Pyman/David Carter	67	75	68	144	354	3,090
Jean Louis Guepy/Michel Besanceney	64	75	70	145	354	3,090
Jamie Spence/Mark Mouland	66	78	65	145	354	3,090
Ross McFarlane/David J. Russell	66	73	68	147	354	3,090
Miles Tunnicliff/Jon Robson	65	77	67	146	355	2,700
Adam Hunter/Gary Orr	65	73	71	147	356	2,550
Paul Curry/Andrew Sherborne	65	72	69	150	356	2,550
Robert Lee/Mark Davis	65	77	73	142	357	2,300
David Howell/Stuart Cage	66	72	75	144	357	2,300
Peter Baker/Paul Broadhurst	67	76	70	144	357	2,300
Steven Richardson/Ricky Willison	68	82	71	139	360	2,050
Ignacio Garrido/Miguel Carrasco	64	74	73	149	360	2,050
Wayne Westner/Malcolm Mackenzie	68	75	70	148	361	1,850
Richard Boxall/Derrick Cooper	70	73	68	150	361	1,850
Mike Harwood/Steve Alker	68	78	67	151	364	1,700
Carl Suneson/Pedro Linhart	64	80	72	150	366	1,600
Jonathan Lomas/Steven Bottomley	69	73	73	152	367	1,500

Alfred Dunhill Cup

Old Course, St. Andrews, Scotland
Par 36-36–72; 7,094 yards

October 16-19
purse, £1,000,000

FIRST ROUND

ENGLAND DEFEATED JAPAN, 3-0
Russell Claydon (E) defeated Tsukasa Watanabe, 70-71; Lee Westwood (E) defeated Nabuhito Sato, 70-73; Mark James (E) defeated Shigemasa Higaki, 73-74.

UNITED STATES DEFEATED ARGENTINA, 2-1
Mark O'Meara (US) defeated Eduardo Romero, 67-67, first extra hole; Angel Cabrera (Arg) defeated Brad Faxon, 68-72; Justin Leonard (US) defeated Jose Coceres, 65-72.

SOUTH AFRICA DEFEATED IRELAND, 2-1
Retief Goosen (SA) defeated Paul McGinley, 70-71; Padraig Harrington (I) defeated David Frost, 67-69; Ernie Els (SA) defeated Darren Clarke, 66-71.

SCOTLAND DEFEATED GERMANY, 2-1
Raymond Russell (Sco) defeated Thomas Gogele, 68-74; Alex Cejka (G) defeated Gordon Brand, Jr., 66-69; Colin Montgomerie (Sco) defeated Sven Struver, 67-73.

SWEDEN DEFEATED CHINESE TAIPEI, 3-0
Joakim Haeggman (Swe) defeated Hsieh Yu-shu, 72-72, first extra hole; Jesper Parnevik (Swe) defeated Lu Hsi-chuen, 65-75; Per-Ulrik Johansson (Swe) defeated Chen Liang-hsi, 71-74.

FRANCE DEFEATED AUSTRALIA, 2-1
Fabrice Tarnaud (F) defeated Robert Allenby, 70-71; Jean Van de Velde (F) defeated Steve Elkington, 71-71, first extra hole; Stuart Appleby (Aus) defeated Marc Farry, 68-71.

ZIMBABWE DEFEATED KOREA, 2-1
Nick Price (Z) defeated Kim Jong-duk, 72-74; Mark McNulty (Z) defeated Mo Joong-kyung, 69-76; Kang Wook-soon (K) defeated Tony Johnstone, 73-73, first extra hole.

NEW ZEALAND DEFEATED SPAIN, 2-1
Steve Alker (NZ) defeated Miguel Angel Martin, 70-73; Frank Nobilo (NZ) defeated Ignacio Garrido, 70-75; Miguel Angel Jimenez (Sp) defeated Michael Long, 71-72.

SECOND ROUND

NEW ZEALAND DEFEATED KOREA, 3-0
Steve Alker (NZ) defeated Mo Joong-kyung, 76-83; Michael Long (NZ) defeated Kim Jong-duk, 75-76; Frank Nobilo (NZ) defeated Kang Wook-soon, 68-70.

ZIMBABWE DEFEATED SPAIN, 2-1
Tony Johnstone (Z) defeated Miguel Angel Martin, 70-74; Mark McNulty (Z) defeated Ignacio Garrido, 70-74; Nick Price conceded match to Miguel Angel Jimenez (Sp) due to injury.

SWEDEN DEFEATED FRANCE, 3-0
Joakim Haeggman (Swe) defeated Fabrice Tarnaud, 70-78; Jesper Parnevik (Swe) defeated Marc Farry, 73-74; Per-Ulrik Johansson (Swe) defeated Jean Van de Velde, 72-73.

AUSTRALIA DEFEATED CHINESE TAIPEI, 2-1
Hsieh Yu-sShu (CT) defeated Robert Allenby, 73-74; Steve Elkington (Aus) defeated Chen Liang-hsi, 76-76, second extra hole; Stuart Appleby (Aus) defeated Lu Hsi-chuen, 77-80.

SCOTLAND DEFEATED IRELAND, 2-1
Paul McGinley (I) defeated Raymond Russell, 69-74; Gordon Brand, Jr. (Sco) defeated Darren Clarke, 73-77; Colin Montgomerie (Sco) defeated Padraig Harrington, 72-76.

SOUTH AFRICA DEFEATED GERMANY, 3-0
Retief Goosen (SA) defeated Thomas Gogele, 73-73, second extra hole; David Frost (SA) defeated Alex Cejka, 74-79; Ernie Els (SA) defeated Sven Struver, 71-72.

UNITED STATES DEFEATED JAPAN, 3-0
Mark O'Meara (US) defeated Tsukasa Watanabe, 70-72; Justin Leonard (US) defeated Nobuhito Sato, 74-82; Brad Faxon (US) defeated Shigemasa Higaki, 73-79.

ARGENTINA DEFEATED ENGLAND, 2-1
Jose Coceres (Arg) defeated Russell Claydon, 71-74; Mark James (E) defeated Eduardo Romero, 71-72; Angel Cabrera (Arg) defeated Lee Westwood, 71-72.

THIRD ROUND

IRELAND DEFEATED GERMANY, 2-1
Darren Clarke (I) defeated Alex Cejka, 68-74; Padraig Harrington (I) defeated Sven Struver, 66-69; Thomas Gogele (G) defeated Paul McGinley, 67-71.

SOUTH AFRICA DEFEATED SCOTLAND, 2-0
David Frost (SA) defeated Raymond Russell, 68-71; Retief Goosen (SA) defeated Gordon Brand, Jr., 67-67, first extra hole; Ernie Els (SA) tied with Colin Montgomerie, 68-68.

UNITED STATES DEFEATED ENGLAND, 3-0
Mark O'Meara (US) defeated Lee Westwood, 67-69; Brad Faxon (US) defeated Russell Claydon, 70-73; Justin Leonard (US) defeated Mark James, 69-72.

ARGENTINA DEFEATED JAPAN, 2-0
Eduardo Romero (Arg) defeated Shigemasa Higaki, 72-73; Angel Cabrera (Arg) defeated Tsukasa Watanabe, 69-73; Jose Coceres (Arg) tied with Nobuhito Sato, 70-70.

SPAIN DEFEATED KOREA, 2-1
Kim Jong-duk (K) defeated Miguel Angel Martin, 70-78; Miguel Angel Jimenez (Sp) defeated Kang Wook-soon, 74-74, second extra hole; Ignacio Garrido (Sp) defeated Mo Joong-kyung, 70-76.

NEW ZEALAND DEFEATED ZIMBABWE, 3-0
Nick Price conceded match to Frank Nobilo (NZ) due to injury; Steve Alker (NZ) defeated Tony Johnstone, 70-75; Michael Long (NZ) defeated Mark McNulty, 67-68.

SWEDEN DEFEATED AUSTRALIA, 2-1
Per-Ulrik Johansson (Swe) defeated Steve Elkington, 72-72, second extra hole; Joakim Haeggman (Swe) defeated Stuart Appleby, 66-69; Robert Allenby (Aus) defeated Jesper Parvenik, 68-70.

FRANCE DEFEATED CHINESE TAIPEI, 3-0
Marc Farry (F) defeated Chen Liang-hsi, 70-73; Fabrice Tarnaud (F) defeated Lu Hsi-chuen, 71-75; Jean Van de Velde (F) defeated Hsieh Yu-shu, 67-76.

SEMI-FINALS

SWEDEN DEFEATED UNITED STATES, 2-1
Mark O'Meara (US) defeated Jesper Parnevik, 68-69; Joakim Haeggman (Swe) defeated Justin Leonard, 68-72; Per-Ulrik Johansson (Swe) defeated Brad Faxon, 71-74.

SOUTH AFRICA DEFEATED NEW ZEALAND, 2-1
Retief Goosen (SA) defeated Michael Long, 67-72; David Frost (SA) defeated Steve Alker, 72-76; Frank Nobilo (NZ) defeated Ernie Els, 66-70.

FINAL

SOUTH AFRICA DEFEATED SWEDEN, 2-1
Retief Goosen (SA) defeated Jesper Parnevik, 70-74; Per-Ulrik Johansson (Swe) defeated David Frost, 71-74; Ernie Els (SA) defeated Joakim Haeggman, 69-72.

	MATCHES WON	INDIVIDUAL GAMES WON (After Round 3)	PRIZE MONEY TEAM	PLAYER
GROUP 1				
United States	3	8	£95,000	£31,666
Argentina	2	5	45,000	15,000
England	1	4	25,500	8,500
Japan	0	0	19,500	6,500
GROUP 2				
Sweden	3	8	150,000	50,000
France	2	5	45,000	15,000
Australia	1	4	25,500	8,500
Chinese Taipei	0	1	19,500	6,500
GROUP 3				
South Africa	3	7	300,000	100,000
Scotland	2	4	45,000	15,000
Ireland	1	4	25,500	8,500
Germany	0	2	19,500	6,500
GROUP 4				
New Zealand	3	8	95,000	31,666
Zimbabwe	2	4	45,000	15,000
Spain	1	4	25,500	8,500
Korea	1	2	19,500	6,500

Oki Pro-Am

Golf La Moraleja I & II, Madrid, Spain
Par 36-36—72; 7,054 yards

October 23-26
purse, £450,000

	SCORES				TOTAL	MONEY
Paul McGinley	66	67	64	69	266	£75,000
Iain Pyman	68	69	69	64	270	50,000
Greg Turner	69	68	67	69	273	28,170
Raymond Russell	66	69	68	71	274	22,500
Howard Clark	70	67	72	66	275	16,103.33
Jose Rivero	65	73	68	69	275	16,103.33
Jonathan Lomas	67	69	69	70	275	16,103.33
Malcolm Mackenzie	70	69	68	69	276	11,250
Peter Baker	69	72	68	68	277	9,110
Miguel Angel Jimenez	67	68	72	70	277	9,110
Stephen Ames	71	67	69	70	277	9,110
Jarmo Sandelin	74	67	70	67	278	6,812.50
Paul Eales	71	69	70	68	278	6,812.50
Angel Cabrera	70	70	69	69	278	6,812.50
Gary Evans	70	67	71	70	278	6,812.50
Jamie Spence	66	72	70	70	278	6,812.50
Juan Carlos Pinero	67	70	68	73	278	6,812.50
Andrew Coltart	74	69	70	66	279	5,220
Pedro Linhart	67	68	74	70	279	5,220
Anders Forsbrand	71	69	69	70	279	5,220
Wayne Riley	71	66	71	71	279	5,220
Padraig Harrington	72	66	69	72	279	5,220
Patrik Sjoland	69	69	69	72	279	5,220
Fernando Roca	65	70	71	73	279	5,220
Richard Boxall	64	72	70	73	279	5,220
Mark Mouland	65	73	74	68	280	4,387.50

	SCORES				TOTAL	MONEY
Paul Curry	71	69	69	71	280	4,387.50
Gary Clark	67	73	69	71	280	4,387.50
Santiago Luna	70	69	68	73	280	4,387.50
Seve Ballesteros	72	70	68	71	281	3,757.50
Jose Sota	69	70	71	71	281	3,757.50
Paul Affleck	69	72	72	68	281	3,757.50
Ignacio Garrido	71	67	70	73	281	3,757.50
Sven Struver	66	73	68	74	281	3,757.50
David Howell	71	71	65	74	281	3,757.50
Dean Robertson	69	70	72	71	282	3,150
Miles Tunnicliff	73	67	72	70	282	3,150
Stuart Cage	70	68	74	70	282	3,150
Alberto Binaghi	67	74	72	69	282	3,150
Peter Mitchell	72	68	70	72	282	3,150
Jim Payne	72	68	70	72	282	3,150
Paul Lawrie	71	66	69	76	282	3,150
Des Smyth	69	67	74	73	283	2,475
Domingo Hospital	67	73	71	72	283	2,475
Massimo Florioli	68	74	70	71	283	2,475
Manuel Pinero	68	72	73	70	283	2,475
Jon Robson	71	72	71	69	283	2,475
Fabrice Tarnaud	69	71	75	68	283	2,475
Miguel Angel Martin	72	69	68	74	283	2,475
Michael Campbell	67	66	75	75	283	2,475
Carl Suneson	68	71	73	72	284	2,025
Gary Orr	72	67	69	76	284	2,025
Jose Coceres	69	70	71	75	285	1,755
David Carter	66	76	70	73	285	1,755
Mark James	71	71	71	72	285	1,755
Ross Drummond	71	68	75	71	285	1,755
Gary Emerson	69	71	71	75	286	1,356.43
Robert Karlsson	70	73	69	74	286	1,356.43
Eduardo Romero	74	68	70	74	286	1,356.43
Thomas Gogele	73	67	74	72	286	1,356.43
David Gilford	69	71	75	71	286	1,356.43
Derrick Cooper	69	71	75	71	286	1,356.43
Diego Borrego	71	71	73	71	286	1,356.43
Jose Maria Canizares	71	69	71	76	287	1,170
Mathias Gronberg	70	73	76	69	288	1,125
Adam Hunter	70	70	76	73	289	675
Jose Rozadilla	75	65	78	74	292	673
Pello Iguaran	72	71	78	76	297	671

Volvo Masters

Montecastillo Hotel & Golf Resort, Jerez, Spain
Par 36-36–72; 7,025 yards
(Fourth round cancelled — thunderstorms.)

October 30-November 2
purse, £1,000,000

	SCORES			TOTAL	MONEY
Lee Westwood	65	67	68	200	£166,000
Padraig Harrington	66	70	67	203	110,000
Jose Maria Olazabal	66	67	71	204	63,000
Robert Karlsson	68	67	70	205	50,600
Peter O'Malley	68	69	69	206	35,966.67
Patrik Sjoland	64	68	74	206	35,966.67
Mark McNulty	64	69	73	206	35,966.67

	SCORES			TOTAL	MONEY
Colin Montgomerie	65	71	71	207	25,000
Eduardo Romero	71	69	68	208	19,833.33
Ian Woosnam	67	69	72	208	19,833.33
Costantino Rocca	69	65	74	208	19,833.33
Michael Long	65	69	75	209	15,866.67
Stephen Ames	67	69	73	209	15,866.67
Jose Coceres	68	69	72	209	15,866.67
Paul Broadhurst	70	66	74	210	13,700
Bernhard Langer	66	70	74	210	13,700
Thomas Bjorn	70	66	74	210	13,700
Darren Clarke	69	64	77	210	13,700
Per-Ulrik Johansson	63	71	76	210	13,700
David Carter	69	68	73	210	13,700
David Howell	70	68	73	211	11,900
Ignacio Garrido	70	66	75	211	11,900
Paul Lawrie	70	65	76	211	11,900
Miguel Angel Jimenez	71	74	67	212	10,500
Phillip Price	69	71	72	212	10,500
Robert Allenby	71	68	73	212	10,500
Brian Davis	70	71	71	212	10,500
Andrew Coltart	68	70	74	212	10,500
Angel Cabrera	72	72	69	213	9,300
Jarmo Sandelin	71	70	72	213	9,300
Seve Ballesteros	72	71	70	213	9,300
Mark Roe	70	73	71	214	7,350
Peter Baker	71	69	74	214	7,350
Anders Forsbrand	70	69	75	214	7,350
Zhang Lian-wei	69	69	76	214	7,350
Peter Mitchell	70	66	78	214	7,350
Joakim Haeggman	72	68	74	214	7,350
Niclas Fasth	71	68	75	214	7,350
Mark James	68	69	77	214	7,350
Sven Struver	72	75	67	214	7,350
Daniel Chopra	71	73	70	214	7,350
David Gilford	68	73	74	215	5,600
Retief Goosen	75	66	74	215	5,600
Greg Turner	72	69	74	215	5,600
Sam Torrance	75	68	73	216	5,200
Dennis Edlund	75	68	74	217	4,442.86
Carl Watts	70	70	77	217	4,442.86
Ronan Rafferty	68	71	78	217	4,442.86
Richard Green	69	73	75	217	4,442.86
Thomas Gogele	65	74	78	217	4,442.86
Paul McGinley	74	67	76	217	4,442.86
Miguel Angel Martin	72	72	73	217	4,442.86
Roger Chapman	68	76	74	218	3,750
Tony Johnstone	71	74	73	218	3,750
Gordon Brand, Jr.	72	72	74	218	3,750
Russell Claydon	74	73	71	218	3,750
Scott Henderson	73	70	76	219	3,400
Wayne Westner	73	71	75	219	3,400
Peter Lonard	72	72	75	219	3,400
Alex Cejka	72	76	72	220	3,200
Clinton Whitelaw	76	72	74	222	3,050
Raymond Russell	71	75	76	222	3,050
Ross McFarlane	72	73	78	223	2,900
Cheng Jun	72	77	77	226	2,800
Michael Jonzon	74	77	76	227	2,650
Mike Harwood	76	73	78	227	2,650

Challenge Tour

Open de Cote D'Ivoire

President Golf Club, Yamoussoukro, Ivory Coast
Par 36-36–72; 6,578 yards

March 5-8
purse, £70,000

	SCORES				TOTAL	MONEY
Knud Storegaard	70	69	68	67	274	£11,370.45
Anssi Kankkonen	71	67	68	68	274	7,575.75
(Storegaard defeated Kankkonen on first extra hole.)						
Francisco Cea	68	65	70	72	275	3,842.48
Markus Brier	69	69	69	68	275	3,842.48
Jose Cantero	74	67	66	70	277	2,463.83
Nicolas Joakimides	69	70	70	68	277	2,463.83
Olivier Edmond	66	68	76	67	277	2,463.83
Jorge Berendt	67	72	71	67	277	2,463.83
David R. Jones	72	70	66	69	277	2,463.83
Emos Korblah	69	70	71	69	279	1,835.93
Chris Williams	70	67	70	72	279	1,835.93
Per Jacobson	72	70	71	67	280	1,332.24
Rob Edwards	72	66	71	71	280	1,332.24
Paul Nilbrink	73	64	74	69	280	1,332.24
Mikko Rantanen	72	68	67	73	280	1,332.24
Peter N'Juru	71	72	66	71	280	1,332.24
Antonio Sobrinho	74	69	73	65	281	854.49
Ricardo Gonzalez	70	70	70	71	281	854.49
Francisco Javier Amatriai	71	69	72	69	281	854.49
Michele Reale	71	70	70	70	281	854.49
Kevin Carissimi	72	71	73	65	281	854.49
Roger Winchester	71	69	73	69	282	743.93
Jesper Kjaerbye	74	69	71	69	283	680.80
Pauli Hughes	72	70	69	72	283	680.80
Scott Watson	69	72	69	73	283	680.80
Buray Kargbo	68	70	71	74	283	680.80
Lee James	69	75	68	72	284	617.67
Paul Lyons	72	71	71	70	284	617.67
Matthew Hazelden	68	71	75	72	286	561.36
Erol Simsek	73	67	72	74	286	561.36
Matthias Debove	74	70	69	73	286	561.36
Martyn Thompson	74	70	70	72	286	561.36

Lonrho Kenya Open

Muthaiga Golf Club, Nairobi, Kenya
Par 35-36–71; 6,729 yards

March 13-16
purse, £65,000

	SCORES				TOTAL	MONEY
Jorge Berendt	70	68	64	66	268	£10,558.28
Sammy Daniels	66	70	68	68	272	7,034.62
Thomas Nielsen	68	73	64	68	273	3,568.02
Michele Reale	69	66	67	71	273	3,568.02

	SCORES				TOTAL	MONEY
Simon Burnell	67	66	72	70	275	2,687.10
Mike Miller	67	67	74	68	276	2,275.17
Michael Scholz	68	66	74	68	276	2,275.17
Mikael Krantz	73	69	66	68	276	2,275.17
Chris Williams	73	67	69	68	277	1,707.96
Eric Carlberg	69	70	70	68	277	1,707.96
Philip Harrison	65	71	72	69	277	1,707.96
Hayo Bensdorp	69	67	67	74	277	1,707.96
Rob Edwards	71	69	69	69	278	1,299.19
David Lynn	72	70	67	69	278	1,299.19
Jose Cantero	66	70	75	68	279	952.21
Chris Van Der Velde	67	71	72	69	279	952.21
Francisco Cea	69	72	69	69	279	952.21
Stewart Cronin	69	69	67	74	279	952.21
David R. Jones	73	67	71	69	280	749.94
Anssi Kankkonen	74	66	71	69	280	749.94
William Guy	71	71	65	73	280	749.94
Francisco Javier Amatriai	72	70	70	69	281	665.44
Kevin Carissimi	68	72	69	72	281	665.44
Tjaart van der Walt	68	69	68	76	281	665.44
Andrew Clapp	70	71	73	68	282	583.05
Malcolm Gregson	71	72	69	70	282	583.05
Anders Haglund	70	70	71	71	282	583.05
Andrew Collison	69	73	69	71	282	583.05
Carlos Duran	73	68	68	73	282	583.05
Emil Madsen	74	69	72	68	283	519.69
Mikko Rantanen	68	73	70	72	283	519.69

Is Molas Challenge

Is Molas Golf Club, Sardinia, Italy
Par 36-36–72; 6,980 yards

April 10-13
purse, £35,000

	SCORES			TOTAL	MONEY
Andrew Collison	71	71	71	68	281	£5,685.23
Thomas Nielsen	73	71	71	71	286	3,787.88
Mark Litton	71	70	75	73	289	1,921.24
Mikael Piltz	70	77	70	72	289	1,921.24
Johan Axgren	73	75	71	71	290	1,280.54
Thomas Levet	73	76	70	71	290	1,280.54
Heinz P. Thul	76	67	72	75	290	1,280.54
Chris Van Der Velde	79	69	68	74	290	1,280.54
Henrik Nystrom	69	72	82	68	291	957.78
Luca Bernardini	75	70	77	69	291	957.78
Nicolas Joakimides	70	77	71	73	291	957.78
Francis Howley	71	74	78	69	292	805.35
Greg Owen	71	75	77	70	293	575.01
Kevin Carissimi	70	76	76	71	293	575.01
Frederic Cupillard	78	71	73	71	293	575.01
Michele Reale	74	73	73	73	293	575.01
Oyvind Rojahn	72	71	74	76	293	575.01
Giuseppe Cali	72	72	73	76	293	575.01
Soren Kjeldsen	74	73	81	66	294	381.06
Bradley Dredge	76	73	76	69	294	381.06
Tony Edlund	74	72	77	71	294	381.06
Ruben Wechgelaer	74	74	74	72	294	381.06
Matthew Hazelden	75	74	73	72	294	381.06

494 / EUROPEAN TOURS

	SCORES	TOTAL	MONEY
Andrea Canessa	71 74 74 75	294	381.06
Marcello Santi	77 69 76 73	295	319.07
Stewart Cronin	73 75 74 73	295	319.07
Simon Burnell	74 74 73 74	295	319.07
Rob Edwards	72 73 73 77	295	319.07
Markus Brier	73 76 77 70	296	273.57
Morten Backhausen	75 74 75 72	296	273.57
Carlos Duran	75 74 73 74	296	273.57
Steve Rey	73 75 73 75	296	273.57
David Tapping	73 75 73 75	296	273.57
Rorbak Petersen	72 72 77 75	296	273.57

Campeonato de Espana de Pro

RCG de Sevilla, Seville, Spain
Par 36-36–72; 6,913 yards

April 10-13
purse, £56,281

	SCORES	TOTAL	MONEY
Ignacio Garrido	69 69 70 72	280	£8,121.75
Francisco Cea	74 68 68 70	280	5,411.25
(Garrido defeated Cea on first extra hole.)			
Jose Carriles	73 71 68 69	281	3,051.75
Juan Pinero	70 72 73 70	285	2,133.63
Juan Quiros	70 71 74 70	285	2,133.63
Santiago Luna	72 72 72 69	285	2,133.63
Andres Jimenez	71 70 76 70	287	1,745.25
Jose Rozadilla	74 74 70 70	288	1,485.25
Bernardo Solanes	74 74 70 70	288	1,485.25
Diego Borrego	71 71 72 74	288	1,485.25
Yago Beamonte	70 78 69 73	290	1,101.75
Inigo Moral	72 78 72 68	290	1,101.75
Rafael Benitez	72 74 67 77	290	1,101.75
Francisco Javier Amatriai	72 74 74 70	290	1,101.75
Ivo Giner	71 68 74 78	291	763.75
Antonio Garrido	72 74 74 71	291	763.75
Jesus Maria Arruti	77 71 69 74	291	763.75
Luis Navarro	76 73 75 68	292	606.13
Ricardo Jimenez	73 73 73 73	292	606.13
Jose Garcia	72 73 74 73	292	606.13
Jose Rodriguez	79 71 73 70	293	550.88
Ander Martinez	71 73 77 73	294	511.88
Alfonso Pinero	74 73 73 74	294	511.88
Jose Sota	70 70 78 76	294	511.88
Manuel Montes	74 75 76 70	295	470.44
Manuel Pinero	72 72 76 75	295	470.44
Carlos Balmaseda	75 74 75 72	296	433.88
Juan Anglada	70 76 76 74	296	433.88
Diego Morito	75 75 74 72	296	433.88
Juan Sanchez	73 74 75 75	297	370.51
Emilio Rodriguez	75 72 77 73	297	370.51
Jose Carro	74 75 76 72	297	370.51
Pedro Portell	73 74 75 75	297	370.51
Alvaro Prat	79 70 77 71	297	370.51
Fernando Roca	73 76 72 76	297	370.51
Felix Ortiz	75 73 73 76	297	370.51
Pello Iguaran	74 75 74 74	297	370.51

Le Pavoniere Superal Challenge

Le Pavoniere Golf Club, Florence, Italy
Par 36-36–72; 7,072 yards

April 16-19
purse, £35,000

	SCORES				TOTAL	MONEY
Andrew Collison	69	68	66	69	272	£5,685.23
Marc Pendaries	69	70	70	67	276	3,787.88
Pauli Hughes	74	70	68	66	278	1,763.13
Mikael Piltz	70	69	70	69	278	1,763.13
Henrik Nystrom	69	68	70	71	278	1,763.13
Knud Storegaard	69	75	67	69	280	1,274.57
Stewart Cronin	69	74	66	71	280	1,274.57
Richard Tinworth	68	72	72	69	281	1,126.13
Anssi Kankkonen	73	73	65	71	282	996.45
Roger Winchester	71	72	67	72	282	996.45
Greg Chalmers	70	72	74	67	283	771.23
Heinz P. Thul	71	74	70	68	283	771.23
Steen Tinning	74	71	69	69	283	771.23
Giorgio Merletti	71	70	71	71	283	771.23
Simon Brown	69	75	72	68	284	534.63
Bryan Ingleby	72	73	70	69	284	534.63
Gordon Sherry	70	73	69	72	284	534.63
Stephen Pullan	73	72	71	69	285	435.10
Juan Ciola	69	72	73	71	285	435.10
Warren Hewlett	68	77	73	68	286	366.28
Mario Tadini	74	70	73	69	286	366.28
Giuseppe Cali	74	73	70	69	286	366.28
Benoit Telleria	73	70	73	70	286	366.28
Sebastien Delagrange	72	71	72	71	286	366.28
Frederic Cupillard	68	75	71	72	286	366.28
Raimo Sjoberg	73	73	71	70	287	313.95
Antonio Sobrinho	72	69	70	76	287	313.95
Lee James	73	69	68	77	287	313.95
Greg Owen	70	76	67	75	288	293.48
Rorbak Petersen	72	74	75	68	289	269.59
Andrea Canessa	75	72	72	70	289	269.59
Rob Edwards	68	74	76	71	289	269.59
Luca Bernardini	72	70	74	73	289	269.59
Patrik Gottfridsson	66	74	73	76	289	269.59

Alianca UAP Challenge

Campo de Golf do Montado, Setubal, Portugal
Par 36-36–72; 6,565 yards

April 24-27
purse, £55,000

	SCORES				TOTAL	MONEY
Anssi Kankkonen	64	63	70	71	268	£8,933.92
Fredrik Lindgren	69	67	66	66	268	4,654.66
Nicolas Vanhootegem	68	67	67	66	268	4,654.66

(Kankkonen defeated Lindgren and Vanhootegem on first extra hole.)

Marcus Wheelhouse	69	69	66	65	269	2,681.25
Per Nyman	69	68	67	66	270	2,273.70
Greg Owen	70	65	71	65	271	2,086.01
Knud Storegaard	69	67	68	68	272	1,919.78
Michele Reale	68	66	69	70	273	1,571.22
Bradley Dredge	69	68	66	70	273	1,571.22
Mike Miller	70	66	69	68	273	1,571.22

	SCORES	TOTAL	MONEY
Gordon J. Brand	68 68 69 68	273	1,571.22
Jorgen Aker	70 70 67 67	274	1,209.25
Andrew Collison	66 71 70 67	274	1,209.25
Simon Brown	66 70 68 71	275	891.52
Gary Marks	65 68 72 70	275	891.52
Patrik Gottfridsson	71 69 67 68	275	891.52
Cameron Clark	71 67 70 67	275	891.52
David A. Russell	66 74 66 70	276	666.74
Mikael Piltz	72 68 68 68	276	666.74
Stephen Dodd	70 69 70 67	276	666.74
Frederic Cupillard	69 69 68 71	277	555.02
Lee James	68 71 68 70	277	555.02
Hans Karlsson	67 67 74 69	277	555.02
Steen Tinning	73 64 71 69	277	555.02
David Lynn	69 72 68 68	277	555.02
Jean-Pierre Cixous	72 67 70 68	277	555.02
Jorge Berendt	67 67 70 74	278	449.68
Daren Lee	68 71 67 72	278	449.68
Per Jacobson	75 66 65 72	278	449.68
Scott Watson	73 66 68 71	278	449.68
Bryan Ingleby	67 70 71 70	278	449.68
Roger Winchester	68 68 72 70	278	449.68
Pauli Hughes	70 70 69 69	278	449.68

Canarias Challenge

Real Golf Club, Las Palmas, Gran Canaria, Spain
Par 35-36–71; 6,221 yards

May 1-4
purse, £49,372

	SCORES	TOTAL	MONEY
Michele Reale	67 69 65 67	268	£8,748.34
Scott Watson	68 67 62 71	268	5,828.73
(Reale defeated Watson on first extra hole.)			
Carlos Sunesson	69 67 67 66	269	2,713.07
Andrew Clapp	68 66 67 68	269	2,713.07
Bradley Dredge	67 64 70 68	269	2,713.07
Antoine Lebouc	69 66 68 67	270	1,885.15
Ivo Giner	69 64 68 69	270	1,885.15
Greg Chalmers	66 67 69 68	270	1,885.15
David A. Russell	69 65 68 69	271	1,473.81
Roger Winchester	65 63 74 69	271	1,473.81
Jose Carriles	67 67 70 67	271	1,473.81
Andrew Collison	70 69 67 66	272	1,130.74
Johan Axgren	66 68 70 68	272	1,130.74
Francisco Javier Amatriai	67 65 69 71	272	1,130.74
Ricardo Gonzalez	70 64 72 67	273	866.43
Patrik Gottfridsson	68 67 69 69	273	866.43
Jesus Maria Arruti	65 69 72 68	274	691.40
Tomas Jesus Munoz	66 72 67 69	274	691.40
Lee James	69 68 70 67	274	691.40
Per Nyman	67 69 69 70	275	573.42
Carlos Balmaseda	68 70 65 72	275	573.42
Francisco Cea	68 68 66 73	275	573.42
Simon Brown	65 67 73 70	275	573.42
Marc Pendaries	70 67 70 68	275	573.42
Jose Rozadilla	67 70 70 69	276	498.86
Morten Backhausen	69 66 71 70	276	498.86

	SCORES				TOTAL	MONEY
Dominique Nouailhac	67	72	69	68	276	498.86
Magnus Persson	69	69	69	70	277	459.47
Fredrik Larsson	65	71	70	71	277	459.47
Steen Tinning	65	70	71	72	278	420.09
Matthew Hazelden	68	68	71	71	278	420.09
Ruben Gonzalez	68	71	72	67	278	420.09
Henrik Nystrom	70	67	71	70	278	420.09

Modena Classic Open

Modena Golf Club, Modena, Italy
Par 36-36–72; 7,024 yards

May 15-18
purse, £35,000

	SCORES				TOTAL	MONEY
Jesus Maria Arruti	65	66	71	69	271	£5,685.23
Mario Tadini	67	68	70	67	272	3,787.88
Greg Chalmers	66	73	69	67	275	1,763.13
Ariel Canete	68	70	66	71	275	1,763.13
Nicolas Joakimides	67	70	66	72	275	1,763.13
Kalle Brink	73	70	70	63	276	1,327.46
Marcello Santi	65	73	71	68	277	1,085.18
Jorge Berendt	67	69	70	71	277	1,085.18
Dimitri Bieri	70	67	69	71	277	1,085.18
Soren Kjeldsen	68	68	68	73	277	1,085.18
Thomas Nielsen	74	64	74	66	278	842.89
Matthew Hazelden	69	68	71	70	278	842.89
Johan Skold	72	68	73	66	279	631.32
Andrea Canessa	69	69	70	71	279	631.32
Frederic Cupillard	70	67	70	72	279	631.32
Markus Rosenlund	71	69	67	72	279	631.32
Marcus Wheelhouse	74	69	71	66	280	449.31
Antoine Lebouc	71	70	70	69	280	449.31
Gianluca Baruffaldi	72	70	69	69	280	449.31
Warren Bennett	73	69	72	67	281	372.64
Lee James	70	73	70	68	281	372.64
Juan Ciola	70	69	72	70	281	372.64
Kevin Carissimi	69	71	71	70	281	372.64
Dominique Nouailhac	73	70	67	71	281	372.64
Mark Foster	69	67	75	71	282	319.07
Pauli Hughes	72	70	69	71	282	319.07
Francisco Cea	70	71	68	73	282	319.07
Eric Carlberg	68	69	71	74	282	319.07
Johan Axgren	71	72	72	68	283	284.38
Bradley Dredge	71	72	71	69	283	284.38
Jean Pierre Sallat	69	69	75	70	283	284.38

Matchmaker Austrian Open

Millstatter See Golf Club, Austria
Par 35-35–70; 6,380 yards

May 22-25
purse, £50,000

	SCORES				TOTAL	MONEY
Erol Simsek	65	68	65	68	266	£8,121.75
Kevin Carissimi	66	67	70	66	269	3,633.50
Steen Tinning	68	68	67	66	269	3,633.50

	SCORES				TOTAL	MONEY
David Lynn	71	68	63	67	269	3,633.50
Mathew Goggin	69	68	68	66	271	2,067
Johan Axgren	69	70	66	67	272	1,820.82
Stephen Gallacher	70	69	64	69	272	1,820.82
Rudi Sailer	72	67	68	66	273	1,608.75
Sebastien Delagrange	67	68	72	67	274	1,423.50
Warren Bennett	66	70	68	70	274	1,423.50
Knud Storegaard	71	68	69	67	275	882.38
Anssi Kankkonen	72	70	67	66	275	882.38
Michele Reale	73	69	67	66	275	882.38
Anders Hansen	72	66	69	68	275	882.38
Nicolas Kalouguine	70	70	67	68	275	882.38
Francisco Cea	69	69	68	69	275	882.38
Brian Davis	69	70	67	69	275	882.38
Per Nyman	71	68	67	69	275	882.38
Henrik Nystrom	73	68	63	71	275	882.38
Thomas Levet	72	69	68	67	276	498.34
Emil Madsen	71	69	69	67	276	498.34
Gary Marks	72	67	71	66	276	498.34
Markus Brier	72	67	68	69	276	498.34
Andrew Barnett	72	70	65	69	276	498.34
Jorge Berendt	71	69	66	70	276	498.34
Ben Tinning	73	67	66	70	276	498.34
Andrew Collison	68	72	64	72	276	498.34
Raphael Jacquelin	68	70	65	73	276	498.34
Niklas Diethelm	69	70	69	69	277	411.94
Simon Burnell	68	69	71	69	277	411.94

Himmerland Open

Himmerland Golf Club, Himmerland, Denmark
Par 36-36–72; 6,837 yards

May 30-June 1
purse, £35,000

	SCORES			TOTAL	MONEY
Mikael Lundberg	69	72	68	209	£5,685.23
Raphael Eyraud	72	70	72	214	3,787.88
Rene Budde	71	70	74	215	1,654.21
Morten Backhausen	68	71	76	215	1,654.21
Frederik Lundgren	71	72	72	215	1,654.21
Knud Storegaard	72	72	71	215	1,654.21
Stephen Gallacher	71	72	73	216	1,085.18
Gary Marks	71	72	73	216	1,085.18
Marcello Santi	71	72	73	216	1,085.18
Johan Rystrom	72	72	72	216	1,085.18
Johan Skold	66	73	78	217	806.49
Hans Karlsson	69	74	74	217	806.49
Paul Nilbrink	71	75	71	217	806.49
Johan Omander	69	72	77	218	631.32
Erik Andersson	72	72	74	218	631.32
Magnus Persson	68	73	78	219	455.91
Thomas Nielsen	70	72	77	219	455.91
Mark Litton	70	72	77	219	455.91
Anders Gillner	72	73	74	219	455.91
Johan Selberg	73	76	70	219	455.91
*Claus Molholm	73	74	72	219	
Per Nyman	70	70	80	220	358.99
Michael Welch	76	71	73	220	358.99

	SCORES			TOTAL	MONEY
Anders Sorensen	72	77	71	220	358.99
Mikko Rantanen	75	74	71	220	358.99
Craig Hainline	74	75	71	220	358.99
Johan Annerfelt	74	71	76	221	290.92
Ivo Giner	72	73	76	221	290.92
Patrik Gottfridsson	68	77	76	221	290.92
Arnaud Langenaeken	71	75	75	221	290.92
Jorgen Aker	74	74	73	221	290.92
Marcus Wheelhouse	72	75	74	221	290.92
Marcus Norgren	70	77	74	221	290.92
Nicolas Joakimides	73	76	72	221	290.92

KB Golf Challenge

Praha Karlstein, Prague, Czech Republic
Par 35-36–71; 6,803 yards

June 5-8
purse, £56,818

	SCORES				TOTAL	MONEY
Alex Cejka	68	70	65	68	271	£9,229.26
Michele Reale	68	68	70	67	273	6,149.15
Marc Pendaries	69	69	68	68	274	3,467.90
Thomas Levet	69	69	69	68	275	2,769.89
Lee James	69	68	70	69	276	2,251.92
Nicolas Vanhootegem	70	70	69	67	276	2,251.92
Greg Chalmers	77	66	66	68	277	1,905.68
Stewart Cronin	65	75	68	69	277	1,905.68
Matthew Hazelden	72	69	67	70	278	1,432.58
Andrew Barnett	70	74	70	64	278	1,432.58
Antoine Lebouc	69	73	67	69	278	1,432.58
Robert Jan Derksen	72	70	69	67	278	1,432.58
Roger Winchester	68	74	69	67	278	1,432.58
Frederick Mansson	71	67	68	73	279	969.46
Patrik Gottfridsson	69	72	68	70	279	969.46
David R. Jones	72	70	70	67	279	969.46
Gary Marks	69	74	66	71	280	664.77
John McHenry	73	69	67	71	280	664.77
Soren Kjeldsen	69	70	71	70	280	664.77
Greg Owen	67	78	66	69	280	664.77
Jonathan Hodgson	73	69	71	67	280	664.77
Niklas Diethelm	70	72	67	71	280	664.77
Francis Howley	67	76	71	66	280	664.77
Patzi Amatriain	70	74	69	68	281	551.21
Markus Brier	73	69	71	68	281	551.21
Marcus Wheelhouse	73	70	69	70	282	501.35
Eric Giraud	69	74	71	68	282	501.35
David Lynn	70	69	74	69	282	501.35
Bradley Dredge	74	71	69	68	282	501.35
Morten Backhausen	71	74	68	70	283	443.19
Mark Pullan	72	73	68	70	283	443.19
Frederic Cupillard	68	71	70	74	283	443.19
Michel Besanceney	70	67	73	73	283	443.19

Siab Open

Soderasen Golf Club, Stockholm, Sweden
Par 71; 6,616 yards

June 5-8
purse, £35,000

	SCORES				TOTAL	MONEY
Joakim Rask	67	71	71	72	281	£5,685.22
Kalle Brink	69	67	73	73	282	3,787.88
Mikael Piltz	76	65	72	72	285	1,921.24
Rene Budde	73	69	76	67	285	1,921.24
Jens Nilsson	74	70	73	70	287	1,446.90
Fredrik Larsson	74	70	75	69	288	1,327.46
Leif Westerberg	75	68	71	75	289	1,173.90
Johan Rystrom	71	73	74	71	289	1,173.90
Carl Magnus Stromberg	72	72	71	75	290	810.71
Tony Edlund	77	69	75	69	290	810.71
Niclas Johnsson	74	72	68	76	290	810.71
Martin Erlandsson	73	75	70	72	290	810.71
Fredrik Lindgren	74	70	69	77	290	810.71
Magnus Persson	71	74	74	71	290	810.71
Magnus Sunesson	71	73	73	73	290	810.71
Joakim Hallberg	70	70	74	77	291	528.94
Mark Litton	70	76	72	74	292	462.39
Jorgen Aker	74	74	72	72	292	462.39
Fredrik Henge	73	67	79	75	294	388.34
Johan Selberg	72	75	72	75	294	388.34
Eric Carlberg	74	72	76	72	294	388.34
Paul Nilbrink	74	75	72	73	294	388.34
Craig Hainline	70	74	79	71	294	388.34
Erik Andersson	76	69	72	78	295	319.07
Henrik Nystrom	75	73	72	75	295	319.07
Mikko Rantanen	74	73	76	72	295	319.07
Don Bell	74	73	79	69	295	319.07
Anssi Kankkonen	75	72	76	72	295	319.07
Anders Sandgren	75	72	74	74	295	319.07
Nils Rorbek	74	74	72	76	296	259.35
Markus Westerberg	76	72	72	76	296	259.35
Ola Eliasson	67	80	72	77	296	259.35
David Lindqvist	76	71	73	76	296	259.35
Birgir Leifur Hafthorsson	71	77	74	74	296	259.35
Frederik Lundgren	73	72	77	74	296	259.35
Fredrik Ekehammar	74	74	76	72	296	259.35
Per Nyman	71	72	75	78	296	259.35

Nedcar National Open

Hoenshuis Golf Club, Hoenshuis, Netherlands
Par 36-36–72; 6,611 yards

June 11-14
purse, £23,649

	SCORES				TOTAL	MONEY
Brian Gee	71	71	73	69	284	£4,054.05
Robert Jan Derksen	70	72	67	77	286	2,533.78
Joost Steenkamer	73	68	73	74	288	1,601.35
*R. Miller	72	72	71	73	288	
Chris Van Der Velde	77	69	73	71	290	1,266.99
John Woof	72	72	75	72	291	1,097.97
*Maarten Van Den Berg	75	72	71	73	291	
*Maarten LaFeber	73	72	71	75	291	

	SCORES	TOTAL	MONEY
Constant Smits Van Wasserghe	72 71 75 77	295	855.85
Stephane Lovey	71 74 73 77	295	855.85
Willem Swart	78 72 67 78	295	855.85
*Rutger Buschow	70 76 73 76	295	
Tim Giles	74 72 76 74	296	709.46
Adrian Morley	70 81 71 76	298	658.78
*Alain Ruiz Fonhoff	75 74 77 72	298	
Ruben Wechgelaer	80 71 73 75	299	557.43
Ruud Bos	75 74 74 76	299	557.43
Mark Metgod	76 80 68 75	299	557.43
*Gaston Metselaar	76 79 70 74	299	

Italian Native Open

Garlenda Golf Club, Garlenda, Italy
Par 35-36–71; 6,532 yards

June 11-14
purse, £49,916

	SCORES	TOTAL	MONEY
Massimo Florioli	67 69 67 69	272	£8,316.73
Emanuele Canonica	70 69 70 70	279	4,332.11
Emanuele Bolognesi	77 72 67 63	279	4,332.11
Federico Bisazza	62 77 68 73	280	2,305.72
Michele Reale	72 69 69 70	280	2,305.72
Alberto Binaghi	70 70 71 72	283	1,942.87
Delio Lovato	73 70 72 69	284	1,787.37
Andrea Canessa	71 73 69 72	285	1,647.22
Alessandro Pissilli	68 73 69 76	286	1,238.61
Marcello Santi	72 68 75 71	286	1,238.61
Maurizio Severa	75 73 68 70	286	1,238.61
Giuseppe Cali	72 72 68 74	286	1,238.61
Andrea Calcari	80 68 67 71	286	1,238.61
Gianluca Baruffaldi	74 70 70 72	286	1,238.61
Gianluca Pietrobono	69 74 74 70	287	823.61
Silvano Locatelli	72 72 70 73	287	823.61
*Joachim Hassan	73 72 68 74	287	
Niccolo Bisazza	74 73 66 75	288	656.58
Luca Bernardini	76 68 70 74	288	656.58
Alessandro Tadini	70 76 71 71	288	656.58
Vittorio Mori	72 72 74 72	290	576.71
Baldovino Dassu	72 75 71 72	290	576.71

STG Coopers & Lybrand ASPG

Montreux Golf Club, Montreux, Switzerland
Par 36-36–72; 6,921 yards

June 12-14
purse, £14,695

	SCORES	TOTAL	MONEY
Juan Ciola	68 68 74	210	£2,608.70
Andre Bossert	71 69 71	211	1,956.52
Christophe Bovet	71 68 74	213	1,521.74
Marcos Moreno	76 67 71	214	1,260.87
Gavin Healy	74 71 70	215	1,086.96
Manolo Garcia	73 72 72	217	913.04
Steve Rey	78 71 70	219	717.39
Marco Scopetta	73 75 71	219	717.39

	SCORES			TOTAL	MONEY
Gianlucca Patuzzo	75	74	72	221	478.26
Karim Baradie	71	75	75	221	478.26
Stefan Gort	75	75	72	222	358.70
Gary Owens	73	76	73	222	358.70
Marc Fluri	75	74	73	222	358.70
Jacques Blatti	71	76	75	222	358.70
Lloyd Freeman	75	75	73	223	282.61
Patrick Kressig	75	75	73	223	282.61
Tim Huyton	76	73	74	223	282.61
Dimitri Bieri	76	77	71	224	228.26
Alain Genoud	69	72	83	224	228.26
Carlos Duran	76	76	73	225	108.70
Yves Auberson	74	78	73	225	108.70

Husqvarna Open

Jonkopings, Husqvarna, Sweden
Par 35-35–70; 6,721 yards

June 13-15
purse, £17,949

	SCORES			TOTAL	MONEY
Mikael Lundberg	66	66	67	199	£3,076.92
Patrik Sjoland	63	71	66	200	2,222.22
Magnus Nilsson	66	68	67	201	1,623.93
Tobias Josefsson	65	66	70	201	1,623.93
Andreas Lindberg	69	68	65	202	1,089.74
Niclas Bjornsson	65	70	67	202	1,089.74
Per Nyman	69	68	66	203	769.23
Morten Hagen	67	68	68	203	769.23
*Daniel Olsson	64	70	69	203	
Peter Henriksson	68	68	68	204	645.30
Anders Haglund	67	71	66	204	645.30
Claes Hovstadius	70	68	67	205	517.09
Petter Jonsson	68	66	71	205	517.09
Mattias Nilsson	68	69	68	205	517.09
Christopher Hanell	66	70	69	205	517.09
Jonas Karlsson	72	66	68	206	341.88
*Johan Andersson	69	69	68	206	
Mikael Persson	69	69	68	206	341.88
Erik Andersson	68	70	68	206	341.88
Bjorn Flygare	70	69	68	207	133.90
Frederik Lundgren	67	70	70	207	133.90
Fredrik Ekehammar	67	68	72	207	133.90
Kalle Brink	67	68	72	207	133.90
Jens Nilsson	67	67	73	207	133.90
Jimmy Kawalec	64	71	72	207	133.90

Championnat de France Pro

Golf D'Arras, St. Omer, France
Par 36-36–72; 6,904 yards

June 12-15
purse, £50,505

	SCORES				TOTAL	MONEY
Raphael Jacqueline	69	70	69	66	274	£8,330
Jean Van de Velde	68	65	74	68	275	5,550
Olivier Edmond	71	68	70	67	276	3,130

	SCORES				TOTAL	MONEY
Bertrand Cornut	72	67	70	69	278	2,310
Thomas Levet	71	67	69	71	278	2,310
Pascal Edmond	70	74	66	69	279	1,945
Dominique Nouailhac	68	66	70	76	280	1,590
Quentin Dabson	70	71	71	68	280	1,590
Raphael Eyraud	67	68	77	68	280	1,590
Fabrice Honnorat	68	75	68	69	280	1,590
Antoine Lebouc	69	68	68	75	280	1,590
Nicolas Kalouguine	71	69	72	69	281	1,235
Nicolas Joakimides	68	65	76	75	284	975
Mikael Dieu	69	73	70	72	284	975
Frederic Cupillard	72	73	67	72	284	975
Pascal Ferran	74	69	70	72	285	737.50
Stephane Lahary	69	67	74	75	285	737.50
Christian Cevaer	68	73	75	70	286	655
Franck Aumonier	68	75	71	73	287	605
Eric Galardi	75	69	72	71	287	605

Lancia Golf Pokal

Rittergut Birkhof, Lancia, Germany
Par 37-36–73; 6,994 yards

June 13-15
purse, £37,879

	SCORES			TOTAL	MONEY
Erol Simsek	69	72	70	211	£6,310.61
Alex Cejka	70	72	70	212	4,204.55
Heinz P. Thul	71	71	73	215	2,371.21
Patrick Platz	75	73	70	218	1,893.94
Torsten Giedeon	75	72	75	222	1,539.77
Oliver Eckstein	73	78	71	222	1,539.77
Kaweh Chirband	73	74	76	223	1,252.52
Uli Zilg	72	69	82	223	1,252.52
Ulrich Eckhardt	71	77	75	223	1,252.52
Thomas Hennig	79	73	73	225	1,060.61
Christian Arenz	78	75	73	226	935.61
Lothar Jahn	69	78	79	226	935.61
Marc Amort	78	72	77	227	814.39
Joerg Vanden Berge	77	74	77	228	700.76
Mark Mattheis	72	78	78	228	700.76
Richard Fries	74	79	76	229	558.71
Christian Von Bonin	73	82	74	229	558.71
Martin Spieckerhoff	81	74	75	230	470.96
Christian Niesing	76	74	80	230	470.96
Gert-Sven Slopianka	72	77	81	230	470.96

Czech Republic

Goplf Club Karlovy Vary, Prague, Czech Republic
Par 36-36–72; 6,701 yards

June 12-15
purse, £8,834

	SCORES			TOTAL	MONEY
Ondrej Trudl	75	70	72	217	£1,329.51
Roman Chudoba	72	71	77	220	887.81
Jifi Janda	76	73	72	221	448.32
Jan Juhaniak	72	73	76	221	448.32

	SCORES	TOTAL	MONEY
Peter Mruzek	74 78 74	226	344.52
Stepan Slezak	73 73 80	226	344.52
Miroslav Janda	75 76 78	229	295.94
Jifi Zavazal, Sr.	75 76 78	229	295.94
Petr Strougal	73 77 79	229	295.94
Karel Skopovy	78 76 76	230	260.60
Bohuslav Syriste	78 80 76	234	251.77
Oldrich Nechanicy	79 78 78	235	242.93
Jiri Kunsta	75 79 82	236	229.68
Karel Cechovsky	79 74 83	236	229.68
Adam Eisner	81 80 77	238	207.60
Martin Dvorak	79 80 79	238	207.60
Jiri Seifert	82 76 80	238	207.60
Miroslav Brtek	85 78 77	240	185.51
Lumir Kainer	80 81 79	240	185.51
Lupos Soukup	82 82 77	241	175.57
Jaraslav Peterka	80 81 80	241	175.57

Team Erhverv Danish Open

Simons Golf Club, Copenhagen, Denmark
Par 36-36–72; 6,780 yards

June 19-22
purse, £80,000

	SCORES	TOTAL	MONEY
David Lynn	70 66 69 69	274	£12,994.80
Robert Jan Derksen	71 71 65 70	277	8,658
Greg Chalmers	69 69 70 70	278	3,781.05
Andrew Clapp	70 70 67 71	278	3,781.05
Mikael Piltz	71 69 68 70	278	3,781.05
Kalle Brink	70 72 67 69	278	3,781.05
Craig Hainline	70 69 70 70	279	2,792.40
Per Jacobson	70 71 69 70	280	2,376.40
Stephen Gallacher	70 68 73 69	280	2,376.40
Antoine Lebouc	67 68 74 71	280	2,376.40
Michele Reale	69 68 75 69	281	2,012.40
Gordon Sherry	71 71 67 73	282	1,213.25
Peter Henriksson	72 70 72 68	282	1,213.25
Rudi Sailer	67 71 73 71	282	1,213.25
Scott Watson	72 68 71 71	282	1,213.25
Rene Budde	71 70 70 71	282	1,213.25
Kevin Carissimi	72 70 66 74	282	1,213.25
Erik Andersson	69 69 72 72	282	1,213.25
Thomas Nielsen	69 74 69 70	282	1,213.25
Knud Storegaard	69 70 73 70	282	1,213.25
Mats Lanner	70 73 69 70	282	1,213.25
Patrik Gottfridsson	70 73 71 68	282	1,213.25
Claes Hovstadius	71 70 72 70	283	790.40
Marcello Santi	69 67 74 73	283	790.40
James Petts	69 72 71 71	283	790.40
Jesus Maria Arruti	71 72 70 71	284	656.07
Mark Plummer	70 72 68 74	284	656.07
John McHenry	74 69 69 72	284	656.07
Anssi Kankkonen	69 74 69 72	284	656.07
Robert Jonsson	70 70 75 69	284	656.07
Henrik Nystrom	72 71 71 70	284	656.07
Markus Brier	73 70 71 70	284	656.07
Jesper Kjaerbye	74 69 70 71	284	656.07
Stephen McAllister	68 71 73 72	284	656.07

Memorial Olivier Barras

Crans-sur-Sierre Golf Club, Crans-sur-Sierre, Switzerland
Par 36-35–71; 6,665 yards
(Third round cancelled — rain.)

June 20-22
purse, £40,000

	SCORES		TOTAL	MONEY
Raphael Jacquelin	68	69	137	£5,391.20
Mario Tadini	71	68	139	1,877
Carlos Duran	70	69	139	1,877
Matthew McGuire	69	70	139	1,877
Denny Lucas	69	70	139	1,877
Gary Marks	69	70	139	1,877
Marcos Moreno	67	72	139	1,877
Bradley Dredge	70	70	140	1,116
Quentin Dabson	73	68	141	922.40
Brandan Pappas	71	70	141	922.40
Sebastien Delagrange	71	70	141	922.40
Giuseppe Cali	67	74	141	922.40
Gianluca Baruffaldi	72	70	142	652
Jeff Hall	70	72	142	652
Laurent Lassalle	70	72	142	652
Alberto Binaghi	69	73	142	652
Stephen Dodd	72	71	143	481.30
Gavin Healey	71	72	143	481.30
Juan Ciola	71	72	143	481.30
George Nikitaidis	74	70	144	409.40
Franck Aumonier	73	71	144	409.40
Dimitri Bieri	73	71	144	409.40
Jiri Janda	70	74	144	409.40
Nicolas Dupuy	68	76	144	409.40
Nicolas Kalouguine	73	72	145	373.60
Nicholas Ludwell	76	70	146	336.60
Bryan Ingleby	76	70	146	336.60
Federico Bisazza	75	71	146	336.60
Arnaud Langenaeken	72	74	146	336.60
Joost Steenkamer	72	74	146	336.60
Bruno Petit	72	74	146	336.60
Christophe Bovet	70	76	146	336.60

Audi Quattro Trophy

Berlin Sporting Club, Berlin, Germany
Par 36-36–72; 7,048 yards

June 26-29
purse, £72,000

	SCORES				TOTAL	MONEY
David A. Russell	67	74	68	70	279	£11,695.32
Greg Chalmers	71	73	67	68	279	7,792.20
(Russell defeated Chalmers on first extra hole.)						
Robert Jonsson	73	72	69	67	281	3,952.26
David Lynn	70	71	67	73	281	3,952.26
Joost Steenkamer	66	75	72	70	283	2,976.48
Kalle Brink	73	72	68	71	284	2,520.18
Nicolas Vanhootegem	71	73	71	69	284	2,520.18
Carlos Duran	69	72	67	76	284	2,520.18
Eric Carlberg	70	72	74	69	285	2,134.08
Roger Winchester	77	67	70	72	286	1,811.16

	SCORES				TOTAL	MONEY
Henrik Nystrom	71	68	71	76	286	1,811.16
Francisco Cea	69	73	71	73	286	1,811.16
Eric Giraud	73	69	73	72	287	1,439.10
Stewart Cronin	71	70	73	73	287	1,439.10
Tony Edlund	72	76	67	73	288	1,228.50
Juan Ciola	74	71	71	73	289	1,035.45
Jorgen Aker	69	72	70	78	289	1,035.45
Mike Miller	74	72	72	72	290	835.38
Greg Owen	73	72	73	72	290	835.38
Lee James	73	71	70	76	290	835.38
Knud Storegaard	72	74	75	69	290	835.38
Steen Tinning	72	73	71	74	290	835.38
Raimo Sjoberg	75	71	73	72	291	700.25
Mark Foster	74	70	71	76	291	700.25
John McHenry	72	75	70	74	291	700.25
Michele Reale	68	73	73	77	291	700.25
Per Jacobson	73	73	74	72	292	605.13
Bryan Ingleby	72	76	73	71	292	605.13
Patrik Gottfridsson	72	76	73	71	292	605.13
Warren Bennett	71	76	74	71	292	605.13
Rudi Sailer	71	72	77	72	292	605.13

Open dei Tessali

Riva dei Tessali, Taranto, Italy
Par 35-36–71; 6,504 yards

June 26-29
purse, £35,000

	SCORES				TOTAL	MONEY
Ivo Giner	70	70	68	72	280	£5,685.23
Stephen Leaney	68	74	72	69	283	3,787.88
Christopher Hanell	73	69	72	70	284	1,921.24
Frederic Cupillard	72	72	71	69	284	1,921.24
Mikko Rantanen	68	74	72	71	285	1,332.01
Alan Lovelace	72	74	66	73	285	1,332.01
Quentin Dabson	70	74	71	70	285	1,332.01
Francesco Guermani	74	72	68	74	288	1,126.13
Marcus Wheelhouse	71	71	79	68	289	919.67
Andrea Canessa	71	69	74	75	289	919.67
Gianluca Baruffaldi	69	73	75	72	289	919.67
Ola Eliasson	75	73	70	71	289	919.67
Stefano Pietrobono	73	74	74	69	290	665.44
Enrico Trentin	76	71	70	73	290	665.44
Euan Little	72	74	75	69	290	665.44
Federico Bisazza	75	72	75	69	291	503.35
Niccolo Bisazza	78	72	69	72	291	503.35
Mark Treleaven	75	74	70	73	292	406.09
Elliot Boult	69	73	72	78	292	406.09
Martin Erlandsson	75	71	70	76	292	406.09
Giuseppe Cali	72	74	73	73	292	406.09
Pauli Hughes	70	73	78	71	292	406.09
Raphael Eyraud	73	73	72	75	293	340.40
Andrew Butterfield	70	79	71	73	293	340.40
Tierri Corte	73	72	77	71	293	340.40
Robert Dickman	72	75	71	75	293	340.40
Chris Van Der Velde	74	70	75	75	294	308.83
Alexandre Balicki	74	73	75	72	294	308.83
Luca Frigerio	72	75	78	70	295	280.68

	SCORES	TOTAL	MONEY
Marco Soffietti	77 71 75 72	295	280.68
Emanuele Lattanzi	72 74 73 76	295	280.68
Gianluca Pietrobono	74 75 76 70	295	280.68

Open des Volcans

Golf des Volcans, Volcans d'Auverge National Park, France
Par 36-36–72; 6,874 yards

July 3-6
purse, £50,505

		SCORES	TOTAL	MONEY
Mark Litton	68	67 73 68	276	£8,203.79
Jose Carriles	67	72 70 67	276	5,465.91
(Litton defeated Carriles on first extra hole.)				
Olivier Edmond	70	70 69 68	277	3,082.58
David A. Russell	65	71 70 73	279	2,275
Warren Bennett	71	68 71 69	279	2,275
John Lawson	69	72 73 66	280	1,915.53
Per Nyman	72	68 68 73	281	1,628.28
Michele Reale	69	69 71 72	281	1,628.28
Scott Watson	68	72 72 69	281	1,628.28
Oyvind Rojahn	70	69 70 73	282	1,324.62
Stephane Lahary	73	70 71 68	282	1,324.62
Emmanuel Dussart	69	71 71 72	283	1,162.12
Craig Hainline	71	72 69 72	284	866.67
Thomas Levet	70	70 69 75	284	866.67
Tim Planchin	71	69 69 75	284	866.67
David Lynn	72	66 76 70	284	866.67
Sebastien Delagrange	66	77 72 69	284	866.67
Frederic Regard	70	67 75 73	285	598.30
Michael Welch	71	73 66 75	285	598.30
Andrew Clapp	72	70 71 72	285	598.30
Marcello Santi	75	69 72 69	285	598.30
Nicolas Vanhootegem	67	72 73 74	286	517.05
Steen Tinning	70	73 71 72	286	517.05
Morten Backhausen	72	68 74 72	286	517.05
Ivo Giner	69	72 72 74	287	460.42
Rene Budde	71	69 72 75	287	460.42
Anders Haglund	74	69 74 70	287	460.42
Stewart Cronin	70	68 75 74	287	460.42
Jean Pierre Sallat	69	75 71 73	288	423.48
Francois Lamare	73	71 69 76	289	398.86
Lee James	70	73 74 72	289	398.86
Greg Chalmers	72	72 73 72	289	398.86

Neuchatel Open

Neuchatel Golf Club, Neuchatel, Switzerland
Par 35-35–70; 6,368 yards

July 4-6
purse, £35,000

	SCORES	TOTAL	MONEY
Erol Simsek	68 68 68	204	£5,685.23
Stephen Leaney	72 68 67	207	3,787.88
Johan Selberg	69 71 68	208	1,763.12
Leif Westerberg	68 71 69	208	1,763.12
Andrew Butterfield	67 72 69	208	1,763.12

	SCORES			TOTAL	MONEY
Gavin Healey	70	71	68	209	1,274.57
Heinz P. Thul	68	70	71	209	1,274.57
Gianluca Pietrobono	73	70	67	210	1,039.67
Steve Rey	72	67	71	210	1,039.67
Christophe Bovet	66	71	73	210	1,039.67
Charles Challen	72	72	67	211	880.42
Dimitri Bieri	69	70	73	212	805.35
Pehr Magnebrant	73	70	70	213	593.78
Rudi Sailer	73	69	71	213	593.78
Elliot Boult	70	71	72	213	593.78
Frederik Lundgren	69	72	72	213	593.78
Ulrich Eckhardt	69	70	74	213	593.78
Tim Huyton	67	76	71	214	481.17
Claes Hovstadius	69	72	73	214	481.17
Warren Hewlett	74	72	69	215	424.13
Jesper Kjaerbye	73	74	68	215	424.13
Jerome Challen	72	73	70	215	424.13
Yves Auberson	71	75	69	215	424.13
Patrik Gottfridsson	71	74	70	215	424.13
Juan Ciola	72	72	71	215	424.13
Marcos Moreno	68	72	75	215	424.13
John Penning	73	72	71	216	392.44
Diego Fiammengo	71	73	72	216	392.44
Lloyd Freeman	74	71	72	217	372.65
Marco Scopetta	73	72	72	217	372.65
Brandan Pappas	72	73	72	217	372.65
Johan Omander	71	72	74	217	372.65
Patrick Kressig	69	75	73	217	372.65

Volvo Finnish Open

Espoo Golf Club, Espoo, Finland
Par 36-36–72; 6,731 yards

July 10-13
purse, £35,000

	SCORES				TOTAL	MONEY
Soren Kjeldsen	70	67	72	67	276	£5,685.23
Thomas Nielsen	72	69	67	71	279	2,962.06
Leif Westerberg	69	69	69	72	279	2,962.06
Nils Rorbek	70	73	71	67	281	1,706.25
Pehr Magnebrant	73	68	71	70	282	1,387.18
Mikael Piltz	71	71	73	67	282	1,387.18
Per Nyman	69	72	72	70	283	1,221.68
Jorgen Aker	69	73	70	72	284	999.87
Warren Hewlett	74	69	73	68	284	999.87
Fredrik Henge	72	71	70	71	284	999.87
Henrik Nystrom	72	70	72	70	284	999.87
Anders Gillner	73	70	69	73	285	769.52
Lars Tingvall	70	71	68	76	285	769.52
Franck Aumonier	74	71	71	70	286	665.44
Per Nyman	71	68	70	78	287	534.63
Gary Marks	72	73	71	71	287	534.63
Pascal Edmond	70	69	75	73	287	534.63
Steven Mattson	73	67	72	76	288	383.48
Rikard Strangert	75	71	69	73	288	383.48
Johan Rystrom	78	66	71	73	288	383.48
Rene Budde	71	71	73	73	288	383.48
Niclas Johnsson	74	70	69	75	288	383.48

	SCORES	TOTAL	MONEY
Ulrik Marcher	72 72 73 71	288	383.48
Marcello Santi	71 69 74 74	288	383.48
Hans Edberg	75 71 72 70	288	383.48
Marcus Norgren	73 73 71 72	289	303.71
Antony Manasson	71 71 73 74	289	303.71
Tomas Jesus Munoz	70 73 76 70	289	303.71
Mika Lehtinen	69 73 73 74	289	303.71
Ola Eliasson	73 70 72 74	289	303.71
*Mikko Manerus	71 70 71 77	289	

Rolex Trophy Pro-Am

Golf Club de Geneve, Geneva, Switzerland
Par 36-36–72; 6,878 yards

July 17-20
purse, £52,174

	SCORES	TOTAL	MONEY
Anssi Kankkonen	66 67 72 71	276	£6,521.74
Thomas Nielsen	70 70 69 68	277	4,130.43
Michele Reale	68 70 70 70	278	3,217.39
Lee James	70 74 69 66	279	2,456.52
Kevin Carissimi	71 72 66 70	279	2,456.52
Kalle Brink	69 71 70 70	280	1,652.17
Ivo Giner	68 72 70 70	280	1,652.17
Thomas Levet	67 69 73 71	280	1,652.17
David Lynn	71 66 71 72	280	1,652.17
Juan Ciola	70 73 69 70	282	1,304.35
Nicolas Joakimides	71 71 66 74	282	1,304.35
Heinz P. Thul	72 70 71 70	283	1,086.96
Markus Brier	70 73 69 71	283	1,086.96
Scott Watson	74 71 64 74	283	1,086.96
Eric Carlberg	71 74 68 71	284	913.04
Jorge Berendt	68 73 71 72	284	913.04
Jesus Maria Arruti	70 70 70 74	284	913.04
Stewart Cronin	70 68 75 74	287	826.09

BTC Slovenian Open

Bled Golf & Country Club, Bled, Slovenia
Par 36-37–73; 6,945 yards

July 24-27
purse, £40,000

	SCORES	TOTAL	MONEY
Kalle Brink	68 67 72 64	271	£6,497.40
Mikael Lundberg	68 71 70 65	274	4,329
Mario Tadini	67 73 68 69	277	2,441.40
Johan Selberg	69 70 71 69	279	1,950
Janeirik Dahlstrom	74 69 70 68	281	1,522.30
Dominique Nouailhac	68 72 68 73	281	1,522.30
Stephane Lahary	71 71 67 72	281	1,522.30
Antony Manasson	70 72 71 69	282	1,098.24
Marcello Santi	69 70 71 72	282	1,098.24
Kevin Carissimi	70 70 72 70	282	1,098.24
Ola Eliasson	72 70 67 73	282	1,098.24
Paul Nilbrink	72 69 72 69	282	1,098.24
Benoit Telleria	75 71 67 70	283	838.50
Younes El Hassani	70 73 69 72	284	648.38

	SCORES	TOTAL	MONEY
Christopher Hanell	69 73 73 69	284	648.38
Mikko Rantanen	70 69 74 71	284	648.38
Mark Treleaven	74 70 73 67	284	648.38
Jeff Hall	69 70 70 76	285	484.90
Niclas Johnsson	73 69 72 71	285	484.90
Frederik Orest	71 69 74 71	285	484.90
Emmanuele Lattanzi	73 71 71 71	286	425.10
Marc Amort	75 63 76 72	286	425.10
Eric Giraud	74 72 69 71	286	425.10
Quentin Dabson	68 68 75 76	287	358.80
Erik Andersson	78 68 67 74	287	358.80
Gary Marks	69 70 73 75	287	358.80
Roberto Zappa	70 71 70 76	287	358.80
Olivier Edmond	72 72 70 73	287	358.80
Jose Sota	71 74 71 71	287	358.80
Andrew Collison	69 72 75 71	287	358.80

Klassis Turkish Open

Klassis Golf & Country Club, Istanbul, Turkey
Par 36-35–71; 6,571 yards

July 31-August 3
purse, £85,000

	SCORES	TOTAL	MONEY
Bradley Dredge	65 72 65 70	272	£13,806.98
Magnus Persson	73 66 68 66	273	9,199.13
Greg Chalmers	71 67 70 67	275	4,017.37
Raphael Jacquelin	71 67 71 66	275	4,017.37
Stephane Lahary	69 68 70 68	275	4,017.37
Nicolas Vanhootegem	73 68 65 69	275	4,017.37
Henrik Nystrom	69 70 67 70	276	2,740.40
Francisco Cea	71 68 67 70	276	2,740.40
Knud Storegaard	68 67 71 70	276	2,740.40
Hans Karlsson	68 65 74 70	277	2,049.09
Roger Winchester	72 68 67 70	277	2,049.09
Bryan Ingleby	69 71 67 70	277	2,049.09
Greg Owen	69 70 67 71	277	2,049.09
Steen Tinning	71 72 67 68	278	1,450.31
Jeremy Robinson	70 71 69 68	278	1,450.31
Erol Simsek	68 71 69 70	278	1,450.31
Frederic Cupillard	71 70 68 70	279	1,091.19
Stephen Leaney	70 72 67 70	279	1,091.19
Patxi Amatriain	70 69 68 72	279	1,091.19
Roberto Zappa	72 70 68 70	280	905
Gary Marks	70 71 70 69	280	905
Marc Pendaries	67 74 70 69	280	905
Michael Watson	70 72 73 65	280	905
Pauli Hughes	72 69 67 72	280	905
Jorgen Aker	73 68 72 68	281	738.77
Soren Kjeldsen	70 70 75 66	281	738.77
Simon Brown	70 70 70 71	281	738.77
Christian Arenz	69 71 72 69	281	738.77
Mark Pullan	71 72 70 68	281	738.77
Warren Bennett	69 70 72 70	281	738.77
Patrik Gottfridsson	65 70 72 74	281	738.77

Challenge Tour Championship

East Sussex National, Uckfield, England
Par 36-36–72; 7,059 yards

August 7-10
purse, £70,000

	SCORES				TOTAL	MONEY
Greg Chalmers	73	68	68	65	274	£11,370.45
Heinz P. Thul	66	71	69	68	274	7,575.75
(Chalmers defeated Thul on second extra hole.)						
Anthony Wall	68	68	70	69	275	4,272.45
Soren Kjeldsen	71	71	71	63	276	3,153.15
Ivo Giner	68	69	69	70	276	3,153.15
Fredrik Larsson	73	67	73	65	278	2,549.14
Robert Wragg	70	68	69	71	278	2,549.14
John Bickerton	70	70	70	69	279	2,252.25
Nicolas Vanhootegem	70	71	70	69	280	1,692.60
Kalle Brink	72	65	72	71	280	1,692.60
Jeremy Robinson	72	68	72	68	280	1,692.60
John McHenry	66	68	73	73	280	1,692.60
Roger Winchester	69	69	70	72	280	1,692.60
Steen Tinning	73	69	71	67	280	1,692.60
Richard Tinworth	69	69	73	70	281	958.92
Stephen Dodd	69	70	72	70	281	958.92
Darren Prosser	72	69	68	72	281	958.92
Kevin Carissimi	69	68	72	72	281	958.92
Fredrik Lindgren	69	72	69	71	281	958.92
Simon Brown	73	65	69	74	281	958.92
Henrik Nystrom	68	71	71	72	282	706.39
Antoine Lebouc	70	72	69	71	282	706.39
Simon Burnell	70	70	66	76	282	706.39
Marc Pendaries	68	70	76	68	282	706.39
Matthew Stanford	71	70	70	71	282	706.39
Raphael Jacquelin	71	70	69	72	282	706.39
Nick Brown	70	68	74	71	283	597.19
Niklas Diethelm	71	69	72	71	283	597.19
Bradley Dredge	66	72	74	71	283	597.19
Gregory Garbero	69	68	77	69	283	597.19

Norwegian PGA Championship

Larvik Golfbane, Larvik, Norway
Par 36-36–72; 6,777 yards

August 14-16
purse, £9,099

	SCORES			TOTAL	MONEY
Morten Hagen	65	73	66	204	£1,774.34
*Don Bell	69	71	65	205	
Thomas Nielsen	72	71	66	209	682.44
*Johan Elgborn	74	69	68	211	
Henrik Bjornstad	71	70	76	217	591.45
Oyvind Rojahn	75	72	72	219	545.95
John Uppard	75	75	70	220	432.21
Derek Crawford	74	73	73	220	432.21
Alan Maxwell	74	72	74	220	432.21
Thor Bockmann	73	75	72	220	432.21
Martin Grythe	80	73	71	224	319.47
Henrik Bjorelind	78	76	71	225	272.98
David Lloyd	76	74	78	228	204.73
Tom Selmer	75	74	79	228	204.73

	SCORES	TOTAL	MONEY
Stig Ronningen	81 76 73	230	154.69
Jorgen Persson	74 79 77	230	154.69
Ross Robertson	84 82 65	231	127.39
Paul Powell	83 78 71	232	100.09
Thomas Hansen	81 78 73	232	100.09
John Drummond	80 80 73	233	72.79

Terracottem Omnium of Belgium

Waregem Happy Golf Club, Waregem, Belgium
Par 36-36–72; 6,603 yards

August 14-17
purse, £25,000

	SCORES	TOTAL	MONEY
*Didier de Vooght	67 71 70 65	273	
*Jerome Theunis	71 70 72 65	278	
*Jack Boeckx	69 69 70 71	279	
*Francois Nicolas	66 68 73 73	280	
Nicolas Vanhootegem	68 71 70 72	281	£4,585
*Nicolas Colsaerts	73 71 68 69	281	
*Frederic de Vooght	76 71 66 69	282	
Gauthier D'Hollander	72 70 68 73	283	2,372.50
Arnaud Langenaeken	74 71 72 66	283	2,372.50
*Bruno Petit	73 73 69 70	285	
*John Penning	74 69 71 72	286	
Philippe Goovaerts	72 74 73 69	288	950
Boris Janjic	73 75 70 70	288	950
Christian Ditlefsen	75 73 69 72	289	785
Dany Vanbegin	70 71 72 76	289	785
Simon Yearsley	71 71 73 74	289	785
*Raf Vanbegin	77 71 72 70	290	
Simon Clough	76 70 71 74	291	682.50
Dave Lebrasseur	75 71 75 70	291	682.50
*Fredrik Olsson	71 73 80 68	292	
David Petrie	74 73 73 72	292	635
*Sebastien De Meurers	73 70 79 71	293	
*Frederik Dejaeghere	76 71 76 70	293	
*Arnoud Beaupain	80 69 72 72	293	

Esbjerg Danish Closed

Esbjerg Golf Club, Esbjerg, Denmark
Par 35-36–71; 6,941 yards

August 15-17
purse, £24,728

	SCORES	TOTAL	MONEY
Knud Storegaard	69 69 69	207	£3,956.48
Rene Budde	71 65 75	211	2,720.08
Soren Rolner	76 69 70	215	2,225.52
Ben Tinning	73 71 72	216	1,730.96
Morten Backhausen	71 73 72	216	1,730.96
Anders Hansen	77 71 70	218	1,338.40
Danny Jorgensen	75 69 74	218	1,338.40
Steen Tinning	73 70 75	218	1,338.40
James Petts	68 74 76	218	1,338.40
Soren Kjeldsen	75 74 70	219	1,081.85
Ole Eskildsen	75 71 73	219	1,081.85

	SCORES	TOTAL	MONEY
Jesper Kjaerbye	77 72 71	220	958.21
Rene Michelsen	75 73 72	220	958.21
Nils Rorbaek	75 76 73	224	834.57
David Philip	73 76 75	224	834.57
Jakob Borregaard	78 73 74	225	741.84
Arne Tinning	78 73 75	226	208.07
Jesper Thuen	72 78 79	229	206.07
John Nielsen	72 79 79	230	204.07

Finnish PGA Championship

Seagolf Cours, Ronnas, Finland
Par 35-36–71; 6,986 yards

August 15-17
purse, £6,667

	SCORES	TOTAL	MONEY
Mikael Piltz	69 76 65	210	£1,673
Pauli Hughes	77 67 66	210	1,292.78
(Piltz defeated Hughes on second extra hole.)			
Mika Lehtinen	72 74 67	213	874.54
*Sakari Saili Aho	71 73 69	213	
Anssi Kankkonen	80 68 70	218	570.34
Erkki Valimaa	73 74 71	218	570.34
Riku Soravuo	74 72 73	219	416.25
Timo Sipponen	74 71 74	219	416.25
Sami Wachter	72 75 73	220	342.21
Mikko Rantanen	77 71 73	221	202.79
Lassi-Pekka Tilander	77 70 74	221	202.79
Juha Selin	74 75 72	221	202.79

Netcom Norwegian Open

Oslo Golf Club, Oslo, Norway
Par 36-36–72; 6,639 yards

August 21-24
purse, £45,000

	SCORES	TOTAL	MONEY
Dimitri Bieri	70 68 65 72	275	£7,309.58
John Bickerton	67 69 72 67	275	4,870.13
(Bieri defeated Bickerton on second extra hole.)			
Steen Tinning	68 69 71 68	276	2,746.58
Patrik Gottfridsson	68 67 72 70	277	2,027.03
Mathew Goggin	75 67 68 67	277	2,027.03
Soren Kjeldsen	66 73 72 67	278	1,706.74
Cameron Clark	69 69 71 70	279	1,570.73
Stewart Cronin	68 73 67 72	280	1,447.88
Mats Lanner	71 70 70 70	281	1,182.43
Marcello Santi	71 72 68 70	281	1,182.43
John Uppard	71 71 71 68	281	1,182.43
Olivier Edmond	72 67 74 68	281	1,182.43
Knud Storegaard	67 72 70 73	282	899.43
Magnus Persson	72 66 72 72	282	899.43
Frederik Lundgren	74 68 71 70	283	687.37
Ivo Giner	70 69 70 74	283	687.37
Ove Sellberg	74 69 73 67	283	687.37
Antoine Lebouc	70 72 72 70	284	511.88
Christopher Hanell	71 72 70 71	284	511.88

	SCORES	TOTAL	MONEY
Mikko Rantanen	71 73 70 70	284	511.88
Hans Karlsson	73 69 72 70	284	511.88
Roger Winchester	74 69 71 70	284	511.88
Gordon Sherry	75 68 72 69	284	511.88
Thomas Nielsen	70 74 73 68	285	416.81
Robert Jonsson	69 69 76 71	285	416.81
Per Nyman	69 72 73 71	285	416.81
Tony Edlund	73 69 71 72	285	416.81
Henrik Nystrom	71 72 71 71	285	416.81
Morten Hagen	72 69 73 72	286	351.73
Eric Carlberg	73 71 68 74	286	351.73
Peter Alabaster	73 70 74 69	286	351.73
Mikael Krantz	69 73 74 70	286	351.73
Duncan Muscroft	71 69 74 72	286	351.73
Stephen Leaney	74 70 72 70	286	351.73

Steelcover Dutch Challenge

Broekpolder Golf Club, Ularrdingue, Holland
Par 36-36–72; 7,019 yards

August 28-31
purse, £60,000

	SCORES	TOTAL	MONEY
Raphael Jacquelin	68 71 68 70	277	£9,746.10
Roger Winchester	66 72 72 70	280	4,360.20
Andrew Butterfield	71 72 69 68	280	4,360.20
Mathew Goggin	68 74 72 66	280	4,360.20
Francisco Cea	70 70 72 69	281	2,283.45
Greg Owen	66 75 69 71	281	2,283.45
Nicolas Joakimides	71 72 70 68	281	2,283.45
Jesus Maria Arruti	71 71 70 70	282	1,782.30
Mats Lanner	68 74 69 71	282	1,782.30
David Lynn	68 68 72 74	282	1,782.30
Gianluca Baruffaldi	71 72 79 61	283	1,382.55
Scott Watson	69 71 73 70	283	1,382.55
Eric Giraud	73 70 69 71	283	1,382.55
Christopher Hanell	71 72 74 67	284	1,023.75
Ariel Canete	68 70 75 71	284	1,023.75
Robert Jan Derksen	71 72 71 70	284	1,023.75
Jean-Pierre Cixous	71 74 72 68	285	750.26
John Bickerton	68 72 73 72	285	750.26
Greg Chalmers	69 76 70 70	285	750.26
Stephen Leaney	69 75 69 72	285	750.26
Tony Edlund	73 72 73 68	286	625.95
Lee James	72 72 72 70	286	625.95
Gordon J. Brand	70 74 71 71	286	625.95
Pauli Hughes	72 73 74 67	286	625.95
Olivier Edmond	73 73 72 69	287	573.30
Angel Franco	70 72 73 73	288	479.17
Gordon Sherry	71 73 69 75	288	479.17
Michele Reale	68 71 73 76	288	479.17
Frederik Andersson	71 69 73 75	288	479.17
Kalle Brink	70 75 77 66	288	479.17
Frederic Cupillard	72 73 72 71	288	479.17
Ivo Giner	72 73 73 70	288	479.17
Elliot Boult	71 75 70 72	288	479.17
Gary Murphy	70 74 70 74	288	479.17
Oyvind Rojahn	75 71 74 68	288	479.17
Mark Foster	72 71 72 73	288	479.17

Toyota PGA Championship

Odensu Eventyr Golf, Odensu, Denmark
Par 36-36–72; 6,754 yards

August 29-31
purse, £40,000

	SCORES			TOTAL	MONEY
Fredrik Henge	65	66	71	202	£6,497.40
Soren Kjeldsen	71	68	65	204	3,385.20
Martin Erlandsson	66	71	67	204	3,385.20
Leif Westerberg	66	69	70	205	1,950
Craig Hainline	70	70	66	206	1,653.60
Stephane Lahary	69	70	68	207	1,456.65
Knud Storegaard	69	70	68	207	1,456.65
Johan Rystrom	70	69	69	208	1,142.70
Francois Lamare	68	70	70	208	1,142.70
Per Nyman	68	70	70	208	1,142.70
Nils Rorbek	66	73	69	208	1,142.70
Don Bell	71	68	70	209	694.76
Rene Budde	70	71	68	209	694.76
Pehr Magnebrant	70	68	71	209	694.76
Nicolas Dupuy	69	71	69	209	694.76
Marcus Norgren	68	71	70	209	694.76
Niklas Diethelm	67	74	68	209	694.76
Roberto Zappa	67	71	71	209	694.76
Jose Garcia	72	69	69	210	420.71
Jesper Bjorklund	71	70	69	210	420.71
Antony Manasson	70	67	73	210	420.71
Steven Mattson	69	70	71	210	420.71
Gary Marks	68	68	74	210	420.71
Lars Tingvall	68	68	74	210	420.71
Charles Challen	67	70	73	210	420.71
Kevin Carissimi	65	75	70	210	420.71
*Mads Vibe-Hastrup	66	74	70	210	
Magnus Persson	73	69	69	211	347.10
Johan Selberg	69	72	70	211	347.10
Per Nyman	67	70	74	211	347.10
*Fredrik Neltoft	70	71	70	211	
Gianluca Pietrobono	72	71	69	212	308.10
David Philp	71	72	69	212	308.10
Henrik Nystrom	70	70	72	212	308.10
Erik Andersson	68	71	73	212	308.10
Daniel Westermark	68	70	74	212	308.10
*Morten Orveland	69	70	73	212	

Sovereign Russian Open

Moscow Golf & Country Club, Moscow, Russia
Par 36-36–72; 7,105 yards

September 3-6
purse, £90,000

	SCORES				TOTAL	MONEY
Michele Reale	73	68	68	71	280	£14,619.15
Heinz P. Thul	72	72	64	72	280	9,740.25
(Reale defeated Thul on second extra hole.)						
Gary Murphy	71	72	70	68	281	4,940.33
Soren Kjeldsen	69	72	70	70	281	4,940.33
Stephen Leaney	72	70	69	71	282	3,567.04
Jorge Berendt	70	67	72	73	282	3,567.04
Anssi Kankkonen	73	71	73	66	283	3,018.60
Nicolas Vanhootegem	71	67	73	72	283	3,018.60

	SCORES	TOTAL	MONEY
Craig Hainline	71 68 69 76	284	2,562.30
Gary Marks	73 67 71 73	284	2,562.30
Henrik Nystrom	71 68 72 74	285	2,073.83
Jesus Maria Arruti	74 71 69 71	285	2,073.83
Warren Bennett	73 69 70 73	285	2,073.83
Frederic Cupillard	71 72 70 73	286	1,458.85
Nicolas Joakimides	70 70 73 73	286	1,458.85
Robert Jan Derksen	73 71 71 71	286	1,458.85
Mikael Lundberg	76 70 71 69	286	1,458.85
Arnaud Langenaeken	72 72 70 73	287	1,118.82
Eric Giraud	73 70 71 73	287	1,118.82
Robert Wragg	65 76 75 72	288	911.51
Kalle Brink	75 71 72 70	288	911.51
Bradley Dredge	72 74 76 66	288	911.51
Benoit Telleria	73 70 76 69	288	911.51
Mikael Piltz	72 69 71 76	288	911.51
Mark Litton	71 71 73 73	288	911.51
Magnus Persson	74 72 70 72	288	911.51
Jeremy Robinson	72 73 72 71	288	911.51
Morten Backhausen	74 72 74 69	289	743.68
Jean Marie Kula	71 70 74 74	289	743.68
Mike Miller	73 70 77 69	289	743.68
Greg Owen	70 71 75 73	289	743.68

Ohrlings Swedish Match Play

Varbergs Golf Club, Himle, Tvaaker, Sweden
Par 37-35–72; 7,037 yards

September 4-7
purse, £50,000

FINAL

Gregory Garbero defeated Elliot Boult, 2 up

(Garbero received £8,121.71; Boult received £5,411.28.)

THIRD-PLACE PLAYOFF

Raimo Sjoberg defeated Fredrick Lindgren, 4 and 2

(Sjoberg received £3,051.71; Lindgren received £2,437.52.)

Perrier European Pro-Am

Golf Club d'Hulencourt
Par 36-36–72; 6,797 yards

September 11-14
purse, £65,000

Royal Waterloo Golf Club, La Marache Course
Par 36-36–72; 6,438 yards

Royal Waterloo Golf Club, Le Lion Course
Par 36-36–72; 6,368 yards
Waterloo, Belgium

	SCORES	TOTAL	MONEY
Craig Hainline	68 71 68 64	271	£10,558.2:
Stephen Leaney	69 68 65 70	272	7,034.6:

	SCORES				TOTAL	MONEY
Greg Owen	68	67	72	67	274	3,967.28
Joakim Gronhagen	67	73	70	66	276	3,168.75
Fredrik Lindgren	69	70	69	69	277	2,687.06
Olivier Edmond	65	73	72	68	278	2,367.06
David A. Russell	70	73	68	67	278	2,367.06
Mark Litton	69	68	69	73	279	1,930.83
Steen Tinning	64	72	72	71	279	1,930.83
Jean Marie Kula	67	69	77	66	279	1,930.83
Antonio Sobrinho	71	69	72	68	280	1,634.67
Paul Nilbrink	68	69	73	71	281	1,364.67
Simon Burnell	72	68	70	71	281	1,364.67
Bradley Dredge	74	71	70	66	281	1,364.67
Tim Planchin	70	69	70	73	282	992.87
Emil Madsen	72	70	70	70	282	992.87
Scott Watson	71	74	69	68	282	992.87
Per Nyman	63	77	71	72	283	830.21
Marc Pendaries	70	74	71	69	284	735.15
Stewart Cronin	72	72	69	71	284	735.15
Jorge Berendt	68	73	73	70	284	735.15
Michele Reale	70	75	72	67	284	735.15
Kalle Brink	72	72	69	72	285	612.63
Markus Brier	71	70	76	68	285	612.63
Raphael Eyraud	72	72	70	71	285	612.63
Robert Jonsson	69	69	74	73	285	612.63
Thomas Nielsen	72	72	71	70	285	612.63
Jose Carriles	67	69	76	73	285	612.63
Morten Backhausen	69	72	70	75	286	521.26
Nils Rorbaek	70	70	73	73	286	521.26
Nicolas Vanhootegem	75	70	74	67	286	521.26
Gianluca Baruffaldi	64	76	72	74	286	521.26

Eulen Open Galea

RSG de Neguri, Vizcaya, Spain
Par 36-36–72; 6,868 yards

September 18-21
purse, £67,322

	SCORES				TOTAL	MONEY
Warren Bennett	67	72	65	67	271	£10,935.44
Tomas Jesus Munoz	72	68	69	71	280	3,727.19
Stephen Leaney	65	72	71	72	280	3,727.19
Per Nyman	73	70	69	68	280	3,727.19
Juan Quiros	71	71	68	70	280	3,727.19
Antoine Lebouc	71	71	69	69	280	3,727.19
Nicolas Joakimides	72	69	71	68	280	3,727.19
Tony Edlund	75	69	69	68	281	1,999.80
Paul Nilbrink	71	69	69	72	281	1,999.80
Mikael Lundberg	67	75	70	69	281	1,999.80
Mats Lanner	73	72	65	72	282	1,483.44
Hans Karlsson	70	74	69	69	282	1,483.44
Greg Owen	72	72	68	70	282	1,483.44
Andrew Butterfield	75	68	71	68	282	1,483.44
Thomas Nielsen	76	67	71	69	283	951.76
Soren Kjeldsen	71	68	73	71	283	951.76
Simon Brown	71	72	74	66	283	951.76
Fredrik Lindgren	67	68	74	74	283	951.76
Heinz P. Thul	72	71	70	70	283	951.76
Steen Tinning	67	70	75	72	284	704.52
Erol Simsek	69	71	72	72	284	704.52

	SCORES				TOTAL	MONEY
Elliot Boult	72	70	71	71	284	704.52
Marc Pendaries	71	71	71	71	284	704.52
Fredrik Larsson	73	71	68	72	284	704.52
Jorge Berendt	72	72	69	71	284	704.52
Markus Brier	72	71	69	73	285	603.88
Henrik Nystrom	72	73	72	68	285	603.88
Jesus Maria Arruti	70	74	66	75	285	603.88
Nicolas Vanhootegem	72	71	68	75	286	512.80
Eric Giraud	71	70	74	71	286	512.80
Ivo Giner	72	73	70	71	286	512.80
David Lynn	71	71	72	72	286	512.80
Fredrik Henge	72	73	69	72	286	512.80
Mariano Aparicio	71	72	69	74	286	512.80
Benoit Telleria	70	71	67	78	286	512.80
Gary Marks	73	71	70	72	286	512.80

BPGT Challenge

Wynyard Hall Golf Club, Newcastle-upon-Tyne, England
Par 36-36–72; 6,851 yards

September 23-26
purse, £35,000

	SCORES				TOTAL	MONEY
Olivier Edmond	69	67	63	68	267	£5,685.23
Craig Hainline	71	64	66	68	269	3,787.88
Russell Hurd	64	68	70	70	272	2,136.23
Gary Murphy	70	71	68	64	273	1,706.25
Warren Bennett	67	72	70	65	274	1,446.90
Charles Challen	71	68	69	67	275	1,178.17
Calvin O'Carroll	65	71	69	70	275	1,178.17
Roger Winchester	68	75	64	68	275	1,178.17
Michael Archer	69	71	67	68	275	1,178.17
Andrew Barnett	63	73	71	69	276	955.50
David R. Jones	71	68	68	70	277	842.89
Stuart Andrew	68	70	69	70	277	842.89
Jeremy Robinson	69	68	71	70	278	699.57
Stephen Leaney	68	70	71	69	278	699.57
Robert Wragg	70	73	69	67	279	512.73
Philip Archer	70	68	71	70	279	512.73
David Valentine	66	74	69	70	279	512.73
Morten Backhausen	71	71	68	69	279	512.73
Duncan Muscroft	73	68	68	71	280	388.34
Matt Deal	67	73	71	69	280	388.34
Paul Lyons	68	72	68	72	280	388.34
David Lynn	72	70	68	70	280	388.34
Jorge Berendt	69	69	71	71	280	388.34
Andrew Butterfield	71	72	69	69	281	313.95
Simon Vale	70	73	70	68	281	313.95
Kevin Carissimi	71	70	72	68	281	313.95
Andrew Clapp	68	72	69	72	281	313.95
Stephen Dodd	72	71	66	72	281	313.95
Neal Briggs	72	70	69	70	281	313.95
Stewart Cronin	70	71	70	70	281	313.95

Telia InfoMedia Grand Prix

Ljunghusens Golf Club, Sweden
Par 36-36–72; 6,115 yards
(First round cancelled — high winds.)

October 2-5
purse, £80,000

	SCORES			TOTAL	MONEY
Fredrik Henge	71	69	65	205	£12,994.80
Steen Tinning	69	68	69	206	8,658
Craig Hainline	72	71	64	207	4,391.40
Marc Pendaries	68	73	66	207	4,391.40
Raphael Jacquelin	68	70	70	208	3,307.20
Greg Owen	72	70	67	209	2,800.20
John Bickerton	72	68	69	209	2,800.20
Antoine Lebouc	65	72	72	209	2,800.20
Gordon J. Brand	71	71	68	210	1,934.40
Heinz P. Thul	71	70	69	210	1,934.40
Jesus Maria Arruti	70	72	68	210	1,934.40
Gregory Garbero	69	71	70	210	1,934.40
Roger Winchester	68	73	69	210	1,934.40
Marten Olander	68	72	70	210	1,934.40
Francisco Cea	72	71	68	211	1,065.26
Thomas Nielsen	72	69	70	211	1,065.26
Fredrik Lindgren	70	71	70	211	1,065.26
Warren Bennett	70	70	71	211	1,065.26
Michele Reale	69	74	68	211	1,065.26
David Lynn	68	75	68	211	1,065.26
Mats Hallberg	68	74	69	211	1,065.26
Andrew Collison	75	67	70	212	767.74
Frederik Lundgren	72	69	71	212	767.74
Michael Campbell	70	73	69	212	767.74
Fredrik Jacobson	70	71	71	212	767.74
Mark Litton	70	67	75	212	767.74
Tim Planchin	69	69	74	212	767.74
Pehr Magnebrant	68	72	72	212	767.74
*Peter Hansson	66	78	68	212	
Erik Andersson	70	72	71	213	659.10
Nicolas Joakimides	69	72	72	213	659.10

San Paolo Vita Open

Margara Golf Club, Margara, Italy
Par 36-36–72; 6,778 yards

October 8-11
purse, £44,156

	SCORES				TOTAL	MONEY
Mathew Goggin	68	70	67	64	269	£7,172.51
Henrik Nystrom	68	66	67	69	270	4,778.81
Francisco Cea	70	67	65	69	271	2,695.07
Kevin Carissimi	66	68	69	69	272	1,884.26
Massimo Florioli	69	71	65	67	272	1,884.26
Markus Brier	71	64	69	68	272	1,884.26
Silvio Grappasonni	68	69	71	66	274	1,481
Nicolas Joakimides	70	68	67	69	274	1,481
John Bickerton	68	68	72	67	275	1,308.79
Olivier Edmond	69	69	67	71	276	1,205.46
Jose Carriles	70	70	67	70	277	1,110.75
Mark Litton	72	67	70	69	278	883.65
Phil Golding	69	70	71	68	278	883.65

	SCORES				TOTAL	MONEY
Heinz P. Thul	70	72	67	69	278	883.65
David R. Jones	70	72	68	68	278	883.65
Marcello Santi	70	67	70	72	279	611.34
Lee James	71	69	71	68	279	611.34
Frederic Cupillard	71	67	72	69	279	611.34
Patxi Amatriain	66	73	72	69	280	520.93
Kalle Brink	72	68	73	67	280	520.93
Andrea Canessa	70	69	73	69	281	438.52
Mike Miller	69	69	67	76	281	438.52
Michele Reale	73	69	68	71	281	438.52
Eric Giraud	71	69	70	71	281	438.52
Jose Sota	69	71	71	70	281	438.52
Roberto Zappa	67	72	70	72	281	438.52
Massimo Scarpa	69	70	73	69	281	438.52
Greg Owen	71	70	70	71	282	383.17
Tim Planchin	69	70	65	79	283	345.14
Stephen Leaney	73	69	68	73	283	345.14
Nicolas Vanhootegem	72	70	70	71	283	345.14
Rudi Sailer	72	70	73	68	283	345.14
Thomas Nielsen	67	73	74	69	283	345.14
Marco Durante	72	69	72	70	283	345.14

Estoril Challenge

Penha Longa, Sintra, Portugal
Par 36-36–72; 6,900 yards

October 16-19
purse, £85,000

	SCORES				TOTAL	MONEY
Jose Carriles	64	70	70	72	276	£13,806.98
Kalle Brink	68	67	72	70	277	9,199.13
Antoine Lebouc	72	64	72	74	282	4,665.87
Neal Briggs	69	73	71	69	282	4,665.87
Patxi Amatriain	69	69	74	72	284	3,368.87
Henrik Nystrom	72	68	75	69	284	3,368.87
Mats Lanner	69	73	74	70	286	2,635.43
Frederic Cupillard	68	70	77	71	286	2,635.43
Andrew Beal	72	67	73	74	286	2,635.43
Daniel Silva	69	73	69	75	286	2,635.43
Nicolas Joakimides	70	68	75	74	287	1,958.61
Roger Winchester	68	70	77	72	287	1,958.61
John Bickerton	69	74	73	71	287	1,958.61
Steen Tinning	74	69	75	70	288	1,533.19
Jose Sota	70	73	73	73	289	1,139.52
Francisco Cea	78	68	72	71	289	1,139.52
Jeff Remesy	70	70	76	73	289	1,139.52
David Lynn	72	68	75	74	289	1,139.52
Nicolas Vanhootegem	70	70	76	73	289	1,139.52
Mathew Goggin	72	73	75	70	290	905
Mikael Lundberg	74	68	75	73	290	905
Mark Litton	72	70	77	71	290	905
Thomas Levet	71	72	76	71	290	905
Kevin Carissimi	72	71	75	72	290	905
Raphael Jacquelin	71	74	75	71	291	738.7
Stephen Leaney	68	71	79	73	291	738.7
Mikael Piltz	71	75	73	72	291	738.7
Mike Miller	74	72	76	69	291	738.7
Anssi Kankkonen	71	75	72	73	291	738.7

	SCORES			TOTAL	MONEY
Robert Jan Derksen	72	74	74	71	291	738.77
Antonio Sobrinho	68	77	76	70	291	738.77

Estoril Grand Final

Club de Golfe do Montado, Setubal, Portugal
Par 36-36–72; 6,603 yards
(Fourth round cancelled — rain.)

October 23-26
purse, £70,000

	SCORES			TOTAL	MONEY
Nicolas Joakimides	69	67	62	198	£11,662
Mikael Lundberg	64	66	69	199	7,770
Per Nyman	69	67	64	200	3,941
Marc Pendaries	68	64	68	200	3,941
Andrew Collison	67	68	67	202	2,732.33
Thomas Levet	66	66	70	202	2,732.33
Stephen Leaney	65	70	67	202	2,732.33
Bradley Dredge	70	65	68	203	2,219
Steen Tinning	69	69	65	203	2,219
Henrik Nystrom	67	68	69	204	1,730.75
Jorge Berendt	71	67	66	204	1,730.75
Kalle Brink	68	70	66	204	1,730.75
Mathew Goggin	70	66	68	204	1,730.75
Olivier Edmond	66	71	68	205	1,295
Francisco Cea	67	66	72	205	1,295
Michele Reale	69	71	66	206	994
Jesus Maria Arruti	69	71	66	206	994
Raphael Jacquelin	70	68	68	206	994
Fredrik Henge	67	68	72	207	812
John Bickerton	69	68	70	207	812
Frederic Cupillard	68	71	68	207	812
Warren Bennett	68	68	71	207	812
Stewart Cronin	71	69	68	208	676.67
Soren Kjeldsen	70	71	67	208	676.67
Jose Carriles	70	68	70	208	676.67
Thomas Nielsen	68	70	70	208	676.67
Nicolas Vanhootegem	68	67	73	208	676.67
Kevin Carissimi	70	67	71	208	676.67
Gregory Garbero	71	66	72	209	554
Knud Storegaard	73	69	67	209	554
Robert Jan Derksen	72	68	69	209	554
Markus Brier	69	68	72	209	554
David Lynn	69	72	68	209	554
Greg Owen	70	70	69	209	554
Morten Backhausen	67	72	70	209	554

Asia/Japan Tours

Mitsubishi Motors - Southwoods Open

Manila Southwoods Golf & Country Club, Masters Course,
Manila, Philippines
Par 36-36–72; 7,132 yards

February 13-16
purse, US$250,000

	SCORES				TOTAL	MONEY
Takao Nogami	66	72	73	70	281	US$41,675
Jim Rutledge	73	72	70	68	283	21,500
Kevin Wentworth	67	75	73	68	283	21,500
John Kernohan	69	74	70	71	284	12,500
Pedro Martinez	69	78	71	67	285	8,666.67
Travis Williams	74	72	70	69	285	8,666.67
Brian Gay	71	73	69	72	285	8,666.67
Gary Rusnak	69	74	71	72	286	5,300
Arjun Atwal	73	71	68	74	286	5,300
Alan Bratton	73	73	70	71	287	4,333.33
David McCampbell	72	73	70	72	287	4,333.33
Uli Zilg	74	69	70	74	287	4,333.33
Tim Straub	72	75	70	71	288	3,800
Kim Jong-duk	70	75	72	71	288	3,800
Joey Snyder III	70	76	70	72	288	3,800
Eric Rustand	74	71	71	72	288	3,800
Ian Leggatt	72	71	73	72	288	3,800
Edward Fryatt	73	75	68	73	289	3,350
Robert Jan Derksen	70	73	73	73	289	3,350
Christian Chernock	71	71	72	75	289	3,350
Peter Alabaster	65	75	71	78	289	3,350
Raul Fretes	72	74	75	69	290	2,950
Jerry Wood	75	71	73	71	290	2,950
Robert Pactolerin	68	75	72	75	290	2,950
Chris McCourt	70	72	73	75	290	2,950
Rob Moss	74	74	75	68	291	2,305.56
Pehr Magnebrant	73	75	72	71	291	2,305.56
Willie De Tomas	69	72	79	71	291	2,305.56
Steve Haskins	71	75	73	72	291	2,305.56
Ray Cragun	70	74	74	73	291	2,305.56
Chris Isackson	72	74	71	74	291	2,305.56
Colin Stoops	73	72	72	74	291	2,305.56
Rick Todd	70	76	70	75	291	2,305.56
Chris Tidland	70	71	72	78	291	2,305.56

Konica U-Bix Manila Open

Wack Wack Golf Club, Manila, Philippines
Par 36-36–72; 7,009 yards

February 20-2
purse, US$200,00

	SCORES				TOTAL	MONEY
Yasuharu Imano	70	74	71	71	286	US$33,340
Kevin Wentworth	72	76	70	70	288	14,800
Pedro Martinez	72	70	74	72	288	14,800

	SCORES				TOTAL	MONEY
Danny Zarate	70	70	75	73	288	14,800
Gustavo Rojas	73	72	69	75	289	7,600
Ian Leggatt	68	73	71	77	289	7,600
Mike Tschetter	72	72	71	75	290	5,600
Raul Fretes	72	74	75	70	291	3,680
Gary Rusnak	75	73	72	71	291	3,680
Robert Pactolerin	68	80	71	72	291	3,680
Edward Fryatt	73	76	68	74	291	3,680
Rob Moss	75	72	70	74	291	3,680
Don Walsworth	69	74	70	78	291	3,680
Hans Albertsson	74	74	71	73	292	3,080
Brad Wilson	75	71	68	78	292	3,080
John Kernohan	75	69	75	74	293	2,880
Miguel Fernandez	73	71	73	76	293	2,880
Grant Masson	72	71	72	78	293	2,880
Takao Nogami	73	77	75	69	294	2,560
Rick Gibson	74	75	73	72	294	2,560
Ron Wuensche	74	74	72	74	294	2,560
Greg Lesher	73	76	70	75	294	2,560
Mars Pucay	73	73	72	76	294	2,560
Brian Wilson	73	75	73	75	296	2,160
Carlos Larrain	73	71	75	77	296	2,160
Dean Wilson	68	74	77	77	296	2,160
Robert Jan Derksen	75	74	69	78	296	2,160
Jim Rutledge	74	75	68	79	296	2,160
Rick Todd	71	77	76	73	297	1,697.14
Chris Tidland	73	74	75	75	297	1,697.14
Joost Steenkamer	74	74	73	76	297	1,697.14
Yurio Akitomi	72	77	71	77	297	1,697.14
Ruben Sasutil	75	72	72	78	297	1,697.14
Danny Mijovic	74	71	73	79	297	1,697.14
Edgar Ababa	71	76	70	80	297	1,697.14

Benson and Hedges Malaysian Open

Saujana Golf & Country Club, Palm Course,
Kuala Lumpur, Malaysia
Par 36-36–72; 7,233 yards

March 6-9
purse, US$300,000

	SCORES				TOTAL	MONEY
Lee Westwood	64	72	69	69	274	US$50,010
Larry Barber	66	70	70	70	276	33,000
Retief Goosen	70	73	69	65	277	18,600
Mike Cunning	69	71	68	70	278	15,000
Brian Gay	72	67	70	70	279	11,400
Harumitsu Hamano	71	67	66	75	279	11,400
Kim Jong-duk	71	73	67	70	281	7,590
Stephen Leaney	71	71	68	71	281	7,590
Dean Wilson	71	73	68	70	282	5,700
Don Walsworth	72	71	68	71	282	5,700
Paul McGinley	69	75	70	69	283	4,980
Darren Clarke	71	72	70	70	283	4,980
Kyi Hla Han	71	72	67	73	283	4,980
Tony Carolan	70	74	71	69	284	4,560
Jim Straub	72	73	66	73	284	4,560
Stewart Ginn	69	72	70	73	284	4,560
Andrew Pitts	72	72	74	67	285	4,140

	SCORES	TOTAL	MONEY
Zhang Liang-wei	71 74 71 69	285	4,140
Arjun Singh	71 73 69 72	285	4,140
Kevin Wentworth	72 71 70 72	285	4,140
Glenn Joyner	73 74 69 70	286	3,540
John Kernohan	72 72 71 71	286	3,540
Mike Tschetter	70 77 67 72	286	3,540
Brett Partridge	72 68 73 73	286	3,540
Ali Kadir	70 70 73 73	286	3,540
David Howell	69 70 73 74	286	3,540
Brian Wilson	72 74 71 70	287	2,760
Chang Tse-peng	71 73 73 70	287	2,760
Ted Gleason	74 72 70 71	287	2,760
Steve Flesch	72 73 71 71	287	2,760
Park Nam-sin	71 72 73 71	287	2,760
Edward Fryatt	71 72 72 72	287	2,760
Craig McClellan	66 76 70 75	287	2,760

Thai Airways International Thailand Open

Sriracha International Golf Club, Pattaya City, Thailand
Par 36-36–72; 6,937 yards

March 13-16
purse, US$300,000

	SCORES	TOTAL	MONEY
Christian Chernock	70 66 68 64	268	US$50,100
Don Walsworth	70 65 69 65	269	33,000
Larry Barber	68 66 70 66	270	18,600
Gary Rusnak	69 70 66 68	273	13,800
Park Nam-sin	70 66 68 69	273	13,800
Gustavo Rojas	69 66 71 68	274	7,356
Tsuneyuki Nakajima	67 67 72 68	274	7,356
Felix Casas	68 68 69 69	274	7,356
Tim Straub	66 70 69 69	274	7,356
Brian Wilson	68 69 65 72	274	7,356
Choi Kyung-ju	70 70 68 67	275	5,070
Greg Lesher	71 71 65 68	275	5,070
Christian Pena	70 70 67 69	276	4,740
Norikazu Kawakami	66 70 69 71	276	4,740
Edward Fryatt	75 67 71 64	277	4,260
Go Higaki	69 70 71 67	277	4,260
Stephen Leaney	73 69 67 68	277	4,260
Kevin Wentworth	69 69 69 70	277	4,260
Banlue Maneerat	68 68 71 70	277	4,260
Philip Jonas	69 68 67 73	277	4,260
Alan Bratton	70 71 71 66	278	3,480
Dean Wilson	69 72 68 69	278	3,480
Ray Cragun	67 73 68 70	278	3,480
Chamnien Chitprasong	70 68 70 70	278	3,480
Grant Masson	67 68 73 70	278	3,480
Oscar Serna	68 69 70 71	278	3,480
Takashi Kanemoto	69 68 68 73	278	3,480
Prayad Marksaeng	71 70 71 67	279	2,760
Randy Wylie	69 72 70 68	279	2,760
Jim Rutledge	69 70 71 69	279	2,760
Hidezumi Shirakata	67 70 72 70	279	2,760
John Riegger	72 66 69 72	279	2,760

Rolex Masters

Singapore Island Country Club, Bukit Course, Singapore
Par 35-36–71; 6,749 yards

March 20-23
purse, US$289,000

	SCORES				TOTAL	MONEY
Kyi Hla Han	67	68	65	68	268	US$48,178.30
Yeh Chang-ting	68	70	68	64	270	24,854
Edward Fryatt	70	69	65	66	270	24,854
Larry Barber	68	70	65	68	271	11,126.50
Gary Rusnak	67	68	68	68	271	11,126.50
Dean Wilson	69	62	71	69	271	11,126.50
Danny Zarate	67	65	68	71	271	11,126.50
Hidezumi Shirakata	67	68	66	71	272	6,631.40
Chung Joon	71	68	69	65	273	5,491
Park Nam-sin	68	68	70	67	273	5,491
Wayne Smith	71	69	67	67	274	4,797.40
Pedro Martinez	70	70	67	67	274	4,797.40
Philip Jonas	70	68	69	67	274	4,797.40
Dino Kwek Beng Kwee	69	68	70	68	275	4,508.40
Kevin Wentworth	70	71	71	64	276	4,161.60
Jim Rutledge	72	67	71	66	276	4,161.60
Tsuneyuki Nakajima	69	72	68	67	276	4,161.60
Felix Casas	72	68	69	67	276	4,161.60
Chang Tse-peng	70	67	68	71	276	4,161.60
Raul Fretes	71	68	69	69	277	3,814.80
Jarrod Moseley	71	70	69	68	278	3,583.60
Don Walsworth	68	69	73	68	278	3,583.60
Brian Gay	65	73	71	69	278	3,583.60
Stuart Holmes	73	69	71	66	279	3,063.40
Jocy Snyder III	71	71	69	68	279	3,063.40
Brian Wilson	72	68	70	69	279	3,063.40
Craig Kamps	69	69	72	69	279	3,063.40
Chris Gray	69	69	71	70	279	3,063.40
Brett Partridge	70	70	68	71	279	3,063.40
Brian Quinn	74	68	69	69	280	2,361.54
Christian Pena	72	68	71	69	280	2,361.54
Greg Lesher	69	70	72	69	280	2,361.54
Mike Cunning	73	69	68	70	280	2,361.54
Randy Wylie	71	68	70	71	280	2,361.54
Eric Epperson	68	71	69	72	280	2,361.54
Poh Eing Cheong	69	68	71	72	280	2,361.54

Classic India Open

Royal Calcutta Golf Club, Calcutta, India
Par 36-36–72; 7,195 yards

March 27-30
purse, US$300,000

	SCORES				TOTAL	MONEY
Edward Fryatt	63	69	67	73	272	US$50,010
Gary Rusnak	70	70	71	67	278	33,000
Christian Pena	68	72	69	70	279	18,600
Dean Wilson	69	73	67	71	280	15,000
Pedro Martinez	65	67	74	75	281	12,600
Tim Straub	69	70	72	72	283	10,200
Hidezumi Shirakata	73	72	68	71	284	7,040
Hans Albertsson	74	66	72	72	284	7,040
Ken Duke	73	68	68	75	284	7,040

	SCORES				TOTAL	MONEY
Marty Schiene	73	72	71	69	285	5,100
Philip Jonas	71	69	74	71	285	5,100
Mike Tschetter	71	69	73	72	285	5,100
Steve Haskins	70	73	69	73	285	5,100
Jerry Wood	72	70	75	69	286	4,500
Craig Jones	71	72	71	72	286	4,500
Brian Wilson	70	70	73	73	286	4,500
Ray Cragun	69	70	71	76	286	4,500
Shaun Haberstroh	75	72	71	69	287	4,080
Takao Nogami	72	73	73	69	287	4,080
Vivek Bhandari	71	70	71	75	287	4,080
Amritinder Singh	74	73	72	69	288	3,660
Uli Zilg	70	76	72	70	288	3,660
Eric Meeks	74	70	73	71	288	3,660
Basad Ali	68	73	72	75	288	3,660
Chris Tidland	73	73	73	70	289	3,180
Andrew Pitts	74	72	70	73	289	3,180
Danny Mijovic	69	77	70	73	289	3,180
Gaurav Ghei	72	71	71	75	289	3,180
*Harmeet Kahlon	68	73	73	75	289	
Rodrigo Cuello	77	70	73	70	290	2,640
Joey Snyder III	71	75	72	72	290	2,640
Larry Barber	74	68	75	73	290	2,640
Joe Lloyd	70	73	72	75	290	2,640
Raul Fretes	70	70	75	75	290	2,640

Mobiline Philippine Open

Camp John Hay Golf Club, Baguio City, Philippines
Par 37-31–68; 5,252 yards

April 17-20
purse, US$300,000

	SCORES				TOTAL	MONEY
Kevin Wentworth	67	62	62	68	259	US$50,010
Tim Straub	65	67	67	63	262	22,200
Mars Pucay	70	65	63	64	262	22,200
Larry Barber	66	62	67	67	262	22,200
Willie De Tomas	68	62	66	67	263	12,600
Steve Haskins	66	66	65	67	264	9,300
Stephen Leaney	65	65	67	67	264	9,300
Ken Duke	70	66	63	66	265	5,835
Hideto Shigenobu	65	69	65	66	265	5,835
Frankie Minoza	68	65	66	66	265	5,835
Dean Wilson	67	63	69	66	265	5,835
Raul Fretes	72	65	65	64	266	4,755
Rodrigo Cuello	71	67	61	67	266	4,755
Felix Casas	68	67	64	67	266	4,755
Robert-Jan Derksen	67	65	65	69	266	4,755
Brian Gay	69	64	67	67	267	4,380
Edward Fryatt	67	65	65	70	267	4,380
Ian Leggatt	69	68	65	66	268	4,080
Norikazu Kawakami	68	68	64	68	268	4,080
Tim Balmer	67	67	65	69	268	4,080
Richard Sinfuego	65	71	67	66	269	3,720
Robert Pactolerin	67	66	69	67	269	3,720
Ted Gleason	68	70	63	68	269	3,720
Periasamy Gunasagaran	70	67	69	64	270	3,360
Christian Chernock	70	68	65	67	270	3,360
Takao Nogami	68	70	65	67	270	3,360

	SCORES	TOTAL	MONEY
Pedro Martinez	72 69 66 64	271	2,940
Mike Tschetter	71 68 68 64	271	2,940
George Olaybar	68 69 68 66	271	2,940
Gary Murphy	70 64 67 70	271	2,940

Maekyung LG Fashion Open

Nam Seoul Golf Club, Seoul, Korea
Par 36-36–72; 6,902 yards
May 1-4
purse, US$400,000

	SCORES	TOTAL	MONEY
Shin Yong-jin	69 67 68 68	272	US$66,680
Tim Balmer	69 67 69 68	273	44,000
Eric Meeks	70 69 69 67	275	22,400
Kevin Wentworth	70 69 66 70	275	22,400
Mike Cunning	69 72 69 66	276	13,866.67
Choi Sang-ho	71 71 66 68	276	13,866.67
Jeev Milkha Singh	65 71 67 73	276	13,866.67
*Kim Hyung-tae	68 70 71 67	276	
Jung Do-man	68 72 68 69	277	7,780
Christian Chernock	69 69 69 70	277	7,780
Choi Kyung-ju	67 66 73 71	277	7,780
Brian Wilson	72 68 65 72	277	7,780
Park Nam-sin	70 70 71 67	278	6,340
Kim Jong-duk	71 70 68 69	278	6,340
Clay Devers	71 70 66 71	278	6,340
Felix Casas	68 71 67 72	278	6,340
Edward Fryatt	71 68 72 68	279	5,920
Raul Fretes	68 70 72 70	280	5,360
Danny Mijovic	65 70 75 70	280	5,360
Gary Rusnak	72 67 70 71	280	5,360
Yoo Jong-ky	66 71 72 71	280	5,360
Gerry Norquist	71 67 70 72	280	5,360
Chang Tse-peng	68 70 67 75	280	5,360
Jim Rutledge	67 75 70 69	281	4,480
Choi Kwang-soo	69 73 69 70	281	4,480
Rob Moss	70 69 72 70	281	4,480
Don Walsworth	71 68 71 71	281	4,480
Park Yeun-tae	70 69 71 71	281	4,480
Lim Jin-han	74 69 71 68	282	3,840
Jerry Wood	70 71 71 70	282	3,840
Kang Wook-soon	68 71 71 72	282	3,840

Volvo China Open

Beijing International Golf Club, Beijing, China
Par 36-36–72; 6,956 yards
May 15-18
purse, US$400,000

	SCORES	TOTAL	MONEY
Cheng Jun	72 70 68 70	280	US$72,000
Adrian Percey	78 74 66 67	285	42,000
Mike Cunning	73 71 72 70	286	24,400
Mo Joong-kyung	72 75 69 70	286	24,400
Jerry Smith	73 76 71 68	287	17,200
Nam Young-woo	76 74 71 67	288	14,400

	SCORES				TOTAL	MONEY
Choi Kyung-ju	74	74	71	69	288	14,400
Justin Cooper	70	79	72	68	289	11,900
David Bransdon	73	73	73	70	289	11,900
Aaron Meeks	75	74	72	69	290	10,200
Christopher Williams	76	72	72	70	290	10,200
Glenn Joyner	74	74	74	69	291	8,200
Kwon Young-suk	74	78	67	72	291	8,200
Raul Fretes	72	75	70	74	291	8,200
Nico van Rensburg	75	77	69	71	292	6,300
Simon Yates	76	71	72	73	292	6,300
Chen Tsang-te	77	74	72	70	293	4,860
Park Nam-sin	74	75	73	71	293	4,860
Fredrick Mansson	75	76	71	71	293	4,860
Christian Chernock	76	76	70	71	293	4,860
Scott Laycock	73	76	72	72	293	4,860
Hsieh Yu-shu	69	74	77	73	293	4,860
Jeff Senior	74	77	73	70	294	3,766.67
Wang Ter-chang	73	76	74	71	294	3,766.67
Steven Alker	73	76	74	71	294	3,766.67
Arjun Singh	75	76	71	72	294	3,766.67
Gerry Norquist	73	74	74	73	294	3,766.67
Dominique Boulet	73	74	73	74	294	3,766.67
Charlie Wi	76	76	73	70	295	2,885.71
Richard Backwell	76	74	74	71	295	2,885.71
Hendrik Buhrmann	76	75	73	71	295	2,885.71
Vivek Bhandari	74	72	77	72	295	2,885.71
Mardan Mamat	77	73	72	73	295	2,885.71
Rob Stephens	72	74	75	74	295	2,885.71
Eric Meeks	72	74	73	76	295	2,885.71

Hyundai Motors Open

Lakeside Country Club, Seoul, Korea
Par 36-36–72; 7,353 yards

May 29-June 2
purse, US$500,000

	SCORES				TOTAL	MONEY
Ian Woosnam	71	74	67	68	280	US$90,000
Sandy Lyle	74	70	67	69	280	50,000
Chung Joon	72	73	69	70	284	34,000
Yasuharu Imano	72	71	70	72	285	22,000
Choi Kyung-ju	68	73	68	76	285	22,000
Park Nam-sin	68	70	74	75	287	18,000
Kang Wook-soon	73	74	71	70	288	14,500
Zhang Lian-wei	72	72	74	70	288	14,500
Richard Lee	75	71	69	73	288	14,500
Prayad Marksaeng	73	72	74	70	289	10,233
Andrew Bonhomme	74	69	75	71	289	10,233
Aaron Meeks	71	73	71	74	289	10,233
Edward Fryatt	75	75	70	70	290	7,800
Shin Yong-jin	74	72	72	72	290	7,800
Yoo Jong-ky	68	75	74	73	290	7,800
Kim Wan-tae	72	74	76	71	293	5,850
Grant Dodd	72	77	72	72	293	5,850
Jarrod Moseley	73	73	73	74	293	5,850
Scott Laycock	71	72	76	74	293	5,850
Jim Rutledge	74	75	75	70	294	4,620
Kwak Hyeung-soo	75	75	73	71	294	4,620
Hong Young-pyo	75	73	74	72	294	4,620

	SCORES	TOTAL	MONEY
Richard Backwell	72 77 71 74	294	4,620
John Senden	73 73 71 77	294	4,620
Kyi Hla Han	73 77 77 68	295	3,950
Jeev Milkha Singh	72 76 74 73	295	3,950
Kim Young-il	72 74 76 73	295	3,950
Kim Jong-duk	74 72 75 74	295	3,950
Greg Hanrahan	70 72 78 75	295	3,950
John Kernohan	70 75 71 79	295	3,950

Chinese Taipei Open

Sunrise Golf & Country Club, Taoyuan, Taiwan
Par 36-36–72; 7,068 yards

July 3-6
purse, US$275,000

	SCORES	TOTAL	MONEY
Tsai Chi-huang	66 66 71 71	274	US$45,842.50
Andre Cruse	72 71 72 66	281	30,250
Jim Rutledge	74 71 70 67	282	17,050
Chou Hung-nan	72 69 71 71	283	13,750
*Su Chin-jung	69 67 71 76	283	
Prayad Marksaeng	71 71 71 71	284	10,450
Hsieh Yu-shu	70 70 72 72	284	10,450
Dean Wilson	74 69 72 70	285	6,957.50
Norikazu Kawakami	71 70 72 72	285	6,957.50
Christian Chernock	77 70 69 70	286	4,829
Eric Meeks	73 71 72 70	286	4,829
Chang Chin-kuo	70 74 71 71	286	4,829
Chen Yuan-chi	70 66 75 75	286	4,829
David Ecob	70 70 70 76	286	4,829
Tim Straub	70 75 73 69	287	4,015
Jeev Milkha Singh	73 72 72 70	287	4,015
Gary Rusnak	72 72 73 70	287	4,015
Andrew Pitts	71 74 70 72	287	4,015
Chang Tse-peng	70 73 71 73	287	4,015
Wang Ter-chang	73 71 69 74	287	4,015
Ho Chung-yuan	75 70 74 69	288	3,410
Robert Stephens	76 71 71 70	288	3,410
Edward Fryatt	76 69 71 72	288	3,410
Charlie Wi	72 72 72 72	288	3,410
Jarrod Moseley	71 69 75 73	288	3,410
Kyi Hla Han	72 77 72 68	289	2,860
Brett Partridge	75 68 74 72	289	2,860
Lai Ying-juh	72 74 70 73	289	2,860
Gerry Norquist	75 66 74 74	289	2,860
Hsu Mong-nan	69 72 74 74	289	2,860

Taiwan PGA Golf Championship

Pearl Heights Golf Club, Taipei, Taiwan
Par 36-36–72; 7,006 yards

July 10-13
purse, US$436,000

	SCORES	TOTAL	MONEY
Gerry Norquist	72 69 69 70	280	US$74,909.09
Chou Hung-nan	70 75 68 67	280	35,454.55
Christian Chernock	70 67 71 72	280	35,454.55

Norquist defeated Chou and Chernock on first extra hole.)

	SCORES	TOTAL	MONEY
Chang Tse-peng	70 71 68 72	281	20,363.64
Jim Rutledge	71 71 71 69	282	16,727.27
Dean Wilson	71 70 71 71	283	12,727.27
Tim Balmer	72 71 64 76	283	12,727.27
Eric Meeks	73 70 71 71	285	8,545.45
Stuart Holmes	71 74 68 72	285	8,545.45
Hideto Shigenobu	71 71 71 72	285	8,545.45
Lucien Tinkler	71 68 73 73	285	8,545.45
Hsieh Yu-shu	72 74 71 69	286	6,618.18
Vivek Bhandari	68 72 74 72	286	6,618.18
Des Terblanche	74 73 72 68	287	5,218.18
Gary Rusnak	72 70 74 71	287	5,218.18
Edward Fryatt	71 71 72 73	287	5,218.18
Jarrod Moseley	75 69 68 75	287	5,218.18
Glenn Joyner	77 72 68 71	288	3,810.91
Chen Liang-hsi	71 77 68 72	288	3,810.91
Lu Hsi-chuen	74 72 69 73	288	3,810.91
Hsieh Min-nan	74 72 68 74	288	3,810.91
Chung Chun-hsing	69 71 73 75	288	3,810.91
Wang Ter-chang	69 77 72 71	289	3,345.45
Aaron Meeks	72 75 73 70	290	3,054.55
Shen Chung-shan	74 70 75 71	290	3,054.55
Hsu Huang-lung	74 74 69 73	290	3,054.55
Kuo Chie-hsiung	70 74 72 74	290	3,054.55
Rodrigo Cuello	73 71 71 75	290	3,054.55
Li Wen-sheng	75 71 68 76	290	3,054.55

Shinhan Donghae Open

Jaeil Country Club, Seoul, Korea
Par 36-36–72; 6,898 yards

September 4-7
purse, US$400,000

	SCORES	TOTAL	MONEY
Edward Fryatt	66 69 68 72	275	US$81,344
Kevin Wentworth	67 69 72 67	275	46,637
(Fryatt defeated Wentworth on first extra hole.)			
Jeev Milkha Singh	72 71 66 68	277	28,199
Takao Nogami	69 66 73 70	278	21,691
Kim Wan-tae	69 69 72 69	279	15,545
Choi Yoon-soo	66 72 72 69	279	15,545
Kim Jin-young	68 71 70 70	279	15,545
Shin Yong-jin	69 70 73 68	280	9,761
Park No-seok	68 72 71 69	280	9,761
Lim Jin-han	69 70 71 70	280	9,761
Kwon Oh-chul	70 70 71 70	281	7,321
Yoo Jae-chul	68 69 72 72	281	7,321
Kim Tae-hoon	73 68 74 67	282	6,507
Ted Oh	73 70 71 69	283	5,233
Lee Myung-chul	73 67 72 71	283	5,233
Kwak Heung-soo	68 74 69 72	283	5,233
Mike Tschetter	69 67 73 74	284	5,233
Chung Joon	73 71 69 71	284	4,229
Ray Cragun	70 72 71 71	284	4,229
*Bae Sung-man	69 72 71 72	284	
Kim Young-il	67 71 72 74	284	4,229
Kim Jong-pil	74 69 73 69	285	3,687
Ahn Joo-hwan	72 71 70 72	285	3,687

	SCORES				TOTAL	MONEY
*Kim Jong-myung	70	70	70	75	285	
Lee Kun-hee	67	76	73	70	286	3,308
Mike Cunning	70	72	70	74	286	3,308
Tim Balmer	69	70	73	74	286	3,308
Richard Backwell	77	70	73	76	286	3,308
Dean Wilson	77	71	80	69	287	2,928
Sin Hee-taek	68	74	74	71	287	2,928
Nam Young-woo	69	74	73	71	287	2,928
*Kim Sung-yoon	74	71	69	73	287	
Yoo Jong-koo	67	74	72	74	287	2,928
Choi Kyung-ju	73	70	69	75	287	2,928

Korea Open

Han Yang Country Club, Goyang City, Korea
Par 36-36–72; 7,021 yards

September 25-28
purse, US$400,000

	SCORES				TOTAL	MONEY
Kim Jong-duk	72	75	67	71	285	US$70,000
Andrew Pitts	72	72	70	71	285	31,000
Choi Kwang-soo	73	72	69	71	285	31,000
Shin Yong-jin	72	68	74	71	285	31,000

(Kim won in extra holes.)

	SCORES				TOTAL	MONEY
Moon Chun-bok	72	76	71	67	286	18,000
Aaron Meeks	76	71	70	70	287	14,000
Park Nam-sin	73	73	71	71	288	10,986
Lim Jin-han	73	70	72	73	288	10,986
John Senden	70	71	73	74	288	10,986
Olle Nordberg	75	72	72	70	289	7,655
Chung Do-man	75	72	70	72	289	7,655
Kwon Oh-chul	73	72	76	69	290	5,698
Cho Chul-sang	76	71	74	69	290	5,698
Martin Schiene	74	74	72	70	290	5,698
Choi Kyung-ju	74	73	73	70	290	5,698
Kwak Heung-soo	72	74	73	71	290	5,698
Jason McCarty	71	71	75	73	290	5,698
Chung Joon	74	71	72	73	290	5,698
Richard Lee	73	72	72	73	290	5,698
Eric Meeks	75	71	69	75	290	5,698
Kazuo Yamamoto	76	67	78	70	291	4,560
Lee Boo-young	75	73	73	70	291	4,560
*Terry Noh	71	77	72	71	291	
Mike Tschetter	76	72	72	71	291	4,560
*Kim Jong-myung	73	71	73	74	291	
Bae Joong-sang	77	70	73	72	292	4,060
Fran Quinn	74	72	74	72	292	4,060
Christian Pena	73	74	72	73	292	4,060
Tim Balmer	75	72	72	73	292	4,060
Amandeep Johl	71	75	71	75	292	4,060
Yoo Jae-chul	73	70	73	76	292	4,060

Mercuries Cup Masters

Tamsui Golf & Country Club, Tamsui, Taipei, Taiwan
Par 36-36–72; 7,121 yards

September 25-28
purse, US$350,000

	SCORES				TOTAL	MONEY
Gerry Norquist	69	70	71	68	278	US$70,175.44
Tsao Chien-teng	71	71	70	71	283	42,105.26
Eric Rustand	76	70	66	72	284	24,561.40
Lu Wen-ter	72	66	71	76	285	12,719.30
Jeev Milkha Singh	72	72	70	71	285	12,719.30
Wang Ter-chang	72	69	72	72	285	12,719.30
Jim Rutledge	71	75	70	69	285	12,719.30
Gary Rusnak	71	69	72	74	286	7,789.47
Yeh Chang-ting	73	68	73	73	287	5,973.68
Paul Friedlander	74	72	70	71	287	5,973.68
Hsieh Chien-sheng	72	69	73	73	287	5,973.68
Yuan Ching-chi	71	73	70	73	287	5,973.68
Thammanoon Sriroj	72	66	76	75	289	4,701.75
Kuo Chie-hsiung	71	72	68	78	289	4,701.75
Chen Liang-hsi	73	72	72	73	290	4,014.04
Craig Kamps	71	69	73	77	290	4,014.04
Chung Chun-hsing	77	72	68	73	290	4,014.04
Hsieh Yu-shu	71	71	75	73	290	4,014.04
Chen Tze-ming	71	72	73	74	290	4,014.04
*Su Ching-jung	71	74	73	72	290	
Chang Chin-kuo	73	72	74	72	291	3,614.04
Lee Wen-sheng	67	80	71	75	293	3,450.28
Tsai Chi-huang	70	71	76	76	293	3,450.28
Kevin Wentworth	74	73	72	74	293	3,450.28
Boonchu Ruangkit	75	72	75	72	294	3,157.89
Chang Tse-peng	74	71	78	71	294	3,157.89
Gaurav Ghei	78	70	73	73	294	3,157.89
Robert Willis	71	69	77	77	294	3,157.89
Hsu Mong-nan	73	77	70	74	294	3,157.89
Dominique Boulet	73	76	73	73	295	2,857.02
Periasamy Gunasegaran	74	74	74	73	295	2,857.02
Lu Chien-soon	72	70	76	77	295	2,857.02
Lai Ying-chu	71	73	72	79	295	2,857.02

Johnnie Walker Super Tour

Emeralda Golf and Country Club, River Course,
Jakarta, Indonesia
Par 36-36–72; 6,475 yards

December 9-14
purse, US$350,000

Panya Indra Golf Club, Bangkok, Thailand
Par 36-36–72; 7,159 yards

Fairways and Bluewater Resort, Manila, Philippines
Par 36-36–72; 6,695 yards

Ta Shee Golf & Country Club, Taipei, Taiwan
Par 36-36–72; 6,807 yards

	SCORES				TOTAL	MONEY
Jesper Parnevik	67	71	68	70	276	US$100,000
Nick Faldo	67	71	72	70	280	65,000

	SCORES				TOTAL	MONEY
Boonchu Ruangkit	72	70	70	70	282	55,000
Ernie Els	69	71	71	72	283	45,000
Felix Casas	70	71	71	73	285	35,000
Hong Chia-yuh	77	77	72	73	299	25,000
Maan Nasim	74	87	68	75	304	15,000
Ian Woosnam	70	74			WD	10,000

China Tour

Volvo Open

Shenzhen Golf Club, Shenzhen
Par 36-36–72; 7,250 yards

April 29-30
purse, US$75,000

	SCORES		TOTAL	MONEY
Adrian Percey	68	69	137	US$13,500
Robin Byrd	69	68	137	8,625

(Percey defeated Byrd on second extra hole.)

	SCORES		TOTAL	MONEY
Chen Tsang-te	68	70	138	4,687.50
Zhang Lian-wei	66	72	138	4,687.50
Jeff Senior	71	68	139	2,681.25
Jose Cantero	71	68	139	2,681.25
Mark Allen	71	68	139	2,681.25
David Bransdon	69	70	139	2,681.25
Glenn Joyner	73	67	140	1,596.43
Cheng Jun	71	69	140	1,596.43
Bill Fung	71	69	140	1,596.43
Charlie Wi	70	70	140	1,596.43
Jyoti Randhawa	70	70	140	1,596.43
Justin Cooper	69	71	140	1,596.43
Robert Herrera	68	72	140	1,596.43
Ali Kadir	73	68	141	1,031.25
Patrick Moore	73	68	141	1,031.25
Liu Wen-the	73	68	141	1,031.25
Euan Mcintosh	71	70	141	1,031.25
Lu Wen-der	71	70	141	1,031.25
S. Murthy	69	72	141	1,031.25
Danny Chia	72	70	142	825
Fredrick Mansson	71	71	142	825
Jerry Smith	70	72	142	825
Chou Hung-nan	69	73	142	825
Wang Ter-chang	68	74	142	825
Liu Guo-jie	74	69	143	600
Unho Park	72	71	143	600
Marimuthu Ramayah	73	70	143	600
Lai Cham-hui	71	72	143	600
Lee Lien-fu	71	72	143	600
Amritinder Singh	70	73	143	600
Ho Chung-yuan	69	74	143	600

Hugo Boss Open

Shenzhen Golf Club, Shenzhen
Par 36-36–72; 7,250 yards

May 2-3
purse, US$75,000

	SCORES		TOTAL	MONEY
Zhang Lian-wei	67	65	132	US$13,500
Jerry Smith	67	66	133	6,937.50
Wang Ter-chang	66	67	133	6,937.50
Euan Mcintosh	68	68	136	3,600
Vivek Chandari	67	69	136	3,600
Amritinder Singh	69	68	137	2,662.50
Chen Yuan-chi	68	69	137	2,662.50
Mark Allen	70	69	139	2,006.25
Robin Byrd	70	69	139	2,006.25
Justin Cooper	68	71	139	2,006.25
Andrew Crerar	68	71	139	2,006.25
Lai Ying-juh	73	68	141	1,320
Fredrick Mansson	72	69	141	1,320
Jeff Senior	71	70	141	1,320
Richard Backwell	71	70	141	1,320
Dino Kwek Beng Kwee	69	72	141	1,320
Andrew Morrow	74	68	142	993.75
Takuhito Nishino	74	68	142	993.75
Tsai Chi-huang	72	70	142	993.75
Darren Echhardt	72	70	142	993.75
Hsu Mong-nan	71	71	142	993.75
Timothy Elliot	71	71	142	993.75
Ali Kadir	74	69	143	693.75
Philip Chapman	73	70	143	693.75
Anthony Kang	73	70	143	693.75
Wu Hung-chu	73	70	143	693.75
Lee Lien-fu	72	71	143	693.75
Poh Eing Chong	72	71	143	693.75
Chris Williams	71	72	143	693.75
David Bransdon	71	72	143	693.75
Chen Tsang-te	70	73	143	693.75
Wayne Bradley	70	73	143	693.75

Coca-Cola Open

Luhu Golf and Country Club, Guangzhou
Par 36-36–72

May 6-7
purse, US$75,000

	SCORES		TOTAL	MONEY
Gustavo Rojas	69	69	138	US$13,500
Charlie Wi	70	70	140	8,625
Chen Tsang-te	71	70	141	4,150
Robin Byrd	70	71	141	4,150
Simon Yates	70	71	141	4,150
Brett Johnson	71	71	142	2,550
Rashid Ismail	70	72	142	2,550
Vivek Chandari	69	73	142	2,550
Wayne Bradley	74	69	143	1,900
Zhang Lian-wei	71	72	143	1,900
Cheng Jun	69	74	143	1,900
Yeh Wei-tze	75	69	144	1,248.21

	SCORES		TOTAL	MONEY
Joseph Gay	74	70	144	1,248.21
Justin Cooper	73	71	144	1,248.21
Euan Mcintosh	71	73	144	1,248.21
Jerry Smith	71	73	144	1,248.21
Bjorn Flygare	69	75	144	1,248.21
Jose Cantero	69	75	144	1,248.21
Jyoti Randhawa	78	67	145	881.25
Ali Kadir	74	71	145	881.25
Anthony Kang	73	72	145	881.25
Glenn Joyner	73	72	145	881.25
Tony Aguilar	73	72	145	881.25
Philip Chapman	72	73	145	881.25
Jeev Milkha Singh	72	73	145	881.25
Raul Fretes	71	74	145	881.25
Hsu Mong-nan	78	68	146	637.50
Andrew Crerar	75	71	146	637.50
Amritinder Singh	74	72	146	637.50
Timothy Elliot	73	73	146	637.50
Zheng Wen-gen	69	77	146	637.50

Founder Open

Sichuan International Golf Club, Chengdu
Par 36-36–72

May 10-11
purse, US$75,000

	SCORES		TOTAL	MONEY
Jerry Smith	66	66	132	US$13,500
Zhang Lian-wei	69	65	134	8,625
Justin Cooper	67	68	135	5,250
Charlie Wi	69	67	136	3,600
Robin Byrd	66	70	136	3,600
Jeev Milkha Singh	72	66	138	2,775
John Wither	71	68	139	2,550
Timothy Elliot	74	66	140	2,006.25
David Bransdon	73	67	140	2,006.25
Joseph Gay	69	71	140	2,006.25
Simon Yates	67	73	140	2,006.25
Euan Mcintosh	70	71	141	1,575
Philip Chapman	74	68	142	1,193.75
Gavin Vearing	73	69	142	1,193.75
Andrew Pitts	71	71	142	1,193.75
Anthony Kang	69	73	142	1,193.75
Raul Fretes	69	73	142	1,193.75
Steven Armstrong	69	73	142	1,193.75
Fredrick Mansson	74	69	143	900
Chen Tsang-te	73	70	143	900
Guy Redford	72	71	143	900
Vivek Chandari	72	71	143	900
Brad Schadewitz	71	72	143	900
Wayne Bradley	70	73	143	900
Lien Yung-sheng	69	74	143	900
Ali Kadir	75	69	144	656.25
Lin Chih-chen	75	69	144	656.25
Tsai Chi-huang	73	71	144	656.25
Hsu Mong-nan	71	73	144	656.25
Richard Backwell	71	73	144	656.25
Chen Yuan-chi	70	74	144	656.25

Japan Tour

Token Corporation Cup

Kedoin Golf Club, Kagoshima
Par 36-36–72; 7,115 yards

March 13-16
purse, ¥100,000,000

	SCORES				TOTAL	MONEY
Masashi Ozaki	71	65	61	72	269	¥18,000,000
Carlos Franco	65	68	69	68	270	9,000,000
Brandt Jobe	71	66	66	69	272	6,120,000
Tsukasa Watanabe	69	64	70	71	274	3,960,000
Eduardo Herrera	73	68	63	70	274	3,960,000
Tateo Ozaki	71	69	67	68	275	3,060,000
Peter Senior	71	67	69	68	275	3,060,000
Hisayuki Sasaki	69	70	66	72	277	2,340,000
Stewart Ginn	69	69	72	67	277	2,340,000
Frankie Minoza	72	69	67	69	277	2,340,000
Teruo Sugihara	69	67	69	73	278	1,656,000
Todd Hamilton	72	68	67	71	278	1,656,000
Peter Teravainen	73	67	69	69	278	1,656,000
Masanobu Kimura	75	68	66	70	279	1,350,000
Hidemichi Tanaka	73	65	69	72	279	1,350,000
Ken Kusumoto	70	71	68	71	280	1,134,000
Shoichi Kuwabara	71	66	74	69	280	1,134,000
Yoshinori Mizumaki	69	69	69	74	281	948,000
Katsunori Kuwabara	70	70	68	73	281	948,000
David Smail	72	68	66	75	281	948,000
Saburo Fujiki	71	71	69	71	282	828,000
Takenori Hiraishi	70	70	68	74	282	828,000
Rick Hartmann	70	68	73	71	282	828,000
Keiji Teshima	69	70	69	75	283	729,000
Toru Suzuki	72	69	71	71	283	729,000
Yasunobu Kuramoto	71	72	71	69	283	729,000
Nobuhito Sato	72	69	75	67	283	729,000
Steve Conran	73	67	72	71	283	729,000
David Ishii	73	69	68	73	283	729,000
Yoshinori Kaneko	71	71	73	69	284	609,750
Katsunari Takahashi	72	71	72	69	284	609,750
Yoshitaka Yamamoto	74	69	72	69	284	609,750
Yoshihiko Terakawa	75	68	69	72	284	609,750
Hirofumi Miyase	72	70	71	71	284	609,750
Naotoshi Nakamura	73	71	70	70	284	609,750
Shusaku Sugimoto	71	71	71	71	284	609,750
Brian Watts	68	74	75	67	284	609,750

Daido Drinko Shizuoka Open

Shizuoka Club, Hamaoka Course, Shizuoka
Par 36-36–72; 6,886 yards

March 20-23
purse, ¥100,000,000

	SCORES				TOTAL	MONEY
Hisayuki Sasaki	71	67	68	68	274	¥18,000,000
Carlos Franco	67	69	71	70	277	9,000,000
Keiji Teshima	66	74	70	69	279	4,032,000
Yoshitaka Yamamoto	70	73	67	69	279	4,032,000
Ryoken Kawagishi	70	73	68	68	279	4,032,000
Keiichiro Fukabori	69	70	70	70	279	4,032,000
Frankie Minoza	69	65	72	73	279	4,032,000
Katsunari Takahashi	69	73	72	66	280	2,475,000
Shigemasa Higaki	69	70	68	73	280	2,475,000
Toshimitsu Izawa	71	71	70	69	281	1,935,000
Shigeki Maruyama	71	69	75	66	281	1,935,000
Seiki Okuda	70	73	69	70	282	1,524,000
Stewart Ginn	69	70	72	71	282	1,524,000
Brandt Jobe	71	72	69	70	282	1,524,000
Tsuyoshi Yoneyama	72	74	71	66	283	1,296,000
Kazuhiro Takami	72	72	72	68	284	1,053,000
Mitsuo Harada	67	70	75	72	284	1,053,000
Katsunori Kuwabara	68	72	75	69	284	1,053,000
Peter McWhinney	69	72	71	72	284	1,053,000
Toru Suzuki	75	71	71	68	285	807,000
Shinichi Yokota	74	68	72	71	285	807,000
Steve Conran	70	73	73	69	285	807,000
Shusaku Sugimoto	72	74	71	68	285	807,000
Peter Senior	70	74	70	71	285	807,000
Rick Todd	69	73	73	70	285	807,000
Peter Teravainen	72	72	72	69	285	807,000
Shigenori Mori	70	76	72	68	286	684,000
Hajime Meshiai	69	74	73	70	286	684,000
Tsukasa Watanabe	73	71	70	72	286	684,000
Shoichi Kuwabara	70	74	72	70	286	684,000
Kazuhiko Hosokawa	71	71	72	72	286	684,000

Just System KSB Open

Kinojo Country Club, Soja, Okoyama
Par 36-36–72; 6,948 yards

March 27-30
purse, ¥70,000,000

	SCORES				TOTAL	MONEY
Keiichiro Fukabori	69	64	69	74	276	¥12,600,000
Toshiaki Odate	71	69	65	73	278	5,292,000
Katsunori Kuwabara	66	67	72	73	278	5,292,000
Nobumitsu Yuhara	73	71	67	68	279	2,772,000
Shoichi Kuwabara	67	69	70	73	279	2,772,000
Tsukasa Watanabe	69	68	70	73	280	2,142,000
Brandt Jobe	67	67	74	72	280	2,142,000
Tsuyoshi Yoneyama	71	71	71	68	281	1,543,500
Shigemasa Higaki	70	72	69	70	281	1,543,500
David Smail	71	71	68	71	281	1,543,500
Carlos Franco	70	67	72	72	281	1,543,500
Teruo Sugihara	71	68	71	72	282	1,108,800
Masayuki Kawamura	70	71	67	74	282	1,108,800
Yutaka Hagawa	71	69	64	79	283	907,200

	SCORES				TOTAL	MONEY
Yoshitaka Yamamoto	72	69	72	70	283	907,200
Kaname Yokoo	67	67	75	74	283	907,200
Hideyuki Sato	71	71	69	73	284	670,320
Seiki Okuda	73	68	69	74	284	670,320
Kenichi Kuboya	70	71	72	71	284	670,320
Rick Gibson	70	74	70	70	284	670,320
Rick Todd	70	72	71	71	284	670,320
Koichi Suzuki	70	65	76	74	285	531,000
Yoshinori Mizumaki	71	70	74	70	285	531,000
Tomohiro Maruyama	70	70	72	73	285	531,000
Yoshikazu Sakamoto	73	68	69	75	285	531,000
Koki Idoki	73	70	71	71	285	531,000
Mitsuo Harada	75	63	66	81	285	531,000
Hirofumi Miyase	73	67	70	75	285	531,000
Yoshimitsu Fukuzawa	71	71	70	74	286	459,900
Yasunobu Kuramoto	71	72	69	74	286	459,900
Taichi Teshima	69	72	71	74	286	459,900
Todd Hamilton	70	71	68	77	286	459,900

Descente Classic

Edosaki Country Club, Ibaragi
Par 36-35–71; 6,831 yards

April 3-6
purse, ¥100,000,000

	SCORES				TOTAL	MONEY
Peter Teravainen	67	67	67	69	270	¥18,000,000
Todd Hamilton	68	68	66	70	272	9,000,000
Shingo Katayama	67	68	69	69	273	6,120,000
Tsuyoshi Yoneyama	70	69	67	69	275	4,320,000
Shigenori Mori	70	69	69	68	276	3,082,000
Ryoken Kawagishi	69	69	69	69	276	3,082,000
Shigemasa Higaki	70	68	69	69	276	3,082,000
David Ishii	75	63	69	69	276	3,082,000
Nobuo Serizawa	69	67	72	69	277	2,070,000
Gohei Sato	67	71	68	71	277	2,070,000
Peter McWhinney	68	70	67	72	277	2,070,000
Hirofumi Miyase	71	66	69	72	278	1,524,000
Shigeki Maruyama	67	69	69	73	278	1,524,000
Samson Gimson	68	67	72	71	278	1,524,000
Nobumitsu Yuhara	71	69	69	70	279	1,068,000
Tsukasa Watanabe	70	72	68	69	279	1,068,000
Masahiro Kuramoto	68	70	74	67	279	1,068,000
Seiichi Koizumi	69	73	69	68	279	1,068,000
Kazuhiko Hosokawa	73	70	66	70	279	1,068,000
Rick Gibson	71	66	71	71	279	1,068,000
Satoshi Higashi	68	71	70	71	280	814,000
Wayne Smith	74	67	70	69	280	814,000
Keiichiro Fukabori	71	70	66	73	280	814,000
Chen Tze-ming	72	70	68	70	280	814,000
Masayuki Kawamura	73	68	70	70	281	693,000
Toshimitsu Izawa	74	66	68	73	281	693,000
Toshikazu Sugihara	70	67	74	70	281	693,000
Hidemichi Tanaka	72	71	69	69	281	693,000
Nobuhito Sato	68	68	72	73	281	693,000
Katsumasa Miyamoto	75	68	68	70	281	693,000
Brandt Jobe	67	68	70	76	281	693,000
Rick Todd	72	69	68	72	281	693,000

Tsuruya Open

Sports Shinko Country Club, Yamanohara Course, Hyogo
Par 36-36–72; 6,842 yards

April 17-20
purse, ¥100,000,000

	SCORES				TOTAL	MONEY
Mitsuo Harada	72	67	72	68	279	¥18,000,000
Shigeki Maruyama	68	70	71	74	283	9,000,000
Tetsu Nishikawa	71	72	73	68	284	6,120,000
Yukihiro Yamamoto	72	74	71	68	285	4,320,000
Hajime Meshiai	74	70	73	69	286	3,082,500
Shoichi Kuwabara	76	70	70	70	286	3,082,500
Katsumasa Miyamoto	68	73	73	72	286	3,082,500
Peter Teravainen	67	71	78	70	286	3,082,500
Tsuneyuki Nakajima	70	73	72	72	287	1,966,500
Seiki Okuda	72	74	72	69	287	1,966,500
Toru Suzuki	73	67	75	72	287	1,966,500
Nobuhito Sato	74	71	69	73	287	1,966,500
Daisuke Serizawa	73	72	71	72	288	1,248,000
Hirofumi Miyase	70	71	72	75	288	1,248,000
Tsutomu Higa	74	70	71	73	288	1,248,000
Stewart Ginn	70	76	72	70	288	1,248,000
Yeh Chang-ting	69	73	75	71	288	1,248,000
David Smail	75	69	72	72	288	1,248,000
Koichi Suzuki	72	70	74	73	289	900,000
Kiyoshi Murota	69	75	71	74	289	900,000
Teruo Sugihara	73	74	71	71	289	900,000
Tateo Ozaki	73	71	71	75	290	758,571
Yoshitaka Yamamoto	74	68	76	72	290	758,571
Ken Kusumoto	76	71	71	72	290	758,571
Hidemichi Tanaka	75	70	71	74	290	758,571
Katsunori Kuwabara	73	71	70	76	290	758,571
Shinichi Akiba	72	74	73	71	290	758,571
Kenichi Kuboya	75	72	71	72	290	758,571
Ryoken Kawagishi	71	73	78	69	291	675,000
David Ishii	72	72	74	73	291	675,000

Kirin Open

Ibaragi Golf Club, West Course, Ibaragi
Par 36-36–72; 7,052 yards

April 24-27
purse, ¥100,000,000

	SCORES				TOTAL	MONEY
Kim Jong-duk	69	73	68	68	278	¥18,000,000
Tateo Ozaki	70	73	71	65	279	6,475,000
Hirofumi Miyase	70	71	68	70	279	6,475,000
Shigeki Maruyama	69	68	67	75	279	6,475,000
Brian Watts	69	70	71	69	279	6,475,000
Hidemichi Tanaka	70	69	69	72	280	2,960,000
Zaw Moe	67	69	69	75	280	2,960,000
Rick Todd	71	72	67	70	280	2,960,000
Carlos Franco	71	68	69	72	280	2,960,000
Edward Fryatt	68	71	71	70	280	2,960,000
Zhang Lian-wei	70	71	70	70	281	2,020,000
Masashi Ozaki	72	72	71	67	282	1,713,333
Satoshi Higashi	69	71	74	68	282	1,713,333
Mike Tschetter	71	73	65	73	282	1,713,333
Tsuneyuki Nakajima	69	72	70	72	283	1,340,000

	SCORES	TOTAL	MONEY
Frankie Minoza	72 68 69 74	283	1,340,000
Stephen Leaney	75 68 67 73	283	1,340,000
*Hidemasa Hoshino	71 70 68 74	283	
Hajime Meshiai	75 70 67 72	284	1,140,000
David Ishii	72 73 68 72	285	1,019,666
Mike Cunning	70 72 70 73	285	1,019,666
Brandt Jobe	74 69 71 71	285	1,019,666
Tsuyoshi Yoneyama	70 73 73 70	286	905,666
Jeev Milkha Singh	72 71 73 70	286	905,666
Dean Wilson	68 73 72 73	286	905,666
Gohei Sato	72 74 73 68	287	829,000
Rick Gibson	74 71 70 72	287	829,000
Peter Senior	69 72 72 74	287	829,000
Christian Chernock	76 68 72 71	287	829,000
Saburo Fujiki	71 74 73 70	288	709,500
Kiyoshi Maita	74 70 72 72	288	709,500
Tetsu Nishikawa	71 73 72 72	288	709,500
Kaname Yokoo	70 72 74 72	288	709,500
Yasuharu Imano	73 68 71 76	288	709,500
Tim Straub	71 72 74 71	288	709,500
Larry Barber	71 73 71 73	288	709,500
Eric Epperson	74 71 74 69	288	709,500

Chunichi Crowns

Nagoya Golf Club, Wago Course, Aichi
Par 35-35–70; 6,455 yards

May 1-4
purse, ¥120,000,000

	SCORES	TOTAL	MONEY
Masashi Ozaki	67 67 66 67	267	¥21,600,000
Brian Watts	67 65 69 68	269	10,800,000
Greg Norman	66 68 67 70	271	7,344,000
Tateo Ozaki	67 68 71 66	272	5,184,000
Nobuo Serizawa	69 68 68 68	273	3,699,000
Kazuhiro Takami	67 67 69 70	273	3,699,000
Stewart Ginn	71 67 71 64	273	3,699,000
Rick Gibson	68 70 67 68	273	3,699,000
Ikuo Shirahama	66 72 68 68	274	2,484,000
Taichi Teshima	62 70 70 72	274	2,484,000
Kaname Yokoo	67 68 72 67	274	2,484,000
Hajime Meshiai	71 70 68 66	275	1,900,800
Nobumitsu Yuhara	71 64 72 68	275	1,900,800
Yoshinori Kaneko	75 68 67 66	276	1,620,000
David Ishii	69 70 69 68	276	1,620,000
Kiyoshi Maita	69 68 70 70	277	1,166,400
Tomohiro Maruyama	72 69 68 68	277	1,166,400
Tsukasa Watanabe	71 70 69 67	277	1,166,400
Masayuki Kawamura	66 71 74 66	277	1,166,400
Mitsuo Harada	70 68 72 67	277	1,166,400
David Smail	66 70 72 69	277	1,166,400
Brandt Jobe	69 67 73 68	277	1,166,400
Eduardo Herrera	70 67 72 69	278	928,800
Tsuyoshi Yoneyama	67 72 69 70	278	928,800
Carlos Franco	70 69 70 69	278	928,800
Kiyoshi Murota	69 65 73 72	279	842,400
Hidemichi Tanaka	70 67 72 70	279	842,400
Shigeki Maruyama	71 68 69 71	279	842,400

	SCORES				TOTAL	MONEY
Corey Pavin	70	68	76	65	279	842,400
Craig Stadler	68	73	72	66	279	842,400

Fuji Sankei Classic

Kawana Hotel Golf Club, Fuji Course, Shizuoka
Par 35-36–71; 6,694 yards

May 8-11
purse, ¥120,000,000

	SCORES				TOTAL	MONEY
Kenichi Kuboya	68	69	73	69	279	¥21,600,000
Masashi Ozaki	70	69	72	69	280	9,072,000
Yoshinori Kaneko	74	70	69	67	280	9,072,000
Carlos Franco	71	70	70	70	281	5,184,000
Tateo Ozaki	73	69	73	68	283	4,320,000
Shigeki Maruyama	71	74	71	68	284	3,888,000
Eiji Mizoguchi	71	69	73	72	285	3,456,000
Toru Nakamura	73	70	70	73	286	2,970,000
Daisuke Serizawa	72	72	70	72	286	2,970,000
Frankie Minoza	72	73	68	74	287	2,484,000
Nobuhito Sato	69	71	73	75	288	2,073,600
Shinichi Yokota	71	77	69	71	288	2,073,600
Kiyoshi Maita	74	72	74	69	289	1,444,114
Hajime Meshiai	74	72	73	70	289	1,444,114
Masanobu Kimura	76	69	71	73	289	1,444,114
Toshiaki Odate	73	71	69	76	289	1,444,114
Shoichi Kuwabara	73	69	76	71	289	1,444,114
Katsunori Kuwabara	71	72	71	75	289	1,444,114
Brian Watts	72	71	74	72	289	1,444,114
Seiichi Kanai	73	74	72	71	290	997,920
Nobuo Serizawa	69	76	71	74	290	997,920
Ken Kusumoto	72	75	69	74	290	997,920
Lin Keng-chi	72	75	74	69	290	997,920
David Smail	73	70	74	73	290	997,920
Joji Furuki	73	73	73	72	291	853,200
Shigenori Mori	73	72	70	76	291	853,200
Seiki Okuda	77	71	69	74	291	853,200
Tsuyoshi Yoneyama	75	72	72	72	291	853,200
Toshimitsu Izawa	80	68	72	71	291	853,200
Chen Tze-chung	76	73	72	70	291	853,200

Japan PGA Championship

Central Golf Club, West Course, Okayama
Par 36-36–72; 7,049 yards

May 15-18
purse, ¥100,000,000

	SCORES				TOTAL	MONEY
Shigeki Maruyama	68	68	69	67	272	¥18,000,000
Shusaku Sugimoto	68	66	69	71	274	9,000,000
Mitsuo Harada	69	70	69	67	275	6,120,000
Masayuki Kawamura	66	68	69	73	276	4,320,000
Toshimitsu Izawa	71	68	70	68	277	3,420,000
Todd Hamilton	69	69	69	70	277	3,420,000
Tsukasa Watanabe	72	66	68	72	278	2,745,000
David Ishii	70	69	69	70	278	2,745,000
Toshiaki Odate	66	74	66	73	279	2,070,000

	SCORES	TOTAL	MONEY
Stewart Ginn	70 69 69 71	279	2,070,000
Shinichi Yokota	68 69 66 76	279	2,070,000
Masanobu Kimura	69 67 73 71	280	1,467,000
Shinichi Akiba	69 71 69 71	280	1,467,000
Kaname Yokoo	69 69 71 71	280	1,467,000
Frankie Minoza	69 71 67 73	280	1,467,000
Yutaka Hagawa	68 71 73 69	281	1,053,000
Hajime Meshiai	71 69 71 70	281	1,053,000
Nobumitsu Yuhara	72 68 74 67	281	1,053,000
Peter Senior	69 69 74 69	281	1,053,000
Tateo Ozaki	72 68 75 67	282	831,600
Yoshinori Kaneko	71 70 71 70	282	831,600
Gohei Sato	70 67 70 75	282	831,600
Katsumasa Miyamoto	72 66 71 73	282	831,600
Brandt Jobe	71 73 68 70	282	831,600
Yasunori Ida	72 68 72 71	283	747,000
Keiichiro Fukabori	69 72 70 72	283	747,000
Satoshi Higashi	72 70 70 72	284	675,000
Saburo Fujiki	68 73 70 73	284	675,000
Kazuhiko Hosokawa	72 69 70 73	284	675,000
Zaw Moe	71 70 69 74	284	675,000
Steve Conran	70 72 73 69	284	675,000
Brian Watts	72 68 74 70	284	675,000

Ube Kosan Open

Ube Country Club, Mannenike Nishi Course, Yamaguchi
Par 35-36–71; 6,935 yards

May 22-25
purse, ¥100,000,000

	SCORES	TOTAL	MONEY
Shigenori Mori	67 64 68 68	267	¥18,000,000
Shigemasa Higaki	65 72 64 70	271	9,000,000
Tsuneyuki Nakajima	70 69 64 69	272	5,160,000
Yoshinori Mizumaki	69 66 69 68	272	5,160,000
Koki Idoki	66 69 68 70	273	3,420,000
Shoichi Kuwabara	68 67 70 68	273	3,420,000
Toru Nakamura	67 69 70 68	274	2,475,000
Takenori Hiraishi	67 68 68 71	274	2,475,000
Toshiaki Odate	67 67 69 71	274	2,475,000
Kaname Yokoo	63 72 70 69	274	2,475,000
Yutaka Hagawa	67 71 68 69	275	1,656,000
Gohei Sato	66 68 73 68	275	1,656,000
Stewart Ginn	68 68 69 70	275	1,656,000
Ikuo Shirahama	71 69 65 71	276	1,116,000
Seiki Okuda	70 67 68 71	276	1,116,000
Hirofumi Miyase	68 70 70 68	276	1,116,000
Satoshi Oide	66 69 68 73	276	1,116,000
Tsutomu Higa	68 71 68 69	276	1,116,000
Taichi Teshima	68 72 68 68	276	1,116,000
Shoichi Miyazato	67 70 67 72	276	1,116,000
Kiyoshi Murota	64 74 66 73	277	846,000
Samson Gimson	66 67 69 75	277	846,000
Koichi Suzuki	68 72 69 69	278	711,000
Akihito Yokoyama	71 68 70 69	278	711,000
Yoshitaka Yamamoto	70 67 71 70	278	711,000
Tsuyoshi Yoneyama	73 66 71 68	278	711,000
Mitsuo Harada	72 67 67 72	278	711,000

	SCORES				TOTAL	MONEY
Yasunobu Kuramoto	68	72	67	71	278	711,000
Hidemichi Tanaka	67	70	68	73	278	711,000
Toru Taniguchi	65	72	68	73	278	711,000
Shinichi Yokota	67	70	71	70	278	711,000
Masashi Shimada	70	69	70	69	278	711,000

Mitsubishi Galant

Taiheiyo Club, Rokko Course, Shizuoka
Par 36-36–72; 7,012 yards

May 29-June 1
purse, ¥120,000,000

	SCORES				TOTAL	MONEY
Masashi Ozaki	70	70	70	68	278	¥21,600,000
Satoshi Higashi	73	69	67	71	280	7,776,000
Toru Nakamura	74	65	69	72	280	7,776,000
Koki Idoki	73	65	70	72	280	7,776,000
Yoshinori Kaneko	72	70	72	67	281	3,699,000
Seiki Okuda	72	70	70	69	281	3,699,000
Eiji Mizoguchi	70	69	72	70	281	3,699,000
Katsumasa Miyamoto	73	72	67	69	281	3,699,000
Ikuo Shirahama	68	73	71	70	282	2,484,000
Tsuneyuki Nakajima	70	71	72	69	282	2,484,000
Yoshinori Mizumaki	70	73	69	70	282	2,484,000
Tateo Ozaki	68	71	70	74	283	1,900,800
Hirofumi Miyase	72	73	68	70	283	1,900,800
Yoshitaka Yamamoto	70	69	73	72	284	1,434,240
Kazuhiro Fukunaga	72	71	70	71	284	1,434,240
Lin Keng-chi	68	71	69	76	284	1,434,240
David Smail	74	62	73	75	284	1,434,240
Todd Hamilton	70	72	71	71	284	1,434,240
Kiyoshi Maita	70	68	75	72	285	988,200
Nobumitsu Yuhara	70	70	72	73	285	988,200
Tsukasa Watanabe	71	72	71	71	285	988,200
Masayuki Kawamura	68	70	75	72	285	988,200
Toshiaki Odate	72	70	68	75	285	988,200
Nobuhito Sato	72	70	71	72	285	988,200
Shinichi Yokota	73	70	70	72	285	988,200
Peter Senior	70	70	69	76	285	988,200
Takenori Hiraishi	74	70	70	72	286	810,000
Daisuke Serizawa	72	68	74	72	286	810,000
Stewart Ginn	73	72	71	70	286	810,000
Ken Tanigawa	70	73	76	67	286	810,000
Kaname Yokoo	68	69	73	76	286	810,000
Hirooki Kikkawa	69	74	72	71	286	810,000

JCB Classic Sendai

Omotezao Kokusai Golf Club, Shibata, Miyagi
Par 36-35–71; 6,651 yards

June 5-8
purse, ¥100,000,000

	SCORES				TOTAL	MONEY
Nobuhito Sato	68	65	64	70	267	¥18,000,000
Naomichi Ozaki	67	68	67	69	271	7,560,000
Toshimitsu Izawa	69	68	67	67	271	7,560,000
Toshiaki Odate	71	65	65	71	272	4,320,000

	SCORES				TOTAL	MONEY
Eduardo Herrera	68	65	71	69	273	3,600,000
Yoshinori Kaneko	67	65	69	74	275	3,240,000
Masashi Ozaki	68	69	68	71	276	2,610,000
Tetsu Nishikawa	66	69	70	71	276	2,610,000
Shoichi Kuwabara	69	68	70	69	276	2,610,000
Taichi Teshima	68	65	73	71	277	2,070,000
Joji Furuki	70	68	69	71	278	1,728,000
Shingo Katayama	70	70	69	69	278	1,728,000
Tateo Ozaki	69	69	70	71	279	1,350,000
Eiichi Itai	68	69	73	69	279	1,350,000
Tsuneyuki Nakajima	69	68	71	71	279	1,350,000
Zaw Moe	69	71	69	70	279	1,350,000
Keiji Teshima	72	70	67	71	280	1,008,000
Naoya Sugiyama	66	69	73	72	280	1,008,000
David Ishii	71	69	68	72	280	1,008,000
Ryoken Kawagishi	71	69	71	70	281	864,000
Hidemichi Tanaka	68	72	72	69	281	864,000
Yeh Chang-ting	67	73	71	70	281	864,000
Tomohiro Maruyama	70	69	69	74	282	774,000
Nobumitsu Yuhara	72	69	70	71	282	774,000
Tsukasa Watanabe	65	71	73	73	282	774,000
Satoshi Higashi	69	68	72	74	283	702,000
Takaaki Fukuzawa	67	71	73	72	283	702,000
Masayuki Kawamura	71	67	72	73	283	702,000
Hitoshi Sasaki	69	72	67	75	283	702,000
Lin Keng-chi	70	70	71	72	283	702,000

Sapporo Tokyu Open

Sapporo Kokusai Country Club,
Shimamatsu Course, Hokkaido
Par 36-36–72; 6,949 yards

June 12-15
purse, ¥100,000,000

	SCORES				TOTAL	MONEY
Hirofumi Miyase	67	70	66	72	275	¥18,000,000
Hajime Meshiai	71	70	69	70	280	9,000,000
Yoshikazu Sakamoto	72	73	69	67	281	6,120,000
Tsuneyuki Nakajima	72	71	71	69	283	3,510,000
Takaaki Fukuzawa	72	73	66	72	283	3,510,000
Frankie Minoza	72	68	67	76	283	3,510,000
Carlos Franco	78	64	70	71	283	3,510,000
Naomichi Ozaki	70	72	73	69	284	2,340,000
Satoshi Higashi	71	69	70	74	284	2,340,000
Katsumasa Miyamoto	72	67	69	76	284	2,340,000
Hideyuki Sato	71	73	70	71	285	1,593,000
Koki Idoki	70	70	72	73	285	1,593,000
Toshiaki Odate	71	69	73	72	285	1,593,000
Katsunori Kuwabara	68	71	72	74	285	1,593,000
Yoshinori Kaneko	68	72	71	75	286	1,101,000
Hisayuki Sasaki	70	71	71	74	286	1,101,000
Shinichi Akiba	73	71	70	72	286	1,101,000
Yeh Chang-ting	69	72	70	75	286	1,101,000
Shigemasa Higaki	71	73	71	71	286	1,101,000
Motomasa Aoki	74	67	70	76	287	819,000
Shigenori Mori	71	73	70	73	287	819,000
Masanobu Kimura	71	72	71	73	287	819,000
Seiki Okuda	74	71	73	69	287	819,000

	SCORES				TOTAL	MONEY
Kaname Yokoo	70	73	72	72	287	819,000
Hirooki Kikkawa	75	69	72	71	287	819,000
Yutaka Hagawa	71	74	71	72	288	702,000
Yoshitaka Yamamoto	74	68	74	72	288	702,000
Tsutomu Higa	70	73	73	72	288	702,000
Shoichi Kuwabara	70	70	68	80	288	702,000
Takeshi Oyama	72	67	72	77	288	702,000

Yomiuri Open

Yomiuri Country Club, Tokyo
Par 36-35–71; 6,987 yards

June 19-22
purse, ¥100,000,000

	SCORES				TOTAL	MONEY
Shigeki Maruyama	67	68	66	66	267	¥18,000,000
Naomichi Ozaki	69	69	66	65	269	9,000,000
Frankie Minoza	71	67	66	67	271	5,220,000
Brandt Jobe	71	68	65	67	271	5,220,000
Toru Suzuki	70	69	69	65	273	3,600,000
Satoshi Higashi	68	68	69	69	274	2,767,500
Yoshinori Mizumaki	72	67	66	69	274	2,767,500
Brian Watts	68	66	70	70	274	2,767,500
Carlos Franco	69	71	66	67	274	2,767,500
Masayuki Kawamura	68	72	65	70	275	2,070,000
Koki Idoki	68	68	73	67	276	1,728,000
Toshiaki Odate	71	71	68	66	276	1,728,000
Katsunari Takahashi	69	69	70	69	277	1,458,000
Keiichiro Fukabori	72	68	67	70	277	1,458,000
Nobuo Serizawa	68	69	68	73	278	1,242,000
Todd Hamilton	69	72	70	67	278	1,242,000
Masanobu Kimura	70	69	71	69	279	1,008,000
Hidemichi Tanaka	72	72	69	66	279	1,008,000
Rick Gibson	72	68	73	66	279	1,008,000
Yutaka Hagawa	68	71	75	66	280	846,000
Saburo Fujiki	70	71	68	71	280	846,000
Yoshitaka Yamamoto	71	69	72	68	280	846,000
Shoichi Kuwabara	69	71	74	66	280	846,000
Yoshimi Niizeki	70	71	70	70	281	729,000
Kiyoshi Murota	71	71	71	68	281	729,000
Shigenori Mori	72	70	69	70	281	729,000
Nobuhito Sato	73	71	70	67	281	729,000
Shusaku Sugimoto	70	72	72	67	281	729,000
Go Higaki	73	68	72	68	281	729,000
Tateo Ozaki	74	69	70	69	282	624,600
Tsuneyuki Nakajima	76	68	68	70	282	624,600
Tsukasa Watanabe	73	70	70	69	282	624,600
Keiji Teshima	69	71	71	71	282	624,600
Mitsutaka Kusakabe	72	68	74	68	282	624,600
Shinichi Yokota	71	72	70	69	282	624,600

Mizuno Open

Tokinodai Country Club, Bijodai Course, Ishikawa
Par 36-36–72; 6,822 yards

June 26-29
purse, ¥100,000,000

	SCORES				TOTAL	MONEY
Brian Watts	69	69	71	69	278	¥18,000,000
Toshimitsu Izawa	72	65	73	70	280	9,000,000
Toru Nakamura	73	71	69	68	281	6,120,000
Shigemasa Higaki	72	70	71	69	282	4,320,000
Hirofumi Miyase	65	72	76	70	283	3,420,000
Rick Gibson	72	72	70	69	283	3,420,000
Hajime Meshiai	69	71	75	70	285	2,475,000
Eiji Mizoguchi	72	74	71	68	285	2,475,000
Shinichi Yokota	69	70	74	72	285	2,475,000
Brandt Jobe	74	69	72	70	285	2,475,000
Zaw Moe	65	72	74	75	286	1,800,000
Tsuneyuki Nakajima	70	71	77	69	287	1,467,000
Kiyoshi Murota	69	76	69	73	287	1,467,000
Stewart Ginn	74	65	76	72	287	1,467,000
Samson Gimson	74	68	76	69	287	1,467,000
Masashi Ozaki	73	69	75	71	288	949,500
Katsunari Takahashi	72	73	70	73	288	949,500
Seiki Okuda	68	73	72	75	288	949,500
Takenori Hiraishi	70	69	73	76	288	949,500
Hiroya Kamide	70	69	76	73	288	949,500
Masayuki Kawamura	71	68	72	77	288	949,500
Taichi Teshima	73	66	74	75	288	949,500
Katsumasa Miyamoto	74	66	74	74	288	949,500
Yoshikazu Sakamoto	70	74	74	71	289	747,000
Ryoken Kawagishi	72	71	69	77	289	747,000
David Ishii	72	70	75	72	289	747,000
Carlos Franco	71	72	73	73	289	747,000
Kazuhiro Takami	74	69	71	76	290	675,000
Hisayuki Sasaki	71	74	70	75	290	675,000
Tsuyoshi Yoneyama	71	74	73	72	290	675,000
Hidemichi Tanaka	72	71	75	72	290	675,000

PGA Philanthropy

Maple Point Country Club, Kitatsuru-gun, Yamanashi
Par 36-35–71; 6,905 yards

July 3-6
purse, ¥70,000,000

	SCORES				TOTAL	MONEY
Naomichi Ozaki	66	64	68	69	267	¥12,600,000
Tsuyoshi Yoneyama	72	67	66	71	276	5,292,000
Eiji Mizoguchi	66	68	70	72	276	5,292,000
Toru Suzuki	72	66	68	71	277	3,024,000
Katsunari Takahashi	67	70	71	71	279	2,394,000
Masanobu Kimura	68	72	67	72	279	2,394,000
Kiyoshi Murota	71	67	68	74	280	1,921,500
Naoya Sugiyama	68	68	72	72	280	1,921,500
Yutaka Hagawa	74	69	68	70	281	1,376,550
Yoshinori Mizumaki	67	66	73	75	281	1,376,550
Hajime Meshiai	72	70	67	72	281	1,376,550
Mitsutaka Kusakabe	72	66	74	69	281	1,376,550
Kazuhiro Takami	71	68	72	71	282	945,000
Daisuke Serizawa	68	66	77	71	282	945,000

	SCORES	TOTAL	MONEY
Chen Tze-ming	68 70 71 73	282	945,000
Todd Hamilton	67 76 69 70	282	945,000
Kiyoshi Maita	70 69 68 76	283	686,700
Toshiaki Odate	72 67 68 76	283	686,700
Hidemichi Tanaka	69 68 70 76	283	686,700
David Smail	70 69 75 69	283	686,700
Teruo Sugihara	70 69 72 73	284	579,600
Hiroyuki Fujita	72 68 72 72	284	579,600
Hirooki Kikkawa	69 72 71 72	284	579,600
Shigeki Maruyama	72 69 68 76	285	535,500
Toru Taniguchi	70 68 75 72	285	535,500
Takaaki Fukuzawa	72 71 70 73	286	497,700
Hirofumi Miyase	67 74 70 75	286	497,700
Tsutomu Higa	72 70 70 74	286	497,700
Chen Tze-chung	68 71 73 74	286	497,700
Akihito Yokoyama	73 68 68 78	287	437,220
Toru Nakamura	72 66 74 75	287	437,220
Koki Idoki	70 72 72 73	287	437,220
Yoshimitsu Fukuzawa	71 71 70 75	287	437,220
Keiichiro Fukabori	71 70 71 75	287	437,220
Kazuhiro Fukunaga	69 65 78 75	287	437,220

Yonex Open Hiroshima

Yonex Country Club, Hiroshima
Par 36-36–72; 6,963 yards

July 10-13
purse, ¥80,000,000

	SCORES	TOTAL	MONEY
Naomichi Ozaki	69 71 68 68	276	¥14,400,000
Hiroyuki Fujita	72 68 70 68	278	7,200,000
Shigemasa Higaki	72 64 67 76	279	4,896,000
Kiyoshi Murota	72 70 70 68	280	3,168,000
Shoichi Kuwabara	70 69 71 70	280	3,168,000
Masanobu Kimura	69 72 72 70	283	2,592,000
Tatsuo Takasaki	72 70 70 72	284	2,196,000
Yoshimitsu Fukuzawa	73 72 68 71	284	2,196,000
Kazuo Kanayama	71 74 68 73	286	1,573,200
Seiki Okuda	71 74 70 71	286	1,573,200
Shingo Katayama	70 73 73 70	286	1,573,200
Todd Hamilton	71 73 69 73	286	1,573,200
Keiji Teshima	72 73 72 70	287	1,080,000
Toru Nakamura	74 72 71 70	287	1,080,000
Kazuhiro Fukunaga	72 72 70 73	287	1,080,000
Hirooki Kikkawa	70 75 71 71	287	1,080,000
Satoshi Higashi	74 71 68 75	288	806,400
Nobumitsu Yuhara	70 75 72 71	288	806,400
Katsunori Kuwabara	74 72 71 71	288	806,400
Hideyuki Sato	74 72 71 72	289	665,280
Takenori Hiraishi	72 72 73 72	289	665,280
Taichi Teshima	71 70 74 74	289	665,280
Yeh Chang-ting	71 68 72 78	289	665,280
Lin Keng-chi	72 74 75 68	289	665,280
Koki Idoki	71 74 71 74	290	604,800
Toji Furuki	74 73 71 73	291	568,800
Tsuyoshi Yoneyama	75 72 74 70	291	568,800
Shinichi Akiba	74 73 75 69	291	568,800
Toshiyuki Hiyama	74 73 70 74	291	568,800

	SCORES	TOTAL	MONEY
Yuji Takagi	74 73 76 69	292	525,600
Mitsuo Harada	72 73 71 76	292	525,600

Nikkei Cup

Dejima Golf Club, Fuji Course, Ibaraki
Par 36-36–72; 6,980 yards

July 24-27
purse, ¥100,000,000

	SCORES	TOTAL	MONEY
Yeh Chang-ting	67 70 67 68	272	¥18,000,000
Tsukasa Watanabe	68 66 69 69	272	9,000,000

(Yeh defeated Watanabe on second extra hole.)

	SCORES	TOTAL	MONEY
Kiyoshi Maita	71 65 67 71	274	5,220,000
Kazuhiko Hosokawa	68 71 66 69	274	5,220,000
Masashi Ozaki	70 66 67 72	275	3,420,000
Satoshi Higashi	64 72 68 71	275	3,420,000
Eiji Mizoguchi	71 66 70 69	276	2,880,000
Toru Suzuki	66 72 73 66	277	2,205,000
Atsushi Takamatsu	70 71 68 68	277	2,205,000
Mitsutaka Kusakabe	69 68 69 71	277	2,205,000
Hidezumi Shirakata	71 69 69 68	277	2,205,000
Yasunori Ida	70 69 68 71	278	1,524,000
Shigemasa Higaki	69 69 68 72	278	1,524,000
David Ishii	69 71 67 71	278	1,524,000
Kazuhiro Takami	71 70 69 69	279	1,101,600
Saburo Fujiki	72 70 68 69	279	1,101,600
Akio Nishizawa	71 64 69 75	279	1,101,600
Keiichiro Fukabori	70 70 68 71	279	1,101,600
David Smail	68 72 68 71	279	1,101,600
Nobuo Serizawa	68 75 68 69	280	900,000
Shoichi Kuwabara	74 69 68 70	281	846,000
Kaname Yokoo	67 70 72 72	281	846,000
Masahiko Akazawa	70 72 67 73	282	774,000
Yuji Takagi	70 66 70 76	282	774,000
Yasunobu Kuramoto	69 72 68 73	282	774,000
Yutaka Hagawa	68 73 70 72	283	729,000
Toru Nakamura	68 73 71 71	283	729,000
Hideyuki Sato	70 71 72 71	284	675,000
Naoki Hattori	68 71 70 75	284	675,000
Kimihiro Matsunaga	73 70 68 73	284	675,000
Toshiaki Odate	70 70 71 73	284	675,000

NST Niigata Open

Forest Golf Club, Niigata, Toyoura
Par 36-36–72; 7,065 yards

July 31-August 3
purse, ¥60,000,000

	SCORES	TOTAL	MONEY
Kazuhiko Hosokawa	71 68 67 71	277	¥10,800,000
Hisayuki Sasaki	71 70 70 67	278	5,400,000
Daisuke Serizawa	70 71 71 68	280	3,672,000
Hisashi Sawada	69 66 74 72	281	2,592,000
Koki Idoki	69 71 71 71	282	2,160,000
Kiyoshi Murota	73 71 69 70	283	1,746,000
Toshiaki Odate	71 71 69 72	283	1,746,000

		SCORES			TOTAL	MONEY
Hidezumi Shirakata	69	73	69	72	283	1,746,000
Tsuneyuki Nakajima	69	72	73	70	284	1,125,360
Toru Suzuki	68	71	71	74	284	1,125,360
Naoki Hattori	73	67	68	76	284	1,125,360
Naoya Sugiyama	67	72	73	72	284	1,125,360
Keiichiro Fukabori	75	69	69	71	284	1,125,360
Toru Nakayama	72	74	69	70	285	669,600
Mitsutaka Kusakabe	74	67	75	69	285	669,600
Gregory Meyer	74	70	71	70	285	669,600
Shinsuke Yanagisawa	72	71	71	71	285	669,600
Nobuhito Sato	70	72	71	72	285	669,600
Yeh Chang-ting	72	71	71	71	285	669,600
Hirooki Kikkawa	73	73	69	70	285	669,600
Hideyuki Sato	73	72	73	69	287	496,800
Gohei Sato	74	70	71	72	287	496,800
Yasunobu Kuramoto	73	73	71	70	287	496,800
Masanobu Kimura	72	72	74	70	288	448,200
Keiji Teshima	76	70	72	70	288	448,200
Shingo Katayama	71	71	71	75	288	448,200
Kazumasa Sakaitani	72	74	74	68	288	448,200
Noboru Sugai	70	65	80	74	289	405,000
Takaaki Fukuzawa	72	70	78	69	289	405,000
Takenori Hiraishi	72	73	72	72	289	405,000
Masayuki Okano	76	69	72	72	289	405,000

Sanko Grand Summer

Sanko 72 Country Club, Gunma
Par 36-36 72; 7,066 yards

August 7-10
purse, ¥100,000,000

		SCORES			TOTAL	MONEY
Shoichi Kuwabara	70	71	64	66	271	¥18,000,000
Taichi Teshima	67	69	68	68	272	7,560,000
Masashi Shimada	67	68	66	71	272	7,560,000
Tsukasa Watanabe	66	71	69	67	273	3,960,000
Nobuhito Sato	66	71	70	66	273	3,960,000
Kiyoshi Maita	67	66	73	68	274	3,240,000
Toru Suzuki	71	70	66	68	275	2,340,000
Kazuhiko Hosokawa	69	69	68	69	275	2,340,000
Yeh Chang-ting	66	73	67	69	275	2,340,000
Shigemasa Higaki	73	70	67	65	275	2,340,000
Frankie Minoza	70	70	68	67	275	2,340,000
Kim Jong-duk	69	69	66	72	276	1,656,000
Kazuo Kanayama	74	63	70	70	277	1,458,000
Kazuhiro Fukunaga	70	71	68	68	277	1,458,000
Tsuneyuki Nakajima	69	69	70	70	278	1,143,000
Hisao Inoue	70	69	71	68	278	1,143,000
Masanobu Kimura	72	69	69	68	278	1,143,000
Shingo Katayama	74	64	70	70	278	1,143,000
Motomasa Aoki	68	70	70	71	279	835,714
Kazuhiro Takami	72	69	66	72	279	835,714
Tomohiro Maruyama	67	73	70	69	279	835,714
Koki Idoki	69	71	72	67	279	835,714
Masayuki Kawamura	73	68	67	71	279	835,714
Ryoken Kawagishi	67	72	70	70	279	835,714
Shinsuke Yanagisawa	72	70	68	69	279	835,714
Hisayuki Sasaki	71	71	71	67	280	711,000

	SCORES				TOTAL	MONEY
Mitsuo Harada	71	71	69	69	280	711,000
Yasunobu Kuramoto	71	70	69	70	280	711,000
Toru Taniguchi	69	70	68	73	280	711,000
Naoya Sugiyama	70	72	68	71	281	624,600
Hidemichi Tanaka	72	69	67	73	281	624,600
Hidezumi Shirakata	70	71	73	67	281	624,600
Ken Tanigawa	69	71	69	72	281	624,600
Shoichi Miyazato	68	69	73	71	281	624,600
Kaname Yokoo	69	73	71	68	281	624,600

Acom International

Seve Ballesteros Golf Club, Izumi Course, Ibaragi
Par 36-36–72; 6,972 yards

August 14-17
purse, ¥100,000,000

	POINTS				TOTAL	MONEY
Kazuo Kanayama	12	11	9	9	41	¥18,000,000
Eduardo Herrera	4	16	11	10	41	9,000,000
(Kanayama defeated Herrera on second extra hole.)						
Taisuke Kitajima	5	9	6	19	39	6,120,000
Hajime Meshiai	5	6	14	11	36	4,320,000
Shoichi Kuwabara	10	4	10	11	35	3,420,000
Kim Jong-duk	9	9	11	6	35	3,420,000
Daisuke Serizawa	10	7	8	9	34	2,880,000
Shingo Katayama	17	5	8	3	33	2,475,000
Mamoru Osanai	7	8	7	11	33	2,475,000
Tateo Ozaki	11	10	10	1	32	2,070,000
Yoshikazu Sakamoto	6	11	5	9	31	1,656,000
Hiroyuki Fujita	11	14	0	6	31	1,656,000
Shigemasa Higaki	11	7	11	2	31	1,656,000
Kiyoshi Maita	5	9	8	8	30	1,404,000
Koichi Suzuki	-4	15	6	11	28	1,143,000
Shigenori Mori	6	5	5	12	28	1,143,000
Eiji Mizoguchi	4	8	10	6	28	1,143,000
Naoki Hattori	13	2	6	8	28	1,143,000
Tatsuo Takasaki	6	6	6	9	27	918,000
Katsunori Kuwabara	7	7	9	4	27	918,000
Masayuki Kawamura	12	6	1	7	26	846,000
Shinichi Yokota	6	11	3	6	26	846,000
Hiroshi Makino	11	10	-1	5	25	756,000
Mitsuo Harada	6	6	2	11	25	756,000
Peter McWhinney	12	10	3	0	25	756,000
Kazuhiro Fukunaga	13	6	1	5	25	756,000
David Smail	5	8	9	3	25	756,000
Ikuo Shirahama	8	3	7	6	24	666,000
Takaaki Fukuzawa	12	3	1	8	24	666,000
Gohei Sato	3	7	5	9	24	666,000
Yukihiro Yamamoto	3	11	3	7	24	666,000
Takanori Hano	10	7	4	3	24	666,000

KBC Augusta

Keya Golf Club, Shima, Fukuoka
Par 36-36–72; 7,154 yards

August 28-31
purse, ¥100,000,000

	SCORES				TOTAL	MONEY
Masashi Ozaki	65	67	67	67	266	¥18,000,000
Takaaki Fukuzawa	69	70	65	74	278	7,560,000
Taichi Teshima	72	70	69	67	278	7,560,000
Steve Conran	71	69	70	69	279	4,320,000
Tateo Ozaki	68	71	69	72	280	3,420,000
Kunihiko Masuda	67	71	73	69	280	3,420,000
Ikuo Shirahama	72	67	72	70	281	2,745,000
Hiroyuki Fujita	72	66	69	74	281	2,745,000
Tsuneyuki Nakajima	70	71	70	71	282	2,340,000
Tomohiro Maruyama	68	72	69	74	283	1,842,000
Tsukasa Watanabe	73	67	72	71	283	1,842,000
Masanobu Kimura	71	72	68	72	283	1,842,000
Kiyoshi Maita	73	70	68	73	284	1,203,428
Hajime Meshiai	73	70	70	71	284	1,203,428
Kazuo Kanayama	71	70	71	72	284	1,203,428
Isamu Sugita	69	73	71	71	284	1,203,428
Norio Hosoya	71	72	72	69	284	1,203,428
Shoichi Kuwabara	68	73	70	73	284	1,203,428
Katsumasa Miyamoto	70	69	72	73	284	1,203,428
Toru Nakamura	71	70	74	70	285	819,000
Yoshihiro Hori	71	70	74	70	285	819,000
Daisuke Serizawa	70	69	75	71	285	819,000
Kimihiro Matsunaga	72	72	74	67	285	819,000
Kazuhiko Hosokawa	69	71	73	72	285	819,000
Brandt Jobe	67	77	68	73	285	819,000
Yoshinori Kaneko	72	68	73	73	286	675,450
Masami Ito	72	71	70	73	286	675,450
Takenori Hiraishi	72	71	71	72	286	675,450
Masayoshi Yamazoe	70	74	73	69	286	675,450
Mitsutaka Kusakabe	69	71	76	70	286	675,450
Toru Taniguchi	73	70	72	71	286	675,450
Lin Keng-chi	68	74	72	72	286	675,450
Yasuharu Imano	70	73	72	71	286	675,450

Japan Match Play

Nidom Classic Course, Hokkaido
Par 36-36–72; 6,941 yards

September 4-7
purse, ¥80,000,000

FIRST ROUND

Naomichi Ozaki defeated Koki Idoki, 1 up
Satoshi Higashi defeated Yoshinori Mizumaki, 1 up
Peter Teravainen defeated Shigenori Mori, 3 and 2
Masanobu Kimura defeated Toru Suzuki, 4 and 2
Shoichi Kuwabara defeated Nobuhito Sato, 1 up, 23 holes
Kazuhiko Hosokawa defeated Kiyoshi Maita, 3 and 2
Todd Hamilton defeated Hajime Meshiai, 2 and 1
Tsukasa Watanabe defeated Taichi Teshima, 3 and 2
Shigeki Maruyama defeated Eiji Mizoguchi, 1 up, 21 holes
Hirofumi Miyase defeated Nobuo Serizawa, 3 and 2
David Ishii defeated Shigemasa Higaki, 3 and 2

Keiichiro Fukabori defeated Yoshinori Kaneko, 2 and 1
Hidemichi Tanaka defeated Brian Watts, 1 up
Katsunori Kuwabara defeated Brandt Jobe, 2 and 1
Mitsuo Harada defeated Hisayuki Sasaki, 2 and 1
Tateo Ozaki defeated Toru Nakamura, 1 up, 19 holes

(Each losing player received ¥400,000.)

SECOND ROUND

Higashi defeated Naomichi Ozaki, 2 and 1
Teravainen defeated Kimura, 1 up, 19 holes
Kuwabara defcated Hosokawa, 2 and 1
Hamilton defeated Watanabe, 1 up
Maruyama defeated Miyase, 3 and 2
Fukabori defeated Ishii, 1 up, 21 holes
Tanaka defeated Kuwabara, 4 and 3
Tateo Ozaki defeated Harada, 5 and 3

(Each losing player received ¥750,000.)

QUARTER-FINALS

Teravainen defeated Higashi, 6 and 5
Kuwabara defeated Hamilton, 4 and 3
Maruyama defeated Fukabori, 2 up
Tateo Ozaki defeated Tanaka, 2 and 1

(Each losing player received ¥1,400,000.)

SEMI-FINALS

Teravainen defeated Kuwabara, 5 and 4
Maruyama defeated Tateo Ozaki, 4 and 3

THIRD-FOURTH PLACE PLAYOFF

Kuwabara defeated Tateo Ozaki, 7 and 6

(Kuwabara received ¥5,200,000; Ozaki received ¥3,800,000.)

FINAL

Maruyama defeated Teravainen, 3 and 2

(Maruyama received ¥25,000,000; Teravainen received ¥11,000,000.)

Suntory Open

Narashino Country Club, Chiba
Par 36-36–72; 7,027 yards

September 11-1⋅
purse, ¥100,000,00⋅

	SCORES				TOTAL	MONEY
Hiroyuki Fujita	68	68	66	72	274	¥18,000,000
Masashi Ozaki	69	68	70	70	277	9,000,000
Hideyuki Sato	73	71	67	69	280	4,680,000
Yoshinori Mizumaki	67	72	69	72	280	4,680,000
David Ishii	66	72	71	71	280	4,680,000
Teruo Sugihara	67	70	73	71	281	2,767,500

	SCORES				TOTAL	MONEY
Stewart Ginn	72	69	68	72	281	2,767,500
Katsumasa Miyamoto	69	72	72	68	281	2,767,500
Carlos Franco	70	74	70	67	281	2,767,500
Tsukasa Watanabe	68	74	72	68	282	1,688,400
Tatsuo Takasaki	66	71	75	70	282	1,688,400
Yasunori Ida	69	72	71	70	282	1,688,400
Eiji Mizoguchi	71	68	76	67	282	1,688,400
Mitsutaka Kusakabe	68	71	67	76	282	1,688,400
Motomasa Aoki	71	73	70	69	283	1,068,000
Yoshinori Kaneko	73	72	68	70	283	1,068,000
Nobuo Serizawa	72	67	73	71	283	1,068,000
Hidemichi Tanaka	70	71	72	70	283	1,068,000
Shinichi Yokota	68	70	75	70	283	1,068,000
Vijay Singh	67	73	71	72	283	1,068,000
Hajime Meshiai	66	76	70	72	284	814,500
Nobumitsu Yuhara	70	72	71	71	284	814,500
Masayuki Kawamura	71	70	69	74	284	814,500
Keiichiro Fukabori	67	76	71	70	284	814,500
Kazuo Kanayama	72	66	76	71	285	693,000
Tsuyoshi Yoneyama	70	71	74	70	285	693,000
Mitsuo Harada	73	69	69	74	285	693,000
Shoichi Kuwabara	69	75	74	67	285	693,000
Shigeki Maruyama	72	72	71	70	285	693,000
Yeh Chang-ting	70	73	71	71	285	693,000
Kevin Wentworth	68	72	71	74	285	693,000
Prayad Marksaeng	71	71	73	70	285	693,000

ANA Open

Sapporo Golf Club, Wattsu Course, Hokkaido
Par 36-36–72; 7,063 yards

September 18-21
purse, ¥100,000,000

	SCORES				TOTAL	MONEY
Shinichi Yokota	68	65	72	68	273	¥18,000,000
Tateo Ozaki	71	69	68	68	276	7,560,000
Zaw Moe	70	66	70	70	276	7,560,000
Shinichi Akiba	68	67	70	76	281	3,960,000
Carlos Franco	71	68	68	74	281	3,960,000
Masashi Ozaki	72	69	72	69	282	3,060,000
Hajime Meshiai	66	73	70	73	282	3,060,000
Hideyuki Sato	69	70	71	73	283	2,475,000
Nobuhito Sato	70	70	71	72	283	2,475,000
Satoshi Higashi	68	72	71	73	284	1,842,000
Toshiaki Odate	71	72	74	67	284	1,842,000
David Ishii	69	71	70	74	284	1,842,000
Hisashi Nakase	73	71	69	72	285	1,404,000
Eiji Mizoguchi	71	70	75	69	285	1,404,000
Shigeki Maruyama	73	69	72	71	285	1,404,000
Kazuhiro Takami	70	73	74	69	286	1,022,400
Nobumitsu Yuhara	72	70	70	74	286	1,022,400
Kazuhiko Hosokawa	69	72	75	70	286	1,022,400
Katsumasa Miyamoto	74	70	73	69	286	1,022,400
Hirooki Kikkawa	73	70	69	74	286	1,022,400
Yuji Takagi	74	71	71	71	287	792,000
Hiroyuki Fujita	71	72	72	72	287	792,000
Taichi Teshima	70	69	72	76	287	792,000
Peter Senior	71	72	73	71	287	792,000

	SCORES				TOTAL	MONEY
Brian Watts	72	68	71	76	287	792,000
Nick Price	71	70	72	74	287	792,000
Koichi Suzuki	70	74	69	75	288	693,000
Katsunari Takahashi	70	71	72	75	288	693,000
Takaaki Fukuzawa	70	71	74	73	288	693,000
Shigenori Mori	71	70	73	74	288	693,000

Jun Classic

Rope Club, Tochigi
Par 36-36–72; 7,116 yards

September 25-28
purse, ¥110,000,000

	SCORES				TOTAL	MONEY
Eduardo Herrera	71	66	69	70	276	¥19,800,000
Toshiaki Odate	70	70	68	69	277	9,900,000
Toru Taniguchi	69	71	71	68	279	6,732,000
Masashi Ozaki	68	70	67	75	280	3,861,000
Tateo Ozaki	72	72	68	68	280	3,861,000
Yukihiro Yamamoto	69	71	73	67	280	3,861,000
Hidemichi Tanaka	69	71	68	72	280	3,861,000
Kiyoshi Maita	69	71	71	70	281	2,722,500
Carlos Franco	66	72	71	72	281	2,722,500
Shigenori Mori	69	72	73	68	282	2,026,200
Shigeki Maruyama	70	67	74	71	282	2,026,200
Hiroyuki Fujita	71	71	71	69	282	2,026,200
Hideyuki Sato	70	70	75	68	283	1,372,800
Eiji Mizoguchi	71	73	68	71	283	1,372,800
Yoshimitsu Fukuzawa	70	75	67	71	283	1,372,800
Katsunori Kuwabara	69	72	69	73	283	1,372,800
Shinichi Yokota	68	76	71	68	283	1,372,800
Frankie Minoza	72	72	69	70	283	1,372,800
Koichi Suzuki	70	74	70	70	284	893,200
Takaaki Fukuzawa	70	73	68	73	284	893,200
Hajime Meshiai	68	75	68	73	284	893,200
Ryoken Kawagishi	73	70	67	74	284	893,200
Keiichiro Fukabori	71	70	68	75	284	893,200
Hidezumi Shirakata	70	75	69	70	284	893,200
Shingo Katayama	72	73	67	72	284	893,200
David Smail	71	73	71	69	284	893,200
Peter Senior	72	71	69	72	284	893,200
Kiyoshi Murota	69	70	72	74	285	742,500
Nobumitsu Yuhara	71	75	68	71	285	742,500
Shoichi Kuwabara	69	75	71	70	285	742,500
Roger Mackay	70	69	75	71	285	742,500

Japan Open

Koga Golf Club, Fukuoka
Par 36-35–71; 6,762 yards

October 2-.
purse, ¥120,000,00

	SCORES				TOTAL	MONEY
Craig Parry	73	73	70	70	286	¥24,000,000
Masashi Ozaki	67	72	77	71	287	9,540,000
Seiki Okuda	70	72	70	75	287	9,540,000
Frankie Minoza	67	74	73	73	287	9,540,000

	SCORES			TOTAL	MONEY
Tateo Ozaki	69	71 75	73	288	5,040,000
Eiji Mizoguchi	70	77 68	74	289	4,080,000
Katsunori Kuwabara	73	73 71	73	290	3,444,000
Shoichi Kuwabara	74	75 68	74	291	3,132,000
Hajime Meshiai	73	75 72	72	292	2,370,000
Masami Ito	76	69 73	74	292	2,370,000
Shigeki Maruyama	76	70 76	70	292	2,370,000
Yoshinori Mizumaki	69	73 78	73	293	1,788,000
Toru Suzuki	73	75 69	76	293	1,788,000
Nobuo Serizawa	75	72 74	73	294	1,449,000
Kazuhiro Takami	75	73 74	72	294	1,449,000
Kiyoshi Maita	72	77 74	71	294	1,449,000
Keiichiro Fukabori	79	70 71	74	294	1,449,000
Masahiko Akazawa	74	71 77	73	295	1,224,000
Katsuyoshi Tomori	71	76 75	73	295	1,224,000
Eduardo Herrera	69	78 76	72	295	1,224,000
Toshiaki Sudo	73	75 74	74	296	1,075,000
Satoshi Higashi	79	74 74	69	296	1,075,000
Hirofumi Miyase	75	71 76	74	296	1,075,000
Yoshimitsu Fukuzawa	73	77 73	73	296	1,075,000
Hidemichi Tanaka	77	74 73	72	296	1,075,000
Peter Senior	69	76 78	73	296	1,075,000
Hidezumi Shirakata	76	73 77	71	297	996,000
Tsukasa Watanabe	79	74 70	75	298	936,000
Tatsuo Takasaki	75	74 74	75	298	936,000
Naoya Sugiyama	78	71 74	75	298	936,000
Kaname Yokoo	78	71 70	79	298	936,000

Tokai Classic

Miyoshi Country Club, Nishi Course, Aichi
Par 36-36–72; 7,050 yards

October 9-12
purse, ¥110,000,000

	SCORES			TOTAL	MONEY
Brandt Jobe	68	72 69	69	278	¥19,800,000
Brian Watts	72	68 69	69	278	9,900,000
(Jobe defeated Watts on first extra hole.)					
Eiji Mizoguchi	72	71 69	71	283	5,742,000
Toru Taniguchi	71	70 70	72	283	5,742,000
Katsuyoshi Tomori	73	70 70	71	284	3,960,000
Shigeki Maruyama	70	71 72	72	285	3,366,000
Frankie Minoza	75	70 67	73	285	3,366,000
Tom Lehman	70	77 69	70	286	2,722,500
Steve Jones	78	70 67	71	286	2,722,500
Hajime Meshiai	71	75 70	71	287	2,277,000
Masami Ito	70	71 74	73	288	1,686,960
Toru Suzuki	75	73 68	72	288	1,686,960
Masatoshi Horikawa	70	71 74	73	288	1,686,960
Hiroyuki Fujita	74	72 73	69	288	1,686,960
Law Moe	72	71 73	72	288	1,686,960
Katsunori Kuwabara	76	73 71	69	289	1,247,400
Jun Kikuchi	73	70 74	72	289	1,247,400
Tateo Ozaki	74	71 72	73	290	1,019,700
Toyoken Kawagishi	74	75 71	70	290	1,019,700
Samson Gimson	70	72 72	76	290	1,019,700
Chusaku Sugimoto	72	74 70	74	290	1,019,700
Taisei Inagaki	71	72 76	72	291	844,800

	SCORES	TOTAL	MONEY
Kazuo Kanayama	75 71 73 72	291	844,800
Yukihiro Yamamoto	74 70 73 74	291	844,800
Naoki Hattori	72 76 71 72	291	844,800
Naoya Sugiyama	68 74 73 76	291	844,800
Hidezumi Shirakata	71 77 71 72	291	844,800
Tsuneyuki Nakajima	69 76 73 74	292	723,360
Yoshinori Mizumaki	70 72 74 76	292	723,360
Yoshitaka Yamamoto	74 73 71 74	292	723,360
Mitsuo Harada	79 70 71 72	292	723,360
Kaname Yokoo	75 73 70 74	292	723,360
Chen Tze-ming	77 70 73 72	292	723,360
*Kintaro Yonekura	72 74 73 73	292	

Golf Digest Tournament

Tomei Country Club, Shizuoka
Par 35-36–71; 6,781 yards

October 16-19
purse, ¥100,000,000

	SCORES	TOTAL	MONEY
Brandt Jobe	68 69 63 67	267	¥18,000,000
Toru Suzuki	67 67 64 69	267	9,000,000
(Jobe defeated Suzuki on first extra hole.)			
Mitsuo Harada	70 67 65 66	268	4,680,000
Katsunori Kuwabara	67 66 67 68	268	4,680,000
Shusaku Sugimoto	67 66 66 69	268	4,680,000
Tsuyoshi Yoneyama	62 66 71 70	269	3,240,000
Keiichiro Fukabori	65 71 66 69	271	2,880,000
Masayuki Kawamura	68 69 65 70	272	2,610,000
Hajime Meshiai	64 69 70 70	273	2,070,000
Seiki Okuda	65 72 67 69	273	2,070,000
Brian Watts	69 70 67 67	273	2,070,000
Yoshinori Kaneko	68 69 68 69	274	1,411,200
Kiyoshi Maita	64 69 69 72	274	1,411,200
Takenori Hiraishi	69 70 66 69	274	1,411,200
Hiroyuki Fujita	67 65 72 70	274	1,411,200
Peter Senior	66 69 71 68	274	1,411,200
Katsuyoshi Tomori	67 67 71 70	275	1,080,000
Kazuhiro Takami	66 68 70 72	276	907,200
Kiyoshi Murota	68 71 70 67	276	907,200
Toru Taniguchi	66 70 68 72	276	907,200
Shingo Katayama	69 66 70 71	276	907,200
Roger Mackay	71 66 68 71	276	907,200
Koichi Suzuki	70 71 71 65	277	729,000
Yoshinori Mizumaki	69 69 69 70	277	729,000
Tomohiro Maruyama	69 70 67 70	277	729,000
Stewart Ginn	69 71 70 67	277	729,000
Shinichi Yokota	70 71 67 69	277	729,000
Kaname Yokoo	69 71 69 68	277	729,000
David Ishii	70 69 66 72	277	729,000
Takao Nogami	69 69 69 70	277	729,000

Bridgestone Open

Sodegaura Country Club, Chiba
Par 36-36–72; 7,151 yards

October 23-26
purse, ¥120,000,000

	SCORES				TOTAL	MONEY
Masashi Ozaki	66	70	71	66	273	¥21,600,000
Tateo Ozaki	68	66	68	72	274	9,072,000
Shigeki Maruyama	71	70	64	69	274	9,072,000
Frankie Minoza	72	64	68	72	276	5,184,000
Yoshinori Kaneko	70	69	67	72	278	3,520,800
Toru Nakamura	71	70	67	70	278	3,520,800
Kazuhiko Hosokawa	69	70	69	70	278	3,520,800
Shingo Katayama	69	70	72	67	278	3,520,800
Bernhard Langer	68	70	73	67	278	3,520,800
Kiyoshi Maita	72	67	68	72	279	2,111,400
Stewart Ginn	71	69	73	66	279	2,111,400
Katsumasa Miyamoto	68	69	69	73	279	2,111,400
Brian Watts	68	70	69	72	279	2,111,400
Ikuo Shirahama	68	71	73	69	281	1,555,200
Katsuyoshi Tomori	73	69	69	70	281	1,555,200
Glen Day	72	68	70	71	281	1,555,200
Yoshimitsu Fukuzawa	67	71	74	70	282	1,177,200
Masatoshi Horikawa	66	73	73	70	282	1,177,200
Hiroyuki Fujita	68	68	73	73	282	1,177,200
Roger Mackay	72	68	69	73	282	1,177,200
Koki Idoki	72	70	72	69	283	993,600
Mitsutaka Kusakabe	70	74	69	70	283	993,600
Peter Senior	68	71	73	71	283	993,600
Naomichi Ozaki	67	72	72	73	284	793,028
Satoshi Higashi	73	71	69	71	284	793,028
Kiyoshi Murota	71	73	69	71	284	793,028
Hajime Meshiai	74	67	73	70	284	793,028
Nobumitsu Yuhara	71	72	73	68	284	793,028
Teruo Sugihara	72	72	71	69	284	793,028
Toru Suzuki	73	68	71	72	284	793,028
Hirofumi Miyase	74	68	70	72	284	793,028
Hidemichi Tanaka	73	66	74	71	284	793,028
Hidezumi Shirakata	71	71	72	70	284	793,028
Shinichi Yokota	71	69	71	73	284	793,028
Kaname Yokoo	71	71	71	71	284	793,028
Chen Tze-chung	71	69	72	72	284	793,028
Carlos Franco	72	69	70	73	284	793,028

Philip Morris Championship

ABC Golf Club, Hyogo
Par 36-36–72; 7,176 yards

October 30-November 2
purse, ¥200,000,000

	SCORES				TOTAL	MONEY
Brian Watts	70	73	67	70	280	¥36,000,000
Kaname Yokoo	73	71	70	68	282	18,000,000
Roger Mackay	73	67	73	70	283	10,440,000
Pete Jordan	70	71	72	70	283	10,440,000
Naomichi Ozaki	72	75	67	70	284	6,480,000
Katsunari Takahashi	72	75	68	69	284	6,480,000
Shigeki Maruyama	72	72	69	71	284	6,480,000
Toru Suzuki	70	76	68	72	286	4,950,000

ASIA/JAPAN TOURS

	SCORES				TOTAL	MONEY
Frankie Minoza	74	73	70	69	286	4,950,000
Masashi Ozaki	71	73	71	72	287	3,376,800
Eiji Mizoguchi	69	74	73	71	287	3,376,800
Hidemichi Tanaka	70	74	73	70	287	3,376,800
Chen Tze-chung	74	74	68	71	287	3,376,800
Todd Hamilton	70	73	73	71	287	3,376,800
Nobumitsu Yuhara	75	69	72	72	288	2,484,000
Yasunori Ida	72	75	73	68	288	2,484,000
Satoshi Higashi	72	72	74	71	289	1,915,200
Tsukasa Watanabe	71	76	75	67	289	1,915,200
Eduardo Herrera	74	71	71	73	289	1,915,200
Peter McWhinney	72	74	71	72	289	1,915,200
Hiroyuki Fujita	72	76	74	67	289	1,915,200
Kazuhiro Fukunaga	74	76	68	72	290	1,596,000
Taichi Teshima	69	77	73	71	290	1,596,000
Shinichi Yokota	74	73	72	71	290	1,596,000
Tateo Ozaki	77	69	72	73	291	1,440,000
Stewart Ginn	72	73	70	76	291	1,440,000
Katsunori Kuwabara	70	76	76	69	291	1,440,000
Kim Jong-duk	73	75	72	71	291	1,440,000
Russ Cochran	73	71	74	73	291	1,440,000
Tsuneyuki Nakajima	77	70	76	70	293	1,249,200
Hajime Meshiai	72	77	72	72	293	1,249,200
Seiki Okuda	69	76	71	77	293	1,249,200
Katsuyoshi Tomori	74	76	74	69	293	1,249,200
Peter Senior	74	75	71	73	293	1,249,200
David Ishii	72	73	73	75	293	1,249,200

Sumitomo Visa Taiheiyo Masters

Taiheiyo Club, Gotemba Course, Shizuoka
Par 36-36–72; 7,072 yards

November 13-16
purse, ¥150,000,000

	SCORES				TOTAL	MONEY
Lee Westwood	68	68	65	71	272	¥27,000,000
Masashi Ozaki	71	65	69	68	273	11,340,000
Naomichi Ozaki	67	68	69	69	273	11,340,000
Toru Suzuki	70	71	67	66	274	5,940,000
Mark O'Meara	69	67	69	69	274	5,940,000
Yoshinori Mizumaki	66	70	70	69	275	4,590,000
Chen Tze-chung	69	69	67	70	275	4,590,000
Taichi Teshima	69	69	68	70	276	3,510,000
Roger Mackay	67	69	72	68	276	3,510,000
Darren Clarke	68	68	69	71	276	3,510,000
Jeff Sluman	71	70	66	70	277	2,592,000
Jose Maria Olazabal	67	70	69	71	277	2,592,000
Peter McWhinney	66	72	71	69	278	2,268,000
Kazuhiko Hosokawa	68	70	69	72	279	2,025,000
Todd Hamilton	71	71	67	70	279	2,025,000
Kiyoshi Maita	70	72	68	70	280	1,579,500
Teruo Sugihara	69	69	74	68	280	1,579,500
Eiji Mizoguchi	72	71	68	69	280	1,579,500
Costantino Rocca	71	73	70	66	280	1,579,500
Nobumitsu Yuhara	70	70	71	70	281	1,323,000
Stewart Ginn	67	74	69	71	281	1,323,000
Kazuhiro Takami	70	72	68	72	282	1,197,000
Katsunori Kuwabara	67	73	73	69	282	1,197,000

	SCORES				TOTAL	MONEY
Brandt Jobe	74	67	73	68	282	1,197,000
Yoshikazu Sakamoto	71	72	72	68	283	1,053,000
Tsuyoshi Yoneyama	68	71	72	72	283	1,053,000
Zaw Moe	69	74	72	68	283	1,053,000
Graham Marsh	72	70	73	68	283	1,053,000
Rick Gibson	71	74	71	67	283	1,053,000
David Ishii	70	69	73	71	283	1,053,000
Carlos Franco	71	73	71	68	283	1,053,000

Dunlop Phoenix Tournament

Phoenix Country Club, Miyazaki
Par 36-35–71; 6,803 yards

November 20-23
purse, ¥200,000,000

	SCORES				TOTAL	MONEY
Tom Watson	70	65	70	70	275	¥36,000,000
Naomichi Ozaki	71	70	71	65	277	18,000,000
Craig Parry	68	68	69	73	278	12,240,000
Jose Maria Olazabal	73	69	67	70	279	7,920,000
Masashi Ozaki	68	71	69	71	279	7,920,000
Shigeki Maruyama	72	68	71	69	280	5,535,000
Carlos Franco	68	71	71	70	280	5,535,000
Retief Goosen	66	72	72	70	280	5,535,000
Costantino Rocca	71	72	68	69	280	5,535,000
David Ishii	74	68	71	68	281	3,384,000
Frankie Minoza	68	70	71	72	281	3,684,000
Darren Clarke	72	70	70	69	281	3,684,000
Jeff Sluman	74	71	68	69	282	2,592,000
Chen Tze-chung	72	73	70	67	282	2,592,000
Satoshi Higashi	68	76	70	68	282	2,592,000
Brandt Jobe	73	72	67	70	282	2,592,000
Miguel Angel Jimenez	72	71	73	66	282	2,592,000
Katsuyoshi Tomori	71	70	70	72	283	1,944,000
Keiichiro Fukabori	68	70	73	72	283	1,944,000
Brian Watts	72	73	69	70	284	1,800,000
Hidemichi Tanaka	67	73	72	73	285	1,605,500
Peter Senior	72	71	71	71	285	1,605,500
Yoshikazu Sakamoto	70	74	72	69	285	1,605,500
Lee Westwood	73	72	70	70	285	1,605,500
Zaw Moe	73	73	71	68	285	1,605,500
Kaname Yokoo	71	70	70	75	286	1,440,000
Shinichi Yokota	74	69	71	72	286	1,440,000
Shigemasa Higaki	75	71	69	71	286	1,440,000
Tateo Ozaki	71	71	70	75	287	1,297,440
Toru Nakamura	74	70	72	71	287	1,297,440
Mark Brooks	75	69	74	69	287	1,297,440
Graham Marsh	70	74	71	72	287	1,297,440
Todd Hamilton	69	74	69	75	287	1,297,440

Casio World Open

Ibusuki Golf Club, Kaimon, Kagoshima
Par 36-36–72; 7,056 yards

November 27-30
purse, ¥150,000,000

	SCORES				TOTAL	MONEY
Mitsutaka Kusakabe	69	68	71	70	278	¥27,000,000
Naomichi Ozaki	67	68	74	70	279	9,720,000
Hirofumi Miyase	69	70	68	72	279	9,720,000
Keiichiro Fukabori	69	71	70	69	279	9,720,000
Masashi Ozaki	67	71	71	71	280	4,185,000
Ryoken Kawagishi	70	71	70	69	280	4,185,000
Shigeki Maruyama	68	74	70	68	280	4,185,000
Brian Watts	70	69	71	70	280	4,185,000
Brandt Jobe	70	71	69	70	280	4,185,000
Miguel Angel Jimenez	71	71	69	69	280	4,185,000
Mark Brooks	70	73	70	68	281	2,592,000
Fred Funk	71	70	74	66	281	2,592,000
Tsukasa Watanabe	71	70	70	71	282	2,025,000
Eduardo Herrera	73	71	69	69	282	2,025,000
David Ishii	68	74	70	70	282	2,025,000
Kim Jong-duk	71	71	71	69	282	2,025,000
Hajime Meshiai	72	68	74	69	283	1,512,000
Stewart Ginn	72	72	70	69	283	1,512,000
Hidemichi Tanaka	70	71	74	68	283	1,512,000
Yoshinori Mizumaki	72	71	70	71	284	1,247,400
Katsuyoshi Tomori	71	73	71	69	284	1,247,400
Toru Nakamura	69	72	72	71	284	1,247,400
Toru Suzuki	73	71	73	67	284	1,247,400
Kazuhiko Hosokawa	70	70	71	73	284	1,247,400
Kazuhiro Takami	73	69	72	71	285	1,093,500
Tsuyoshi Yoneyama	72	72	74	67	285	1,093,500
Taichi Teshima	75	68	71	71	285	1,093,500
Rick Gibson	71	67	75	72	285	1,093,500
*Taichiro Kiyota	71	70	75	69	285	
Tsuneyuki Nakajima	71	70	75	70	286	999,000
Retief Goosen	71	73	72	70	286	999,000
Chris Smith	67	74	73	72	286	999,000

Japan Series of Golf

Tokyo Yomiuri Country Club, Tokyo
Par 35-36–71; 6,983 yards

December 4-7
purse, ¥100,000,000

	SCORES				TOTAL	MONEY
Shigeki Maruyama	70	63	68	67	268	¥30,000,000
Tateo Ozaki	67	67	71	65	270	13,000,000
Eduardo Herrera	68	65	68	70	271	6,100,000
Craig Parry	68	62	71	70	271	6,100,000
Naomichi Ozaki	68	68	66	71	273	3,363,333
Tsukasa Watanabe	69	68	68	68	273	3,363,333
Keiichiro Fukabori	65	70	66	72	273	3,363,333
Brian Watts	68	70	68	68	274	2,450,000
Mitsuo Harada	67	71	69	69	276	2,100,000
Shoichi Kuwabara	71	70	66	70	277	1,650,000
Hiroyuki Fujita	71	70	67	69	277	1,650,000
Nobuhito Sato	69	69	71	68	277	1,650,000
Carlos Franco	71	69	68	70	278	1,400,000

	SCORES				TOTAL	MONEY
Yeh Chang-ting	68	75	66	70	279	1,300,000
Hirofumi Miyase	66	68	73	73	280	1,200,000
Eiji Mizoguchi	69	70	71	71	281	1,065,000
Kazuhiko Hosokawa	72	70	69	70	281	1,065,000
Toru Suzuki	70	72	69	71	282	935,000
Kim Jong-duk	70	75	68	69	282	935,000
Kenichi Kuboya	74	75	67	67	283	835,000
Brandt Jobe	73	69	69	72	283	835,000
Frankie Minoza	74	68	70	72	284	770,000
Shigenori Mori	73	72	69	71	285	730,000
Kazuo Kanayama	74	71	70	71	286	670,000
Mitsutaka Kusakabe	73	72	68	73	286	670,000
Peter Teravainen	71	72	73	71	287	620,000
Shinichi Yokota	75	69	71	73	288	590,000
Hisayuki Sasaki	76	69	73	71	289	560,000
Shigemasa Higaki	74	73	72	71	290	530,000
Hajime Meshiai	71	69	71	80	291	500,000

Daikyo Open

Daikyo Country Club, Okinawa
Par 36-35–71; 6,308 yards

December 11-14
purse, ¥120,000,000

	SCORES				TOTAL	MONEY
Kenichi Kuboya	66	64	68	65	263	¥21,600,000
Katsunori Kuwabara	65	68	70	61	264	9,072,000
Brian Watts	66	66	66	66	264	9,072,000
Toru Suzuki	71	66	61	69	267	5,184,000
Hirofumi Miyase	66	65	70	67	268	4,104,000
David Ishii	63	66	69	70	268	4,104,000
Mitsutaka Kusakabe	68	65	67	69	269	3,294,000
Shigemasa Higaki	68	65	67	69	269	3,294,000
Hiroshi Makino	66	69	69	66	270	2,646,000
Yeh Chang-ting	71	65	66	68	270	2,646,000
Masahiro Kuramoto	72	64	67	69	272	1,911,600
Keiichiro Fukabori	68	64	71	69	272	1,911,600
Atsushi Takamatsu	69	67	66	70	272	1,911,600
Peter McWhinney	67	66	69	70	272	1,911,600
Kaname Yokoo	66	72	69	66	273	1,490,400
Kiyoshi Maita	69	67	69	68	273	1,490,400
Kikuo Arai	70	68	69	67	274	1,209,600
Nick Gibson	70	67	69	68	274	1,209,600
Ryoken Kawagishi	63	71	68	72	274	1,209,600
Shinichi Yokota	70	69	70	66	275	997,920
Stewart Ginn	70	69	70	66	275	997,920
Toshitaka Yamamoto	72	68	68	67	275	997,920
Kazumasa Sakaitani	73	63	72	67	275	997,920
Shigeki Maruyama	66	70	67	72	275	997,920
Masakazu Noritake	70	67	75	64	276	874,800
Yusaku Sugimoto	66	70	73	67	276	874,800
Hiroyuki Fujita	67	71	70	68	276	874,800
Hideki Kase	68	68	70	70	276	874,800
Peter Teravainen	72	67	72	66	277	788,400
Eiji Mizoguchi	71	68	68	70	277	788,400
Frankie Minoza	70	67	70	70	277	788,400
Taichi Teshima	69	66	70	72	277	788,400

Omega Tour

Asian Honda Classic

Thai Country Club, Bangkok, Thailand
Par 36-36–72; 7,016 yards

February 6-9
purse, US$300,000

	SCORES				TOTAL	MONEY
Tiger Woods	70	64	66	68	268	US$48,450
Mo Joong-kyung	70	70	70	68	278	33,390
Jim Rutledge	69	75	72	63	279	15,200
Carlos Espinosa	68	68	74	69	279	15,200
Chang Tse-peng	69	68	71	71	279	15,200
Yeh Chang-ting	72	69	72	67	280	9,000
Brad Andrews	68	73	70	69	280	9,000
Mike Cunning	69	70	70	71	280	9,000
Arjun Atwal	73	70	69	69	281	6,345
Frank Nobilo	70	68	70	73	281	6,345
Steve Elkington	71	71	71	69	282	5,160
Curtis Strange	68	74	71	69	282	5,160
Greg Hanrahan	70	66	70	76	282	5,160
Masayoshi Yamazoe	72	74	70	67	283	4,230
Felix Casas	71	75	70	67	283	4,230
Marimuthu Ramayah	70	73	72	68	283	4,230
Paul Foley	75	66	73	69	283	4,230
Danny Zarate	72	72	68	71	283	4,230
Prayad Marksaeng	67	73	73	71	284	3,610
Edward Fryatt	68	69	74	73	284	3,610
Zaw Moe	74	69	65	76	284	3,610
Hsieh Yu-shu	71	69	71	74	285	3,420
Jerry Smith	73	71	71	71	286	3,105
Zhang Lian-wei	70	71	74	71	286	3,105
Takao Nogami	69	72	71	74	286	3,105
Christian Pena	71	70	71	74	286	3,105
Clay Devers	67	75	68	76	286	3,105
Lee Petters	66	70	73	77	286	3,105
Cheng Jun	71	74	74	68	287	2,700
Jeff Senior	71	74	72	70	287	2,700
Larry Barber	71	71	72	73	287	2,700

Vietnam Open

Vietnam Golf & Country Club, Ho Chi Minh City, Vietnam
Par 36-36–72; 7,021 yards

March 27-3
purse, US$200,000

	SCORES			TOTAL	MONEY
Andrew Bonhomme	68	70	66	69	273	US$32,300
Chang Tse-peng	70	64	69	71	274	22,260
Mike Cunning	69	69	71	67	276	12,400
Wang Ter-chang	67	72	67	71	277	10,000
Christopher Williams	72	67	68	71	278	8,000
Scott Laycock	70	71	68	71	280	6,500
Grant Dodd	70	68	70	72	280	6,500

	SCORES				TOTAL	MONEY
Prayad Marksaeng	71	69	71	71	282	5,000
Akinori Tani	70	75	70	68	283	4,230
Derek Fung	74	70	67	72	283	4,230
Gerry Norquist	72	69	72	71	284	3,552
Eric Rustand	72	68	72	72	284	3,552
Danny Zarate	74	69	71	71	285	3,072
Thaworn Wiratchant	70	72	71	72	285	3,072
Jamnian Chitprasong	75	71	66	73	285	3,072
Cesar Ababa	74	72	74	66	286	2,700
Hsieh Yu-shu	71	75	70	70	286	2,700
Cho Chul-sang	73	68	73	72	286	2,700
Simon Yates	71	74	72	70	287	2,313.33
John Kernohan	70	74	72	71	287	2,313.33
Rob Willis	71	70	73	73	287	2,313.33
Kyi Hla Han	73	70	70	74	287	2,313.33
Jerry Smith	70	72	70	75	287	2,313.33
John Senden	72	68	71	76	287	2,313.33
Mamoru Takahashi	68	78	70	72	288	2,010
Chua Guan Soon	72	73	69	74	288	2,010
Boonchu Ruangkit	72	69	73	74	288	2,010
Norio Matsuke	71	69	73	75	288	2,010
Nam Young-woo	72	75	73	69	289	1,720
Madasamy Murugiah	74	74	70	71	289	1,720
Yurio Akitomi	76	71	70	72	289	1,720
Craig Kamps	69	74	73	73	289	1,720
Andy Wada	71	71	71	76	289	1,720
Hendrik Buhrmann	69	73	70	77	289	1,720

London Myanmar Open

City Golf Resort, Yangon, Myanmar
Par 36-36–72; 6,638 yards

April 3-6
purse, US$200,000

	SCORES				TOTAL	MONEY
Boonchu Ruangkit	72	65	68	68	273	US$32,300
John Senden	73	71	63	66	273	22,260
(Boonchu defeated Senden on first extra hole.)
Theodore Purdy	72	69	64	70	275	12,400
Jamnian Chitprasong	69	67	68	72	276	10,000
Yasuhiro Taguchi	71	70	69	67	277	7,500
Hendrik Buhrmann	69	71	67	70	277	7,500
Mynt Thaung	68	72	70	68	278	5,500
Jeev Milkha Singh	69	69	71	69	278	5,500
Adrian Percey	68	70	72	69	279	4,230
Kyaw Moe	68	75	67	69	279	4,230
Lu Wen-teh	72	70	75	63	280	3,552
Nam Young-woo	67	68	70	75	280	3,552
Jerry Smith	71	67	71	72	281	3,009
Scott Laycock	69	71	69	72	281	3,009
Craig Kamps	68	73	66	74	281	3,009
Prayad Marksaeng	68	67	72	74	281	3,009
Andrew Bonhomme	72	68	74	69	283	2,540
Rob Stephens	72	70	71	70	283	2,540
Arjun Atwal	65	72	74	72	283	2,540
Christopher Williams	69	70	70	74	283	2,540
Lee Eagleton	71	76	68	69	284	2,250
Simon Yates	71	73	70	70	284	2,250
Madasamy Murugiah	71	69	73	71	284	2,250

	SCORES	TOTAL	MONEY
Chawalit Plaphol	69 69 71 75	284	2,250
Soe Kyaw Naing	73 70 72 70	285	2,040
Lee Petters	71 72 71 71	285	2,040
Tsai Chi-huang	73 71 67 74	285	2,040
Robert Huxtable	70 74 76 66	286	1,830
Brad Andrews	72 72 71 71	286	1,830
Cheng Jun	74 69 71 72	286	1,830
Mardan Mamat	72 68 73 73	286	1,830

DFS Galleria Guam Open

Leo Palace Resort, Manenggon Hills, Guam
Par 36-36–72; 6,757 yards
(Fourth round cancelled — typhoon.)

April 17-20
purse, US$250,000

	SCORES	TOTAL	MONEY
Gerry Norquist	74 69 67	210	US$40,375
Mike Cunning	73 71 69	213	27,825
Jerry Smith	73 73 68	214	14,000
Jim Rutledge	71 74 69	214	14,000
Theodore Purdy	73 70 72	215	9,375
Tsai Chi-huang	69 70 76	215	9,375
John Senden	74 76 66	216	6,875
Aaron Meeks	69 75 72	216	6,875
Craig Kamps	77 74 67	218	5,287.50
Akinori Tani	76 75 67	218	5,287.50
Simon Yates	77 73 69	219	4,299.67
Christopher Williams	75 70 74	219	4,299.67
Prayad Marksaeng	71 74 74	219	4,299.67
Grant Dodd	73 75 72	220	3,825
Vivek Bhandari	82 70 69	221	3,380
Mo Joong-kyung	78 73 70	221	3,380
Chikara Nagata	74 75 72	221	3,380
Brad Andrews	73 74 74	221	3,380
Hendrik Buhrmann	74 72 75	221	3,380
Arjun Atwal	75 77 70	222	2,775
Goo Ja-hoon	70 80 72	222	2,775
Jeff Senior	77 73 72	222	2,775
Yasuo Sone	81 69 72	222	2,775
Koji Sato	79 70 73	222	2,775
Nico van Rensburg	78 71 73	222	2,775
Scott Laycock	77 72 73	222	2,775
Leith Wastle	78 74 71	223	2,325
Dinesh Chand	76 75 72	223	2,325
Chen Jung-hsin	73 78 72	223	2,325
Masakuzu Noritake	73 77 73	223	2,325
Yoshio Funiyama	74 76 73	223	2,325

Satelindo Indonesia Open

Jagorawi Golf & Country Club, Jakarta, Indonesia
Par 36-36–72; 6,322 yards

April 24-
purse, US$250,00

	SCORES	TOTAL	MONEY
Craig Parry	67 70 74 69	280	US$44,412.
Des Terblanche	69 70 73 70	282	30,607.

	SCORES				TOTAL	MONEY
Gerry Norquist	71	69	69	74	283	17,050
Nozomi Kawahara	69	70	73	73	285	13,750
Jeff Senior	71	70	70	75	286	11,000
Clay Devers	72	74	71	70	287	8,250
Arjun Singh	73	73	68	73	287	8,250
Charlie Wi	70	72	70	75	287	8,250
Mark Calcavecchia	70	73	76	69	288	5,559.58
Prayad Marksaeng	76	71	72	69	288	5,559.58
Mo Joong-kyung	72	72	72	72	288	5,559.58
Greg Hanrahan	74	74	71	71	290	4,348.44
Paul Foley	70	71	75	74	290	4,348.44
Rob Willis	72	75	68	75	290	4,348.44
Poh Eing Cheong	72	72	71	75	290	4,348.44
Mardan Mamat	72	74	74	71	291	3,510.83
Grant Dodd	71	74	75	71	291	3,510.83
Simon Owen	69	76	74	72	291	3,510.83
Jerry Smith	70	74	75	72	291	3,510.83
John Wither	72	77	69	73	291	3,510.83
Kenny Walker	74	69	74	74	291	3,510.83
Tadashi Ezure	76	71	75	70	292	2,928.75
Andrew Bonhomme	74	76	70	72	292	2,928.75
Rafael Ponce	77	72	71	72	292	2,928.75
John Senden	70	72	77	73	292	2,928.75
Kasiadi	71	76	70	75	292	2,928.75
Theodore Purdy	67	74	76	75	292	2,928.75
Craig Kamps	72	75	76	70	293	2,598.75
Lucas Parsons	73	72	75	73	293	2,598.75
Jun Tae-hyun	73	74	73	74	294	2,392.50
Thaworn Wiratchant	73	74	73	74	294	2,392.50
Hendrik Buhrmann	72	73	70	79	294	2,392.50

Sabah Masters

Sabah Golf & Country Club, Kota Kinabalu, Malaysia
Par 36-36–72; 6,970 yards

August 7-10
purse, US$200,000

	SCORES				TOTAL	MONEY
Des Terblanche	73	72	70	66	281	US$32,300
Thammanoon Sriroj	72	71	65	73	281	22,260

(Terblanche defeated Thammanoon on third extra hole.)

	SCORES				TOTAL	MONEY
Paul Foley	71	69	69	73	282	12,400
Kasiadi	75	70	69	70	284	7,750
Zhang Lian-wei	72	71	70	71	284	7,750
Chawalit Plaphol	72	70	70	72	284	7,750
Mardan Mamat	71	69	70	74	284	7,750
Rodrigo Cuello	74	70	67	74	285	4,730
Ian Quinn	69	71	69	76	285	4,730
Chang Tse-peng	70	69	76	71	286	4,000
Prayad Marksaeng	73	72	72	70	287	3,670
Gerry Norquist	72	71	75	70	288	3,236.67
Simon Owen	73	71	74	70	288	3,236.67
Thaworn Wiratchant	75	71	71	71	288	3,236.67
Lee Petters	72	71	73	73	289	2,760
Ali Kadir	72	72	71	74	289	2,760
Rob Stephens	70	70	74	75	289	2,760
Ian Rutledge	74	69	70	76	289	2,760
Kenny Walker	75	72	72	71	290	2,375

	SCORES				TOTAL	MONEY
Ramon Brobio	73	74	72	71	290	2,375
Madasamy Murugiah	70	76	72	72	290	2,375
John Kernohan	73	73	68	76	290	2,375
Wayne Bradley	73	77	72	69	291	2,040
Christian Pena	72	72	78	69	291	2,040
Marciano Pucay	78	69	72	72	291	2,040
Craig Kamps	72	74	73	72	291	2,040
Aaron Meeks	68	73	78	72	291	2,040
Suppacheep Meesom	73	74	71	73	291	2,040
Marimuthu Ramayah	73	70	69	79	291	2,040
Felix Casas	71	79	71	71	292	1,648.57
Mike Cunning	74	73	71	74	292	1,648.57
Periasamy Gunasegaran	72	73	73	74	292	1,648.57
Rob Willis	73	71	74	74	292	1,648.57
George Olaybar	75	69	74	74	292	1,648.57
Carlos Espinosa	74	72	71	75	292	1,648.57
Scott Laycock	69	76	72	75	292	1,648.57

SingTel Ericsson Singapore Open

Jurong Country Club, Singapore
Par 36-36–72; 6,568 yards

August 14-17
purse, US$500,000

	SCORES				TOTAL	MONEY
Zaw Moe	67	69	69	72	277	US$80,750
Fran Quinn	69	73	70	68	280	55,650
Jeev Milkha Singh	73	68	71	69	281	23,375
Rafael Ponce	71	68	71	71	281	23,375
Gerry Norquist	70	71	69	71	281	23,375
Boonchu Ruangkit	69	70	70	72	281	23,375
Simon Owen	68	74	70	70	282	10,635.7
Rodney Pampling	69	68	73	72	282	10,635.7
Felix Casas	71	73	66	72	282	10,635.7
Carlos Espinosa	70	69	70	73	282	10,635.7
Grant Dodd	68	70	71	73	282	10,635.7
Kasiadi	68	69	72	73	282	10,635.7
Edward Fryatt	69	65	75	73	282	10,635.7
Brad Andrews	72	69	75	67	283	6,908.3
Marty Schiene	69	73	72	69	283	6,908.3
Peter Fowler	72	71	70	70	283	6,908.3
Clay Devers	72	72	69	70	283	6,908.3
Justin Cooper	72	70	69	72	283	6,908.3
Leith Wastle	67	72	71	73	283	6,908.3
Kevin Wentworth	70	75	70	69	284	5,625
Mike Tschetter	68	69	77	70	284	5,625
Aaron Meeks	72	70	72	70	284	5,625
Jim Rutledge	72	70	72	70	284	5,625
John Kernohan	70	74	70	70	284	5,625
Soe Kyaw Naing	67	72	73	72	284	5,625
Eric Meeks	69	73	73	70	285	4,650
Prayad Marksaeng	70	71	73	71	285	4,650
Kenny Walker	71	71	72	71	285	4,650
Scott Laycock	68	70	75	72	285	4,650
Craig Jones	71	71	71	72	285	4,650
Stephen Leaney	71	74	68	72	285	4,650
Ali Kadir	68	69	73	75	285	4,650

Philip Morris Asia Cup

Woo Jung Hills Country Club, A-san City, Korea
Par 36-36–72; 7,051 yards

August 21-24
purse, US$500,000

		SCORES			TOTAL	MONEY
Park No-seok	71	71	66	71	279	US$80,750
Park Nam-sin	69	71	68	72	280	55,650
Choi Kyung-ju	74	70	72	68	284	25,333.33
John Kernohan	73	69	71	71	284	25,333.33
Kang Wook-soon	69	72	72	71	284	25,333.33
Jee Tae-hwa	76	70	74	65	285	16,250
Brad Andrews	73	72	72	68	285	16,250
Choi Sang-ho	71	70	71	75	287	11,825
Lim Jin-han	76	68	67	76	287	11,825
Prayad Marksaeng	69	73	76	70	288	9,253.33
Choi Kwang-soo	71	70	76	71	288	9,253.33
Paul Foley	75	72	70	71	288	9,253.33
Chae Young-tae	71	71	76	71	289	8,040
Clay Devers	74	73	73	70	290	6,662.50
Kim Wan-tae	71	75	73	71	290	6,662.50
Charlie Wi	74	76	69	71	290	6,662.50
Yoo Jong-ky	73	74	71	72	290	6,662.50
Chawalit Plaphol	69	74	75	72	290	6,662.50
Kim Tae-hoon	75	74	69	72	290	6,662.50
Eric Rustand	74	73	70	73	290	6,662.50
Choi Yoon-soo	71	71	73	75	290	6,662.50
Tadashi Ezure	70	77	74	70	291	5,475
Ted Purdy	74	76	71	70	291	5,475
Kyi Hla Han	71	76	71	73	291	5,475
Jeev Milkha Singh	74	71	71	75	291	5,475
Craig Kamps	76	71	74	71	292	4,650
Chang Tse-peng	70	75	75	72	292	4,650
Marciano Pucay	68	78	74	72	292	4,650
Bran Quinn	76	74	70	72	292	4,650
Chung Joon	70	75	74	73	292	4,650
Paul Friedlander	73	69	77	73	292	4,650
Jerry Smith	71	72	75	74	292	4,650

Asia Pacific Ericsson Masters

Bintan Lagoon Golf & Beach Resort, Bintan, Indonesia
Par 36-36–72; 7,050 yards

September 11-14
purse, US$500,000

		SCORES			TOTAL	MONEY
Darren Cole	72	64	68	71	275	US$80,750
Jeev Milkha Singh	66	69	68	72	275	55,650
(Cole defeated Singh on first extra hole.)						
Mike Cunning	70	71	70	66	277	28,000
Wayne Bradley	71	69	65	72	277	28,000
Kim Young-woo	71	69	70	68	278	18,750
Arjun Atwal	65	70	67	76	278	18,750
Ted Purdy	74	68	67	70	279	12,162.50
Kevin Coles	72	69	68	70	279	12,162.50
Craig Kamps	71	67	69	72	279	12,162.50
Nico van Rensburg	68	66	71	74	279	12,162.50
Bran Quinn	74	69	71	66	280	9,175
John Kernohan	75	69	72	65	281	8,091.67

	SCORES				TOTAL	MONEY
Doug Dunakey	68	71	69	73	281	8,091.67
Brett Partridge	71	68	67	75	281	8,091.67
Peter Fowler	69	69	74	70	282	7,350
Paul Foley	73	71	70	69	283	6,490
Edward Fryatt	70	72	70	71	283	6,490
Jim Rutledge	71	72	69	71	283	6,490
Paul Devenport	71	71	69	72	283	6,490
John Senden	70	67	73	73	283	6,490
Matthew Ecob	74	71	70	69	284	5,700
Mark Allen	72	70	71	71	284	5,700
Des Terblanche	73	68	70	73	284	5,700
Marciano Pucay	69	73	73	70	285	4,950
Madasamy Murugiah	70	72	71	72	285	4,950
David McKenzie	71	73	68	73	285	4,950
Chris Gray	70	74	68	73	285	4,950
Lucas Parsons	74	68	70	73	285	4,950
Michael Long	73	71	67	74	285	4,950
Scott Laycock	72	70	67	76	285	4,950

Mild Seven Kuala Lumpur Open

Saujana Golf & Country Club, Kuala Lumpur, Malaysia
Par 36-36–72; 7,233 yards

September 18-21
purse, US$300,000

	SCORES				TOTAL	MONEY
Charlie Wi	67	73	69	68	277	US$48,450
Zhang Lian-wei	71	73	70	67	281	25,995
Lu Wen-teh	75	67	70	69	281	25,995
Clay Devers	73	69	73	69	284	12,500
Jun Tae-hyun	73	72	70	69	284	12,500
Kyi Hla Han	74	71	69	70	284	12,500
Jim Rutledge	71	72	72	70	285	8,250
Felix Casas	72	69	72	72	285	8,250
Marimuthu Ramayah	75	71	71	69	286	5,634
Thaworn Wiratchant	71	74	71	70	286	5,634
Rafael Ponce	72	74	70	70	286	5,634
Prayad Marksaeng	72	72	68	74	286	5,634
Chou Hong-nan	69	70	71	76	286	5,634
Andrew Bonhomme	74	74	71	68	287	4,230
Hsieh Yu-shu	70	76	69	72	287	4,230
Soe Kyaw Naing	71	75	68	73	287	4,230
Kenny Walker	72	70	72	73	287	4,230
Craig Kamps	70	69	74	74	287	4,230
Rob Stephens	71	72	76	69	288	3,516
Chen Liang-hsi	71	75	71	71	288	3,516
Lee Petters	71	72	72	73	288	3,516
Aaron Meeks	74	69	71	74	288	3,516
Choi Kyung-ju	66	76	72	74	288	3,516
Jyoti Randhawa	72	73	75	69	289	2,880
Marciano Pucay	72	76	71	70	289	2,880
Chung Joon	74	70	74	71	289	2,880
Gerry Norquist	74	70	74	71	289	2,880
Mardan Mamat	71	70	76	72	289	2,880
Lai Ying-juh	69	74	74	72	289	2,880
Nam Young-woo	73	73	71	72	289	2,880
Danny Zarate	75	73	68	73	289	2,880
Rob Willis	73	71	71	74	289	2,880

Yokohama Singapore PGA

Raffles Country Club, Singapore
Par 36-36–72; 6,829 yards

October 2-5
purse, US$200,000

	SCORES				TOTAL	MONEY
Prayad Marksaeng	71	71	65	70	277	US$32,300
Kasiadi	69	69	71	69	278	22,260
Eric Meeks	72	69	67	71	279	11,200
Thammanoon Sriroj	67	67	73	72	279	11,200
Jyoti Randhawa	76	69	72	65	282	8,000
Grant Dodd	67	72	74	70	283	6,500
Craig Kamps	69	72	72	70	283	6,500
Fran Quinn	72	69	75	68	284	4,282
Aaron Meeks	69	73	72	70	284	4,282
Mike Cunning	66	74	73	71	284	4,282
Wayne Bradley	70	73	65	76	284	4,282
Leith Wastle	72	70	74	69	285	3,434
Zaw Moe	71	74	73	68	286	3,072
Paul Foley	72	77	68	69	286	3,072
Nico van Rensburg	70	74	67	75	286	3,072
Myint Thaung	73	73	70	71	287	2,820
Toru Kinoshita	72	69	77	70	288	2,500
Jeev Milkha Singh	71	72	75	70	288	2,500
Lin Chien-bing	74	70	73	71	288	2,500
Thaworn Wiratchant	70	74	72	72	288	2,500
Ted Purdy	74	71	70	73	288	2,500
Lee Petters	76	72	72	70	290	2,220
Adrian Percey	74	69	75	72	290	2,220
Paul Friedlander	73	73	71	73	290	2,220
Chris Williams	74	74	72	71	291	1,890
Wang Ter-chang	75	74	70	72	291	1,890
Rafael Ponce	74	74	71	72	291	1,890
Chang Tse-peng	75	73	70	73	291	1,890
Brad Andrews	72	72	73	74	291	1,890
Yeh Wei-tze	68	77	71	75	291	1,890
Scott Laycock	69	73	74	75	291	1,890
Yasuhiro Taguchi	68	71	76	76	291	1,890

ABN-AMRO Pakistan Masters

Karachi Golf Club, Karachi, Pakistan
Par 36-36–72; 7,010 yards

October 16-19
purse, US$200,000

	SCORES				TOTAL	MONEY
Thammanoon Sriroj	67	70	68	69	274	US$32,300
Scott Laycock	68	65	70	71	274	22,260

(Thammanoon defeated Laycock on second extra hole.)

Peter Fowler	69	66	74	70	279	11,200
John Senden	69	68	70	72	279	11,200
Wayne Bradley	72	72	68	68	280	7,500
Prayad Marksaeng	67	70	68	75	280	7,500
Jim Rutledge	71	70	72	68	281	5,500
Nico van Rensburg	67	68	73	73	281	5,500
Mardan Mamat	69	73	70	71	283	4,043.33
Taimur Hussain	69	74	69	71	283	4,043.33
Arjun Singh	68	72	71	72	283	4,043.33
Jyoti Randhawa	70	69	72	73	284	3,434

	SCORES				TOTAL	MONEY
Craig Kamps	73	71	70	71	285	3,072
Paul Foley	72	72	69	72	285	3,072
Kim Holden	73	69	69	74	285	3,072
Choi Kyung-ju	76	69	74	67	286	2,514.29
Ramon Brobio	71	68	77	70	286	2,514.29
Suppacheep Meesom	70	74	72	70	286	2,514.29
Gaurav Ghei	71	75	69	71	286	2,514.29
Vivek Bhandari	70	74	71	71	286	2,514.29
Jun Tae-hyun	74	68	71	73	286	2,514.29
Lee Petters	72	71	69	74	286	2,514.29
Robert Herrera	74	71	73	69	287	2,100
Eric Meeks	69	72	75	71	287	2,100
Yoshio Fumiyama	69	72	75	71	287	2,100
Greg Hanrahan	75	72	69	71	287	2,100
Boonchu Ruangkit	75	69	70	73	287	2,100
Supha. Veerawut	75	72	73	68	288	1,860
Chris Williams	72	77	70	69	288	1,860
Carito Villaroman	74	71	73	70	288	1,860

Dubai Creek Open

Dubai Creek Golf & Yacht Club, Dubai
Par 36-36–72; 6,789 yards

October 22-25
purse, US$250,000

	SCORES				TOTAL	MONEY
Adrian Percey	69	68	66	69	272	US$40,375
Des Terblanche	69	72	64	68	273	27,825
Ted Purdy	66	72	68	71	277	15,500
Boonchu Ruangkit	70	67	72	69	278	9,687.50
Chawalit Plaphol	72	71	66	69	278	9,687.50
Paul Foley	72	69	68	69	278	9,687.50
Dominique Boulet	67	68	71	72	278	9,687.50
Charlie Wi	69	70	69	72	280	5,608.33
Imdad Hussain	69	72	65	74	280	5,608.33
Craig Kamps	69	69	68	74	280	5,608.33
Eric Meeks	77	70	66	68	281	4,299.67
Ramon Brobio	73	70	68	70	281	4,299.67
Kenny Walker	72	71	65	73	281	4,299.67
Ho Chung-yuan	74	73	66	69	282	3,675
Lu Wen-teh	69	75	68	70	282	3,675
Scott Laycock	70	67	68	77	282	3,675
Thammanoon Sriroj	71	70	70	72	283	3,375
Jeev Milkha Singh	67	76	73	68	284	3,062.50
Grant Dodd	73	69	69	73	284	3,062.50
Gaurav Ghei	69	71	71	73	284	3,062.50
Kwon Young-suk	72	69	66	77	284	3,062.50
Simon Owen	74	70	72	69	285	2,700
Wang Ter-chang	69	73	73	70	285	2,700
Aaron Meeks	73	71	69	72	285	2,700
Brad Andrews	69	73	71	72	285	2,700
Chang Tse-peng	70	70	71	74	285	2,700
Leith Wastle	76	70	70	70	286	2,325
Kyi Hla Han	74	70	71	71	286	2,325
Vivek Bhandari	74	71	68	73	286	2,325
Arjun Singh	68	73	72	73	286	2,325
Nico van Rensburg	70	71	71	74	286	2,325

Hero Honda Masters

Delhi Golf Club, Delhi, India
Par 36-36–72; 6,888 yards

October 30-November 2
purse, US$200,000

	SCORES				TOTAL	MONEY
Ted Purdy	72	68	66	71	277	US$32,300
Gaurav Ghei	71	68	72	67	278	22,260
Jim Rutledge	72	71	72	64	279	12,400
Bjorn Flygare	74	69	70	67	280	8,333.33
Arjun Atwal	72	69	71	68	280	8,333.33
Mike Cunning	73	66	71	70	280	8,333.33
Lu Wen-teh	67	73	73	68	281	6,000
Ho Chung-yuan	73	72	66	71	282	5,000
Jerry Smith	69	68	77	69	283	4,043.33
Craig Kamps	71	69	69	74	283	4,043.33
Jeev Milkha Singh	68	69	72	74	283	4,043.33
Scott Laycock	70	72	73	69	284	3,325
Basad Ali	73	73	67	71	284	3,325
Chang Tse-peng	74	70	72	69	285	2,940
Taimur Hussain	72	71	72	70	285	2,940
Vivek Bhandari	76	69	68	72	285	2,940
Gerry Norquist	69	77	69	71	286	2,640
Aaron Meeks	70	73	71	72	286	2,640
Park Unho	75	69	71	72	287	2,440
Grant Dodd	72	71	71	73	287	2,440
Mo Joong-kyung	71	72	73	72	288	2,280
Adrian Percey	73	71	71	73	288	2,280
Charlie Wi	73	73	67	75	288	2,280
Peter Fowler	71	73	75	70	289	2,100
Leith Wastle	73	71	73	72	289	2,100
Uttam Singh Mundy	75	68	74	72	289	2,100
Mukesh Kumar	75	71	77	67	290	1,920
Lee Tae-hwa	77	70	76	67	290	1,920
Wang Ter-chang	71	78	69	72	290	1,920
Kenny Walker	72	72	76	71	291	1,770
*Harmeet Kahlon	72	74	74	71	291	
Amritinder Singh	70	72	76	73	291	1,770

Ta Shee Open

Ta Shee Golf & Country Club, Taiwan
Par 36-36–72; 6,901 yards

November 6-9
purse, US$250,000

	SCORES				TOTAL	MONEY
Wang Ter-chang	71	70	70	71	282	US$40,375
Leith Wastle	71	74	68	70	283	21,662.50
Eric Meeks	69	71	72	71	283	21,662.50
Hsieh Yu-shu	70	73	72	69	284	11,250
Chen Liang-hsi	71	71	72	70	284	11,250
Mike Cunning	71	73	69	72	285	8,750
Christian Pena	75	73	70	68	286	6,081.25
Lin Wen-teng	73	72	70	71	286	6,081.25
Lin Chih-chen	70	71	73	72	286	6,081.25
Jerry Smith	70	72	72	72	286	6,081.25
Gerry Norquist	75	71	73	68	287	4,439.50
Tai Ying-juh	73	70	73	71	287	4,439.50
Simon Yates	72	74	75	67	288	3,468.13

	SCORES	TOTAL	MONEY
Lu Wen-teh	75 73 72 68	288	3,468.13
Aaron Meeks	74 76 68 70	288	3,468.13
Lin Keng-chi	71 76 70 71	288	3,468.13
Yoshitaka Yamamoto	74 71 71 72	288	3,468.13
Mardan Mamat	72 70 73 73	288	3,468.13
Eric Rustand	71 73 70 74	288	3,468.13
Koki Idoki	72 72 70 74	288	3,468.13
Dominique Boulet	70 79 69 71	289	2,887.50
Chen Tze-chung	70 75 70 74	289	2,887.50
Chung Chun-hsing	73 75 70 72	290	2,700
Chen Yuan-chi	73 73 71 73	290	2,700
Tseng Wen-chi	71 69 71 79	290	2,700
Mo Joong-kyung	76 72 71 72	291	2,437.50
Andy Wada	75 69 74 73	291	2,437.50
Clay Devers	73 73 71 74	291	2,437.50
Mitsuo Harada	73 72 71 75	291	2,437.50
Ho Chia-feng	72 77 73 70	292	2,034.38
Shen Chung-shan	75 72 73 72	292	2,034.38
Greg Hanrahan	74 72 73 73	292	2,034.38
Kuo Chie-hsiung	71 74 74 73	292	2,034.38
Jeff Senior	71 72 76 73	292	2,034.38
Chen Tsang-te	71 72 76 73	292	2,034.38
Jee Tae-hwa	72 72 74 74	292	2,034.38
Chawalit Plaphol	73 76 68 75	292	2,034.38

Volvo Masters of Malaysia

Kelab Golf Sultan Abdul Aziz Shah,
Kuala Lumpur, Malaysia
Par 36-36—72; 6,711 yards

November 13-16
purse, US$200,000

	SCORES	TOTAL	MONEY
Christian Pena	69 70 68 69	276	US$32,300
Hsieh Yu-shu	72 65 70 70	277	22,260
Craig Kamps	70 71 68 69	278	12,400
Kwon Young-suk	71 71 69 68	279	9,000
Simon Yates	70 67 69 73	279	9,000
Jyoti Randhawa	72 70 69 70	281	7,000
Lai Ying-juh	73 71 71 67	282	5,153.33
Chang Tse-peng	74 69 69 70	282	5,153.33
Vivek Bhandari	73 69 70 70	282	5,153.33
Park Nam-sin	73 71 72 67	283	3,835
Chawalit Plaphol	71 70 71 71	283	3,835
Rafael Ponce	70 75 70 69	284	3,236.67
Ramon Brobio	72 70 72 70	284	3,236.67
Thammanoon Sriroj	73 67 72 72	284	3,236.67
Yeh Wei-tze	73 70 74 68	285	2,940
Kenny Walker	73 74 70 69	286	2,553.33
Mo Joong-kyung	73 70 73 70	286	2,553.33
Eric Meeks	73 73 70 70	286	2,553.33
Hsu Mong-nan	70 71 73 72	286	2,553.33
Mardan Mamat	72 73 68 73	286	2,553.33
Dino Kwek Beng Kwee	71 68 73 74	286	2,553.33
Soe Kyaw Naing	72 73 73 70	288	2,250
Zhang Lian-wei	72 73 67 76	288	2,250
Shaifubari Muda	76 71 73 69	289	2,010
Periasamy Gunasegaran	70 74 74 71	289	2,010

	SCORES				TOTAL	MONEY
Marciano Pucay	72	74	70	73	289	2,010
Jeev Milkha Singh	68	72	76	73	289	2,010
Greg Hanrahan	71	72	72	74	289	2,010
Danny Zarate	73	68	71	77	289	2,010
Kang Wook-soon	72	77	72	69	290	1,692
Poh Eng Wah	74	72	72	72	290	1,692
Cho Chul-sang	72	72	74	72	290	1,692
Wang Ter-chang	71	71	73	75	290	1,692
George Olaybar	74	71	69	76	290	1,692

Lexus International

Bangpoo Country Club, Bangkok, Thailand
Par 36 36–72; 7,048 yards

November 20-23
purse, US$200,000

	SCORES				TOTAL	MONEY
Prayad Marksaeng	70	69	65	66	270	US$32,300
Arjun Atwal	67	69	68	67	271	22,260
Kyi Hla Han	67	67	73	67	274	11,200
Kenny Walker	66	68	73	67	274	11,200
Mike Cunning	69	65	71	71	276	8,000
Greg Hanrahan	68	71	70	68	277	6,500
Vivek Bhandari	67	70	71	69	277	6,500
Chawalit Plaphol	64	70	73	71	278	5,000
Simon Yates	69	71	68	71	279	4,460
Park Nam-sin	70	72	71	67	280	3,701.33
Shaifubari Muda	71	70	68	71	280	3,701.33
Lai Ying-juh	71	68	70	71	280	3,701.33
Lu Wen-teh	69	67	71	74	281	3,216
Yasuhiro Taguchi	72	70	71	69	282	2,940
Rodrigo Cuello	71	74	68	69	282	2,940
Hsu Mong-nan	72	69	68	73	282	2,940
Jyoti Randhawa	75	71	71	66	283	2,586.67
Yeh Wei-tze	71	73	70	69	283	2,586.67
Chang Tse-peng	71	72	69	71	283	2,586.67
Lee Yong-hee	69	75	72	68	284	2,280
Nozomi Kawahara	75	70	70	69	284	2,280
Gavin Vearing	68	73	71	72	284	2,280
Eric Meeks	70	67	74	73	284	2,280
Craig Kamps	71	70	69	74	284	2,280
Marciano Pucay	73	66	78	68	285	2,010
Christian Pena	70	71	73	71	285	2,010
Jeff Senior	71	73	68	73	285	2,010
Toru Kinoshita	69	71	71	74	285	2,010
Preecha Senaprom	72	74	74	66	286	1,830
Rangsan Raksomchi	69	76	70	71	286	1,830

Tugu Pratama PGA

Damai Indah Golf and Country Club, Jakarta, Indonesia
Par 36-36–72; 7,145 yards

November 27-30
purse, US$300,000

	SCORES				TOTAL	MONEY
Clay Devers	69	69	68	70	276	US$48,450
Kwon Young-suk	70	71	70	66	277	22,330

	SCORES				TOTAL	MONEY
Mike Cunning	67	72	70	68	277	22,330
Paul Friedlander	67	62	75	73	277	22,330
Jim Rutledge	68	73	70	67	278	12,000
Kasiadi	74	72	66	67	279	8,422.50
Christian Pena	69	75	66	69	279	8,422.50
Simon Owen	71	68	69	71	279	8,422.50
Ted Purdy	71	69	68	71	279	8,422.50
Prayad Marksaeng	73	70	71	66	280	5,370
Craig Kamps	72	68	71	69	280	5,370
Chang Tse-peng	66	72	72	70	280	5,370
Mardan Mamat	74	66	69	71	280	5,370
Kenny Walker	71	71	71	68	281	4,320
Gavin Vearing	68	72	72	69	281	4,320
Kyi Hla Han	72	73	67	69	281	4,320
Jeff Senior	71	67	72	71	281	4,320
Boonchu Ruangkit	70	73	69	70	282	3,870
Soe Kyaw Naing	71	75	67	70	283	3,610
Stephen Atako-Lindskog	70	70	73	70	283	3,610
Chawalit Plaphol	66	71	74	72	283	3,610
Jun Tae-hyun	70	75	72	67	284	3,375
Ilyasyak	76	69	71	68	284	3,375
Simon Yates	77	70	69	69	285	3,015
Wayne Bradley	71	74	71	69	285	3,015
Bachtlar Sanja	69	71	75	70	285	3,015
Chua Guan Soon	71	73	69	72	285	3,015
Lee Yong-hee	71	69	72	73	285	3,015
Brad Andrews	67	71	73	74	285	3,015
Lee Joon-suk	74	73	68	71	286	2,505
Dominique Boulet	71	71	73	71	286	2,505
Eric Meeks	71	73	71	71	286	2,505
Thaworn Wiratchant	73	71	69	73	286	2,505
Supha. Veerawut	72	72	69	73	286	2,505
Richard Kaplan	71	72	69	74	286	2,505

Andersen Consulting Hong Kong Open

Hong Kong Golf Club, Fanling, N.T., Hong Kong
Par 35-36–71; 6,672 yards

December 4-7
purse, US$350,000

	SCORES				TOTAL	MONEY
Frank Nobilo	67	66	66	68	267	US$58,345
Kang Wook-soon	67	69	67	69	272	38,500
Tim Straub	68	64	70	72	274	21,700
Zhang Lian-wei	68	68	68	71	275	16,100
Lin Keng-chi	67	70	66	72	275	16,100
Lu Wen-teh	70	71	67	68	276	11,900
Choi Gwang-soo	72	68	69	68	277	9,800
Jim Rutledge	72	69	70	67	278	7,910
Scott Rowe	72	70	72	65	279	6,440
Wayne Bradley	71	68	69	71	279	6,440
Mike Cunning	71	66	71	71	279	6,440
Vivek Bhandari	71	73	65	71	280	5,474
Edward Fryatt	70	67	72	71	280	5,474
Costantino Rocca	67	68	73	72	280	5,474
Barry Lane	69	66	73	72	280	5,474
Richard Kaplan	67	68	69	76	280	5,474
Eric Meeks	72	71	67	71	281	4,760

	SCORES	TOTAL	MONEY
Ian Leggatt	69 68 73 71	281	4,760
Greg Hanrahan	69 71 69 72	281	4,760
Rodrigo Cuello	68 68 73 72	281	4,760
Nam Young-woo	69 70 68 74	281	4,760
Carlos Espinosa	69 70 73 70	282	4,270
Park No-seok	70 75 66 71	282	4,270
Shin Yong-jin	70 75 69 69	283	3,850
Daniel Chopra	76 69 67 71	283	3,850
Tang Man-kee	69 73 70 71	283	3,850
Nico van Rensburg	70 70 71 72	283	3,850
Robert Coles	69 69 77 69	284	3,036.25
Clay Devers	71 74 69 70	284	3,036.25
Craig Kamps	71 73 70 70	284	3,036.25
Gerry Norquist	70 71 73 70	284	3,036.25
Hsieh Yu-shu	71 73 68 72	284	3,036.25
David Frost	69 72 71 72	284	3,036.25
Hsu Mong-nan	68 74 69 73	284	3,036.25
Dean Wilson	66 71 73 74	284	3,036.25

Omega PGA Championship

Clearwater Bay Golf & Country Club,
Sai Kung, Hong Kong
Par 35-35–70; 6,115 yards

December 11-14
purse, US$500,000

	SCORES	TOTAL	MONEY
Rodrigo Cuello	70 69 65 66	270	US$80,750
Lu Wen-teh	64 71 69 67	271	55,650
Park No-seok	64 72 68 69	273	31,000
Craig Kamps	67 71 68 68	274	22,500
Kenny Walker	68 67 66 73	274	22,500
Brad Andrews	72 67 72 64	275	15,000
Jim Rutledge	70 68 69 68	275	15,000
Zaw Moe	66 69 69 71	275	15,000
Zhang Lian-wei	71 71 68 66	276	9,727.50
Leith Wastle	64 74 71 67	276	9,727.50
Lai Ying-juh	67 71 70 68	276	9,727.50
Arjun Atwal	70 70 68 68	276	9,727.50
Dominique Boulet	66 69 74 68	277	7,522.50
Cheng Jun	72 69 67 69	277	7,522.50
Jyoti Randhawa	68 69 68 72	277	7,522.50
Chris Williams	68 71 66 72	277	7,522.50
Kim Jong-duk	68 74 67 69	278	6,600
Chen Liang-hsi	66 72 70 70	278	6,600
Toru Kinoshita	70 72 70 67	279	5,860
Christian Pena	72 70 68 69	279	5,860
Ted Purdy	67 72 70 70	279	5,860
Takeshi Oyama	70 71 67 71	279	5,860
Choi Gwang-soo	66 71 69 73	279	5,860
Kim Young-il	71 69 70 70	280	5,325
Chang Tse-peng	70 71 64 75	280	5,325
Nico van Rensburg	73 68 68 72	281	4,725
Aaron Meeks	71 68 70 72	281	4,725
Hendrik Buhrmann	68 72 68 73	281	4,725
Mino Kwek Beng Kwee	66 69 72 74	281	4,725
Gerry Norquist	71 68 67 75	281	4,725
Choi Kyung-ju	65 65 72 79	281	4,725

Volvo Asian Match Play

Mimosa Golf & Country Club, Subic Bay, Philippines
7,214 yards

December 17-20
purse, US$250,000

FIRST ROUND

Jerry Smith defeated Paul Foley, 1 up
Des Terblanche defeated Boonchu Ruangkit, 4 and 3
Felix Casas defeated Gerry Norquist, 1 up
Edward Fryatt defeated Craig Kamps, 4 and 2
Brett Partridge defeated Adrian Percey, 2 and 1
Scott Laycock defeated Larry Barber, 4 and 3
Zaw Moe defeated Christian Pena, 2 and 1

SECOND ROUND

Ted Purdy defeated Smith, 2 up
Terblanche defeated Peter Mitchell, 4 and 3
Casas defeated Rodrigo Cuello, 1 up
Fryatt defeated Park Nam-sin, 1 up
Cheng Jun defeated Christian Chernock, 5 and 4
Partridge defeated Zhang Lian-wei, 5 and 4
Laycock defeated Prayad Marksaeng, 1 up
Moe defeated Mike Cunning, 1 up

QUARTER-FINALS

Terblanche defeated Smith, 3 and 2
Casas defeated Fryatt, 4 and 3
Partridge defeated Cheng, 5 and 3
Moe defeated Laycock, 1 up

SEMI-FINALS

Terblanche defeated Casas, 4 and 3
Partridge defeated Moe, 1 up

FINAL

Terblanche won when Partridge conceded match on 27th hole, withdrawing because of injury

(Terblanche received US$46,500.)

Australasian Tour

Victorian Open

Victoria Golf Club, Melbourne, Victoria
Par 36-36–72; 6,801 yards

January 9-12
purse, A$200,000

		SCORES			TOTAL	MONEY
Stephen Leaney	64	72	72	72	280	A$36,000
Darren Cole	72	70	68	71	281	16,950
Euan Walters	69	69	72	71	281	16,950
*Geoff Ogilvy	68	74	68	72	282	
Peter Lonard	70	74	68	70	282	9,600
Robert Allenby	71	71	73	68	283	7,600
Stephen Allan	72	69	71	71	283	7,600
Leith Wastle	69	74	68	73	284	6,100
Anthony Painter	71	70	70	73	284	6,100
Lucas Parsons	73	73	73	66	285	4,700
Rodney Pampling	71	68	77	69	285	4,700
Michael Long	69	74	73	69	285	4,700
Steve Alker	70	72	70	73	285	4,700
Pierre Fulke	72	71	73	70	286	3,500
Tim Elliott	72	69	74	71	286	3,500
Stephen Collins	69	71	78	69	287	2,581.66
Robin Byrd	71	75	71	70	287	2,581.66
Gavin Coles	69	74	74	70	287	2,581.66
Peter Fowler	74	72	70	71	287	2,581.66
Mike Clayton	71	70	74	72	287	2,581.66
Philip Chapman	74	71	69	73	287	2,581.66
Matthew Goggin	72	75	71	70	288	2,040
Chris Gray	73	71	73	71	288	2,040
Jarrod Moseley	73	68	74	73	288	2,040
Martyn Roberts	73	69	79	68	289	1,567.50
Elliot Boult	71	74	75	69	289	1,567.50
Paul Moloney	70	76	73	70	289	1,567.50
Jean Van de Velde	69	77	73	70	289	1,567.50
Stuart Cage	72	69	77	71	289	1,567.50
*Brad Lamb	68	77	72	72	289	
Richard Green	73	71	72	73	289	1,567.50
Ben Jackson	72	74	70	73	289	1,567.50
Gary Evans	71	70	74	74	289	1,567.50

Johnnie Walker Classic

Hope Island Golf Club, Gold Coast, Queensland
Par 36-36–72; 7,074 yards

January 23-26
purse, A$1,400,000

		SCORES			TOTAL	MONEY
Ernie Els	70	68	71	69	278	A$271,844.64
Peter Lonard	69	69	69	72	279	127,993.51
Michael Long	68	68	71	72	279	127,993.51
Anthony Painter	67	73	67	75	282	62,423.58
Fred Couples	68	76	67	71	282	62,423.58

578 / AUSTRALASIAN TOUR

	SCORES				TOTAL	MONEY
Nick Faldo	70	72	70	70	282	62,423.58
Michael Campbell	70	71	74	68	283	37,324.70
Peter O'Malley	73	68	74	68	283	37,324.70
David Howell	69	72	75	67	283	37,324.70
Bernhard Langer	73	72	69	69	283	37,324.70
Robert Allenby	73	73	70	67	283	37,324.70
Stephen Leaney	69	72	75	67	283	37,324.70
Marc Farry	72	70	72	69	283	37,324.70
Ian Woosnam	74	70	71	69	284	25,674.21
Joakim Haeggman	72	71	70	72	285	21,848.25
Colin Montgomerie	71	74	73	67	285	21,848.25
*Hong Chia-yuh	72	74	70	69	285	
Craig Jones	68	76	72	70	286	17,141.31
Alex Cejka	73	67	73	73	286	17,141.31
Phillip Price	76	70	68	72	286	17,141.31
Paul Broadhurst	74	70	72	71	287	14,131.60
Gary Orr	71	75	70	71	287	14,131.60
David Carter	67	75	72	73	287	14,131.60
Steve Alker	68	73	73	73	287	14,131.60
Stephen Ames	72	74	72	69	287	14,131.60
Steve Conran	67	75	73	72	287	14,131.60
Raymond Russell	74	69	73	71	287	14,131.60
Frank Nobilo	70	73	72	73	288	10,496.22
Padraig Harrington	71	73	73	71	288	10,496.22
Anders Forsbrand	74	72	73	69	288	10,496.22
Andrew Sherborne	71	73	75	69	288	10,496.22

Heineken Classic

The Vines Resort, Perth, Western Australia
Par 36-36–72; 7,101 yards

January 30-February 2
purse, A$1,200,000

	SCORES				TOTAL	MONEY
Miguel Angel Martin	70	67	65	71	273	A$216,000
Fred Couples	68	70	69	67	274	122,400
Frank Nobilo	66	69	70	70	275	62,200
Jean Van de Velde	69	69	69	68	275	62,200
Marc Farry	72	66	69	68	275	62,200
Ian Woosnam	72	69	69	66	276	40,800
Wayne Riley	71	66	69	70	276	40,800
Katsuyoshi Tomori	69	68	69	71	277	32,400
Ernie Els	73	71	68	65	277	32,400
Robert Allenby	70	68	71	68	277	32,400
Greg Turner	65	71	72	70	278	22,320
Greg Chalmers	70	72	71	65	278	22,320
Paul Eales	70	69	67	72	278	22,320
Padraig Harrington	70	63	73	72	278	22,320
Rodney Pampling	68	73	66	71	278	22,320
Peter O'Malley	68	69	71	71	279	16,440
Rodger Davis	71	72	68	68	279	16,440
David Carter	71	69	70	70	280	13,335
Kenny Druce	71	69	72	68	280	13,335
Peter Senior	69	71	70	70	280	13,335
Roger Chapman	70	69	73	68	280	13,335
Colin Montgomerie	70	72	72	67	281	11,920
Andrew Coltart	71	72	69	69	281	11,920
Stephen Leaney	72	71	69	69	281	11,920

	SCORES				TOTAL	MONEY
Darren Clarke	70	69	71	72	282	9,810
Darren Cole	73	71	68	70	282	9,810
Thomas Bjorn	69	70	74	69	282	9,810
Paul Broadhurst	70	69	70	73	282	9,810
Shane Tait	71	70	73	69	283	7,410
Wayne Grady	67	72	73	71	283	7,410
Rick Gibson	70	70	70	73	283	7,410
Miles Tunnicliff	67	72	72	72	283	7,410
Jon Robson	72	67	70	74	283	7,410
Paul McGinley	72	65	69	77	283	7,410
Stuart Cage	69	73	71	70	283	7,410
Carl Suneson	69	72	71	71	283	7,410

Ford Open

Kooyonga Golf Club, Adelaide, South Australia
Par 37-35–72; 6,717 yards

February 6-9
purse, A$300,000

	SCORES				TOTAL	MONEY
Steve Alker	71	67	70	65	273	A$54,000
Wayne Grady	72	66	66	70	274	30,600
Michael Long	69	66	72	68	275	14,362.50
Brett Ogle	68	71	67	69	275	14,362.50
Craig Parry	68	69	69	69	275	14,362.50
Tom Lehman	68	69	66	72	275	14,362.50
Shane Tait	67	69	70	70	276	9,150
Peter O'Malley	69	69	67	71	276	9,150
Rick Gibson	75	65	71	68	279	6,720
Kenny Druce	70	69	70	70	279	6,720
Robert Allenby	70	71	68	70	279	6,720
David Smail	72	70	66	71	279	6,720
Greg Chalmers	71	67	67	74	279	6,720
Elliot Boult	71	71	69	70	281	4,740
Gary Simpson	67	70	71	73	281	4,740
Mike Harwood	70	65	72	74	281	4,740
Grant Kenny	72	70	71	69	282	3,447
David Ecob	69	74	68	71	282	3,447
Anthony Painter	76	68	66	72	282	3,447
Martin Peterson	74	67	68	73	282	3,447
Doug Dunakey	70	68	70	74	282	3,447
Grant Dodd	67	74	72	70	283	2,838
Paul Devenport	71	72	69	71	283	2,838
Rodney Pampling	72	70	70	71	283	2,838
Chris Gray	71	72	68	72	283	2,838
Jean Louis Guepy	69	70	70	74	283	2,838
Jon Evans	76	67	70	71	284	2,340
Craig Jones	73	71	72	69	285	2,040
Peter Lonard	74	68	72	71	285	2,040
David Hill	70	71	73	71	285	2,040
Stephen Scahill	72	71	70	72	285	2,040
Scott Laycock	71	72	69	73	285	2,040

Ericsson Australian Masters

Huntingdale Golf Club, Melbourne, Victoria
Par 36-37–73; 6,994 yards

February 13-16
purse, A$750,000

	SCORES				TOTAL	MONEY
Peter Lonard	69	69	69	69	276	A$135,000
Peter O'Malley	65	66	73	72	276	76,500
(Lonard defeated O'Malley on second extra hole.)						
Shane Tait	68	67	74	68	277	43,312.50
Wayne Grady	70	67	69	71	277	43,312.50
Lucas Parsons	64	67	74	73	278	30,000
Mike Weir	67	72	70	70	279	27,000
Robert Allenby	70	66	70	76	282	24,000
Larry Mize	68	70	72	73	283	20,250
Tiger Woods	68	70	72	73	283	20,250
Rodger Davis	72	65	72	74	283	20,250
Steve Alker	72	70	73	69	284	13,950
Andrew Bonhomme	70	75	70	69	284	13,950
Lyndsay Stephen	73	69	72	70	284	13,950
Leith Wastle	71	69	73	71	284	13,950
Simon Owen	68	72	73	71	284	13,950
Grant Moorhead	69	75	72	69	285	10,800
Steve Conran	70	75	68	73	286	9,062.50
Rick Gibson	67	68	77	74	286	9,062.50
Brett Partridge	70	71	71	74	286	9,062.50
Kenny Druce	70	71	77	69	287	7,153.12
Marcus Wheelhouse	69	74	75	69	287	7,153.12
Mike Clayton	70	73	73	71	287	7,153.12
David Ecob	71	68	76	72	287	7,153.12
Craig Parry	73	70	70	74	287	7,153.12
Rodney Pampling	73	71	69	74	287	7,153.12
Shigenori Mori	71	71	70	75	287	7,153.12
Peter Senior	69	68	74	76	287	7,153.12
Jay Townsend	73	70	75	70	288	5,000
*Geoff Ogilvy	73	72	72	71	288	
Scott Laycock	73	69	74	72	288	5,000
Shane Robinson	69	72	75	72	288	5,000
Stephen Allan	70	74	72	72	288	5,000
Richard Green	70	75	71	72	288	5,000
Doug Dunakey	68	72	72	76	288	5,000

Canon Challenge

Terrey Hills Country Club, Sydney, New South Wales
Par 36-36–72; 7,019 yards

February 20-23
purse, A$450,000

	SCORES				TOTAL	MONEY
Peter Senior	68	70	66	70	274	A$81,000
Steve Alker	67	70	72	65	274	45,900
(Senior defeated Alker on fourth extra hole.)						
Peter Lonard	68	69	72	67	276	25,987.50
Robert Allenby	70	69	69	68	276	25,987.50
Nobuhito Sato	71	71	68	69	279	17,100
David Smail	68	72	72	67	279	17,100
Tsuyoshi Yoneyama	69	72	68	71	280	14,400
Marcus Wheelhouse	69	71	75	67	282	11,587.50
Craig Parry	75	68	71	68	282	11,587.50
Mike Weir	70	74	70	68	282	11,587.50

	SCORES				TOTAL	MONEY
Stuart Bouvier	68	73	68	73	282	11,587.50
David Ecob	70	67	69	77	283	9,000
Paul Devenport	75	71	71	67	284	7,357.50
Wayne Smith	73	73	70	68	284	7,357.50
Chris Gray	66	71	72	75	284	7,357.50
Lucas Parsons	67	71	71	75	284	7,357.50
Paul Gow	72	72	71	70	285	5,437.50
Stephen Allan	69	74	70	72	285	5,437.50
Jean Louis Guepy	71	71	69	74	285	5,437.50
Peter Teravainen	73	73	71	69	286	4,860
Brett Partridge	73	70	77	67	287	4,680
Terry Price	72	73	71	72	288	4,017.85
Robert Stephens	69	68	78	73	288	4,017.85
Simon Owen	71	73	71	73	288	4,017.85
Darren Cole	71	71	72	74	288	4,017.85
Grant Kenny	68	73	73	74	288	4,017.85
Anthony Gilligan	76	69	69	74	288	4,017.85
Tony Carolan	69	73	71	75	288	4,017.85
Peter McWhinney	73	71	76	69	289	2,880
Anthony Painter	71	72	74	72	289	2,880
Rob Willis	71	75	71	72	289	2,880
Jeff Senior	71	74	70	74	289	2,880
Adrian Percey	73	70	71	75	289	2,880
Doug Dunakey	73	73	74	69	289	2,880

MasterCard PGA Championship

New South Wales Golf Club, Sydney, New South Wales
Par 36 36–72; 6,850 yards

November 20-23
purse, A$500,000

	SCORES				TOTAL	MONEY
Andrew Coltart	72	71	66	76	285	A$94,735
Stuart Appleby	67	73	74	73	289	44,605
Steve Allan	69	71	74	75	289	44,605
Rodger Davis	70	73	74	73	290	23,160
Paul Devenport	72	71	72	75	290	23,160
Robert Allenby	73	70	72	76	291	18,950
Jean-Louis Guepy	72	71	77	72	292	16,053
Martin Peterson	76	71	73	72	292	16,053
Craig Spence	73	73	72	74	293	10,903
Shane Robinson	73	73	71	75	293	10,903
Darin Anderson	75	69	81	68	293	10,903
Peter O'Malley	76	72	72	73	293	10,903
David Diaz	74	69	76	74	293	10,903
Steve Conran	73	67	78	75	293	10,903
David Smail	74	73	71	75	293	10,903
Neil Kerry	73	75	70	75	293	10,903
Shane Robinson	73	73	71	76	293	10,903
David Howell	75	69	72	77	294	6,170
Robin Byrd	76	69	74	75	294	6,170
Terry Price	76	70	71	77	294	6,170
Anthony Edwards	75	74	68	77	294	6,170
Gavin Coles	73	73	69	79	294	6,170
Richard Green	72	69	77	76	294	6,170
Stuart Thompson	73	73	79	70	295	4,467
Byron Clarkson	72	74	78	71	295	4,467
Shane Tait	75	71	76	73	295	4,467
Greg Chalmers	74	72	74	75	295	4,467

	SCORES	TOTAL	MONEY
Tim Elliott	74 75 71 75	295	4,467
Steve Leaney	76 70 72 77	295	4,467
Matthew Ecob	73 73 78 72	296	3,016
Nicholas O'Hern	74 73 75 74	296	3,016
Wayne Grady	70 75 76 75	296	3,016
Brad King	76 73 72 75	296	3,016
Peter Lonard	73 71 76 76	296	3,016
Chris Gray	73 74 73 76	296	3,016
David Ecob	72 75 73 76	296	3,016
Anthony Gilligan	73 71 74 78	296	3,016
Stewart Hardiman	73 73 72 78	296	3,016

Holden Australian Open

Metropolitan Golf Club, Melbourne, Victoria
Par 36-36–72; 7,031 yards

November 27-30
purse, A$1,000,000

	SCORES	TOTAL	MONEY
Lee Westwood	68 66 68 72	274	A$189,470
Greg Norman	68 67 66 73	274	107,370
(Westwood defeated Norman on fourth extra hole.)			
Craig Parry	70 70 70 65	275	71,050
Stephen Leaney	66 72 72 67	277	50,530
Nick O'Hern	67 66 74 72	279	42,110
Andrew Coltart	65 74 70 71	280	37,900
Robert Allenby	68 74 74 66	282	30,876
Vijay Singh	73 69 69 71	282	30,876
Phil Mickelson	69 68 73 72	282	30,876
Steve Allan	66 70 75 72	283	24,740
Paul Devenport	69 70 70 74	283	24,740
Jean-Louis Guepy	72 72 71 69	284	21,050
Peter Senior	68 73 74 70	285	18,425
Robert Damron	68 72 70 75	285	18,425
Greg Chalmers	70 72 72 72	286	15,226
Peter Lonard	63 77 73 73	286	15,226
Stuart Appleby	67 70 73 74	286	15,226
Don Fardon	72 73 71 71	287	12,630
David Smail	70 74 75 69	288	11,225
Shane Robinson	69 76 73 70	288	11,225
Shane Tait	68 76 72 72	288	11,225
Darren Clarke	72 71 71 74	288	11,225
Robert Stephens	71 72 76 70	289	9,176
Robert Willis	71 74 73 71	289	9,176
Craig Spence	67 75 75 72	289	9,176
Brian Davis	71 73 73 72	289	9,176
Justin Cooper	71 71 74 73	289	9,176
Rodney Pampling	70 75 70 74	289	9,176
Rodger Davis	72 71 78 69	290	6,274
Scott Laycock	72 74 73 71	290	6,274
Phil Tataurangi	73 73 73 71	290	6,274
Mark Calcavecchia	69 73 76 72	290	6,274
Chris Gray	71 73 74 72	290	6,274
David Howell	70 75 73 72	290	6,274
Brett Partridge	67 70 80 73	290	6,274
Lucas Parsons	70 75 72 73	290	6,274
Kim Felton	73 73 70 74	290	6,274
Stuart Bouvier	70 76 67 77	290	6,274
Wayne Grady	71 74 73 72	290	6,274

ANZ Players Championship

Royal Queensland Golf Club, Brisbane, Queensland
Par 36-36–72; 6,921 yards

December 4-7
purse, A$1,012,500

	SCORES				TOTAL	MONEY
Greg Chalmers	71	70	67	68	276	A$142,102
Peter Lonard	68	74	67	68	277	80,527
Robert Allenby	70	65	69	74	278	53,287
Scott Wearne	72	74	64	69	279	32,634
Stuart Appleby	68	68	68	75	279	32,634
Russell Swanson	72	66	70	71	279	32,634
Jean-Louis Guepy	70	70	70	70	280	24,078
Stephen Scahill	72	68	69	71	280	24,078
Craig Spence	76	70	67	68	281	21,315
Cameron Howell	70	69	72	71	282	17,632
Andrew Coltart	74	69	68	71	282	17,632
Robert Stephens	67	70	73	72	282	17,632
Chris Gray	71	69	68	75	283	13,818
Chris McCourt	70	68	68	77	283	13,818
Nick O'Hern	72	72	72	68	284	9,907
Kenny Druce	73	71	72	68	284	9,907
Hadyn Morgan	72	70	73	69	284	9,907
Peter McWhinney	75	68	72	69	284	9,907
Brad King	76	69	69	70	284	9,907
Rodney Pampling	72	69	71	72	284	9,907
Matthew King	66	72	73	73	284	9,907
Craig Jones	70	70	75	70	285	7,659
David Bransdon	73	70	72	70	285	7,659
Lucas Parsons	72	68	73	72	285	7,659
Tony Carolan	70	67	75	73	285	7,659
Rodger Davis	69	72	73	72	286	6,712
John Senden	72	72	72	71	287	5,742
Stuart Thompson	69	70	74	72	287	5,742
Steve Alker	73	69	71	74	287	5,742
Greg Norman	73	68	71	75	287	5,742

AMP - Air New Zealand Open

Auckland Golf Club, Auckland, New Zealand
Par 36-36–72; 6,787 yards

December 11-14
purse, NZ$500,000

	SCORES				TOTAL	MONEY
Greg Turner	69	69	71	69	278	NZ$94,735
Jean-Louis Guepy	76	67	75	67	285	38,158
Andrew Coltart	71	70	75	69	285	38,158
Lucas Parsons	72	65	73	75	285	38,158
Frank Nobilo	72	71	73	70	286	20,002
Brett Partridge	72	71	69	74	286	20,002
Phil Tataurangi	71	73	74	69	287	15,438
Paul Gow	73	76	68	70	287	15,438
Craig Parry	73	71	70	73	287	15,438
Neil Kerry	73	73	71	71	288	12,370
Paul Devenport	74	74	69	71	288	12,370
Peter O'Malley	73	70	75	73	291	10,000
David McKenzie	72	74	72	73	291	10,000
Elliott Boult	73	76	71	72	292	8,316
Peter Lonard	72	75	71	74	292	8,316

	SCORES				TOTAL	MONEY
Steve Alker	71	74	72	75	292	8,316
Richard Lee	77	72	73	71	293	6,190
Craig Spence	72	76	73	72	293	6,190
John Senden	72	73	73	75	293	6,190
Ben Ferguson	72	69	76	76	293	6,190
Richard Backwell	76	69	78	71	294	4,796
Terry Price	75	71	77	71	294	4,796
Scott Wearne	70	74	76	74	294	4,796
Rodger Davis	72	71	76	75	294	4,796
Anthony Edwards	75	75	69	75	294	4,796
Peter Fowler	71	73	74	76	294	4,796
Danny Vera	71	75	72	76	294	4,796
Justin Cooper	75	73	70	76	294	4,796
Bob Charles	73	73	78	71	295	3,309
David Somervaille	76	70	74	75	295	3,309
Anthony Christie	73	76	71	75	295	3,309
Kenny Druce	75	74	71	75	295	3,309
Gavin Coles	75	74	71	75	295	3,309
David Frost	70	71	78	76	295	3,309
Matthew Goggin	72	71	76	76	295	3,309
Marcus Wheelhouse	75	71	70	79	295	3,309

Schweppes Coolum Classic

Hyatt Coolum Resort, Coolum, Queensland
Par 36-36—72; 6,853 yards

December 18-21
purse, A$275,000

	SCORES				TOTAL	MONEY
Craig Parry	70	68	71	67	276	A$52,104
Robert Allenby	70	70	73	66	279	29,526
Shane Tait	72	70	69	72	283	19,538
Kenny Druce	71	72	71	70	284	11,966
Lucas Parsons	68	69	76	71	284	11,966
Wayne Smith	69	73	73	69	284	11,966
Craig Jones	73	68	71	73	285	8,828
Robin Byrd	69	73	72	71	285	8,828
Robert Willis	70	73	73	70	286	7,526
Payne Stewart	69	77	72	68	286	7,526
Craig Spence	71	74	72	70	287	6,078
Nick O'Hern	77	68	72	70	287	6,078
Peter Lonard	71	72	77	68	288	5,066
Matthew Goggin	72	76	69	71	288	5,066
Gary Evans	74	70	72	73	289	4,631
Grant Dodd	77	74	73	66	290	3,665
David McKenzie	71	77	75	67	290	3,665
Darin Anderson	74	73	73	70	290	3,665
Terry Price	77	73	70	70	290	3,665
Brad King	73	71	78	69	291	2,833
Peter O'Malley	71	77	73	70	291	2,833
Michael Barry	73	71	75	72	291	2,833
Rodney Pampling	76	74	69	72	291	2,833
Michael Long	76	74	69	72	291	2,833
Grant Kenny	74	77	66	74	291	2,833
Tony Carolan	72	75	69	75	291	2,833
Daniel Chopra	73	75	76	68	292	2,105
John Senden	76	72	75	69	292	2,105
Jarrod Moseley	74	71	75	72	292	2,105
David Ecob	71	72	76	73	292	2,105

African Tours

San Lameer South African Masters

San Lameer Country Club, Margate, South Africa
Par 36-36–72; 5,581 yards

January 16-19
purse, R750,000

	SCORES				TOTAL	MONEY
Mark McNulty	71	68	70	67	276	R118,500
Adilson de Silva	67	71	72	70	280	86,250
Deane Pappas	73	72	69	72	286	44,362.50
Bruce Vaughan	74	75	67	70	286	44,362.50
Gavin Levenson	72	70	77	68	287	28,762.50
Van Phillips	71	74	73	69	287	28,762.50
Retief Goosen	73	72	74	69	288	22,125
Ronnie McCann	79	70	69	71	289	16,450
Sean Pappas	72	70	74	73	289	16,450
Mark Wiltshire	72	71	74	72	289	16,450
Graeme van der Nest	75	69	74	72	290	13,425
Desvonde Botes	76	65	75	75	291	11,493.75
Ian Palmer	75	73	71	72	291	11,493.75
Dean van Staden	80	68	73	70	291	11,493.75
Chris Williams	76	72	70	73	291	11,493.75
Jeff Hawkes	72	73	73	74	292	10,350
Ashley Roestoff	75	76	71	71	293	9,787.50
Wayne Westner	72	77	76	68	293	9,787.50
Darren Fichardt	75	74	73	72	294	8,367.85
Ben Fouchee	71	75	77	71	294	8,367.85
Lan Gooch	76	72	74	72	294	8,367.85
Nic Henning	75	73	75	71	294	8,367.85
Philip Jonas	72	76	73	73	294	8,367.85
Richard Kaplan	77	73	71	73	294	8,367.85
Nico van Rensburg	80	72	72	70	294	8,367.85
Trevor Dodds	79	71	73	72	295	6,975
Warrick Druian	76	74	70	75	295	6,975
Tom Gillis	82	69	74	70	295	6,975
Brad Ott	72	74	75	74	295	6,975
Fran Quinn	75	78	72	70	295	6,975

Nashua Wild Coast Sun Challenge

Wild Coast Sun County Club, Port Edward, South Africa
Par 35-35–70; 5,310 yards

January 23-26
purse, R750,000

	SCORES				TOTAL	MONEY
Mark McNulty	66	68	70	66	270	R118,500
Justin Hobday	68	73	71	67	279	86,250
James Kingston	71	68	70	71	280	44,362.50
Ronnie McCann	70	76	68	66	280	44,362.50
Chris Williams	71	71	72	67	281	30,975
A.P. Botes	69	67	75	71	282	22,375
Desvonde Botes	66	66	76	74	282	22,375
Warren Schutte	69	70	74	69	282	22,375

	SCORES				TOTAL	MONEY
Tom Gillis	69	66	81	67	283	13,275
Lan Gooch	69	74	72	68	283	13,275
Marco Gortana	70	68	76	69	283	13,275
Ian Palmer	70	71	75	67	283	13,275
Wayne Westner	70	70	73	70	283	13,275
Clinton Whitelaw	66	68	81	68	283	13,275
Trevor Dodds	68	73	75	68	284	10,650
Don Gammon	71	70	73	71	285	9,787.50
Jeff Hawkes	69	72	77	67	285	9,787.50
Stuart Hendley	72	67	77	69	285	9,787.50
Graeme van der Nest	70	73	73	69	285	9,787.50
John McHenry	72	70	69	75	286	8,575
Deane Pappas	70	69	77	70	286	8,575
Steve van Vuuren	69	70	75	72	286	8,575
Noel Maart	70	67	74	76	287	7,987.50
John Mellor	71	72	70	74	287	7,987.50
Hugh Baiocchi	70	69	78	71	288	7,425
Paul Blaikie	70	76	74	68	288	7,425
Van Phillips	69	71	74	74	288	7,425
Hendrik Buhrmann	71	75	73	70	289	6,862.50
Mark Wiltshire	70	74	78	67	289	6,862.50
Michael du Toit	71	71	77	71	290	6,000
Retief Goosen	69	72	76	73	290	6,000
Alan McLean	70	72	78	70	290	6,000
Alan Mitchell	71	70	79	70	290	6,000
Brad Ott	68	72	75	75	290	6,000
Sean Pappas	69	72	79	70	290	6,000
Ashley Roestoff	71	74	76	69	290	6,000
Bruce Vaughan	69	74	75	72	290	6,000

FNB Players Championship

Durban Country Club, Durban, South Africa
Par 36-36–72; 6,642 yards

January 30-February 2
purse, R750,000

	SCORES				TOTAL	MONEY
Warren Schutte	69	71	69	65	274	R118,500
Nico van Rensburg	67	69	73	67	276	86,250
Andre Cruse	70	66	72	71	279	51,900
Richard Kaplan	66	70	74	70	280	36,825
Hugh Baiocchi	71	73	70	67	281	22,860
Marco Gortana	72	71	71	67	281	22,860
Jeff Hawkes	68	67	77	69	281	22,860
Deane Pappas	72	73	72	64	281	22,860
Tjaart van der Walt	72	68	74	67	281	22,860
Wayne Bradley	70	70	72	70	282	12,690
Trevor Dodds	73	65	72	72	282	12,690
Mark McNulty	71	69	74	68	282	12,690
Brad Ott	72	68	75	67	282	12,690
Andrew Pitts	71	69	75	67	282	12,690
Darren Fichardt	73	71	70	69	283	10,325
Don Gammon	71	70	72	70	283	10,325
Retief Goosen	72	67	47	70	283	10,325
Tom Gillis	71	70	71	72	284	8,910
Michael Green	70	66	75	73	284	8,910
Nic Henning	71	71	72	70	284	8,910
Ian Hutchings	69	68	76	71	284	8,910

	SCORES				TOTAL	MONEY
Bruce Vaughan	71	68	74	71	284	8,910
Mark Barry Foster	76	69	69	71	285	7,650
Philip Jonas	71	69	77	68	285	7,650
Andrew McLardy	73	68	71	73	285	7,650
Roger Wessels	70	72	73	70	285	7,650
Chris Williams	71	69	74	71	285	7,650
Warrick Druian	72	68	74	72	286	6,656.25
John Mellor	72	73	73	68	286	6,656.25
Fran Quinn	74	71	71	70	286	6,656.25
Clinton Whitelaw	68	71	76	71	286	6,656.25

South African Open

Glendower Country Club, Johannesburg, South Africa
Par 36-36–72; 7,408 yards

February 6-9
purse, R3,375,000

	SCORES				TOTAL	MONEY
Vijay Singh	69	66	66	69	270	R529,300
Nick Price	72	66	65	68	271	385,250
Fulton Allem	66	71	71	67	275	178,220
Ernie Els	66	72	67	70	275	178,220
Mark McNulty	69	69	68	69	275	178,220
Retief Goosen	72	67	72	67	278	118,590
David Gilford	69	66	74	70	279	90,617.50
Ian Woosnam	66	75	69	69	279	90,617.50
Sven Struver	70	71	71	68	280	65,995
Jean Van de Velde	68	69	73	70	280	65,995
Clinton Whitelaw	74	66	74	66	280	65,995
Eamonn Darcy	67	69	73	72	281	51,338.75
Gary Evans	68	72	72	69	281	51,338.75
Andrew McLardy	72	71	69	69	281	51,338.75
Wayne Westner	69	70	73	69	281	51,338.75
*Hennie Otto	74	68	68	72	282	
Fran Quinn	69	72	72	69	282	46,230
Thomas Bjorn	66	69	75	74	284	42,880
Trevor Dodds	72	70	71	71	284	42,880
Adam Hunter	71	68	70	75	284	42,880
Wayne Bradley	65	70	75	75	285	38,860
Ignacio Garrido	70	73	71	71	285	38,860
Andre Bossert	73	69	73	71	286	35,175
Bobby Lincoln	71	69	72	74	286	35,175
Phillip Price	71	68	76	71	286	35,175
Ashley Roestoff	74	68	72	72	286	35,175
Warren Schutte	74	69	72	71	286	35,175
Warrick Druian	70	74	70	73	287	31,657.50
Padraig Harrington	72	73	73	69	287	31,657.50
Anders Forsbrand	70	72	70	76	288	29,256.66
Thomas Gogele	71	71	80	66	288	29,256.66
Justin Hobday	72	68	73	75	288	29,256.66

Dimension Data Pro-Am

Gary Player Country Club, Sun City, South Africa
Player Course: Par 36-36–72; 7,484 yards
Lost City Course: Par 36-36–72; 7,236 yards

February 13-16
purse, £400,000

	SCORES				TOTAL	MONEY
Nick Price	67	66	66	69	268	£63,384.19
David Frost	69	65	71	71	276	46,155.87
Thomas Bjorn	67	67	71	72	277	27,765.64
Mark McNulty	71	66	69	73	279	14,455.76
Wayne Westner	72	66	70	71	279	14,455.76
Stephen Ames	69	69	70	71	279	14,455.76
Padraig Harrington	70	66	68	75	279	14,455.76
Ronnie McCann	65	73	71	70	279	14,455.76
Desvonde Botes	69	67	70	74	280	8,293.63
Tony Johnstone	67	71	70	72	280	8,293.63
Lee Westwood	70	69	71	72	282	6,263.63
Daniel Chopra	72	67	71	72	282	6,263.63
Costantino Rocca	67	72	73	70	282	6,263.63
Hugh Baiocchi	72	68	73	69	282	6,263.63
Ian Garbutt	69	72	68	73	282	6,263.63
Paul McGinley	68	72	72	70	282	6,263.63
Chris Williams	69	69	70	75	283	5,208.56
Iain Pyman	70	67	74	72	283	5,208.56
Retief Goosen	71	68	72	72	283	5,208.56
Des Smyth	73	68	71	72	284	4,727.77
Trevor Dodds	69	72	70	73	284	4,727.77
Chris Davison	74	67	75	69	285	4,407.24
Anders Hansen	67	74	70	74	285	4,407.24
Katsuyoshi Tomori	71	68	77	69	285	4,407.24
Phil Golding	71	68	73	74	286	3,859.68
Peter Baker	73	71	69	73	286	3,859.68
Roger Wessels	73	71	70	72	286	3,859.68
Brett Liddle	67	77	69	73	286	3,859.68
Eamonn Darcy	70	74	73	69	286	3,859.68
Sven Struver	70	68	74	74	286	3,859.68

Alfred Dunhill South African PGA

Houghton Golf Club, Johannesburg, South Africa
Par 36-36–72; 7,035 yards

February 20-23
purse, £300,000

	SCORES				TOTAL	MONEY
Nick Price	67	66	70	66	269	£47,319.16
David Frost	69	63	66	71	269	34,457.44
(Price defeated Frost on first extra hole.)						
Nico van Rensburg	68	68	66	68	270	20,728.31
Retief Goosen	65	66	70	71	272	14,716.20
Marco Gortana	70	67	67	69	273	10,618.40
Greg Petersen	71	69	65	68	273	10,618.40
Wayne Westner	68	66	71	68	273	10,618.40
Max Anglert	68	67	69	70	274	6,288.78
Mathew Goggin	69	69	69	67	274	6,288.78
Katsuyoshi Tomori	67	67	67	73	274	6,288.78
Niclas Fasth	66	69	68	71	274	6,288.78
Greg Chalmers	70	68	71	66	275	4,725.93
Craig Kamps	68	68	68	71	275	4,725.93

		SCORES			TOTAL	MONEY
Sven Struver	71	69	65	70	275	4,725.93
Desvonde Botes	68	72	67	69	276	4,032
Bob May	66	68	72	70	276	4,032
Tony Johnstone	70	69	67	70	276	4,032
Trevor Dodds	68	72	68	68	276	4,032
Ignacio Garrido	69	69	67	71	276	4,032
Van Phillips	70	64	74	69	277	3,290.21
Mark McNulty	69	69	67	72	277	3,290.21
Paul McGinley	71	67	71	68	277	3,290.21
Gordon Sherry	69	68	71	69	277	3,290.21
Fulton Allem	69	69	69	70	277	3,290.21
Carl Watts	69	69	69	70	277	3,290.21
Michael Archer	68	68	74	67	277	3,290.21
Ian Hutchings	67	71	68	72	278	2,757.79
James Kingston	69	71	71	67	278	2,757.79
Brad Ott	68	69	67	74	278	2,757.79
Mark Murless	66	69	69	74	278	2,757.79
Ashley Roestoff	67	70	69	72	278	2,757.79

Hollard Insurance Royal Swazi Sun Open

Royal Swazi Sun Golf Club, Mbabane, Swaziland
Par 36-36–72; 5,609 yards

February 27-March 2
purse, R500,000

		SCORES			TOTAL	MONEY
Warrick Druian	70	64	65	70	269	R79,000
Chris Davison	67	67	69	67	270	46,050
Nic Henning	66	66	69	69	270	46,050
Bobby Lincoln	72	67	68	65	272	22,600
Michael Scholz	71	70	67	64	272	22,600
Derek Crawford	71	70	64	68	273	16,225
Pelop Panagopoulos	67	72	67	67	273	16,225
Tjaart van der Walt	69	66	70	69	274	12,300
Desvonde Botes	63	73	69	70	275	10,800
Craig Kamps	73	65	68	70	276	9,375
Ashley Roestoff	73	68	68	67	276	9,375
Wayne Bradley	71	68	67	71	277	8,100
Callie Swart	66	69	71	71	277	8,100
Marco Gortana	70	69	71	68	278	7,000
Justin Hobday	66	71	69	72	278	7,000
Brad Ott	69	68	69	72	278	7,000
Des Terblanche	71	67	71	69	278	7,000
Alan McLean	70	70	68	71	279	6,037.50
Mark Murless	71	65	73	70	279	6,037.50
Fran Quinn	69	72	70	68	279	6,037.50
Bradford Vaughan	69	71	69	70	279	6,037.50
Nico van Rensburg	67	72	73	68	280	5,400
Bruce Vaughan	68	72	69	71	280	5,400
Steve Woods	71	73	68	68	280	5,400
Hugh Baiocchi	72	71	69	69	281	4,875
Hendrik Buhrmann	69	69	75	68	281	4,875
Wallie Coetsee	73	69	68	71	281	4,875
Ronnie McCann	68	71	69	73	281	4,875
Brett Liddle	70	68	75	69	282	4,312.50
Hennie Otto	73	69	69	71	282	4,312.50
Greg Petersen	70	72	69	71	282	4,312.50
Steve van Vuuren	66	73	75	69	282	4,312.50

Kalahari Classic

Sishen Golf Club, Kathu, South Africa
Par 36-36–72; 6,988 yards

April 10-12
purse, R75,000

	SCORES			TOTAL	MONEY
Sean Pappas	67	73	69	209	R11,625
Justin Hobday	71	70	69	210	6,625
Andrew McLardy	73	70	67	210	6,625
Tjaart van der Walt	74	69	67	211	6,625
Wallie Coetsee	69	70	73	212	4,500
James Kingston	72	75	66	213	3,600
Mark Murless	71	71	71	213	3,600
Brett Liddle	73	72	69	214	2,850
Noel Maart	72	73	70	215	2,400
Jannie le Grange	73	68	75	216	1,800
Titch Moore	69	76	71	216	1,800
Ashley Roestoff	71	72	74	217	1,425
Steve van Vuuren	73	73	71	217	1,425
Ian Hutchings	70	74	74	218	1,200
Warren Abery	71	72	76	219	1,046.25
Wimpie Botha	74	73	72	219	1,046.25
Alan McLean	77	68	74	219	1,046.25
Schalk van der Merwe	71	77	71	219	1,046.25
Johan Krugel	78	70	72	220	870
David Owen	75	70	75	220	870
Martyn Proctor	75	70	75	220	870
Hennie Swart	73	72	75	220	870
Roger Wessels	72	76	72	220	870
Darren Fichardt	74	71	76	221	765
Adriaan van Pletzen	72	72	77	221	765
Michael Boshoff	71	73	78	222	720
Richard Fulford	72	75	75	222	720
Charl van Heyningen	73	73	76	222	720
Michael du Toit	75	71	77	223	682.50
Mellette Hendrikse	76	70	77	223	682.50

Vodacom Series: Eastern Cape

Humewood Golf Club, Port Elizabeth, South Africa
Par 36-36–72; 6,732 yards

June 25-27
purse, R150,000

	SCORES			TOTAL	MONEY
Des Terblanche	75	68	68	211	R23,550
Andre Cruse	72	69	72	213	17,250
Desvonde Botes	76	69	70	215	12,000
Sean Pappas	72	69	75	216	9,450
Bobby Lincoln	78	69	71	218	6,375
Hennie Walters	71	74	73	218	6,375
Sammy Daniels	75	70	74	219	4,425
Darren Fichardt	82	69	68	219	4,425
Neil Homann	78	69	73	220	3,300
Keith Horne	71	75	74	220	3,300
James Kingston	79	67	74	220	3,300
Chris Williams	77	71	72	220	3,300
Grant Muller	74	72	75	221	2,775
Robbie Stewart	81	72	68	221	2,775
Andrew McLardy	75	71	76	222	2,400

	SCORES	TOTAL	MONEY
Ashley Roestoff	76 68 78	222	2,400
Colin Sorour	73 78 71	222	2,400
Graeme van der Nest	75 76 71	222	2,400
Hendrik Buhrmann	80 71 72	223	1,972.50
Mellette Hendrikse	79 71 73	223	1,972.50
James Loughnane	74 76 73	223	1,972.50
Andrew Plunkett	78 69 76	223	1,972.50
Steve van Vuuren	79 71 73	223	1,972.50
Bradford Vaughan	78 72 73	223	1,972.50
Warren Abery	77 73 74	224	1,695
Vaughn Groenewald	80 70 74	224	1,695
Titch Moore	76 73 76	225	1,575
Ian Palmer	76 73 76	225	1,575
Gerry Coetsee	74 73 79	226	1,395
Justin Hobday	76 73 77	226	1,395
Sean Ludgater	77 74 75	226	1,395
John Mashego	76 76 74	226	1,395
Pelop Panagopoulos	79 73 74	226	1,395

Bosveld Classic

Mogol Golf Club, Ellisras, South Africa
Par 36-36–72; 6,581 yards

July 3-5
purse, R80,000

	SCORES	TOTAL	MONEY
Desvonde Botes	66 72 67	205	R15,700
Darren Fichardt	66 73 69	208	11,500
James Kingston	67 70 72	209	6,333.33
Sean Pappas	70 71 68	209	6,333.33
Steve van Vuuren	68 71 70	209	6,333.33
Jannie le Grange	68 74 68	210	3,800
Neil Homann	72 69 70	211	2,783.33
Noel Maart	70 73 68	211	2,783.33
Chris Williams	69 76 66	211	2,783.33
Wayne Bradley	69 72 71	212	1,960
Craig Kamps	69 72 71	212	1,960
Andrew McLardy	73 72 67	212	1,960
John Nelson	68 75 69	212	1,960
Ashley Roestoff	72 68 72	212	1,960
Kevin Stone	71 70 71	212	1,960
Wallie Coetsee	70 74 69	213	1,630
Marc Cayeux	72 72 70	214	1,446
Sammy Daniels	76 70 68	214	1,446
Colin Sorour	73 71 70	214	1,446
Callie Swart	74 70 70	214	1,446
Schalk van der Merwe	73 69 72	214	1,446
Warren Abery	71 72 72	215	1,240
Alan Michell	74 73 68	215	1,240
Robbie Stewart	71 70 74	215	1,240
Dion Fourie	72 72 72	216	1,034.28
Justin Hobday	73 71 72	216	1,034.28
Brett Liddle	71 69 76	216	1,034.28
John Mashego	74 71 71	216	1,034.28
Pelop Panagopoulos	75 72 69	216	1,034.28
Graeme van der Nest	73 73 70	216	1,034.28
Bradford Vaughan	72 70 74	216	1,034.28

Vodacom Series: Mpumalanga

White River Country Club, Nelspruit, South Africa
Par 36-35–71; 6,539 yards

July 10-12
purse, R150,000

	SCORES			TOTAL	MONEY
Robbie Stewart	65	68	69	202	R23,550
Steve van Vuuren	65	69	69	203	17,250
Sean Pappas	69	66	71	206	12,000
Andrew McLardy	70	67	70	207	8,250
Callie Swart	67	70	70	207	8,250
Bradford Vaughan	73	67	68	208	5,700
Michiel Bothma	75	67	67	209	3,351.66
Sammy Daniels	69	68	72	209	3,351.66
Bradley Davison	69	70	70	209	3,351.66
Darren Fichardt	72	68	69	209	3,351.66
Dion Fourie	69	67	73	209	3,351.66
James Loughnane	69	75	65	209	3,351.66
Ian Palmer	69	68	72	209	3,351.66
Pelop Panagopoulos	72	69	68	209	3,351.66
Kevin Stone	68	68	73	209	3,351.66
Keith Horne	68	69	73	210	2,445
Wallie Coetsee	72	70	69	211	2,208.75
Justin Hobday	70	71	70	211	2,208.75
James Kingston	65	76	70	211	2,208.75
Gavin Levenson	68	71	72	211	2,208.75
Michael Green	70	69	73	212	1,830
Brett Liddle	68	73	71	212	1,830
Alan Michell	69	68	75	212	1,830
Mark Murless	73	70	69	212	1,830
Chad Ransby	72	72	68	212	1,830
Mark Wiltshire	67	73	72	212	1,830
Russell Fletcher	73	68	72	213	1,605
Cliffie Botha	70	68	76	214	1,466.25
John Mashego	68	72	74	214	1,466.25
Adriaan van Rensburg	69	74	71	214	1,466.25
Graeme van der Nest	74	69	71	214	1,466.25

Trustbank Gauteng Classic

Randburg Golf Club, Randburg, South Africa
Par 36-36–72; 7,373 yards

July 24-26
purse, R120,000

	SCORES			TOTAL	MONEY
Bradford Vaughan	73	66	70	209	R18,840
Des Terblanche	69	71	70	210	13,000
Brett Liddle	71	73	68	212	8,580
Ashley Roestoff	68	74	70	212	8,580
Grant Muller	75	69	69	213	5,100
Michael Scholz	68	74	71	213	5,100
Darren Fichardt	69	72	73	214	3,540
James Kingston	75	70	69	214	3,540
Warren Abery	72	69	74	215	2,940
Bobby Lincoln	72	73	71	216	2,700
Michiel Bothma	72	73	72	217	2,460
Darran Warner	71	74	72	217	2,460
Sammy Daniels	76	70	72	218	2,020
Nic Henning	71	75	72	218	2,020

	SCORES			TOTAL	MONEY
Neil Homann	72	74	72	218	2,020
Andrew McLardy	71	77	70	218	2,020
John Nelson	72	75	71	218	2,020
Steve van Vuuren	70	75	73	218	2,020
Jannie le Grange	76	72	71	219	1,698
David Riddle	70	76	73	219	1,698
Richard Fulford	71	70	79	220	1,464
John Mashego	68	77	75	220	1,464
Alan Michell	74	73	73	220	1,464
Sean Pappas	73	73	74	220	1,464
Robbie Stewart	74	75	71	220	1,464
Mark Wiltshire	72	74	74	220	1,464
Desvonde Botes	70	77	74	221	1,157.14
Andre Cruse	73	74	74	221	1,157.14
Bradley Davison	72	73	76	221	1,157.14
Justin Hobday	72	76	73	221	1,157.14
Gavin Levenson	74	71	76	221	1,157.14
Mark Murless	74	75	72	221	1,157.14
Callie Swart	73	74	74	221	1,157.14

Vodacom Series: Gauteng

Royal Johannesburg Golf Club, Johannesburg, South Africa
Par 36-36–72; 7,394 yards
August 7-9
purse, R150,000

	SCORES			TOTAL	MONEY
John Nelson	71	68	72	211	R23,550
John Mashego	70	71	71	212	14,625
Bradford Vaughan	70	71	71	212	14,625
James Kingston	74	68	71	213	9,050
Robbie Stewart	74	67	73	214	7,050
Andre Cruse	75	72	68	215	4,850
Darren Fichardt	69	70	76	215	4,850
Schalk van der Merwe	74	71	70	215	4,850
Wimpie Botha	71	72	73	216	3,300
Michael Green	74	72	70	216	3,300
Nic Henning	71	74	71	216	3,300
Noel Maart	73	69	74	216	3,300
Michiel Bothma	70	76	71	217	2,580
Justin Hobday	74	72	71	217	2,580
Grant Muller	72	72	73	217	2,580
Ian Palmer	71	73	73	217	2,580
Colin Sanderson	73	73	71	217	2,580
Desvonde Botes	77	68	73	218	1,976.25
Jannie le Grange	71	71	76	218	1,976.25
Gavin Levenson	71	76	71	218	1,976.25
Bobby Lincoln	67	78	73	218	1,976.25
Mark Murless	75	72	71	218	1,976.25
David Owen	71	74	73	218	1,976.25
Michael Scholz	73	71	74	218	1,976.25
Kevin Stone	75	72	71	218	1,976.25
Warren Abery	75	71	73	219	1,605
Brett Liddle	72	72	75	219	1,605
Steve van Vuuren	72	74	73	219	1,605
Andrew McLardy	78	71	71	220	1,485
Alan Michell	74	73	74	221	1,395
Trevor Sidley	75	74	72	221	1,395
Phil Simmons	70	75	76	221	1,395

FNB Botswana Open

Gaborone Golf Club, Gaborone, Botswana
Par 36-35–71; 6,750 yards

August 29-31
purse, R150,000

	SCORES			TOTAL	MONEY
Nasho Kamungeremu	72	65	68	205	R23,550
Marc Cayeux	70	66	70	206	17,250
Justin Hobday	69	63	75	207	9,500
James Kingston	69	73	65	207	9,500
Hennie Otto	66	70	71	207	9,500
Ian Palmer	67	72	69	208	5,212.50
Chris Williams	68	70	70	208	5,212.50
Des Terblanche	66	74	69	209	4,125
Colin Sanderson	68	65	77	210	3,525
Mark Wiltshire	70	68	72	210	3,525
Bradley Davison	68	71	72	211	3,150
Warren Abery	68	71	73	212	2,925
Robbie Stewart	70	69	73	212	2,925
Wimpie Botha	71	69	73	213	2,410
Brett Liddle	73	70	70	213	2,410
David Owen	71	70	72	213	2,410
Ashley Roestoff	69	70	74	213	2,410
Schalk van der Merwe	73	66	74	213	2,410
Mike Williams	69	72	72	213	2,410
Desvonde Botes	67	74	73	214	1,833.75
Wallie Coetsee	70	73	71	214	1,833.75
Dion Fourie	71	69	74	214	1,833.75
Noel Maart	71	68	75	214	1,833.75
Andrew McLardy	70	72	72	214	1,833.75
Kevin Stone	72	67	75	214	1,833.75
Steve van Vuuren	71	69	74	214	1,833.75
Nico van Rensburg	73	69	72	214	1,833.75
Grant Muller	67	68	80	215	1,545
Michael du Toit	68	72	76	216	1,395
Neil Homann	73	70	73	216	1,395
Jannie le Grange	70	71	75	216	1,395
Titch Moore	71	68	77	216	1,395
Bradford Vaughan	71	70	75	216	1,395

FNB Namibia Open

Windhoek Country Club, Windhoek, Namibia
Par 36-35–71; 7,002 yards

September 11-13
purse, R150,000

	SCORES			TOTAL	MONEY
Wallie Coetsee	69	69	65	203	R23,560
Brett Liddle	69	67	68	204	17,250
James Kingston	68	66	71	205	10,725
Bradford Vaughan	66	71	68	205	10,725
Justin Hobday	70	69	68	207	7,050
Nasho Kamungeremu	70	68	70	208	5,212.50
Robbie Stewart	72	71	65	208	5,212.50
Warrick Druian	69	67	73	209	3,900
Hennie Otto	67	72	70	209	3,900
Wimpie Botha	70	69	71	210	2,869.28
Sean Farrell	70	70	70	210	2,869.28
Neil Homann	69	69	72	210	2,869.28

	SCORES			TOTAL	MONEY
Grant Muller	75	69	66	210	2,869.28
Ashley Roestoff	74	67	69	210	2,869.28
Kevin Stone	71	68	71	210	2,869.28
Steve van Vuuren	73	70	67	210	2,869.28
Ian Hutchings	68	71	72	211	2,340
Sammy Daniels	74	68	70	212	2,088
Wayne de Haas	72	70	70	212	2,088
Paul Marks	72	70	70	212	2,088
Andrew McLardy	72	70	70	212	2,088
Graeme van der Nest	77	66	69	212	2,088
Adilson da Silva	71	70	72	213	1,728
Richard Fulford	72	70	71	213	1,728
Francois Hanekom	73	68	72	213	1,728
Mawonga Nomwa	70	72	71	213	1,728
Darran Warner	73	70	70	213	1,728
Mone Haasbroek	71	72	71	214	1,490
Bobby Lincoln	74	69	71	214	1,490
Charl van Heyningen	69	74	71	214	1,490

Bearing Man Highveld Classic

Witbank Golf Club, Witbank, South Africa
Par 36-36–72; 6,764 yards
September 19-21
purse, R75,000

	SCORES			TOTAL	MONEY
Darren Fichardt	65	66	69	200	R15,700
Sean Pappas	66	67	69	201	11,500
Wallie Coetsee	67	65	70	202	7,150
Ashley Roestoff	69	66	67	202	7,150
Michael Green	62	70	71	203	3,883.33
Noel Maart	69	65	69	203	3,883.33
Bradford Vaughan	70	66	67	203	3,883.33
John Nelson	67	71	66	204	2,750
Justin Hobday	69	68	68	205	2,083.33
Ian Hutchings	67	65	73	205	2,083.33
James Kingston	68	70	67	205	2,083.33
Mark Murless	71	66	68	205	2,083.33
Schalk van der Merwe	68	69	68	205	2,083.33
Chris Williams	70	66	69	205	2,083.33
Pelop Panagopoulos	67	71	68	206	1,670
Brenden Pappas	67	68	71	206	1,670
Andre Cruse	69	68	70	207	1,530
Hennie Otto	71	68	68	207	1,530
Ryan Dreyer	72	68	68	208	1,183.33
Neil Homann	72	66	70	208	1,183.33
Brett Liddle	67	68	73	208	1,183.33
Sean Ludgater	72	68	68	208	1,183.33
John Mashego	72	65	71	208	1,183.33
Lyall McNeill	68	69	71	208	1,183.33
Titch Moore	70	70	68	208	1,183.33
Kevin Stone	71	69	68	208	1,183.33
Callie Swart	70	66	72	208	1,183.33
Steve van Vuuren	66	70	72	208	1,183.33
Darran Warner	70	70	68	208	1,183.33
Douglas Wood	68	68	72	208	1,183.33

Vodacom Series: Free State

Bloemfontein Golf Club, Bloemfontein, South Africa
Par 36-36–72; 7,202 yards

October 9-11
purse, R150,000

	SCORES			TOTAL	MONEY
Dean van Staden	67	69	69	205	R23,550
Roger Wessels	64	71	72	207	17,250
Nico van Rensburg	68	71	69	208	12,000
Ian Hutchings	74	66	69	209	9,450
Jams Kingston	67	73	70	210	7,050
Justin Hobday	69	71	71	211	4,320
Neil Homann	71	69	71	211	4,320
Noel Maart	68	72	71	211	4,320
Andrew McLardy	68	72	71	211	4,320
Steve van Vuuren	73	68	70	211	4,320
Richard Fulford	67	74	71	212	3,150
Wimpie Botha	73	67	73	213	2,712
Bobby Lincoln	75	68	70	213	2,712
Ashley Roestoff	73	70	70	213	2,712
Bradford Vaughan	70	71	72	213	2,712
Clinton Whitelaw	71	71	71	213	2,712
Mark Wiltshire	72	71	71	214	2,340
Michiel Bothma	70	74	71	215	2,165
Mark Murless	76	70	69	215	2,165
Callie Swart	70	73	72	215	2,165
Sammy Daniels	70	76	70	216	1,935
Nic Henning	73	69	74	216	1,935
Jannie le Grange	71	75	70	216	1,935
Desvonde Botes	76	69	72	217	1,695
Brett Liddle	70	72	75	217	1,695
Langley Perrins	69	73	75	217	1,695
Colin Sorour	70	74	73	217	1,695
Wallie Coetsee	70	74	74	218	1,443
Gavin Levenson	73	70	75	218	1,443
Ian Palmer	71	72	75	218	1,443
Sean Pappas	76	71	71	218	1,443
Chris Williams	70	72	76	218	1,443

Vodacom Series: Western Cape

Rondebosch Golf Club, Cape Town, South Africa
Par 36-36–72; 6,633 yards

October 16-18
purse, R150,000

	SCORES			TOTAL	MONEY
Desvonde Botes	69	66	68	203	R23,550
Dean van Staden	67	68	68	203	17,250
(Botes defeated van Staden on first extra hole.)					
Brenden Pappas	71	69	65	205	12,000
Bobby Lincoln	68	72	68	208	9,450
James Kingston	71	67	71	209	5,825
Schalk van der Merwe	69	70	70	209	5,825
Bradford Vaughan	69	70	70	209	5,325
Ian Palmer	70	69	71	210	4,125
Wimpie Botha	70	70	71	211	3,125
Brett Liddle	68	70	73	211	3,125
Mark Murless	69	67	75	211	3,125
Sean Pappas	71	70	70	211	3,125

	SCORES			TOTAL	MONEY
Ashley Roestoff	69	70	72	211	3,125
Roger Wessels	69	70	72	211	3,125
Alan McLean	69	71	72	212	2,565
Michael Green	72	68	73	213	2,256
Justin Hobday	73	69	71	213	2,256
Jannie le Grange	68	75	70	213	2,256
John Mashego	72	70	71	213	2,256
Robbie Stewart	68	73	72	213	2,256
Wallie Coetsee	70	70	74	214	1,935
Sean Farrell	73	72	69	214	1,935
Nasho Kamungeremu	67	73	74	214	1,935
James Loughnane	72	70	73	215	1,725
Pelop Panagopoulos	73	72	70	215	1,725
Callie Swart	70	70	75	215	1,725
Bradley Davison	72	68	76	216	1,470
Ryan Dreyer	73	72	71	216	1,470
Keith Horne	67	75	74	216	1,470
Richard Kaplan	70	71	75	216	1,470
Colin Sorour	69	72	75	216	1,470
Graeme van der Nest	71	73	72	216	1,470

Vodacom Series: Kwazulu-Natal

Selborne Country Club, South Coast, South Africa
Par 36-36–72; 6,543 yards
October 23-25
purse, R150,000

	SCORES			TOTAL	MONEY
Grant Muller	71	70	70	211	R23,550
Hennie Otto	72	70	74	216	17,250
Brett Liddle	74	69	74	217	8,550
Bobby Lincoln	75	72	70	217	8,550
Brenden Pappas	72	69	76	217	8,550
Darran Warner	73	74	70	217	8,550
Justin Hobday	69	74	75	218	4,425
Roger Wessels	72	69	77	218	4,425
Ashley Roestoff	72	73	74	219	3,675
Andre Cruse	74	68	78	220	3,093.75
Keith Horne	74	75	71	220	3,093.75
Nasho Kamungeremu	78	70	72	220	3,093.75
Gavin Levenson	70	72	78	220	3,093.75
Ryan Dreyer	73	72	76	221	2,460
Alan Michell	73	74	74	221	2,460
Steve van Vuuren	73	70	78	221	2,460
Bradford Vaughan	75	75	71	221	2,460
Mark Wiltshire	73	73	75	221	2,460
Nic Henning	79	67	76	222	2,122.50
Jannie le Grange	75	73	74	222	2,122.50
Warren Abery	72	75	76	223	1,897.50
James Kingston	71	73	79	223	1,897.50
John Mashego	77	70	76	223	1,897.50
Colin Sanderson	69	77	77	223	1,897.50
Michael du Toit	79	70	75	224	1,695
Ian Palmer	71	68	85	224	1,695
Douglas Clayton	74	73	78	225	1,575
Wallie Coetsee	76	73	76	225	1,575
Ian Basson	71	72	77	226	1,395
Bradley Davison	72	76	78	226	1,395

	SCORES	TOTAL	MONEY
James Loughnane	75 73 78	226	1,395
Andrew McLardy	74 72 80	226	1,395
Pelop Panagopoulos	72 78 76	226	1,395

Lombard Tyres Classic

Krugersdorp Golf Club, Krugersdorp, South Africa
Par 36-36–72; 7,166 yards

October 29-November 1
purse, R120,000

	SCORES	TOTAL	MONEY
Andrew McLardy	71 66 66 70	273	R19,625
Justin Hobday	69 68 68 69	274	14,375
Wallie Coetsee	66 72 69 70	277	5,218.75
Jeff Hawkes	70 70 68 69	277	5,218.75
Nic Henning	72 67 72 66	277	5,218.75
Alan Michell	69 66 73 69	277	5,218.75
Ashley Roestoff	69 70 73 65	277	5,218.75
Dean van Staden	73 68 66 70	277	5,218.75
Steve van Vuuren	68 68 67 74	277	5,218.75
Mark Wiltshire	69 67 69 72	277	5,218.75
Andre Cruse	72 70 67 69	278	2,500
James Kingston	75 67 70 66	278	2,500
Hennie Otto	64 75 72 67	278	2,500
Gavin Levenson	68 69 69 73	279	2,141.66
Sean Pappas	72 71 66 70	279	2,141.66
Nico van Rensburg	72 71 69 67	279	2,141.66
John Bele	71 68 70 71	280	1,875
Ryan Dreyer	72 70 68 70	280	1,875
Alan McLean	72 71 66 71	280	1,875
Sammy Daniels	71 70 73 68	282	1,643.75
Darren Fichardt	70 70 72 70	282	1,643.75
Brenden Pappas	69 67 71 75	282	1,643.75
Schalk van der Merwe	72 68 72 70	282	1,643.75
Bradford Vaughan	72 68 71 72	283	1,487.50
Brett Liddle	76 66 69 73	284	1,337.50
Bobby Lincoln	71 73 66 74	284	1,337.50
Grant Muller	69 74 68 73	284	1,337.50
Hennie Swart	70 73 73 68	284	1,337.50
Roger Wessels	70 70 70 74	284	1,337.50
Warren Abery	73 68 72 72	285	1,143.75
Chris Davison	73 72 72 68	285	1,143.75
Michael du Toit	71 67 76 71	285	1,143.75
Bryan Prytz	71 65 74 75	285	1,143.75

Hassan II Trophy

Royal Golf Dar-es-Salam, Red Course, Rabat, Morocco
Par 36-37–73; 7,350 yards

November 13-16
purse, US$415,000

	SCORES	TOTAL	MONEY
Colin Montgomerie	73 68 67 69	277	US$100,000
Henrik Nystrom	68 71 71 70	280	40,000
David Howell	67 73 72 68	280	40,000
Donnie Hammond	72 69 71 69	281	24,000
Tom Lehman	73 71 69 69	282	18,500

	SCORES			TOTAL	MONEY
Ignacio Garrido	73 69 70 70			282	18,500
Mark Roe	72 67 69 75			283	14,000
David Sutherland	70 74 69 70			283	14,000
Roger Chapman	72 73 72 68			285	11,000
P.H. Horgan III	72 74 71 68			285	11,000
Tom Pernice	73 69 72 71			285	11,000
Ronan Rafferty	70 76 69 72			287	9,000
Younes El Hassani	74 71 72 73			290	8,000
Clinton Whitelaw	73 73 71 73			290	8,000
Carl Suneson	76 71 76 68			291	6,450
Alex Cejka	74 74 73 70			291	6,450
Malcolm Mackenzie	72 75 70 74			291	6,450
Dave Rummells	73 71 74 73			291	6,450
Tony Johnstone	75 67 77 74			293	5,700
Joe Daley	70 78 71 76			295	5,500
Anders Forsbrand	78 74 74 72			298	5,000
Mohamed Makroune	73 76 78 73			300	5,000
Marc Farry	74 71 77 79			301	5,000
Carlo Blanchard	80 72 76 78			306	5,000
Bobby Casper	74 76 78 78			306	5,000
Wayne Westner	77 72 73 85			307	5,000
Billy Casper	82 76 77 77			312	5,000
Mohammed Sayeh	81 72 82 77			312	5,000
Ismail Bendiab	81 76 78 81			316	5,000
Arnaud Langenaeken	86 86 78 80			330	5,000

Leopard Rock Classic

Leopard Rock Country Club, Mutare, Zimbabwe
Par 36-35–71; 6,678 yards

November 14-16
purse, R100,000

	SCORES			TOTAL	MONEY
Adilson da Silva	64 69 66			199	R23,550
Mark Murless	70 67 66			203	14,625
Sean Pappas	64 69 70			203	14,625
Andre Cruse	69 67 68			204	9,450
Marc Cayeux	69 71 67			207	5,400
Bradley Davison	65 71 71			207	5,400
James Kingston	70 69 68			207	5,400
Brenden Pappas	69 69 69			207	5,400
Warren Abery	67 68 73			208	3,400
Richard Fulford	69 69 70			208	3,400
Bradford Vaughan	68 70 70			208	3,400
Keith Horne	68 70 71			209	2,925
Chris Williams	76 66 67			209	2,925
Wayne de Haas	73 68 69			210	2,632.50
Brett Liddle	72 69 69			210	2,632.50
Lee Bromley	71 69 71			211	2,345
Sean Farrell	70 72 69			211	2,345
Hennie Walters	71 70 70			211	2,345
Darren Fichardt	70 72 70			212	2,160
Ryan Dreyer	71 73 69			213	1,935
Sean Ludgater	68 67 78			213	1,935
Alan Michell	72 69 72			213	1,935
Ashley Roestoff	75 68 70			213	1,935
Steve van Vuuren	73 70 70			213	1,935
Neil Homann	72 69 73			214	1,665

	SCORES			TOTAL	MONEY
Hendre Jacobs	71 71 72			214	1,665
Grant Muller	69 73 72			214	1,665
Paul Cuningham	71 70 74			215	1,466.25
Jannie le Grange	72 69 74			215	1,466.25
Mawonga Nomwa	69 74 72			215	1,466.25
Rudy Whitfield	70 73 72			215	1,466.25

Zambia Open

Lusaka Golf Club, Lusaka, Zambia
Par 37-36–73; 7,159 yards

November 20-23
purse, R250,000

	SCORES				TOTAL	MONEY
James Loughnane	71	65	66	71	273	R39,250
Colin Sorour	70	70	68	66	274	28,750
Hennie Otto	72	71	70	63	276	20,000
Warren Abery	71	66	73	67	277	13,000
Andre Cruse	72	69	69	67	277	13,000
Alan Michell	66	65	77	70	278	8,750
Wallie Coetsee	71	73	63	72	279	6,250
James Kingston	75	68	67	69	279	6,250
Brenden Pappas	70	69	70	70	279	6,250
Chris Williams	70	69	71	69	279	6,250
Ryan Dreyer	75	67	74	64	280	4,575
Michael Green	69	70	71	70	280	4,575
Brett Liddle	71	71	72	66	280	4,575
Ashley Roestoff	68	75	66	71	280	4,575
Sammy Daniels	71	70	72	68	281	3,925
Nasho Kamungeremu	68	72	68	73	281	3,925
Titch Moore	72	70	73	66	281	3,925
Andy Bean	71	71	71	69	282	3,312.50
Grant Muller	68	66	75	73	282	3,312.50
Len O'Kennedy	72	71	71	68	282	3,312.50
Steve van Vuuren	70	70	71	71	282	3,312.50
Tjaart van der Walt	70	66	71	75	282	3,312.50
Bradford Vaughan	72	68	69	73	282	3,312.50
Sean Farrell	72	72	69	70	283	2,800
Darren Fichardt	69	68	71	75	283	2,800
Lyall McNeill	72	69	71	71	283	2,800
Jan Basson	74	68	73	69	284	2,430
Michiel Bothma	71	73	68	72	284	2,430
Jannie le Grange	73	67	73	71	284	2,430
Sean Pappas	73	71	73	67	284	2,430
Adrian Wadey	70	71	73	70	284	2,430

Zimbabwe Open

Chapman Golf Club, Harare, Zimbabwe
Par 36-36–72; 7,064 yards

November 27-30
purse, R400,000

	SCORES				TOTAL	MONEY
Nick Price	68	67	66	68	269	R70,650
Mark McNulty	68	68	66	69	271	43,875
Brenden Pappas	70	67	68	66	271	43,875
Tjaart van der Walt	68	69	65	70	272	24,750

	SCORES				TOTAL	MONEY
Andre Cruse	70	68	67	68	273	18,900
James Kingston	65	67	75	67	274	15,840
Nasho Kamungeremu	68	74	65	68	275	13,590
Wallie Coetsee	69	68	68	72	277	11,790
Hennie Swart	72	67	64	75	278	10,440
Dean van Staden	71	68	71	69	279	8,550
Tony Johnstone	71	71	68	69	279	8,550
Mark Murless	66	70	73	70	279	8,550
Darren Fichardt	67	64	73	75	279	8,550
Warren Abery	69	71	71	69	280	6,570
Ryan Dreyer	73	71	68	68	280	6,570
Adilson da Silva	72	71	67	70	280	6,570
Steve van Vuuren	70	70	69	71	280	6,570
Kevin Stone	71	69	68	72	280	6,570
Roger Wessels	71	70	71	69	281	5,670
Michael Green	72	70	66	73	281	5,670
Bradford Vaughan	71	69	69	72	281	5,670
Philip van den Berg	72	72	70	68	282	5,130
Alan Michell	73	68	70	71	282	5,130
Neil Homann	71	69	70	72	282	5,130
Pelop Panagopoulos	67	69	75	72	283	4,747.50
Ian Hutchings	72	71	72	68	283	4,747.50
Mervyn Galant	71	68	70	75	284	4,477.50
Wimpie Botha	74	69	72	69	284	4,477.50
Lyall McNeill	69	71	74	71	285	4,140
Michael Scholz	71	71	69	74	285	4,140
Noel Maart	73	71	71	70	285	4,140

Nedbank Million Dollar Challenge

Gary Player Country Club, Sun City, South Africa
Par 36-36–72; 7,597 yards

December 4-7
purse, US$2,510,000

	SCORES				TOTAL	MONEY
Nick Price	71	68	68	68	275	$1,000,000
Davis Love III	68	67	74	67	276	225,000
Ernie Els	69	70	70	67	276	225,000
Phil Mickelson	67	68	69	73	277	175,000
Bernhard Langer	69	70	67	72	278	150,000
Justin Leonard	74	72	67	68	281	125,000
Tom Lehman	74	74	69	69	286	105,000
Colin Montgomerie	78	68	69	71	286	105,000
Jesper Parnevik	70	70	79	70	289	100,000
Nick Faldo	73	73	71	74	291	100,000
Mark O'Meara	76	71	69	75	291	100,000
Ian Woosnam	74	73	72	73	292	100,000

Mycom Mafunyane Trophy

Hans Merensky Country Club, Phalaborwa, South Africa
Par 36-36–72; 6,637 yards

December 11-14
purse, R200,000

	SCORES			TOTAL	MONEY
Kevin Stone	69	70	64	203	R23,550
Gavin Levenson	68	67	70	205	14,625
Brenden Pappas	68	66	71	205	14,625
Nasho Kamungeremu	69	68	69	206	8,250
Roger Wessels	69	68	69	206	8,250
Ryan Dreyer	73	65	69	207	4,556.25
Simon Hobday	71	68	68	207	4,556.25
Bobby Lincoln	72	69	66	207	4,556.25
Ashley Roestoff	68	72	67	207	4,556.25
Richard Fulford	71	68	69	208	3,262.50
Callie Swart	70	69	69	208	3,262.50
Andre Cruse	70	71	68	209	2,850
Pelop Panaglopoulos	71	71	67	209	2,850
Tjaart van der Walt	68	68	73	209	2,850
Marc Cayeux	72	68	70	210	2,307.50
Michael Green	69	69	72	210	2,307.50
Nic Henning	70	72	68	210	2,307.50
Hennie Otto	66	71	73	210	2,307.50
Gregory Reid	69	70	71	210	2,307.50
Bradford Vaughan	72	68	70	210	2,307.50
Wimpie Botha	69	73	69	211	1,897.50
Sammy Daniels	70	72	69	211	1,897.50
Justin Hobday	71	70	70	211	1,897.50
Paul Marks	72	69	70	211	1,897.50
Andrew Barnard	70	71	71	212	1,665
Desvonde Botes	68	71	73	212	1,665
Alan McLean	71	71	70	212	1,665
Warren Abery	71	70	72	213	1,443
Ian Hutchings	74	67	72	213	1,443
James Kingston	65	76	72	213	1,443
Grant Muller	75	66	72	213	1,443
Trevor Sidley	71	70	72	213	1,443

Senior Tours

MasterCard Championship

Hualalai Golf Club, Kailua-Kona, Hawaii
Par 36-36–72; 6,850 yards

January 17-19
purse, $1,000,000

	SCORES			TOTAL	MONEY
Hale Irwin	73	68	68	209	$186,000
Gil Morgan	72	69	70	211	110,000
Bob Charles	74	69	69	212	90,000
Jim Colbert	75	70	69	214	61,666.67
Jay Sigel	80	67	67	214	61,666.67
Al Geiberger	76	68	70	214	61,666.66
Vicente Fernandez	74	72	69	215	42,500
Graham Marsh	74	72	69	215	42,500
John Bland	77	68	71	216	29,600
Dave Eichelberger	73	70	73	216	29,600
Raymond Floyd	77	72	67	216	29,600
Jimmy Powell	74	72	70	216	29,600
Tom Weiskopf	75	70	71	216	29,600
Charles Coody	78	73	67	218	21,666.67
Jack Nicklaus	78	72	68	218	21,666.67
Jim Dent	77	69	72	218	21,666.66
Gibby Gilbert	76	76	67	219	19,000
Dave Stockton	73	74	72	219	19,000
Isao Aoki	75	71	74	220	17,500
Dale Douglass	78	72	71	221	16,500
Mike Hill	76	74	72	222	15,500
Bob Murphy	78	75	71	224	14,750
Lee Trevino	79	73	72	224	14,750
Walter Morgan	86	72	72	230	14,000

Royal Caribbean Classic

Crandon Park Golf Club, Key Biscayne, Florida
Par 35-36–71; 6,754 yards

January 31-February 2
purse, $850,000

	SCORES			TOTAL	MONEY
Gibby Gilbert	70	66	66	202	$127,500
David Graham	71	67	68	206	74,800
Isao Aoki	71	67	69	207	56,100
John Schroeder	71	69	67	207	56,100
Bob Charles	74	69	65	208	35,133.34
Frank Conner	72	67	69	208	35,133.33
Tony Jacklin	70	70	68	208	35,133.33
Vicente Fernandez	72	69	68	209	22,440
Jerry McGee	71	68	70	209	22,440
Jay Sigel	73	68	68	209	22,440
Bruce Summerhays	68	73	68	209	22,440
DeWitt Weaver	71	67	71	209	22,440
Dave Eichelberger	70	67	73	210	17,000
Jim Albus	75	68	68	211	14,875

	SCORES			TOTAL	MONEY
John Bland	74	68	69	211	14,875
Larry Gilbert	71	68	72	211	14,875
Graham Marsh	74	67	70	211	14,875
Jim Colbert	70	69	73	212	11,623.75
Jack Kiefer	68	71	73	212	11,623.75
Chi Chi Rodriguez	67	75	70	212	11,623.75
Rocky Thompson	72	69	71	212	11,623.75
Hubert Green	73	66	74	213	9,158.75
Simon Hobday	73	71	69	213	9,158.75
Calvin Peete	73	71	69	213	9,158.75
Gary Player	72	72	69	213	9,158.75
Jim Dent	73	73	68	214	7,395
Larry Laoretti	76	70	68	214	7,395
Will Sowles	71	69	74	214	7,395
Steven Veriato	74	70	70	214	7,395
Buddy Whitten	73	70	71	214	7,395
Mike Hill	72	69	74	215	5,992.50
Gil Morgan	76	71	68	215	5,992.50
Bob Panasik	71	72	72	215	5,992.50
Larry Ziegler	71	71	73	215	5,992.50
Al Geiberger	71	74	71	216	4,896
Harold Henning	71	72	73	216	4,896
Walter Morgan	72	73	71	216	4,896
Leonard Thompson	72	73	71	216	4,896
Kermit Zarley	69	74	73	216	4,896
J.C. Snead	68	74	75	217	4,335

LG Championship

Bay Colony Golf Club, Naples, Florida
Par 36-36—72; 6,811 yards

February 7-9
purse, $1,000,000

	SCORES			TOTAL	MONEY
Hale Irwin	70	66	65	201	$150,000
Bob Murphy	68	69	65	202	88,000
Vicente Fernandez	67	69	68	204	72,000
David Graham	67	71	67	205	54,000
Jack Kiefer	68	68	69	205	54,000
Dave Stockton	68	67	71	206	40,000
Jim Colbert	70	69	68	207	36,000
Mike Hill	70	70	68	208	30,000
Jerry McGee	68	69	71	208	30,000
Jim Albus	71	68	70	209	23,000
John Bland	68	72	69	209	23,000
Gibby Gilbert	73	69	67	209	23,000
J.C. Snead	68	73	68	209	23,000
Graham Marsh	69	71	70	210	18,000
Bruce Summerhays	69	68	73	210	18,000
Lee Trevino	74	69	67	210	18,000
Bud Allin	71	73	67	211	13,716.67
Isao Aoki	67	74	70	211	13,716.67
John Jacobs	72	70	69	211	13,716.67
Gil Morgan	72	70	69	211	13,716.67
Charles Coody	69	71	71	211	13,716.66
Chi Chi Rodriguez	67	71	73	211	13,716.66
Tom Knapp	72	73	67	212	10,750
Bobby Stroble	69	70	73	212	10,750

	SCORES			TOTAL	MONEY
Frank Conner	70	70	73	213	9,325
Dave Eichelberger	73	74	66	213	9,325
Rocky Thompson	67	72	74	213	9,325
Tom Wargo	71	74	68	213	9,325
Bob Charles	71	72	71	214	7,725
Dennis Coscina	72	71	71	214	7,725
Jim Dent	72	73	69	214	7,725
Larry Gilbert	69	74	71	214	7,725
Bob Dickson	72	73	70	215	6,166.67
Mike McCullough	74	71	70	215	6,166.67
Gary Player	72	72	71	215	6,166.67
Buddy Whitten	71	73	71	215	6,166.67
Terry Dill	68	75	72	215	6,166.66
Tom Shaw	71	69	75	215	6,166.66
Dale Douglass	70	75	71	216	5,000
Al Geiberger	66	77	73	216	5,000
John Morgan	74	71	71	216	5,000
Calvin Peete	71	73	72	216	5,000

GTE Classic

TPC of Tampa Bay at Cheval, Lutz, Florida
Par 35-36–71; 6,638 yards

February 14-16
purse, $900,000

	SCORES			TOTAL	MONEY
David Graham	71	68	65	204	$135,000
Bob Dickson	69	71	67	207	79,200
Raymond Floyd	72	66	70	208	54,000
Hubert Green	69	73	66	208	54,000
Bruce Summerhays	73	68	67	208	54,000
Isao Aoki	70	69	70	209	32,400
Bob Eastwood	71	65	73	209	32,400
Gil Morgan	68	69	72	209	32,400
Lee Trevino	70	71	69	210	24,300
Tom Wargo	70	68	72	210	24,300
John Bland	69	69	73	211	18,540
Frank Conner	71	70	70	211	18,540
Jim Dent	74	71	66	211	18,540
Graham Marsh	74	68	69	211	18,540
Tom Shaw	70	69	72	211	18,540
George Archer	71	71	70	212	14,400
Brian Barnes	71	68	73	212	14,400
Simon Hobday	71	69	72	212	14,400
Jim Colbert	69	73	71	213	11,542.50
Gene Littler	69	74	70	213	11,542.50
Jay Sigel	71	72	70	213	11,542.50
Dave Stockton	73	71	69	213	11,542.50
Vicente Fernandez	73	74	67	214	8,627.15
J.C. Snead	68	75	71	214	8,627.15
Bud Allin	72	71	71	214	8,627.14
Bill Hall	69	72	73	214	8,627.14
Jack Nicklaus	71	72	71	214	8,627.14
David Ojala	72	69	73	214	8,627.14
Larry Ziegler	72	71	71	214	8,627.14
Mike Hill	70	71	74	215	6,780
Jerry McGee	70	72	73	215	6,780
Bob Murphy	70	73	72	215	6,780

	SCORES			TOTAL	MONEY
Bruce Crampton	75	72	69	216	5,438.58
Miller Barber	74	72	70	216	5,438.57
Bob Charles	72	70	74	216	5,438.57
Larry Gilbert	73	73	70	216	5,438.57
David Oakley	72	73	71	216	5,438.57
John Schroeder	67	75	74	216	5,438.57
Leonard Thompson	70	74	72	216	5,438.57
Tony Jacklin	75	70	72	217	4,410
Calvin Peete	74	74	69	217	4,410
Rocky Thompson	73	73	71	217	4,410

American Express Invitational

TPC at Prestancia, Sarasota, Florida
Par 36-36—72; 6,763 yards

February 21-23
purse, $1,200,000

	SCORES			TOTAL	MONEY
Bud Allin	68	68	69	205	$180,000
Jim Colbert	68	71	67	206	105,600
Jim Albus	69	70	69	208	72,000
Mike Hill	73	66	69	208	72,000
Bruce Summerhays	71	70	67	208	72,000
Isao Aoki	70	69	70	209	43,200
Simon Hobday	68	73	68	209	43,200
Lee Trevino	70	70	69	209	43,200
Bob Charles	72	68	71	211	28,800
Frank Conner	71	71	69	211	28,800
Dale Douglass	70	70	71	211	28,800
Hubert Green	69	71	71	211	28,800
Graham Marsh	72	67	72	211	28,800
George Archer	71	70	71	212	21,600
John Morgan	73	71	68	212	21,600
Gary Player	75	70	67	212	21,600
Rick Acton	70	70	73	213	18,040
John Bland	71	72	70	213	18,040
Charles Coody	71	69	73	213	18,040
Butch Baird	68	72	74	214	13,095
Bruce Crampton	71	74	69	214	13,095
Jerry McGee	73	70	71	214	13,095
Gil Morgan	71	73	70	214	13,095
Chi Chi Rodriguez	70	74	70	214	13,095
John Schroeder	72	70	72	214	13,095
Bobby Stroble	74	68	72	214	13,095
Kermit Zarley	72	70	72	214	13,095
Bob Eastwood	73	66	76	215	9,960
Hale Irwin	71	73	71	215	9,960
Don January	75	71	69	215	9,960
Bob Dickson	69	77	70	216	7,920
Terry Dill	74	73	69	216	7,920
Larry Gilbert	78	68	70	216	7,920
John Jacobs	72	74	70	216	7,920
Jack Kiefer	71	78	67	216	7,920
Calvin Peete	76	69	71	216	7,920
Will Sowles	70	72	74	216	7,920
Brian Barnes	72	71	74	217	6,120
Deane Beman	73	69	75	217	6,120
Jim Dent	77	71	69	217	6,120

	SCORES	TOTAL	MONEY
David Graham	76 73 68	217	6,120
Larry Ziegler	71 74 72	217	6,120

Senior Slam

Palmilla Golf Club, San Jose del Cabo, Mexico
Par 36-36–72; 6,841 yards

February 24-25
purse, $500,000

	SCORES	TOTAL	MONEY
Hale Irwin	65 66	131	$250,000
Dave Stockton	72 68	140	125,000
Raymond Floyd	70 71	141	75,000
Jack Nicklaus	73 70	143	50,000

Toshiba Senior Classic

Newport Beach Country Club,
Newport Beach, California
Par 35-36–71; 6,598 yards

March 14-16
purse, $1,000,000

	SCORES	TOTAL	MONEY
Bob Murphy	65 70 72	207	$150,000
Jay Sigel	69 68 70	207	88,000
(Murphy defeated Sigel on ninth extra hole.)			
Isao Aoki	68 71 69	208	60,000
Bob Charles	68 68 72	208	60,000
Gil Morgan	69 69 70	208	60,000
Bruce Crampton	66 73 70	209	34,000
David Graham	65 69 75	209	34,000
Hubert Green	72 68 69	209	34,000
Lee Trevino	68 69 72	209	34,000
Don Bies	72 68 70	210	23,000
Jim Dent	70 72 68	210	23,000
Dick Hendrickson	74 68 68	210	23,000
Leonard Thompson	68 70 72	210	23,000
Bud Allin	69 72 70	211	16,516.67
Jack Kiefer	71 70 70	211	16,516.67
J.C. Snead	65 74 72	211	16,516.67
Dave Stockton	71 71 69	211	16,516.67
Chi Chi Rodriguez	73 67 71	211	16,516.66
Walter Zembriski	71 67 73	211	16,516.66
John Bland	70 72 70	212	11,171.43
Simon Hobday	69 74 69	212	11,171.43
Hale Irwin	72 70 70	212	11,171.43
Gary Player	69 72 71	212	11,171.43
Bruce Summerhays	71 72 69	212	11,171.43
Rocky Thompson	69 72 71	212	11,171.43
David Oakley	69 71 72	212	11,171.42
Jim Albus	71 71 71	213	8,116.67
Bob Eastwood	67 75 71	213	8,116.67
Walter Morgan	70 73 70	213	8,116.67
Buddy Whitten	70 73 70	213	8,116.67
Dick Acton	73 69 71	213	8,116.66
Brian Barnes	72 70 71	213	8,116.66
Dennis Coscina	74 73 67	214	6,042.86

	SCORES	TOTAL	MONEY
Jim Ferree	71 71 72	214	6,042.86
John Morgan	71 74 69	214	6,042.86
Tom Shaw	69 73 72	214	6,042.86
Bobby Stroble	72 74 68	214	6,042.86
Bob Dickson	74 68 72	214	6,042.85
Dale Douglass	70 70 74	214	6,042.85
Butch Baird	72 73 70	215	4,800
Charles Coody	71 73 71	215	4,800
Tony Jacklin	73 72 70	215	4,800
John Jacobs	71 71 73	215	4,800

Liberty Mutual Legends of Golf

PGA West, Palmer Course, La Quinta, California
Par 36-36–72; 6,723 yards

March 21-23
purse, $1,100,000

	SCORES	TOTAL	MONEY (Each)
John Bland/Graham Marsh	63 64 65	192	$100,000
Hubert Green/Gil Morgan	65 63 67	195	50,000
Tom Wargo/Calvin Peete	67 64 65	196	29,166.66
Tony Jacklin/David Graham	67 64 65	196	29,166.66
Gibby Gilbert/J.C. Snead	65 63 68	196	29,166.66
Mike Hill/Lee Trevino	69 63 65	197	17,000
Gene Littler/Don January	63 65 69	197	17,000
Bruce Crampton/Jim Dent	66 64 68	198	14,250
Dave Stockton/Al Geiberger	65 63 70	198	14,250
Bob Murphy/Jim Colbert	65 65 69	199	12,500
Miller Barber/Jim Ferree	64 69 67	200	12,000
Bob Wynn/Dave Hill	69 66 66	201	9,500
Homero Blancas/Tom Shaw	66 66 69	201	9,500
Dale Douglass/Charles Coody	71 64 66	201	9,500
Gary Player/Lee Elder	65 69 68	202	7,000
Don Bies/Bruce Devlin	67 68 67	202	7,000
Simon Hobday/George Archer	67 69 66	202	7,000
Chi Chi Rodriguez/Harold Henning	68 66 69	203	6,000
Bobby Nichols/Butch Baird	66 68 71	205	5,250
Roberto De Vicenzo/Larry Mowry	70 66 69	205	5,250
Bud Allin/Tommy Aaron	66 70 70	206	4,500
Billy Casper/Gay Brewer	70 68 69	207	4,000
Orville Moody/Jimmy Powell	69 67 72	208	3,500
Johnny Pott/Tommy Jacobs	71 69 70	210	3,000
Bob Toski/Mike Fetchick	70 74 73	217	3,000
Don Massengale/Frank Beard	73 71 74	218	3,000
Ken Still/Dow Finsterwald	71 78 74	223	3,000
Billy Maxwell/Bob Goalby	75 76 72	223	3,000
Lou Graham/Bob Lunn	75 75 75	225	2,500
Paul Harney/Mike Souchak	75 77 74	226	2,500
Lionel Hebert/Al Balding	75 77 75	227	2,500

Southwestern Bell Dominion

Dominion Country Club, San Antonio, Texas
Par 36-36–72; 6,814 yards

March 28-30
purse, $800,000

	SCORES			TOTAL	MONEY
David Graham	68	69	69	206	$120,000
John Jacobs	67	71	69	207	70,400
John Bland	70	71	67	208	52,800
Raymond Floyd	73	66	69	208	52,800
Chi Chi Rodriguez	69	67	73	209	35,200
Dave Stockton	69	66	74	209	35,200
Vicente Fernandez	69	70	72	211	27,200
Jay Sigel	70	71	70	211	27,200
Graham Marsh	67	72	73	212	22,400
Bud Allin	73	66	74	213	17,200
Larry Gilbert	68	70	75	213	17,200
Jack Kiefer	70	69	74	213	17,200
Mike McCullough	70	71	72	213	17,200
Walter Morgan	74	69	70	213	17,200
Leonard Thompson	69	70	74	213	17,200
Butch Baird	74	69	71	214	11,693.34
Tom Shaw	72	69	73	214	11,693.34
Bob Dickson	72	68	74	214	11,693.33
Terry Dill	71	68	75	214	11,693.33
John Morgan	71	69	74	214	11,693.33
J.C. Snead	72	68	74	214	11,693.33
John Schroeder	70	74	71	215	9,040
Rocky Thompson	68	75	72	215	9,040
Isao Aoki	75	68	73	216	8,000
Bruce Crampton	69	72	75	216	8,000
Jerry McGee	73	71	72	216	8,000
Dick Hendrickson	70	73	74	217	6,800
Jimmy Powell	71	73	73	217	6,800
Bruce Summerhays	78	71	68	217	6,800
Tom Wargo	71	72	74	217	6,800
Frank Conner	71	69	78	218	5,520
Bob Eastwood	69	73	76	218	5,520
Fritz Gambetta	74	73	71	218	5,520
Robert Landers	73	71	74	218	5,520
Bobby Stroble	71	75	72	218	5,520
Tommy Aaron	72	72	75	219	4,088.89
Rick Acton	72	74	73	219	4,088.89
Jim Albus	72	74	73	219	4,088.89
Miller Barber	74	72	73	219	4,088.89
Harold Henning	78	71	70	219	4,088.89
Tony Jacklin	73	71	75	219	4,088.89
Bob E. Smith	72	73	74	219	4,088.89
Steven Veriato	74	71	74	219	4,088.89
Lee Elder	72	71	76	219	4,088.88

The Tradition

Golf Club at Desert Mountain, Cochise Course,
Scottsdale, Arizona
Par 36-36–72; 6,891 yards

April 3-6
purse, $1,200,000

	SCORES				TOTAL	MONEY
Gil Morgan	66	66	67	67	266	$180,000
Isao Aoki	66	68	70	68	272	105,600
John Jacobs	66	68	70	70	274	86,400
Larry Gilbert	70	71	68	67	276	72,000
Jay Sigel	72	70	68	67	277	57,600
Jim Dent	69	68	70	72	279	45,600
Graham Marsh	68	69	69	73	279	45,600
George Archer	68	70	70	72	280	34,400
Terry Dill	67	67	71	75	280	34,400
Bob Eastwood	72	70	67	71	280	34,400
Jimmy Powell	69	74	71	67	281	27,600
Tom Wargo	71	69	70	71	281	27,600
Hale Irwin	72	71	69	70	282	23,400
J.C. Snead	66	71	73	72	282	23,400
Walter Morgan	69	70	75	69	283	21,000
Dave Stockton	71	74	67	71	283	21,000
Bob Charles	68	72	72	73	285	18,600
Mike McCullough	70	71	75	69	285	18,600
Raymond Floyd	69	75	69	73	286	16,380
Mike Hill	74	74	69	69	286	16,380
Charles Coody	74	69	73	71	287	14,000
Dave Eichelberger	72	72	72	71	287	14,000
David Graham	72	74	71	70	287	14,000
Brian Barnes	73	69	73	73	288	12,600
John Bland	72	69	72	76	289	10,700
Jerry McGee	73	74	72	70	289	10,700
Jack Nicklaus	67	74	75	73	289	10,700
Bob E. Smith	73	73	71	72	289	10,700
Bruce Summerhays	70	70	78	71	289	10,700
Lee Trevino	74	74	71	70	289	10,700
Miller Barber	71	77	71	71	290	8,640
Simon Hobday	66	74	74	76	290	8,640
John Schroeder	68	72	79	71	290	8,640
Butch Baird	71	74	72	74	291	7,380
Jack Kiefer	72	75	72	72	291	7,380
Tom Shaw	72	74	73	72	291	7,380
Dan Wood	77	73	73	68	291	7,380
Rick Acton	74	71	73	74	292	6,480
Kermit Zarley	75	68	76	73	292	6,480
Tony Jacklin	68	72	77	76	293	5,880
Larry Mowry	70	72	77	74	293	5,880
Buddy Whitten	79	77	69	68	293	5,880

PGA Seniors' Championship

PGA National Golf Club, Champion Course,
Palm Beach Gardens, Florida
Par 36-36–72; 6,869 yards

April 17-20
purse, $1,200,000

		SCORES			TOTAL	MONEY
Hale Irwin	69	65	72	68	274	$216,000
Dale Douglass	70	76	71	69	286	105,000
Jack Nicklaus	71	72	73	70	286	105,000
Gibby Gilbert	69	73	74	71	287	55,000
Jack Kiefer	72	72	73	70	287	55,000
John Morgan	71	72	72	72	287	55,000
John Bland	67	77	71	73	288	40,000
Bob Charles	71	70	75	72	288	40,000
Larry Gilbert	74	69	70	75	288	40,000
Walter Morgan	74	75	69	71	289	30,000
David Graham	75	75	70	70	290	19,625
Tommy Horton	72	76	69	73	290	19,625
John Schroeder	70	74	73	73	290	19,625
Kermit Zarley	76	75	72	67	290	19,625
Bud Allin	76	69	74	72	291	15,000
Seiichi Kanai	72	76	74	69	291	15,000
Gil Morgan	70	73	73	75	291	15,000
Dave Stockton	72	76	73	70	291	15,000
DeWitt Weaver	75	74	70	72	291	15,000
Isao Aoki	70	79	70	73	292	13,000
Graham Marsh	72	75	71	74	292	13,000
Gary Player	70	77	75	70	292	13,000
Brian Barnes	76	73	73	71	293	11,500
Jerry McGee	76	74	71	72	293	11,500
Bruce Summerhays	72	76	76	69	293	11,500
J.C. Snead	73	79	71	71	294	10,500
Jim Albus	72	78	74	71	295	9,000
Bob Murphy	73	72	75	75	295	9,000
Calvin Peete	75	72	73	75	295	9,000
Lee Trevino	75	73	72	75	295	9,000
Chi Chi Rodriguez	74	70	75	76	295	9,000
Gay Brewer	75	75	74	72	296	7,000
Jim Colbert	76	73	74	73	296	7,000
Jim Jewell	72	74	74	76	296	7,000
Hugh Baiocchi	77	71	75	74	297	5,000
Jose Maria Canizares	73	76	75	73	297	5,000
Vicente Fernandez	73	77	70	77	297	5,000
Raymond Floyd	75	73	79	70	297	5,000
Mike Hill	73	73	74	77	297	5,000
Steve Benson	74	78	72	74	298	3,200
Bob Dickson	73	77	72	76	298	3,200
Dana Quigley	75	71	75	77	298	3,200
Dick Rhyan	74	71	76	77	298	3,200
Jay Sigel	79	72	71	76	298	3,200
Bob E. Smith	73	76	75	74	298	3,200

Las Vegas Senior Classic

TPC at The Canyons, Las Vegas, Nevada
Par 36-35–71; 6,762 yards

April 25-27
purse, $1,000,000

	SCORES			TOTAL	MONEY
Hale Irwin	70	65	72	207	$150,000
Isao Aoki	66	71	71	208	89,000
Jim Colbert	72	66	73	211	66,900
John Jacobs	70	67	74	211	66,900
Raymond Floyd	70	69	74	213	44,800
Walter Morgan	76	69	68	213	44,800
Gibby Gilbert	73	74	67	214	34,800
Gil Morgan	66	73	75	214	34,800
J.C. Snead	71	71	73	215	28,000
Kermit Zarley	73	69	73	215	28,000
Charles Coody	75	71	70	216	19,875
Bruce Crampton	76	70	70	216	19,875
Bob Dickson	73	74	69	216	19,875
David Graham	71	72	73	216	19,875
Graham Marsh	71	68	77	216	19,875
Chi Chi Rodriguez	72	73	71	216	19,875
Lee Trevino	72	70	74	216	19,875
Walter Zembriski	72	72	72	216	19,875
Vicente Fernandez	72	73	72	217	14,000
Jack Kiefer	74	75	68	217	14,000
John Schroeder	73	69	75	217	14,000
Larry Gilbert	75	75	68	218	10,533.34
Simon Hobday	76	72	70	218	10,533.34
John Bland	70	72	76	218	10,533.33
Bob Charles	73	68	77	218	10,533.33
Jay Sigel	77	68	73	218	10,533.33
Dave Stockton	75	68	75	218	10,533.33
Tommy Aaron	74	74	71	219	7,625
Miller Barber	77	74	68	219	7,625
Brian Barnes	77	69	73	219	7,625
Terry Dill	75	71	73	219	7,625
Bob Murphy	72	71	76	219	7,625
Jimmy Powell	72	71	76	219	7,625
Bruce Summerhays	75	68	76	219	7,625
Tom Wargo	72	73	74	219	7,625
George Archer	73	74	73	220	5,412.50
Dale Douglass	74	77	69	220	5,412.50
Hubert Green	76	71	73	220	5,412.50
Tony Jacklin	74	75	71	220	5,412.50
Don January	72	76	72	220	5,412.50
Orville Moody	70	72	78	220	5,412.50
Bobby Stroble	74	71	75	220	5,412.50
Rocky Thompson	75	69	76	220	5,412.50

Bruno's Memorial Classic

Greystone Golf Club, Hoover, Alabama
Par 36-36–72; 6,967 yards

May 2-
purse, $1,150,00

	SCORES			TOTAL	MONEY
Jay Sigel	68	67	70	205	$172,500
Gil Morgan	67	72	69	208	101,200

	SCORES			TOTAL	MONEY
Isao Aoki	69	71	70	210	82,800
Bob Eastwood	70	68	73	211	69,000
Walter Morgan	70	73	69	212	55,200
Chi Chi Rodriguez	72	69	72	213	46,000
Harold Henning	73	69	72	214	39,100
Hale Irwin	71	68	75	214	39,100
Brian Barnes	75	67	73	215	31,050
J.C. Snead	72	68	75	215	31,050
Jim Colbert	70	72	74	216	21,706.25
Jim Dent	75	70	71	216	21,706.25
Larry Gilbert	72	70	74	216	21,706.25
Graham Marsh	72	70	74	216	21,706.25
John Schroeder	70	70	76	216	21,706.25
Dave Stockton	72	73	71	216	21,706.25
Bruce Summerhays	71	75	70	216	21,706.25
Steven Veriato	71	73	72	216	21,706.25
Dave Eichelberger	76	70	71	217	13,953.34
Jack Kiefer	73	72	72	217	13,953.34
Bob Charles	68	73	76	217	13,953.33
Terry Dill	73	71	73	217	13,953.33
Tony Jacklin	72	69	76	217	13,953.33
John Morgan	69	72	76	217	13,953.33
Al Geiberger	70	74	74	218	11,212.50
Bob Murphy	72	70	76	218	11,212.50
George Archer	79	68	72	219	9,775
Hubert Green	73	76	70	219	9,775
Jerry McGee	74	75	70	219	9,775
Tom Shaw	68	74	77	219	9,775
Miller Barber	73	70	77	220	8,280
Vicente Fernandez	72	74	74	220	8,280
DeWitt Weaver	71	75	74	220	8,280
Will Sowles	75	71	75	221	6,653.58
Tommy Aaron	72	72	77	221	6,653.57
John Bland	75	73	73	221	6,653.57
Gibby Gilbert	75	73	73	221	6,653.57
Mike Hill	73	75	73	221	6,653.57
John Jacobs	75	73	73	221	6,653.57
Rocky Thompson	72	73	76	221	6,653.57

Home Depot Invitational

TPC at Piper Glen, Charlotte, North Carolina
Par 36-36–72; 6,774 yards

May 9-11
purse, $900,000

	SCORES			TOTAL	MONEY
Jim Dent	68	70	70	208	$135,000
Larry Gilbert	68	70	70	208	72,000
Lee Trevino	70	71	67	208	72,000

(Dent defeated Gilbert on first and Trevino on second extra hole.)

Hugh Baiocchi	70	71	68	209	41,400
John Bland	70	69	70	209	41,400
Jay Sigel	73	68	68	209	41,400
Kermit Zarley	69	69	71	209	41,400
John Morgan	66	71	73	210	25,800
Walter Morgan	70	67	73	210	25,800
DeWitt Weaver	68	66	76	210	25,800
Mike Hill	70	72	69	211	20,700

	SCORES			TOTAL	MONEY
Don January	72	66	73	211	20,700
Bob Duval	69	72	71	212	18,000
David Oakley	71	72	70	213	16,200
Jimmy Powell	72	71	70	213	16,200
Will Sowles	68	73	72	213	16,200
Jose Maria Canizares	71	75	68	214	11,995.72
David Graham	73	72	69	214	11,995.72
Mike McCullough	74	72	68	214	11,995.72
Isao Aoki	71	70	73	214	11,995.71
Don Bies	68	74	72	214	11,995.71
Tony Jacklin	68	74	72	214	11,995.71
Jack Kiefer	70	72	72	214	11,995.71
Bruce Crampton	71	70	74	215	8,797.50
Gibby Gilbert	71	71	73	215	8,797.50
Dick Rhyan	69	73	73	215	8,797.50
Bob Wynn	70	72	73	215	8,797.50
Rick Acton	71	73	72	216	6,975
Bob Dickson	72	75	69	216	6,975
Vicente Fernandez	71	74	71	216	6,975
Simon Hobday	76	68	72	216	6,975
Greg Powers	71	70	75	216	6,975
John Schroeder	71	73	72	216	6,975
Jim Colbert	72	76	69	217	5,418
Jerry McGee	72	70	75	217	5,418
J.C. Snead	70	74	73	217	5,418
Leonard Thompson	73	75	69	217	5,418
Rocky Thompson	72	73	72	217	5,418
Charles Coody	70	74	74	218	4,500
Dale Douglass	72	77	69	218	4,500
Orville Moody	72	74	72	218	4,500
Bob E. Smith	70	73	75	218	4,500

Cadillac NFL Classic

Upper Montclair Country Club, Clifton, New Jersey
Par 36-36–72; 6,816 yards

May 16-18
purse, $950,000

	SCORES			TOTAL	MONEY
Bruce Crampton	76	67	67	210	$142,500
Hugh Baiocchi	71	70	69	210	83,600
(Crampton defeated Baiocchi on third extra hole.)					
Dave Stockton	74	67	71	212	68,400
Isao Aoki	77	68	68	213	51,300
Lee Trevino	75	72	66	213	51,300
Rik Massengale	72	68	74	214	29,450
Walter Morgan	73	71	70	214	29,450
J.C. Snead	75	69	70	214	29,450
Bruce Summerhays	74	70	70	214	29,450
Leonard Thompson	75	70	69	214	29,450
Kermit Zarley	76	70	68	214	29,450
Bunky Henry	77	71	67	215	20,900
George Archer	67	72	77	216	17,575
Bob Eastwood	75	71	70	216	17,575
Mike McCullough	71	76	69	216	17,575
Bob Murphy	75	70	71	216	17,575
Larry Gilbert	73	72	72	217	14,725
Jimmy Powell	73	74	70	217	14,725

	SCORES			TOTAL	MONEY
Dick Hendrickson	74	75	70	219	13,395
Rick Acton	77	73	70	220	10,877.50
Bob Charles	74	71	75	220	10,877.50
Terry Dill	73	70	77	220	10,877.50
Raymond Floyd	76	71	73	220	10,877.50
Hubert Green	80	69	71	220	10,877.50
Jerry McGee	78	70	72	220	10,877.50
Dale Douglass	79	69	73	221	8,265
Dave Eichelberger	74	72	75	221	8,265
Orville Moody	76	76	69	221	8,265
Will Sowles	73	75	73	221	8,265
Walter Zembriski	78	71	72	221	8,265
Butch Baird	79	74	69	222	6,697.50
Jim Colbert	75	74	73	222	6,697.50
Mike Hill	78	72	72	222	6,697.50
David Ojala	79	74	69	222	6,697.50
Bob Dickson	75	75	73	223	5,066.67
Lee Elder	76	74	73	223	5,066.67
David Oakley	75	76	72	223	5,066.67
Calvin Peete	80	71	72	223	5,066.67
Bob E. Smith	78	73	72	223	5,066.67
Dan Wood	75	77	71	223	5,066.67
Deane Beman	73	76	74	223	5,066.66
DeWitt Weaver	78	70	75	223	5,066.66
Buddy Whitten	77	71	75	223	5,066.66

Bell Atlantic Classic

Chester Valley Golf Club, Malvern, Pennsylvania
Par 35-35–70; 6,608 yards
(Third round cancelled — rain.)

May 23-25
purse, $1,000,000

	SCORES		TOTAL	MONEY
Bob Eastwood	66	69	135	$150,000
John Bland	67	69	136	80,000
Bob E. Smith	69	67	136	80,000
Dana Quigley	69	69	138	60,000
Bob Dickson	67	72	139	48,000
Brian Barnes	71	70	141	36,000
Raymond Floyd	68	73	141	36,000
Mike McCullough	71	70	141	36,000
Hugh Baiocchi	71	71	142	24,000
Jack Kiefer	69	73	142	24,000
Walter Morgan	70	72	142	24,000
Calvin Peete	71	71	142	24,000
Jimmy Powell	73	69	142	24,000
Tommy Aaron	75	68	143	15,144.45
Ed Hayes	71	72	143	15,144.45
Larry Laoretti	75	68	143	15,144.45
Buddy Whitten	72	71	143	15,144.45
Bud Allin	71	72	143	15,144.44
Jim Colbert	71	72	143	15,144.44
Jerry McGee	71	72	143	15,144.44
Bob Murphy	71	72	143	15,144.44
Roy Vucinich	69	74	143	15,144.44
Bobby Gilbert	71	73	144	10,500
Chi Chi Rodriguez	72	72	144	10,500

	SCORES	TOTAL	MONEY
Jay Sigel	73 71	144	10,500
Dennis Coscina	71 74	145	8,137.50
Bruce Devlin	73 72	145	8,137.50
Dale Douglass	72 73	145	8,137.50
Dave Hill	76 69	145	8,137.50
Gil Morgan	75 70	145	8,137.50
John Schroeder	73 72	145	8,137.50
Austin Straub	75 70	145	8,137.50
Bobby Stroble	71 74	145	8,137.50
Charles Coody	74 72	146	5,354.55
Terry Dill	76 70	146	5,354.55
Rives McBee	74 72	146	5,354.55
Tony Perla	76 70	146	5,354.55
Dave Stockton	74 72	146	5,354.55
Tom Wargo	75 71	146	5,354.55
Billy Casper	74 72	146	5,354.54
Bob Charles	72 74	146	5,354.54
Bruce Crampton	73 73	146	5,354.54
John Morgan	73 73	146	5,354.54
Leonard Thompson	73 73	146	5,354.54

Ameritech Senior Open

Kemper Lakes Golf Course, Long Grove, Illinois
Par 36-36–72; 6,830 yards

May 30-June 1
purse, $1,200,000

	SCORES	TOTAL	MONEY
Gil Morgan	67 69 74	210	$180,000
Hale Irwin	71 66 74	211	105,600
Bob Eastwood	70 71 71	212	86,400
Mike Hill	72 71 71	214	72,000
David Graham	71 70 74	215	52,800
J.C. Snead	73 70 72	215	52,800
Hugh Baiocchi	68 73 75	216	36,600
John Bland	71 71 74	216	36,600
Dave Stockton	71 76 69	216	36,600
DeWitt Weaver	72 70 74	216	36,600
Bob Charles	72 73 72	217	24,720
Raymond Floyd	71 74 72	217	24,720
Jerry McGee	71 68 78	217	24,720
Jimmy Powell	73 73 71	217	24,720
Jay Sigel	70 72 75	217	24,720
Walter Morgan	72 70 76	218	19,800
Tom Shaw	70 70 78	218	19,800
Miller Barber	74 73 72	219	16,920
Bob Dickson	73 67 79	219	16,920
Graham Marsh	72 72 75	219	16,920
Gary Player	73 72 75	220	14,400
Chi Chi Rodriguez	74 75 71	220	14,400
Dennis Coscina	71 72 78	221	12,900
Terry Dill	71 75 75	221	12,900
Bud Allin	74 75 73	222	11,440
John Jacobs	70 76 76	222	11,440
Mike McCullough	73 71 78	222	11,440
George Archer	71 78 74	223	9,504
Brian Barnes	70 73 80	223	9,504
Dick Hendrickson	72 72 79	223	9,504
Dana Quigley	74 73 76	223	9,504

	SCORES	TOTAL	MONEY
Dan Wood	75 74 74	223	9,504
Tony Jacklin	70 77 77	224	7,920
Don January	74 77 73	224	7,920
Tom Wargo	71 75 78	224	7,920
Don Bies	75 73 77	225	6,624
Gay Brewer	75 75 75	225	6,624
Frank Conner	77 76 72	225	6,624
Bruce Crampton	75 74 76	225	6,624
Jack Kiefer	71 72 82	225	6,624

BellSouth Senior Classic

Springhouse Golf Club, Nashville, Tennessee
Par 36-36–72; 6,783 yards

June 6-8
purse, $1,300,000

	SCORES	TOTAL	MONEY
Gil Morgan	69 66 67	202	$195,000
John Bland	69 67 68	204	114,400
Larry Gilbert	70 68 68	206	93,600
Hale Irwin	71 68 68	207	70,200
Tom Wargo	69 70 68	207	70,200
Brian Barnes	71 66 71	208	46,800
Graham Marsh	68 74 66	208	46,800
Jay Sigel	71 71 66	208	46,800
Isao Aoki	70 69 71	210	30,116.67
Vicente Fernandez	71 71 68	210	30,116.67
David Graham	67 73 70	210	30,116.67
Bruce Summerhays	70 71 69	210	30,116.67
John Jacobs	68 70 72	210	30,116.66
Dave Stockton	70 67 73	210	30,116.66
Mike Hill	71 71 69	211	20,215
Jimmy Powell	71 67 73	211	20,215
Chi Chi Rodriguez	73 68 70	211	20,215
J.C. Snead	67 72 72	211	20,215
Rocky Thompson	70 72 69	211	20,215
Lee Trevino	69 71 71	211	20,215
George Archer	69 74 69	212	14,430
Frank Conner	70 70 72	212	14,430
Jerry McGee	71 71 70	212	14,430
Walter Morgan	64 77 71	212	14,430
Bob Wynn	70 72 70	212	14,430
Walter Zembriski	74 69 70	213	10,808.58
Jim Dent	70 70 73	213	10,808.57
Dave Eichelberger	70 71 72	213	10,808.57
John Morgan	73 71 69	213	10,808.57
Calvin Peete	69 73 71	213	10,808.57
Bob E. Smith	70 70 73	213	10,808.57
DeWitt Weaver	70 73 70	213	10,808.57
Larry Laoretti	74 71 69	214	8,580
Larry Mowry	70 72 72	214	8,580
David Oakley	70 73 71	214	8,580
Hubert Green	68 75 72	215	7,041.67
Don January	70 73 72	215	7,041.67
Leonard Thompson	71 74 70	215	7,041.67
Buddy Whitten	72 71 72	215	7,041.67
Terry Dill	74 72 69	215	7,041.66
Will Sowles	74 72 69	215	7,041.66

du Maurier Champions

St. George's Golf & Country Club, Etobicoke, Ontario
Par 35-36–71; 6,797 yards

June 12-15
purse, $1,100,000

	SCORES				TOTAL	MONEY
Jack Kiefer	65	67	69	68	269	$165,000
Jim Colbert	65	65	70	71	271	96,800
Graham Marsh	65	66	70	72	273	79,200
John Bland	68	69	69	68	274	66,000
Jerry McGee	68	69	68	70	275	48,400
Walter Morgan	68	70	72	65	275	48,400
Frank Conner	73	69	67	68	277	33,550
Dave Eichelberger	72	67	68	70	277	33,550
Gary Player	70	68	69	70	277	33,550
Tom Wargo	69	70	69	69	277	33,550
Vicente Fernandez	68	68	70	72	278	25,300
Bob Wynn	69	70	72	67	278	25,300
Brian Barnes	70	70	69	70	279	20,350
Larry Gilbert	71	67	70	71	279	20,350
David Oakley	70	71	68	70	279	20,350
Leonard Thompson	72	67	67	73	279	20,350
Bob Eastwood	67	70	74	70	281	17,050
David Graham	69	71	70	71	281	17,050
George Archer	71	71	71	69	282	14,107.50
Terry Dill	70	74	68	70	282	14,107.50
John Jacobs	72	71	69	70	282	14,107.50
J.C. Snead	71	66	72	73	282	14,107.50
Bob Charles	71	71	71	70	283	11,550
Bruce Crampton	70	72	68	73	283	11,550
Dick Hendrickson	68	72	70	73	283	11,550
Bob Duval	71	72	70	71	284	9,570
David Ojala	69	71	73	71	284	9,570
Calvin Peete	66	78	70	70	284	9,570
Lee Trevino	74	66	74	70	284	9,570
DeWitt Weaver	72	71	71	70	284	9,570
Deane Beman	69	71	72	73	285	8,085
Mike McCullough	71	72	74	68	285	8,085
Homero Blancas	73	73	68	72	286	7,260
John Irwin	74	71	70	71	286	7,260
John Morgan	75	69	72	70	286	7,260
Bob Betley	72	75	71	69	287	5,845.72
Dale Douglass	71	73	72	71	287	5,845.72
Tom Shaw	74	74	68	71	287	5,845.72
Rick Acton	69	71	71	76	287	5,845.71
Bob Dickson	72	70	73	72	287	5,845.71
Larry Laoretti	70	76	68	73	287	5,845.71
Ben Smith	72	75	69	71	287	5,845.71

Nationwide Championship

Golf Club of Georgia, Lakeside Course,
Alpharetta, Georgia
Par 36-36–72; 6,777 yards

June 20-2?
purse, $1,300,000

	SCORES			TOTAL	MONEY
Graham Marsh	67	68	70	205	$195,000
Hale Irwin	68	69	69	206	114,400

	SCORES	TOTAL	MONEY
David Graham	68 72 69	209	93,600
Bob Charles	66 72 72	210	78,000
George Archer	72 70 69	211	50,700
Butch Baird	72 72 67	211	50,700
Bob Dickson	71 70 70	211	50,700
Bob Murphy	64 73 74	211	50,700
Isao Aoki	70 72 70	212	32,500
Raymond Floyd	73 70 69	212	32,500
Larry Gilbert	69 71 72	212	32,500
Jay Sigel	69 70 73	212	32,500
Dale Douglass	72 73 68	213	24,050
Mike Hill	74 68 71	213	24,050
Simon Hobday	70 70 73	213	24,050
Jerry McGee	71 70 72	213	24,050
Gibby Gilbert	71 73 70	214	19,543.34
Jim Colbert	73 69 72	214	19,543.33
Tom Shaw	73 71 70	214	19,543.33
Dave Eichelberger	71 72 72	215	17,160
Jack Kiefer	76 70 70	216	14,083.34
Bobby Stroble	72 73 71	216	14,083.34
John Bland	70 73 73	216	14,083.33
Vicente Fernandez	75 68 73	216	14,083.33
Hubert Green	75 70 71	216	14,083.33
J.C. Snead	73 71 72	216	14,083.33
Tommy Aaron	75 74 68	217	9,685
Rick Acton	70 72 75	217	9,685
Frank Conner	77 70 70	217	9,685
Terry Dill	71 75 71	217	9,685
Lee Elder	70 76 71	217	9,685
Larry Laoretti	77 67 73	217	9,685
Orville Moody	72 76 69	217	9,685
John Morgan	74 75 68	217	9,685
Chi Chi Rodriguez	73 74 70	217	9,685
John Schroeder	72 75 70	217	9,685
Don Bies	71 72 75	218	6,500
Jose Maria Canizares	76 70 72	218	6,500
Jim Dent	73 75 70	218	6,500
Bob Irving	71 73 74	218	6,500
Buddy Whitten	76 73 69	218	6,500
Kermit Zarley	77 71 70	218	6,500
Walter Zembriski	73 72 73	218	6,500
Larry Ziegler	72 75 71	218	6,500

U.S. Senior Open

Olympia Fields Country Club, Olympia Fields, Illinois
Par 35-35–70; 6,841 yards

June 26-29
purse, $1,300,000

	SCORES	TOTAL	MONEY
Graham Marsh	72 67 67 74	280	$232,500
John Bland	69 70 69 73	281	137,500
Gil Morgan	69 74 71 68	282	73,320.50
Tom Wargo	69 70 73 70	282	73,320.50
Hugh Baiocchi	73 71 69 71	284	39,938
Dave Eichelberger	70 69 70 75	284	39,938
Hale Irwin	73 74 70 67	284	39,938
Jack Nicklaus	73 72 70 69	284	39,938

	SCORES				TOTAL	MONEY
Leonard Thompson	70	72	70	72	284	39,938
Jose Maria Canizares	73	74	66	72	285	29,412.50
Jay Sigel	74	68	74	69	285	29,412.50
Hubert Green	72	71	68	75	286	25,118
Dana Quigley	71	71	71	73	286	25,118
Bruce Summerhays	71	75	69	71	286	25,118
Frank Conner	71	74	73	69	287	21,155.33
Larry Laoretti	71	73	72	71	287	21,155.33
Lee Trevino	75	69	73	70	287	21,155.33
Bud Allin	74	73	70	71	288	17,876.33
Bob Charles	73	68	72	75	288	17,876.33
Jimmy Powell	72	68	78	70	288	17,876.33
Gibby Gilbert	73	73	74	69	289	13,349
Walter Morgan	75	75	71	68	289	13,349
Gary Player	76	72	71	70	289	13,349
Chi Chi Rodriguez	71	72	74	72	289	13,349
Tom Shaw	72	76	72	69	289	13,349
Rocky Thompson	74	72	72	71	289	13,349
Kermit Zarley	69	69	80	71	289	13,349
Bob Duval	76	69	70	75	290	9,512.67
John Morgan	73	69	73	75	290	9,512.67
Bobby Stroble	73	73	69	75	290	9,512.67
Bruce Crampton	74	71	76	70	291	8,752
Butch Baird	72	73	73	74	292	7,655.75
Hank Cooper	74	71	71	76	292	7,655.75
Vicente Fernandez	72	70	74	76	292	7,655.75
Bob Murphy	77	73	70	72	292	7,655.75
Calvin Peete	76	70	70	76	292	7,655.75
J.C. Snead	75	73	72	72	292	7,655.75
Steven Veriato	69	72	73	78	292	7,655.75
Dan Wood	73	70	79	70	292	7,655.75
David Graham	74	74	74	71	293	6,507
John Jacobs	71	76	72	74	293	6,507

Kroger Senior Classic

Golf Center at Kings Island, Grizzly Course, Mason, Ohio
Par 36-35–71; 6,628 yards

July 4-6
purse, $1,000,000

	SCORES			TOTAL	MONEY
Jay Sigel	66	63	66	195	$150,000
Isao Aoki	68	67	67	202	88,000
Larry Gilbert	68	66	70	204	60,000
John Jacobs	68	71	65	204	60,000
David Ojala	65	68	71	204	60,000
Mike McCullough	69	70	66	205	32,400
Jimmy Powell	66	68	71	205	32,400
John Schroeder	67	68	70	205	32,400
Bruce Summerhays	72	65	68	205	32,400
Leonard Thompson	68	66	71	205	32,400
Bud Allin	69	68	69	206	23,000
Bob Eastwood	65	72	69	206	23,000
Frank Conner	69	65	73	207	18,000
Terry Dill	69	72	66	207	18,000
Dave Eichelberger	70	69	68	207	18,000
Simon Hobday	69	72	66	207	18,000
Bob Murphy	69	71	67	207	18,000

	SCORES	TOTAL	MONEY
Hubert Green	67 69 72	208	14,100
Jerry McGee	71 67 70	208	14,100
Kermit Zarley	70 68 70	208	14,100
Gibby Gilbert	68 68 73	209	11,100
Graham Marsh	69 70 70	209	11,100
John Morgan	71 73 65	209	11,100
Larry Mowry	72 67 70	209	11,100
J.C. Snead	68 69 72	209	11,100
Brian Barnes	70 70 70	210	8,500
Dale Douglass	68 73 69	210	8,500
Dick Hendrickson	71 68 71	210	8,500
Calvin Peete	67 71 72	210	8,500
Bob E. Smith	71 70 69	210	8,500
Tom Wargo	70 69 71	210	8,500
Bob Charles	70 73 68	211	6,450
Jim Dent	68 69 74	211	6,450
Bob Dickson	70 70 71	211	6,450
Al Geiberger	67 71 73	211	6,450
Larry Laoretti	69 73 69	211	6,450
Will Sowles	70 70 71	211	6,450
Tommy Aaron	70 71 71	212	4,800
Dennis Coscina	69 70 73	212	4,800
Walter Hall	71 69 72	212	4,800
Bunky Henry	71 69 72	212	4,800
Jack Kiefer	73 68 71	212	4,800
Bobby Nichols	71 71 70	212	4,800
David Oakley	72 73 67	212	4,800
Rocky Thompson	74 67 71	212	4,800

Ford Senior Players Championship

TPC of Michigan, Dearborn, Michigan
Par 36-36–72; 6,876 yards

July 10-13
purse, $1,800,000

	SCORES	TOTAL	MONEY
Larry Gilbert	67 68 72 67	274	$270,000
Isao Aoki	70 68 71 68	277	120,600
Bob Dickson	72 66 69 70	277	120,600
Jack Kiefer	72 70 67 68	277	120,600
Dave Stockton	68 70 69 70	277	120,600
John Jacobs	71 66 72 70	279	68,400
Gil Morgan	70 71 69 69	279	68,400
Graham Marsh	70 69 69 72	280	54,000
Jack Nicklaus	69 67 72 72	280	54,000
Hugh Baiocchi	74 68 67 72	281	39,960
John Bland	68 70 69 74	281	39,960
David Graham	76 70 68 67	281	39,960
Hubert Green	71 70 70 70	281	39,960
Jay Sigel	70 69 71 71	281	39,960
Vicente Fernandez	69 70 73 70	282	32,400
Bob Charles	70 69 69 75	283	28,800
Larry Laoretti	73 72 68 70	283	28,800
Steven Veriato	72 67 69 75	283	28,800
George Archer	74 70 66 74	284	21,291.43
Raymond Floyd	70 68 73 73	284	21,291.43
Hale Irwin	73 70 68 73	284	21,291.43
Walter Morgan	74 71 72 67	284	21,291.43

	SCORES	TOTAL	MONEY
John Schroeder	69 69 78 68	284	21,291.43
Lee Trevino	75 69 67 73	284	21,291.43
Frank Conner	72 71 66 75	284	21,291.42
Gibby Gilbert	70 69 70 77	286	16,380
Jimmy Powell	71 67 79 69	286	16,380
Dana Quigley	67 75 70 74	286	16,380
Bruce Crampton	74 69 71 73	287	13,608
Jim Dent	71 69 71 76	287	13,608
Bob E. Smith	72 74 72 69	287	13,608
Bobby Stroble	75 69 69 74	287	13,608
Leonard Thompson	71 72 74 70	287	13,608
Terry Dill	72 69 74 73	288	10,836
Dale Douglass	73 71 72 72	288	10,836
Chi Chi Rodriguez	74 74 69 71	288	10,836
Bruce Summerhays	74 69 72 73	288	10,836
Kermit Zarley	75 70 68 75	288	10,836
Al Geiberger	72 73 77 67	289	9,180
Tom Wargo	77 70 72 70	289	9,180
Walter Zembriski	72 71 74 72	289	9,180

Burnet Senior Classic

Bunker Hills Golf Club, Coon Rapids, Minnesota
Par 36-36–72; 6,909 yards

July 18-20
purse, $1,350,000

	SCORES	TOTAL	MONEY
Hale Irwin	65 68 66	199	$202,500
Lee Trevino	66 68 67	201	118,800
Larry Gilbert	65 71 68	204	97,200
John Bland	68 67 70	205	54,900
Bob Eastwood	68 72 65	205	54,900
Graham Marsh	66 71 68	205	54,900
Walter Morgan	68 71 66	205	54,900
Bob Murphy	66 69 70	205	54,900
Jay Sigel	67 70 68	205	54,900
Gil Morgan	68 71 67	206	35,100
Jim Dent	72 66 69	207	29,700
Jerry McGee	71 69 67	207	29,700
Jimmy Powell	64 74 69	207	29,700
Jim Albus	73 66 69	208	22,950
Terry Dill	69 70 69	208	22,950
Vicente Fernandez	71 69 68	208	22,950
Larry Laoretti	74 68 66	208	22,950
Bobby Stroble	67 73 68	208	22,950
Charles Coody	69 71 69	209	16,821
Raymond Floyd	68 69 72	209	16,821
Al Geiberger	71 73 65	209	16,821
David Graham	70 69 70	209	16,821
Mike McCullough	69 69 71	209	16,821
Dave Eichelberger	71 69 70	210	13,500
Tony Jacklin	73 69 68	210	13,500
DeWitt Weaver	72 66 72	210	13,500
Bob Dickson	70 71 70	211	10,957.50
Hubert Green	71 69 71	211	10,957.50
Harold Henning	71 71 69	211	10,957.50
Dave Stockton	69 69 73	211	10,957.50
Leonard Thompson	71 69 71	211	10,957.50

	SCORES			TOTAL	MONEY
Tom Wargo	70	72	69	211	10,957.50
Bud Allin	70	71	71	212	8,707.50
Ray Arinno	69	73	70	212	8,707.50
Frank Conner	70	74	68	212	8,707.50
Bob Wynn	71	68	73	212	8,707.50
George Archer	67	73	73	213	7,020
Miller Barber	73	71	69	213	7,020
Dennis Coscina	68	73	72	213	7,020
Bruce Crampton	68	72	73	213	7,020
Don January	72	73	68	213	7,020
Chi Chi Rodriguez	70	71	72	213	7,020

Franklin Quest Championship

Park Meadows Golf Club, Park City, Utah
Par 36-36–72; 7,026 yards

July 25-27
purse, $1,000,000

	SCORES			TOTAL	MONEY
Dave Stockton	69	64	68	201	$150,000
Kermit Zarley	67	69	67	203	88,000
Hugh Baiocchi	67	71	66	204	66,000
Larry Ziegler	70	70	64	204	66,000
Graham Marsh	71	68	66	205	44,000
Tom Shaw	67	69	69	205	44,000
DeWitt Weaver	68	70	68	206	36,000
Dale Douglass	70	70	67	207	30,000
Vicente Fernandez	68	70	69	207	30,000
Jimmy Adams	68	69	71	208	23,000
Bob Duval	70	68	70	208	23,000
Walter Morgan	71	67	70	208	23,000
Bob E. Smith	72	69	67	208	23,000
Al Geiberger	74	67	68	209	17,500
Simon Hobday	72	68	69	209	17,500
Mike McCullough	67	69	73	209	17,500
Jerry McGee	69	68	72	209	17,500
Don Bies	69	70	71	210	12,225
Frank Conner	67	69	74	210	12,225
Jack Kiefer	70	70	70	210	12,225
Larry Laoretti	68	73	69	210	12,225
Leonard Thompson	74	70	66	210	12,225
Lee Trevino	71	72	67	210	12,225
Steve Veriato	71	72	67	210	12,225
Dan Wood	69	75	66	210	12,225
Don January	69	69	73	211	9,500
Miller Barber	71	73	68	212	7,942.86
Bob Betley	70	72	70	212	7,942.86
Tony Jacklin	70	73	69	212	7,942.86
Bruce Summerhays	69	73	70	212	7,942.86
Walter Zembriski	74	71	67	212	7,942.86
Bud Allin	70	66	76	212	7,942.85
Dennis Coscina	73	69	70	212	7,942.85
John Paul Cain	69	76	68	213	6,020
David Lundstrom	68	70	75	213	6,020
John Schroeder	72	71	70	213	6,020
Jay Sigel	68	69	76	213	6,020
Bobby Stroble	67	69	77	213	6,020
Rick Acton	68	71	75	214	4,900

	SCORES			TOTAL	MONEY
Bruce Crampton	69	73	72	214	4,900
Bob Dickson	76	73	65	214	4,900
Will Sowles	74	66	74	214	4,900
Austin Straub	70	75	69	214	4,900

BankBoston Classic

Nashawtuc Country Club, Concord, Massachusetts
Par 36-36–72; 6,787 yards

August 1-3
purse, $1,000,000

	SCORES			TOTAL	MONEY
Hale Irwin	69	67	67	203	$150,000
Jerry McGee	68	70	67	205	80,000
Bob Wynn	71	68	66	205	80,000
Tom Wargo	69	68	69	206	60,000
Bob Betley	70	66	71	207	48,000
Hubert Green	70	73	65	208	36,000
Bob Murphy	71	71	66	208	36,000
Dana Quigley	68	72	68	208	36,000
John Bland	72	69	68	209	24,000
Frank Conner	68	73	68	209	24,000
John Jacobs	68	71	70	209	24,000
Tom Shaw	71	71	67	209	24,000
Dan Wood	69	70	70	209	24,000
Walter Morgan	69	71	70	210	17,000
Larry Mowry	69	73	68	210	17,000
Leonard Thompson	70	73	67	210	17,000
Lee Trevino	70	71	69	210	17,000
Kermit Zarley	66	75	69	210	17,000
DeWitt Weaver	72	69	70	211	13,650
Buddy Whitten	73	68	70	211	13,650
Bob Charles	74	71	67	212	10,350
Bob Dickson	76	67	69	212	10,350
Bob Duval	71	68	73	212	10,350
David Graham	70	70	72	212	10,350
Simon Hobday	71	73	68	212	10,350
Tony Jacklin	69	70	73	212	10,350
Bob E. Smith	71	71	70	212	10,350
J.C. Snead	71	69	72	212	10,350
Jim Albus	72	68	73	213	7,900
Hugh Baiocchi	70	70	73	213	7,900
Vicente Fernandez	72	69	72	213	7,900
Tommy Aaron	73	70	71	214	6,750
Butch Baird	74	70	70	214	6,750
Miller Barber	73	72	69	214	6,750
Dave Eichelberger	73	71	70	214	6,750
Ted Hayes	70	73	72	215	5,850
Mike Hill	72	72	71	215	5,850
Rick Acton	68	78	70	216	4,600
Gay Brewer	68	72	76	216	4,600
Bruce Crampton	70	73	73	216	4,600
Terry Dill	73	71	72	216	4,600
Jack Kiefer	76	70	70	216	4,600
Mike McCullough	73	72	71	216	4,600
David Ojala	72	69	75	216	4,600
Jay Sigel	69	72	75	216	4,600
Bobby Stroble	71	71	74	216	4,600
Walter Zembriski	74	70	72	216	4,600

Northville Long Island Classic

Meadow Brook Club, Jericho, New York
Par 36-36–72; 6,842 yards

August 8-10
purse, $1,000,000

	SCORES			TOTAL	MONEY
Dana Quigley	67	67	70	204	$150,000
Jay Sigel	68	70	66	204	88,000
(Quigley defeated Sigel on third extra hole.)					
Jose Maria Canizares	64	70	71	205	60,000
Raymond Floyd	70	69	66	205	60,000
Hubert Green	65	70	70	205	60,000
Bob Duval	67	70	69	206	38,000
Leonard Thompson	68	69	69	206	38,000
Mike Hill	67	74	66	207	28,666.67
John Schroeder	71	68	68	207	28,666.67
Lee Trevino	66	72	69	207	28,666.66
Brian Barnes	69	70	69	208	21,250
Bob Charles	70	72	66	208	21,250
Walter Hall	66	68	74	208	21,250
Walter Morgan	68	72	68	208	21,250
Hugh Baiocchi	71	68	70	209	17,000
John Bland	73	71	65	209	17,000
Vicente Fernandez	68	70	71	209	17,000
Frank Conner	72	68	70	210	14,550
Dick Hendrickson	70	72	68	210	14,550
Charles Coody	70	73	68	211	11,171.43
Terry Dill	72	71	68	211	11,171.43
John Jacobs	67	73	71	211	11,171.43
Jack Kiefer	69	71	71	211	11,171.43
Bob E. Smith	70	70	71	211	11,171.43
Bobby Stroble	68	71	72	211	11,171.43
Jim Dent	72	68	71	211	11,171.42
Butch Baird	69	72	71	212	8,300
Al Geiberger	70	67	75	212	8,300
Larry Gilbert	72	71	69	212	8,300
Bob Murphy	68	72	72	212	8,300
Tom Shaw	72	69	71	212	8,300
Miller Barber	72	72	69	213	6,450
Tony Jacklin	71	70	72	213	6,450
Mike McCullough	70	72	71	213	6,450
Arnold Palmer	73	70	70	213	6,450
J.C. Snead	70	72	71	213	6,450
Walter Zembriski	69	69	75	213	6,450
Bunky Henry	70	71	73	214	4,900
Larry Laoretti	70	70	74	214	4,900
Bobby Nichols	68	72	74	214	4,900
Calvin Peete	71	72	71	214	4,900
Tom Wargo	74	73	67	214	4,900
DeWitt Weaver	71	73	70	214	4,900
Kermit Zarley	70	74	70	214	4,900

First of America Classic

Egypt Valley Country Club, Ada, Michigan
Par 36-36–72; 6,909 yards

August 15-17
purse, $1,000,000

	SCORES			TOTAL	MONEY
Gil Morgan	69	67	71	207	$150,000
Bob Duval	68	70	70	208	88,000
John Morgan	68	73	69	210	72,000
Dave Eichelberger	70	70	71	211	54,000
Mike Hill	71	72	68	211	54,000
Hugh Baiocchi	71	73	68	212	36,000
Bunky Henry	73	69	70	212	36,000
Dave Stockton	74	71	67	212	36,000
Jim Albus	71	70	72	213	24,000
Isao Aoki	76	67	70	213	24,000
Jose Maria Canizares	77	69	67	213	24,000
Larry Gilbert	71	69	73	213	24,000
Lee Trevino	73	70	70	213	24,000
Bob Dickson	79	66	69	214	18,000
Jerry McGee	69	72	73	214	18,000
Dana Quigley	71	70	73	214	18,000
Brian Barnes	70	77	68	215	13,716.67
John Bland	76	68	71	215	13,716.67
Frank Conner	74	72	69	215	13,716.67
Mike McCullough	72	73	70	215	13,716.67
Dan Wood	69	73	73	215	13,716.66
Bob Wynn	71	70	74	215	13,716.66
Bruce Crampton	73	69	74	216	10,250
Gibby Gilbert	72	68	76	216	10,250
Gary Player	74	68	74	216	10,250
Bruce Summerhays	73	71	72	216	10,250
Fritz Gambetta	73	72	72	217	8,116.67
Bobby Stroble	75	70	72	217	8,116.67
Tom Wargo	76	71	70	217	8,116.67
Kermit Zarley	71	72	74	217	8,116.67
David Graham	73	68	76	217	8,116.66
Tony Jacklin	74	68	75	217	8,116.66
Ted Hayes	72	73	73	218	6,750
Leonard Thompson	76	69	73	218	6,750
David Ojala	72	72	75	219	5,875
John Schroeder	72	75	72	219	5,875
Steve Veriato	71	74	74	219	5,875
Buddy Whitten	69	77	73	219	5,875
George Archer	78	72	70	220	5,200
John Jacobs	76	73	71	220	5,200

Saint Luke's Classic

Loch Lloyd Country Club, Belton, Missouri
Par 35-35–70; 6,539 yards

August 22-24
purse, $1,000,000

	SCORES			TOTAL	MONEY
Bruce Summerhays	63	71	65	199	$150,000
Hugh Baiocchi	63	65	71	199	88,000
(Summerhays defeated Baiocchi on second extra hole.)					
Dave Stockton	68	68	64	200	72,000
Bob Eastwood	67	67	67	201	54,000

	SCORES			TOTAL	MONEY
Bobby Stroble	68	68	65	201	54,000
Calvin Peete	67	67	68	202	38,000
Jay Sigel	65	64	73	202	38,000
John Jacobs	67	67	69	203	32,000
Jimmy Powell	68	69	67	204	22,428.58
John Bland	68	66	70	204	22,428.57
Bruce Crampton	66	70	68	204	22,428.57
Dave Eichelberger	67	67	70	204	22,428.57
Hale Irwin	70	67	67	204	22,428.57
Jack Kiefer	70	67	67	204	22,428.57
Larry Laoretti	69	64	71	204	22,428.57
Brian Barnes	67	69	69	205	16,000
Tom Wargo	68	67	70	205	16,000
DeWitt Weaver	68	67	70	205	16,000
Rick Acton	70	67	69	206	12,460
Jimmy Adams	67	68	71	206	12,460
Jim Albus	68	70	68	206	12,460
David Graham	68	68	70	206	12,460
Kermit Zarley	71	66	69	206	12,460
Isao Aoki	68	68	71	207	10,250
Gibby Gilbert	69	67	71	207	10,250
Bob Dickson	69	65	74	208	9,100
Bob Duval	69	70	69	208	9,100
Walter Morgan	66	69	73	208	9,100
George Archer	68	69	72	209	7,900
Mike McCullough	66	72	71	209	7,900
Larry Ziegler	68	68	73	209	7,900
Charles Coody	70	68	72	210	6,600
Dennis Coscina	71	66	73	210	6,600
Dana Quigley	72	71	67	210	6,600
Tom Shaw	70	69	71	210	6,600
Robert Zimmerman	70	69	71	210	6,600
Bud Allin	71	70	70	211	5,100
Ray Arinno	69	72	70	211	5,100
Larry Gilbert	71	69	71	211	5,100
Bunky Henry	67	72	72	211	5,100
Don January	70	72	69	211	5,100
David Oakley	71	71	69	211	5,100
David Ojala	72	66	73	211	5,100

Pittsburgh Senior Classic

Quicksilver Golf Club, Midway, Pennsylvania
Par 36-36–72; 6,896 yards

August 29-31
purse, $1,100,000

	SCORES			TOTAL	MONEY
Hugh Baiocchi	70	70	66	206	$165,000
Bob Duval	68	68	70	206	96,800
(Baiocchi defeated Duval on sixth extra hole.)					
Walter Morgan	69	72	66	207	79,200
John Bland	71	70	67	208	50,600
John Jacobs	68	70	70	208	50,600
Gil Morgan	71	71	66	208	50,600
J.C. Snead	70	70	68	208	50,600
Vicente Fernandez	72	68	69	209	35,200
Mike Hill	70	72	68	210	30,800
George Archer	73	69	69	211	25,300

	SCORES	TOTAL	MONEY
David Graham	70 68 73	211	25,300
Tom Wargo	70 68 73	211	25,300
Buddy Whitten	71 71 69	211	25,300
Ray Arinno	72 67 73	212	19,250
Brian Barnes	71 72 69	212	19,250
Dave Eichelberger	69 70 73	212	19,250
Hubert Green	74 67 71	212	19,250
Jim Albus	70 75 68	213	14,171.67
Frank Conner	71 73 69	213	14,171.67
Bob Eastwood	71 70 72	213	14,171.67
Bruce Summerhays	70 73 70	213	14,171.67
John Rech	68 72 73	213	14,171.66
Leonard Thompson	70 70 73	213	14,171.66
Rick Acton	69 74 71	214	10,285
Harold Henning	72 72 70	214	10,285
Larry Laoretti	75 66 73	214	10,285
John Schroeder	72 73 69	214	10,285
Dan Wood	68 76 70	214	10,285
Kermit Zarley	68 73 73	214	10,285
Bud Allin	73 73 69	215	8,112.50
Isao Aoki	74 71 70	215	8,112.50
Terry Dill	73 74 68	215	8,112.50
Roy Vucinich	72 71 72	215	8,112.50
Homero Blancas	72 73 71	216	6,622
Bruce Crampton	71 76 69	216	6,622
Jim Dent	69 71 76	216	6,622
David Oakley	72 71 73	216	6,622
Bob E. Smith	70 72 74	216	6,622
Charles Coody	72 71 74	217	5,500
Tony Jacklin	70 75 72	217	5,500
Jack Kiefer	72 73 72	217	5,500
Dave Stockton	70 73 74	217	5,500

Bank One Classic

Kearney Hill Links, Lexington, Kentucky
Par 36-36—72; 6,760 yards

September 5-7
purse, $800,000

	SCORES	TOTAL	MONEY
Vicente Fernandez	67 69 67	203	$120,000
Isao Aoki	72 65 67	204	70,400
Walter Hall	66 71 68	205	52,800
Buddy Whitten	72 67 66	205	52,800
Hugh Baiocchi	70 70 66	206	38,400
Al Geiberger	68 67 72	207	30,400
Jay Sigel	68 68 71	207	30,400
Jack Kiefer	71 70 67	208	22,933.34
Dave Eichelberger	73 67 68	208	22,933.33
David Graham	71 68 69	208	22,933.33
John Schroeder	71 70 68	209	19,200
Bob Duval	69 71 70	210	15,360
Gibby Gilbert	72 70 68	210	15,360
Simon Hobday	69 71 70	210	15,360
Tom Shaw	71 71 68	210	15,360
Kermit Zarley	70 69 71	210	15,360
Miller Barber	68 71 72	211	11,660
Frank Conner	68 72 71	211	11,660

	SCORES			TOTAL	MONEY
Dale Douglass	71	71	69	211	11,660
Bob E. Smith	72	69	70	211	11,660
Dan Wood	72	70	70	212	9,333.34
Tom Wargo	70	70	72	212	9,333.33
Hubert Green	69	71	72	212	9,333.33
Bunky Henry	68	72	73	213	7,150
Chi Chi Rodriguez	71	72	70	213	7,150
Will Sowles	70	74	69	213	7,150
Bruce Summerhays	70	69	74	213	7,150
Robert Thomas	73	71	69	213	7,150
Leonard Thompson	69	70	74	213	7,150
DeWitt Weaver	70	70	73	213	7,150
Bob Wynn	73	71	69	213	7,150
Jim Dent	72	74	68	214	5,160
Terry Dill	69	77	68	214	5,160
Mike Hill	69	71	74	214	5,160
Mike McCullough	72	72	70	214	5,160
Jimmy Powell	71	71	72	214	5,160
Robert Zimmerman	72	72	70	214	5,160
Dick Hendrickson	75	72	68	215	4,240
Ben Smith	69	73	73	215	4,240
Bobby Stroble	74	71	70	215	4,240

Boone Valley Classic

Boone Valley Golf Club, Augusta, Missouri
Par 36-35–71; 6,670 yards

September 12-14
purse, $1,300,000

	SCORES			TOTAL	MONEY
Hale Irwin	70	65	65	200	$195,000
Gil Morgan	70	67	65	202	114,400
John Bland	69	68	68	205	93,600
David Graham	67	68	71	206	78,000
Dave Eichelberger	68	70	69	207	62,400
Mike Hill	75	64	70	209	49,400
Mike McCullough	67	72	70	209	49,400
Hugh Baiocchi	69	71	70	210	39,000
Rocky Thompson	66	74	70	210	39,000
George Archer	73	70	68	211	31,200
Dick Hendrickson	71	68	72	211	31,200
Lee Trevino	68	71	72	211	31,200
Dale Douglass	68	69	75	212	24,700
Bob Duval	69	71	72	212	24,700
Raymond Floyd	74	71	67	212	24,700
Bud Allin	68	76	69	213	17,923.75
Miller Barber	73	71	69	213	17,923.75
Jack Kiefer	74	71	68	213	17,923.75
Larry Nelson	69	70	74	213	17,923.75
Dana Quigley	72	69	72	213	17,923.75
Dave Stockton	74	69	70	213	17,923.75
Bruce Summerhays	68	74	71	213	17,923.75
Tom Wargo	72	73	68	213	17,923.75
Walter Hall	74	71	69	214	11,885.72
David Oakley	73	72	69	214	11,885.72
Jay Sigel	73	74	67	214	11,885.72
Frank Conner	73	68	73	214	11,885.71
Kurt Cox	69	72	73	214	11,885.71

	SCORES			TOTAL	MONEY
Terry Dill	73	68	73	214	11,885.71
Bobby Stroble	72	70	72	214	11,885.71
Al Geiberger	75	70	70	215	8,970
Graham Marsh	70	73	72	215	8,970
John Morgan	75	70	70	215	8,970
Chi Chi Rodriguez	73	71	71	215	8,970
Leonard Thompson	74	68	73	215	8,970
Tommy Aaron	72	70	74	216	7,176
Bob Charles	71	71	74	216	7,176
Jim Dent	69	75	72	216	7,176
John Jacobs	75	70	71	216	7,176
Bob Murphy	72	69	75	216	7,176

Comfort Classic

Brickyard Crossing Golf Club, Speedway, Indiana
Par 36-36–72; 6,760 yards

September 19-21
purse, $1,050,000

	SCORES			TOTAL	MONEY
David Graham	67	68	65	200	$157,500
Bud Allin	70	65	66	201	84,000
Larry Nelson	69	65	67	201	84,000
Jim Dent	69	69	65	203	63,000
Raymond Floyd	69	66	70	205	50,400
John Jacobs	70	70	66	206	37,800
Gil Morgan	71	66	69	206	37,800
Bob Murphy	68	69	69	206	37,800
Bob Eastwood	70	69	68	207	27,300
Graham Marsh	68	72	67	207	27,300
Tom Wargo	71	70	66	207	27,300
Jimmy Powell	71	70	67	208	21,350
J.C. Snead	74	71	63	208	21,350
Dave Stockton	71	68	69	208	21,350
Dana Quigley	66	73	70	209	18,900
Bob Duval	69	75	66	210	15,813
Dick Hendrickson	71	68	71	210	15,813
Bobby Stroble	70	69	71	210	15,813
Bruce Summerhays	68	71	71	210	15,813
Rocky Thompson	70	68	72	210	15,813
Al Geiberger	68	72	71	211	11,375
Gibby Gilbert	73	66	72	211	11,375
Simon Hobday	65	76	70	211	11,375
Hale Irwin	68	73	70	211	11,375
Jerry McGee	69	72	70	211	11,375
Walter Morgan	74	71	66	211	11,375
Vicente Fernandez	73	69	70	212	9,135
Mike Hill	73	70	69	212	9,135
Chi Chi Rodriguez	70	70	72	212	9,135
Jim Albus	75	71	67	213	7,743.75
Jack Kiefer	73	70	70	213	7,743.75
Mike McCullough	71	68	74	213	7,743.75
John Morgan	66	75	72	213	7,743.75
Miller Barber	72	70	72	214	5,958.75
John Bland	70	72	72	214	5,958.75
John Paul Cain	76	69	69	214	5,958.75
Larry Laoretti	72	72	70	214	5,958.75
Pat O'Brien	70	72	72	214	5,958.75

	SCORES			TOTAL	MONEY
David Ojala	75	68	71	214	5,958.75
Will Sowles	69	71	74	214	5,958.75
DeWitt Weaver	74	67	73	214	5,958.75

Emerald Coast Classic

The Moors Golf Club, Milton, Florida
Par 35-35–70; 6,719 yards

September 26-28
purse, $1,100,000

	SCORES			TOTAL	MONEY
Isao Aoki	71	60	65	196	$165,000
Gil Morgan	64	68	64	196	96,800
(Aoki defeated Morgan on first extra hole.)					
Bob Duval	66	66	68	200	60,500
Simon Hobday	67	63	70	200	60,500
Hale Irwin	65	66	69	200	60,500
Jay Sigel	69	66	65	200	60,500
Dave Eichelberger	72	63	66	201	37,400
Vicente Fernandez	63	67	71	201	37,400
Hugh Baiocchi	70	68	64	202	28,600
Bob Eastwood	68	64	70	202	28,600
David Graham	66	68	68	202	28,600
Mike Hill	72	66	65	203	20,533.34
Larry Laoretti	67	71	65	203	20,533.34
Hubert Green	72	64	67	203	20,533.33
Larry Nelson	64	69	70	203	20,533.33
Chi Chi Rodriguez	69	66	68	203	20,533.33
Buddy Whitten	67	69	67	203	20,533.33
John Bland	68	67	69	204	14,586
Bob Murphy	66	68	70	204	14,586
J.C. Snead	73	65	66	204	14,586
Bobby Stroble	64	71	69	204	14,586
Kermit Zarley	66	68	70	204	14,586
Butch Baird	69	65	71	205	11,022
Bruce Crampton	72	63	70	205	11,022
Dale Douglass	66	65	74	205	11,022
John Jacobs	69	68	68	205	11,022
Rocky Thompson	70	67	68	205	11,022
Charles Coody	69	70	67	206	8,525
Raymond Floyd	66	70	70	206	8,525
Dick Hendrickson	72	63	71	206	8,525
John Morgan	67	67	72	206	8,525
Dana Quigley	71	66	69	206	8,525
DeWitt Weaver	70	65	71	206	8,525
Bud Allin	69	65	73	207	6,765
Gary Player	70	67	70	207	6,765
Dave Stockton	71	64	72	207	6,765
Leonard Thompson	70	65	72	207	6,765
George Archer	70	67	71	208	5,500
Brian Barnes	69	71	68	208	5,500
Jim Dent	70	65	73	208	5,500
Bob Dickson	70	68	70	208	5,500
Graham Marsh	68	70	70	208	5,500
Jimmy Powell	65	74	69	208	5,500

Vantage Championship

Tanglewood Park, Championship Course,
Clemmons, North Carolina
Par 36-36–72; 6,680 yards

October 3-5
purse, $1,500,000

	SCORES			TOTAL	MONEY
Hale Irwin	64	62	69	195	$225,000
Dave Eichelberger	66	68	62	196	132,000
Larry Nelson	66	65	69	200	108,000
Gil Morgan	67	70	65	202	90,000
Isao Aoki	69	66	68	203	66,000
Jose Maria Canizares	65	69	69	203	66,000
John Bland	67	67	71	205	45,750
Frank Conner	68	70	67	205	45,750
Bob Murphy	68	69	68	205	45,750
Jay Sigel	68	68	69	205	45,750
David Graham	70	68	68	206	30,900
Walter Hall	70	68	68	206	30,900
Mike Hill	68	69	69	206	30,900
Dave Stockton	67	69	70	206	30,900
DeWitt Weaver	71	65	70	206	30,900
Bruce Summerhays	73	70	64	207	25,500
Mike McCullough	73	68	67	208	23,250
Jerry McGee	68	70	70	208	23,250
Brian Barnes	71	70	68	209	18,690
Larry Laoretti	67	71	71	209	18,690
Graham Marsh	72	71	66	209	18,690
Bobby Stroble	69	72	68	209	18,690
Tom Wargo	68	73	68	209	18,690
Al Geiberger	71	70	69	210	15,000
Dana Quigley	67	72	71	210	15,000
Kermit Zarley	68	69	73	210	15,000
Dale Douglass	72	70	69	211	11,914.29
Vicente Fernandez	69	72	70	211	11,914.29
John Jacobs	68	74	69	211	11,914.29
J.C. Snead	70	72	69	211	11,914.29
Gibby Gilbert	70	65	76	211	11,914.28
John Morgan	69	71	71	211	11,914.28
Walter Zembriski	69	71	71	211	11,914.28
Walter Morgan	70	71	71	212	9,225
Gary Player	68	72	72	212	9,225
Lee Trevino	70	71	71	212	9,225
Dan Wood	71	71	70	212	9,225
Jim Albus	74	70	69	213	7,200
Bud Allin	73	73	67	213	7,200
George Archer	72	70	71	213	7,200
Bob Dickson	73	71	69	213	7,200
Simon Hobday	72	70	71	213	7,200
Jack Kiefer	75	69	69	213	7,200
Jimmy Powell	69	72	72	213	7,200
Larry Ziegler	72	70	71	213	7,200

The Transamerica

Silverado Country Club, Napa, California
Par 35-37–72; 6,632 yards

October 10-12
purse, $800,000

	SCORES			TOTAL	MONEY
Dave Eichelberger	67	68	70	205	$120,000
Frank Conner	72	70	67	209	53,600
Terry Dill	68	70	71	209	53,600
John Jacobs	67	70	72	209	53,600
DeWitt Weaver	69	67	73	209	53,600
Jimmy Powell	68	69	73	210	30,400
Dan Wood	71	71	68	210	30,400
Bob Duval	71	71	69	211	22,000
Hubert Green	71	70	70	211	22,000
Larry Nelson	64	74	73	211	22,000
Chi Chi Rodriguez	69	71	71	211	22,000
Bruce Crampton	71	71	70	212	14,933.34
Bruce Summerhays	70	72	70	212	14,933.34
Isao Aoki	68	72	72	212	14,933.33
Jim Dent	71	71	70	212	14,933.33
Graham Marsh	69	68	75	212	14,933.33
David Ojala	70	71	71	212	14,933.33
Bob Charles	73	66	74	213	12,000
Don January	73	71	70	214	10,260
John Morgan	73	72	69	214	10,260
J.C. Snead	69	72	73	214	10,260
Will Sowles	72	70	72	214	10,260
Jerry McGee	70	76	69	215	8,016
Johnny Miller	70	75	70	215	8,016
Bob Murphy	75	71	69	215	8,016
Tom Shaw	72	72	71	215	8,016
Rocky Thompson	69	75	71	215	8,016
Gary Player	73	72	71	216	6,068.58
Butch Baird	72	71	73	216	6,068.57
Bob Eastwood	73	69	74	216	6,068.57
Simon Hobday	73	69	74	216	6,068.57
Bob E. Smith	72	71	73	216	6,068.57
Leonard Thompson	72	69	75	216	6,068.57
Walter Zembriski	71	70	75	216	6,068.57
Bud Allin	72	69	76	217	4,350
Don Bies	72	73	72	217	4,350
John Paul Cain	70	74	73	217	4,350
Ray Carrasco	71	73	73	217	4,350
Al Geiberger	75	70	72	217	4,350
Tony Jacklin	72	72	73	217	4,350
Tom Wargo	72	73	72	217	4,350
Buddy Whitten	73	74	70	217	4,350

Hyatt Regency Maui Kaanapali Classic

Kaanapali Resort, North Course, Kaanapali, Hawaii
Par 35-36–71; 6,590 yards

October 17-19
purse, $850,000

	SCORES			TOTAL	MONEY
Hale Irwin	67	63	70	200	$127,500
Mike Hill	70	64	69	203	68,000
Bruce Summerhays	64	65	74	203	68,000

	SCORES	TOTAL	MONEY
Rocky Thompson	68 65 71	204	51,000
Bob Charles	67 66 72	205	40,800
Walter Hall	67 69 70	206	34,000
Isao Aoki	71 70 66	207	28,900
Kermit Zarley	70 64 73	207	28,900
Frank Conner	68 69 71	208	21,250
Jack Kiefer	73 67 68	208	21,250
Chi Chi Rodriguez	66 70 72	208	21,250
DeWitt Weaver	66 69 73	208	21,250
Rick Acton	71 66 72	209	16,150
Bob Duval	74 69 66	209	16,150
J.C. Snead	64 73 72	209	16,150
Bud Allin	71 68 71	210	12,801
Simon Hobday	68 73 69	210	12,801
Dana Quigley	71 69 70	210	12,801
Jay Sigel	68 71 71	210	12,801
Dave Stockton	71 69 70	210	12,801
Jim Albus	68 69 74	211	9,668.75
John Jacobs	69 69 73	211	9,668.75
Graham Marsh	72 69 70	211	9,668.75
Jerry McGee	70 73 68	211	9,668.75
Terry Dill	75 66 71	212	7,926.25
Ted Hayes	73 69 70	212	7,926.25
Walter Morgan	73 70 69	212	7,926.25
Leonard Thompson	68 70 74	212	7,926.25
George Archer	70 68 75	213	6,715
Bob Eastwood	74 70 69	213	6,715
Robert Thomas	73 72 68	213	6,715
Will Sowles	72 72 70	214	5,367.15
Buddy Whitten	70 73 71	214	5,367.15
Hugh Baiocchi	70 70 74	214	5,367.14
Homero Blancas	68 75 71	214	5,367.14
Jim Colbert	72 66 76	214	5,367.14
Dale Douglass	72 68 74	214	5,367.14
Bobby Stroble	71 70 73	214	5,367.14
Charles Coody	71 71 73	215	4,250
Dave Eichelberger	69 71 75	215	4,250
Dick Hendrickson	71 71 73	215	4,250
Bunky Henry	70 73 72	215	4,250

Raley's Gold Rush Classic

Serrano Country Club, El Dorado Hills, California
Par 36-36–72; 6,772 yards

October 24-26
purse, $900,000

	SCORES	TOTAL	MONEY
Bob Eastwood	67 69 68	204	$135,000
Rick Acton	73 65 68	206	79,200
Jim Dent	69 69 70	208	59,400
John Jacobs	71 70 67	208	59,400
Jerry McGee	74 67 69	210	39,600
Jimmy Powell	73 67 70	210	39,600
Brian Barnes	70 73 68	211	26,280
Raymond Floyd	76 69 66	211	26,280
Mike Hill	72 71 68	211	26,280
Tom Wargo	69 71 71	211	26,280
Buddy Whitten	72 70 69	211	26,280

	SCORES			TOTAL	MONEY
John Bland	74	69	69	212	16,800
Vicente Fernandez	74	70	68	212	16,800
Jack Kiefer	74	65	73	212	16,800
Gil Morgan	74	66	72	212	16,800
Bruce Summerhays	69	69	74	212	16,800
Rocky Thompson	71	72	69	212	16,800
Al Geiberger	73	73	67	213	12,307.50
Dana Quigley	72	71	70	213	12,307.50
Bob E. Smith	72	69	72	213	12,307.50
DeWitt Weaver	75	69	69	213	12,307.50
Ray Arinno	72	70	72	214	9,255
Hugh Baiocchi	73	73	68	214	9,255
Charles Coody	75	68	71	214	9,255
Terry Dill	77	69	68	214	9,255
Gibby Gilbert	76	68	70	214	9,255
Gary Player	69	69	76	214	9,255
Bob Charles	74	71	70	215	7,290
Jim Colbert	71	71	73	215	7,290
Gene Littler	74	73	68	215	7,290
Leonard Thompson	75	72	68	215	7,290
Butch Baird	73	71	72	216	5,940
Don January	71	74	71	216	5,940
John Morgan	69	74	73	216	5,940
Walter Morgan	75	68	73	216	5,940
Bobby Stroble	77	71	68	216	5,940
David Graham	78	71	68	217	5,040
Mike McCullough	75	71	71	217	5,040
Bruce Crampton	75	73	70	218	4,410
Lee Elder	78	72	68	218	4,410
Chi Chi Rodriguez	74	71	73	218	4,410
John Schroeder	74	70	74	218	4,410
Larry Ziegler	72	74	72	218	4,410

Ralphs Senior Classic

Wilshire Country Club, Los Angeles, California
Par 35-36–71; 6,571 yards

October 31-November 2
purse, $1,000,000

	SCORES			TOTAL	MONEY
Gil Morgan	67	66	65	198	$150,000
George Archer	67	68	64	199	88,000
Jimmy Powell	68	67	68	203	72,000
Larry Nelson	66	71	67	204	60,000
Jim Colbert	65	65	75	205	48,000
Hubert Green	68	70	68	206	40,000
Dick Hendrickson	71	71	65	207	34,000
Graham Marsh	67	69	71	207	34,000
Frank Conner	69	72	67	208	25,000
Hale Irwin	63	72	73	208	25,000
Bob E. Smith	69	69	70	208	25,000
Leonard Thompson	67	70	71	208	25,000
Miller Barber	70	69	70	209	18,500
John Bland	69	70	70	209	18,500
David Oakley	74	67	68	209	18,500
Gary Player	68	69	72	209	18,500
Chi Chi Rodriguez	73	70	67	210	13,328.57
Hugh Baiocchi	74	67	69	210	13,328.58

	SCORES	TOTAL	MONEY
Al Geiberger	68 71 71	210	13,328.57
Harold Henning	72 69 69	210	13,328.57
Simon Hobday	69 71 70	210	13,328.57
Don January	74 67 69	210	13,328.57
Will Sowles	70 68 72	210	13,328.57
Bud Allin	69 69 73	211	8,937.50
Isao Aoki	69 73 69	211	8,937.50
John Paul Cain	71 69 71	211	8,937.50
Charles Coody	67 70 74	211	8,937.50
Vicente Fernandez	73 66 72	211	8,937.50
Mike McCullough	73 66 72	211	8,937.50
Jerry McGee	74 71 66	211	8,937.50
Bobby Stroble	68 72 71	211	8,937.50
Bob Charles	69 72 71	212	6,314.29
John Schroeder	77 70 65	212	6,314.29
Lee Trevino	71 70 71	212	6,314.29
Tom Wargo	74 70 68	212	6,314.29
Raymond Floyd	71 70 71	212	6,314.28
David Graham	70 71 71	212	6,314.28
Dave Stockton	64 72 76	212	6,314.28
Brian Barnes	71 71 71	213	4,800
Terry Dill	77 70 66	213	4,800
Dale Douglass	73 66 74	213	4,800
John Jacobs	74 70 69	213	4,800
David Ojala	72 70 71	213	4,800
Dana Quigley	72 67 74	213	4,800

Energizer Senior Tour Championship

The Dunes Golf & Beach Club, Myrtle Beach, South Carolina
Par 36-36–72; 6,815 yards

November 6-9
purse, $1,850,000

	SCORES	TOTAL	MONEY
Gil Morgan	69 66 66 71	272	$328,000
Hale Irwin	68 67 68 71	274	187,000
Isao Aoki	70 69 73 67	279	154,000
Hugh Baiocchi	69 69 71 71	280	105,666.67
Lee Trevino	69 72 69 70	280	105,666.67
Jay Sigel	69 72 68 71	280	105,666.66
Bob Duval	69 66 74 72	281	73,000
Hubert Green	67 73 68 73	281	73,000
Dave Eichelberger	69 69 70 74	282	58,500
Raymond Floyd	74 71 69 68	282	58,500
Jim Dent	71 71 68 74	284	48,166.67
Vicente Fernandez	72 70 71 71	284	48,166.67
Bob Murphy	66 72 71 75	284	48,166.66
David Graham	70 70 70 75	285	38,666.67
Bruce Summerhays	68 74 70 73	285	38,666.67
Mike Hill	69 70 69 77	285	38,666.66
Walter Morgan	71 74 69 72	286	33,000
Tom Wargo	73 70 71 72	286	33,000
Bob Eastwood	72 70 75 70	287	29,000
Dave Stockton	73 71 73 70	287	29,000
Jim Colbert	72 71 76 69	288	26,500
John Bland	71 72 72 74	289	24,250
Jimmy Powell	70 76 73 70	289	24,250

	SCORES	TOTAL	MONEY
Jack Kiefer	72 73 73 73	291	22,000
Graham Marsh	74 72 71 74	291	22,000
Bob Charles	69 76 73 75	293	20,500
John Jacobs	70 75 74 75	294	20,000
Frank Conner	72 73 74 76	295	19,250
Jerry McGee	71 79 76 69	295	19,250
Bud Allin	74 74 76 75	299	18,500

Diners Club Matches

PGA West, Nicklaus Course, La Quinta, California
Par 36-36–72; 6,700 yards

December 11-14
purse, $700,000

FIRST ROUND

Gil Morgan and Jay Sigel defeated John Jacobs and Gary Player, 1 up
Jack Kiefer and Bob Duval defeated Bruce Summerhays and Vicente Fernandez, 3 and 2
Dave Stockton and Larry Nelson defeated Chi Chi Rodriguez and David Graham, 2 and 1
Bob Eastwood and Walter Morgan defeated Bob Murphy and Jim Colbert, 1 up

SECOND ROUND

Gil Morgan and Sigel defeated Kiefer and Duval, 1 up
Summerhays and Fernandez defeated Jacobs and Player, 2 and 1
Rodriguez and Graham defeated Murphy and Colbert, 4 and 2
Eastwood and Walter Morgan defeated Stockton and Nelson, 2 and 1

THIRD ROUND

Summerhays and Fernandez defeated Gil Morgan and Sigel, 2 up
Kiefer and Duval defeated Jacobs and Player, 1 up
Eastwood and Walter Morgan defeated Rodriguez and Graham, 2 up
Stockton and Nelson defeated Murphy and Colbert, 2 up

FINAL ROUND

Gil Morgan and Sigel defeated Eastwood and Walter Morgan, 1 up

(Gil Morgan and Sigel received $110,000 each; Eastwood and Walter Morgan received $60,000 each.)

European Seniors Tour

Beko Turkish Seniors Open

National Golf Club, Antalya, Turkey
Par 36-36–72; 6,761 yards

May 8-10
purse, £150,000

	SCORES			TOTAL	MONEY
Tommy Horton	69	70	69	208	£25,503.66
Maurice Bembridge	69	72	69	210	16,956.65
Joe Carr	68	74	69	211	9,508.55
Snell Lancaster	72	72	70	214	7,089.43
Antonio Garrido	70	72	72	214	7,089.43
Jan Bjornsson	70	72	73	215	5,657.31
Jan Dorrestein	74	66	75	215	5,657.31
Harry Flatman	74	70	71	215	5,657.31
David Creamer	72	75	69	216	4,151.40
Brian Huggett	71	73	72	216	4,151.40
Bill Brask	75	72	69	216	4,151.40
Brian Waites	71	74	71	216	4,151.40
Randall Vines	74	72	71	217	2,950.76
Gordon Parkhill	71	75	71	217	2,950.76
Renato Campagnoli	71	75	71	217	2,950.76
Chick Evans	69	74	75	218	2,266.48
Bob Menne	76	74	68	218	2,266.48
Helmuth Schumacher	74	76	69	219	2,045.18
Norman Wood	72	71	77	220	1,785.71
Malcolm Gregson	72	74	74	220	1,785.71
Bill Hardwick	72	75	73	220	1,785.71
Noel Ratcliffe	74	76	71	221	1,579.67
Paul Leonard	72	77	72	221	1,579.67
Hugh Inggs	74	73	75	222	1,338.74
Vincent Tshabalala	72	75	75	222	1,338.74
Jim Rhodes	72	76	74	222	1,338.74
Ken Fulton	74	76	72	222	1,338.74
Matt McCrorie	73	74	75	222	1,338.74
David Butler	73	73	76	222	1,338.74
DeRay Simon	77	73	72	222	1,338.74

AIB Irish Seniors Open

St. Margarets Golf Club, Dublin, Ireland
Par 36-36–72; 6,555 yards

May 16-18
purse, £75,000

	SCORES			TOTAL	MONEY
Tommy Horton	71	69	68	208	£12,100
Noel Ratcliffe	66	72	72	210	7,900
Malcolm Gregson	71	72	69	212	4,600
Maurice Bembridge	70	71	72	213	3,176.67
Bob Menne	71	73	69	213	3,176.67
Ian Richardson	71	75	67	213	3,176.67
Norman Wood	71	74	69	214	2,570

	SCORES			TOTAL	MONEY
Antonio Garrido	70	72	73	215	1,946.67
Bobby Verwey	71	72	72	215	1,946.67
David Creamer	71	72	72	215	1,946.67
Peter Townsend	74	69	72	215	1,946.67
Alberto Croce	73	72	70	215	1,946.67
Renato Campagnoli	73	74	68	215	1,946.67
Tony Jacklin	74	74	68	216	1,515
Vincent Tshabalala	73	72	74	219	1,342.50
Guy Hunt	73	73	73	219	1,342.50
Liam Higgins	74	72	73	219	1,342.50
John Fourie	73	76	70	219	1,342.50
David Huish	72	73	75	220	993.57
Chick Evans	74	72	74	220	993.57
Harry Flatman	74	72	74	220	993.57
Neil Coles	73	75	72	220	993.57
Brian Huggett	75	74	71	220	993.57
Randall Vines	74	75	71	220	993.57
Hugh Inggs	74	75	71	220	993.57
J.R. Delich	75	72	74	221	745
Tienie Britz	74	73	74	221	745
Jim Rhodes	74	75	72	221	745
Roberto Bernardini	77	71	74	222	682
Brian Waites	80	69	73	222	682

Philips PFA Golf Classic

Marriott St. Pierre Hotel & Country Club,
Chepstow, Wales
Par 35-36–71; 6,688 yards

May 30-June 1
purse, £80,000

	SCORES			TOTAL	MONEY
DeRay Simon	69	69	74	212	£12,500
Tommy Horton	69	72	77	218	8,300
Jim Rhodes	69	74	76	219	3,640
Malcolm Gregson	71	72	76	219	3,640
Antonio Garrido	72	73	74	219	3,640
Tienie Britz	76	70	73	219	3,640
Brian Huggett	72	74	73	219	3,640
Brian Waites	73	70	77	220	2,333.33
Liam Higgins	72	73	75	220	2,333.33
Vincent Tshabalala	76	73	71	220	2,333.33
Snell Lancaster	70	74	77	221	1,800
Roberto Bernardini	72	74	75	221	1,800
Neil Coles	70	74	78	222	1,345
Norman Wood	74	71	77	222	1,345
J.R. Delich	75	71	76	222	1,345
Stewart Adwick	72	77	73	222	1,345
Doug Dalziel	73	75	75	223	971
Roger Fidler	74	74	75	223	971
Hugh Inggs	73	75	75	223	971
Paul Leonard	74	75	74	223	971
John Fourie	74	76	73	223	971
David Creamer	73	70	81	224	785
Ian Richardson	76	75	73	224	785
Alberto Croce	70	75	80	225	720
Bernard Hunt	74	74	77	225	720
Agim Bardha	72	77	76	225	720
Arnold O'Connor	74	77	74	225	720

	SCORES	TOTAL	MONEY
Bill Hardwick	69 76 81	226	630
Renato Campagnoli	75 72 79	226	630
Noel Ratcliffe	75 72 79	226	630
Harry Flatman	73 76 77	226	630
David Snell	76 73 77	226	630

Jersey Seniors Open

La Moye Golf Club, Jersey
Par 36-36–72; 6,664 yards

June 6-8
purse, £100,000

	SCORES	TOTAL	MONEY
Tommy Horton	69 67 68	204	£15,000
Craig Defoy	71 70 69	210	10,000
Jose Maria Canizares	71 70 72	213	5,070
Paul Leonard	69 70 74	213	5,070
Malcolm Gregson	71 73 70	214	3,850
Ian Richardson	70 71 73	214	3,850
Brian Waites	73 71 71	215	3,400
Antonio Garrido	70 77 69	216	2,800
Liam Higgins	71 71 74	216	2,800
Jim Rhodes	73 72 71	216	2,800
David Creamer	72 69 76	217	2,200
Bobby Verwey	74 73 70	217	2,200
Guy Hunt	77 68 74	219	1,740
David Huish	71 72 76	219	1,740
Randall Vines	69 74 76	219	1,740
John Garner	73 74 73	220	1,480
John Fourie	77 72 72	221	1,330
Noel Ratcliffe	74 71 76	221	1,330
DeRay Simon	73 78 71	222	1,086.67
Gordon Parkhill	73 75 74	222	1,086.67
Bill Hardwick	75 74 73	222	1,086.67
Hugh Boyle	75 71 77	223	840
Alberto Croce	73 77 73	223	840
Chick Evans	73 75 75	223	840
Bryan Carter	77 73 73	223	840
Bob Menne	74 75 74	223	840
Norman Wood	76 75 73	224	710
Matt McCrorie	74 72 78	224	710
David Snell	73 77 74	224	710
Doug Dalziel	71 77 76	224	710

De Vere Hotels Seniors Classic

Belton Woods Golf Club, Grantham, England
Par 36-36–72; 6,564 yards

June 13-15
purse, £80,000

	SCORES	TOTAL	MONEY
T.R. Jones	68 73 71	212	£13,350
Tommy Horton	71 70 72	213	8,900
Arnold O'Connor	70 72 72	214	4,143.33
David Creamer	71 70 73	214	4,143.33
Noel Ratcliffe	69 71 74	214	4,143.33
David Huish	69 73 73	215	3,200

	SCORES			TOTAL	MONEY
Hugh Jackson	72	74	70	216	2,835
Jim Rhodes	72	73	71	216	2,835
Eddie Polland	72	73	72	217	2,490
Agim Bardha	69	74	75	218	1,803.33
Randall Vines	72	72	74	218	1,803.33
Peter Townsend	68	76	74	218	1,803.33
John Garner	72	74	72	218	1,803.33
Malcolm Gregson	77	74	67	218	1,803.33
Guy Hunt	78	70	70	218	1,803.33
Jose Cabo	70	74	75	219	1,050.83
Jan Bjornsson	72	73	74	219	1,050.83
Ian Richardson	75	70	74	219	1,050.83
Brian Waites	73	72	74	219	1,050.83
Bob Menne	71	70	78	219	1,050.83
DeRay Simon	75	71	73	219	1,050.83
Paul Leonard	77	71	72	220	806.25
Bobby Verwey	74	73	73	220	806.25
Howell Fraser	70	76	74	220	806.25
Doug Dalziel	73	74	73	220	806.25
Roberto Bernardini	69	74	78	221	725
Renato Campagnoli	72	75	75	222	676.67
Graham Burroughs	73	75	74	222	676.67
Norman Wood	74	71	77	222	676.67
Wally Armstrong	72	76	75	223	625
Stewart Adwick	74	74	75	223	625
Bill Hardwick	71	77	75	223	625

Ryder Collingtree Seniors Classic

Collingtree Park ETC, Northampton, England
Par 36-36–72; 6,704 yards

June 20-22
purse, £90,000

	SCORES			TOTAL	MONEY
Neil Coles	68	71	69	208	£15,000
Antonio Garrido	72	75	68	215	7,845
Brian Waites	69	72	74	215	7,845
Agim Bardha	70	71	76	217	4,225
Doug Dalziel	71	73	73	217	4,225
Tommy Horton	71	74	73	218	3,550
Jim Rhodes	72	76	70	218	3,550
Ian Richardson	71	77	71	219	3,100
Maurice Bembridge	76	72	72	220	2,800
Hugh Jackson	73	76	72	221	2,300
Hugh Inggs	75	72	74	221	2,300
Randall Vines	74	71	76	221	2,300
Graham Burroughs	75	71	76	222	1,810
Billy Casper	70	76	76	222	1,810
Malcolm Gregson	72	75	76	223	1,285.71
DeRay Simon	76	74	73	223	1,285.71
Noel Ratcliffe	74	75	74	223	1,285.71
Peter Townsend	74	76	73	223	1,285.71
David Snell	77	74	72	223	1,285.71
Bill Hardwick	72	73	78	223	1,285.71
Harry Flatman	71	75	77	223	1,285.71
Lloyd Monroe	70	74	80	224	860
Matt McCrorie	69	75	80	224	860
Bryan Carter	76	74	74	224	860

	SCORES			TOTAL	MONEY
Renato Campagnoli	75	76	73	224	860
Fred Boobyer	76	75	74	225	740
Jan Bjornsson	72	75	78	225	740
John Fourie	74	73	78	225	740
Paul Leonard	76	74	76	226	666
David Creamer	73	73	80	226	666
Liam Higgins	73	74	79	226	666
Rafe Botts	73	75	78	226	666
Alberto Croce	73	77	76	226	666

Manadans Affarer Seniors

Fagelbro Golf Club, Stockholm, Sweden
Par 71; 7,060 yards

June 26-28
purse, £75,000

	SCORES			TOTAL	MONEY
Noel Ratcliffe	69	67	68	204	£12,000
Stephen Wild	67	68	76	211	7,850
Norman Wood	68	72	72	212	4,600
Brian Waites	72	70	72	214	3,600
Bobby Verwey	71	74	70	215	3,120
Roger Fidler	77	70	69	216	2,830
Jim Rhodes	72	73	72	217	2,490
Guy Hunt	75	71	71	217	2,490
Lloyd Monroe	75	74	69	218	2,023.33
Kenneth Magnusson	70	77	71	218	2,023.33
Tienie Britz	70	80	68	218	2,023.33
John Fourie	72	78	69	219	1,571.25
Stewart Adwick	73	76	70	219	1,571.25
Hugh Inggs	72	73	74	219	1,571.25
Chick Evans	74	73	72	219	1,571.25
Jan Bjornsson	70	74	76	220	1,325
David Creamer	70	77	73	220	1,325
Eddie Polland	72	75	74	221	1,200
David Huish	73	74	74	221	1,200
DeRay Simon	76	71	75	222	1,110
Liam Higgins	73	73	77	223	936
Peter Butler	73	77	73	223	936
Harry Flatman	76	71	76	223	936
Antonio Garrido	74	75	74	223	936
Alberto Croce	73	80	70	223	956
Renato Campagnoli	77	75	74	226	780
David Butler	75	72	78	225	735
Roberto Bernardini	73	77	75	225	735
Doug Dalziel	80	75	71	226	690
John Garner	75	77	74	226	690
David Snell	77	72	77	226	690

Lawrence Batley Seniors

Huddersfield Golf Club, West Yorkshire, England
Par 35-36–71; 6,463 yards

July 3-5
purse, £80,000

	SCORES			TOTAL	MONEY
Antonio Garrido	70	68	68	206	£13,000
Renato Campagnoli	70	68	69	207	8,440
Malcolm Gregson	68	72	68	208	4,043.33
Bill Hardwick	70	71	67	208	4,043.33
Brian Waites	71	65	72	208	4,043.33
Brian Huggett	68	68	73	209	2,733.33
DeRay Simon	70	71	68	209	2,733.33
David Huish	70	69	70	209	2,733.33
Bobby Verwey	71	68	71	210	2,037.50
Noel Ratcliffe	69	68	73	210	2,037.50
Hugh Inggs	72	69	69	210	2,037.50
Tienie Britz	69	73	68	210	2,037.50
Harry Flatman	70	71	70	211	1,650
Liam Higgins	70	68	73	211	1,650
Norman Wood	71	71	71	213	1,475
John Fourie	72	71	70	213	1,475
Jim Rhodes	71	74	70	215	1,300
Paul Leonard	75	68	72	215	1,300
David Jones	69	76	70	215	1,300
Stephen Wild	73	69	74	216	1,125
Guy Hunt	71	73	72	216	1,125
Bernard Hunt	74	73	70	217	890.67
Neil Coles	68	73	76	217	890.67
Bryan Carter	75	70	72	217	890.67
Roger Fidler	74	74	69	217	890.67
David Creamer	73	71	73	217	890.67
Alberto Croce	71	72	74	217	890.67
Vincent Tshabalala	75	68	75	218	744
Randall Vines	73	71	75	219	712
David Butler	75	73	72	220	700
Maurice Bembridge	75	74	71	220	700

Senior German Open

Owingen-Uberlingen Golf Club, Lake Constance, Germany
Par 36-36–72; 6,478 yards

July 11-13
purse, £100,000

	SCORES			TOTAL	MONEY
Noel Ratcliffe	66	69	69	204	£16,660
David Creamer	72	69	65	206	11,100
David Jones	67	69	71	207	6,260
Maurice Bembridge	69	71	70	210	4,620
Renato Campagnoli	70	68	72	210	4,620
Lloyd Monroe	73	70	68	211	3,590
Tommy Horton	71	69	71	211	3,590
Tienie Britz	69	69	73	211	3,590
Harry Flatman	77	70	65	212	2,806.67
Agim Bardha	70	72	70	212	2,806.67
Eddie Polland	70	69	73	212	2,806.67
Bobby Verwey	73	70	71	214	2,255
Neil Coles	69	68	77	214	2,255
Craig Defoy	69	76	70	215	1,400

	SCORES	TOTAL	MONEY
Wally Armstrong	71 74 70	215	1,400
Ian Richardson	75 71 69	215	1,400
Sandy Walker	71 73 71	215	1,400
Brian Waites	71 73 71	215	1,400
J.R. Delich	69 74 72	215	1,400
David Huish	72 71 72	215	1,400
Doug Dalziel	70 73 72	215	1,400
John Garner	72 71 72	215	1,400
Roger Stern	73 72 71	216	1,030
Antonio Garrido	75 71 70	216	1,030
Jose Cabo	75 72 70	217	950
Skip Pratt	69 75 73	217	950
Malcolm Gregson	71 73 73	217	950
Fred Whitfield	72 73 73	218	836
Kenneth Magnusson	72 74 72	218	836
Guy Hunt	72 74 72	218	836
Graham Burroughs	74 72 72	218	836
Jim Rhodes	70 74 74	218	836

Senior British Open

Royal Portrush Golf Club, Portrush, Northern Ireland
Par 36-36–72; 6,692 yards

July 24-27
purse, £350,000

	SCORES	TOTAL	MONEY
Gary Player	68 70 72 68	278	£58,330
John Bland	66 72 70 70	278	38,850
(Player defeated Bland on second extra hole.)			
Noel Ratcliffe	70 65 75 69	279	19,705
Jim Rhodes	69 71 71 68	279	19,705
Bobby Verwey	71 71 72 68	281	14,840
Tom Wargo	71 70 69 72	282	11,375
Jose Maria Canizares	76 72 68 66	282	11,375
Dave Eichelberger	68 71 75 69	283	8,295
Walter Hall	75 70 71 67	283	8,295
Paul Leonard	72 70 74 69	285	6,720
Tommy Horton	71 72 72 70	285	6,720
T.R. Jones	70 76 73 67	286	5,671.67
Brian Waites	73 68 76 69	286	5,671.67
Roy Vucinich	72 71 72 71	286	5,671.67
David Jones	74 74 72 67	287	4,732
Malcolm Gregson	72 76 70 69	287	4,732
Ian Richardson	71 75 71 70	287	4,732
John Fourie	74 69 71 73	287	4,732
Bill Brask	75 71 75 66	287	4,732
Maurice Bembridge	73 72 71 72	288	4,200
Liam Higgins	69 74 74 72	289	4,000
Bill Hardwick	73 71 74 71	289	4,000
Kenny Stevenson	75 73 71 70	289	4,000
Neil Coles	72 72 73 73	290	3,750
David Huish	73 74 71 72	290	3,750
Antonio Garrido	72 72 78 69	291	3,400
Norman Wood	73 74 74 70	291	3,400
Brian Huggett	73 71 75 72	291	3,400
John Morgan	74 71 76 70	291	3,400
Craig Defoy	74 72 71 74	291	3,400

Shell Wentworth Senior Masters

Wentworth Club, Edinburgh Course, Surrey, England
Par 36-36–72; 6,573 yards

August 1-3
purse, £125,000

	SCORES			TOTAL	MONEY
Gary Player	69	68	70	207	£20,830
David Creamer	69	68	71	208	10,845
Jose Maria Canizares	72	68	68	208	10,845
Terry Gale	72	72	65	209	6,250
Jose Maria Roca	71	70	69	210	4,691.25
David Jones	69	73	68	210	4,691.25
Tommy Horton	68	73	69	210	4,691.25
Guy Hunt	70	68	72	210	4,691.25
Eddie Polland	70	74	68	212	3,800
Antonio Garrido	74	70	69	213	3,225
Hugh Jackson	67	73	73	213	3,225
Brian Waites	71	69	73	213	3,225
Brian Huggett	74	70	70	214	2,315
Jose Cabo	71	73	70	214	2,315
Norman Wood	74	72	68	214	2,315
Alberto Croce	73	73	68	214	2,315
Noel Ratcliffe	72	74	69	215	1,646.67
Neil Coles	73	71	71	215	1,646.67
Malcolm Gregson	72	72	71	215	1,646.67
Walt Sauer	70	73	73	216	1,442.50
Vincent Tshabalala	73	71	72	216	1,442.50
DeRay Simon	71	72	74	217	1,288.75
Hugh Inggs	73	72	72	217	1,288.75
Renato Campagnoli	74	71	72	217	1,288.75
Tienie Britz	72	75	70	217	1,288.75
Stewart Adwick	71	73	74	218	1,137.50
Craig Defoy	72	74	72	218	1,137.50
Bob Menne	73	73	72	218	1,137.50
Liam Higgins	72	75	71	218	1,137.50
Agim Bardha	71	73	75	219	953.75
Peter Butler	73	75	71	219	953.75
John Garner	70	77	72	219	953.75
David Huish	71	74	74	219	953.75
Arnold O'Connor	71	73	75	219	953.75
Howell Fraser	72	75	72	219	953.75
John Fourie	72	73	74	219	953.75
Jim Rhodes	75	71	73	219	953.75

Credit Suisse Private Banking Seniors Open

Bad Ragaz Golf Club, Zurich, Switzerland
Par 35-35–70; 5,740 yards

August 8-10
purse, £100,000

	SCORES			TOTAL	MONEY
Brian Waites	63	69	71	203	£16,660
Malcolm Gregson	68	69	66	203	11,100
(Waites defeated Gregson on second extra hole.)					
Noel Ratcliffe	64	70	70	204	5,630
Hugh Inggs	64	69	71	204	5,630
Neil Coles	67	70	68	205	3,752.50
Tommy Horton	70	69	66	205	3,752.50
Jim Rhodes	68	68	69	205	3,752.50

646 / SENIOR TOURS

	SCORES			TOTAL	MONEY
Paul Leonard	65	73	67	205	3,752.50
Terry Gale	69	70	67	206	2,920
Renato Campagnoli	67	67	72	206	2,920
Alberto Croce	74	69	64	207	2,260
DeRay Simon	71	67	69	207	2,260
Skip Pratt	69	72	66	207	2,260
Bill Hardwick	71	66	70	207	2,260
Kenneth Magnusson	67	71	70	208	1,450
Antonio Garrido	68	71	69	208	1,450
David Huish	68	71	69	208	1,450
Harry Flatman	72	68	68	208	1,450
Lloyd Monroe	72	69	67	208	1,450
Steve Wild	74	67	68	209	1,133.33
Snell Lancaster	72	67	70	209	1,133.33
John Garner	70	69	70	209	1,133.33
Chick Evans	68	69	73	210	1,030
Francisco Abreu	67	77	66	210	1,030
Graham Burroughs	68	73	70	211	878.75
Jose Maria Roca	71	72	68	211	878.75
Craig Defoy	69	73	69	211	878.75
Vincent Tshabalala	70	69	72	211	878.75
Brian Huggett	73	68	70	211	878.75
David Jones	69	70	72	211	878.75
Eddie Polland	70	69	72	211	878.75
Jose Cabo	69	74	68	211	878.75

The Belfry PGA Seniors Championship

The Belfry, North Warwickshire, England
Par 36-36–72; 7,177 yards

August 22-25
purse, £150,000

	SCORES				TOTAL	MONEY
Walter Hall	69	69	69	70	277	£25,000
Tommy Horton	68	71	73	68	280	16,640
Antonio Garrido	68	70	69	75	282	8,365
Jose Maria Canizares	68	74	72	68	282	8,365
David Jones	69	73	72	71	285	6,440
John Garner	71	72	74	69	286	5,780
Terry Gale	75	70	72	69	286	5,780
David Huish	71	71	70	75	287	4,900
Iain Clark	72	73	73	69	287	4,900
Renato Campagnoli	71	71	75	74	291	4,060
Bob Menne	73	70	75	73	291	4,060
John Morgan	74	73	72	73	292	3,360
Ian Richardson	75	73	72	72	292	3,360
Noel Ratcliffe	68	76	76	73	293	2,490
Guy Hunt	72	73	73	75	293	2,490
Jim Rhodes	76	70	75	72	293	2,490
Lloyd Monroe	76	71	74	72	293	2,490
DeRay Simon	75	71	77	71	294	1,930
Bill Hardwick	72	76	74	72	294	1,930
Kenneth Magnusson	72	78	71	74	295	1,720
Liam Higgins	73	72	76	75	296	1,630
Don McCart	77	72	72	75	296	1,630
Brian Huggett	73	74	79	71	297	1,510
Brian Waites	75	73	76	73	297	1,510
Norman Wood	73	74	74	77	298	1,335

	SCORES	TOTAL	MONEY
Eddie Polland	75 72 78 73	298	1,335
Maurice Bembridge	74 74 79 71	298	1,335
Malcolm Gregson	76 75 73 74	298	1,335
Peter Townsend	71 71 78 79	299	1,186.67
Jose Cabo	76 72 75 76	299	1,186.67
Snell Lancaster	71 78 76 74	299	1,186.67

Motor Senior Classic

Marriott Goodwood Park Hotel & Country Club, England
Par 36-36–72; 6,458 yards

August 29-31
purse, £75,000

	SCORES	TOTAL	MONEY
Ian Richardson	70 67 71	208	£12,500
Eddie Polland	66 70 73	209	6,497.50
DeRay Simon	67 73 69	209	6,497.50
Noel Ratcliffe	70 71 69	210	3,455
John Morgan	72 68 70	210	3,455
Renato Campagnoli	73 69 69	211	2,780
David Jones	74 69 68	211	2,780
Norman Wood	72 69 70	211	2,780
Tienie Britz	70 73 69	212	2,230
Maurice Bembridge	72 70 70	212	2,230
Jose Maria Roca	73 69 71	213	1,468.57
Arnold O'Connor	74 68 71	213	1,468.57
David Creamer	70 73 70	213	1,468.57
Terry Gale	71 71 71	213	1,468.57
Matt McCrorie	72 70 71	213	1,468.57
Hugh Inggs	73 68 72	213	1,468.57
Brian Waites	72 69 72	213	1,468.57
Gordon Parkhill	72 71 71	214	905
John Fourie	72 72 70	214	905
John Garner	73 71 70	214	905
Malcolm Gregson	72 73 69	214	905
Rafe Botts	71 66 78	215	755
Peter Townsend	73 71 71	215	755
Craig Defoy	72 73 70	215	755
Graham Burroughs	72 70 73	215	755
Harry Flatman	72 75 69	216	632
Snell Lancaster	71 72 73	216	632
Randall Vines	69 71 76	216	632
Bill Hardwick	74 70 72	216	632
Hugh Boyle	76 70 70	216	632

Scottish Seniors Open

Newmachar Golf Club, Aberdeen, Scotland
Par 36-36–72; 6,514 yards
(Tournament shortened to two rounds.)

September 5-7
purse, £100,000

	SCORES	TOTAL	MONEY
Tommy Horton	70 62	132	£16,660
J.R. Delich	72 69	141	11,100
Michael Murphy	69 74	143	5,166.67
Jose Maria Roca	73 70	143	5,166.67

	SCORES	TOTAL	MONEY
Jim Rhodes	73 70	143	5,166.67
Andrew Brooks	73 71	144	3,452.50
Alberto Croce	74 70	144	3,452.50
Brian Waites	70 74	144	3,452.50
Vincent Tshabalala	72 72	144	3,452.50
Gordon Parkhill	75 70	145	2,472.50
Paul Leonard	74 71	145	2,472.50
Antonio Garrido	73 72	145	2,472.50
Ian Richardson	72 73	145	2,472.50
Eddie Polland	71 75	146	1,750
John Garner	73 73	146	1,750
Peter Townsend	72 74	146	1,750
Jan Bjornsson	73 74	147	1,252
John Hudson	76 71	147	1,252
Snell Lancaster	72 75	147	1,252
Hugh Inggs	75 72	147	1,252
David Huish	75 72	147	1,252
Steve Wild	74 74	148	984.29
Neil Coles	76 72	148	984.29
Guy Hunt	74 74	148	984.29
David Creamer	71 77	148	984.29
Renato Campagnoli	73 75	148	984.29
Liam Higgins	73 75	148	984.29
Roberto Bernardini	74 74	148	984.29
Phil Ferranti	72 77	149	791.43
Gordon Gray	76 73	149	791.43
Lloyd Monroe	75 74	149	791.43
Maurice Bembridge	76 73	149	791.43
Norman Wood	72 77	149	791.43
Bobby Verwey	75 74	149	791.43
Mike Hoyle	74 75	149	791.43

Clubhaus Seniors Classic

Benton Hall, Essex, England
Par 36-36–72; 6,500 yards

September 12-14
purse, £75,000

	SCORES	TOTAL	MONEY
Tommy Horton	68 71 64	203	£12,450
David Jones	69 68 68	205	8,250
Malcolm Gregson	68 71 68	207	4,650
Liam Higgins	68 71 70	209	3,680
Renato Campagnoli	68 76 67	211	3,110
Steve Wild	70 69 72	211	3,110
Andrew Brooks	74 68 70	212	2,760
Guy Hunt	67 73 73	213	2,220
Brian Huggett	71 69 73	213	2,220
Antonio Garrido	67 71 75	213	2,220
Joe Carr	74 72 67	213	2,220
Harry Flatman	71 73 71	215	1,670
Jim Rhodes	75 71 69	215	1,670
Jan Bjornsson	71 77 68	216	1,283.33
Alberto Croce	72 73 71	216	1,283.33
Norman Wood	66 75 75	216	1,283.33
Hugh Inggs	70 74 73	217	936
Jose Maria Roca	73 72 72	217	936
J.R. Delich	74 70 73	217	936

	SCORES			TOTAL	MONEY
Roger Stern	73	69	75	217	936
John Garner	74	72	71	217	936
Tienie Britz	74	75	69	218	700.71
Peter Butler	77	70	71	218	700.71
Arnold O'Connor	70	76	72	218	700.71
David Creamer	73	72	73	218	700.71
Fred Whitfield	72	75	71	218	700.71
Stewart Adwick	72	76	70	218	700.71
Noel Ratcliffe	72	75	71	218	700.71
Vincent Tshabalala	75	70	74	219	581.25
Ian Richardson	72	79	68	219	581.25
Neil Coles	74	70	75	219	581.25
Geoffrey King	77	73	69	219	581.25

Senior Tournament of Champions

Buckinghamshire Golf Club, Denham, England
Par 36-36–72; 6,662 yards

October 17-19
purse, £120,000

	SCORES			TOTAL	MONEY
Tommy Horton	69	67	68	204	£20,000
Jose Maria Canizares	68	66	73	207	13,300
Alberto Croce	76	69	67	212	6,750
David Huish	70	70	72	212	6,750
Eddie Polland	74	68	71	213	4,866.67
Neil Coles	74	73	66	213	4,866.67
Noel Ratcliffe	73	73	67	213	4,866.67
Malcolm Gregson	73	73	68	214	4,200
Maurice Bembridge	74	73	68	215	3,900
J.R. Delich	69	74	73	216	3,400
Brian Huggett	74	71	71	216	3,400
Paul Leonard	72	74	70	216	3,400
Norman Wood	71	73	73	217	2,700
Renato Campagnoli	79	66	72	217	2,700
Ian Richardson	72	73	72	217	2,700
Antonio Garrido	75	69	73	217	2,700
Bill Hardwick	74	72	72	218	2,116.67
T.R. Jones	72	73	73	218	2,116.67
Jim Rhodes	73	75	70	218	2,116.67
Terry Gale	74	72	73	219	1,755
Steve Wild	68	76	75	219	1,755
Craig Defoy	76	72	71	219	1,755
Hugh Inggs	73	74	72	219	1,755
John Fourie	76	71	73	220	1,401.67
Bob Menne	74	72	74	220	1,401.67
John Garner	77	72	71	220	1,401.67
DeRay Simon	74	75	71	220	1,401.67
David Jones	76	69	75	220	1,401.67
David Creamer	79	70	71	220	1,401.67
Tienie Britz	72	77	72	221	1,200
Liam Higgins	75	73	73	221	1,200

// / SENIOR TOURS

Japan Senior Tour

Daiichi Seimei Cup

Tomisato Golf Club, Sanmu, Chiba
Par 36-36–72; 6,428 yards

May 23-25
purse, ¥50,000,000

	SCORES			TOTAL	MONEY
Gary Player	69	68	71	208	¥7,500,000
Teruo Sugihara	71	71	66	208	3,125,000
Terry Gale	69	71	68	208	3,125,000
(Player defeated Sugihara and Gale on second extra hole.)					
Hsieh Min-nan	70	70	71	211	2,000,000
Kesahiko Uchida	70	74	68	212	1,625,000
Lee Trevino	68	71	73	212	1,625,000
Tadao Nakamura	65	77	71	213	1,116,666
Katsuji Hasegawa	73	71	69	213	1,116,666
Ichiro Teramoto	74	70	69	213	1,116,666
Kikuo Arai	71	70	73	214	833,750
Seiichi Kanai	69	73	72	214	833,750
Mitsuhiro Kitta	69	77	68	214	833,750
Kuo Chie-hsiung	67	74	73	214	833,750
Shoji Kikuchi	71	73	71	215	750,000
Namio Takasu	70	73	72	215	750,000
Kiyotaka Hochida	75	69	71	215	750,000
Akira Kawamata	69	72	75	216	712,500
Toru Nakayama	73	70	73	216	712,500
Hisao Inoue	74	72	71	217	675,000
Mitoshi Tomita	75	69	73	217	675,000
Norihiko Matsumoto	70	72	75	217	675,000
Hideo Jibiki	68	75	75	218	622,500
Tetsuhiro Ueda	74	70	74	218	622,500
Shigeru Uchida	74	74	70	218	622,500
Kenichi Tsurumoto	70	76	72	218	622,500
Fumio Tanaka	73	70	76	219	580,000
Yutaka Suzuki	70	73	76	219	580,000
Ichiro Togawa	68	74	77	219	580,000
Masaru Amano	74	72	74	220	545,000
Takahiro Takeyasu	73	71	76	220	545,000
Ryosuke Ota	74	72	74	220	545,000
Hisashi Suzumura	75	70	75	220	545,000

TPC Starts Senior Golf

Narita Golf Club, Ibaragi
Par 36-36–72; 6,905 yards

June 5-8
purse, ¥50,000,000

	SCORES				TOTAL	MONEY
Seiji Ogawa	69	71	69	71	280	¥7,500,000
Seiichi Kanai	71	72	70	68	281	3,500,000
Toru Nakayama	70	68	70	74	282	2,750,000
Haruo Yasuda	71	71	70	72	284	2,000,000

	SCORES				TOTAL	MONEY
Masaru Amano	71	72	71	71	285	1,750,000
Fujio Kobayashi	72	73	68	73	286	1,425,000
Shoji Kikuchi	70	73	69	75	287	1,150,000
Teruo Sugihara	76	73	69	70	288	1,000,000
Masaji Kusakabe	72	73	74	70	289	850,000
Ichiro Teramoto	72	75	70	72	289	850,000
Fumio Tanaka	70	75	73	72	290	775,000
Mitoshi Tomita	69	79	69	73	290	775,000
Akira Kawamata	68	71	73	79	291	716,666
Katsuji Hasegawa	72	73	72	74	291	716,666
Toshiharu Horimoto	68	71	76	76	291	716,666
Kesahiko Uchida	75	74	73	70	292	662,500
Hsieh Min-nan	72	76	71	73	292	662,500
Joji Yokoi	72	71	71	78	292	662,500
Hisashi Suzumura	75	71	73	73	292	662,500
Ryosuke Ota	73	71	71	78	293	610,000
Yasuhiro Daio	73	76	70	74	293	610,000
Hsu Chie-san	72	75	74	72	293	610,000
Isao Matsui	70	76	72	76	294	553,000
Mitsuhiro Kitta	74	73	69	78	294	553,000
Masao Harashima	68	73	80	73	294	553,000
Kuo Chie-hsiung	78	70	74	72	294	553,000
Terry Gale	75	73	73	73	294	553,000
Fukuji Kikuchi	72	75	72	76	295	505,000
Akira Yabe	75	74	74	72	295	505,000
Teruo Suzumura	73	77	71	74	295	505,000
Masayoshi Toda	74	75	72	74	295	505,000

Castlehill Senior Open

Castlehill County Club, Hoi-gun, Aichi
Par 36-36–72; 6,644 yards

June 13-15
purse, ¥30,000,000

	SCORES			TOTAL	MONEY
Toru Nakayama	69	70	69	208	¥4,500,000
Ichiro Teramoto	76	73	70	209	2,100,000
Hiroshi Kazami	69	72	69	210	1,650,000
Akira Yabe	74	68	69	211	1,200,000
Katsuji Hasegawa	71	72	71	214	1,050,000
Seiichi Kanai	74	71	70	215	770,000
Shigeru Uchida	72	72	71	215	770,000
Terry Gale	70	72	73	215	770,000
Ichiro Ino	73	72	71	216	548,000
Teruo Suzumura	69	72	75	216	548,000
Norihiko Matsumoto	75	69	72	216	548,000
Shoji Kikuchi	73	71	73	217	472,000
Yutaka Suzuki	68	72	77	217	472,000
Mitoshi Tomita	74	73	70	217	472,000
Hisao Kinoshita	71	72	75	218	436,500
Mitsuhiro Kitta	73	71	74	218	436,500
Akio Toyoda	74	68	76	218	436,500
Katsumi Hara	71	76	71	218	436,500
Ryosuke Ota	74	70	75	219	409,500
Kiyotaka Hochida	70	75	74	219	409,500
Fujio Kobayashi	73	71	76	220	391,500
Wataru Horiguchi	78	71	71	220	391,500
Eiji Ogawa	71	70	80	221	378,000

	SCORES	TOTAL	MONEY
Hsieh Min-nan	76 71 75	222	364,500
Tetsuhiro Ueda	71 78 73	222	364,500
*Yahei Goto	72 74 76	222	
Sadao Ogawa	77 73 73	223	330,000
Hiroshi Kumazawa	75 75 73	223	330,000
Fumio Tanaka	72 76 75	223	330,000
Koji Nakajima	76 72 75	223	330,000
Chouji Noguchi	78 73 72	223	330,000
Izuru Taka	74 71 78	223	330,000
Yoshihiro Takada	75 74 74	223	330,000
Kenichi Tsurumoto	75 73 75	223	330,000
Tadao Furuichi	72 75 76	223	330,000

Japan Media System Cup

Tsu Country Club, Tsu City, Mie
Par 36-36–72; 6,742 yards
(Event shortened due to typhoon.)

July 25-26
purse, ¥30,000,000

	SCORES	TOTAL	MONEY
Katsuji Hasegawa	71	71	¥4,500,000
Koji Nakajima	71	71	2,200,000
(Hasegawa defeated Nakajima on first extra hole.)			
Fumio Tanaka	72	72	1,425,000
Akira Yabe	72	72	1,425,000
Fujio Kobayashi	73	73	785,000
Hiroshi Kazami	73	73	785,000
Isao Matsui	73	73	785,000
Shigeru Uchida	73	73	785,000
Seiichi Kanai	74	74	468,180
Shoji Kikuchi	74	74	468,180
Masaharu Ohshima	74	74	468,180
Toshiki Matsui	74	74	468,180
Kuo Chie-hsiung	74	74	468,180
Hsieh Min-nan	75	75	388,800
Hideyo Sugimoto	75	75	388,800
Hiroyuki Nagai	75	75	388,800
Tetsuhiro Ueda	75	75	388,800
Kenji Ueda	75	75	388,800
Hisashi Suzumura	75	75	388,800
Takuo Terashima	75	75	388,800
Toru Nakayama	76	76	352,350
Norihiko Matsumoto	76	76	352,350
*Kiyou Mitsuhioe	76	76	
Kiyokumi Kimoto	77	77	316,912
Hiro Sakai	77	77	316,912
Takahiro Takeyasu	77	77	316,912
Tadao Nakamura	77	77	316,912
Wataru Horiguchi	77	77	316,912
Mitsuhiro Kitta	77	77	316,912
Izuru Taka	77	77	316,912
Akio Toyoda	77	77	316,912

HTB Senior Classic

Mitsui Kanko Iris Golf Club, Hokkaido
Par 36-36–72; 6,442 yards

September 13-14
purse, ¥15,000,000

	SCORES		TOTAL	MONEY
Kesahiko Uchida	69	69	138	¥2,500,000
Toru Nakayama	72	68	140	950,000
Hiroshi Ishii	70	70	140	950,000
Ichiro Ino	71	71	142	500,000
Fujio Kobayashi	75	68	143	265,000
Jun Nobechi	72	71	143	265,000
Namio Takasu	73	71	144	220,000
Hiroshi Tahara	74	71	145	207,500
Toshiki Matsui	71	74	145	207,500
Kenichi Yamada	72	74	146	197,500
Ryosuke Ota	71	75	146	197,500
Seiji Ogawa	77	70	147	187,000
Masaji Kusakabe	74	73	147	187,000
Yasuo Kuninaka	74	73	147	187,000
Koji Nakajima	76	71	147	187,000
Tadao Nakamura	76	71	147	187,000
Akira Yabe	71	76	147	187,000
Mitoshi Tomita	72	75	147	187,000
Hideyo Sugimoto	76	73	149	171,500
Teruo Suzumura	73	76	149	171,500
Ichiro Togawa	75	74	149	171,500
Norihiko Matsumoto	71	78	149	171,500
Tetsuhiro Ueda	73	77	150	158,500
Shozo Miyamoto	77	73	150	158,500
*Masanori Yoshimizu	77	73	150	
Fukuji Kikuchi	75	76	151	156,000
Isao Matsui	77	74	151	156,000
Kenichi Tsurumoto	76	75	151	156,000
*Mitsuo Ueda	79	72	151	
*Iwao Yang	76	76	152	
*Toshiaki Ishioka	73	79	152	

Komatsu Nagoya TV Open

Hananoki Golf Club, Aichi
Par 36-36–72; 6,771 yards

September 19-21
purse, ¥40,000,000

	SCORES			TOTAL	MONEY
Seiji Ogawa	68	69	72	209	¥6,000,000
Toru Nakayama	69	71	70	210	2,800,000
Seiichi Kanai	74	68	69	211	1,900,000
Katsuji Hasegawa	73	68	70	211	1,900,000
*Yukio Imada	76	67	68	211	
Yamotsu Ito	74	66	73	213	1,120,000
Akira Kawamata	72	69	72	213	1,120,000
Hsieh Min-nan	72	71	70	213	1,120,000
Wataru Horiguchi	72	72	69	213	1,120,000
Osano Kasugai	72	70	71	213	
Mitoshi Tomita	74	69	71	214	800,000
Masaji Kusakabe	72	72	71	215	656,000
Hiroshi Kazami	75	70	70	215	656,000
Haruo Yasuda	73	70	72	215	656,000

	SCORES	TOTAL	MONEY
Hisao Inoue	75 66 74	215	656,000
Ichiro Teramoto	72 71 72	215	656,000
Kikuo Arai	74 69 73	216	594,000
Hideo Hashimoto	80 67 69	216	594,000
Fumio Tanaka	76 69 72	217	570,000
Izuru Taka	74 72 71	217	570,000
Takahiro Takeyasu	73 73 72	218	505,333
Kenichi Yamada	75 70 73	218	505,333
Shigeru Uchida	74 75 69	218	505,333
Syunji Kanazawa	77 71 70	218	505,333
Yutaka Suzuki	72 74 72	218	505,333
Katsumi Hara	75 71 72	218	505,333
Norihiko Matsumoto	74 70 74	218	505,333
Osamu Watanabe	79 67 72	218	505,333
Terry Gale	72 68 78	218	505,333
Hiroshi Ishii	75 71 73	219	452,000
Toshikazu Izumi	73 72 74	219	452,000

Japan PGA Senior Championship

Shimoakima Country Club, Aichi
Par 36-36–72; 6,823 yards

October 9-12
purse, ¥50,000,000

	SCORES	TOTAL	MONEY
Ichiro Teramoto	73 69 72 72	286	¥7,500,000
Toru Nakayama	71 71 69 79	290	3,500,000
Hsieh Min-nan	73 72 72 76	293	2,750,000
Masaru Amano	78 71 74 73	296	1,875,000
Fumio Tanaka	75 69 72 80	296	1,875,000
Seiichi Kanai	75 77 74 71	297	1,425,000
Terry Gale	77 74 72 75	298	1,150,000
Hisashi Suzumura	71 75 73 80	299	1,000,000
Shichiro Enomoto	72 68 76 84	300	900,000
Yomio Ishii	79 74 74 74	301	800,000
Akira Kawamata	75 77 78 72	302	761,666
Katsuji Hasegawa	75 79 73 75	302	761,666
Masao Harashima	77 77 75 73	302	761,666
Kikuo Arai	75 76 74 78	303	707,500
Yoshikazu Izumi	75 76 73 79	303	707,500
Shizuo Hiyoshi	77 74 75 78	304	647,500
Mitsugi Maruyama	74 77 74 79	304	647,500
Hiroshi Yorikawa	77 73 79 75	304	647,500
Hisao Inoue	76 72 76 80	304	647,500
Mitsuhiro Kitta	74 75 74 81	304	647,500
Teruo Sugihara	75 71 74 84	304	647,500
Fujio Kobayashi	78 71 79 77	305	595,000
Ichiro Ino	79 73 78 76	306	553,000
Takahiro Takeyasu	78 75 78 75	306	553,000
Haruo Yasuda	78 75 72 81	306	553,000
Ryosuke Ota	79 71 76 80	306	553,000
Osamu Watanabe	75 74 78 79	306	553,000
Katsuji Murakami	76 73 78 80	307	505,000
Tooru Kurihara	76 74 80 77	307	505,000
Sukree Onchan	77 76 76 78	307	505,000
Mitsuo Iwata	72 72 79 84	307	505,000

Japan PGA Senior Open

Morinaga Takataki County Club, Ichihara, Chiba
Par 36-36–72; 6,787 yards
(Third round cancelled — rain.)

November 27-30
purse, ¥50,000,000

	SCORES			TOTAL	MONEY
Isao Aoki	70	69	71	210	¥7,500,000
Hiroshi Ishii	71	70	74	215	2,750,000
Teruo Sugihara	68	73	74	215	2,750,000
Graham Marsh	73	74	68	215	2,750,000
Isao Inoue	73	71	72	216	1,441,666
Toshiki Matsui	72	74	70	216	1,441,666
Kenichi Tsurumoto	72	71	73	216	1,441,666
Takashi Kurihara	73	72	73	218	900,000
Toru Nakayama	76	73	69	218	900,000
Katsuji Hasegawa	74	75	69	218	900,000
Kumio Tanaka	75	69	75	219	775,000
Akira Yabe	78	71	70	219	775,000
Hitoshi Tomita	73	71	76	220	716,666
Katsumi Hara	71	73	74	220	716,666
Osamu Watanabe	74	76	70	220	716,666
Akira Kawamata	72	76	73	221	632,500
Ujio Kobayashi	74	76	71	221	632,500
Hsieh Min-nan	70	73	78	221	632,500
Hiroshi Tahara	77	73	71	221	632,500
Tadao Nakamura	73	75	73	221	632,500
Teruo Suzumura	72	75	74	221	632,500
Kuo Chie-Hsiung	71	77	73	221	632,500
Jerry Gale	73	74	74	221	632,500
Eiji Ogawa	75	76	71	222	535,833
Eiichi Kanai	72	74	76	222	535,833
Koji Kikuchi	74	72	76	222	535,833
Toru Kurihara	76	71	75	222	535,833
Haruo Yasuda	74	77	71	222	535,833
Toshikazu Izumi	70	72	80	222	535,833
Ryuzo Shimatani	76	77	69	222	

›
South Africa Senior Tour

Vodacom Senior Classic

Dainfern Country Club, Johannesburg, South Africa
Par 36-36–72; 6,894 yards

November 14-16
purse, R400,000

	SCORES			TOTAL	MONEY
Simon Hobday	71	65	69	205	R62,800
Hugh Baiocchi	69	67	70	206	46,000
Allan Henning	68	71	69	208	32,000
Gary Player	68	73	68	209	22,000
John Bland	72	72	66	210	16,800
Bob Charles	70	70	71	211	14,080
Tony Jacklin	70	70	74	214	12,080
Hugh Inggs	74	72	70	216	10,480
Joe Dlamini	74	71	72	217	8,880
John Howie	73	72	72	217	8,880
Orville Moody	74	72	72	218	7,840
Gabriel Putsoe	69	70	80	219	7,280
Geoffrey King	73	75	72	220	6,600
Solly Sepeng	71	74	75	220	6,600
Jonathan Fourie	76	71	76	223	6,000
Vincent Tshabalala	73	74	77	224	5,800
Bobby Verwey	74	75	77	226	5,600
John Mabe	71	77	80	228	5,300
Daddy Naidoo	76	78	74	228	5,300
Donald Knight	75	77	78	230	4,960
Tony Rice	73	77	80	230	4,960
Muss Gammon	74	77	83	234	4,490
Peter Mkata	79	76	79	234	4,490
Absolom Nkosi	78	78	78	234	4,490
Terry Westbrook	77	81	76	234	4,490
Tony Finlayson	77	80	78	235	4,100
Obed Matlou	77	81	77	235	4,100
George Burns	78	84	75	237	3,860
Shadrack Molefe	72	81	84	237	3,860
Terry Bloom	80	83	76	239	3,620
David Burd	81	81	77	239	3,620

Templeton South African Senior Open

Houghton Golf Club, Johannesburg, South Africa
Par 36-36–72; 6,946 yards

November 20-22
purse, R125,000

	SCORES			TOTAL	MONEY
John Bland	71	72	69	212	R25,000
Allan Henning	73	74	71	218	18,750
Bobby Verwey	74	74	71	219	13,750
Hugh Baiocchi	74	72	74	220	8,750
Tommy Horton	72	75	73	220	8,750
Simon Hobday	77	71	78	226	5,208.3
Tony Jacklin	76	76	74	226	5,208.3
Orville Moody	74	74	78	226	5,208.3
Gabriel Putsoe	77	72	79	228	3,750

	SCORES			TOTAL	MONEY
Solly Sepeng	76	72	81	229	3,125
David Burd	78	75	77	230	2,291.66
Jonathan Fourie	81	75	74	230	2,291.66
Vincent Tshabalala	78	79	73	230	2,291.66
Tony Rice	79	77	75	231	1,875
Gert van Biljon	79	78	74	231	1,875
*Adriaan van Niekerk	77	77	77	231	
Bob Vosloo	78	79	74	231	1,875
Joe Dlamini	78	75	79	232	1,562.50
Peter Mkata	78	78	76	232	1,562.50
*Mike Kerby	83	76	76	235	
*Richard Lyon	78	80	77	235	
Tony Finlayson	81	78	77	236	1,312.50
Bobby Jones	82	79	75	236	1,312.50
*Ray Earle	80	81	76	237	
*Peter Loeb	78	83	76	237	
Thomas Ntebele	78	81	78	237	1,100
Tommy O'Neill	82	74	81	237	1,100
Geoffrey King	80	75	83	238	900
M. Mbele	76	81	81	238	900
Zacharia Mayundla	78	82	79	239	737.50

ICI John Bland Invitational

Royal Johannesburg Golf Club, Johannesburg, South Africa
Par 37-35–72; 6,985 yards
November 26-28
purse, R100,000

	SCORES			TOTAL	MONEY
Tommy Horton	69	69	68	206	R20,000
John Bland	71	67	69	207	15,000
Hugh Baiocchi	72	68	70	210	9,500
Allan Henning	70	68	72	210	9,500
Joe Dlamini	71	73	68	212	6,000
Simon Hobday	73	75	70	218	5,000
Tony Finlayson	78	72	69	219	3,750
Gabriel Putsoe	74	72	73	219	3,750
Solly Sepeng	76	72	72	220	3,000
Hugh Inggs	73	74	75	222	2,250
Bobby Verwey	73	73	76	222	2,250
Geoffrey King	77	72	75	224	1,750
Vincent Tshabalala	78	74	72	224	1,750
Jonathan Fourie	74	77	74	225	1,600
John Howie	77	74	76	227	1,500
Thomas Ntebele	71	77	81	229	1,400
Daddy Naidoo	77	77	76	230	1,250
Tony Rice	75	76	79	230	1,250
John Mabe	78	73	80	231	1,050
Terry Westbrook	80	78	73	231	1,050
Zacharia Mayundla	77	77	78	232	920
Donald Knight	78	74	81	233	800
Peter Mkata	77	76	80	233	800
Peter Matkovich	80	77	77	234	640
Shadrack Molefe	77	79	78	234	640
Ranjith Singh	82	74	79	235	570
Gert van Biljon	80	76	79	235	570
Aduetse Masilo	79	75	83	237	540
Graham Henning	77	80	81	238	510
Emmanuel Maabane	76	81	81	238	510

Women's Tours

Chrysler-Plymouth Tournament of Champions

Weston Hills Country Club, Ft. Lauderdale, Florida
Par 36-36–72; 6,151 yards

January 9-12
purse, $700,000

	SCORES				TOTAL	MONEY
Annika Sorenstam	72	66	68	66	272	$115,000
Karrie Webb	69	68	69	70	276	72,000
Barb Mucha	72	66	69	70	277	52,500
Michelle McGann	73	72	72	68	285	37,050
Nancy Lopez	73	73	68	71	285	37,050
Nanci Bowen	77	72	68	69	286	21,010
Rosie Jones	73	69	75	69	286	21,010
Beth Daniel	72	73	70	71	286	21,010
Caroline Pierce	72	71	72	71	286	21,010
Dottie Pepper	73	72	69	72	286	21,010
Jenny Lidback	73	72	72	70	287	14,670
Dawn Coe-Jones	72	73	67	75	287	14,670
Laura Davies	73	75	72	68	288	12,933
Alison Nicholas	73	73	72	70	288	12,933
Kathryn Marshall	76	74	71	68	289	11,758
Betsy King	76	70	71	73	290	10,783
Barb Whitehead	72	69	75	74	290	10,783
Val Skinner	75	71	76	69	291	10,032
Patty Sheehan	75	72	73	71	291	10,032
Liselotte Neumann	73	71	76	72	292	9,223
Becky Iverson	77	73	69	73	292	9,223
Dale Eggeling	74	76	70	73	293	8,640
Kelly Robbins	75	76	74	69	294	8,155
Chris Johnson	76	72	73	73	294	8,155
Mary Beth Zimmerman	75	74	77	70	296	7,552
Tracy Kerdyk	79	72	74	71	296	7,552
JoAnne Carner	79	72	74	71	296	7,552
Meg Mallon	80	74	71	73	298	6,853
Julie Piers	75	76	71	76	298	6,853
Pat Bradley	72	75	71	80	298	6,853

HealthSouth Inaugural

Walt Disney World, Lake Buena Vista Course,
Orlando, Florida
Par 36-36–72; 6,336 yards

January 17-1*
purse, $600,00*

	SCORES			TOTAL	MONEY
Michelle McGann	66	72	69	207	$90,000
Karrie Webb	68	70	69	207	55,855
(McGann defeated Webb on first extra hole.)					
Beth Daniel	69	72	70	211	40,759
Jane Geddes	72	72	69	213	31,702
Barb Mucha	69	73	72	214	23,398
Joanne Morley	68	72	74	214	23,398

	SCORES	TOTAL	MONEY
Dottie Pepper	72 72 71	215	16,756
Nancy Lopez	74 69 72	215	16,756
Marianne Morris	73 74 70	217	13,435
Deb Richard	73 69 75	217	13,435
Catriona Matthew	74 73 71	218	9,476
Meg Mallon	73 73 72	218	9,476
Chris Johnson	73 73 72	218	9,476
Tina Barrett	73 73 72	218	9,476
Laura Davies	71 74 73	218	9,476
Jan Stephenson	69 76 73	218	9,476
Charlotta Sorenstam	74 70 74	218	9,476
Penny Hammel	74 76 69	219	6,571
Dawn Coe-Jones	74 76 69	219	6,571
Anna Acker-Macosko	74 74 71	219	6,571
Emilee Klein	74 73 72	219	6,571
Cindy Schreyer	71 76 72	219	6,571
Renee Heiken	74 72 73	219	6,571
Alicia Dibos	72 74 73	219	6,571
Dana Dormann	70 75 74	219	6,571
Jill Briles-Hinton	75 75 70	220	4,821
Mayumi Hirase	76 73 71	220	4,821
Karen Weiss	76 72 72	220	4,821
Nanci Bowen	71 77 72	220	4,821
Patty Sheehan	74 72 74	220	4,821
Mitzi Edge	74 72 74	220	4,821
Jenny Lidback	71 74 75	220	4,821
Kim Williams	69 75 76	220	4,821
Vicki Fergon	68 76 76	220	4,821

Diet Dr. Pepper National Pro-Am

Ibis Golf & Country Club, Legend Course,
West Palm Beach, Florida
Par 36-36–72; 6,323 yards

February 6-9
purse, $500,000

	SCORES	TOTAL	MONEY
Kelly Robbins	66 69 69 67	271	$75,000
Emilee Klein	71 67 70 63	271	46,546
(Robbins defeated Klein on second extra hole.)			
Chris Johnson	68 73 67 67	275	33,966
Kate Golden	67 71 70 68	276	26,418
Vicki Goetze	70 69 68 72	279	19,499
Jane Geddes	73 64 69 73	279	19,499
Pat Bradley	70 72 69 70	281	13,250
Dottie Pepper	69 68 74 70	281	13,250
Juli Inkster	68 69 71 73	281	13,250
Lorie Kane	71 71 71 69	282	10,064
Val Skinner	68 70 74 70	282	10,064
Kathryn Marshall	73 71 71 68	283	8,554
Michele Redman	72 71 70 70	283	8,554
Betsy King	73 70 70 72	285	7,799
Dale Eggeling	72 73 75 66	286	5,839
Liselotte Neumann	71 73 74 68	286	5,839
Lori West	71 73 72 70	286	5,839
Eva Dahllof	71 73 72 70	286	5,839
Missie Berteotti	68 73 75 70	286	5,839
Catrin Nilsmark	72 71 72 71	286	5,839

	SCORES				TOTAL	MONEY
Alison Nicholas	71	73	70	72	286	5,839
Jane Crafter	69	71	74	72	286	5,839
Mayumi Hirase	69	72	72	73	286	5,839
Tracy Hanson	71	68	72	75	286	5,839
Laurel Kean	70	69	68	79	286	5,839
Terry-Jo Myers	74	68	76	69	287	4,503
Martha Nause	76	68	70	73	287	4,503
Becky Iverson	70	72	76	70	288	4,201
Donna Andrews	71	71	74	72	288	4,201
Kristi Albers	71	68	80	70	289	3,703
Mitzi Edge	74	69	75	71	289	3,703
Cindy Rarick	73	69	75	72	289	3,703
Tracy Kerdyk	73	71	70	75	289	3,703
Penny Hammel	70	70	71	78	289	3,703

Los Angeles Women's Championship

Oakmont Country Club, Glendale, California
Par 36-36—72; 6,276 yards

February 14-16
purse, $650,000

	SCORES			TOTAL	MONEY
Terry-Jo Myers	74	66	66	206	$97,500
Annika Sorenstam	66	69	73	208	60,510
Alicia Dibos	71	73	67	211	29,698
Kelly Robbins	73	69	69	211	29,698
Catrin Nilsmark	73	69	69	211	29,698
Donna Andrews	68	73	70	211	29,698
Ellie Gibson	69	69	73	211	29,698
Jane Geddes	71	72	69	212	14,636
Emilee Klein	70	72	70	212	14,636
Liselotte Neumann	71	70	71	212	14,636
Amy Fruhwirth	70	71	71	212	14,636
Michelle Dobek	73	72	65	213	10,793
Lorie Kane	70	73	70	213	10,793
Jenny Lidback	70	71	72	213	10,793
Penny Hammel	73	72	69	214	8,749
Cindy Figg-Currier	73	70	71	214	8,749
Mayumi Hirase	72	70	72	214	8,749
Stephanie Maynor	72	69	73	214	8,749
Juli Inkster	74	70	71	215	6,690
Barb Whitehead	73	71	71	215	6,690
Cristie Kerr	73	71	71	215	6,690
Missie McGeorge	71	73	71	215	6,690
Cathy Johnston-Forbes	73	70	72	215	6,690
Hollis Stacy	72	71	72	215	6,690
Wendy Ward	72	71	72	215	6,690
Renee Heiken	71	72	72	215	6,690
Luciana Bemvenuti	73	68	74	215	6,690
Aki Takamura	76	71	69	216	5,265
Mardi Lunn	72	74	70	216	5,265
Tina Barrett	73	72	71	216	5,265
Leta Lindley	73	66	77	216	5,265

Cup Noodles Hawaiian Ladies Open

Kapolei Golf Course, Kapolei, Oahu, Hawaii
Par 36-36–72; 6,056 yards

February 20-22
purse, $650,000

	SCORES			TOTAL	MONEY
Annika Sorenstam	67	66	73	206	$97,500
Meg Mallon	69	68	70	207	60,510
Betsy King	67	72	69	208	44,156
Gail Graham	71	68	71	210	34,344
Marnie McGuire	74	69	68	211	20,474
Chris Johnson	73	68	70	211	20,474
Laura Davies	70	70	71	211	20,474
Pat Hurst	69	70	72	211	20,474
Kelly Robbins	67	72	72	211	20,474
Amy Read	74	69	69	212	11,756
Missie McGeorge	74	69	69	212	11,756
Amy Fruhwirth	72	71	69	212	11,756
Donna Andrews	72	69	71	212	11,756
Kristal Parker-Gregory	70	71	71	212	11,756
Mayumi Murai	72	70	71	213	8,628
Moira Dunn	71	71	71	213	8,628
Wendy Ward	71	70	72	213	8,628
Kim Saiki	71	70	72	213	8,628
Barb Whitehead	69	70	74	213	8,628
Karen Weiss	72	70	72	214	6,604
Michelle Estill	71	71	72	214	6,604
Alison Nicholas	75	66	73	214	6,604
Kris Tschetter	74	67	73	214	6,604
Mayumi Hirase	73	68	73	214	6,604
Nancy Ramsbottom	71	70	73	214	6,604
Michiko Hattori	71	69	74	214	6,604
Cindy Rarick	70	70	74	214	6,604
Patty Sheehan	72	72	71	215	4,888
Nancy Harvey	72	72	71	215	4,888
Jan Stephenson	71	73	71	215	4,888
Eva Dahllof	75	68	72	215	4,888
Hollis Stacy	72	71	72	215	4,888
Dana Dormann	70	73	72	215	4,888
Marianne Morris	70	73	72	215	4,888
Suzuko Maeda	75	67	73	215	4,888
Ok-Hee Ku	70	72	73	215	4,888

Welch's/Circle K Championship

Randolf North Golf Course, Tucson, Arizona
Par 35-37–72; 6,222 yards

March 13-16
purse, $500,000

	SCORES				TOTAL	MONEY
Donna Andrews	68	67	70	68	273	$75,000
Tina Barrett	68	70	67	69	274	46,546
Dale Eggeling	68	71	67	69	275	30,192
Annika Sorenstam	67	68	69	71	275	30,192
Anna Acker-Macosko	70	71	70	65	276	21,386
Chris Johnson	71	70	68	69	278	17,612
Karrie Webb	71	72	68	68	279	11,463
Cindy Schreyer	72	69	69	69	279	11,463
Liselotte Neumann	64	73	73	69	279	11,463

	SCORES	TOTAL	MONEY
Michele Redman	69 72 68 70	279	11,463
Tracy Hanson	70 68 70 71	279	11,463
Julie Piers	65 72 70 72	279	11,463
Hiromi Kobayashi	73 70 69 68	280	7,593
Charlotta Sorenstam	71 71 69 69	280	7,593
Nancy Lopez	73 68 69 70	280	7,593
Susie Redman	70 70 68 72	280	7,593
Penny Hammel	70 70 75 66	281	6,335
Kris Tschetter	68 70 76 67	281	6,335
Suzanne Strudwick	73 69 71 68	281	6,335
Kristal Parker-Gregory	69 71 72 70	282	5,461
Stefania Croce	71 71 69 71	282	5,461
Jan Stephenson	69 70 70 73	282	5,461
Juli Inkster	68 70 71 73	282	5,461
*Marisa Baena	73 67 69 73	282	
Emilee Klein	71 71 71 70	283	4,624
Michelle McGann	74 69 69 71	283	4,624
Deb Richard	70 72 70 71	283	4,624
Jane Geddes	69 68 74 72	283	4,624
Joan Pitcock	71 66 70 76	283	4,624
Marianne Morris	67 75 72 70	284	3,950
Betsy King	72 70 71 71	284	3,950
Alicia Dibos	68 69 74 73	284	3,950
Pam Wright	71 69 69 75	284	3,950

Standard Register PING

Moon Valley Country Club, Phoenix, Arizona
Par 36-37—73; 6,435 yards

March 20-23
purse, $850,000

	SCORES	TOTAL	MONEY
Laura Davies	70 69 70 68	277	$127,500
Kelly Robbins	67 68 73 69	277	79,129
(Davies defeated Robbins on first extra hole.)			
Laurie Brower	69 72 70 70	281	51,327
Barb Mucha	65 70 73 73	281	51,327
Becky Iverson	72 73 67 71	283	33,148
Karrie Webb	71 68 70 74	283	33,148
Cindy Figg-Currier	70 69 74 71	284	22,526
Kris Tschetter	69 69 74 72	284	22,526
Karen Weiss	68 69 75 72	284	22,526
Michele Redman	68 70 73 74	285	17,964
Nancy Lopez	73 74 70 69	286	14,200
Lorie Kane	78 69 68 71	286	14,200
Chris Johnson	72 73 69 72	286	14,200
Jane Geddes	72 73 68 73	286	14,200
Mardi Lunn	69 68 74 75	286	14,200
Dina Ammaccapane	73 73 72 69	287	10,264
Elaine Crosby	73 72 73 69	287	10,264
Alicia Dibos	71 72 73 71	287	10,264
Juli Inkster	75 69 70 73	287	10,264
Mayumi Hirase	72 70 72 73	287	10,264
Amy Benz	69 71 73 74	287	10,264
Dawn Coe-Jones	66 70 74 77	287	10,264
Tammie Green	72 73 72 71	288	8,311
Donna Andrews	73 71 72 72	288	8,311
Cristie Kerr	71 72 71 74	288	8,311

	SCORES				TOTAL	MONEY
Betsy King	71	74	75	70	290	7,399
Marianne Morris	76	69	73	72	290	7,399
Tina Barrett	73	70	75	72	290	7,399
Alison Nicholas	71	71	73	75	290	7,399
Michelle McGann	78	69	73	71	291	6,079
Tracy Hanson	71	73	75	72	291	6,079
Rachel Hetherington	73	72	73	73	291	6,079
Sally Little	74	69	74	74	291	6,079
Meg Mallon	72	72	72	75	291	6,079
Melissa McNamara	68	73	74	76	291	6,079
Hiromi Kobayashi	71	69	73	78	291	6,079

Nabisco Dinah Shore

Mission Hills Country Club, Rancho Mirage, California
Par 36-36–72; 6,460 yards

March 27-30
purse, $900,000

	SCORES				TOTAL	MONEY
Betsy King	71	67	67	71	276	$135,000
Kris Tschetter	66	76	66	70	278	83,783
Amy Fruhwirth	69	70	68	72	279	54,346
Kelly Robbins	70	67	68	74	279	54,346
Nanci Bowen	70	74	70	68	282	35,097
Lisa Hackney	70	72	72	68	282	35,097
Tina Barrett	70	71	70	72	283	26,720
Mary Beth Zimmerman	75	74	72	63	284	21,285
Hiromi Kobayashi	72	69	71	72	284	21,285
Annika Sorenstam	70	72	68	74	284	21,285
Marianne Morris	71	75	72	67	285	15,065
Donna Andrews	73	71	72	69	285	15,065
Jane Geddes	68	75	72	70	285	15,065
Jane Crafter	70	71	72	72	285	15,065
Dottie Pepper	69	70	71	75	285	15,065
Tammie Green	72	73	71	70	286	10,898
Juli Inkster	72	74	69	71	286	10,898
Michelle McGann	74	70	71	71	286	10,898
Liselotte Neumann	74	71	69	72	286	10,898
Pat Hurst	74	69	71	72	286	10,898
Laura Davies	70	70	74	72	286	10,898
Kathryn Marshall	66	73	73	74	286	10,898
Cindy Schreyer	72	74	73	68	287	8,690
Jenny Hammel	76	72	67	72	287	8,690
Trish Johnson	70	72	73	72	287	8,690
Nancy Lopez	70	74	69	74	287	8,690
Marisa Baena	74	71	73	69	287	
Barb Mucha	71	72	73	72	288	8,000
Carrie Webb	69	74	71	75	289	7,728
Ayumi Hirase	70	77	72	71	290	6,940
Michelle Estill	72	73	73	72	290	6,940
Dawn Coe-Jones	73	72	72	73	290	6,940
Deb Richard	68	75	74	73	290	6,940
Dale Eggeling	68	72	75	75	290	6,940

Longs Drugs Challenge

Twelve Bridges Golf Club, Lincoln, California
Par 36-36–72; 6,412 yards

April 3-6
purse, $500,000

	SCORES				TOTAL	MONEY
Annika Sorenstam	73	68	71	73	285	$75,000
Pamela Kometani	71	77	67	70	285	46,546
(Sorenstam defeated Kometani on second extra hole.)						
Jan Stephenson	74	70	70	72	286	30,192
Juli Inkster	72	68	73	73	286	30,192
Alicia Dibos	73	69	72	73	287	21,386
Barb Mucha	72	70	74	72	288	17,612
Amy Fruhwirth	71	73	78	68	290	13,250
Danielle Ammaccapane	73	74	71	72	290	13,250
Donna Andrews	75	70	70	75	290	13,250
Cindy Schreyer	77	73	71	71	292	10,072
Tammie Green	70	73	77	72	292	10,072
Pat Hurst	78	72	72	71	293	8,319
Dale Eggeling	75	74	71	73	293	8,319
Kim Saiki	75	76	68	74	293	8,319
Charlotta Sorenstam	76	73	72	73	294	6,608
Patty Sheehan	74	74	71	75	294	6,608
Lorie Kane	72	73	74	75	294	6,608
Deb Richard	74	74	70	76	294	6,608
Kris Tschetter	72	72	73	77	294	6,608
Chris Johnson	77	73	72	73	295	5,325
Sherri Turner	75	71	74	75	295	5,325
Vickie Odegard	72	74	74	75	295	5,325
Stephanie Maynor	74	71	75	75	295	5,325
Sharon Barrett	70	72	77	76	295	5,325
Sherri Steinhauer	74	72	72	78	296	4,747
Mitzi Edge	76	74	75	72	297	4,218
Wendy Ward	73	76	76	72	297	4,218
Brandie Burton	73	78	73	73	297	4,218
Karen Weiss	72	76	73	76	297	4,218
Dana Dormann	73	72	76	76	297	4,218
Mayumi Hirase	75	69	76	77	297	4,218

Susan G. Komen International

Wachesaw Plantation East Golf Club,
Murrells Inlet, South Carolina
Par 36-36–72; 6,248 yards

April 17-2
purse, $500,00

	SCORES				TOTAL	MONEY
Karrie Webb	72	72	66	66	276	$75,000
Lorie Kane	72	70	67	69	278	35,643
Cathy Johnston-Forbes	69	73	66	70	278	35,643
Nanci Bowen	65	73	70	70	278	35,643
Michelle McGann	69	73	68	69	279	21,386
Maggie Will-Halpin	69	72	71	68	280	17,612
Erika Hayashida	74	72	69	66	281	13,250
Brandie Burton	69	72	72	68	281	13,250
Rosie Jones	70	73	66	72	281	13,250
Mayumi Hirase	68	75	72	67	282	9,644
Charlotta Sorenstam	70	73	69	70	282	9,644
Tina Barrett	68	72	72	70	282	9,644

	SCORES				TOTAL	MONEY
Pam Wright	72	75	70	66	283	7,008
Cindy Schreyer	72	70	72	69	283	7,008
Laura Davies	68	76	69	70	283	7,008
Colleen Walker	72	72	68	71	283	7,008
Pat Bradley	71	73	68	71	283	7,008
Patty Sheehan	69	71	72	71	283	7,008
Juli Inkster	70	72	69	72	283	7,008
Annika Sorenstam	68	74	70	72	284	5,787
Hiromi Kobayashi	72	74	72	67	285	5,291
Lisa Kiggens	66	79	73	67	285	5,291
Sherri Steinhauer	68	78	70	69	285	5,291
Cindy Figg-Currier	69	78	71	68	286	4,805
Lisa Hackney	68	74	71	73	286	4,805
Pat Hurst	70	78	70	69	287	4,201
Natascha Fink	73	73	70	71	287	4,201
Betsy King	71	74	71	71	287	4,201
Carin Hj Koch	69	75	72	71	287	4,201
Helen Alfredsson	69	72	75	71	287	4,201
Nancy Harvey	66	78	69	74	287	4,201

Chick-fil-A Charity Championship

Eagle's Landing Country Club, Stockbridge, Georgia
Par 36-36–72; 6,187 yards
(Shortened to 36 holes — rain.)

April 25-27
purse, $550,000

	SCORES		TOTAL	MONEY
Nancy Lopez	71	66	137	$82,500
Tina Barrett	70	69	139	39,208
Deb Richard	69	70	139	39,208
Karrie Webb	69	70	139	39,208
Lorie Kane	68	72	140	23,524
Kelly Robbins	71	70	141	14,206
Leigh Ann Mills	71	70	141	14,206
Alicia Dibos	71	70	141	14,206
Jill Briles-Hinton	70	71	141	14,206
Susie Redman	69	72	141	14,206
Hiromi Kobayashi	69	72	141	14,206
Jan Stephenson	72	70	142	8,579
Dale Reid	72	70	142	8,579
Laurel Kean	70	72	142	8,579
Laura Davies	70	72	142	8,579
Judy Dickinson	69	73	142	8,579
Juli Inkster	73	70	143	6,780
Jane Geddes	73	70	143	6,780
Alison Nicholas	71	72	143	6,780
Emilee Klein	71	72	143	6,780
Kris Tschetter	73	71	144	5,511
Annika Sorenstam	72	72	144	5,511
Catrin Nilsmark	72	72	144	5,511
Jenny Lidback	71	73	144	5,511
Susan Veasey	71	73	144	5,511
Barb Mucha	70	74	144	5,511
Luciana Bemvenuti	75	70	145	3,809
Helen Alfredsson	75	70	145	3,809
Missie McGeorge	74	71	145	3,809
Brandie Burton	74	71	145	3,809

	SCORES	TOTAL	MONEY
Noelle Daghe	74 71	145	3,809
Betsy King	73 72	145	3,809
Amy Benz	73 72	145	3,809
Nancy Harvey	72 73	145	3,809
Dana Dormann	72 73	145	3,809
Dina Ammaccapane	72 73	145	3,809
Elaine Crosby	71 74	145	3,809
Mardi Lunn	71 74	145	3,809
Katie Peterson-Parker	70 75	145	3,809
Danielle Ammaccapane	70 75	145	3,809
Marianne Morris	69 76	145	3,809

Sprint Titleholders Championship

LPGA International, Daytona Beach, Florida
Par 36-36–72; 6,393 yards

May 1-4
purse, $1,200,000

	SCORES				TOTAL	MONEY
Tammie Green	66	67	69	72	274	$180,000
Annika Sorenstam	71	69	70	66	276	111,711
Cindy Schreyer	69	71	70	67	277	65,416
Kelly Robbins	72	67	69	69	277	65,416
Karrie Webb	68	71	69	69	277	65,416
Nancy Lopez	70	70	66	72	278	42,268
Sherri Steinhauer	71	70	68	70	279	33,513
Dawn Coe-Jones	70	71	68	70	279	33,513
Pat Hurst	72	72	70	66	280	24,455
Meg Mallon	72	67	70	71	280	24,455
Kris Monaghan	68	68	71	73	280	24,455
Kristal Parker-Gregory	71	65	69	75	280	24,455
Missie Berteotti	69	71	72	69	281	19,927
Emilee Klein	70	69	74	69	282	16,303
Wendy Doolan	70	72	70	70	282	16,303
Chris Johnson	72	68	72	70	282	16,303
Juli Inkster	71	70	70	71	282	16,303
Laura Davies	73	68	68	73	282	16,303
Lisa Hackney	67	70	70	75	282	16,303
Brandie Burton	70	70	72	71	283	12,740
Kate Golden	68	72	72	71	283	12,740
Patty Sheehan	70	69	70	74	283	12,740
Dottie Pepper	68	69	71	75	283	12,740
Kris Tschetter	67	67	70	79	283	12,740
Liselotte Neumann	73	70	71	70	284	10,808
Nanci Bowen	70	73	70	71	284	10,808
Deb Richard	69	72	71	72	284	10,808
Colleen Walker	69	71	70	74	284	10,808
Lorie Kane	74	70	73	68	285	9,214
Joan Pitcock	72	71	68	74	285	9,214
Hollis Stacy	73	69	69	74	285	9,214
Michelle Estill	68	71	71	75	285	9,214
Betsy King	71	65	74	75	285	9,214

Sara Lee Classic

Hermitage Golf Course, Old Hickory, Tennessee
Par 36-36–72; 6,290 yards

May 9-11
purse, $675,000

	SCORES			TOTAL	MONEY
Terry-Jo Myers	70	67	70	207	$101,250
Laurel Kean	69	72	66	207	54,345
Nancy Harvey	67	72	68	207	54,345

(Myers defeated Harvey on second and Kean on fifth extra hole.)

Dale Eggeling	71	69	68	208	32,267
Kelly Robbins	70	66	72	208	32,267
Dana Dormann	71	71	68	210	21,908
Jan Stephenson	70	72	68	210	21,908
Lisa Kiggens	73	72	66	211	13,982
Erika Wicoff	71	74	66	211	13,982
Amy Read	73	69	69	211	13,982
Alicia Dibos	72	68	71	211	13,982
Helen Alfredsson	66	74	71	211	13,982
Kim Saiki	70	69	72	211	13,982
Chris Johnson	70	73	69	212	9,850
Nancy Lopez	71	70	71	212	9,850
Tina Tombs	69	72	71	212	9,850
Kris Tschetter	72	73	68	212	9,850
Marianne Morris	73	71	69	213	7,387
Barb Mucha	72	72	69	213	7,387
Kris Monaghan	72	72	69	213	7,387
Becky Iverson	72	71	70	213	7,387
Tammie Green	71	72	70	213	7,387
Amy Fruhwirth	71	71	71	213	7,387
Amy Benz	71	69	73	213	7,387
Michelle McGann	69	70	74	213	7,387
Cindy Figg-Currier	71	66	76	213	7,387
Lorie Kane	72	74	68	214	4,848
Kim Williams	73	71	80	214	4,848
Mardi Lunn	71	73	70	214	4,848
Rosie Jones	70	74	70	214	4,848
Sherri Steinhauer	73	70	71	214	4,848
Deb Richard	72	71	71	214	4,848
Joan Pitcock	72	71	71	214	4,848
Kathy Postlewait	72	70	72	214	4,848
Jane Geddes	70	72	72	214	4,848
Carin Hj Koch	74	67	73	214	4,848
Cathy Johnston-Forbes	73	68	73	214	4,848
Donna Andrews	71	70	73	214	4,848
Alison Nicholas	71	70	73	214	4,848

McDonald's LPGA Championship

Du Pont Country Club, Wilmington, Delaware
Par 35-36–71; 6,386 yards

May 15-18
purse, $1,200,000

	SCORES				TOTAL	MONEY
Chris Johnson	68	73	69	71	281	$180,000
Leta Lindley	72	69	69	71	281	111,711

(Johnson defeated Lindley on second extra hole.)

Annika Sorenstam	70	73	72	67	282	81,519
Laura Davies	67	75	74	68	284	57,365

		SCORES			TOTAL	MONEY
Sherri Steinhauer	68	71	73	72	284	57,365
Gail Graham	69	79	71	66	285	38,947
Dawn Coe-Jones	70	75	71	69	285	38,947
Trish Johnson	70	73	72	71	286	31,400
Karrie Webb	71	79	70	67	287	26,871
Barb Mucha	68	73	72	74	287	26,871
Kelly Robbins	73	74	74	67	288	20,047
Pat Bradley	70	75	76	67	288	20,047
Brandie Burton	71	73	76	68	288	20,047
Dana Dormann	70	73	75	70	288	20,047
Judy Dickinson	75	72	68	73	288	20,047
Wendy Doolan	74	72	74	69	289	15,397
Lorie Kane	73	74	71	71	289	15,397
Donna Andrews	73	71	73	72	289	15,397
Kim Saiki	68	75	69	77	289	15,397
Amy Fruhwirth	72	75	73	70	290	13,586
Jennifer Wyatt	73	75	71	71	290	13,586
Mardi Lunn	72	77	75	67	291	12,176
Meg Mallon	72	76	73	70	291	12,176
Tina Barrett	69	77	75	70	291	12,176
Dale Reid	74	75	73	70	292	10,446
Wendy Ward	72	78	71	71	292	10,446
Catriona Matthew	71	75	75	71	292	10,446
Missie McGeorge	73	74	73	72	292	10,446
Alicia Dibos	71	76	73	72	292	10,446
Cindy Figg-Currier	71	76	72	73	292	10,446

Corning Classic

Corning Country Club, Corning, New York
Par 36-36—72; 6,062 yards

May 22-25
purse, $650,000

		SCORES			TOTAL	MONEY
Rosie Jones	72	69	71	65	277	$97,500
Tammie Green	71	70	67	69	277	60,510
(Jones defeated Green on first extra hole.)						
Helen Dobson	73	70	68	67	278	44,156
Karen Weiss	75	67	70	68	280	28,346
Kathryn Marshall	72	71	68	69	280	28,346
Michele Redman	71	69	70	70	280	28,346
Pat Bradley	73	72	69	67	281	18,152
Penny Hammel	72	73	68	68	281	18,152
Patty Sheehan	74	68	69	71	282	15,373
Joan Pitcock	74	68	72	69	283	13,083
Helen Alfredsson	70	73	68	72	283	13,083
Denise Killeen	77	72	69	66	284	10,793
Patti Liscio	72	72	69	71	284	10,793
Colleen Walker	72	71	70	71	284	10,793
Catriona Matthew	73	74	70	68	285	8,749
Tina Barrett	73	72	72	68	285	8,749
Caroline Pierce	70	75	70	70	285	8,749
Kris Monaghan	74	69	70	72	285	8,749
Barb Mucha	73	74	70	69	286	7,523
Anne Marie Palli	76	70	70	70	286	7,523
Deb Richard	73	70	72	71	286	7,523
Mitzi Edge	76	71	70	70	287	6,721
Nancy Ramsbottom	72	73	71	71	287	6,721

	SCORES	TOTAL	MONEY
Sharon Barrett	77 72 73 66	288	6,050
Mardi Lunn	69 74 72 73	288	6,050
Michelle Mackall	75 70 69 74	288	6,050
Sally Little	75 68 71 74	288	6,050
Dawn Coe-Jones	78 69 73 69	289	5,462
Janice Gibson	72 77 69 71	289	5,462
Amy Read	77 73 74 66	290	4,402
Charlotta Sorenstam	78 71 73 68	290	4,402
Heather Drew	76 72 74 68	290	4,402
Vickie Odegard	72 73 75 70	290	4,402
Missie McGeorge	78 71 70 71	290	4,402
Laurel Kean	76 73 70 71	290	4,402
Karen Noble	75 74 70 71	290	4,402
Ellie Gibson	79 69 70 72	290	4,402
Kim Williams	74 72 71 73	290	4,402
Michelle Dobek	73 70 73 74	290	4,402

Michelob Light Classic

Forest Hills Country Club, St. Louis, Missouri
Par 36-36–72; 6,350 yards

May 29-June 1
purse, $600,000

	SCORES	TOTAL	MONEY
Annika Sorenstam	70 69 66 72	277	$90,000
Hiromi Kobayashi	69 68 69 74	280	55,855
Karrie Webb	70 71 71 72	284	40,759
Lisa Hackney	74 71 69 71	285	31,702
Kathryn Marshall	72 71 72 71	286	25,663
Wendy Doolan	72 75 70 70	287	19,473
Penny Hammel	69 73 73 72	287	19,473
Erika Wicoff	71 71 76 70	288	14,190
Karen Weiss	70 74 72 72	288	14,190
Nancy Ramsbottom	73 68 73 74	288	14,190
Nancy Harvey	70 75 73 71	289	10,710
Catriona Matthew	73 73 71 72	289	10,710
Kate Golden	73 71 73 72	289	10,710
Tina Barrett	73 75 70 72	290	9,099
Chris Johnson	72 73 70 75	290	9,099
Janice Gibson	73 74 73 71	291	7,740
Pam Wright	77 71 71 72	291	7,740
Amy Fruhwirth	73 74 71 73	291	7,740
Nanci Bowen	73 74 67 77	291	7,740
Rachel Hetherington	74 76 73 69	292	6,540
Lorie Kane	72 77 73 70	292	6,540
Cathy Johnston-Forbes	75 71 69 77	292	6,540
Dottie Pepper	70 74 71 77	292	6,540
Nancy Scranton	76 74 71 72	293	5,717
Laurel Kean	69 78 72 74	293	5,717
Jan Stephenson	72 75 70 76	293	5,717
Anna Acker-Macosko	75 74 75 70	294	5,174
Luciana Bemvenuti	72 76 76 70	294	5,174
Se Ri Pak	74 74 74 72	294	5,174
Dale Reid	72 75 78 70	295	4,333
Mitzi Edge	75 75 72 73	295	4,333
Jane Crafter	71 76 75 73	295	4,333
Emilee Klein	74 72 75 74	295	4,333
Mary Beth Zimmerman	73 76 71 75	295	4,333

	SCORES	TOTAL	MONEY
Vicki Goetze-Ackerman	71 74 73 77	295	4,333
Jody Anschutz	68 73 74 80	295	4,333

Oldsmobile Classic

Walnut Hills Country Club, East Lansing, Michigan
Par 36-36–72; 6,191 yards

June 5-8
purse, $600,000

	SCORES	TOTAL	MONEY
Pat Hurst	68 70 71 70	279	$90,000
Juli Inkster	69 70 71 70	280	55,855
Kim Saiki	73 68 71 69	281	36,230
Susie Redman	70 70 70 71	281	36,230
Elaine Crosby	68 72 70 72	282	23,398
Lisa Hackney	68 71 68 75	282	23,398
Leta Lindley	68 69 76 70	283	15,096
Michelle McGann	73 67 72 71	283	15,096
Cathy Johnston-Forbes	74 64 73 72	283	15,096
Jenny Lidback	71 71 68 73	283	15,096
Chris Johnson	72 68 73 71	284	11,075
Caroline Pierce	70 72 70 72	284	11,075
Karrie Webb	70 73 74 68	285	9,112
Hollis Stacy	72 69 74 70	285	9,112
Dina Ammaccapane	73 72 68 72	285	9,112
Kelly Robbins	71 64 78 72	285	9,112
Donna Andrews	72 73 73 68	286	7,300
Suzanne Strudwick	74 71 72 69	286	7,300
Vicki Goetze-Ackerman	71 69 76 70	286	7,300
Liselotte Neumann	72 66 75 73	286	7,300
Barb Whitehead	70 72 70 74	286	7,300
Vickie Odegard	73 72 72 70	287	6,143
Tammie Green	72 72 70 73	287	6,143
Tina Barrett	68 73 72 74	287	6,143
Angie Ridgeway	69 76 73 70	288	5,458
Cathy Mockett	70 72 73 73	288	5,458
Laura Baugh	70 67 78 73	288	5,458
Dana Dormann	73 69 71 75	288	5,458
Barb Mucha	75 70 74 70	289	4,505
Nanci Bowen	71 75 72 71	289	4,505
Pat Bradley	74 70 72 73	289	4,505
Dale Eggeling	72 72 72 73	289	4,505
Betsy King	75 70 70 74	289	4,505
Leslie Spalding	74 69 71 75	289	4,505
Debbi Koyama	71 72 71 75	289	4,505

Edina Realty Classic

Rush Creek Golf Club, Maple Grove, Minnesota
Par 36-36–72; 6,342 yards

June 13-15
purse, $600,000

	SCORES	TOTAL	MONEY
Danielle Ammaccapane	70 70 68	208	$90,000
Hiromi Kobayashi	69 70 70	209	38,494
Jane Geddes	70 67 72	209	38,494
Catriona Matthew	69 68 72	209	38,494

	SCORES			TOTAL	MONEY
Mayumi Hirase	69	68	72	209	38,494
Kris Tschetter	68	70	72	210	19,473
Brandie Burton	67	68	75	210	19,473
Susie Redman	70	72	69	211	12,922
Cindy Rarick	70	72	69	211	12,922
Pat Bradley	70	71	70	211	12,922
Erika Wicoff	68	70	73	211	12,922
Michelle McGann	67	70	74	211	12,922
Stefania Croce	71	73	68	212	8,227
Cindy Figg-Currier	73	70	69	212	8,227
Tracy Hanson	68	75	69	212	8,227
Vicki Fergon	74	68	70	212	8,227
Donna Andrews	71	71	70	212	8,227
Moira Dunn	69	72	71	212	8,227
Michelle Estill	74	66	72	212	8,227
Pat Hurst	67	71	74	212	8,227
Leslie Spalding	75	71	67	213	6,116
Missie Berteotti	70	74	69	213	6,116
Kelly Robbins	70	73	70	213	6,116
Jenny Lidback	69	74	70	213	6,116
Dana Dormann	72	69	72	213	6,116
Mary Beth Zimmerman	76	69	69	214	4,709
Kristi Albers	75	70	69	214	4,709
Rachel Hetherington	72	73	69	214	4,709
Sally Little	69	76	69	214	4,709
Emilee Klein	71	73	70	214	4,709
Michele Redman	72	71	71	214	4,709
Jill McGill	72	71	71	214	4,709
Sherri Steinhauer	72	70	72	214	4,709
Nancy Harvey	71	70	73	214	4,709
Juli Inkster	71	70	73	214	4,709

Rochester International

Locust Hill Country Club, Pittsford, New York
Par 35-37–72; 6,162 yards

June 19-22
purse, $600,000

	SCORES				TOTAL	MONEY
Penny Hammel	71	70	70	68	279	$90,000
Tammie Green	71	71	70	68	280	43,589
Dottie Pepper	69	69	71	71	280	43,589
Nanci Bowen	68	67	74	71	280	43,589
Kim Saiki	71	72	68	70	281	21,948
Wendy Doolan	72	68	70	71	281	21,948
Allison Finney	70	69	69	73	281	21,948
Joan Pitcock	71	71	68	72	282	16,000
Donna Andrews	71	70	74	68	283	14,461
Catriona Matthew	73	71	71	69	284	11,384
Patty Sheehan	69	73	71	71	284	11,384
Amy Fruhwirth	70	74	68	72	284	11,384
Gail Graham	69	74	66	75	284	11,384
Michelle McGann	66	72	78	69	285	8,307
Leta Lindley	73	69	73	70	285	8,307
Susie Redman	73	70	71	71	285	8,307
Rachel Hetherington	72	69	73	71	285	8,307
Jennifer Wyatt	70	71	73	71	285	8,307
Kris Monaghan	71	71	71	72	285	8,307

	SCORES				TOTAL	MONEY
Stephanie Maynor	76	70	72	68	286	6,769
Brandie Burton	73	71	73	69	286	6,769
Liselotte Neumann	72	71	73	70	286	6,769
Anne Marie Palli	71	74	74	68	287	5,603
Michele Redman	74	69	75	69	287	5,603
Erika Hayashida	74	70	72	71	287	5,603
Sherri Steinhauer	69	71	76	71	287	5,603
Debbi Koyama	71	70	74	72	287	5,603
Nancy Scranton	67	68	79	73	287	5,603
Amy Read	75	68	70	74	287	5,603
Nancy Ramsbottom	68	76	75	69	288	4,529
Karen Weiss	71	72	74	71	288	4,529
Danielle Ammaccapane	70	74	72	72	288	4,529
Sherrin Smyers	74	67	74	73	288	4,529
Cindy Schreyer	69	69	76	74	288	4,529

ShopRite Classic

Greate Bay Resort & Country Club,
Somers Point, New Jersey
Par 36-35–71; 6,235 yards

June 27-29
purse, $900,000

	SCORES			TOTAL	MONEY
Michelle McGann	72	65	64	201	$135,000
Annika Sorenstam	65	68	71	204	85,384
Juli Inkster	71	69	66	206	62,307
Cindy Schreyer	68	72	67	207	34,245
Patty Sheehan	67	71	69	207	34,245
Dottie Pepper	69	67	71	207	34,245
Caroline Blaylock	66	70	71	207	34,245
Jane Geddes	67	68	72	207	34,245
Kathryn Marshall	72	66	70	208	21,692
Karrie Webb	71	70	68	209	17,691
Tina Barrett	69	71	69	209	17,691
Amy Fruhwirth	69	68	72	209	17,691
Jody Anschutz	72	72	66	210	13,476
Pat Hurst	72	69	69	210	13,476
Sherri Steinhauer	72	68	70	210	13,476
Sally Little	68	72	70	210	13,476
Vickie Odegard	67	68	75	210	13,476
Kelly Kuehne	73	70	68	211	10,392
Martha Nause	72	71	68	211	10,392
Vicki Fergon	71	72	68	211	10,392
Dana Dormann	71	71	69	211	10,392
Catriona Matthew	69	70	72	211	10,392
Donna Andrews	67	72	72	211	10,392
Sherrin Smyers	71	70	71	212	8,399
Colleen Walker	71	69	72	212	8,399
Allison Finney	72	67	73	212	8,399
Rosie Jones	68	71	73	212	8,399
Wendy Doolan	69	69	74	212	8,399
Liselotte Neumann	73	70	70	213	6,922
Lisa Hackney	72	71	70	213	6,922
Amy Alcott	70	73	70	213	6,922
Maggie Will-Halpin	72	70	71	213	6,922
Caroline Pierce	71	69	73	213	6,922
Alicia Dibos	70	70	73	213	6,922

Jamie Farr Kroger Classic

Highland Meadows Golf Club, Sylvania, Ohio
Par 34-37–71; 6,319 yards

July 3-6
purse, $700,000

		SCORES			TOTAL	MONEY
Kelly Robbins	67	64	67	67	265	$105,000
Tammie Green	67	69	70	67	273	65,165
Nancy Lopez	68	66	71	69	274	47,553
Vickie Odegard	67	71	67	71	276	36,985
Terry-Jo Myers	70	71	69	67	277	27,298
Karrie Webb	65	68	71	73	277	27,298
Alicia Dibos	74	70	70	64	278	20,782
Helen Alfredsson	71	70	66	72	279	17,435
Missie McGeorge	70	67	70	72	279	17,435
Brandie Burton	71	71	74	64	280	12,210
Hiromi Kobayashi	70	71	72	67	280	12,210
Kris Monaghan	71	72	69	68	280	12,210
Joan Pitcock	76	69	66	69	280	12,210
Susie Redman	70	71	69	70	280	12,210
Tracy Hanson	68	72	70	70	280	12,210
Dana Dormann	72	71	68	70	281	9,158
Juli Inkster	69	74	68	70	281	9,158
Amy Benz	71	71	68	71	281	9,158
Amy Fruhwirth	70	74	70	68	282	7,461
Cindy Figg-Currier	68	73	72	69	282	7,461
Kathryn Marshall	72	72	68	70	282	7,461
Rachel Hetherington	70	73	68	71	282	7,461
Sally Little	68	71	72	71	282	7,461
Tina Barrett	74	67	68	73	282	7,461
Laurie Rinker-Graham	66	74	68	74	282	7,461
Dina Ammaccapane	73	70	72	68	283	6,093
Carin Hj Koch	71	70	74	68	283	6,093
Jody Anschutz	73	72	68	70	283	6,093
Kristal Parker-Gregory	70	73	69	71	283	6,093
Kristi Albers	72	71	72	69	284	5,095
Pat Bradley	74	70	70	70	284	5,095
Cathy Johnston-Forbes	68	73	73	70	284	5,095
Marianne Morris	68	71	73	72	284	5,095
Nanci Bowen	69	71	71	73	284	5,095
Penny Hammel	70	69	71	74	284	5,095

U.S. Women's Open

Pumpkin Ridge Golf Club, Cornelius, Oregon
Par 36-35–71; 6,365 yards

July 10-13
purse, $1,300,000

		SCORES			TOTAL	MONEY
Alison Nicholas	70	66	67	71	274	$232,500
Nancy Lopez	69	68	69	69	275	137,500
Kelly Robbins	68	69	74	66	277	86,708
Karrie Webb	73	72	65	68	278	60,432
Stefania Croce	72	69	71	67	279	46,159
Lisa Hackney	71	70	67	71	279	46,159
Tammie Green	74	70	71	65	280	37,542
Michele Redman	74	67	70	69	280	37,542
Patty Sheehan	72	71	71	68	282	28,769
Chris Johnson	72	68	73	69	282	28,769

	SCORES				TOTAL	MONEY
Dawn Coe-Jones	72	67	73	70	282	28,769
Donna Andrews	74	71	66	71	282	28,769
Akiko Fukushima	71	71	69	71	282	28,769
Brandie Burton	73	72	69	70	284	21,287
Dottie Pepper	72	70	72	70	284	21,287
Juli Inkster	72	66	76	70	284	21,287
Liselotte Neumann	67	70	76	71	284	21,287
Deb Richard	68	70	73	73	284	21,287
Trish Johnson	69	74	71	71	285	17,407
Kim Williams	71	71	67	76	285	17,407
Kelly Kuehne	72	73	74	67	286	13,800
Karen Weiss	74	72	72	68	286	13,800
Se Ri Pak	68	74	75	69	286	13,800
Pat Hurst	72	74	70	70	286	13,800
Luciana Bemvenuti	73	71	72	70	286	13,800
Caroline Pierce	71	71	73	71	286	13,800
Catriona Matthew	76	69	70	72	287	10,961
Sherrin Smyers	71	71	75	71	288	9,188
Pat Bradley	72	71	73	72	288	9,188
Kathryn Marshall	72	71	73	72	288	9,188
Betsy King	74	72	69	73	288	9,188
Joan Pitcock	71	69	75	73	288	9,188

JAL Big Apple Classic

Wykagyl Country Club, New Rochelle, New York
Par 35-36–71; 6,161 yards

July 17-20
purse, $750,000

	SCORES				TOTAL	MONEY
Michele Redman	64	67	71	70	272	$112,500
Annika Sorenstam	71	68	67	69	275	69,819
Meg Mallon	71	70	67	68	276	50,949
Chris Johnson	68	73	69	67	277	35,853
Karrie Webb	66	73	68	70	277	35,853
Lorie Kane	71	68	72	67	278	24,342
Wendy Doolan	73	67	69	69	278	24,342
Betsy King	70	71	69	69	279	17,738
Tina Barrett	69	67	71	72	279	17,738
Barb Mucha	68	68	70	73	279	17,738
Laura Davies	71	66	72	71	280	14,366
Helen Alfredsson	66	70	72	73	281	12,856
Rachel Hetherington	69	69	69	74	281	12,856
Terry-Jo Myers	69	71	70	72	282	11,724
Caroline Pierce	70	76	69	68	283	10,340
Catrin Nilsmark	70	72	71	70	283	10,340
Dina Ammaccapane	69	72	71	71	283	10,340
Sally Little	69	73	75	67	284	8,893
Hollis Stacy	68	73	72	71	284	8,893
Jan Stephenson	72	67	69	76	284	8,893
Cindy Schreyer	66	68	73	77	284	8,893
Kim Saiki	70	74	73	69	286	7,383
Juli Inkster	70	70	76	70	286	7,383
Janice Gibson	73	71	69	73	286	7,383
Missie McGeorge	68	75	70	73	286	7,383
Alicia Dibos	71	67	75	73	286	7,383
Stephanie Maynor	72	73	71	71	287	6,327
Danielle Ammaccapane	71	72	72	72	287	6,327

	SCORES	TOTAL	MONEY
Rosie Jones	69 73 72 73	287	6,327
Lisa Hackney	71 69 72 75	287	6,327

Giant Eagle Classic

Avalon Lakes Golf Course, Warren, Ohio
Par 36-36–72; 6,308 yards

July 25-27
purse, $600,000

	SCORES	TOTAL	MONEY
Tammie Green	64 71 68	203	$90,000
Laura Davies	67 66 70	203	55,855
(Green defeated Davies on fifth extra hole.)			
Cindy Figg-Currier	67 69 70	206	40,759
Barb Mucha	71 68 68	207	24,078
Charlotta Sorenstam	70 69 68	207	24,078
Hiromi Kobayashi	68 69 70	207	24,078
Brandie Burton	65 66 76	207	24,078
Kathy Guadagnino	68 72 68	208	13,511
Dina Ammaccapane	71 68 69	208	13,511
Nancy Lopez	70 66 72	208	13,511
Moira Dunn	67 68 73	208	13,511
Penny Hammel	69 71 69	209	10,265
Kim Saiki	70 69 70	209	10,265
Wendy Ward	68 72 70	210	8,332
Cindy Schreyer	70 69 71	210	8,332
Janice Gibson	69 69 72	210	8,332
Suzanne Strudwick	69 69 72	210	8,332
Catriona Matthew	71 65 74	210	8,332
Jan Stephenson	75 70 66	211	6,175
Pat Hurst	72 73 66	211	6,175
Amy Read	70 73 68	211	6,175
Nancy Ramsbottom	71 71 69	211	6,175
Tina Tombs	71 69 71	211	6,175
Lorie Kane	69 70 72	211	6,175
Erika Wicoff	68 71 72	211	6,175
Dottie Pepper	70 68 73	211	6,175
Emilee Klein	69 69 73	211	6,175
Dana Dormann	70 75 67	212	4,380
Donna Andrews	72 71 69	212	4,380
Liselotte Neumann	72 70 70	212	4,380
Joan Pitcock	69 73 70	212	4,380
Jody Anschutz	73 68 71	212	4,380
Anna Acker-Macosko	64 77 71	212	4,380
Karen Weiss	71 69 72	212	4,380
Tracy Hanson	74 65 73	212	4,380
Heather Drew	69 70 73	212	4,380
Lisa Walters	68 70 74	212	4,380

du Maurier Classic

Glen Abbey Golf Club, Oakville, Ontario, Canada
Par 36-37–73; 6,367 yards

July 31-August 3
purse, $1,200,000

	SCORES				TOTAL	MONEY
Colleen Walker	68	72	73	65	278	$180,000
Liselotte Neumann	71	67	73	69	280	111,711
Betsy King	71	69	72	69	281	72,461
Kelly Robbins	71	65	73	72	281	72,461
Cindy Figg-Currier	69	74	69	70	282	46,797
Juli Inkster	70	69	71	72	282	46,797
Emilee Klein	73	70	71	69	283	33,513
Rosie Jones	69	71	71	72	283	33,513
Lisa Hackney	73	69	75	67	284	26,871
Chris Johnson	70	72	72	70	284	26,871
Jane Geddes	74	69	74	68	285	21,335
Donna Andrews	71	69	76	69	285	21,335
Brandie Burton	69	75	66	75	285	21,335
Helen Alfredsson	75	70	69	72	286	18,114
Tina Barrett	71	71	70	74	286	18,114
Rachel Hetherington	73	72	74	68	287	14,197
Kris Tschetter	72	73	74	68	287	14,197
Hiromi Kobayashi	71	73	72	71	287	14,197
Laura Davies	73	70	73	71	287	14,197
Danielle Ammaccapane	71	75	69	72	287	14,197
Deb Richard	72	73	70	72	287	14,197
Kim Saiki	75	69	71	72	287	14,197
Wendy Ward	72	71	72	72	287	14,197
Sherri Steinhauer	72	73	73	70	288	11,351
Tracy Hanson	72	69	76	71	288	11,351
Barb Mucha	71	75	70	72	288	11,351
Dottie Pepper	72	75	73	69	289	10,264
Helen Dobson	74	69	73	73	289	10,264
Karrie Webb	71	72	70	76	289	10,264
Jill Briles-Hinton	77	70	73	70	290	8,583
Jackie Gallagher-Smith	76	69	73	72	290	8,583
Jane Crafter	70	73	74	73	290	8,583
Kathryn Marshall	68	75	74	73	290	8,583
Lorie Kane	74	72	70	74	290	8,583
Susie Redman	72	72	72	74	290	8,583
Meg Mallon	74	70	71	75	290	8,583

Friendly's Classic

Crestview Country Club, Agawam, Massachusetts
Par 36-36–72; 6,381 yards

August 7-1
purse, $550,00

	SCORES				TOTAL	MONEY
Deb Richard	72	70	68	67	277	$82,500
Chris Johnson	68	72	70	68	278	51,201
Brandie Burton	73	70	69	68	280	37,363
Pat Hurst	70	69	73	71	283	29,060
Dana Dormann	73	72	69	70	284	21,448
Betsy King	73	69	69	73	284	21,448
Amy Fruhwirth	70	75	70	70	285	15,359
Nancy Harvey	73	68	69	75	285	15,359
Emilee Klein	73	72	71	70	286	13,008

	SCORES				TOTAL	MONEY
Karrie Webb	69	72	75	71	287	10,615
Allison Finney	71	73	70	73	287	10,615
Cathy Mockett	72	71	71	73	287	10,615
Denise Killeen	74	71	69	74	288	8,865
Luciana Bemvenuti	73	71	70	74	288	8,865
Carin Hj Koch	71	72	77	69	289	6,967
Wendy Ward	74	74	71	70	289	6,967
Martha Nause	71	76	72	70	289	6,967
Cindy Schreyer	73	71	74	71	289	6,967
Noelle Daghe	72	75	70	72	289	6,967
Kim Saiki	70	74	72	73	289	6,967
Dottie Pepper	71	70	74	74	289	6,967
Barb Whitehead	74	68	77	71	290	5,317
Kris Tschetter	71	71	76	72	290	5,317
Meg Mallon	74	70	73	73	290	5,317
Kristi Albers	72	69	76	73	290	5,317
Elaine Crosby	77	66	73	74	290	5,317
Sherri Steinhauer	70	72	72	76	290	5,317
Kim Williams	73	72	75	71	291	4,547
Tina Tombs	76	70	73	72	291	4,547
Lisa Kiggens	72	73	73	73	291	4,547

Star Bank Classic

Country Club of the North, Beavercreek, Ohio
Par 36-36–72; 6,331 yards

August 22-24
purse, $550,000

	SCORES			TOTAL	MONEY
Colleen Walker	67	69	67	203	$82,500
Terry-Jo Myers	72	67	66	205	51,201
Laura Davies	71	68	67	206	27,330
Tammie Green	68	70	68	206	27,330
Kim Williams	69	67	70	206	27,330
Dottie Pepper	68	66	72	206	27,330
Rosie Jones	72	67	69	208	15,359
Karen Weiss	68	69	71	208	15,359
Michelle Dobek	73	69	67	209	10,437
Hollis Stacy	70	71	68	209	10,437
Hiromi Kobayashi	71	69	69	209	10,437
Chris Johnson	68	70	71	209	10,437
Luciana Bemvenuti	70	67	72	209	10,437
Kelly Robbins	69	67	73	209	10,437
Juli Inkster	70	71	69	210	7,269
Marianne Morris	70	71	69	210	7,269
Nancy Ramsbottom	69	72	69	210	7,269
Tracy Hanson	70	70	70	210	7,269
Cristie Kerr	69	69	72	210	7,269
Page Dunlap	73	70	68	211	5,556
Jane Geddes	71	72	68	211	5,556
Lisa Walters	71	71	69	211	5,556
Donna Andrews	71	71	69	211	5,556
Cristi Albers	71	71	69	211	5,556
Renee Heiken	72	68	71	211	5,556
Jackie Gallagher-Smith	71	69	71	211	5,556
Betsy King	71	67	73	211	5,556
Martha Nause	75	69	68	212	4,321
Smriti Mehra	74	69	69	212	4,321

	SCORES			TOTAL	MONEY
Barb Mucha	72	70	70	212	4,321
Lorie Kane	71	71	70	212	4,321
Kathryn Marshall	69	70	73	212	4,321
Brandie Burton	66	72	74	212	4,321

State Farm Rail Classic

Rail Golf Club, Springfield, Illinois
Par 36-36–72; 6,403 yards

August 30-September 1
purse, $600,000

	SCORES			TOTAL	MONEY
Cindy Figg-Currier	69	63	68	200	$90,000
Kris Tschetter	68	68	64	200	48,307
Lorie Kane	67	68	65	200	48,307
(Figg-Currier defeated Tschetter and Kane on first extra hole.)					
Donna Andrews	69	66	67	202	24,078
Jane Crafter	67	67	68	202	24,078
Sherri Steinhauer	65	69	68	202	24,078
Kim Williams	69	64	69	202	24,078
Nancy Lopez	68	68	67	203	14,190
Page Dunlap	67	69	67	203	14,190
Kathryn Marshall	72	62	69	203	14,190
Helen Dobson	65	73	66	204	11,075
Michelle McGann	69	67	68	204	11,075
Kristi Albers	71	67	67	205	9,112
Rachel Hetherington	68	69	68	205	9,112
Lisa Hackney	70	66	69	205	9,112
Dana Dormann	65	71	69	205	9,112
Mitzi Edge	70	71	65	206	6,866
Annette DeLuca	70	71	65	206	6,866
Allison Finney	69	72	65	206	6,866
Alicia Dibos	71	69	66	206	6,866
Barb Whitehead	69	71	66	206	6,866
Jackie Gallagher-Smith	69	70	67	206	6,866
Moira Dunn	69	68	69	206	6,866
Jenny Murdock	67	69	70	206	6,866
Barb Mucha	68	73	66	206	6,866
Jean Zedlitz	72	68	67	207	5,100
Dina Ammaccapane	70	68	69	207	5,100
Pat Bradley	69	69	69	207	5,100
Tina Barrett	66	72	69	207	5,100
Leta Lindley	69	68	70	207	5,100
Wendy Doolan	67	70	70	207	5,100
Stephanie Maynor	69	67	71	207	5,100

Safeway Golf Championship

Columbia Edgewater Country Club, Portland, Oregon
Par 36-36–72; 6,300 yards

September 5-
purse, $550,00

	SCORES			TOTAL	MONEY
Chris Johnson	70	70	66	206	$82,500
Kim Saiki	69	72	66	207	44,282
Lisa Hackney	68	69	70	207	44,282
Shani Waugh	67	69	72	208	29,060

	SCORES			TOTAL	MONEY
Juli Inkster	71	71	67	209	19,741
Kim Williams	68	72	69	209	19,741
Dawn Coe-Jones	69	69	71	209	19,741
Susie Redman	69	72	69	210	13,007
Kelly Robbins	68	73	69	210	13,007
Karrie Webb	67	70	73	210	13,007
Karen Weiss	71	70	70	211	9,828
Denise Killeen	69	72	70	211	9,828
Tina Barrett	70	69	72	211	9,828
Suzanne Strudwick	73	69	70	212	7,688
Emilee Klein	72	69	71	212	7,688
Sherri Steinhauer	68	72	72	212	7,688
Carin Hj Koch	69	70	73	212	7,688
Dana Dormann	66	72	74	212	7,688
Annika Sorenstam	73	73	67	213	6,276
Barb Whitehead	72	71	70	213	6,276
Maggie Will-Halpin	69	71	73	213	6,276
Cindy Schreyer	66	73	74	213	6,276
Luciana Bemvenuti	73	71	70	214	5,007
Katie Peterson-Parker	72	72	70	214	5,007
Barb Mucha	68	76	70	214	5,007
Alicia Dibos	68	76	70	214	5,007
Wendy Doolan	70	73	71	214	5,007
Helen Dobson	67	75	72	214	5,007
Susan Veasey	72	69	73	214	5,007
Brandie Burton	71	68	75	214	5,007

Safeco Classic

Meridian Valley Country Club, Kent, Washington
Par 36-36–72; 6,241 yards

September 11-14
purse, $550,000

	SCORES				TOTAL	MONEY
Karrie Webb	67	67	71	67	272	$82,500
Annika Sorenstam	67	71	66	69	273	51,201
Patty Sheehan	69	68	65	75	277	37,363
Kelly Robbins	72	69	69	68	278	26,292
Dale Reid	67	72	68	71	278	26,292
Lorie Kane	70	72	68	69	279	16,697
Colleen Walker	72	70	67	70	279	16,697
Liselotte Neumann	68	70	70	71	279	16,697
Brandie Burton	72	66	71	71	280	13,008
Cindy Figg-Currier	69	72	67	73	281	10,635
Michelle McGann	68	70	70	73	281	10,635
Jenny Lidback	68	70	70	73	281	10,635
Jane Crafter	70	72	70	71	283	8,895
Laurie Brower	69	71	69	74	283	8,895
Dawn Coe-Jones	72	70	76	66	284	7,289
Michele Redman	71	72	73	68	284	7,289
Cindy Schreyer	69	73	72	70	284	7,289
Lisa Hackney	74	70	68	72	284	7,289
Nani Waugh	68	70	73	73	284	7,289
Donna Andrews	69	74	72	70	285	5,995
Dana Dormann	70	70	73	72	285	5,995
Wendy Ward	68	75	69	73	285	5,995
Angie Ridgeway	71	71	70	73	285	5,995
Emilee Klein	73	69	75	69	286	4,992

	SCORES				TOTAL	MONEY
Deb Richard	72	72	72	70	286	4,992
Luciana Bemvenuti	69	74	73	70	286	4,992
Nancy Harvey	71	71	71	73	286	4,992
Karen Weiss	71	71	71	73	286	4,992
Rachel Hetherington	69	71	73	73	286	4,992
Helen Dobson	72	71	77	67	287	4,042
Jackie Gallagher-Smith	72	72	75	68	287	4,042
Amy Read	74	71	73	69	287	4,042
Rosie Jones	75	70	72	70	287	4,042
Sherri Turner	68	77	70	72	287	4,042
Sherri Steinhauer	72	71	72	72	287	4,042

Welch's Championship

Blue Hill Country Club, Canton, Massachusetts
Par 36-36–72; 6,137 yards

September 18-21
purse, $550,000

	SCORES				TOTAL	MONEY
Liselotte Neumann	67	70	69	70	276	$82,500
Nancy Harvey	67	68	71	73	279	51,201
Karrie Webb	69	70	71	72	282	37,363
Sherri Steinhauer	71	72	67	74	284	29,060
Brandie Burton	69	78	66	72	285	18,404
Angie Ridgeway	69	70	73	73	285	18,404
Carin Hj Koch	70	69	72	74	285	18,404
Rachel Hetherington	72	66	72	75	285	18,404
Kris Tschetter	75	70	71	70	286	11,208
Laurie Brower	69	74	72	71	286	11,208
Muffin Spencer-Devlin	73	71	69	73	286	11,208
Deb Richard	73	69	70	74	286	11,208
Leigh Ann Mills	72	74	69	72	287	8,302
Chris Johnson	71	70	73	73	287	8,302
Dottie Pepper	68	73	73	73	287	8,302
Becky Iverson	74	69	70	74	287	8,302
Colleen Walker	68	73	76	71	288	6,503
Tammie Green	72	71	73	72	288	6,503
Shani Waugh	69	70	77	72	288	6,503
Michelle Estill	69	75	71	73	288	6,503
Cathy Johnston-Forbes	68	72	74	74	288	6,503
Catriona Matthew	76	68	68	76	288	6,503
Patti Liscio	74	71	73	71	289	4,957
Betsy King	72	75	70	72	289	4,957
Jill Briles-Hinton	73	70	74	72	289	4,957
Leslie Spalding	72	68	77	72	289	4,957
Erika Hayashida	71	75	70	73	289	4,957
Leta Lindley	73	72	71	73	289	4,957
Cindy Schreyer	71	74	71	73	289	4,957
Mitzi Edge	73	71	72	73	289	4,957

Fieldcrest Cannon Classic

Peninsula Club, Charlotte, North Carolina
Par 36-36–72; 6,318 yards

September 25-28
purse, $550,000

	SCORES				TOTAL	MONEY
Wendy Ward	66	65	64	70	265	$82,500
Jane Geddes	69	66	67	65	267	44,282
Rosie Jones	67	69	65	66	267	44,282
Kristal Parker-Gregory	68	68	68	66	270	29,060
Donna Andrews	69	68	69	65	271	17,324
Dottie Pepper	67	67	71	66	271	17,324
Meg Mallon	70	66	68	67	271	17,324
Juli Inkster	67	67	69	68	271	17,324
Betsy King	67	68	66	70	271	17,324
Trish Johnson	70	66	68	69	273	10,609
Kelly Robbins	66	69	68	70	273	10,609
Liselotte Neumann	66	66	71	70	273	10,609
Lorie Kane	70	66	69	69	274	8,856
Tina Barrett	69	68	67	70	274	8,856
Nancy Harvey	72	68	67	68	275	7,403
Shani Waugh	68	70	69	68	275	7,403
Cristie Kerr	69	64	72	70	275	7,403
Jackie Gallagher-Smith	70	66	68	71	275	7,403
Martha Nause	69	71	69	67	276	6,642
Becky Iverson	70	72	67	68	277	5,956
Michelle McGann	70	67	72	68	277	5,956
Sherri Steinhauer	71	69	68	69	277	5,956
Joanne Morley	70	69	68	70	277	5,956
Tammie Green	69	70	72	67	278	4,870
Erika Wicoff	76	66	68	68	278	4,870
Dana Dormann	72	67	71	68	278	4,870
Helen Dobson	70	68	72	68	278	4,870
Stefania Croce	72	69	68	69	278	4,870
Barb Mucha	68	69	72	69	278	4,870
Leta Lindley	68	71	68	71	278	4,870

CoreStates Betsy King Classic

Berkleigh Country Club, Kutztown, Pennsylvania
Par 35-37–72; 6,075 yards

October 2-5
purse, $600,000

	SCORES				TOTAL	MONEY
Annika Sorenstam	70	67	68	69	274	$90,000
Kelly Robbins	72	69	65	70	276	55,855
Wendy Doolan	70	72	69	66	277	29,814
Juli Inkster	70	72	68	67	277	29,814
Catriona Matthew	67	70	70	70	277	29,814
Betsy King	70	68	67	72	277	29,814
Denise Killeen	73	67	73	66	279	15,096
Vickie Odegard	74	66	70	69	279	15,096
Mardi Lunn	71	69	70	69	279	15,096
Trish Johnson	69	70	70	70	279	15,096
Dale Reid	73	71	70	66	280	9,742
Chris Johnson	70	73	69	68	280	9,742
Lorie Kane	74	66	70	70	280	9,742
Tammie Green	72	68	70	70	280	9,742
Kim Bauer	72	68	67	73	280	9,742

	SCORES	TOTAL	MONEY
Jackie Gallagher-Smith	70 66 71 73	280	9,742
Cindy Schreyer	72 69 72 68	281	7,125
Laurel Kean	69 72 72 68	281	7,125
Tina Barrett	68 71 72 70	281	7,125
Karrie Webb	72 68 68 73	281	7,125
Dale Eggeling	70 65 73 73	281	7,125
Maggie Will-Halpin	70 67 70 74	281	7,125
Dottie Pepper	71 68 73 70	282	5,993
Cathy Mockett	73 69 69 71	282	5,993
Dana Dormann	72 73 68 70	283	5,163
Kim Saiki	73 71 69 70	283	5,163
Cindy Figg-Currier	71 71 70 71	283	5,163
Alicia Dibos	70 71 71 71	283	5,163
Gail Graham	71 70 68 74	283	5,163
Shani Waugh	70 70 69 74	283	5,163
Deb Richard	74 68 66 75	283	5,163

Samsung World Championship of Women's Golf

Lakeside Country Club, West Course, Seoul, Korea
Par 36-36–72; 6,395 yards

October 16-19
purse, $525,000

	SCORES	TOTAL	MONEY
Juli Inkster	67 74 72 67	280	$131,000
Kelly Robbins	69 74 68 69	280	62,500
Helen Alfredsson	70 71 66 73	280	62,500
(Inkster defeated Robbins and Alfredsson on first extra hole.)			
Donna Andrews	75 71 66 69	281	35,000
Chris Johnson	68 73 67 74	282	27,000
Annika Sorenstam	70 76 67 70	283	21,750
Alison Nicholas	71 71 71 70	283	21,750
Betsy King	72 72 70 70	284	17,375
Karrie Webb	67 74 72 71	284	17,375
Colleen Walker	75 71 70 71	287	15,000
Rosie Jones	73 71 70 74	288	14,500
Laura Davies	73 71 71 74	289	14,000
Michelle McGann	71 74 70 76	291	13,500
Liselotte Neumann	76 70 72 74	292	13,000
Mi-Hyun Kim	71 78 72 76	297	12,500
Ikuyo Shiotani	79 74 74 77	304	12,000

ITT LPGA Tour Championship

Desert Inn Golf Club, Las Vegas, Nevada
Par 36-36–72; 6,373 yards

November 20-23
purse, $750,000

	SCORES	TOTAL	MONEY
Annika Sorenstam	72 68 67 70	277	$160,000
Lorie Kane	71 68 71 67	277	75,000
Pat Hurst	72 64 73 68	277	75,000
(Sorenstam defeated Hurst on first and Kane on third extra hole.)			
Karrie Webb	72 66 72 69	279	40,250
Kelly Robbins	73 66 69 71	279	40,250
Nancy Lopez	69 68 71 72	280	32,500

	SCORES				TOTAL	MONEY
Donna Andrews	69	73	67	72	281	25,000
Juli Inkster	69	70	70	72	281	25,000
Chris Johnson	72	71	68	71	282	19,163
Colleen Walker	72	69	68	73	282	19,163
Hiromi Kobayashi	70	76	70	69	285	14,264
Tammie Green	72	72	69	72	285	14,264
Liselotte Neumann	72	69	72	72	285	14,264
Deb Richard	71	69	72	73	285	14,264
Dottie Pepper	70	75	73	68	286	11,452
Laura Davies	71	71	72	72	286	11,452
Cindy Figg-Currier	74	75	67	71	287	10,577
Barb Mucha	75	71	73	70	289	9,389
Sherri Steinhauer	71	73	71	74	289	9,389
Brandie Burton	71	71	72	75	289	9,389
Rosie Jones	71	68	75	75	289	9,389
Michelle McGann	71	74	71	74	290	8,577
Terry-Jo Myers	74	72	75	70	291	7,952
Alison Nicholas	71	74	75	71	291	7,952
Betsy King	72	69	79	71	291	7,952
Michele Redman	75	72	71	73	291	7,952
Tina Barrett	76	73	72	71	292	7,327
Kris Tschetter	73	78	73	69	293	7,052
Jane Geddes	69	72	79	73	293	7,052
Lisa Hackney	69				DQ	

Diners Club Matches

PGA West, Nicklaus Course, La Quinta, California
Par 36-36–72; 6,383 yards

December 11-14
purse, $700,000

FIRST ROUND

Alison Nicholas and Helen Alfredsson defeated Karrie Webb and Kelly Robbins, 19 holes
Nancy Lopez and Laura Davies defeated Tammie Green and Donna Andrews, 4 and 3
Annika Sorenstam and Michelle McGann defeated Colleen Walker and Brandie Burton, 1 up
Juli Inkster and Dottie Pepper defeated Betsy King and Chris Johnson, 5 and 4

SECOND ROUND

Lopez and Davies defeated Webb and Robbins, 1 up
Green and Andrews defeated Nicholas and Alfredsson, 20 holes
Inkster and Dottie Pepper defeated Sorenstam and McGann, 3 and 1
King and Johnson defeated Walker Brandie Burton, 4 and 3

THIRD ROUND

Webb and Robbins defeated Green and Andrews, 1 up
Lopez and Davies defeated Nicholas and Alfredsson, 2 up
Sorenstam and McGann defeated King and Johnson, 2 up
Inkster and Pepper defeated Walker and Burton, 4 and 3

FINAL ROUND

Inkster and Pepper defeated Lopez and Davies, 3 and 2

Pepper and Inkster received $110,000 each; Lopez and Davies received $60,000 each.)

Women's European Tour

Estoril Ladies' Open

Clube de Golf do Estoril, Estoril, Portugal
Par 34-35–69; 5,333 yards

May 9-11
purse, £90,000

	SCORES			TOTAL	MONEY
Mandy Sutton	63	68	71	202	£13,500
Karina Orum	66	66	71	203	9,135
Shani Waugh	68	73	66	207	6,300
Diane Barnard	67	75	66	208	3,631.50
Lora Fairclough	66	67	75	208	3,631.50
Helen Wadsworth	69	70	69	208	3,631.50
Anne-Marie Knight	69	70	69	208	3,631.50
Anna-Carin Jonasson	68	69	72	209	2,133
Joanne Mills	72	68	69	209	2,133
Maria Hjorth	73	71	66	210	1,668
Pernilla Sterner	70	74	66	210	1,668
Myra Murray	72	71	67	210	1,668
Federica Dassu	74	69	68	211	1,338
Marie-Laure de Lorenzi	69	73	69	211	1,338
Karen Lunn	74	70	67	211	1,338
Marie-Therese Pistolet	68	65	78	211	1,338
Petra Rigby-Jinglov	71	71	69	211	1,338
Johanna Head	69	71	71	211	1,338
Patricia Meunier Lebouc	69	72	71	212	1,158.75
Valerie Michaud	72	71	69	212	1,158.75
Vibeke Stensrud	74	69	69	212	1,158.75
Elizabeth Bowman	68	73	71	212	1,158.75
Xonia Wunsch-Ruiz	72	71	70	213	1,035
Sophie Gustafson	76	68	69	213	1,035
Charlotta Eliasson Wharton	71	71	71	213	1,035
Jane Leary	74	73	66	213	1,035
Kristel Mourgue d'Algue	73	71	69	213	1,035
Rae Hast	71	73	70	214	886.50
Wendy Dicks	74	67	73	214	886.50
Natascha Fink	69	74	71	214	886.50
Raquel Carriedo	72	71	71	214	886.50
Nicola Moult	73	69	72	214	886.50
Fiona Pike	69	71	74	214	886.50

American Express Tour Players' Classic

The Tytherington Club, Macclesfield, Cheshire, England
Par 36-36–72; 6,049 yards

May 15-18
purse, £100,000

	SCORES				TOTAL	MONEY
Karen Lunn	74	67	71	71	283	£15,000
Patricia Meunier Lebouc	75	69	66	74	284	8,575
Tina Fischer	69	69	73	73	284	8,575
Helen Wadsworth	74	67	72	75	288	5,400

	SCORES				TOTAL	MONEY
Anna-Carin Jonasson	75	70	70	74	289	4,240
Marie-Laure de Lorenzi	72	73	74	72	291	3,000
Janet Soulsby	75	70	70	76	291	3,000
Marina Arruti	76	76	66	73	291	3,000
Estefania Knuth	78	69	74	71	292	2,120
Sara Melin	74	75	70	73	292	2,120
Stephanie Dallongeville	75	70	72	76	293	1,680
Myra Murray	72	80	71	70	293	1,680
Anne-Marie Knight	71	74	74	74	293	1,680
Vibeke Stensrud	69	76	69	79	293	1,680
Mette Hageman	77	71	69	77	294	1,460
Sophie Gustafson	73	71	74	76	294	1,460
Kristel Mourgue d'Algue	73	76	71	74	294	1,460
Lisa Jensen	77	72	75	71	295	1,290
Amaia Arruti	73	79	68	75	295	1,290
Natascha Fink	74	74	75	72	295	1,290
Catherine Schmitt	78	70	72	75	295	1,290
Anna Radford	75	73	72	75	295	1,290
Sara Forster	74	73	74	74	295	1,290
Sarah Bennett	74	73	74	75	296	1,120
Valerie Van Ryckeghem	78	75	74	69	296	1,120
Charlotta Eliasson Wharton	72	74	75	75	296	1,120
Iben Tinning	77	73	72	74	296	1,120
Karolina Andersson	77	75	71	73	296	1,120
Diane Barnard	79	74	71	73	297	925
Maria Hjorth	73	80	71	73	297	925
Mary Grace Estuesta	76	76	75	70	297	925
Valerie Michaud	74	73	73	77	297	925
Susan Farron	77	73	74	73	297	925
Jane Leary	76	74	73	74	297	925
Fiona Pike	73	75	73	76	297	925
Julie Castanier	75	74	71	77	297	925

Ford-Stimorol Danish Open

Vejle Golf Club, Vejle, Denmark
Par 36-36–72; 5,667 yards

June 6-8
purse, £90,000

	SCORES			TOTAL	MONEY
Laura Davies	68	70	69	207	£13,500
Maria Hjorth	73	73	64	210	9,135
Marie-Laure de Lorenzi	72	69	72	213	5,580
Karen Lunn	73	71	69	213	5,580
Valerie Michaud	73	75	66	214	3,483
Johanna Head	73	71	70	214	3,483
Lara Tadiotto	69	72	74	215	2,322
Patricia Meunier Lebouc	71	70	74	215	2,322
Pernilla Sterner	69	74	72	215	2,322
Jane Leary	73	74	69	216	1,800
Anne-Marie Knight	74	74	69	217	1,656
Anna-Carin Jonasson	70	75	73	218	1,464
Mandy Sutton	73	72	73	218	1,464
Lynnette Brooky	75	72	71	218	1,464
Susan Elliott	73	75	71	219	1,260
Linda Ericsson	75	76	68	219	1,260
Mia Lojdahl	70	74	75	219	1,260
Lora Fairclough	79	70	70	219	1,260

	SCORES	TOTAL	MONEY
Iben Tinning	75 71 73	219	1,260
Sara Forster	75 74 70	219	1,260
Diane Barnard	75 73 72	220	1,089
Nadene Gole	74 72 74	220	1,089
Wendy Dicks	76 68 76	220	1,089
Sophie Gustafson	73 77 70	220	1,089
Nicola Moult	72 74 74	220	1,089
Federica Dassu	73 75 73	221	927
Gillian Stewart	71 75 75	221	927
Tracey Craik	71 74 76	221	927
Laura Navarro	71 76 74	221	927
Martina Koch	76 73 72	221	927
Sandrine Mendiburu	74 72 75	221	927
Samantha Head	74 74 73	221	927

Deesse Ladies' Swiss Open

Golf Club de Lausanne, Lausanne, Switzerland
Par 36-36–72; 6,236 yards

June 12-15
purse, £90,000

	SCORES	TOTAL	MONEY
Marie-Laure de Lorenzi	72 68 70 70	280	£13,500
Trish Johnson	68 73 70 69	280	9,135
(De Lorenzi defeated Johnson on first extra hole.)			
Karen Lunn	66 71 73 72	282	6,300
Anna-Carin Jonasson	72 70 72 70	284	4,338
Anna Berg	70 68 75 71	284	4,338
Sara Melin	71 73 72 70	286	3,150
Karina Orum	72 69 76 70	287	2,700
Joanne Morley	67 74 74 73	288	2,250
Federica Dassu	69 74 75 71	289	1,908
Lynnette Brooky	78 69 72 70	289	1,908
Susan Farron	74 70 71 75	290	1,656
Diane Barnard	75 71 74 71	291	1,464
Alison Nicholas	73 70 74 74	291	1,464
Shani Waugh	73 72 76 70	291	1,464
Joanne Mills	68 75 76 73	292	1,332
Katharina Poppmeier	72 73 76 71	292	1,332
Loraine Lambert	76 72 71 74	293	1,192.50
Anna Radford	68 77 70 78	293	1,192.50
Jane Leary	69 74 77 73	293	1,192.50
Katharina Larsson	74 72 73 74	293	1,192.50
Julie Castanier	75 67 75 76	293	1,192.50
Caroline Blaylock	74 73 71 75	293	1,192.50
Laurette Maritz	74 71 74 75	294	1,062
Dale Reid	73 72 73 76	294	1,062
Sarah Carbon	74 72 75 73	294	1,062
Maureen Madill	74 73 74 74	295	940.50
Wendy Dicks	70 76 77 72	295	940.50
Stephanie Dallongeville	73 74 73 75	295	940.50
Raquel Carriedo	72 76 75 72	295	940.50
Tina Fischer	73 73 75 74	295	940.50
Pernilla Sterner	72 74 78 71	295	940.50

Evian Masters

Royal Golf Club Evian, Evians-les-Bains, France
Par 36-36–72; 5,938 yards

June 18-21
purse, £425,000

	SCORES				TOTAL	MONEY
Hiromi Kobayashi	69	67	69	69	274	£63,750
Alison Nicholas	68	68	68	70	274	43,031.25
(Kobayashi defeated Nicholas at first extra hole.)						
Marie-Laure de Lorenzi	73	69	71	67	280	29,750
Joanne Morley	67	67	74	74	282	22,865
Carin Hj Koch	71	71	73	68	283	14,051.56
Shani Waugh	70	69	72	72	283	14,051.56
Amy Alcott	67	70	72	74	283	14,051.56
Charlotta Sorenstam	74	69	71	69	283	14,051.56
Laura Davies	74	70	70	71	285	7,987.87
Trish Johnson	70	76	67	72	285	7,987.87
Kathryn Marshall	72	71	69	73	285	7,987.87
Helen Alfredsson	72	70	70	73	285	7,987.87
Pernilla Sterner	71	72	72	70	285	7,987.87
Estefania Knuth	73	71	68	75	287	6,527.29
Lisa Hackney	71	70	73	73	287	6,527.29
Fiona Pike	76	72	70	69	287	6,527.29
Annika Sorenstam	74	74	70	70	288	6,056.25
Lynnette Brooky	71	75	70	72	288	6,056.25
Loraine Lambert	76	70	69	73	288	6,056.25
Mardi Lunn	71	73	76	69	289	5,514.37
Martina Koch	73	70	72	74	289	5,514.37
Val Skinner	72	68	77	72	289	5,514.37
Anne-Marie Knight	75	71	72	71	289	5,514.37
Laurette Maritz	76	72	73	70	291	4,845
Gillian Stewart	78	70	72	71	291	4,845
Patricia Meunier Lebouc	77	67	75	72	291	4,845
Julie Forbes	72	73	73	73	291	4,845
Caroline Blaylock	74	67	71	79	291	4,845
Lora Fairclough	74	70	74	74	292	4,324.37
Katharina Poppmeier	72	76	74	70	292	4,324.37

Guardian Irish Open

Luttrellstown Castle Golf & Country Club,
Castleknock, Dublin, Ireland
Par 36-36–72; 6,179 yards

June 26-29
purse, £110,000

	SCORES				TOTAL	MONEY
Patricia Meunier Lebouc	74	70	69	71	284	£16,500
Laura Navarro	73	73	70	69	285	11,165
Alison Nicholas	73	74	70	69	286	7,700
Natascha Fink	74	71	70	73	288	5,940
Lora Fairclough	72	72	73	72	289	4,664
Sarah Carbon	74	72	72	72	290	3,300
Asa Gottmo	73	74	70	73	290	3,300
Jane Leary	66	79	71	74	290	3,300
Nicola Moult	75	75	69	72	291	2,332
Joanne Morley	74	71	73	73	291	2,332
Corinne Dibnah	76	71	73	72	292	1,808.40
Karen Lunn	73	70	76	73	292	1,808.40
Sally Prosser	75	73	74	70	292	1,808.40

	SCORES				TOTAL	MONEY
Karen Pearce	73	71	78	70	292	1,808.40
Jenny Lee	81	71	68	72	292	1,808.40
Maureen Madill	74	75	69	75	293	1,562
Laurette Maritz	74	72	77	70	293	1,562
Anna Berg	74	72	72	75	293	1,562
Diane Barnard	76	77	71	70	294	1,348.87
Federica Dassu	71	73	74	76	294	1,348.87
Gillian Stewart	76	74	71	73	294	1,348.87
Karina Orum	75	74	72	73	294	1,348.87
Maria Hjorth	75	76	71	72	294	1,348.87
Anna-Carin Jonasson	73	73	72	76	294	1,348.87
Nicola Murray	76	72	73	73	294	1,348.87
Johanna Head	73	74	70	77	294	1,348.87
Janet Soulsby	76	69	76	74	295	1,116.50
Caryn Louw	76	74	72	73	295	1,116.50
Amaia Arruti	75	74	73	73	295	1,116.50
Petra Rigby-Jinglov	75	75	72	73	295	1,116.50
Kristel Mourgue d'Algue	75	76	72	72	295	1,116.50
Marlene Hedblom	75	75	68	77	295	1,116.50

Ladies' German Open

Marriott Hotel Treudelberg Golf & Country Club, July 24-27
Hamburg, Germany purse, £100,000
Par 36-37–73; 6,200 yards

	SCORES				TOTAL	MONEY
Joanne Mills	71	71	70	71	283	£15,000
Lynnette Brooky	68	74	70	71	283	10,150
(Mills defeated Brooky on second extra hole.)						
Joanne Morley	72	68	70	74	284	7,000
Dale Reid	72	70	69	74	285	5,400
Trish Johnson	72	73	71	70	286	4,240
Maria Hjorth	70	74	71	72	287	3,250
Jane Leary	68	71	76	72	287	3,250
Diane Barnard	78	68	72	70	288	2,060
Gillian Stewart	70	71	73	74	288	2,060
Asa Gottmo	70	75	73	70	288	2,060
Deni Booker	70	71	70	77	288	2,060
Lora Fairclough	70	75	73	70	288	2,060
Marie-Laure de Lorenzi	72	73	72	72	289	1,508
Karen Lunn	71	72	72	74	289	1,508
Sally Prosser	72	70	72	75	289	1,508
Sophie Gustafson	70	69	73	77	289	1,508
Julie Forbes	71	71	74	73	289	1,508
Lara Tadiotto	73	73	70	74	290	1,340
Sara Melin	65	73	74	78	290	1,340
Loraine Lambert	71	66	74	79	290	1,340
Caryn Louw	72	71	70	78	291	1,195
Wendy Dicks	72	68	73	78	291	1,195
Raquel Carriedo	71	75	72	73	291	1,195
Helen Wadsworth	73	71	72	75	291	1,195
Pernilla Sterner	72	73	74	72	291	1,195
Iben Tinning	71	68	76	76	291	1,195
Isabella Maconi	72	70	74	76	292	1,075
Marie-Josee Rouleau	67	76	71	78	292	1,075
Regine Lautens	74	70	76	73	293	955
Tracey Craik	72	71	73	77	293	955

	SCORES	TOTAL	MONEY
Shelly Rule	77 71 75 70	293	955
Lisa Jensen	71 75 70 77	293	955
Marie-Therese Pistolet-Boselli	70 73 76 74	293	955
Lotte Greve	74 74 73 72	293	955

McDonald's WPGA Championship of Europe

The Gleneagles Hotel, King's Course, Perthshire, Scotland
Par 37-35–72; 6,007 yards

August 7-10
purse, £300,000

	SCORES	TOTAL	MONEY
Helen Alfredsson	74 65 67 70	276	£45,000
Charlotta Sorenstam	74 68 70 68	280	25,725
Kathryn Marshall	70 69 71 70	280	25,725
Marie-Laure de Lorenzi	68 70 71 73	282	13,140
Trish Johnson	67 73 68 74	282	13,140
Lora Fairclough	66 72 70 74	282	13,140
Alison Nicholas	69 71 72 71	283	7,740
Rachel Hetherington	72 67 72 72	283	7,740
Lisa Hackney	75 70 72 66	283	7,740
Dale Reid	70 66 70 78	284	5,232
Maria Hjorth	71 73 73 67	284	5,232
Helen Wadsworth	69 72 72 71	284	5,232
Pernilla Sterner	71 72 67 74	284	5,232
Caroline Pierce	70 72 70 72	284	5,232
Diane Barnard	72 71 70 72	285	4,380
Laura Davies	71 68 69 77	285	4,380
Catriona Matthew	67 71 73 74	285	4,380
Karen Lunn	69 71 76 70	286	4,080
Kirsty Taylor	70 70 73 73	286	4,080
*Janice Moodie	69 72 73 72	286	
Liselotte Neumann	71 69 76 71	287	3,765
Sally Prosser	74 67 74 72	287	3,765
Pamela Wright	76 71 71 69	287	3,765
Shani Waugh	72 75 68 72	287	3,765
Natascha Fink	75 71 74 68	288	3,450
Lynnette Brooky	72 71 77 68	288	3,450
Marie-Josee Rouleau	75 70 72 71	288	3,450
Barbara Pestana	74 69 77 69	289	3,135
Mandy Sutton	73 72 70 74	289	3,135
Patricia Meunier Lebouc	72 76 71 70	289	3,135
Joanne Morley	71 71 72 75	289	3,135

Weetabix Women's British Open

Sunningdale Golf Club, Sunningdale, England
Par 36-36–72; 6,255 yards

August 14-17
purse, £525,000

	SCORES	TOTAL	MONEY
Karrie Webb	65 70 63 71	269	£82,500
Rosie Jones	70 70 66 71	277	52,000
Annika Sorenstam	72 70 69 67	278	36,750
Brandie Burton	73 69 71 67	280	27,000
Catriona Matthew	70 70 70 71	281	20,000
Lisa Hackney	74 69 67 71	281	20,000

690 / WOMEN'S TOURS

		SCORES			TOTAL	MONEY
Wendy Doolan	74	70	68	70	282	14,000
Tina Barrett	70	72	70	70	282	14,000
Chris Johnson	71	71	73	68	283	11,500
Charlotta Sorenstam	71	70	72	71	284	10,100
Betsy King	71	72	68	73	284	10,100
Liselotte Neumann	68	75	71	71	285	7,414.28
Jenny Lidback	71	74	70	70	285	7,414.28
Kathryn Marshall	70	68	73	74	285	7,414.28
Helen Dobson	73	69	69	74	285	7,414.28
Mayumi Hirase	76	65	74	70	285	7,414.28
Barb Mucha	72	67	73	73	285	7,414.28
Juli Inkster	69	71	73	72	285	7,414.28
Corinne Dibnah	72	71	70	73	286	5,837.50
Alicia Dibos	71	72	70	73	286	5,837.50
Carin Hj Koch	76	71	71	68	286	5,837.50
Loraine Lambert	70	73	73	70	286	5,837.50
Laura Davies	74	73	69	71	287	5,300
Rachel Hetherington	75	70	71	71	287	5,300
Kris Tschetter	73	70	72	72	287	5,300
Emilee Klein	69	74	70	75	288	5,000
Lynnette Brooky	72	73	72	72	289	4,475
Joanne Morley	75	69	76	69	289	4,475
Helen Alfredsson	69	76	72	72	289	4,475
Susan Farron	72	75	75	67	289	4,475
Janice Moodie	74	71	71	73	289	4,475
Barb Whitehead	71	74	77	67	289	4,475

Compaq Open

Osterakers Golf Club, Stockholm, Sweden
Par 36-36–72; 6,115 yards

August 21-24
purse, £300,000

		SCORES			TOTAL	MONEY
Annika Sorenstam	67	67	73	70	277	£45,000
Catrin Nilsmark	71	72	69	71	283	30,450
Nancy Lopez	66	71	74	74	285	21,000
Helen Alfredsson	71	74	70	71	286	16,200
Karrie Webb	74	69	74	70	287	12,720
Alison Nicholas	71	72	72	74	289	9,000
Lisa Hackney	70	75	73	71	289	9,000
Susan Farron	76	71	75	67	289	9,000
Karen Lunn	71	69	75	76	291	5,850
Laurette Maritz	75	72	71	73	291	5,850
Liselotte Neumann	75	75	69	72	291	5,850
Karen Pearce	69	79	72	71	291	5,850
Asa Gottmo	71	76	69	76	292	4,660
Helen Wadsworth	77	72	68	75	292	4,660
Anna Berg	71	77	77	67	292	4,660
Marie-Laure de Lorenzi	74	74	71	74	293	4,320
Joanne Morley	74	76	68	75	293	4,320
Corinne Dibnah	73	72	76	74	295	3,918
Wendy Dicks	77	75	74	69	295	3,918
Maria Hjorth	76	72	70	77	295	3,918
Charlotta Sorenstam	70	73	74	78	295	3,918
Catherine Schmitt	73	71	77	74	295	3,918
Dale Reid	78	72	69	77	296	3,540
Xonia Wunsch-Ruiz	75	73	72	76	296	3,540
Patricia Meunier Lebouc	75	76	71	74	296	3,540

	SCORES	TOTAL	MONEY
Julie Forbes	78 75 72 72	297	3,360
Stephanie Dallongeville	74 75 75 74	298	3,180
Loraine Lambert	74 71 78 75	298	3,180
Vibeke Stensrud	75 73 70 80	298	3,180
Debbie Dowling	75 78 72 74	299	2,865
Lynnette Brooky	70 84 68 77	299	2,865
Raquel Carriedo	77 77 71 74	299	2,865
Joanne Mills	71 73 80 75	299	2,865
*Isabelle Rosberg	76 70 73 80	299	

Ladies' French Open

Paris International Club, Paris, France
Par 36-36–72; 6,003 yards

September 4-7
purse, £100,000

	SCORES	TOTAL	MONEY
Karen Lunn	72 70 69 70	281	£15,000
Laurette Maritz	72 70 70 73	285	10,150
Trish Johnson	74 69 72 71	286	7,000
Joanne Mills	75 70 69 75	289	5,400
Loraine Lambert	71 75 70 74	290	4,240
Marie-Laure de Lorenzi	74 72 75 70	291	3,250
Helene Koch	75 72 71 73	291	3,250
Stephanie Dallongeville	76 68 73 76	293	2,246.66
*Ludivine Kreutz	71 74 76 72	293	
Patricia Meunier Lebouc	72 74 75 72	293	2,246.66
Lora Fairclough	74 77 73 69	293	2,246.66
Barbara Pestana	73 74 75 72	294	1,780
Fiona Pike	73 76 72 73	294	1,780
Valerie Michaud	73 72 78 72	295	1,553.33
Anna Berg	73 69 77 76	295	1,553.33
Samantha Head	72 75 71 77	295	1,553.33
Susan Farron	71 78 72 75	296	1,460
Lynnette Brooky	79 69 76 73	297	1,400
Iben Tinning	75 77 73 72	297	1,400
Janice Arnold	73 76 72 77	298	1,256.66
Laura Davies	74 72 76 76	298	1,256.66
Debbie Dowling	72 76 75 75	298	1,256.66
Susan Moon	78 71 71 78	298	1,256.66
Susan Elliott	76 76 73 73	298	1,256.66
Mia Lojdahl	78 74 72 74	298	1,256.66
Amaia Arruti	70 78 73 78	299	1,090
Laura Navarro	75 76 75 73	299	1,090
Katharina Larsson	78 73 72 76	299	1,090
Marlene Hedblom	72 76 73 78	299	1,090
Sara Forster	73 77 76 73	299	1,090

Hennessy Cup

Golf und Land-club Koln, Koln, Germany
Par 36-36–72; 6,297 yards

September 18-21
purse, £300,000

	SCORES	TOTAL	MONEY
Laura Davies	75 71 68 74	288	£45,000
Anne-Marie Knight	74 74 69 72	289	30,400

	SCORES				TOTAL	MONEY
Alison Nicholas	74	70	72	74	290	16,616.66
Helen Alfredsson	72	71	75	72	290	16,616.66
Lisa Hackney	71	75	72	72	290	16,616.66
Sally Prosser	73	72	76	70	291	9,000
Maria Hjorth	67	74	76	74	291	9,000
Natascha Fink	72	72	72	75	291	9,000
Marie-Laure de Lorenzi	74	74	73	72	293	6,350
Raquel Carriedo	75	73	72	73	293	6,350
Karen Pearce	67	71	82	74	294	5,335
Helen Wadsworth	73	76	71	74	294	5,335
Laurette Maritz	74	76	74	71	295	4,600
Wendy Dicks	72	73	75	75	295	4,600
Sophie Gustafson	77	74	69	75	295	4,600
Asa Gottmo	76	73	77	69	295	4,600
Patricia Meunier Lebouc	75	71	77	72	295	4,600
Tina Fischer	74	71	75	76	296	4,215
Anna Berg	73	75	72	76	296	4,215
Barbara Pestana	77	77	72	71	297	3,830
Catherine Schmitt	72	76	77	72	297	3,830
Joanne Mills	71	74	75	77	297	3,830
Martina Koch	75	71	77	74	297	3,830
Fiona Pike	75	74	73	75	297	3,830
Dale Reid	71	75	74	78	298	3,450
Pernilla Sterner	76	70	77	75	298	3,450
Federica Dassu	73	73	74	79	299	3,100
Caryn Louw	75	72	76	76	299	3,100
Amaia Arruti	76	74	76	73	299	3,100
Stephanie Dallongeville	73	75	76	75	299	3,100
Kathryn Marshall	75	70	78	76	299	3,100

Sicilian/Italian Open

Il Picciolo Golf Club, Sicily, Italy
Par 36-37–73; 5,608 yards

October 2-5
purse, £100,000

	SCORES				TOTAL	MONEY
Valerie Van Ryckeghem	72	65	75	76	288	£15,000
Patricia Gonzalez	70	71	68	79	288	10,150
(Van Ryckeghem defeated Gonzalez on first extra hole.)						
Marie-Laure de Lorenzi	71	73	74	71	289	6,200
Karina Orum	73	74	71	71	289	6,200
Samantha Head	71	72	75	72	290	4,240
Laurette Maritz	75	67	75	74	291	2,648
Alison Nicholas	75	72	75	69	291	2,648
Tracey Craik	69	73	74	75	291	2,648
Nicola Moult	74	71	73	73	291	2,648
Helen Alfredsson	71	71	78	71	291	2,648
*Silvia Cavalleri	72	74	70	75	291	
Karen Pearce	72	75	75	70	292	1,780
Marika Preti	72	72	73	75	292	1,780
Sara Melin	71	73	73	76	293	1,580
Tina Fischer	71	73	73	76	293	1,580
Gillian Stewart	71	70	76	77	294	1,440
Helen Hopkins	69	73	78	74	294	1,440
Barbara Pestana	76	73	72	73	294	1,440
Jane Leary	73	72	77	72	294	1,440
Lora Fairclough	72	77	72	74	295	1,340

	SCORES				TOTAL	MONEY
Natascha Fink	71	74	75	76	296	1,285
Helen Wadsworth	74	72	77	73	296	1,285
Karen Lunn	74	70	77	76	297	1,225
Valerie Michaud	76	70	78	73	297	1,225
Maria Hjorth	77	71	74	76	298	1,150
Patricia Meunier Lebouc	72	74	73	79	298	1,150
Anna Radford	74	74	73	77	298	1,150
Asa Gottmo	69	76	73	81	299	1,030
Nicola Murray	79	69	75	76	299	1,030
Sandrine Mendiburu	72	71	80	76	299	1,030
*Monica Cosenza	72	74	73	80	299	
Sara Eklund	76	78	74	71	299	1,030
Lisa Educate	77	70	77	75	299	1,030

Air France Madame Open

New Golf de Deauville, Deauville, France
Par 35-36–71; 5,998 yards

October 24-26
purse, £60,000

	SCORES			TOTAL	MONEY
Loraine Lambert	71	73	69	213	£9,000
Alison Nicholas	73	69	73	215	6,090
Shani Waugh	67	77	72	216	3,720
Valerie Michaud	70	72	74	216	3,720
Debbie Dowling	75	72	70	217	2,148
Gillian Stewart	72	68	77	217	2,148
Sandrine Mendiburu	70	75	72	217	2,148
Marie-Laure de Lorenzi	73	75	70	218	1,287
Sally Prosser	68	78	72	218	1,287
Patricia Meunier Lebouc	72	72	74	218	1,287
Laura Navarro	71	71	76	218	1,287
Amaia Arruti	75	69	76	220	1,032
Catherine Schmitt	74	73	74	221	948
Nicola Moult	75	75	71	221	948
Janet Soulsby	76	73	73	222	876
Barbara Pestana	78	72	72	222	876
Helen Wadsworth	75	75	72	222	876
Susan Moon	74	72	77	223	804
Mia Lojdahl	71	76	76	223	804
Jane Leary	76	73	74	223	804
Pernilla Sterner	79	71	74	224	735
Kirsty Taylor	75	74	75	224	735
Marina Arruti	73	75	76	224	735
Iben Tinning	77	77	70	224	735
Patricia Gonzalez	76	77	72	225	672
Laurette Maritz	77	73	75	225	672
Marie-Therese Pistolet-Boselli	72	79	74	225	672
Karen Pearce	77	74	75	226	627
Anna Berg	77	77	72	226	627
Sara Melin	78	76	73	227	582
Nicola Murray	74	74	79	227	582
Raquel Carriedo	76	78	73	227	582

Princess Lalla Meriem Cup

Royal Golf Dar-es-Salam, Red Course, Rabat, Morocco
Par 73; 6,400 yards

November 14-16
purse, US$70,000

	SCORES			TOTAL	MONEY
Diane Barnard	71	75	71	217	US$13,000
Amaia Arruti	75	73	73	221	9,100
Gillian Stewart	79	71	72	222	5,865
Lora Fairclough	74	75	73	222	5,865
Sally Prosser	76	70	77	223	3,800
Federica Dassu	72	76	77	225	3,120
Susan Moon	77	74	75	226	2,813
Helen Wadsworth	75	73	78	226	2,813
Xonia Wunsch-Ruiz	74	76	76	226	2,813
Mounia Amalou	77	78	74	229	2,600
Valerie Michaud	82	73	74	229	2,600
Sandrine Mendiburu	78	76	77	231	2,500
Regine Lautens	76	77	80	233	2,500
Sofia Gronberg	77	78	79	234	2,500
Kristel Mourgue d'Algue	76	84	80	240	2,500
Sophie Gustafson	83	79	78	240	2,500
Veronique Palli	78	84	84	246	2,500

Praia D'El Rey European Cup

Praia D'El Rey Golf & Country Club, Obidos, Portugal
Par 36-36–72; 6,094 yards

November 14-16
purse, £150,000

FIRST DAY
Foursomes

Marie-Laure de Lorenzi and Kathryn Marshall defeated Jose Maria Canizares and Antonio Garrido, 2 up
Alison Nicholas and Trish Johnson defeated Noel Ratcliffe and Maurice Bembridge, 3 and 1
David Creamer and Malcolm Gregson defeated Laurette Maritz and Shani Waugh, 7 and 5
Brian Waites and Jim Rhodes defeated Patricia Meunier Lebouc and Maria Hjorth, 1 up
Karen Lunn and Joanne Morley halved with Tommy Horton and John Morgan

POINTS: WPG European Tour 2½, PGA European Seniors Tour 2½

SECOND DAY
Fourball

Canizares and Garrido defeated Nicholas and Johnson, 6 and 4
Gregson and Waites defeated Waugh and Maritz, 3 and 2
Creamer and Bembridge defeated Hjorth and Meunier Lebouc, 3 and 2
Morgan and Rhodes defeated Lunn and Morley, 5 and 4
Ratcliffe and Horton defeated De Lorenzi and Marshall, 7 and 6

POINTS: PGA European Seniors Tour 7½, WPG European Tour 2½

THIRD DAY
Singles

Johnson defeated Garrido, 2 and 1
De Lorenzi defeated Creamer, 3 and 1
Ratcliffe defeated Nicholas, 1 up
Lunn defeated Rhodes, 1 up
Marshall defeated Bembridge, 1 up
Hjorth halved with Waites
Canizares defeated Morley, 3 and 2
Gregson defeated Maritz, 3 and 2
Morgan defeated Meunier Lebouc, 3 and 1
Horton defeated Waugh, 2 and 1

TOTAL POINTS: PGA European Seniors Tour 13, WPG European Tour 7

(Each member of PGA European Seniors Tour team received £10,000; each member of WPG European Tour team received £5,000.)

Women's Australasian Tours

Republic of China Open

Chang Gung Golf Club, Taipei, Taiwan
Par 36-36–72; 6,215 yards

January 30-February 1
purse, US$120,000

	SCORES			TOTAL	MONEY
Ai-Yu Tu	71	78	69	218	US$16,500
Jean Bartholomew	77	71	72	220	9,625
Huang Hui-Fan	70	75	75	220	9,625
Mette Hageman	75	73	73	221	6,600
Nicola Moult	75	72	75	222	4,180
Wen-Lin Li	74	73	75	222	4,180
Kiyoe Yamazaki	75	76	73	224	3,080
Mei-Chi Cheng	76	74	74	224	3,080
Kozue Azuma	75	72	77	224	3,080
Ming-Yeh Wu	72	76	77	225	2,107
Elizabeth Bowman	72	76	77	225	2,107
Sarah Nicklin	74	73	78	225	2,107
Huang Yu-Chen	71	74	80	225	2,107
Sachiko Ohshima	75	76	75	226	1,865
Sarah Bennett	77	73	76	226	1,865
Laree Pearl Sugg	77	76	74	227	1,672
Mie Hasegawa	76	76	75	227	1,672
Yumi Kokubo	77	74	76	227	1,672
Chen Li-Ying	74	77	76	227	1,672
Jodi Renner	71	78	78	227	1,672
Tai Yu-Hsia	77	77	74	228	1,370
Yoshiko Ito	79	74	75	228	1,370
Camie Hoshino	77	75	76	228	1,370

	SCORES	TOTAL	MONEY
Lu Shu-Mien	72 80 76	228	1,370
Bie-Shyun Huang	75 76 77	228	1,370
Caroline Hall	74 72 82	228	1,370
Julie Forbes	78 76 75	229	1,007
Masako Ishihara	78 76 75	229	1,007
Susan Farron	78 75 76	229	1,007
Debbie Dowling	75 78 76	229	1,007
Mika Ishijima	77 75 77	229	1,007
Hisako Ohgane	75 77 77	229	1,007
Chieko Amanuma	79 71 79	229	1,007
Yu-Chuan Tai	74 75 80	229	1,007

Toyota Philippine Open

Sta. Elena Golf Club, Laguna, Manila, Philippines
Par 36-36–72; 6,081 yards

February 6-8
purse, US$110,000

	SCORES	TOTAL	MONEY
Pernilla Sterner	75 68 73	216	US$15,000
Asa Gottmo	72 70 75	217	10,000
Anna Carin Jonasson	71 72 75	218	7,500
Michie Ohba	73 71 76	220	6,000
Masako Ishihara	78 72 72	222	3,800
Loraine Lambert	75 73 74	222	3,800
Kim Shipman	69 73 81	223	3,100
Elizabeth Bowman	77 73 74	224	2,342
Lee Chiou-Yann	77 72 75	224	2,342
Stephanie Comstock	78 70 76	224	2,342
Harumi Sakagami	74 73 77	224	2,342
Tina Fischer	79 75 71	225	1,695
Kiyoe Yamazaki	76 76 73	225	1,695
Xonia Wunsch-Ruiz	76 76 73	225	1,695
Jean Bartholomew	75 77 73	225	1,695
Nicole Jeray	76 74 75	225	1,695
Liz Earley	73 76 76	225	1,695
Joanne Mills	78 76 72	226	1,420
Alison Munt	78 73 75	226	1,420
Kelly Crawford	76 73 77	226	1,420
Julie Forbes	75 73 78	226	1,420
Sarah Bennett	78 77 72	227	1,073
Hitomi Notsu	77 78 72	227	1,073
Kozue Azuma	78 74 75	227	1,073
Lara Tadiotto	77 75 75	227	1,073
Martina Koch	75 77 75	227	1,073
Sara Melin	73 79 75	227	1,073
Kerryn Starr	70 81 76	227	1,073
Asayo Ito	76 75 76	227	1,073
Nicole Lowein	74 77 76	227	1,073
Jodi Renner	76 74 77	227	1,073
Sylvia Torres	76 74 77	227	1,073

Thailand Open

Natural Park Hill Golf Club, Pattaya, Thailand
Par 36-36–72; 5,860 yards

February 12-14
purse, US$120,000

	SCORES			TOTAL	MONEY
Sophie Gustafson	72	72	70	214	US$16,500
Tseng Hsiu-Feng	74	72	69	215	9,625
Jean Bartholomew	70	70	75	215	9,625
Sachiko Ohshima	72	73	72	217	5,610
Mayumi Ishii	71	74	72	217	5,610
Julie Forbes	72	73	73	218	3,575
Karen Lunn	71	70	77	218	3,575
Michie Ohba	73	73	73	219	2,750
Mikiko Furuya	71	75	73	219	2,750
Alison Munt	71	72	76	219	2,750
Xonia Wunsch-Ruiz	71	76	73	220	2,057
Hisako Ohgane	75	72	74	221	1,974
Tina Fischer	73	73	75	221	1,974
Sarah Bennett	79	71	72	222	1,864
Janet Soulsby	75	74	73	222	1,864
Laree Pearl Sugg	74	73	76	223	1,754
Nicole Jeray	73	73	77	223	1,754
Pernilla Sterner	76	74	74	224	1,562
Aideen Rogers	76	73	75	224	1,562
Debbie Dowling	71	78	75	224	1,562
Stephanie Comstock	74	74	76	224	1,562
Fusako Nagata	73	71	80	224	1,562
Loraine Lambert	77	76	72	225	1,287
Malin Burstrom	77	76	72	225	1,287
Kiyoe Yamazaki	74	78	73	225	1,287
Hiromi Kaneda	78	72	75	225	1,287
Yumi Kokubo	72	74	79	225	1,287
Lara Tadiotto	72	81	73	226	928
Mary Grace Estuesta	76	75	75	226	928
Mette Hageman	74	77	75	226	928
Kim Shipman	76	73	77	226	928
Jodi Renner	76	73	77	226	928
Megumi Matsuo	77	73	76	226	928
Hiroko Tanabe	75	75	76	226	928
Mika Ishijima	72	78	76	226	928
Hitomi Notsu	80	69	77	226	928
Sadae Kumagai	75	73	78	226	928

JAL Malaysian Open

Glenmarie Golf & Country Club, Subang, Malaysia
Par 36-36–72; 6,120 yards

February 20-22
purse, US$90,000

	SCORES			TOTAL	MONEY
Petra Rigby-Jinglov	66	74	71	211	US$12,750
Masako Ishihara	70	70	72	212	8,500
Tina Fischer	74	71	70	215	6,375
Jean Bartholomew	71	74	71	216	3,548
Katharina Poppmeier	74	70	72	216	3,548
Sofie Eriksson	75	66	75	216	3,548
Pernilla Sterner	73	68	75	216	3,548
Sophie Gustafson	75	75	67	217	2,380

	SCORES	TOTAL	MONEY
Jodi Renner	76 74 68	218	1,611
Maureen Madill	69 80 69	218	1,611
Mary Grace Estuesta	74 74 70	218	1,611
Anna Carin Jonasson	73 74 71	218	1,611
Kayo Segawa	72 75 71	218	1,611
Hisako Ohgane	75 71 72	218	1,611
Malin Burstrom	73 72 73	218	1,611
Lim Siew Ai	72 70 76	218	1,611
Sarah Bennett	74 76 69	219	1,228
Moon Woo Hae	74 75 70	219	1,228
Camie Hoshino	74 75 70	219	1,228
Tseng Hsiu-Feng	74 72 73	219	1,228
Diane Irvin	74 72 73	219	1,228
Kelly Crawford	73 73 73	219	1,228
Susan Farron	75 74 71	220	1,015
Shelly Rule	71 75 74	220	1,015
Asa Gottmo	71 75 74	220	1,015
Loraine Lambert	74 70 76	220	1,015
Takako Kuniyoshi	76 75 70	221	845
Wendy Dicks	76 73 72	221	845
Joanne Mills	73 75 73	221	845
Harumi Sakagami	73 75 73	221	845

Indonesian Open

Pondok Cabe Golf & Country Club, Tangerang, Jawa Barat, Indonesia
Par 36-36–72; 6,112 yards

February 26-28
purse, US$110,000

	SCORES	TOTAL	MONEY
Pernilla Sterner	72 67 76	215	US$15,000
Wendy Dicks	72 74 69	215	10,000
(Sterner defeated Dicks in extra holes.)			
Laree Pearl Sugg	75 72 69	216	7,500
Sofie Eriksson	74 73 70	217	4,175
Debbie Dowling	72 74 71	217	4,175
Jean Bartholomew	73 72 72	217	4,175
Lara Tadiotto	72 72 73	217	4,175
Nicola Moult	74 72 72	218	2,160
Diane Irvin	76 69 73	218	2,160
Stephanie Comstock	73 72 73	218	2,160
Shelly Rule	71 74 73	218	2,160
Asa Gottmo	69 76 73	218	2,160
Lim Siew Ai	70 71 77	218	2,160
Camie Hoshino	76 75 68	219	1,620
Julie Forbes	74 74 71	219	1,620
Kayo Segawa	75 72 72	219	1,620
Sarah Nicklin	74 73 72	219	1,620
Mary Grace Estuesta	71 72 76	219	1,620
Masako Ishihara	74 76 70	220	1,445
Kim Kyung Boon	75 71 74	220	1,445
Hideko Maeda	76 73 72	221	1,320
Sarah Bennett	74 74 73	221	1,320
Sara Melin	74 71 76	221	1,320
Ji Hyun Suh	77 76 69	222	1,220
Elizabeth Bowman	78 71 74	223	1,070
Kelly Crawford	76 73 74	223	1,070

	SCORES			TOTAL	MONEY
Xonia Wunsch-Ruiz	74	75	74	223	1,070
Mika Ishijima	70	79	74	223	1,070
Petra Rigby-Jinglov	70	76	77	223	1,070
Hiromi Kaneda	77	76	71	224	806
Sylvia Torres	76	75	73	224	806
Megumi Higuchi	79	75	73	227	806
Aideen Rogers	75	76	73	224	806
Kim Myung Hee	79	70	75	224	806
Irene Yeoh	75	74	75	224	806
Nicole Jeray	77	71	76	224	806
Liz Earley	75	71	78	224	806

Alpine Australian Ladies Masters

Royal Pines Resort, Gold Coast, Queensland
Par 37-35–72; 6,250 yards

February 27-March 2
purse, A$650,000

	SCORES				TOTAL	MONEY
Gail Graham	66	68	71	68	273	A$97,500
Karrie Webb	69	66	66	73	274	61,666
Laura Davies	69	72	68	66	275	45,000
Jane Geddes	70	71	68	68	277	35,000
Sophie Gustafson	72	68	69	70	279	28,333
Se Ri Pak	72	66	73	70	281	21,499
Val Skinner	70	72	68	71	281	21,499
Karen Weiss	68	75	69	70	282	16,499
Cindy Figg-Currier	67	71	73	71	282	16,499
Chris Johnson	69	71	71	72	283	14,000
Marnie McGuire	69	73	73	69	284	11,476
Meg Mallon	71	75	68	70	284	11,476
Corinne Dibnah	70	70	71	73	284	11,476
Charlotta Sorenstam	66	71	71	76	284	11,476
Sherri Turner	75	73	70	67	285	8,615
Kelly Robbins	75	72	71	67	285	8,615
Joanne Morley	72	74	72	67	285	8,615
Lisa Hackney	73	74	70	68	285	8,615
Michele Redman	70	75	70	70	285	8,615
Alison Munt	68	76	69	72	285	8,615
Jill Briles-Hinton	74	73	69	70	286	7,393
Betsy King	74	72	70	71	287	6,667
Stephanie Maynor	72	69	72	74	287	6,667
Luciana Bemvenuti	68	69	75	75	287	6,667
Kristal Parker-Gregory	75	68	68	76	287	6,667
Amy Fruhwirth	74	71	74	69	288	5,826
Hollis Stacy	76	72	69	71	288	5,826
Tina Barrett	73	73	70	72	288	5,826
Helen Dobson	72	72	71	73	288	5,826
Fiona Pike	75	72	72	70	289	4,966
Kathryn Marshall	74	74	70	71	289	4,966
Alice Ritzman	74	68	73	74	289	4,966
Susie Redman	72	71	71	75	289	4,966
Vicki Goetze	72	70	71	76	289	4,966

Toyota Australian Women's Open

Yarra Yarra Golf Club, Melbourne, Victoria
Par 37-36–73; 5,958 yards

November 13-16
purse, A$350,000

	SCORES				TOTAL	MONEY
Jane Crafter	65	72	72	70	279	A$52,500
Joanne Mills	70	74	70	68	282	35,000
Kang Soo-Yun	75	68	69	71	283	21,000
Wendy Doolan	69	77	70	70	286	17,500
Karrie Webb	74	75	72	68	289	14,000
Corinne Dibnah	74	72	74	71	291	13,300
Rachel Hetherington	71	73	74	74	292	11,900
Mi Hyun Kim	72	76	73	72	293	10,500
Anne-Marie Knight	77	77	72	69	295	7,700
Alison Munt	74	70	76	75	295	7,700
Hyun Soon Park	72	78	70	75	295	7,700
*Kate MacIntosh	74	71	74	76	295	
Liselotte Neumann	69	74	75	77	295	7,700
Susan Farron	73	74	77	73	297	5,390
Mardi Lunn	72	76	74	75	297	5,390
Catriona Matthew	72	79	71	76	298	4,900
Jennifer Dammeyer	76	76	73	74	299	4,515
Nadene Gole	73	77	75	74	299	4,515
*Michelle Ellis	72	80	77	71	300	
Sarah Carbon	72	76	76	76	300	4,200
Fiona Pike	72	79	80	70	301	3,850
Jan Stephenson	75	75	76	75	301	3,850
Jane Leary	67	76	81	77	301	3,850
*Nadina Taylor	78	74	76	74	302	
Karen Pearce	72	81	74	75	302	3,570
*Toni Clatworthy	72	76	78	76	302	
Karina Orum	77	78	75	73	303	3,360
*Natalie Parkinson	73	79	77	74	303	
Jung Sook Nam	75	76	71	81	303	3,360
*Dayle Linnertson	74	74	75	81	304	
*Adele Bannerman	76	76	77	75	304	

Japan LPGA Tour

Daikin Orchid Ladies

Ryukyu Golf Club, Okinawa
Par 36-36–72; 6,260 yards

March 7-9
purse, ¥60,000,000

	SCORES			TOTAL	MONEY
Woo-Soon Ko	69	68	69	206	¥10,800,000
Ok-Hee Ku	72	66	68	206	5,280,000
(Ko defeated Ku on second extra hole.)					
Ikuyo Shiotani	70	64	74	208	4,200,000
Aki Takamura	68	73	68	209	2,580,000
Natsuko Noro	70	67	72	209	2,580,000
Marnie McGuire	69	71	69	209	2,580,000
Atsuko Kikuchi	70	70	69	209	2,580,000
Fumiko Muraguchi	70	68	71	209	2,580,000
Kumiko Hiyoshi	70	69	71	210	1,350,000
Kaori Harada	66	72	72	210	1,350,000
Mayumi Murai	69	72	70	211	1,104,000
Hisako Takeda	70	71	71	212	954,000
Ayako Okamoto	70	69	73	212	954,000
Mayumi Hirase	72	71	69	212	954,000
Yu-Chuan Tai	70	71	71	212	954,000
Akane Ohshiro	68	70	75	213	744,000
Michiko Hattori	70	71	72	213	744,000
Mikino Kubo	67	74	72	213	744,000
Yuko Moriguchi	72	71	71	214	594,000
Patty Sheehan	70	76	68	214	594,000
Hiroko Inoue	72	71	72	215	546,000
Etsuko Kawakami	77	68	70	215	546,000
Nayoko Yoshikawa	74	72	70	216	486,000
Chieko Nishida	75	72	69	216	486,000
Michiko Okada	70	73	73	216	486,000
Akemi Yamaoka	70	74	72	216	486,000
Mitsuyo Hirata	72	73	71	216	486,000
Yuri Kawanami	72	71	73	216	486,000
Young-Me Lee	70	75	71	216	486,000
Kasumi Fujii	71	74	71	216	486,000

Saishunkan Ladies

Kumamoto Kukoh Country Club, Kumamoto
Par 36-36–72; 6,470 yards

March 21-23
purse, ¥60,000,000

	SCORES			TOTAL	MONEY
Chikayo Yamazaki	73	69	73	215	¥10,800,000
Yuko Moriguchi	72	72	72	216	4,360,000
Huang Yu-Chen	76	69	71	216	4,360,000
Ikuyo Shiotani	74	70	72	216	4,360,000
Chieko Nishida	72	75	71	218	3,000,000
Ritsu Imahori	72	76	71	219	2,250,000

	SCORES	TOTAL	MONEY
Fuki Kido	68 78 73	219	2,250,000
Ok-Hee Ku	77 75 68	220	1,800,000
Toshiko Fujisaki	74 73 74	221	1,266,000
Woo-Soon Ko	73 73 75	221	1,266,000
Aki Takamura	72 72 77	221	1,266,000
Michiko Hattori	74 77 71	222	948,000
Yuko Ogura	74 75 73	222	948,000
Fumiko Muraguchi	75 74 73	222	948,000
Mayumi Murai	72 73 77	222	948,000
Toshimi Kimura	77 73 73	223	738,000
Young-Me Lee	78 73 72	223	738,000
Norimi Terasawa	79 69 75	223	738,000
Michiko Okada	72 78 74	224	555,600
Kasumi Fujii	73 76 75	224	555,600
Nayoko Yoshikawa	74 74 76	224	555,600
Miyuki Shimabukuro	75 73 76	224	555,600
Rie Mitsuhashi	72 73 79	224	555,600
Yuri Kawanami	77 73 75	225	468,000
Marnie McGuire	76 74 75	225	468,000
Keiko Arai	74 75 76	225	468,000
Ai-Yu Tu	74 75 76	225	468,000
Aiko Takasu	75 74 76	225	468,000
Mikako Kanamori	76 72 77	225	468,000
Akane Ohshiro	74 74 77	225	468,000
Fumiko Omata	76 71 78	225	468,000

Yellow Hat Tokyo Ladies Open

Wakasu Golf Links, Tokyo
Par 36-36–72; 6,360 yards

March 28-30
purse, ¥50,000,000

	SCORES	TOTAL	MONEY
Suzuko Maeda	70 76 68	214	¥9,000,000
Mikino Kubo	74 71 70	215	3,080,000
Woo-Soon Ko	70 72 73	215	3,080,000
Yuko Saitoh	74 67 74	215	3,080,000
Kyoko Ono	72 69 74	215	3,080,000
Akane Ohshiro	69 72 74	215	3,080,000
Natsuko Noro	75 72 70	217	1,500,000
Fuki Kido	73 73 71	217	1,500,000
Jennifer Sevil	71 73 73	217	1,500,000
Toshimi Kimura	75 73 70	218	883,750
Yuko Moriguchi	74 74 70	218	883,750
Akemi Yamaoka	73 71 74	218	883,750
Ikuyo Shiotani	73 71 74	218	883,750
Young-Me Lee	69 76 74	219	620,000
Michiko Hattori	75 71 73	219	620,000
Ae-Sook Kim	74 71 74	219	620,000
Keiko Arai	69 75 75	219	620,000
Kasumi Adachi	74 71 74	219	620,000
Kayo Yamada	74 70 75	219	620,000
Yuri Kawanami	78 69 73	220	410,000
Hisako Takeda	72 75 73	220	410,000
Aki Takamura	75 72 73	220	410,000
Miyuki Shimabukuro	72 74 74	220	410,000
Ok-Hee Ku	71 75 74	220	410,000
Misayo Fujisawa	70 75 75	220	410,000

	SCORES	TOTAL	MONEY
Kumiko Hiyoshi	71 73 76	220	410,000
Marnie McGuire	73 70 77	220	410,000
Norimi Terasawa	75 71 75	221	350,000
Huang Yu-Chen	72 73 76	221	350,000
Junko Yasui	74 76 71	221	350,000
Tseng Hsiu-Feng	73 70 78	221	350,000

Kenshoen Ladies

Dohgo Golf Club, Ehime
Par 36-36–72; 6,271 yards

April 11-13
purse, ¥50,000,000

	SCORES	TOTAL	MONEY
Kaori Harada	71 72 73	216	¥9,000,000
Mitsuyo Hirata	70 71 75	216	4,400,000
(Harada defeated Hirata on sixth extra hole.)			
Hisako Takeda	74 75 68	217	3,500,000
Ae-Sook Kim	74 70 74	218	2,750,000
Yuko Motoyama	73 71 74	218	2,750,000
Mikino Kubo	71 71 77	219	1,750,000
Yuko Saitoh	68 74 77	219	1,750,000
Aiko Takasu	72 73 74	219	1,750,000
Keiko Arai	71 75 74	220	877,500
Mitsuko Hamada	71 76 73	220	877,500
Akiko Fukushima	70 76 74	220	877,500
Jae-Sook Won	72 73 75	220	877,500
Kumiko Hiyoshi	73 75 72	220	877,500
Bie-Shyun Huang	75 74 71	220	877,500
Ok-Hee Ku	75 72 73	220	877,500
Yuko Moriguchi	71 75 74	220	877,500
Jennifer Sevil	75 76 70	221	486,666
Yu-Chuan Tai	74 73 74	221	486,666
Fumiko Muraguchi	74 74 73	221	486,666
Miyuki Shimabukuro	69 78 74	221	486,666
Young-Me Lee	73 75 73	221	486,666
Reiko Kashiwado	77 73 71	221	486,666
Kayo Fukumoto	76 71 74	221	486,666
Kasumi Fujii	74 74 73	221	486,666
Fuki Kido	75 73 73	221	486,666
Aki Takamura	74 73 75	222	395,000
Ayako Okamoto	72 76 74	222	395,000
Woo-Soon Ko	71 76 75	222	395,000
Mikako Kanamori	71 74 77	222	395,000
Tseng Hsui-Feng	75 73 75	223	355,000
Junko Yasui	72 78 73	223	355,000
Nayoko Yoshikawa	74 75 74	223	355,000
Chieko Nishida	75 75 73	223	355,000

Mitsukoshi Cup Ladies Open

Segovia Golf Club, Chiyoda, Ibaraki
Par 37-36–73; 6,161 yards

April 17-20
purse, ¥60,000,000

	SCORES				TOTAL	MONEY
Akemi Yamaoka	71	70	72	71	284	¥10,800,000
Akiko Fukushima	73	71	71	69	284	5,280,000
(Yamaoka defeated Fukushima on first extra hole.)						
Michiko Hattori	73	72	74	69	288	4,200,000
Fusako Nagata	71	73	71	74	289	3,300,000
Keiko Arai	72	72	69	76	289	3,300,000
Suzuko Maeda	71	72	76	71	290	1,800,000
Wen-Lin Li	75	73	71	71	290	1,800,000
Atsuko Kikuchi	72	69	75	74	290	1,800,000
Kyoko Ono	73	73	69	75	290	1,800,000
Kumiko Hiyoshi	72	70	72	76	290	1,800,000
Kaori Harada	73	68	78	72	291	1,044,000
Yuko Saitoh	73	72	73	73	291	1,044,000
Ayako Okamoto	72	75	70	74	291	1,044,000
Misayo Fujisawa	73	71	77	71	292	834,000
Hiromi Takamura	75	72	72	73	292	834,000
Yuko Motoyama	71	73	74	74	292	834,000
Bie-Shyun Huang	71	77	68	76	292	834,000
Yuko Moriguchi	74	75	71	73	293	582,000
Miyuki Shimabukuro	71	73	75	74	293	582,000
Sachiko Ohshima	76	69	74	74	293	582,000
Ok-Hee Ku	73	74	72	74	293	582,000
Kaori Higo	75	73	71	74	293	582,000
Kasumi Fujii	72	72	74	75	293	582,000
Aiko Takasu	72	73	77	72	294	498,000
Aki Takamura	69	75	76	74	294	498,000
Jean Bartholomew	74	72	74	74	294	498,000
Marnie McGuire	71	69	78	76	294	498,000
Ae-Sook Kim	74	73	76	72	295	462,000
Junko Yasui	73	75	73	74	295	462,000
Hiromi Hirakata	74	74	79	69	296	420,000
Hisako Takeda	73	76	76	71	296	420,000
Tseng Hsui-Feng	74	75	77	70	296	420,000
Kozue Azuma	74	75	74	73	296	420,000
Woo-Soon Ko	70	76	72	78	296	420,000

Nasu Ogawa Ladies

Nasu Ogawa Golf Club, Tochigi
Par 36-36–72; 6,138 yards

April 25-27
purse, ¥50,000,000

	SCORES			TOTAL	MONEY
Woo-Soon Ko	72	72	69	213	¥9,000,000
Marnie McGuire	71	71	72	214	4,400,000
Ikuyo Shiotani	70	79	67	216	3,250,000
Kumiko Hiyoshi	70	74	72	216	3,250,000
Nayoko Yoshikawa	71	74	72	217	2,500,000
Ae-Sook Kim	76	71	71	218	2,000,000
Fumiko Muraguchi	73	74	72	219	1,290,000
Akiko Fukushima	73	73	73	219	1,290,000
Kikuko Shibata	71	74	74	219	1,290,000
Junko Yoshida	74	72	73	219	1,290,000

	SCORES			TOTAL	MONEY
Misayo Fujisawa	74	70	75	219	1,290,000
Akemi Yamaoka	76	74	70	220	800,000
Kiriko Nishizawa	73	74	73	220	800,000
Natsuko Noro	74	73	73	220	800,000
Jae-Sook Won	73	73	74	220	800,000
Mikino Kubo	72	68	80	220	800,000
Kayo Fukumoto	77	71	73	221	545,000
Chikayo Yamazaki	73	75	73	221	545,000
Kaori Harada	73	74	74	221	545,000
Michiko Okada	74	73	74	221	545,000
Aki Nakano	71	73	77	221	545,000
Michiko Hattori	74	71	76	221	545,000
Yu-Chuan Tai	69	79	74	222	450,000
Junko Yasui	76	73	73	222	450,000
Tomoko Ueda	73	74	75	222	450,000
Yuko Moriguchi	74	73	75	222	450,000
Toshiko Fujisaki	73	70	79	222	450,000
Ok-Hee Ku	73	76	74	223	405,000
Kaori Higo	73	74	76	223	405,000
Kyoko Ono	74	73	76	223	405,000
Hisako Takeda	75	69	79	223	405,000

Katokichi Queen's Cup

Sakaide Country Club, Kagawa
Par 36-36–72; 6,319 yards

May 2-4
purse, ¥50,000,000

	SCORES			TOTAL	MONEY
Jae-Sook Won	66	75	69	210	¥9,000,000
Chieko Nishida	66	72	74	212	4,400,000
Hiromi Takamura	71	70	72	213	3,000,000
Yuri Kawanami	69	71	73	213	3,000,000
Toshimi Kimura	67	73	73	213	3,000,000
Jennifer Sevil	73	74	69	216	1,625,000
Mariko Watanabe	70	74	72	216	1,625,000
Kumiko Hiyoshi	70	74	72	216	1,625,000
Kyoko Ono	71	71	74	216	1,625,000
Suzuko Maeda	74	72	71	217	917,500
Fumiko Muraguchi	71	72	74	217	917,500
Ae-Sook Kim	73	71	73	217	917,500
Hisako Takeda	70	71	76	217	917,500
Kikuko Shibata	76	72	70	218	715,500
Nayoko Yoshikawa	70	74	74	218	715,500
Young-Me Lee	71	73	74	218	715,500
Woo-Soon Ko	71	70	77	218	715,500
Aiko Takasu	72	74	73	219	525,000
Ai-Yu Tu	69	75	75	219	525,000
Mitsuko Hamada	72	72	75	219	525,000
Marnie McGuire	70	71	78	219	525,000
Chihiro Furukawa	77	70	73	220	440,000
Toshiko Fujisaki	71	75	74	220	440,000
Fusako Nagata	74	73	73	220	440,000
Akane Ohshiro	72	74	74	220	440,000
Bie-Shyun Huang	71	74	75	220	440,000
Huang Yu-Chen	69	76	75	220	440,000
Ikuyo Shiotani	70	72	78	220	440,000
Aki Nakano	71	77	73	221	385,000

	SCORES	TOTAL	MONEY
Natsuko Noro	74 74 73	221	385,000
Miyuki Shimabukuro	73 73 75	221	385,000
Hiromi Hirakata	71 71 79	221	385,000

Gunze Cup World Ladies

Tokyo Yomiuri Golf Club, Tokyo
Par 36-36–72; 6,411 yards

May 8-11
purse, ¥60,000,000

	SCORES	TOTAL	MONEY
Tseng Hsui-Feng	73 75 69 74	291	¥10,800,000
Michiko Okada	73 74 72 72	291	5,280,000
(Tseng defeated Okada on first extra hole.)			
Ikuyo Shiotani	74 74 73 71	292	3,900,000
Natsuko Noro	78 73 69 72	292	3,900,000
Akiko Fukushima	79 73 73 68	293	3,000,000
Toshimi Kimura	79 69 72 74	294	2,250,000
Fumiko Muraguchi	78 71 72 73	294	2,250,000
Mei-Chi Cheng	72 74 77 73	296	1,650,000
Junko Yasui	75 73 74 74	296	1,650,000
Mitsuko Hamada	79 74 73 71	297	1,050,000
Yuko Saitoh	79 71 76 71	297	1,050,000
Mayumi Murai	80 72 74 71	297	1,050,000
Yuri Fudoh	77 72 76 72	297	1,050,000
Ae-Sook Kim	80 72 72 73	297	1,050,000
Liselotte Neumann	81 72 70 74	297	1,050,000
Bie-Shyun Huang	78 75 73 72	298	780,000
Fuki Kido	79 73 73 73	298	780,000
Aiko Takasu	78 71 74 75	298	780,000
Yu-Chuan Tai	77 76 75 71	299	630,000
Emilee Klein	75 76 74 74	299	630,000
Kaori Higo	82 70 75 73	300	558,000
Kiyoe Yamazaki	78 74 75 73	300	558,000
Laura Navarro	76 75 76 73	300	558,000
Nayoko Yoshikawa	80 72 74 74	300	558,000
Chie Yoshida	78 77 76 69	300	558,000
Yuko Motoyama	74 73 76 77	300	558,000
Akane Ohshiro	78 76 75 72	301	510,000
Misayo Fujisawa	77 73 73 78	301	510,000
Rie Mitsuhashi	80 75 74 73	302	492,000
Huang Yu-Chen	75 77 76 75	303	468,000
Keiko Arai	76 77 74 76	303	468,000
Kayo Yamada	78 72 79 74	303	468,000

Yakult Ladies

Fukuoka Kokusai Country Club, Fukuoka
Par 36-36–72; 6,279 yards

May 16-18
purse, ¥60,000,000

	SCORES	TOTAL	MONEY
Tomiko Ikebuchi	67 70 70	207	¥10,800,000
Aki Takamura	65 70 73	208	5,280,000
Toshimi Kimura	68 73 68	209	3,900,000
Akiko Fukushima	71 70 68	209	3,900,000
Fumiko Muraguchi	72 66 73	211	3,000,000

	SCORES			TOTAL	MONEY
Hiromi Hirakata	71	69	72	212	2,250,000
Aiko Takasu	69	71	72	212	2,250,000
Marnie McGuire	73	71	69	213	1,800,000
Mayumi Murai	74	72	68	214	1,270,000
Natsuko Noro	73	72	69	214	1,270,000
Fuki Kido	73	70	71	214	1,270,000
Shin Sora	74	72	69	215	990,000
Michie Ohba	72	70	73	215	990,000
Wen-Lin Li	70	71	74	215	990,000
Yuko Moriguchi	73	71	72	216	780,000
Kyoko Ono	72	71	73	216	780,000
Akane Ohshiro	74	69	73	216	780,000
Atsuko Kikuchi	70	71	75	216	780,000
Tamayo Ueda	73	71	73	217	600,000
Miyuki Shimabukuro	73	70	74	217	600,000
Ok-Hee Ku	72	75	71	218	504,000
Ikuyo Shiotani	73	74	71	218	504,000
Woo-Soon Ko	75	71	72	218	504,000
Huang Yu-Chen	73	73	72	218	504,000
Nayoko Yoshikawa	74	72	72	218	504,000
Ae-Sook Kim	73	72	73	218	504,000
Akemi Yamaoka	71	74	73	218	504,000
Suzuko Maeda	72	72	74	218	504,000
Yuko Saitoh	73	71	74	218	504,000
Tseng Hsui-Feng	71	72	75	218	504,000

Chukyo TV Bridgestone Ladies

Kasugai Country Club, Aichi
Par 36-36–72; 6,237 yards

May 23-25
purse, ¥50,000,000

	SCORES			TOTAL	MONEY
Aki Takamura	72	69	71	212	¥9,000,000
Bie-Shyun Huang	66	72	75	213	4,400,000
Natsuko Noro	72	72	70	214	3,000,000
Mitsuko Hamada	67	75	72	214	3,000,000
Woo-Soon Ko	68	73	73	214	3,000,000
Tseng Hsui-Feng	72	71	72	215	1,875,000
Young-Me Lee	70	72	73	215	1,875,000
Chieko Nishida	73	70	73	216	1,500,000
Ae-Sook Kim	78	70	69	217	981,000
Toshiko Fujisaki	74	73	70	217	981,000
Kyoko Ono	74	71	72	217	981,000
Yumi Kokubo	72	72	73	217	981,000
Ikuyo Shiotani	71	71	75	217	981,000
Yuko Saitoh	72	76	70	218	660,000
Ok-Hee Ku	75	73	70	218	660,000
Suzuko Maeda	70	77	71	218	660,000
Yuri Kawanami	76	71	71	218	660,000
Huang Yu-Chen	72	71	75	218	660,000
Michie Ohba	70	72	76	218	660,000
Yoko Inoue	73	76	70	219	470,000
Kumiko Hiyoshi	74	74	71	219	470,000
Mayumi Murai	73	74	72	219	470,000
Hisako Takeda	73	71	75	219	470,000
Fumiko Omata	77	71	72	220	430,000
Michiko Okada	71	76	73	220	430,000

	SCORES			TOTAL	MONEY
Jae-Sook Won	73	73	74	220	430,000
Yuko Moriguchi	74	71	75	220	430,000
Kayo Yamada	72	76	73	221	385,000
Keiko Arai	73	73	75	221	385,000
Kiyoe Yamazaki	73	73	75	221	385,000
Kaori Higo	75	72	74	221	385,000
Michiko Hattori	70	74	77	221	385,000

Toto Motors Ladies

Toto Hannoh Country Club, Saitama
Par 36-36—72; 6,183 yards

May 30-June 1
purse, ¥50,000,000

	SCORES			TOTAL	MONEY
Yoko Inoue	66	70	72	208	¥9,000,000
Kaori Higo	69	66	74	209	4,400,000
Kumiko Hiyoshi	71	71	68	210	3,250,000
Woo-Soon Ko	65	73	72	210	3,250,000
Fuki Kido	69	68	74	211	2,500,000
Yumiko Akagi	71	68	74	213	1,875,000
Shin Sora	70	69	74	213	1,875,000
Michie Ohba	72	72	70	214	1,035,714
Chikayo Yamazaki	71	73	70	214	1,035,714
Masako Ishihara	70	73	71	214	1,035,714
Kaori Harada	71	72	71	214	1,035,714
Natsuko Noro	73	70	71	214	1,035,714
Akane Ohshiro	70	72	72	214	1,035,714
Kayo Fukumoto	73	69	72	214	1,035,714
Yuko Motoyama	74	70	71	215	625,000
Jae-Sook Won	71	72	72	215	625,000
Harumi Sakagami	70	71	74	215	625,000
Akiko Fukushima	71	71	73	215	625,000
Yueh-Chyn Huang	70	69	76	215	625,000
Kozue Azuma	72	68	75	215	625,000
Kikuko Shibata	72	72	72	216	430,000
Rie Mitsuhashi	75	69	72	216	430,000
Michiko Hattori	71	73	72	216	430,000
Tatsuko Morimoto	69	75	72	216	430,000
Ok-Hee Ku	73	72	71	216	430,000
Suzuko Maeda	74	71	71	216	430,000
Takayo Bandoh	73	72	71	216	430,000
Junko Kitajima	74	71	71	216	430,000
Junko Yasui	72	73	71	216	430,000
Akemi Kuwashima	71	74	71	216	430,000
Hisako Takeda	70	72	74	216	430,000
Misayo Fujisawa	73	73	70	216	430,000
Rie Fujiwara	71	71	74	216	430,000

Mitsubishi Denki Ladies

Kitarokkoh Country Club, Hyogo
Par 36-37–73; 6,300 yards

June 6-8
purse, ¥50,000,000

	SCORES			TOTAL	MONEY
Akiko Fukushima	70	70	69	209	¥9,000,000
Junko Yasui	68	73	70	211	3,950,000
Young-Me Lee	70	69	72	211	3,950,000
Fuki Kido	73	72	68	213	2,500,000
Kaori Harada	70	72	71	213	2,500,000
Kaori Higo	71	70	72	213	2,500,000
Misayo Fujisawa	71	74	69	214	1,750,000
Akemi Yamaoka	72	72	71	215	1,375,000
Kyoko Ono	71	71	73	215	1,375,000
Aki Nakano	73	74	69	216	917,500
Kumiko Hiyoshi	72	73	71	216	917,500
Miyuki Shimabukuro	70	74	72	216	917,500
Woo-Soon Ko	72	72	72	216	917,500
Toshimi Kimura	74	74	69	217	765,000
Michiko Hattori	73	77	67	217	765,000
Mie-Chi Cheng	74	74	71	219	590,000
Hisako Takeda	72	74	73	219	590,000
Yu-Chuan Tai	70	75	74	219	590,000
Yuko Moriguchi	72	74	73	219	590,000
Yumi Kokubo	73	70	76	219	590,000
Keiko Arai	73	75	72	220	460,000
Yuko Motoyama	75	75	70	220	460,000
Natsuko Noro	74	73	73	220	460,000
Yuri Kawanami	72	74	74	220	460,000
Nayoko Yoshikawa	70	73	77	220	460,000
Man-Soo Kim	76	72	73	221	405,000
Rie Mitsuhashi	74	74	73	221	405,000
Yuka Shiroto	78	70	73	221	405,000
Tomiko Ikebuchi	75	74	72	221	405,000
Junko Yoshida	71	78	72	221	405,000
Kasumi Adachi	73	74	74	221	405,000

We Love Kobe Suntory Ladies Open

Arima Royal Golf Club, Hyogo
Par 36-36–72; 6,259 yards

June 12-15
purse, ¥50,000,000

	SCORES				TOTAL	MONEY
Ikuyo Shiotani	70	64	66	72	272	¥9,000,000
Miyuki Shimabukuro	71	69	72	67	279	3,950,000
Chikayo Yamazaki	70	73	71	65	279	3,950,000
Toshimi Kimura	67	72	72	70	281	3,000,000
Kaori Harada	72	68	72	70	282	2,250,000
Jae-Sook Won	74	66	71	71	282	2,250,000
Young-Me Lee	72	71	71	69	283	1,750,000
Junko Yasui	71	72	71	70	284	1,162,500
Akemi Yamaoka	75	69	68	72	284	1,162,500
Hisako Takeda	71	72	73	68	284	1,162,500
Fuki Kido	71	70	69	74	284	1,162,500
Ae-Sook Kim	71	70	71	73	285	725,000
Yuko Motoyama	70	73	69	73	285	725,000
Mie-Chi Cheng	67	73	73	72	285	725,000

	SCORES				TOTAL	MONEY
Hiromi Takamura	73	70	72	70	285	725,000
Mayumi Murai	72	69	72	72	285	725,000
Junko Kitajima	75	67	71	72	285	725,000
Yuko Moriguchi	72	70	71	73	286	550,000
Kiyoe Yamazaki	75	71	69	72	287	430,000
Woo-Soon Ko	71	68	75	73	287	430,000
Ray Bell	68	75	69	75	287	430,000
Kyoe Fumihira	74	70	72	71	287	430,000
Kyoko Isoda	72	70	71	74	287	430,000
Kaori Higo	74	70	70	73	287	430,000
Kayo Yamada	70	72	70	75	287	430,000
Kayo Segawa	68	76	70	73	287	430,000
Marnie McGuire	71	73	73	71	288	375,000
*Hee-Won Han	73	72	71	72	288	
Syoko Asano	70	76	72	70	288	375,000
Nayoko Yoshikawa	73	72	67	77	289	345,000
Mitsuyo Hirata	70	74	74	71	289	345,000
Fusako Nagata	73	72	72	72	289	345,000
Yuri Kawanami	74	69	73	73	289	345,000

Dunlop Twin Lakes Ladies Open

Twin Lakes Country Club, Gunma
Par 36-36–72; 6,293 yards
(Second round cancelled — rain.)

June 19-22
purse, ¥50,000,000

	SCORES			TOTAL	MONEY
Ok-Hee Ku	72	72	67	211	¥6,750,000
Young-Me Lee	73	69	71	213	2,962,500
Toshiko Fujisaki	72	68	73	213	2,962,500
Hiromi Takamura	72	72	70	214	2,062,500
Yukiyo Haga	72	70	72	214	2,062,500
Toshimi Kimura	74	73	68	215	1,406,250
Michie Ohba	73	72	70	215	1,406,250
Michiko Okada	72	72	72	216	937,500
Keiko Motoyama	69	72	75	216	937,500
Akane Ohshiro	74	68	74	216	937,500
Syoko Asano	76	72	69	217	682,500
Tseng Hsui-Feng	75	68	74	217	682,500
Natsuko Noro	72	74	72	218	551,250
Aki Takamura	71	74	73	218	551,250
Kayo Yamada	73	70	75	218	551,250
Nayoko Yoshikawa	70	73	75	218	551,250
Marnie McGuire	73	70	75	218	551,250
Akemi Yamaoka	73	76	70	219	381,750
Yuko Motoyama	76	73	70	219	381,750
Yueh-Chyn Huang	72	74	73	219	381,750
Chihiro Furukawa	75	71	73	219	381,750
Mayumi Murai	73	72	74	219	381,750
Miyuki Shimabukuro	73	75	72	220	330,000
Ikuyo Shiotani	73	74	73	220	330,000
Kanako Tago	73	74	73	220	330,000
Mineko Nasu	73	74	73	220	330,000
Yuka Shiroto	76	73	72	221	288,750
Junko Yasui	71	77	73	221	288,750
Kayoko Ikoma	76	71	74	221	288,750
Kayo Fukumoto	73	75	73	221	288,750

	SCORES	TOTAL	MONEY
Junko Ishii	73 74 74	221	288,750
Fuki Kido	75 72 74	221	288,750
Woo-Soon Ko	71 74 76	221	288,750

Japan Women's Open

Higashi-Hirono Golf Club, Hyogo
Par 36-36–72; 6,306 yards

June 26-29
purse, ¥70,000,000

	SCORES	TOTAL	MONEY
Ayako Okamoto	78 71 73 73	295	¥14,000,000
Akiko Fukushima	77 75 75 71	298	7,700,000
Kumiko Hiyoshi	74 77 75 73	299	5,425,000
Tomoko Ueda	72 79 76 73	300	3,255,000
Mayumi Murai	77 75 74 74	300	3,255,000
Kaori Higo	78 76 76 71	301	2,227,000
Marnie McGuire	77 77 74 73	301	2,227,000
Ikuyo Shiotani	73 85 75 70	303	1,734,000
*Hee-Won Han	76 74 76 77	303	
Toshimi Kimura	75 78 74 76	303	1,734,000
Nayoko Yoshikawa	76 78 78 72	304	1,290,666
Aki Takamura	76 80 75 73	304	1,290,666
Michiko Hattori	74 77 78 75	304	1,290,666
Bie-Shyun Huang	79 75 80 71	305	927,750
Yukiyo Haga	78 82 73 72	305	927,750
Yuri Fudoh	80 72 78 75	305	927,750
Mikino Kubo	82 77 71 75	305	927,750
Ae-Sook Kim	82 77 76 71	306	721,500
Fuki Kido	79 74 77 76	306	721,500
Young-Me Lee	75 77 77 77	306	721,500
Ok-Hee Ku	76 76 71 83	306	721,500
Norimi Terasawa	78 77 80 72	307	589,000
Hisako Takeda	74 85 76 72	307	589,000
Akane Ohshiro	77 77 78 75	307	589,000
Yuko Motoyama	79 80 72 76	307	589,000
Woo-Soon Ko	81 77 72 77	307	589,000
Atsuko Hikage	74 79 75 79	307	589,000
Mie-Chi Cheng	74 80 74 79	307	589,000
Yuri Kawanami	80 75 73 79	307	589,000
Yoko Inoue	80 76 78 74	308	519,000
Kikuko Shibata	85 73 76 74	308	519,000
Chieko Nishida	76 75 76 81	308	519,000

Tohato Ladies

Oak Village Golf Club, Chiba
Par 36-36–72; 6,402 yards

July 4-6
purse, ¥50,000,000

	SCORES	TOTAL	MONEY
Suzuko Maeda	67 72 74	213	¥9,000,000
Kozue Azuma	70 80 72	222	4,400,000
Mayumi Murai	70 79 76	225	3,500,000
Nayoko Yoshikawa	73 77 76	226	2,500,000
Kaori Harada	74 73 79	226	2,500,000
Kumiko Hiyoshi	69 76 81	226	2,500,000

	SCORES			TOTAL	MONEY
Toshiko Fujisaki	74	76	78	228	1,500,000
Kyoko Ono	74	74	80	228	1,500,000
Ok-Hee Ku	71	74	83	228	1,500,000
Marnie McGuire	73	82	74	229	972,500
Yuri Kawanami	72	76	81	229	972,500
Ikuyo Shiotani	75	79	76	230	820,000
Chihiro Furukawa	76	77	77	230	820,000
Huang Yu-Chen	74	77	79	230	820,000
Mitsuyo Hirata	77	73	80	230	820,000
Man-Soo Kim	77	79	75	231	539,444
Yuka Irie	75	80	76	231	539,444
Hiromi Takamura	71	81	79	231	539,444
Kaori Higo	74	78	79	231	539,444
Toshimi Kimura	72	80	79	231	539,444
Shin Sora	75	77	79	231	539,444
Yuko Motoyama	75	76	80	231	539,444
Kiriko Nishizawa	71	79	81	231	539,444
Kikuko Shibata	72	77	82	231	539,444
Natsuko Noro	72	83	77	232	435,000
Young-Me Lee	74	81	77	232	435,000
Aki Takamura	73	75	84	232	435,000
Yoko Inoue	72	82	79	233	405,000
Akemi Yamaoka	75	79	79	233	405,000
Kayo Fukumoto	74	77	82	233	405,000

Toyo Suisan Ladies Hokkaido

Kosaido Sapporo Country Club, Hokkaido
Par 36-36–72; 6,412 yards

July 11-13
purse, ¥50,000,000

	SCORES			TOTAL	MONEY
Kaori Higo	69	68	67	204	¥9,000,000
Marnie McGuire	72	69	69	210	4,400,000
Chieko Nishida	70	73	70	213	3,000,000
Keiko Arai	70	71	72	213	3,000,000
Ok-Hee Ku	72	70	71	213	3,000,000
Fumiko Muraguchi	74	72	68	214	1,875,000
Ikuyo Shiotani	71	69	74	214	1,875,000
Yuko Moriguchi	73	73	69	215	1,500,000
Aki Nakano	77	71	68	216	1,017,500
Tomiko Ikebuchi	77	70	69	216	1,017,500
Yuri Kawanami	75	72	69	216	1,017,500
Kyoko Isoda	77	70	69	216	1,017,500
Hiromi Takamura	74	74	69	217	810,000
Man-Soo Kim	73	74	70	217	810,000
Mieko Nomura	75	74	69	218	635,000
Miyuki Shimabukuro	71	75	72	218	635,000
Yoko Inoue	72	74	72	218	635,000
Kumiko Hiyoshi	75	71	72	218	635,000
Mikino Kubo	74	69	75	218	635,000
Natsuko Noro	75	75	69	219	460,000
Kayo Fukumoto	72	77	70	219	460,000
Mayumi Murai	76	74	69	219	460,000
Ming-Yeh Wu	73	75	71	219	460,000
Ayako Okamoto	72	75	72	219	460,000
Kayo Yamada	69	77	73	219	460,000
Michiko Hattori	77	73	70	220	405,000

	SCORES	TOTAL	MONEY
Masako Ishihara	74 76 70	220	405,000
Syoko Asano	71 77 72	220	405,000
Junko Yoshida	76 72 72	220	405,000
Suzuko Maeda	73 74 73	220	405,000

Resort Trust Ladies

St. Creek Golf Club, Aichi
Par 36-36–72; 6,402 yards

July 18-20
purse, ¥50,000,000

	SCORES	TOTAL	MONEY
Fumiko Muraguchi	66 69 69	204	¥9,000,000
Yuri Kawanami	69 70 68	207	4,400,000
Mayumi Murai	71 70 68	209	3,500,000
Miyuki Shimabukuro	72 69 71	212	3,000,000
Woo-Soon Ko	73 67 74	214	2,500,000
Jae-Sook Won	67 75 74	216	2,000,000
Mikino Kubo	71 76 70	217	1,290,000
Ikuyo Shiotani	71 76 70	217	1,290,000
Yuri Fudoh	73 73 71	217	1,290,000
Aki Takamura	68 74 75	217	1,290,000
Natsuko Noro	72 71 74	217	1,290,000
Young-Me Lee	76 71 71	218	875,000
Kumiko Hiyoshi	73 73 72	218	875,000
Akemi Yamaoka	71 77 71	219	725,000
Ann Wilson	70 73 76	219	725,000
Kiyoe Yamazaki	74 72 73	219	725,000
Harumi Hyodoh	72 69 78	219	725,000
Michiko Okada	74 73 73	220	600,000
Syoko Asano	71 78 72	221	474,444
Yuko Motoyama	74 75 72	221	474,444
Michiko Hattori	74 74 73	221	474,444
Kaori Higo	73 74 74	221	474,444
Aki Nakano	72 74 75	221	474,444
Jean Bartholomew	75 70 76	221	474,444
Kayo Yamada	72 71 78	221	474,444
Toshiko Fujisaki	71 71 79	221	474,444
Mina Nishikawa	73 67 81	221	474,444
Yuko Moriguchi	72 76 74	222	405,000
Tomiko Ikebuchi	73 75 74	222	405,000
Mineko Nasu	75 73 74	222	405,000
Chieko Nishida	75 72 75	222	405,000

Golf 5 Ladies

Mizunami Country Club, Gifu
Par 36-36–72; 6,419 yards

August 1-3
purse, ¥50,000,000

	SCORES	TOTAL	MONEY
Akiko Fukushima	67 67 71	205	¥9,000,000
Chieko Nishida	66 69 71	206	4,400,000
Marnie McGuire	68 71 69	208	3,500,000
Ikuyo Shiotani	67 71 71	209	3,000,000
Nayoko Yoshikawa	69 71 71	211	2,500,000
Akane Ohshiro	71 70 72	213	1,875,000

	SCORES			TOTAL	MONEY
Mikiyo Nishizuka	69	70	74	213	1,875,000
Kayo Yamada	74	68	72	214	1,375,000
Toshimi Kimura	70	70	74	214	1,375,000
Ok-Hee Ku	75	70	70	215	972,500
Miyuki Shimabukuro	71	70	74	215	972,500
Yoko Inoue	73	74	69	216	895,000
Hiromi Takamura	75	73	69	217	770,000
Aiko Takasu	71	72	74	217	770,000
Tseng Hsui-Feng	73	71	73	217	770,000
Yuri Kawanami	73	69	75	217	770,000
Aki Nakano	70	78	70	218	529,285
Yuri Fudoh	75	73	70	218	529,285
Jae-Sook Won	73	73	72	218	529,285
Michiko Hattori	70	75	73	218	529,285
Michiko Okada	74	69	75	218	529,285
Natsuko Noro	73	70	75	218	529,285
Junko Yasui	71	71	76	218	529,285
Toshiko Fujisaki	71	76	72	219	440,000
Kayo Fukumoto	70	76	73	219	440,000
Kyoe Fumihira	71	75	73	219	440,000
Harumi Sakagami	71	74	74	219	440,000
Junko Yoshida	73	74	73	220	400,000
*Mayumi Nakajima	74	73	73	220	
Mie-Chi Cheng	75	71	74	220	400,000
*Kimiyo Yoshida	69	76	75	220	
Syoko Asano	68	77	75	220	400,000
Kasumi Fujii	70	72	78	220	400,000

Mizuno Ladies

Asahikokusai Hamamura Onsen Golf Club, Tottori
Par 36-36–72; 6,309 yards

August 8-10
purse, ¥60,000,000

	SCORES			TOTAL	MONEY
Aiko Takasu	69	72	70	211	¥10,800,000
Yoko Inoue	72	70	70	212	5,280,000
Jean Bartholomew	71	72	70	213	4,200,000
Huang Yu-Chen	71	73	70	214	3,600,000
Ok-Hee Ku	73	73	70	216	2,700,000
Marnie McGuire	72	72	72	216	2,700,000
Kaori Higo	73	69	75	217	2,100,000
Lee Oh-Soon	73	72	73	218	1,800,000
Mariko Watanabe	72	74	73	219	1,350,000
Yuri Kawanami	73	71	75	219	1,350,000
Akane Ohshiro	77	73	70	220	948,000
Ai-Yu Tu	73	76	71	220	948,000
Yuko Motoyama	76	73	71	220	948,000
Miyuki Shimabukuro	74	74	72	220	948,000
Young-Me Lee	75	73	72	220	948,000
Mikiyo Nishizuka	72	74	74	220	948,000
Harumi Hyodoh	75	72	73	220	948,000
Bie-Shyun Huang	77	74	70	221	588,000
Yuri Fudoh	71	78	72	221	588,000
Toshimi Kimura	73	75	73	221	588,000
Shin Sora	72	76	73	221	588,000
Kasumi Fujii	74	73	74	221	588,000
Yukiyo Haga	73	74	74	221	588,000

	SCORES	TOTAL	MONEY
Yuka Irie	75 70 76	221	588,000
Junko Yasui	71 71 79	221	588,000
Chikayo Yamazaki	73 76 73	222	498,000
Jae-Sook Won	73 76 73	222	498,000
Toshiko Fujisaki	76 73 73	222	498,000
Nobuko Kizawa	74 74 74	222	498,000
Ae-Sook Kim	74 76 73	223	450,000
Hiromi Takamura	74 74 75	223	450,000
Masako Ishihara	74 73 76	223	450,000
Mikako Kanamori	75 72 76	223	450,000

NEC Karuizawa 72

Karuizawa 72 Golf Club, Nagano
Par 36-36–72; 6,440 yards
(Shortened to 45 holes — dense fog.)

August 15-17
purse, ¥60,000,000

	SCORES	TOTAL	MONEY
Yuka Irie	75 70 36	181	¥10,800,000
Akiko Fukushima	77 72 33	182	3,696,000
Kasumi Fujii	74 73 35	182	3,696,000
Nobuko Kizawa	72 75 35	182	3,696,000
Sachiko Ohshima	71 75 36	182	3,696,000
Marnie McGuire	70 73 39	182	3,696,000
Akane Ohshiro	71 77 35	183	1,543,200
Ok-Hee Ku	72 75 36	183	1,543,200
Ai-Yu Tu	73 74 36	183	1,543,200
Hiromi Takamura	72 74 37	183	1,543,200
Kyoko Isoda	73 72 38	183	1,543,200
Mitsuyo Hirata	73 77 34	184	936,000
Jean Bartholomew	75 74 35	184	936,000
Huang Yu-Chen	74 74 36	184	936,000
*Mayumi Nakajima	74 73 37	184	
Yuko Motoyama	76 71 37	184	936,000
Toshiko Fujisaki	73 73 38	184	936,000
Suzuko Maeda	75 73 37	185	645,600
Jeanne Kei	76 71 38	185	645,600
Ayako Okamoto	72 74 39	185	645,600
Kasumi Adachi	74 72 39	185	645,600
Bie-Shyun Huang	73 73 39	185	645,600
Syoko Asano	75 76 35	186	510,000
Mie-Chi Cheng	76 75 35	186	510,000
Yoko Inoue	77 74 35	186	510,000
Yu-Chuan Tai	73 77 36	186	510,000
Natsuko Noro	74 75 37	186	510,000
Chieko Nishida	72 76 38	186	510,000
Rie Fujiwara	74 73 39	186	510,000
Yukiyo Haga	70 77 39	186	510,000

Shin Caterpillar Mitsubishi Ladies

Grand Fields Country Club, Shizuoka
Par 36-36–72; 6,389 yards

August 22-24
purse, ¥60,000,000

	SCORES			TOTAL	MONEY
Takayo Bandoh	70	72	69	211	¥10,800,000
Yuri Fudoh	72	70	72	214	5,280,000
Huang Yu-Chen	69	71	75	215	4,200,000
Ok-Hee Ku	72	73	71	216	3,300,000
Mikino Kubo	71	73	72	216	3,300,000
Kayo Fukumoto	77	69	71	217	2,250,000
Yumiko Akagi	71	73	73	217	2,250,000
Chikako Matsuzawa	75	74	69	218	1,405,500
Ikuyo Shiotani	73	75	70	218	1,405,500
Nayoko Yoshikawa	71	74	73	218	1,405,500
Mikiyo Nishizuka	77	68	73	218	1,405,500
Toshiko Fujisaki	70	78	71	219	882,000
Tseng Hsui-Feng	74	74	71	219	882,000
Keiko Arai	73	74	72	219	882,000
Norimi Terasawa	75	73	71	219	882,000
Aki Takamura	73	73	73	219	882,000
Kaori Higo	74	72	73	219	882,000
Aki Nakano	77	67	75	219	882,000
Harumi Sakagami	75	74	71	220	612,000
Akemi Yamaoka	74	73	73	220	612,000
Woo-Soon Ko	77	72	72	221	528,000
Kyoko Ono	73	75	73	221	528,000
Yukiyo Haga	74	74	73	221	528,000
Michiko Hattori	76	71	74	221	528,000
Yuri Kawanami	72	74	75	221	528,000
Young-Me Lee	73	73	75	221	528,000
Mitsuyo Hirata	74	72	75	221	528,000
Yuko Motoyama	75	69	77	221	528,000
Michie Ohba	77	72	73	222	456,000
Akane Ohshiro	76	73	73	222	456,000
Yumi Kokubo	73	75	74	222	456,000
Kyoe Fumihira	74	74	74	222	456,000

Goyo Kensetsu Ladies

The Privilege Golf Club, Chiba
Par 36-36–72; 6,227 yards

August 29-31
purse, ¥60,000,000

	SCORES			TOTAL	MONEY
Michiko Hattori	67	66	71	204	¥10,800,000
Yuri Kawanami	71	69	65	205	5,280,000
Akiko Fukushima	66	68	72	206	4,200,000
Yuri Fudoh	69	69	70	208	3,600,000
Natsuko Noro	67	70	73	210	3,000,000
Ikuyo Shiotani	68	72	71	211	1,950,000
Miki Furuya	70	69	72	211	1,950,000
Huang Yu-Chen	68	70	73	211	1,950,000
Hiromi Takamura	68	68	75	211	1,950,000
Junko Yoshida	73	70	70	213	1,200,000
Mineko Nasu	74	69	71	214	1,074,000
Harumi Hyodoh	71	72	71	214	1,074,000
Toshiko Fujisaki	72	70	72	214	1,074,000

	SCORES			TOTAL	MONEY
Mieko Nomura	72	72	71	215	750,000
Hisako Takeda	73	71	71	215	750,000
Chikako Matsuzawa	73	70	72	215	750,000
Mikino Kubo	69	72	74	215	750,000
Nobuko Kizawa	67	74	74	215	750,000
Mikiyo Nishizuka	70	71	74	215	750,000
Kozue Azuma	71	69	75	215	750,000
Sachiko Ohshima	70	69	76	215	750,000
Yumi Kokubo	75	70	71	216	540,000
Kaori Harada	71	72	73	216	540,000
Miyuki Shimabukuro	70	72	74	216	540,000
Young-Me Lee	68	72	76	216	540,000
Kikuko Shibata	70	70	76	216	540,000
Ayako Shibata	70	70	76	216	540,000
Norimi Terasawa	74	71	72	217	480,000
Kayo Yamada	72	72	73	217	480,000
Fuki Kido	70	73	74	217	480,000
Mitsuyo Hirata	72	68	77	217	480,000

Fuji Sankei Ladies Classic

Fujizakura Country Club, Yamanashi
Par 35-36–71; 6,291 yards

September 5-7
purse, ¥60,000,000

	SCORES			TOTAL	MONEY
Aki Takamura	69	71	71	211	¥10,800,000
Yu-Chuan Tai	70	73	68	211	5,280,000
(Takamura defeated Tai at fourth extra hole.)					
Mitsuyo Hirata	72	73	69	214	3,600,000
Mayumi Murai	71	71	72	214	3,600,000
Fumiko Muraguchi	72	70	72	214	3,600,000
Yukiyo Haga	70	73	72	215	2,400,000
Chihiro Furukawa	74	70	72	216	1,800,000
Debbi Koyama	71	71	74	216	1,800,000
Yukiko Ishiguro	73	68	75	216	1,800,000
Junko Yasui	73	71	73	217	1,128,000
Akemi Yamaoka	70	73	74	217	1,128,000
Natsuko Noro	71	71	75	217	1,128,000
Miyuki Shimabukuro	74	73	71	218	822,000
Yuri Fudoh	74	71	73	218	822,000
Kaori Higo	74	71	73	218	822,000
Mie-Chi Cheng	73	71	74	218	822,000
Yumiko Akagi	75	69	74	218	822,000
Nayoko Yoshikawa	73	69	76	218	822,000
Ikuyo Shiotani	70	70	78	218	822,000
Ayako Okamoto	73	75	71	219	546,000
Akiko Fukushima	71	73	75	219	546,000
Jenny Sevil	71	73	75	219	546,000
Ok-Hee Ku	71	73	75	219	546,000
Fusako Nagata	74	70	75	219	546,000
Toshiko Fujisaki	71	72	76	219	546,000
Fuki Kido	71	70	78	219	546,000
Tseng Hsui-Feng	77	70	73	220	480,000
Syoko Asano	75	71	74	220	480,000
Tomoko Ueda	73	72	75	220	480,000
Yoko Inoue	72	71	77	220	480,000

Japan LPGA Championship

Fuji Country Club, Syuga, Gifu
Par 36-37–73; 6,532 yards

September 11-14
purse, ¥70,000,000

	SCORES				TOTAL	MONEY
Akiko Fukushima	72	69	70	72	283	¥12,600,000
Miyuki Shimabukuro	72	75	72	69	288	6,160,000
Fumiko Muraguchi	73	74	71	72	290	4,900,000
Huang Yu-Chen	74	69	72	77	292	4,200,000
Aki Nakano	76	72	78	67	293	2,712,500
Akemi Yamaoka	75	71	74	73	293	2,712,500
Natsuko Noro	73	72	75	73	293	2,712,500
Toshimi Kimura	73	71	75	74	293	2,712,500
Ae-Sook Kim	72	73	72	77	294	1,750,000
Nayoko Yoshikawa	74	73	75	73	295	1,246,000
Junko Yasui	74	74	72	75	295	1,246,000
Yuko Motoyama	74	73	72	76	295	1,246,000
Ok-Hee Ku	76	73	73	74	296	994,000
Aki Takamura	72	76	74	74	296	994,000
Harumi Sakagami	76	72	73	75	296	994,000
Debbi Koyama	79	69	76	73	297	784,000
Young-Me Lee	71	76	75	75	297	784,000
Kumiko Hiyoshi	74	73	73	77	297	784,000
Ai-Yu Tu	72	76	77	73	298	571,200
Ikuyo Shiotani	73	76	74	75	298	571,200
Yuri Fudoh	75	70	75	78	298	571,200
Man-Soo Kim	74	74	73	77	298	571,200
Mikino Kubo	72	74	74	78	298	571,200
Harumi Kawano	75	75	75	74	299	518,000
Kanako Tago	76	75	76	73	300	476,000
Mayumi Murai	75	75	75	75	300	476,000
Keiko Arai	73	75	76	76	300	476,000
Wen-Lin Li	73	73	76	78	300	476,000
Yuko Moriguchi	70	74	77	79	300	476,000
Fumiko Omata	74	76	77	74	301	386,909
Yu-Chuan Tai	73	74	79	75	301	386,909
Michie Ohba	77	72	77	75	301	386,909
Mitsuyo Hirata	77	71	77	76	301	386,909
Shin Sora	74	75	76	76	301	386,909
Kasumi Fujii	76	73	76	76	301	386,909
Mikako Kanamori	72	78	75	76	301	386,909
Ayako Okamoto	76	75	74	76	301	386,909
Hiromi Takamura	74	74	76	77	301	386,909
Yueh-Chyn Huang	73	74	76	78	301	386,909
Hitomi Notsu	76	73	74	78	301	386,909

Yukijirushi Ladies Tokai Classic

Ryosen Golf Club, Mie
Par 36-36–72; 6,351 yards

September 19-21
purse, ¥60,000,000

	SCORES			TOTAL	MONEY
Akiko Fukushima	75	66	70	211	¥10,800,000
Ikuyo Shiotani	70	71	73	214	5,280,000
Yoko Inoue	72	72	71	215	4,200,000
Kaori Higo	78	69	70	217	3,000,000
Natsuko Noro	75	70	72	217	3,000,000

	SCORES	TOTAL	MONEY
Kaori Harada	71 72 74	217	3,000,000
Yuko Nakamura	78 71 69	218	2,100,000
Yuko Motoyama	78 73 68	219	1,650,000
Young-Me Lee	77 73 69	219	1,650,000
Suzuko Maeda	76 74 70	220	1,167,000
Chikako Matsuzawa	74 72 74	220	1,167,000
Fumiko Muraguchi	77 74 70	221	1,014,000
Yuko Moriguchi	78 72 71	221	1,014,000
Miyuki Shimabukuro	79 71 71	221	1,014,000
Woo-Soon Ko	75 75 72	222	744,000
Kayo Yamada	76 73 73	222	744,000
Aki Nakano	75 73 74	222	744,000
Kumiko Fuchi	74 73 75	222	744,000
Tseng Hsui-Feng	73 73 76	222	744,000
Chieko Nishida	73 72 77	222	744,000
Ayako Shibata	79 73 71	223	564,000
Akemi Yamaoka	75 76 72	223	564,000
Kumiko Hiyoshi	77 74 72	223	564,000
Man-Soo Kim	76 72 75	223	564,000
Jean Bartholomew	79 73 72	224	516,000
Michiko Okada	80 71 73	224	516,000
Yuri Kawanami	76 74 74	224	516,000
Debbi Koyama	78 72 74	224	516,000
Mayumi Murai	80 72 73	225	450,000
Rie Fujiwara	78 73 74	225	450,000
Ok-Hee Ku	78 73 74	225	450,000
Wen-Lin Li	76 73 76	225	450,000
Michie Ohba	79 70 76	225	450,000
Aki Takamura	78 71 76	225	450,000
Ae-Sook Kim	73 73 79	225	450,000

Miyagi TV Cup Ladies Open

Hananomori Golf Club, Miyagi
Par 36-36–72; 6,329 yards
(Third round cancelled — bad weather.)

September 26-28
purse, ¥50,000,000

	SCORES	TOTAL	MONEY
Michiko Hattori	67 75	142	¥6,750,000
Aki Takamura	72 72	144	2,725,000
Yumi Kokubo	71 73	144	2,725,000
Chieko Nishida	69 75	144	2,725,000
Keiko Arai	73 73	146	1,453,125
Michie Ohba	73 73	146	1,453,125
Tseng Hsui-Feng	76 70	146	1,453,125
Kaori Harada	70 76	146	1,453,125
Asayo Itoh	74 73	147	740,250
Aki Nakano	72 75	147	740,250
Mitsuko Hamada	71 76	147	740,250
Ok-Hee Ku	72 75	147	740,250
Fuki Kido	71 76	147	740,250
Harumi Sakagami	74 74	148	456,250
Natsuko Noro	74 74	148	456,250
Shin Sora	74 74	148	456,250
Fumiko Omata	73 75	148	456,250
Yukiyo Haga	72 76	148	456,250
Akemi Yamaoka	72 76	148	456,250

	SCORES	TOTAL	MONEY
Kyoko Ono	72 76	148	456,250
Mayumi Murai	76 72	148	456,250
Kaori Higo	69 79	148	456,250
Etsuko Kawakami	73 76	149	303,750
Yuko Motoyama	75 74	149	303,750
Kyoko Isoda	75 74	149	303,750
Rie Fujiwara	73 76	149	303,750
Wen-Lin Li	73 76	149	303,750
Yuko Moriguchi	75 74	149	303,750
Akane Ohshiro	73 76	149	303,750
Kanako Tago	72 77	149	303,750
Matsuko Maekawa	72 77	149	303,750
Woo-Soon Ko	72 77	149	303,750
Sachiko Ohshima	72 77	149	303,750
Syoko Asano	71 78	149	303,750
Mitsuyo Hirata	70 79	149	303,750

Kosaido Ladies Golf Cup

Chiba Kosaido Country Club, Chiba
Par 36-36—72; 6,257 yards

October 3-5
purse, ¥60,000,000

	SCORES	TOTAL	MONEY
Akiko Fukushima	69 72 70	211	¥10,800,000
Kyoko Ono	70 72 71	213	5,280,000
Suzuko Maeda	71 73 70	214	4,200,000
Mie-Chi Cheng	71 75 69	215	2,580,000
Ae-Sook Kim	70 74 71	215	2,580,000
Yuri Fudoh	72 71 72	215	2,580,000
Nayoko Yoshikawa	74 68 73	215	2,580,000
Mikino Kubo	70 72 73	215	2,580,000
Kyoe Fumihira	75 70 71	216	1,270,000
Ai-Yu Tu	71 73 72	216	1,270,000
Ayako Okamoto	74 69 73	216	1,270,000
Natsuko Noro	71 72 74	217	1,020,000
Yumiko Akagi	73 71 73	217	1,020,000
Nobuko Kizawa	73 75 70	218	840,000
Akemi Yamaoka	73 74 71	218	840,000
Kasumi Adachi	72 72 74	218	840,000
Toshiko Fujisaki	74 70 74	218	840,000
Kaori Harada	75 73 71	219	612,000
Kaori Higo	72 73 74	219	612,000
Tseng Hsui-Feng	70 74 75	219	612,000
Sachiko Ohshima	72 72 75	219	612,000
Fumiko Muraguchi	74 75 71	220	522,000
Junko Yasui	76 73 71	220	522,000
Kumiko Hiyoshi	72 76 72	220	522,000
Man-Soo Kim	69 77 74	220	522,000
Kayo Yamada	71 74 75	220	522,000
Kikuko Shibata	73 76 72	221	474,000
Pernilla Sterner	75 74 72	221	474,000
Kyoko Isoda	76 73 72	221	474,000
Aiko Takasu	74 75 73	222	420,000
Jae-Sook Won	76 73 73	222	420,000
Kiyoe Yamazaki	72 76 74	222	420,000
Mayumi Murai	72 76 74	222	420,000
Hiromi Takamura	75 72 75	222	420,000
Yumi Kokubo	74 73 75	222	420,000

TaKaRa World Invitational

Caledonian Golf Club, Chiba
Par 36-36–72; 6,238 yards

October 9-12
purse, ¥80,000,000

	SCORES				TOTAL	MONEY
Liselotte Neumann	69	68	73	72	282	¥14,400,000
Yuko Motoyama	67	73	75	69	284	7,040,000
Kyoe Fumihira	74	76	73	69	292	4,800,000
Emilee Klein	73	77	72	70	292	4,800,000
Akemi Yamaoka	71	74	74	73	292	4,800,000
Kaori Higo	77	74	73	69	293	2,800,000
Hisako Takeda	75	74	72	72	293	2,800,000
Ae-Sook Kim	74	71	72	76	293	2,800,000
Kaori Harada	71	74	80	69	294	1,620,000
Keiko Arai	72	73	78	71	294	1,620,000
Debbi Koyama	73	72	77	72	294	1,620,000
Aki Takamura	73	72	76	73	294	1,620,000
Akane Ohshiro	69	74	78	74	295	1,280,000
Marnie McGuire	71	76	74	74	295	1,280,000
Laura Davies	75	78	73	70	296	1,000,000
Toshiko Fujisaki	74	72	79	71	296	1,000,000
Mikino Kubo	75	71	75	75	296	1,000,000
Tseng Hsui-Feng	73	72	76	75	296	1,000,000
Jennifer Sevil	75	74	71	76	296	1,000,000
Toshimi Kimura	77	75	72	73	297	752,000
Leta Lindley	75	75	72	75	297	752,000
Catriona Matthew	77	75	75	71	298	712,000
Ok-Hee Ku	76	75	74	73	298	712,000
Yuri Fudoh	72	73	77	76	299	712,000
Jean Bartholomew	76	76	75	72	299	672,000
Ayako Okamoto	76	72	74	77	300	672,000
Nayoko Yoshikawa	76	75	77	72	300	608,000
Man-Soo Kim	75	74	79	72	300	608,000
Mayumi Murai	76	75	76	73	300	608,000
Aiko Takasu	75	71	80	74	300	608,000
Masako Ishihara	76	71	78	75	300	608,000
Natsuko Noro	74	73	77	76	300	608,000

Fujitsu Ladies

Hamano Golf Club, Chiba
Par 36-36–72; 6,403 yards

October 17-19
purse, ¥60,000,000

	SCORES			TOTAL	MONEY
Aiko Takasu	70	72	68	210	¥10,800,000
Hiromi Kobayashi	72	69	71	212	5,280,000
Ok-Hee Ku	72	70	71	213	3,900,000
Kayo Yamada	72	69	72	213	3,900,000
Norimi Terasawa	71	70	73	214	3,000,000
Akane Ohshiro	71	73	72	216	1,800,000
Yuki Kido	70	73	73	216	1,800,000
Yuko Motoyama	72	72	72	216	1,800,000
Natsuko Noro	71	70	75	216	1,800,000
Keiko Arai	72	69	75	216	1,800,000
Kyoko Ono	73	70	74	217	1,140,000
Nobuko Kizawa	72	73	73	218	960,000
Suzuko Maeda	71	73	74	218	960,000

	SCORES	TOTAL	MONEY
Kikuko Shibata	75 69 74	218	960,000
Akemi Yamaoka	71 72 75	218	960,000
Mikino Kubo	69 71 78	218	960,000
Kumiko Hiyoshi	75 72 72	219	690,000
Jennifer Sevil	73 72 74	219	690,000
Junko Yasui	74 69 76	219	690,000
Ann Wilson	71 69 79	219	690,000
Young-Me Lee	71 76 73	220	558,000
Akemi Kuwashima	76 71 73	220	558,000
Toshimi Kimura	73 74 73	220	558,000
Jae-Sook Won	69 76 75	220	558,000
Ae-Sook Kim	71 72 77	220	558,000
Tomiko Ikebuchi	68 71 81	220	558,000
Kasumi Fujii	75 72 74	221	480,000
Fumiko Muraguchi	73 74 74	221	480,000
Kiriko Nishizawa	75 72 74	221	480,000
Yuri Fudoh	74 73 74	221	480,000
Lee Oh-Soon	71 75 75	221	480,000
Junko Yoshida	73 72 76	221	480,000
Mika Horiba	71 72 78	221	480,000

Higuchi Hisako Kibun Classic

Manju Golf Club, Nara
Par 36-36–72; 6,369 yards

October 23-26
purse, ¥70,000,000

	SCORES	TOTAL	MONEY
Annika Sorenstam	72 70 73 72	287	¥12,600,000
Natsuko Noro	69 71 75 73	288	5,530,000
Ok-Hee Ku	72 68 71 77	288	5,530,000
Takayo Bandoh	72 71 74 73	290	3,850,000
Young-Me Lee	72 68 73 77	290	3,850,000
Junko Yasui	71 70 75 75	291	2,625,000
Akiko Fukushima	72 69 74 76	291	2,625,000
Miyuki Shimabukuro	77 68 73 74	292	2,100,000
Ae-Sook Kim	71 75 72 75	293	1,575,000
Fuki Kido	70 70 74 79	293	1,575,000
Yuri Fudoh	69 70 74 81	294	1,316,000
Chikayo Yamazaki	69 74 74 78	295	1,246,000
Man-Soo Kim	71 75 76 74	296	1,106,000
Yuko Motoyama	73 75 74 74	296	1,106,000
Hiromi Kobayashi	75 72 73 76	296	1,106,000
Yukiyo Haga	76 71 74 76	297	826,000
Michiko Hattori	74 70 76 77	297	826,000
Norimi Terasawa	71 72 77 77	297	826,000
Rie Mitsuhashi	75 73 71 78	297	826,000
Yuka Shiroto	69 75 74 79	297	826,000
Mikino Kubo	70 71 82 75	298	651,000
Kasumi Fujii	76 73 74 75	298	651,000
Kayo Yamada	74 75 74 75	298	651,000
Toshiko Fujisaki	73 70 74 81	298	651,000
Michie Ohba	75 73 75 76	299	595,000
Mitsuko Hamada	74 72 76 77	299	595,000
Yueh-Chyn Huang	72 73 75 79	299	595,000
Yuko Moriguchi	75 70 73 81	299	595,000
Kozue Azuma	69 74 81 76	300	546,000
Suzuko Maeda	70 70 80 80	300	546,000
Aki Nakano	76 73 72 79	300	546,000

Nichirei International

Tsukuba Country Club, Ibaragi
Par 36-36–72; 6,294 yards

October 31-November 2
purse, US$675,000

FIRST DAY
Better Ball

Jane Geddes and Cindy Figg-Currier (USA) defeated Miyuki Shimabukuro and Mayumi Murai, 65-68.
Deb Richard and Colleen Walker (USA) defeated Kaori Higo and Natsuko Noro, 66-67.
Liselotte Neumann and Kelly Robbins (USA) tied Fumiko Muraguchi and Ikuyo Shiotani, 68-68.
Hiromi Kobayashi and Pat Hurst (USA) defeated Toshimi Kimura and Kumiko Hiyoshi, 63-65.
Gail Graham and Terry-Jo Myers (USA) defeated Marnie McGuire and Yoko Inoue, 64-67.
Michele Redman and Tina Barrett (USA) defeated Michiko Hattori and Aki Takamura, 61-67.
Rosie Jones and Lorie Kane (USA) defeated Suzuko Maeda and Chieko Nishida, 67-69.
Kaori Harada and Akiko Fukushima (Japan) defeated Chris Johnson and Kris Tschetter, 61-64.
Alison Nicholas and Lisa Hackney (USA) defeated Woo-Soon Ko and Akemi Yamaoka, 63-67.

POINTS: United States 7½, Japan 1½

SECOND DAY
Better Ball

Geddes and Figg-Currier (USA) defeated Kimura and Hiyoshi, 66-71.
Richard and Walker (USA) tied McGuire and Inoue, 68-68.
Neumann and Robbins (USA) tied Hattori and Takamura, 65-65.
Kobayashi and Hurst (USA) tied Shimabukuro and Murai, 67-67.
Graham and Myers (USA) defeated Higo and Noro, 64-66.
Redman and Barrett (USA) defeated Maeda and Nishida, 69-71.
Muraguchi and Shiotani (Japan) defeated Jones and Kane, 65-66.
Johnson and Tschetter (USA) tied Ko and Yamaoka, 67-67.
Harada and Fukushima (Japan) defeated Nicholas and Lisa Hackney, 67-69.

POINTS: United States 12½, Japan 5½

THIRD DAY
Singles

Shiotani (Japan) defeated Geddes, 71-72.
Hurst (USA) tied Hiyoshi, 73-73.
Robbins (USA) defeated Nishida, 72-76.
Walker (USA) defeated Maeda, 74-75.
Noro (Japan) defeated Myers, 70-71.
Richard (USA) defeated Muraguchi, 73-74.
Figg-Currier (USA) defeated Harada, 70-75.
Murai (Japan) defeated Tschetter, 70-71.
Kobayashi (USA) defeated Shimabukuro, 71-73.
Neumann (USA) defeated Higo, 72-73.
Yamaoka (Japan) defeated Redman, 70-72.
Kane (USA) defeated Ko, 74-75.
Hackney (USA) defeated Hattori, 67-72.
Barrett (USA) defeated Kimura, 72-75.

McGuire (Japan) defeated Graham, 72-73.
Takamura (Japan) defeated Nicholas, 72-76.
Inoue (Japan) defeated Jones, 72-73.
Johnson (USA) defeated Fukushima, 68-70.

TOTAL POINTS: United States 23, Japan 13

(Each member of USA team received US$24,000; each member of Japanese team received US$13,500.)

Toray Japan Queen's Cup

Seta Golf Course, Otsu-shi, Shiga
Par 36-36–72; 6,423 yards

November 7-9
purse, US$750,000

	SCORES			TOTAL	MONEY
Liselotte Neumann	68	70	67	205	US$112,500
Lorie Kane	70	69	67	206	69,819
Lisa Hackney	69	71	67	207	45,288
Chris Johnson	67	72	68	207	45,288
Laura Davies	72	69	67	208	21,198
Jane Geddes	71	70	67	208	21,198
Kyoko Ono	70	71	67	208	21,198
Mayumi Murai	72	67	69	208	21,198
Helen Alfredsson	70	69	69	208	21,198
Michele Redman	69	69	70	208	21,198
Sherri Steinhauer	67	71	70	208	21,198
Catriona Matthew	71	68	70	209	12,144
Toshimi Kimura	69	70	70	209	12,144
Kris Tschetter	68	71	70	209	12,144
Leta Lindley	71	65	73	209	12,144
Suzuko Maeda	70	69	71	210	9,880
Yuko Moriguchi	67	72	71	210	9,880
Yoko Inoue	68	69	73	210	9,880
Yuri Kawanami	73	68	70	211	8,748
Kris Monaghan	69	72	70	211	8,748
Charlotta Sorenstam	68	73	70	211	8,748
Gail Graham	72	72	68	212	7,189
Helen Dobson	67	76	69	212	7,189
Jae-Sook Won	70	72	70	212	7,189
Tina Barrett	69	73	70	212	7,189
Karen Weiss	70	71	71	212	7,189
Wendy Doolan	69	72	71	212	7,189
Rosie Jones	71	68	73	212	7,189
Kim Williams	73	72	68	213	5,728
Alison Nicholas	73	72	68	213	5,728
Fumiko Muraguchi	72	72	69	213	5,728
Hiromi Kobayashi	71	72	70	213	5,728
Akiko Fukushima	70	68	75	213	5,728
Jane Crafter	69	68	76	213	5,728

Itoen Ladies

Great Island Club, Chiba
Par 36-36–72; 6,388 yards

November 14-16
purse, ¥80,000,000

	SCORES			TOTAL	MONEY
Helen Alfredsson	68	71	69	208	¥10,800,000
Akemi Yamaoka	72	67	69	208	5,280,000
(Alfredsson defeated Yamaoka on first extra hole.)					
Kaori Higo	68	67	75	210	4,200,000
Ae-Sook Kim	72	68	71	211	3,600,000
Yuko Nakamura	74	69	69	212	3,000,000
Chie Yoshida	76	69	68	213	2,100,000
Aki Nakano	70	72	71	213	2,100,000
Yuko Moriguchi	70	71	72	213	2,100,000
Marnie McGuire	73	70	71	214	1,114,000
Harumi Sakagami	72	71	71	214	1,114,000
Ok-Hee Ku	73	70	71	214	1,114,000
Keiko Arai	72	69	73	214	1,114,000
Ikuyo Shiotani	75	65	74	214	1,114,000
Kikuko Shibata	70	70	74	214	1,114,000
Nayoko Yoshikawa	73	73	69	215	756,000
Norimi Terasawa	73	72	70	215	756,000
Michiko Okada	76	69	70	215	756,000
Masako Ishihara	74	70	71	215	756,000
Laura Davies	72	74	70	216	543,600
Junko Yoshida	73	72	71	216	543,600
Fuki Kido	72	72	72	216	543,600
Yuri Fudoh	70	74	72	216	543,600
Nahoko Hirao	72	71	73	216	543,600
Kumiko Hiyoshi	71	76	70	217	468,000
Toshimi Kimura	72	72	73	217	468,000
Tatsuko Morimoto	74	70	73	217	468,000
Wen-Lin Li	71	72	74	217	468,000
Yuri Kawanami	74	70	73	217	468,000
Young-Me Lee	70	71	76	217	468,000
Junko Yasui	75	73	70	218	420,000
Tomiko Ikebuchi	74	73	71	218	420,000

Daio Seishi Elleair Ladies Open

Elleair Golf Club, Matsuyama, Kagawa
Par 36-36–72; 6,245 yards

November 21-23
purse, ¥65,000,000

	SCORES			TOTAL	MONEY
Ok-Hee Ku	69	69	67	205	¥11,700,000
Takayo Bandoh	69	68	72	209	5,720,000
Tseng Hsui-Feng	68	70	72	210	4,550,000
Rie Fujiwara	70	71	70	211	3,006,250
Kasumi Adachi	71	69	71	211	3,006,250
Man-Soo Kim	70	70	71	211	3,006,250
Yukiyo Haga	65	73	73	211	3,006,250
Kaori Higo	72	74	66	212	1,456,000
Yuko Moriguchi	69	73	70	212	1,456,000
Natsuko Noro	69	72	71	212	1,456,000
Aki Nakano	68	71	73	212	1,456,000
Akemi Yamaoka	68	71	73	212	1,456,000
Harumi Sakagami	77	68	68	213	1,007,500
Kasumi Fujii	69	73	71	213	1,007,500

	SCORES	TOTAL	MONEY
Norimi Terasawa	72 70 71	213	1,007,500
Jean Bartholomew	70 70 73	213	1,007,500
Yuko Oda	71 72 71	214	845,000
Akiko Fukushima	72 73 70	215	650,000
Yuko Nakamura	74 70 71	215	650,000
Vicki Goetze	73 71 71	215	650,000
Marnie McGuire	70 73 72	215	650,000
Carin Hj Koch	70 73 72	215	650,000
Kyoko Ono	73 70 72	215	650,000
Hiromi Takamura	71 71 73	215	650,000
Kyoko Isoda	72 70 73	215	650,000
Suzuko Maeda	73 72 71	216	552,500
Ikuyo Shiotani	68 77 71	216	552,500
Kaori Harada	73 71 72	216	552,500
Fumiko Omata	70 76 70	216	552,500
Yuri Fudoh	72 73 72	217	487,500
Fumiko Muraguchi	70 74 73	217	487,500
Ae-Sook Kim	74 72 71	217	487,500
Yoshiko Itoh	78 68 71	217	487,500
Ming-Yeh Wu	70 73 74	217	487,500
Shin Sora	68 75 74	217	487,500

JLPGA Meiji Nyugyo Cup

Aoshima Golf Club, Miyazaki
Par 36-36–72; 6,437 yards

November 27-30
purse, ¥60,000,000

	SCORES	TOTAL	MONEY
Akiko Fukushima	70 70 70 73	283	¥10,800,000
Yuko Motoyama	71 70 73 71	285	5,400,000
Mayumi Murai	72 76 68 70	286	3,600,000
Akane Ohshiro	75 70 70 72	287	2,550,000
Ikuyo Shiotani	70 68 75 74	287	2,550,000
Junko Yasui	72 73 71 73	289	1,980,000
Marnie McGuire	73 77 70 70	290	1,860,000
Mei-Chi Cheng	72 73 72 74	291	1,740,000
Young-Me Lee	76 73 73 70	292	1,520,000
Ok-Hee Ku	74 72 74 72	292	1,520,000
Kaori Higo	74 76 70 72	292	1,520,000
Ae-Sook Kim	73 77 67 76	293	1,380,000
Man-Soo Kim	72 75 74 73	294	1,290,000
Wen-Lin Li	71 74 72 77	294	1,290,000
Natsuko Noro	76 73 77 69	295	1,140,000
Chikayo Yamazaki	72 77 74 72	295	1,140,000
Ayako Okamoto	72 79 71 73	295	1,140,000
Miyuki Shimabukuro	75 76 76 69	296	990,000
Toshimi Kimura	76 75 74 71	296	990,000
Yuko Moriguchi	73 78 74 72	297	870,000
Woo-Soon Ko	78 72 73 74	297	870,000
Fuki Kido	73 79 70 75	297	870,000
Aiko Takasu	75 74 75 74	298	780,000
Nayoko Yoshikawa	73 76 72 77	298	780,000
Yoko Inoue	72 75 73 78	298	780,000
Yuka Irie	75 73 74 77	299	690,000
Yuri Kawanami	74 74 72 79	299	690,000
Jae-Sook Won	73 72 71 83	299	690,000
Yukiyo Haga	73 79 75 73	300	600,000
Hiromi Takamura	73 77 72 78	300	600,000